REFERENCE

DO NOT REMOVE FROM LIBRARY

SOUTH COLLEGE
709 Mall Blvd.
Savannah, GA 31406

# BRITISH WRITERS
*Selected Authors*

# BRITISH WRITERS

*Selected Authors*

IAN SCOTT-KILVERT

General Editor

EDITED UNDER THE AUSPICES OF THE BRITISH COUNCIL

VOLUME II

CHARLES SCRIBNER'S SONS

Macmillan Library Reference USA

Simon & Schuster Macmillan

New York

Simon & Schuster and Prentice Hall International

London   Mexico City   New Delhi   Singapore   Sydney   Toronto

Copyright © 1997 by the British Council and Charles Scribner's Sons

All articles copyright by the British Council except:
Arthur Conan Doyle
Daphne du Maurier
John le Carré
C. S. Lewis
Alan Paton
Mary Shelley
J. R. R. Tolkien
P. G. Wodehouse

All rights reserved. No part of this book may be reproduced or transmitted in any form or by any means, electronic or mechanical, including photocopying, recording, or by any information storage or retrieval system, without permission in writing from the publisher.

1 3 5 7 9 11 13 17 19  20 18 16 14 12 10 8 6 4 2

LIBRARY OF CONGRESS CATALOGING-IN-PUBLICATION DATA

British Writers, selected authors / Ian Scott-Kilvert, general editor.
    p. cm.
    Edited under the auspices of the British Council.
    Includes bibliographical references and index.
    ISBN 0-684-80518-9 (set: alk. paper).—ISBN 0-684-80515-4  (v. 1: alk. paper).
    —ISBN 0-684-80516-2 (v. 2 : alk. paper).—ISBN 0-684-80517-0  (v. 3 : alk. paper)
    1. English literature—Dictionaries.  2. English literature—Biobibliography—Dictionaries.
    3. Authors, English—Biography—Dictionaries.  I. Scott-Kilvert, Ian. II. British Council.
    PR19.B68  1997
    820.9′0003—dc21
    [B]                                                                                                97-15303
                                                                                                              CIP

0-684-80518-9 (Set)
0-684-80515-4 (Vol. I)
0-684-80516-2 (Vol. II)
0-684-80517-0 (Vol. III)

Printed in the United States of America

The paper in this publication meets the requirements of ANSI / NISO Z39.48-1992 (Permanence of Paper).

# Contents

| | |
|---|---|
| HENRY FIELDING / John Butt | 497 |
| E. M. FORSTER / Philip Gardner | 511 |
| WILLIAM GOLDING / Stephen Medcalf | 529 |
| GRAHAM GREENE / Bernard Bergonzi | 557 |
| THOMAS HARDY / R. A. Scott-James and C. Day Lewis | 577 |
| GERARD MANLEY HOPKINS / Graham Storey | 599 |
| A. E. HOUSMAN / Ian Scott-Kilvert | 621 |
| ALDOUS HUXLEY / Focelyn Brooke | 635 |
| SAMUEL JOHNSON / S. C. Roberts | 647 |
| BEN JONSON / J. B. Bamborough | 665 |
| JAMES JOYCE / F. I. M. Stewart | 683 |
| JOHN KEATS / Miriam Allott | 701 |
| RUDYARD KIPLING / A. G. Sandison | 729 |
| D. H. LAWRENCE / Alastair Niven | 771 |
| JOHN LE CARRÉ / George J. Leonard | 811 |
| DORIS LESSING / Michael Thorpe | 833 |
| C. S. LEWIS / Sanford Schwartz | 855 |
| SIR THOMAS MALORY / M. C. Bradbrook | 877 |
| KATHERINE MANSFIELD / Ian A. Gordon | 891 |
| W. SOMERSET MAUGHAM / Anthony Curtis | 905 |
| JOHN MILTON / E. M. W. Tillyard | 925 |
| GEORGE ORWELL / Tom Hopkinson | 947 |
| ALAN PATON / Randy Malamud | 963 |
| HAROLD PINTER / John Russell Taylor | 985 |
| ALEXANDER POPE / Ian Jack | 1001 |
| WILLIAM SHAKESPEARE / Stanley Wells | 1013 |

# Contents of Other Volumes

## Volume I

| | |
|---|---|
| *Historical Chronology* | xi |
| W. H. AUDEN / Richard Hoggart | 1 |
| JANE AUSTEN / Brian Southam | 23 |
| SAMUEL BECKETT / Jean-Jacques Mayoux | 47 |
| THE ENGLISH BIBLE / Donald Coggan | 69 |
| WILLIAM BLAKE / F. B. Beer | 89 |
| JAMES BOSWELL / P. A. W. Collins | 111 |
| THE BRONTËS / Winifred Gérin | 129 |
| ELIZABETH BARRETT BROWNING / Alethea Hayter | 179 |
| ROBERT BROWNING / Philip Drew | 193 |
| JOHN BUNYAN / Henri A. Talon | 215 |
| ROBERT BURNS / David Daiches | 231 |
| GEORGE GORDON, LORD BYRON / Macolm Kelsall | 245 |
| THOMAS CARLYLE / Ian Campbell | 269 |
| GEOFFREY CHAUCER / Nevill Coghill | 283 |
| SAMUEL TAYLOR COLERIDGE / R. L. Brett | 313 |
| JOSEPH CONRAD / C. B. Cox | 331 |
| DANIEL DEFOE / James Sutherland | 349 |
| CHARLES DICKENS / Barbara Hardy | 363 |
| JOHN DONNE / Frank Kermode | 397 |
| ARTHUR CONAN DOYLE / Bernard Benstock | 415 |
| DAPHNE DU MAURIER / Nina Auerbach | 435 |
| GEORGE ELIOT / Lettice Cooper | 453 |
| T. S. ELIOT / M. C. Bradbrook | 469 |

## Volume III

| | |
|---|---|
| GEORGE BERNARD SHAW / Margery M. Morgan | 1053 |
| MARY SHELLEY / Anne K. Mellor | 1085 |
| PERCY BYSSHE SHELLEY / G. M. Matthews | 1105 |
| EDMUND SPENSER / Alastair Fowler | 1121 |
| SIR RICHARD STEELE and JOSEPH ADDISON / A. R. Humphreys | 1145 |
| ROBERT LOUIS STEVENSON / G. B. Stern | 1161 |
| TOM STOPPARD / C. W. E. Bigsby | 1177 |
| JONATHAN SWIFT / A. Norman Feffares | 1195 |
| ALFRED, LORD TENNYSON / Brian Southam | 1219 |
| WILLIAM MAKEPEACE THACKERAY / John Carey | 1237 |
| DYLAN THOMAS / Leslie Norris | 1261 |
| J. R. R. TOLKIEN / Karl Kroeber | 1277 |
| ANTHONY TROLLOPE / Hugh Sykes Davies | 1295 |
| EVELYN WAUGH / William Myers | 1311 |
| H. G. WELLS / Kenneth Young | 1331 |
| OSCAR WILDE / John Stokes | 1353 |
| P. G. WODEHOUSE / David Damrosch | 1377 |
| VIRGINIA WOOLF / Bernard Blackstone | 1395 |
| WILLIAM WORDSWORTH / F. R. Watson | 1419 |
| WORLD WAR I POETS / John Press | 1445 |
| WILLIAM BUTLER YEATS / G. S. Fraser | 1473 |
| *Chronological List of Subjects* | 1493 |
| *List of Contributors* | 1497 |
| *Complete Listing of Subjects in Parent Set* | 1501 |
| *Index* | 1507 |

# HENRY FIELDING
(1707-1754)

## *John Butt*

### I

To say that the English novel began in the 1740's with the work of Samuel Richardson and Henry Fielding is to invite refinement, if not contradiction. The Elizabethans had plenty of novels to read, by Thomas Nashe, Robert Greene, Thomas Lodge, and Thomas Deloney; in the latter half of the seventeenth century, there were numerous translations and imitations of the French romance; and Aphra Behn, Daniel Defoe, and Mary Manley all have some claim upon the historian of the novel. Yet there is something in the broad contention that Richardson and Fielding, for all their differences, would have approved. Recalling the circumstances of his writing *Pamela* (1740), Richardson claimed, in a letter to a friend, that he had hit upon "a new species of writing," and Fielding was equally confident that *Joseph Andrews* (1742) was a "kind of writing, which I do not remember to have seen hitherto attempted in our language." At least some of their readers were prepared to acknowledge the claim. Samuel Johnson, writing in 1750, when *Clarissa*, *Tom Jones*, and Tobias Smollett's *Roderick Random* had been published, was able to distinguish one important difference between the new style of fiction and the old. In *Rambler* No. 4 he remarks:

> The works of fiction, with which the present generation seems more particularly delighted, are such as exhibit life in its true state, diversified only by accidents that daily happen in the world, and influenced by passions and qualities which are really to be found in conversing with mankind.... Its province is to bring about natural events by easy means, and to keep up curiosity without the help of wonder: it is therefore precluded from the machines and expedients of the heroick romance, and can neither employ giants to snatch away a lady from the nuptial rites, nor knights to bring her back from captivity; it can neither bewilder its personages in deserts, nor lodge them in imaginary castles.

Such, Johnson would have us believe, were the themes and incidents of the older style of fiction. All the writer had to do was "let loose his invention, and heat his mind with incredibilities; a book was thus produced without fear of criticism, without the toil of study, without knowledge of nature, or acquaintance with life." Very different, in Johnson's opinion, was the equipment of the modern novelist. Besides "learning which is to be gained from books," he must have "experience which . . . must arise from general converse and accurate observation of the living world." His books will then be not merely "just copiers of human manners," but will also serve as "lectures of conduct, and introductions into life."

Perhaps Johnson was not altogether fair to the older style of fiction. Many novelists since the time of Sir Philip Sidney had been interested in providing "lectures of conduct," and many besides Defoe (whom Johnson seems to have overlooked) were acquainted with life. But one of the principal differences between the old and the new is made very clear in his emphasis upon "accidents that daily happen in the world." The men and women in the novels of Fielding—and Richardson—act "in such scenes of the universal drama as may be the lot of any other man" or woman. That is true of neither Sidney nor Defoe. A young man might imagine himself feeling like Sidney's Musidorus or acting like Robinson Crusoe, but he could never expect to share their experiences, as he might expect to share the experiences of Tom Jones. A young woman might well believe all that Moll Flanders reports had happened to her, but she could scarcely say of Moll, as she could say of Amelia or even of Clarissa, "there but for the grace of God go I."

But when Fielding, Richardson, and Johnson insisted that such accidents as "daily happen in the world" must be the staple of the new style of fiction, they were writing not at the beginning, but toward the end, of a critical tradition. The marvelous had long been losing esteem, and writers of romances in the previous century had been accustomed to discuss in their prefaces to what use historical incidents might be put. Thus Sir George Mackenzie, in the preface to his *Aretina* (1660), had censured those who have "stuffed their Books with things impracticable, which because they were above the reach of man's power, they should never have fallen within the circle of his observation"; and Robert Boyle took credit for having chosen an episode from history for his *Theodore* (1687), since:

> True Examples do arm and fortify the mind far more efficaciously than Imaginary or Fictitious ones can do; and the fabulous labours of *Hercules*, and Exploits of *Arthur of Britain*, will never make men aspire to Heroick Vertue half so powerfully, as the real Examples of Courage and Gallantry afforded by *Jonathan*, *Caesar*, or the *Black Prince*.

These novelists were following in the steps of Georges de Scudéry, the most famous of the French romance writers, whose *Ibrahim* (1642) had been translated into English in 1652. In the preface to that work, Scudéry claimed that he had observed

> the Manners, Customs, Religions, and Inclinations of People: and to give a more true resemblance to things, I have made the foundations of my work Historical, my principal Personages such as are marked out in the true History for illustrious persons.

Even though the practice of these writers did not always accord with their theory, it is easy to see how in time the desire for "a more true resemblance to things" could lead the author of *Robinson Crusoe* to declare that "the Editor believes the thing to be a just History of Fact; neither is there any Appearance of Fiction in it." The innocent deception of passing off fiction as history or biography is perpetrated on several title pages. Thus the reader is offered *The Life and Strange Surprising Adventures of Robinson Crusoe, of York, Mariner. Written by Himself* and *The Fortunes and Misfortunes of the Famous Moll Flanders. Who Was Born in Newgate, Was Twelve Year a Thief, Eight Year a Transported Felon in Virginia. Written from Her Memorandums.* Twenty years later the novelists were less concerned for the success of their deceptions. *Pamela. Or, Virtue Rewarded* (1740) is merely *A Narrative Which Has Its Foundations in Truth and Nature*, but the tradition of offering "a more true resemblance to things" is maintained in such titles as *The History of the Adventures of Joseph Andrews and of His Friend Mr. Abraham Adams* (1742); *Clarissa. Or, The History of a Young Lady* (1747-1748); and *The History of Tom Jones, a Foundling* (1749).

In choosing to let their novels pass as histories or biographies, these writers were aware of what they might adopt in structure and narrative technique from a well-established literary "kind," and it is not surprising that they should search for profitable analogies in other forms of narrative as well. It was certainly to be expected that they would have an eye to the epic in particular, since this was a form of paramount reputation and much critical thought had been given to the analysis of its constituent parts. Sidney had long ago declared that the *Theagenes and Chariclea* of Heliodorus was not prevented from exerting influence as a heroic poem though it was written in prose, and he had set an example when revising his *Arcadia* to make its structure conform more truly to epic principles. Scudéry again had emphasized what valuable lessons a novelist might learn from the epic, and possibly the most successful of modern epics, François Fénelon's *Les aventures de Télémaque*, had been written in prose. Thus, when Fielding told his readers that *Joseph Andrews* was to be regarded as "a comic epic poem in prose" and that, moreover, it was a "kind of writing which I do not remember to have seen hitherto attempted in our language," the novelty of his claim lay not so much in the notion of a prose epic, nor even of a comic epic poem—for this everyone recognized in Alexander Pope's *Dunciad*—but in a conflation of the two. The act of conflation required the spark of Fielding's genius, and the critical temper of the day was prepared to see such a spark fly.

II

Fielding was well prepared for this new venture by his experience of men and books and by his previous career as a writer. Born near Glastonbury on 27 April 1707, he came of a family of small landowners in the West Country related to the earls of Denbigh. Among his immediate forebears were men who had risen to positions of some distinction in the learned professions. It might be suspected that the novelist derived his inclination toward the law from his mother's father, who was a justice of the Queen's Bench, and that to his paternal grandfather, an archdeacon of Salisbury, he owed both his love of learning and the strong bent toward Christian moral teaching that characterize his novels. Though we need not pay too much attention to such surmises nor inquire what traits of character were inherited from his somewhat feckless father, Lieutenant General Edmund Fielding, it is at least clear in what rank of society he was bred.

After a boyhood spent on his mother's Dorsetshire estates, Fielding joined his father in London. In 1728, at the age of twenty-one, he wrote his first play, *Love in Several Masques*, a comedy of manners. No doubt owing partly to the patronage of his cousin, Lady Mary Wortley Montagu, the play was performed at the Drury Lane Theatre, and ran for four nights. But though he was to lead a busy life as a dramatist and theater manager between 1730 and 1737, Fielding now decided not to pursue his moderate success but to enroll as a student in the Faculty of Letters at the University of Leiden under the redoubtable critic Peter Burmann. In later years he was to mock Burmann's editorial manner in the notes to his burlesque tragedy *Tom Thumb*, but it is probable that he now received his first instruction in critical theory and began to obtain his extensive knowledge of classical literature. Certainly he was later to own a remarkable library of classical and modern texts, and his novels show that he possessed what Dr. Johnson considered the primary equipment of the modern novelist: "learning which is to be gained from books."

At the age of thirty-five, when he began to write *Joseph Andrews*, Fielding had had sufficient opportunity to acquire the second item in Johnson's equipment, "experience which . . . must arise from general converse and accurate observation of the living world." If we did not know this from *Joseph Andrews* itself, we should know it from the plays written during the seven years following his return from Leiden in 1730 and from his journalistic essays. These serve to show something of the range of that experience as well as to indicate how the experience might be used by the future novelist.

Writing for the stage had taught him how to manipulate dialogue and to devise speech rhythms for distinguishing a country squire from a man-about-town or a modish lady from a young miss. It had taught him to contrive a concatenation of incidents by which the principal characters are brought together in the final scene of play or novel for the unraveling of the knot. It seems also to have accustomed him to imagine some of his scenes in terms of a drawing room set on a stage of limited dimensions, and to offer in the novel scenes that experience told him would be effective in the theater. His plays abound in scenes where characters are interrupted by an unexpected entry that disturbs and perplexes their existing relationship. Thus in Act III of *The Temple Beau* (1730), an early play, young Wilding is pretending to make love to Lady Lucy Pedant and has just taken her in his arms when they are interrupted by the entry of her husband ("Hoity-toity? Hey-day! What's here to do? Have I caught you, gentlefolks. . . .") and, immediately after, of Wilding's father, who has lately discovered his son's deceptions. This use of the unexpected entry is more skillfully developed in *Tom Jones* (XV.5), in a scene where Lord Fellamar's unwanted attentions to Sophia in Lady Bellaston's house are interrupted by the entry of Squire Western, who has at last discovered where Sophia has taken refuge. Western is followed by Lady Bellaston, who joins him in representing to Sophia the advantages of agreeing to a proposal of marriage. Lord Fellamar, being assured that his suit was favored by Lady Bellaston and assuming that it must also be favored by Western, decides to take advantage of the new turn in the situation:

Coming up therefore to the squire, he said, "Though I have not the honour, sir, of being personally known to you; yet, as I find I have the happiness to have my proposals accepted, let me intercede, sir, in behalf of the young lady, that she may not be more solicited at this time."

"You intercede, sir!" said the squire; "why, who the devil are you?"

"Sir, I am Lord Fellamar," answered he, "and am the happy man, whom I hope you have done the honour of accepting for a son-in-law."

"You are the son of a b——," replied the squire, "for all

your laced coat. You my son-in-law, and be d——n'd to you!"

"I shall take more from you, sir, than from any man," answered the lord; "but I must inform you, that I am not used to hear such language without resentment."

"Resent my a——," quoth the squire. "Don't think I am afraid of such a fellow as thee art! because hast got a spit there dangling at thy side. Lay by your spit, and I'll give thee enough of meddling with what doth not belong to thee. I'll teach you to father-in-law me. I'll lick thy jacket."

"It's very well, sir," said my lord, "I shall make no disturbance before the ladies. I am very well satisfied. Your humble servant, sir; Lady Bellaston, your most obedient."[1]

There can be little doubt that in this episode Fielding has made use of his theatrical experience, as he has also done in scenes involving the use of stage properties, even though the number of these is meager. The most notable example in his plays is perhaps to be found in Act III of *The Letter Writers* (1731), where Mrs. Wisdom and her gallant Rakel are disturbed by the arrival of Mrs. Softly, and Rakel, wishing to protect Mrs. Wisdom's reputation, hides under the table. Mrs. Softly is followed by Mr. Wisdom and a nephew who, in a drunken fit, overturns the table and discovers Rakel. This is the prototype of more memorable discoveries: of Lady Bellaston discovering Mrs. Honour hiding behind the bed in Jones's room (XV.7), and of Jones discovering the philosopher Square behind a rug in Molly Seagrim's bedchamber (V.5). It is surprising that after his early experiment in *The Letter Writers*, Fielding should not have improved upon the device in a subsequent play. The hint was to be taken by Richard Brinsley Sheridan, who in *The School for Scandal* shows, in the scene of Sir Peter Teazle's discovery of his wife behind a screen in Joseph Surface's library, that he had learned something from each of the episodes in *Tom Jones*, for he there combined the embarrassment of Square's discovery and the reversal of fortune that sprang from Mrs. Honour's.

During his career as a dramatist, Fielding had attempted a considerable number of forms. He had written witty comedies of intrigue in the Restoration manner, farces, ballad operas with political implications, burlesques, comedies reflecting upon modern manners, and satirical comedies on the pattern of the duke of Buckingham's *Rehearsal* (1671), in which an absurd play is rehearsed with comments from the author, a critical acquaintance, and the players. Two of the last of these, *Pasquin* (1736) and *The Historical Register* (1737), were among the most successful of his plays; and the device he there employed, accompanying the action with critical comment from the wings, may have suggested to him the "prolegomenous" chapters of *Tom Jones*, which, on a more serious level, serve the same purpose. Equally significant is his early experience of burlesque in *Tom Thumb* (1730) and *The Covent-Garden Tragedy* (1732) where, by burlesquing an old-fashioned "kind," he produced a new "kind," as it were, by mutation. Though the burlesque of epic is not so prominent in *Joseph Andrews* and its successors as the burlesque of tragedy in *Tom Thumb*, it is by a similar process of "mutation" that the novels arose.

Fielding's experience as a journalist was scarcely less useful to his future career than his experience in the theater. From 1739 to 1741 he was the leader of a group of writers responsible for conducting an opposition newspaper called *The Champion*. To this journal Fielding contributed a number of essays modeled on *The Spectator*. Just as Joseph Addison had invented a Spectator Club and had defined the persona of one member of the club who should write his lucubrations, aided and abetted by his fellow members, so Fielding assumed the persona of Captain Hercules Vinegar, whose business it was to write about the issues of the day, aided by his wife Joan and their two sons. Also like Addison he varied the form of his articles: now character sketches, now lay sermons or letters from imaginary correspondents, visions, critical papers, essays in installments, and Saturday papers on religious matters. These essays reveal a more serious-minded Fielding than one might suppose, judging from the plays alone. Here he is seen formulating his views on the moral problems that form the staple of his three novels and illustrating those problems by anecdotes and character sketches. He was also unwittingly practicing what was regarded as an important part of the novelist's duty. The novelist was expected to provide, in Johnson's phrase, "lectures of conduct." He was not merely to edify by the story he told, but to make sure that his

---

[1] Quotations are from the Everyman's Library edition of *Tom Jones* (London, 1963).

lesson was understood. Hence the pithy and summary comment upon manners, common both to the novelist and the essayist.

### III

For much of his future work, Fielding was well prepared both in theory and in practice. It is not surprising, therefore, that from the beginning his command was assured, even though his approach was haphazard, even accidental. If it had not been for Richardson's *Pamela*, he might never have become a novelist. This story deals with a young woman's marriage outside her station in life. When a young man and a young woman of different social classes fell in love, it was generally assumed that their association could only be illegitimate. "Why, what is all this, my dear," says Sir Simon Darnford, one of Richardson's characters, to his wife, "but that our neighbour has a mind to his mother's waiting maid! And if he takes care she wants for nothing, I don't see any great injury will be done her. He hurts no *family* by this." And Parson Williams reports the opinion of Parson Peters that this was "too common and fashionable a case to be withstood by a private clergyman or two." What makes this particular case uncommon is that Pamela resists her would-be seducer, yet cannot help loving him in spite of his ill treatment; and that Mr. B. expects to be able to seduce Pamela, yet, in spite of favorable circumstances, is won by her behavior and, against the opinion of the world, offers her marriage.

Thus Pamela's virtue is rewarded. But though Richardson emphasizes that aspect of his story in his subtitle, there is much more to the novel. Had that been all, we might have expected that her virtue would be rewarded by marriage in the last chapter. But the ceremony takes place two-thirds of the way through, and yet we read on, since it is not merely Pamela's chastity but the integrity of her personality that is tested. She must also be shown preserving her humility, her thankfulness, her piety, and her intelligence in her new station. Hers is indeed a most difficult task. She is required to loathe Mr. B.'s behavior, yet to love him; to be content with her lowly position, yet to aspire to Mr. B.'s hand; to be humble, yet to reprobate aristocratic vice; to be meek, yet outspoken; to be simple, yet quick-witted; to be innocent, yet wide awake and on her guard. It would seem almost impossible that Richardson should succeed in steering so intricate a path. But each incident is related with such careful attention to detail, Pamela's letters give so powerful a sense of immediacy, and Richardson himself preserves such an unhesitating belief in Pamela's word and in the truth of appearances, that he almost persuades us to believe too. Almost, but not quite. Many contemporaries were persuaded, but others saw that a different interpretation was possible. Among the latter was Fielding.

To convey this alternative interpretation, Fielding called upon his experience in burlesque and produced, pseudonymously, *An Apology for the Life of Mrs. Shamela Andrews. In Which, the Many Notorious Falshoods and Misrepresentations of a Book Called Pamela, Are Exposed and Refuted; and All the Matchless Arts of That Young Politician, Set in a True and Just Light. Together with a Full Account of All That Passed Between Her and Parson Arthur Williams; Whose Character is Represented in a Manner Something Different from That Which He Bears in Pamela. The Whole Being Exact Copies of Authentick Papers Delivered to the Editor.* It is a riotous travesty, in which Pamela is shown as a shameless and designing hussy, yet ready to talk for "a full Hour and a half, about my Vartue" or "of honourable Designs till Supper-time," and Mr. B.'s full name is discovered to be Booby. And just as the rehearsed plays in *Pasquin* and *The Historical Register* had been enclosed within a framework of commentary from the supposed author and his friend, so these authentic letters are sent by Parson Oliver, who knew the facts, to Parson Tickletext, who had taken *Pamela* at Richardson's valuation.

If any moral is to be drawn, it is that the distinction between being and seeming must be recognized. No exponent of the comedy of manners could fail to draw such a distinction, and Fielding's plays are especially rich in characters who are not what they seem, from Lady Gravely, the affected prude of *The Temple Beau*, to the false and grasping Valences of *The Fathers*. But Fielding had more than a professional dramatist's interest in unmasking appearances. He returned to the subject in an essay on the pursuit of reputation, published in *The Champion* on 4 March 1740. In it he showed that folly and vice "are continually industrious to disguise themselves," and wear the habits of virtue and wisdom, "which the world, always judging by the outside, easily suffers them to accomplish." The irony of *The Life of Mr. Jonathan Wild the Great* is sustained—tediously, it must be admitted—to prove that the Great Man, properly considered, is no better than a gangster.

The distinction between being and seeming is the guiding principle of *Joseph Andrews*. In the preface to his novel, Fielding explains that the ridiculous is his province, that the only source of the true ridiculous is affectation, and that affectation "proceeds from one of these two causes, Vanity or Hypocrisy." To display the ridiculous he has devised this new kind of writing, the comic epic poem in prose, observing the best epic practice in such matters as fable and characters. But whereas the epic fable is customarily grave and solemn, his will be light and ridiculous, and whereas epic characters are of the highest, his will mostly be of inferior rank and manners. The difficulty is to see how Fielding interprets the representation of the fable in action. Fortunately he is more explicit in the preface he wrote for his sister's novel, *David Simple* (1744). There, after referring to his preface to *Joseph Andrews*, he mentions the two great originals of all epic writing, the *Iliad* and the *Odyssey*, which

differ principally in the action, which in the *Iliad* is entire and uniform; in the *Odyssey*, is rather a series of actions, all tending to produce one great end.

The followers of Homer have observed this principal difference, whether their imitations were serious or comic. And so we see that just as Pope in *The Dunciad* fixed on one action, Samuel Butler and Miguel de Cervantes fixed on a series. Fielding's sister's work belongs to the latter category: "The fable consists of a series of separate adventures, detached from and independent of each other, yet all tending to one great end."

The same may be seen in *Joseph Andrews*. It too is an Odyssean epic, "consisting of a series of separate adventures, detached from and independent of each other, yet all tending to one great end." And it may be observed that just as the *Odyssey* relates the adventures of Odysseus in finding his way home and the hardships that befell him after incurring the wrath of Poseidon, so Fielding relates the adventures of Joseph Andrews and Parson Adams in finding their way home and the hardships that befell them after Joseph had incurred the wrath of Lady Booby. Perhaps contemporary readers might have noticed an even closer application of the burlesque. The critic Andrew Ramsay had pointed out that in Fénelon's *Aventures de Télémaque* it is the hatred of Venus, rather than the wrath of Poseidon, that supplies the cause of the action, and in his *La Vie de Fénelon* that "the Hatred of *Venus* against a young Prince, that despises Pleasure for the Sake of Virtue, and subdues his Passions by the Assistance of Wisdom, is a Fable drawn from Nature, and at the same Time includes the sublimest Morality." No reader could fail to relish the notion of the lascivious Lady Booby in the role of Venus, whose desire for her handsome footman Joseph Andrews is turned to hatred when that young prince despises pleasure for the sake of virtue, and subdues his passions with the assistance of his sister Pamela's wisdom.

But what is the great end to which all the separate adventures are tending? Why, surely, the display of the ridiculous, of those affectations that arise from vanity and hypocrisy. This is the characteristic common to Lady Booby, Mrs. Slipslop, and Mrs. Grave-airs, all of them women who pretend to more modesty, more learning, or more gentility than they possess. And this is the characteristic of the innkeepers and their wives who can make a show of human kindness once they are satisfied of the standing of their guests, of the soldiers who pretend to valor, of the justices who pretend to a knowledge of the law, and of the parsons who pretend to godliness. Even Parson Trulliber can make a show of Methodism, when he is satisfied that Adams has not come to buy his pigs: "Get out of my doors," he cries, when Adams tells him that, in addition to faith, he must perform the good works of giving to the needy. "Fellow, dost thou speak against faith in my house? I will no longer remain under the same roof with a wretch who speaks wantonly of faith and the Scriptures."

The two interpolated stories fall into place in this pattern. The unfortunate jilt is a story of pretense to affection, and the story of Mr. Wilson is a tale of the pretenses practiced in London life. Vanity of vanities is Mr. Wilson's theme as he recalls his experiences of life in the Temple among smart fellows who drank with lords they did not know and intrigued with women they never saw, and of town coquettes animated solely by vanity who sometimes have a whim to affect wisdom, wit, good nature, politeness, and health, but are also affected to put on ugliness, folly, nonsense, ill nature, ill breeding, and sickness in their turns.

Such are Mr. Wilson's reflections. Far from being an idle digression, they are highly appropriate to Fielding's scheme and purpose; for his action, by confining him to the high road and the inn, precludes him from commenting upon London life; it is a sample of London society that Mr. Wilson's story exposes.

But these at worst are transient characters, and at best they are minor. What of Parson Adams himself? He too has his vanities—innocent vanities, indeed—his learning and his power as a preacher. His role is that of a modern Don Quixote, a man of good sense, good parts, and good nature, as Fielding declares, but "as entirely ignorant of the ways of this world as an infant just entered into it could possibly be." His book reading did not, like his illustrious prototype's, lead him to mistake windmills for giants or inns for castles; it led him instead to expect on every hand an honest, undesigning, Christian behavior. He is therefore constantly the victim of deceit. But he never loses our affection, partly because his expectations are noble and partly because (like Don Quixote) he hurls himself upon the oppressor, thinking only of the blows his fists or his crabstick will deliver, and nothing of those he will receive. It is not merely in such episodes as the fight at the inn, which interrupts the story of the unfortunate jilt, or the "roasting" of Adams by the fox-hunting squire (which recalls the treatment of Don Quixote at the hands of the duke and duchess), or the midnight tussle with Mrs. Slipslop, in which Adams believes himself bewitched, that the reader recognizes the justice of the assertion on the title page of *Joseph Andrews* that it is "Written in Imitation of the Manner of Cervantes."

But there are two sides to the relationship of being and seeming. While most of the men and women in *Joseph Andrews* are worse than they seem, others are better. And though the bedraggled appearance of the worthy Adams is the most prominent example, Fielding asks us to notice that the man who lends all but sixpence of the sum needed to pay the stranded travelers' bill is not the wealthy Parson Trulliber but "a fellow who had been formerly a drummer in an Irish regiment, and now travelled the country as a pedlar"; that when Joseph lies sick at the Tow-wouses' inn, it is not the surgeon or the parson or the innkeeper who looks after him, but Betty the chambermaid, whose morals are no better than they should be; and that when Joseph has been found wounded and naked in a ditch, it is not any of the fine ladies in a passing coach who takes pity on him, but the postilion:

(a lad who hath been since transported for robbing a henroost), [who] voluntarily stript off a greatcoat, his only garment, at the same time swearing a great oath (for which he was rebuked by the passengers), "that he would rather ride in his shirt all his life than suffer a fellow-creature to lie in so miserable a condition."[2]

To some extent this anatomy of the ridiculous is a counterblast to *Pamela*, and by recalling certain incidents in that novel and introducing one or two of its characters, Fielding made sure that we should keep *Pamela* in view. Richardson had placed an implicit trust in the truth of appearances. But that way lies self-deception. It is only by the most careful scrutiny that we can see beneath appearances and find the true springs of human action.

IV

YET appearances are important too. "It is not enough," Fielding writes, "that your designs, nay that your actions, are intrinsically good; you must take care that they shall appear so"; for "prudence and circumspection are necessary even to the best of men." The passage occurs in one of those chapters of *Tom Jones* (III.7) "in which the author himself makes his appearance on the stage," and it is close to the heart of the novel. The theme is in fact announced in similar terms in the dedication:

I have endeavoured strongly to inculcate, that virtue and innocence can scarce ever be injured but by indiscretion; and . . . it is this alone which often betrays them into the snares which deceit and villainy spread for them.

To illustrate this idea, Fielding chose a hero as typical of his own order of society as the epic hero was of his. We are asked to recognize that Tom, in spite of some lack of prudence and circumspection, and in spite of some contraventions of the moral code, is essentially a good man. It might be said of Tom, as Ramsay had said of Fénelon's Telemachus: "Our Poet does not lift *Telemachus* above Humanity; he makes him fall into such Weaknesses, as are

[2]Quotations are from the Everyman's Library edition of *Joseph Andrews* (London, 1962).

compatible with a sincere Love of Virtue." Young Mr. Blifil, on the other hand, with whom Tom is brought up in Mr. Allworthy's household, has more than enough of prudence and circumspection, but his love of virtue is on a par with the affectations that Fielding exposed in *Joseph Andrews*. The distinction is one that Sheridan was to make familiar when he contrasted the brothers Charles and Joseph Surface in *The School for Scandal*.

The best critical theory of the day stated that an epic should have a beginning, a middle, and an end; that the beginning should deal with the causes of the action; and that in the causes might be observed two opposite "designs," the hero's and the design of those who opposed him. In adopting these sensible precepts, Fielding provided an introductory section of six books in which numerous incidents open Tom's character and reveal the designs of Blifil and his two tutors, Thwackum and Square, who sought to prejudice Tom in the eyes of Mr. Allworthy and to prevent him from marrying Sophia and inheriting Squire Western's estate. Tom is shown (IV.6) to have "somewhat about him, which, though I think writers are not thoroughly agreed in its name" (the third earl of Shaftesbury had called it the "moral sense")

> ... doth certainly inhabit some human breasts; whose use is not so properly to distinguish right from wrong, as to prompt and incite them to the former, and to restrain and withhold them from the latter.... Though he did not always act rightly, yet he never did otherwise without feeling and suffering for it.

Thus the boy is incited to sell the little horse that Mr. Allworthy had given him so as to prevent the family of a dismissed servant from starving, and he is prompted to risk his neck in recovering Sophia's pet bird, which Blifil had maliciously allowed to escape. And if he is prompted to fornication with the gamekeeper's daughter, he is prepared to deal honorably with her until he discovers that he was not the first to seduce her; and if he was drunk and disorderly in Mr. Allworthy's house, it was because he had already been thrown into an "immoderate excess of rapture" on hearing that Mr. Allworthy was recovering from his dangerous illness. Allworthy summarizes (V.7) what Fielding wishes us to think of Tom when he says to him on his sickbed: "I am convinced, my child, that you have much goodness, generosity, and honour, in your temper: if you will add prudence and religion to these, you must be happy."

But in spite of his conviction, Allworthy allows his mind to be poisoned by the malicious insinuations of Blifil and turns Tom out of his house and into a series of adventures on the high road, corresponding to those of Joseph Andrews and Parson Adams. They fill the second six books of the novel and correspond, in epic terms, to "the Shipping off of *Aeneas*, his Voyages, his Battels, and all the Obstacles he met with," which (in the words of René Le Bossu, the chief authority on epic structure at that time) "compose a just Middle; [for] they are a Consequence of the Destruction of Troy ... and these same Incidents require an End."

The high road leads to London, and on it are not only Tom and Partridge (his Sancho Panza) but also Sophia, who has fled from her father's house to escape being forced into marriage with Blifil. As in *Joseph Andrews*, the high road and the inn provide a suitable scene for the testing of character, the recognition of bad nature masquerading as good, and of good nature concealed or tainted by imprudence. Tom has something to learn even from the Man of the Hill, who, like Mr. Wilson and like many a character in epic, is permitted to interrupt the narrative with his story. The Man of the Hill provides further instances of imprudence, in particular of incautiousness in placing his affections, as a result of which he had become a misanthrope and a hermit. But, as Tom permits himself to comment (VIII.15), "What better could be expected in love derived from the stews, or in friendship first produced and nourished at the gaming table?" One must not think evil of the rest of mankind on that account, for, as Tom continues, enunciating Fielding's doctrines of the good-natured man and the deceptiveness of appearances:

> If there was, indeed, much more wickedness in the world than there is, it would not prove such general assertions against human nature, since much of this arrives by mere accident, and many a man who commits evil is not totally bad and corrupt in his heart.
>
> (VIII.15)

Sophia is learning as much as Tom, directly in such scenes as that at the inn at Upton, and by proxy as she listens to Mrs. Fitzpatrick's cautionary tale of her imprudent marriage, which is interrupted by appeals to Sophia to declare how she would have acted in like circumstances.

The lovers reach London independently, and the

final section of six further books begins. Tom's good nature is as clear as ever, notably in his generous treatment of the highwayman who is driven by penury to attack him and in his chivalrous championship of Mrs. Miller's daughter. His imprudence is clearer still in "the ignominious circumstance of being kept" by Lady Bellaston. Fielding never asks his readers to overlook Tom's misdemeanors. His worst offense is most severely punished, for his relations with Lady Bellaston cannot be forgiven by Sophia. We see him at the end of the sixteenth book at the nadir of his fortunes, rejected by Sophia, dismissed from Allworthy's favor, and imprisoned on a charge of murdering his opponent in a duel. "Such," Fielding muses (XVII.1), "are the calamities in which he is at present involved, owing to his imprudence . . . that we almost despair of bringing him to any good; and if our reader delights in seeing executions, I think he ought not to lose any time in taking a first row at Tyburn."

Readers of the epic will recognize that the time is ripe for a discovery or a reversal of fortune, perhaps even for both, and they will recall that it was not unusual for the author to invoke divine aid for rescuing a hero in distress. Fielding has prepared both for his discovery—that was allowed for in making Tom a foundling—and for his reversal of fortune, but he disdains to employ the marvelous. It is true that luck is on Tom's side when his victim in the duel recovers from his wound and when the facts of his parentage (concealed by Blifil) are discovered, but in other respects the reader is asked to recognize that Tom has worked his passage. He has cast his bread upon the waters in acts of abundant good nature, and by the assistance of Mrs. Miller's representations to Mr. Allworthy, he finds it after many days. His virtue is rewarded by restoration into the favor of Allworthy and the good graces of Sophia. Since he is now discovered to be Allworthy's nephew and heir, Squire Western has no further objections to bestowing his daughter upon him; they marry and "preserve the purest and tenderest affection for each other, an affection daily increased and confirmed by mutual endearments and mutual esteem."

This is a pious hope that the reader may find it difficult to share, for it rests upon the assumption that Tom has ceased to be indiscreet. He is at best a good-natured man, and though endowed with a well-developed moral sense, he must, on Allworthy's evidence, add religion as well as prudence to his good nature. Even if we allow that he has become prudent, there is nothing to show that he has become religious.

Some such reflections seem to have occurred to Fielding, for his next novel, *Amelia* (1751), begins where *Tom Jones* leaves off. Captain and Mrs. Booth also entertain the purest and tenderest affection for each other and confirm it by mutual endearments and mutual esteem, yet various accidents befall them, owing partly to Booth's character, and it is with these accidents and with their effect upon this worthy couple that the novel is concerned.

V

THE decision to deal with the accidents of domestic life set Fielding some new problems in structure. The high road and the inn could have no place here, since married folk are not usually nomadic. Consequently we miss the Odyssean-Quixotic episodes that in the earlier novels provided him with so many shining opportunities for unmasking affectation and testing character. He had also to decide how to relate the earlier history of his couple, a problem he had not been required to face before. But the comic adaptation of epic conventions was available here, as it had been at the beginning of *Joseph Andrews*. Just as Aeneas was stranded on the coast of Carthage, was succored there by Dido, related to her his story, and consummated his furtive love in a cave; so Captain Booth was stranded in Newgate Prison, was succored there by Miss Matthews, a high-class courtesan, related to her his story, and consummated his furtive love in a superior kind of cell. Nor is this merely an ingenious piece of burlesque. Booth's misdemeanor with Miss Matthews, which he is ashamed to confess to Amelia, dogs him throughout the novel, and the somberness of the opening scenes in Newgate sets the tone of the book. Fielding takes care to show us the squalor and oppression that were the lot of the penniless prisoner and the relative comfort to be had at the price of a bribe. He also describes the coarse and depraved ruffians, male and female, the tricksters and sharpers, who molest and prey upon the weak, the unfortunate, and even the innocent who have come there through a miscarriage of justice.

This is the scene in which we first discover Booth, whose previous history shows him to be imprudent, liable to deception, with "very slight and uncertain" notions of religion, yet essentially good-natured. He will not return to Newgate, but he will always be in danger of return. And when he escapes, the reader recognizes that Newgate was only a somewhat more lurid epitome of society outside, where merit counts for nothing, where civil and military places go by influence exerted for a bribe, where those in high places have rogues, pimps, and bawds in their pay, and where gallantry is a cover for fornication and adultery. Fielding had said as much in his play *The Modern Husband* (1731), and had repeated it in *Jonathan Wild*. And if *Joseph Andrews* and *Tom Jones* appear lighter in tone than *Amelia*, it is only because the scene is laid more frequently in the country. London is the breeding place for such creatures as Lord Fellamar and Lady Bellaston, and Mr. Wilson anticipated Booth in finding that in London "poverty and distress, with their horrid train of duns, attorneys, bailiffs, haunted me day and night. My clothes grew shabby, my credit bad, my friends and acquaintance of all kinds cold."

The scene is in fact so somber that a tragic conclusion seems inevitable. Even a stronger and a better man than Booth could scarcely escape that fate. In considering the conclusion to which he was leading his "worthy couple," Fielding is likely to have paid attention to the best critical teaching available. The consensus among commentators upon the epic pointed to a conclusion favorable to the hero. But Le Bossu could discover no reason why that should be so:

"Yet if any heed be given to Authority," he concluded, "I do not know any one Instance of a Poet, who finishes his Piece with the Misfortunes of his Heroe. . . . The *Epick Poem's* Action is of a larger Extent than that of the Theatre; [and] it would perhaps be less satisfactory to the Reader, if, after so much Pains and so long Troubles with which this kind of Poem is always fill'd, it should at last bring them to a doleful and unhappy End."

(*Traité du poème épique*)

The easiest way of bringing the Booths to a happy end might well have been to repeat the formula of *Tom Jones* and show the eventual reward of the hero's virtuous actions. But Fielding seems to have been no longer content with such teaching. It was Booth's mistake to believe that since men "act entirely from their passions, their actions can have neither merit or demerit." If a man's ruling passion happened to be benevolence, he would relieve the distress of others, but if it were avarice, ambition, or pride, other men's miseries would have no effect upon him. Booth is eventually corrected of an error, which to Amelia seems little better than atheism, by reading a volume of Isaac Barrow's sermons while detained in the bailiff's house, but in the meanwhile Fielding allows him little opportunity for charity. The reader notices instead how his imprudence in the use of what little money he has reduces Amelia to penury and how his ill-placed trust and his single act of fornication endanger her chastity. She, on the other hand, shows herself to be on all occasions a model of wifely prudence, constancy, obedience, forgiveness, and love.

"To retrieve the ill consequences of a foolish conduct, and by struggling manfully with distress to subdue it, is one of the noblest efforts of wisdom and virtue." That is all that Fielding asks of his worthy couple, and having displayed their struggles, he is not averse to rescuing them by an epic discovery (that Amelia is an heiress) and an epic reversal of fortune, which enables a now prudent and Christian Booth to retire to a country estate.

In *Amelia*, as in *Tom Jones*, Fielding implies that at the end of the book the hero is in some respects an altered man without persuading us of the fact. Charles Dickens was the first novelist to succeed in such persuasion and George Eliot the first to specialize in showing the modifying effect of incident upon character. These Victorian successes have made demands that the modern reader is inclined to impose upon earlier novelists and earlier dramatists without perhaps reflecting whether changes in character are necessary or always important. *Amelia*, like *Tom Jones*, deals with wider issues than the modification of character. It has to do not merely with Booth and his wife but also with miseries and distresses typical of mid-eighteenth-century London life. No other novel provides such a wide panorama of London society or better conveys what it was like to live in London in the 1750's.

VI

In a paper that he wrote for the last of his periodicals, *The Covent Garden Journal* (28 January 1752), Fielding declared that he would not trouble the world with any more novels. He had not been entirely committed to the profession of letters since the abrupt termination of his career as a dramatist. The severity of his attack upon Walpole's government in *Pasquin* had led directly to the Licensing Act of 1737 and to the closure of all theaters but Drury Lane and Covent Garden. Fielding's Little Theatre in the Haymarket was the principal victim, and his chief source of income was thus removed. He thereupon began a serious study of the law, was called to the bar in 1740, and practiced for some time on the Western Circuit. Shortly after completing *Tom Jones* in 1748 and before its publication, he had been appointed a police court magistrate at Bow Street, and his jurisdiction was soon extended to the whole of the county of Middlesex. He was also appointed justice of the peace for Westminster in the same year. As a magistrate he was exceptionally industrious and did much to break up the gangs of thieves that infested London. His *Enquiry into the Causes of the Late Increase of Robbers* (1751), dedicated to the lord chancellor, the earl of Hardwicke, shows both an extensive knowledge of the law and an intimate acquaintance with the evil and its origin. His energies might have been directed more and more to clearing up the criminal underworld if his health had not broken down. In the summer of 1754, he undertook a sea trip to Lisbon with his wife and daughter in a desperate search for health, and whiled away his time in keeping a diary. This he revised, and the manuscript was posthumously published as *The Journal of a Voyage to Lisbon* (1755). Not the least of its merits is the picture it gives us of the man himself, affectionately considerate to his family, patiently suffering from an incurable disease, yet observing with undiminished zest the oddities of human behavior and seizing such opportunities as incidents offered for social or political comment. The book is prefaced by a disquisition on travel literature comparable in kind with the disquisition on the comic epic poem in prose that prefaces *Joseph Andrews*. Once again Fielding declares that he is laying down the rules for a kind of writing that had not been properly undertaken before (except by Lord George Anson in the published account of his circumnavigation, 1740–1744), for travelers seem to have fallen either into the fault of "filling their pages with monsters which nobody hath ever seen, and with adventures which never have, nor could possibly have happened to them," or, on the other hand, they

waste their time and paper with recording things and facts of so common a kind, that they challenge no other right of being remembered than as they had the honour of having happened to the author.[3]

This opportunity of reforming travel literature was as haphazard as the chance Fielding took of reforming the novel, but even if he had lived longer—he died at Lisbon on 8 October 1754, at the age of forty-seven—it was not likely that he would have had occasion to write more in this kind. It is easy, however, to see that his theories might have been profitably applied to biography and that he was well equipped by imagination, a reverence for truth, judgment, and a sense of proportion to succeed in that kindred form.

But this is idle speculation. Even though Fielding may have felt that he had outgrown the novel, it is there that his achievement lies, and it is an achievement typical of an age that relished the mock epics of Pope and the ballad operas of John Gay. Like those poets, Fielding brought literary experience gained in other writing and a wealth of critical learning to bear upon the production of a new form, but a form that constantly recalls older, well-tried forms and adapts them to the spirit and use of his own times. He showed himself, in Johnson's words, one of those "just copiers of human manners," who could offer "lectures of conduct and introductions into life."

### SELECTED BIBLIOGRAPHY

I. COLLECTED WORKS. A. Murphy, ed., *The Works*, 4 vols. (London, 1762); *The Dramatic Works*, 4 vols. (London, 1783); A. Chalmers, ed., *The Works*, 10 vols. (London, 1806); Sir W. Scott, ed., *The Novels*, 10 vols. (London, 1821); T. Roscoe, ed., *The Novels* (London, 1831–1832); T. Roscoe, ed., *The Works* (London, 1840); L. Stephen, ed., *The Works*, 10 vols. (London, 1893); G. Saintsbury, ed., *The Works*, 12 vols. (London, 1893); E. Gosse, ed., *The Works*, 12 vols. (London, 1899); W. E. Henley et al., eds., *The Complete Works*, 16 vols. (London, 1903); *Fielding's Novels*, 10 vols. (Oxford, 1926). A new collected ed. is being published by the Wesleyan

---

[3]Quotation from the Everyman's Library edition of *The Journal of a Voyage to Lisbon* (New York–London, 1932).

University Press and the Oxford University Press. The first vol. to appear is M. C. Battestin, ed., *Joseph Andrews* (London–Middletown, Conn., 1967); H. K. Miller, ed., *Miscellanies* (London, 1972); F. Bowers, ed., *Tom Jones* (London, 1975); W. B. Coley, ed., *The Jacobite Journal and Related Writings* (London, 1975).

II. SELECTED WORKS. H. Fielding, *Miscellanies*, 3 vols. (London, 1743), vol. I: poems and essays, vol. II: *A Journey from This World to the Next* and plays, vol. III: *The Life of Mr. Jonathan Wild the Great*; H. Fielding, *The Beauties of Fielding* (London, 1782); J. P. Browne, ed., *Miscellanies and Poems* (London, 1872); G. H. Geroulde, ed., *Selected Essays* (New York, 1905); G. Saintsbury, ed., *Fielding* (London, 1909); L. Rice-Oxley, ed., *Fielding* (Oxford, 1923).

III. SEPARATE WORKS. *Love in Several Masques, a Comedy* (London, 1728); *The Temple Beau, a Comedy* (London, 1730); *The Author's Farce* (London, 1730); *Tom Thumb, a Tragedy* (London, 1730), rev. ed., with annotations, titled *The Tragedy of Tragedies; or, The Life and Death of Tom Thumb the Great* (London, 1731), both texts repr. in J. T. Hillhouse, ed. (New Haven, Conn., 1918); *Rape upon Rape; or, The Justice Caught in His Own Trap, a Comedy* (London, 1730); *The Letter-Writers: or, A New Way to Keep a Wife at Home, a Farce* (London, 1731); *The Welsh Opera: or, The Grey Mare the Better Horse* (London, 1731), drama; *The Lottery, a Farce* (London, 1732); *The Modern Husband, a Comedy* (London, 1732); *The Old Debauchees, a Comedy* (London, 1732); *The Covent-Garden Tragedy* (London, 1732); *The Mock Doctor; or, The Dumb Lady Cur'd. A Comedy, Done from Molière* (London, 1732); *The Miser. A Comedy, Taken from Plautus and Molière* (London, 1733); *The Intriguing Chambermaid, a Comedy* (London, 1734); *Don Quixote in England, a Comedy* (London, 1734), contains the famous songs "When Mighty Roast Beef Was the Englishman's Food" and "The Dusky Night Rides Down the Sky"; *An Old Man Taught Wisdom: or, The Virgin Unmask'd, a Farce* (London, 1735); *The Universal Gallant: or, The Different Husbands, a Comedy* (London, 1735); *Pasquin, a Dramatick Satire upon the Times* (London, 1736); *Tumble-down Dick: or, Phaeton in the Suds. A Dramatick Entertainment* (London, 1736); *Eurydice, a Farce* (London, 1737); *The Historical Register for the Year 1736* (London, 1737), drama, also contains *Eurydice Hiss'd*, "a very merry Tragedy."

*The Champion* (15 November 1739–19 June 1740), 2 vols. (London, 1741), essays, also edited by S. J. Sackett as *The Voyages of Mr. Job Vinegar* (Los Angeles, 1958); *Of True Greatness* (London, 1741), poem; *The Vernoniad* (London, 1741), poem; *An Apology for the Life of Mrs. Shamela Andrews* (London, 1741), repr. with essays by R. B. Johnson, ed. (London, 1926), also in B. W. Downs, ed. (London, 1930), S. W. Baker, Jr., ed. (Berkeley, Calif., 1953), and I. Watt, ed. (Los Angeles, 1956), the Watt ed. being considered the most reliable; *The Crisis, a Sermon* (London, 1741); *The History of the Adventures of Joseph Andrews and of His Friend Mr. Abraham Adams*, 2 vols. (London, 1742), repr. in the World's Classics ed. with preface by L. Rice-Oxley (London, 1919), J. P. de Castro, ed. (London, 1929), Everyman's Library ed. with preface by A. R. Humphreys (London, 1962), and M. C. Battestin, ed. (London, 1965), the last being annotated and including *Shamela*; *Miss Lucy in Town, a Farce* (London, 1742); *Plutus, the God of Riches. A Comedy, Translated from the Original Greek of Aristophanes* (London, 1742); *Some Papers Proper to be Read Before the Royal Society* (London, 1743), satirical pamphlets; *The Wedding-Day, a Comedy* (London, 1743); *The Life of Mr. Jonathan Wild the Great* (London, 1743; new ed., with corrections and additions, 1754), also in the World's Classics ed., text of 1743 with variants of 1754 in appendix (London, 1951), first published in *Miscellanies*; *A Serious Address to the People of Great Britain* (London, 1745), political tract; *A Dialogue Between the Devil, the Pope, and the Pretender* (London, 1745), political tract; *The True Patriot* (5 November 1745–17 June 1746), essays; *Ovid's Art of Love Paraphrased* (London, 1747), reiss. as *The Lover's Assistant* (London, 1959), also in C. E. Jones, ed. (Los Angeles, 1961), a prose travesty; *The Jacobite's Journal* (5 December 1747–5 November 1748), essays; *The History of Tom Jones, a Foundling*, 6 vols. (London, 1749), repr. in Everyman's Library ed., with intro. by A. R. Humphreys, 2 vols. (London, 1963), R. P. C. Nutter, ed. (London, 1966), the last being considered the best annotated ed.; *A Charge Delivered to the Grand Jury* (London, 1749), legal work; *A True State of the Case of Bosavern Penlez* (London, 1749), legal work.

*An Enquiry into the Causes of the Late Increase of Robbers* (London, 1751), legal work; *Amelia*, 4 vols. (London, 1752), also in Everyman's Library ed., with intro. by A. R. Humphreys (London, 1962), Fielding's revised text first published in Murphy's ed. of *The Works*; *A Plan of the Universal Register Office* (London, 1752), essay; *Examples of the Interposition of Providence in the Detection and Punishment of Murder* (London, 1752), treatise; *A Proposal for Making an Effectual Provision for the Poor* (London, 1753), essay; *A Clear State of the Case of Elizabeth Canning* (London, 1753), legal work; *The Journal of a Voyage to Lisbon* (London, 1755), also in A. Dobson, ed. (London, 1892; 1907), J. H. Lobban, ed. (London, 1913), and H. E. Pagliaro, ed. (New York, 1963), a full ed. published in 1755 and suppressed, also repr. with *Jonathan Wild* in Everyman's Library (London–New York, 1932); *The Father's; or, The Good-Natur'd Man, a Comedy* (London, 1778); E. L. McAdam, "A New Letter from Fielding," in *Yale Review*, 28 (1949).

IV. BIOGRAPHICAL AND CRITICAL STUDIES. W. C. Hazlitt, *Lectures on the English Comic Writers* (London, 1819); Sir W. Scott, *Lives of the Novelists* (London, 1825); W. M. Thackeray, *The English Humourists of the Eighteenth Cen-*

*tury* (London, 1853); A. Dobson, *Fielding* (London, 1883), and *Eighteenth Century Vignettes* (1st ser., London, 1892; 2nd ser., 1896); Sir W. A. Raleigh, *The English Novel* (London, 1894); G. M. Godden, *Henry Fielding: A Memoir* (London, 1910); W. L. Cross, *The History of Henry Fielding*, 3 vols. (New Haven, Conn., 1910), the standard biography, with a valuable bibliography; A. Digeon, *Les Romans de Fielding* (Paris, 1923), also an English translation (London, 1925); F. T. Blanchard, *Fielding the Novelist* (New Haven, Conn., 1926), a study of Fielding's reputation; F. W. Bateson, *English Comic Drama 1700-50* (Oxford, 1929); E. M. Thornbury, *Henry Fielding's Theory of the Comic Prose Epic* (Madison, Wis., 1931); F. O. Bissell, *Fielding's Theory of the Novel* (Ithaca, N.Y., 1933); B. M. Jones, *Henry Fielding, Novelist and Magistrate* (London, 1933); G. Sherborn, "Fielding's *Amelia*: An Interpretation," in *Journal of English Literary History*, 3 (1936), an outstanding essay; K. C. Slagle, *The English Country Squire as Depicted in English Prose Fiction from 1740 to 1800* (Philadelphia, 1938).

W. R. Irwin, *The Making of Jonathan Wild* (New York, 1941); B. Willey, *The Eighteenth Century Background* (London, 1946); M. P. Willcocks, *A True Born Englishman: Being the Life of Henry Fielding* (London, 1947); E. Jenkins, *Henry Fielding* (London, 1947); J. A. Work, ed., "Henry Fielding, Christian Censor," in F. W. Hilles, ed., *The Age of Johnson: Essays Presented to Chauncey Brewster Tinker* (New Haven, Conn., 1949); F. H. Dudden, *Henry Fielding: His Life, Works, and Times*, 2 vols. (Oxford, 1952), useful on the social background; R. S. Crane, "The Concept of Plot and the Plot of *Tom Jones*," in Crane's *Critics and Criticism Ancient and Modern* (Chicago, 1952); A. R. Humphreys, *The Augustan World* (London, 1954); J. M. Murry, *Unprofessional Essays* (London, 1956), contains a masterly defense of Fielding against some modern denigrations; A. D. McKillop, *The Early Masters of English Fiction* (Lawrence, Kans., 1956); I. Watt, *The Rise of the Novel* (London, 1957); W. Empson, "Tom Jones," in *Kenyon Review*, 20 (1958); M. C. Battestin, *The Moral Basis of Fielding's Art: A Study of Joseph Andrews* (Middletown, Conn., 1959; repr., 1964); J. Loftis, *Comedy and Society from Congreve to Fielding* (Stanford, Calif., 1959).

W. C. Booth, *The Rhetoric of Fiction* (Chicago, 1961); M. Johnson, ed., *Fielding's Art of Fiction: Eleven Essays on "Shamela," "Joseph Andrews," and "Amelia"* (Philadelphia, 1961); H. K. Miller, *Essays on Fielding's Miscellanies* (Princeton, N.J., 1961); R. Paulson, ed., *Fielding: A Collection of Critical Essays* (Englewood Cliffs, N.J., 1962), an intro. followed by thirteen essays by modern critics, including those by Sherburn, Murry, and Empson mentioned above; S. Sacks, *Fiction and the Shape of Belief: A Study of Fielding* (Berkeley, Calif., 1964); A. E. Dyson, *The Crazy Fabric* (London, 1965); I. Ehrenpreis, *Fielding: Tom Jones* (London, 1965); A. Wright, *Henry Fielding: Mask and Feast* (London-Berkeley, Calif., 1965); R. D. Spector, ed., *Essays on the Eighteenth-Century Novel* (London, 1965); M. Golden, *Fielding's Moral Psychology* (Amherst, Mass., 1966); J. Preston, "The Ironic Mode: A Comparison of 'Jonathan Wild' and 'The Beggar's Opera,'" in *Essays in Criticism*, 16 (1966); M. Irwin, *Henry Fielding: The Tentative Realist* (Oxford, 1967); G. R. Levine, *Henry Fielding and The Dry Mock: A Study of the Techniques of Irony in His Early Works* (The Hague, 1967); R. Alter, *Fielding and the Nature of the Novel* (Cambridge, Mass., 1968); M. C. Battestin, ed., *Tom Jones: A Collection of Critical Essays* (Englewood Cliffs, N.J., 1968); G. W. Hatfield, *Henry Fielding and the Language of Irony* (Chicago, 1968); R. Paulson and T. Lockwood, eds., *Fielding: The Critical Heritage* (London, 1968); C. J. Rawson, *Henry Fielding* (London, 1968), contains short bibliography; H. Goldberg, *The Art of Joseph Andrews* (Chicago-London, 1969); J. Compton, ed., *Henry Fielding's "Tom Jones": A Casebook* (London, 1970); C. J. Rawson, *Henry Fielding and the Augustan Ideal Under Stress* (London, 1972).

# E. M. FORSTER
(1879-1970)

## Philip Gardner

*I*

IN addition to being one of the finest novelists of his generation—and of this century—E. M. Forster was also the longest-lived. When he died, on 8 June 1970, he was in his ninety-second year. His longevity assisted official recognition of the enduring quality of his work: in 1953 he was made a Companion of Honour, in 1968 appointed to the Order of Merit. In Forster's case, these honors seem also to be tokens of collective esteem for the man himself, revealed by his writings to be a liberal humanist, sensitive and tolerant (though not lacking a salutary astringency), concerned with the individual conscience and the individual heart.

But, as Forster said in a broadcast in 1940, "by the time writers have become eminent they have usually done their best work." Forster's novels, on which his major reputation rests, belong to the first half of his life, and *A Passage to India*, the last and best of them, appeared in 1924. Between then and 1951, the year of *Two Cheers for Democracy*, Forster continued to respond eloquently to the world about him, to the pressures of book, person, and event, but in the form of lectures, essays, and broadcasts rather than by means of the deeper and more wide-ranging transformations of fiction. His last two books, *The Hill of Devi* (1953) and *Marianne Thornton* (1956), though often fascinating and never less than interesting, are evocations of the past consisting largely of letters written many years earlier. They are in effect a return by Forster to his origins: to those Indian experiences that he had so memorably transmuted into fiction, and to the families from which he sprang and the great-aunt whose generous legacy made his career as a writer possible.

Part of Forster's reason for abandoning fiction (as to all appearances he had) was no doubt indicated in the answers he gave, always kindly, to those whose regret prompted them to question him about it. As he put it to me: the postwar world was not one in which his imagination felt at home—too much had changed. One such change, which he lamented in 1946, was the sudden expansion of Stevenage into a large new satellite town of London; it was near that erstwhile village—in the house that was the original for *Howards End* (1910)—that he had spent his happiest childhood years. But there was something else, as became clear after his death with the publication in 1971 of *Maurice* (written in 1914) and in 1972 of *The Life to Come*, of which seven stories had been written after *A Passage to India* (the last in 1958): not many, but enough to show that Forster had not in fact dried up. But the homosexual content of these stories and of *Maurice* understandably kept Forster from publishing them when the law was hostile and the public likely to be intolerant. Forster's recognition of this central aspect of himself seems eventually (for a sense of impatience with conventional human configurations shows itself as early as a diary entry of 1911) to have prevented his imagination from setting it aside in exchange for publication. His problem may perhaps be expressed by a sentence from *Aspects of the Novel* (1927): "It is a pity that Man cannot be at the same time impressive and truthful." If Forster could not publish fiction as a homosexual, he would not publish it as if he were not one.

The posthumous appearance of *Maurice* and *The Life to Come* was thus for the majority of Forster's readers like the shaking of a kaleidoscope, substituting new patterns for old, or at least altering their proportions and perspectives. Since then, the immense extensions to our knowledge of Forster made by the scrupulous Abinger editions of Oliver Stallybrass, by the unemphatic frankness of Forster's biographer P. N. Furbank, and not least by Forster's own manuscripts and papers, left by him to King's College, Cambridge, have provided a larger context than existed in Forster's lifetime within which the various elements present in his fiction may perhaps be brought into steady focus. This necessarily brief survey cannot hope to be more than an attempt to do so.

II

EDWARD MORGAN FORSTER was born on 1 January 1879 in a house in London near Marylebone Station: 6 Melcombe Place, Dorset Square. He chose as a writer to be known by his initials, but to family and friends he was always Morgan, his second Christian name preferred to the first possibly because that was intended to have been Henry—an early instance, as John Colmer has pointed out, of the phenomenon of "muddle" that often crops up in his novels. Another phenomenon there, sudden death, may have been suggested by the death from consumption of Forster's father in October 1880, at the early age of thirty-three.

The consequence of his father's death was that Forster's childhood was dominated by women: by his mother, Alice (Lily) Clara Whichelo, to whom he was very close and with whom he lived until her death in 1945; and to a lesser extent by his maternal grandmother (on whom he modeled one of his most likable women characters, Mrs. Honeychurch, in *A Room with a View*, 1908), and by his paternal great-aunt, Marianne Thornton. The latter on her death in 1887 left him £8,000, which provided for his education, his early travels, and his start as a writer. Forster may have derived much of his high-minded humanism from the Thorntons, influential nineteenth-century bankers and philanthropists with strong Evangelical connections. From his mother's family, poorer but more artistic than the Thorntons, and from his father, an architect, came the seeds of his creativity and the value he attached to form.

Forster was eventually to live in a house built by his father, West Hackhurst, near Abinger in Surrey, but this was not until 1925. In 1883 he and his mother moved into a former farmhouse, of faded red brick, set in the rolling Hertfordshire countryside near Stevenage; it can still be glimpsed to the left as one hurtles down the Great North Road from Baldock—photographs do not do justice to its charm. This house his mother named Rooksnest, after the tiny hamlet in which it lay, and in it and its adjacent meadow, orchard, and garden (with its tall wychelm tree) Forster enjoyed a happy only childhood.

His earliest surviving piece of writing is a detailed description, dating from 1894, that reveals Rooksnest as the blueprint for *Howards End*; to this Forster added in 1901 a note on his friendship with one of the garden boys there, "my beloved Ansell," the memory of whom he partly fictionalized in an early short story ("Ansell") and in *Maurice,* and whose name he borrowed for a character in *The Longest Journey* (1907).

By 1894 Forster's unregimented years in the country had ended. From 1890 to 1893 he had boarded at a small preparatory school in Eastbourne, where he was told that "school is the world in miniature." In 1893, the lease on Rooksnest having expired, he found himself uprooted into a suburban world of narrow-minded, snobbish gentility and insensitive heartiness to which he later gave the name "Sawston"—a choice that, though evocative of sawdust and "wise saws," seems unfair to the real village of that name near Cambridge. In plain terms, Forster and his mother went to live at Tonbridge in Kent, and later at Tunbridge Wells, so that he could attend Tonbridge School as a day boy. As his descriptions in *The Longest Journey* indicate (there is something of Forster in A. C. Varden, the boy whose ears are pulled, as well as in Rickie Elliot), he and the school—which "aimed at producing the average Englishman," characterized by Forster elsewhere as having a well-developed body, a fairly developed mind, and an undeveloped heart—did not suit each other. The first half of his time there was acutely unhappy, and he was glad enough to leave in the summer of 1897.

King's College, Cambridge, where he spent the next four years reading first classics and then history (he gained second-class honors in both), was an altogether different, open-minded world, a harmonious society of undergraduates and dons. It inspired in Forster "the only unforced loyalty I have ever experienced." With two of his teachers he formed close and lasting friendships: the energetic, unconventional Nathaniel Wedd, his tutor in classics, who first encouraged him to write; and Goldsworthy Lowes Dickinson, the political scientist, Hellenophile, and author of *The Greek View of Life,* whose biography Forster published in 1934. There, as well as in *The Longest Journey*, he recorded his love for Cambridge and his gratitude for its liberating influence. Among other things Cambridge revealed to Forster his homosexual nature: the Platonic relationship between Maurice Hall and Clive Durham is partly based on his love for his fellow Kingsman H. O. Meredith, through whom in his final year Forster was elected to the eminent Cambridge debating society known as the Apostles (at some of whose meetings homosexuality was freely discussed). It was to Meredith ("H.O.M.") that Forster dedicated *A Room with a View*, the first notes for which, made late in 1901, carried his initials in the list of projected characters.

Having graduated from Cambridge, Forster expanded his horizons further, adding gradually to the stock of raw material that, once fructified by his developing imagination, was to issue in short stories and his first three novels. Much of 1901 and 1902 he spent traveling in Italy, Sicily, and Greece, experiencing not only the curious, insular life of the English middle classes abroad (particularly at a pension in Florence), but also the unmediated freshness and challenge of Europe—Italian painting and opera, the historic hill towns of Tuscany (like San Gimignano, the original of Monteriano), and the Pan-haunted landscapes of the south that thrust straight into his mind two of his earliest short tales, "The Story of a Panic" and "The Road from Colonus." By the time, in 1904, that the itinerant Forster and his mother had found another English home (an unlovely house in Weybridge in which they lived until 1925), Forster had built up a confidence in his literary powers that helped to keep the conventionalities of Sawston at bay, a sense of larger intellectual and spiritual values to set against them, and a context of character and incident within which to embody the struggle between the two. It is to Forster the writer that I now turn.

### III

SINCE Forster began his career in fiction as a writer of short stories, it is convenient to mention them first, though they overlap with four prewar novels. His earliest published story, "Albergo Empedocle," a fine mixture of poetry and ironic observation, appeared in *Temple Bar* in 1903 and was inexplicably not seen again until after his death. The others, spanning 1902 to 1912, were published (or reprinted from the Liberal *Independent Review*, jointly edited by Dickinson and Wedd) in two widely separated collections, *The Celestial Omnibus* (1911) and *The Eternal Moment* (1928). As revealed by these volumes (Forster's homosexual stories, written from 1922 onward, are of a different type and are treated later), the short story was useful to Forster as a more poetic, more "fantastic" vehicle for his feelings and ideas than he allowed his novels to be.

In his use of fantasy, that "muddling up of the actual and the impossible" that permits a horse bus driven by Dante and Sir Thomas Browne to ply between Surbiton and Heaven, and a girl harassed by her conventional fiancé to turn into a tree ("Other Kingdom"), Forster was in part influenced by his admiration for Samuel Butler's *Erewhon* (1872). But what one feels more strongly is his own belief in the individual's need for freedom, whether attained through literature (an allegorical Heaven inaccessible to those who, like the culture-snob Mr. Bons, cannot abandon *baldanza*—self-importance) or expressed in the metaphors of mythology: the transformation of Daphne; the liberating influence of Pan ("The Story of a Panic" and "The Curate's Friend"); the song of the Siren, which may bring inspiration, total understanding, or death. For if most of Forster's early stories—short but not lightweight, their tone ranging from the whimsical to the mystical—celebrate various kinds of liberating encounter (such as that of Mr. Lucas in "Colonus"), they also intimate a sense that extinction, or separation from others (as with Harold's final insanity in "Albergo Empedocle"), may be the price that needs to be paid for illumination. The "supreme transfiguring event" that Mr. Lucas is deprived of by not staying at Colonus turns out to be death; and the "escape" of Eustace into the primitive energy of nature, at the end of "The Story of a Panic," is accompanied by the death of the Italian boy Gennaro, who in a sense dies to save him.

Less ambiguous, more straightforwardly powerful, is Forster's only exercise in science fiction, "The Machine Stops" (1909), a reaction against Wellsian views of progress. Here, against first an ironic and then a despairing vision of a civilization that has banished direct awareness of people and nature, Forster asserts his belief that "Man is the measure" and that his divine essences are his soul and body, "those five portals by which we can alone apprehend."

Stimulating as Forster's fantasies are ("Co-ordination" is the only one that falls flat), they are not entirely satisfactory. Their fables and metaphors, didactic in apparent intention, tend to outrun literal application, and it is sometimes hard to distinguish imaginative subtlety from obscurity. In my view, the best of the stories, the most austere and controlled, is "The Eternal Moment" (1905), whose investigation of the power of emotion to transfigure everyday experience takes place in a beautifully realized and entirely real world. Revisiting, with Miss Raby, the town of Vorta, in which the most important event of her life has occurred, we are in fact entering the world of Forster the novelist, who also, in his first novel, depicted the collision between England and Italy.

*Where Angels Fear to Tread* (1905) was referred to by Forster as "my novelette," but it is in fact an astonishingly accomplished first performance. It originated in a scrap of gossip Forster overheard on his travels in Italy, about an English tourist who contracted a misalliance with an Italian. Out of this he spun a complex plot that he handles with great skill; the crucial part of it concerns the attempts of a middle-class Sawston family, the Herritons, to gain possession of a baby, sole fruit of the hasty and short-lived union between their widowed daughter-in-law, Lilia, and the much younger Gino Carella, the son of a small-town Italian dentist.

The wish to be free of narrow Sawston respectability has made Lilia susceptible to the charm of Italy and led her to fall in love with a man who, though handsome and impetuous, takes a decidedly conventional, male-chauvinist view of his role as a husband. The breakdown of the marriage, from which Lilia pathetically and ineffectually tries to escape, is powerfully conveyed in chapter 4, at the end of which Lilia dies in giving birth to Gino's son. (It is remarkable how often the motif of remarriage, as well as that of sudden death, occurs in Forster's novels.)

The Herritons' attempt to get hold of the baby (their reasons, described in chapter 5, are a muddled mixture of rivalry, the need to appear respectably concerned, and a little genuine feeling for Irma, Lilia's daughter by Charles Herriton) ends in disaster. Though Philip Herriton and Caroline Abbott, a family friend, at last realize the extent of Gino's elemental pride in his fatherhood (splendidly rendered in chapter 7), the obsessional bigotry of Philip's sister, Harriet, causes her to steal the baby when Gino is out. The carriage in which she takes it to the station goes too fast in the darkness and overturns on the muddy road; the baby is thrown out and killed. If this seems melodramatic in a summary, it is not so in the novel. Nor is the following scene, in which Philip, taking the blame for Harriet's action on himself, has his arm (broken in the accident; Forster broke his own arm in Italy) painfully twisted by Gino and is methodically half-strangled. This sadistic vengefulness on Gino's part has been prepared for much earlier by his silent but terrifying reaction to Lilia's suggestion that she can keep him in order by denying him money. Now, at any rate, he has the nobler motive of grief. But there is more to the scene than Gino's paternal feelings. There is a sexual element in this physical confrontation in the dark room ("You are to do what you like with me, Gino," Philip says) that Forster recognized many years later; and the fundamentally sympathetic relationship between Philip and Gino adumbrates the closer one (emphasized by a closer family link) between Rickie and Stephen in *The Longest Journey*, a novel to which the words of Gino's friend Spiridione—"Sono poco simpatiche le donne" (Women are not very likable)— apply particularly well.

The scene ends with the reconciliation of the brothers-in-law, which is brought about by the intervention of Caroline Abbott, the first of those women in Forster's novels who are given not only intuition but an aura of the superhuman—both Philip and Gino in their different ways worship her. But she is a woman, not a goddess, revealing as she and Philip return with Harriet to England that she has all along been physically in love with Gino. Details of her earlier behavior, once puzzling, are suddenly made clear, and one again appreciates Forster's skill in preparing revelations. Philip, by now in love with her, is surprised by the news, but he has been so matured by the climactic events of the novel that he can silently rise above personal disappointment. As Caroline has helped him earlier, so he helps her now, and the novel ends on a note of "great friendliness," a phrase that, though chasteningly not "love" (Forster's supreme absolute), conveys the hard-earned value of personal relations. The novel also ends with protective tolerance toward those less able to respond to life's opportunities for self-enlargement, as Philip and Caroline return to their railway carriage "to close the windows lest the smuts get into Harriet's eyes," as they had done also when, some hundred pages earlier, she had opened the window to clear the air of "filthy foreigners" as the train passed through the San Gotthard tunnel on the outward journey.

The novel's title has some aptness: the Herritons' interference in Gino's love for his child, "something greater than right or wrong," is partly a case of fools rushing in. But Forster did not like the title, which was his publisher's choice. His own was "Monteriano," which emphasized the importance of the Italian town in which, by the end, "all the wonderful things had happened." It is in Monteriano that the narrow and joyless, if dutiful, Sawston conformities are confronted by something more vibrant, if more vulgar. This is not to say that Gino Carella is not a conformist too, in his own man-centered world, nor that Forster feels Italy to be perfect; but what Monteriano has is an instinctive sense of the importance of the emotions and of human relationships that Sawston either lacks or smothers. Mrs. Herriton's concealment from Irma of the fact that she has a "lital brother" contrasts with Gino's unthinking but more natural attempt to establish an awareness of him in the girl's mind by sending picture postcards.

The people of Monteriano are capable of wholehearted, unembarrassed enjoyment, displayed in chapter 6 at the performance of *Lucia di Lammermoor* (an opera Forster himself had heard in Italy). Music always plays a significant part in Forster's novels, and this scene is particularly rich. While for Harriet the opera is "culture," demanding a reverent silence, for the Italians it is life, to be actively entered into. And to Philip it brings "an access of joy" that "promised to be permanent," opening his heart to the later experiences that turn him from an ineffectual, priggish aesthete with a merely romantic, spectator's view of Italian history and art into a full human being.

For Forster, indeed, "the object of the book is the improvement of Philip," and Philip, though based in some details on Forster's Cambridge friend E. J. Dent (later a renowned musicologist), is more essentially a portrait of Forster himself, as the wry description at the start of chapter 5 suggests. There is a strong feeling in the book that action, even if it involves mistakes, is preferable to observation; and that mistakes can themselves lead to right action. Philip's "improvement," subtly charted and culminating in his painful confrontation with Gino, which Forster in 1905 called "sacramental," causes him to learn the truth of the text that he preaches so glibly to Lilia at the beginning: "Love and understand the Italians, for the people are more marvellous than the land." The novel begins and ends with a train journey, the first an unthinking departure, the second a sadder but wiser return.

Forster once said that he had learned from Jane Austen "the possibilities of domestic humour." Comedy is not the dominant mode of *Where Angels Fear to Tread*, though—a mixed approach to life being characteristic of Forster—neither is tragedy. But there is certainly a sharpness in his observation of the two contrasting, close-knit societies of Sawston and Monteriano, together with an overall crispness and economy of presentation, that Austen may well have taught him. In his first novel Forster is obviously writing about matters of great moment to him, but he seems to hold them at a distance: it is a minor masterpiece of artistic detachment. *The Longest Journey* is a fuller, heavier book, and a more pressingly personal one. It is neither neat nor altogether clear; nevertheless, in later life Forster described it not only as the novel "I am most glad to have written" but as the one in which "I have got nearer . . . to saying what I wanted than I have elsewhere."

It is appropriate at this point to suggest thematic concerns in terms of which Forster's novels may all be seen. Three seem particularly important: the individual's search for and achievement of self-realization; the attempt to harmonize different life-styles and schemes of value; and the individual life as set against something larger than itself—a country, the universe, the human urge for continuance or expansion. The first two concerns carry with them a sense of the primacy of personal relations and the inner life; the last sometimes involves the suspicion (as in the mind of Mrs. Moore in *A Passage to India*) that the individual may be of small account. All of them may be unified under one single heading, Forster's epigraph to *Howards End* (1910): "Only connect." His key characters are shown trying to connect with themselves, substituting intellectual and emotional honesty for catchwords and conventional stances; with other people (they may succeed or fail); and with some spiritual reality sensed behind and beyond human life. It is perhaps because *The Longest Journey* shows these connections being painfully sought by a character admitted by Forster to be very close to himself—Rickie Elliot—that Forster valued the book so highly. It is to a large extent a working out of his own inner tensions, a projection of conflicting aspects of himself into different characters and life-styles. It is also, next to *A Passage to India*, his most mystical book, and one in which symbolism reinforces plot.

The novel's title is taken from a passage in Percy Bysshe Shelley's poem "Epipsychidion" in which the poet contrasts his own preference, the love of mankind (or of a wide range of friends), with the habit of most people of taking one mate and thus narrowing their horizons. Marriage, for Shelley, is "the dreariest and the longest journey." Forster's novel is divided into three sections—Cambridge, Sawston, Wiltshire—that partly represent chronological stages in Rickie Elliot's clouded pilgrimage, in the increasingly uncongenial company of his wife, Agnes Pembroke, a woman older and less imaginative than himself, toward death and a vicarious immortality. More important, the three divisions represent three ways of life that Rickie is offered and in none of which he is completely at home. Each of these ways (two good, one bad) is epitomized by a character who is narrower yet tougher than Rickie and who survives: Stewart Ansell, Agnes Pembroke, and Stephen Wonham. Rickie, who seems to have the potential to comprehend them all, fails through some weakness (objectified in his lameness, but its source never made quite clear) to make much of his life. Through his attitudes, the novel seems to recommend the impulse toward tolerance, but through his experience, to suggest its dangers. This is surely what is meant by Rickie's "Primal Curse," which is "not the knowledge of good and evil, but the knowledge of good-and-evil."

Forster described *The Longest Journey* as being "about reality and the need for accepting it." For Rickie, an orphan devoted to the memory of his mother and detesting (rightly) that of his father, the problem of reality—of discovering what is really there and what is illusory—becomes bound up with discovering his own deepest nature and to whom he is related: specifically, with acknowledging his illegitimate half-brother, Stephen Wonham, who has been brought up in Wiltshire and stands for the life of simple emotion and instinct. Rickie's journey begins in Cambridge, which in the person of his uncompromising friend Stewart Ansell stands for the life of the mind, the search for the central reality. (Ansell was modeled on Forster's fellow Apostle, the argumentative, pipe-smoking Alfred Ainsworth.) To the clarity of this life Rickie is attracted but not suited, by reason of his romantic imagination (he writes short stories, one of them obviously Forster's own "Other Kingdom"). This leads him, unfortunately, to invest ordinary people with qualities they do not possess and to expect more of them than they can perform.

It is in such an idealizing spirit that Rickie comes to marry Agnes Pembroke (who for the rude but perceptive Ansell is "not really there") and enter the world of Sawston, the ambitious minor public school in which her brother Herbert has full scope for his meaningless activities of organization and regulation. Forster called the Pembrokes a "compensation device" for his unhappy school days, and the world of petty pomposity and hypocrisy that he builds around them is devastating and memorable. Nevertheless, he is too fair-minded entirely to condemn them ("For Agnes also has her tragedy": chapter 24), and one may see Rickie's spiritual ruin and sense of unreality at Sawston as the result partly of values false in themselves and partly of his simply marrying a woman who is as wrong for him as she had been right for Gerald Dawes, her athletic fiancé most improbably "broken up in the football match" in chapter 5.

Rickie's emancipation from Sawston is brought about by Ansell. In chapter 1 Ansell has been described drawing squares inside circles ad infinitum: reality is "the one in the middle of everything." This image becomes a symbol in chapter 13, when the fact that Rickie has a half-brother is gradually revealed to him by his paternal aunt, the clever but cold Mrs. Failing, as they walk through the two concentric circles of "Cadbury Rings" (Figsbury Rings, an Iron Age earthwork near Salisbury). That Stephen is his half-brother dawns on Rickie just as they reach the central tree; but this basic "real thing" immediately changes for Rickie into an image of his hated father, whose illegitimate son he assumes Stephen to be. Partly because of this, partly because Agnes' concern for respectability is stronger than his desire for truth, Rickie conceals the relationship (of which Stephen at this point is unaware) for two years. But then Stephen is thrown out of Cadover, Mrs. Failing's home; and Ansell, happening to meet him and learning his story (this is less merely coincidental than it seems), determines that the truth shall be heard, not only by Rickie but by a whole dining hall full of Sawston boys. (We believe in this scene because of its theatrical appropriateness rather than its likelihood; Rickie's complacency badly needs shaking up by now.) In the process Rickie learns something he has not bargained for: Stephen is the son of his idolized mother. The reader, also kept in ignorance, is enlightened by the flashback of chapter 29, whereas Rickie's reaction—the shock to his rather priggish illusions—is conveyed by the beautiful extended metaphor of chapter 28: the soul's "coinage," its bankruptcies, its chances of recovery.

But although in the final section Rickie leaves his false life with Agnes and sees that Sawston values had "ignored personal contest, personal truces, personal love," such as he now feels in relation to Stephen, he still errs by idealizing: Stephen is to him not simply a man, whose virtues and faults (he is prone to drunkenness) are alike earthy, but the reborn image of his mother, "a symbol for the vanished past." On his ride through Wiltshire with Stephen he feels "confirmed by the earth" (sufficiently to reject Mrs. Failing's assertion of the majesty of conventions), but his lately gained sense of reality is so precarious that it cannot withstand the discovery that Stephen, a "hero," has broken his promise and got drunk. A second time (Agnes was the first) he is bankrupted of his belief in the reality of people, and though one is sorry for his weakness, one also sympathizes with the "chill of disgust" that passes over Leighton, Mrs. Failing's manservant and Stephen's less sensitive friend. Finding Stephen sprawled over the level crossing (whose dangerousness has been mentioned many times in the novel), Rickie "wearily" pulls him to safety but is unable to save himself. Nor, one feels, does he wish to.

Yet the conclusion of this confused but moving book (which may in crude terms be said to show the survival of the fittest, and perhaps is Forster's burning in effigy of flaws in himself) is not pessimistic. Overlaid on Rickie's pathetic story of failure—which rises, however "wearily," to self-sacrifice at the end—is a mystical sense of continuance. Not only does Rickie achieve some posthumous reputation with his short stories; it is as if, in the last few paragraphs, some of his sensitivity passes into the stronger and now maturer Stephen, through whom and through whose small daughter, "to whom he had given the name of their mother," he gains a portion of immortality.

The last three paragraphs of *The Longest Journey*, which crystallize Forster's feeling for the Wiltshire landscape whose endurance underlies the human life of the novel, are among the most beautiful in his work. Their poignant tranquillity is foreshadowed by the last paragraph of chapter 33, in which Rickie and Stephen launch a burning paper boat into a stream. It is a brilliant poetic symbol of their difference and their unity, and perhaps the high point of the novel:

The paper caught fire from the match, and spread into a rose of flame. "Now gently with me," said Stephen and they laid it flower-like on the stream. Gravel and tremulous weeds leapt into sight, and then the flower sailed into deep water, and up leapt the two arches of a bridge. "It'll strike!" they cried; "no, it won't; it's chosen the left," and one arch became a fairy tunnel, dropping diamonds. Then it vanished for Rickie; but Stephen, who knelt in the water, declared that it was still afloat, far through the arch, burning as if it would burn for ever.

*A Room with a View* (which Forster unjustly called "slight, unambitious and uninteresting") is a simpler and sunnier book, beginning in Florence with the discovery of love and, after an interval of "muddle," ending there with what promises to be a happy marriage. Forster's third published novel, it was in fact the first he started, and it took its origin from his experiences, in 1901, at a boardinghouse in Florence very like the Pension Bertolini in the novel. It progressed through two drafts, the first a rather pedestrian notation of tourist manners and Italian art called "Lucy"; the second, begun at the end of 1903, a more lively and more emotional story called "New Lucy," which ended with George Emerson being killed by a falling tree while cycling to meet Lucy at Summer Street and elope with her. (This version also contains a scene in which the liberal-minded parson, Mr. Beebe, talks to George Emerson at night in a wood and calls him "irresistible"; there is a homosexual tinge in this that may provide an alternative explanation to that of the published novel for Mr. Beebe's sudden hostility when he learns that Lucy loves George.)

Though Forster rejected his earlier unhappy ending, *A Room with a View* by no means lacks seriousness. Mostly deft and light in its handling, and blending in its social comedy the spirit of Jane Austen and that of George Meredith, it is committed no less than *The Longest Journey* and *Where Angels Fear to Tread* to the idea that life is a battleground of conflicting impulses, with naturalness, truth, and "greatness" as the prizes to be gained by right choices and lost by wrong ones. As Caroline Abbott says to Philip Herriton: "There's never any knowing . . . which of our actions, which of our idlenesses, won't have things hanging on it for ever." The conflict in *A Room with a View* is summed up in its title, which from the start of Lucy Honeychurch's acquaintance with Italy and with the unconventionally truthful Emersons takes on symbolic overtones. Rooms stand for social conventions, deadening by themselves; views for naturalness, freedom, whatever makes it possible for the spirit to breathe and expand. Like *Where Angels Fear to Tread*, *A Room with a View* is about the improvement of its protagonist, and it too uses Italy ("the eternal league of Italy with youth") as the place where that improvement can be begun. Lucy, though subject to the conventional restraints of her prim spinster chaperone,

Charlotte Bartlett, has come to Italy not from Sawston but from a house with the promising name Windy Corner and a wide view of the Weald of Sussex. She has already shown to one sympathetic observer, the clergyman Mr. Beebe, the capacity for greatness in her playing of Beethoven. It is his hopeful prophecy that the novel fulfills, though his belief in celibacy cannot tolerate the form of its fulfillment: "If Miss Honeychurch ever takes to live as she plays, it will be very exciting."

She takes a long time to do so, even though it is soon apparent to the reader that she responds instinctively to the melancholy, lower-class George Emerson, who is awkward of speech but physically direct and eloquent. The first important encounter comes about as a result of a stabbing in the Piazza Signoria, when Lucy faints and George holds her in his arms; it is a tacit assertion of youth and life in the face of death. The second takes place on a hillside covered with violets and with a panoramic view of Florence and the Arno Valley: here George, the "good man" to whom the percipient Italian cab driver has directed her, suddenly kisses her—the lyrical climax to a delightful chapter whose message is that spring in nature and spring in man are the same. But the spell is broken by Charlotte Bartlett, "brown against the view," and before Lucy has had time to respond, Charlotte's propriety and Lucy's own unwillingness to face her feelings have created "a shame-faced world of precautions and barriers" in which good form triumphs over the stirrings of love.

Part II, set in Lucy's English village, where Forster gradually contrives the reassembly of most of the pension cast, shows Lucy's slow realization—in all senses—of what Italy and George Emerson have so simply offered her. Her path to love, freedom, and truth (which for Forster are all bound up together) is the more tortuous since she must first perceive the imperfections of Cecil Vyse, the supercilious aesthete to whom in her unadmitted retreat from George she has become engaged. It is plain to the reader that George's criticisms of Cecil lead Lucy to reject him, and equally plain that Cecil, essentially ascetic, is less physically attractive to Lucy than George, whom she encounters after the naked bathing scene in chapter 12, "barefoot, barechested, radiant and personable"; but, tangled in a web of petty lies, social embarrassment, and sexual inhibition, Lucy still refuses to admit that she loves George, and for a time joins what Forster, in one of those judgment-passing asides characteristic of his work, calls "the armies of the benighted, who follow neither the heart nor the brain" and have "sinned against passion and truth." It is the intuitive penetration and passionate honesty of old Mr. Emerson —whose ideas resemble those of Samuel Butler— that finally burn through Lucy's conventional armor, equip her instead with "courage and love," and save her from the fate of such as Charlotte Bartlett. The novel ends with Lucy and George united and back in Florence, looking out of their room at the view and listening to "the river, bearing down the snows of winter into the Mediterranean." They have gained happiness, but there is no doubt that it has been touch and go.

Shortly before *A Room with a View* was published, Forster wrote to Nathaniel Wedd that he was "getting much more interested in public affairs"; at the end of 1908 he repeated the sentiment in his diary. Hitherto his novels had mostly concerned themselves with the individual's inner life and its development; the pretensions of the great world offered little of which Forster could approve. But in *Howards End,* whose appearance established Forster's reputation with a larger public, he made a concerted effort to determine whether the life of feeling and imagination could run in double harness with the life of business, action, and convention. Behind the book lies a desire to "see life steadily and see it whole," and with this in mind Forster expands his canvas to include the poor clerk Leonard Bast as well as two contrasting middle-class families, the intellectual and artistic Schlegels and the commercial Wilcoxes, and wills himself to perceive merit in an unimaginative world that had seemed, in *The Longest Journey,* almost wholly uncongenial.

By *Howards End* Forster clearly thought of himself as the creator of a fictional empire, since the reader's attention is directed to other of his novels. In chapter 13 Tibby Schlegel's lack of interest in a profession is discussed in terms of a "weedy" Mr. Vyse and an admirably industrious Mr. Pembroke; and chapter 9 mentions a piano-playing Miss Quested, who will play a more important part in *A Passage to India.*

*Howards End* is a consciously "big" book, with a wide range of incidents and interests (one of these, the position of women, is carried over from *A Room with a View*). The unfolding of its action is leisurely, too complex to summarize, and covers a longer period of time than that of any other Forster novel except

*Maurice*; indeed, the passing of time, and the concomitant gradual encroachment of London, "a tract of quivering grey," on the countryside around, is an important aspect of it. Its two major elements, however, and those on which the story turns, are indicated by the title and the epigraph. Howards End, the house in Hertfordshire that Forster based down to the smallest detail on Rooksnest, has an indefinable numinous quality that transcends not only the materialism of the Wilcoxes (father and children) but the intellectualism of the Schlegels. Like its owner, the retiring, intuitive Mrs. Wilcox, it represents permanence, suggests the "unseen," and is the spiritual touchstone of the novel. Here the story begins, with the impressionable Helen Schlegel visiting and falling briefly in love with Paul Wilcox; here it ends, with Margaret Schlegel at last in possession of the home Mrs. Wilcox had left her so many chapters before, only to be disregarded by her "sensible" family. The passage in chapter 11 where her wishes are set aside is perhaps Forster's finest authorial judgment: with scrupulous fairness he marshals the arguments in favor of the Wilcoxes' action, then adds with steely finality the one that surely outweighs them: "They did neglect a personal appeal. The woman who had died did say to them, 'Do this,' and they answered, 'We will not.'"

Howards End, like Wiltshire in *The Longest Journey*, is Forster's symbol of England, an immemorial rural England resisting the "red rust" of advancing suburbia and opposed to the impersonal flux of London, where "month by month things were stepping livelier, but to what goal? The population still rose, but what was the quality of the men born?" England is symbolized also by Oniton Grange, remote at the western edge of Shropshire; another house loved by Margaret, it means nothing to its casual Wilcox owners and they mean nothing to it: "It is not their ghosts that sigh among the alders at evening." In large part, *Howards End* is a fair-minded novelist's attempt to answer, through the detailed texture of representative human lives, the question about England that his poetic alter ego poses at the end of chapter 19, as Helen Schlegel watches the sunset from the downs between Swanage and Poole Harbour. There is perhaps rather too much of a catch in his voice, but his words are moving nonetheless:

England was alive, throbbing through all her estuaries, crying for joy through the mouths of all her gulls, and the north wind, with contrary motion, blew stronger against her rising seas. What did it mean? For what end are her fair complexities, her changes of soil, her sinuous coast? Does she belong to those who have moulded her and made her feared by other lands, or to those who have added nothing to her power, but have somehow seen her, seen the whole island at once, lying as a jewel in a silver sea, sailing as a ship of souls, with all the brave world's fleet accompanying her towards eternity?

The epigraph, "Only connect . . . ," is a quotation from the novel itself, and appears in its full form in chapter 22: "Only connect the prose and passion, and both will be exalted, and human love will be seen at its height." The idea of "connection" recurs throughout the novel; its meaning ranges from being honest with oneself (as by avoiding the hypocrisy of the sexual "double standard," which Mr. Wilcox in the climactic scene between himself and Margaret in chapter 38 shows himself unable to do), to bringing together in one partnership the Wilcox outer life of business, practicality, and imperialism and the Schlegel inner life of culture, personal relations, and individual responsibility. Forster's conscious urge toward this imagined wholeness (which stems partly from the honest liberal intellectual's refusal to spurn the practical world in which he functions, and partly from loss of nerve, the fear that, by themselves, "personal relations lead to sloppiness in the end") is embodied in Margaret Schlegel, the elder of the two sisters—she is twenty-nine when the novel begins, which was Forster's age when he started to write it. But it is hard to feel either that her relationship with Henry Wilcox succeeds in building a "rainbow bridge" or that the love that keeps it going is more than a requirement of plot and theme. Henry is a cut above his brusque and hidebound son, Charles, but Margaret is too clear-sighted not to notice his lack of imagination, his conventionality of response, his lapses from honesty. In his depiction of their relationship Forster's instincts pull strongly against his intentions, and the reader resists Margaret's over-tolerant progress toward what seems a decidedly arranged marriage.

Margaret's aim is worthwhile, certainly, and Margaret herself is an admirable character, sensitive as well as reasonable. But it is her younger, prettier, and more impulsive sister, Helen, whom the reader may find more sympathetic. If Margaret makes one think of a less vulnerable Rickie, Helen is something of a less single-minded Ansell. It is she who first responds to the apparent masculine strength of the

Wilcoxes, who are "keen on all games" and "put everything to use"; but she soon discovers, behind their life of "telegrams and anger," no resources for dealing with emotion, and regains her conviction that only personal relations matter. Where they are missing, as she is reminded in chapter 5, listening in the Queen's Hall to the third movement of Beethoven's Fifth Symphony, there is only "panic and emptiness."

Leonard Bast, who enters the novel at this point as an insignificant but aspiring clerk who goes to concerts and reads "improving" authors like Ruskin (meanwhile his flat is dark, as well as stuffy), grows in importance and stature as the novel proceeds. Forster describes his life with tartness yet compassion: he had spent some time teaching in London at the Working Men's College. From being a deserving case taken up by the liberal Miss Schlegel, he becomes vital not only to the plot but to the novel's theme of connection. Leonard loses his job as an indirect result of bad advice from Henry Wilcox; and Helen's simultaneous failure to right matters and her discovery that Leonard's older wife, Jacky, was once Wilcox's mistress cause her to give herself to Leonard. (Some critics have found this unconvincing; on the basis of the descriptions in chapters 40 and 41, I disagree.) Out of that brief half-hour of love at Oniton come Helen's pregnancy (a revelation Forster dramatically withholds, while Helen is absent in Germany); Margaret's realization of the hollowness of her marriage; the moving reunion of the sisters at Howards End, despite the self-righteous and "unconnecting" prohibition of Henry Wilcox; and the death of Leonard himself, through heart disease and Charles Wilcox's notions of chivalrous behavior.

It is not for nothing, however, that Leonard's death ("They laid Leonard, who was dead, on the gravel; Helen poured water over him") has a likeness to baptismal rebirth. Though Margaret's kindness keeps her with Henry, who needs her support now that his son has been imprisoned by a law "made in his own image," all her efforts have failed to make a bridge between her world and that of her husband. Howards End is hers, belatedly, but it is to the illegitimate child of Leonard and Helen—the fruit of impulse, the "connection" of middle-class culture and working-class aspiration—that it will pass, thus in a sense restoring the urban, uprooted Leonard to the land from which his agricultural forebears sprang. There is no facile optimism in Forster's pastoral ending; the "shiver" of Margaret and the "infectious joy" of Helen are too closely juxtaposed for that. But the inner life has won a kind of victory, and what Forster many years later called "the possession of England" has been achieved by those who have deserved it.

*Howards End* is a remarkable piece of work and enlarges the area of contemporary life on which Forster comments (making his heroines half-German seems partly a device allowing him to use impressions gathered while in Pomerania in 1905, as tutor to the daughters of the countess von Arnim, the Elizabeth of *Elizabeth and Her German Garden*). But it is not entirely characteristic of him, this liberal intellectual's excursion (as he later felt it to be) into the realistic, essentially metropolitan world of Galsworthy and Wells; at times the novel moves heavily, at times Forster's addresses to the reader lack his usual authority and aplomb (in the last paragraph of chapter 2, for instance), and it is perhaps symptomatic that he chooses to educate Tibby Schlegel not at his own Cambridge but at Oxford, which "wants its inmates to love it rather than to love one another." Where the novel is Forsterian is in its defense of the inner life, its preference of the country to the city, its transcendence of materialism (the Wilcox world of motorcars and money) by an awareness of greater values—all that is implied by Helen Schlegel's cryptic and visionary phrase, "Death destroys a man; the idea of Death saves him."

In 1911 Forster started a new novel that he called "Arctic Summer." (The title refers to the aim of one of its protagonists, a successful civil servant named Martin Whitby, who wants a "new era . . . in which there will be time to get something really important done.") It was again intended to contrast, and apparently to bring together, two human types, the civilized intellectual and, this time, the romantic, chivalrous "man of instinct," represented by a fair-haired young officer, Clesant March. Forster later salvaged this name for his stories "Dr. Woolacott" and "The Other Boat"; but the novel, which opened promisingly with a vivid scene at Basle station and proceeded to Italy, was abandoned in 1912 because he "had not settled what was going to happen."

In October 1912 Forster set off on the first of his two visits to India. He stayed for six months and traveled widely: to Aligarh to see his Muslim friend Syed Ross Masood, whom he had first met in Weybridge in 1906, tutored for Oxford entrance, and fallen in love with; to the native state of Dewas

Senior near Indore, where his Cambridge friend Malcolm Darling was tutor to the young maharajah; to Bankipore in Bengal (the original of Chandrapore) and the nearby Barabar Caves. On this visit he drafted the first seven chapters of *A Passage to India* and parts of the novel up to the outing to the Marabar Caves; he knew that something important was to happen there but (as with "Arctic Summer") not yet what. But this, at least, eventually became clear, some ten years later.

Meanwhile, a visit that Forster paid in September 1913 to the sixty-year-old thinker Edward Carpenter realized in him the wish and the ability to write directly about homosexuality. Carpenter (himself a homosexual who shared his "simple life" with a young working-class man) had written courageously on sexual matters, and in his essay "The Intermediate Sex" there is a description of the male homosexual that fits Forster well enough: he "tends to be of a gentle, emotional disposition," and his mind "is generally intuitive and instinctive in its perceptions, with more or less of artistic feeling." To this feminine temperament, expressed indirectly in the heterosexual framework of his conventional novels, may be credited both his heroes' response to other men (even Rickie's marriage to Agnes seems partly a vicarious possession of Gerald) and his empathy toward his heroines. It is not too fanciful to see in the sisterly tenderness of Helen and Margaret (chapters 37 and 40 of *Howards End*) another kind of love relationship, and in their embattled unity against Wilcox maleness a declaration by their creator. One may also sense in Margaret's defense of "eternal differences" (chapter 14) a meaning beyond the immediate context, an increasing pressure within Forster himself: "people are far more different than is pretended. All over the world men and women are worrying because they cannot develop as they are supposed to develop. Here and there they have the matter out, and it comforts them." It was in *Maurice*, begun immediately after his visit to Carpenter and finished in July 1914, that Forster "had the matter out," though factors external and personal delayed the publication of his fictional catharsis until after his death.

The four parts into which *Maurice* is symmetrically divided can be considered virtually as two, each dealing with one of Maurice's relationships: his intense but Platonic one with his fellow undergraduate Clive Durham, and his frankly physical one with the gamekeeper Alec Scudder. The two large sections are related by motifs; in each occurs the yearning invocation "Come!" and both relationships reach fulfillment by means of contrasted entries at windows, Maurice leaping up to Clive's, Alec climbing into Maurice's. But counterpointed against the chronological four-part or two-part structure of the novel—which charts Maurice's "improvement" through self-realization—is another, thematic, one, tripartite and akin to that of *The Longest Journey*: one may call it "Sawston, Cambridge, Wiltshire." Though, as a distancing device, Forster makes Maurice in some externals unlike himself—he is the son of a stockbroker, has sisters, is fairly good at games, and is not an intellectual—Maurice's discoveries are Forster's and give him the opportunity to present the plight of the homosexual in an unsympathetic and largely uncomprehending world: the portraits of Dr. Barry, Dr. Lasker-Jones, and the clergyman, Mr. Borenius, are notable additions to his gallery of minor characters. Nor, while rendering sympathetically Maurice's loneliness and his search for the friend of his boyhood dream, does Forster's honesty fail to record the seamier side of his experience, in the earlier chapters of part III.

Maurice's journey begins in the pleasant but clouded world of suburbia—mother-dominated home, preparatory school (at the seaside, like Forster's), public school (here called Sunnington) —where he has fitful intimations of his homosexual nature, inherited from his father. He moves on to Cambridge, where his mind is progressively liberated: by the perception that talk can matter (Risley, the garrulous Trinity B.A., is based on Lytton Strachey), by music (Tchaikovsky's "Pathetic" Symphony, which recurs as an example of homosexual composition), by the reading of Plato's *Symposium*, and finally by the realization that he returns the love of the more intellectual Clive Durham. Their relationship is a mixture of tenderness, high-minded restraint, and youthful ragging, its perfection beautifully caught in chapter 13, the motorcycle excursion that ends in the fens beyond Ely, and is both ordinary and outside time and society. But for Clive, inheritor of a country estate, homosexuality proves only a phase, and his terse announcement from Greece, "Against my will I have become normal," plunges Maurice into "the abyss where he had wandered as a boy." Only an iron effort of will that involves a total separation of his public and his private personalities keeps him going.

It is from Penge, Clive's estate "on the Wiltshire

and Somerset border," that Maurice's salvation eventually comes, in the form of Alec Scudder, an under-gamekeeper. Scudder is at first a shadowy, barely articulate figure, a servant in a middle-class world; but by a number of slight touches (some literal) Forster makes credible his intuitive response to Maurice's need, which is now physical as well as emotional. But it is not until class differences and class mistrust have been fully confronted (in the tense British Museum scene, extensively revised in 1932, and the chapter following, added then) that a real relationship between two people is established—one which, after Alec has decided not to sail for Argentina on the *Normannia*, can survive only if he and Maurice drop out of stratified society and take like outlaws to "the greenwood." The final scene, in which Maurice confronts Clive and then seems almost to vanish poetically into air, is thus a declaration both of sexual and of social nonconformity, of ideal freedom, the world well lost for love; an ending that, in the words of Edward Carpenter, "though improbable is not impossible." (The 1914 text contained an epilogue, removed by 1932, in which Maurice's sister Kitty comes across her brother and Alec working as woodcutters somewhere in Yorkshire—a life of "connection" that "combined daily work with love." It was the sort of life Carpenter had himself achieved on his farm near Sheffield.)

Though it lacks the complexity and symbolism of other Forster novels (its simple forward thrust gives it some likeness to *A Room with a View*), and though it chooses to emphasize the sexual psychology of its hero above other possible aspects of his life, *Maurice* is not thinly disguised autobiography or wish fulfillment but a created fictional world. Forster's style, whether in lively or in somber mood, is admirably terse, adapted both to express Maurice's character and to keep a difficult subject under control. If the occasional phrase embarrasses, one needs to remember that Forster was breaking new ground, an incidental indication of his difficulties being given in chapter 16: "No convention settled what was poetic, what absurd." But in general the novel's presentation of the many aspects of homosexuality is illuminating and moving.

Forster spent most of World War I (from late 1915 to early 1919) in Alexandria, collecting information from the wounded as a search officer for the Red Cross. He also contributed articles to the *Egyptian Mail* under the pen name Pharos (the famous lighthouse of ancient Alexandria), compiled a very comprehensive *History and Guide* that was published there in 1922, and wrote a number of essays on aspects of Alexandria, classical and modern, that appeared in England in 1923 under the title *Pharos and Pharillon*. Among them is one on the Alexandrian poet C. P. Cavafy, whose work Forster consistently championed; others reveal an interest in byways of the early Christian church and an awareness of Alexandria as a historic meeting point of West and East.

In 1921 Forster revisited India, acting for six months as private secretary to the maharajah of Dewas Senior. This fascinating experience (fully documented in 1953 in *The Hill of Devi*) gave Forster the material for the final section of *A Passage to India*, but he was able to continue work on the book only when he had returned from the country it "purported to describe," and it was completed with difficulty and self-doubt.

*A Passage to India* was eventually published in 1924, to a chorus of praise that may have allayed Forster's worries about its adequacy as a picture of the country. Even for an Anglo-Indian critic, who pointed out technical inaccuracy in the trial scene and in the portrayal of the collector and other officials, there was no lack of emotional verisimilitude (it should be said that, in political terms, the novel—in the words of K. Natwar-Singh—"depicts a pre-1914 India"). Though much of its material is disturbing, Forster's handling of it is not, and the novel has an impressive air both of authority and of truth.

The comments of T. E. Lawrence, comparing it with his own *Seven Pillars of Wisdom*, are particularly illuminating: "If excellence of materials meant anything, my book would have been as good as yours: but it stinks of me: whereas yours is universal: the bitter hopeless picture a cloud might have painted, of man in India." The last three words, and their juxtaposition, are significant. Forster's novels have always dealt with people, and *A Passage to India* does so too, finding in the misunderstandings and rapprochements of English and Indians both a new and special example of human relationships and a final metaphor for their general difficulty. They have also presented human development, people reexamining themselves in relation to a country or the sense of one, and here India takes the place of an invigorating Italy or a quietly enduring England. But in *A Passage to India* the variety of races and types—English, Anglo-Indian, Indian (Moslem and

Hindu)—is so much wider that "men" become "man"; and the country is so much bigger, so much more deeply challenging in its diverse religions and manifestations of the unseen, so baffling a mixture of mystery and muddle, that it comes to represent the universe itself, against which man's values seem so uncertain and man's activities so trivial.

It is this contrast that makes *A Passage to India* such a profound and poignant book: despite the pessimism voiced by (and through) Mrs. Moore, people matter in it, but nothing could be less true than D. H. Lawrence's statement that Forster here sees "people, people and nothing but people." The novel's detachment is twin to its universality and is demonstrated in two specific differences from its predecessors: it contains virtually no authorial asides, no glosses on its characters' behavior, which is left to explain itself; and it begins (as do its second and third sections) not with people talking but with a description of the context in which they exist: city and sky; dry hills and caves; God. Without denigrating the earlier novels, one may say of Forster in *A Passage to India* what he says in chapter 26 about the symbolically named Adela Quested, the transplanted denizen of the cultured London of *Howards End*: "she was no longer examining life, but being examined by it."

*A Passage to India* is a realistic and a symbolic novel, of such rich and even texture, so successfully doing so many things at once, that it is difficult to separate its varied strands without falsifying the total impression it gives. Out of the confrontation between the English and India, and the simple but gripping plot that dramatizes it, Forster makes his most comprehensive statement of human possibilities and limitations. The drama is played out against a larger, and in some sense divine, background that is suggested by the book's division into three sections named after vital elements of the Indian experience: "Mosque," "Caves," "Temple." The outer sections represent the Moslem world of Dr. Aziz and the Hindu world of Professor Godbole respectively, and are broadly positive in tone. But the central one, which in terms of action displays the worst attitudes of the British Raj and sets them against the open mistrust and dislike of the Indian governed, represents the enigmatic and frightening side of spiritual experience, the sense of chaos and nothingness whose effects spill over and make the conclusion of the novel equivocal. The sections are also, however, appropriate seasons of the year, states of mind, and stages in an evolving pattern: coolness, rationality, the search for understanding; heat and dryness, climactic hysteria, loss of faith, hostility, fragmentation; rain, rebirth, a kind of reconciliation. (The movement from "Caves" to "Temple" suggests a possible link between Forster's novel and T. S. Eliot's *The Waste Land*, published two years earlier.)

"Mosque" is concerned with building up a scene, with human interaction, and with certain particular relationships, rather than with anything as definite as plot. But its splendid opening chapter (one of Forster's best pieces of writing) presents a clear indication of the novel's scope, describing first the two worlds of Chandrapore—shapeless Indian town and neat British civil station—linked only by the "overarching sky"; and ending, with apparent casualness yet a touch of foreboding, with a mention of the distant "fists and fingers" of the Marabar Hills, "containing the extraordinary caves." The adjective (which recurs like a leitmotif in chapters 12 and 32) has its original, literal force in this novel: the caves—outside nature, superhuman—are the ground where the ordinary, the familiar, the positive will be tested and strained. While they wait, Forster with a multitude of small details and lively touches shows the failure of "official" relations between British and Indians at Mr. Turton's "bridge party" (Forster does not like the group mentality of Anglo-India—especially that of the memsahibs—but he is by no means as blindly hostile to it as is sometimes supposed), and the more successful attempts at communication between individuals. The most important of these is between the mild and humane principal of the Government College, Cyril Fielding (whose response in chapter 32 to Venice's "beauty of form" makes him seem an older Martin Whitby), and the volatile, poetic Moslem doctor, Aziz, whose impetuosity is brilliantly rendered by the opening of chapter 2. Aziz also establishes an instinctive relationship, through their meeting in the mosque, with Mrs. Moore, who believes in goodwill and, in her intuitive capacity, resembles Mrs. Wilcox. It is through her that the religious uneasiness of the novel is transmitted, first by her puzzlement when the Christian "God is love" is faced by Godbole's Hindu god who "refuses" or "neglects to come," then through her terrifying experience of "panic and emptiness" in the Marabar Caves.

Here, on the expedition planned by Aziz to cement his friendship with the two visiting English ladies, things fall apart. The introductory chapter of

"Caves" contains a perfect natural symbol for attempted union (with fellow man, or perhaps with God) in its description of the striking of a match in the polished interior chamber: "Immediately another flame rises in the depths of the rock and moves towards the surface like an imprisoned spirit. . . . The two flames approach and strive to unite, but cannot, because one of them breathes air, the other stone."

But on Adela and Mrs. Moore the caves (sacred places in India) have a totally malign effect, destructive of human friendship and of sustaining faith. Their claustrophobic atmosphere causes the former to imagine she has been assaulted by Aziz (she has not, but what has happened cannot be dismissed by the easy term "hallucination") and sets off all the latent hostility of rulers and ruled, its last reverberations—after the trial—even upsetting the mutual trust and generosity of Aziz and Fielding. For Mrs. Moore it is the cave's dull, monotonous echo, "bououm" or "ou-boum," that generates horror: "It had managed to murmur, 'Pathos, piety, courage—they exist, but are identical, and so is filth. Everything exists, nothing has value.'" The echo, it is important to notice, is heard by Mrs. Moore "at a time when she chanced to be fatigued," and so its message of futility and blankness can hardly be taken as Forster's final vision of life, particularly in view of the end of chapter 23; but its pessimism lurks at the edges of human endeavor in this novel. It is present in Adela's statement to Fielding, in chapter 29, that "all these personal relations we try to live by are temporary"; and (though here the effect is ironic and humbling rather than disillusioning) in Forster's use, as a frame for the fiasco of the trial scene, of the untouchable punkah-wallah, to whom nothing has any meaning and who, when it is all over, continues "to pull the cord of his punkah, to gaze at the empty dais and the overturned special chairs, and rhythmically to agitate the clouds of descending dust."

"Temple," the mystical concluding section—in which the quality of Forster's writing, as if borne on some hidden current of understanding, touches what he called "prophecy"—offers a knitting-together, a reconciliation, as well as the "scene of separation" that Forster had recommended in 1906, in a lecture entitled "Pessimism in Literature," as the only close to a novel that offered "rest with honour." Fielding and Aziz come together again not in British India but in the native state of Mau (actually Dewas Senior), whose function in the novel resembles that of Oniton in *Howards End*: a place enduring "somewhere else," where something mysterious and good goes on. They compose their differences, the misunderstanding about Adela (whom Aziz supposes Fielding to have married) is cleared up, the two are friends again; but "socially they had no meeting-place," and we are made to feel that for them, "here" and "now," parting is inevitable—a condition not merely of India but, it seems, of human life. Yet around them, in the rainy season, the lovingly described sacred and funny rituals of Gokul Ashtami—the festival of the birth of Krishna—are going on: a topsy-turvy world of "God is love" in which, as Godbole sings his song of appeal and holds within his mind both Mrs. Moore and a wasp (like the one she had called "pretty dear" in chapter 3), it may be said that everything exists and everything has value. The dead Mrs. Moore is also present through her daughter, Stella (whom Fielding has married), and through her son, Ralph, quick to sense the nuances of human feeling and thus "an Oriental," as Aziz calls him in the identical phrase he had used to Mrs. Moore herself. All of them seem comprised within the divine chaos of the Hindu festival, and in the collision of their two boats with each other and with the mud replica of Krishna's village of Gokul as it is carried into the waters of the tank, Forster offers a magnificent natural symbol of baptismal rebirth, as humans touch each other and what is beyond them. Thus, though the last ride of Aziz and Fielding takes sad note of "the divisions of daily life" and the particular obstacles to friendship in India, we are able to sense in the final negatives "not yet" and "not there" the presence, the possibility, of "sometime" and "somewhere."

IV

AFTER *A Passage to India* Forster published no more fiction in his lifetime. Had he actually written no more (and he wrote little enough), the technical mastery of his last novel, and the feeling of completeness it gives, would be enough in themselves to account for his silence: it is hard to see how *A Passage to India* could be bettered as a statement of the human experience sub specie aeternitatis. But we now know, from Forster's correspondence and private papers, and from the stories of *The Life to Come*, both that he retained the wish to express the homosexual outlook on life and that, from time to time, he succeeded in doing so. He felt unable, however either to publish the results or to suppress the wish (or express it in a form compatible with censorship, as to some extent his earlier novels had done, the friendship of Fielding and Aziz being perhaps the last, though very faint, example). His dilemma is suggested by a letter of 1928 that he and Virginia Woolf addressed to the *Nation and Athenaeum* in connection with Radclyffe Hall's lesbian novel *The Well of Loneliness:* "The sense that there is a taboo list [of prohibited or prohibitable subjects] will work on [the novelist], and will make him alert and cautious instead of surrendering himself to his creative impulses." For Forster, the effect was to separate his career after 1924 into two pieces, the public and the private.

In 1927 he gave the Clark lectures at Trinity College, Cambridge. These were published as *Aspects of the Novel* and express with admirable lucidity and organization a host of insights into the ways in which novels work, some of them—particularly the notions of pattern, rhythm, expansion, and the affinity between fiction and music—being invaluable as indications of Forster's own aims as a novelist. Forster's essays of many years were collected in *Abinger Harvest* (1936) and *Two Cheers for Democracy* (1951): they are obviously the work of a man who loved writing, and who valued it not only as a way of expressing delight and giving language permanence, but as a weapon in the fight against the darker tendencies of the twentieth-century world. It is in his essays that Forster most clearly appears as a liberal humanist, concerned for the life of the individual and of the spirit, against philistinism, intolerance, and any kind of political totalitarianism. His later writings have a largely retrospective flavor, that of a man less and less at home in the organized world about him, and feeling piety and gratitude toward the past: toward the tradition of the countryside in his pageant play, *England's Pleasant Land* (1940), toward individuals in his biographies, *Goldsworthy Lowes Dickinson* (1934) and *Marianne Thornton* (1956), and toward a vanished India, "the great opportunity of my life," in *The Hill of Devi*. As great an opportunity had been furnished by his undergraduate years at King's College, Cambridge, and some return to that life was offered when, in 1945, King's made him an honorary fellow and invited him, unusually, to reside. There he spent his last twenty-five years: it was an appropriate conclusion, and one as beneficial to others as to himself.

But Forster had not entirely given up fiction, as the publication in 1972 of *The Life to Come* made clear. At the International Writers' Congress in Paris in 1935 he had complained again about censorship and declared that "sex is a subject for serious treatment and also for comic treatment." In his eight homosexual short stories, written between 1922 and 1958, both methods are used. "The Obelisk" (1939) is the best of the comic ones, but it is not merely a phallic joke. The suggestive double entendre at the end ("It's fallen into the landslip upside-down, the tip of it's gone in ever so far") is extremely funny, as is Hilda's dawning realization that if she and her handsome sailor did not reach the obelisk, then neither did her husband, Ernest, and his odd one. But it is also a genuinely happy and liberating story, in which the secret dreams of husband and wife are satisfied (both, in another sense, reach the obelisk), and a tacit appeal for equal tolerance of the two routes to it, homosexual as well as heterosexual. The more fanciful, Ruritanian "What Does It Matter?" is also such an appeal (though less well executed), an attempt to deflate the pressure of sexual intolerance by laughing at it.

The serious stories admit the pressure and powerfully convey the unhappiness it brings. "Arthur Snatchfold" (1928), the story of a brief but not sordid weekend encounter between a rich businessman and a milkman, emphasizes the vindictiveness of the law and suggests the dignity of homosexual feeling by associating it with self-sacrifice—that of the working-class partner: it is as if *Maurice* had taken a grimmer turn at the end. "The Life to Come" (1922), with its bleak, tragic misunderstanding between a missionary and a native chief, and between two kinds of love, is strangely imaginative and haunting, and ends in a violence that, Vithobai hopes, will unite him with Paul Pinmay beyond the grave. But the violence that ends the finest, longest, and most physically explicit of all these stories, "The Other Boat" (begun in 1913 and finished in 1957–1958), is surely that of defiance and despair. Set in the second decade of the century, on a boat bound for India (the *Normannia*, as in *Maurice*), the story brilliantly creates the two worlds of Lionel March: that of convention and racial superiority in which as a young army officer he appears to belong, and that below decks which he shares with the half-caste, "Cocoanut," his childhood playmate on the boat going the other way, and now his lover. The complex tension between his loyalties, public and personal, and between his knowledge of his real nature and his orthodox revulsion from it, lead to his strangling Cocoanut at the point of orgasm and then to his suicide, jumping into the sea "naked and with the seeds of love on him." It is a magnificent and terrible climax, and suggests—particularly coming from a man of nearly eighty—Forster's frustration as a writer unable to express his full self publicly. Such was the price he paid for reticence. When he wrote on the final text (1960) of *Maurice* the wry comment "Publishable—but worth it?" (which—if it is not mere tautology—means "Is it worth stirring up a fuss?"), he indicated that he did not wish to pay whatever price frankness in his lifetime might involve. In view of the public and legal attitude to homosexuality as late as the early 1960's (as evidenced, for instance, by the contemporary British film *Victim*, 1961), criticism of Forster's choice seems out of place.

The conclusion of a short essay like this, on a writer as complex and subtle as Forster, can be no more than the précis of a précis. He is both an intellectual novelist and a poetic one. He moves easily from the realistic into the symbolic and the mystical. Beneath a sometimes comic manner he is profoundly serious. Aesthetically, his novels have pattern, harmony, order. To the mind they offer more wisdom than most; in both mind and emotions they generate a sense of liberation and excitement, and go on doing so. Forster has his blind spots and his prejudices, but his conscientious fairness strives to reduce them. He is occasionally clumsy and unconvincing. But here we should remember what he said, in *Aspects of the Novel*, about Sir Walter Scott: "If he had passion he would be a great writer—no amount of clumsiness or artificiality would matter then." Unlike Scott, Forster has much more than "a temperate heart and gentlemanly feelings and an intelligent affection for the countryside." Forster has passion, and is a great writer.

## SELECTED BIBLIOGRAPHY

I. BIBLIOGRAPHY. B. J. Kirkpatrick, *A Bibliography of E. M. Forster* (London, 1965; rev. ed., 1968); F. P. W. McDowell, "E. M. Forster: An Annotated Secondary Bibliography," *English Literature in Transition* 13, 2 (1970), very comprehensive.

II. COLLECTED WORKS. Uniform Edition (London, 1924), *A Passage to India* first published in this edition, 1926; Pocket Edition: novels (London, 1947), *Aspects of the Novel* (London, 1949), *Goldsworthy Lowes Dickinson* (London, 1962); *Collected Short Stories* (London, 1947; repr. 1966), intro. by Forster; O. Stallybrass, ed., Abinger Edition (London, 1972-     ).

III. SEPARATE WORKS. *Where Angels Fear to Tread* (London, 1905), novel, Abinger ed. (1975); *The Longest Journey* (London, 1907), novel, World's Classics ed. (London, 1960), with intro. by Forster; *A Room with a View* (London, 1908), novel, Abinger ed. (1977); *Howards End* (London, 1910), novel, Abinger ed. (1973); *The Celestial Omnibus and Other Stories* (London, 1911; repr. 1920 and 1924), contains "The Story of a Panic," "The Other Side of the Hedge," "The Celestial Omnibus," "Other Kingdom," "The Curate's Friend," "The Road from Colonus."

*The Story of the Siren* (London, 1920), short story; *The Government of Egypt: Recommendations by a Committee of the International Section of the Labour Research Department* (London, 1920), includes "Notes on Egypt" by Forster; *Alexandria: A History and a Guide* (Alexandria, 1922), repr. with new intro. by author (New York, 1961; Gloucester, Mass., 1968; Woodstock, N. Y., 1974); *Pharos and Pharillon* (London, 1923; repr. 1926, 1961), essays; *A Passage to India* (London, 1924), novel; *Aspects of the Novel* (London, 1927), criticism, the Clark lectures, Cambridge, Abinger ed. (London, 1974); *The Eternal Moment, and Other Stories* (London, 1928), contains "The Machine Stops," "The Point of It," "Mr. Andrews," "Co-ordination," "The Story of the Siren," "The Eternel Moment"; *Goldsworthy Lowes Dickinson* (London, 1934), biography, Abinger ed. (London, 1973), with intro. by W. H. Auden; *Abinger Harvest* (London, 1936), sixty assorted pieces contributed to various journals from 1903 to 1934.

*Nordic Twilight* (London, 1940), political essay, Macmillan War Pamphlet no. 3; *England's Pleasant Land; A Pageant Play* (Toronto-London, 1940); *Virginia Woolf* (Cambridge, 1942), criticism, the Rede lecture, Cambridge, 1941, repr. in *Two Cheers for Democracy*; *The Development of English Prose Between 1918 and 1939* (Glasgow, 1945), the W. P. Ker Memorial lecture, Glasgow, 1944, repr. and rev. in *Two Cheers for Democracy*; *Two Cheers for Democracy* (London, 1951), sixty-seven essays and reviews from 1925 to 1951, Abinger ed. (London, 1972); *The Hill of Devi: Being Letters from Dewas State Senior* (London, 1953); *Marianne Thornton, 1797-1887: A Domestic Biography* (London, 1956).

A. Gishford, ed., *Tribute to Benjamin Britten on His Fiftieth Birthday* (London, 1963), contains "Arctic Summer: Fragment of an Unfinished Novel" by Forster; *Maurice* (New York-London, 1971), novel, intro. by P. N. Furbank; *Albergo Empedocle and Other Writings* (London, 1971), ed. with intro. and notes by G. H. Thompson, contains Forster's earliest published story and other uncollected essays and reviews from 1900 to 1915; *The Life to Come, and Other Stories* (New York-London, 1972), Abinger ed., contains "Ansell," "Albergo Empedocle," "The

Purple Envelope," "The Helping Hand," "The Rock," "The Life to Come," "Dr. Woolacott," "Arthur Snatchfold," "The Obelisk," "What Does It Matter? A Morality," "The Classical Annex," "The Torque," "The Other Boat," "Three Courses and a Dessert"; *The Lucy Novels: Early Sketches for "A Room with a View"* (London, 1977), Abinger ed.

IV. SHORTER PIECES. "'Reflections in India—Too Late,' by our Indian correspondent [E. M. F.]," *Nation and Athenaeum* (21 January 1922), 614-615; E. Fay, *Original Letters from India 1779-1815* (London, 1925), intro. and notes by Forster; G. Beith, ed., *Edward Carpenter: In Appreciation* (London, 1931), includes "Some Memories" by Forster, pp. 74-81; A. W. Lawrence, ed., *T. E. Lawrence by His Friends* (London, 1937), includes section by Forster, pp. 282-286; A. Craig, *The Banned Books of England* (London, 1937)), intro. by Forster; "The Ivory Tower," *London Mercury* (Christmas 1938), 119-130; "The Art of Fiction I: E. M. Forster," *Paris Review* (Spring 1953), 28-41, interview by P. N. Furbank and F. J. H. Haskell; "Indian Entries," *Encounter* 18 (January 1962), 20-27, extracts from Forster's diary describing his first visit to India (8 October 1912 to 2 April 1913).

V. BIOGRAPHICAL AND CRITICAL STUDIES. V. Woolf, "The Novels of E. M. Forster," *Atlantic Monthly* 115, no. 5 (November 1927), repr. in *The Death of the Moth and Other Essays* (London, 1942); D. M. Hoare, *Some Studies in the Modern Novel* (London, 1938), contains ch. on Forster; R. Macaulay, *The Writings of E. M. Forster* (London, 1938); L. Trilling, *E. M. Forster: A Study* (Norwalk, Conn., 1943); E. K. Brown, "The Revival of E. M. Forster," *Yale Review* 33 (June 1944), 668-681; P. Ault, "Aspects of E. M. Forster," *Dublin Review* (October 1946), 109-134; D. Cecil, *Poets and Story Tellers* (London, 1949), contains essay on Forster; R. Warner, *E. M. Forster* (London, 1950), rev. by J. Morris (London, 1960); J. K. Johnstone, *The Bloomsbury Group* (London, 1954), a study of Forster, Strachey, Woolf, and their circle; J. McConkey, *The Novels of E. M. Forster* (Ithaca, N.Y., 1957).

H. J. Oliver, *The Art of E. M. Forster* (Melbourne, 1960); J. B. Beer, *The Achievement of E. M. Forster* (London, 1962); F. C. Crews, *E. M. Forster: The Perils of Humanism* (Oxford, 1962); K. W. Gransden, *E. M. Forster* (Edinburgh, 1962); V. A. Shahane, *E. M. Forster: A Reassessment* (Allahabad, India, 1962); K. Natwar-Singh, ed., *E. M. Forster: A Tribute, with Selections from His Writings on India* (New York, 1964), with intro. by ed.; A. Wilde, *Art and Order: A Study of E. M. Forster* (New York, 1964; London, 1965); H. T. Moore, *E. M. Forster* (New York-London, 1965); D. Shusterman, *The Quest for Certitude in E. M. Forster's Fiction* (Bloomington, Ind., 1965); M. Bradbury, *Forster: A Collection of Critical Essays* (Englewood Cliffs, N. J., 1966), repr. of essays by D. S. Savage, F. R. Leavis, I. A. Richards, P. Burra, and E. K. Brown; W. Stone, *The Cave and the Mountain: A Study of E. M. Forster* (Stanford, 1966); G. H. Thompson, *The Fiction of E. M. Forster* (Detroit, 1967); N. Kelvin, *E. M. Forster* (Carbondale, Ill., 1967); L. Brander, *E. M. Forster: A Critical Study* (London, 1968); D. Godfrey, *E. M. Forster's Other Kingdom* (Edinburgh-London, 1968); F. P. W. McDowell, *E. M. Forster* (New York, 1969); O. Stallybrass, ed., *Aspects of E. M. Forster: Essays and Recollections Written for His Ninetieth Birthday* (London, 1969); H. H. Anniah Gowda, ed., *A Garland for E. M. Forster* (Mysore, 1969), includes letters from Forster to R. C. Trevelyan.

J. R. Ackerley, *E. M. Forster: A Portrait* (London, 1970); E. Barger, "Memories of Morgan," *New York Times Book Review* (16 August 1970); J. P. Levine, *Creation and Criticism: A Passage to India* (London, 1971); E. Ellem, "E. M. Forster's 'Arctic Summer,'" *Times Literary Supplement* (21 September 1973), 1087-1089; P. Gardner, ed., *E. M. Forster: The Critical Heritage* (Boston-London, 1973); J. Colmer, *E. M. Forster: The Personal Voice* (London, 1975); J. S. Martin, *E. M. Forster: The Endless Journey* (London, 1976); I. Stephens, *Unmade Journey* (London, 1977), ch. 55 treats Forster; J. L. Pinchin, *Alexandria Still: Forster, Durrell and Cavafy* (Princeton, N. J., 1977); P. N. Furbank, *E. M. Forster: A Life* (New York, 1978; pbk. ed., 1981).

# WILLIAM GOLDING
(1911–    )

## Stephen Medcalf

*I*

WILLIAM GOLDING was born in Cornwall on 19 September 1911 into a world "of sanity and logic and fascination." "My life is passed in a condition of ravished astonishment!," the exclamation he gives to the experimental scientist in his play *The Brass Butterfly,* might have been, and perhaps was, spoken by his father, Alec Golding. But the first memory that he has given us of his childhood, in the autobiographical fragment "The Ladder and the Tree," is of terror and darkness: darkness and indescribable terror made objective in the flint-walled cellars of their fourteenth-century house in Marlborough, and in the graveyard by which it stood.

He offers a social cause for this contact with darkness:

Had my mother perhaps feared this shadowy house and its graveyard neighbour when she went there with me as a baby? She was Cornish and the Cornish do not live next to a graveyard from choice. But we had very little choice. My father was a master at the local grammar school, so that we were all the poorer for our respectability.

(*The Hot Gates,* p. 167)

But clearly this matter of class is not a cause but only part of the conditions for a personal plight. It seems less important, so to speak, to Golding that Marlborough was an inward-looking, snobbish, provincial town than that it is at the edge of the "prehistoric metropolis [whose cathedral] was Stonehenge.... To spend your life here in Wessex, as I have done, is to live where archaeology is as natural, or at least as usual, as gardening," he says in "Digging for Pictures": and the archaeologist, the explorer of the darkness under the earth, has, he suggested in a review of Grahame Clarke's *World Prehistory* (1961), replaced as culture-hero the "wise men, at once distinguished and responsible, who emerge from the Admiralty or Government background of Buchan's novels."

The key event that marked loss of faith in the wise men he dates in the same review to the time when he was an infant. "I remember my mother once confiding to me that her awareness of the world as an exhilarating but risky place dated from the day on which she heard that the *Titanic* had sunk. She could not say why. She only knew that the years before that had been sunny and placid, while the years that came after seemed by nature full of storm": that is, after mid-April, 1912.

By the time Golding was seven he had begun to connect the darkness, although not the storm, with the ancient Egyptians. From them he learned, or onto them he projected, mystery and symbolism, a habit of mingling life and death, and an attitude of mind skeptical of the scientific method that descends from the Greeks. Already as a child, he says in "Egypt from My Inside":

I know about symbols without knowing what I know. I understand that neither their meaning nor their effect can be described, since a symbol is that which has an indescribable effect and meaning. I have never heard of levels of meaning, but I experience them. In my notebook, the scarab, the ankh, the steps, the ladder, the *thet,* are drawn with a care that goes near to love.

(*The Hot Gates,* p. 74)

He tried to find a focus to stare into the eyes of a carved face on a sarcophagus, "the face prepared to go down and through, in darkness." And therefore,

though I admire the Greeks, I am not one of them. . . . I am, in fact, an Ancient Egyptian, with all their unreason, spiritual pragmatism and capacity for ambiguous belief. And if you protest on the evidence of statistical enquiry they were not like that, I can only answer in the jargon of my generation, that for me they have projected that image.

(pp. 81–82)

In all this, if not necessarily cause, there is at any rate a picture of Golding's present genius—of a way of writing existing at the edge between an acutely skeptical and organizing consciousness and a powerful awareness of the darkness beneath consciousness. It is proper too that he lives near Stonehenge, the temple of astronomy almost Greek in its entasis[1] and proportion, whose effect, he once pointed out in conversation, partly lies in the way that weathering, lichens, and the channels worn by rain have made it seem like something emerging from unhuman nature.

His first book, the *Poems* (1934), published when he was twenty-two, reveals something of this only to hindsight and meditation. He has called the poems "poor, thin things," but curiosity about them is immediately aroused by his remark: "The novelist is a displaced person, torn between two ways of expression.... You might say I write prose because I can't write poetry."

In fact, they are not so bad. They deal with emotions—as they come out in the poems, rather easy emotions—of loss and grief, reflected in nature and the seasons. The beauty of the world, in several not unmemorable pieces, suggests loss. There is satire, some cheap and some good. The rhythms are traditional, on the whole conventional. The book is, by and large, very Georgian, echoing Edward Thomas, Walter de la Mare, A. E. Housman, and Siegfried Sassoon.

But when it is put in a Georgian context, a kind of crack appears, letting in something visionary, something Blakean although not derived from Blake:

> The phoenix rose again and flew
> With crest and plume and pinion
> In splendour from grey ashes flashing
> Like a jewel turned beneath the sun.
>
> In cities and in palaces,
> Or toiling through the hot dumb sand
> Bare-footed in the barren hills,
> Men saw—and would not understand.
>
> But some there were among the fields
> That let the swerving plough jolt on
> And stood and gazed against the light
> Through wide eyes filled with tears as bright,
> Until the burning bird was gone.

> Oh Phoenix! did they hear as I
> The agony, the lonely cry
> Of mateless, mateless, mateless Beauty
> Echoing in the desert sky?
>     ("The Phoenix Rose Again")

In general the poems—another example is "Isobel"

> The worm that the scythe bites,
> The flower in the grass,
> Shadows and sunlight that
> Flutter and pass,
>
> Thunder that mutters,
> Brooklets that murmur,
> Are words that she utters,
> And runes to confirm her.

—suggest an attempt to do what de la Mare did, but missing de la Mare's supreme mastery of the auditory imagination.

Between the *Poems* and *Lord of the Flies* (1954), Golding experienced two things that he counts the greatest influences on his writing—first, the war and his service in the navy, and second, in the same years, his learning ancient Greek. The former confirmed for him the process, begun with the sinking of the *Titanic*, of shattering the liberal and optimistic image of man. The latter perhaps had large effects on his style. There is something dynamic, concrete, and living about Greek to which one may guess he responded. It is (as Owen Barfield has observed[2]) a language in which we find ourselves not so much conscious of having long hair as "conscious *in* the growing of our hair, [feeling] it as *movement* in something the same way that we still feel our breathing as movement"; in which we do not say "So and so—is—young," but "So and so blossoms" or "blooms" without any necessary consciousness of metaphor; and in which even abstractions acquire a concrete and substantial quality. The war and Greek literature together perhaps confirmed the dissociation from current and ephemeral affairs which makes Golding say that if the novelist "has a serious, an Aeschylean, preoccupation with the human tragedy ... he is committed to looking for the root of the disease instead of describing the symptoms" ("The Writer in His Age").

It is illuminating to approach his prose by con-

---

[1] An almost imperceptible swelling of the shaft of a column, used in ancient Greek architecture to counter the effect of optical distortion.

[2] *Romanticism Comes of Age*, London, 1944.

sidering what he does *not* do in his poems. Clearly it is not by mastery of elusive and delicate effects of tune and sound in their relation to meaning that he moves us in his poems. Yet he is a master of words; and he says that from childhood he has had the poet's "passion for words in themselves, and collected them like stamps or bird's eggs" ("Billy the Kid"). It is perhaps permissible to guess that his feeling for words has something synaesthetic, something visual rather than auditory about it. That is, the words stand out in his prose much as one would expect if he sometimes feels as his Jocelin does in *The Spire*:

"When you hear things, do you see them?"
He lay in his nowhere, turning his headache from side to side as though he could shake it off. Footsteps walked past the window, and the looped line of cheerful whistling. Drearily in his head, he watched the whistling disappear round a corner.

(*The Spire,* p. 195)

The description of the same feeling in *Pincher Martin* sounds very like a metaphorical account of the style: "Words and sounds were sometimes visible as shapes.... They did not vibrate and disappear. When they were created they remained as hard enduring things like the pebbles."

This synaesthetic faculty would perhaps accompany, as it does for Jocelin, Martin, and Lok in *The Inheritors,* the intense visual imagination that Golding recounts from his childhood: "I had no doubt that if one frowned long enough at the page it would brighten and come alive. Indeed, it did. The words and paper vanished. The picture emerged. Details were there to be heard, seen, touched."

Elusive effects of words become subsidiary to vivid, dynamic, and detailed imagination. This does not apply only to sound. Golding's words tend not to have meanings of the incantatory kind that exploit the whole spider's web of developed connotation and association, as they would have to do if he were to be a poet of the kind of de la Mare or T. S. Eliot. Instead he tends to use words in unexpected disjunctive combinations, which allow only the single meaning he wants. Perhaps this is part of the reason for his love not only for ancient Greek but also for Old English—the fact that in both the words are relatively clean of association, hard and sharp.

This kind of attitude toward meaning rests in its turn on the whole approach of his books to experience. His genius seems to lie in pushing already formed and distinct conceptualization back to the point where it is just experience: on the largest scale, some of his books, for all their originality, began as parodies, as *Lord of the Flies* is a parody of *The Coral Island.* This again might disqualify him for the elusive de la Mare kind of poetry that he attempted, a poetry in which all depends on catching the experience before any distinct conceptualization has taken place.

Golding might have learned some of this pushing of concept back to percept from the concreteness of ancient Greek. But he has given his own image for the mental process involved, in "Fable":

I remember, many years ago, trying to bore a hole with a drilling machine through armour plate.... In my extreme ignorance, I put the drill in the chuck, held by half an inch of its extreme end. I seized the handle and brought the revolving drill down on the armour. It wobbled for a second; then there was a sharp explosion, the drill departed in every direction.... Wiser now, I held the next drill deep in the chuck so that only the point protruded, held it mercilessly in those steel jaws and brought it down on the armour with the power behind it of many hundred horses. This operation was successful. I made a small red-hot hole in the armour, though of course I ruined the drill. If this small anecdote seems fatuous, I assure you that it is the best image I know for one sort of imaginative process. There is the same merciless concentration, the same will, the same apparently impenetrable target, the same pressure applied steadily to one small point.

(*The Hot Gates,* p. 97)

He has also given a word for it when he asks what future, if the sense of value is impaired, there can be "for the novel which tries to look at life anew, ... for intransigence."

II

GOLDING's novels therefore move at the level of phenomena, of things happening in the physical or spiritual worlds, and develop their own forms for experience. One consequence of this is that, perhaps more than with any other novelist, the process of reading a Golding novel is overwhelmingly important. You ought not to be the same person at the end of one of them as at the beginning, and the book itself therefore ought not to be the same. Golding's usual way of achieving this effect involves a process of reinterpretation which begins approximately as soon as the first picture of what is happening has been established—let us say after the first chapter. At some point the reader finds himself so involved in the principal character's perceptions that his own judgment of what is happening is swallowed up. The second interpretation forces itself more and more upon the first, grows more and more toward covering all the phenomena; when this is complete, the book moves suddenly into a more normal world, and ends. Golding once rashly used the word "gimmick" for this way of ending, and readers who feel resentfully that they have been fooled have used it against him. But the whole structure of the book depends on the process of reinterpretation, and the shift to normality is needed to drive it home.

But although the change in the ending is not a mere gimmick, the effect of a Golding novel is marred if one knows how it is reinterpreted before the first reading: by existing over and above the text, the reader misses an involvement that affects his subsequent readings also. It is especially unwise, therefore, to read about one of these novels before reading it.

At the beginning of *Lord of the Flies*, the reader has two forms of reality offered him, one in the text, the other in the title. The text begins with a well-known sort of story: boys making their own lives on an island, apart from adults. The immediate model is made clear enough: Robert Michael Ballantyne's *The Coral Island* (1858), in which three adolescents, Ralph, Jack, and Peterkin, create a happy simple life on a Pacific island. But one can feel many others of the genre hovering about the story, notably Arthur Ransome's *Swallows and Amazons* and even more his *Secret Water*, in which a naval officer's children play at explorers in the marshy islands behind Walton-on-the-Naze in Essex until confronted by local children whose game is to be a savage tribe with corroboree, ritual dance, and mock human sacrifice. But the children are all very nice and responsible children, and everything remains at the level of game.

Ballantyne's names, Ralph and Jack, are those of the two principals in Golding's book; and the first chapter differs from Ballantyne's and Ransome's shape for the world only in Golding's peculiar, detailed, almost hallucinatory awareness of physical reality. But for a year before the war and from its end until 1961 he was a schoolmaster, and he draws on this experience both to enlarge (the behavior and language of the boys is accurate enough) and to alter this shape. Another schoolmaster, F. McEachran, has said, "If you want to understand the spirit of Nazism, make a class of adolescents, with teeth clenched, bellow out Hitler's sentence 'Niemand hat je gesagt, ich wäre feig gewesen' (No one has ever said I was a coward)."[3] The first real intimation of change in *Lord of the Flies* comes at the end of the first chapter when—trying to repel his own horrified inhibition against cutting into living flesh, even a pig's—Jack responds like one of McEachran's boys. He "snatched his knife out of the sheath and slammed it into a tree trunk. Next time there would be no mercy. He looked round fiercely, daring them to contradict" (p. 41).

But instead of disappearing, the timidity that has to be rebutted actually grows. The smaller boys are frightened of their own nightmares of the island, and presently Jack admits that "in the forest . . . when you're on your own . . . you can feel as if you're not hunting but being hunted; as if something's behind you all the time in the jungle" (p. 67). Fear denied, blood lust let loose, and projection of both these spread among nearly all the boys until at the end they are at the point of sacrificing Ralph to the Beast that for them haunts the island.

From the beginning, the title of the book suggested a world in which something like this would happen. For a reader who does not know its hidden reference, the name *Lord of the Flies* provides a haunting, an unease that comes to light when the head of the first pig killed, spiked on a stick and offered to the Beast, speaks to the visionary boy Simon. The flies that swarm around it "were black and iridescent green and without number; and in front of Simon, the Lord of the Flies hung on his stick and grinned" (p. 171). Simon's sense of "mankind's essential illness" speaks through it: "I'm part of you? Close, close, close! I'm the reason why it's no go?"

Concept is now reduced to sheer experience. The concept so treated, Golding declares in "Fable," may "seem trite, obvious and familiar in theological terms. Man is a fallen being. He is gripped by original sin. . . . I accept the theology and admit the triteness; but what is trite is true." But the book

[3]*Spells*, Oxford, 1954, p. 41.

presents sheer religious experience, sheer phenomenon as close to unmediated experience as the descriptions of the island are to unconstructed physical sensation; so much so that we may even venture to disagree with this reformulation of it.

If the book were about original sin—about a state of alienation from good by which all mankind is equally gripped from birth—there would be no propriety in the boys' apparent innocence at the beginning, in the evident continuing innocence of Simon and the commonsensical Piggy, nor in the resistance to evil put up by Ralph. These things may be factually compatible with believing that the three also are alienated at heart, but they are not shown to be so in the novel. Again, original sin might lead one to expect some dealing with the mysterious ways out from it that are offered under names like grace and redemption. (In fact, Golding eschews these in his first three books; there are hints of them in *Free Fall* and *The Spire*, but they are not dealt with centrally until *Darkness Visible* and *The Paper Men*.) The sense in *Lord of the Flies* of struggle with something itself wholeheartedly corrupt suggests something different. Matthew Arnold (when he suggested in *Literature and Dogma* that the Bible should be regarded as written in an experiential and unconceptualized way, such as Golding's essentially is) used for the word and concept "God" the empirical sensation of the "power not ourselves making for righteousness." What speaks through the pig's head sounds analogous to that—namely a power not ourselves, but in ourselves, making for corruption. As the title suggests, then, the book is about the experience behind the biblical name for God's adversary, Beelzebub, which does indeed mean "Lord of the Flies." It is proper enough that the boys who are killed in sacrifice to him should be the innocents, and the one about to be sacrificed at the end, the resister. Golding gives the passage in which the Lord of the Flies speaks to Simon as his example of what happens when imagination concentrates like the drill on armor-plate. "The point of the fable under imaginative consideration does not become more real than the real world, it shoves the real world on one side. The author becomes a spectator, appalled or delighted, but a spectator." It is at this point that for the reader also the book re-forms. For a while we forget that we are reading about boys and identify ourselves with the mere human being in his predicament: the human being faced with that which it is a mistake to name—because we then commit the boys' own error of projection—but a greater mistake not to recognize, the error of Piggy, the one boy who remains true to what he understands of liberalism.

Simon commits neither error. There is something sitting on the mountain in the middle of the island which the boys believe to be the Beast. Simon insists on climbing the mountain to find out what it is. Against the boys' derision he says, and against the warning of the Lord of the Flies he repeats, "What else is there to do?" His intransigence in climbing the mountain, his insistence on understanding, is a metaphor for what the book itself does.

In the new world of the Lord of the Flies, Simon is no longer only a helpful boy who likes praying in the forest where Jack finds only terror, no longer even what the connection of his name with Peterkin, the third of Ballantyne's heroes, would suggest, Simon called Peter, "the Rock." A Christ figure, he has Christ's reward. Going down the mountain to tell the rest that the thing on it is the fallen corpse of an airman, he is killed by them because they think he is the Beast.

In the world where they are humanity confronted by evil, the boys behave with as much fitness as they do if they are considered only as silly little boys. I have heard two young Germans arguing whether corruption spreads from Jack or is latent in all the boys, and they knew that they were arguing about Hitler, *Führerprinzip*, and the German nation. The book's realism allows both explanations.

It even allows that the corruption need not absolutely have taken place. The rule of the Lord of the Flies is not total. There are two points in the book, both associated with the swell of the ocean, that pierce beyond him. In one, when Ralph, on the other side of the island, where there are no "filmy enchantments of mirage," feels clamped down before the ocean, Simon suddenly, inexplicably, and rightly says, "You'll get back to where you came from." In the second, Simon's broken body is described in a passage of deliberate beauty as moving out in obedience to the pull of the tide toward the open sea, "a silver shape beneath the steadfast constellations." It is a kind of resurrection. Some kind of factuality in the world is other and greater than evil.

Within the ordinary human and diabolic world, the book moves toward its climax, the second point where the reader totally identifies with one of the characters; this is where we see Ralph, hiding in the forest from the rest,

> looking straight into the savage's eyes.
> Don't scream.
> (p. 245)

Simon's words, the assurance from beyond the world in which he is trapped, suddenly well up, like a spring so deeply buried that it is almost not seen: "You'll get back." Then Ralph bursts out, "hopeless fear on flying feet, rushing through the forest . . . rolling over and over in the warm sand, crouching with arm up to ward off, trying to cry for mercy."

At once he dwindles back into little boy. A naval officer looks down on him. In one way this is rescue, properly and ironically accounted for; the boys had tried earlier and unsuccessfully to attract ships with the smoke of a bonfire, and now, by setting fire to the whole island in the attempt to smoke out Ralph, they have succeeded. But in another way, the naval officer and his cruiser remind us at the end of the book (like the crash landing of the boys at the beginning and the fall of the airman in the middle) that the boys are themselves escaping from a world war. The shift of viewpoint from child to man only drives home what we learned among the children, the things Ralph weeps for, "the end of innocence" and "the darkness of man's heart."

The end of innocence, a fall of man, does take place after the first chapter of *Lord of the Flies*. To begin with, the boys are afraid of shedding blood, but they are at home in the forest. Presently, they create rituals and an embryonic society that centers on hunting and killing, but they project their own fears and bloodlust onto a presence in the woods. It is partly from this contrast that the *The Inheritors* (1955) develops. In it, Golding's prose reaches perhaps its highest achievement in expressing the consciousness of primitive man, of a man who conceptualizes very little and knows little of chains of reasoning, only that some imaginative pictures help in forming others—the consciousness of a man as he feels in words such as he could never have imagined. The book is consequently in a way the finest of the novels (in fact Golding's own favorite), but also the hardest to read. Unless one's visualization is constant and intense, one is apt to miss what is going on.

The people not only do not conceptualize, they know nothing of art; their religion is devoid of ritual, although they pray and make offering before Oa, who brought forth the earth from her belly and is present where Awe is. Since art and ritual are, like conceptualization, a kind of shaping of experience, and a projection and division of the self, it is understandable that they should go together. But the people have other qualities, which seem obscurely connected with these first three. They are like the boys at the beginning of *Lord of the Flies*, innocent, usually mutually affectionate, excited by their world; they are at home in their forest; and, although they are omnivorous, they will not eat meat unless something else has killed it and sucked the blood. Even then they feel guilty about it and make excuses ("The meat is for Mal who is sick") to cover their guilt. Yet perhaps if they feel guilt, it is wrong to call them "unfallen." They live on the edge of the Fall—just as in physical actuality they live on a ledge above a fall of water. Their evil is perhaps latent, and held in check by their innocent lack of consciousness.

Although they are conceived in sharp reaction to the nastier fancies of some believers in survival of the fittest—of aggressive, contentious, competitive weapon-users—one is apt to think that they must be our early ancestors. The epigraph from the most brilliant of monuments to the belief in progress, H. G. Wells's *The Outline of History* (1919–1920), warns us that the subject of the book will be the encounter between *Homo sapiens* and Neanderthal man with a quotation from Sir Harry Johnston: "The dim racial remembrance of such gorilla-like monsters, with cunning brains, shambling gait, hairy bodies, strong teeth, and possibly cannibalistic tendencies, may be the germ of the ogre in folklore."

Nevertheless, it is a long time before one is finally convinced that the people through whom we see are Neanderthal men, and the "other," by whom they are at first attracted and eventually destroyed, our own forerunners. Neanderthal man has something in common with our unfallen ancestors, as mythically imagined in a reaction against Wells and rationalism similar to Golding's by C. S. Lewis in *The Problem of Pain* (1940), a book Golding was moved by when it came out during the war:

All that experience and practice can teach he had still to learn: if he chipped flints, he doubtless chipped them clumsily enough. He may have been utterly incapable of expressing in conceptual form his paradisal experience. . . . If the Paradisal man could now appear among us, we should regard him as an utter savage, a creature to be exploited, or, at best, patronized. Only one or two, and those the holiest among us, would glance a second time at the naked, shaggy-bearded, slow-spoken creature: but they, after a few minutes, would fall at his feet.

(ch. 5)

But in form Lewis's description is really closer to Wells's, a fable. And although both Golding himself and his critics have applied the word "fable" to his novels, they really are not that. Lewis and Wells begin with a concept of primitive man viewed from outside in terms of their respective value systems—Lewis's belief in the Fall, Wells's in survival; and their concepts, however much they flesh them out, remain externally drawn shapes. In all Golding's novels valuing is essential, is part of the "intransigence" he demands; but he begins his imagining from the inside out. He has criticized Stevenson's *Treasure Island,* saying "the island as it stuck out of the sea, the reason for it being there, and the relationship between the parts, escapes me even when I used the overrated chart. An island must be built, and have an organic structure like a tooth." This may not be quite fair to Stevenson, but it is good analysis of Golding. The island of *Lord of the Flies* and the way in which the minds of Lok and Fa are drawn in *The Inheritors* have mythic purposes, their final shape is strongly value-laden; but they are built up from inside with an organic structure, like a tooth. We live in Lok's mind, Lok exists to that extent, as Wells's and Lewis's men do not.

This unity of some of the qualities of fable with the method of inner exploration is the special quality of a Golding novel. In *The Inheritors,* as in *Lord of the Flies,* part of the way it is achieved is the shift at the end, once the reader is completely involved in a new world, to a more normal one: the naval officer's grown-up view in one, and in the other the viewpoint of the Inheritors, Homo sapiens, our own ancestors. And they, we realize, are unquestionably fallen. Like the boys at the end of *Lord of the Flies* they kill freely, have hunting rituals, and project their own evil onto the forest. "They are frightened of the air where there is nothing," says the Neanderthal woman Fa.

Above all, they project their own evil onto the Neanderthalers. When Tuami, the artist among the new men, draws pictures of the first men at the bidding of the witch doctor Marlan, it is Marlan at his most evil they resemble. "The hair stood out round the head as though the figure were in the act of some frantic cruelty . . . as the hair of the old man had stood out when he was enraged or frightened." Indeed Marlan becomes more like his own projected evil side; when we see him through Tuami's eyes, he has acquired the Neanderthaler's red hair and the tense posture and blind eyes of the pictures: "The sun was blazing on the red sail and Marlan was red. His arms and legs were contracted, his hair stood out and his beard, his teeth were wolf's teeth and his eyes like blind stones"; and later, in a moment of terror, "his eyes were glaring like stones"—Golding's use of repetition at its most intense and obsessive.

H. G. Wells's view of the Neanderthalers is that of the new men: the vision of our own projected evil selves. So far as that view contains facts, it is true, even to the cannibalism. The Neanderthalers' old leader, Mal, asks as he dies, "Do not open my head and my bones. You would only taste weakness." It is evidently nothing sinister, but a posthumous act of love. But the new men eat a Neanderthal girl, Liku, because they are hungry and do not care to eat the fungi and other things the Neanderthalers eat. Golding makes use of a further detail that Wells mentions, which points the other way from the contrast of ogrelike Neanderthaler and amiable Homo sapiens. The Neanderthaler's "canine teeth were *less* marked, *less* like dog-teeth, than ours," says Wells—our "teeth that remembered wolf," as Golding's Neanderthalers see them; Marlin's "wolf's teeth," as Tuami sees them.

But to Wells and to the new men, the Neanderthalers are devils who live in the darkness under the trees. In between the world as seen by the Neanderthalers and the world of the new men, Golding sets a passage in detached authorial style, visual, avoiding words of value or emotion. In context, because we know the "red creature" it describes is Lok, and see his discovery of the death of Liku, his tears, and presently his own death, the detached style makes it one of the most poignant passages in Golding's works; and the projection of evil onto Lok is the more pathetic and appalling. In Golding's first draft, this was the last chapter, and by itself corresponded to the shift of consciousness at the end of *Lord of the Flies.* But in the published version he doubled the shift. We now learn about the projection of evil through the mind of Tuami, the artist, and find it bound up with the capacity of the new men to conceptualize and to perform developed magical rituals that center on art, the painting of the stag they would kill and of the Neanderthaler they fear. The new men can distance themselves from themselves and can therefore live in self-deception. Their power of conceptualization is, in short, bound up with their fallenness. In this, Golding is closer than C. S. Lewis to the biblical myth. For Lewis, the Fall can only have been men's wish to exist independently of God, "to be on their own, to take care for their own future, to plan for pleasure and for security, to have a *meum* . . . which . . . was theirs not His."

Golding pushes fallenness back to the division in the self, the awareness of oneself over against everything else, which is the precondition of Lewis's fallen wishes. Fa has dim pictures—that shoots might grow nearer the shelter and water be carried in shells—which approach Lewis's notion, but she has not enough detachment from her pictures to see how to do it; and the Old Woman of her people warns her off even from these as if from poison. And we do not even see that the people prepare flint tools for future use (as the Neanderthalers known to archaeology did), although they use the stones they find. They seem therefore to be unaware even of the means "to be on their own." Lewis has the classicist's notion that in paradisal man there was already a division between will and appetites, although the appetites obeyed the will; Golding, the romantic's idea of a man in whom will and appetite are innocent and undivided. His Neanderthalers are not divided even from one another. "One of the deep silences fell on them, that seemed so much more natural than speech, a timeless silence in which there were at first many minds in the overhang; and then perhaps no mind at all." The new men only get drunk together and make savage love. They have done what the Bible perhaps expresses in the eating of the fruit of the tree of *knowledge* of good and evil, when Adam and Eve first knew that they were naked.

It is possible, though, that after all the fall is not complete. The first people may be among our ancestors. For the new men carry a stolen Neanderthal baby with them as they flee from their own fears. Moreover, Golding's fall has something of the paradoxical idea of the Fortunate Fall. Golding's first draft of *The Inheritors* had no place for the physical symbol of the fall, the fall of water. It came to him as a symbol of the law of entropy, the dissipation of energy in the physical universe against which Life, concentrating and organizing energy, must move. It sweeps away the innocent: but the new people, the Inheritors, are "people of the fall." They struggle against entropy, and although in so doing they fall morally, they do make headway against it. They move upstream. At the end of the book, when in Golding's second ending we are given access to Tuami's mind, it is not the Neanderthalers with whom we would prefer to be, but Tuami, with the conceptualization and art that Lok thought was "like Oa." Tuami is making an ivory knife to murder Marlan. But as he sees the rump of the Neanderthal baby devil against the head of the spoiled, lustful woman Vivani, he forgets the knife's use. "The rump and the head fitted each other and made a shape you could feel with your hands. They were waiting in the rough ivory of the knife-hilt that was so much more important than the blade. They were an answer, the frightened, angry love of the woman, and the ridiculous, intimidating rump." Tuami's art is honest, strips projection off, is inclusive and looks toward something new. In all this it is an image of the novel itself. We turn away from the Neanderthalers, whose happiest thought is "Today is like yesterday and tomorrow," to peer forward with Tuami, even though it is into an image of darkness like that at the end of *Lord of the Flies*, "to see what lay at the other end of the lake, but it was so long, and there was such a flashing from the water that he could not see if the line of darkness had an ending."

*Pincher Martin* (1956) also has a root in *Lord of the Flies*, as can be seen in the moment when Ralph stands on the other side of the island and, in contrast to the mirages, the hopes of rescue, and the defending shield of the lagoon by which the boys usually stay, finds that "faced by the brute obtuseness of the ocean, the miles of division, one was clamped down, one was helpless, one was condemned, one was—." Martin, lost at sea in the war and struggling to survive on the island he believes to be Rockall, shares both the fact of isolation and the mirages of rescue and defense. The identification of reader with character is overwhelmingly important in this book. It is made very easy for us, with the strong sensuous impact of the sea and (once again built up organically like a tooth) the island, its rocks, waters, and sea vegetation.

We are given a strong sense of what it is like to

be *in* Martin's body, feeling his specific pains and looking out through the orbs of his eyes. It is made easy, too, by the familiarity and detail of the reminiscence, to live Martin's memories of his earlier life through. Golding gave to Martin more of the external conditions of his own life than to any other of his characters, from Oxford (so far as can be made out, Golding's own college of Brasenose) through a period of acting and theater life to a commission in the wartime navy. And behind all this is the emotional pressure of many myths of man suffering, building his fate, defying the elements. Martin himself invokes Atlas, Ajax, Lear, Prometheus; and others are present: the sailors cast up on Prospero's island, Milton's Lycidas whelmed beyond the Hebrides, and, above all, Robinson Crusoe. We cannot but share in the desperate ingenuity of Martin's work to survive, to which Golding gives all his own love of technical device. We applaud, as we share in, his will to conquer, to continue his life; so much so that we excuse, and even identify ourselves with, the gradually apparent fact that he is an unusually evil man.

Of the three parts we know of his life, it is the acting that is strongest in Martin: with all his will to conquer, he is a hollow person, with few characteristics other than that will. He is a series of masks. He contrasts with his own manipulation of his face people whose expressions rise "spontaneously from the conjectural centre behind the face," people like his friend Nathaniel Lovell, who *is* what he offers, who has a character without division, a face that immediately incarnates his spirit. Pincher, divided between will and attitudes, the true survivor, is also at the opposite extreme from the Neanderthalers. In his memory the cheats, seductions, and thefts involved in his conquering—which end with murder—so pile up that at some point the whole thing begins to reverse. In place of excusing his selfish will by the good use he makes of it to survive, we begin to feel that the appetite for survival, one of H. G. Wells's prime values, is itself evil. The whole ethic of Robinson Crusoe, the ethic of the entrepreneur and possessive individualist, begins to reverse itself—to reverse itself exactly, since there are traces in Defoe's *Robinson Crusoe* of an ethic that condemns Crusoe for his willful discontent and makes his adventures a punishment for his contempt for the life he has deserted like the prodigal son. But Defoe was carried away by his hero's patience, courage, and enterprise, and the suggestion of allegorical condemnation that is implied in the prodigal son image tends to be swallowed up in what Crusoe actually did.

One might say that the epoch of mercantile capitalism in life and realism in literature that *Crusoe* heralded is given its discharge in *Pincher Martin*. But this would not go nearly deep enough. It is not man of any particular epoch who is being criticized, but man himself. Crusoe was not the world's first sailor, wanderer, possessive individualist—all of which are only images for man as survivor. Martin's first ancestor in literature seems to be Odysseus. One might trace his appearance, cast up on his rock, with "the bleached wrinkles" of his hand and the "corrugations at the finger tips" to one of Golding's childhood visual imaginings:

When he was washed up in Phaeacia his hands were white and corrugated and his nails bled—not because of the rocks but because he bit them . . . I saw him . . . while he peered at the dark, phantom dangers. . . . The wily, the great-hearted, the traveller, the nail-biter.
(*The Hot Gates*, p. 172)

But although Martin is related to Homer's Odysseus, he seems to be Dante's even more—the wicked counsellor of the twenty-sixth canto of the *Inferno* who, abandoning the loves he owed his son, father, and wife, told his crew that it is man's business to break all horizons, and took them with him into the Atlantic, until they went down before the rock of Purgatory, "as pleased Another."

It becomes increasingly clear that it is something like this rock that Martin is on, and that he is in conflict with the same Other—God. The laudatory images of man building his fate that come into Pincher's mind are classical or Renaissance, but in the general pattern of what happens to him they are dominated by medieval and condemnatory images—not only of Ulysses but also of Judas Iscariot, whom in Irish legend Saint Brendan saw reprieved from Hell on an Atlantic rock. Pincher's fellow actors, moreover, in a morality play find for him the part of Greed. Yet in his conflict with God, evil as he is, he is also Everyman. Golding has given him something more out of his own autobiography, his childhood fear of the darkness of the cellar and the coffin ends crushed in the walls from the graveyard outside. The darkness universalizes him. It becomes increasingly but always properly laden with symbolism: the darkness of the thing that cannot examine itself, the observing ego; the darkness of the unconscious; the darkness of sleep, of death, and beyond death, heaven. "Take us as we are now," his friend Nathaniel told Martin at Oxford, "and heaven would be sheer negation. Without form and void. You see? A sort of black lightning destroying everything that we call life."

But heaven is also God, and Martin, as he is forced to face that Other, hears "the cellar door swinging to behind a small child who must go down, down in his sleep to meet the thing he turned from when he was created." Golding made these symbols explicit in a letter to John Peter, in which he says that the cellar suggests "that God is the thing we turn away from into life, and therefore we hate and fear him and make a darkness there. . . . Pincher is running away all the time, always was running, from the moment he had a *persona* and could say 'I.' " But it is clear enough in the book, when the imagery and events are put together. The fourteenth-century mystic Walter Hilton has the same philosophy in his *Ladder of Perfection:* if you abstract your mind from all images of physical sensation and look within, he says, you will find nothing. "This 'nothing' is none else than darkness of mind. . . . Were the roots of sin greatly reduced and dried up in you, then if you looked into your heart you would not find nothing. You would find Jesus."[4]

Martin sees God in his own body, with a bloodshot eye, in seaman's clothes. He says to it:

"You are a projection of my mind. But you are a point of attention for me. Stay there."

. . .

"Have you had enough, Christopher?"

. . .

"I could never have invented that."

(p. 194)

Perhaps Golding has taken a hint here from a passage he admires in C. S. Lewis's science-fiction novel *Perelandra,* where a man—a philologist—faced with the necessity to do something he cannot bear to do argues with a presence in the darkness that surrounds him until it says:

[4]Walter Hilton, *The Ladder of Perfection* 1.53, L. Sherley-Price, trans., London, 1957.

"It is not for nothing that you are named Ransom."
And he knew that this was no fancy of his own. He knew it for a very curious reason—because he had known for many years that his surname was derived not from *Ransom* but from *Ranolf's son*. It would never have occurred to him thus to associate the two words. To connect the name Ransom with the act of ransoming would have been for him a mere pun.

(p. 168)

There is a similar pun in the way Martin is addressed—Christopher, "the Christ bearer." But Pincher Martin will not recognize it; it is not this that makes him recognize that he is speaking to God, but the questioning of the prime urge of his being:

"Enough of what?"
"Surviving. Hanging on."

. . .

"I hadn't considered."
"Consider now."

. . .

"I will not consider! I have created you and I can create my own heaven."
"You have created it."

(pp. 195–196)

He has created it. The fear of facing the darkness within himself, where his self comes to an end in God, made him once take refuge in aggression: "I climbed away from the cellar over the bodies of used and defeated people, broke them to make steps on the road away from you." Now, he has taken refuge in solipsism. The rock, the whole business of survival, is nothing but his own mirage, blotting out God. (In *Perelandra* the waves of the sea suggest self-abandonment to divine providence,[5] and the rock the desire "to make sure—to be able on one day to command, where I should be the next and what should happen to me." This idea seems closer in *Pincher Martin* than in *The Inheritors*.) Before the presence of God everything surrounding Martin vanishes, and he himself is left nothing but a center of consciousness and a pair of claws against which the black lightning of heaven plays, "prying for a weakness, wearing them away in a compassion that was timeless and without mercy."

[5]The title of a book by J. P. de Caussade, 1861.

This terrific epiphany is not the end. In *Pincher Martin,* as in the first two books, we shift from this wholly remade world into a more ordinary consciousness. On the Hebrides, a Mr. Campbell asks a naval officer come to examine Martin's corpse if there is any survival. The officer, not comprehending that this is a question about personal immortality, responds, "Don't worry about him. You saw the body. He didn't even have time to kick off his seaboots."

But this was the first thing Martin did: we saw him do it on the fourth page of the first chapter. Not a part, but the whole of his effort to survive was hallucination, indeed deliberate self-deception. When one rereads the book one realizes that from very early on Martin was fighting against a series of realizations, among them that the rock and the other rocks breaking the impact of the waves on it are nothing but his own teeth, a barrier against the outside world, the "wall of the teeth" of which Homer speaks. The whole story took place either in the moment of death, or after death in eternity—the latter, it would seem, for there is no break as Martin's imaginings surrender to the compassion that is timeless.

No doubt some readers pick up the hallucinatory nature of Martin's experiences relatively soon. I can only record that at first reading the last sentence left me trembling.

The novella "Envoy Extraordinary" (1956) was published along with stories by John Wyndham and Mervyn Peake, all three sharing the theme of someone disruptive coming on a static or dying society. It reveals in Golding a skeptical and ironic commentator on the themes of his own novels, one who treats the same ideas as the darkly mystical, Ancient Egyptian Golding, lightheartedly, satirically, and externally, with little question of identification with any of the characters. The intellect, imagination, and drive toward conquest of the universe that Tuami and Pincher Martin had, together with the confident enlightenment of Piggy, are given to the charming Phanocles, whose ecstatic proclamation of absorption in science is quoted at the beginning of this essay. He produces in the late Roman Empire a confusion with his invention of the steamship that is only put right, disastrously, by his second invention of high explosives. Before the third, the printing press, can take effect, the emperor packs him off as ambassador to China. For he comes up against men with other ruling passions—Postumus, heir to the empire, whom we have met before as Jack, with the lust for power; the emperor, whose passion is memory, to recover the intense enjoyments of youth, and who welcomes steam only for the sake of the recovery of flavor in the pressure cooker—but whose headmasterly wisdom points out a certain selfishness in Phanocles' irresponsible urges; and Mamillius, who being still young has no ruling passion until he falls in love with Phanocles' sister Euphrosune. She is silent, perhaps the only unselfish person in the story, since she has no ruling passion; she is also perhaps the most intelligent, since she saves the situation that the others have made for themselves. In the excellent witty play, *The Brass Butterfly* (1958), made from the story, she is given her own ruling passion, a youthfully ecstatic Christianity. I think this an improvement. The play remains Shavianly ironic: Golding's preface describes the ruling passions as Sacred Cows or Unexamined Beliefs.

*Free Fall* (1959) returns from ironic and skeptical comment—what Golding in an essay on "Thinking as a Hobby" called Grade Two Thinking—to Grade One Thinking, the passionate enquiry after truth. It attempts both a new structure and a new style in obedience to a question left hanging in *Lord of the Flies:* whether the end was necessitated by the beginning, the savage tribe already potential in the schoolboys, the moment when Roger kills Piggy latent in the moment when Ralph pretended to machine-gun him. In spite of the implicit presence of the Fall in *The Inheritors* and *Pincher Martin,* no transition was shown. If we reject the idea of states of being that either do not change, or develop inevitably one from another, if we believe with the Jews and Christians that there are times of total free will, how do we express this in a novel? How indeed do we recognize such a moment in our own lives?

This is not a question for the first reading of a Golding novel of the classic shape. Such a novel, moreover, cannot take the question-begging way out, of simply portraying one state as suddenly existing where there was another a paragraph before; this must not happen except at the point where our self-identification with the text is to be disturbed. Sammy Mountjoy, the autobiographer of *Free Fall,* questions his memory like a critic reading a classic Golding novel for the second time, going back to see where one interpretation superimposed itself on another, one self on another, the end of the process on the beginning. He circles about his life until he finds the very moment of fall; and he returns to the present to find, in a passage like the final twist of the earlier novels, what the consequences of his fall were. But self-consciousness is an endlessly involuting thing, and Sammy finds himself rather like T. S. Eliot in the *Four Quartets*, especially "Burnt Norton," looking for an answer to the problem of freedom, not in the loss of freedom but in the moment when he found himself detached enough from time and process to look at them from outside. So reading *Free Fall* is not only like rereading *Pincher Martin* with an eye to Martin's memories. In a sense a structure of the classic Golding two-worlds kind is superimposed on the structure that Sammy Mountjoy at first creates as he explores his past experience. But a reinterpreting of the questioning itself occupies the place of the taking over of one world view by another. So that now we must ask how the questioning itself changed; and that means one more shift of viewpoint in the final paragraph.

In fact, reading the book is not as complicated as that, because like the paths in *Alice in Wonderland* the questioning shakes itself and becomes one question. At the beginning Sammy finds himself living in two worlds, the mystical and moral world of the spirit and the world of sense and matter. To the end, he is looking for a bridge between them. Since we can speak of responsibility and freedom there must be such a bridge; but can it be expressed in the language of either world?

This problem is that which Dante wrote the *Divine Comedy* to solve. Dante, like Sammy, came to himself in the middle of his life, in a dark wood, unable to remember how he came there, "so full of sleep are we in the instant at which we leave the right way." His only way out is to see the world whole and himself in its light. Hell, purgatory, and heaven are revealed to him directly, himself and this world of sense in glimpses from the standpoint of divine justice and eternity. Golding took something like this course in *Pincher Martin*; in *Free Fall* his intent is to show this world directly, the other in hints and guesses. He is involved therefore in showing directly the moment of fall at which Dante only hints. He has a hero without reference points, who therefore lives in the vertigo of free fall, reproachful of an age in which those who have a morality or a system softly refuse to insist on them; a hero for whom no system he has will do, but who is looking for his own unity in the world —and that, the real world, is "like nothing, because it is everything." Golding, however, has the advantage of being able to bring Dante's world in by allusion; and he does so with a Paradise Hill on which a Beatrice is met.

Dante's style is answerable to his vision: pure, but capable of moving from high to low in a moment. Sammy begins his book in a divided style that harshly yokes the two worlds in the uncertain glory of "I have walked by stalls in the market place where books, dog-eared and faded from their purple, have burst with a white hosanna." He feels himself too divided to effect a union; fallen, like Pincher Martin, split between a too undetermined inner self—"the unnameable, unfathomable and invisible darkness . . . at the centre . . . always different from what you believe it to be"—and a self wholly determined, unfree.

When he goes on to tell about his childhood, he and his style are assured enough, as certain that he was free then as Dr. Johnson with his massive probity ever was; he almost echoes Johnson's "Sir, we *know* our wills are free, and *there's* an end on't." He looks for no excuses there for his later life, in his fatherless life in a rural slum or the overwhelming personalities of his mother and of his friend Evie, and the queer longing he receives from them to be a girl. His style moves easily in an undivided world from his mother on the bog to the Trahernian picture of a tree in moonlight in the general's garden on Paradise Hill. "There was one tree between me and the lawns, the stillest tree that ever grew, a tree that grew when no one was looking. . . . Later, I should have called the tree a cedar and passed on, but then, it was an apocalypse." He was tough enough and a bully, but his actions were innocent because unreflective, and set up no permanent division, no habit of fallenness.

From the last moment when he knows this was true, at the end of childhood and his mother's death, he overleaps the doubtful time of transition to the first moment when he knows he was unfree. He is in love with Beatrice, he has already interpreted this love as a need to possess and subdue, he possesses, subdues, deserts her. She is like the main object of Pincher Martin's jealousy, Mary Lovell who married Nathaniel; but he is too possessed with the wish to break out of his ego to be all

Pincher Martin to her. His childhood wish to be a girl transforms itself into the wish to know what it is like to be Beatrice. She is innocent and possesses a unity, a transparency of matter to spirit like Nat's or Mary Lovell's. But although she is in this sense a symbol, she has no words to explain what it is like to be a symbol. Further, Sammy says, "I was not wise enough to know that a sexual sharing was no way of bringing us together.... We had had our revelation of each other." He goes to queer byways of sadism to find her out, but in a way he knows her all the time. "After the last and particularly degrading step of her degradation," he paints her; and his imagination is a real artist's, not like Martin's, the means of his self-deception. He is not Martin but Tuami. He can still make the truth he cannot recognize. In his painting, Beatrice lies in gold "scattered from the window . . . looking out of the window as though she had been blessed."

In a German prison camp, the psychologist Dr. Halde singles Sammy out as someone weak enough to tell the Gestapo what he is sensitive enough to know, which of his fellow prisoners has the temperament for trying to escape. Halde puts him blindfolded into a dark cupboard to be left for torture to his imagination.

The narrative moves back to the end of childhood to find that Sammy began to be afraid of the dark when he lost the "way of seeing, which was a part of innocence"; when transferred from his slum to a lonely rectory he felt the "certain want and horror . . . beyond imagination" that Thomas Traherne also describes as happening at the end of childhood's vision.[6] Golding has endowed Sammy, like Martin, with his own childhood terror of the dark. But what Martin resisted, Sammy surrenders to: his imagination drives him onward toward every torture the Gestapo may have in store for him, and he screams for help. The recognition of the need for help changes him: "The thing that screamed left all living behind and came to the entry where death is close as darkness against eyeballs. And burst that door."

He does not say on what the door opened—perhaps on God. But he comes out of the cupboard reduced to a child again: silly and blessed; dead and resurrected. He finds the world transfigured. He draws his fellow prisoners in the image of cigarette cards he collected as a boy, "the haggard unshaven kings of Egypt in their glory." He knows as ego what he always knew as artist, that the substance of the world is love. Pincher Martin's cosmos is turned inside out. In the light of the transfigured world Sammy sees his "center" free, defying the determinist's "law of the conservation of energy," creative of endless shapes of evil.

Like Dante in the dark wood, he rediscovers the memory of Beatrice and sees her transfigured, in her "clear absence of being," a fullness that had "once shone out of her face." He goes back now to the transition period, the bridge between childhood and guilt; remembers himself at school, dominated by two teachers, Miss Pringle in whose room he was told that "as a sign to Moses that the Lord was present, the bush burned with fire but was not consumed away," and Mr. Shales next door, who says, "Matter can neither be destroyed nor created." He is offered a bridge between them when Beatrice sits for the class as a model and Sammy in the act of drawing her is born as an artist. "I saw there . . . a metaphorical light that none the less seemed to me to be an objective phenomenon." But he has already chosen Mr. Shales's universe because Mr. Shales is a good man, a saintly Phanocles, although that universe provides no context for his saintliness. The light then can only be reduced to the brute fact of sex. Sammy discovers, looking back, the day on which his headmaster told him that there is such a thing as the ruling passion; and he chose for his ruling passion his lust for Beatrice, changed into the need for her abjection if she denied him total possession of her. He has found the moment of fall at last.

Returned from his vision in Germany, he meets Beatrice again on Paradise Hill, an idiot in a lunatic asylum, sent there by his treatment of her, although quite possibly her cool, dumb self-possessedness would have issued in idiocy anyway. Once again he can see no bridge; the book almost ends in the statement of his belief in two separate worlds. But the last paragraph returns to a German Commandant letting him out of the darkness. It functions partly as a shower of cold normal consciousness on Sammy's transports, since the darkness is only a cupboard; partly, like others of Golding's endings, to stress the reality of the now distanced abnormal consciousness. Yet in both worlds a door has opened. Golding himself has

---

[6]Thomas Traherne, *Centuries of Meditations* 3.23.

remarked that the opening of the cell door is like the "handprint on the canvas that changes the whole thing," and that when he saw that, it became "the first genuine passion I felt about the book."[7] But this is not convincingly conveyed, if only because Sammy has already told us that the "Commandant came late and as a second string." Nevertheless, Sammy clings as to a bridge between the two worlds to the Commandant's saying, "The Herr Doctor does not know about peoples." Whatever realization happened in the cupboard—and that is still only obliquely known—finds some response in this, perhaps because it declares that the way of putting nature to the test by torment and questions, the way the psychologist took with him and he with Beatrice, is not the way to knowing what is there. But the resolution remains thick and uncertain; and, perhaps because Sammy has already tried to do it for us, the second reading of the book provides nothing new. Alone among Golding's novels, *Free Fall* is more of a puzzle fragmentarily solved than a mystery to be known, although it has long, illuminated stretches.

In the same year as *Free Fall*, Golding also published a short story, "The Anglo-Saxon," which deserves resuscitation from its back number of *The Queen*. A story trying to express the world of a downland drover who has a language of 650 words hung in the "dark, angry cupboard" of his head, who is confronted with a world of laws, new men, and new exigencies that he does not understand, it goes closely with *The Inheritors* and might be bound up with it in case anyone takes from the novel the notion that inarticulateness necessarily means unfallenness.

Golding's two short stories are like the later ones of Rudyard Kipling, in that by omission and obliquity they try to convey in a very short length the emotional intensity of a novel. His other one, "Miss Pulkinhorn," written in 1951, was not published until 1960, after appearing as one of his two radio plays in the same year. The radio plays, in contrast, having in regard the difficulty of a form only heard and not to be reread, are explicit in their buildup. "Miss Pulkinhorn" is one of the rare pieces in which one feels Golding at his full intensity while dealing with a situation neither of the past nor on a distant island, but in twentieth-century England. Both the setting, a cathedral and its close, and the peculiar emotions involved are eccentric to the age, however, although the ultimate theme—the uncompromising strangeness of the religious passion—is universal. That passion takes the form of the dependency of an Anglo-Catholic (that is, a strongly sacramental Anglican) on the reserved sacrament of Christ's body, the consecrated bread kept for the communion of the sick and adored by some, and the violent hatred that this adoration can arouse. Anglo-Catholicism is a peculiarly experiential religion; its adherents, who have, unlike traditional Roman Catholics, little repose on the authority of the Church, find their repose instead in the Holy Communion; and some will center so intensely on the experience that it is a common Anglo-Catholic claim that there is a recognizable difference between a church that has the presence of the reserved sacrament and one that has not. Golding, who once observed that hearing a great line of Shakespeare is a moment "no more to be defined than taking a Sacrament, or bearing a child, or falling in love," is well fitted to present this kind of perceptual and experiential religion; indeed we have seen similar things in *Lord of the Flies* and elsewhere.

In the radio play the emotion is presented at length. It is first prepared for in the awe of the cathedral, then in the devotion of an old, crazy, holy man and emphasized by the intense repugnance of Miss Pulkinhorn; and given a ground of more widely shared emotion in the repetition in cathedral services of Christ's words, "Take, eat. This is my Body which is given for you"; and one more widely shared still in Gustav von Holst's setting of the carol in which Christ says:

Sing O my love, O my love, O my love, my love
This have I done for my true love.

This in its turn has a context in human falling in love, as a boy repeats it to his girlfriend. The words, however, also suggest that religious feeling in the man and in Miss Pulkinhorn may not be free of unconscious sexuality. We are well prepared when the man says, "They'll light the light, just as though I needed a light to tell me He's there . . . I'll see Him . . . and He'll see me—and I shall whisper 'Hosannah' just as we did in Jerusalem"; and, when on an evening when the Sacrament has been

---

[7] V. Tiger, *William Golding: The Dark Fields of Discovery*, p. 160.

removed to communicate a dying person, Miss Pulkinhorn relights the light that is the sign of the presence of Christ's body, we can fully comprehend the enormous violation done to the man as, while he adores something that is not there, the verger puts out the light. We can believe both in his subsequent death and the breaking down of Miss Pulkinhorn by her realization of what she has done, until she kneels before the light herself; and feel the force of her still declaring, "My conscience is perfectly clear."

In the story the buildup is absent; the old man does not speak and remains ambiguous. The emotions are seen to happen; but unless one knows them at first hand, they remain, as it were, in a foreign language. Tauter and finer than the play, intensely moving to those who know its emotions, the story remains relatively inaccessible, the purest example of the merits and defects of Golding's intransigence. It sets in fact a problem of exposition that he solves in *The Spire,* to which "Miss Pulkinhorn" is related as "The Anglo-Saxon" is to *The Inheritors.* The emotion and ambiguity of "This have I done for my true love" in the play; and the old man's assertion, using Christ's justification for his shout of Hosanna, "If these held their peace, the very stones would cry out," again in the play; and in the story the assertion that the old man has the posture of Abraham in one of the cathedral windows—images of the strangeness of the religious passion—all find their place in the novel.

The second radio play, "Break My Heart" (1966), is very pure radio drama. It is essentially a quasi-documentary of a day in the life of a country school in the late 1950's. But the welter of voices gradually centers on the problem of Malcolm Smith, until this term an unexceptionable and happy boy, now apparently stupid and "against everybody." At the very end of the play, we find, in between two attempts to teach him one of Hamlet's soliloquies, that he is in Hamlet's situation, his mother committing adultery with his father's brother. When *Break My Heart* is read in script, something of a conflict appears between the themes of the opacity of man's heart and the incomprehension of society. Smith's situation as presented seems even too explicable, the masters' incomprehension a matter largely of overwork. The strong stresses needed for radio are apparent here: the play is said to make excellent listening.

In *The Spire* (1964) the interest is all in the opacity of the man and in a further exploration of man's all-sacrificing will. Jocelin, dean of a cathedral about 1330, is first seen with the light exploding in his face through a window that pictures Abraham sacrificing Isaac. In theme and intensity the book is one to put alongside Søren Kierkegaard's treatment of Abraham in *Fear and Trembling* (1843). Jocelin says, listing Noah, Job, Hosea, and Abraham among the God-possessed figures of the Old Testament:

"Even in the old days God never asked men to do what was reasonable. Men can do that for themselves. They can buy and sell, heal and govern. But then out of some deep place comes the command to do what makes no sense at all—to build a ship on dry land; to sit among the dunghills; to marry a whore; to set their son on the altar of sacrifice. Then, if men have faith, a new thing comes."
(p. 121)

Genesis takes the reality of the command from God as an assumption. Kierkegaard thought that the ruling passion is self-justifying, if it is the thing inexplicable to anyone else that every man has as the heart of his individuality, his unique relation to God. It may be possible to make a mistake, but a man who makes a mistake in this is a monster. Even so, no one can know enough to judge such a man except himself and God.

It is the possibility of mistake, and the dubiety of the whole concept of self that follows, which Golding explores. He returns to the classic Golding shape to do so. The first chapter, however, differs from this shape in that while we are not told as in *Free Fall* that the innocent world presented is less than the whole story, still the noises of warning are louder than in the three earliest novels. Jocelin is to give his cathedral a new spire. The life of the cathedral is serene and ordered. It is the day of the new beginning. He is full of joy, looks with love on everyone, very gently rebukes two young men for talking uncharitably, feels a warmth at his back as he prays. And if there is doubt about the strength of the cathedral's foundations, faith answers that God will provide.

This may be well enough. But the reader picks up the suggestions that it is not only the physical foundations that are at fault, but the foundations of Jocelin's personality. Jocelin is blameably ignorant in having no notion that the young men may be talking about him; that his affection for his daughter in God, the wife of Pangall the sexton, may be not quite unmixed; that Pangall is bitterly unhappy because he is impotent and the workmen mock him for it; that his unassertive chaplain Father Adam (being under obedience) will stand indefinitely if not countermanded; and that the money to build the spire which comes from his aunt, the late king's mistress, is not only tainted but unpaid for: for she wants in return a tomb in the cathedral, which he will not give her.

It is hard therefore for the reader to identify himself with Jocelin. What we do identify ourselves with is the work. Jocelin's Abrahamic single will is not imposing itself on something that, like Pincher Martin's imagination, it can only falsify. Form is being imposed on matter, matter that resists, but that also is the potential substance of what is to be made. All Golding's delight in technical contrivance is brought into play in the shifts of Roger the mason in his impossible task; all his brilliance of sensuous imagination in rendering the resistance opposed to it—a resistance which does not seem to be that of dead matter, but of life being tamed. Under the strain imposed on them, the pillars sing and pebbles move on the earth like "some form of life: that which ought not to be seen or touched, the darkness under the earth, turning, seething, coming to the boil."

Simon's climbing the mountain, Tuami's carving the knife, Sammy's drawing Beatrice, were images within each book of the whole of each book. Pincher Martin's falsifying imagination was an image of half the book—the book at first reading, so to speak. But the whole of *The Spire* is an image of the writing of it: the reader shares in the drill biting into the armor plate, the intransigence.

The book's tendency therefore is to abandon the original sense that it is about the religious will for the sense that it is about art. That it never finally does so is due, first, to the fact that Jocelin and Roger Mason both remain in our eye, both necessary to each other. Jocelin has not only the will but the idea of what Roger does, so much so that Roger falls in love with Pangall's wife; and Jocelin assents in him to a passion he does not even recognize in himself because it will keep Roger at the work. Roger in turn—and therefore Jocelin—is involved in the actions of his men: what he thinks is what they do. They murder Pangall and put his body under the spire as a good luck offering. But because it is Jocelin's consciousness that we inhabit, a consciousness now (like Martin's) cut off from reality, except for his dependence on Roger Mason who must keep in touch with reality, we learn about Pangall's death only as it forces itself on Jocelin's mind, after he has seen, from the spire, fires of pagan offering on Midsummer Eve in the valley of the Hanging Stones: Stonehenge. Spire and Stonehenge recognize each other as places of sacrifice.

The other reason why religion and art, idea and means, are never separated, Golding partly owes to the fourteenth century. A cathedral is itself symbolic, is worship, and may be, as it is in Golding's hands, the whole of a man. Jocelin lays hands on himself when he lays hands on the cathedral, and in stirring up the darkness under the earth, begins to see the darkness within himself.

It seems to be all one process, therefore, that as Jocelin pushes the spire up by Roger's means he realizes that his urgency to build the spire is connected with his love for Pangall's wife—even obscurely that the spire is phallic, a club brandished in the sky toward the constellation called Berenice's hair; and that the warmth of the angel at his back is tuberculosis—that the vision in which he felt his body as the cathedral with the spire growing from it was deception. From it follow debts, the church deserted, discord, the murder of Pangall, the death of Pangall's wife bearing Roger's stillborn child, the despair and destruction of Roger and Jocelin themselves, and an "ungainly crumbling" spire. "This have I done for my true love" means only that visionary religion is repressed sexuality, and God exists if anywhere "lying between people and to be found there."

Thus Golding succeeds in bringing a philosophy of 1964 into the language of 1330: fittingly, since the century of Walter Hilton, already quoted, and of William Langland and the author of *The Cloud of Unknowing*, understood better than any other the ambiguity of religious vision. And ambiguity remains: there are two interpretations still to come. In "Miss Pulkinhorn," the narrator observes that his visionary was not a saint. "Read about the saints, even the least spectacular among them, and somewhere in their characters you'll come across steel, sheer adamant, something that can't be driven." This is realized in *The Spire* in a sudden revelation of the character of the least spectacular of its people, Father Adam. It is he who explains to Jocelin that his vision is a result of the capacity for visualizing that goes along with seeing sounds when one hears them—and with a beautiful unshakeability consoles Jocelin as one who was never taught to pray, since it is part of the science of prayer that such visions as his are encouragements only "just above vocal prayer." "Your prayer was a good prayer certainly: but not very."

But something so dry and undramatic finds little comprehension in Jocelin. His vision must be either all, his spire pierce all the stages of prayer, or nothing. He has a momentary comfort seeing an appletree—like the terrible tree that is his image for all the consequences of his will, like the Tree of Knowledge, but with more than one branch and a real tree. "It was there beyond the wall, bursting up with cloud and scatter, laying hold of the earth and the air, a fountain, a marvel, an appletree"; and near it "all the blue of the sky" is condensed into the flash of a kingfisher. But he only reacts into a depressed version of Father Adam's comment: "I make too much fuss among the appletrees and the kingfishers."

Only, as he dies, he sees his spire, dividing "the blue of the sky." It is beautiful, it astonishes, it glitters "like an upward waterfall" defying entropy, and his work culminates in it: "The substance was one thing that broke all the way to infinity in cascades of exultation that nothing could trammel." After all, we are doing something in building and praying. Whatever the cause (Jocelin thinks with a text from Christ's entry into Jerusalem, Luke 19:40), "our very stones cry out." And Jocelin dies, crying out at the very limits of language: *"It's like the appletree!"*

This is *The Spire*'s utmost reach into what cannot be expressed and Golding's most aspiring raid so far on poetry. In 1977 he was to refer to the final image in conversation as a symbol for a novel that succeeds. "It's a single activity, it's a beautiful thing, it's like the appletree growing out of a seed." Most certainly this is true of *The Spire;* and novel, spire, and appletree, if they are like the Tree of Knowledge, are like it as the tree of the Fortunate Fall. What Jocelin's cry does lack is the steel of the vision of God in *Pincher Martin*. And that is supplied in the last sentence: "Father Adam, leaning down, could hear nothing. But he saw a tremor of the lips that might be interpreted as a cry of: *God! God! God!* So of the charity to which he had access, he laid the Host on the dead man's tongue."

*"It's like the appletree!" "God! God! God!"*—alternative expressions; charity and the action of giving the Sacrament; and a silence between Jocelin's cry of *"the appletree"* and Father Adam's response, which may be like the shifts of consciousness in the earlier novels but can be felt as holding the mysterious fullness intended by the opening of the door at the end of *Free Fall*. Golding achieves something like the silences in Eliot's *Four Quartets*, revelatory silences, bridges into another world.

But he did not raid further into poetry for fifteen years, except in the articles and autobiographical fragments, some of which are assembled in *The Hot Gates* (1965), which we have already sampled. They make one wish for more autobiography. *The Pyramid* (1967) was, indeed, at first reading a disappointment to anyone who had acquired the taste for strong Golding. But no more than the others is it the same book at the end as at the beginning. At the beginning it seems to be a mixture of *Bildungsroman* and class novel. The title suggests the "social pyramid," a phrase out of *Free Fall;* the epigraph, also Egyptian—"If thou be among people make for thyself love, the beginning and end of the heart"—seems to refer to the emotional education of Oliver growing up between the wars in Stilbourne (more or less Marlborough). The episodes give his contact with three twisted lives—Evie Babbacombe, lower class, sexy, and exploitable, particularly as relief from Oliver's dreamlike infatuation for the middle-class Imogen; Mr. Evelyn de Tracy, a homosexual whom Oliver fails to understand, but who gives him his release from Imogen; and Bounce Dawlish, his music teacher, in frustrated love with Henry Williams, who introduced cars and garages to Stilbourne, and going mad. At this stage the book seems pleasantly written, but in low key. It seems only a defect in its fulfilling of its aims that there is no special subtlety in observing the marks of social differentiation, and that after all the social structure has little to do even with the fate of Evie —would she, or Oliver's feelings for her, have been strikingly different if she too had been a dispenser's child?—and nothing at all with those of Mr. de Tracy or Miss Dawlish. And the one flash of strong Golding at the end seems only an anomaly, as Oliver stands by the tomb of Clara Cecilia

Dawlish, 1890–1960, with the inscription "Heaven is Music":

> It was here, close and real, two yards away as ever, that pathetic, horrible, unused body, with the stained frills and Chinese face. This was a kind of psychic ear test before which nothing survived but revulsion and horror, childishness and atavism, as if unnameable things were rising round me and blackening the sun.
>
> (p. 213)

But then the whole book moves into a new key as Oliver realizes for the first time: "I was afraid of you, and so I hated you. It is as simple as that. When I heard you were dead I was glad." Finally he finds burned and smashed in Miss Dawlish's garden all her music books and papers, her father's metronome, a bust of Beethoven, and her father's photograph. The only person who could have done this was Bounce herself: in rebellion against her father and his phrase "Heaven is Music." Paying Henry Williams for petrol, Oliver sees Williams and himself as people who will pay a reasonable price to help others; but never more than a reasonable price.

After all, the book is not a picture of Oliver's emotional development; at most, a development to the point where he realizes our failure in emotion, the difficulty of making for ourselves love. In fact, in its original context in *The Maxims of Ptah-hotep,* "make for thyself love" is likely to have the merely prudential sense "make yourself liked": and that becomes likely too to be its sense for Oliver's life. As for *The Pyramid,* it seems that a better title might have been that originally given to the story of Bounce—*Inside a Pyramid:* her body in the image of Marlborough graveyard, in the darkness where Golding's childhood imagination began.

When the first meaning of pyramid becomes tomb, a chill is sent back through the whole book. Bounce was entombed all her life long—except for some years in which she was relaxed, smiling, and actually mad. And though the idea of social ascent is still present, it is penetrated by the coldness of the little town, the shut-inness of every house surrounding the square, the deathliness.

We know now too that the horrible pathos of Bounce's life issued from the beatings and discipline given her by her thwarted father; and this reflects back violently onto Evie's life, a girl brought up to masochism from a guessed-at early relationship with her father. And the general theme of the pathos of music, the reflection of a harmony that no one achieves, takes up even the partly comic episode of *The King of Hearts* as produced by the Stilbourne Operatic Society under Evelyn de Tracy. Not Evie's singing voice, nor the opera, nor Oliver's practice, nor the Savoy Orpheans (a radio orchestra) to whom Oliver compares Evie, nor any relationship described in the book offer what Sir Thomas Browne talked of:

> Even that vulgar and Tavern-Musick, which makes one man merry, another mad, strikes in me a deep fit of Devotion ... it is ... such a melody to the Ear as the whole world well understood would afford the understanding ... a sensible fit of that harmony which intellectually sounds in the Ears of God.[8]

Music serves as a metaphor once again for the achievement of the novel: but the harmony of art is in the end a chilly thing beside love.

*The Pyramid* has the obliquity of Golding's short stories—it is not explicit that it was Bounce who destroyed her music, and Evie's sexual relationships are also not made plain. In *The Scorpion God* (1971), he returned to the more relaxed satiric novella. It seems to be built around the previously published "Envoy Extraordinary": in place of the original stories by Peake and Wyndham, Golding puts two of his own, making a trio concerned with what one might call the beginning of history. "The Scorpion God" itself presents the beginning of political history as we understand it, for the first historic Pharaoh of united Egypt was called "The Scorpion." The culture of predynastic Egypt and the hot, bright country itself are re-created with an odd, vivid mixture of satire and love. The opening description of the Heb-Sed race (by which the Pharaohs proved their strength and consequent capacity to rule) reads like historical clairvoyance. And simultaneously the first page majestically echoes the sculptural world of the older gods at the opening of Keats's *Hyperion*—the numinous stillness that Keats embodied in light seeds on feathered grass, a leaf that falls and does not stir, the voiceless river, the Naiad among her reeds and Saturn in his fall, is marvelously, and detail for detail, paralleled. But gradually the story shifts key, following a suggestion out of Herodotus that the Egyptians do every-

[8]*Religio Medici,* II§9.

thing the opposite way from other nations, to become a clever satire, not unlike Wells's *Mr Blettsworthy on Rampole Island,* on the modern age. The Scorpion, a comic version or parody of Pincher Martin, in Egypt, which believes that to die is to begin to live, refuses to join the Pharaoh in "life," indeed kills a number of people to avoid it, and at the end is clearly about to destroy the traditional assumptions of Egypt—he seems to be a Greek—by marrying the dead Pharaoh's wife, Pretty Flower, and becoming Pharaoh. The chief minister, a physician of the soul who works on opposite principles from those of our psychoanalysts, says of him, "He has a death wish." Myth has been transformed into history. "Clonk Clonk," set long before the beginning of history, presents the advantages of being a misfit in traditional society once again: a man whose weak ankle goes "clonk," giving him something of the disadvantages of a woman who cannot hunt, and a woman whose mind (she says) goes "clonk," giving her the forebodings and tendency to poetry proper only to men. They marry, to each other's great advantage, and happily nothing further happens, the woman's forebodings being unfulfilled. In this context, "Envoy Extraordinary" joins with the other two stories in presenting the silliness and comfort of the three disturbed societies and a vivid, sensuous re-creation of heat which makes the excessive activity of the three heroes particularly obnoxious.

The skeptical, rationalistic Greeks of "Egypt from My Inside" seemed to have defeated the imaginative, spiritually pragmatic Egyptians in Golding's work: the relatively detached satiric style of *The Scorpion God* fits its skeptical heroes. And he published no more imaginative writing until 1979.

III

From the eight years' silence, it was Egypt that called Golding back. When in 1976 he went for the first time in geographical reality to Egypt, his imagination was caught by the Colossi of Memnon—the pair of giant statues of Amenophis III whose faces, he said in a lecture a few months later,

have been struck away as if blasted by some fierce heat and explosion. All that is visible there is shadow. Their heads preserve nothing but a sense of gaze, their bodies nothing but the rubble of posture on a royal throne. Here might be an image of a humanity indomitable but contrite because history has broken its heart ... of a creature maimed yet engaged to time and our world and enduring it with a purpose no man knows and an effect that no man can guess.

(*A Moving Target,* p. 168)

What he describes bears more than a little resemblance to the broken body with "the ruin of a face" of the airman in *Lord of the Flies,* which became the Beast; to his exegesis of it in *Fable* as suggesting the inescapableness of human history; to the "terrible knees and feet of black stone" of the gods in the cellar in *Pincher Martin;* and to "the haggard unshaven Kings of Egypt in their glory" in *Free Fall.* The stone Pharaohs embody history, and the destructiveness of history, and some purpose more than human in history. But this description adds new elements: contrition (in significant contrast with Simon's idea of the Beast "a human at once heroic and sick," there is "humanity indomitable but contrite") and fire.

It is fairly clear that this perception became the nucleus of what is perhaps the most remarkable single passage in Golding's works, the opening eight pages of *Darkness Visible.* It is a passage that works like the overture of an opera, announcing themes and images in what amounts to a symbol of great intensity and complexity, and in so doing finds a way of developing the raid on poetry of the kind that happened at the end of *The Spire.*

The Egyptian statues merge with the archetype of the burning babe, which one can find as a picture of Christ in Thomas Campion's poem on Christmas day; which smites itself into the host in Thomas Malory's description of the mass of the Grail at Carbonek; which is implicit in the three children in the fiery furnace in the book of Daniel; and which is seen as it were in manhood at the beginning of the Apocalypse, the Son of Man with eyes and feet like fire, a face like the sun, and a two-edged sword coming from his mouth.

With this weight of meaning behind him, but himself speechless, Matty walks, a child maimed and with his face blasted by heat and fire, out of the blitz on London on a night of full moon when the water mains broke. What he comes out of has many more significances: the tower of Babel struck down by fire from heaven when the languages of mankind were divided; the burning bush; the infernal city; the ruins of Pompeii; the pillars of smoke and fire that went before the Israelites at the Exodus, but here are seen as sacred to the moon. The scene is also a vivid and concrete evocation of a night in the blitz. The final note is perfectly built up to—the grief of the captain of firemen who sees Matty's appearance, "not for the maimed child but for himself, a maimed creature whose mind had touched for once on the nature of things."

The work of *Darkness Visible* is to fit the mythic and symbolic figure of Matty into a realistic novel. As regards Matty himself, it perfectly succeeds. Matty comes out of mystery and fire, and goes back into mystery and fire at the end, when he is for a second time in contact with an exploding bomb and comes burning from it—to rescue another small boy, a figure like himself of destiny, from probable murder. The book is haunted by the sense that he is a visitant from the other side of things; a little before his death he comes to that sense of himself. But for most of the book he is what was adumbrated in the Lovells in *Pincher Martin* and in Beatrice Ifor in *Free Fall,* the literal side only of a symbol that stretches into mystery. He is in fact a pathologically literal person, whether he is reading the Bible with a reverence that includes the verse numbers or responding to other people's ironic remarks; and he is besides driven by compulsions, which a psychiatrist might class as neurotic but which he identifies, like Jocelin in *The Spire,* with the compulsive symbolic actions of the possessed men and prophets of the Bible. Left maimed in mind and body by the fire, in his isolation he asks first "Who am I?" then "What am I?" and finally "What am I for?," wandering like the biblical Abraham in search of an answer to the other side of the world. In 1965, however, he begins to have visions and to record them in a journal, in which we follow him between then and 1978, growing up to them so that, for example, the "spirits," one of whom is "in red with a hat on," while the other "in blue had a hat too but not as expensive," become "red and blue elders" who "took off their crowns and threw them down 'before' the white spirit with the circle of the sun round his head."

Matty throughout is both scapegoat and visionary, like Simon and like Nathaniel Lovell. He is shown "the seamy side where the connections are," and through him it is shown to others. Here again is something that his visit to Egypt seems to have enlarged in Golding's attention. He says in the superb essay he wrote in 1977 as a twin for "Egypt from My Inside," "Egypt from My Outside," that the mythology of ancient Egypt, the "beautiful, wise, malevolent and insane language of the wall-paintings," possessed his mind in a way that brought a verse of the psalms with it: "Day unto day uttereth speech and night unto night sheweth knowledge" (19:2). For, he adds, "I believe that life is central to the cosmos and that there are some times for some people when the deeps of that cosmos like the deeps of our minds open out."

For Matty, day does utter speech to day. His visions are of light and of things that are not within himself—a glass ball filled with sunlight on a dull day, Orion seen in Australia "with his dagger bursting fiery up," even the elders who—as the change in their description shows—are as objective as a pure vision can be. The one vision that someone has as a result of meeting him that is described in detail is of the palm of his own hand "made of light."

Matty is a saint translated into a language that is plausible for a late-twentieth-century realistic novel. "The knowledge that night shews to night" is given to the other principal character of the book, Sophy, who is in the same kind of translation a diabolist, a witch. She is as pretty and clever as Matty is ugly and half-witted; she has the same capacity for vision of the other side of things, and perhaps—though this is never quite unambiguously said of either—shares with him a capacity for miracles. Both Matty and the elders recognize her as the same kind of being as himself. Early in their lives, both have done something that they regard as a miracle—Matty cursed a boy who seemed to threaten his teacher, Mr. Pedigree, and the boy died. Sophy threw a stone at a dabchick and hit it. Pedigree is blamed for the boy's death and tells Matty, "It's all your fault": Matty accepts Mr. Pedigree's guilt as well as his own, and spends the rest of his life in contrition. Sophy, moved partly by an intense, in the end incestuous, jealousy over her father, thinks she has learned that she must follow the rhythms behind the universe, and in the end identifies those rhythms with entropy, the unraveling of the world into black nothing, symbolized in *The Inheritors* by falling water, and now by fire, which it is her nature to urge on by outrage. Matty, who comes out of the burning bush, a symbol here as in *Free Fall* of what burns and is not consumed, and therefore of what is not subject to entropy, sees that behind himself and behind every human being is "a spirit like the rising of the sun." Sophy knows that there is blackness in her, at the mouth of which she lies, and chooses to identify herself with that blackness.

The book is at once prolific of patterns and bursting with untidy life. The only passage that matches Matty's first epiphany in its intensity is that in which Sophy deliriously abandons herself, as a final outrage, to an imagination of knifing the boy whom in fact Matty has already saved from her by the burnt offering of his death. But that passage also drives home the parallel between her and Pedigree, who like her obeys an entropic rhythm, the rhythm of his pederasty, but in the end dies resisting it when he feels it driving him to the point where he will find himself murdering a boy. And the passage describing Pedigree's death is the closing movement of the book, which partly answers to the overture: it is Matty who brings Pedigree both the help, which is death, and the love that he needs. Matty is transfigured in ways that again draw on Egypt—Pedigree's dying vision of him begins with the sun with many golden hands, like the sundisc that the Pharaoh Akhnaton worshiped, and Matty himself is seen transformed to burning gold with the face—though this not made explicit—of a Pharaonic coffin. The epilogue has neither the intensity nor the complex overtones of the overture, and the reader is not lost in it; we do not forget it is a vision given only to Pedigree, are indeed continually reminded of this in the narration.

This is characteristic of the novel. The practice of the earlier novels of identifying the reader with a consciousness within the novel is, except in Sophy's horrid fantasy of murder, subjected to a distancing. We do indeed see the inwardness of Matty, Sophy, Pedigree, and a little of a fourth narrative eye, Sim Goodchild, an old bookseller who begins, in a kind of further parallel to Pedigree, with a muted passion for Sophy as a child, but ends as Matty's disciple; but we see this inwardness at the same kind of distance as in reading someone's journal, as in literal truth we do Matty's. This fits one of the minor themes of the novel, the partitions between people, and Matty's power momentarily to break them down. There is an almost Dickensian frequency of minor characters of whose inwardness we see nothing—most tantalizingly in the case of Antonia, Sophy's twin, who may well be a closer parallel than Sophy is to Matty, since she is capable of commitment: once, like Matty, to Jesus; later to a destructive political terrorism. Almost certainly she is a much more interesting person than Sophy, but Sophy naturally does not think so, and we see her only through Sophy's eyes. All the other characters—the twins' father, Sophy's men, Matty's employers, the inhabitants of the town where most of the story happens—serve severally to define the four whose inwardness we see, and collectively to give a satiric and somewhat hyperbolic account of England's and civilization's development in Matty's and Sophy's lifetimes.

The novel's fertility in characters adds a sense of compulsive growth to its compulsive parallelisms, which matches the compulsions of Pedigree, Sophy, and Matty. This compulsiveness is suggested by the novel's epigraph, which is from Virgil's invocation at the beginning of his description of the underworld, in the sixth book of the *Aeneid*, "Sit mihi fas audita loqui" (May it be lawful for me to say what I have heard), as if the book is the author's record of visions like Matty's visions. Something of the same meaning is given to the title by Sophy's reflecting on her "desire for the impossibilities of the darkness and the bringing of them into being to disrupt the placid normalities of the daylight world."

But this, the knowledge that night gives to night, is only half the book. C. G. Jung remarked that "one does not become enlightened by imagining figures of light, but by making the darkness conscious." This would be a suitable description of what Golding seems to be doing in all his earlier novels, and in Sophy's side of *Darkness Visible*. But it is Matty's side, the knowledge that day gives to day, which is victorious in the total story. In the set of lectures that includes "Egypt from My Outside," Golding tentatively suggests that novelists may have "a tincture" of the inexplicable perception of character possessed by some saints, notably —although he was "near enough a half-wit"—by the curé d'Ars. Matty, less consciously intelligent still, has that power. And Golding, as it were mimicking the character whom he created, is compelled to try to see the central characters of the book and to break down the partitions between them as Matty does. Thus the image that, like others of Golding's novels, it carries of itself within itself is not Sophy's witchcraft but the principal symbol that Matty brings from the other side of things, his legacy to Sim Goodchild, his journal.

Thus *Darkness Visible*, like Matty's journal within it, might be said to be a prophetic symbol. If so, what it prophetically warns of is the final decay of Western civilization. The title, from *Paradise Lost*, and the epigraph from the *Aeneid* are balanced at the end by a tag from their common predecessor, Homer's *Iliad*. Sebastian Pedigree's outwardly squalid pederasty is compassionated and dignified by the words τηλίκου ὥς περ ἐγών (old, as I am), which compare his longings to Priam's when he begs Achilles to give him the corpse of his son Hector. This quotation in the general narration perhaps justifies Pedigree's own more terrible and pitiful appropriation, in the Greek of the Bible, of Christ's cry on the cross, "Διψῶ Διψάω" (I thirst). Cumulatively, the four quotations in the—now less and less understood—original languages, from the Bible and the three great epics, claim for *Darkness Visible* in the whole great tradition of Western literature a place they may be at once a consummation and—so far as Sophy's experience, the knowledge that night gives to night, goes—a degradation. The sword that proceeds from the mouth of the Word in both the Apocalypse and the novel, and that gives Matty the message of his death, is also promised to Matty himself by the elders. But his mouth is "not intended for speaking," and part of his message is against "reproduced words." He knows that words other than prophetic words distort experience. *Darkness Visible* embodies a crisis of faith in language and literature familiar in modernism and deals with it in a way that continually brings to mind Eliot's *Little Gidding*, looking like that poem for a new birth, out of pentecostal fire, of a spiritual language.

Within a year of *Darkness Visible* Golding published a novel, *Rites of Passage*, that in relation to it is like the other half of a diptych. It is mirrorlike on the one hand in having set within it the journal of a visionary, a scapegoat, and a wanderer, driven by unknown compulsions and undergoing a terrible rite of passage—the name anthropologists give to rituals that mark out and declare the meaning of a passage from one state of life, one identity, to another—on his way to the other side of the world. But on the other hand it is contrasted in being classic and formally composed, whereas *Darkness Visible* is romantic and riotous in growth; a historical novel set in about 1813–1814, whereas *Darkness Visible* ends in 1978, about a year before the date of publication; having its mythic qualities concealed in overtones and its social satire in the foreground, whereas *Darkness Visible* scarcely keeps its myth in bounds and its social satire is only scene setting; set in water whereas *Darkness Visible* is set in fire.

The nucleus of *Rites of Passage* is an anecdote—told by Elizabeth Longford in her biography of the Duke of Wellington, out of William Hickey's *Memoirs*.[9] A young "member of the 'higher classes'" called Blunt, a clergyman whom Hickey in 1797 persuaded Wellington—then named Colonel Wellesley—to take as chaplain on an expedition from Bengal against the Philippines, "got abominably drunk" and rushed naked from his cabin among the crew, talking and singing obscenities. Thereafter, shutting himself in his cabin in shame, he refused to eat. Colonel Wellesley himself rowed across to Blunt's ship. "He told him," says Hickey, "that what had passed was not of the least consequence, as no one would think the worse of him for the little irregularities committed in a moment of forgetfulness. . . . In short Colonel Wellesley laboured to reconcile Mr Blunt to himself, treating the circumstances as by no means calling for the deep contrition expressed and felt by him." But Blunt's contrition killed him in ten days.

This extraordinary confrontation between the code of a broadminded man of the world and violent religious emotion remains the essence of *Rites of Passage*. But Golding has made three conspicuous alterations. First, he has made the chaplain a peasant, with the look of a medieval peasant from the border of a psalter, risen from the laboring classes. This is part of the general structure of the book, which clearly intends to make the ship in which the Reverend Mr. Colley dies a microcosm of English society. The microcosm is drawn with elegance and wit; and yet, as in *The Pyramid*, one wonders if the concern with class does not distract from the real issue. It is not unfair to refer back to the actual incident, which confirms that Colley might have behaved in the same way even had he not

---

[9]*Wellington: The Years of the Sword* (London, 1969), p. 51.

been persistently humiliated for his plebeian unease in society. And a chance was rejected for a different and perhaps profounder comment on class, for the Reverend Mr. Blunt was of the same family that in Wilfred Scawen Blunt during the nineteenth century, and Anthony Blunt during the twentieth, produced two further examples of reacting against one's society from, even because of, a situation of ease and privilege within it.

The dramatic advantage of the change is that Blunt was not, but Colley is, isolated from the beginning. And this fits into a context with the second change, the small but important shift in date that brings the events into the hightide of the romantic age. Colley, although a religious man, is not like Matty a prophetic and mystical visionary and solitary, but rather a romantic one, whose romanticism is a compound of ecstasy in nature and evangelicalism. He dies as a kind of scapegoat, like Matty, and that too is drawn into the romantic age by being related to Samuel Taylor Coleridge's great myth of the fall in the killing of the albatross by the Ancient Mariner. And Colley's journal contrasts with the general narration of the book, which is also a journal, not like Matty's as mystical to secular, but as romantic and evangelical to Whiggish, classic, and of the Enlightenment. The keeper of this outer, covering journal is of the historical Mr. Blunt's social status, but not of his temperament, a young gentleman named Talbot under the patronage of a noble and influential godfather, for whom indeed the journal is kept. It is Talbot, naturally, who tried as long as possible to reduce the reasons for Colley's ruin to class and society; who, while Colley is in the process of shaming himself and the sailors are mocking him, reflects that "the civilized world has had cause to lament the results of indiscipline among the Gallic Race."

Third, there is a geographic change that subtly enhances the mythic element in the story. This is not any voyage, but the great voyage like the Ancient Mariner's across the equator to the other side of the world. As they cross the equator, Colley, at the edge of his humiliation in a mock rite of passage that itself prepares for his final shame and crisis, sees, with the eye of romantic religion, the sun and moon hanging level like the scales of God's justice. Talbot whimsically notes that the captain (who plays a large part in Colley's humiliations, but whose own birth in England was humiliating) has, when he turns away from the gardening of plants in his cabin that provides his only release for affection, "the stony or sullen face . . . of the expelled Adam." In the destinies of both Colley and the captain, there is as it were a myth of an English fall at the beginning of the history of modern Australia.

Yet the book is a little hopeful. There is in it the rarest of creations by any novelist, a convincing and likeable good man, Lieutenant Summers, who tells Talbot that either Colley's "wits are gone or he knows nothing of his own religion . . . a Christian *cannot* despair!" Hopeful in itself, this remark casts a doubt on Colley's earlier romantic piety. And yet again, at the end, Talbot—who at the moment of crossing the equator was farcically seducing an actress, and one of whose irresponsible words was probably the cause of the death of his servant—has by reading Colley's journal had his own rite of passage: he has grown up a little. It is only a very little; two pages from the end he makes the telltale mistake that Jocelin makes in the first chapter of *The Spire:* hearing two people talk unkindly about himself, he reflects on their uncharity but assumes it is directed against someone else. But two shifts in his consciousness happen in those last two pages. First, he realizes that Colley had actually done something to make him die of shame, and what it was; and with the realization comes further recognition and shame at his own implication in Colley's ruin. Second, having with a touch still of his Whiggish orotundity written that "men can die of shame," he shows in his final sentence how deeply he has been affected by reading Colley's vision of the sun and moon as the scales of God, how much his sense of both the human and the natural world has been enlarged: "With lack of sleep and too much understanding, I grow a little crazy, I think, like all men at sea who live too close to each other and too close thereby to all that is monstrous under the sun and moon."

Here, as throughout the book, sea, sun, and moon seem ambiguously to increase the claustrophobia of human society and to suggest that outside it there is something better—the sense provided by the steadfast constellations and the tide for Simon's transformed body in *Lord of the Flies.* They reinforce too the haunting presence of Coleridge; perhaps the changes of light suggest something like Coleridge's comparison of the power of poetry to "the sudden charm... which moon-light or sunset diffused over a known and familiar landscape."[9] At any rate, some of these ideas were brought together in the magnificent and rather Coleridgean lecture "Belief and Creativity," which Golding delivered about the time of the completion of *Rites of Passage* and published in *A Moving Target*:

It may be—I hope it is—redemption to guess and perhaps perceive that the universe, the hell which we see, for all its beauty, vastness, majesty is only a part of a whole which is quite unimaginable.... The act of human creativity, a newness starting into life at the heart of confusion and turmoil... I guess... is a signature scribbled in the human soul, sign that beyond the transient horrors and beauties of our hell there is a Good which is ultimate and absolute.

("Belief and Creativity")

At the beginning of "Belief and Creativity," however, Golding sets a contrasting picture of himself as novelist peering out of the wrappings that have been tightened on him by the reading public in "a process of literary mummification." In his next novel, *The Paper Men*, he explores how far literary mummification and the power of words to displace experience can go. Here the journal form pushes out the external narrative of *Darkness Visible* and the observing exterior journal of *Rites of Passage*. In *The Paper Men* we have only the journal written and observe the world seen by a successful but deeply self-indulgent novelist, whose books have titles—*Coldharbour, All We like Sheep, The Birds of Prey, The Endless Plain, Horses at the Spring*—that recall not William Golding but Malcolm Lowry's *Hear Us O Lord from Heaven Thy Dwelling Place* or *The Forest Path to the Spring*. The theme of wandering becomes that of mere flight, of the novelist—Wilfred Barclay—from his critic, Rick L. Tucker; the rite of passage becomes the humiliation of Tucker, which Barclay performs as a seal to what he dramatizes as his own moral ruin. The visionary side of the journal remains, but has severe doubt cast on it by the hysterical and suggestible side of Barclay's imagination. Almost as soon as we encounter Barclay, he tells us that on him a placebo has all the power of an aphrodisiac: seeing Padre Pio's stigmata he thinks they are something of the sort, and by the end of the book he has pains in his own hands and feet which he interprets as his own stigmata. The deliberate diminishing of reality, not sublime like that in *Pincher Martin* but nevertheless telling, reaches its term when we discover that the journal was written by one kind of paper man, the novelist Barclay, for the other, the critic Tucker; and that we, the readers, are taking Tucker's part. As in Golding's previous experiments in the journal form, we remain a little distanced from Barclay, and we are only diminished in humanity and reality by acting like Tucker.

What strikes one as real, what momentarily identifies the reader's consciousness with Barclay's, is his suffering. When that appears, his style, which is normally choked with allusion and quotation, simplifies and intensifies. His memories are "like worms eating into the flesh, Rick pursuing, worms eating"—"the red hot worms under my carapace"—heat and a strain in his chest building up until the moment on an island off Sicily when he sees a silver statue of Christ "striding forward like an archaic Greek statue. It was crowned and its eyes were rubies or garnets or carbuncles or plain red glass that flared like the heat in my chest." He falls down with a stroke in front of it and wakes to know himself "created by that ghastly intolerance in its own image," one of the predestinate damned. He hints of it to Rick, tells him it was real and a rite of passage just before he pettily humiliates him as a further rite.

Thereafter he has a continual dream of walking across hot sand, and of protecting his burning feet by digging holes so deep and black that they are "sickening, like a hole in the universe." The digging is also "writing a strange language or making pictures." His novel-writing he now calls "hippityhop"—part of the grotesque attempt to escape the hot sand. He writes novels for the same reason he drinks, to find oblivion. But in the first chapter and again in the fifth he has used what the reader took then as an easy cliché, "footpaths in the sands of time," to describe all his writings, literary or otherwise, the biographical evidence mixed up with his sense of guilt, which Tucker wants to explore. Now the cliché has turned real for him, with the implication that in digging his holes he is only increasing his involvement with his guilt and the hot sand. And this is perhaps grotesquely confirmed by the next step in the dream logic—his hands and feet begin to hurt even when he is awake, the sensation he takes to be equivalent to having the stigmata.

[9] S. T. Coleridge, *Biographia Literaria*, 1817, ch. 19.

All this comes to the reader with the force of reality. Barclay's next vision is of an atonement, of being led down steps to a dark, calm sea—"since I have nothing to speak with but metaphor. Also there were creatures in the sea that sang. For the singing and the song I have no words at all." To Barclay this means that the boil of his strain and suffering has burst; the pain in his hands and feet is still there but feels "as if a doctor had put some sort of salve on them that hurt because it would heal." He goes home to try to make some reconciliation with his wife, his daughter, and even Rick L. Tucker.

But the most powerful of the strokes with which external reality breaks in on his monologue is to come. His wife dies, and when at the funeral he tells the local vicar he has the stigmata, the vicar "with a grin of quite unclerical teeth" says, "After all. There were three crosses." Barclay takes this as the gift of the peace "of knowing myself a thief," of no longer having to compare himself to Christ. The reader may be reminded of the remark Samuel Beckett attributed to Saint Augustine (it is actually bleaker and more arbitrary than anything Augustine says): "Do not despair: one of the thieves was saved. Do not presume: one of the thieves was damned." And with that remark one may find a parallel for *The Paper Men*—for Barclay's imagery of clowning, his dreams of the desert, and the novel's total ambiguity of hope and despair—in the play Beckett said was related to that epigram, *Waiting for Godot*.

The end of the book is, at least, peaceful. Barclay wonders why, if he has the wounds in the hands and feet, or the sensation of them, he has not the wound in the side that is peculiar to Christ and certified him dead. While Barclay wonders if the intolerance, which an orthodox theologian might call the justice, of God has let go of him, and records his intention to show his own kind of mercy to Tucker by giving him the journal, he receives the last wound, the death, which like Mr. Pedigree he wants.

The book is a successfully comic treatment of the themes of the traditional doctrine of the atonement. Guilt is done away with by suffering imaged in the crucifixion. And when death breaks in on Barclay's solipsistic discourse and the reader returns to ordinary reality by finishing the story, one might recognize a sad and ironic version of the psalm that traditionally is held to proclaim the atonement: "Mercy and truth are met together: righteousness and peace have kissed each other" (85:10). Golding once remarked that "any novelist is forgiving his own sins. If he has luck, he forgives other people's too." Perhaps Barclay succeeds in this, if not as novelist, at any rate as journal-writer.

It is as if in *Rites of Passage* and *The Paper Men* Golding were gnawing at the question left unanswered by Plato at the end of the *Symposium*: whether the master artist of tragedy, which Golding has certainly shown himself to be, is also the master artist of comedy. The comedy, although funny and at times farcical, remains sad. Afterward, however, Golding paid a second visit to Egypt and wrote a fourth journal of wandering, which brings gentleness, self-mockery, nonsense, an enjoyment of the process of things, and events that come to unassuming happy endings successfully together in a happier humor.

*An Egyptian Journal* is straightforwardly autobiographical; or rather Golding, having transformed himself for the length of *The Paper Men* into the sadly comic unreality of Wilfred Barclay, seems now determined on another comic quest for reality in the country that had already provided much of the stuff of his imagination. The conditions for reality are set oddly high, as when he says of the tombs of Beni Hassan:

Unless you are a professional archaeologist there is more interest to be found in an illustrated book of a tomb than in the comfortless, rock-hewn thing itself. There is a primary degree of experience which lies in a touch of the hand on rock, as with the pyramids for example, and the realisation that *I am here!* After that, what is most of interest is the unexpected, and all the unforeseen surroundings of an unexpected event.

(pp. 56–57)

Context at least is more important than the first part of this passage suggests, as indeed the latter part goes far toward saying. And the contrast between the two essays "Egypt from My Inside" and "Egypt from My Outside," together with the very existence of *Darkness Visible*, tells the opposite story about the impact of the monuments of Egypt on Golding at his other visit.

The result of this peculiar dislocation of and quest for reality is that *An Egyptian Journal* remarkably fills the gap left for comedy in Golding's oeuvre. It would be less surprising under the name of Eric Newby or Evelyn Waugh; it belongs in their tradition, the tradition of the English author as incompetent traveler, conveying obliquely even though his own miscomprehensions a good deal of truth and vivid reality. There is of course much of the earlier Golding of vivid dreams (Memphis on All Souls Night) and just sensuous description (Dawn on the Nile): but perhaps the real triumphs are in the farce (the unspeakable lavatory that is rendered sweet only by the failure of the steering) and in the slightly, but how memorably, drawn crew—above all the deeply touching Said, who, having worked in the Suez area forty years earlier, hates the English and begins by making Golding feel hated. After much shared struggle against "the unexpected," and attempts to establish communication which culminate in Golding's success in obtaining honey by sticking his thumbs in his ears and waggling his fingers, "meanwhile making a buzzing noise," Said says goodbye in the words: "English troubles all long time away." I should not enjoy *An Egyptian Journal* if I were a humorless Egyptian incapable of understanding the role given to the narrator, but Egyptians with a sense of humor must enjoy the indirect compliment to their country immensely. The narrator's archetype is Chaucer on the road to Canterbury.

These last four books with their repeated concern for the state of England, like Golding's first response to the news of receiving the Nobel prize, that he saw it as an honor for England, make apparent what was implicit in the earlier novels, that he is English of the English: the reading apparent in his books is that of the intelligent nonintellectual Englishman—apart from Anglo-Saxon, Greek, Egyptology, and Dante, it is Arthur Mee's *Children's Encyclopaedia*, childhood stories from the *Odyssey*, the *Aeneid* and medieval romance, H. G. Wells, Jules Verne, Arthur Ransome, R. M. Ballantyne, Stevenson, Defoe, C. S. Lewis, John Buchan, the Bible, Keats, Coleridge, Milton, Shakespeare, and Edgar Allan Poe. Yet his work is rootedly European. He claims the Greek tragedians as the greatest influence after Homer on his work; and Nietzsche's judgment in *The Birth of Tragedy* on them fits him: here the form-giver, Apollo, works in perfect balance with the urge out of darkness, Dionysus, unless the ironic intellect, Socrates, interposes. But in Golding the moral passion of the Hebrews is at least equally present, united with their awareness of the transcendent God. Naturally these urges center on a continual attempt in his books to describe something more specifically Christian, a symbol, an incarnation, a figure in human form who embodies the transcendent.

Perhaps this Graeco-Hebraic and Christian union of forces is why, if one wants to place him in English literature, the nearest writers are those of post-Puritan New England, Herman Melville and Nathaniel Hawthorne; perhaps one might think of Charles Williams also, or the Conrad of *Heart of Darkness*. But really his books relate primarily to themselves. The intransigence, the concern for truth, the fitting together of image and image into patterns of great constancy, the reduction of concept to experience, and the re-creation of language make something as new in English literature as there has ever been. One might well hope that he will be the father of a recovered freshness in the English language and its literature, and of something like his own intransigence in our approach to religion and human nature.

## SELECTED BIBLIOGRAPHY

I. BIBLIOGRAPHY. V. Tiger, *William Golding: The Dark Fields of Discovery* (London, 1974), contains bibliography of works by and on Golding, including essays, reviews, and chapters in general studies, up to 1972.

II. SEPARATE WORKS. *Poems* (London, 1934); *Lord of the Flies: A Novel* (London, 1954); *The Inheritors* (London, 1955), novel; *Pincher Martin* (London, 1956), novel, reiss. in America as *The Two Deaths of Christopher Martin* (New York, 1957); *Sometime, Never: Three Tales of Imagination* (London, 1956), contains "Envoy Extraordinary," by Golding, "Consider Her Ways," by J. Wyndham, and "Boy in Darkness," by M. Peake; *The Brass Butterfly: A Play in Three Acts* (London, 1958), dramatized version of "Envoy Extraordinary"; *Free Fall* (London, 1959), novel; "The Anglo-Saxon," in the *Queen* (22 December 1959), short story; "Miss Pulkinhorn," in *Encounter* (August 1960), short story, repr. in C. Bradby and A. Ridler, eds., *Best Stories of Church and Clergy* (London, 1966) and presented as a radio play on BBC radio (20 April 1960); "Before the Beginning," in the *Spectator* (26 May 1961), review of G. Clark's *World Prehistory* (London, 1961); "Party of One: Thinking as a Hobby," in *Holiday* (Philadelphia), 30 (August 1961); *The Spire* (London, 1964), novel; *The Hot Gates, and Other Occasional Pieces* (London, 1965), reviews and articles, includes "The Ladder and the Tree," "Digging for Pictures," "Egypt from My Inside," "Fable," "Billy the Kid," and other autobiographical pieces; "Break My

Heart," unpub. radio play from 1966 available at Broadcasting House, London, in typescript; *The Pyramid* (London, 1967), novel; *The Scorpion God: Three Short Novels* (London, 1971), includes "The Scorpion God," "Clonk Clonk," and "Envoy Extraordinary"; "Survival," in the *Guardian* (9 May 1974), review of P. P. Read, *Alive* (London, 1974); *Darkness Visible* (London, 1979), novel; *Rites of Passage* (London, 1980), novel; *A Moving Target* (London, 1982), reviews and articles, includes "Egypt from My Outside"; *The Paper Men* (London, 1984), novel; *An Egyptian Journal* (London, 1985).

III. INTERVIEWS. O. Webster, "Living with Chaos," in *Books and Art* (March 1958); F. Kermode, "The Meaning of It All," in *Books and Bookmen,* 5 (October 1959); J. W. Aldridge, "William Golding," in the *New York Times Book Review* (10 December 1961); D. M. Davis, "Conversation with Golding," in the *New Republic* (4 May 1963); B. F. Dick, "The Novelist Is a Displaced Person," in *College English,* 26 (March 1965); J. I. Biles, *Talk: Conversations with William Golding* (New York, 1970); *William Golding Talks to Stephen Medcalf* (London, 1977), British Council recording and pamphlet.

IV. CRITICAL STUDIES. F. Kermode, *Puzzles and Epiphanies: Essays and Reviews, 1958–1961* (London, 1962), includes ch. on Golding; W. Nelson, *William Golding's "Lord of the Flies": A Source Book* (New York, 1963), contains most of the good articles on Golding's work up to 1963; C. B. Cox, *The Free Spirit* (London, 1963), pp. 172–184; S. Hynes, *William Golding* (New York, 1964; 2nd ed., 1968), Columbia Essays on Modern Writers, excellent short study of the six novels; J. R. Baker, *William Golding: A Critical Study* (New York, 1965), argues that Golding is more a classical than a Christian moralist; B. S. Oldsey and S. Weintraub, *The Art of William Golding* (New York, 1965), reads Golding in the light of his sources and analogues; H. Talon, *Le mal dans l'oeuvre de William Golding* (Paris, 1966); I. Gregor and M. Kinkead-Weekes, *William Golding: A Critical Study* (London, 1967; rev. ed., 1984), excellent study of the first five novels in relation to the nature of fiction; P. Elmen, *William Golding: A Critical Essay* (Grand Rapids, Michigan, 1967), short critique in the Contemporary Writers in Christian Perspective series; B. F. Dick, *William Golding* (New York, 1967), surveys all Golding's writing up to *The Pyramid;* L. Hodson, *William Golding* (Edinburgh, 1970), a biographical and critical study; J. S. Whitley, *Golding: "Lord of the Flies"* (London, 1970), in the Studies in English Literature series; G. Josipovici, *The World and the Book: A Study of Modern Fiction* (London, 1971), see ch. 10, "Golding: The Hidden Source"; E. Smith, *Some Versions of the Fall* (London, 1973), see pt. 3, "The Way of the Personal Myth"; V. Tiger, *William Golding: The Dark Fields of Discovery* (London, 1974), discusses all Golding's fiction as the creation in the reader of a confrontation with the spiritual world; J. I. Biles and R. O. Evans, eds., *William Golding: Some Critical Considerations* (Lexington, Ky., 1978); D. Crompton and J. Briggs, *A View from the Spire: William Golding's Later Novels* (Oxford, 1985); N. Page, ed., *William Golding: Novels, 1954–67* (London, 1985); J. Carey, ed., *William Golding: The Man and His Books* (London, 1986).

# GRAHAM GREENE
(1904–    )

## *Bernard Bergonzi*

*I*

GRAHAM GREENE has had an exceptionally long literary career, extending over sixty years. In 1925 he published a volume of undergraduate verse. It was succeeded by more than twenty novels as well as collections of short stories, several plays, and miscellaneous books of travel writing, biography, essays, and film criticism. In 1984, when he reached his eightieth birthday, he published *Getting to Know the General,* an autobiographical work about his friendship with Omar Torrijos, sometime president of Panama. It was followed in 1985 by a literary curiosity in the shape of a short novel, *The Tenth Man,* which had been written forty years earlier as the basis for a film and then forgotten. Greene's long life as man and writer makes it more appropriate to refer to his successive careers rather than a single unified one. In Greene's and the century's eighties he looks a different kind of writer from the figure he presented in the 1950's, when critics first began to take him seriously.

Despite his work in other genres, it is as a novelist that Greene is primarily known and admired. And as a novelist he has passed through several stages: as a writer of quasi-thrillers that are cinematic in technique and melodramatic in story and atmosphere; as an explorer of tormenting religious dilemmas and extreme situations in the so-called Catholic novels that made him internationally famous after World War II; as a cool observer of political violence and ideological dramas in the Third World; and, most recently, as a fictional joker, sometimes sinister, sometimes genial. Greene's appeal is unusually wide, since he commands a large popular readership as well as being increasingly a focus of academic critical attention.

Despite the many phases of Greene's work, the task of discussing it as a totality is made easier by the persistence of an unmistakable literary personality. There are certain qualities—of sensibility, style, narrative device, forms of characterization—that mark out a Greene novel, early or late. Critics attempt to sum them up by using the shorthand term "Greeneland"; it has become a cliché, and one that Greene understandably finds irritating, though there is some evidence that he colluded with it in the past; but it is so convenient that it is hard to avoid.

Greene has always been very reticent about himself. He has produced a number of autobiographical writings that say quite a lot about his childhood and adolescence and very little about his personal life as an adult. They continually loop back to his novels, their genesis and circumstances of composition; the man is in a sense created by the writings rather than the other way around. There are certain characteristics that Greene shares with other British writers of his generation. He came from the English professional classes, his father being headmaster of a minor "public" (that is, private) school at Berkhamsted, a few miles to the north of London. Born on 2 October 1904, he was old enough to be aware of World War I but too young to fight in it; it was remembered as a shadow over his later childhood, as it was for other writers of what Samuel Hynes has called the "Auden generation." The salient personal facts about Greene that have affected his entire career as a writer can be reduced to three: he had a happy childhood followed by a bored, unhappy adolescence, when he underwent psychoanalysis; in 1926 he entered the Catholic Church on the occasion of his marriage to a Catholic; and he has lived out of England for much of his life.

Two important aspects of Greene the writer, opposed but covertly related, are the melodramatist and the joker. They combine in a bizarre form in a very late novel, *Doctor Fischer of Geneva or the Bomb Party,* but they recur throughout his work, early and late. Certain themes continually appear, like a pattern in a carpet: betrayal, duplicity, pursuit. For Greene, betrayal and childhood are closely related. His volume of essays, *The Lost Childhood* (1951), carries an epigraph from the Irish poet George Russell, who wrote as "A.E.": "In the lost boyhood of Judas/Christ was betrayed." The idea that childhood is betrayed as the shades of the adult prison-house close round is a romantic literary theme, and in *Brighton Rock* it is said of Pinkie, the teenage gangster, "hell lay around him in his infancy," in a deliberate distortion of Wordsworth's "Immortality Ode." In Greene's fiction, and particularly in his short stories, children are often betrayed—by other children, by adults, by life itself. "The Basement Room" (1935) is a poignant study of a child who unwittingly betrays his adult friend. Throughout his life Greene has been fascinated by the figure of the betrayer and of the traitor, as is apparent in his sympathetic presentation of the spy Maurice Castle in *The Human Factor*, and, in real life, in his admiration for the British spy Kim Philby, whom he had known in World War II and whom he continued to regard as a friend after his exposure and defection to the Soviet Union.

Greene's first novel, *The Man Within* (1929), is untypical of his later work insofar as it is a historical costume drama, set among Sussex smugglers at the beginning of the nineteenth century. But his major themes or obsessions are already in evidence. The central figure, Andrews, is a smuggler who is reluctantly following the trade of his swaggering, bullying father. Andrews is on the run from his comrades, whom he has betrayed to the law. He is given sanctuary by a beautiful, pure, remote young woman called Elizabeth, who persuades him to give evidence against the other smugglers in court. She is the first of the madonna types who recur in Greene's fiction; the other woman in the novel is Lucy, the mistress of the prosecuting counsel, Sir Henry Merriman. She embodies the opposed type of the whore, who also recurs, if less frequently. The contrast between madonna and whore recalls a familiar Catholic typological opposition: that of the Virgin Mary and Mary Magdalene. In Greene's case its roots are probably temperamental, reinforced by the masters of fictional romance, such as Robert Louis Stevenson and Joseph Conrad, who heavily influenced *The Man Within* and his other early novels. *The Man Within* is a little too carefully written, and its literary effects are overcalculated.

As an adventure story it moves forward vigorously and the suspense is well sustained; in these ways it points to Greene's later novels of betrayal and pursuit. Its epigraph, from Sir Thomas Browne, reflects his abiding fascination with doubleness or duplicity: "There's another man within me that's angry with me." There were to be a succession of such double men in Greene's fiction: the Third Man, Our Man in Havana, the Tenth Man.

In this early novel the melodramatist is dominant, but the joker makes what looks in hindsight like a small appearance. Sir Henry Merriman bears Greene's own name—he was christened Henry Graham—and is the first of a succession of male characters called "Henry"; later ones include Henry Scobie, the tragic hero of *The Heart of the Matter*, the cuckolded civil servant Henry Miles in *The End of the Affair*, and Henry Pulling, the retired bank manager who is the narrator of *Travels with My Aunt*. Most recently, Greene's one-act play *Yes and No* invokes a dramatist called "Henry Privet." Greene has been an active practical joker in life, and he is fond of jokey self-reference in his fiction, notwithstanding his reticence about direct autobiographical revelation. Philip Stratford has written of Greene's long preoccupation with things that are green or colored green (like "Privet" in the instance just referred to) and with the proper names "Greene" or "Green"; he is also, it seems, drawn to the chromatic opposite of green, shown in the recurrence of the girls' names "Rose" and "Coral" (reinforced in *Brighton Rock* by the union of Rose and Pinkie). There is a revealing small instance of this sly playing with names in Greene's novel of 1934, *It's a Battlefield*, where a character of working-class London origins is doubly burdened in life by the possession of "brains" and the outlandish Christian name of "Conrad." When he asks his parents why he was christened so oddly, they can only say that he was called after a merchant seaman of that name who once lodged in the house and of whom they can remember nothing remarkable. As Greene himself acknowledged, *It's a Battlefield* is a novel in which the influence of Joseph Conrad, who was once a merchant seaman, is excessively strong. Other echoes and repetitions of names in Greene's fiction may be significant but remain inexplicable; why, for instance, should the principal male and female characters in both *The End of the Affair* and *The Human Factor* be called Maurice and Sarah?

Greene followed *The Man Within* with two more romantic novels, *The Name of Action* (1930) and *Rumour at Nightfall* (1931), set, respectively, in modern Germany and nineteenth-century Spain. Greene has suppressed them both and never allowed them to be reprinted. In his second volume of autobiography, *Ways of Escape* (1980), he has written: "Both books are of a badness beyond the power of criticism properly to evoke—the prose flat and stilted and in the case of *Rumour at Nightfall* pretentious (the young writer had obviously been reading again and alas! admiring Conrad's worst novel, *The Arrow of Gold*), the characterisation non-existent." *Rumour at Nightfall* is of some interest for the pattern of Greene's entire career because it provides an early example of his interest in the Hispanic world, which shows in many of his later novels.

In 1932 Greene published *Stamboul Train* (U.S. title, *Orient Express*), in which he finally hit on a subject matter and treatment that he was able successfully to develop for the rest of the 1930's. Although Greene himself has tended to dismiss his prewar novels and they are sometimes regarded by critics as no more than apprentice work, I believe them to be an important part of his literary achievement. In these books Greene wrote about the contemporary world in a striking combination of public and personal idioms. In their public dimensions they are representative of their period. Greene continually focuses on significant images of the age, particularly those of the British urban scene; as a writer of observant fictional documentary he has something in common with other novelists of his generation who emerged in the early 1930's, such as George Orwell and Christopher Isherwood. Greene was, at this stage, an intensely cinematic writer; many passages in his early novels, such as the opening paragraph of *Stamboul Train*, recall the films of the time:

The purser took the last landing-card in his hand and watched the passengers cross the grey wet quay, over a wilderness of rails and points, round the corners of abandoned trucks. They went with coat-collars turned up and hunched shoulders; on the tables in the long coaches lamps were lit and glowed through the rain like a chain of blue beads. A giant crane swept and descended, and the clatter of the winch drowned for a moment the pervading sounds of water, water falling from the overcast sky, water washing against the sides of channel steamer and quay. It was half-past four in the afternoon.

It is worth noting that Greene was a professional film critic between 1935 and 1940, and his collected film reviews, *The Pleasure Dome* (1974), is a volume of considerable and many-faceted interest. It has much to say about the films of the 1930's and is very revealing of the myths and images of the age; it also conveys, obliquely, quite a lot about Greene's state of mind. In his distaste for the products and culture of Hollywood, we see the origins of Greene's anti-Americanism. The film reviews illuminate the novels he was writing at the time by showing his familiarity with cinematic techniques; there are places where the fiction seems to echo the film criticism, and vice versa. (I have said more about this in my book *Reading the Thirties*.) A curious incidental point about Greene's film reviews is that some of them were ghost-written by his friend, the late Kenneth Allott—poet, critic, and subsequently co-author of one of the first critical books on Greene. He had evidently absorbed Greene's style very effectively, and there is no surviving evidence to show which reviews Allott in fact wrote.

The extent to which Greene's fiction of the 1930's was directly influenced by the cinema is complicated by other factors, particularly the literary influence of Conrad, who was a strongly cinematic writer virtually before the cinema existed (passages in *The Secret Agent* are as filmlike as anything in Greene). In their "public" dimensions these novels are immersed in the popular culture of the 1930's, not only the cinema but also the thriller and the detective novel. The thriller was a natural vehicle for Greene's perennial theme of the hunted man. He was also conscious of the radio and gramophone and the resultant dissemination of dance music and popular songs. Nearly all his prewar novels contain snatches of song lyrics composed by Greene in a skillful pastiche of the sophisticated or sentimental productions of Cole Porter or Ira Gershwin (again, a topic discussed at some length in *Reading the Thirties*). Aspects of these novels anticipate what was later formulated, with reference to painting and sculpture, as "pop art," where a serious artist makes deliberate use of the artifacts of mass culture for his own aesthetic ends. It is significant that *Stamboul Train* was first published not as a novel but as an "entertainment," as were *A Gun for Sale* and *The Confidential Agent*. Greene originally made the distinction because he regarded his novels as artistically serious and his entertainments as mere pot-boilers written for money. It was, from the beginning, a rather factitious distinction; although the entertainments may be a little closer to the genres of popular fiction, they are not less well written than the novels and are just as pervaded by Greene's personal vision of life. *Brighton Rock*, which I take to be Greene's most substantial novel of the 1930's, was originally described in the first American edition as an entertainment; Greene has dropped the distinction in the collected edition of his work. During the 1970's and 1980's the generic distinctions among kinds of fiction, which may have seemed clear-cut in the 1930's, have become blurred.

In their "public" aspects Greene's prewar novels are very much of their time in their concern with social documentary, thrillers, films, and popular music. But in their "personal" aspects they are uniquely and unmistakably by Greene. This is most evident in their style, which is elaborately, sometimes extravagantly, metaphorical in a way that immediately distinguishes it from the flat, laconic, descriptive manner of contemporaries such as Orwell, Isherwood, and the early Anthony Powell. Greene's impulse toward figurative language shows itself in startling similes, in which the abstract is seen in minutely concrete terms: "Camaraderie, good nature, cheeriness fell like shutters before a plate glass window"; or, "his sympathy didn't belong, it could be peeled off his eyes like an auction ticket from an ancient flint instrument." Occasionally Greene reverses the process, presenting the concrete in terms of the abstract: "He drank the brandy down like damnation." In his autobiography Greene has deplored these rhetorical devices, blaming them on his early taste for the Metaphysical poets of the seventeenth century and their elaborate conceits. A contemporary influence may have been the fanciful similes in the poetry of W. H. Auden, whom Greene greatly admired. Sometimes, it is true, Greene's similes are too bizarre to be effective, but when they work they import a poetic dimension into the urban realism of the fiction, as K. W. Gransden has shown. In *Brighton Rock*, in particular, the similes rise to a strange surrealistic intensity that goes beyond the registration of unexpected resemblances. Consider, for instance, the description of the face of the young girl Rose when she is in a stubborn mood: "The bony and determined face stared back at her: all the fight there was in the world lay there—warships cleared for action and bombing fleets took flight between the set eyes and the stubborn mouth. It was like the map of a campaign marked with flags." The girl's features are transformed into a montage of 1930's newsreel shots. These images are both public and private and evidently had an obsessional significance for Greene, for he repeats some of them in his next novel, *The Confidential Agent:* "bombing planes took flight from between his eyes, and in his brain the mountains shook with shell-bursts." Another stylistic device to which Greene was much addicted is the tripartite list of items in apposition without conjunctions (known in classical rhetoric, as Gransden points out, as "tricolon in asyndeton"): " 'I've seen you with him,' she lied: a courtyard, a sewing wench beside the fire, the cock crowing"; "He preferred the distrust, the barbarity, the betrayals"; "the broken bridge, the torn-up track, the horror of seventy years ahead"; and "It had the furtiveness of lust, the sombreness of religion, the gaiety of stolen cigarettes."

Such things make Greene's style, in his novels of the 1930's and early 1940's, instantly recognizable and easily parodyable. Yet more is involved than a personal manner that can be idiosyncratic to the point of affectation, though there is some point to that charge. If the style is the man, then Greene's rhetorical devices may arise from something in the depths of his temperament. The essence of metaphor is to compare one thing with another; a further term is always involved, a pointing beyond the immediate fact or experience, which is why figurative devices are unusual in the fiction of realistic description. Greene's extensive use of simile seems to reflect his desire for significance, a word that includes the idea of the "sign" and denotes a pointing beyond the immediately given. Greene explores this need for significance in his essays of the 1930's and 1940's; it can, of course, be related to his Catholic beliefs, but its roots seem deeply temperamental, recalling his lifelong struggle against boredom and his need for "ways of escape," to quote the title of his second volume of autobiography.

Although *Stamboul Train* is a minor novel, it shows Greene coming to terms with the contemporary world and turning from the romance model to a fictional formula popular in the early 1930's. It is the kind of novel that brings together a cosmopolitan and heterogeneous collection of people in the arbitrary confines of a luxury hotel or international express train. (Agatha Christie's *Murder in the Calais Coach,* published a year after *Stamboul Train,* is a classically famous detective story that also uses the formula.) *Stamboul Train* was filmed, though the film version was rather overshadowed by other "train" films such as *Shanghai Express, Rome Express,* and the Russian *Turksib.* In Greene's novel a variegated group of passengers, mainly English, travel across Europe on the Orient Express to Istanbul. They include a young Jewish businessman, Carleton Myatt, who is a complex neurotic character, and a young chorus girl, Coral Musker, with whom he is briefly involved; she is one of Greene's recurring female types, innocent, waiflike, vulnerable. Others on the journey and in the story are Dr. Czinner, a Yugoslav political refugee returning to participate in a revolution in his native country, and Mabel Warren, a lesbian journalist. With the possible exception of Myatt, they are types rather than characters, and though this might suggest a deficiency in Greene's art, if one assumes him to be aspiring toward total fictional realism, it is worth recalling that he has more than once gone on record as favoring the "type" over the "fully rounded" fictional character. This may have been making a virtue of necessity, but it had some basis in his world view.

Aspects of *Stamboul Train* faintly look forward to scenes and episodes of Greene's later fiction. Dr. Czinner and his revolutionary aspirations represent a sketchy gesture toward the political contexts of the 1930's, an interest much more fully developed in Greene's fictional explorations of repression and resistance in the Third World from the 1950's onward. In *Stamboul Train* Dr. Czinner is captured at the Yugoslav frontier, and the ideological exchanges between him and his captor, the chief of police, Colonel Hartrep, anticipate later debates, notably those between the priest and the lieutenant in *The Power and the Glory.*

In his next novel, *It's a Battlefield* (1934), Greene turned to contemporary London. It is a technically complex work, and I agree with Roger Sharrock's judgment that it is Greene's most accomplished novel before *Brighton Rock* and one of the best novels of its period. The central situation of the plot is simple. A London bus driver, Jim Drover (who never appears in the action), has killed a policeman at a political demonstration and is under sentence of death for murder. There is widespread agitation for a reprieve, and suspense is generated throughout the novel by uncertainty if it will be granted. The central characters are Jim's wife, Milly; his brother, Conrad, an embittered white-collar worker (the one burdened with "brains" and an outlandish Christian name); and Milly's sister, Kay, an extrovert factory girl with a cheerfully amoral attitude toward sex. Set apart from the other characters is the Assistant Commissioner of the police, a lonely, unnamed figure who moves across the scenes of the action and whose reflections embody much of Greene's view of the world. His origin in Conrad's *The Secret Agent* is unmistakable, and the influence of this novel on Greene's is uncomfortably strong. Nevertheless, what Greene writes is more than pastiche, and he is able to adapt Conrad to his own purposes. Other influences may be the panoramic urban visions of James Joyce's *Ulysses* and Virginia Woolf's *Mrs. Dalloway.*

The strength of *It's a Battlefield* is not so much in its rather commonplace story nor in its characterization, which is still strongly typological, but in what Sharrock has called its urban poetry, with which Greene fuses the public and the personal. The camera eye moves continually over London in cinematic ranging shots and occasional close-ups. The language and presentation are pervaded by Greene's obsessional perceptions. His vision of London, and by extension of life itself, is of a battlefield, and a battlefield like that of Inkerman in the Crimean War, which was fought in mist so that groups of soldiers were isolated from each other, ignorant of the general progress of the battle. Greene's urban poetry emerges from what looks like the extremity of realism; the images of the modern city succeed each other like shots in a film, or are juxtaposed in the random fashion of a newspaper:

The man who tears paper patterns and the male soprano were performing before the pit queues, the shutters of the shops had all gone up, the prostitutes were moving west. The feature pictures had come on the second time at the super-cinemas, and the taxi ranks were melting and re-forming. In the Café Français in Little Compton Street a man at the counter served two coffees and sold a packet of "Weights." The match factory in Battersea pounded out the last ten thousand boxes, working overtime. The cars in the Oxford Street fun-fair rattled and bounced, and the evening papers went to press for the last edition—"The Streatham Rape and Murder. Latest Developments," "Mr. MacDonald Flies to Lossiemouth," "Disarmament Conference Adjourns," "Special Service for Footballers," "Family of Insured Couple Draw £10,000. Insure Today." At each station on the Outer Circle a train stopped every two minutes.

(ch. 1)

At the end of this seemingly objective survey Greene the joker reveals himself. There never has been a section of the London underground railway system called the "Outer Circle"; what is now the "Circle Line" would have been known in the 1930's as the "Inner Circle." But Dante refers to the outer circle of Hell in the *Inferno,* and this forms a recurring motif in Greene's novel. In the preceding paragraph the Assistant Commissioner, visiting a prison, thinks: "He had a dim memory that someone had once mapped hell in circles, and as the searchlight swooped and touched and passed, and the bell ceased clanging for Block C to go to their cells, he thought, 'this is only the outer circle.'"

In *It's a Battlefield* Greeneland is put on the map for the first time. It is a dismal urban wasteland, stalked by evil and betrayal; but it is also the modern world, lit up, literally or figuratively, by the glittering images of mass culture, whose fascination the author reluctantly acknowledges. The inescapable, recurring adjective for Greeneland is seedy. It has been used to excess by Greene's critics, but he employed it frequently himself in his fiction and film reviews of the 1930's. Greeneland has two aspects: if one is the modern city, the other is the jungle, the desert, the so-called savage places in remote parts of the globe. In *It's a Battlefield* the Assistant Commissioner frequently compares London with the African jungle, where he had previously served, preferring the natural to the urban jungle. Greene's own quest for significance made him feel increasingly that modern English civilization was a hollow shell and that authentic existence was more likely to be discovered in the real jungle, or some other lawless topography. Within a few years this quest was to take him to West Africa and Mexico; much further ahead lay many more visits to Africa, Indochina, and Latin America.

Greene's next novel, *England Made Me* (1935; U.S. title, *The Shipwrecked*), is one of which he has said, in *Ways of Escape,* he has "a soft spot in [his] heart for," although, as he acknowledges, this taste has not been shared by the public at large. It represents a move toward the mainstream realistic novel, involving a theme of some psychological depth and complexity, with characters rather than types at the center of the action. It is set in Stockholm, a city that Greene confesses he knew very little of at the time. The central characters are a sister and brother, Kate and Anthony Farrant. Anthony is a charming but feckless man in his thirties, an ex-public-school ne'er-do-well, a type Greene has often portrayed in fiction; Kate is the secretary and mistress of Krogh, a shady Swedish tycoon. The central human interest is the incestuous affection between Kate and Anthony, of which they themselves are not fully aware. Greene tends to be distracted from this weighty and sensitive topic by other concerns, such as his presentation of Krogh as an evil, scheming financial genius, another recurring type in the demonology of the 1930's; as Greene later acknowledged, Krogh refused to come alive as a character. This may have been because Greene had no opportunity really to get to know someone like Krogh or his milieu. On the other hand, an originally very minor figure, Minty, the inevitably seedy expatriate Anglo-Catholic journalist, became (as Greene has described) altogether too alive and commanding for the balance of the book. The most memorable things in *England Made Me* are, on the whole, marginal to the main theme, such as the character of Minty and the description of a flight made by Krogh's henchman, Fred Hall, from Amsterdam to Stockholm, which gives a vivid sense of what civil flying was like in the Europe of over fifty years ago. But in its major themes and treatment *England Made Me* sags, and Greene's attempt at a Joycean stream of consciousness is half-hearted. The Stockholm setting, too, is thin compared with the rich evocation of London in Anthony's consciousness. Notwithstanding the novel's aspiration toward straightforward realism, it reveals Greene the melodramatist. Below the realistic surface there are hints of Jacobean tragedy in the incest theme and in the surrounding gallery of villains and grotesques. In his book *British Dramatists* Greene wrote about John Webster's *Duchess of Malfi* in terms of high praise, suggesting a temperamental affinity. But the long-term effect of *England Made Me* may have been to spoil Greene's chances of receiving the Nobel Prize for Literature. Some members of the Swedish Academy may well have disliked his treatment of Sweden in this early novel.

With *A Gun for Sale* (U.S. title, *This Gun for Hire*), published in 1936 as an entertainment, Greene returned to the subject with which he was most at home. It embodies his central theme of the hunted man, drawing on the conventions of the thriller and the gangster movie. The settings are entirely English and urban, moving from London to the Midland city of Nottwich (based on Nottingham, where Greene lived as a young man). The central figure, Raven, is like a malcontent from Jacobean drama. He is a professional killer, his life has been warped by a wretched childhood, and he is physically disfigured by a harelip. At the beginning of the novel he murders a prominent European statesman who is working for peace. He is then cheated by his paymasters, who pay him in forged notes, and he has to flee from the police. Raven is a depraved creature, but he attracts the reader's reluctant sympathy. *A Gun for Sale* is pervaded by Greene's urban poetry and shows the world in cinematic gray or black. It is very conscious of its historical moment; war threatens, and a mock air raid plays a part in the plot. The sinister figure of the arms magnate, Sir Marcus Stein, who is very old and sick but still powerful—it is he who wanted the statesman murdered—is a familiar type from the demonology of the 1930's; a caricature, perhaps, but done with more conviction than Krogh in *England Made Me*.

Greene's other entertainment of the 1930's, *The Confidential Agent* (1939), has the generic qualities that its title suggests and also reflects contemporary history. The hero is another man on the run, and like some other Greene characters he has no name, being known only as D. (There may have been some influence here of Franz Kafka, who was beginning to be read in England at the time.) D. comes from an unnamed foreign country where a civil war is raging; the Spanish Civil War is clearly intended though not identified as such. D. is a scholar in normal life, now working for his government on a special mission to purchase coal. Once in England he is ruthlessly pursued by enemy agents, and his life is in danger. *The Confidential Agent* is, of course, more than just a thriller, for it raises Greene's perennial themes of trust, loyalty, and betrayal; in *Ways of Escape* he refers to the way the book enacts "the predicament of the agent with scruples, who is not trusted by his own party and who realises that his party is right not to trust him." In further reflections in *Ways of Escape*, Greene remarks on the way in which *The Confidential Agent* anticipated features of English life, such as holiday camps, which did not become familiar until much later. Closer both to history and to Greene's own art is the moment when D. listens to a radio talk on the Problem of Indochina. In 1938 there was no visible unrest in that region, but it was to preoccupy the postwar world for decades and to provide the subject of one of Greene's major novels of the 1950's, *The Quiet American*. Indeed, there is an uncanny quality of anticipation in Greene, which made him write *Our Man in Havana* before the Cuban missile crisis, *A Burnt-Out Case* before the Congo civil war, and *The Honorary Consul* before a British ambassador was kidnapped by Uruguayan revolutionaries.

Between *A Gun for Sale* and *The Confidential Agent* Greene published *Brighton Rock* (1938), which was originally conceived as an entertainment, but is, in my judgment, his most substantial and rewarding novel of the decade. It is not, indeed, a work of conventional realism, for it is a novel of multiple genres. As a thriller it is superbly tense and fast-moving. It is indeed realistic in the cinematic accuracy with which it presents Brighton low and high life, though the realism is mediated by Greene's idiosyncratic, metaphorical prose, whose stylistic devices here run to a considerable degree of baroque or surrealistic elaboration. It is also the first of his novels in which Catholic themes play any part, and so has elements of the moral or religious fable. The theme of the hunted man is announced in the arresting opening sentence: "Hale knew, before he had been in Brighton three hours, that they meant to murder him." Hale is indeed murdered, or at least dies in a way that looks like murder, and the focus shifts to his murderer, the seventeen-year-old gangster, Pinkie. Pinkie is one of Greene's most memorable figures, though he cannot be described as a conventionally realistic fictional character. He is a fuller version of the doomed and damned Raven. Pinkie is undoubtedly a creation of Greene the melodramatist; he possesses a strange combination of purity and wickedness. There is some division in Greene's implied attitude toward his character: does Pinkie's depravity arise from the wretched conditions of a slum childhood, when the sight of his parents' sexual activity made him loathe the idea of sex, or is Pinkie essentially evil —a dark angel whose nature has nothing to do with his social origins? This division or indecision in Greene is apparent in his writings of this period. He sometimes seems to adopt the left-wing political attitudes common in the Auden generation, and in some respects they have remained constant in his fiction, notably in the postwar books set in Latin America. At other times he expresses a conviction in the realities of evil and hell, and a skepticism about progress and reform, which spring from a Catholic-conservative pessimism about human nature.

*Brighton Rock* is a transitional work. It is the best of Greene's novels of the decade, exploring the

English urban dimension of Greeneland in a characteristic combination of the cinematic and the poetic. It can also be seen as the first of a "Catholic" sequence continued in *The Power and the Glory, The Heart of the Matter,* and *The End of the Affair.* It is worth recalling that Greene had been a Catholic for twelve years before he published *Brighton Rock,* and there had been no previous hint of his religious convictions in his fiction. However, in an essay called "Henry James: The Religious Aspect," first published in 1933, we find him praising James for a sense of supernatural evil that had affinities with Catholic beliefs and for being at least a religious novelist manqué. Greene quoted from T. S. Eliot's well-known essay on Charles Baudelaire in which Eliot asserts that man's glory can be seen in his capacity for damnation as well as his capacity for salvation; the dire thing about the modern world is that many of its inhabitants are not men enough to be damned. Greene sees James as possessing a much stronger sense of damnation than of salvation, having this much in common with Baudelaire; his own character, Pinkie, is in the same situation. Pinkie is indelibly marked by his Catholic origins, though for him Hell is a much stronger possibility than Heaven.

This early essay by Greene is more illuminating about its author than about James, and it provides clues for understanding how Catholicism works in his novels. There was much discussion in the 1940's, particularly among Catholics, of the theological implications of Greene's fiction, and to what extent his Catholicism was Augustinian or Jansenistic or actually heretical. Catholic readers tended to take sides about it; the difficulty arose from not understanding the dangers of trying to extract coherent doctrine from works of fiction. It is now evident, in the light of his later work, that Catholicism in Greene's fiction, like his picture of modern England, was mediated by a temperament that enjoyed melodramatic extremes and oppositions, and for whom the realities of hell and damnation were a way of alleviating the boredom generated by a secular bourgeois world. Greene's interest in Catholicism was dramatic rather than doctrinal; life seemed more real when people were poised between salvation and damnation. It is relevant to recall the line from Robert Browning's "Bishop Blougram's Apology," which Greene has quoted more than once and which could serve as an epigraph to all his fiction, Catholic or secular: "Our interest's on the dangerous edge of things" (1.395). Greene is a very literary writer and a very well-read one, and it was natural that he looked to literary models for his newfound sense of religious melodrama. Henry James provided one, as did Eliot's version of Baudelaire; and from Baudelaire, Greene moved on to a number of French Catholic writers, not all entirely orthodox, of the late nineteenth and twentieth centuries, whom he wrote about or alluded to or drew on for the epigraphs of his novels: Léon Bloy, Charles Péguy, Georges Bernanos, François Mauriac. Here Greene found reinforcement for his sense of life as an intense and dangerous spiritual drama. What looked to English readers like dangerous religious dilemmas and speculations arose not from theology but from a particular, exotic literary tradition.

Pinkie, it has to be repeated, is not a realistic fictional character. As I have suggested, it is easy to point to his disparate aspects: he is a psychopathically disturbed, underprivileged youth, a victim of social deprivation; he is also an embodiment of pure diabolic will and energy, harking back beyond the French Catholic literary tradition to Fyodor Dostoevsky. At the same time, he also belongs in a native tradition; like Raven, he recalls the villains of Jacobean drama, beyond whom lay the more remote figure of the Vice in the old morality plays, about which Greene has written with informed admiration. In his presentation of Pinkie, Greene reflects something of the modernist dismissal of stable, consistent literary characters. Pinkie's vitality is unmistakable, while his plausibility is more arguable; many readers will sympathize with Orwell's complaint that *Brighton Rock*

presupposes that the most brutishly stupid person can, merely by having been brought up a Catholic, be capable of great intellectual subtlety. Pinkie, the race course gangster, is a species of satanist, while his still more limited girl friend understands and even states the difference between the categories "right and wrong" and "good and evil."

(*Collected Essays, Journalism and Letters,* vol. 4, p. 500)

There are times, certainly, when Pinkie loses all credibility, as when he distorts the Latin words of the Creed to "Credo in unum Satanum." The difference between "good and evil" and "right and wrong" to which Orwell refers is central to the literary-theological frame of reference within which Greene was working. It presupposes an absolute opposition between the divine and the human, or between grace and nature. Good and evil are God-given absolutes, whereas right and wrong are merely humanistic substitutes for these transcendental values. In *Brighton Rock* Rose and Pinkie understand the former because of the superior knowledge that their Catholic upbringing has given them, whereas the cheerful, promiscuous Ida Arnold, full of sentimental decencies and with a heart of gold, understands only the latter. Ida's values seem to be dismissed in the novel, yet it is she who triumphs in the end, when she pursues Pinkie to a horrible death, "doubled up in appalling agony: it was as if the flames had literally got him." In terms of later, more humanistic developments in Catholic theology, the opposition between the two sets of values has no real foundation; "right and wrong" represent a real if imperfect apprehension of "good and evil." *Brighton Rock* cannot be satisfactorily read for its doctrine or as a realistic novel; if it works—and this author thinks it does—it is as a kind of poem.

## II

THE 1930's were a busy decade for Greene. As well as the nine novels he published between 1929 and 1939, he wrote a collection of short stories, along with critical essays, book reviews, and film reviews, many of them preserved in his *Collected Essays* (1969) and *The Pleasure Dome*. A curiosity, showing the breadth of his interests, is a biography of the Restoration poet Lord Rochester, which was written in 1934 but remained unpublished until 1974. More significantly, there are Greene's travel books *Journey Without Maps* (1936) and *The Lawless Roads* (1939; U.S. title, *Another Mexico*) about his visits to, respectively, Liberia and Mexico. The travel book was a popular form of the period, when authors would obtain publishers' advances to write accounts of faraway places. Greene, however, was more than a detached recorder of the exotic splendors of nature or the oddities of native life. He believed, like the Assistant Commissioner in *It's a Battlefield*, that authentic existence was more likely to be found in supposedly savage places than in the tedium of modern civilization. These travel books contain some of his most deeply personal writing.

In West Africa Greene experienced much discomfort and some danger, which he conveys vividly, though whatever he saw and felt is colored by his obsessive consciousness. Greene claimed that he loathed West Africa, but there is an undercurrent of affection, renewed during World War II when he was an intelligence officer in Sierra Leone. In *Journey Without Maps* Greene presents himself as though he were a solitary traveler, apart from his African servants and bearers. In fact, he was accompanied by his cousin Barbara Greene, who later published her own account of the journey. When he visited Mexico, Greene was concerned with spiritual as well as physical extremity, for the immediate purpose of his journey was to investigate the fierce persecution of the Catholic Church by an antireligious government. Greene was fascinated as well as repelled by the harshness of the landscape and the intensities of human deprivation and suffering that he found in Mexico. The immediate result of this visit was the novel that many readers regard as his best, *The Power and the Glory* (1940; U.S. title, *The Labyrinthine Ways*). By the end of the 1930's Greeneland was moving away from urban England to new locations in Africa and Latin America.

*The Power and the Glory* is the most Catholic of Greene's novels and the most accessible of his so-called Catholic novels. The abiding themes of his fiction are very apparent: pursuit, suffering, betrayal, the clash of innocence and experience. *The Power and the Glory* is also a study of sanctity and failure, seeing the two as intimately related. Its central figure, the "whiskey priest," is a more psychologically complex character than anyone in Greene's earlier novels; to this extent *The Power and the Glory* is closer to traditional realistic fiction. But it still has elements of the morality play, that early dramatic form so admired by Greene, particularly in the typological opposition of the priest and the atheistic police lieutenant. The priest has depth and arouses sympathy, but he is never named, like the duchess in Greene's favorite Jacobean play, *The Duchess of Malfi*. In the eyes of the world and the conventionally pious, he seems unworthy, an almost complete failure. He is an alcoholic who has abandoned much of his priestly practice, and he has fathered a child. Nevertheless, in a part of Mexico where the persecution of religion is fiercest and where the penalty for being a priest is death, he persists in trying, in secret, to say mass and bring the sacraments to the people. He is the archetypal man on the run, partly inspired by the Jesuit missionaries in Elizabethan England who were also trying to carry out their priestly functions while being hunted by the agents of the state, with a price on their heads. The broad appeal of such a situation has made the book popular among those who do not share Greene's religious world view. As John Spurling has written: "For non-Catholic readers it is precisely the personal, dogged, earthbound nature of the priest's faith, the fact that the religious sense is not objectified in anything so out-of-the way as even 'a presence above a croquet lawn' [the reference is to an account, in *The Lawless Roads*, of a religious experience in childhood], which makes the book credible and sympathetic" (*Graham Greene*, p. 36).

*The Power and the Glory* has much in common with Greene's earlier novels, particularly the restless, ranging cinematic eye and the metaphorical prose. But the Mexican setting is new and strange, though it seems as much a projection from within the author's consciousness as the impact of an objective, alien reality. The priest and the lieutenant, the hunted and the hunter, are the central figures, though there are many lesser ones, some of them significant Greenian types. There is the young girl, Coral, innocent but clear-sighted, the child of an English expatriate family, who shelters the priest when he is on the run; in contrast to her is the priest's daughter, Brigitta, prematurely corrupted by the world. There are the upright German-American couple, the Lehrs, whose Protestant innocence or ignorance is contrasted with Catholic understanding; they are an early embodiment in Greene's fiction of his conviction that Americans do not know enough about life and that this ignorance can be harmful. The most vicious character in the book is another man on the run, the American gangster Calver. At the end of the novel the priest, having crossed the border to safety in a state where Catholicism is tolerated and not actively persecuted, deliberately goes back to the dying Calver, who he has been told is a Catholic and wants a priest. Calver dies impenitent and the priest is finally captured by his pursuer, the lieutenant of police, to face a death sentence.

The "border" (Browning's "the dangerous edge of things") is a central concept in Greene's literary imagination. He reflects on it at some length in *The Lawless Roads* as he describes crossing the frontier, metaphorical as well as literal, between the United States and Mexico. As a boy Greene had been in the unsettling and anomalous position of attending as a weekly boarder the school where his father was headmaster, but returning to the family home in the same building for weekends; this meant passing through a green baize door from the cold institutionalized severity and minor cruelties of the school to the warm and happy environment of home. Such divisions in experience continued to fascinate him, and they ramify in his fiction.

*The Power and the Glory* deserves its high reputation, and there are some memorable scenes in it, one of the finest occurring when the priest, arrested on the minor charge of possessing liquor and not yet identified as a priest, spends a night in a crowded prison cell full of assorted human types. Yet there is a certain weakness in the novel in that it is too diagrammatic, notably in the opposition between lieutenant and priest, atheist and believer, dedicated respectively to progress and salvation. Greene tries to be fair to the lieutenant, who is a good man in humanistic terms but altogether too schematic and two-dimensional. *The Power and the Glory* is an implicitly conservative book ideologically, in that it accepts the poverty of the Mexican Indians as a fact of nature and even a positive aid to their ultimate salvation; in later novels with a Latin American setting, such as *The Comedians* and *The Honorary Consul*, Greene implies that revolutionary struggle for human betterment is right and unavoidable. In *The Power and the Glory* the drama remains wholly individual. It is a moving demonstration of how a sinner can be a saint and how spiritual strength can arise from physical weakness, but it is still a little too much of a demonstration.

*The Ministry of Fear* (1943) is the last of Greene's entertainments, and it is a more obscure and confusing book than its predecessors, partly, perhaps, because its central character's mind is supposed to be out of focus. Arthur Rowe has been acquitted of the mercy killing of his sick wife, but he lives with the guilt of this action. It is wartime and his memory has been affected by the explosion of a bomb. He gets inadvertently caught up with a Nazi spy ring and is accused of a murder he did not commit. In *A Gun for Sale* and *The Confidential Agent* war had been a threat in the background; in *The Ministry of Fear* it is a present reality. A strong element of the novel is its vivid evocation of the bombing of London. (Greene set down his experience of that time in the brief journal "London 1940–41" in *Ways of Escape*.) In a more subjective way the novel reflects Greene's perennial interest in dreams and the importance of childhood experience; a green baize door appears as a physical entity. *The Ministry of Fear* remains a minor part of Greene's oeuvre, written during his period in West Africa on secret-service work. He went there late in 1941 and during the voyage wrote a short book, *British Dramatists* (1942) —in fact an illustrated, bound pamphlet for a series called Britain in Pictures. It is of some interest in obliquely illustrating Greene's attitudes of the early 1940's to life as well as to literature. He writes of his admiration for *Everyman* and *The Duchess of Malfi*. He says that William Shakespeare's great tragic figures are as much the embodiment of qualities and passions in the Morality tradition as satisfying "characters": "Here is the watershed between the morality and the play of character: the tension between the two is perfectly kept: there is dialectical perfection. After Shakespeare, character —which was to have its dramatic triumphs—won a too-costly victory." It is perhaps worth noting that when Pinkie, toward the end of his desperate career in *Brighton Rock*, says, "It's no good stopping now. We got to go on . . . ," he is in effect paraphrasing Macbeth's words: "I am in blood/Stepp'd in so far that, should I wade no more,/Returning were as tedious as go o'er" (*Macbeth*, III.4). Greene continued to be suspicious of character as an end in itself, mainly, it seems, because it lacks the transcendental significance given by a religious view of life; a few years later he applied a similar argument to fiction, saying that with the death of Henry James the religious sense was lost to the English novel and that "the characters of such distinguished writers as Mrs. Virginia Woolf and Mr. E. M. Forster wandered like cardboard symbols through a world that was paper-thin" ("François Mauriac," *Collected Essays*). This was the aesthetic that sustained Greene in his "Catholic" phase.

In West Africa he found himself, if not at home, at least in familiar territory, where the wild inner landscape of his imagination acquired a tangible form. Greene has written of it in *Ways of Escape*: "Greeneland perhaps: I can only say it is the land in which I have passed much of my life." In Sierra Leone Greene absorbed the experience of place and atmosphere that was to appear, several years later, in his next novel, *The Heart of the Matter*. His work for the secret service also gave him an understanding of the stratagems and techniques of intelligence work that he was to treat farcically in *Our Man in Havana* and seriously in *The Human Factor*.

Greene returned to England in 1944 with the pattern of his life radically changed. For many years he had been a busy, London-based man of letters working as a novelist, critic, and reviewer. Picking up the threads of life again, he found himself working for the cinema as a scriptwriter; curiously, when Greene began writing for the films his prose became less cinematic. One of the first products of this new phase of Greene's life had a strange history. In 1944 he wrote, in the form of a novella, the outline for a film set in France under the German occupation. This material was never used, and for forty years it lay forgotten in the archives of a film company. In 1985, after its discovery, it was published as *The Tenth Man*, with an introduction by Greene. *The Tenth Man* is a good vintage Greene narrative with the familiar themes of betrayal and pursuit and deception. A number of hostages in a prison are ordered to be shot by the Nazis. One of them, a wealthy lawyer, persuades another prisoner to take his place, in exchange for his country house and all his wealth. This man agrees, and before he is shot makes a will leaving everything to his mother and sister. After his release from prison the lawyer, now penniless, makes his way to what was once his ancestral home and meets the dead man's sister. *The Tenth Man* is a taut and powerful tale, with the qualities of a legend or fable; it makes good use of the traditional folklore motif of the doppelgänger, when a stranger turns up claiming to be the real survivor. In his introduction Greene records his reaction to the rediscovered story: "What surprised and aggravated me most of all was that I found this forgotten story very readable— indeed I prefer it in many ways to *The Third Man*." I am inclined to agree with Greene: *The Tenth Man* is more substantial than *The Third Man*, though that is his most famous work of fiction written for the cinema. Inevitably one's reading of *The Third Man* is affected by the stark images of Carol Reed's famous film set in the ruins of postwar Vienna, and by Orson Welles's memorable performance as Harry Lime, the last of Greene's quasi-Jacobean melodramatic villains.

After the war Greene's literary production proceeded at a slower pace than in the 1930's, and *The Heart of the Matter* did not appear until 1948. This is the most notorious of his Catholic novels; it is at the same time far more of a conventional novel than *Brighton Rock* or *The Power and the Glory*. Its central figure, Major Scobie, is more of a traditional fictional character, less of a type than the whiskey priest or Pinkie. Major Scobie is a good but flawed man, like a traditional tragic hero, and *The Heart of the Matter* has something of the largeness of scope and forward drive of a classical tragedy. Its story is too complicated to be easily summarized; what one most remembers about the book is not the plot or Scobie's torturing dilemmas but its setting and atmosphere. It is set in West Africa during World War II, and Greene achieves a fine distillation of his memories of that time and place, mixed with elements taken from his visit to Liberia in 1934. It is the familiarly exotic Greeneland but more richly rendered, in the intensities of heat, the rats and cockroaches, and the prevailing sense of physical and moral corruption. Scobie is a middle-aged Catholic police officer, a man of celebrated rectitude who is a fuller version of the Assistant Commissioner in *It's a Battlefield*. Yet Scobie's life is a mess; he no longer loves his ailing, neurotic, intellectually pretentious wife; but he pities her, and pity, the novel implies, is a dangerous virtue. Greene's mistrust of pity was first apparent in *The Ministry of Fear*; it is contrasted with the more profound virtue of compassion, though the difference is not altogether easy to grasp. But pity undoubtedly leads to Scobie's undoing, as he moves on to adultery and compliance in corruption—even, perhaps, in murder—and then to receiving Communion in a state of mortal sin, and on to the ultimate and technically unforgivable sin of suicide. If *The Heart of the Matter* is a tragedy, it is also a Christian tragedy, a form that some critics have said cannot exist; Scobie moves inexorably on, not merely to temporal death or disaster, but to damnation. Whether Scobie is actually damned is a topic that has attracted much discussion among Catholic readers. Among non-Catholics the argument has tended to be about the contradictions within Scobie: is he a self-deceiving neurotic, or is he a genuinely good man for whom everything goes wrong, and who is tragically trapped in a course of action from which in human terms there is no escape? It is not surprising that critics have interpreted him in quite different ways. He is a remarkably humble man, almost to the point of lacking any sense of self-worth; but he also, and perhaps for the same reason, can seem strangely arrogant, particularly at the end of his sad life, when, from pitying his wife and his mistress, he goes on to pity God.

*The Heart of the Matter* lacks the broad human appeal of *The Power and the Glory* despite its greater psychological depth. In the perspective of Greene's later work the novel has a new emphasis. It still reflects the French literary Catholic tradition, as in its invocation in an epigraph of Péguy's claim that the sinner himself is at the heart of Christianity, and in placing the possibility of damnation as the climax of the story. Yet in its presentation of Scobie it shows that Greene was more sympathetic to the humanistic ideal of character than he had once been. And though a theological frame of reference is still explicit, there is also a sense that it is being tested to destruction.

Greene's next novel, *The End of the Affair* (1951), still looked very Catholic, with a paradoxical epigraph from the melodramatic French Catholic novelist Léon Bloy: "Man has places in his heart which do not yet exist, and into them enters suffering, in order that they may have existence." God is more overtly a character than in *The Heart of the Matter*, even to the point of intervening in the action; there are suggestions of actual miracles, which Greene had never approached in his earlier Catholic fiction. At the same time, it is a different kind of novel from anything he had previously written, formally and thematically. It is a first-person narrative told by Maurice Bendrix, who is a novelist and an unbeliever, and the essence of his story is how he lost his lover, Sarah Miles, the wife of a civil servant, to God, whom he ultimately acknowledges as a rival and a more powerful maker of plots. Bendrix is in the fullest sense a complex character, revealing himself as his narrative unfolds as a real and understandable if not very likable man. In the skillful development of Bendrix's account of himself, Greene is evidently indebted to Ford Madox Ford's *The Good Soldier*, a novel he greatly admires. *The End of the Affair* treats time fluidly, but most of it takes place toward the end of the war when London was under attack from flying bombs, and in the early months of peace. The presentation of London is more direct and prosaic than in Greene's fiction of the 1930's; the metaphorical urban poetry and the cinematic effects have now gone. Henceforth, as Roger Sharrock has shown, Greene's prose is soberly aphoristic rather than poetic. Bendrix is a new type in Greene's fiction, though one that is to become familiar. He is an isolated figure like Pinkie and the whiskey priest and Scobie, but he is not a Catholic, and he does not exist in their spiritually problematic dimension. Rather, he looks forward to the lonely, cynical, sometimes embittered observers of the human scene who are to provide the central consciousness of Greene's novels from the 1950's onward: Fowler in *The Quiet American,* Query in *A Burnt-Out Case,* Brown in *The Comedians.* Bendrix is a man of stronger passions than them, however, and his narrative is full of intensities of feeling; David Lodge has remarked on the frequency with which the words "love" and "hate" recur in the book.

Sexual love is at the heart of the action in a way that is new in Greene's fiction, and his central female character, Sarah, is a Magdalene-like figure who moves from sin to sanctity, from human love to divine love. It is her capacity for the former, it is implied, that impels her to seek the latter. She dies of pneumonia, and after her death strange things happen to people she had been involved with: a small boy instantly recovers from a grave illness, and an atheist preacher who had been in love with her is suddenly and inexplicably cured of a disfiguring birthmark. These events may, of course, be medical improbabilities, not impossibilities; or they may be what the faithful regard as miracles, works wrought by the intercession of Sarah, now a saint in heaven. Such things still mark *The End of the Affair* as a Catholic novel, disconcertingly so for some humanist readers, just as the emphasis on sex disturbs some of Greene's devout Catholic readers. Yet the emphasis on salvation rather than damnation is a new note, and there is no longer an absolute opposition between belief and unbelief. Maurice Bendrix ends the novel still an unbeliever, but his last words form a kind of bleak prayer: "O God, You've done enough, You've robbed me of enough, I'm too tired and old to learn to love, leave me alone for ever." For several years Greene's fictional practice and his personal aesthetic had been predicated on an absolute opposition between the religious and the human orders. In *The End of the Affair* the two orders have become inextricably mixed, with the love of man leading potentially to the love of God. This short, austere work remains one of Greene's most impressive achievements in fiction.

III

WITH *The End of the Affair* Greene's Catholic fiction came to an end, though he pursued some of its characteristic themes—adultery, loss of faith, suicide—in his first two plays, *The Living Room* (1953) and *The Potting Shed* (1957). Ten years after *The End of the Affair* Greene did indeed publish another novel concerned with Catholic questions, *A Burnt-Out Case,* though its treatment of them is very different from the earlier novels that had made him famous as a Catholic novelist, a description he always rejected, preferring to call himself a Catholic who wrote novels. The heavily Catholic phase of his fiction lasted no more than thirteen years, from 1938 to 1951. *The Quiet American,* which came out in 1955, opened a new phase that has, in effect, lasted for thirty years. Henceforth, Greene appeared as a writer more concerned with politics than with religion, setting his fiction in what we conventionally call the Third World: Indochina at a time when the French were still the imperial power, in *The Quiet American;* and different parts of Latin America in *Our Man in Havana, The Comedians, Travels with My Aunt, The Honorary Consul,* and *Getting to Know the General,* which emerged as a memoir instead of the novel that Greene wanted to write but was unable to. These parts of the world are still recognizably Greeneland, but the picture of them is significantly different from its earlier manifestations, whether the London of the 1930's or the Mexico of *The Power and the Glory* and the West Africa of *The Heart of the Matter.* Greene's vision of those places was obsessional and haunted, rendered with elaborate rhetoric and metaphor. In his postwar books he observes the world with the sharp but weary eye of the practiced traveler or the cynical reporter, like the journalist Fowler in *The Quiet American.* And the prose is correspondingly cooler and flatter. Greene himself took on a number of assignments as a foreign correspondent during the 1950's, in Indochina, where he gathered the material for *The Quiet American,* and in Kenya, during the Mau-Mau insurrection. The political sympathies implied in these novels are on the side of popular movements of liberation and against imperialism, usually American. To some extent they show a continuity with one aspect of Greene's writing of the 1930's: the intermittently left-wing sympathies that made Orwell think that Greene might be the first Catholic fellow traveler of the Communists. On the other hand the spiritual quietism with which Greene regards the poverty and deprivation of the Mexican Indians in *The Power and the Glory* has been replaced by an activist spirit of social justice (in some measure paralleling developments in official Catholic attitudes).

*The Quiet American* and Greene's next novel, *Our Man in Havana*, both have memorable titles that have generated a variety of journalistic clichés ("the something American" or "our man in . . ."). *The Quiet American* has things in common with *The End of the Affair;* like the earlier novel it is formally tight and carefully planned, sober in tone and language; and its central consciousness, Harry Fowler, has something of Maurice Bendrix's sour view of life. But he lacks Bendrix's passionate intensities; indeed, for much of the novel he shows little capacity for real feelings of any kind, and God is absent from the action. As a historical text, *The Quiet American* vividly documents the desperate attempt by the French in the 1950's to maintain their colonial rule in Indochina, and it anticipates the many bitter years that lay ahead when the Americans replaced the French and Indochina became known as Vietnam. The English journalist Harry Fowler is, at first, cynically indifferent to the fortunes of either side. In some respects, he recalls a stock Hollywood type, the tough journalist—a Bogart figure, perhaps—who is concerned only about doing a good professional job without sentiment getting in the way. But Harry Fowler's life is complicated by the young American secret agent, Alden Pyle. He is for Greene an embodiment of a kind of American innocence that he believes to be dangerous and ultimately destructive. In the novel Pyle is working to set up a third force between the French and Communists, and his endeavors end in death and destruction. Fowler is shaken from his detachment and is instrumental in helping to eliminate Pyle.

Schematically, the novel is polarized in a Jamesian way between the European experience of Fowler and the American innocence of Pyle, and there is no doubt that Greene favors the former. However much of a realist and reporter he appears to be, he remains a very literary writer whose early immersion in Henry James has colored his later apprehensions of America. In *The Quiet American* Greene's anti-Americanism becomes explicit, although it had been anticipated by his presentation of the Lehrs in *The Power and the Glory*, the kindly but stupid couple who are too innocent or too ignorant to have any real understanding of Mexico or Catholicism. This attitude is an understandable irritant and stumbling block for American readers of Greene, but it is worth unraveling its causes and constituents. Politically, Greene's anti-Americanism is directed against American imperialism, particularly in Latin America. But in Greene's case this position is the product of more than political radicalism. His attitudes originated in the 1930's and were apparent in his days as a film critic, when he continually expressed scorn and derision for the products of Hollywood and the cultural attitudes that underlay them. One aspect, at least, of Greene's anti-Americanism is rooted in the European conservative's distaste for American mass culture. There is also a purely personal consideration. Because Greene was for a very short time a member of the Communist party as an undergraduate, he was for several years refused entry to the United States or was permitted only a restricted entry visa. This petty restriction was eventually revoked, but Greene has never forgiven it, and the joker in him loses no opportunity to embarrass official America, as he shows in *Getting to Know the General*.

However critical Greene is of official American attitudes, he can be equally scathing and satirical about the British establishment. This is very evident in his next novel, *Our Man in Havana* (1958), which represented a move by Greene into sardonic comedy. Mr. Wormold, the humble representative in Havana of a vacuum-cleaner company, is casually recruited into the British secret service. Having nothing in particular to report, he invents fictional stories of ever-increasing ingenuity, culminating in the discovery of alleged rocket installations in the mountains of the Cuban interior. The supposedly authenticating photographs are in fact of parts of a vacuum cleaner. Greene is here interestingly anticipating the Cuban missile crisis of 1962, albeit in a farcical way. *Our Man in Havana* is set in the last days of the Batista regime, and although the Cuban revolution looms vaguely in the background, there is no hint of the advent of Fidel Castro, which took place a few months after the book was published, and of his transforming effect on the Western hemisphere. Still, Greene was not trying to write a serious political novel of the kind he later produced in *The Comedians* and *The Honorary Consul*. What he did produce is a highly entertaining and readable farce that mocks the kind of secret-service operations with which he had become familiar in West Africa during World War II.

Catholic themes treated in a quite new way reappear in *A Burnt-Out Case* (1961). It was foreshadowed by a short story called "A Visit to Morin," published in 1957, in which a young Englishman on holiday in France visits a distinguished elderly French Catholic writer whose books he knows and admires. He discovers that this man, Morin, is no longer a Catholic; at least he has lost his overt belief in Catholicism, though in some unexplained, paradoxical way faith remains. This story might be seen as indicating a crisis in Greene's own relationship to the Catholic Church and as marking a farewell to the French Catholic tradition of Bloy, Bernanos, and Mauriac that had inspired his own earlier Catholic novels. Morin is a fictional character, of course, not a persona for Greene; but it is worth noting that the distinction between belief, seen as a matter of conscious adherence to doctrine, and faith, as a deeper stratum of commitment, is acknowledged by Greene in his conversations with Marie-Françoise Allain, in the latter's book *The Other Man*. The central figure of *A Burnt-Out Case*, Querry, is another of Greene's new-style weary, cynical protagonists; he is an eminent Catholic architect, famous for his churches and cathedrals, who has lost his faith and retreated to a leper colony, in the depths of what was then still the Belgian Congo, in order to get away from his admirers and recover his peace of mind. It would be too simple to assume that the famous Catholic architect necessarily equals the famous Catholic novelist, but there are elements in Querry's rather thin and schematic story that point in that direction; both the character and author have received similar acclamations, even to the point of having their pictures on the cover of *Time*.

On the face of it, *A Burnt-Out Case* repudiates the values of Greene's earlier Catholic novels, and some Catholic readers were disconcerted by it, such as his friend Evelyn Waugh, who took it as indicating an actual loss of faith on Greene's part. In a subsequent interview Greene briskly disposed of Waugh's objection to the book in a slightly disingenuous fashion: "I hadn't lost faith, my character Querry lost *his* faith. Nothing to do with me." It is certainly true that *A Burnt-Out Case* is pervaded by a much more humanistic kind of Catholicism than one finds in Greene's previous novels or their French antecedents, which are so conscious of the division between nature and grace. Querry argues with the Father Superior of the leper settlement— Greene's taste for debates in fiction is one thing carried over from the earlier phase—about the separation between religious and human virtues. Querry, though no longer a believing Catholic, still thinks in the old categories, though he sees them from outside: "You try to draw everything into the net of your faith, father, but you can't steal all the virtues. Gentleness isn't Christian, self-sacrifice isn't Christian, charity isn't, remorse isn't." But the Father Superior asserts the exact opposite; preaching to his flock he tells them that when they love or are merciful, it is Jesus who does these things in them. This reflects later developments in Catholic theology, which stress that all good things come from God, that nature and grace are interdependent, and that there is a virtual and implicit Christianity as well as a doctrinally informed and committed Christianity. As ideas these are interesting and congenial, but they do not make *A Burnt-Out Case* a particularly convincing work of fiction; it seems a much thinner work than the antihumanistic *Brighton Rock*.

Five years later Greene published what is undoubtedly one of his finest novels, *The Comedians* (1966), set in the francophone black republic of Haiti under the odious dictatorship of François "Papa Doc" Duvalier. Haiti as Greene describes it is appallingly cruel and corrupt, an extreme and peculiar region of Greeneland. At the same time, the novel is good-humored in a way new in Greene's fiction; Greene as joker is present in the way the three main characters are given the most common surnames in English: Brown, Smith, and Jones. Brown is the central consciousness, a worldweary, cynical observer in the mold of Fowler and Querry, but he has more of a sense of humor, and he shares the action with other protagonists of a different temperament. Roger Sharrock has written well of the fresh direction Greene took in *The Comedians*, and his words are worth quoting at some length:

Yet there is a difference in *The Comedians*, and the difference marks a decisive change in tone and emphasis which is felt in all of Greene's subsequent novels. The scene is open, not oppressively enclosed, and laughter is possible even in the dark night of Haiti; sometimes it is critical laughter, sometimes a quite disinterested sympathetic humour. The comedy that Greene had demonstrated in asides, and in ancillary characters and episodes, and to which he had given fuller rein in some of the entertainments (*Loser Takes All* and *Our Man in Havana* are cases in point), now moves nearer to the centre of the stage in a major novel.... The strength of *The Comedians, The Honorary Consul,* and their successors, resides in the broad, tolerant range of a vision that is at once comic and intensely serious. To quote Brown again, invoking the absent God in whom he no longer believes, "all are driven by an authoritative practical joker towards the extreme point of comedy."

(*Saints, Sinners and Comedians,* pp. 222–223)

There are unambiguously admirable characters in *The Comedians,* like the Marxist doctor, Dr. Magiot, engaged in resistance against Duvalier's dictatorship, and a visiting American couple, the Smiths. They are crusading vegetarians and upholders of a wide assortment of good causes—Mr. Smith has the hazy distinction of once having stood as a candidate for the United States presidency on the ticket of the Vegetarian party. They have the naiveté that we expect of Greene's Americans, and to some extent they are more developed versions of the Lehrs in *The Power and the Glory*. There is a peculiar innocence about their efforts to advance the vegetarian cause amid the poverty and violence of Haiti. But their innocence lacks the destructive quality to be found in Greene's earlier fictional Americans, Alden Pyle in particular. They are basically good people, with the quality of being able to learn from their experience. The Smiths stand as a reminder that Greene can portray Americans sympathetically; so does the elderly, unsuccessful American expatriate on a Caribbean island who appears in one of his best short stories, "Cheap in August."

Greene's next novel, *Travels with My Aunt* (1969), culminates in another grim part of Latin America, the Paraguay of General Stroessner, but the treatment is determinedly comic. Henry Pulling, a retired bank manager of quiet habits, reluctantly agrees to set out on picaresque travels with his fun-loving, bohemian, septuagenarian Aunt Augusta and her black lover, Wordsworth. Greene has said that this novel reflects the manic side of a manic-depressive writer—the depressive side was represented eight years earlier by *A Burnt-Out Case* —and called it, in *Ways of Escape,* the only book he has written for the fun of it. There are some good comic moments in *Travels with My Aunt,* but much of the comedy strikes me as forced or merely facetious; Greene without doubt has a sense of humor, but he is not enough of a purely comic writer to sustain that spirit through a whole novel without the contrasting presence of different qualities. The literary joker is much in evidence as he engages in self-allusions, invoking earlier novels such as *Stamboul Train* and *Brighton Rock.*

In Greene's next novel, *The Honorary Consul* (1973), we are once more in South America, this time in a remote province of northern Argentina. This is a "serious" political novel, though there are elements of comedy, particularly in the presentation of the eponymous honorary consul, Charley Fortnum. He is a British businessman, a dim and rather absurd figure who is the local honorary consul for Britain (though he has, strictly, no longer any legal right to the title). He is kidnapped by some inept revolutionaries in mistake for the American ambassador. Much of the novel focuses on Eduardo Plarr, a local doctor of partly British origins who is one of Greene's familiar later types: lonely, cynical, and wary of much human engagement. However, he is a decent man and a dedicated doctor, illustrating the tendency of people in Greene's later novels to be rather better as people than are the characters in his early books. After the kidnapping of his friend Charley, Plarr gets tangled up with the revolutionaries; their leader, Leon, is an old acquaintance, a former priest who is now a guerrilla fighter. In the latter part of the novel there is a long debate between Plarr and Leon. It goes on throughout the night in a village hut, while their lives are in danger from the police. Both are ex-Catholics but the idea of God is still real to them, and they argue at length about religion and ideology and revolution, in a more elaborate version of earlier debates in Greene's fiction: between the priest and the lieutenant in *The Power and the Glory;* between Querry and the Father Superior and Dr. Collin in *A Burnt-Out Case.* This debate goes on too long, but *The Honorary Consul* is a generally successful work, among the best of Greene's postwar novels.

Its successor, *The Human Factor* (1978), is, I think, one of his weakest. In more than one sense it represents a return to Greene's origins. As a novel about spies and secret agents it goes back to the models of his earliest fiction, as well as drawing on his own experience in World War II. Its central figure, Maurice Castle, lives in Berkhamsted, the small Hertfordshire town just outside London where Greene grew up and which was the scene of the formative childhood experiences described in his autobiographical writings. And it is the first of Greene's novels to be set wholly in England since *The End of the Affair*. Maurice Castle works for British intelligence; he is also, in a small way, a Soviet agent. He does this not out of great ideological commitment to communism or the Soviet Union—like most of Greene's major characters he is a skeptic about ideologies—but out of gratitude to the Communists who had helped his black wife escape from South Africa as a political refugee. *The Human Factor* is a tired book, lacking conviction, and it suggests that the vein of the secret-agent story that had served Greene well for many years was finally running out. The fictional texture is thin, and the rendering of London is perfunctory, in contrast to the intimate sense of the city that Greene had conveyed so well in the 1930's. Indeed, there is much about *The Human Factor* that reminds us that Greene, who lives in the south of France, has been physically cut off from day-to-day English life for many years. It is full of missed opportunities, like the conversation between two of its characters, Hargreaves and the richly sinister Dr. Percival, after lunch at the Reform Club, which ought, somehow, to be more blackly comic than it is.

*The Human Factor* raises the larger question of Greene's apparent sympathy for communism. This undoubtedly exists, though it takes an idiosyncratic form; Greene has never shown any great regard for the Soviet Union and has protested against the Soviet persecution of writers, but he is on the side of the Marxist revolutionaries of Latin America. Such people are sympathetically portrayed in his novels (Dr. Magiot in *The Comedians* and Luis in *The Honorary Consul*); and in *Getting to Know the General* Greene writes warmly of the Sandinista government in Nicaragua. There are a number of related attitudes involved: a compassionate and idealistic identification with the poor and oppressed; a conviction that Marxist-led revolution is the only likely way to improve their lot; and a degree of Greene's perennial anti-Americanism. Nevertheless, Greene's political vision remains extremely individualistic, in some respects naive. He has more than once expressed his conviction that "disloyalty" is a necessary human quality, particularly for the writer. This attitude leads to paradoxes and, ultimately, contradictions. Greene has expressed admiration for his old friend and colleague, the British spy and traitor Kim Philby, saying that Philby was a man who remained loyal throughout his life to his belief in Soviet communism. For Greene this kind of loyalty is somehow preferable to Philby's disloyalty to his country. The issue is raised in *The Human Factor,* where Castle's personally motivated disloyalty is sympathetically regarded. Roger Sharrock remarks in his discussion of this book on Greene's "peculiar belief in the entirely personal valuation of action, as if decisions were taken quite apart from group codes or inherited standards." Again, Greene's long physical absence from British life may be a factor. Sharrock's insight suggests both the strengths and weaknesses of Greene's fictional treatment of the human condition. Greene is undoubtedly liable to political confusions. In his conversations with Marie-Françoise Allain he admits that present-day Soviet realities are far removed from the ideal of "communism with a human face" to which he has aspired, and he confesses to being of two minds about Castro: "I admire his courage and his efficiency, but I question his authoritarianism" (*The Other Man,* p. 111). Greene does, however, assert an admirable principle when he invokes Tom Paine's maxim: "We must guard even our enemies against injustice."

IV

IN 1980 Greene made one of his surprising fresh starts when he published *Doctor Fischer of Geneva or the Bomb Party*. This short novel is a moral fable and a fantasy; it has some of the qualities of a dream, recalling how often Greene has described dreams in his fiction and drawn on them for literary effect. Doctor Fischer is one of his most magnificently horrible creations; he is a Swiss millionaire with a totally negative view of human nature. He is surrounded by a circle of greedy, sycophantic disciples —one could hardly call them "friends"—who are willing to endure any amount of humiliation at the hands of Fischer so as to acquire the riches he cynically bestows upon them. Fischer manipulates the world in a kind of monstrous parody of divine providence. He also embodies the idea of the novelist-as-joker, which has always fascinated Greene.

The narrator is Jones, a hard-up, middle-aged Englishman who works as a translator of business correspondence in a Geneva chocolate factory, and who lost his right hand in the bombing of London —a disability that leads us back to the air raids that form the background of *The Ministry of Fear* and Greene's wartime journal. There is Fischer's beautiful and gentle daughter, Anna-Louise, who is the opposite of her father in all possible ways. She falls in love with Jones and braves her father's anger by marrying him; they are idyllically happy for a short time, before she is killed in a skiing accident. And there is the elderly clerk, Steiner, who had been innocently in love with Fischer's wife and was ruined by him in revenge. At the end of the story Fischer too is dead, by his own hand, in an ultimate triumph of pure negation. It is a sad and sometimes shocking novel, but it is also a comedy, in the grim robust vein of Ben Jonson's dramatic exposures of human greed and folly. And the stuff of folklore lies not far below the surface. After the weariness of *The Human Factor*, Greene triumphantly renewed his art in an unpredictable way.

*Doctor Fischer* was followed by another, more genial comedy, *Monsignor Quixote* (1982). This is a serene, playful book, where Greene the joker is in a gentler mood. He plays with the idea of fiction, with the opposed systems of Catholicism and Marxism, even with his own reputation. It is a reflective and self-reflective story that looks back over more than fifty years of fiction making. The book is presented as a latter-day *Don Quixote* about the picaresque adventures of a humble Spanish priest, Monsignor Quixote, who is a direct descendant of Cervantes' character, or so we are told. From the beginning Greene raises questions about the relation of fact to fiction, and a few pages into the novel a sophisticated Italian bishop remarks, "perhaps we are all fictions, Father, in the mind of God." *Monsignor Quixote* is Greene's culminating treatment of the Hispanic world with which he has been concerned for so long, and it is a return to Spain itself after the many fictional explorations of Latin America. In *Ways of Escape* Greene refers to the debt his religious thinking owes to the great Spanish philosopher Miguel de Unamuno. He remarks that as a young man he read Unamuno's *Life and Death of Don Quixote* and then appeared to have forgotten about the book. But it had a long-term hidden effect, working in what Greene calls "the cellars of the unconscious." He concludes, "At the end of a long journey, without myself knowing the course which I had been taking, I found myself in 'A Visit to Morin' and *A Burnt-Out Case* in that tragi-comic region of La Mancha where I expect to stay." Monsignor Quixote is Greene's conscious tribute to Catholic quixotry in a work deliberately imitative of Cervantes' great original, not only in reproducing some of the same adventures but even in the style and chapter headings.

When the story opens Father Quixote behaves with simple Christian charity to a visiting Italian bishop whose car has broken down in his village. The grateful bishop proves to be an influential Vatican dignitary, and before long word comes from Rome that Father Quixote is to be promoted to the rank of monsignor. This does not please his own bishop, who has little time for him and believes that the pope must have taken leave of his senses to bestow such an honor. The newly elevated monsignor decides to take a little holiday and sets out in his battered old Seat 600 car, nicknamed Rocinante, accompanied by his friend and adversary, Sancho, the Communist ex-mayor of the village, who has just lost his post in an election and feels the need for a holiday himself. Their shared adventures in the footsteps of Cervantes' archetypal couple provide the action, but much of the interest comes from their arguments. Quixote and Sancho are doughty upholders of the causes of Catholicism and communism, respectively, eager to score points off each other. But when they are really at ease, after a little wine, each is prepared to admit that his conviction is not quite absolute, and that belief is sometimes mingled with doubt. These debates echo the many previous ones in Greene's fiction, particularly those in *The Power and the Glory*, to which novel Greene inserts some clues. At one point Monsignor Quixote refuses another glass of wine, saying, "I fear if I'm not careful I shall become what I've heard called a whiskey priest," and later he says he has no relatives except a second cousin in Mexico. But the world of Monsignor Quixote is not divided between opposed absolutes. Greene's priest and Communist are presented as good men, united by more than what divides them, struggling to live decently and help humanity as best they can without the comfort of absolute and unreflecting convictions. At the end, an undogmatic love triumphs. *Monsignor Quixote* is a serenely good-humored book—the fruit of a long life of experience and reflection—and it contains some of Greene's best comic writing.

In his excellent discussion of this novel Roger Sharrock shows how it brings together and reconciles some of the major themes of the earlier fiction: the remoteness of man from God without the dynamic of love; the debate between Catholicism and humanism, leading on to a shared commitment; and the effect of the experience of a fallen world on an innocent mind. In *Monsignor Quixote* we see Greene taking what appears to be a Prospero-like farewell to his life and art; to say this is not to rule out the possibility of Greene's writing another novel, just as Shakespeare continued to write plays after the apparent valediction in *The Tempest*.

The sheer length of Greene's career continues to be one of the most important things about it. Looked at in one way, it has been marked by remarkable variety; although primarily a novelist, he has written in many literary and journalistic forms. Even in the primary form of the novel, he has shown great variety of subject and treatment, from the early romances and the urban poetry of the thrillerlike entertainments to the spiritual dilemmas of the Catholic novels. After these came the shift of direction when Greene appeared primarily as a novelist of political interests writing about revolution and struggle in the Third World, particularly Latin America. After seeming for many years to be a writer without much sense of humor (apart from the "grim grin" that appears in one distorted version of his name), he then emerged as something of a comic novelist. And in the latest phase of his career, he has turned to fable and fantasy. Greene has not wholly escaped the dangers of self-imitation that attend the popular writer with an extensive career. But they have been more than compensated for by his capacity for self-renewal and the trying of fresh options; and his self-imitations, or perhaps one should say self-allusions, are increasingly deliberate and conscious, in the spirit of the intertextual joker. Greene has been a Catholic all his adult life, and his conversations with Marie-Françoise Allain make it clear that he still regards himself as one, though his relationship with the institutional church is not what it once was. But the distance between the bleak Augustinian absolutes that polarized *Brighton Rock*, his first overtly Catholic novel, and the humanistic, self-doubting, undogmatic Catholicism that is sympathetically presented in *Monsignor Quixote*, is immense.

Yet underlying the variety there is continuity. His preoccupation with solitude, pursuit, betrayal, and deception recurs in different forms from the early novels to the late. Roger Sharrock has even referred to "a fresh disguise for the single novel he is writing all the time." Greene is the most private of writers and has always discouraged speculation about his personality; but it is evident that the conflict between innocence and experience goes very deep in him. It is a theme often present in Henry James, who was one of Greene's earliest literary admirations, though in existential and personal terms it is evidently rooted in his own childhood experience, about which he has written much more explicitly than about his later life, and to which his psychoanalysis in adolescence is clearly relevant. Related to this conflict is a sense of guilt and complicity in guilt, considerations that dominate the Catholic fiction. When in the 1950's he moved from religious to political themes he engaged in what Sharrock calls "a reshuffling of the cards, not the introduction of a new pack. . . . Greene has changed the field of interest of his fiction without departing from its essential concern with the agony of moral decision" (pp. 130, 197). The personality may be elusive, but its obsessions are unmistakable.

Greene's favorite Browning line, "Our interest's on the dangerous edge of things," frequently comes to mind when one contemplates his career. Within the novels there is a recurring fascination with things that are drawn to their apparent opposites: the sinner who becomes, or may become, a saint; the atheist who is conscious of God; the revolutionary who was once a priest; the Catholic and the Communist who have a mutual dependence. Similar paradoxical oppositions occur when we try to get a sense of the kind of novelist Greene is. It is evident he is not a modernist; he has not followed in the aesthetic tracks of Joyce or William Faulkner or Samuel Beckett, and he has a wide readership among those who look for the traditional satisfactions of narrative rather than artistic innovation. Greene is a practitioner of what Roland Barthes has called the "classic realist text"; he works in a tradition of nineteenth-century realism, using the novel form to provide information about remote parts of the globe; he has not hesitated to bring a reportorial dimension into his fiction; there are places that Greene has, in several senses, put on the map for his readers: Brighton or West Africa or Haiti, for instance. Yet Greene's realism is not solid or unreflecting, and it is continually on the edge of other literary or dramatic forms: the adventure story, the thriller, the morality play, the gangster film, the dream-fantasy, the fable. He is not so easily categorized as some of his contemporaries. He is, indeed, like a realist of an earlier generation in being popular; whatever else Greene is, he is an outstanding storyteller, and his general reputation seems assured. With academic critics his reputation is less certain; for some, at least, his popularity puts him on a dangerous edge of things. Greene remains sufficiently individual to resist canonization; he is a survival from a time when literary culture was less divided. He may not be a great writer, ready for insertion into an academic canon; but he is an extraordinarily good one.

## SELECTED BIBLIOGRAPHY

I. BIBLIOGRAPHY. R.A. Wobbe, *Graham Greene: A Bibliography and Guide to Research* (New York and London, 1979).

II. COLLECTED WORKS. *Collected Essays* (London, 1969); *Triple Pursuit* (New York, 1971); J. R. Taylor, ed., *Graham Greene on Film: Collected Film Criticism* (New York, 1972); *Collected Stories* (London, 1972); P. Stratford, ed., *The Portable Graham Greene* (New York, 1973; rev. ed., 1977); *Shades of Greene* (London, 1975); *Collected Plays* (Harmondsworth, 1985).

III. SELECTED WORKS. *Babbling April* (Oxford, 1925), poems; *The Man Within* (London, 1929); *The Name of Action* (London, 1930); *Rumour at Nightfall* (London, 1931); *Stamboul Train* (London, 1932), U.S. title, *Orient Express; It's a Battlefield* (London, 1934); *The Bear Fell Free* (London, 1935); *England Made Me* (London, 1935), U.S. title, *The Shipwrecked; A Gun for Sale* (London, 1936), U.S. title, *This Gun for Hire; Journey Without Maps* (London, 1936), travel; *Brighton Rock* (London, 1938); *The Lawless Roads* (London, 1939), U.S. title, *Another Mexico,* travel; *The Confidential Agent* (London, 1939).

*The Power and the Glory* (London, 1940), U.S. title originally *The Labyrinthine Ways; British Dramatists* (London, 1942), criticism; *The Ministry of Fear* (London, 1943); *The Heart of the Matter* (London, 1948); *The Third Man and the Fallen Idol* (London, 1950); *The Lost Childhood* (London, 1951); *The End of the Affair* (London, 1951); *The Living Room* (London, 1953), play; *The Quiet American* (London, 1955); *Loser Takes All* (London, 1955); *The Potting Shed* (London, 1957), play; *Our Man in Havana* (London, 1958); *A Burnt-Out Case* (London, 1961); *In Search of a Character: Two African Journals* (London, 1961), travel; *The Comedians* (London, 1966); *Travels with My Aunt* (London, 1969); *A Sort of Life* (London, 1971), autobiography; *The Honorary Consul* (London, 1973); *Lord Rochester's Monkey* (London, 1974), biography; *The Human Factor* (London, 1978); *Ways of Escape* (London, 1980), autobiography; *Doctor Fischer of Geneva or the Bomb Party* (London, 1980); *J'Accuse, the Dark Side of Nice* (London, 1982), polemic; *Monsignor Quixote* (London, 1982); *Getting to Know the General* (London, 1984), memoir; *The Tenth Man* (London, 1985).

IV. BIOGRAPHICAL AND CRITICAL STUDIES. K. Allott and M. Farris, *The Art of Graham Greene* (London, 1951); D. O'Donnell (C. C. O'Brien), *Maria Cross; Imaginative Patterns in a Group of Catholic Writers* (London, 1953); S. O'Faoláin, *The Vanishing Hero* (London, 1956); J. Atkins, *Graham Greene* (London, 1952; rev. ed., 1966); R. W. B. Lewis, *The Picaresque Saint* (Philadelphia, 1959); P. Stratford, "Unlocking the Potting Shed," in the *Kenyon Review* (Winter 1962); F. Kermode, *Puzzles and Epiphanies* (London, 1962); D. Pryce-Jones, *Graham Greene* (Edinburgh, 1963; rev. ed., 1973); W. Allen, *Tradition and Dream: The English and American Novel from the Twenties to Our Time* (London, 1964); P. Stratford, *Faith and Fiction: Creative Process in Greene and Mauriac* (Notre Dame, Ind., 1964); J. M. Ross, *Memoirs of the Forties* (London, 1965); R. O. Evans, ed., *Graham Greene: Some Critical Considerations* (Lexington, Ky., 1967); G. Orwell, *Collected Essays, Journalism and Letters* (Harmondsworth, 1968), ed. by S. Orwell and I. Angus; D. Lodge, *The Novelist at the Crossroads* (Ithaca, N.Y., and London, 1971); S. Hynes, ed., *Graham Greene: A Collection of Critical Essays* (Englewood Cliffs, N.J., and London, 1973); G. D. Phillips, *Graham Greene: The Films of His Fiction* (New York and London, 1974); S. Hynes, *The Auden Generation* (New York and London, 1976); J. P. Kulshrestha, *Graham Greene: The Novelist* (Delhi, India, 1977); B. Bergonzi, *Reading the Thirties: Texts and Contexts* (London, 1978); K. W. Gransden, "Graham Greene's Rhetoric," in *Essays in Criticism* (January 1981); M.-F. Allain, *The Other Man: Conversations with Graham Greene* (New York, 1983); D. Gallagher, ed., *The Essays, Articles and Reviews of Evelyn Waugh* (Boston and London, 1983); J. Spurling, *Graham Greene* (New York and London, 1983); R. Sharrock, *Saints, Sinners and Comedians: The Novels of Graham Greene* (Notre Dame, Ind., and Tunbridge Wells, England, 1984); P. French, "Greene on the Screen," in *Encounter* (July–August 1985).

# THOMAS HARDY
## (1840-1928)

### R. A. Scott-James and C. Day Lewis

#### THE NOVELS

Suddenly an unexpected series of sounds began to be heard in this place up against the sky. They had a clearness which was to be found nowhere in the wind, and a sequence which was to be found nowhere in nature. They were the notes of Farmer Oak's flute.

SUCH were the notes that set the key in chapter 2 of *Far from the Madding Crowd* (1874). They are the same notes that were heard as distinctly in *Under the Greenwood Tree* (1872), the first of Thomas Hardy's novels to win the attention of a large public, though the second in order of appearance. That book introduces us to a place, a scene, set in a region the particularities of which were to be gradually unfolded in a series of novels, a region to become familiar in the mind's eye as the "Wessex of Thomas Hardy," centered in the hamlets, villages, towns, woods, meadows, and heathland of Dorset, and overflowing into the adjoining counties. It is a countryside inhabited by country people living, for the most part, under the conditions that prevailed when Hardy was a boy. The character of the region and still more the habits of the people have suffered many changes since then; and these outer and inner changes, already perceptibly beginning a hundred years ago, are again and again linked with the tragedies of his heroes and heroines. But the memory of the Wessex described by Hardy is fixed for posterity as long as English fiction continues to be read. It lives in the imagination more distinctly than any other region described by an English writer, perhaps any writer. Not thus do we know even the Scottish country described by Walter Scott. The Lake country associated with William Wordsworth is to Hardy's Wessex as a poetic symbol is to a human reality—a reality charged with all that is intimate and poignant in human experience. Not only have we been made to see the wild expanse of Egdon Heath, the rich meadowland of Talbothays, where Tess milked her cows and Angel Clare made love to her, the fir plantations and orchards of the Hintocks among which moved Giles Winterbourne and Marty South, the houses and streets and cornmarket of Casterbridge, frequented by all the farmers of the neighborhood; but also we have become aware of these places as influences subtly entering into the lives of the men and women born and bred there, who inherit memories, habits, and instincts handed on through the centuries. Those born in the Hintocks, with

an almost exhaustive biographical or historical acquaintance with every object, animate and inanimate, within the observer's horizon ... know all about those invisible ones of the days gone by, whose feet have traversed the fields which look so grey from the window; recall whose creaking plough has turned those sods from time to time; whose hands planted the trees that form a crest to the opposite hill; whose horses and hounds have torn through that underwood; what birds affect that particular brake; what bygone domestic dramas of love, jealousy, revenge, or disappointment have been enacted in the cottages, the mansions, the street or on the green.
(*The Woodlanders*, ch. 17)

This Wessex country, inhabited by simple people and the ghosts of their ancestors, and no less by animals, trees, and grasses,[1] is the background never wholly absent in Hardy's work, fiction or poetry.

What he says of Clym Yeobright, walking on Egdon Heath in *The Return of the Native* (1878), might have been said of himself:

If anyone knew the heath well, it was Clym. He was permeated with its scenes, with its substance, with its odours. He might be said to be its product. His eyes had first opened thereon; with its appearance all the first images

---

*In this essay R. A. Scott-James wrote the sections The Novels and The Dynasts; C. Day Lewis wrote The Lyrical Poetry.

[1] It is curious that songbirds occur rarely in the novels.

of his memory were mingled; his estimate of life had been coloured by it; his toys had been the flint knives and arrowheads which he found there, wondering why stones should "grow" to such odd shapes; his flowers, the purple bells and yellow gorse; his animal kingdom, the snakes and croppers; his society, its human haunters.

(bk. III, ch. 2)

Hardy was born in 1840 in Higher Bockhampton, in the parish of Stinsford. His father was a stonemason and builder who inherited from the grandfather a love of instrumental music and the care of the church choir; carol singing at Christmas, as described in *Under the Greenwood Tree*, and festive occasions celebrated with jigs, hornpipes, reels, and other country dances, lived in the memory of the novelist; again and again in his novels his style acquires a wonderful liveliness where he tells the story of a dance. As a small child, Florence Hardy says, he was "of ecstatic temperament, extraordinarily sensitive to music"; he was so moved by some of the tunes that he had to dance on to conceal his weeping. In his childhood his life was never far from that of the folk; he lived continuously in Dorset until he was twenty-two, attending first the village school, then schools at Dorchester. At the age of sixteen he began to study architecture under an architect much of whose work was concerned with church restoration. He read books omnivorously, studied Latin and French, and later, with the help of a friend, Greek; and he wrote poetry. It was in Dorchester that he came to know William Barnes, who as pedagogue gave him advice on grammar, and as poet stimulated his poetic interest in Dorset.

In literature, poetry was Hardy's first love, as it was his last. When he went to London at the age of twenty-two to pursue his profession of architecture, he worked conscientiously at it but continued to write poetry, though he had no success in getting it published. He was by no means unpractical. His supreme interest, he felt, lay in the composition of poetry, and throughout his earlier and middle creative period he constantly wrote verse to please himself; but he did not turn his back on the necessity of earning a living. He continued his regular work as an architect until he had made sure he could succeed in literature. In the field of literature, since the editors and publishers did not want his poems but did, in time, come to demand his novels, he gave his energies to fiction and found there his means of self-expression. He was to prove that a poet could write fiction in prose and would do it the better for being a poet. But often the task was irksome. Many of his novels had to be written on schedules to suit the journals in which they were published serially. When he was at the height of his powers (by the age of forty-six), he complained that his novel writing was "mere journeywork," and in later years he was impatient with those who did not think his verse superior to his fiction. But one need not overstress this self-criticism. Earlier, he was dissatisfied with cramping conditions; later, enjoying freedom, he remembered years when he had written under duress. Again and again he spoke seriously enough of his art, meaning the art of fiction, as when he wrote on 3 January 1886: "My art is to intensify the expression of things, as is done by Crivelli, Bellini, etc., so that the heart and inner meaning is made vividly visible."

Nonetheless, one must remember that for more than twenty years, during most of his novel-writing period, Hardy was, in a certain sense, writing for a living; that is to say, he was not in a position to rest on his oars and stop writing. This means that though we shall see him developing his essential powers and writing from inner necessity, we shall also find him producing work in which he is below himself, in books parts at least of which are irrelevant to his genius. His first venture in fiction, "The Poor Man and the Lady" (1867–1868), was never published, though a much shortened version of it was printed later in a magazine. It was read and criticized by two publishers' readers, none other than John Morley and George Meredith, the latter advising him, probably rightly, against publication, but less rightly telling him how to set about the writing of a novel. Hardy took the advice and exaggerated it in the thrills and surprising episodes that he heaped one on another in *Desperate Remedies* (1871)—a clever experiment in fiction, but not what we have come to think of as characteristic of Hardy.

Yet in the very next book, *Under the Greenwood Tree*, the real Hardy is present unmistakably. Already we strike the authentic note. No one could have done this book but Hardy, and, for what it is, it could scarcely have been done better. Here we have not yet reached the philosophy of Hardy; there is no sense of overwhelming destiny, no note of tragedy, no deep hint of the tears of things. It is not one of his greater books, yet I should profoundly regret it if he had not written it. It is a picture, an idyll, of Dorset country life as the author remembered it from his boyhood and before reflection had tinged it with bitterness. Here is Wessex—the Dorset country and people, the fir trees sobbing in the breeze, the ash hissing, the beeches rustling, the procession of villagers proceeding in the dark to the tranter's cottage, the rustic choir singing under Fancy Day's window, the dancing, the lovemaking that goes awry and ends gaily—all of this, the lovely raw material of rustic life as it might have been if no Spirit Sinister had left its mark, no "viewless, voiceless Turner of the Wheel" had been discerned working havoc. It is the Garden of Eden before Adam fell; and if Fancy Day had ever so little of Eve's naughtiness, it was not more than enough to make her human. The scenes are real, the characters true to life; yet the book is not so much a novel as an idyll of English country life, a pastoral poem in prose.

The next book was to be a more ambitious essay in fiction, but far less satisfying. *A Pair of Blue Eyes* (1873) has received from many critics higher praise than I am able to give it. The total impression that this book leaves does not carry for me the unmistakable, unforgettable note of the essential Hardy. Several critics have divided Hardy's novels into three or four classes, and Hardy himself distinguished between kind and kind. Thus, Lionel Johnson, the earliest important critic of the novels, arranged them into three groups: the tragic; the idyllic; and the comic, ironic, satiric, romantic, extravagant. This division is well enough, but takes no account of a distinction that in my opinion is more important—a distinction of quality between the books that spring from Hardy's essential genius and those that do not. The former come from the inner core of his creative imagination; the latter are fabricated. In the first he is possessed by his subject; in the second he is using his inventive talent to carry him as best it can through an ingenious story.

From first to last, Hardy—observant, percipient, sensitive, and thoughtful as he was—was a person of great simplicity. There was something of the peasant in him that sophistication did not wholly eliminate. He grew up to know, as only an observant, percipient, and sensitive person could have known, a world of a certain kind, filled with a certain life, human and natural—to know it in all its beauty, its contrariness, and its perplexing painfulness. That life, as he had known it from his childhood, he absorbed imaginatively, and it became the raw material of his art. He would never be at his best except when near to the life that he had thus absorbed, though he was to transcend it and put it into a vaster context. Even as a boy and young man he was being modified by his reading of English literature, the classics, and history, by his careful study of architecture, by his interest in pictures and in acting, by his disturbing contacts with Charles Darwin, Herbert Spencer, and Arthur Schopenhauer, and by his puzzled study of the Oxford Movement theologians and their opponents. As a man he became more and more uneasy with innovations that were displacing rustic customs and with social ideas at variance with the older codes of life. He found evils aggravated by the intolerant judgment of society, as if there were not enough that are beyond human control and inherent in human life. Percipient, meditative, contemplative, he remained simple, a peasant burdened with knowledge that magnified the problems, heightened the significance of the emotions, and enlarged the objects of perception until they seemed to be coexistent with all the world and the infinite. The problems that were thus revealed were to become insoluble and almost unbearable, and the more so as men and women—the raw material of life, continuing their plodding existence with primitive passions and developing consciousness—were converted into tragicomic realities of the imagination. "The business of the poet and novelist," he wrote on 19 April 1885, two days after he had written the last page of *The Mayor of Casterbridge* (1886), "is to show the sorriness underlying the grandest things, and the grandeur underlying the sorriest things."

The people and the countryside of what he called Wessex, seen through the prism of a romantic imagination, provided for Hardy the archetypal forms of human existence. During the whole of his novel-writing period, the life of this kind that he portrayed became, when he was at his best, like the notes and chords in an orchestral composition moving from theme to theme as the motive dictated. He might be clumsy in individual passages, the plot might creak under the excessive use of coincidence, but the essence of the movement is there, the sureness of the motive unerring. Hardy is possessed by his subject. His assimilating and constructive imagination is engaged. And this is just as true in the case of a slight masterpiece, such as *Under the Greenwood Tree*, as in the grand tragedy of *The Return of the Native*, or *Tess of the d'Urbervilles* (1891), or *The Mayor of Casterbridge*. But it was not always thus. At one moment, as we have seen, Hardy was diverted from his inclination by advice offered by the great Meredith. At another time, as Mrs. Hardy says, when "he was committed by circumstances to novel-writing as a regular trade," he felt constrained to look about for material in social and fashionable life; his "gloomy misgivings" on this score were confirmed in a talk with Anne Isabella Thackeray, who told him that "a novelist must necessarily like society." Moreover, the "journeywork" of writing thrust upon him commitments to editors of magazines demanding that he write another book before his creative imagination was ready for the task. Under these circumstances it is easy to understand that he should have written a number of books that, though they would have been creditable to a lesser novelist, lack the mark of the real Hardy. The sum total of his work would not be much impoverished if we removed altogether *A Pair of Blue Eyes, The Hand of Ethelberta* (1876), *A Laodicean* (1881), and *Two on a Tower* (1882)—books that were interspersed among the finest of his novels.

This is not to say that there are not many excellencies in these books, and passages in which the writer reveals his distinctive power. *A Pair of Blue Eyes* commands the reader's interest from beginning to end. The theme is that of a woman's inconstancy, one not likely to be dully treated by Hardy, who idealized the opposite quality, that of long-suffering constancy in love, in Tess, Giles Winterbourne, Marty South, Gabriel Oak, the Trumpet-Major. Hardy found the making of much tragedy in the possession or lack of that virtue. In *Jude the Obscure* (1895), passion for Sue began with "the love of being loved"; for Elfride in *A Pair of Blue Eyes*, it began in "the love of admiration." In retrospect there is the memory of a first entanglement, the young man whom she had kissed at the tomb; he had died. In the early part of this book she becomes secretly engaged to the young architect, for he is of humble origin; she runs away to be married, but does not marry. In the next phase she succumbs to the superior qualities of her lover's rather priggish friend. By a series of accidents the third lover discovers all that has happened, suspects more, and leaves her. Lovers number two and three travel together to Elfride's village on a train, and find that it carries a hearse and her body. She had married a fourth lover and then died. Thus baldly outlined, the story sounds melodramatic and absurd, and in fact it is not without these defects. Yet Elfride is done well enough to gain our sympathy, and Knight to earn our dislike. The narrative is alive and often exciting, as in the episode on The Cliff without a Name; and though the scene is in Cornwall, and not in Hardy's more intimately known Dorset, there are passages of description that show he had already intuitively discovered a way of conveying through the medium of words what a painter conveys in a picture, but by devices appropriate to the art of letters. Hardy knows that by writing you cannot "paint" a scene; to attempt to do by successive words what a painter does by coexistent images in a picture is merely to bewilder the reader, as by a catalog; he prefers to describe through action, to show things moving, breathing, appearing; to give us as much that can be *heard* as *seen*; to record the effect left on the mind of a spectator. Though we can find much finer passages in Hardy's other books, this power of literary description is exhibited many times in *A Pair of Blue Eyes*, as thus in chapter 24, when Stephen stands at the door of the church porch looking for Elfride:

The faint sounds heard only accentuated the silence. The rising and falling of the sea, far away along the coast, was the most important. A minor sound was the scurr of a distant night-hawk. Among the minutest where all were minute were the light settlement of gossamer fragments floating in the air, a toad humbly labouring along through the grass near the entrance, the crackle of a dead leaf which a worm was endeavouring to pull into the earth, a waft of air, getting nearer and nearer, and expiring at his feet under the burden of a winged insect.

In such passages as that we have the authentic note that is Hardy's.

*The Hand of Ethelberta* is one of those books that I have spoken of as being "fabricated." When he wrote it, Hardy was taking Miss Thackeray's advice—he was entering society, describing a life that he could report but not build up through his own vision. It is incidentally interesting as affording an example of Hardy's consciousness of class distinction, discernible in greater or lesser degree in most of his novels.

*A Laodicean* is generally, and rightly, spoken of as the worst of his novels. Much of it was written when he was ill but under contract to provide chapters month by month for an editor. Hardy had doubtless intended to write a book illustrating the contrast between the ancient and the modern, the inherited and the acquired, the dignity of the old order and the indignity of modern progress. He produced in fact a crudely thrilling melodrama in which villainy, blackmail, eavesdropping, and violence produce a succession of reversals of fortune ending happily in marriage. Hardy sufficiently described the book himself in the preface to the 1896 edition: "*A Laodicean* may perhaps help to while away an idle afternoon of the comfortable ones whose lines have fallen to them in pleasant places; above all, of that large and happy section of the reading public which has not yet reached ripeness of years."

*Two on a Tower* is not very much better than *A Laodicean*, though a series of coincidences that thwart hero and heroine is less absurd. It concerns a love affair between a young man of peasant birth who is becoming a brilliant astronomer, and a lady of aristocratic family who has been deserted by her husband; and the love scenes take place on a lonely tower where the young man introduces Lady Constantine to the fixed stars. "This slightly-built romance," wrote Hardy thirteen years later, "was the outcome of a wish to set the emotional history of two infinitesimal lives against the stupendous background of the stellar universe."

The books of which I have just been speaking may be considered minor episodes in Hardy's work. Like his other and greater books they are love stories depending for their development on the external incidents of plot. Hardy firmly believed that a novel should tell a story, and with him the story always turned upon actual events in the lives of his personages. He spoke slightingly about Henry James's preoccupation with "the minutiae of manners": "James's subjects are those one could be interested in at moments when there is nothing larger to think of." What Hardy sought was an action exhibiting the simple, elemental emotions, such as had been chosen by the Greek tragedians and Shakespeare. In the lesser books, where his imagination was not fully engaged, the story is just a story, ingeniously contrived, whose incidents afford occasions for exhibiting individual characters; but the characters do not stand in symbolic relationship to a pattern of life. The poet in him asserted itself from time to time, but did not control the situation. He told his story with a sort of ingenuous fidelity to his task, and that was all. But when the grand moment came, Hardy the poet-novelist took charge. The dividing line between his greater work and his lesser is absolute. To the former belong unmistakably *Under the Greenwood Tree*, *Far from the Madding Crowd*, *The Return of the Native*, *The Trumpet-Major* (1880), *The Mayor of Casterbridge*, *The Woodlanders* (1887), *Tess of the d'Urbervilles*, and *Jude the Obscure*.

Hardy had the mind of a poet. He was reading and writing poetry through all the years of his novel writing, and he turned finally to poetry when he had said his say in the appropriate form of fiction and came to the grand summing-up. He had the imagination of Samuel Taylor Coleridge's creative poet who seeks to externalize all the world that he is aware of in terms of his understanding of it. That being so, his art was from its nature progressive, revealing the successive stages of his discovery of life. No author's work reveals a clearer pattern, moving on stage by stage in the elucidation of life, not by argument or teaching, but by exhibiting life itself, human beings in action, driven by forces they do not understand. It begins with the simpler material of human life, men and women shown under stress of emotion, generally in a rustic setting. It ends with all history in time, all the universe in space, and the Kosmos, which includes all space and time and the possible beyond. His real creative work shows a steady progression from perception of an individual to perception of the Universal. In the latter case it is *perception*, not *conception*, for even the Universal is individualized and perceived through the eye of the artist.

Each of Hardy's finer novels may be taken as a projection of his state of awareness at a certain stage of his development; its material is the world that he felt to be real. The content of that world, when he wrote *Under the Greenwood Tree*, was that Wessex life of which I have spoken and all the memories of youth it included. It was still such that it could be presented idyllically, with the rhythmic pattern of a pastoral poem. If the course of true love is not quite smooth, it is only so little troubled as to make the smoothing pleasant. The village, which is the scene of action, stands for all the English villages where life is cast in the traditional mold. But Hardy has moved on when he comes two years later to *Far from the Madding Crowd*. The country life is in essentials the same, though we see it on a larger scale. It is more consciously conceived as something that does not change, remaining "ancient" when so much else is becoming "modern."

In Weatherbury three or four score years were included in the mere present, and nothing less than a century set a mark on its face or tone. Five decades hardly modified the cut of a gaiter, the embroidering of a smock-frock, by the breadth of a hair. Ten generations failed to alter the turn of a single phrase.

(ch. 22)

The more important persons, with one exception, might have behaved as they do here a century or two ago. The exception is Bathsheba herself, the first example that Hardy gives us of a partly emancipated woman, who farms her own farm and demands equal status with the men when she goes to Casterbridge market. The story, as in most of Hardy's novels, is essentially a love story. It touches a deeper note that has the quality of tragedy, but the disturbance arises not, as we are to feel later, from any cruelty in the nature of things, but from the conflict between the characters and their responses to impulse or to those accidents that play too frequent a part in all Hardy's plots. For Hardy, love is always treated as the major passion in life, and constancy in love is shown as the major virtue, accompanied by other excellencies that it implies. Gabriel Oak stands side by side with John Loveday, Giles Winterbourne, Marty South, and the Reddleman among the heroes and heroines whose love is proof against all shocks.

Farmer Oak is slow, deliberate, moving with quiet energy, though if occasion demanded he could "do or think a thing with as mercurial a dash as can the man of towns . . . his special power, morally, physically, and mentally, was static, owing little or nothing to momentum. . . ." When he looked at the sky he drew practical conclusions about the time and the weather, but "being a man not without a frequent consciousness that there was some charm in this life he led, he stood still after looking at the sky as a useful instrument, and regarded it in an appreciative spirit, as a work of art supremely beautiful" (chapter 2). He does not hesitate to criticize Bathsheba when she has offended his sense of right, and can help her as none other can in moments of crisis, yet he has not that sort of masterfulness that would compel her to love him. He will not, like Farmer Boldwood, press his claims because she has flirted with him. He is not the man to plead where he is not wanted. Bathsheba, for all her strength and good sense, proves to be at the mercy of her own impetuosity where the heart is involved, and falls all too easy a prey to the handsome, adventurous seducer, Troy. Once again, however, it is an accident that plays its part in leading her to marry him. The story pursues its way rhythmically through incidents that stir the emotions of three men and a girl amid the rustic events of sheepshearing, stacking, marketing, in calm and in storm, to a running commentary of gossip from the chorus of workers. The ending is a compromise between that of tragedy and comedy. Gabriel marries Bathsheba, but not until his rivals have been tragically removed.

*Far from the Madding Crowd* established Hardy's reputation, but it was to be followed disappointingly by *The Hand of Ethelberta* and then by a masterpiece, *The Return of the Native*. But first, a word about *The Trumpet-Major*, a novel that might well have come before rather than just after *The Return of the Native* in Hardy's natural development. We know from his memoranda that in 1875, five years before *The Trumpet-Major* was published and three years before *The Return of the Native*, Hardy's mind was moving toward the theme that was to become that of *The Dynasts* (1903–1904; 1906; 1908). "Mem:" he wrote at that time, "a Ballad of the Hundred Days. Then another of Moscow. Others of earlier campaigns—forming altogether an Iliad of Europe from 1789 to 1815." And two years later he wrote, "Consider a grand drama, based on the wars with Napoleon, or some one campaign (but not as Shakespeare's historical dramas). It might be called 'Napoleon' or 'Josephine,' or by some other person's name." But long before then Hardy had been deeply interested in the recollections of old persons whom he had known in childhood, who had been eyewitnesses of the events that occurred in Dorset when the invasion of England by Napoleon was daily expected. As a boy he had studied the "casual relics" of the preparations for defense—"a heap of bricks and clods on a beacon-hill," "worm-eaten shafts and iron heads of pikes," "ridges on the down thrown up during the encampment, fragments of volunteer uniform, and other such lingering remains." These discoveries profoundly affected the imagination of the young Hardy, and gave him an insight into the condition of England at the time of the Battle of Trafalgar (1805). This early knowledge was to be extended later by close study of the history of the period. Already, before he wrote *The Trumpet-Major*, Hardy was imaginatively seeing the history of his native district in the larger perspective of England and Napoleon's Europe, just as so often in his stories of individuals living in a Wessex homestead we find the pressure of a wider humanity surging round and beyond. "A certain provincialism of feeling is invaluable," he wrote in the very year of *The Trumpet-Major*. "It is the essence of individuality, and is largely made up of that crude enthusiasm without which no great thoughts are thought, no great deeds done."

And so it is with *The Trumpet-Major*. Though in a certain sense it is the story of love affairs written in the spirit of light comedy, its lightness is that of the provincial scenes in *The Dynasts*—it is the relief to a vaster background of historic events; it is the village commentary on life the day before the battle. The slight love story will stand on its own merits, but it becomes something more when it is an interlude in a world conflict. Not that Hardy presses upon us these sterner reflections. In this historical novel we are much nearer to *Under the Greenwood Tree* than to *Jude*. There is enough to entertain us in the succession of lively pictures that Hardy draws—the cavalry soldiers on their bulky gray chargers, ascending the down and preparing the camp, while the romantic Anne looks on from the miller's cottage; the excitement in the village; the party at the miller's; the behavior of the solid John Loveday, the soldier, and his lively, mercurial brother, Bob; the King's visit to Budmouth; the false alarm when the beacon is lit; and the ups and downs of Bob's affections. There are touches of melodrama, such as when the bully Festus has too many opportunities for playing the villain or when Matilda exceeds herself as the scarlet woman. But it is all part of the play—vigorous, zestful—whose romance takes a deeper note when it describes the simple fidelity of John to his unattainable beloved and his unstable brother. Though not a major novel, this has its place in the sequence of Hardy's works in which he is genuinely possessed by his subject.

The five greater novels, which it remains to consider, are all tragedy—tragedy on the grand scale. They are all of them love stories, as before, but the men and women who suffer this passion in its extremity, individual as they are, become also representatives of the human race. We are to see them through Hardy's eyes, as Aeschylus saw Prometheus chained to a rock, against a vast background of nature, the victim of "the President of the Immortals." His magnificent beginning of *The Return of the Native*, showing in the description of Egdon Heath what sort of place it is in which the persons are to suffer, creates an impression of nature more somber than we have had before, indeed a nature that appears to share the suffering of men. "Fair prospects wed happily with fair times; but alas, if times be not fair. . . . Haggard Egdon appealed to a subtler and scarcer instinct, to a more recently learnt emotion . . . wearing a sombreness distasteful to our race when it was young." "The storm was its lover, and the wind its friend." It could become "the home of strange phantoms." "Like man, slighted and enduring," it was "colossal and mysterious in its swarthy monotony." In *The Woodlanders*, too, though there are some gentler pictures, "the bleared white visage of a sunless winter day emerged like a dead-born child," and in the wood we observe "the Unfulfilled Intention, which makes life what it is," working havoc underground—"the leaf was deformed, the curve was crippled, the taper was interrupted; the lichen ate the vigour of the stalk and the ivy slowly strangled to death the promising sapling." Though nature assumes a far sweeter aspect at Talbothays during those months when Tess and Clare are working among the cows and the meadows, the sweetness of it becomes a foil to the horrors that are to follow.

Hardy peoples this alternately lovely and sinister world with men and women, the more ordinary of whom play the chorus. The exceptional ones, some capable of intense emotion, others, in a worse plight, equally emotional but also acutely conscious and self-conscious, sense in themselves what Tess "was expressing in her own native phrases—assisted a little by her Sixth Standard training—feelings which might almost have been called those of the age—the ache of modernism." In *The Return of the Native* Clym Yeobright's face reflects "the view of life as a thing to be put up with, replacing that zest for existence which was so intense in early civilizations." Henchard in *The Mayor of Casterbridge* perceives more simply but passionately. The shape of his ideas in time of affliction was simply "a moody 'I am to suffer, I perceive'"; his superstitious nature led to the grim conclusion that his misfortunes were due to "some sinister intelligence bent on punishing him." In *Jude the Obscure* the perception of the new type of human being reaches an extremity where it is unbearable. Even as a boy Jude showed that he was "the sort of man who was born to ache"; he was at moments "seized with a sort of shuddering." As a man he is a victim of "the modern vice of unrest." Sue—the ethereal, the fine-nerved, the idealist—has the same sensitiveness and becomes almost masochistic in her love of suffering. Hardy pursues the theme to a point where it becomes almost horrible in reproducing the affliction of the parents in their children. "I ought not to be born, ought I?" says Little Father Time, working himself up to the mood that ends in his hanging himself and his baby brother and sister. "The doctor," it is reported, "says there are such boys springing up amongst us—boys of a sort unknown in the last generation. . . . It is the beginning of the coming universal wish not to live."

These five books are not to be taken as a statement of Hardy's philosophy. But in giving body to human life, as this meditative man finds it, a pattern appears, a pattern in accordance with which human nature manifests itself; the pattern yields a philosophy, imposed on Hardy by his intuitive reading of experience. There emerges a sort of theory of society into which the facts, as he sees them, fit; it widens into nothing less than a view of the universe. Already in *The Return of the Native* we are faced with the problem of a young man of bucolic origin moving too quickly to intellectual and sophisticated aims, reaching a condition of unbalance between the two elements in himself. In *The Mayor of Casterbridge* we have in Lucetta the half-emancipated woman—"I'll love whom I choose." The old superstition still strong in her, however, she shrinks and withers to her death before the terrors of the skimmington-ride. In *The Woodlanders* we are introduced to the deficiencies of the divorce laws; in *Tess* to the cruelty of public opinion toward those who have offended against its decrees; and in *Jude* Sue Bridehead, so clear-sighted in vision, though so unreasonable in action, makes her explicit protest against "the social moulds civilization fits us into," and asks whether a marriage ceremony is a religious thing or "only a sordid contract, based on material convenience in householding, rating, and taxing, and the inheritance of land and money by children." "When people of a later age look back upon the barbarous customs and superstition of the times that we have the unhappiness to live in, what *will* they say?" she exclaims. And before then even Jude, with his more conventional views, finding his life ruined by marriage with the coarse, dissolute Arabella, had reflected on the fundamental error of "having based a permanent contract on a temporary feeling."

In these, Hardy's subtlest and most tragic books, we have a searching criticism of modern life and finally of all life. We have still the chorus of ordinary men and women, with rustic minds not yet unhinged, accepting life and judging it, gaily or sadly, in accordance with the older standards. But in the forefront we have others, born in the same milieu, who have come to put everything to the question; who have acquired the self-consciousness that is the distinctive characteristic of modern man; who question the fundamentals of the society we live in, the rightness of social conventions, the sanctity of the marriage contract, the goodness of a progress and a civilization that bring so much misery to man, and finally, the benevolence or the omnipotence of the power that rules the universe. Clym Yeobright saw "the whole creation groaning and travailing in pain." Henchard feared "some sinister intelligence." Tess supposed that we live on a star that is "a blighted one"; she questioned the "use of learning," though she added, "I shouldn't mind learning why—why the sun do shine on the just and the unjust alike.... But that's what books will not tell me." Sue Bridehead had once imagined that "the world resembled a stanza or melody composed in a dream," but her fully awakened intelligence concluded that "the First Cause worked automatically like a somnambulist, and not reflectively like a sage." "All the ancient wrath of the Power above us has been vented upon us, His poor creatures, and we must submit." Sue comes near to expressing the developed cosmology of *The Dynasts*. The characters, more sinned against than sinning, are those of human beings set in a framework of universal destiny.

Hardy did not set out to give us a pessimistic philosophy. He did set out to show how certain persons, selected because they were interesting and had certain characters, would behave under certain circumstances, arbitrarily conceived, but not impossible. In bringing them to disaster he is prone to weight the chances against their prosperity by too many coincidences. His frequent use of the unlucky accident is a blemish in nearly all of his plots—the accident that Giles Winterbourne should fail to notice the writing that Grace chalked on his wall, or that grim mishap in *The Return of the Native* that prevents the opening of the door when Clym's mother had made her dreary journey over the heath to be reconciled with her son and his wife: "'Tis too much, Clym. How can he bear to do it? He is at home; and yet he lets her shut the door against me!" Hope turns to gloom and disaster.

It has been claimed, and I think rightly, that Hardy has elevated the function of the novel, and succeeded in placing it among the greatest of the literary art forms. He has told in each case a tale, and in that respect it stands on the merits proper to a tale. Each also contains characters who are faithfully and subtly exhibited. But that is not all. The action is significant. It moves according to a pattern that is part of the pattern of all life, and so yields an account of the world and the universe we live in. This visible tract of life unfolded before our eyes springs from Hardy's vision of life as a whole; it is nothing less than his conception of the universe expressing itself at given moments of time and in a given place, and the time and even the place itself participate in his cosmic conceptions. Just as Shakespeare calls upon the whole of his imagination when he makes a Macbeth or a Lear, and Milton in his quite different way when he presents the Archangels at War, so does Hardy when he shows Mrs. Yeobright striving to overcome her prejudices, or Michael Henchard proceeding headlong to a doom brought down on him by his own arrogance and obstinacy, or poor Tess harassed and killed by the avenging Furies of conventional opinion.

The tragedy, however, does not always follow the Aristotelian rules. A good plot (in spite of the coincidences); characters, serious and deserving of our attention; action, calling forth pity and fear; all of these are present. But Hardy sometimes violates the rule that forbids the shocking spectacle of a virtuous person brought through no fault of his or her own from prosperity to adversity. In *Jude the Obscure*, Hardy goes to extremes in showing men and women pursued relentlessly by a cruel "Universe" through no fault of their own. This novel, I think, immense as it is in dissecting the problems of Jude and Sue and in describing their relationship, does leave a sense of horror at the end that is incompatible with the highest art, but in this case alone. In *The Return of the Native* the two characters who matter are Clym and his mother, Mrs. Yeobright. The tragedy is brought about by the error of Clym, who misconceives his mission in life, and above all by Mrs. Yeobright, whose prejudice and obstinacy are not atoned for by her gestures of forgiveness. In *The Mayor of Casterbridge* it is the recklessness, the pride, the unforgiving obstinacy of Henchard's nature that cause his downfall. His tragedy, like Lear's, is the tragedy of his own soul.

There is no comparable fault or error in the protagonists of *The Woodlanders* or *Tess*; yet we are not disgusted, unless it be by the violence with which Tess's life is ended. If in these cases we are not shocked, but on the contrary are profoundly moved by the behavior of the persons and the sublimity of the scene, I think we shall discover that that is because the disaster is not complete. Destiny may seem pitiless and cruel, but the nobility of the characters facing it with courage and sympathy toward one another evokes a compensating admiration. In *The Woodlanders* the devotion of Giles to Grace is unfailing, and at the end the tragedy of his death is softened by the triumph of his self-sacrifice for her sake, and beautified by the unfailing and apparently unrewarded love of Marty South. Marty's patient love, serenely in the background throughout the story, breathed only to the young larches, is immortalized in the book's silences and in the lyrical whispered cry with which it ends.

Even in *Tess*, when "'Justice' was done, and the President of the Immortals, in Aeschylean phrase, had ended his sport with Tess," and had shown the last of her so grimly on the gallows, the penultimate scene had its compensation. It brought happiness—Tess called it happiness—in the final reunion and understanding between herself and Clare. When the pursuers at last find them at Stonehenge, "'It is as it should be,' she murmured. 'Angel, I am almost glad—yes, glad! This happiness could not have lasted. It was too much.'" She faces the end with her habitual courage. "'I am ready,' she said quietly."

Hardy is pessimistic about the governance of the universe, but not about human beings. In his lesser books there are villains playing their melodramatic parts, but in his greater novels there are no villains. There are weak, and volatile, and selfish people like Wildeve or Fitzpiers; but they are not simply scoundrels. There can be a coarse, unscrupulous creature like Arabella, but even she is not wholly bad. The chorus of ordinary men and women is full of good humor and the milk of human kindness. The heroes and heroines have noble and lovable qualities; they stand in sublime contrast to the supreme powers. Giles Winterbourne, "born and bred among the orchards," who "looked and smelt like Autumn's very brother," is endowed with the qualities that Christians have allotted to the saints. And with what wonderful words does Mrs. Cuxsom reveal both herself and the dead woman of whom she speaks.

"And she was as white as marble-stone. And likewise such a thoughtful woman, too—ah, poor soul—that a' minded every little thing that wanted tending. 'Yes,' says she, 'when I'm gone, and my last breath's blowed, look in the top drawer o' the chest in the back room by the window, and you'll find all my coffin clothes; a piece of flannel—that's to put under me, and the little piece is to put under my head; and my new stockings for my feet—they are folded alongside, and all my other things. And there's four ounce pennies, the heaviest I could find, a-tied up in bits of linen, for weights—two for my right eye and two for my left,' she said. 'And when you've used 'em, and my eyes don't open no more, bury the pennies, good souls, and don't ye go spending 'em, for I shouldn't like it. And open the windows as soon as I am carried out, and make it as cheerful as you can for Elizabeth-Jane.'"
(*The Mayor of Casterbridge*, ch. 18)

The grimly comic is not lacking when she tells how Christopher Coney dug up and spent the pennies. The passage ends with one of those lyrical sayings that abound in the prose of this poet:

"Well poor soul, she's helpless to hinder that or anything else now," answered Mother Cuxsom. "And all her shining keys will be took from her, and her cupboards opened; and little things a' didn't wish seen, anybody will see; and her wishes and ways will all be as nothing."

Hardy, a meditative poet, gave to the novel a sublimity which in his own country it had not attained before. His procedure is architectural. Out of all the elements in life that he knows, he builds up, through a series of novels, a whole that embraces the kind of men and women he has observed, the beautiful English country they have lived in, the memory of the past that has haunted them, and the whole panorama of life and earth filled with love and jealousy, ambition, fear, and unfulfilled ideals. His style moves for the most part slowly and cumbrously, sometimes awkwardly, like Gabriel Oak's walk. He has no scholarly fastidiousness of language; yet in moments of excitement or tension or deep emotion it breaks through its impediments, becoming now vivacious, now brilliant, now lovely in its still depths. But for the most part the effects are cumulative; he assembles piece by piece the elements that go to the making of a vast panorama.

## THE DYNASTS

I have said that Hardy's art was progressive, revealing the successive stages in his discovery of life. When he had written *Jude*, he probably felt that he had said all that he had to say in novel form. The torrent of invective that the book drew down upon him from the critics was an experience that, he said seventeen years later, completely cured him of further interest in novel writing. But the invective can scarcely be the whole or even the main reason for his abandoning prose fiction. He had always known himself to be a poet, and he was a poet whether he wrote in prose or verse; and he was now free to follow his bent. But there were overwhelming reasons, inherent in his own development, why he should turn from novels to the epic drama of *The Dynasts*. He had spent twenty-five years in the effort to state life in terms of life; the novels were an objective expression of the raw material of experience; his gradual discovery of what life consists of led to those novels; experience, intuition, meditation gave birth to those tracts of human experience there exposed; and already, before he had done with them, they were revealing themselves in a wider context: the history of the human race and its place in the universe. It remained for him to state his conclusions—not philosophically, for his mind worked imaginatively, but in a poem. *The Dynasts* is the summing-up of all that he had done before.

"Ay; begin small, and so lead up to the greater. It is a sound dramatic principle." Thus the Spirit Sinister in *The Dynasts* replies to the Spirit of the Years, who had called the attention of the assembled Spirits to some human beings traveling in a stagecoach over a ridge in Wessex in March 1805. Hardy's own literary work had proceeded in this way, beginning small with light poems and *Under the Greenwood Tree*, gaining volume and depth as the novels progressed, and culminating in his great epic drama. He had for many years been preparing himself for the subject he treats here, "the Great Historical Calamity, or Clash of Peoples" in the Napoleonic wars, for the use of verse as a literary medium, and for a cosmological survey of the human race. I have already alluded to his studies of the Napoleonic wars, which he used in the small beginnings of *The Trumpet-Major*, and of his growing interest in the scheme of an epic of Napoleon. It was natural that he should link this up with his studies of individual human beings whom he had observed tragically out of harmony with the "social moulds" of modern life and as the victims of a fate that appeared to dog them senselessly and pitilessly.

In form *The Dynasts* is both epic and drama. It uses both narrative and dialogue, mainly in verse, but partly in prose. Its subject in the narrower sense is that of the Napoleonic wars from 1805 to 1815 (followed in strict accord with historic evidence), with special reference to the part played by England in the European conflict. There are many scores of persons, conspicuous among them Napoleon, William Pitt (the Younger), Horatio Nelson, George III, Pierre Villeneuve, the emperors Francis and Alexander, the empress Josephine, Lady Hester Stanhope, and many admirals, marshals, politicians, priests, court ladies, and humble sailors, soldiers, burgesses, beacon-watchers, and rustics seen and heard on the continent of Europe, in England, or at sea. Regarded as historic epic the work presents a colossal, and I believe accurate, historic pageant of the leaders and common people of Europe in the greatest human conflict prior to the two world wars. But it is much more than that; it follows the classic examples of Homer's *Iliad* and Milton's *Paradise Lost* in introducing extraterrestrial powers, and allotting to them an integral part in the action. But there are significant differences, corresponding to the differences in thought, which put a gulf between Hardy and the poets of less skeptical ages. The gods in Homer are like men and intervene in their affairs; the Archangels of Milton are also anthropomorphically conceived and intervene benevolently or malignly in the affairs of men. The Immanent Will of *The Dynasts*, however, from the nature of its being cannot appear at all as a person or a speaker. As for the Spirits—the Ancient Spirit and Chorus of the Years, the Spirit and Chorus of the Pities, the Shade of the Earth, the Spirits Sinister and Ironic with their Choruses, and the Rumours, Spirit-Messengers, and Recording Angels—they do not, with two or three exceptions, interfere at all in the human sphere; they are observers, recorders, commentators. We are to discover that it is not we human beings who are primarily the audience, the spectators, of the drama. The play is played to the Spirits; it is they who watch it, they who judge it and express their sympathy or indifference. The vast panoramic struggle is thrown as it were on a terrific screen that embraces the whole of Europe and seen through the eyes of nonhuman Intelligence. Behind all is the Immanent Will and its designs:

> It works unconsciously, as heretofore,
> Eternal artistries in Circumstance,
> Whose patterns, wrought by rapt aesthetic rote,
> Seen in themselves Its single listless aim,
> And not their consequence.
> (Fore Scene)

"In the Foretime," adds the Spirit of the Years,

> Nothing appears of shape to indicate
> That cognizance has marshalled things terrene,
> Or will (such is my thinking) in my span.
> Rather they show that, like a knitter drowsed,
> Whose fingers ply in skilled unmindfulness,
> The Will has woven with an absent heed
> Since life first was; and ever will so weave.
> (Fore Scene)

The Spirit of the Years, aloof and passionless, presides among the Spirits as the play goes on before them; the Pities, as Hardy pointed out, approximate what August von Schlegel called "the Universe Sympathy of human nature—the Spectator idealized" of the Greek chorus. The speeches of the Spirits constitute a sublime play beyond the play; they are in strong, rhythmic, sonorous verse appropriate to their dignity, the vocabulary strangely compounded of long Latin words and terse, pithy Anglo-Saxon words such as

> You'll mark the twitchings of this Bonaparte
> As he with other figures foots his reel,
> Until he twitch him into his lonely grave.
> (Fore Scene)

The stage descriptions embrace all Europe and the scene gives us people in millions. "The nether sky opens, and Europe is disclosed as a prone and emaciated figure, the Alps shaping like a backbone, and the branching mountain-chains like ribs, the peninsula plateau of Spain forming a head...." "The peoples, distressed by events which they did not cause, are seen writhing, crawling, heaving, and vibrating in their various cities and nationalities." What a foreglimpse, in 1903, of the world wars to follow, as seen from the onlookers' stall.

The human play is methodically pursued, with varying power. Some of the "small" things are among the best, where Hardy, in appropriate prose, writes of his Wessex folk, talking with their native humor in the vernacular; or Wessex soldiers, fighting in Spain, recalling their old loves at home; or French soldiers, in their distracted retreat from Moscow. His love of the gruesome comes out in the *Mad Soldier's Song* (sung in the retreat):

> What can we wish for more?
> Thanks to the frost and flood
> We are grinning crones—thin bags of bones
> Who once were flesh and blood.
> So foolish life adieu
> And ingrate leader too.
> —Ah, but we loved you true!
> Yet—he-he-he! and ho-ho-ho!—
> We'll never return to you.
> (pt. III, I.xi)[2]

To meet the ends of an action that covers so wide a field, in so many representative scenes, the language varies in power and dignity. The verse is always vigorous, but not always at a high level of poetry. But who before has attempted in verse the task of reporting a parliamentary debate? Even so, Pitt in

[2] References are to part, act, and scene.

one of his speeches talks in successful verse almost as Winston Churchill talked in prose.

> The strange fatality that haunts the times
> Wherein our lot is cast, has no example.
> Times are they fraught with peril, trouble, gloom;
> We have to mark their lourings, and to face them.
> (pt. I, I.iii)

The speeches of Napoleon are usually rhetorical, but there are vivacity and force in the rhetoric. The strategists, statesmen, and courtiers all talk in character. The action proceeds from scene to scene with swiftness and unfailing energy, and we can read on as we would read a story, eager to follow the thrilling narrative, and stirred by the dark adventures and bold exhibitions of character. Sometimes—even on the battlefield of Waterloo—we are gripped by the poetic sense of the continuing life of the earth, the earth that Hardy knows in Wessex, but here grimly threatened by the human conflict:

> Yea, the coneys are scared by the thud of hoofs,
> And their white scuts flash at their vanishing heels,
> And swallows abandon the hamlet-roofs.
> (pt. III, VI.vii)

It is a singular fact that in this drama of a European war Hardy should so write that we can never forget that Wessex coast and the people who live in the Wessex villages. Though Hardy is a good world citizen, and once said that the sentiment of "foreignness" should "attach only to other planets and their inhabitants, if any," we feel nonetheless that he is stirred by English patriotism, that he admires the patriotic sentiments that Pitt expresses, and loves the innate and ineradicable patriotism—provincialism, if you like—of the English countryman. Though he is completely objective in his treatment of friends and enemies of the English and rejects nationalism in his sympathy and in his pity for human beings, nonetheless the pulse of the poet seems to beat a little faster when he exhibits the reflections of a Pitt, the emotions of a Nelson, or the sentiment and humor of the English rustic. He has not set himself to praise England as Vergil in the *Aeneid* sang the praises of Rome; nonetheless there emerges in the course of the epic a sort of personality, which is that of the English people, with qualities very dear to the poet, compounded of good and bad, serious and comic, but, in the sum, both noble and lovable. But these qualities are also those of the human race. Much of the tragic irony lies in this contrast between the essential goodness and kindliness of human beings and the blank indifference, the unkindness, of the irresistible universe. The Spirit of the Pities recalls the words of Sophocles, who

> . . . dubbed the Will "the gods." Truly said he,
> "Such gross injustice to their own creation
> Burdens the time with mournfulness for us,
> And for themselves with shame."
> (pt. I, V.iv)

*The Dynasts* is a large-scale action, planned to project the situation of the whole human race, which consists of individuals possessing a sense of justice and noble aspirations, frustrated, as it seems to them, by an irresistible and indifferent destiny. The whole is an imaginative picture, not a set of dogmas; but it yields the conclusion that arises irresistibly from those samples of life Hardy has given in the novels.

The novels are as full of poetry as is this epic. The epic itself contains many prose passages, and some of the speeches written in verse would have been equally, sometimes more, satisfactory in prose. Hardy traverses the low ground of less distinguished speech and high ground where his verse becomes equal to the strain and exhibits extreme vigor and sometimes a rare and forceful imagery that touches the higher peaks of poetry. He is not a fastidious writer with a sure touch in the use of words, and yet in a few passages the words could not be bettered—that occurs when he is fully possessed by the emotional content of his theme, and the words seem to pour from him irresistibly in their own right.

*The Dynasts* is the indispensable culmination of his work. It is as necessary as *War and Peace* is to Leo Tolstoy, combining, as that book does, the individual and the universal. The private tragedies, which in Tolstoy were interwoven with the world catastrophe, are more subtly treated by the Russian and more poignant. Tolstoy's individuals are more individual, more alive. But all this, the human side of life, had already been presented by Hardy in his novels with less aloofness but with consummate power. *The Dynasts* has an advantage over *War and Peace* in its unity and orchestration. It is the finale of the great body of work that had begun in his youth, matured in his middle age, and concluded itself here. He had surpassed any other English novelist in using the novel as an artistic vehicle for projecting life in its totality realistically, emotionally, meditatively; in doing with it what hitherto only poetry had done; and in fitting it into a structure sublimely conceived and capable of summary in a final work that, in form as well as substance, is poetic.

## THE LYRICAL POETRY

It is related of Thomas Hardy's infancy that, one hot afternoon, his mother returned to the cottage at Higher Bockhampton to find the baby asleep in his cradle, with "a large snake curled up upon his breast, comfortably asleep like himself." It had come in, no doubt, from the wild country nearby, which he would immortalize one day as Egdon Heath. To strangle snakes in his cradle is a very proper symbol for the future hero of action. For one destined to be a hero of another kind—a contemplative who saw less good than evil in the human condition, but, by taking that evil to heart, by accepting it into his poetry, disarmed or purified it a little; a man of great compassion, a man who preserved through journeywork, fame, obloquy, and disillusionment a singular innocence—for such a hero the image of the sleeping snake on the infant's breast is strangely fitting.

Personalities, as a rule, should be kept out of the criticism of poetry. But it is extraordinarily difficult, and possibly undesirable, to dissociate Hardy's poetry from his character. Those who knew him best have all borne witness to his patience and modesty, his tenderness, and the magnanimity that gave grandeur to a somber cast of mind. We know about the moral courage without which a mind so sensitive as his might well have closed up against experience in despair and the integrity that insisted that what seemed true of life, however terrible, should not be excluded from art. We have human witnesses to these qualities; but we do not need them, for they are manifest in the poems themselves. But in other respects we may misinterpret or undervalue the poems unless we realize the complicated nature, so oddly compounded of naiveté and erudition, ardor and melancholy, that produced them. For example, if we ignore the inherited peasant streak in Hardy, we shall fail to catch the countryman's raw humor and his love of a story for its own sake.

There is another reason why personality must enter any discussion of Hardy's verse. Almost all his finest poems are deeply, nakedly personal: the love poems of 1912–1913, for example, or the meditations in old age—"Surview," "Afterwards," "An Ancient to Ancients." It is the tone of such poems that, perhaps more than any other facet of his genius, awakes in the reader a feeling of affectionate veneration for the man who wrote them. Hardy put everything he felt, everything he noticed, everything he was into his poetry. As a result he wrote many indifferent poems; but because what he gave so unreservedly were the impressions of a magnanimous heart—the thoughts of a mind closely engaged in the problems of its own time and possessed of a strong historical sense, the experience of a man thoroughly versed in human suffering—his poetry has that breadth of matter and manner that only a major poet can compass.

We must not, however, be led by the importance of the personal in Hardy's verse to judge him as a sort of well-meaning, ham-handed titan who somehow blundered into poetry now and then by sheer force of personality. This is a superficial judgment, albeit a common one still. Though I sympathize with F. R. Leavis' feelings of dismay at Hardy's "gaucherie, compounded of the literary, the colloquial, the baldly prosaic, the conventionally poetical, the pedantic and the rustic," I believe that, in common with other critics who do not write verse, he has failed to notice the great technical skill that Hardy commanded and the amount of experiment in versification that he undertook. Often, it is true, Hardy seems to lose all touch with his medium, and will dress up his subjects in the shoddiest, hand-me-down verse. But it is of the utmost significance that whenever he comes to write of something near to his heart, of personal experience, he finds his touch again, and his technique becomes masterly. Consider this enchanting picture of his childhood home:

> Here is the ancient floor,
> Footworn and hollowed and thin,
> Here was the former door
> Where the dead feet walked in.
>
> She sat here in her chair,
> Smiling into the fire;
> He who played stood there,
> Bowing it higher and higher.
>
> Childlike, I danced in a dream;
> Blessings emblazoned that day;
> Everything glowed with a gleam;
> Yet we were looking away!
>                ("The Self-Unseeing")

This lilting, serious, elegant poem illustrates several of the salient qualities in Hardy's lyrical poetry. We see here, for example, what has been justly termed his "natural piety"—the "he" and the "she" are his father and mother. We notice how the subject of beloved things in retrospect calls out here, as it seldom failed to do, the poet's lyrical tenderness. The poem illustrates, too, that love of music and the dance that affected Hardy from an early age and clearly influenced his style. It shows his delicate skill in suffusing pathos with gaiety, his sense of the transient haunting all scenes of present happiness. Although it is not strongly marked by his well-known idiosyncrasies of manner, it could not be mistaken for any other poet's writing—"Blessings emblazoned that day;/Everything glowed with a gleam" has the authentic Hardy ring.

The first thing we notice about Hardy's manner is that he seems to have been born with it. It can be detected in his earliest surviving poem, "Domicilium." Hardy wrote a fair number of poems during his young manhood, very few in his middle novel-writing period, and returned happily to verse—the medium he had always preferred—after the publication of *Jude the Obscure* and *The Well-Beloved* (1897). It was during the last thirty years of his life that the bulk of his verse, including *The Dynasts*, was written. His first volume of verse, *Wessex Poems*, was not published until 1898. Here, as in each subsequent volume, he included a number of earlier poems with poems composed at more recent dates. The former he sometimes, but not always, dated. His development would therefore have to be traced by internal evidence for the most part: luckily for the critic, there was no development in the sense of a change from one style to another or from one field of subject matter to another. Throughout, he was chiefly concerned with love, transience, death, and what the newspapers would call "human-interest stories." If we compare the poems dated between 1865 and 1875 with those poems of a later date, we find little alteration in manner: what we do notice is that most of the earlier ones are in the iambic ten-syllable meter, and many of them sonnets. It seems that Hardy did not experiment widely in the complex stanza forms and flexible rhythms that represent his greatest technical achievement until he returned to poetry in his late fifties.

Not only in idiosyncrasy but in more general aspects of style Hardy's poetry shows little alteration through the years. We know he read Vergil when young, admired Crabbe, Shelley, Keats, Scott, and, of his contemporaries, Barnes, Swinburne, Meredith, and Browning. But it is extremely difficult to detect any stylistic influence that these writers had upon him other than his use of certain of Barnes's stanza forms and his affinity with Browning. Browning is the only poet whose idiom is strongly echoed from Hardy's own verse. For example, these famous lines ironically sum up Hardy's attitude to life:

> Let him in whose ears the low-voiced Best is killed by
>   the clash of the First,
> Who holds that if way to the Better there be, it exacts
>   a full look at the Worst,
> Who feels that delight is a delicate growth cramped
>   by crookedness, custom, and fear,
> Get him up and be gone as one shaped awry; he
>   disturbs the order here.
>              ("In Tenebris II," st. 4)

The shyness that prevented Hardy from meeting Browning and other contemporaries during his young days in London may well have contributed to the persistence of his own early idiom; certainly, had he met them, he might have become a more self-critical poet. But he gained more than he lost by not being thrown, so young and immature as he was then, into the deep end of literary society. For Hardy's is a classic example, if ever there was one, of the self-made manner: not just a manner made largely out of his self, and in that sense full of character, full of flavor; but also as it were a self-taught manner with the roughness, the naiveté, the vigor, the uncertainty of taste that we might infer from the term "self-made." He was not, however, altogether uncritical about his own work: for instance, when his first wife died, he wrote a considerable number of poems about their past: of these he selected twenty-one to appear in *Satires of Circumstance* (1914) as "Poems of 1912–13"; the remainder we find scattered about in later publications. If we compare these with the original twenty-one, we find that the latter are noticeably superior: his first choice was, in fact, a sound one; and to have chosen so well from a body of poems so intimately personal as these surely argues a genuine critical detachment.

We learn something about his attitude to poetry from Hardy's own *Life of Thomas Hardy*. He approved Leslie Stephen's judgment that "the ultimate aim of the poet should be to touch our hearts by showing his own; and not to exhibit his learning, or his fine taste, or his skill in mimicking the notes of his predecessors." Elsewhere he says, "To find beauty in ugliness is the province of the poet." He made "quantities of notes on rhyme and metre: with outlines and experiments in innumerable original measures," his tendency being always against too regular a beat. Again, writing of his prose method, he says:

The whole secret of a living style and the difference between it and a dead style, lies in not having too much style—being, in fact, a little careless, or rather seeming to be, here and there. . . . It is, of course, simply a carrying into prose the knowledge I have acquired in poetry—that inexact rhymes and rhythms now and then are far more pleasing than correct ones.

Hardy's poems are less rich than his novels in fresh, attentive description of natural objects; nor, except in *The Dynasts*, do we often find the panoramic views that form the great poetic images of his novels. In another respect, however, the novelist and the poet were one. Nothing was too small to escape Hardy's notice, or too great to daunt his powers, whether it was a hedgehog crossing a lawn at night or Europe's armies on the march. In his poetry no less than in his novels, he shows a genius for focusing together the great and the small, for feeling and revealing "infinite passion, and the pain/Of finite hearts that yearn," through some little glimpse or brief episode that, prosaic or trivial on the surface, he transmutes into a moment of vision.

Much has been written about Hardy's philosophy. He himself was at pains, though he spoke of the poet's task as "the application of ideas to life," to contradict those who found a philosophy of life in his work. What critics called his philosophical tenets were, he said, only "impressions" or rationalizations of moods. He vigorously disclaimed the title of pessimist, preferring to be thought of as a meliorist, and showing in his idea of an emergent consciousness in the universe a certain affinity with the doctrine of Emergent Evolution. It is, indeed, not difficult to sympathize with critics who found the deepest-dyed pessimism in his work. But we must not coagulate a poet's moods into a philosophical system, anymore than we must demand consistency from his ideas. Nor should we disregard the more positive and brighter aspect of Hardy's beliefs. He himself gave us the ideal groundwork of his art when he said that human nature is "neither ghastly, hateful, nor ugly; neither commonplace, unmeaning, nor tame, but . . . slighted and enduring; and withal singularly colossal and mysterious"; or when he jotted down in his diary of August 1882: "An ample theme: the intense interests, passions, and strategy that throb through the commonest lives." We may disagree with this generous humanism of his, but if we disregard it, we shall lose much of the value of his poetry. For it is part of the pattern as he saw it, about which he said in a note for *The Dynasts:* "The human race to be shown as one great network or tissue which quivers in every part when one point is shaken, like a spider's web if touched."

In the compass of this essay, I shall confine my remarks to the shorter poems. They are the ones that put the greatest strain upon our allegiance to Hardy: often trivial, grotesque, or merely quaint in subject, these potted melodramas are all the more difficult to take because they tend to be written in a sort of album verse that ranges between the inept and the perfunctory. Moreover, they are apt to get laughs in the wrong places:

> "Then, where dwells the Canon's kinswoman,
>     My friend of aforetime?"
> I asked, to disguise my heart-heavings
>     And new ecstasy.

or

> We late-lamented, resting here,
>     Are mixed to human jam. . . .

There is a certain monotony of theme in these poems, and we feel that the poet is all the time shepherding his characters remorselessly toward the tomb. Once or twice, as in 'The Trampwoman's Tragedy," Hardy deepens the implications of an episode and tautens the verse form, so that we get powerful poetry. But too often he found a story so absorbing as gossip that he could not or would not see any necessity for heightening it poetically. To a friend who remonstrated with him about one such poem, Hardy replied, "Oh, but it was a true story." Again and again this interest in gossip lures Hardy on to blithely tackling the most intractable subjects. Such narratives—and there are dozens of them—are not the products merely of idle curiosity about folktales and provincial contretemps: they show us how Hardy was touched by the little accidents that change human lives; and therefore, though they are often laughable, the laughter they provoke in us is affectionate.

Sympathy like this is the seed of poetic imagination. We get the full harvest in the vast imaginative vistas of *The Dynasts*, but one of the shorter poems offers us in miniature the same grandeur: "The Convergence of the Twain," subtitled "Lines on the Loss of the *Titanic*." It describes how the Immanent Will shapes an iceberg, "a sinister mate" for the great liner, and designs them to be "twin halves of one august event."

> In a solitude of the sea
> Deep from human vanity,
> And the Pride of Life that planned her, stilly couches she.
>
> Steel chambers, late the pyres
> Of her salamandrine fires,
> Cold currents thrid, and turn to rhythmic tidal lyres.
>
> Over the mirrors meant
> To glass the opulent
> The sea-worm crawls—grotesque, slimed, dumb, indifferent.
>
> Jewels in joy designed
> To ravish the sensuous mind
> Lie lightless, all their sparkles bleared and black and blind.
>
> Dim moon-eyed fishes near
> Gaze at the gilded gear
> And query: "What does this vaingloriousness down here?"...
>
> Well: while was fashioning
> This creature of cleaving wing
> The Immanent Will that stirs and urges everything
>
> Prepared a sinister mate
> For her—so gaily great—
> A Shape of Ice, for the time far and dissociate.
>
> And as the smart ship grew
> In stature, grace and hue,
> In shadowy silent distance grew the Iceberg too.
>
> Alien they seemed to be:
> No mortal eye could see
> The intimate welding of their later history,
>
> Or sign that they were bent
> By paths coincident
> On being anon twin halves of one august event,
>
> Till the Spinner of the Years
> Said "Now!" And each one hears
> And consummation comes, and jars two hemispheres.

Theme, language, and rhythm are perfectly congruous here; the weird submarine imagery of the opening stanzas deepens the imaginative reach of the subject. It is one of those poems, like Tennyson's "The Kraken" or Browning's "Childe Roland to the Dark Tower Came," that, although they are recognizably in the poet's idiom, seem to lie outside his canon and compel us to speculate how different that canon might be had the poet explored this particular vein more persistently.

But Hardy, in his shorter poems, evoked his genius most successfully through the personal and the lyrical. His lyrics are seldom pure; they are nearly always clouded by personal experience, and, even when the poem seems to be a pure distillation, it almost certainly had its sources in some real incident or flesh-and-blood person. The exquisite poem "To Lizbie Browne," for instance, is not addressed to any ideal or composite rustic charmer: Lizbie Browne was a gamekeeper's daughter with whom Hardy fell in love as a boy.

In his old age Hardy said that "his only ambition, as far as he could remember, was to have some poem or poems in a good anthology like the Golden Treasury." The model he had set before himself was "Drink to Me Only," by Ben Jonson. We remember that Hardy from childhood was devoted to music, could tune a fiddle at the age of six, and learned to refine in his verse rhythms the lilting, pausing, lolloping measures he had first loved in country dance tunes. So it is not after all very surprising if he took the Ben Jonson poem as his model. What is remarkable is that he should have written so many of his most beautiful lyrics in old age. If Hardy's mind was born old, his heart remained young:

> But Time, to make me grieve,
> Part steals, lets part abide,
> And shakes this fragile frame at eve
> With throbbings of noontide.
> ("I Look into My Glass")

The idealisms of his youth were never quite extinguished. They can be heard in the wistful last stanzas of "The Oxen" and "The Darkling Thrush," both of which are strainings after "some blessed Hope" in a bleak world. The passion that moves behind his love poems is the passion of young manhood seen through a golden haze of retrospect. We must allow that this backward-looking stance is vulnerable to criticism. Nostalgia, we are told, is an enervating emotion, likely to corrupt a poet's work. I can readily believe it; indeed any emotion is dangerous to a poem: there is only one thing more dangerous—the lack of it. The poet has somehow to distance himself from his emotions and the objects that gave rise to them without losing touch with them altogether. Hardy distanced himself by the simple device of writing most of his poetry in old age: he kept in touch because—again I can think of no more scientific phrase for it—his heart remained young; also, he evidently had what we might call a good sensuous memory. He was a nostalgic, both in the strict sense of one who feels homesickness—this is part of the emotional tone of his natural piety toward his parents, friends, and places of his youth—and in the looser sense of brooding constantly over the past. But the verse in which he embodies such brooding seldom shows the tenuousness or oversweetness that are signs of a morbid nostalgia. It is saved from them partly by deliberate roughness of technique and his habit of weaving homely images and colloquial phrases into the poetical texture, partly by sheer force of sincerity.

There are times, indeed, when we feel that the sense of the transience of things has become a monomania with Hardy; but at least his variations on this theme are extremely diverse, ranging from some of the best of the intimate poems to such unusual lyrics as "The Five Students" or "During Wind and Rain." Both of these offer us a subtle use of refrain, a technical device that Hardy employed in a masterly way to underline the pathos and inevitability of things passing. In both, the romantic and plangent refrain lines are balanced by the hard, factual, forthright imagery of the lines that precede them.

Another technical skill can be seen in Hardy's blending of the gay and the humorous with the poignant, an extremely difficult thing to do without breaking up the legato of the poem or ruining its texture. A good example of this is "He Revisits His First School":

> I should not have shown in the flesh,
> I ought to have gone as a ghost;
> It was awkward, unseemly almost,
> Standing solidly there as when fresh,
>     Pink, tiny, crisp-curled,
>     My pinions yet furled
> From the winds of the world.
>
> After waiting so many a year
> To wait longer, and go as a sprite
> From the tomb at the mid of some night

> Was the right, radiant way to appear;
>     Not as one wanzing[3] weak
>     From life's roar and reek,
> His rest still to seek:
>
> Yea, beglimpsed through the quaint quarried glass
> Of green moonlight, by me greener made,
> When they'd cry, perhaps, "There sits his shade
> In his olden haunt—just as he was
>     When in Walkingame he
>     Conned the grand Rule-of-Three
> With the bent of a bee."
>
> But to show in the afternoon sun,
> With an aspect of hollow-eyed care,
> When none wished to see me come there,
> Was a garish thing, better undone.
>     Yes; wrong was the way;
>     But yet, let me say,
> I may right it—some day.

That charming poem, with so much of his personality in it, brings us to the most personal of all his poems—and the best. A little must be said about the human situation behind them. Hardy's first marriage went wrong. There were faults, very possibly, on his side that made him a difficult man to live with. When the glamour of their Cornish courtship faded, his wife was seen to be snobbish, small-minded, and incapable of living gracefully in the shadow of Hardy's genius. But a greater shadow fell upon her and darkened their relationship. Some mental derangement of hers has been hinted at, and veiled references may be found in a number of the poems: for instance, "Near Lanivet," "The Blow," "The Interloper," "The Man with a Past," or here, in "The Division":

> But that thwart thing betwixt us twain,
>     Which nothing cleaves or clears,
> Is more than distance, Dear, or rain,
>     And longer than the years!

Whatever "that thwart thing" may have been, his wife's death when the poet was seventy-two[4] swept away the long estrangement there had been between them, releasing a gush of reminiscence and poetry. I believe the best of these 1912–1913 poems to be some of the finest love poetry in our language: indeed, one

---

[3] Wanzing: wasting, diminishing.
[4] Two years later Hardy married his second wife, Florence Emily Dugdale, who was also a writer.

may wonder if there is in any language a parallel to this winter flowering of a poetry or sentiment that had lain dormant in the poet's heart throughout the summer of his age. The emotional range of the poems is remarkable, from the agony of bereavement and remorse in "The Going" to the almost ecstatic acceptance of "After a Journey"; from the delicate pathos of "The Haunter," in which the dead wife is speaking, to the no less delicate melancholy, strengthened by sinewy phrasing and a few clear-cut images, that makes "At Castle Boterel" so haunting a farewell to love. The variety of emotion is equaled by that of stanza form: it is as though the diverse molds had been preparing through a lifetime, and now those scenes from the past ran freely into them, each recognizing its own. Tricks of technique, which had at times been wasted on inferior material or had called too much attention to themselves, now came into their own—such as the triplet rhyming of "The Voice":

> Woman much missed, how you call to me, call to me,
> Saying that now you are not as you were
> When you had changed from the one who was all to me,
> But as at first, when our day was fair.
>
> Can it be you that I hear? Let me view you, then,
> Standing as when I drew near to the town
> Where you would wait for me: yea, as I knew you then,
> Even to the original air-blue gown!

Beneath their grace and appealing diversity, the 1912–1913 poems have good bone, formed by the sincerity, the refusal to overstate an emotion or falsify a situation, that we have noticed before. There might so forgivably have been flecks of self-pity, or sentimentality, even, in the best of these poems. That there are none is due not to the carefulness of a poet who has feared to give too much of himself away lest it muddy the stream of his verse but to the unselfconscious recklessness with which Hardy did give himself. The moral quality of that self may be gauged, I believe, by the poetic quality of what was thus created:

> Hereto I come to view a voiceless ghost;
>    Whither, O whither will its whim now draw me?
> Up the cliff, down, till I'm lonely, lost,
>    And the unseen waters' ejaculations awe me.
> Where will you next be there's no knowing,
>    Facing round about me everywhere,
>       With your nut-coloured hair,
> And grey eyes, and rose-flush coming and going.

> Yes: I have re-entered your olden haunts at last;
>    Through the years, through the dead scenes I have tracked you;
> What have you now found to say of our past—
>    Scanned across the dark space wherein I have lacked you?
> Summer gave us sweets, but autumn wrought division?
>    Things were not lastly as firstly well
>       With us twain, you tell?
> But all's closed now, despite Time's derision.
>
> I see what you are doing: you are leading me on
>    To the spots we knew when we haunted here together,
> The waterfall, above which the mist-bow shone
>    At the then fair hour in the then fair weather,
> And the cave just under, with a voice still so hollow
>    That it seems to call out to me from forty years ago,
>       When you were all aglow,
> And not the thin ghost that I now frailly follow!
>
> Ignorant of what there is flitting here to see,
>    The waked birds preen and the seals flop lazily;
> Soon you will have, Dear, to vanish from me,
>    For the stars close their shutters and the dawn whitens hazily.
> Trust me, I mind not, though Life lours,
>    The bringing me here; nay, bring me here again!
>       I am just the same as when
> Our days were a joy, and our paths through flowers.
>                                    ("After a Journey")

Such, then, is the tenderness of Thomas Hardy. I do not know any other English poet who strikes that note of tenderness so firmly and so resonantly. With Hardy at his best, it is the poem—the whole poem, not any high spots in it—that makes the impression. We shall be offended by his frequent use of archaic, uncouth, or stock-poetic words if we detach them from their contexts—words such as "domicile," "denizenship," "subtrude," "thuswise," "hodiernal," "fulgid," "lippings," "unbe." But if we allow the momentum of the poem to carry us over them, as often it can, they will seem very small obstacles; and without them his poetry would lose something of its characteristic flavor. It cannot, of course, be denied that the massive deployment of a simple idea, though apt enough for a work on the scale of *The Dynasts*, becomes in a short poem grandiose and cumbrous: circumlocution is a serious danger to Hardy's lyrics. Yet he often, by a secret formula in which craft and innocence are somehow combined, manages to absorb his circumlocutions in the body of the poem. One can think of few less promising lines to start a poem—or more ponderous ways of saying "When I am dead"—than "When the Present has latched its postern behind my tremulous stay": yet the poem it begins is one of Hardy's finest. The language of poetry is, after all, an artificial language, whether the poet uses a poetic diction throughout a poem or whether he varies it with colloquial phrases. The only question is, has he achieved balance and congruence; and the final test of this is whether the poem survives as a whole or in fragments.

I believe that where personal poetry is concerned the wholeness of a poem must depend not only upon technical skill, not even upon technical skill backed by imaginative power, but also—and perhaps most—on a certain wholeness in the poet himself. Great poems have been written by immature, flawed, or unbalanced men; but not, I suggest, great personal poetry; for this, ripeness, breadth of mind, charity, honesty are required: that is why great personal poetry is so rare. It is an exacting medium: false humility, egotism, or emotional insincerity cannot be hidden in such poetry; they disintegrate the poem. Thomas Hardy's best poems do seem to me to offer us images of virtue; not because he moralizes, but because they breathe out the truth and goodness that were in him, inclining our own hearts toward what is lovable in humanity:

> When the Present has latched its postern behind my tremulous stay,
>   And the May month flaps its glad green leaves like wings,
> Delicate-filmed as new-spun silk, will the neighbours say,
>   "He was a man who used to notice such things"?
>
> If it be in the dusk when, like an eyelid's soundless blink,
>   The dewfall-hawk comes crossing the shades to alight
> Upon the wind-warped upland thorn, a gazer may think,
>   "To him this must have been a familiar sight."
>
> If I pass during some nocturnal blackness, mothy and warm,
>   When the hedgehog travels furtively over the lawn,
> One may say, "He strove that such innocent creatures should come to no harm,
>   But he could do little for them, and now he is gone."
>
> If, when hearing that I have been stilled at last, they stand at the door,
>   Watching the full-starred heavens that winter sees,
> Will this thought rise on those who will meet my face no more,
>   "He was one who had an eye for such mysteries"?
>
> And will any say when my bell of quittance is heard in the gloom,
>   And a crossing breeze cuts a pause in its outrollings,
> Till they rise again, as they were a new bell's boom,
>   "He hears it not now, but used to notice such things"?
>
> ("Afterwards")

## SELECTED BIBLIOGRAPHY

I. BIBLIOGRAPHY. C. Wilson, ed., *A Descriptive Catalogue of the Grolier Club Centenary Exhibition* (Waterville, Me., 1940); C. J. Weber, *The First Hundred Years of Thomas Hardy, 1840-1940* (Waterville, Me., 1942), a centenary bibliography of Hardiana; R. L. Purdy, *Thomas Hardy: A Bibliographical Study* (London, 1954); K. Carter, comp., *Thomas Hardy Catalogue* (Dorchester, 1968), a list of the books by and about Hardy in the Dorset County Library.

II. COLLECTED WORKS. *Works in Prose and Verse*, 20 vols. (London, 1895-1913); *The Writings of Thomas Hardy in Prose and Verse*, 21 vols. (New York–London, 1895-1903), the Anniversary ed.; *Works in Prose and Verse*, 25 vols. (London, 1906-1919), the Pocket ed.; *Works in Prose and Verse*, 23 vols. (London, 1912-1913), the Wessex ed.; *Works in Prose and Verse*, 37 vols. (London, 1919-1920), the Mellstock ed.; *Poetical Works*, 2 vols. (London, 1919-1921), vol. I: *Poems*, vol. II: *The Dynasts*; the 2nd and subsequent eds., each in one vol., do not include *The Dynasts*; the first one-vol. ed. of *The Dynasts* was published in 1910, and there is a deluxe ed. in three vols. (1927); *Short Stories* (London, 1928); *The Novels* (London, 1949-1952); J. Gibson, ed., *Complete Poems* (London, 1974), the New Wessex ed.

III. SELECTED WORKS. G. M. Young, ed., *Selected Poems* (London, 1940); W. E. Williams, ed., *Selected Poems* (London, 1960); J. C. Ransom, ed., *Selected Poems* (New York, 1961); C. J. Weber, ed., *Love Poems* (London, 1963); P. N. Furbank, ed., *Selected Poems* (London, 1964); J. Wain, ed., *Selected Shorter Poems* (London, 1966); J. Wain, ed., *Selected Stories* (London, 1966); G. Grigson, ed., *Choice of Poems* (London, 1969); T. R. M. Creighton, ed., *A New Selection* (London, 1974); J. Gibson, ed., *Chosen Short Stories* (London, 1976); J. Moynahan, ed., *The Portable Thomas Hardy* (London, 1979); D. Wright, ed., *Selected Poems* (London, 1979).

IV. SEPARATE WORKS. *Desperate Remedies*, 3 vols. (London, 1871), novel, first published anonymously; *Under the Greenwood Tree: A Rural Painting of the Dutch School*, 2 vols. (London, 1872), novel, first published anonymously; "A New Edition with a Portrait of the Author and Fifteen Illustrations" [by Thomas Hardy] was published in 1891; *A Pair of Blue Eyes: A Novel*, 3 vols. (London, 1873); *Far from the Madding Crowd*, 2 vols. (London, 1874), novel; *The Hand of Ethelberta: A Comedy in Chapters*, 2 vols. (London, 1876), novel; *The Return of the Native*, 3 vols. (London, 1878), novel; *The Trumpet-Major: A Tale*, 3 vols. (London, 1880), novel; *A Laodicean, or, The Castle of the De Stancys: A Story of To-day*, 3 vols. (London, 1881), novel; *Two on a Tower: A Romance*, 3 vols. (London, 1882), novel; *The Dorset Farm Labourer Past and Present* (Dorchester, 1884), essay; *The Romantic Adventures of a Milkmaid* (New York, 1884), short story; *The Mayor of Casterbridge: The Life and Death of a Man of Character*, 2 vols. (London, 1886), novel; *The Woodlanders*, 3 vols. (London, 1887), novel; *Wessex Tales: Strange, Lively and Commonplace*, 2 vols. (London, 1888), short stories.

*Tess of the d'Urbervilles: A Pure Woman Faithfully Presented*, 3 vols. (London, 1891), novel; *A Group of Noble Dames* (London, 1891), short stories; *The Three Wayfarers: A Pastoral Play in One Act* (London, 1893), a dramatization of the short story "The Three Strangers"; *Life's Little Ironies. A Set of Tales with Some Colloquial Sketches Entitled "A Few Crusted Characters"* (London, 1894), includes "The Melancholy Hussar," first printed in *Three Notable Stories* (London, 1890), and "To Please His Wife," first printed in *Stories from "Black and White"* (London, 1893); *Jude the Obscure* (London, 1895), novel; "The Spectre of the Real," short story written in collaboration with F. Henniker, printed in *In Scarlet and Grey* by F. Henniker (London, 1896); *The Well-Beloved: A Sketch of a Temperament* (London, 1897), novel; *Wessex Poems and Other Verses* (London, 1898), with thirty illustrations by Hardy.

*Poems of the Past and Present* (London, 1901); *The Dynasts: A Drama of the Napoleonic Wars*, 3 parts (London, 1903–1904, 1906, 1908), J. Wain, ed. (paperback) (London–New York, 1965), verse drama; *Time's Laughingstocks and Other Verses* (London, 1909), verse; *A Changed Man, The Waiting Supper, and Other Tales* (London, 1913), short stories; *Satires of Circumstance: Lyrics and Reveries* (London, 1914), verse; *Moments of Vision, and Miscellaneous Verses* (London, 1917), verse.

*Late Lyrics and Earlier. With Many Other Verses* (London, 1922), verse; *The Famous Tragedy of the Queen of Cornwall at Tintagel in Lyonness* (London, 1923), verse drama; *Compassion: An Ode* (London, 1924), verse; *Human Shows, Far Phantasies, Songs and Trifles* (London, 1925), verse; *Life and Art* (New York, 1925), essays and letters, not previously printed in book form, ed. with intro. by E. Brennecke; *Winter Words, in Various Moods and Metres* (London, 1928), verse; *Old Mrs. Chundle* (New York, 1929), short story not in the collected short stories; *An Indiscretion in the Life of an Heiress* (London, 1934), short novel, adapted by the author from his first novel, "The Poor Man and the Lady," it was privately printed in a limited edition for Mrs. Hardy (London, 1934), first published separately (Baltimore, 1935) with an intro. by C. J. Weber; *The Intruder* (Fairfield, Me., 1938), short story not in the collected short stories.

*Revenge Is Sweet: Two Short Stories* (Waterville, Me., 1940), this limited edition contains "Destiny and a Blue Cloak" and "The Doctor's Legend," previously unpublished in book form; *Maumbury Ring* (Waterville, Me., 1942), essay, limited edition, not published elsewhere; *Our Exploits at West Poley* (London, 1952), story; E. Hardy, ed., *Notebooks, and Some Letters from Julia Augusta Martin* (London, 1955); C. J. Weber, ed., *Dearest Emmie* (London, 1963), letters from Hardy to his first wife; *The Architectural Notebook* (Dorchester, 1966), with intro. by C. J. P. Beatty; H. Orel, ed., *Thomas Hardy's Personal Writings* (Lawrence, Kans., 1967).

V. LETTERS. R. L. Purdy and M. Millgate, eds., *Collected Letters*, vol. I: *1840–1892* (London, 1978), vol. II: *1893–1901* (London, 1980).

VI. BIOGRAPHICAL AND CRITICAL STUDIES. L. P. Johnson, *The Art of Thomas Hardy* (London, 1894; rev. ed., 1923), the latter adds new material, also contains a bibliography by J. Lane of 1st eds. to 1922 and an added ch. on the poetry by J. E. Barton; C. G. Harper, *The Hardy Country: Literary Landmarks of the Wessex Novels* (London, 1904); F. O. Saxelby, *A Thomas Hardy Dictionary* (London, 1911); L. Abercrombie, *Thomas Hardy: A Critical Study* (London, 1912); D. H. Lawrence, "Study of Thomas Hardy," in *Phoenix* (London, 1914); H. Child, *Thomas Hardy* (London, 1916); H. D. Duffin, *Thomas Hardy: A Study of the Wessex Novels* (Manchester, 1916).

J. M. Murry, *Aspects of Literature* (London, 1920); J. W. Beach, *The Technique of Thomas Hardy* (London, 1922); E. Brennecke, *Thomas Hardy's Universe: A Study of a Poet's Mind* (London, 1924); R. Williams, *The Wessex Novels* (London, 1924); E. Brennecke, *Life of Thomas Hardy* (London, 1925); H. B. Brimsditch, *Character and Environment in the Novels of Thomas Hardy* (London, 1925); M. Chase, *Thomas Hardy, from Serial to Novel* (Minneapolis, 1927; repr., New York, 1962); A. Symons, *A Study of Thomas Hardy* (London, 1927); P. Braybrooke, *Thomas Hardy and His Philosophy* (London, 1928); V. H. G. Collins, *Talks with Thomas Hardy at Max Gate 1920–1922* (London, 1928); P. d'Exideuil, *Le Couple humain dans l'oeuvre de Thomas Hardy* (Paris, 1928), English translation from rev. text by F. W. Crosse, with an intro by H. Ellis (London, 1930), the French ed. contains a list of French translations of Hardy's works; F. E. Hardy, *The Early Life of Thomas Hardy, 1840–1891* (London, 1928); H. M. Tomlinson, *Thomas Hardy* (New York, 1929).

F. E. Hardy, *The Later Years of Thomas Hardy, 1892–*

1928 (London, 1930), this work and the previous one of 1928, which purport to be by Hardy's widow, were actually written by Hardy himself, a fact that he went to some lengths to conceal; the two books were repr. in one vol. entitled *The Life of Thomas Hardy, 1840–1928* (London, 1962); F. L. Lucas, *Eight Victorian Poets* (London, 1930); A. S. MacDowall, *Thomas Hardy: A Critical Study* (London, 1931); F. R. Leavis, *New Bearings in English Poetry* (London, 1932); A. C. Chakravarty, *The Dynasts and the Post-War Age in Poetry* (London, 1938); W. R. Rutland, *Thomas Hardy* (Oxford, 1938).

C. J. Weber, *Hardy of Wessex: His Life and Literary Career* (New York, 1940; rev. and exp., 1965); E. Blunden, *Thomas Hardy* (London, 1941); D. Cecil, *Hardy the Novelist: An Essay in Criticism* (London, 1943), the Clark Lectures, 1942; C. Clemens, *My Chat with Thomas Hardy* (Webster Groves, Mo., 1944), with an intro. by C. J. Weber; C. M. Bowra, *The Lyrical Poetry of Thomas Hardy* (Nottingham, 1946), the Byron Lecture, 1946; J. G. Southworth, *The Poetry of Thomas Hardy* (New York, 1947); H. C. Webster, *On a Darkling Plain: The Art and Thought of Thomas Hardy* (Chicago, 1947); A. J. Guerard, *Thomas Hardy: The Novels and Stories* (London, 1949).

D. Hawkins, *Thomas Hardy* (London, 1950), although the ed. bears this date, publication was in the following year; R. A. Scott-James, *Fifty Years of English Literature, 1900–1950* (London, 1951), contains an assessment of Hardy as a lyric poet; see also Scott-James's *Modernism and Romance* (London, 1908); C. Day Lewis, *The Poetry of Thomas Hardy* (London, 1951), a lecture delivered before the British Academy, June 1951, and published in the *Proceedings*; J. Holloway, *The Victorian Sage* (London, 1953); W. Allen, *The English Novel* (London, 1954); M. D. Brown, *Thomas Hardy* (London, 1954; 2d ed., rev., 1961); E. Hardy, *Thomas Hardy: A Critical Biography* (London, 1954); C. M. Bowra, *Inspiration and Poetry* (London, 1955); J. O. Bailey, *Thomas Hardy and the Cosmic Mind: A New Reading of The Dynasts* (Chapel Hill, N. C., 1956); G. Ford, ed., *The Pelican Guide to English Literature*, vol. VI: *Dickens to Hardy* (London, 1958).

J. Paterson, *The Making of "The Return of the Native"* (Berkeley-London, 1960); Emma Hardy, *Some Recollections*, Evelyn Hardy and R. Gittings, eds. (London, 1961), recollections of Hardy's first wife, together with fourteen of Hardy's poems that inspired them; S. Hynes, *The Pattern of Hardy's Poetry* (London, 1961); M. D. Brown, *Hardy: The Mayor of Casterbridge* (London, 1962), a close critical analysis of the novel; J. S. Cox, *Monographs on the Life, Times and Works of Thomas Hardy* (St. Peter Port, Guernsey, 1962–), a large collection of memorabilia by various authors; A. J. Guerard, *Hardy: A Collection of Critical Essays* (Englewood Cliffs, N. J., 1963); H. Orel, *Thomas Hardy's Epic Drama: A Study of "The Dynasts"* (Lawrence, Kans., 1963); J. I. M. Stewart, *Eight Modern Writers*, Oxford History of English Literature, vol. XII (Oxford, 1963); G. Wing, *Hardy* (London, 1963); R. C. Carpenter, *Thomas Hardy* (New York, 1964); L. Dacon, *Hardy's Sweetest Image: Thomas Hardy's Poetry for His Lost Love, Tryphena* (Chagford, 1964); R. Morell, *Thomas Hardy: The Will and the Way* (Kuala Lumpur, 1965); D. Lodge, *Language of Fiction* (London, 1966); A. Kettle, *Hardy the Novelist: A Reconsideration* (Swansea, 1967); H. Orel, ed., *Thomas Hardy: Personal Writings* (London, 1967); E. Gosse, *Thomas Hardy, O.M.*, R. Knight, ed. and annot. (Bulpham, 1968); I. Howe, *Thomas Hardy* (London, 1968); T. Johnson, *Thomas Hardy* (London, 1968); L. Lerner and J. Holmstrom, eds., *Thomas Hardy and His Readers: A Selection of Contemporary Reviews* (London, 1968), with commentary; F. B. Pinion, *A Hardy Companion: A Guide to the Works of Thomas Hardy and Their Background* (London, 1968); D. Daiches, *Some Late Victorian Attitudes* (London, 1969); K. Marsden, *The Poems of Thomas Hardy* (London, 1969).

J. O. Bailey, *The Poetry of Thomas Hardy* (Chapel Hill, N. C., 1970); R. G. Cox, ed., *Hardy: The Critical Heritage* (London, 1970); J. H. Miller, *Thomas Hardy: Distance and Desire* (Cambridge, Mass., 1970); M. Millgate, *Thomas Hardy, His Career as a Novelist* (London, 1971); F. R. Southerington, *Hardy's Vision of Man* (London, 1971); J. I. M. Stewart, *Thomas Hardy: A Critical Biography* (London, 1971); F. E. Halliday, *Thomas Hardy: His Life and Work* (Bath, 1972); E. Hardy and F. B. Pinion, *One Rare Fair Woman* (London-Coral Gables, Fla., 1972); P. Meisel, *Thomas Hardy: The Return of the Repressed* (New Haven, Conn.-London, 1972); M. Williams, *Thomas Hardy and Rural England* (London-New York, 1972); D. Davis, *Thomas Hardy and British Poetry* (London, 1973); F. B. Pinion, ed., *Thomas Hardy and the Modern World* (London, 1974); P. Vigar, *The Novels of Thomas Hardy: Illusion and Reality* (London, 1974); M. Drabble, ed., *The Genius of Thomas Hardy* (London, 1975); R. P. Draper, ed., *Hardy: The Tragic Novels. A Casebook* (London, 1975); R. Gittings, *The Young Thomas Hardy* (London, 1975); D. Kramer, *Thomas Hardy: The Forms of Tragedy* (London, 1975); G. Thurley, *The Psychology of Hardy's Novels: The Nervous and the Statuesque* (St. Lucia, Queensland, 1975); D. Hawkins, *Thomas Hardy: Novelist and Poet* (Newton Abbot-New York-Vancouver, 1976); H. Orel, *The Final Years of Thomas Hardy* (London, 1976); T. O'Sullivan, *Thomas Hardy: An Illustrated Biography* (London, 1976); F. B. Pinion, *A Commentary on the Poems of Thomas Hardy* (London, 1976); L. St. J. Butler, *Thomas Hardy After Fifty Years* (London, 1977); F. B. Pinion, *Thomas Hardy: Art and Thought* (London, 1977); J. Bayley, *Essay on Hardy* (Cambridge, 1978); R. Gittings, *The Older Hardy* (London, 1978); A. Enstice, *Thomas Hardy: Landscapes of the Mind* (London-New York, 1979); R. Gittings, *The Second Mrs. Hardy* (London, 1979); J. Grundy, *Hardy and the Sister Arts* (London, 1979); D. Kramer, *A Critical Approach to the Fiction of Thomas Hardy* (London, 1979); D. K. Robinson, *The First*

Mrs. Thomas Hardy (London, 1979); A. Smith, ed., The Novels of Thomas Hardy (London, 1979); P. Boumelha, Thomas Hardy and Women: Sexual Ideology and Narrative Form (Sussex, 1982).

### LIST OF SHORT STORIES

(The title in italics refers to the volume in which the story appears.)

"Absent-Mindedness in a Parish Choir," *Life's Little Ironies*; "Alicia's Diary," *A Changed Man*; "Andrey Satchel and the Parson and Clerk," *Life's Little Ironies*; "Anna, Lady Braxby," *A Group of Noble Dames*; "Barbara of the House of Grebe," *A Group of Noble Dames*; "A Changed Man," *A Changed Man*; "A Committee-Man of 'The Terror,'" *A Changed Man*; "The Distracted Preacher," *Wessex Tales*; "The Duchess of Hamptonshire," *A Group of Noble Dames*; "The Duke's Reappearance," *A Changed Man*; "Enter a Dragoon," *A Changed Man*.

"Fellow-Townsmen," *Wessex Tales*; "A Few Crusted Characters," *Life's Little Ironies*; "The Fiddler of the Reels," *Life's Little Ironies*; "The First Countess of Wessex," *A Group of Noble Dames*; "For Conscience' Sake," *Life's Little Ironies*; "The Grave by the Handpost," *A Changed Man*; "The History of the Hardcomes," *Life's Little Ironies*; "The Honourable Laura," *A Group of Noble Dames*; "An Imaginative Woman," *Life's Little Ironies* (first published in *Wessex Tales*); "Incident in the Life of Mr. George Crookhill," *Life's Little Ironies*; "Interlopers at the Knapp," *Wessex Tales*; "The Lady Icenway," *A Group of Noble Dames*; "Lady Mottisfont," *A Group of Noble Dames*; "The Lady Penelope," *A Group of Noble Dames*.

"The Marchioness of Stonehenge," *A Group of Noble Dames*; "Master John Horseleigh, Knight," *A Changed Man*; "The Melancholy Hussar of the German Legion," *Wessex Tales* (first published in *Life's Little Ironies*); "A Mere Interlude," *A Changed Man*; "Netty Sargent's Copyhold," *Life's Little Ironies*; "Old Andrey's Experience as a Musician," *Life's Little Ironies*; "On the Western Circuit," *Life's Little Ironies*; "The Romantic Adventures of a Milkmaid," *A Changed Man*; "The Son's Veto," *Life's Little Ironies*; "Squire Petrick's Lady," *A Group of Noble Dames*; "The Superstitious Man's Story," *Life's Little Ironies*.

"The Three Strangers," *Wessex Tales*; "Tony Kytes, the Arch-Deceiver," *Life's Little Ironies*; "To Please His Wife," *Life's Little Ironies*; "A Tradition of Eighteen Hundred and Four," *Wessex Tales* (first published in *Life's Little Ironies*); "A Tragedy of Two Ambitions," *Life's Little Ironies*; "A Tryst at an Ancient Earthwork," *A Changed Man*; "The Waiting Supper," *A Changed Man*; "What the Shepherd Saw," *A Changed Man*; "The Winters and the Palmleys," *Life's Little Ironies*; "The Withered Arm," *Wessex Tales*.

# GERARD MANLEY HOPKINS
(1844-1889)

## *Graham Storey*

### INTRODUCTION AND EARLY POEMS

JUDGED by the lives of most English nineteenth-century poets, Gerard Manley Hopkins' life was outwardly uneventful. He was born on 28 July 1844 into a prosperous and cultivated home near London and spent his boyhood in Hampstead. He received a conventional middle-class education that culminated in four, mainly very happy, years at Balliol College, Oxford, where he took first classes in classics. His conversion to Roman Catholicism in 1866 was much more of a crisis to his family, teachers, and friends than it would be today. Two years later he entered the Society of Jesus, and after the rigorous Jesuit training, he spent the remainder of his relatively short life (he died on 8 June 1889) carrying out the mission and teaching duties of a Jesuit priest.

This outward life—much of it inevitably isolated—conceals the remarkable intensity of his inner life, of his solitary experience, an intensity that, transmuted into poetry, has moved and excited a vast number of twentieth-century readers. Hopkins' admirers are, I think, most impressed by his remarkable technical originality, by his constant innovations in language, rhythm, and syntax, and by the exhilarating sense of freedom such experimenting brings. For this, they are fully willing to face the linguistic difficulties that inevitably arise. They are impressed too by his energy, both aesthetic and intellectual; by the fineness and self-exactingness of his mind; by his remarkable sensitivity to detail, to the minutiae of nature (a sensitivity that he shares particularly with Samuel Taylor Coleridge); and by his power to express extremes of feeling, uncharted—or not so courageously charted—by other Victorian poets. Few poets have communicated so strongly both excitement at natural beauty and its opposite, intimate knowledge of the terrors of despair. Hopkins above all communicates the mystery of selfhood, both of the experiencing self and of the objects experienced. All of his poetry is religious; but it appeals strongly to an immense number of readers who do not share his faith.

The canon of Hopkins' mature poems is small: between the end of 1875, the year of "The Wreck of the Deutschland," his first great mature poem, and his death in 1889, he wrote only forty-nine finished poems. The poems and fragments that he wrote as an undergraduate, following a few as a schoolboy, are in fact more numerous, but their chief interest now is in showing how excitedly he responded to other poets, particularly to the young John Keats. Hopkins' three earliest known poems, "The Escorial," which won a school prize when he was only fifteen, "A Vision of the Mermaids" (which he illustrated with a pen-and-ink drawing), and "Winter with the Gulf Stream" (published in *Once a Week* on 14 February 1863, when he was eighteen—one of the few poems published in his lifetime), all show his absorption of Keats. It is Keatsian color that enriches the envisioned mermaids:

> clouds of violet glow'd
> On prankèd scale; or threads of carmine, shot
> Thro' silver, gloom'd to a blood-vivid clot.[1]

Later, undergraduate poems chart the religious doubts that led to the crisis of his conversion; and many of these poems again draw for their tone on accepted Victorian models: Christina Rossetti, John Henry Cardinal Newman, Matthew Arnold. Such absorption—or, in some cases, clear imitation—makes the totally new and original voice of "The Wreck" all the more remarkable. Two of the early poems, of 1865 and 1866, are particularly interesting

---

[1] All poems are quoted from W. H. Gardner and N. H. MacKenzie, eds., *Poems of Gerard Manley Hopkins*, 4th ed. (Oxford, 1967).

for the light they throw on Hopkins' inner conflicts and hopes. Both the symbolism of "The Alchemist in the City" and the alchemist's sense of isolation and wasted effort point to a similar sense of separateness and failure in Hopkins himself. "The Habit of Perfection" ("Elected Silence, sing to me") asks for a total denial of the senses, but it expresses the senses, in their imagined denial, with a sensuousness that is still Keatsian:

> O feel-of-primrose hands, O feet
> That want the yield of plushy sward....

That sharp clash of sensuousness (with its intimate grasp on nature) and asceticism is perhaps the most striking characteristic of the young Hopkins' temperament.

Some of Hopkins' undergraduate essays—in particular, the longest of them, "On the Origin of Beauty: A Platonic Dialogue" (1865), which owes much to John Ruskin—show how consciously he was now searching for an aesthetic of his own. "The Probable Future of Metaphysics," written two years later, goes beyond both Ruskin and Walter Pater (who had been his tutor): a belief in Platonic "Ideal Forms" behind every form in nature is now the only alternative to "a philosophy of flux." Hopkins was now moving to the two famous terms he coined the following year in some notes on the early Greek philosopher Parmenides: "inscape" and "instress." Their importance for him was both philosophical and aesthetic; they pointed again to Plato's Ideal Forms; and they provided the objective criteria for both the beauty and reality that he was seeking. "Inscape" he used to denote the distinctive pattern that expresses an object's inner form, gives it its selfhood. "Instress" he used in two senses: (1) for the energy that "upholds" an object's inscape, gives it its essential being, and (2) for the force that the inscape exerts on the perceiver. How important these concepts were for his mature poetry a letter to his friend Robert Bridges of 15 February 1879 shows explicitly:

But as air, melody, is what strikes me most of all in music and design in painting, so design, pattern or what I am in the habit of calling "inscape" is what I above all aim at in poetry.[2]

Not only do his poems aim at "catching" the inscapes of things ("I caught this morning morning's minion . . ."), but the individual poem itself is an inscape; a pattern of sound and shape as well as of meaning.

Ironically (as it must seem to us now), while Hopkins was developing his all-important poetic criteria, he was writing no poetry. In May 1868, the month in which he made his decision to become a Jesuit, he decided both to burn the poems he had already written ("Slaughter of the innocents" is his 11 May journal entry)[3] and to write no more, "as not belonging to my profession" (as he later told Canon Richard Watson Dixon). Little now unknown was probably destroyed, but his self-imposed poetic silence was kept for over seven years. Instead, his powers of minute observation, his constant search for distinctive beauty, went into the journal he kept faithfully from 1866 to 1875. The journal is in a great many ways a workshop for the poems that were to follow it.

But to persuade himself that the writing of poetry would not interfere with his vocation as a priest, Hopkins needed far more than aesthetic justification. He needed a spiritual fiat, a conviction that, as a poet, he could serve God. It was this that the *Spiritual Exercises* of St. Ignatius Loyola, the meditations that are the central study and practice of every Jesuit, undoubtedly provided. We know what a profound effect they had on him. His most important spiritual writing was the beginning of a commentary on them; its opening, the celebration of selfhood, is his finest piece of sustained prose. Ignatius' favorite image, of the Jesuit as Christ's dedicated soldier, pervades many of his poems. The opening section of "The Wreck of the Deutschland" was inspired by his first experience of the *Exercises* as a novice seven years before. And, for Hopkins, they gave the most compelling of all reasons to rededicate himself as a poet. "Man was created to praise," the *Spiritual Exercises* open; in "Further Notes" on that opening Foundation Exercise, Hopkins wrote: "This world then is word, expression, views of God.... the world, man, should after its own manner give God being in return for the being he has given it." The poet, then, has his own place in this sacramental view of nature: the "being" he renders back to God is

---

[2] All letters to Robert Bridges are quoted from C. C. Abbott, ed., *The Letters of Gerard Manley Hopkins to Robert Bridges*, rev. ed. (London, 1955).

[3] See H. House, ed., *The Journals and Papers of Gerard Manley Hopkins*, 2nd ed., completed by G. Storey (London, 1959), pp. 537–539. All quotations from the journals are taken from this ed.

not only himself but the poem he has created, in its distinctive form another of God's works.

Moreover, in August 1872, while studying philosophy at Stonyhurst, Hopkins discovered the thirteenth-century Franciscan philosopher John Duns Scotus.

> At this time, I had first begun to get hold of the copy of Scotus on the Sentences in the Baddely library and was flush with a new stroke of enthusiasm. It may come to nothing or it may be a mercy from God. But just then when I took in any inscape of the sky or sea I thought of Scotus.
> (journal, August 1872)

Hopkins' enthusiasm was justified. Duns Scotus believed in the "principle of individuation," that the mind could come to know the universal (the *summum* of all medieval philosophy) through apprehending an individual object's "this-ness" (*haecceitas*) and that such apprehensions ultimately reveal God. Hopkins had intuitively believed this earlier, as a famous journal entry shows:

> I do not think I have ever seen anything more beautiful than the bluebell I have been looking at. I know the beauty of our Lord by it. It[s inscape] is [mixed of][4] strength and grace.
> (journal, 18 May 1870)

Duns Scotus gave philosophical and, above all, religious support for Hopkins' own theories of inscape and instress. It is not surprising that several of the mature poems show Duns Scotus' strong influence and that one, "Duns Scotus's Oxford" (1879), is a deeply felt tribute to him.

## "THE WRECK OF THE DEUTSCHLAND"

IN December 1875, when Hopkins read the account of the wreck of the *Deutschland* and the Rector of St. Beuno's, with whom he was studying theology, told him that "he wished someone would write a poem on the subject," he was ready to break his seven years' poetic silence. What is remarkable is that the poem he wrote should be so utterly different from all the poems he had written before—in language, rhythm, and structure. "The Wreck of the Deutschland" displays all his technical innovations, already in their most sustained form. Of these, the best-documented is his use of "sprung rhythm," of which, explaining the origins of "The Wreck" to Canon Dixon on 5 October 1878, he wrote: "I had long had haunting my ear the echo of a new rhythm which now I realized on paper."[5] But he had been equally concerned over the past two years with poetic language and, above all, its attainment of stress and emphasis: this had been the main subject of lectures on rhetoric he had given, as part of his training, at Manresa House, Roehampton, in 1873–1874. And the excitement of being sent to St. Beuno's, of learning Welsh, and of reading Welsh classical poetry undoubtedly played its part. In the letter to Dixon already quoted, he went on to mention "certain chimes suggested by the Welsh poetry I had been reading (what they call *cynghanedd*)." So an extraordinary confidence in a quite new poetic technique came together with a conviction that he now had a spiritual fiat for writing poetry again, and the result was one of the great religious poems in the English language.

"The Wreck of the Deutschland," Hopkins' longest and, for many, his greatest work, is at once an occasional poem—the central stanzas follow very closely the reports of the wreck in the *Times* (London), 8–13 December 1875—a religious ode, celebrating God's mastery and mercy; and a deeply personal spiritual autobiography: "What refers to myself in the poem is all strictly and literally true and did all occur," Hopkins told Bridges; "nothing is added for poetical padding." It is a complex and difficult poem, and a brief summary may help toward the understanding necessary for its great rewards.

Part I (stanzas 1–10) gives us Hopkins' own spiritual crisis: first, the agony of his own "shipwreck," as he submits to God's mastery ("Thou mastering me/God!"), then the grace of God's mercy, mediated to him through Christ's presence in the Communion (the second half of stanza 3). God's mastery and mercy are developed now almost as in a fugue: first, experienced personally in stanzas 4 ("I am soft sift/In an hourglass") and 5 ("I kiss my

---

[4]Hopkins' brackets.

[5]All letters to Canon Dixon are quoted from C. C. Abbott, ed., *The Correspondence of Gerard Manley Hopkins and R. W. Dixon*, rev. ed. (London, 1965).

hand/To the stars"), then as the paradox of Christ's Incarnation and Passion (stanzas 6 and 7), which demands our acceptance in the striking image of a ripe sloe bursting in our mouths. Stanzas 9 and 10 bring the two qualities together:

> Make mercy in all of us, out of us all
> Mastery, but be adored, but be adored King.

In their asking for "wrecking" and "storm," the fulfillment of God's double purpose, they link up with part II.

Part II (stanza 11 to the end) gives us the narrative of the shipwreck and of "the tall nun," introduced by stanza 11, proclaiming the inevitability of death ("The sour scythe cringe, and the blear share come") and ending with a prayer to Christ that completes and deepens the theme of part I. The sailing of the *Deutschland* from Bremen, the storm, and the wreck of the ship on the Kentish Knock occupy only six stanzas (12–17); the tall nun is dramatically introduced at the end of stanza 17 ("a lioness arose breasting the babble"); and after four stanzas (20–23) describing the nuns' exile and their dedication to the martyred St. Francis, we reach the center of the poem in stanza 24, the tall nun's cry, "'O Christ, Christ, come quickly.'" In the next three stanzas Hopkins puts forward, only to reject, possible motives for her cry. It was not that she wished to become more like "her lover" Christ, nor that she wanted a martyr's crown in heaven, nor even that she was driven to ask for ease by the "electrical horror" of the storm. No, it was the daily burden of a life of constant self-sacrifice ("The jading and jar of the cart,/Time's tasking") that made her cry out (stanza 27). Stanza 28, the climax of the poem, gives us the true meaning of the nun's cry: the ellipses ("But how shall I . . . make me room there . . .") show that it is all but inexpressible. The nun has *seen* Christ himself walking across the water. He will take her to him. Stanza 29 praises her for her understanding. In uttering the cry, the word kept within her, she has, as it were, given Christ a new birth: hence the significance of this night being the eve of the feast of the Immaculate Conception (stanza 30). There is yet a further miracle: the nun's cry has providently startled the lost sheep, the other passengers, the "Comfortless unconfessed," back to the fold—is not "the shipwreck then a harvest?" (stanza 31). The next two stanzas renew Hopkins' praise of God's mastery and mercy, the theme of part I, and the poem ends with two prayers. The first is to Christ, to "burn" anew, having "royally" reclaimed "his own," and the second is to the tall nun, "Dame, at our door/Drowned," to intercede in heaven for the return of Christ to England.

What gives such a poem, written in two formal parts and thirty-five eight-line stanzas, its compelling sense of unity is, above all, its symbolism. The suffering of the tall nun in the shipwreck (part II) mirrors Hopkins' own spiritual suffering in *his* "shipwreck" (part I); both ultimately mirror Christ's suffering and Crucifixion, so that the poem ends as a paean of praise to Christ himself. T. K. Bender, in *Gerard Manley Hopkins: The Classical Background* (1966), went further and, claiming that Hopkins wrote in the tradition of Pindar, the greatest of the Greek writers of odes, saw him, like Pindar, as holding the poem together through the power of an unstated but key image. The image he sees as unifying the poem is that of water, with its double powers of healing and destruction. The destruction, in a shipwreck poem, we expect, but few poets have given to the sea the almost apocalyptic power that Hopkins gives to it here:

And the sea flint-flake, black-backed in the regular blow,
Sitting Eastnortheast, in cursed quarter, the wind;
   Wiry and white-fiery and whirlwind-swivellèd snow
Spins to the widow-making unchilding unfathering deeps.

(st. 13)

Yet, at the same time, the sea brings the five martyred nuns to their salvation; they

> Are sisterly sealed in wild waters,
> To bathe in his fall-gold mercies, to breathe in his all-fire glances.

(st. 23)

Throughout the rest of the poem, water, the flushing of liquid, melting are images of divine mercy and help:

> Stroke and a stress that stars and storms deliver,
> That guilt is hushed by, hearts are flushed by and melt—

(st. 6)

And, in the great vision of Christ's return to earth, in the penultimate stanza, the analogy is again with water, a refreshing shower:

Not a dooms-day dazzle in his coming nor dark as
   he came;
      Kind, but royally reclaiming his own;
A released shower, let flash⁶ to the shire, not a
   lightning of fire hard-hurled.
                                                (st. 34)

The image of water, then, as Bender says, seems to be a key symbol that points to the poem's ultimate subject, the paradox of suffering.

But, if such use of imagery was traditional, Hopkins' use of language and sprung rhythm was daringly experimental. The sprung rhythm shocked his friend Robert Bridges, an orthodox prosodist ("the dragon in the gate," he later called "The Wreck" in his edition of Hopkins' poems); and it was too much for Fr. Henry Coleridge, editor of the Jesuit journal *The Month*, who, as Hopkins said, "dared not publish" the poem. Sprung rhythm, in fact, was vital to what Hopkins was trying to do in poetry by employing speech rhythms to give the words their maximum sound-impact and stress. He explained it to Canon Dixon very simply: "To speak shortly, it consists in scanning by accents or stresses alone, without any account of the number of syllables, so that a foot may be one strong syllable or it may be many light and one strong" (5 October 1878). In a later letter (27 February 1879) he was simpler still: "This then is the essence of sprung rhythm: *one stress makes one foot*, no matter how many or few the syllables."

The stressing throughout "The Wreck" is the same except that in part I the first line of each stanza has two stresses and in part II three; thereafter the number of stresses in each stanza is 3-4-3-5-5-4-6. As Harold Whitehall showed convincingly in an essay in *The Kenyon Critics* (1937), most of Hopkins' distinctive poetic devices—alliteration, internal rhyming, "chiming" of consonants—all that he defended as achieving "more brilliancy, starriness, quain, margaretting," help us to know which are the strong stresses (Whitehall suggested that this was in fact their main purpose). We quickly see how, as Hopkins intended, they both "fetch out" the meaning (his own phrase) and intensify it. The stressing of stanza 2, for example, is an integral part of the spiritual crisis as Hopkins reexperiences it:

   I did say yes
   O at lightning and lashed rod;
   Thou heardst me truer than tongue confess

⁶Here in its meaning "as a rush of water."

   Thy terror, O Christ, O God;
Thou knowest the walls, altar and hour and night:
   The swoon of a heart that the sweep and the
      hurl of thee trod
      Hard down with a horror of height:
And the midriff astrain with leaning of, laced with fire
   of stress.

The terror of that is strongly physical too: "a heart . . . trod/Hard down," "the midriff astrain": the strong stresses reenact the violence, and they almost compel us to read the words aloud as Hopkins pleaded to Bridges again and again to do: "Take breath and read it with the ears, as I always wish to be read, and my verse becomes all right." For Hopkins, poetry, like every art, had to have its proper "performance." As he wrote much later (1885) to his youngest brother Everard: "poetry, the darling child of speech, of lips and spoken utterance . . . must be spoken; *till it is spoken it is not performed*, it does not perform, it is not itself."

The shock of "The Wreck" to Bridges, and no doubt to Fr. Coleridge, too, was not only its new rhythm but its language. Hopkins was equally aware of what he was aiming to do here. He wrote to Bridges on 14 August 1879:

For it seems to me that the poetical language of an age shd. be the current language heightened, to any degree heightened and unlike itself, but not (I mean normally: passing freaks and graces are another thing) an obsolete one. This is Shakespeare's and Milton's practice and the want of it will be fatal to Tennyson's Idylls and plays, to Swinburne, and perhaps to Morris.

The reference to Shakespeare is as important as the comment on his contemporaries. From "The Wreck" onward, Hopkins' use of language *is* Shakespearean: he employs the resources of words to their utmost, makes them work urgently and physically. The words, as he claimed, are "current"; they are also, as he allowed, too, "to any degree heightened" to make their dramatic effect.

For Milton, and particularly for Milton's prosody, Hopkins had the highest possible admiration. "His achievements are quite beyond any other English poet's, perhaps any modern poet's," he wrote to Bridges on 3 April 1877; and to Dixon the following year (5 October): "His verse as one reads it seems something necessary and eternal. . . . I have paid a good deal of attention to Milton's versification and collected his later rhythms. . . . I found his most advanced effects in the *Paradise Regained* and, lyrically, in the *Agonistes*." Milton's verse remained a constant subject in Hopkins' letters to both Bridges and Dixon; and it is clear that, as a highly conscious innovator himself, he derived immense encouragement from the poet he saw as the greatest innovator in English prosody.

In stanza 27 of "The Wreck," Hopkins finds, after several attempts, the true reason for the tall nun's cry of "O Christ, Christ, come quickly":

> No, but it was not these.
> The jading and jar of the cart,
> Time's tasking, it is fathers that asking for
> ease
> Of the sodden-with-its-sorrowing
> heart,
> Not danger, electrical horror; then further it finds
> The appealing of the Passion is tenderer in prayer
> apart:
> Other, I gather, in measure her mind's
> Burden, in wind's burly and beat of endragonèd seas.

The key words here were, and are, in current use (though "electrical" was audacious in 1875); the alliteration and assonance of "jading and jar," "Time's tasking," and "sodden-with-its-sorrowing" heighten and deepen an experience, grounded in the difficulties of a life of constant self-sacrifice, that Hopkins knew only too well.

Rhythm, language, and the inner relationship between the two parts of the poem give "The Wreck" its sense of unity. But critics have been worried by two apparent digressions: stanzas 20–23, describing the birthplace of the five nuns and their relationship to St. Francis, and the final stanza, asking the drowned nun to pray for the conversion (or reconversion) of England to Rome. "The Wreck of the Deutschland" is both a profoundly Catholic and a daringly apocalyptic poem. The exile of the nuns from Germany under the anti-Catholic Falck Laws, their martyrdom in the wreck, even their number, five, mirroring St. Francis' five stigmata, are all central to the poem's true subject, the paradox that suffering brings salvation. The final stanza extends the miracle of the tall nun's vision to the prayed-for miracle of England's conversion. It was Elisabeth Schneider, in "*The Wreck of the Deutschland*: A New Reading" (1966), who first claimed that, for Hopkins, the tall nun actually *saw* Christ as a miraculous presence—hence the virtual impossibility of expressing her experience at the poem's climax:

> But how shall I . . . make me room there:
> Reach me a . . . Fancy, come faster—
> Strike you the sight of it? look at it loom there,
> Thing that she . . . There then! the Master,
> *Ipse*, the only one, Christ, King, Head:
> He was to cure the extremity where he had cast her;
> Do, deal, lord it with living and dead;
> Let him ride, her pride, in his triumph, despatch and have
> done with his doom there.
>
> (st. 28)

Christ has come to the tall nun at the climax of the storm; the poem's ultimate prayer—made through her intercession—is that this should prophesy his second coming, to restore England to his flock. The worship of Christ in the magnificently chiming and interlocking final two lines completes His dominant presence throughout the whole poem:

> Pride, rose, prince, hero of us, high-priest,
> Our hearts' charity's hearth's fire, our thoughts' chivalry's
> throng's Lord.
>
> (st. 35)

### POEMS, 1877–1882

HOPKINS followed "The Wreck of the Deutschland" with ten sonnets, all written in Wales ("Always to me a mother of Muses") during 1877, his final year at St. Beuno's, leading up to his ordination that September. They include some of his best-known and best-loved poems: "God's Grandeur," "The Starlight Night," "The Windhover," "Hurrahing in Harvest." A stanza from part I of "The Wreck," "I Kiss my hand/To the stars" (stanza 5), provides the key to the most exultant of them: the finding, "instressing," of God's mystery in the wonders of nature. In a sense, then, these are poems of meditation, celebrating the created world in all its beauty and wildness—and in all its detailed texture and color—as embodying God; and Louis Martz, in *The Poetry of Meditation* (1954), has claimed that Hopkins belongs to that great seventeenth-century tradition. What is peculiar to Hopkins is the astonishing energy with which, time and again, the meditation is made to lead to a call for spiritual action.

"The Starlight Night," the second of these sonnets (dated 24 February 1877), embodies just this pattern. The octet gives us all the beauty of the star world, its order ("bright boroughs," "circle-citadels"), mystery, and movement (like rippling leaves or doves in flight). It also insists on the excitement with which we should experience it:

> Look at the stars! look, look up at the skies!
> O look at all the fire-folk sitting in the air!

There is an excitement intensified by the imperatives and exclamations and by the use of a sprung line:

> Look at the|stars!|look, look|up at the skies!

Then the sestet insists on the action we must take to make all this beauty our own:

> Buy then! bid then!—What?—Prayer, patience, alms, vows.

The reward, moreover, is even higher—"within-doors house/The shocks [the sheaves of the harvest]" . . . "Christ and his mother" and all the saints.

"God's Grandeur," the sonnet written the day before, introduces a new note, the shaming contrast between the beauty of nature and man's sin or ugliness. The sonnet begins exultantly:

> The world is charged with the grandeur of God.

It moves to one of Hopkins' most intimate, movingly vulnerable apprehensions of nature's secret life:

> There lives the dearest freshness deep down things.

But in between there is the cry against man's instinct to spoil (it loses none of its strength by going back to William Blake and William Wordsworth), emphasized by the lines' repetition and assonance:

Generations have trod, have trod, have trod;
   And all is seared with trade; bleared, smeared with toil;
   And wears man's smudge and shares man's smell: the soil
Is bare now, nor can foot feel, being shod.

It is a note we hear in several more poems: in another of this group of sonnets, "The Sea and The Skylark," written at Rhyl, the North Welsh sea resort, the lark's pure and fresh song shames "this shallow and frail town"; in "Duns Scotus's Oxford," Oxford's "base and brickish skirt" confounds "Rural rural keeping—folk, flocks, and flowers"; and in "Ribblesdale" (1882), industrialist man, "heir/To his own selfbent so bound," thoughtlessly spoils "Thy lovely dale."

In "Pied Beauty" ("Glory be to God for dappled things—") Hopkins brings together all the "dappled" distinctive life he so loved—particularly the multitudinous detail of color, texture, and shape:

> For skies of couple-colour as a brinded cow;
>    For rose-moles all in stipple upon trout that swim;
> Fresh-firecoal chestnut-falls; finches' wings;

then in the final two lines he puts them in their proper created order and calls for the action that, alone for him, can save his and our souls:

> He fathers-forth whose beauty is past change:
>                 Praise him.

Such an ending points to the inadequacy of T. S. Eliot's description of Hopkins as essentially a "nature-poet."

The two most exultant of these sonnets of 1877 are "The Windhover," written in May, and "Hurrahing in Harvest," written the following September, three weeks before his ordination. Hopkins later described "The Windhover" to Bridges as "the best thing I ever wrote." Despite the controversies about its meaning, almost all readers of Hopkins have agreed on its poetic greatness. The octet wonderfully catches every movement of the kestrel in his soaring and gliding flight; sprung rhythm and imagery (the riding-school, the "skate's heel") add to his beauty and power. But the dedication "To Christ our Lord," added by Hopkins, is all-important. "I caught," the sonnet's opening words—"I caught this morning morning's minion"—shows Hopkins seizing the inscape of the kestrel; but the images from chivalry ("minion," "kingdom," "dauphin"), taken from the great meditation on the kingdom of Christ in the *Spiritual Exercises*, make it clear that he sees too the presence of Christ in the bird's beauty and mastery, the "achieve of, the mastery of the thing!"

The meaning of the sestet and of "My heart in hiding" from the end of the octet (line 7) has aroused continuing controversy. Some critics, notably I. A. Richards and William Empson, have seen "My heart in hiding" as a cry of envy for the sensuous life symbolized by the kestrel; and they interpret the whole poem as one of inner friction, a subconscious conflict between priest and poet. Conflict there must certainly be in any life of self-sacrifice, and "The Wreck of the Deutschland" shows how intensely Hopkins had dedicated himself to that life. But he never wavered in his vocation, and an unforgettable phrase he used to his agnostic friend Alexander Baillie on 10 April 1871 shows what the Jesuit life meant to him: "this life here [at Stonyhurst] though it is hard is God's will for me as I most intimately know, which is more than violets knee-deep."[7] Hopkins had dedicated himself to the "hidden life"; and the two key images of the sonnet's final three lines stress ("No wonder of it") that the heart dedicated to such service ultimately shines brightest. The "shéer plód" (Hopkins' own stress marks) of the horse makes the ploughshare shine down the furrow ("sillion"); and the "blue-bleak embers" of a dying fire, as they split apart, blaze out gold and orange-red. The final line, "Fall, gall themselves, and gash gold-vermilion," suggests strongly Christ's three crises on His way to the Crucifixion.

This still leaves the sonnet's crux, the meaning of "Buckle" in the second line of the sestet:

> Brute beauty and valour and act, oh, air, pride, plume, here
>     Buckle! AND the fire that breaks from thee then, a billion
> Times told lovelier, more dangerous, O my chevalier!

Acceptance of the life of self-sacrifice must support its commonest meaning of "collapse, give way under strain"; and the "AND" (thus capitalized) points to the paradox that, though the kestrel's plumage apparently crumples as it swoops down, the light that flashes from it is then at its loveliest. *This* is the paradox of sacrifice. But, as several critics have pointed out, the kestrel's wings do *not* in fact crumple as it dives. "Buckle" has in fact two other meanings: (a) "fasten, buckle on" (*transitive*) and (b) "grapple, prepare for action" (*intransitive*). If either of these was intended, the mood of "buckle" is imperative. In (a) the cry is to Christ, to buckle on to his heart ("here"—stressed in the line) the kestrel's beauty and power; in (b) the cry is to the kestrel's qualities themselves, to come to his heart and prepare themselves for action. It is part of the richness and tension of the poem that no one of these meanings totally and certainly excludes the other two.

"Hurrahing in Harvest" was the outcome, Hopkins wrote to Bridges, "of half an hour of extreme enthusiasm as I walked alone one day from fishing in the Elwy." Hopkins' rapture is intense but precise; the vision is of "our Saviour" Himself, present in the cornfields. Such a presence needs one of his most daring and original images to express it—"as a stallion stalwart, very-violet-sweet!" (we remember the "violets knee-deep" of his letter to Baillie); and its force on him, the beholder, a final, most striking image of immense physical and spiritual energy:

> The heart rears wings bold and bolder
> And hurls for him, O half hurls earth for him off under his feet.

The moment of understanding, the experience's "instress," has been transformed into pure, visionary activity.

"Spring," written in May 1877, shows us another of nature's "inscapes" that most moved Hopkins, its "wildness and wet," as he called it in the later poem "Inversnaid." Here we have

> When weeds, in wheels, shoot long and lovely and lush . . .

("wheels," in particular, is exact—their coiling shape—and exuberant). But the sestet first questions the scene's meaning:

> "What is all this juice and all this joy?"

And then, characteristically, Hopkins transforms it to innocent human beauty—"Innocent mind and Mayday in girl and boy"—and sees it as threatened:

> . . . Have, get, before it cloy,
> Before it cloud, Christ, lord, and sour with sinning.

This feeling for innocence threatened by corruption is the major theme of a group of poems inspired by Hopkins' experiences as a priest: "The Handsome Heart" and "The Bugler's First Communion," both written at Oxford in 1879 when he was serving at St. Aloysius' Church; and "Brothers," based on a scene that touched him at Mount St. Mary's College, Chesterfield (where he was "sub-minister" in 1877–1878), but not completed until 1880. With "Felix Randal," written in April 1880 at Liverpool, where he was priest at St. Francis Xavier's, these are almost his only poems describing incidents in his relations with others. Poetically, the first three seem to have obvious weaknesses; if some readers have been drawn to their delicacy and pathos, others have dismissed

---

[7] C. C. Abbott, ed., *Further Letters of Gerard Manley Hopkins* (London, 1938).

them as indulgent and sentimental. And the main reason for such reservations, if we share them, is that, in terms of what we are accustomed to from Hopkins, the incidents they recount—a boy's "gracious answer," a bugler's first Communion, a man's response to his younger brother's acting—seem too simple; we miss the urgency and complexity of the poems about himself. But we cannot miss the ardor of the prayers that end the first two:

> . . . Only . . . On that path you pace
> Run all your race, O brace sterner that strain!
> ("The Handsome Heart")

Recorded only, I have put my lips on pleas
Would brandle[8] adamantine heaven with ride and jar,
　　did Prayer go disregarded:
Forward-like, but however, and like[9] favourable heaven
　　heard these.
　　　　　　　("The Bugler's First Communion")

Nor the sudden, happy recognition of the goodness of human nature that ends "Brothers":

> There dearly thén, deárly,
> Dearly thou canst be kind.

The sonnet "Felix Randal" ("Felix Randal the farrier, O is he dead then? my duty all ended") is a far greater poem; to many it is one of Hopkins' most memorable. More powerfully than in any of his other poems, it brings together priest and poet. It is concerned with an adult, not children—a blacksmith, one of his Liverpool flock, who has just died. It is an elegy but the strong feeling it contains goes both ways. Hopkins' ministrations have comforted Felix, but the blacksmith's need of them has equally comforted Hopkins:

This seeing the sick endears them to us, us too it endears.

Hopkins makes Felix's attraction for him quite clear ("his mould of man, big-boned and hardy-handsome"); and as this becomes the accepted love of and for the priest at the sickbed, the poet can address Felix directly and through his imagination conjure up Felix's marvelously boisterous life in the past:

How far from then forethought of, all thy more boisterous
　years,

[8] Shake.
[9] Most likely.

When thou at the random grim forge, powerful amidst
　peers,
Didst fettle for the great grey drayhorse his bright and
　battering sandal!

Meanwhile, the year before, at Mount St. Mary's College, Hopkins had written his second long narrative poem, "The Loss of the Eurydice." Like "The Wreck of the Deutschland," it is an occasional poem: the *Eurydice* had just foundered off the Isle of Wight and many details of the disaster are taken from reports in the *Times* (London), 25–27 March 1878. Like "The Wreck," it is an explicitly religious poem; Hopkins sees the wreck, with its loss of three hundred young lives, as an analogy for England's lapse from Roman Catholicism. But there the resemblances end. It is a much simpler poem than "The Wreck," with none of the urgency or complexity of his own close spiritual involvement. This lack of complexity is underlined by the far simpler prosodic structure: four-line stanzas, each line bearing three stresses. "The scanning runs on without break to the end of the stanza, so that each stanza is rather one long line rhymed in passage than four lines with rhymes at the end," runs a note Hopkins added to his manuscript. But the rhymes "in passage" make, at times, considerable demands on us:

> Some asleep unawakened, all un-
> 　warned, eleven fathoms fallen
> 　　　　　　　(st. 1)

> But what black Boreas wrecked her? he
> Came equipped, deadly-electric
> 　　　　　　　(st. 6)

There is not the powerful symbolism of "The Wreck" to give "The Eurydice" that kind of unity. But the description of the storm itself—the sudden quickening of the language, the alliteration, the stresses of the sprung rhythm—suggests an apocalyptic violence:

> A beetling baldbright cloud thorough England
> Riding: there did storms not mingle? and
> 　Hailropes hustle and grind their
> 　Heavengravel? wolfsnow, worlds of it, wind there?
> 　　　　　　　(st. 7)

The picture of the young drowned sailor is as good as anything Hopkins did in its kind:

> Look, foot to forelock, how all things suit! he
> Is strung by duty, is strained to beauty,
>     And brown-as-dawning-skinned
> With brine and shine and whirling wind.
>                              (st. 20)

And stanzas 22–26, in which he contemplates the loss of young life and equates it with England's lapse from Rome, show, movingly, Hopkins' real concern:

> Only the breathing temple and fleet
> Life, this wildworth blown so sweet,
>     These daredeaths, ay this crew, in
> Unchrist, all rolled in ruin—
>                              (st. 24)

The prayer that ends the poem—like that which ends "The Wreck" and so many of the poems of this period—shows how intensely Hopkins hopes, through his poetry, to awaken men to God's providence:

> But to Christ lord of thunder
> Crouch; lay knee by earth low under:
>                              (st. 28)

Oxford, where Hopkins was a priest at St. Aloysius' Church from December 1878 to October 1879, proved an exceptionally fruitful place and time for his poetry. In all, he wrote nine poems there—besides the two already discussed, "Binsey Poplars," "Duns Scotus's Oxford," "Henry Purcell," "The Candle Indoors," "Morning, Midday, and Evening Sacrifice," "Andromeda," and "Peace." Of these, many would claim "Henry Purcell" to be among his finest—if most difficult—sonnets. Both it and, expectedly, "Duns Scotus's Oxford," owe a great deal to Scotus. The latter poem is more than a tribute; in its celebration of the distinctiveness of Oxford, its *haecceitas* ("Towery city and branchy between towers"), it follows Scotist principles; hence the despair that Scotus' own city, where he traditionally both studied and taught, should have betrayed its past beauty:

> Thou hast a base and brickish skirt there, sours
> That neighbour-nature thy grey beauty is grounded
> Best in; . . .

Yet, for Hopkins, Scotus' presence still haunts Oxford; and the sonnet ends with a moving and heartfelt acknowledgment of what he owes to him:

> Yet ah! this air I gather and I release
> He lived on; these weeds and waters, these walls are what
> He haunted who of all men most sways my spirits to peace;
>
> Of reality the rarest-veinèd unraveller . . .

That last phrase, in its giving to Scotus true insight into the reality of things, links closely with "Henry Purcell," written the following month, and particularly with the important epitaph Hopkins gave to it: that Purcell's music has "uttered in notes the very make and species of man as created both in him and in all men generally."

"Henry Purcell," then, again both explores and celebrates distinctiveness; not only of the genius of Purcell's music but, ultimately through that music, of "the very make and species of man," of selfhood itself:

> It is the forgèd feature finds me; it is the rehearsal
> Of own, of abrúpt sélf there so thrusts on, so
>     throngs the ear.

This is the essence of Purcell's music: "forgèd" has the force of being beaten out on the anvil, beaten to the right shape, to utter Purcell's "abrúpt sélf" (the stress marks are Hopkins' own). The sestet then seeks to find an exact analogy in nature to bring this insight home, and Hopkins finds it in one of his boldest and most majestic images, that of the "great stormfowl":

> . . . so some great stormfowl, whenever he has walked his while
>
> The thunder-purple seabeach, plùmed purple-of-thunder,
> If a wuthering of his palmy snow-pinions scatter a colossal smile
> Off him, but meaning motion fans fresh our wits with wonder.

The image is difficult, as Robert Bridges found the whole sonnet. But, because of that, Hopkins explained the meaning of almost every phrase in letters to him; and, as he showed, the analogy between Purcell and the "great stormfowl" is an exact one: "It is as when a bird thinking only of soaring spreads its wings: a beholder may happen then to have his attention drawn by the act to the plumage displayed" (4 January 1883). In the same way, Purcell, in his music, shows us unawares its distinctive ("arch-especial") beauty. It is one of the poems Hopkins most liked himself ("one of my very best pieces," he told Bridges); and its richness and complexity (especially of the final image) fully justify the prosodic innovation he made in it: it is his first sonnet in alexandrines, six-feet lines with a stress to each foot—a meter to which he returned in "Felix Randal."

A third sonnet, "As kingfishers catch fire," given neither title nor date by Hopkins, is an even stronger expression of the belief he shared with Duns Scotus in the fulfilling of individuality. The striking similarity of its imagery to a passage from his December 1881 commentary on the *Spiritual Exercises* suggests that Hopkins may have written it at Roehampton, during his tertianship, a period of renewal after the horrors of his missions in Liverpool and Glasgow. It is a very much simpler sonnet than "Henry Purcell"; but its simplicity is that of absolute confidence, as he moves from the "selving" (his own word) of animate and even inanimate objects—kingfishers, dragonflies, stones, bells—to the "selving" of "the just man" who, by fulfilling himself, becomes, through grace, another Christ:

> Acts in God's eye what in God's eye he is—
> Christ. For Christ plays in ten thousand places,
> Lovely in limbs, and lovely in eyes not his
> To the Father through the features of men's faces.

But another note enters increasingly the poems he wrote, after his ten months at Oxford, in Lancashire, either in Liverpool, while serving at St. Francis Xavier's, or at Stonyhurst, where he taught classics for two years, 1882–1884. It is a strong sense of transience, a conviction that the beauty he so loved in the world would pass, however cherished. Almost ten years earlier, on 17 April 1873, when an ash tree was felled in the garden at Stonyhurst, he had recorded in his journal:

> . . . there came at that moment a great pang and I wished to die and not to see the inscapes of the world destroyed any more.

It is this feeling of wretchedness at the loss of natural beauty that gives such poignancy to "Binsey Poplars"—felled while he was in Oxford in 1879, a poignancy transmuted by the musical repetitions:

> Ten or twelve, only ten or twelve
> Strokes of havoc únselve
> The sweet especial scene,
> Rural scene, a rural scene,
> Sweet especial rural scene.

During this period, Hopkins was beginning to write music, mostly airs to his own, Bridges', and Canon Dixon's poems.[10] To some degree, as in this poem, the clear musical concern, while seeming to intensify the feeling, also serves to transmute it, to make it more bearable. This is certainly the effect of the first part of "The Leaden Echo and the Golden Echo," the Maidens' song from his projected verse drama "St. Winefred's Well," written at Stonyhurst in October 1882, of which he wrote to Dixon on 23 October 1886: "I never did anything more musical." Both parts employ musical repetition more than any other poem Hopkins wrote. "The Leaden Echo" ends on the key word "despair" conjured up by the passing of beauty, but its repetition again seems to transmute, to distance it; while "The Golden Echo," although finding the only answer, for Hopkins, to mortal beauty's loss:

> Give beauty back, beauty, beauty, beauty, back
>    to God, beauty's self and beauty's giver,

still has two lines that face personal feelings head on, in words and rhythm that seem frighteningly undistanced:

> O then, weary then whý should we tread? O why are we
>    so haggard at the heart, so care-coiled, care killed,
>    so fagged, so flashed, so cogged, so cumbered,
> When the thing we freely fórfeit is kept with fonder a
>    care. . . .

Those two lines alone of the comparatively few poems of 1880–1882 seem to look forward uncompromisingly to the later poems of desolation. But almost all of them have some sense of loss, of blight, of "unselving" (to use Hopkins' own word from "Binsey Poplars"), even though that is far from the total—or even major—tone of the poem. Much the most delicate and subtle of them—indeed one of the most delicate and subtle of all Hopkins' poems—is "Spring and Fall," addressed to a young child ("Márgarét, are you grieving/Over Goldengrove unleaving?"), composed on his way back from Lydiate, in Lancashire, to Liverpool, in September 1880. The sharp but gentle questioning goes to the roots of all sorrow; and one phrase in particular shows Hopkins' skill in using the full resources of words:

[10]For a full account of Hopkins as musician, see H. House and G. Storey, eds., *The Journals and Papers of Gerard Manley Hopkins* (Oxford, 1959), pp. 457–497.

> Though worlds of wanwood leafmeal lie;

where "wan" fuses both "dismal" and, as an obsolete prefix, "deficient" or "lost." The end of the poem is perhaps the finest expression we have of Hopkins' belief in the true wisdom of the heart and the spirit ("ghost"):

> Nor mouth had, no nor mind, expressed
> What heart heard of, ghost guessed:
> It ís the blight man was born for,
> It is Margaret you mourn for.

Two other poems, written in the autumns of 1881 and 1882, are, at first sight and sound, celebrations, though in very different moods, of the countryside Hopkins so loved—"Inversnaid" of the Scottish Highlands, "Ribblesdale" of the Lancashire dale in which Stonyhurst College lies. But each ends with a warning not to destroy such inscapes. "Inversnaid" describes the movement of the Scottish burn so happily and excitedly that we might miss the sudden menace of the whirlpool:

> Of a pool so pitchblack, féll-frówning,
> It rounds and rounds Despair to drowning.

And no one can miss Hopkins' cry in the final stanzas:

> What would the world be, once bereft
> Of wet and of wildness? Let them be left,
> O let them be left, wildness and wet;
> Long live the weeds and the wilderness yet.

just as no one can miss Hopkins' fear, in the sestet of "Ribblesdale," that man, "the heir/To his own selfbent so bound," will despoil "Thy lovely dale."

### POEMS OF DESOLATION, 1884–1885

THE very intensity of the six "terrible sonnets" (as Bridges called them) of 1885—one of them, as Hopkins told Bridges, "written in blood" (17 May 1885)—has led many to believe that the entire five years of Hopkins' time in Dublin—from February 1884, when he took up his appointment as Professor of Greek at University College and Fellow of the Royal University of Ireland, to his death on 8 June 1889 from typhoid—were years of unrelieved wretchedness. This is not confirmed by the other poems he wrote in Ireland: the other two sonnets of 1885—"To what serves Mortal Beauty?" and "The Soldier"—and most of the varied poems, some unfinished, he wrote from 1887 to within six weeks of his death. Nor is it shown by Hopkins' other remarkably wide-ranging signs of intellectual energy, including his projected books on Homer and on "the Dorian Measure or on Rhythm in general" (of which virtually nothing, sadly, remains); letters to Bridges on prosody and John Milton; to R. W. Dixon, on Dixon's own poems and on poetry in general; to Coventry Patmore, giving him detailed criticism for a new edition of his *Collected Poems*; and to his old friend Alexander Baillie on possible early relations between Egypt and Greece. In addition, he was writing a lot of music, and in the year before his death, he began drawing again.

But there can be no doubt of the paralyzing desolation that Hopkins felt in the winter of 1884 (to which the first drafts of "Spelt from Sybil's Leaves" belong) and for more than a year afterward. The "terrible sonnets" themselves document his feelings of isolation, of intense inner struggle, and, paradoxically (since they are, to many readers, his finest sonnets), of frustration at his inability to create. Many factors certainly contributed to such feelings: bad health and nervous depression, increased by the strain on his eyes of almost continuous reading of examination papers; his sense of being an exile, exacerbated by the Irish nationalism he detested. And, perhaps, there were less conscious conflicts: the residual, and perhaps for him, inevitable conflict between priest and poet; the suppression of strong, possibly homosexual, feelings; and, most likely, the exaggeration, in his search for sanctity, of the distinction between his "affective" will, his love of beauty (including poetic beauty), and his "elective will," his desire for duty and holiness (an explanation put forward very convincingly by Fr. Christopher Devlin in *The Sermons and Devotional Writings of Gerard Manley Hopkins*, 1959).

"Spelt from Sybil's Leaves," to which Hopkins returned during the first six months of 1885, shows his powers at their finest. It is the only one of his sonnets to use an eight-stress line (marked by a strong caesura after four stresses); he described it to Bridges as "the longest sonnet ever made" and wrote to him on 11 December 1886:

Of this long sonnet above all remember what applies to all my verse, that it is, as living art should be, made for performance and that its performance is not reading with the eye but loud, leisurely, poetical (not rhetorical) recitation, with long rests, long dwells on the rhyme and other marked syllables, and so on. This sonnet shd. be almost sung: it is most carefully timed in *tempo rubato* [irregular rhythm].

It is a poem of prophecy, of warning, drawing its title from both Vergil's Cumaean Sybil, who guided Aeneas to the underworld (*Aeneid* 6), and the *Dies irae*, "The Day of Wrath," of the Roman Catholic Burial Mass: "As David and the Sybil testify . . . what terror shall affright the soul when the judge comes."[11] In the terrible description of the war within, with which it ends:

> . . . a rack
> Where, selfwrung, selfstrung, sheathe-|and shelterless,|
>    thóughts agaínst thoughts ín groans grínd,

it prophesies the major theme of the six "terrible sonnets"; but its warning is much more comprehensive. The analogy of the haunting picture of the descent of night, in the first half of the sonnet, is the ending of all "selving," of all the "dappled things" Hopkins loved, of all distinctiveness:

> For earth|her being was unbound; her
>    dapple is at an end, as-
> tray or aswarm, all throughther, in throngs; self ín self
>    steepèd and páshed—qúite
> Disremembering, dismémbering|áll now. . . .

What is deeply impressive in the poem is not only the power of each analogy, each set of images, but the felt exactitude of their parallelism. The straining of evening to be night *becomes* the total blanketing-out of earth's individual features, now lit only by the last rays of the dying sun ("Her fond yellow hornlight wound to the west"); the loss of each object's true shape and meaning, its inscape ("self ín self steepèd and páshed") *becomes*—the warning is in line 7 ("Heart, you round me right/With")—the nightmare alternative, where the trees have the shape of dragons and the "bleak light" the texture of a Damascene-worked sword. And this again is "Óur tale," the dire prophecy of the poem's title: once we let earth's multiplicity go—her "once skéined stained véined varíety"—once we attempt to reduce life to absolute moral judgment—"black, white;|right, wrong"—we shall experience the self-torturing, self-wringing rack of the poem's last line. But the final analogy carries the direst warning: "párt, pen, páck" refers to Christ's separation of the sheep from the goats at the Last Judgment (Matt. 25: 31-33). On one level, fear of this judgment lies behind the image in the final line of unprotected conscience on the rack, from which there can be no escape.

Hopkins' description of "Sibyl's Leaves" to Bridges as "living art . . . made for performance"—his totally justified pride in it as a sonnet—must strongly modify our sense of its apparently bleak pessimism. "To what serves Mortal Beauty?" written during a retreat at Clongowes on 23 August 1885—very near in time to the final draft of "Sibyl's Leaves"—shows how gracefully and relaxedly Hopkins could treat the conflict that Fr. Christopher Devlin has suggested is central to the desolate sonnets of this year, his "affective will," his love of beauty, versus his "elective will," his duty to God. The famous story of Pope Gregory the Great sending Augustine to convert England, after seeing the handsome English slaves ("*Non Angli sed Angeli*"),[12] is one example of the higher use of mortal beauty:

> Those lovely lads once, wet-fresh|windfalls of war's storm,
> How then should Gregory, a father,|have gleanèd else from
>    swarm-
> èd Rome? But God to a nation|dealt that day's dear chance.

The sonnet's ending, the hope to "Merely meet" mortal beauty and to wish for it, as for all outward beauty, spiritual beauty, "God's better beauty, grace," presents the Christian "use" of beauty and does so with no sign of conflict or strain.

A sense of strain is dominant in the six desolate (although in differing degrees) sonnets that, insofar as we can date them, were written in 1885, the strain, above all, of isolation, of feeling deserted by God, of being certain that his creative capacity was dead. But we cannot miss either the energy, the determination to resist despair, or the authenticity, the equal determination to be utterly true to his own feelings, however self-tortured and self-torturing. Formally, these sonnets are the antitheses of "Spelt from Sybil's Leaves": the language is stark, bare, stripped, to ex-

---

[11]Paul L. Mariani has also shown how close the poem is to some of Hopkins' Retreat notes for the meditation on Hell from the *Spiritual Exercises* (*A Commentary on the Complete Poems of Gerard Manley Hopkins* [Ithaca, N. Y., 1970], pp. 199 ff.).

[12]"Not Angles, but Angels."

press the essentials of the experience recorded, the resultant pitch of concentration a powerful new rhetoric.

Our only keys to dating them are letters and retreat notes. We know Hopkins' state of mind in the spring of 1885 from a letter to Alexander Baillie: his constitutional melancholy, he wrote, was becoming

> ... more distributed, constant, and crippling.... when I am at the worst, though my judgment is never affected, my state is much like madness.

But two letters to Bridges help us to identify and date the sonnets themselves. In May 1885 Hopkins wrote to him, "I have after long silence written two sonnets, which I am touching: if ever anything was written in blood one of these was." And in September of the same year, "I shall shortly have some sonnets to send you, five or more. Four of these came like inspirations unbidden and against my will." Bridges thought the sonnet "written in blood" was "Carrion Comfort"; the more desolate "No worst, there is none," written on the same manuscript page as a revised version of "Carrion Comfort," seems more likely.[13] There can be little doubt that the "five or more" sonnets mentioned in the September letter—neither these nor the one "written in blood" were in fact sent to Bridges—were the "terrible sonnets" and thus very probably written in 1885.

"Carrion Comfort" has the greatest energy of these sonnets. It is generated at once in the opening line, in the refusal to "feast" on despair:

> Not, I'll not, carrion comfort, Despair, not feast on thee;

(there are three more repeated "nots" in the first quatrain). The energy is increased by all the physical images of wrestling, and it is felt strongly again in the successive questions Hopkins asks of his terrible and mysterious adversary. The "underthought" of the sonnet (Hopkins' own word for the "often only half realised" source of a poem's images) combines the Book of Job with Gen. 32: 24–30, Jacob's wrestling with God; but, in turn, the adversary becomes Christ the winnower and finally Christ the Master. By kissing His rod and hand, Hopkins seems to have recovered: "my heart lo! lapped strength, stole joy, would laugh, chéer." But the sonnet ends on an agonizedly questioning note: the only certainty now is that the initial struggle with despair has become a wrestling bout with God Himself, scrupulously and bitterly documented:

> That night, that year
> Of now done darkness I wretch lay wrestling with
>     (my God!) my God.

The poem "No worst, there is none" creates—or re-creates—an extraordinarily intense sense of physical and mental pain, mainly through imagery, sound, and rhythm, but also through an "underthought" that combines the most intense works of suffering, all of which Hopkins knew intimately: the Book of Job (the "whirlwind"), Aeschylus' *Prometheus Bound* (Prometheus chained to his mountain), *King Lear* (the sonnet's final two lines). In the very first line, "Pitched past pitch of grief" suggests an inexpressible degree of pain; "More pangs ... schooled at forepangs, wilder wring" turns the grief into something horrifyingly active. The image of the lowing herd of cattle turns the pain into sorrow; but the anvil wincing and singing and Fury's shrieking force the sense of physical pain on us again and turn the screw tighter. Throughout the octet, repetitions and sound accentuate the experience; a mark that Hopkins made in his manuscript connecting "sorrow" with "an" in line 6, thus putting four of the line's five stresses on "áge-old anvil wince and sing," shows how sprung rhythm could "fetch out" his meaning.

The sestet begins with one of Hopkins' most striking images, painfully relevant to the states of near-madness he described in his letters:

> O the mind, mind has mountains; cliffs of fall
> Frightful, sheer, no-man-fathomed. Hold them cheap
> May who ne'er hung there....

It ends with clear references to the Book of Job, *King Lear*, and *Macbeth* that not only deepen the experience but universalize it. After the intense pain of the sonnet, the resigned acceptance of the final line seems the only course left open:

>                                                 all
> Life death does end and each day dies with sleep.

"To seem the stranger lies my lot" records both Hopkins' loneliness as a Roman Catholic in Ireland

---

[13]Norman MacKenzie has recently argued for "I wake and feel" as being the most likely in *A Reader's Guide to G. M. Hopkins* (London, 1981), pp. 171–172.

and his conviction that he can no longer create. The power of the first ten lines is that of direct, simple statement: his grief is poignant, but restrained. That restraint makes the clotted movement of lines 11–13, mirroring his bewildered frustration, the more powerful:

> . . . Only what word
> Wisest my heart breeds dark heaven's baffling ban
> Bars or hell's spell thwarts. . . .

Many years ago F. R. Leavis compared these lines to Macbeth's speech, "My thought, whose murder yet is but fantastical," as a "rendering of the very movement of consciousness";[14] and the judgment still holds. Hopkins' bafflement is at his inability to create (seen, as so often in this period, as a natural sexual process: "my heart breeds"); and, as we know from his letters, this sense of frustration extended to all his activities, musical and scholarly as well as poetic. Whether we read the sonnet's last sad phrase, "a lonely began," as a verb following an omitted relative pronoun or as a coined noun, its economy and poignancy fit perfectly the tone of the whole sonnet; its honesty demands our respect.

"I wake and feel the fell of dark" is, for most readers, probably the most desolate of these sonnets. The multiple meanings of the opening image, "the fell of dark" ("animal hide," "fierce," and "having fallen" are perhaps the key ones), dominate the octet.[15] All of them powerfully suggest the physical oppressiveness of the night's experience and carry that oppressiveness back, as the "black hoürs" "mean years, mean life." The image of "dead" (i.e., undelivered) letters sent to an unhearing God completes the sense of total lostness.

The sestet adds physical nausea to Hopkins' state: "gall" is poison as well as bitterness. In line 11 the bones, blood, and flesh that he praised God for binding in him in the first stanza of "The Wreck of the Deutschland" are now part of God's curse on him:

Bones built in me, flesh filled, blood brimmed the curse.

There are two ambiguities in the sonnet's last three lines. Either "selfyeast" or "a dull dough" can be the subject of "Selfyeast of spirit a dull dough sours": either way, the right, healthy process—the leavening of body by spirit—has been soured, perverted. The second ambiguity should not be there: both theology and the syntax of the final two lines assert that the agonies of the damned in hell must be worse than his. Yet the doubt persists: "but worse" *could* mean that his torments were worse than theirs. The possibility of that is an index of the sonnet's authenticity:

With witness I speak this.

We believe Hopkins is at his lowest ebb; and in the final two of these Dublin sonnets, "Patience, hard thing!" and "My own heart let me more have pity on," we can readily believe that at last some light has dawned for him. In each he seeks a way out of his misery; but in neither does he belittle the difficulties. The prayer for patience is totally realistic; it means he must continue to endure, to accept "war" and "wounds" and, worse still, the inner conflicts, the grating and bruising of his heart on itself. But patience offers consolations absent from the more tormented sonnets. Like ivy, "Natural heart's ivy," she "masks / Our ruins of wrecked past purpose" (the "beginnings of things, ever so many, which it seems to me might well have been done, ruins and wrecks," as Hopkins described his many unfinished projects in a letter to Baillie); and there, in an image of ivy's purple berries and liquid-green leaves, at once precise and hauntingly beautiful,

> . . . she basks
> Purple eyes and seas of liquid leaves all day.
> ("Patience, hard thing!")

But the final emblem of patience is God Himself. It is He who distills kindness, as a bee distills honey, and fills His honeycomb with it, "and that comes those ways we know."

The description of his own state in the octet of "My own heart let me more have pity on" is more complex and superbly, if difficultly, rendered. Hopkins knows that his torment is self-caused and at that stage is sure that there is no way out. The dense syntax and imagery perfectly mirror his bewilderment:

> I cast for comfort I can no more get
> By groping round my comfortless, than blind
> Eyes in their dark can day or thirst can find
> Thirst's all-in-all in all a world of wet.

---

[14] *New Bearings in English Poetry* (London, 1932), p. 170.
[15] Norman MacKenzie has discussed the many possible meanings of "fell" in *Hopkins* (Edinburgh, 1968), pp. 88–90.

We have to understand "world" after "comfortless," so as to parallel "dark" in the next line, and to appreciate that thirst itself seeks water (as the Ancient Mariner did, surrounded by the sea) just as blindness seeks light. As with Shakespeare and the seventeenth-century metaphysical poets, the effort forces us to share the writer's experience.

But the tone of the sestet, like that of the sonnet's first two lines, is self-reproaching, more relaxed, has even a touch of humor:

> Soul, self; come, poor Jackself, I do advise
> You, jaded, let be . . .

Bewilderment has now become self-exhortation: "leave comfort root-room" (let it expand like a plant); "let joy size" (let it grow—at God's will); trust unpredictable moments of happiness. The final coined verb ("as skies/Betweenpie mountains": as patches of sky seen between them dapple the mountains) suggests, in its very idiosyncrasy, at least a momentary restoration of Hopkins' faith in his own creativity.

## FINAL POEMS, 1887–1889

Most of the poems that Hopkins wrote in the last two years of his life—including the unfinished "Epithalamion"—show, despite his often harrowing letters, how poetically alive he was until his final illness. They also show his constant technical experimentation. Of his three extended sonnets with codas, only one, "Tom's Garland" (September 1887), his one attempt to write a political poem "upon the Unemployed," did not work as he had hoped: he had to confess to Bridges that it was "in point of execution very highly wrought, too much so, I am afraid"; and most modern readers have agreed with him. Each of the other two, "Harry Ploughman" and "That Nature is a Heraclitean Fire," totally justifies, in its own individual way, Hopkins' experimenting. But during the same period he was also deliberately reverting almost to the opposite style, to the "Miltonic plainness and severity" that he told Bridges he had aimed at in "Andromeda," written almost ten years earlier at Oxford. It is this experiment in style, his admiration for John Dryden, "the most masculine of our poets" as he put it, and his hope "to be more intelligible, smoother, and less singular" (letter to Bridges, 25 September 1888) that lie behind the other sonnets of these two years, however different their concerns: "St. Alphonsus Rodriguez," "Thou art indeed just, Lord," and "To R.B.," his last poem, written six weeks before his death and addressed to Bridges. The fourth of these sonnets, "The Shepherd's Brow" (3 April 1889), Bridges excluded from the canon as "thrown off one day in a cynical mood." It is in fact the last of five full drafts; but a note of something near hysteria in its despair makes it, as a poem, much less impressive than either the earlier desolate sonnets or the three "plainer" sonnets of Hopkins' last year.

On 6 November 1887 Hopkins wrote to Bridges of "Harry Ploughman," written at Dromore two months before: "I want Harry Ploughman to be a vivid figure before the mind's eye; if he is not that the sonnet fails." On 11 October, he had written to Bridges that the sonnet was "altogether for recital not for perusal" and its rhythm was "very highly studied." He also thought that the sonnet was a "very good one." It is in fact an astonishingly vivid picture of a ploughman in action, "fetched out" by the sprung rhythm (in one of the two manuscripts Hopkins gives seven "reading-marks" to help the reader)[16] and by the five extra "burden-lines" (which Hopkins thought might be recited by a chorus). The octet—increased to eleven lines by the three "burden-lines"—gives us Harry himself, as Hopkins saw or imagined him in his strength and almost sculptured handsomeness:

> Hard as hurdle arms, with a broth of goldish flue,
> Breathed round; the rack of ribs; the scooped flank . . .

The bodily details accumulate; but they form a unity, the vital inscape of a man ready for action, all his limbs perfectly disciplined:

> By a grey eye's head steered well, one crew, fall to;
> Stand at stress. . . .

Hence the dominant images of the serving sailor or soldier: "one crew," "as at a rollcall, rank," "His sinew-service."

In the sestet the ploughing itself takes over; and now plough and ploughman, his curls lifted and laced by the wind, his feet racing behind the plough-

---

[16] Reproduced in *The Poems of Gerard Manley Hopkins*, 4th ed., p. 293.

share and the upturned shining earth, form a new unity, the inscape of work well done. Ploughing as a symbol of work has a long history, both pagan and Christian; and Hopkins greatly admired one contemporary painting of it, Frederick Walker's *The Plough* (Royal Academy, 1870), which he thought "a divine work" (letter to Dixon, 30 June 1886).[17]

The poem's syntax throughout is difficult, as Hopkins himself confessed to Bridges, and words are used in unusual senses, demanding a leap of understanding from the reader, to make—as they do—the maximum impact. The two word-coinages in line 16, "Churlsgrace, too, child of Amansstrength" (the first from "churl," peasant), sum up the two qualities, grace and strength, that have combined to create this powerfully active figure.

"That Nature is a Heraclitean Fire and of the Comfort of the Resurrection" was written on 26 July 1888, near Dublin, "one windy bright day between floods," Hopkins told Dixon. Both technically and imaginatively it is one of his finest sonnets, fully justifying its great length (it is in alexandrines and has three codas). Hopkins was pleased with what he called its distillation of "early Greek philosophical thought," but prouder of its originality: "The effect of studying masterpieces is to make me admire and do otherwise," he wrote to Bridges two months after its composition.

Heraclitus (*ca.* 535 B.C.–*ca.* 475 B.C.) believed that all nature would ultimately resolve itself into fire. Everything was in a state of flux; not even man's body or soul could escape destruction. This relentless process is the subject of the central section of the sonnet's three sections, lines 10–16. But before this, the sonnet's opening section, lines 1–9, gives us one of Hopkins' most dynamic, excited pictures of nature in movement: racing clouds, light, and boisterous wind play together in apparent abandon:"Heavenroysterers, in gay gangs⎪they throng." Then, suddenly, Hopkins sees them as part of the Heraclitean process; the wind turns the floods into earth and ooze; then all, as in Heraclitus, becomes fire:

   . . . Million-fuelèd, nature's bonfire burns on.

But man's toiling footprints have been obliterated, too, leading Hopkins to the dramatic change of tone in the second section, as he contemplates the loss of man's mind and soul, communicated in three highly expressive word-coinages: man's "firedint," the spark his being gives out; his "Manshape," his inscape or essence; his "disseveral" being, his individual selfhood. All these "death blots black out"; all traces of his precious individuality "vastness blurs and time⎪beats level."

But the change of tone in the final section is more dramatic still. "Enough! the Resurrection" is, for Hopkins, a complete answer to Heraclitus. There is no balking of man's frailties and almost comic inadequacies: he is still "This Jack, joke, poor potsherd,⎪patch, matchwood," but Christ has promised his ultimate survival; he is therefore, too, "immortal diamond." The echo of the last short line makes certainty, for Hopkins, more certain.

"Epithalamion," Hopkins' unfinished ode for his youngest brother Everard's wedding in April 1888, deserves to be better known. It was only a collection of fragments that Bridges, with the greatest skill, put together; and there is little success in the faltering attempt at the end to make the scene, of the boys bathing, apply allegorically to marriage—or indeed in the rather absurd picture of the "listless stranger" (Hopkins himself?) undressing and taking off his boots. But there are marvelous lines that communicate to the full Hopkins' joy in re-creating such a remembered scene and his technical skills in doing so. Of the boys bathing:

With dare and with downdolphinry and bellbright bodies
    huddling out,
Are earthworld, airworld, waterworld thorough hurled,
    all by turn and turn about;

of the pool, surrounded by his favorite trees:

Fairyland; silk-beech, scrolled ash, packed sycamore, wild
    wychelm, hornbeam fretty overstood
By. Rafts and rafts of flake leaves light, dealt so, painted
    on the air, . . .

And of the strangely shaped rocks that we know, from his journal and some of his drawings, he was so fond of:

. . . a coffer, burly all of blocks
Built of chancequarrièd, selfquainèd, hoar-huskèd
    rocks
And the water warbles over into, filletèd⎪with glassy
    grassy quicksilvery shivès and shoots. . . .

---

[17] It is reproduced in R. K. R. Thornton, ed., *All My Eyes See: The Visual World of G. M. Hopkins* (Sunderland, 1975), p. 105.

However diverse the concern, of the three "plain" sonnets written in Ireland during his last year, they share certain new qualities of tone. They are, in form and meter, a return to tradition after the long, experimental sonnets they follow. Letters to Bridges, sending him earlier, finally rejected drafts of "St. Alphonsus Rodriguez," show how deliberate this return was; and one comment on it, however ironically framed, shows how desperate he was to be understood: "The sonnet (I say it snorting) aims at being understood." He called its sestet "both pregnant and exact"; the near-classical claim is justified by all three sonnets. They are also, all three, very personal, related intimately to his spiritual trials and, above all, to what he felt keenly—and, as the poems themselves show, wrongly—as poetic sterility. And to objectify that personal tone, to give it a new, quiet dignity, they have, each of them in different ways, a near-ironic self-awareness.[18]

"St. Alphonsus Rodriguez" was "written to order" in autumn 1888 in honor of a recently canonized sixteenth-century Jesuit hall porter in Majorca. The quiet irony comes from the clear identification of his own state in Dublin, apparently fruitless and inactive, with that of Alphonsus. The sonnet celebrates "the war within" as against the outward martyrdom of "exploit," the inner trials Alphonsus suffered:

> Those years and years . . . of world without event
> That in Majorca Alfonso watched the door.

The God "who, with trickling increment, / Veins violets," is the God he trusts, despite his sense of aridity, to bring him slowly but firmly to fulfillment.

In "Thou art indeed just, Lord" (17 March 1889), that trust is sorely tried. The epigraph, from Jer. 12: 1, "Why do the ways of the wicked prosper?" partly paraphrased in the sonnet's opening three lines, is bitter enough: Hopkins' tone, emphasized by the repeated "Sir," turns it into a dignified plea. The poignant picture of returning spring in the sestet— "fretty chervil," "fresh wind," and nesting birds— contrasted with his own sense of sterility reinforces the personal bitterness: the image of the straining eunuch comes in both a letter to Bridges and a private retreat-note of the same year. But the prayer of the final line,

> Mine, O thou lord of life, send my roots rain

in which the "Mine" must surely govern both "lord of life" and "roots," both reacknowledges God's power over him and at least posits a new intimacy between them. The cry of sterility has produced one of his most beautifully structured and tonally delicate sonnets.

Hopkins' last poem, "To R.B.," dated 22 April 1889, six weeks before his death, and sent to Bridges with his last letter to him, again laments his flagging inspiration. But bitterness is now muted. What we have instead is a confident control of the Conception and birth image in the octet and the perfect mirroring of the explanation of his "un-creativity" in the movement and sound of the last four lines:

> O then if in my lagging lines you miss
>
> The roll, the rise, the carol, the creation,
> My winter world, that scarcely breathes that bliss
> Now, yields you, with some sighs, our explanation.

## JOURNAL AND LETTERS

HOPKINS kept a journal from May 1866, his third year at Oxford, to February 1875, six months after he had begun studying theology at St. Beuno's College in North Wales. It has been of great use to biographers in giving details of outward events— and some more inward events—in Hopkins' life: the exact day, so far as he could record it, of his conversion; his feelings about the various Jesuit institutions in which he lived during his training; two occasions on which he broke down when hearing passages from the lives of Catholics read aloud; the first time he read Duns Scotus and its effect on him.

But its greatest interest is that it covers all but the last ten months of his seven years' "poetic silence," for it was Hopkins' journal that became the outlet for his remarkable powers of observation and for his hypersensitive response to the minutiae of nature. Its most vivid writing is therefore a splendid gloss on the mature poems that were to follow: the trees, skies, clouds, mountains, rushing water, rocks, flowers that were to become the subjects and images of so many of the poems are all recorded here. The journal is full of "wildness and wet," "the weeds and the wilderness." It is also full of unusual words—dialect,

---

[18]Paul L. Mariani, in his *Commentary on the Complete Poems*, stresses the irony (including "The Shepherd's Brow" in his discussion) and claims that "these last sonnets amount to a new direction in lyrical poetry" (pp. 299, 316).

archaic, sometimes coined—which he sought out, as in his poems, to express the inscapes that gave him such delight: "brindled and hatched," "knopped," "pelleted," "ruddled" (of clouds); "dappled with big laps and flowers-in-damask" (of the sun in rain); "They look like little gay jugs by shape when they walk, strutting and jod-jodding with their heads" (of pigeons), to cite only a few. It is in the journal that we have almost all the explicit examples of "inscape" and "instress," used for objects in nature, paintings, even buildings, from 1868 onward: "Query has not Giotto the instress of loveliness" (27 June 1868, on a visit to the National Gallery) is the first; "Swiss trees are, like English, well inscaped—in quains [coigns, wedge-shaped blocks]" (7 July 1868, in Switzerland), the second.

The comments on contemporary paintings in the journal are extremely interesting.[19] Like Ruskin, Hopkins made notes on the exhibitions he visited: during the nine years covered by the journal he went whenever he could to the main exhibitions of the Royal Academy, the National Gallery, and the Society of Painters in Water-Colours, as well as to two special loan exhibitions of National Portraits. On all these he made notes, sometimes only jottings, as well as commenting on them in letters. As we might expect, a great many paintings are judged in terms of their inscape (or instress) or lack of it. As an undergraduate, he had greatly admired the Pre-Raphaelites; the painters in whom he took the most delight or critical interest during these years were Sir John Everett Millais, Frederick Leighton, Frederick Walker, Sir Lawrence Alma-Tadema, and the sculptor Sir Hamo Thornycroft. In 1863, as an undergraduate, he had described Millais as "the greatest English painter, one of the greatest of the world." At the Royal Academy exhibition in May and June 1874 he is more critical, but still highly appreciative:

Millais—*Scotch Firs*; "*The silence that is in the lonely woods*"—No such thing, instress absent, firtrunks ungrouped, four or so pairing but not markedly, true bold realism but quite a casual install of woodland with casual heathertufts, broom with black beanpods and so on, but the master shewn in the slouch and toss-up of the firtreehead in near background, in the tufts of fir-needles, and in everything. So too *Winter Fuel:* "*Bare ruined choirs*" etc—almost no sorrow of autumn; a rawness (though I felt this less the second time), unvelvety papery colouring, especially in raw silver and purple birchstems, crude rusty cartwheels, aimless mess or minglemangle of cut underwood in under-your-nose foreground; aimlessly posed truthful child on shaft of cart; but then most masterly Turner-like outline of craggy hill, silver-streaked with birchtrees, which fielded in an equally masterly rust-coloured young oak, with strong curl and seizure in the dead leaves.
(journal, 23 May 1874)

Such a passage illustrates well the vigor, observation, and freshness of the best of Hopkins' journal-writing; it also shows the search for significant detail and for the unusual word in which to capture it that will play such a part in his mature poems.

Hopkins' letters fill three volumes, all edited by C. C. Abbott. There are letters to his undergraduate friends, including the famous letter to Alexander Baillie of 10 September 1864 on the "three kinds" of poetic language; much later letters to Baillie on possible early relations between Egypt and Greece; letters to his family, mainly to his mother; both sides of his correspondence with two fellow poets, Canon R. W. Dixon and Coventry Patmore; and letters to his most intimate friend, the future poet laureate, Robert Bridges. These three contemporary poets, however much they may have lacked understanding of Hopkins' own poetry—and particularly of his technical innovations—were his only regular readers in his lifetime: his "public," as he called Bridges. The letters to Dixon and Patmore are mainly interesting for the detailed comments on poetry utterly different from Hopkins' own: they show what a meticulous and sympathetic critic Hopkins was. And it is in his letters to Dixon that we find the explanation for Hopkins' seven years' poetic silence, when he became a Jesuit; the account of how "The Wreck of the Deutschland" came to be written; the clearest explanation of sprung rhythm; and his antipathy after the Jesuit *Month*'s rejection of both "The Wreck" and "The Loss of the Eurydice" toward further attempts at publication.

But it is the letters to Bridges that reveal most of Hopkins as a man and add considerably to his stature both as a poet and as a critic, perhaps almost as much as the letters of Keats, whom Hopkins so persistently admired, add to his stature. Dixon was twelve years older than Hopkins, Patmore twenty-two: in a Victorian ambience, that gap made the letters between them necessarily formal. Hopkins and Bridges were the same age, undergraduates at Oxford together, and by 1865 close friends. Despite

---
[19]They are the subject of a chapter by Norman White in *All My Eyes See: The Visual World of G. M. Hopkins*, pp. 89–106, that reproduces many of the paintings that particularly interested Hopkins.

Bridges' dislike of Roman Catholicism and his lack of sympathy with Hopkins' poetic experiments, they remained close friends to the end of Hopkins' life. For Hopkins, the friendship was vital. After he had become a Jesuit, they met only about a dozen times. Hence the reliance on letters: there are 172 (including a few cards) of Hopkins'; Bridges destroyed his own letters after his friend's death.

Hopkins' letters make wonderful reading. The best of them are vivid, candid, spontaneous, and often sharply comic. They show his capacity to laugh at himself, which we would hardly have expected from the poems. A great many of them, as we would expect, discuss in detail his own and Bridges' poems. Frequently under attack for "obscurities" and "eccentricities," Hopkins is often on the defensive: but the line-by-line explanations he consequently gave Bridges provide the best running commentary we have on his poetry (a commentary often used in earlier sections of this essay). It is to Bridges' questioning of individual effects that we owe some of Hopkins' best-known defenses of both his practice and poetic beliefs:

> Why do I employ sprung rhythm at all? Because it is the nearest to the rhythm of prose, that is the native and natural rhythm of speech, the least forced, the most rhetorical and emphatic of all possible rhythms. . . .
> (21 August 1877)

The above letter was written after Bridges had called the verse of "The Wreck of the Deutschland" "presumptious [sic] jugglery."

> To do the Eurydice any kind of justice you must not slovenly read it with the eyes but with your ears, as if the paper were declaiming it at you. For instance the line "she had come from a cruise training seamen" read without stress and declaim is mere Lloyd's Shipping Intelligence; properly read it is quite a different thing. Stress is the life of it.
> (21 May 1878)

He answered Bridges' charge of "queerness" against the first three lines of the sestet of "The Lantern out of Doors."

> . . . as air, melody, is what strikes me most of all in music and design in painting, so design, pattern or what I am in the habit of calling "inscape" is what I above all aim at in poetry. Now it is the virtue of design, pattern, or inscape to be distinctive and it is the vice of distinctiveness, to become queer. This vice I cannot have escaped.
> (15 February 1879)

> This leads me to say that a kind of touchstone of the highest or most living art is seriousness; not gravity but the being in earnest with your subject—reality.
> (1 June 1886)

In his criticism of Bridges' own poems, so unlike his own, Hopkins is generous, meticulous, exact in both praise and dispraise. He can be sharp when he wants to be:

> "Disillusion" does exist, as typhus exists and the Protestant religion. The same "brutes" say "disillusion" as say "standpoint" and "preventative" and "equally as well" and "to whomsoever shall ask."
> (26 January 1881)

And his affection never blurs what he sees as blemishes in character:

> You seem to want to be told over again that you have genius and are a poet and your verses beautiful. . . . You want perhaps to be told more in particular. I am not the best to tell you, being biassed by love, and yet I am too. . . . If I were not your friend I should wish to be the friend of the man who wrote your poems.
> (22 October 1879)

But there is a great deal more than criticism of each other's poetry in these letters. The two friends shared many other interests: the classics, Milton, music, language, prosody, contemporary writers and painters. Hopkins writes on all of them, sharply and individually. Above all, he can write of his feelings when he most needed a confidant in his last five difficult years in Dublin.

Bridges has been much criticized: for his delay of thirty years in publishing the poems (which he scrupulously kept); for the charges of obscurity and lapses of taste he leveled at some of them in his preface, when he finally edited them in 1918; and for his often tactlessly expressed dislike of Hopkins' Roman Catholicism. Almost all modern readers and critics, with one or two noted exceptions (recorded in the bibliography), are firmly on Hopkins' side. What these letters show, besides the remarkable distinctiveness of a far-ranging mind fully engaged in whatever it touched, is how essential Bridges was to Hopkins' emotional stability; and how important poetry, the other "vocation," remained to the dedicated Jesuit priest.

A final point must be made. Hopkins could never have been accepted as a major poet by his own contemporaries: his innovations were too extreme, his aims—to the temper of his time—too independent. Only comparatively few readers were ready for him in 1918: Bridges' edition of his poems (750 copies only) took twelve years to sell. He has had no obvious followers. But from the 1930's onward his impact has been immense in many countries of the world. His technical innovations in rhythm and language have been endlessly debated and almost universally admired. The challenge he offers appeals strongly to the twentieth-century reader. In this important regard, the thirty years' delay in publication of his poems has in fact worked in Hopkins' favor.

## SELECTED BIBLIOGRAPHY

I. BIBLIOGRAPHY. The Kenyon Critics, *Gerard Manley Hopkins: A Critical Symposium* (Norfolk, Conn., 1945; repr. New York, 1975), contains a bibliography; M. Charney, "A Bibliographical Study of Hopkins Criticism, 1918-1949," Thought, 25 (June 1950), 297-326; E. H. Cohen, *Works and Criticism of Gerard Manley Hopkins: A Comprehensive Bibliography* (Washington, D. C., 1969); G. Watson, ed., *The New Cambridge Bibliography of English Literature*, vol. III (Cambridge, 1969), entry for Hopkins by G. Storey; T. Dunne, *Gerard Manley Hopkins: A Comprehensive Bibliography* (Oxford, 1976). Note: The Hopkins Research Bulletin carried annual bibliographies, 1970-1976.

II. COLLECTED WORKS. R. Bridges, ed., *Poems of Gerard Manley Hopkins* (Oxford, 1918), with preface and notes; C. Williams, ed., *Poems of Gerard Manley Hopkins*, 2nd ed. (Oxford, 1930), with additional poems and a critical intro.; W. H. Gardner, ed., *Poems of Gerard Manley Hopkins*, 3rd ed. (Oxford, 1948), with notes and a biographical intro.; W. H. Gardner and N. H. MacKenzie, eds., *Poems of Gerard Manley Hopkins*, 4th ed. (Oxford, 1967; repr. 1970), with additional notes, a foreword on the revised text, and a new biographical and critical intro., the authoritative ed., incorporating all known poems and fragments.

III. LETTERS AND JOURNALS. C. C. Abbott, ed., *The Letters of Gerard Manley Hopkins to Robert Bridges* (Oxford, 1935; rev. ed., 1955); C. C. Abbott, ed., *The Correspondence of Gerard Manley Hopkins and R. W. Dixon* (Oxford, 1935; rev. ed. London, 1955); H. House, ed., *The Note-Books and Papers of Gerard Manley Hopkins* (Oxford, 1937), with notes and a preface by House, the first publication of Hopkins' early notebooks and journal, with a selection of devotional writings and drawings; C. C. Abbott, ed., *Further Letters of Gerard Manley Hopkins* (Oxford, 1938; enl. 2nd ed., 1956), contains letters to Hopkins' family and friends, and his correspondence with Coventry Patmore; H. House, ed., *The Journals and Papers of Gerard Manley Hopkins*, 2nd ed., rev. and enl., and completed by G. Storey (Oxford, 1959), contains Hopkins' full journal, music, and a large selection of his drawings; C. Devlin, S.J., ed., *The Sermons and Devotional Writings of Gerard Manley Hopkins* (Oxford, 1959), contains all of Hopkins' known spiritual writings with Fr. Devlin's intros.

IV. SEPARATE WORKS. "Winter with the Gulf Stream," in *Once a Week*, 8 (14 February 1863), p. 210; "Barnfloor and Winepress," in *Union Review*, 3 (1865), p. 579; A. H. Miles, ed., *The Poems and the Poetry of the Century* (London, 1893), vol. VIII contains eleven poems by Hopkins (including a partial text of "A Vision of the Mermaids"), with a short intro. by R. Bridges; H. C. Beeching, sel. and arr., *Lyra Sacra* (London, 1895), contains five poems by Hopkins; R. Bridges, ed., *The Spirit of Man* (London, 1916), contains six poems by Hopkins (including partial texts of "Spring and Fall" and "The Habit of Perfection" and stanza 1 of "The Wreck of the Deutschland," as amended by Bridges).

V. SELECTED WORKS. W. H. Gardner, ed., *Poems and Prose of Gerard Manley Hopkins* (London, 1953; rev. ed., 1969); J. Pick, ed., *A Hopkins Reader* (Oxford, 1953; rev. and enl. ed., Garden City, N. Y., 1966); J. Reeves, ed., *Selected Poems of Gerard Manley Hopkins* (London, 1953; ppbk. ed., 1967); G. Storey, ed., *Hopkins: Selections* (Oxford, 1967); N. H. MacKenzie, ed., *Poems by Gerard Manley Hopkins* (London, 1974), Folio Society.

VI. BIOGRAPHICAL AND CRITICAL STUDIES. K. Brégy, "Gerard Hopkins: An Epitaph and an Appreciation," in *Catholic World*, 88 (January 1909), pp. 433-447, one of the first critical essays written from a strong Catholic viewpoint; J. Keating, "Impressions of Father Gerard Hopkins, S.J.," in the Month, 114 (July, August, and September 1909), pp. 59-68, 151-160, and 246-258, early biographical essays; I. A. Richards, "Gerard Hopkins," in the Dial (New York), 81 (September 1926), pp. 195-203, highly influential early critical essay; W. Empson, *Seven Types of Ambiguity* (London, 1930), contains two important sections on Hopkins; G. F. Lahey, S.J., *Gerard Manley Hopkins* (Oxford, 1930), the first biography; F. R. Leavis, *New Bearings in English Poetry* (London, 1932; repr. 1950), contains an important and appreciative chapter on Hopkins; E. Phare, *The Poetry of Gerard Manley Hopkins* (Cambridge, 1933); B. Kelly, *The Mind and Poetry of Gerard Manley Hopkins* (Ditchling, 1935; repr. New York, 1971); *New Verse*, 14 (April, 1935), contains essays on Hopkins by A. Bremond, C. Devlin, L. W. Griffith, G. Grigson, H. House, L. MacNeice, and C. Madge.

D. Daiches, *Poetry and the Modern World* (Chicago,

1940), contains a section on Hopkins; J. Pick, *Gerard Manley Hopkins: Priest and Poet* (Oxford, 1942; rev. ppbk. ed., 1966); W. H. Gardner, *Gerard Manley Hopkins (1844-1889): A Study of Poetic Idiosyncrasy in Relation to Poetic Tradition*, 2 vols. (London, 1944 and 1949; rev. ed., Oxford, 1966), the fullest, if discursive, critical study of Hopkins as a poet; The Kenyon Critics, *Gerard Manley Hopkins: A Critical Symposium* (Norfolk, Conn., 1945; repr. New York, 1973), contains essays by M. McLuhan, H. Whitehall, J. Miles, A. Warren, R. Lowell, and A. Mizener; M. M. Holloway, *The Prosodic Theory of Gerard Manley Hopkins* (Washington, D. C., 1947); W. A. M. Peters, S.J., *Gerard Manley Hopkins: A Critical Essay Towards the Understanding of his Poetry* (Oxford, 1948; repr. 1970), stresses the effects on Hopkins' poetry of his theories of inscape; N. Weyand, S.J., and R. V. Schoder, S.J., eds., *Immortal Diamond* (London, 1949), contains essays by twelve Jesuit critics; F. R. Leavis, *The Common Pursuit* (London, 1952), contains an influential ch. on Hopkins; D. Davie, *Purity of Diction in English Verse* (London, 1952; 2nd ed., 1967), contains "Hopkins as a Decadent Critic," including some strictures on his language; G. H. Hartman, *The Unmediated Vision* (New Haven, Conn., 1954), contains an essay on Hopkins; L. L. Martz, *The Poetry of Meditation* (New Haven, Conn., 1954; rev. ed., 1962), shows Hopkins' debt to this tradition; G. Grigson, *Gerard Manley Hopkins* (London, 1955), for the British Council, Writers and their Work, no. 59 (rev. ed., 1962), a particularly perceptive study on Hopkins as a nature-poet; A. Heuser, *The Shaping Vision of Gerard Manley Hopkins* (Oxford, 1958).

D. A. Downes, *Gerard Manley Hopkins: A Study of His Ignatian Spirit* (London, 1960), stresses the sacramental nature of Hopkins' poetry; J.-G. Ritz, *Robert Bridges and Gerard Hopkins, 1863-1889: A Literary Friendship* (Oxford, 1960); R. Boyle, S.J., *Metaphor in Hopkins* (Chapel Hill, N. C., 1961), includes a detailed analysis of "The Windhover"; Y. Winters, *The Function of Criticism* (London, 1962), repr. his well-known attack on Hopkins from the *Hudson Review* (1949); T. K. Bender, *Gerard Manley Hopkins: The Classical Background and Critical Reputation of His Work* (Baltimore, 1966); G. H. Hartman, ed., *Hopkins: A Collection of Critical Essays* (Englewood Cliffs, N. J., 1966), includes essays by M. McLuhan, J. Wain, F. R. Leavis, F. O. Matthiessen, A. Warren, W. J. Ong, and others; F. N. Lees, *Gerard Manley Hopkins* (New York, 1966); E. W. Schneider, "The Wreck of the Deutschland: A New Reading," in *PMLA* (March 1966), 110–122; D. McChesney, *A Hopkins Commentary* (London, 1968), detailed commentary on the main poems; N. H. MacKenzie, *Hopkins* (Edinburgh, 1968), Writers and Critics series, an excellent general intro.; E. W. Schneider, *The Dragon in the Gate: Studies in the Poetry of G. M. Hopkins* (Berkeley, 1968); A. Thomas, S.J., *Hopkins the Jesuit: The Years of Training* (Oxford, 1969), based on Jesuit archives, contains a previously unpublished journal kept by Hopkins while he was a Jesuit novice.

P. L. Mariani, *A Commentary on the Complete Poems of Gerard Manley Hopkins* (Ithaca, N. Y., 1970); P. M. Ball, *The Science of Aspects: The Changing Role of Fact in the Work of Coleridge, Ruskin and Hopkins* (London, 1971); A. G. Sulloway, *Gerard Manley Hopkins and the Victorian Temper* (London, 1972); H. W. Fulweiler, *Letters from the Darkling Plain: Language and the Grounds of Knowledge in the Poetry of Arnold and Hopkins* (Columbia, Missouri, 1972); R. K. R. Thornton, *Gerard Manley Hopkins: The Poems* (London, 1973), a short, helpful intro. in the Studies in English Literature series; M. Bottrall, ed., *Gerard Manley Hopkins: Poems—A Casebook* (London, 1975), contains essays by H. Read, T. S. Eliot, H. House, G. Grigson, E. Jennings, P. A. Wolfe, and others; P. Milward, S.J. (text), and R. V. Schoder, S.J. (photographs), *Landscape and Inscape: Vision and Inspiration in Hopkins's Poetry* (London, 1975); R. K. R. Thornton, ed., *All My Eyes See: The Visual World of G. M. Hopkins* (Sunderland, 1975), examines the visual aspect of Hopkins' life, illus. by his own, his brothers', and his contemporaries' work; P. Milward, S.J., and R. V. Schoder, S.J., eds., *Readings of "The Wreck": Essays in Commemoration of the Centenary of G. M. Hopkins' "The Wreck of the Deutschland"* (Chicago, 1976); B. Bergonzi, *Gerard Manley Hopkins* (London, 1977), an up-to-date, succinct biography in the Masters of World Literature series; J. Milroy, *The Language of Gerard Manley Hopkins* (London, 1977); J. Robinson, *In Extremity: A Study of Gerard Manley Hopkins* (Cambridge, 1978); N. H. MacKenzie, *A Reader's Guide to G. M. Hopkins* (London, 1981). Note: Periodicals containing valuable regular contributions about Hopkins include *The Hopkins Research Bulletin*, 1970-1976, and *The Hopkins Quarterly*, 1974- , Guelph, Ontario. The Hopkins Society Annual Lectures, 1970- , are distributed to its members by the Society.

# A. E. HOUSMAN

(1859-1936)

## Ian Scott-Kilvert

### INTRODUCTION

"Cambridge has seen many strange sights," remarked Housman when he bade farewell to University College, London, to become Kennedy Professor of Latin. "So the University which once saw Wordsworth drunk and once saw Porson sober will see a better scholar than Wordsworth, and a better poet than Porson, betwixt and between." The two names at first sight might appear only to emphasize how impassable a gulf is fixed between the achievements of poet and scholar at the level of genius. There have been, of course, other scholarly poets in English literature. Milton, Gray, Landor, Arnold, FitzGerald, and Bridges were not only erudite men; their lives were molded by a certain precision of mind and detachment from worldly affairs that mark the scholar, and the character of their poetry reflects these qualities. But their learning was wide rather than deep, and their scholarship scarcely more than an adjunct to their poetic gifts.

Housman, on the other hand, aspired to the life of learning as early as a man can discover such an aptitude in himself. He is one of the very few English scholars to attain a European stature and the only one who is also a poet of consequence. If we can isolate a single element common to both fields, it is surely that Housman was a master of words of a very rare order. His scholarship is seldom concerned with general ideas or literary judgments: its special achievement is to concentrate his unrivaled knowledge of the classical tongues and his poetic sensibility upon the narrow front of textual criticism. His talk arrested the few who were privileged to hear it by the extraordinary aptness and penetration of the phrases he could command, when his interest overcame his reserve. His verse was deliberately limited to a few themes, which are among the most universal and timeworn in poetic currency; what strikes home immediately is the compelling power of the language, the quality of something inevitably and rightly said.

But Housman was also one of those who are born to mystify their fellows by their attitude to the human condition. In this sense he has been compared to Jonathan Swift and to T. E. Lawrence, as men gifted far above the common lot, who show themselves at once contemptuous of the admiration of others, eager for fame on their own terms, and strangely indifferent to the gift of life itself. Both in his scholarship and in his view of human relationships, Housman was a perfectionist, tormented by any falling short of his ideal, and it is the vehemence of this protest that distinctively tunes and tautens his poetry. In it the satirist, the man moved by horror and scorn and indignation, is constantly at the elbow of the love poet, and his suffering seems to spring not so much from any particular circumstance as from the very nature of human association. If Housman's life provokes a curiosity extending beyond his work, a curiosity that exceeds anything we want to know concerning most modern poets, it is not a matter of unearthing clues to his emotional experience. It is because his achievement, charged as it is with the sense of something missed and desired, raises questions that human nature is never tired of exploring, the question, for example, of what prevents such a man from rising to his full height, and of the use that men make of great gifts.

### EARLY LIFE

Alfred Edward Housman was born on 26 March 1859, the eldest of seven children, near Bromsgrove in Worcestershire, where his father practiced as an attorney. His mother's family was connected with the Drakes of Devon, and the Drakes's motto, *Aquila non capit muscas* (The eagle does not catch flies), could hardly have been better chosen to epitomize Housman's attitude to the world. Shropshire was never his home, nor did he at any period spend much time there. But the Shropshire hills had formed the western horizon of his childhood, and they imprinted themselves upon his memory as an imaginary world beyond the setting sun and the frontiers of everyday life. For the very reason that he did not know the county too intimately, it could later supply him with a rustic mythology and the music of place names, which served to evoke both memory and fantasy.

Housman was educated at Bromsgrove School and won a scholarship to St. John's College, Oxford. Here his true bent began to show itself, though at first with disastrous results. He was already devoted to exact and specialized study, and he could not bring himself to absorb the Greats curriculum,[1] with its widely spread interests.

One lecture from the celebrated Benjamin Jowett was enough to make him abandon the course in disgust at the professor's disregard for minutiae. Having obtained a first-class grade in the preliminary examination for Litterae Humaniores (Moderations), he may well have found the temptation irresistible to anticipate his degree and embark upon the work of a qualified scholar. At any rate when he sat for his finals his preparations proved quite inadequate, he could return only scrappy answers to some of the papers, and the examiners had no choice but to exclude him from an honors degree.

Housman's debacle at Oxford was a crucial episode in his career and resulted in the enforced relegation of his cherished classical studies to his spare time and an exile of eleven years before he could regain a position in academic life. It also offers some important clues to the austere personality he later developed, that of a man early disillusioned with the human lot, a controversialist who gave no quarter, a figure reserved and sardonic even to his closest friends, yet also capable of unexpected impulses of generosity and compassion.

Housman's biographer George L. Watson has argued persuasively that this academic disaster and its aftermath coincided and was linked with other critical stresses that had been developing for some time. Housman had been devoted to his mother, who had died on his twelfth birthday, and had become acutely conscious of the increasing incapacity of his father (who had failed in his chosen profession of attorney) to play his part as head of the family, and hence of his own responsibilities as the eldest of seven children. The crisis in his personal life centered on his fellow undergraduate and lifelong friend, Moses Jackson. This was a friendship of opposites, Jackson being a strongly extravert "all-rounder," who rowed for Oxford and took a first-class degree in science; he was a frank and steadfast friend, but one incapable of sharing the kind of emotional intimacy that the poet's nature sought. The differences that separated them are aptly summed up in these posthumously published verses:

> Because I liked you better
> Than suits a man to say,
> It irked you, and I promised
> To throw the thought away.
> (*More Poems*, XXXI)

Whether this frustrated attachment contributed to the disastrous examination result can only be a matter for conjecture. But certainly Housman must have seen clearly the distress that his failure had brought upon his stricken family, and from this moment the desire to retrieve it became a consuming ambition.

After setting aside such money as he could spare for his family, Housman decided to leave home, take the civil service examination, and settle in London. Through the help of Jackson, with whom he now felt able to resume his friendship on a more pragmatic basis, he obtained a post in the patent office and moved into rooms he shared with Jackson and the latter's younger brother, Adalbert. The patent office was not an exacting employer, and Housman's main energies could now be devoted to his classical reading at the British Museum, where he proceeded to lay the foundations of his scholarship. Thus in the years when most men form their most lasting ties, his naturally reserved and solitary disposition was set in a still more inhibiting mold. According to his closest friends, his coldness of manner was imposed upon a nature that secretly craved affection, but the natural consequence was to secure his independence rather than his happiness.

Gradually his classical work began to bear fruit and his contributions to learned journals to attract attention. Finally the Chair of Latin at University College, London, fell vacant. Housman applied and was now able to support his candidature with seventeen testimonials from British, American, and German scholars. He did not fail to include the phrase, "In 1881 I failed to obtain Honours in the final

---

[1] The honors school of Litterae Humaniores, which involved the study of Greek and Roman literature, history, and philosophy.

School of Litterae Humaniores." Fortunately, the electors were unmoved, and in 1892 he took up the professorship he was to hold for nineteen years until his election to the Kennedy Chair of Latin at Cambridge.

### CLASSICAL SCHOLARSHIP

HOUSMAN's appointment to Cambridge gave him the leisure and the higher standard of teaching that his gifts required for their full development. During these years he became recognized as the most eminent Latinist of the century and his name was ranked with Richard Porson's as the greatest of English scholars after Richard Bentley. Still, the nature of Housman's achievement is sufficiently remote from the interests of the general reader to require some explanation.

In the present age of mass education the public has come to expect that the distinguished scholar should, to some extent, act as a popularizer in his own field. He should not, it is held, address himself exclusively to his fellow experts. He should also communicate something of his enjoyment of his studies or pass judgment on them as literature, or relate them to the spirit or the preoccupations of his own times. The work of Gilbert Murray or C. M. Bowra might be taken as representative of this kind of scholarship. Housman's genius was of a different order. It belongs to the older, more austere tradition of scholarship, where it is assumed that the reader can supply his own appreciation and needs only to be furnished with the best possible text. The scholar, for his part, never ventures an aesthetic or moral judgment and limits himself strictly to the role of editor and to the perennial task of detecting and removing errors in the surviving manuscripts. Ideally, this work can absorb an almost unlimited measure of intellectual power, linguistic skill, and poetic sensibility: how far the results may justify the expense of so much talent is another question.

Housman upheld this point of view in his introductory lecture delivered to the combined faculties of University College in 1892. It is an eloquent address, warmer in sentiment, less waspish than his later prose, but its conclusions will fall strangely upon modern ears. The study of the arts and the sciences, he tells us, is often defended by unreal arguments. Science is not necessarily the most serviceable kind of knowledge and its true aim is not to be judged by utilitarian standards. On the other hand, the humanities are praised for their power to transform our inner natures. But in practice only a tiny fraction of the human race can profit from them and they can do so "without that minute and accurate study of the classical tongues which affords Latin professors their only excuse for existence." The only genuine justification for any of these studies, he concludes, is that in their different ways they satisfy man's desire for knowledge, and this innate human appetite is part of man's duty to himself.

The reader is left to conclude that any department of knowledge is of equal value with any other. Housman evidently assumes that the classics will continue to be read, but he does not find it necessary to explain how a work becomes or remains a classic, or why, if a severe philological discipline is the sole raison d'être for professors, it would not be equally valuable for them to study the poetry of the Mayas or the Tibetans.

This, at any rate, was the narrow frame from which Housman's own work never departed. It is true, of course, that the textual expert is often ill-equipped for making literary judgments and, if a warning had been necessary, Housman always had before him the fearful precedent of Bentley's edition of *Paradise Lost* (1732).[2] But in fact Housman was keenly aware of the frontier between textual and appreciative criticism, and the intellectual pride that appears so consistently throughout his classical writings made him a relentless judge of his performance as a literary critic. He wrote explicitly on this point when he declined an invitation to deliver the Clark Lectures on English literature:

I do regard myself as a connoisseur: I think I can tell good from bad in literature. But literary criticism, referring opinions to principles and setting them forth so as to command assent, is a high and rare accomplishment and quite beyond me.... And not only have I no talent for producing the genuine article, but no taste or inclination for producing a substitute....

Since he thus disqualified himself from discussing poetry, his classical writings are of distinctly

---

[2]Bentley put forward the idea that Milton had employed both an amanuensis and an editor, who were held to be responsible for the clerical errors, alterations, and interpolations that Bentley professed to have found in the text.

specialized interest. The most important are the prefaces to his editions of Juvenal, Lucan, and Manilius, in which he sets out his editorial principles; a series of articles on the manuscripts of Propertius; and a paper given in 1921 to the Classical Association and ironically entitled "The Application of Thought to Textual Criticism." Besides these, he published well over a hundred articles in learned journals, notably on the Greek tragedians and on Propertius, Horace, Ovid, and Martial. Most of these papers consist of discussions of isolated textual problems. They are fragmentary reading in themselves, but to read even a few consecutively is a revelation of the intellectual discipline through which Housman developed his gifts. They display the immense range of his knowledge of the classical tongues and of the history of words, his vigilance in detecting corruption, his dexterity and insight in proposing remedies, and, above all, his unrivaled accuracy and patience, which can only have been acquired by a supreme effort of control over a brain so swift in reaching its conclusions.

While he was at the patent office, Housman published as much on Greek as on Latin poetry; after his appointment to University College he virtually ceased to write on Greek. His explanation was that he found he "could not attain to excellence in both" languages. This definition of excellence was all his own, for he certainly possessed more Greek than many professed Hellenists. What he demanded, as the bare essentials, was a complete mastery of grammar and of metrical and verbal usage, a comprehensive knowledge of manuscript history, and, beyond this, the capacity to absorb, year after year, a mass of minute detail bearing directly or indirectly on the chosen field. Judged by these standards, and remembering the far greater complexity of the Greek language and its literature, it becomes easier to understand his decision; and it must be remembered that for Housman's particular talents Latin poetry offered the more tempting prospects. For his choice of the authors he was to edit was influenced more by the ambition to build himself a monument in scholarship than by his personal literary taste.

Housman's approach to editorial problems is sketched in the paper on textual criticism already mentioned, probably the most brilliant outline of the subject that has yet been written in English. Textual criticism, he insists, is by no means a professional mystery, as it is sometimes represented, but a matter of reason and common sense. But he is equally emphatic that it is not an exact science, and nothing angered him more than the so-called scientific approach to manuscript problems, which attempted to solve by a system of rules difficulties that required an independent and flexible judgment:

A textual critic . . . is not at all like Newton investigating the motions of the planets: he is much more like a dog hunting for fleas. If a dog hunted for fleas on mathematical principles, basing his researches on statistics of area and population, he would never catch a flea except by accident. They require to be treated as individuals; and every problem which presents itself to the textual critic must be regarded as possibly unique.
("On the Application of Thought to Textual Criticism," *Selected Prose*, pp. 132–133)

The simile is characteristic. Housman was fond of testing academic generalizations by translating them into some homely and sensuous analogy, because, as he put it, the human senses have had a much longer history than the human intellect and are far less easy to deceive. Another target he singled out was the then fashionable dogma of the supreme authority of the oldest manuscript. According to this theory, the editor, having selected the earliest, is then bound to defend all its readings, unless they are hopelessly corrupt. Housman attacked it unmercifully, and he was among the first to understand, obvious though the truth may seem today, that such a doctrine was bound to become the standby of the laziest and least competent scholars.

When we come to his own editions, many lovers of the classics have found it inexplicable that a man who cared so passionately for poetry could choose for the main object of his life's work an author so little rewarding as Manilius. Lucan, we are told, was selected for him, while Juvenal is a poet entirely worthy of his gifts, whose influence on the tone of Housman's own poetry has perhaps never been fully appreciated. But Manilius, who composed a treatise on astronomy and astrology in the first century A.D., is an author whose poetic merit is less than second-rate and whose scientific value is almost nonexistent, who presents in fact the minimum of interest from any point of view but the professional scholar's. On the other hand, as Andrew Gow tells us, Housman saw in Manilius' text a better prospect "of approaching finality in the solution of the problems presented." He was an ambitious scholar, and it was no coincidence that he chose a poet previously edited by Julius Caesar Scaliger, whose Manilian commentary had been one of the most dazzling achievements of Renaissance scholarship, and by Bentley, the greatest of Housman's predecessors in England. From this point of view, he was taking up a challenge that could extend his powers to the full. This will not prevent many readers from regarding his choice as wayward and eccentric, especially since it involved the sacrifice of a commentary on Propertius, on whose text Housman had done much preliminary work and for whose poetry he cared far more.

Still, it would be wrong to suppose that Housman's poetic sensibility was shut out from his classical work. He possessed a talent excessively rare among scholars, an instinctive familiarity with the way in which poets handle words, and he succeeded in extending this so as to think poetically in the dead languages. In this way he was able to restore or to purify many lines of poetry and to perceive the deeper meaning of phrases obscured for centuries by the errors of scribes and scholiasts. Such a gift, controlled as Housman controlled it, is surely the quality that distinguishes the great from the merely competent textual critic and that guided Housman to many of his most brilliant emendations. Edmund Wilson has noted as a typical example a passage from Juvenal, where in place of the generally accepted reading, *Perditus ac vilis sacci mercator olentis* (The reckless merchant [on a stormy voyage] whose life is cheap [to himself], with his odorous bag of saffron), whose sense, if any, is obscure and labored, Housman by a small change suggests an immediately striking satirical image: *Perditus ac similis sacci mercator olentis* (The reckless merchant . . . turns as yellow as his odorous bag of saffron).

This power of responding to and recreating classical poetry found another outlet in his rare translations. Latin verse, which served as so admired a model to the Augustans, had seldom been translated by the romantics or by their Victorian successors; nor, with the exception of Landor, had it notably influenced their style. Housman's best translation is of the seventh ode of Horace's fourth book, in which his own idiom and diction, conspicuously Saxon though they are, seem perfectly matched to the original:

> The snows are fled away, leaves on the shaws
>   And grasses in the mead renew their birth,
> The river to the river-bed withdraws,
>   And altered is the fashion of the earth. . . .
>
> But oh, whate'er the sky-led seasons mar,
>   Moon upon moon rebuilds it with her beams:
> Come *we* where Tullus and where Ancus are,
>   And good Aeneas, we are dust and dreams. . . .
>         (*More Poems*, V, "Diffugere Nives")

Housman has preserved the peculiarly Roman gift for expressing poetic commonplaces in monumental style, but his verses, while remarkably exact in their rendering, evoke a different kind of response, biblical in their vocabulary and romantic in the melody of their rhymed quatrains. The Latin speaks with a poignancy unusual in Horace, and Housman's language carries an emotional tension rarely achieved in Augustan translations.

Housman's eminence is inseparable from the moral passion that infused his studies. He possessed to a very high degree the scholar's willingness to sacrifice the present to the future; nothing could have proved this more forcibly than his career at Oxford. He put so much more into scholarship than is commonly understood by the term, making it an ideal that absorbed many of the loyalties and emotions that most men reserve for the world outside. "The faintest of human passions," he once wrote, "is the love of truth": for himself he could genuinely claim the contrary.

In consequence, his high ideal left little room for moderation. For several generations past, the elucidation of the classics had been treated as a subject deserving a calm, urbane, and tolerant approach. Housman did not see the matter in this light. He considered accuracy not a virtue but a duty. He regarded careless or lazy work as an insufferable affront to the dignity of learning, and he could seldom restrain his anger at what seemed to him the organized sloth and complacency of average scholarship. When an editor assigned to Propertius a metrically faulty line, he commented: "This is the mood in which Tereus ravished Philomela: concupiscence concentrated on its object and indifferent to all beside." And he kept a notebook in which shafts of this kind were stored up to be launched at the first deserving recipient. The layman coming fresh to his writings might feel that he was back in the age of pamphleteering, aptly described by Lytton Strachey, when "erudition was gigantic, controversies frenzied, careers punctuated by brutal triumphs, wild temerities and dreadful mortifications."

Housman was as certain of the importance of his work as he was of the rightness of his opinions, and he writes of the operations of scholars in the language of a historian surveying a line of princes:

> [Palmer's] talent, like that of Heinsius, resided in felicity of instinct: it did not proceed, like Madvig's, from the perfection of intellectual power. Now the class which includes Heinsius includes also Gilbert Wakefield; and Palmer's rank in the class is nearer to Wakefield than to Heinsius. His inspiration was fitful, and when it failed him he lacked the mental force and rightness which should have filled its place. His was a nimble but not a steady wit: it could ill sustain the labour of severe and continuous thinking; so he habitually shunned that labour.... He had much natural elegance of taste, but it was often nullified by caprice and wilfulness, so that hardly Merkel himself has proposed uncouther emendations....
> ("Palmer's 'Heroides' of Ovid," *Selected Prose*, p. 91)

Though he refrains from passing judgment on the classical poets, he likes to sit as a Rhadamanthus of the world of learning, issuing elaborately qualified verdicts upon dead or living scholars:

> Say what you will, he [Jacob] has contributed to the *Astronomica* . . . a body of corrections not only considerable in number but often of the most arresting ingenuity and penetration. Yet the virtues of his work are quenched and smothered by the multitude and monstrosity of his vices.... Not only had Jacob no sense for grammar, no sense for coherency, no sense for sense, but being himself possessed by a passion for the clumsy and the hispid he imputed this disgusting taste to all the authors whom he edited; and Manilius, the one Latin poet who excels even Ovid in verbal point and smartness, is accordingly constrained to write the sort of poetry which might have been composed by Nebuchadnezzar when he was driven from men and did eat grass as oxen.
> ("Prefaces," Manilius I, *Selected Prose*, p. 33)

Housman's supremacy within the limits he set for himself is beyond dispute. The depth of his learning and his capacity to focus it upon minute details, the force of his intellect and the scrupulous honesty with which he applied it (a virtue for which the great Bentley was not conspicuous)—these qualities place him in the front rank of scholars.

Concerning the ultimate value of his approach to the classics, there is less agreement. Scholarship, after all, is not an end in itself; it presupposes an original literature worth preserving, and its tasks may vary greatly from one age to another. A scholar such as Petrarch seeks above all to make discoveries, to stimulate and to fertilize, and at such a moment in history it may be more valuable to kindle enthusiasm than to enforce accuracy. In Bentley's day, the first requirement was a sustained and methodical criticism, to set in order the immense classical inheritance brought to light by the three preceding centuries. In our own age, we are faced with an ominous breakdown in communication between the expert and the layman. The latter is apt to feel that the classics have no relevance for the contemporary world, while the former disdains to make that relevance felt. In such times it is arguable that the greatest need is for scholars to check the fragmentation of our culture, to concentrate upon interpretation and skilled translation as much as on specialized research. Yet to assert this, to speak of "what the age demands," is to speak of lesser men. One might argue that had Housman lived in an earlier century his talents would have produced a richer harvest. But it is idle to regret that a scholar of his caliber, who set himself the highest standards and satisfied them, did not develop differently. At any rate, in the preface to his last volume of Manilius, published very near the end of his life, the question is faced in as uncompromising a fashion as we might expect: "Perhaps there will be no long posterity for learning: but the reader whose good opinion I desire and have done my utmost to secure is the next Bentley or Scaliger who may chance to occupy himself with Manilius."

## FAME AND HONORS

It would be misleading to leave the impression that Housman spent his life in unrelieved seclusion. His early years in London were no doubt a painful and lonely experience. But later his growing fame and the duties of academic life imposed more social demands and enriched his circle of acquaintance. At University College he showed himself a formidable debater and impromptu speaker. He wrote light verse, which includes his "Fragment of a Greek Tragedy"—a brilliant parody of the Greek tragic idiom that is unique in English—and a number of excellent nonsense rhymes. Although he was notoriously averse to small talk, he took pleasure in conversation that challenged his interests, and at Cambridge he was at his best in the intimate society of a dining club. He became a renowned connoisseur of wine and his letters speak of travels in Italy, Turkey, and France.

It was in fact the contrast between all that life appeared to offer him, including fame, security, and congenial work, and what he was prepared to make of its rewards that perplexed all who knew him. With scarcely any exceptions Housman kept his friends at arm's length, and his distrust of his fellow men's judgment was not relaxed even when they desired to honor him. "You should be welcome to praise me if you did not praise one another," he once wrote, and this was evidently the motive that inclined him to refuse the doctorates and degrees that many universities offered him. The final honor he declined was the Order of Merit, on the ground that it was not always given to those who deserved it, and in particular that it was already held by an author for whose work Housman felt an extreme distaste. In his letter to the king's secretary, Housman, after respectfully declining the proposed award, went on to quote the words of Admiral William Cornwallis on a similar occasion: "I am, unhappily, of a turn of mind that would make my receiving that honour the most unpleasant thing imaginable."

## POETRY AND CRITICISM

WHEN *A Shropshire Lad* first appeared in 1896, it had been rejected by several publishers, among them Macmillan on the advice of John Morley, and it was finally issued at the poet's own expense. At first it was slow to attract attention, but after the Boer War, and indeed for the first quarter of the present century, its reputation grew immensely. It appealed to the sophisticated no less than to a far larger public, for whom the greater part of contemporary verse was a closed book. By the time that *Last Poems* was published in 1922, Housman probably commanded, with the exception of Rudyard Kipling, a wider audience than any contemporary poet in our language. Indeed, on the strength of *A Shropshire Lad* alone, Sir Walter Alexander Raleigh had already referred to him as the greatest living English poet.

Such success did not take Housman unawares, but neither did it alter a mode of life in which his poetry remained a submerged activity. He scarcely ever published in periodicals, and he consistently refused to allow *A Shropshire Lad* to appear in anthologies. He neither wrote about the poetry of others nor expounded his own creative processes, and even in his correspondence, to judge by what his brother has published, poetry is scarcely ever seriously discussed. His one public pronouncement on these subjects, *The Name and Nature of Poetry* (1933), was delivered almost at the end of his life, and then not without severe misgiving before and self-reproach after the event.

Because of this reticence it was generally believed that he had suppressed or destroyed a large number of poems, and it is not surprising that the legend should have grown up of the great scholar sternly disciplining his lyrical gifts and rejecting all but the most perfectly finished products of his muse. In reality, it seems clear that the creative impulse visited him only at rare intervals, and now that all his verses are in print, we may be equally surprised at the inferiority of some of the poems he published and the excellence of others he held back.

During his lifetime, Housman's poetic career presented as much of an enigma as his personal history, and his own actions served to deepen the mystery. The quality of the verse that he consented to publish was unusually consistent both in its merits and its limitations, so that until his unpublished poems were issued posthumously, it was extremely difficult to trace any pattern of development in his work.

The poet himself stated that most of *A Shropshire Lad* was composed during a period "of continuous excitement in the early months of 1895," and that the whole book had been finished at full stretch over eighteen months. Recently, however, the remains of Housman's verse notebooks have been completely and minutely scrutinized by American scholars, and their findings tell a different story. According to his friend Dr. Percy Withers, Housman first set himself seriously to write poetry soon after he had settled in London, his preparation consisting less in practicing versification than in an intensive study of his chosen models, mainly the Border Ballads, the songs of Shakespeare, and the lyrics of Heinrich Heine. For four or five years progress was painfully slow, but the notebooks suggest that his inspiration had begun to move freely as far back as 1890. The first five months of 1895 thus represent the climax of his creative power during which twenty-three of the sixty-three *Shropshire Lad* lyrics were drafted or finished; 1895, in fact, was his *annus mirabilis*, for in its later months were written not only the remaining third of *A Shropshire Lad* but drafts of some half-dozen pieces which later appear in *Last Poems*, and a still larger number good enough to be preserved for the posthumous *More Poems* (1936). There followed a prolonged aftermath of six years, during which fewer and fewer new poems were begun, and after 1902 the creative flow dwindled to a trickle until, apparently under the excitement of preparing *Last Poems*, it returned briefly in 1922.

Grant Richards, Housman's publisher after 1897, quoted him as saying early in their association, "I am not a poet by trade. I am a professor of Latin." Behind this statement one may read something other than modesty—namely, a disinclination to commit himself to the spiritual and material hazards of a career dedicated to poetry. His creative period had flung him, we are told, into an intense emotional disturbance whose recurrence he dreaded, and after it he may well have felt that poetry for him must be an accomplishment, not a vocation, a gift to be used as circumstances might allow, not a continually dominating presence with power to shape his life according to the changing stresses of experience.

The chronology of his poetry, so far as it can be established, confirms the impression that his style was formed early and that his verses at sixty or later display almost exactly the same qualities, marvelously unimpaired and yet undeveloped, as those he wrote as a young man. There are differences in tone and in his attitude to his material, but it is difficult to fasten upon any single composition as a landmark in his development, particularly since a number of the poems that appeared after *A Shropshire Lad* contain revisions carried out at widely separate periods. Reading the posthumously published poems, one often comes upon identical epithets or turns of phrase echoed with equally striking effects in a different context, and in this sense his poetry resembles a single perpetual "work in progress."

At present Housman's verse is passing through a necessary critical revaluation; 1922 saw the appearance both of *Last Poems* and of *The Waste Land*, and the year might serve, crudely, to mark an end and a beginning in English poetry, with Housman's work standing on the far side of the rift in poetic idiom that the modern movement has produced. For the very reason that Housman presents none of the difficulties of later poets, his work has suffered from uncritical admiration and all too frequent imitation, and when a poetic revolution takes place, the penalty for contemporary popularity of this kind is apt to be overpaid.

Housman began to write at a time when the romantic tradition, as inherited by the major Victorian poets, had all but exhausted its resources, and he felt strongly how stale the current poetic jargon had become in the hands of writers such as Andrew Lang and Arthur O'Shaughnessy.[3] Yet in the light of what was to come, his own approach might be called backward looking. He did not feel the need for fresh patterns of verbal association nor for changes in poetic structure: in later life he never became sympathetic to experiments in free verse nor to the abandonment of rhyme, and he regarded Bridges's praise of Hopkins' poetry, cautious though that was, as no more than a personal foible.

Today it is easier to recognize the traces in his work of the spirit of the 1890's; in particular the fastidiousness of expression—was there ever a period in which men trimmed and pared their writing so assiduously?—the choice of minor poetic forms and the note of weary disillusionment, the view of life as something to be endured:

> When shall this slough of sense be cast,
> This dust of thoughts be laid at last,
> The man of flesh and soul be slain
> And the man of bone remain?
> ("The Immortal Part,"
> *A Shropshire Lad*, XLIII)

And it is noticeable that the five-line rhyming stanza of "Bredon Hill" and other lyrics was a favorite meter of Ernest Dowson's.

Housman himself, however, remained severely aloof from the poetic coteries that flourished in London at this time. He was older than Lionel Johnson, Dowson, and most of the members of the Rhymers' Club, and in any case the leanings of this group toward ritualism combined with a Bohemian life on the Parisian model must have been thoroughly antipathetic to his temperament. Many years afterward, replying to an editor who sought permission to include him in an anthology of the period, Housman wrote that it would be as technically correct and as essentially inappropriate to reprint his poems in such a collection as to include Lot in a book on the cities of the plain.

Certainly what most impressed the early readers of *A Shropshire Lad* was its *unlikeness* to the prevailing idiom. Here apparently was a poet who could voice the familiar passions of humanity with a strange, death-dealing sweetness in sharp contrast to the current urban poetry of languor and exotic sensibility. The contrast is striking enough, yet the

---

[3]See *The Name and Nature of Poetry* (London, 1933), p. 23.

simplicity is deceptive. The primitive ballad meters, which Housman revived, are employed for a poetry not of action but of introspection. The diction is natural at some moments, artificial at others, a curious yet assured blend of the archaic and the colloquial. In Housman's hands these were genuine achievements, but they were also poetic ventures that none but he could execute—a mile farther, says William Butler Yeats of *A Shropshire Lad*, and all had been marsh.

In his early style there are echoes of the shorter poems of Bridges and of the martial measures of Kipling and William Ernest Henley, and an affinity, which cannot have been conscious, to the rustic lyrics of Thomas Hardy. Housman's poem "The Sage to the Young Man" is remarkably reminiscent of Bridges's "O Youth whose hope is high," but one has only to see the two side by side to feel the far stronger impact of the former. It is this power to communicate direct and personal emotion, through a language that lodges instantly in the brain, that distinguishes Housman from all the poets of this period.

The comparison with Hardy is more illuminating. Housman also, it might appear, sought his inspiration in a part of England that still pursued the traditions of country life, uncontaminated by the Industrial Revolution. Like Hardy, too, he had been led by the scientific materialism of the age to form a deeply pessimistic view of human destiny, judging it to be ruled by forces absolutely indifferent to moral values. But Housman's gift for exquisite description of nature has obscured the difference between his poetry and that of a genuinely rural writer such as Hardy or John Clare. Housman was not a countryman, nor did he enjoy talking or mingling with rustics. It is easily forgotten that he spent the years between twenty-three and fifty-two almost continuously in London, and that the scenes of *A Shropshire Lad* were the product of his inward eye as he walked on Hampstead Heath. His friends have noted that he was indifferent to country landscape, though he was peculiarly sensitive to the shape and characteristics of trees. When he writes of them in a poem such as "The orchards half the way," the force and beauty of his language serve not so much to describe as to intensify them as dramatic symbols of a particular state of emotion.

Thus, at first glance, *A Shropshire Lad* is written in the character of a country youth uprooted from his surroundings and exiled to a hostile metropolis where he clings to his memories of a simpler life. But it is soon clear that "Shropshire" is not a native heath with a solid existence such as Hardy's Wessex. It is rather a personification of the writer's memories, dreams, and affections. In order to make his emotions articulate, Housman apparently needed an imaginary setting and a central character who could at once be himself and not himself.

This need to construct a personal world of the imagination, perhaps as a defense against the overwhelming inhumanity of city life, seems to have been shared by other poets of the same period. The gaslit and theatrical Bohemia of Arthur Symons and Dowson, the engine room of Kipling, the world of childhood and the supernatural of Walter de la Mare are sufficiently diverse instances of the same process. Housman found his mythology in the local tragedies of rustic life, the ballads of the country youths whose sweethearts die young or desert them, who are hanged in Shrewsbury jail for crimes of passion, or who commit suicide or take the queen's shilling[4] to march away and fall on fields forgotten. In such episodes he could express his indignation at the injustice of human destiny, and he did so by infusing into the pastoral convention a new note of irony. Pastoral poetry traditionally makes its appeal by invoking a countryside where youth seems eternal, and the calm and simplicity of nature are praised by contrast with the feverish corruption of a great capital. Housman's Shropshire is a blighted Arcadia, in which the poet is constantly reminded of the limitations of mortality. Here the beauty of the countryside only intensifies the pain of his experience, since Nature, he feels, is utterly indifferent to the emotions she arouses in him. Love, which alone might redeem our lives, does no more than beguile us with hope; then it proves to be unrequited or is cut short by a harsh fate:

> His folly has not fellow
> Beneath the blue of day
> That gives to man or woman
> His heart and soul away.
> (XIV)

The brave and the true gain nothing from their virtue, and indeed they are best out of a world that will never reward their qualities:

---

[4] A recruit was paid the bounty of one shilling when he signed on. This practice continued until 1879.

> Be still, be still, my soul; it is but for a season:
> Let us endure an hour and see injustice done.
>     (LVIII)

Apart from this commerce with the outer world, Shropshire represents a more inward experience. The Shropshire hills, as we have seen, formed the western boundary of Housman's childhood, and the memory of them suggests to him a lost state of innocence and happiness. At its simplest, this feeling is communicated in the poems that lament his separation from the countryside:

> Oh tarnish late on Wenlock Edge,
>     Gold that I never see;
> Lie long, high snowdrifts in the hedge
>     That will not shower on me.
>     (XXXIX)

It is pursued less overtly in a group of poems that seem to gather up the various themes of the book and to form its keystone; Housman lights upon the exact metaphor for this state of mind when he discovers, with a sharp thrust of irony, that the very recollection of the countryside serves no longer to invigorate but only to torment:

> Into my heart an air that kills
>     From yon far country blows;
> What are those blue remembered hills,
>     What spires, what farms are those?
>
> That is the land of lost content,
>     I see it shining plain,
> The happy highways where I went
>     And cannot come again.
>     (XL)

*Last Poems* represents the gleanings of several harvests. Most of its poems date from the *Shropshire Lad* period and its immediate aftermath, while a few others are associated with the Edwardian decade and World War I. In 1920 Housman decided to set in order the work of twenty-five years, and the effort of revising and completing his drafts set him writing again. Some of these late lyrics—"Eight o'clock," for example—are an astonishing echo of his youthful style; others, such as "Tell me not here, it needs not saying," inspired by his declared farewell to poetry, touch a note of elegiac tenderness richer than anything he had written before. Compared to *A Shropshire Lad*, the book appears uneven in quality; it contains some of Housman's tritest pieces, such as "Grenadier" or "Lancer," and it leaves an impression of less sustained power. Yet the style is more completely Housman's own, and the language at its best still more inevitable, so that the reader at times is scarcely conscious of description, so completely are the words identified with the mood and scene they create:

> When the eye of day is shut,
>     And the stars deny their beams,
> And about the forest hut
>     Blows the roaring wood of dreams,
>
> From deep clay, from desert rock,
>     From the sunk sands of the main,
> Come not at my door to knock,
>     Hearts that loved me not again.
>     (XXXIII)

Here also one meets for the first time several poems on astronomical subjects. Such imagery intensified Housman's sense of the power and indifference of the surrounding universe and of man's insignificance upon his turning planet. In "Revolution" the poet watches the alternations of day and night with the eye of a celestial mechanic:

> See, in mid heaven the sun is mounted; hark,
> The belfries tingle to the noonday chime.
> 'Tis silent, and the subterranean dark
> Has crossed the nadir, and begins to climb.
>     (XXXVI)

Cold and disciplined, these are among the most faultless of Housman's poems, approaching unexpectedly close to the territory of wit, which he professed to abhor in poetry. There are echoes of them in a successor whose work bears other traces of Housman's influence, W. H. Auden.

Laurence Housman, as literary executor, was authorized to print all the finished poems that he considered not inferior to the average of those already published, and, thanks to his editorial tact, another seventy-two poems have been preserved. This collection defines the full range of Housman's verse and, since his earlier poems often take their effect in hit-or-miss fashion, it illustrates more clearly, by means of other similar attempts, the nature of his successes and failures. The full range, of course, is still a very narrow one. Housman is a repetitive writer and he was clearly right to publish only a selection of his poetry to avoid diluting its effect. *More Poems* and the "Additional Poems" (eighteen poems that have not been published separately but are included in his *Collected Poems*) consist of pieces that either could not be fitted into his thematic arrangement or that he felt echoed what he had already published. Yet both categories contain lyrics that can stand beside his finest work. It is difficult to understand why he could not find room for such truly classical pieces as "Crossing alone the nighted ferry" or the beautiful poem on Hero and Leander, "Tarry delight, so seldom met." Others, such as the "Easter Hymn" or his farewell to Venice, provoke regret that his themes are normally so restricted. Those poems devoted to battlefields and soldiers' graves, on the other hand, almost suggest a parody of his manner. Certainly the instinct to suppress these was sound, but it is impossible not to be struck by the unsureness with which Housman writes of this subject.

War is one of the dominant themes in his poetry, and the life of physical action clearly held a special excitement for him, no less strong because it was so remote from his own. In his early poems he takes pride in the martial virtues as a part of his rural heritage, and they are linked too with his feeling that youth is the supreme testing time of life. In *A Shropshire Lad*, written in an era of apparently endless peace and security, war is merely a heroic fantasy, a rumble that falls thrillingly upon the ears of rustic lovers but never approaches nearer than the frontiers of empire:

> On the idle hill of summer,
>   Sleepy with the flow of streams,
> Far I hear the steady drummer
>   Drumming like a noise in dreams.
>                     (XXXV)

*Last Poems*, besides several excessively literary pieces on the same theme, contains others directly inspired by the Boer War and World War I. For these he chose a formal, epigrammatic style reminiscent of the classic military epitaphs of Simonides, though the tone is quite distinct:

> For pay and medals, name and rank,
>   Things that he has not found,
> He hove the Cross to heaven and sank
>   The pole-star underground.
>                ("Astronomy," XVII)

So Housman wrote of his younger brother killed in South Africa, and this note of irony is sounded still more decisively in the famous "Epitaph on an Army of Mercenaries":

> Their shoulders held the sky suspended;
>   They stood, and earth's foundations stay;
> What God abandoned, these defended,
>   And saved the sum of things for pay.
>                     (XXXVII)

A Greek poet could use understatement in this context because it epitomized the Spartan code, which was the Hellenic military ideal, but the homage that Simonides wishes to communicate is quite unreserved. It is difficult for a modern poet to praise war so unequivocally. Hardy, in his Boer War poem "Drummer Hodge," is moved above all by the pathos of the ignorant country boy who never knew the meaning of the broad Karoo and the southern stars. Housman, not wishing to pay a conventional tribute, strengthens his effect by stressing the element for which all can agree the sacrifice was *not* made. War, or the trade of man, as he calls it, remained for him a subject that, at worst, demanded a certain decorum of treatment: it never presented itself, as it did to other poets, as a target for satire, yet his irony still preserves the edge of his poem, after more explicit denunciations have lost much of theirs.

Housman is often praised as a "classical" writer, but this verdict needs a good deal of qualification. He is a poet who borrows freely, though with distinction, and his style is more strongly influenced by the language of the Old Testament and of Shakespeare than by the Greek or Latin poets. The classical element, in fact, is more apparent in the outward form than in the spirit of his verse. His poems often suggest the effect of a vase painting, of a clear-cut design dexterously executed within narrow limits, and the strictness of his versification, his inversions of word order, and his skill in placing his isolated, significant epithets all strengthen this impression. Certainly classical history and mythology often enrich his imagery and provide a core for his poems. "The Oracles," for example, follows closely Herodotus' description of the Spartan sang-froid before Thermopylae, and its seven-foot lines echo the rough hexameters in which the Delphic Oracle uttered its prophecies. And the epigram on the Boer War,

> Here dead lie we because we did not choose
>   To live and shame the land from which we sprung.

> Life, to be sure, is nothing much to lose;
> But young men think it is, and we were young.
> *(More Poems,* XXXVI)

has a possible ancestor in the epitaph attributed to Simonides on the Athenian dead at Chalcis:

> A gift desired, for youth is sweet
> And youth we gave, nor turned away,
> Though sharp the tide of battle beat,
> That darkened all our day.

Where Housman parts company from the classical spirit is in the emotional appeal of many of his poems. Though he rejects any belief in an afterlife, at the same time he rails against the very conditions of human existence. The classical poets, though they may warn us to count no man happy until he is dead, have nonetheless come to terms with the mortal state: suffering is not for them to be softened into a yearning for death, nor do they undervalue the gift of life itself:

> The joys I have possessed, in spite of fate, are mine.
> Not Heaven itself upon the past has power;
> But what has been, has been, and I have had my hour.
> (Dryden trans., Horace, *Odes* III. 29.8)

John Dryden's verses are an utterance of the classical spirit; in Housman, on the contrary, we find that aspiration constantly outruns fulfillment. There are exceptions, but these, significantly, are mostly found among those poems that he did not publish. His poetry in fact occupies an ambiguous position between two worlds of feeling; this lends them a special poignancy but also leaves them peculiarly exposed to the dangers of false or facile sentiment.

Housman works always to a simple and distinctly conceived idea of the form a poem should take. His verse is almost brutally explicit and quite contradicts the ideal of pure poetry that he upholds in *The Name and Nature of Poetry*, perhaps because he did not possess the gift of sustained melody. His poetry often came to him in snatches, the gaps having to be filled in by conscious effort, and to write in this way he needed a regular metrical framework. He has been censured for the monotony of his versification, and there is force in this criticism, for he lacks the metrical subtlety of Yeats or de la Mare. His meters are primitive and his pauses heavy, at times even mechanical. But they are appropriate for the particular tones that he wished to render, for most of his lyrics are tinged with an element of the dramatic or the rhetorical. The four-line rhymed stanza, with the lines alternating between eight and six beats, is pressed so strongly into this service that it comes to represent the typical mood and cadence of a Housman poem, in which the note of challenge is sounded in the longer line and subsides in negation in the shorter:

> June suns, you cannot store them
> To warm the winter's cold,
> The lad that hopes for heaven
> Shall fill his mouth with mould.
> *(More Poems,* XXII)

The characteristic effects are those of paradox, sudden poignancy, unexpected irony, and to achieve these, the ear needs to be led on by a smooth versification to the epithet or rhyme that is the point of stress. For this purpose too he employs a closely knit syntax in which nouns and verbs carry the main weight of his images:

> Or beeches strip in storms for winter
> And stain the wind with leaves.
> *(Last Poems,* XL)

Their effect is often reinforced by alliteration, which creates a peculiar harmony and interdependence of sound and sense. He uses epithets sparingly, but when he does they are often inspired inventions: such phrases as "light-leaved spring," "felon-quarried stone," "the bluebells of the listless plain" perfectly combine a decorative with an emotional value in their context. His brother has pointed out how frequently Housman's capacity for self-criticism improved his poetry; how, for example, in the poem "Be still, my soul," the alternatives—vex, plague, tear, wrench, rend, wring, break, and pierce—were all rejected before the line took its final shape: "All thoughts to *rive* the heart are here, and all are vain."

The lecture on *The Name and Nature of Poetry* provoked, partly for fortuitous reasons, a considerable stir when it was delivered. Housman's personal distinction and the fact that this was his first and only venture into literary criticism had aroused high expectations. The poetic values that it defends, which Housman had long held, might be described as an extension of the position established by Matthew Arnold, and this part of the lecture, uttered twenty or even ten years earlier, would hardly have excited much comment. But by 1933 the shift in critical opinion, which had received such an impetus from Eliot, was already well under way, so that Housman's words were naturally interpreted as something of a counterattack in defense of the romantic conception of poetry. Looking back, however, and particularly in view of his avowed difficulty in writing the lecture, it seems unlikely that he was consciously entering upon controversy. In any case it is important to remember that this is a lecture, not a treatise, and that its virtues are those which belong to a formal public utterance of limited length. It is superbly phrased, it possesses wit, provocative emphasis, and felicity of quotation. It gives the verdict of a great classical scholar upon the English neoclassical poets, and it modifies Arnold's superficial and evasive estimate of Dryden and Alexander Pope. But it is not a fully developed critical position. Housman once more disclaims the office of critic, and what he offers, far from being a twentieth-century Poetics, is no more than a statement of what poetry meant to him.

He is more confident that he can feel poetry than that he can define it. He offers, in passing, various tentative definitions, none of which can be pressed very closely—"poetry seems to me more physical than intellectual," "meaning is of the intellect, poetry is not." But he is categorical in laying down what is *not* poetry, and here his taste excludes metaphysical poetry and the bulk of the verse produced between Milton's *Samson Agonistes* (1671) and William Wordsworth and Samuel Taylor Coleridge's *Lyrical Ballads* (1798). The most poetical of all writers for him is William Blake who, he says, gives us poetry "adulterated with so little meaning that nothing except poetic emotion is perceived and matters."

In saying this, Housman places himself with those critics who identify the poetic process with communication rather than with expression. He is also tacitly following the modern tendency to pass over architectonic qualities in poetry and to regard the lyric as somehow intrinsically more poetical than dramatic or narrative poetry. This point of view, he freely admits, is influenced by his own experience of composition. His description of how his own poetry came to be produced is the best-known part of the lecture, and his normal reticence gives what he had to say on this subject an authority all the more commanding. But it is plain that the process he describes could apply only to the composition of lyrics and not to the major literary forms, in which construction, balance, and sustained creative energy have an important part to play.

In the end, the only infallible criterion that Housman admits is the instinctive reaction that poetry produced upon his physical and nervous system. This verdict is startling, coming from a scholar whom one would suppose to be steeped in the teaching of Plato, Aristotle, and Horace on the moral basis of poetry; on the other hand, Housman had given warning that he regarded true literary criticism as the rarest of gifts, and any other kind as possessing no more authority than personal taste. It is not very profitable, in short, to analyze his lecture in detail. A poet often works by intuitions that he cannot explain any more satisfactorily than anyone else, and *The Name and Nature of Poetry* is best read as a statement not of critical doctrine but of a poet's instincts.

When a decisive change takes place in poetic taste, such as has been experienced in the last sixty years, not only a poet's virtues and vices, but even his aims and much that he has taken for granted, come to be differently regarded. Few writers of so slender an output can have satisfied so fully—for a time even molded—the poetic ideals of their generation as did Housman; in the event, he has suffered the fate of a minor poet thrust by popularity into the role of a major one, in that his verse has been acclaimed as much for its message as for its strictly poetic excellence, and its imperfections overlooked. In judging his work today, it is surely an advantage that our sensibility has turned to a different, more complex ideal of poetic art and that the shortcomings of Housman's pessimistic philosophy have become more apparent.

Housman's original inspiration sprang from the emotions of youth, the period when untried ideals and untutored desires at their strongest first encounter a hostile or indifferent world. At his best, he can voice these passions with an extraordinary force, with a sensuous yet cold fury—"fire and ice within me fight"—in which feeling, language, and meter are completely fused. But at this stage of emotional development he stops short. The rest of his experience is measured by the same standards, and indeed much of the emotion of his later poetry springs precisely from this vehement refusal to come to terms with life's demands and disillusionments. His choice is to reject the cup, to condemn the human situation proudly and without compromise. He would not have conceded, as Yeats could do:

I am content to live it all again
And yet again, if it be life to pitch
Into the frog-spawn of a blind man's ditch....

These limitations in Housman's outlook and choice of material are familiar enough. There remain his superb powers of expression, the capacity to write verses of great poetry, if not to be a great poet. In his prose and verse alike, Housman is limited to the short flight and the minor form; but for the strength and purity of his expression, he can take his place in the company of the acknowledged masters of the English tongue. In an age of constant confusion and debasement of speech he has stood forth as one of the true heirs of the language, in whom its latent riches, the passionate simplicity of Anglo-Saxon, the splendor and eloquence of Latin, have once more found a voice. At his best he possesses the indefinable poetic faculty of conferring on words a new life, so that one turns eagerly to any new Housman fragment not so much for a fresh poetic experience as for some sudden felicity of language. Much was sacrificed for these ideals, but he possesses them securely; the command of words and the proud integrity with which he practiced it are his greatest gifts.

## SELECTED BIBLIOGRAPHY

I. BIBLIOGRAPHY. J. Carter and J. Sparrow, *A. E. Housman: An Annotated Handlist* (London, 1952), annotations contain important biographical material.

II. COLLECTED AND SELECTED WORKS. *Collected Poems* (London, 1939), repr. in the Cape paperback series (1967); *Collected Poems* (London, 1956), in the "Penguin Poets" series; J. Carter, ed., *Selected Prose* (London, 1961), contains lectures mentioned below, several of Housman's most important papers on classical subjects, including critical prefaces to his eds. of Manilius and Juvenal, "On the Application of Thought to Textual Criticism," and selection of reviews, letters to the press, and other occasional writings; F. C. Horwood, ed., *Poetry and Prose: A Selection* (London, 1971).

III. SEPARATE WORKS. *Introductory Lecture*, University College, London (London, 1892; privately repr. 1933; repr. 1937); *A Shropshire Lad* (London, 1896), verse; *Last Poems* (London, 1922); A. Platt, *Nine Essays* (London, 1927), contains important preface by Housman; *The Name and Nature of Poetry* (London, 1933), the 1933 Leslie Stephen Lecture; *More Poems* (London, 1936); *The Confines of Criticism* (London, 1969), complete text of Housman's Cambridge Inaugural Lecture, 1911, with notes by J. Carter; J. Diggle and F. R. D. Goodyear, eds., *The Classical Papers of A. E. Housman*, 3 vols. (London, 1972).

IV. CLASSICAL TEXTS. *M. Manilii: Astronomicon*, 5 vols. (London, 1903–1930), repr. in 1 vol. (1932); *D. Ivnii Ivvenalis: Satvrae* (London, 1905; 2nd ed., corrected, 1931); *M. Annaei Lucani: Belli Civilis Libri Decem* (Oxford, 1926; 2nd ed., corrected, 1927).

V. LETTERS. T. B. Haber, ed., *Thirty Letters to Witter Bynner* (New York, 1957); H. Maas, ed., *The Letters of A. E. Housman* (London, 1971).

VI. BIOGRAPHICAL AND CRITICAL STUDIES. H. W. Garrod, *The Profession of Poetry* (London, 1929), includes lecture on Housman as poet and scholar; A. S. F. Gow, *A. E. Housman* (London, 1936), sketch with definitive handlist of Housman's contributions to classical scholarship, and other prose papers; "The Bromsgrovian": *Housman Memorial Supplement* (London, 1936), this supplement to Housman's old school magazine contains reminiscences and appreciations by his brother, his sister, and other hands, published in book form (New York, 1937); L. Housman, *A. E. H.: Some Poems, Some Letters and a Personal Memoir* (London, 1937), includes quotations from Housman's letters and notebooks and 18 additional poems never published separately but contained in *Collected Poems*; E. Wilson, *The Triple Thinkers* (London, 1938), contains essay on Housman's scholarship; R. W. Chambers, *Man's Unconquerable Mind* (London, 1939), contains sketch of Housman's career at University College, London; H. W. Garrod, "Housman: 1939," in *Essays and Studies*, XXV (London, 1939); P. Withers, *A Buried Life* (London, 1940); G. Richards, *Housman: 1897–1936* (London, 1941), biographical study by Housman's first publisher, includes appendix by G. B. Fletcher analyzing classical influences in Housman's poetry; C. Connolly, *The Condemned Playground* (London, 1945), contains article on Housman and the subsequent controversial letters in response, repr. from the *New Statesman*; T. B. Haber, *The Manuscript Poems of A. E. Housman* (London, 1955), publishes for the first time a large number of fragments and lines from Housman's MS notebooks (previously excluded from publication by Laurence Housman under the terms of his brother's will) in the Library of Congress; also discusses chronology of the poems; G. L. Watson, *A. E. Housman: A Divided Life* (London, 1957); N. Marlow, *A. E. Housman: Scholar and Poet* (London, 1958), sensitive study of biographical rather than critical interest; T. B. Haber, *A. E. Housman* (New York, 1967); C. Ricks, ed., *A. E. Housman: A Collection of Critical Essays* (London, 1969), in the Twentieth Century Views series; B. J. Leggett, *Housman's Land of Lost Content: A Critical Study of A Shropshire Lad* (Lincoln, Nebr., 1970); B. J. Leggett, *The Poetic Art of A. E. Housman* (Lincoln, Nebr., 1978); R. P. Graves, *A. E. Housman. The Scholar Poet* (London, 1979).

# ALDOUS HUXLEY
## (1894-1963)

### Jocelyn Brooke

ANY comparison between Aldous Huxley and H. G. Wells must seem, at first glance, impossibly arbitrary and far-fetched: for surely no two writers—considered merely as writers—could be more dissimilar. Yet such a comparison is, I think, not only justified but, as a matter of literary history, almost unavoidable.

For those who came to maturity during the first two decades of the present century, the most potent intellectual influence was probably that of Wells; it was an influence that might be resisted but could hardly be ignored by any up-to-date young man of the period. Wells was not only the first and greatest of the scientific popularizers; he was also a prophet and a revolutionary, and his perky, disrespectful attitude to "respectable" institutions, combined with an immensely readable style, seemed to his younger contemporaries to typify the intellectual climate of the time.

How different, it may well be objected, was the case of Huxley: aloof, fastidious, and, by contrast with Wells's bouncing optimism, profoundly a pessimist; upper-class both by birth and disposition, whereas Wells was plebeian and proud of it; preoccupied largely with problems of pure aesthetics and, latterly, with mysticism, for both of which Wells would have felt little but an amused contempt. Yet, viewed in a wider context, the similarities between the two men can be seen to outweigh their differences: for Huxley was also a popularizer, not only of aesthetic and philosophic ideas, but also (like Wells) of scientific ones; he too—though in a somewhat different sense—was both a revolutionary and a prophetic writer; and, most notably, he was, like Wells before him, the "typical" writer of his generation, and a major influence upon the young intelligentsia of his time.

His importance, in this last respect, can hardly be exaggerated, though there is a very natural tendency among the youngest generation to underestimate it. For those who, like the writer of the present essay, were growing up during the 1920's, Aldous Huxley seemed unquestionably the most stimulating and exciting writer of the day: his style in itself was a novelty—highly wrought yet extremely readable, deriving from unfamiliar models, and providing a refreshing contrast to that of such older writers as John Galsworthy, Arnold Bennett, and Wells himself. Huxley was gay, sophisticated, and (for those days) agreeably shocking; but more important for his young readers was the impact of an alert, penetrating, and widely ranging intelligence. By comparison, most other contemporary writers seemed stuffy, unenlightened, and old-fashioned.

The effect was intoxicating: like the great Knockespotch, that imaginary genius described in *Crome Yellow* (1921), Huxley had "delivered us from the dreary tyranny of the realistic novel"; like Knockespotch, again, he preferred to study the human mind, not "bogged in a social plenum," but "freely and sportively bombinating":

"Oh those Tales—those Tales! [exclaims the eloquent Mr. Scogan]. How shall I describe them? Fabulous characters shoot across his pages like gaily dressed performers on the trapeze. There are extraordinary adventures and still more extraordinary speculations. Intelligences and emotions, relieved of all the imbecile preoccupations of civilised life, move in intricate and subtle dances, crossing and recrossing. . . . An immense erudition and an immense fancy go hand in hand. . . . The verbal surface of his writing is rich and fantastically diversified. The wit is incessant."

(ch. 14)

This description, one felt at the time, could well have been applied to the tales of Huxley himself. The combination of wit and erudition is an uncommon one in English fiction, and one has to go back to Thomas Love Peacock (by whom Huxley was much influenced) to find a comparable example. Huxley's erudition was, even in his earlier works, encyclopedic; yet he wore his learning lightly, with an offhand, man-of-the-world air that was entirely disarming. He was often, in those days, accused of intellectual snobbery, and it is true that he was capable, on occasion, of referring to such comparatively recondite figures as, say, Crébillon *fils* or Notker Balbulus with an air of casual omniscience that somewhat suggested the style of the contemporary gossip writer ("Lady So-and-so, who *of course* . . ."). The trick, one suspects, was consciously employed, partly from a sense of mischief, partly from an amiable desire to flatter his readers. In the essay *Vulgarity in Literature* (1930), he remarks of Paul Morand that he "has a wonderfully airy, easy way of implying that he has looked into everything—absolutely everything, from God and the Quantum Theory to the slums of Baku (the world's most classy slums—didn't you know it?)." Here, one feels, Huxley is having a sly dig not only at Morand but at himself.

If Huxley had written nothing after 1925, it is probable that he would be remembered today merely as a brilliant and somewhat eccentric minor writer comparable in stature, say, with Ronald Firbank. Judged by those early works, his subsequent development is astonishing: not only was he one of the most prolific of living English writers (his published works number between fifty and sixty volumes); he was also one of the most versatile. Novels, poetry, drama, travel books, short stories, biography, essays—there is almost no literary form that he did not, at one time or another, attempt. His writings, moreover, cover an enormous range not only of form but of subject matter: apart from his purely creative work, he wrote learnedly and perceptively about painting, music, science, philosophy, religion, and a dozen other topics. Yet, considering the breadth of his interests and the magnitude of his output, his work, examined as a whole, has a surprising homogeneity; nor, despite the temptations that could beset a successful author, did he ever seriously compromise his intellectual integrity. Though a bestseller, he remains, paradoxically, an essentially unpopular writer.

His development falls roughly into three phases. The earlier stories and novels are mainly satirical and (like the historical studies of Lytton Strachey) are largely concerned with the debunking of accepted ideas and standards. Like T. S. Eliot, James Joyce, Wyndham Lewis, and others of his own or a slightly earlier generation, he was profoundly affected by the progressive breakdown of nineteenth-century ideals that had culminated in World War I, and his predicament is reflected in these early volumes, in which the surface gaiety serves only to emphasize his underlying pessimism. Religion, conventional morality, romantic love—all are subjected to a cynical and ruthless mockery. The world of *Antic Hay* (1923) has much in common with that of Eliot's *The Waste Land* (which had appeared in the previous year); it is a world of "broken images," where "the dead tree gives no shelter, the cricket no relief." Only in the realm of pure art (it is implied) can one hope, perhaps, to discover some kind of established order to set against the prevailing anarchy. Yet the fin de siècle doctrine of art for art's sake could never have proved finally satisfying to a man of Huxley's lively and speculative intelligence; and there is soon apparent a growing preoccupation not only with the more advanced theories of modern science, but also with psychology, ethics, and philosophy.

This second phase may be said to have begun with the publication of *Proper Studies* (1927), the first of his books to be explicitly serious in intention. Thenceforward, though he continued to write novels and short stories, he assumed a more responsible role—that of the teacher, the professional philosopher—and one can no longer regard him as primarily a novelist, whose chief purpose is to entertain. During the 1930's he developed an increasing interest in politics and, more particularly, in the contemporary cult of pacifism; at the same time, he began to turn his attention to the Eastern mystics, and the third and final stage in his development can already be inferred from the works of this period.

Though by temperament a skeptic, Huxley always, one imagines, recognized within himself the need for some kind of religious approach to the universe; moreover, throughout his career as a writer, he showed a recurrent interest in the phenomena of mysticism. Others among his contemporaries, though sharing his initial skepticism, subsequently became converted to one form or another of the Christian faith; Huxley, with greater intellectual resistance, refused to abandon his empirical attitude in such matters, and the approach to his later philosophical position was cautious in the extreme. His prolonged study of the mystics convinced him that the mystical experience itself—the individual's direct union with the Godhead—is an objective fact that can be experimentally verified; and his last works are almost all concerned, directly or indirectly, with an attempt to synthesize the existing evidence into a comprehensive system, to which he gave the name "the Perennial Philosophy."

One can say, then, that Huxley progressed from a purely aesthetic, through a politico-ethical, to a predominantly religious point of view. This, of course, is a drastic simplification. In reality, his development was far more complex—for, as I shall try to show in this essay, most of the beliefs that he embraced in his maturity are latent in his earliest published works.

Aldous Leonard Huxley was born at Godalming, Surrey, on 26 July 1894, a son of Leonard Huxley (editor of the *Cornhill* magazine) and grandson of T. H. Huxley, the illustrious scientist; Sir Julian Huxley, the biologist, was his brother. His mother was an Arnold, and he was thus connected on both the paternal and maternal sides with that distinguished intellectual aristocracy which was so dominant a force in late-nineteenth-century England. He was educated at Eton and at Balliol College, Oxford; after leaving the university, he taught for a while at Eton (an incongruous interlude to which he refers, disrespectfully, in *Antic Hay*), but soon decided to devote himself to writing. He married comparatively early, to Maria Nys in 1919,[1] and spent much of his time during the 1920's in France and Italy. He traveled widely, not only in Europe but in the East and in America, and lived in California for many years before his death there on 22 November 1963.

His first published work was a small volume of poems; and this is perhaps a good moment to note that Huxley, though less known as a poet than as a prose writer, was an extremely accomplished writer of verse. These early poems are chiefly remarkable today for being so wholly unlike the average product of the contemporary Georgian school.[2] Huxley, like Eliot before him, had plainly been much influenced by the French symbolists; his third collection of verse, *The Defeat of Youth* (1918), is an admirable translation of Stéphane Mallarmé's *L'Après-midi d'un faune*. Sometimes there are echoes of a rather eighteen-ninetyish romanticism:

> Shepherd, to yon tall poplars tune your flute:
>   Let them pierce, keenly, subtly shrill,
>   The slow blue rumour of the hill;

> Let the grass cry with an anguish of evening gold,
>   And the great sky be mute.
>
>       ("Song of Poplars")

Many of these early poems are, however, satirical or epigrammatic; and in the volume called *Leda* (1920) the more memorable pieces, apart from the title poem (an ambitious and on the whole successful work in rhymed couplets), are of a similar character—for example, the "Fifth Philosopher's Song":

> A million million spermatozoa,
>   All of them alive:
> Out of their cataclysm but one poor Noah
>   Dare hope to survive.
>
> And among that billion minus one
>   Might have chanced to be
> Shakespeare, another Newton, a new Donne—
>   But the One was Me.
>
> Shame to have ousted your betters thus,
>   Taking ark while the others remained outside!
> Better for all of us, froward Homunculus,
>   If you'd quietly died!

A third volume, *The Cicadas* (1931), shows the same verbal felicity, but with a leaning toward more serious (and more formal) verse. Two or three of the poems there reprinted appeared originally in the novel *Those Barren Leaves* (1925), where, significantly, they were attributed to one of the leading characters, Francis Chelifer, who has more than a little in common with Huxley himself.

Huxley's first prose work, *Limbo*, appeared in 1920, the same year as *Leda*; this is a collection of stories, one of which—"Farcical History of Richard Greenow"—is in fact a short novel or long tale and occupies almost half the volume. This story is one of Huxley's most hilarious and successful essays in ironic comedy; the hero is a "spiritual hermaphrodite," a Jekyll-and-Hyde personality in whom are combined an overfastidious intellectual and a vastly successful lady novelist. Rereading it today, one is still astonished by its intellectual maturity and by the richness of Huxley's comic invention. Among the other six stories in the book, all extremely accomplished, may be mentioned "Happily Ever After," in which one of Huxley's chief preoccupations becomes for the first time apparent. Guy Lambourne, the hero of the story, is the prototype of many subsequent Huxley heroes—the young lover who is tortured by an irreconcilable conflict between romantic passion and physical sexuality. In later

---

[1] Huxley's first wife died of cancer in 1955; the next year he married his second wife, Laura Archera, an Italian concert violinist and psychotherapist.

[2] So called in reference to the series of anthologies, *Georgian Poetry*, edited by the late Sir Edward Marsh.

works this dichotomy will become almost obsessional, for Huxley had much of Jonathan Swift's hatred for bodily functions, combined with a lively appreciation of the pleasures to be obtained therefrom.

In 1921 appeared Huxley's first novel, *Crome Yellow*, and with it he established his reputation. In many ways it remains—on a purely aesthetic level—his most successful achievement. Like *Limbo*, it is an extraordinarily mature production for a young man still in his twenties, yet it has, too, all the freshness and spontaneity one associates with an "early" work. It is Huxley's gayest and happiest book; the graver, more responsible attitude of his later years can already be detected, as it were, in embryo, but the novel as a whole is a thoroughly lighthearted affair, enormously readable and, in parts, extremely amusing.

The structure of *Crome Yellow* owes much to Thomas Peacock: a number of people are gathered together at a house party; there is plenty of incident—the characters dance, go swimming, attend a garden fete, fall in love; but above all they talk—brilliantly, wittily, and almost without stopping. The book is a conversation piece in which the characters, though sharply drawn and clearly differentiated, are employed primarily as vehicles for the prolific and highly imaginative ideas of their creator. It is a useful device that Huxley was to adopt again in subsequent books, though seldom quite so successfully as he employs it here. The danger of such a method is that the action of the novel—and the characters themselves—will be swamped by the stream of conversation; in *Chrome Yellow*, however, the balance is almost perfectly maintained, and Mr. Scogan, for example, though irrepressibly eloquent, is never allowed to become a bore.

In *Chrome Yellow* Huxley presents a gallery of characters many of whom will be resuscitated, with slight variations (and under different names), in his later novels. For instance, there is Denis, the "hero" (it is difficult to refer to Huxley's very unheroic heroes without the ironic qualification of quotation marks), the typically Huxleyan young man, burdened (as he complains) by "twenty tons of ratiocination," romantically in love yet sexually inhibited and profoundly convinced of the futility of life and of himself. There is Mary Bracegirdle, with her bobbed hair like "a bell of elastic gold about her cheeks," the too-intelligent ingenue whose practical experience of sex is so sadly disproportionate to her theoretical knowledge of it. In sharp contrast is Anne—uninhibited, hedonistic, sexually sophisticated—in whom one recognizes the forerunner of Mrs. Viveash and Lucy Tantamount, the femmes fatales who play so prominent a part in the more mature works.

In *Chrome Yellow*, as I have already hinted, one can detect the germs of several ideas that will be developed in later books: a good example is Mr. Scogan's prophetic description of a scientific Utopia:

"An impersonal generation will take the place of Nature's hideous system. In vast state incubators, rows upon rows of gravid bottles will supply the world with the population it requires. The family system will disappear; society, sapped at its very base, will have to find new foundations; and Eros, beautifully and irresponsibly free, will flit like a gay butterfly from flower to flower through a sunlit world."
(ch. 5)

This passage contains, in essence, an idea that Huxley developed and elaborated eleven years later in *Brave New World*. Mr. Scogan himself, despite his loquacity, is one of Huxley's best-conceived characters, and the scene in which he impersonates Madame Sesostris, the Sorceress of Ecbatana, is one of the most richly comic episodes in a novel that, apart from its other merits, is certainly among the funniest in modern English fiction. *Crome Yellow* derives, as I have pointed out, from Peacock; one guesses, too, that Huxley was also influenced at this period by Norman Douglas' *South Wind*, and perhaps to a lesser extent by the novels of Ronald Firbank.

*Crome Yellow* was followed, in 1922, by *Mortal Coils*, another volume of short stories. During the subsequent decade the short (or long-short) story accounted for a considerable proportion of Huxley's output, and it will be convenient at this point to consider his achievement in the form.

In the opinion of many critics, these shorter pieces are Huxley's most successful contribution to fiction. In his novels he is too apt to use the form merely as a vehicle for the presentation of his own ideas; in the short stories he shows a greater respect for his medium and, whereas his novels tended to become longer, more serious, and more diffuse, his shorter tales retained much of the gaiety and compactness of form that one finds in *Chrome Yellow*. Among a large output may be mentioned "Nuns at Luncheon" (*Mortal Coils*, 1922), "Little Mexican" (in the volume of that name, 1924), and "The Claxtons" (*Brief Candles*, 1930)—all admirably written in Huxley's best comic vein. The title story in *Two or Three Graces* (1926) is also noteworthy, partly as a fascinating character study of a woman afflicted by *bovarysme* and partly for its portrait of D. H. Lawrence ("Kingham"), which may be compared instructively with the very different version of Lawrence in *Point Counter Point* (1928).

During this period Huxley established himself as a master of the short essay, a form that has tended to decline sharply in popularity during the last fifty years or so. His first collection, *On the Margin* (1923), consisted mainly of pieces contributed to weekly reviews. This was followed at intervals by half a dozen other volumes, among which may be mentioned *Proper Studies*, Huxley's first serious excursion into the realm of sociology and philosophy, and *Do What You Will* (1929), especially memorable for the perceptive essay on Charles Baudelaire. Among other miscellaneous writings of this period are the two excellent travel books, *Jesting Pilate* (1926) and *Beyond the Mexique Bay* (1934), besides *The World of Light* (1931), a satirical comedy about spiritualism. The drama is not a form at which one would have expected Huxley to excel, yet *The World of Light* is not only highly entertaining to read, but also extremely good theater, as the present writer, who saw the original production at the Royalty Theatre in 1931, is able to testify. ("The Gioconda Smile," in the volume *Mortal Coils*, has also been successfully dramatized.)

Huxley's second novel, *Antic Hay*, appeared in 1923 and created a considerable sensation, owing to its frank and detailed treatment of sexual matters. Today, this would hardly arouse comment, but at that time *Antic Hay* acquired an undeserved reputation for "obscenity," and several of the more respectable libraries refused to stock it. It is a considerably longer and more ambitious work than *Crome Yellow* and, though it has much of the high spirits of the previous book, is more serious in intention. The scene is set mainly in London, and the characters are drawn largely from the artistic and intellectual coteries of the time; many of them are thinly disguised portraits of real persons, among others the composer Philip Heseltine (known as Peter Warlock), who is easily recognizable in the character of Coleman. In structure the book is loose and episodic, though the story plays a more important part than in *Crome Yellow*; conversations are frequent and often prolonged, but here they are for the most part subordinated to the narrative. The hero, Theodore Gumbril, is an older, more worldly version of Denis in *Crome Yellow*, and serves to illustrate once again the predicament of the modern intellectual torn between his youthful idealism and the inconvenient promptings of *l'homme moyen sensuel* (the average sensual man). The book is an odd mixture of broad farce and a kind of ironic realism, but one feels at times that the two elements are not perfectly fused: thus, the episode of Gumbril's "patent smallclothes" and his farcical disguise as the Rabelaisian "Complete Man," though extremely funny in themselves, strike one as curiously out of key with the more serious passages.

Yet *Antic Hay*, if it lacks the structural perfection of *Crome Yellow*, is in many respects a more important book. Of all Huxley's novels, it is the one that is most "alive": the characters are presented more vividly and their relation to their background is more authentic than in any previous or subsequent work. Mr. Mercaptan, Mrs. Viveash, Lypiatt, Shearwater—they remain in the memory as living entities, not as mere mouthpieces for Huxley's erudite and witty disquisitions. In this novel, too—in spite of its predominantly comic theme—it is noticeable that Huxley strikes a more emotional note than is usual with him: there are passages in which he betrays a feeling of romantic nostalgia (though tempered by a habitual irony) that one seldom finds elsewhere in his work. It should be noted, too, that in *Antic Hay* he is already beginning to employ a technique that in his next few books becomes increasingly important—the technique of describing one form of experience in terms of another and of uniting a number of apparently diverse phenomena into a logical and self-contained unity. In the following passage Gumbril is lying in bed with his (platonic) mistress, Emily:

Very gently, he began caressing her shoulder, her long slender arm, drawing his finger tips lightly and slowly over her smooth skin; slowly from her neck, over her shoulder, lingeringly round the elbow to her hand. Again, again: he was learning her arm. The form of it was part of the knowledge, now, of his finger tips; his fingers knew it as they knew a piece of music, as they knew Mozart's Twelfth Sonata, for example. And the themes that crowd so quickly one after another at the beginning of the first movement played themselves aerially, glitteringly in his mind; they became a part of the enchantment.

(ch. 13)

Love in terms of music—music in terms of love: it is a typically Huxleyan transposition of terms, and is greatly elaborated in the next two novels. One may add that *Antic Hay*, like *Crome Yellow*, sometimes strikes a prophetic note—as, for instance, in the passage in chapter 22 where Gumbril is soliloquizing after luncheon to the somnolent Mrs. Viveash: "'I have a premonition,' he went on, 'that one of these days I may become a saint. An unsuccessful flickering sort of saint, like a candle beginning to go out.'"

Without disrespect to Huxley, I think one can infer from Gumbril's flippant words a faint adumbration of his creator's future progress toward the philosophy of nonattachment.

*Those Barren Leaves*, the next novel, was published in 1925. Here, as in *Crome Yellow*, Huxley adopts the Peacockian device of the house party. The background, in this case, is a villa on the Italian Riviera, but the characters have a good deal in common with those of the earlier book. Thus, the would-be sophisticated Mary Bracegirdle reappears as Irene, the niece of the hostess, Mrs. Aldwinkle (who, like the hostess of *Crome Yellow*, is largely a comic character); Mr. Scogan is replaced by Mr. Cardan, no less loquacious, cultured, and concupiscent than his predecessor; the romantic Ivor of *Crome Yellow* becomes Calamy, the handsome young philanderer; and so on. In this novel, as in *Antic Hay*, Huxley introduces a number of grotesque episodes, but here they are more closely integrated with the rest of the book. For example, the story of Mr. Cardan's betrothal to a lunatic heiress and her subsequent death from food poisoning is, if sufficiently fantastic, at least more plausible than Gumbril's pneumatic trousers, and the whole episode is a vividly imagined essay in the farcical-macabre.

Again, love plays a considerable part; here, however, a new element enters, foreshadowing the direction in which Huxley is moving. In *Antic Hay*, his attitude to sexual relations is one of almost Proustian pessimism: sexuality, he seems to imply, is inherently squalid and disgusting, but it is unavoidable. The philosopher, therefore, must accept it with a shrug and make the best of it. In *Those Barren Leaves*, however, he makes the young lover, Calamy, willingly renounce his affair with a fellow guest and retire to a mountaintop where, significantly, he spends his time in philosophic meditation.

"And what [asks the skeptical Mr. Cardan] will happen at the end of three months' chaste meditation when some lovely young temptation comes toddling down this road . . . ? What will happen to your explorations of the inward universe then, may I ask? . . . Perhaps you'll find that you can explore simultaneously both the temptation and the interior universe."

Calamy shook his head. "Alas, I'm afraid that's not practicable."

(Conclusions, ch. 4)

I mentioned Proust in another connection, and it is noticeable that in *Those Barren Leaves* Huxley shows signs of Proustian influences, not so much in the matter of style (though this indeed is more elaborate than in the earlier books) as in his delineation of character: Mrs. Aldwinkle, for instance, with her proprietary attitude to her "view," and to Italy in general, owes much to Mme. Verdurin; and Miss Thriplow's reminiscences, prompted by the smell of a bay leaf, also have a suggestive Proustian flavor.

If *Those Barren Leaves* owes something to Proust, its successor, *Point Counter Point*, is even more heavily indebted to another French writer, Andre Gide, from whose novel *Les Faux-monnayeurs* Huxley has frankly borrowed a number of technical devices. *Point Counter Point* is one of Huxley's longest and most ambitious novels and, I should say, the most perfectly constructed—though the intricacy of its form entails a certain loss of spontaneity; admirable though it is, it lacks some of the force and vitality of *Crome Yellow* and *Antic Hay*.

The title provides a clue to Huxley's intention, which is to present, by a method analogous to counterpoint in music, a kind of multiple vision of life, in which the diverse aspects of experience can be observed simultaneously. (The technique has already been hinted at, as I have pointed out, in earlier novels.) The method is best described in the words of one of the characters, Philip Quarles. Quarles is a novelist and keeps a journal in which he discusses, at considerable length, the novelist's technique (this device of the novelist-within-a-novel is borrowed from *Les Faux-monnayeurs*):

The musicalization of fiction. Not in the symbolist way, by subordinating sense to sound. . . . But on a large scale, in the construction. Meditate on Beethoven. The changes of moods, the abrupt transitions. (Majesty alternating with a joke, for example, in the first movement of the B flat major Quartet. . . .) . . . A theme is stated, then developed, pushed out of shape, imperceptibly deformed, until, though still recognizably the same, it has become quite different. . . . All you need is a sufficiency of characters and parallel, contrapuntal plots. While Jones is murdering a wife, Smith is wheeling the perambulator in the park.

(ch. 22)

*Point Counter Point* is precisely the kind of novel that Quarles contemplated writing. The contrapuntal method resolves itself, in practice, into a system of elaborate and judicious "cutting," comparable to the technique of the cinema; many other writers have employed it subsequently (Graham Greene, for example), but seldom on so large a scale or so successfully as Huxley.

So far as its moral and philosophical implications are concerned, *Point Counter Point* seems to indicate a partial regression to Huxley's earlier pessimism; the promise (implied in the closing pages of *Those Barren Leaves*) of a possible escape from the "wearisome condition of humanity" is not fulfilled, and Huxley's habitual cynicism takes on a harsher, more ferocious quality. A new preoccupation with violence is noticeable—the murder of Webley the fascist, for example (one of Huxley's few attempts at melodrama and a not wholly successful one); death and suffering, in one form or another, pervade the book—for example, old Bidlake's duodenal ulcer and the death of Quarles's little boy. With few exceptions, the characters are even more unsympathetic than Huxley's previous creations: Webley the fascist, Spandrell the ineffectual diabolist, Lucy Tantamount, a typically Huxleyan femme fatale, though less perfectly characterized than some of her predecessors.

The most vividly drawn character in the book—and in many ways the most significant—is Spandrell, a modern incarnation of Baudelaire (whose personality Huxley had always found fascinating). The Baudelairean situation is reproduced almost exactly—the child's adoration for the widowed mother, the mother's remarriage to an elderly army officer, the boy's revulsion and his subsequent cult for debauchery and the "artificial paradises" of drugs and alcohol. Yet Spandrell is more than a mere echo of Baudelaire, for he represents (in a fictitious and, of course, exaggerated form) an aspect of Huxley himself to which I have already drawn attention —the perpetually recurring conflict between sensuality and asceticism. In Spandrell's case the conflict is presented in its most extreme and perverse form. Debauchery has become, as it were, a moral compulsion, a prolonged and unremitting protest against the mother's defection; Spandrell is filled with a passionate hatred not only for all moral values but even for, among other things, the beauties of nature. This is well illustrated in the following passage (Spandrell has taken out an elderly and ill-favored prostitute for a day in the country):

"Lovely, lovely," was Connie's refrain. The place, the day reminded her, she said, of her childhood in the country. She sighed.

"And you wish you'd been a good girl," said Spandrell sarcastically. "'The roses round the door make me love mother more,' I know, I know." . . .

"Oh, the foxgloves!" cried Connie, who hadn't even been listening. She ran toward them, grotesquely unsteady on her high heels. Spandrell followed her.

"Pleasingly phallic," he said, fingering one of the spikes of unopened buds. And he went on to develop the conceit profusely.

"Oh, be quiet, be quiet," cried Connie. "How can you say such things?" She was outraged, wounded. "How can you—here?"

"In God's country," he mocked. "How can I?" And raising his stick he suddenly began to lay about him right and left, slash, slash, breaking one of the tall proud plants at every stroke. The ground was strewn with murdered flowers.

"Stop, stop!" She caught at his arm. Silently laughing, Spandrell wrenched himself away from her and went on beating down the plants. . . .

"Down with them," he shouted, "down with them." . . . Connie was in tears.

"How could you?" she said. "How could you do it?"

. . . "Serves them right," he said. "Do you think I'm going to sit still and let myself be insulted? The insolence of the brutes! Ah, there's another!" He stepped across the glade to where one last tall foxglove stood as though hiding among the hazel saplings. One stroke was enough. The broken plant fell almost noiselessly.

(ch. 29)

As in the other novels, many of the characters in *Point Counter Point* are drawn from living models—notably Mark Rampion, a full-length portrait of D. H. Lawrence. It is significant that the previous sketch of Lawrence in *Two or Three Graces* is extremely unsympathetic, not to say malicious; Rampion, on the other hand, is drawn with great sympathy, even with affection, and one feels that he is the only character in the book of whom Huxley almost wholly approves. The contrast between the two portraits is probably due to the fact that in the intervening period Huxley had become increasingly sympathetic to Lawrence's ideas. One would have supposed the two men to be poles apart—and in many respects they were; yet a strong friendship united them during the latter years of Lawrence's life, and Huxley, though never quite prepared to accept Lawrence's philosophy in its entirety, was certainly profoundly influenced by it. Himself (as he often confessed) a prisoner of the intellect, debarred by his temperament from a complete and satisfying participation in the life of the senses, Huxley doubtless saw in Lawrence's "philosophy of the blood" a possible means of escape from his own predicament. After Lawrence's death, however, he seems finally to have rejected (if somewhat reluctantly) the instinctual approach to life, and in his subsequent works the Lawrentian influence became less and less noticeable. (It should be mentioned, however, that Huxley's introduction to Lawrence's letters[3] is one of the fairest and most balanced assessments of Lawrence and his work.)

*Point Counter Point* suffers from its overelaborate construction; some of the old gaiety has gone, and in the quality of the prose itself one notes a tendency to overfacility, a lack of tautness, and an increasing use of certain rather irritating mannerisms. Yet there can be little doubt that, technically speaking, *Point Counter Point* is Huxley's most considerable achievement in fiction. The interest of his subsequent novels is mainly one of content rather than of form: henceforward he concentrated less upon problems of pure technique and tended more and more to use the novel merely as a convenient medium for the expression of his ideas. I propose, therefore, to deal with the remaining novels rather more briefly.

*Brave New World* (1932) is a "novel of the future," and might be described as the reverse of the Wellsian medal. "Homo *au naturel*—" remarks Mr. Mercaptan in *Antic Hay*, "ça pue. And as for Homo à la H. G. Wells—*ça ne pue pas assez.*" Huxley's Utopia, like that of Wells, "doesn't stink enough," and besides being hygienically odorless it is in other respects modeled largely on its Wellsian prototype; the difference between *Men Like Gods* (1923) and *Brave New World* lies chiefly in the point of view of the two writers. For Huxley the Wellsian Utopia, far from being a desirable state of affairs, represents the triumph of all that he most fears and dislikes, for it is a world in which humanity has been dehumanized, a world in which scientific progress has been produced, so to speak, to the *n*th degree. Mr. Scogan's

[3]*The Letters of D. H. Lawrence* (London, 1932).

prophecy in *Crome Yellow* has been more than fulfilled: babies are incubated in bottles and a system of strictly scientific conditioning ensures that each individual shall perform automatically his allotted function within the community. It is a totalitarian and quasi-theocratic world; its gods are Karl Marx and Henry Ford—the latter referred to on pious occasions as Our Ford (or occasionally as Our Freud). In an artificially inseminated society, the most obscene word is "mother" and hygiene has become the ultimate moral value (the children are taught such variants of old-fashioned nursery rhymes as "Streptocock-Gee to Banbury T, to see a fine bathroom and W.C.").

The theme is developed with inexorable logic and with much of Huxley's characteristically ironic humor. The end, however, is tragic—the story culminates with the suicide (in a lighthouse in Surrey) of a "savage" imported from one of the few remaining native reservations, where life remains on a purely primitive (and pre-Fordian) level. *Brave New World*, if stylistically inferior to his previous novels, is one of Huxley's most spirited performances. Its main weakness lies, I think, in the fact that Huxley argues from an arbitrarily chosen set of premises and ignores a number of present tendencies that are quite as likely to influence the future as the ones with which he chooses to deal. Thus—as he himself admitted in a new preface to the book—there is no mention of nuclear fission, which had, as he says, "been a popular topic of conversation for years before the book was written." *Brave New World* may profitably be compared with George Orwell's *1984*, which, allowing for the fact that it was written nearly twenty years later, seems a far more plausible (and even more depressing) vision of the future than Huxley's.

The same year saw the publication of *Texts and Pretexts*, a personal anthology in which the verse extracts are interspersed with notes and short essays by Huxley himself. Besides testifying to his wide knowledge of English and French literature, the book also shows Huxley in one of his happiest roles—that of literary critic and "interpreter."

*Brave New World* is Huxley's nearest approach to popular fiction and probably served to introduce him to a far wider public. In his next novel, *Eyeless in Gaza* (1936), he reverts to an earlier and more characteristic manner. The first section describes the leading character looking at an album of photographs; his memory shifts to and fro over the past, as each photograph evokes a different scene or episode; thereafter the novel shifts backward and forward in time, the successive chapters being arranged unchronologically—thus, from 1933 we jump to 1934, thence back to 1933, then to 1902, and so on. The method probably owes something to Christopher Isherwood's *The Memorial* (1932), which is constructed on a very similar plan; and politics plays a far larger part in this book than in the previous novels—a fact that again suggests that Huxley may have been affected by politically minded writers of a younger generation.

The world of *Eyeless in Gaza* is still, very largely, the world of *Point Counter Point*, and the same kinds of characters and situations recur; there is, however, an increasing interest not only in politics (more especially in the political aspects of pacifism) but in the doctrines of mystical philosophy. Huxley's final convictions are as yet only implicit; but the philosophical outlook implied in *Eyeless in Gaza* is already very different from that of *Point Counter Point*. It is interesting to note that the further Huxley progressed toward his ultimate goal of nonattachment, the more preoccupied he seemed to become with the more unpleasant aspects of the human body. One would have expected the reverse to happen; yet in this novel and its successors there are a number of passages in which his "nastiness" seemed, to many readers, almost gratuitously offensive. In his earlier books one could attribute such lapses to mere youthful high spirits and a desire to shock bourgeois sensibilities; recurring in his maturity, they are perplexing, and one can only assume that the progressive heightening of his spiritual vision in some way intensified, retrospectively, his old Swiftian loathing for the body and its functions. The only good life, he seems to imply, is the spiritual life; but we are "born under one law, to another bound," and since we are condemned to live in a world of lust and excretion, of enemas and halitosis, we should do well not to forget the fact.

Many of the political and philosophic ideas in *Eyeless in Gaza* are further elaborated, in a more systematic form, in *Ends and Means* (1937), a long essay that appeared in the following year. Here Huxley's main thesis is that, in political as in individual behavior, the means condition the end and that therefore the much-invoked dictum "the end justifies the means" is demonstrably fallacious; the point is surely an important one and Huxley's elucidation of it is a valuable contribution to political thought.

*Ends and Means* cannot, however, be regarded as a mere political tract for the times: it is, among other things (as Huxley says), a kind of "cookbook" of reform and supplies an extremely comprehensive survey of the contemporary intellectual scene. The ideal goal of human effort has, as he says, been a matter of general agreement for the last thirty centuries: "From Isaiah to Karl Marx the prophets have spoken with one voice. In the Golden Age to which they look forward there will be liberty, peace, justice, and brotherly love." The trouble is—as Huxley sees it—that there has been no such general agreement about the means by which this ideal is to be attained: "Here unanimity and certainty give place to utter confusion, to the clash of contradictory opinions, dogmatically held and acted upon with the violence of fanaticism." Huxley's own solution of the problem (insofar as he attempts a solution) is in essence a religious one—the doctrine of complete nonattachment. Whether or not one agrees with Huxley's conclusions is hardly a matter of great importance; the chief value of *Ends and Means* lies in the attempt to evolve some kind of synthesis from the political, ethical, and religious confusions of our age. And, as Huxley modestly remarks in his closing words, "even the fragmentary outline of a synthesis is better than no synthesis at all."

*After Many a Summer* (1939) is a comedy of longevity set in Hollywood: a scientist, attempting to prolong human life by artificial means, is confronted by an actual bicentenarian who has anticipated his own discoveries a century and a half before. Much of the novel is in Huxley's best comic manner, but the philosophic divagations are inserted somewhat arbitrarily and tend to destroy the balance of the book. The same might be said of *Time Must Have a Stop* (1944), perhaps the least successful of Huxley's novels; in it he attempts the difficult feat of describing the mental processes of a man already dead, but the experiment can hardly be said to succeed.

Apart from fiction, Huxley's most substantial work to appear during World War II was *Grey Eminence* (1941), a detailed and scholarly biography of Father Joseph, the confidential adviser of Cardinal Richelieu. This is a model of its kind and makes one wish that Huxley's excursions into historiography had been more frequent. His researches into the life and times of Father Joseph may well have drawn his attention to the events related in *The Devils of Loudon* (1952). This is a detailed psychological study of an extraordinary case of demonic possession in seventeenth-century France. It is of great interest, but here again—as so often in his later work—Huxley seems overpreoccupied with the more unpleasant physiological aspects of his subject. There is, for instance, a description of the monstrous enemas employed as aids to exorcism that recalls certain comparable passages in *Eyeless in Gaza* and would seem to suggest that for Huxley the subject had a recurrent and somewhat morbid fascination.

During the last twenty years or so of Huxley's life, his output was hardly less prolific than formerly, and the works of this period show a remarkable diversity. Essays and belles lettres on the whole predominated over fiction, but three novels were published after 1945, and it will be convenient to consider these together. *Ape and Essence* (1948) is a short book, hardly more than a novella. It is a postatomic vision of the future, and though the theme may seem to justify Huxley's melodramatic treatment of it, the most gloating relish with which he piles on the horrors somewhat diminishes the total impact of the story. *The Genius and the Goddess* (1955) explores a situation that Huxley had more than once dealt with before: the frequent combination of intellectual preeminence with a total inability to cope with the emotional (and, as often as not, the purely practical) demands of life. Henry Maartens is a physicist of genius, married to a beautiful wife who runs his life for him. The story is told by his younger assistant, Rivers, to the narrator, a novelist. Rivers had become the lover of Maartens' wife, Katy, at a moment when Maartens was dangerously ill; the young man is tortured by guilt at having betrayed his adored master, yet his act restores to Katy what Huxley calls the quality of "grace," and she is thus enabled, by a kind of psychosomatic miracle, to save her husband's life. The situation, with its neat reversal of ethical cause and effect, has a typically Huxleyan irony. "*Le Cocu Miraculé.* What a subject for a French farce!" comments the narrator; but, as Rivers points out, Oedipus or Lear could equally well be conceived in farcical terms.

In *Island* (1962) Huxley returns once again to the theme of Utopia. A remote island, Pala, is populated by a community whose principles of government are founded, basically, upon Tantric Buddhism and an uninhibited but rational attitude to sex. In contrast with *Brave New World*, this later Utopian fantasy portrays a way of life many aspects of which, it may be supposed, its author would have found congenial. But Huxley, though he may have preferred the world of Pala to that of *Brave New World*, came to realize that such earthly paradises must prove finally helpless against the assault of industrialism and modern scientific techniques. This novel is, even for Huxley—who had never taken a very hopeful view of the future—a profoundly pessimistic one.

The more significant of Huxley's later writings were nonfictional. In 1945 appeared *The Perennial Philosophy*, a kind of anthology with an extensive running commentary, drawn from the writings of the mystics. Huxley's purpose was to extract from the manifold aspects of the subject a kind of highest common denominator, a system of philosophy that would include yet transcend the various methods by which men have sought to attain direct communication with God. As Huxley himself admitted, the mystical experience is, and must remain, finally incommunicable; many will dispute the validity of the mystic's claims, but whether one agrees or disagrees with Huxley's conclusions may be largely a matter of temperament. On the other hand, there can be no doubt whatsoever about the intellectual integrity of Huxley himself. His conversion (if one can use the word in this context) involved no intellectual surrender, no sudden act of faith; it was the result, rather, of a prolonged and critical investigation of the available evidence conducted with the caution and objectivity of a scientist.

*The Perennial Philosophy* was followed by two studies dealing with the effects of mescaline and lysergic acid (LSD): *The Doors of Perception* (1954) and *Heaven and Hell* (1956). Huxley maintains that the hallucinatory states produced by these drugs are hardly to be distinguished from the beatific vision of the mystics. This leads him to some interesting speculations as to the relationship between mind and body. Mescaline, for example, is allied to adrenochrome, which, it is thought, may occur spontaneously in the human organism. "In other words," writes Huxley, "each one of us may be capable of manufacturing a chemical, minute doses of which are known to cause profound changes in consciousness." The mystical state, therefore, may prove to be a mere function of the adrenal glands.

*Adonis and the Alphabet* (1956) is a volume of essays, all of which show that Huxley was a master of this form. The essay has become unpopular in an age of mass communications, but it was always well suited to the didactic strain in Huxley that he perhaps inherited from his grandfather. In this volume the title piece may be singled out as particularly characteristic. It describes a visit to Syria and Lebanon and relates the myth of Adonis to that unknown Phoenician who "about thirty-five centuries ago . . . invented, or at least perfected, the ABC." Here Huxley is in his best vein, and the witty, erudite writing recalls the lighthearted mood of such early travel books as *Jesting Pilate* and *Beyond the Mexique Bay*.

*Brave New World Revisited* (1958) is a long essay in which Huxley reconsiders his prophetic novel of 1932. He points out that many of his predictions came true very much sooner than he expected and the outlook gives little cause for optimism; yet it is our duty, he says, to resist the forces that menace our freedom, even though we may be (and probably are) fighting a losing battle.

It is a far cry from *Limbo* to *The Perennial Philosophy*, yet Huxley's works, considered as a whole, reveal a remarkably consistent pattern of development. His earliest books, apparently so slight and even frivolous, contain the germs of his later and more serious productions. This internal cohesion is the more surprising in view of Huxley's enormous range of interests; one could instance many modern writers whose work has the same kind of unity, but for the most part they are writers whose ideas operate within far narrower limits or who have some specific ax to grind. Huxley never ground an ax in his life—unless his unremitting and disinterested search for truth may be so described; yet, despite the homogeneity of his writings, he remains a strangely paradoxical figure: an intellectual who profoundly distrusted the intellect, a sensualist with a deep-seated loathing for bodily functions, a naturally religious man who remained an impenitent rationalist.

## SELECTED BIBLIOGRAPHY

I. BIBLIOGRAPHY. H. R. Duval, *Aldous Huxley: A Bibliography* (New York, 1939); C. J. Eschelbach and J. L. Schober, *Aldous Huxley: A Bibliography 1916-1959* (Berkeley, Calif., 1961).

II. COLLECTED WORKS. *Twice Seven: Fourteen Collected Stories* (London, 1944); *The Collected Edition* (London, 1946-1960); *Collected Short Stories* (London, 1957); *Collected Essays* (New York, 1959); D. Watt, ed., *The Collected Poetry of Aldous Huxley* (London, 1969); *Collected Works* (London, 1970-    ).

III. SELECTED WORKS. *Selected Poems* (Oxford, 1925); *Essays New and Old* (London, 1926); *Rotunda* (London, 1932), a general selection; *Stories, Essays and Poems* (London, 1937); *Verses and a Comedy* (London, 1946); M. Philipson, ed., *On Art and Artists* (London, 1960); H. Raymond, ed., *Selected Essays* (London, 1961); C. J. Rolo, ed., *The World of Aldous Huxley: An Omnibus of His Fiction and Nonfiction Over Three Decades* (New York, 1957); G. Smith, ed., *Letters of Aldous Huxley* (London, 1969).

IV. SEPARATE WORKS. *The Burning Wheel* (Oxford, 1916), verse; *Jonah* (Oxford, 1917), verse; *The Defeat of Youth and Other Poems* (Oxford, 1918).

*Leda and Other Poems* (London, 1920); *Limbo* (London, 1920), short stories; *Crome Yellow* (London, 1921), novel; *Mortal Coils* (London, 1922), short stories; *Antic Hay* (London, 1923), novel; *On the Margin* (London, 1923), essays; *The Discovery* (London, 1924), drama, adaptation of F. Sheridan's play; *Little Mexican* (London, 1924), short stories; *Along the Road* (London, 1925), travel; *Those Barren Leaves* (London, 1925), novel; *Jesting Pilate* (London, 1926), travel; *Two or Three Graces* (London, 1926), short stories; *Proper Studies* (London, 1927), essays; *Point Counter Point* (London, 1928), novel; *Arabia Infelix* (London, 1929), verse; *Do What You Will* (London, 1929), essays; *Holy Face, and Other Essays* (London, 1929).

*Brief Candles* (London, 1930), short stories; *This Way to Paradise* (London, 1930), dramatization of *Point Counter Point* by C. Dixon, preface by Huxley; *Vulgarity in Literature* (London, 1930), criticism; *The Cicadas and Other Poems* (London, 1931); *Music at Night* (New York, 1931), essays; *The World of Light* (London, 1931), drama; *Brave New World* (London, 1932), novel; *Texts and Pretexts* (London, 1932), anthology; *Thomas Henry Huxley as a Man of Letters* (London, 1932), criticism; *Beyond the Mexique Bay* (London, 1934), travel; *Eyeless in Gaza* (London, 1936), novel; *The Olive Tree* (London, 1936), essays; *What Are You Going to Do About It? The Case for Constructive Peace* (London, 1936), commentary; *Ends and Means* (London, 1937), commentary; *The Elder Pieter Breugel* (New York, 1938), art criticism; *The Most Agreeable Vice* (Los Angeles, 1938); *After Many a Summer* (London, 1939), novel.

*Words and Their Meanings* (Los Angeles, 1940); *Grey Eminence* (London, 1941), biography; *The Art of Seeing* (London, 1942), essay; *Time Must Have a Stop* (London, 1944), novel; *The Perennial Philosophy* (New York, 1945), commentary; *Science, Liberty and Peace* (New York, 1946), commentary; *Ape and Essence* (New York, 1948), novel; *The Gioconda Smile* (London, 1948), drama, adapted from a story in *Mortal Coils*; *Food and People* (London, 1949), with Sir John Russell; *The Prisons* (London, 1949), criticism.

*Themes and Variations* (London, 1950), essays; *The Devils of Loudon* (London, 1952), biography; *Joyce the Artificer: Two Studies of Joyce's Method* (London, 1952), with S. Gilbert; *The Doors of Perception* (London, 1954), essay; *The Genius and the Goddess* (London, 1955), novel;

*Adonis and the Alphabet* (London, 1956), essays; *Heaven and Hell* (London, 1956), essay, sequel to *Doors of Perception*; *Brave New World Revisited* (New York–London, 1958), essay.

*On Art and Artists* (London, 1960), anthology; *Island* (London, 1962), novel; *Literature and Science* (London, 1963), essay; *The Crows of Pearblossom* (London, 1967), children's story.

V. Translations and Introductions. R. de Gourmont, *A Virgin Heart* (New York, 1921), trans. from French by Huxley; C. P. de Crébillon, *The Opportunities of a Night* (London, 1925), trans. by E. Sutton, intro. by Huxley; *The Autobiography and Memoirs of Benjamin Robert Haydon* (London, 1926), intro. by Huxley; J. H. Burns, *A Vision of Education* (London, 1929), intro. by Huxley; *The Letters of D. H. Lawrence* (London, 1932), intro. by Huxley; A. Huxley, ed., *An Encyclopedia of Pacifism* (London, 1937); *The Song of God: Bhagavad-Gita* (Hollywood, 1944), trans. by S. Prabhavanda and C. Isherwood, intro. by Huxley.

VI. Biographical and Critical Studies. G. Vann, *On Being Human: St. Thomas and Mr. Aldous Huxley* (London, 1933); A. J. Henderson, *Aldous Huxley* (London, 1935); A. Gérard, *À la rencontre de Aldous Huxley* (Paris, 1947); S. Chatterjee, *Aldous Huxley: A Study* (Calcutta, 1955); J. Atkins, *Aldous Huxley: A Literary Study* (London, 1956).

S. Ghose, *Aldous Huxley: A Cynical Salvationist* (London, 1962); J. Huxley, ed., *Aldous Huxley, 1894–1963: A Memorial Volume* (London, 1965); S. J. Greenblatt, *Three Modern Satirists: Waugh, Orwell and Huxley* (London, 1965); R. W. Clark, *The Huxleys* (London, 1968); P. Bowering, *Aldous Huxley: A Study of the Major Novels* (London, 1968); L. A. Huxley, *This Timeless Moment: A Personal View of Aldous Huxley* (New York, 1968); J. Meckier, *Aldous Huxley: Satire and Structure* (London, 1969); D. P. Scales, *Aldous Huxley and French Literature* (London, 1969).

C. M. Holmes, *Aldous Huxley and the Way to Reality* (Bloomington, Ind., 1970); L. Brander, *Aldous Huxley: A Critical Study* (London, 1970); G. Woodcock, *Dawn and the Darkest Hour: A Study of Aldous Huxley* (London, 1972); K. May, *Aldous Huxley* (London, 1972); P. Firchow, *Aldous Huxley, Satirist and Novelist* (Minneapolis, 1972); S. Bedford, *Aldous Huxley*, 2 vols. (London, 1974, 1979); R. E. Kuehn, ed., *Aldous Huxley: A Collection of Critical Essays* (Englewood Cliffs, N. J., 1974).

C. S. Ferns, *Aldous Huxley, Novelist* (London, 1980); K. Gandhi, *Aldous Huxley* (London, 1981).

# SAMUEL JOHNSON
(1709-1784)

## S. C. Roberts

### I

"SAMUEL JOHNSON is more vivid to us in a book written by another man than in any of the books that he wrote himself." Such is the penalty of being the subject of the greatest biography in the language, with the further result that many readers tend to separate Johnson the writer from Johnson the man as displayed by James Boswell.

Fundamentally, the distinction is unsound. It was Johnson's writings that first attracted Boswell, and if the reader wishes to recapture the Boswellian aura, he must do as Boswell did and study the works of the man who became known as the Great Moralist and the Great Lexicographer while Boswell was still a schoolboy. This simple chronological reminder is the best critical antidote to the ancient fallacy that Johnson was made by Boswell. Of course, Boswell's ultimate triumph in "Johnsonizing the land" was supreme. But the old view that "it was the object of Boswell's life to connect his own name with that of Johnson" contains little more than a dangerous half-truth. Boswell wished his name to be associated with many other famous names besides that of Johnson, and his wish was fulfilled. But among all his schemes for the attainment of literary fame, there remained at the back of his mind the possibility of a magnum opus, and for the subject of his culminating work he chose Johnson. Why? The answer, or the foundation of an answer, can best be found in a contemplation of Johnson's early career and of his position in the world of letters at the time of Boswell's introduction to him in 1763.

### II

WHEN Johnson came to try his fortune in London, he was twenty-eight years old. The son of a not very successful bookseller in Lichfield, he had left Oxford after four terms, without a degree. Poverty and ill health made his prospects poor. After an unhappy experience as an assistant teacher in a grammar school, he moved to Birmingham, where he chanced upon some hackwork (notably the translation of Jeronimo Lobo's[1] *Voyage to Abyssinia*) and also upon a wife, "a widow, the relict of Mr. Porter, a mercer," and Johnson's senior by twenty years. The bride brought a modest fortune with her, and near his old home at Lichfield Johnson determined to set up an academy where young gentlemen could be "boarded and taught the Latin and Greek languages." An elaborate classical curriculum was prepared, but the school failed and Johnson made his final choice of life—"to become an author by profession."

It was a profession that could be followed only in London, and so Johnson went there in 1737. He was, as he said, "an adventurer in literature," and he brought one of his pupils, David Garrick, with him:

> The two fellow-travellers had the world before them, and each was to choose his road to fortune and to fame. They brought with them genius, and powers of mind, peculiarly formed by nature for the different vocations to which each of them felt himself inclined. They acted from the impulse of young minds, even then meditating great things, and with courage anticipating success. . . . In three or four years afterwards Garrick came forth with talents that astonished the publick . . . Johnson was left to toil in the humble walks of literature.

For many years the walks were humble indeed. A newly founded journal, the *Gentleman's Magazine*, edited by Edward Cave, was the medium of Johnson's first contributions to periodical literature.

---

[1] Portuguese Jesuit missionary (1593–1678) in India and Abyssinia whose manuscript account of his travels was translated into French: *Voyage Historique d'Abissinie* (1728).

Odes, epigrams, epitaphs, reviews, short biographies, and other pieces were accepted by Cave, who quickly recognized Johnson's quality as a journalist. In particular, he employed his new contributor to revise and embellish the reports of debates in Parliament that formed an important feature of his magazine. They were not the verbatim reports to which the modern reader of *Hansard's House of Commons Journal* is accustomed. They were written with a fervor that "bordered upon enthusiasm" and with a particular determination "that the Whig dogs should not have the best of it." In later years Johnson had some compunction in looking back upon these *Debates* and warned historians not to quote them. After listening to the praises poured upon a famous speech of William Pitt beginning "Sir, the atrocious crime of being a young man . . . " he broke in with "That speech I wrote in a garret in Exeter street."

But while he faced the necessity of "writing for bread" Johnson preserved also the legitimate ambition of a man of letters. As a young man, he had written of

> . . . the young author panting for a name
> And fir'd with pleasing hope of endless fame

and early in 1738 he submitted his poem "London" to Cave for publication. It was a poem of more substance than his customary contributions to the magazine and Cave arranged for its publication by Robert Dodsley. "London" is at once an illustration of the literary fashion of its time and an individual expression of Johnson's scholarship. It was written in imitation of Juvenal's third satire and *saeva indignatio* is turned against the lawlessness of the streets:

> Here malice, rapine, accident conspire,
> And now a rabble rages, now a fire;
> Their ambush here relentless ruffians lay,
> And here the fell attorney prowls for prey;
> Here falling houses thunder on your head,
> And here a female atheist talks you dead,[2]
> (13-18)

against the corruption and cowardice of the government:

[2]Quotations are from the Yale edition of *The Works of Samuel Johnson* (New Haven, 1958), still in progress.

> Here let those reign, whom pensions can incite
> To vote a patriot black, a courtier white;
> Explain their country's dear-bought rights away
> And plead for pirates in the face of day
> (51-54)

and, more personally, against the poor man's lot:

> Of all the griefs that harrass the distress'd,
> Sure the most bitter is a scornful jest;
> Fate never wounds more deep the gen'rous heart
> Than when a blockhead's insult points the dart. . . .
> This mournful truth is ev'ry where confess'd,
> SLOW RISES WORTH, BY POVERTY DEPRESS'D. . . .
> (165-168; 176-177)

In form, "London" may be regarded as a Latinist's exercise; in substance, it comes from the heart of Grub Street and from the heart of the writer. The poem was published anonymously, but its quality was recognized. "Here," people said, "is an unknown poet, greater even than Pope," and Pope himself, being informed that the author was an unknown man named Johnson, declared: "He will soon be *déterré*." Johnson's monetary reward was ten guineas.

So the hackwork continued and sometimes more than hackwork: the *Life* of his friend Richard Savage, for instance, of which he wrote forty-eight pages at a sitting, and the *Observations on Macbeth* (1745), to which were appended *Proposals* for an edition of Shakespeare. For his old pupil, David Garrick, he wrote a prologue for the opening of the Drury Lane Theatre in 1747, surveying in rapid review the history of the English stage since Shakespeare's time. His comment on the Restoration was essentially that of the moralist:

> The Wits of *Charles* found easier Ways to Fame,
> Nor wish'd for Jonson's Art or Shakespeare's Flame;
> Themselves they studied, as they felt, they writ,
> Intrigue was Plot, Obscenity was Wit.
> Vice always found a sympathetic Friend;
> They pleas'd their age and did not aim to mend.
> (17-22)

Two years later Johnson came forward himself as a playwright. In the early days of his marriage he had drafted a tragedy based on the story, as told by Richard Knolles in his *Generall Historie of the Turkes*, of Mahomet II and the beautiful Greek maiden, Irene, who was taken captive at the fall of

Constantinople. The play, *Irene: A Tragedy*, was finished soon after his arrival in London. For some years his efforts to have it either published or acted were fruitless; but when Garrick came into power at Drury Lane, he determined to do his best for his old schoolmaster. The play was produced "with a display of eastern magnificence" on 6 February 1749 and ran for nine nights. It has never been revived. One contemporary critic remarked that "to instance every moral which is inculcated in this performance would be to transcribe the whole." From Johnson's point of view, the heart of the matter is Irene's failure to resist the appeals of Mahomet and to hold fast to her religion. To her friend, Aspasia, she puts the question:

> Upbraid me not with fancy'd Wickedness
> I am not yet a Queen, or an Apostate.
> But should I sin beyond the Hope of Mercy,
> If, when Religion prompts me to refuse,
> The Dread of instant Death restrains my Tongue?
> (III. viii. 21-25)

to which Aspasia answers:

> Reflect that Life and Death, affecting Sounds,
> Are only varied Modes of endless Being:
> Reflect that Life, like ev'ry other Blessing,
> Derives its Value from its Use alone;
> Not for itself but for a nobler End
> Th' Eternal gave it, and that End is Virtue....
> (III. viii. 26-31)

And when Irene hints at the benefit her own country might derive from her apostasy:

> O! did Irene shine the Queen of *Turkey*,
> No more should *Greece* lament those prayers rejected.
> Again should golden Splendour grace her Cities....
> (III. viii. 51-53)

the reply is prompt and uncompromising:

> By virtuous Ends pursued by virtuous Means,
> Nor think th' Intention sanctifies the Deed:
> That Maxim publish'd in an Impious Age,
> Would loose the wild Enthusiast to destroy,
> And fix the fierce Usurper's bloody Title.
> The Bigotry might send her Slaves to War,
> And bid Success become the Test of Truth.
> (III. viii. 57-63)

As a dramatic production, *Irene*, in spite of Garrick's efforts, was not a success; but it is one of the many evidences of Johnson's preoccupation with the proper tests of truth. Primarily, it was the work of a "young author panting for a name," but in Johnson's hands the story of Irene quickly became a reflection of the continuing struggles in his own mind. A man at once of strong passions and of deep dependence upon an ultimate faith, he pointed the moral of Irene's apostasy with all the fervor of a Christian moralist. It would be idle to pretend that *Irene* left any permanent mark upon the history of English drama; but a few of its lines are preserved in footnotes to chapter 68 of Edward Gibbon's *Decline and Fall of the Roman Empire*.

Just before the production of his play, Johnson had, with greater success, published his second satire, "The Vanity of Human Wishes," the first work to be issued with the author's name on the title page. Like "London," the poem was written in imitation of Juvenal, but the treatment is much freer. The theme of the young author is developed, and the lot of the struggling scholar is presented in lines that have become part of the English literary tradition:

> Deign on the passing world to turn thine eyes
> And pause awhile from letters, to be wise;
> There mark what ills the scholar's life assail,
> Toil, envy, want, the patron and the gaol.
> (158-161)

But the poem is much more than a personal complaint. Thomas Cardinal Wolsey, Charles XII of Sweden, and others are cited to demonstrate the impermanence of human fame and the hollowness of martial triumph:

> The festal blazes, the triumphal show,
> The ravish'd standard, and the captive foe,
> The senate's thanks, the gazette's pompous tale.
> With force resistless o'er the brave prevail.
> Such bribes the rapid Greek o'er Asia whirl'd,
> For such the steady Romans shook the world;
> For such in distant lands the Britons shine,
> And stain with blood the Danube or the Rhine;
> This pow'r has praise, that virtue scarce can warm
> Till fame supplies the universal charm.
> Yet Reason frowns on War's unequal game,
> Where wasted nations raise a single name,
> And mortgag'd states their grand-sires' wreaths regret,
> From age to age in everlasting debt;

Wreaths which at last the dear-bought right convey
To rust on medals, or on stones decay.
(175-190)

Here is no transient satire upon current events, but "the high seriousness which comes from absolute sincerity," though Matthew Arnold would never have put this hallmark on the work of an Augustan poet.

Meanwhile, Johnson was too good a realist to imagine that satire in verse would enable him to make a living; but he was now coming to be recognized as a competent man of letters, and he sought for some more solid and more scholarly task than weekly journalism could provide. So, when a syndicate of booksellers approached him with a proposal for a dictionary of the English language, he accepted the offer and produced his plan in 1747. He was drawn forward, he said, by the prospect of employment that, though not splendid, would be useful. The plan was addressed to Lord Chesterfield, whose initial neglect and subsequent attempts to make amends provoked the most famous of all Johnson's letters. At the outset, even Johnson was "frighted" at the extent of the work he had undertaken. But on the top floor of his house in Gough Square he organized his six amanuenses (five of them from Scotland, as Boswell is careful to point out) and the "harmless drudgery" went forward.

Johnson made no complaint about the sum the booksellers paid him, but, even so, the prospective fame of lexicography would not keep the wolf from the door. Accordingly, he decided to embark upon a weekly paper, which he entitled the *Rambler*. In general form it followed the pattern of the *Spectator* and the *Tatler*, and Johnson had an especially high opinion of Joseph Addison's prose. The *Rambler* was not conceived as a series of papers to provide weekly entertainment. It was deliberately the work of a "majestic teacher of moral and religious wisdom" and Johnson embarked upon it with a prayer: "Grant, I beseech Thee, that in this undertaking thy Holy Spirit may not be withheld from me, but that I may promote Thy glory and the salvation of myself and others."

An appreciation of the nature and the circumstances of the production of the *Rambler* is fundamental to an understanding of Johnson's position in the world of letters. To later critics it has been a stumbling block. Thomas Macaulay grumbles at "Johnsonese"; Hippolyte Taine complains that the essays are no more and no less than sermons; Leslie Stephen notes that a moralist must not aim at originality in his precepts; and readers, as a whole, put the *Rambler* aside and go back to Boswell. But they do not always reflect upon Boswell's own attitude. In his early reading he had nowhere found "more bark and steel for the mind" than in the *Rambler*; in his early meetings with Johnson his culminating pride was in the fact that he had spent an evening not with the great clubman, not with the Great Lexicographer, but with the author of the *Rambler*. Unlike readers today, Boswell was primarily drawn to Johnson by the "amazing universality" of his genius as a writer. The highest compliment he could pay to his conversation was to put it on a level with his written works. Here it must be remembered that when Johnson took a pen in his hand, he deliberately adopted a style and a standard that were quite distinct from his tavern chair manner. Talking and writing were for him quite separate arts:

As many please [he wrote] by extemporary talk, though utterly unacquainted with the more accurate method and more laboured beauties which composition requires; so it is very possible that men wholly accustomed to works of study may be without that readiness of conception and affluence of language always necessary to colloquial entertainment.
(*Rambler* No. 14)

If the *Times* (London), as we know it, had existed in Johnson's day, he would have made an admirable lead editorial writer; but he would not have been commissioned to write the light commentaries. Accordingly, the reader of the *Rambler* must not look for "colloquial entertainment"; but he will be a dull reader if he does not occasionally derive pleasure, as well as instruction, from its pages. Unlike his successors of today, Johnson never "complied with contemporary curiosity" and rarely "exemplified his assertions by living characters." Consequently, the *Rambler* is not a day-to-day commentary on the political, social, or literary events of the time. If, on occasion, Johnson had individual characters or particular events in mind, he was careful to generalize them. Yet, nowhere can a better picture of the journalist's lot be found than in the *Rambler* No. 145:

It has formerly been imagined that he who intends the entertainment or instruction of others must feel in himself some peculiar impulse of genius.... But the authors whom I am now endeavouring to recommend have been too long hackneyed in the ways of men to indulge the chimerical ambition of immortality; they have seldom any claim to the trade of writing, but that they have tried some other without success, they perceive no particular summons to composition, except the sound of the clock . . . and about the opinion of posterity they have little solicitude, for their productions are seldom intended to remain in the world longer than a week.

This is but one of several shrewd reflections on the profession of literature, and when Johnson wrote of Grub Street he wrote of what he knew. But in fact only a small proportion of the *Rambler* is devoted to literary topics. Many of the essays are character sketches; one of them, that of Suspirius, was used by Oliver Goldsmith for the making of Croaker in *The Good Natur'd Man*, and it was Croaker who made the play a success. Domestic relationships provided material for many essays, and it is legitimate to conjecture that in the *Rambler* No. 112 the description of the fussy housewife and the grumbling male may reflect some features of Johnson's own experience. Solemnity is by no means the pervading quality of the *Rambler*, but it is certainly evident in the treatment of such subjects as the death sentence for robbery. Here, and not only here, Johnson's opinions were in advance of his time:

Death is. . . . of dreadful things the most dreadful. . . . To equal robbery with murder is to reduce murder to robbery, to confound in common minds the gradations in iniquity and incite the commission of a greater crime to prevent the detection of a less.

(*Rambler* No. 114)

The *Rambler*, in short, abounds in passages that are an essential complement to Johnson's utterances as preserved in Boswell's record, and, let it be repeated, it was on the *Rambler* that Boswell's admiration was initially based.

Johnson's second series of periodical essays (the *Idler*) were contributed to the *Universal Chronicle*, a weekly publication, between 1758 and 1760, and to anyone who still protests that Johnson is unreadable, there is no better answer than to confront him with a selection of *Idler* papers. Boswell himself is curiously apologetic. The *Idler*, he says, has less body and more spirit than the *Rambler*, and he comes as near to censure as a hero worshiper can when he reflects upon Johnson's wantonness of disquisition and his failure to suppress his power of sophistry—and all this because Johnson made fun of the opinion "that our mental facilities depend, in some degree, upon the weather," in an essay beginning:

It is commonly observed that when two Englishmen meet, their first talk is of the weather; they are in haste to tell each other, what each must already know, that it is hot or cold, bright or cloudy, windy or calm. . . .

(*Idler* No. 11)

Some of the *Idler* papers, as Boswell is pleased to remark, approximate in "profundity of thought" and "labour of language" to the *Rambler* standard; but others display a lighter touch and a remarkable freshness. On newswriters in wartime, for instance:

In a time of war . . . the task of news-writers is easy: they have nothing to do but to tell . . . that a battle has been fought, in which we and our friends, whether conquering or conquered, did all, and our enemies did nothing. Scarcely anything awakens attention like a tale of cruelty. . . .

(*Idler* No. 30)

Or this description of a bargain hunter:

I am the unfortunate husband of *a buyer of bargains* . . . whatever she thinks cheap, she holds it the duty of an economist to buy; in consequence of this maxim, we are encumbered on every side with useless lumber. The servants can scarcely creep to their beds through the chests and boxes that surround them. The carpenter is employed once a week in building closets, fixing cupboards and fastening shelves. . . .

(*Idler* No. 35)

But perhaps the most revealing essay is that in which Johnson purports to display the character of his old friend Sober:

Sober is a man of strong desires and quick imagination, so exactly balanced by the love of ease, that they can seldom stimulate him to any difficult undertaking; they have, however, so much power, that they will not suffer him to lie quite at rest; and though they do not make him sufficiently useful to others, they make him at least weary of himself.

Mr. Sober's chief pleasure is conversation; there is no end of his talk or his attention; to speak or to hear is equally pleasing. . . . But there is one time at night when he must go home, that his friends may sleep; and another time in the morning, when all the world agrees to shut out interruption. These are the moments of which poor Sober trembles at the thought....

(*Idler* No. 31)

It is Johnson's *apologia pro vita sua*.

### III

BEFORE the series of *Idler* papers was completed, Johnson heard that his mother, now ninety years old, was gravely ill at Lichfield. On 13 January 1759 he contrived to send her twelve guineas. A week later he wrote in terms of deep affection and distress and on the same day he also wrote to William Strahan, the printer, telling him that he had written a new work for which he would need an immediate advance of £30. The work was *The History of Rasselas Prince of Abyssinia* and Johnson had written it in the evenings of a week. His mother died a few days after he had delivered the copy, but at least he had earned some money for the expenses of her funeral. Apart from the circumstances of its production, *Rasselas* is important in relation not only to Johnson's philosophy of life but also to eighteenth-century taste. Neither the *Rambler* nor the *Idler* had achieved more than a succès d'estime, but *Rasselas* was immediately welcomed and was, indeed, the one work of Johnson's that won solid popularity during the author's lifetime. As Boswell says, it was "extensively diffused over Europe" in a variety of translations, and readers of Elizabeth Gaskell's *Cranford* will remember that in the middle of the nineteenth century old-fashioned ladies still regarded it as a more reliable kind of fiction than the new-fangled and sensational stuff then being produced by Charles Dickens.

The eighteenth century loved a moral tale ("impressive truth, in splendid fiction drest") and *Rasselas* is Johnson's culminating work as a social and ethical philosopher. The setting of the tale, but little else, was no doubt taken from Lobo's *Voyage to Abyssinia*. Rasselas and his sister, "wearying of the soft vicissitudes of pleasure and repose," leave their happy valley with a determination to gain experience of the varying conditions of human existence and to make their choice of life. They meet and talk with young men and old, with professors, astronomers, shepherds, and poets. Their conclusion ("in which nothing is concluded") is similar to that of the author of *Ecclesiastes*, and so they resolve to return to Abyssinia. No work of Johnson's is more relevant to the study of the author's temperament and outlook than *Rasselas*. It is addressed, at the outset, to those "who listen with credulity to the whispers of fancy and pursue with eagerness the phantoms of hope; who expect that age will perform the promises of youth and that the deficiencies of the present day will be supplied by the morrow," and the discussions between Rasselas and his companions range over many of the fundamental issues of art and life. Are the Europeans happier than we? Rasselas asks. Imlac, in reply, describes their many advantages and Rasselas feels that with all their conveniences and ease of communication they must surely be happy. Then comes Imlac's—and Johnson's—final verdict: "The Europeans are less unhappy than we, but they are not happy. Human life is every where a state in which much is to be endured, and little to be enjoyed."

In whatever context it is sought, happiness continues to be elusive. The poet sets himself so high a standard ("the interpreter of nature . . . the legislator of mankind . . . a being superior to time and place") that Rasselas protests himself convinced that no human being can ever be a poet. The hermit, after fifteen years of solitude, resolves to return to the world, convinced that "the life of a solitary man will be certainly miserable, but not certainly devout." The way to be happy, says the philosopher, is to live according to nature. What is life according to nature? asks Rasselas. "To live according to nature," is the reply, "is to act always with due regard to the fitness arising from the relations and qualities of causes and effects: to concur with the great and unchangeable scheme of universal felicity; to co-operate with the general disposition and tendency of the present system of things." Upon which Rasselas appropriately concluded that "this was one of the sages whom he should understand less as he heard him longer."

Similarly, after an earnest discussion of the problems of family life, the conclusion is reached that "marriage has many pains, but celibacy has no pleasures"; and a visit to the Great Pyramid leads Imlac to observe: "I consider this mighty structure as a monument of the insufficiency of human enjoyments."

From all this we may understand Boswell's feeling when he wrote: "The fund of thinking which this work contains is such that almost every sentence of it may furnish a subject of long meditation." Boswell did not comment on Johnson's conjecture that someday man might use "the swifter migration of wings"; but it may still provoke prolonged meditation:

What would be the security of the good, if the bad could at pleasure invade them from the sky? Against an army sailing through the clouds, neither walls, nor mountains, nor seas could afford any security. A flight of northern savages might hover in the wind, and light at once with irresistible violence upon the capital of a fruitful region that was rolling under them.
(*Rasselas*, ch. 6)

Meanwhile Johnson's work in another field had been going steadily forward. "This is a great work, William Sir," said Dr. Adams, master of Johnson's old college. "How can you do this in three years?" To which Johnson said, "Sir, I have no doubt that I can do it in three years." And when told that the forty members of the Académie Française had taken forty years to compile their dictionary, he replied, "Sir, thus it is. This is the proportion. Let me see; forty times forty is sixteen hundred. As three to sixteen hundred, so is the proportion of an Englishman to a Frenchman." This was Johnson talking for victory, and in fact he was engaged upon his task for eight years. In the plan of 1747 it is characteristic that, although the work was to bring him a degree, it was not undertaken merely as an academic thesis:

The value of a work must be estimated by its use; it is not enough that a dictionary delights the critick, unless, at the same time, it instructs the learner, as it is to little purpose that an engine amuses the philosopher by the subtilty of its mechanism, if it requires so much knowledge in its application as to be of no advantage to the common workman.
(*The Plan of a Dictionary of the English Language*)

The two massive folios that appeared in 1755 may well have seemed a formidable tool to be used by the common workman of literature. But Johnson was a pioneer in lexicography. Even the most rapid and casual comparison of Johnson's handling of a familiar English word with the scanty definitions given by his immediate predecessor, Nathaniel Bailey, is enough to demonstrate the quality and magnitude of Johnson's achievement. Conscious alike of the "scholar's reverence for antiquity" and the "grammarian's regard to the genius of our tongue," he realized that words were not museum pieces to be cataloged, but symbols subject to continual change and adaptation. He realized also that if he followed every byway of research, he would never finish his work:

I saw one inquiry only gave occasion to another, that book referred to book, that to search was not always to find, and to find was not always to be informed. . . . I then contracted my design, determining to confide in myself.
(*ibid.*)

It was a confidence well placed. No one before Johnson had attempted to analyze the finer variations of meaning that a simple word might have acquired in different authors and in different contexts;[3] and the wealth of illustrative quotation was the fruit of his own wide reading and tenacious memory. That the work would contain "a few wild blunders and risible absurdities" Johnson was well aware. Even Boswell admits that his definition of "network" ("Anything reticulated or decussated, at equal distances, with interstices between the intersections") was quoted with sportive malignity; and today it is the grim little jokes in the definitions of "oats" and "excise" and "lexicographer" that are remembered by the ordinary reader. Such is the inevitable work of time, which "antiquates antiquities and hath an art to make dust of all things." But Johnson's *Dictionary* has not come to dust. The late editor in chief of the *Oxford English Dictionary*, Sir James Murray, described it as "a marvellous piece of work to accomplish in eight and a half years"; and it remains a battered, but enduring, milestone in the history of English lexicography.

So, in 1755, Johnson became the Great Lexicographer, and he had the further satisfaction of being able to add the letters A.M. (*Artium Magister*) after his name on the title page. But the ground on which he was recommended for an Oxford degree is significant: he had "very eminently distinguished himself by the publication of a series of essays, ex-

---

[3] The word "go," for instance, is defined by Bailey as "to walk, move about, etc." Johnson distinguishes sixty-seven senses of the word, with illustrations from the Bible, Shakespeare, Locke, Dryden, Swift, and many others.

cellently calculated to form the manners of the people, and in which the cause of religion and morality is everywhere maintained by the strongest powers of argument and language." In 1775 the University of Oxford awarded him the higher degree of Doctor of Civil Law. But ten years earlier he had been made LL.D. (*Legum Doctor*) by Trinity College, Dublin, and it should not be forgotten that it was an Irish university that first created "Doctor Johnson." In the preface to the *Dictionary* can be found some of the best examples of Johnson's prose:

In this work, when it shall be found that much is omitted, let it not be forgotten that much likewise is performed; and though no book was ever spared out of tenderness to the author, and the world is little solicitous to know whence proceeded the faults of that which it condemns; yet it may gratify curiosity to inform it, that the English Dictionary was written with little assistance of the learned, and without any patronage of the great; not in the soft obscurities of retirement, or under the shelter of academick bowers, but amidst inconvenience and distraction, in sickness and in sorrow.

One of Johnson's principal sorrows had been the death of his wife in 1752, just after the issue of the last *Rambler*. "Remember me in your prayers," Johnson wrote to his friend Dr. John Taylor, "for vain is the help of man," and while Mrs. Johnson in her lifetime may well have provoked a certain measure of domestic irritation by her "particular preference for cleanliness," there can be no doubt of Johnson's devotion to the memory of his dear Tetty. Although the scholastic triumph of the *Dictionary* in 1755 marked the final stage of Johnson's emergence from hackwork to literary eminence, it was not until 1762 that he was delivered from the labor and anxiety of "writing for bread." In that year, to his surprise, he was informed that His Majesty King George III was graciously pleased to award him a pension of three hundred pounds a year. Johnson was staggered. Had he not written in "London" of those "whom pensions can incite/To vote a patriot black, a courtier white"? Had he not defined "pension" as "pay given to a state hireling for treason to his country"? Conscious of all this, Johnson hesitated to accept the honor; but his friends reassured him and, in particular, Lord Bute, the prime minister, overcame his scruples by telling him: "It is not given you for any thing you are to do, but for what you have done."

## IV

Such were a few of the events in Johnson's career before his first meeting with Boswell, but enough, perhaps, to indicate the celebrity he had achieved by 1763. In a diary of the previous year, Boswell had recorded how, after reading some *Rambler* papers to the company assembled in a country house, he delivered his opinion that Johnson was "a man of much philosophy, extensive reading and real knowledge of human life" and when, on 19 September 1762, he beheld the City of London from Highgate Hill, his soul "bounded forth to a certain prospect of happy futurity." On 18 December he was delighted to accept an invitation to meet Johnson at dinner with Tom Davies the bookseller, on Christmas Day. Unfortunately, Johnson decided to go to Oxford for Christmas, but Boswell had the pleasure of meeting Oliver Goldsmith and seized the opportunity of discussing the *Rambler* and *Idler* with him. The famous first meeting in Tom Davies' shop, on 16 May 1763, was in fact accidental, but it was the beginning of one of the most famous associations in history. Boswell had two principal ambitions: to be the friend of famous men and to be a famous author himself. Among the celebrities whom he wished to meet in London in 1763, Johnson stood very high, and when Boswell found himself supping on easy terms of intimacy with him and realized that the quality of Johnson's talk was equal to that of his writings, he rejoiced at his good fortune and immediately began to make notes of their conversations. ("We sat till between one and two and finished a couple of bottles of port. I went home in high exultation.")[4] But the *Life* was not an isolated achievement; it was, as has already been observed, the final triumph of a career of literary ambition and effort.

Johnson, for his part, was immediately captivated by Boswell's ingenuous charm. To the end of his life, he looked upon every day in which he did not make a new acquaintance as being lost. Boswell was a superb listener, and nothing could have been more flattering to a lonely scholar than to be eagerly admired by someone thirty years his junior. During the summer of 1763 the friendship developed. There were suppers at the Mitre Tavern and excursions on the Thames, but the most strik-

[4] Quotations of Boswell are from the Everyman's Library edition of his *Life of Samuel Johnson* (London, 1949).

ing proof of Johnson's attachment was his decision to accompany Boswell to Harwich at the end of his London visit. There Boswell received good advice on a variety of subjects. He was bound for Holland, where he was to continue his study of law, and Johnson bade him kneel in the church and commend himself to his Creator and Redeemer. When they came out of the church, Johnson demonstrated his contempt for the Berkeleian theory of matter by "striking his foot with mighty force against a large stone." He also warned Boswell of the folly of pretending indifference to food and of using big words for little matters. As they parted they promised to write to each other. Boswell expressed the hope that Johnson would not forget him. "Nay, Sir," Johnson replied, "it is more likely you should forget me than that I should forget you." It was the reply of one who loved the acquaintance of young people; young acquaintances, he said, lasted longest.

To Johnson a club was one of the first necessities of life. In his *Dictionary* he defined it as "an assembly of good fellows meeting under certain conditions." As early as 1749 he founded the Ivy Lane Club, where he would "pass those hours in a free and unrestrained interchange of sentiments, which otherwise had been spent at home in painful reflection." It was not a purely literary gathering; three members of the club were physicians (including Johnson's very dear friend Richard Bathurst, who could not tolerate fools or rogues or Whigs and was, in short, "a very good hater"). There were John Hawkesworth, editor of the *Adventurer*, John Payne, publisher of the *Rambler*, Samuel Salter, formerly archdeacon of Norfolk, and Sir John Hawkins, for whom Johnson was afterward driven to coin the word "unclubable."

More famous was the Club, founded in 1764. It was Sir Joshua Reynolds who first suggested its formation to Johnson, and among the original members were Edmund Burke, Topham Beauclerk, Bennet Langton, and Goldsmith. Boswell was admitted later, after some hesitation on the part of certain members. Johnson told Boswell the story of his election with characteristic candor: "Sir, they knew that if they refused you, they'd probably never have got in another. I'd have kept them all out." Posterity is heavily indebted to Johnson's dictatorship. Meetings of the Club provided Boswell with material for some of his most brilliant reporting. Good company, good food, and good conversation constituted the primary solace of Johnson's life, and now that he was relieved of the necessity of earning his living by his pen, he was free to take his pleasures—but not always with a good conscience. On Easter Eve 1764 he recorded:

My indolence, since my last reception of the Sacrament, has sunk into grosser sluggishness, and my dissipation spread into wilder negligence. . . . A kind of strange oblivion has overspread me, so that I know not what has become of the last year. . . . This is not the life to which heaven is promised.

(*Life of Johnson*, vol. I, p. 300)

On Easter Day, he went to church (coming in "at the first of the Psalms"), and in his prayers he recommended his dear Tetty as well as his father, mother, brother, and Bathurst, "so far as it might be lawful." As he received the Sacrament at the altar, he resolved to repel sinful thoughts, to study eight hours daily, to go to church every Sunday, and to read the Scriptures. After putting his shilling in the plate, he saw a poor girl at the Sacrament in a bedgown and gave her, privately, a crown. He then prayed earnestly for amendment and repeated his prayer at home. This account of Easter 1764 is no isolated record. It is typical of Johnson's self-examination at Easter, or on his birthday, or on New Year's Day, over a long period of years.

There was one delay that weighed with particular force on Johnson's mind. In 1756 he had published his *Proposals* for an edition of Shakespeare, hoping to complete the work by the end of the following year. It was a mark of editorial optimism not peculiar to Johnson or his period. But after six years it provoked some raillery:

> He for subscribers baits his hook
> And takes your cash; but where's the book?

When the eight volumes at length appeared in 1765, the subscribers' names were not included in them. For this omission Johnson gave what he described as two cogent reasons—he had lost the names and spent the money.

After the *Dictionary*, the edition of Shakespeare is the most valuable legacy of Johnson's scholarship. Every generation produces its quota of Shakespearean editors and critics and, in 1908, Walter Raleigh remarked that while Johnson had been neglected and depreciated in the nineteenth century he would probably be respected in the twentieth. This

# SAMUEL JOHNSON

forecast has been fulfilled; and a modern editor of Shakespeare was not ashamed to entitle the first chapter of his book on Falstaff "Back to Johnson."[5]

Throughout his life Johnson had been a devoted student of Shakespeare; he began at so early an age that the speech of the Ghost in *Hamlet* terrified him when he was alone. His first work as an anonymous commentator (*Miscellaneous Observations on the Tragedy of Macbeth*) was published in 1745, with a postscript on the recent edition of Sir Thomas Hanmer, which was weighed in the balance and found wanting:

> Its pomp recommends it more than its accuracy. There is no distinction made between the ancient reading and the innovations of the editor; there is no reason given for any of the alterations which are made; the emendations of former critics are adopted without any acknowledgment, and few of the difficulties are removed which have hitherto embarrassed the readers of Shakespeare.

To this devastating summary of editorial failure Johnson appended proposals for an edition of his own; but copyright difficulties arose and it was not until after the publication of the *Dictionary*, which abounds in quotations from Shakespeare, that he issued his more elaborate *Proposals*. Here, the justification of a new edition and the primary obligations of an editor are set out in positive form: first, it is his business to correct what is corrupt, and the circumstances of the writing of Shakespeare's plays made this a difficult task, since the plays were "vitiated by the blunders of the penman... changed by the affectation of the player... and printed without the concurrence of the author"; secondly, Shakespeare presented many obscurities that it was the commentator's duty to elucidate, especially the obscurities inherent in Shakespeare's common colloquial language with its "allusive, elliptical and proverbial" phrases; finally, in order to appreciate Shakespeare's use of his sources, the editor must read the story "in the very book which Shakespeare consulted." As to the occurrence of obsolete diction in the plays, Johnson claimed, not immodestly, that he had had more motives to consider the whole extent of the English language than any other man.

Philology apart, Johnson was too honest a critic not to "confess the faults of our favourite to gain credit to our praise of his excellencies," and his fundamental criticism of Shakespeare was the criticism of the Christian moralist:

> His precepts and axioms drop casually from him; he makes no just distribution of good and evil... he carries his persons indifferently through right and wrong and at the close dismisses them without further care, and leaves their examples to operate by chance. This fault the barbarity of his age cannot extenuate: for it is always a writer's duty to make the world better.
> (*Preface to Shakespeare*, p. 71)

There speaks the Rambler, and by any argument for the artist's primary duty of self-expression he would have been unshaken.

Another characteristic mark of Johnson's approach was that he had a greater relish for the printed than the spoken word. Many of the plays, he thought, and particularly the tragedies, were the worse for being acted, and he was insensitive to dramatic illusion:

> The truth is that the spectators are always in their senses and know, from the first act to the last, that the stage is only a stage and that the players are only players. They come to hear a certain number of lines recited with just gesture and elegant modulation.
> (*ibid.* p. 77)

Here Johnson reveals his fundamentally bookish attitude to the drama. What good actor is content with recitation? What good playgoer with elegant modulation? And yet Johnson realized, as clearly as any modern critic, that it was for the playgoer that the plays were written:

> Shakespeare regarded more the series of ideas, than of words; and his language not being designed for the reader's desk, was all that he desired it to be, if it conveyed his meaning to the audience.
> (*ibid.* p. 97)

But it was at his reader's desk that Johnson absorbed, and was absorbed by, Shakespeare's series of ideas. By the great tragedies he was deeply moved. He was so shocked by Cordelia's death in *King Lear* that he could not bring himself to read again the last scenes of the play until he undertook to revise them as an editor; and on the murder of Desdemona in *Othello*, he wrote: "I am glad that I have ended my revisal of this dreadful scene. It is not to be endured."

---

[5] J. Dover Wilson, *The Fortunes of Falstaff* (London, 1943).

In his treatment of the comedies Johnson shows clearly how the Rabelaisian and the moralist were constantly striving for mastery within them. Thus, the one great fault that he found in *The Merry Wives of Windsor* was the frequency of profane expressions; "there are laws of higher authority than those of criticism." At the end of *As You Like It*, Shakespeare had "lost an opportunity of exhibiting a moral lesson."

But to Falstaff, Johnson made a complete surrender. Despicable as he might be from the moralist's point of view, he was saved "by the most pleasing of all qualities, perpetual gaiety, by an unfailing power of exciting laughter." No one was more keenly aware than Johnson of the virtue of cheerfulness. His first observation on the characters of *The Tempest* is that Gonzalo, being the only good man who appears with the king, is the only man who preserves his cheerfulness in the wreck.

Like all critics, Johnson had his prejudices and his limitations; but he never forgot the stature of the poet whom he was editing: "The stream of time, which is continually washing the dissoluble fabricks of other poets, passes without injury by the adamant of Shakespeare." Johnson's criticism, too, has its adamantine qualities.

For the last twenty years of his life Johnson liked to regard himself as a professional writer who had won his discharge. "I wonder, Sir," said Boswell, "you have not more pleasure in writing than in not writing." "Sir," said Johnson, "you *may* wonder." Nevertheless, circumstances led him to produce two works of substance. In 1773 Boswell persuaded him to make a tour in Scotland. Starting from Edinburgh, the travelers followed the east road and turned westward through Banff and Inverness. At Anoch, Johnson found himself seated on a bank, "such as a writer of Romance might have delighted to feign":

I had indeed no trees to whisper over my head, but a clear rivulet streamed at my feet. The day was calm, the air soft, and all was rudeness, silence and solitude. Before me, and on either side, were high hills, which by hindering the eye from ranging, forced the mind to find entertainment for itself. Whether I spent the hour well I know not: for here I first conceived the thought of this narration.
(*A Journey to the Western Islands of Scotland*, p. 40)

The narration was published in 1775 and was entitled *A Journey to the Western Islands of Scotland*. By all except professed students of Johnson it is commonly neglected in favor of Boswell's *Journal of a Tour to the Hebrides* (1785). The preference is natural. The *Tour* was, in fact, the first installment of the *Life*, and Boswell had Johnson's authority for saying that it was a very exact picture. It was not only exact but brilliant. "Let me not be censured," he wrote, "for mentioning minute particulars"; and it is this particularity, based upon acute observation and continuous industry, that has won the admiration and the affection of the great company of Boswellians. Johnson's own account was different. He was concerned primarily to describe a country and a society that were new to him. Himself fundamentally urban, he thought it worthwhile to record his impression of the religion, language, education, agriculture, and daily life of a society he had long desired to visit. At an early age he had read Martin Martin's *Description of the Western Islands* (1703) and in one respect he was disappointed. Since the second Jacobite rebellion of 1745, the Highlanders had been tamed:

We came hither too late to see what we expected, a people of peculiar appearance and a system of antiquated life. The clans retain little now of their original character, their ferocity of temper is softened, their military ardour is extinguished, their dignity of independence is depressed, their contempt of government subdued, and the reverence of their Chiefs abated.
(*ibid.* p. 57)

Nevertheless, he rejoiced to find a vigorous patriarchal life at Raasay:

Raasay has little that can detain a traveller, except the Laird and his family; but their power wants no auxiliaries. Such a seat of hospitality, amidst the winds and waters, fills the imagination with a delightful contrariety of images. Without is the rough ocean and the rocky land, the beating billows and the howling storm: within is plenty and elegance, beauty and gaiety, the song and the dance. In Raasay, if I could have found an Ulysses, I had fancied a Phaeacia.
(*ibid.* p. 66)

Not all of Johnson's comments are so favorable. He was interested in everything he saw and did not shrink from blunt criticism. But he realized clearly his limitations as a city dweller and modestly reflected that his thoughts on national manners were the thoughts of one who had seen but little.

Apart from his edition of Shakespeare, the other

major work of Johnson's later life is the one that is best known, or least neglected, today—*The Lives of the Poets*. Like the *Dictionary*, the scheme for the *Lives* originated with a group of booksellers who were planning an elegant and uniform edition on the English poets and invited Johnson to write a short life of each poet. For once Johnson undertook the work without hesitation. An introduction to a literary work was one of the things he felt confident he could do well, and he had at first no intention to give more than a short account of each poet. But the "honest desire of giving useful pleasure" led him to write more when he felt so disposed, and his essays on such poets as Abraham Cowley, John Dryden, and Alexander Pope have become classics of English criticism. For many less eminent writers Johnson felt that "little lives, and little criticism" would serve and appealed to his friends for biographical facts. He wrote, for instance, to Dr. Richard Farmer to inquire whether there might be useful material at Cambridge, and offered to inspect such material himself, "for who that has once experienced the civilities of Cambridge would not snatch the opportunity of another visit?" Similarly he wrote to William Sharp for information about Isaac Watts, whose name he had always held in veneration. "I wish to distinguish Watts," he wrote, "a man who never wrote but for a good purpose." When he came to write the *Life*, he counseled his readers to imitate Watts "in all but his nonconformity." For a short life of George Lyttelton, whom he did not like, Johnson applied to his brother, Lord Westcote: "My desire is to avoid offence, and to be totally out of danger." On the other hand, the help given by his old friend Gilbert Walmsley in the *Life* of Edmund Smith led Johnson to include a tribute to Walmsley himself, which is as splendid as it is irrelevant:

He was a Whig, with all the virulence and malevolence of his party; yet difference of opinion did not keep us apart. I honoured him, and he endured me.

He had mingled with the gay world, without exemption from its vices or its follies, but had never neglected the cultivation of his mind; his belief of Revelation was unshaken; his learning preserved his principles; he grew first regular, and then pious.... His acquaintance with books was great; and what he did not immediately know, he could at least tell where to find. Such was his amplitude of learning, and such his copiousness of communication, that it may be doubted whether a day now passes in which I have not some advantage from his friendship.

This paragraph sheds no additional light or luster on the poetry of Edmund Smith, but it is a good example of the obiter dicta that serve to enhance the charm of *The Lives of the Poets*. "Sir," said Johnson, "the biographical part of literature is what I love most," and in these *Lives* he was concerned at least as much with fact and anecdote as with theories of poetry. He made no attempt to separate the poetry from the personality of the poet, and if he disliked the personality, he frankly colored his criticism with his dislike. The two best-known instances of this are the *Lives* of John Milton and Thomas Gray.

About the greatness of the author of *Paradise Lost* Johnson had no doubts:

The characteristic quality of his poem is sublimity. He sometimes descends to the elegant, but his element is the great.... He can please when pleasure is required; but it is his peculiar power to astonish.

As an epic poet, Milton displayed all the qualities that Johnson sought—knowledge, morality, piety, grandeur; and his confession that "we read Milton for instruction . . . and look elsewhere for recreation" is, in effect, a tribute to the intellectual and emotional effort that a proper appreciation of *Paradise Lost* demands. Even Johnson's notorious prejudice against blank verse is forgotten in the sublimity of Milton's subject: "I cannot prevail on myself to wish that Milton had been a rhymer; for I cannot wish his work to be other than it is." Such is Johnson's considered verdict on a poem that is "not the greatest of heroic poems only because it is not the first." They are the concluding words of a long essay, but much earlier the reader will, no doubt, have been astonished by the two devastating pages on "Lycidas." Why should Johnson have condemned the diction as harsh, the rhymes as uncertain, the numbers as unpleasing? Why should he have set his mind so stubbornly against an appreciation of such lines as:

We drove a field and both together heard
What time the Gray-fly winds her sultry horn,
Battening our flocks with the fresh dews of night

and commented, like a fractious child: "We know that they never drove a field and that they had no flocks to batten"? Part of the answer must be sought in the biographical portion of the essay, in which Milton's religious and political opinions are ruthlessly denounced:

He has not associated himself with any denomination of Protestants; we know rather what he was not, than what he was. He was not of the Church of Rome; he was not of the Church of England. To be of no church is dangerous. . . . Milton, who appears to have had full conviction of the truth of Christianity . . . yet grew old without any visible worship.

To Johnson, a good Church of England man who preferred the papists to the Presbyterians because the latter body had no church or apostolical ordination, any kind of undenominationalism was exasperating. Similarly, in politics:

His political notions were those of an acrimonious and surly republican. . . . Milton's republicanism was, I am afraid, founded in an envious hatred of greatness and a sullen desire of independence. . . . He hated monarchs in the State and prelates in the Church; for he hated all whom he was required to obey.

"Lycidas" was in the form of a pastoral ("easy, vulgar and therefore disgusting"); but in spite of such epithets, Johnson could take pleasure in a pastoral poem, provided it was genuinely descriptive of country life. Years before, in a *Rambler* essay, he had declared it to be an improper medium of political or ecclesiastical criticism. Furthermore, "Lycidas" mingled "trifling fictions" with "the most awful and sacred truths" and so became the target of Johnson's exaggerated scorn. His criticism of the poem is distorted by his fundamental distrust of the anarchical temperament of the poet—but it did not weaken his belief in Milton's greatness.

Against Gray, Johnson was less violently prejudiced. Here again, he paid full tribute to the "Elegy," but he had little patience with the fastidious productions of the scholar who asked for leisure to be good and wrote only when the humor took him. He also disliked what he regarded as Gray's affectation in his tricks of inversion and in the use of antiquarian epithets. In the *Lives* of Milton and Gray it is possible to detect some slight bitterness on Johnson's part as he compared their academic careers with his own four terms at Oxford, followed by the long years in Grub Street. The mythological imagery of "Lycidas," he observes, "is such as a college easily supplies" and the even tenor of Milton's life appeared to be attainable only in colleges. Gray's plea, made from college rooms, that he could write only when he was in the right mood Johnson dismissed as "fantastick foppery."

The Rambler had produced his paper twice a week, whatever his mood.

There are some, perhaps, who feel about Johnson's writings as Johnson felt about Milton. They recognize the element of greatness in them and read them as a matter of duty; but for recreation and companionship they turn elsewhere—and most naturally to Boswell. They may recognize that Johnson's own works were, historically, the foundation of the *Life*, but the brilliance of Boswell's superstructure, with its superb record of conversation and its convincing picture of the social scene, has inevitably monopolized their interest. But for Boswell it was always the Rambler who argued and declaimed. Whether at the Mitre, the Club, or Mrs. Thrale's dining table, Boswell looked for instruction at least as much as for entertainment—indeed, he was slightly shocked whenever Johnson indulged his capacity for pure fun. At Corricatachin, for instance, Boswell found it "highly comick" to see the grave philosopher—the Rambler—toying with a Highland beauty (and a married woman, too) upon his knee; when Johnson "exulted in his own pleasantry" at the expense of Bennet Langton, Boswell felt that it was not such as might be expected from the author of the *Rambler*. But whether the evening's conversation had been grave or gay, there came, inevitably, "the one time at night when he must go home," and at home Johnson would be left to his reflections and his melancholy—the melancholy not merely of loneliness but of penitence. For to Johnson the doctrine of the sinfulness of man and of man's redemption by the passion of Jesus Christ was fundamental. Year after year he recited his sins of omission—his failure to read good books (and particularly the Bible); to rise early; to worship regularly; to keep a journal; to avoid idleness. On his birthday in 1764 he deplored that he had spent fifty-five years in resolving but had done nothing. It was his conscience as a scholar that especially troubled him. He knew that he had been endowed with a scholar's talents, but how had he used them? "O God," he prayed, "make me to remember that *the night cometh when no man can work.*"

At Easter 1779, he found little good of himself to report except the publication of the first part of the *Lives of the Poets* and "a little charity." The last phrase is significant. Johnson sought the companionship he needed to make life endurable not only in distinguished clubs and fashionable drawing rooms, but among the poor and the unfortunate, and to several of these he offered a refuge in his own house. Among them were Anna Williams, the blind lady to whose "variety of knowledge" he was indebted for thirty years; Mrs. Desmoulins, the daughter of his godfather (Dr. Swinfen), to whom he made an allowance of half a guinea a week; Francis Barber, his black servant, whom he sent to school at Bishop's Stortford; and Robert Levet, "an obscure practiser of physick amongst the lower people," who shared Johnson's penny loaf at breakfast. In the great panorama of Boswell's narrative there are many minor figures who have attained immortality by a single phrase or incident. Of these, the best known perhaps is Oliver Edwards, who remarked, "You are a philosopher, Dr. Johnson. I have tried too in my time to be a philosopher; but I don't know how, cheerfulness was always breaking in." But Robert Levet's immortality was conferred upon him by Johnson himself in a tribute that came straight from the heart of a man who had lost his friend:

> Condemn'd to hope's delusive mine,
> As on we toil from day to day,
> By sudden blasts, or slow decline,
> Our social comforts drop away.
>
> Well try'd, through many a varying year,
> See LEVET to the grave descend;
> Officious, innocent, sincere,
> Of ev'ry friendless name the friend.
> . . .
> In misery's darkest cavern known,
> His useful care was ever nigh,
> Where hopeless anguish pour'd his groan
> And lonely want retir'd to die.
>
> No summons, mock'd by chill delay,
> No petty gain, disdain'd by pride;
> The modest wants of ev'ry day
> The toil of ev'ry day supply'd.
>
> His virtues walk'd their narrow round,
> Nor made a pause, nor left a void;
> And sure th' Eternal Master found
> The single talent well employ'd.
> ("On the Death of Dr. Robert Levet,"
> 1–8; 16–28)

Here, as Walter Raleigh suggests, the reader may find at least a partial explanation of Johnson's failure to appreciate "Lycidas" as a lament for a friend.

Johnson's treatment of Francis Barber was prompted not only by personal affection but by his persistent hatred of the slave trade. How is it, he asked, that we hear the loudest yelps for liberty among the drivers of Negroes? Johnson disliked yelps for liberty wherever they came from, but when Macaulay described him as "a Tory . . . from mere passion such as inflamed the Capulets against the Montagues," he was seeking too easy an answer. It is true that Johnson was inflamed by passion; but it was a passion not for a party but for order in church and state and society. The first Whig was the Devil, who had upset the order of Heaven, and Whig talk about liberty in the abstract infuriated him, especially when it championed a man of the character of John Wilkes. As to the American colonists, Johnson regarded them simply as English subjects who had voluntarily crossed the ocean and left their voting rights behind them; they still enjoyed the protection of the armed forces of the crown, and for that protection it was right that they should pay. But, whatever his views on current controversy, Johnson was no supporter of absolute power:

> When I say that all governments are alike, I consider that in no government power can be abused long. Mankind will not bear it. If a sovereign oppresses his people to a great degree, they will rise and cut off his head.
> (*Life of Johnson*, vol. I, p. 424)

So he regarded the Irish situation of his own time with profound misgiving. "The Irish," he said, "are in a most unnatural state; for we see there the minority prevailing over the majority." In France he deplored the lack of a healthy middle class between the magnificence of the rich and the misery of the poor. A decent provision for the poor was, he said, the true test of civilization—and by a decent provision he meant something more than the bare necessities. "What signifies," said someone, "giving halfpence to common beggars? they only lay it out in gin and tobacco." "And why," thundered Johnson, "should they be denied such sweeteners of their existence?"

V

THUS the study of Samuel Johnson is something more than the enjoyment of a great clubman and a great diner-out whose conversational exploits have been uniquely described by a great literary artist.

# SAMUEL JOHNSON

Johnson's personality presents many facets and many paradoxes. The man whose character and opinions have delighted, and continue to delight, great multitudes of readers was a man to whom life was something to be endured rather than enjoyed; and those against whom he displayed his most violent prejudices—Whigs, Americans, atheists, Scots—are among his most faithful worshipers. When Goldsmith proposed some additions to the Club, since the existing members had traveled over one another's minds, Johnson flashed out: "Sir, you have not travelled over *my* mind, I assure you."

Nor, perhaps, have we.

### SELECTED BIBLIOGRAPHY

I. BIBLIOGRAPHY. W. P. Courtney and D. N. Smith, *A Bibliography of Samuel Johnson* (Oxford, 1915; reiss., 1968), supplement by R. W. Chapman and A. T. Hazen, Oxford Bibliographical Society (1938); *The R. B. Adam Library, Relating to Dr. Samuel Johnson and His Era*, 4 vols. (London, 1929-1930); J. L. Clifford, *Johnsonian Studies 1887-1950* (Minneapolis, 1951), supplement 1950-1960 by J. L. Clifford and D. J. Greene in M. Wahta, ed., *Johnsonian Studies* (Cairo, 1962); J. D. Freeman, *A Preliminary Handlist of Documents and Manuscripts of Samuel Johnson*, Oxford Bibliographical Society (Oxford, 1968).

II. COLLECTED WORKS. [G. Kearsley], ed., *The Poetical Works* (London, 1785; enl. ed., 1789); J. Hawkins, ed., *The Works*, 11 vols. (London, 1787), with two additional vols. by J. Stockdale, ed. (1787); A. Murphy, ed., *The Works*, 12 vols. (London, 1792), new ed. by A. Chalmers (1806); R. Anderson, ed., *The Poetical Works* (Edinburgh, 1795), vol. XI: *The Poets of Great Britain*; F. W. Blagdon, ed., *The Poems* (London, 1808); A. Chalmers, ed., *The Poems* (London, 1810), vol. XVI: *The Works of the English Poets*; *The Works*, 11 vols. (London, 1825), Oxford English Classics series; R. Lynam, ed., *The Works*, 6 vols. (London, 1825); G. Gilfillan, ed., *The Poetical Works of Johnson, Parnell, Gay, Etc.* (Edinburgh, 1855); T. M. Ward, ed., *Poems* (London, 1905), includes Goldsmith, Gray, and Collins; D. N. Smith and E. L. McAdam, eds., *The Poems* (Oxford, 1941); *Works*, the Yale ed., in progress, comprises: E. L. McAdam, Jr., and D. and M. Hyde, eds., vol. I, *Diaries, Prayers and Annals* (New Haven, 1958); W. J. Bate, J. M. Bullitt, and L. F. Powell, eds., vol. II, *The Idler and The Adventurer* (1963); E. L. McAdam, Jr., ed., vol. VI, *Poems* (1964); A. Sherbo, ed., vols. VII and VIII, *Johnson on Shakespeare* (1968).

III. SELECTED WORKS. *The Beauties of Johnson* (London, 1781), and later eds.; S. Howard, ed., *The Beauties of Johnson* (London, 1833); G. B. Hill, ed., *Wit and Wisdom of Samuel Johnson* (London, 1888); G. B. Hill, ed., *Select Essays*, 2 vols. (London, 1889); C. G. Osgood, ed., *Selections from Johnson* (New York, 1909); A. Meynell and G. K. Chesterton, eds., *Samuel Johnson* (London, 1911); R. W. Chapman, ed., *Johnson, Prose and Poetry* (Oxford, 1922); R. W. Chapman, ed., *Selected Letters* (Oxford, 1925), in the World's Classics ed.; S. C. Roberts, ed., *Samuel Johnson, Writer* (London, 1926); J. E. Brown, ed., *The Critical Opinions of Samuel Johnson* (Princeton, N. J., 1926); A. T. Hazen, ed., *Samuel Johnson's Prefaces and Dedications* (London, 1937); M. Wilson, ed., *Johnson, Prose and Poetry* (London, 1950); E. L. McAdam, Jr., and G. Milne, *Johnson's Dictionary: A Modern Selection* (London, 1963); R. T. Davies, ed., *Samuel Johnson: Selected Writings* (London, 1965); P. Cruttwell, ed., *Samuel Johnson: Selected Writings* (London, 1968), with intro. and notes.

IV. LETTERS. H. L. Piozzi, ed., *Letters to and from Samuel Johnson*, 2 vols. (London, 1788); G. B. Hill, ed., *Letters of Samuel Johnson*, 2 vols. (Oxford, 1892); Marquess of Lansdowne, ed., *Johnson and Queeney* (London, 1932), letters to Queeney Thrale; and *The Queeney Letters* (London, 1934); R. W. Chapman, ed., *The Letters of Samuel Johnson*, 3 vols. (Oxford, 1952), the standard ed.

V. SEPARATE WORKS. *Lobo. A Voyage to Abyssinia* (London, 1735), also in H. Morley, ed. (London, 1887); *London: A Poem* (London, 1738), also in T. S. Eliot, ed. (London, 1930); *Marmor Norfolciense* (London, 1739); *A Compleat Vindication of the Licensers of the Stage* (London, 1739); *Life of Mr. Richard Savage* (London, 1744), repr. in *Lives of the Poets*; *Miscellaneous Observations on Macbeth* (London, 1745); *The Plan of a Dictionary of the English Language* (London, 1747); *The Vanity of Human Wishes* (London, 1749), also in E. J. Payne, ed. (Oxford, 1876) and T. S. Eliot, ed. (London, 1930); *Irene: A Tragedy* (London, 1749); *Rambler* (London, 1750-1752), some selections in W. H. White, ed. (London, 1907); *A Dictionary of the English Language*, 2 vols. (London, 1755); *A Dictionary of the English Language*, 2 vols. (London, 1756), abstracted from the folio ed.; *The History of Rasselas Prince of Abyssinia*, 2 vols. (London, 1759), also in G. B. Hill, ed. (London, 1887) and R. W. Chapman, ed. (Oxford, 1927); *Idler*, 2 vols. (London, 1761), papers from *Idler* in S. C. Roberts, ed. (Cambridge, 1921); *The Plays of William Shakespeare*, 8 vols. (London, 1765; 10 vols., 1773), with notes by Johnson and Steevens; Johnson's proposals, preface, and notes are conveniently assembled in Sir W. A. Raleigh, *Johnson on Shakespeare* (London, 1908); *The False Alarm* (London, 1770); *Thoughts on the Late Transactions Respecting Falkland's Islands* (London, 1771); *Patriot* (London, 1774); *Taxation No Tyranny* (London, 1775); *A Journey to the Western Islands of Scotland* (London, 1775), also, with Boswell's *Tour*, in R. W. Chapman, ed. (Oxford, 1924); *Prefaces to the Works of the English Poets*, 10 vols.

(London, 1779-1781), reiss. as *The Lives of the English Poets*, 4 vols. (London, 1781), also in A. Napier, ed., 3 vols. (London, 1890), A. Waugh, ed., World's Classics ed., 6 vols. (London, 1896), G. B. Hill, ed., 3 vols. (London, 1905), L. A. Hind, ed., Everyman's Library ed., 2 vols. (London, 1925); the six chief lives—Milton, Dryden, Swift, Addison, Pope, Gray—edited by Matthew Arnold (London, 1878); a more recent selection is S. C. Roberts, ed. (London, 1963); G. Strahan, ed., *Prayers and Meditations* (London, 1785), also in G. B. Hill, ed., *Johnsonian Miscellanies* (London, 1897), and in H. Higgins, ed. (London, 1904) and H. E. Savage, ed. (Lichfield, 1927); *Debates in Parliament*, 2 vols. (London, 1787); R. Wright, ed., *An Account of the Life of Dr. Samuel Johnson from His Birth to His Eleventh Year, Written by Himself* (London, 1805); R. Duppa, ed., *A Diary of a Journey into North Wales in the Year 1744* (London, 1816), repr. in A. M. Broadley, *Dr. Johnson and Mrs. Thrale* (London, 1910); M. Tyson and H. Guppy, eds., *The French Journals of Mrs. Thrale and Dr. Johnson* (Manchester, 1932).

VI. BIOGRAPHICAL AND CRITICAL STUDIES. *The Life of Samuel Johnson, LLD* (London, 1785), attributed to William Cooke; *Memoirs of the Life and Writings of the Late Dr. Samuel Johnson* (London, 1785), attributed to William Shaw; J. Boswell, *The Journal of a Tour to the Hebrides with Samuel Johnson* (London, 1785), also in J. W. Croker, ed. (London, 1831), R. Carruthers, ed. (London, 1851), A. Napier, ed. (London, 1884), G. B. Hill, ed. (London, 1887), R. W. Chapman, ed. (London, 1924), with Johnson's *Journey*, F. A. Pottle and C. H. Bennett, eds. (London, 1936), from the MS; H. L. Piozzi, *Anecdotes of the Late Samuel Johnson* (London, 1786), also in S. C. Roberts, ed. (London, 1925); J. Hawkins, *The Life of Samuel Johnson* (London, 1787); J. Boswell, *The Life of Samuel Johnson* (London, 1791), also in J. W. Croker, ed., 5 vols. (London, 1831), R. Carruthers, ed., 4 vols. (London, 1851-1852), A. Napier, ed., 5 vols. (London, 1884), G. B. Hill, ed., 6 vols. (Oxford, 1887), includes the *Tour*, reedited by L. F. Powell (London, 1934-1940), the standard ed. for scholars, R. Ingpen, ed., 2 vols. (London, 1907), notable for its illustrations; other reprints by Oxford, Globe, and Everyman's Library; A. Murphy, *An Essay on the Life and Genius of Samuel Johnson* (London, 1792); R. Anderson, *The Life of Samuel Johnson* (London, 1795); T. B. Macaulay, "Croker's Edition of Boswell's *Life of Johnson*," in *Edinburgh Review* (Sept. 1831); T. Carlyle, "Boswell's *Life of Johnson*," in *Fraser's Magazine* (May 1832); Dr. T. Campbell, *A Diary of a Visit to England in 1775*, edited by S. Raymond (Sydney, 1854), also in J. L. Clifford, ed. (London, 1947), from the newly discovered MS; T. B. Macaulay, "Samuel Johnson," in *Encyclopaedia Britannica*, 8th ed., vol. XII (London, 1856); G. B. Hill, *Dr. Johnson: His Friends and His Critics* (London, 1870); L. Stephen, *Samuel Johnson* (London, 1878), in the English Men of Letters series; A. Napier, ed., *Johnsoniana* (London, 1884); F. Grant, *Life of Samuel Johnson* (London, 1887), with a bibliography by J. P. Anderson; G. B. Hill, ed., *Johnsonian Miscellanies* (Oxford, 1897; facs. ed., 2 vols., London, 1968); G. Whale and J. Sargeaunt, eds., *Johnson Club Papers* (London, 1899; 2nd ser., 1920); T. Seccombe, *The Age of Johnson* (London, 1889); J. A. H. Murray, *The Evolution of English Lexicography* (London, 1900); A. L. Reade, *The Reades of Blackwood Hill and Dr. Johnson's Ancestry* (London, 1906), and *Johnsonian Gleanings*, 11 vols. (London, 1909-1952), an encyclopedia of Johnson's family and of his early life; J. T. Raby, ed., *Bi-centenary of the Birth of Dr. Samuel Johnson* (London, 1909); Sir W. A. Raleigh, *Six Essays on Johnson* (London, 1910), an important restatement, correcting Macaulay's views; J. Bailey, *Dr. Johnson and His Circle* (London, 1913); S. C. Roberts, *The Story of Dr. Johnson* (London, 1919); P. H. Houston, *Dr. Johnson: A Study in Eighteenth-Century Humanism* (Cambridge, Mass., 1923); C. Hollis, *Doctor Johnson* (London, 1928); R. Lynd, *Doctor Johnson and Company* (London, 1928); D. N. Smith, R. W. Chapman, and L. F. Powell, *Johnson and Boswell Revisited* (Oxford, 1928); S. C. Roberts, *Doctor Johnson* (London, 1934); J. W. Krutch, *Samuel Johnson* (London, 1944); S. C. Roberts, *Samuel Johnson* (London, 1944), British Academy lecture; B. H. Bronson, *Johnson Agonistes and Other Essays* (London, 1944); R. W. Chapman, *Johnsonian and Other Essays and Reviews* (Oxford, 1953); W. J. Bate, *The Achievements of Samuel Johnson* (New York, 1955); J. L. Clifford, *The Young Samuel Johnson* (London, 1955); E. A. Bloom, *Samuel Johnson in Grub Street* (Providence, 1957); S. C. Roberts, *Doctor Johnson and Others* (London, 1958); F. W. Hilles, ed., *New Light on Dr. Johnson* (New Haven, 1959); D. J. Greene, *The Politics of Samuel Johnson* (New Haven, 1960); R. Voitle, *Samuel Johnson the Moralist* (Cambridge, Mass., 1961); M. J. C. Hodgart, *Samuel Johnson and His Time* (London, 1962); M. J. Quinlan, *Samuel Johnson, A Layman's Religion* (Madison, Wis., 1964); D. J. Greene, ed., *Samuel Johnson* (Englewood Cliffs, N. J., 1965), the Twentieth-Century Views series, *Johnson, Boswell and Their Circle* (Oxford, 1965), essays by various hands presented to L. F. Powell in honor of his eighty-fourth birthday; A. Sachs, *Passionate Intelligence: Imagination and Reason in the Works of Samuel Johnson* (Baltimore-London, 1967); F. E. Halliday, *Doctor Johnson and His World* (London, 1968), contains illustrations with accompanying text; J. P. Hardy, ed., *The Political Writings of Dr. Johnson* (London, 1968); J. T. Boulton, ed., *Samuel Johnson: The Critical Heritage* (London, 1971); F. Grant, *Time, Form and Style in Boswell's "Life of Johnson"* (New Haven, 1971); G. Irwin, *Samuel Johnson: A Personality in Conflict* (Wellington, New Zealand, 1972); A. Passler, *Life of Samuel Johnson* (London, 1972); R. B. Schwartz, *Samuel Johnson and the New Science* (Madison, Wis., 1972); D. J. Greene, *The Politics* of *Samuel Johnson* (Port Washington, N. Y., 1973); A. T. Hazen, *Samuel Johnson: Prefaces and Dedications* (Port Washington, N. Y., 1973); C. McIntosh, *Samuel Johnson and the World of Fiction* (New Haven, 1973); R. Stock, *Samuel Johnson and Neo-classical Dramatic Theory* (Lincoln, Nebr., 1973); J. Wain, ed., *Johnson as Critic* (London, 1973); J. H. Sledd and G. J. Kolb, *Dr. Johnson's Dictionary: Essays in the Biography of a Book* (Chicago, 1974); J. Wain, *Samuel Johnson* (London, 1974); M. Lane, *Samuel Johnson and His World* (London, 1975); R. B. Schwartz, *Samuel Johnson and the Problem of Evil* (Madison, Wis., 1975); J. Wain, ed., *Johnson on Johnson* (London, 1976), in the Everyman's Library; W. Edinger, *Samuel Johnson and Poetic Style* (Chicago, 1977); R. Folkenflik, *Samuel Johnson, Biographer* (Ithaca, N. Y., 1978); W. J. Bate, *Samuel Johnson* (London, 1978).

# BEN JONSON
(ca. 1572-1637)

## J. B. Bamborough

I

BEN JONSON suffered the worst fate that can overtake a creative writer. Himself a man of great talent or minor genius—his real place is on the frontier where the terms become virtually indistinguishable—he had the misfortune to live and work at the same time and in the same field as a genius acknowledged by the world as supreme—William Shakespeare. However devotedly his admirers have labored to rescue him from this position, their efforts have never succeeded in saving him from being overcast by that mighty shadow. For a time, in the seventeenth century, he was considered Shakespeare's equal—even, by some, his superior—but from the time of Dryden onward his reputation has become more and more eclipsed. It must seem very unjust and unfair to his ghost, and also very irritating. Not that he did not admire Shakespeare; although he occasionally made fun of him, Jonson wrote about Shakespeare more warmly than he wrote about any other contemporary writer. Yet his love for Shakespeare was, as he said himself, "this side idolatry." He thought that Shakespeare had many faults and made many mistakes; above all, he thought that Shakespeare had not reflected deeply enough on the nature and purpose of drama, nor taken sufficient care to observe its laws. To find himself ranked below a writer seemingly so careless and unserious would have been a very bitter pill to swallow. Yet however hard we try to avoid it, we almost automatically find ourselves comparing the two, and Jonson nearly always comes off the worse.

In some respects the comparison is illuminating. Their social origins were not dissimilar: Shakespeare's father was a tradesman; Jonson's father, who died before Jonson was born, was a priest, but his mother soon married again, and her second husband was a bricklayer or builder. Both, then, belonged to the lower middle class, that vast and rather ill-defined reservoir of talent from which so many English writers have come. But Shakespeare was a countryman, and his knowledge and love of the country are shown in countless images in his poetry from country life; Jonson, at least from early years, was a Londoner, and his interests and memories were predominantly urban. We know nothing of Shakespeare's education (although modern research has shown that he possessed more book learning than he was at one time given credit for); Jonson was educated at Westminster, one of the largest and most important English public schools, under William Camden, the greatest Elizabethan scholar and antiquary, and there he acquired not only an impressive store of knowledge—mainly, of course, of classical literature—but scholarly habits of mind that never deserted him. In later life he was able to consort on equal terms with the most famous scholars of his age, men like Sir Walter Ralegh (to whose son he acted as tutor), Sir Robert Cotton, and John Selden, and he thought of himself as a scholar as much as a creative writer.

When he left Westminster, Jonson did not proceed, as he might have been expected to do, to one of the universities. Perhaps his family was too poor; indeed, according to one not very well supported story, he did spend a few weeks at Cambridge, but had to leave for lack of money. Instead he worked for a time as a bricklayer in his stepfather's firm; then, tiring of this, he volunteered as a soldier, and went in one of the English expeditionary forces to the Netherlands, fighting the Spanish; this would have been in the early 1590's. After this he appears to have become an actor, possibly in one of the second-rate touring companies which traveled around England putting on shows in town halls, marketplaces, or gentlemen's houses—wherever they could find an audience; and from this he graduated to playwriting. This again is rather what Shakespeare did, but there is an important difference. Shakespeare, at least by the time he was thirty, had established himself not only as an actor and playwright, but as a "sharer" or partner in the activities of one particular theatrical company with which he became identified and for which he wrote all his plays. Jonson never took part in the business side of the theater, and always maintained his position as a freelance writer. Indeed, for the greater part of his life his income came as much from the king or noble patrons as from the popular audience, and he always made it clear that he was a playwright from necessity rather than from choice. There is little doubt that he would have preferred to earn his living another way, if he had not been hampered by his lack of powerful connections and by his religion; for a long period of his life he was a Roman Catholic, and this in itself prevented him from taking up certain kinds of employment. The stage was really the only opening for him if he was to win his independence by his pen, but he never forgot, as he put it later in life in *Ode to Himself*, written when one of his plays had been hissed off the stage by the audience (it begins: "Come, leave the loathéd Stage!"), that

They were not meant for thee, less, thou for them,

and he always preferred to be regarded as a gentleman who happened to write for the stage rather than as a professional playwright. (One of the charges made against him by his enemies was that he was always boasting of his grand friends.)

There is still one more important comparison between Shakespeare and Jonson to be made. Shakespeare was born in 1564, Jonson probably in the summer of 1572; and that difference of eight years meant a great deal. Shakespeare was 25 in 1589 and probably began his work in the theater about the same time. At that period the great literary figures were Sidney and Spenser, and in the theater the big names were Lyly, Kyd, Marlowe, and the rest of the so-called university wits; the influence of all these men can be seen in Shakespeare's early work. Jonson reached maturity in 1597, which is also the year in which he is first recorded as writing for the stage, and his generation was that of Donne, Middleton, Webster, and Marston. The mere mention of these names indicates the quite different atmosphere in which Jonson was working. The earlier generation had been high-minded and courtly, sometimes flamboyant and extravagant, but always idealistic and romantic. By the middle of the 1590's a new kind of writer had appeared; one is tempted to call them the Elizabethan "angry young men," and the comparison is not without point. Like their predecessors, the "university wits," they were intellectuals; but unlike Marlowe and his friends they were not natural bohemians, politically suspect, and accustomed to living only one jump ahead of the bailiff. Instead, they were the sons of professional men or of the minor gentry, and many of them had been trained as lawyers in the Inns of Court, the legal colleges in London that formed almost a third university in England. Instead of being high-minded and idealistic, they were down-to-earth, flippant, sometimes cynical in their approach to life; at the same time they were scholars and fundamentally serious-minded (many of them ended in the church). Above all their mood was satirical; what they most wanted to do was to attack society, to puncture pretense and reveal folly and corruption. Jonson readily absorbed their tone. He had in any case, we may suspect, the irascibility, the strong sense of the ridiculous, and the deep conviction of his own rightness that go to the making of the born satirist, but in addition the time was ripe for his development. His home in Westminster was not far from the Inns of Court, many of the students were old schoolfellows of his, and his first major success, *Every Man in His Humor* (staged in 1598), was very much to their taste. We know that before this he had written or had a share in writing several other plays, but this was the first he saw fit to preserve, and clearly he regarded his career as a playwright as beginning with it. In the following year he followed it with his second important play, *Every Man out of His Humor*. Put on, like its predecessor, by Shakespeare's company (according to tradition it was Shakespeare who first recognized Jonson's gifts and urged his fellows to employ him), *Every Man out of His Humor* had an even greater success. Jonson made it something like a manifesto of his artistic intentions, and published it in 1600—the first of his plays to see print—with the air of offering a sample of a new art form. From that time onward his position as a major dramatist was recognized, though not for a long time was it unchallenged.

## II

JONSON was a proud and self-confident man. Circumstances might force him to take up playwriting, a despised occupation looked down on by the scholars and gentlemen among whom he felt his right place to be; very well, he would make it his business to render it an accepted and valued profession. Time and again he asserts the high place of poetry, which for him meant all forms of creative writing. One of the earliest and also one of his finest defenses occurs in the original version of *Every Man in His Humor*. A father tries to dissuade his son from writing by pointing out to him how low a place poets and poetry hold in the world's opinion, and the son bursts out:

> Opinion? O God let gross opinion
> Sink and be damned as deep as Barathrum.[1]
> If it may stand with your most wished content,
> I can refell opinion, and approve
> The state of poesy, such as it is,
> Blessed, eternal, and most true divine:
> Indeed if you will look on poesy,
> As she appears in many, poor and lame,
> Patched up in remnants and old worn rags,
> Half starved for want of her peculiar food,
> Sacred invention, then I must confirm,
> Both your conceit and censure of her merit.
> But view her in her glorious ornaments,
> Attirèd in the majesty of art,
> Set high in spirit with the precious taste
> Of sweet philosophy, and which is most,
> Crowned with the rich traditions of a soul,
> That hates to have her dignity profaned,
> With any relish of an earthly thought;
> Oh then how proud a presence doth she bear.
> Then is she like her self, fit to be seen
> Of none but grave and consecrated eyes.
> (V. iii. 312–333)

[1] The pit of Hell.

Bad poets might have brought poetry into disrepute, and given cause for her enemies to attack her; it was Jonson's aim to

> raise the despised head of *poetry* again, and stripping her out of those rotten and base rags, where with the times have adulterated her form, restore her to her primitive habit, feature and majesty, and render her worthy to be embraced, and kissed of all the great and master-spirits of our world.

It was a bold claim, but Jonson had no doubts of his ability to fulfill it. A man who could write a play for presentation before the queen, and end it with the injunction:

> By God 'tis good, and if you lik't, you may!

did not suffer from lack of self-confidence.

One aspect of Jonson's resolve to raise the status of his art was his determination that his plays should be considered as literature. Elizabethan plays were usually thought of as acting vehicles only, and were printed, if at all, as an afterthought. Jonson wrote his plays with his eye on the reader as much as on the spectator, and he had them printed with remarkable (and unique) care. The crowning point of his campaign came in 1616, when a collection of his plays, masques, and poems was printed in folio—a format hitherto reserved for serious works of learning—as *The Works of Benjamin Jonson*. This caused great mirth: for a writer to call his plays "works" was absurd—"works" meant works of philosophy, theology, or science. Even thirty years later Sir John Suckling made fun of Jonson by representing him as claiming his right to be crowned by Apollo above other poets:

> For his were called works, where others were but plays.

Yet Jonson carried his point. Not only did his example cause a general rise in the standard of printing plays (and very likely gave Heming and Condell the idea of collecting Shakespeare's works in folio); since his time nobody has seriously denied the right of plays to be considered as literature.

Jonson had not merely to establish plays as literature; he had to demonstrate the correct way of writing them. He knew quite well what was wrong with the plays of his contemporaries. Wherever he looked he saw them full of errors: they were badly written, stuffed with stale jokes and senseless bombast, marred by obscenity and blasphemy—"all licence of offence to God and man"; their plots were absurd, full of improbabilities and coincidences, and such stale tricks as mistaken identity and the "cross-wooing" of dukes, duchesses, and their servants (as in *Twelfth Night*); their characters were incredible and there were too many clowns and servant-monsters (such as Caliban); they contained far too many violent, pointless, and noisy incidents—battles, storms, shipwrecks, and so on. All this was partly the fault of authors, partly of the audience, whose poor taste Jonson frequently reproved (no dramatist, not even Shaw, has been so consistently rude to his audience as Jonson was). Jonson's audiences could expect none of all this; instead, they were to be given models of correctly formed, correctly written drama. Late in life Jonson wrote a prologue for a play by a former servant of his, Richard Brome. In it he congratulates Brome on having achieved success

>By observation of those comic laws
>Which I, your master, first did teach the age,

and it was as a lawgiver, a pioneer in drama, that he saw himself.

This did not mean, as it so often meant in the later Renaissance, that he was a slave to the "laws of drama" derived by neoclassical theorists from Aristotle and the practice of the ancient dramatists. Jonson was very firm about this. The ancients, he said, were there as guides, not masters, and just as they had modified and improved their own drama, so it was open to modern dramatists to modify their practice and improve upon them. This is why arguments as to whether Jonson is more correctly regarded as a "classical" writer on the Continental model or as a "romantic" English writer are beside the point. In fact he was both; he deliberately set out to combine the best in both traditions. He wished to have the seriousness of purpose, the polish, the concentration, and the precise construction of the classics, without losing the richness, the vitality, and the raciness of the freer English native drama. Because of this he may seem, to a critic accustomed to the loose, often haphazard, architecture of other Elizabethan drama, to be very classical; while to a French critic, brought up on the severity of Corneille and Racine, he will seem characteristically English and undisciplined.

Jonson observed the rules as far as he thought necessary, and ignored them when he thought fit. One thing he did absorb from his study of classical and neoclassical drama, and that was the beautiful articulation of his plots. No praise can be too high for the construction of his comedies. Nothing in them happens by chance and no loose ends are ever left dangling; it is not too much to say that every character who appears is given an intelligible motive for his actions, and his every entrance and exit is accounted for. Alongside the plays of his contemporaries, which often seem like heaps of broken parts, Jonson's plays resemble well-oiled, smoothly running machines.

More important to Jonson, however, than the formal qualities of drama was the aim which it shared with all literature, that of being morally instructive. No tag is more frequently quoted by him than Horace's dictum that poetry should either instruct or delight, or, as it was usually taken by the Renaissance, should instruct *and* delight. This was the justification for the high place which Jonson claimed for poetry and also why he so many times insisted that to be a good poet it was first necessary to be a good man. He saw it as his duty to instruct his audience, and he carried out that duty. As a comic writer it was not his place to give examples of right behavior—that was more the function of tragedy—and in fact there are very few characters in his comedies who are held up for admiration. His mode was satire, and his method of teaching was to attack the faults he saw in men, and by ridicule to shame them out of their vices and follies. In *Every Man out of His Humor* the character Asper (who to some extent is Jonson himself) proclaims his intention:

>with an arméd and resolvéd hand
>I'll strip the ragged follies of the time,
>Naked, as at their birth . . .
>. . . and with a whip of steel,
>Print wounding lashes in their iron ribs.

I fear no mood stamped in a private brow,
When I am pleased t' unmask a public vice:
I fear no strumpet's drugs, nor ruffian's stab,
Should I detect their hateful luxuries:
No broker's, usurer's, or lawyer's gripe,
Were I disposed to say, they're all corrupt.
(Ind., 16–26)

This bold and independent attitude made Jonson famous, but it also made him many enemies. Other writers resented his arrogant suggestion that only he was truly moral and only he knew how to write comedies, and not long after the publication of this play he found himself attacked in plays and pamphlets. He tried to ward off these attacks by writing a play—*Poetaster*, staged in 1601—in which he parodied his opponents and defended his methods; this had some success, but in the end Jonson was defeated. He retreated from the theater in a huff, loudly proclaiming that the age was not capable of understanding his drama, and for the next few years he wrote no comedies. When he resumed in 1605, with *Volpone*, his tone was noticeably more moderate, though no less self-assured.

Although in effect he abandoned his claim to be the sole censor or moral conscience of his age, Jonson never gave up his didactic purpose. All his life he was engaged in attacking affectation and pretentiousness, and the eccentricities which the age called "humors." Strictly speaking, the humors were the four secretions which the human body was thought to contain—blood, phlegm, choler, and "black bile." A man's "temperament" depended on which of these was present in the greatest quantity in him: if it was blood, then he would be sanguine; if phlegm, phlegmatic; if choler, choleric; and if black bile predominated, then he would be melancholy. We still use these terms, of course, to mean very much what they meant in Jonson's day. By the end of the sixteenth century, however, "humor" was being used as a slang term very much as "complex" is used today. A man would say that it was his humor to dislike cats, or that it was his humor to trim his beard in a particular way. Jonson objected to this use of the term, and also to the belief that it was smart to have a particular affectation. At the beginning of *Every Man out of His Humor* he introduces three characters called Asper, Cordatus, and Mitis. Asper afterward takes a part in the play, while Cordatus and Mitis remain on the stage and act as a kind of chorus, commenting for the benefit of the audience on Jonson's purpose and technique. At their first appearance one of them happens to use the word "humor" and Asper immediately picks the term up. He gives a little lecture on what the word really means, and then goes on to describe some of the silly habits that get dignified by the popular use of the word:

But that a rook, in wearing a pied feather,
The cable hat-band, or the three-piled ruff,
A yard of shoetie, or the Switzer's knot
On his French garters, should affect a humor!
O, 'tis more than most ridiculous.
(Ind., 110–114)

He finishes by threatening to expose these fops:

Well I will scourge those apes;
And to these courteous eyes oppose a mirror,
As large as is the stage, whereon we act:
Where they shall see the time's deformity
Anatomized in every nerve, and sinew,
With constant courage and contempt of fear.
(Ind., 117–122)

When Jonson called his plays "comedies of humors," then, he did not mean that he was only going to represent the humors in their limited medical sense; if he had, he would have had a total cast of only four characters. What he meant was that he was going to satirize the follies and affectations of his age, and this he certainly did; there are in his plays a vast number of foolish, vain, affected, and pretentious people, as well as a few who are not quite sane, like Morose in *Epicoene* (Morose's "humor" is that he cannot bear noise, and his servants have to communicate with him by gesture only). All of them, by the end of the plays in which they appear, have been taken "out of their humor"—that is, ridiculed or shocked into realizing their folly, and cured of it. The danger of this, of course, is that it may strike us today as rather out of date; it is not very easy to get excited over an exposure of the absurdities of people's behavior three hundred and fifty years ago. Some critics have also felt that Jonson spent so much time attacking stupidity that he neglected much more serious faults. This is not quite fair, for he does deal in several plays with important human sins—pride, luxury, ambition, and greed, for example—although it is true that there are some failings which he hardly mentions at all. The real object of Jonson's attack, however, was deception, including deception of oneself. Like Swift (though perhaps not as bitterly as Swift) he resented all the means we use in order to feed our vanity and disguise from ourselves that our real value depends on our moral worth and nothing else. His aim was to bring man to a sense of his real nature, and to make him realize that right action can only be based on reason and a recognition of truth. To see vanity and folly as ridiculous is a first step in the right direction.

III

BUT it is, after all, not for his moral teaching that we are likely to value a comic writer. Rightly or wrongly (wrongly, in Jonson's eyes), we are more interested in delight than in instruction, more concerned with the sugar than with the pill. What has Jonson to offer us in his comedies? In the first place, great energy and exuberance. We usually associate seriousness of artistic purpose and scrupulous attention to form with thinness of inspiration and content, but this is not so with Jonson. He always provides a multitude of characters and a variety of incidents, and his humor is lively and boisterous, sometimes even rough and crude. He has a liking for practical jokes; at the end of *Poetaster*, for example, he brings on his chief enemy, the poet and playwright John Marston, and the other characters give him a pill which makes him vomit up specimens of his vocabulary, which Jonson thought pedantic and obscure. It is hardly a refined scene, but it is a very funny one, as Marston with difficulty regurgitates words like "turgidous," "bolatrant," "furibund," and "prorumped." There is no use in coming to Jonson's plays looking for refinement and delicacy of feeling, for he had little; on the other hand he was rarely bitter or mean in his ridicule.

The wealth of character and incident makes Jonson's plays sometimes rather difficult to read and follow, but when they are put on the stage this difficulty disappears, and his skill in handling a mass of material is revealed. His most remarkable achievement in this respect is *Bartholomew Fair*, which has a cast of over forty speaking parts, and really requires a large number of "extras" as well if it is to be properly staged. Its plot is quite impossible to describe briefly; in fact it is built up not so much around a plot as by interlocking a large number of episodes. The scene is the great yearly fair at Smithfield, near London; some of the characters are the showmen and stallholders of the fair, and the others are the visitors to whom they sell their trumpery wares (and whose pockets they pick). The whole play is full of color, movement, and excitement, and it comes wonderfully alive on the stage; it might be even more successful as a film.

Jonson had an acute sense of the theater—he had, after all, been an actor himself—and a good many scenes which one hardly notices in reading his plays are very effective on the stage. In *Every Man in His Humor* the intriguing servant Brainworm makes the lawyer's clerk Formal drunk, and steals his clothes. When Formal sobers up, all he can find to put on is an old suit of rusty armor, in which he later makes an entrance. The eye may easily slip over this on the printed page, but in the theater Formal clanking on with great difficulty, with his pale face peering out of a battered helmet, makes a very happy moment. Jonson's comic scenes, however, are not usually simple like this one, but complex and cumulative. In *The Alchemist*, one of his best plays, Face the servant is left in charge of the house while his master has gone to the country to escape the plague. He brings in two accomplices—Subtle, whose speciality is to masquerade as a magician or alchemist, and a girl, Doll Common—and between them they defraud a wide selection of "gulls" of their money. The action of the play only covers a few hours and everything takes place at great speed, as the victims arrive hot on each other's heels. Face, Subtle, and Doll display breathtaking virtuosity in taking advantage of every opportunity. One customer brings a load of scrap metal which he wants turned into gold, and they promptly sell this to another customer as goods belonging to some poor orphans; a country squire arrives to be taught the manners of the town, bringing his sister with him, and in no time they are offering her favors to another customer, who has come in the belief that they are running a bawdyhouse. Trick is piled on trick until eventually Face's master returns unexpectedly, and the whole house of cards collapses.

In *Epicoene* the surly Morose, who hates noise, decides to get married in order to disinherit his nephew, whom he detests. The problem is to find a woman who will not upset him by her chatter. One is produced who is reported never to talk at all, and he marries her; as soon as they are married, however, she finds her voice and nags him all the time, and, what is more, invites all her friends to a noisy party. In despair, Morose sends for a lawyer and a priest to see if they can find some way of declaring his marriage invalid. In fact they are Otter and Cutberd, both frauds, sent along by his nephew, and they argue with each other in a wonderful mixture of dog-Latin and sheer gibberish:

Ott. Your *impotentes*, I should say, are *minime apti ad contrahenda matrimonium*.
True. Matrimonium! we shall have most unmatrimonial Latin with you: *matrimonia*, and be hanged.
Daup. You put them out, man.
Cut. But then there will arise a doubt, master parson, in our case, *post matrimonium*: that *frigid itate proeditus*—do you conceive me, sir?
Ott. Very well, sir.
Cut. Who cannot *uti uxore pro uxore*, may *habere eam pro sorore*.
Ott. Absurd, absurd, absurd, and merely apostatical!
Cut. You shall pardon me, master parson, I can prove it.
Ott. You can prove a will, master doctor, you can prove nothing else. Does not the verse of your own canon say

*Haec socianda vetant connubia, facta retractant?*

Cut. I grant you; but how do they *retractare*, master parson?
Mor. O, this was it I feared.
Ott. *In aeternum*, sir.
Cut. That's false in divinity, by your favor.
Ott. 'Tis false in humanity to say so. Is he not *prorsus inutilis ad thorum?* Can he *proestare fidem datam?* I would fain know.
Cut. Yes; how if he do *convalere?*
Ott. He cannot *convalere*, it is impossible.
(V. iii. 188–213)

This quarrel is funny in itself; it is also torture for Morose, across whom the disputants are shouting. The real point, however, as some at least of the audience will have guessed (and the rest will shortly find out), is that Morose's "wife" is not a woman at all, but a boy planted on him by his nephew, and the whole business is absolutely absurd because he has never been married at all.

This cumulative effect seems to be the result of the way Jonson worked—deliberately and carefully, rather than impulsively and by inspiration. He seems to have been a slow writer; indeed his enemies taunted him that his brain, like an elephant, took a year to gestate. His method appears to have been to hit upon the original idea or theme for a play and then work over it at leisure, building it up piece by piece into a whole. The strength of the constructions made in this way is always noticeable, and also their originality, notwithstanding the fact that he borrowed much from other writers—mainly from the classics. This was no crime in his day, when imitation was a recognized and accepted method of writing; the only rule was that one should always try to improve on one's original. This Jonson nearly always succeeds in doing: as Dryden said, "he invades authors like a monarch, and what would be theft in other poets is only victory in him." In fact he transformed all he took, and if we read his plays without looking up any notes (or better still, see them on the stage), what strikes us most is how much of a piece they seem, and how unlike any other comedies. One never feels with Jonson, as one sometimes does with Molière, that he is merely engaged in reshuffling plots and characters that have been the common stock of European comedy for centuries.

Just as Jonson's comic effects depend on piling up incident upon incident, his characteristic style is the result of an accumulation of words and phrases. He is not a witty writer in the sense that Congreve or Sheridan or Wilde is witty; he does not have the unexpected adroitness of phrasing that causes a single remark to be greeted with a shout of laughter in the theater and remain fixed in the memory. Nor for that matter does he have (and this is a great relief) more than a little of the tiresome wordplay and still more tedious obscenity which mar so many Elizabethan comedies; in fact he disapproved strongly of both. His habit is to let his characters overwhelm us with a flood of words, and he is happiest with a quarrel or a tirade. He seems to have been fascinated by contemporary tricks of speech, and particularly by the cant or jargon of different professions. In *The Alchemist*, for example, Subtle holds forth at great length on the mysteries of alchemy in speeches which modern producers usually cut—wisely, for although they are technically remarkable, they go on rather too long. The same play, however, begins with a splendid quarrel between Face and Subtle, with Doll vainly trying to restrain them:

*Face:* Do but 'collect, sir, where I met you first.
*Subtle.* I do not hear well.
*Face.*                      Not of this, I think it.
But I shall put you in mind, sir, at Pie Corner,[2]
Taking your meal of steam in from cooks' stalls,
Where, like the father of hunger, you did walk
Piteously costive, with your pinched-horn-nose,
And your complexion, of the Roman wash,[3]
Stuck full of black and melancholic worms,
Like powder corns,[4] shot, at th'artillery-yard.[5]
*Subtle.* I wish, you could advance your voice, a little.
*Face.* When you went pinned up, in the several rags,
You'd raked, and picked from dunghills, before day,
Your feet in mouldy slippers, for your kibes,[6]
A felt of rug,[7] and a thin threaden cloak,
That scarce would cover your no-buttocks—
*Subtle.*                                    So, sir!
*Face.* When all your alchemy, and your algebra,
Your minerals, vegetals, and animals,
Your conjuring, cozening, and your dozen of trades,
Could not relieve your corpse,[8] with so much linen
Would make you tinder, but to see a fire;
I ga' you countenance, credit for your coals,
Your stills, your glasses, your materials,
Built you a furnace, drew you customers,
Advanced all your black arts; lent you, beside,
A house to practice in—
*Subtle.*                         Your master's house?
*Face.* Where you have studied the more thriving skill
Of bawdry, since.
                    . . .
*Face.*                    I will have
A book, but barely reckoning thy impostures,
Shall prove a true philosopher's stone, to printers.
*Subtle.* Away, you trencher-rascal.
*Face.*                    Out you dog-leech,
The vomit of all prisons—
*Doll.*                    Will you be
Your own destructions, gentlemen?
*Face.*                    still spewed out
For lying too heavy o' the basket.[9]
*Subtle.* Cheater.
*Face.*        Bawd.
*Subtle.*           Cow-herd.
*Face.*                  Conjurer.
*Subtle.*                    Cut-purse.
*Face.*                         Witch.
(I. i. 23–49; 100–107)

As well as this gift for vituperation, Jonson had a fine vein of nonsense. In *Bartholomew Fair* Justice Overdo, the central character, in order to keep an eye on the criminals at the fair, disguises himself as a lunatic called Mad Arthur of Bradley, and in this disguise he delivers a sermon against ale and tobacco (in the original this is broken up by interruptions from the other characters on the stage):

Thirst not after that frothy liquor, ale; for who knows when he openeth the stopple, what may be in the bottle? Hath not a snail, a spider, yea, a newt been found there? Thirst not after it, youth; thirst not after it. . . . Neither do thou lust after that tawny weed, tobacco. . . . whose complexion is like the Indian's

---

[2] A well-known inn near Smithfield.
[3] Swarthy; a hint also of a lotion for skin disease.
[4] Grains of powder.
[5] A public place for weapon practice.
[6] Chilblains.    [7] Coarse hat.
[8] Body.
[9] Alludes to the greed of prisoners who seize more than their share of the scraps of food sent in by basket.

that vents [sells] it. . . . and who can tell, if before the gathering and making up thereof, the alligator hath not pissed thereon? . . . The creeping venom of which subtle serpent, as some late writers affirm, neither the cutting of the perilous plant, nor the drying of it, nor the lighting or burning, can any way persway [mitigate] or assuage. . . . Hence it is that the lungs of the tobacconist [smoker] are rotted, the liver spotted, the brain smoked like the backside of the pig-woman's booth here, and the whole body within, black as her pan you saw e'en now, without.

(II. vi. 11–44)

Much of the vitality and excitement of Jonson's comedies resides precisely in these glittering heaps of words, but they are by no means careless and haphazard effusions. Jonson was very much concerned with language and style; indeed he wrote one of the first English grammars. Since he meant his plays to be read as literature, he was extremely careful in writing them. There was another reason for this care, for he believed that character was revealed most clearly in speech; in his notebooks he jotted down the tag from Quintilian: "Speech most shews a man; Speak, that I may know thee." He portrays his characters more through what they say than what they do, and this is why he took so much interest in contemporary colloquial speech. In his portrayal of character Jonson was much influenced by the Renaissance principle of decorum, which (in brief) laid it down that the persons of a drama must always be types, with the typical characteristics belonging to their age, sex, social class, profession, and so on, and that they must never do anything which a person of their type would not do. The result is not that his characters never impress us as individuals, for this they frequently do, but it does mean that they often strike us as one-sided and limited. Bobadil, the boastful, cowardly soldier in *Every Man in His Humor*, is one of Jonson's best creations, but he is far less complex and rounded than Falstaff, who belongs to the same general type. A better way of putting it would be to say that Bobadil is a vivid representation of the type, while Falstaff can surprise us with some of the things he says and does; Bobadil cannot and does not. Decorum also demanded that characters should be consistent from their first appearance to their last, and this means that Jonson's people never develop in the course of the plays in which they appear. It is this fact, together with their tendency to have some marked idiosyncrasy or "humor," that led Coleridge to remark that they were like "the hopeless patients of a mad doctor." This is overstating the case, but it is true that Jonson's characterization lacks subtlety and depth. Yet he was wonderfully faithful to the appearance and manners of his contemporaries and in "holding the mirror up to Nature"; in his plays we have, as Dryden said of *The Canterbury Tales*, "our forefathers and great-grandames all before us."

What *is* difficult is to feel much affection for Jonson's characters, and this is the direct result of his decision to instruct by ridicule. There are few really likable people in Jonson's plays, and curiously enough those that are most likable are very often rogues—which hardly assists his moral purpose. This makes his comedies different from most English comedies, and they are different, too, in that they contain almost no mixture of the pathetic or tragic. This again was a matter of principle; it was the business of comedy to deal only with laughable events, or as Jonson put it, to

Sport with human follies, not with crimes;

anything more serious was the province of tragedy. Only once, in his greatest play, does Jonson verge on the tragic in a comedy. In *Volpone* the hero is a magnifico of Venice and a rich man, but he delights in adding to his wealth by pretending to be sick and dying, thus inducing other rich men to give him presents in the hope of being made his heirs. One of these suitors is even persuaded to prostitute his wife to Volpone in the hope of cutting out his rivals, and the scene in which Volpone tries to seduce the shrinking girl is more like what we expect to find in Elizabethan tragedy than anything else in Jonson. The speech in which she begs for mercy is truly moving:

If you have ears that will be pierced; or eyes,
That can be opened; a heart, may be touched;
Or any part, that yet sounds man, about you:
If you have touch of holy saints, or heaven,
Do me the grace, to let me scape. If not,
Be bountiful, and kill me. You do know,
I am a creature, hither ill betrayed,
By one, whose shame I would forget it were.

If you will deign me neither of these graces,
Yet feed your wrath, sir, rather than your lust;
(It is a vice, comes nearer manliness)
And punish that unhappy crime of nature,
Which you miscall my beauty: flay my face,
Or poison it, with ointments, for seducing
Your blood to this rebellion. Rub these hands,
With what may cause an eating leprosy,
E'en to my bones, and marrow: anything,
That may disfavour[10] me, save in my honour.
And I will kneel to you, pray for you, pay down
A thousand hourly vows, sir, for your health,
Report, and think you virtuous—
                    (III. vii. 240–260)

This is fine, but it is quite untypical of Jonson, and elsewhere he restricted himself to what he considered the true matter of comedy. To an Englishman, accustomed to the pathetic, often sentimental, comedy of Chaucer, Shakespeare, or Dickens, Jonson as a result often seems strange and un-English, despite the raciness of his scenes and characters. His is a hard, tough, quite unsentimental comedy, and it belongs more in the tradition of European comedy than to the peculiarly English stream. In that tradition it takes a high place; not perhaps as high as Molière's, but nearly so; and that is in itself no mean achievement.

## IV

JONSON's comedies, however, are only part of his work, although to us by far the most important part. He himself would have put equal or greater weight on his masques and tragedies, to say nothing of his nondramatic verse. The masque was a dramatic form which in England reached its peak in the reign of King James, and Jonson was its foremost practitioner. Magnificently spectacular, it was also inordinately expensive—too expensive for the frugal Elizabeth. James was naturally extravagant, and felt it part of his duty as a great prince to have these "shows" staged for the entertainment of his court. Jonson wrote his first court masque in 1605; it was a great success, and from then onward his services were in steady demand. He produced an average of one masque a year until King James's death in 1625. Writing these masques not only provided him with a good income, it gave him enhanced social position and literary prestige. He was able to regard himself as "the King's poet," and there is evidence that he hoped to be given the (as yet nonexistent) post of poet laureate. So secure did he feel that for ten years, from 1616 to 1626, he gave up writing for the public stage altogether and devoted himself entirely to poetry and to his work for the court and his noble patrons. This must have seemed to him the crown of his career, after his early struggles to make his name and the period from 1605 to 1616 in which he was consolidating his reputation (and in which, as we now see, he was writing his greatest plays). The death of King James, however, broke his connection with the court. Although he wrote a few more masques, he was never as highly regarded by Charles I as by his father, and in consequence he had to turn back to the public stage in order to support himself. The three or four plays he wrote from 1626 onward were unkindly described by Dryden as his "dotages"; the description is unduly harsh, but not quite unjustified, for they undeniably represent a decline of his great powers. When he wrote them he was in sickness and in poverty, not without friends but surrounded by powerful enemies, and whatever we may think of these last plays as literature, it is impossible not to admire the courage with which he maintained a bold and confident front. He went on writing up to his death in 1637—at least a manuscript of a half-finished play was found among his papers after he died, and curiously enough this (*The Sad Shepherd*) is one of his most serene, light-hearted, and beautiful works.

It is more pleasant to turn back to Jonson at the height of his success. Yet even here there is an element of sadness in watching Jonson devoting his gifts to so transitory and ephemeral an art form as the masque. For all their great cost, and the splendor of their scenery and costumes, the masques were very rarely staged more than once, and in the performance of them there must have been something of the air of brief glory that hangs over a great ball. Jonson captured this feeling of pathos and finality at the end of *Oberon*, one of his best masques; Phosphorus, the Day Star, appears and bids the dancers end their revels:

[10] Disfigure.

# BEN JONSON

To rest, to rest; the herald of the day,
Bright Phosphorus commands you hence; obey.
The moon is pale, and spent; and wingéd night
Makes head-long haste, to fly the morning's sight:
Who now is rising from her blushing wars,
And, with her rosy hand, puts back the stars.
Of which my self, the last, her harbinger,
But stay, to warn you, that you not defer
Your parting longer. Then, do I give way,
As night hath done, and so must you, to day.

*After this, they danced their last dance, into the work. And with a full song, the star vanished, and the whole machine closed.*

### SONG
O yet, how early, and before her time,
The envious morning up doth climb,
    Though she not love her bed!
What haste the jealous sun doth make
His fiery horses up to take,
    And once more shew his head!
Lest, taken with the brightness of this night,
The world should with it last, and never miss his
    light.     (434–455)

Moreover, the poet's part in the masque was not all-important. The scenery and the costumes, which were the work of the designer (usually, in Jonson's masques, Inigo Jones), the music, and above all the dances, which were performed by members of the court (including, on occasion, some of the royal family), were the main source of interest to the audience, and all the poet was required to do was to provide a story and some speeches which would hold everything together. Despite the pomp of their staging, the masques were really amateur theatricals (though some professionals took part in them), and what could be printed was only a fragment of the whole. What is left to us of Jonson's masques, in fact, is something like the libretto of a grand opera. Yet they illuminate aspects of his genius which we would hardly guess at from his comedies—above all, a gift of delicate lyrical grace and fantasy. Here as an example is a song sung by the Nymphs in *Pan's Anniversary*, a minor masque written to celebrate one of the king's birthdays (James is figured under the name of Pan, the god of shepherds):

Thus, thus, begin the yearly rites
Are due to Pan on these bright nights;
His morn now riseth, and invites
To sport, to dances, and delights:
    All envious and profane, away,
    This is the shepherds' holiday.

Strew, strew, the glad and smiling ground
With every flower, yet not confound
The primrose drop, the spring's own spouse,
Bright daisies, and the lips of cows,
    The garden-star, the queen of May,
    The rose, to crown the holiday.

Drop, drop, you violets, change your hues,
Now red, now pale, as lovers use;
And in your death go out as well
As when you lived, unto the smell;
    That from your odor all may say,
    This is the shepherds' holiday.     (5–24)

This is far removed from the boisterousness of Jonson's comedies, and many similar passages could be quoted; they are a useful corrective to the tendency to think of Jonson as a purely urban writer.

Less need be said of Jonson's two tragedies, *Sejanus* and *Catiline*. They were failures when they were first staged, and they have never found many admirers since, although *Catiline* enjoyed a brief run of popularity at the time of the Restoration. It is not difficult to account for their lack of success. Jonson made them monuments to his scholarship; they are very accurate re-creations of Roman life, and in the original editions their margins are studded with references to the Roman historians and other authorities. They are also serious studies of the effects of ambition, corruption, and power-lust in the state, and their moral intention is always apparent. Their characters are powerfully and clearly drawn, but they are also, unfortunately, verbose and static; they have a marked tendency to orate at each other without getting anything done. This is especially true of *Catiline*, where whole scenes are taken up with translations of Cicero's orations. We know that these bored the Jacobean audience, and we cannot but sympathize with them; no amount of seriousness of purpose or obedience to the formal rules of drama will make up for sheer dullness. But to us a more deep-seated failing is a failing in the writing itself, and it could be expressed by saying that Jonson failed because he tried to write poetic tragedy without writing poetry.

This is to oversimplify grossly, yet there is truth in it. As a poet Jonson had many gifts. He was excelled only by Shakespeare in the art of playing off the rhythms of colloquial speech against the regular beat of blank verse, and his best dramatic poetry is clear, strong, and full of movement. Here is a character in one of his later and less well-known plays speaking on that common Elizabethan theme, the wickedness of luxury:

> Who can endure to see
> The fury of men's gullets, and their groins?
> What fires, what cooks, what kitchens might be spared,
> What stews, ponds, parks, coopes, garners, magazines,
> What velvets, tissues, scarfs, embroideries,
> And laces they might lack! They covet things—
> Superfluous still; when it were much more honor
> They could want necessary! What need hath nature
> Of silver dishes, or gold chamberpots?
> Of perfumed napkins, or a numerous family
> To see her eat? Poor and wise, she requires
> Meat only; hunger is not ambitious:
> Say, that you were the emperor of pleasures,
> The great dictator of fashions, for all Europe,
> And had the pomp of all the courts, and kingdoms,
> Laid forth unto the show? to make your self
> Gazed, and admired at? You must go to bed
> And take your natural rest: then, all this vanisheth.
> Your bravery was but shown; 'twas not possessed:
> While it did boast it self, it was then perishing.
> (*The Staple of News*, III. iv. 45–66)

This is flexible, sinewy, athletic writing, but in no way exceptional in Jonson; and it is a great contrast to the flaccid and nerveless verse of many of his contemporaries in the drama. In the same play the hero describes his emotions at first meeting his mistress:

> My passion was clear contrary, and doubtful,
> I shook for fear, and yet I danced for joy,
> I had such motions as the sunbeams make
> Against a wall, or playing on a water,
> Or trembling vapour of a boiling pot
> (II. v. 63–67)

Simple, vivid images of this kind abound in Jonson's plays; even in the somber, more rhetorical verse of the tragedies there come snatches like this, in which one character describes how the conspiring senators whisper together:

> Ay, now their heads do travail, now they work;
> Their faces run like shuttles, they are weaving
> Some curious cobwebs to catch flies.
> (*Sejanus*, III. 22–24)

Jonson's dramatic verse, like his prose, is always meaningful and pointed, never empty or conventional.

Of his poems outside his plays Jonson himself valued his epigrams most highly, but to us the best are found among his vigorous odes, his grave and manly verse letters:

> Tonight, grave sir, both my poor house, and I
> Do equally desire your company:
> Not that we think us worthy such a guest,
> But that your worth will dignify our feast,
> (*Inviting a Friend to Supper*, 1–4)

and in a handful of lovely lyrics. *Drink to Me Only with Thine Eyes* is too familiar to need quotation; this *Hymn to Diana* from *Cynthia's Revels* is less well known, and equally good:

> Queen and huntress, chaste, and fair,
> Now the sun is laid to sleep,
> Seated, in thy silver chair,
> State in wonted manner keep:
>   Hesperus entreats thy light,
>   Goddess, excellently bright.
>
> Earth, let not thy envious shade
> Dare itself to interpose;
> Cynthia's shining orb was made
> Heaven to clear, when day did close:
>   Bless us then with wishèd sight,
>   Goddess, excellently bright.
>
> Lay thy bow of pearl apart,
> And thy crystal-shining quiver;
> Give unto the flying hart
> Space to breathe, how short soever:
>   Thou, that mak'st a day of night,
>   Goddess, excellently bright.

It was the exquisite finish and smoothness of this type of lyric that Jonson handed on to his "sons," the group of younger poets—the best known of them is Herrick—who accepted him as their master.

Yet for all the vigor, dignity, polish, and sweetness of which Jonson's poetry is capable, we become in the end aware of something lacking in it. It is not merely that he shows a marked preference for concrete images, drawn (sometimes awkwardly) from everyday life, and avoids anything vague, exotic, or "romantic." This indeed should be of positive value to him today, when the vaguely "poetic" is so much out of favor. It is not even that his poetry for the most part is passionless, and lacks urgency. The later seventeenth-century critics always note, when they are discussing Jonson, that he was surprisingly unsuccessful as a love poet, and he himself began his verse collection, *The Forest*, with a little humorous poem called *Why I write not of Love*. As a matter of fact this is not quite true, for he wrote several love poems, and some of them are very fine—for instance this, one of a group of poems in *The Underwood* dedicated to a lady he called Charis:

See the chariot at hand here of Love
  Wherein my lady rideth!
Each that draws, is a swan, or a dove,
  And well the car Love guideth.
As she goes, all hearts do duty
    Unto her beauty;
And enamoured, do wish, so they might
    But enjoy such a sight,
That they still were, to run by her side,
Thorough swords, thorough seas, whither she would
  ride.

Do but look on her eyes, they do light
  All that Love's world compriseth!
Do but look on her hair, it is bright
  As Love's star when it riseth!
Do but mark her forehead's smoother
    Than words that sooth her!
And from her archèd brows, such a grace
    Sheds itself through the face,
As alone there triumphs to the life
All the gain, all the good, of the elements' strife.

Have you seen but a bright lily grow,
  Before rude hands have touched it?
Ha' you marked but the fall o' the snow
  Before the soil hath smutched it?
Ha' you felt the wool o' the beaver,
  Or swansdown ever?
Or have smelt o' the bud o' the briar,
  Or the nard in the fire?
Or have tasted the bag of the bee?
O so white! O so soft! O so sweet is she!

*(Her Triumph)*

Yet although this is exciting and moving, it is not exactly personal—certainly not in the way that Donne's and Burns's love lyrics are personal, and this is generally true of Jonson's poetry. He put a good deal of himself into his poems, but always with a certain reserve and a sense of himself as a public figure speaking in public. There is never any question of Jonson's pouring forth his full heart in profuse strains of unpremeditated art; he is always the conscious artist fully in control of his medium.

This restraint can indeed be a great advantage, as it is, for example, in Jonson's elegies, particularly the poems he wrote on his two eldest children, who died young, and in his *Epitaph on Salomon Pavy*. Pavy was a boy actor (he acted in *Cynthia's Revels*) who died before he grew up; it is a subject which would lend itself very easily to sentimentality, but Jonson with his exquisite control makes his poem tender, yet never in the least mawkish:

> Weep with me all you that read
>   This little story,
> And know, for whom a tear you shed,
>   Death's self is sorry.
> 'Twas a child, that so did thrive
>   In grace and feature,
> As Heaven and Nature seemed to strive
>   Which owned the creature.
> Years he numbered scarce thirteen
>   When Fates turned cruel,
> Yet three filled zodiacs had he been
>   The stage's jewel;
> And did act (what now we moan)
>   Old men so duly,
> As, sooth, the Parcae[11] thought him one,
>   He played so truly.
> So, by error, to his fate
>   They all consented,
> But viewing him since (alas, too late)
>   They have repented;
> And have sought (to give new birth)
>   In baths to steep him;
> But, being so much too good for earth,
>   Heaven vows to keep him.
>
> *(Epigram CXX)*

[11] Fates.

# BEN JONSON

This is a poem that can hardly be faulted, and in the face of it, it is perhaps churlish to wish that Jonson had sometimes been prepared to drop his guard and speak more directly from his heart.

But Jonson's main limitation as a poet lies elsewhere, and much nearer to the heart of poetry. It is, quite simply, that while Jonson's use of words is always precise, vigorous, and meaningful, he almost always brings into play only their immediate denotatory or dictionary significance, and only rarely calls up their complete range of suggestion, evocation, or emotive power. His verse, that is, lacks texture or richness of overtone and verbal harmony, and it is this that distinguishes it so sharply from the work of most of our major poets, and especially from the poetry of Shakespeare. This is the major reason why Jonson's tragedies are failures: unlike Shakespeare's they fail to establish through their poetry an atmosphere in which their characters can have their being, and they do not stir us imaginatively and emotionally. In comedy this limitation is less severe, and it is not so apparent in the masques, but it imposes throughout an all-important restriction on the praise which can be given Jonson as a master of language.

Here again qualification is necessary. There are indeed passages of poetry in Jonson of a profoundly moving kind; one of them—Celia's plea for mercy—has already been quoted. Characteristically, however, they are passages expressing two emotions not usually thought of as "poetic"—scorn and greed. In vituperation Jonson's manipulation of language is really creative or (to use Coleridge's term) esemplastic, and here, too, his sharp sense of the realistic and the sordid strengthens his vigor (see, for example, Face's description of Subtle in his poverty, given above). He has yet finer passages which communicate the desire for possession or power. At the beginning of *Volpone* the hero expounds his credo, rejoicing that he does not, as other men do, win wealth by toil or by the oppression of others, but by the exercise of a superior intelligence, and delivers a paean of praise to his idol, gold:

Good morning to the day; and, next, my gold!
Open the shrine, that I may see my saint.
Hail the world's soul, and mine! More glad than is
The teeming earth to see the longed-for sun
Peep through the horns of the celestial Ram,
Am I, to view thy splendor, darkening his;
That, lying here, amongst my other hoards,
Show'st like a flame, by night; or like the day
Struck out of Chaos, when all darkness fled
Unto the center. O, thou sun of Sol,
But brighter than thy father, let me kiss,
With adoration, thee, and every relic
Of sacred treasure, in this blessed room.
Well did wise Poets, by thy glorious name
Title that age, which they would have the best;
Thou being the best of things; and far transcending
All style of joy in children, parents, friends,
Or any other waking dream on earth.
Thy looks when they to Venus did ascribe,
They should have given her twenty thousand Cupids;
Such are thy beauties, and our loves! Dear saint,
Riches, the dumb god, that giv'st all men tongues;
That canst do nought, and yet mak'st men do all things;
The price of souls; even hell, with thee to boot,
Is made worth heaven! Thou art virtue, fame,
Honor and all things else!

(I. i. 1–26)

This is powerful poetry, but it should be noticed that part at least of its power comes from its subject; it is about something which stirs some of our strongest if not our most noble feelings—wealth and the possession of wealth. In a subtle way, then, it is the same sort of poetry as the song about Charis, and also the Nymphs' *Song from Pan's Anniversary*; in all of them the subject—the gold, the woman, the flowers—moves us in itself, of its own nature. The subject, that is, is giving force to the verse, rather than the verse to the subject. We may doubt whether Jonson could through his language alone make poetry about something to which we previously have felt indifferent (as Coleridge claimed that Wordsworth did), and it is not an accident that the two emotions, desire and scorn, which Jonson found it easiest to communicate, demand the actual presence of people or things in themselves desirable or contemptible. Jonson, that is, is a poet of the actual, the real, solid world about us, and not often of the inner world of hopes and ideals, velleities and doubts.

## V

Dryden concluded his famous comparison between Jonson and Shakespeare in his *Essay of Dramatic Poesy* by saying "I admire him, but I love Shakespeare," and this has been the common response to Jonson. He certainly did not lack "personality"—indeed he lives for us in his work as a singularly vivid, robust, and even aggressive figure—but he did lack charm, and not many readers have taken him to their hearts. To the general public, in fact, he is known, if at all, as a literary figure rather similar to (and, one suspects, sometimes confused with) his namesake Samuel Johnson. Yet his best plays—*Volpone, Epicoene, The Alchemist,* and *Bartholomew Fair*—are always successful whenever they are performed. No other playwright except Shakespeare and Shaw has added so many plays to the national repertory, and it is not irrelevant to wonder how many of Shaw's plays will still be holding the stage in three hundred years' time. If Jonson must be thought of as a considerable rather than as a great poet, he did at least write one of the best-known lyrics in the English language, and he is a prose writer of very great distinction—a fact which is not always recognized. His range as a master of prose is wide, from the racy, colloquial dialogue of the comedies to the grave, dignified, harmonious prose of some of his prefaces and of the descriptive passages in the masques, and just as his poetry had a profound influence on the development of much later seventeenth-century verse, he had a part to play in the reformation of English prose style. Without ever losing the vigor of Elizabethan language, that is, he looked forward to the clear, smooth, yet pointed English of the eighteenth century. He has considerable importance, too, as a critic. Much of his criticism is incidental to his plays, but he left behind a critical notebook—*Timber, or Discoveries*—in which he had set down from time to time his considered thoughts on literature. These observations show him as virtually the first Englishman to have thought deeply about writing as a craftsman and practitioner rather than as a grammarian or moralist, and in this he anticipates Dryden. We have, too, some notes of his everyday conversation, made by the Scots poet Drummond of Hawthornden, whom Jonson visited in 1619; they form an odd mixture of scraps of gossip, anecdotes, and pieces of biographical information, but among them there are many snap judgments of men and books. No doubt Jonson would be horrified to find some of them quoted solemnly by scholars and literary historians, as they often are today, but they reveal much of his mind, and from them one thing emerges clearly: although he was often harsh and brusque in his condemnation of bad writing, he was very ready to praise what he thought good, and he recognized quality when he saw it.

Jonson answers better than most English writers to the description of a man of letters—that is, a writer who has thought deeply and read widely about his art, and tries to carry out his work according to his own principles. The English tend to prefer wilder and less self-conscious geniuses, and to associate artistic care with aestheticism and effeteness. Nothing could be less true of Jonson. He cared as much for his art as any other English writer, and more than all but a few, but there is nothing in him of the *petit maître*. Together with his fine sense of form and love of solid construction went a great vitality and creative vigor, and the two together give him his unique power. He belongs, as Milton does, to that class of serious and dedicated artists of whom Virgil (whom he admired so much) is the supreme example, and if he is not among the greatest, he is not unworthy of their company.

### SELECTED BIBLIOGRAPHY

I. Bibliography. H. L. Ford, *Collation of the Ben Jonson Folios, 1616–31–1640* (London, 1932); S. A. Tannenbaum, *Ben Jonson: A Concise Bibliography* (New York, 1938), Elizabethan Bibliographies, Supplement (New York, 1947), supplement no. 3 to the series adds a section on Jonson covering the years 1947–1965, compiled by G. R. Goffey (London, 1968); W. W. Greg, *A Bibliography of the English Printed Drama to the Restoration*, 4 vols. (Oxford, 1940–1959); D. Heyward Brock and J. M. Welsh, *Ben Jonson: A Quadricentennial Bibliography, 1947–1971* (Metuchen, N.J., 1974); S. Wells, ed., *English Drama (excluding Shakespeare)*, Select Bibliographical Guides (London, 1975), ch. 5.

II. Collected Works, First Folio. *The Workes* (1616), contains (date of first performance in parentheses): *Every Man in His Humor* (1598); *Every Man out of His Humor* (1599), *Cynthias Revells* (1600); *Poetaster* (1601); *Sejanus* (1603); *Volpone* (1605); *Epicoene* (1609); *The Alchemist* (1610); *Catiline* (1611); *Part of the Kings Entertainment* (15 March 1604); *A Panegyre on the Happie Entrance of James* (19 March 1604); *Entertainment at Althrope* (25 June 1603); *Entertainment at Highgate* (1 May 1604); *The Masque of Blackness* (6 Jan. 1605); *Hymenaei* (3 Jan. 1606); *Entertainment of the King of Denmark* (24 July 1606); *Entertainment at Theobalds* (22 May 1607); *The Masque of Beautie* (10 Jan. 1608); *Lord Haddington's Masque* (9 Feb. 1608); *The Masque of Queenes* (2 Feb. 1609); *Prince Henry's Barriers* (6 Jan. 1610); *Oberon* (1 Jan. 1611); *Love Freed from Ignorance and Folly* (3 Feb. 1611); *Love Restored* (6 Jan. 1612); *A Challenge at Tilt* (1 Jan. 1614); *The Irish Masque* (9 Dec. 1613); *The Golden Age Restor'd* (6 Jan. 1615); *Mercury Vindicated* (1 Jan. 1616); *Epigrammes*; *The Forrest* (poems).

III. COLLECTED WORKS, SECOND FOLIO. *The Workes*, 2 vols. (1640), vol. I reprints the First Folio, vol. II adds (date of first performance in parentheses) *Bartholomew Fayre* (31 Oct. 1614); *The Divell Is an Asse* (1616); *The Staple of News* (1626); *The Magnetick Lady* (1632); *A Tale of a Tub* (1633); *The Sad Shepherd* (unfinished); *Christmas His Masque* (1616); *Lord Hay's Masque (Lovers Made Men)* (22 Feb. 1617); *The Vision of Delight* (6 Jan. 1617); *Pleasure Reconciled to Virtue* (6 Jan. 1618); *For the Honour of Wales* (17 Feb. 1618); *Newes from the New World Discover'd in the Moon* (17 Jan. 1620); *Pans Anniversarie* (19 June 1620); *The Gypsies Metamorphos'd* (3 Aug. 1621); *The Masque of Augures* (6 Jan. 1622); *Time Vindicated* (19 Jan. 1623); *Neptunes Triumph* (planned for 6 Jan. 1624 but never performed); *The Masque of Owles* (19 Aug. 1624); *The Fortunate Isles* (9 Jan. 1625); *Loves Triumph through Callipolis* (9 Jan. 1631); *Chloridia* (22 Feb. 1631); *Entertainment at Welbeck* (21 May 1633); *Love's Welcome at Bolsover* (30 July 1634); *Underwoods* (poems); *Mortimer His Fall* (an unfinished tragedy); *Horace, His Art of Poetrie* (translation); *The English Grammar*; *Timber, or Discoveries* (critical notes).

IV. OTHER COLLECTED WORKS. W. Gifford, ed., *Works*, 9 vols. (London, 1816), repr. with corrections by F. Cunningham, 9 vols. (London, 1875); F. E. Schelling, ed., *Complete Plays*, 2 vols. (London 1910), in Everyman's Library. C. H. Herford, P. Simpson, and E. M. Simpson, eds., *Works*, 11 vols. (Oxford, 1925–1952), the definitive ed. with ample intro. and full critical and textual notes, a masterpiece of scholarship; A. B. Kernan and R. B. Young, eds., *The Yale Ben Jonson*, (New Haven, 1962–    ).

V. SELECTED WORKS. M. Castelain, ed., *Timber; or Discoveries* (London, 1889; Paris, 1906); G. B. Harrison, ed. (London, 1923); H. Morley, ed., *Masques and Entertainments* (London, 1890); B. Nicholson, ed., *Ben Jonson*, 3 vols. (London, 1893–1894), with intro. by C. H. Herford, Mermaid Dramatists Series, contains *Every Man in His Humour*; *Every Man out of His Humour*; *Poetaster*; *Bartholomew Fair*; *Cynthia's Revels*; *Sejanus*; *Volpone*; *Epicoene*; *The Alchemist*; B. H. Newdigate, ed., *The Poems* (Oxford, 1936), I. Donaldson, ed., Oxford Standard Authors (Oxford, 1975), G. Parfitt, ed., Penguin modern spelling ed. (Harmondsworth, 1975); H. Levin, ed., *Selected Works* (New York, 1938); *Five Plays* (Oxford, 1953), in the World's Classics Series, contains *Every Man in His Humour*; *Sejanus*; *Volpone*; *The Alchemist*; *Bartholomew Fair*; S. Orgel, ed., *The Complete Masques* (New Haven-London, 1969).

VI. SEPARATE WORKS. *The Comicall Satyre of Every Man out of His Humour* (1600), comedy, facs. rep. of the first of the quarto eds. of 1600, W. W. Greg and F. P. Wilson, eds., Malone Society (London, 1920); *Every Man in His Humour* (1601), comedy, the quarto ed. revised by Jonson before inclusion in the First Folio, Facsimile, H. H. Carter, ed. (New Haven, 1921), M. Seymour-Smith, ed., New Mermaids Series (London, 1966), J. W. Lever, ed., Regents Renaissance Drama Series (London, 1972); *The Fountain of Self-Love, or, Cynthia's Revels* (1601), comedy, edited from the quarto of 1601 by W. Bang and L. Krebs (Louvain, 1908); *Poetaster, or, the Arraignment* (1602), comedy, H. de Vocht, ed. (Louvain, 1934); *Part of King James His Royal and Magnificent Entertainment . . . also, a Brief Panegyre of His Majesties Entrance to Parliament . . . (together with) the Entertainment of the Queene and Prince to Althrope* (1604), masque; *Sejanus His Fall* (1605), tragedy, H. de Vocht, ed. (Louvain, 1935), W. F. Bolton, ed., New Mermaids Series (London, 1968); *Hymenaei* (1606), masque; *Volpone, or, The Foxe* (1607), comedy, H. de Vocht, ed. (Louvain, 1937), P. Brockbank, ed., New Mermaids Series; *The Characters of Two Royall Masques, the One of Blackness, the Other of Beautie* (1608); *The Description of the Masque . . . Celebrating the Happy Marriage of . . . Viscount Haddington* (1609), F. E. Schelling, ed. (New York, 1926); *The Case Is Alter(e)d* (1609), comedy, not included in the First Folio, first included in *Works*, P. Whalley, ed. (1756), W. E. Selin, ed. (New Haven, 1919); *The Masque of Queens* (1609), facs. with Inigo Jones's designs, G. Chapman, ed. (London, 1930); *Catiline His Conspiracy* (1611), tragedy, W. F. Bolton and J. F. Gardner, eds., Regents Renaissance Drama Series (London, 1973); *The Alchemist* (1612), comedy, Noel Douglas Replicas (London, 1927), D. Brown, ed., New Mermaids Series (London, 1966), F. H. Mares, ed., Revels Plays (London, 1967); *Lovers Made Man* (1617), masque; *Epicoene, or, the Silent Woman* (1620), comedy, R. Beaurline, ed. (London, 1967), Regents Renaissance Drama Series (London, 1967); *The Masque of Augures* (1621); *Time Vindicated* (1623), masque; *The Fortunate Isles and Their Union* (1624), masque; *Neptunes Triumph* (1625), masque; *Loves Triumph Through Callipolis* (1630), masque; *Chloridia* (1630), masque; *The New Inne, or, the Light Heart* (1631); *Bartholomew Fair: A Comedy* (1631), E. A. Horsman, ed., Revels Plays (London, 1960), E. B. Partridge, ed., Regents Renaissance Drama Series (London, 1964), M. Hussey, ed., New Mermaids Series (London, 1964); *Execration Against Vulcan . . . Epigrams* (1640), verse; *The Masque of Gypsies* (1640), W. W. Greg, ed. (London, 1952); *The Divell Is an Asse: A Comedie* (1641).

VII. SOME BIOGRAPHICAL AND CRITICAL STUDIES. R. F. Patterson and G. B. Harrison, eds., *Conversation with William Drummond* (London, 1623), a Scottish poet's notes on the visit Jonson paid him at Hawthornden in 1618; B. Duppa, ed., *Jonsonus Virbius*, (London, 1638), memorial verses by some of Jonson's friends; J. Dryden, *An Essay of Dramatick Poesie* (London, 1668), contains critical remarks on Jonson, and an "Examen" of *Epicoene, or, the Silent Woman*; W. Hazlitt, *Lectures on the English Comic Writers* (London, 1819), includes an essay "On Shakespeare and Ben Jonson"; S. T. Coleridge, *Literary Remains*, vol. I (London, 1836); A. C. Swinburne, *A Study of Ben Jonson* (London, 1889); F. E. Schelling, *Ben Jonson and the Classical School* (Baltimore, 1898); M. Castelain, *Ben Jonson: L'homme et L'oeuvre* (Paris, 1907); G. G. Smith, *Ben Jonson* (London, 1919), in English Men of Letters Series; T. S. Eliot, *The Sacred Wood* (London, 1920), includes an essay on Ben Jonson, repr. in *Selected Essays* (London, 1932); E. Welsford, *The Court Masque: A Study in the Relationship Between Poetry and the Revels* (Cambridge, 1927); J. Palmer, *Ben Jonson* (1934); R. G. Noyes, *Ben Jonson on the English Stage 1660–1776* (Cambridge, Mass., 1935); U. M. Ellis-Fermor, *The Jacobean Drama: An Interpretation* (London, 1936; 2nd ed., 1947; 3rd ed., 1953); F. R. Leavis, *Revaluation* (London, 1936); L. C. Knights, *Drama and Society in the Age of Jonson* (London, 1937); O. J. Campbell, *Comicall Satyre and Shakespeare's "Troilus and Cressida"* (San Marino, Calif., 1938); A. H. King, *The Language of the Satirized Characters in "Poetaster": A Socio-stylistic Analysis*, Lund Studies in English, no. 10 (London, 1941); G. E. Bentley, *Shakespeare and Jonson: Their Reputations in the 17th Century Compared*, 2 vols. (Chicago, 1945); G. B. Johnson, *Ben Jonson: Poet* (New York, 1945); F. L. Townsend, *Apologie for Bartholomew Fayre: The Art of Jonson's Comedies* (New York, 1947); A. H. Sackton, *Rhetoric as a Dramatic Language in Jonson* (New York, 1948); E. V. Pennanen, *Chapters on the Language of Ben Jonson's Dramatic Works* (Turku, Finland, 1951); Edmund Wilson, *The Triple Thinkers* (2nd ed., 1952), includes an essay, "Morose Ben Jonson"; A. C. Partridge, *Studies in the Syntax of Jonson's Plays* (Cambridge, 1953); A. C. Partridge, *The Accidence of Jonson's Plays, Masques and Entertainments* (Cambridge, 1953); M. Chute, *Ben Jonson of Westminster* (New York, 1953; London, 1954); M. C. Bradbrook, *The Growth and Structure of Elizabethan Comedy* (London, 1955); P. Simpson, *Studies in Elizabethan Drama* (Oxford, 1955); G. Walton, *Metaphysical to Augustan: Studies in Tone and Sensibility in the Seventeenth Century* (Cambridge, 1955); J. J. Enck, *Jonson and the Comic Truth* (Madison, 1957); E. B. Partridge, *The Broken Compass: A Study of the Major Comedies of Ben Jonson* (London, 1958); W. T. Furniss, *Ben Jonson's Masques*, Yale Studies in English, no. 138 (New Haven–London, 1958), pp. 89–179; J. A. Barish, *Ben Jonson and the Languages of Prose Comedy* (Cambridge, Mass., 1960); W. Trimpi, *Ben Jonson's Poems: A Study of the Plain Style* (Stanford, 1962); J. A. Barish, *Ben Jonson: A Collection of Critical Essays* (Englewood Cliffs, N.J., 1963); C. G. Thayer, *Ben Jonson: Studies in the Plays* (Norman, Okla., 1963); R. E. Knoll, *Ben Jonson's Plays: An Introduction* (Lincoln, Neb., 1964); S. K. Orgel, *The Jonsonian Masque* (Cambridge, Mass., 1965); J. C. Meagher, *Methods and Meaning in Jonson's Masques* (Notre Dame–London, 1966); B. Gibbons, *Jacobean City Comedy: A Study of Satiric Plays by Jonson, Marston and Middleton* (London, 1968); G. B. Jackson, *Vision and Judgement in Ben Jonson's Drama*, Yale Studies in English, no. 166 (New Haven–London, 1968); J. G. Nichols, *The Poetry of Ben Jonson* (London, 1969); J. B. Bamborough, *Ben Jonson* (London, 1970); Ian Donaldson, *The World Upside-Down* (Oxford, 1970); Ian Donaldson, "Ben Jonson," in *English Drama to 1710*, edited by C. Ricks, Sphere History of Literature in the English Language, vol. 3 (London, 1971); H. C. Dessen, *Jonson's Moral Comedy* (Evanston, Ill., 1971); J. A. Bryant, Jr., *The Compassionate Satirist* (Athens, Ga., 1972); G. Parfitt, *Ben Jonson: Public Poet and Private Man* (London, 1976); L. A. Beaurline, *Ben Jonson and Elizabethan Comedy* (San Marino, Calif., 1978).

# JAMES JOYCE
(1882-1941)

## J. I. M. Stewart

### I

JAMES JOYCE was born on 2 February 1882 in Dublin, where his father was sufficiently prosperous to send him to a fashionable Jesuit boarding school and sufficiently improvident to be virtually penniless a few years later. Partly because of the steady decline in his family's fortunes, and partly because he himself was a little disposed to fudge the evidence, it is difficult to place Joyce tidily in a social class. Virginia Woolf, distressed by the milieu of *Ulysses* (1922), concluded that its author must be "a self-taught working man." Wyndham Lewis (who was educated at Rugby) made fun of Joyce's fictional alter ego, Stephen Dedalus, for his anxiety to appear a gentleman. Perhaps the Joyces became shabby more pronouncedly than they remained genteel. But class consciousness is not important with Joyce, as it is with the other great novelist of the age, D. H. Lawrence. Priest, artist, citizen are Joyce's categories, not gentle and simple.

Nevertheless, what may be called the George Gissing aspect of his youth—the precariousness of his slender degree of privilege, the cultural poverty of life around him—marked him deeply. He grew up arrogant and aloof, contemptuous of all proposals, whether political or artistic, for the regeneration of his country, proud of his precocious knowledge of contemporary continental literature. He renounced the Catholic church, and in 1904 he left Ireland for good, taking with him a young woman named Nora Barnacle, whom he subsequently married. Miss Barnacle was not literary, but a certain pungency attends some of her recorded utterances. "I guess the man's genius," she said of Joyce, "but what a dirty mind he has, hasn't he?" At least she had found a good husband and a devoted father of their two children. To support his family Joyce labored for many years as a teacher of English in Trieste and Zurich; it was only during his later life, when benefactions and his first substantial royalties enabled him to maintain a modest establishment in Paris, that the threat of destitution ceased to hang over him. He appears to have been very sure of his genius. He resisted the discouragements of poverty, neglect, moral censorship, and a grave disease of the eyes. By the time he died in 1941 there was little responsible literary opinion in either Europe or America that failed to acknowledge him as one of the most significant writers of the age. At the same time he attracted much foolish adulation, and his books suffered what they certainly invite, much extravagant exegesis.

### II

THE first of Joyce's works to appear in book form was *Chamber Music* (1907), a collection of thirty-six poems. It was completed in 1904 but had to wait three years for a publisher, and in the interval Joyce ceased to feel much regard for it. There is nothing surprising in this. His life's task, if abundantly egotistical, was wholly serious, a presenting of himself and his immediate environment to the world in fictions laying claim to the highest representative significance. With that task, to which he had already addressed himself in the apparently unpublishable *Dubliners* (1914), the poems in *Chamber Music* have nothing to do. They are serious only in a restricted aesthetic sense, which Joyce's genius transcended from the first. He had read Elizabethan lyrics with attention, and his own verses may best be described as consummate imitations of the older poets as they appeared through a fin de siècle haze. They are unchallengeably lyrical; like the best of the Elizabethan, each seems to sigh for its accordant air:

> Who goes amid the green wood
> With springtide all adorning her?

> Who goes amid the merry green wood
>   To make it merrier?
>
> Who passes in the sunlight
>   By ways that know the light footfall?
> Who passes in the sweet sunlight
>   With mien so virginal?
> > (*Chamber Music*, VIII, st. 1–2)

The range is narrow, and one would never guess that these elegant dabblings and paddlings in familiar shallows preluded some of the farthest voyages ever achieved over the wide waters of the word.

Yet of poetry when sufficiently broadly defined all Joyce's work was to be full. From Stephen Dedalus' early turnings-over of words—"a day of dappled seaborne clouds"—on to the last cadence of *Finnegans Wake* (1939):

> There's where. First. We pass through grass behush the bush to. Whish! A gull. Gulls. Far calls. Coming, far! End here. Us then. Finn, again! Take. Bussoftlhee, mememormee! Till thousendsthee. Lps. The keys to. Given! A way a lone a last a loved a long the

we hear this poetry plainly; and Joyce's own readings from his work as preserved on phonograph records are astonishing achievements in verbal music. Moreover, his prose is "poetic" in more ways than this. When Stephen is looking out from the Martello tower at the beginning of *Ulysses*, we read:

> Woodshadows floated silently by through the morning peace from the stairhead seaward where he gazed. Inshore and farther out the mirror of water whitened, spurned by lightshod hurrying feet. White breast of the dim sea. The twining stresses, two by two. A hand plucking the harpstrings merging their twining chords. Wavewhite wedded words shimmering on the dim tide.

This is consciously presented as poetry; and it is challengingly, not fortuitously, that it comes immediately after a quotation from Yeats. But we are not merely charmed by a cadence. Why—we find ourselves asking—"wavewhite wedded words"? Joyce is concerned with language as *language*; he is never solely concerned with melopoetic effect.

Modern criticism has taught us to recognize in linguistic compressions and ambiguities a range of resources characteristic of poetry proper. At its most effective, Joyce's developed prose was to combine musical suggestion with a hitherto unexampled power to scramble effectively the connotations of words. In *Finnegans Wake* there is a sort of prayer for the River Liffey that runs: "haloed be her eve, her singtime sung, her rill be run, unhemmed as it is uneven!"—thus echoing, enchantingly if profanely, the Lord's Prayer: "Hallowed be Thy Name. Thy kingdom come. Thy will be done in earth. As it is in heaven." It is reasonable to believe that Joyce's peculiar prose has been responsible for a good deal of modern poetry, and for some reinterpretation of older poetry as well. At least it is the work of a writer notably in command of instruments that the present age in particular has considered a large part of the essential endowment of the poet. Yet when Joyce addressed himself, quite simply, to metrical composition, all his largeness and boldness left him.

*Pomes Penyeach*, the self-consciously depreciatory title of a volume diminutive to the point of affectation, which he published in 1927, shows a mild technical development in consonance with the ideas of the imagists, and is the better—as so much of the century's poetry is the better—from the writer's acquaintance with Ezra Pound. But the poet's properties remain gray, wan, pale, frail, and démodé:

> The moon's greygolden meshes make
> All night a veil,
> The shorelamps in the sleeping lake
> Laburnum tendrils trail.
> The sly reeds whisper to the night
> A name—her name—
> And all my soul is a delight,
> A swoon of shame.
> > ("Alone")

When these lines were written, *Ulysses* was well under way.

### III

*Exiles* (1918), a play written in 1914 or 1915, is another work of minor interest. Striking as is Joyce's lifelong obsession with Dublin and Dubliners, he was determinedly and from the first a European before he was an Irishman, and in Ibsen he found an international figure who could be held up to point a contrast with the provinciality, as Joyce conceived it, of the Irish literary movement. But *Exiles* is not merely a counterblast, opposing to the theater of Yeats and Synge and Lady Gregory an aggressively naturalistic dramatic convention. It is the work of a writer who has a real if limited temperamental affinity with Ibsen; and it contrives to treat, at once with a bleak painful intensity and a large measure of obscurity, a theme very much from the world of *A Doll's House* and *Hedda Gabler*. We are certainly shown, in one cautious commentator's words, "a puzzling series of dilemmas concerning the limits of freedom, the demands of love, and the possessiveness inherent in marriage." And it seems probable that Joyce proposed to give us something yet closer to Ibsen than this, the spectacle of a harsh ethical absolutism at work in a fatally egotistical personality.

Richard Rowan is an Irish writer who has lived abroad for a number of years with Bertha, a simple and unintellectual girl whom he has been unable or indisposed to marry. They return to Dublin, where an old friend, Robert Hand, is determined that Rowan shall be appointed to a chair of romance literature. But Hand is also determined to seduce Bertha; and presently we find, in a scene of neat theatrical surprise, that Bertha, while passively accepting the successive stages of this advance and even accepting an assignation with Hand, is regularly reporting the developing situation to Rowan. Rowan will not in any degree bind, guide, or support her. He imagines her dead and says to Hand:

I will reproach myself then for having taken all for myself because I would not suffer her to give to another what was hers and not mine to give, because I accepted from her her loyalty and made her life poorer in love. That is my fear. That I stand between her and any moments of life that should be hers, between her and you, between her and anyone, between her and anything. I will not do it. I cannot and I will not. I dare not.

(Act II)

We are shown Bertha presenting again her former passive face to Hand's eventual wooing in his secluded cottage, and then the curtain descends at an ambiguous moment. In the last act Bertha returns to Rowan with an earnest protestation that she has been true to him. But he declares that he now has a deep, deep wound of doubt in his soul, and that this wound tires him. "He stretches himself out wearily along the lounge," and the play closes upon Bertha murmuring a passionate prayer for the return of their earliest days as lovers.

The characters in *Exiles* are very poorly realized. Rowan is represented as a lover but seems not to have the stuff of a lover in him. He constantly demands that he himself be understood, seen for what he is, and so accepted. But he virtually denies that a beloved, or any other person, is knowable. And he never himself contrives to notice this contradiction. We thus feel him to be the projection of a serious but imperfect self-analysis; and this feeling is fatal to any impression of a fullness of dramatic life. A small indication of the extent to which Joyce was here self-absorbed and self-tormented as he worked is the early percolation into the play of talk about Rowan's dead mother and the fact or calumny of his having in some way slighted her. This has no relevance to the action and is a spillover from Joyce's more openly autobiographical writing in the history of Dedalus.

IV

If the intellectual and emotional pressures that bore upon the young Joyce neither inform his poetry nor fortify his play, they are brought under fruitful artistic control in *Dubliners*. When eventually published in 1914, this volume contained fifteen sketches or short stories, about which Joyce had written thus to a prospective publisher nine years before:

My intention was to write a chapter of the moral history of my country and I chose Dublin for the scene because the city seemed to me the centre of paralysis. I have tried to present it to the indifferent public under four of its aspects: childhood, adolescence, maturity and public life. The stories are arranged in this order. I have written it for the most part in a style of scrupulous meanness and with the conviction that he is a very bold man who dares to alter in the presentment, still more to deform, whatever he has seen and heard.

This is a little manifesto of naturalism; but its most significant phrase is "moral history." And we are not far advanced in *Dubliners* before we realize that Joyce does not differ from other young writers in having as his chief stock-in-trade a set of powerful moral responses before the spectacle of fallen humanity. It is urged upon us that almost every aspect of Dublin life is pitiful or degraded, and that to the effective asserting of this the artist must bend all his cunning. Joyce will allow no half measures. His book is about paralysis—both the word and the thing fascinate a small boy on the first page—and paralysis is uncompromisingly asserted as something to make the flesh creep.

Each one of the stories cries out against the frustration and squalor of the priest-ridden, pub-besotted, culturally decomposing urban lower-middle-class living it depicts. An elderly priest dies in a state of mental and perhaps moral degeneration, and a child to whom he has given some instruction learns from whispering women that the trouble began when he dropped and broke a chalice. Two boys play truant and have a casual encounter with an ineffective pervert. A coarse amorist, to the admiration of a less accomplished friend, gets money out of a servant girl. A drunken clerk is scolded by a bullying employer and humiliated in a public house; he goes home and flogs his son. In another public house a traveler in tea falls down the steps of a lavatory and injures himself. While convalescent he is visited by friends, who talk tediously and ignorantly about ecclesiastical matters, and then endeavor to reform him by taking him to hear a sermon for businessmen. It is recorded by Joyce's brother that lavatory, bedside, and church in this story are designed in a ludicrous correspondence to Dante's Inferno, Purgatorio, and Paradiso.

We may well agree that the style in which such incidents as these are recounted should be "scrupulously mean." And a great part of their effect lies in Joyce's virtuosity here. It is largely a matter of the tact with which a mimetic or semiventriloquial technique is employed. In "Eveline," the story of a very simple girl, we read: "One time there used to be a field there in which they used to play every evening with other people's children. Then a man from Belfast bought the field and built houses in it." And similarly with the adults. The quality of their living is defined in "Two Gallants" by the language:

One said that he had seen Mac an hour before in Westmoreland Street. At this Lenehan said that he had been with Mac the night before in Egan's. The young man who had seen Mac in Westmoreland Street asked was it true that Mac had won a bit over a billiard match. Lenehan did not know: he said that Holohan had stood them drinks in Egan's.

Even an exclamation mark may be made to do this sort of work: "Just as they were naming their poisons who should come in but Higgens!" Higgens, thus acclaimed, is a cipher; he has not appeared before and will not appear again. Such effects would be wearisome if unrelieved; and so the texture of the prose is unobtrusively varied. The first story, that of the priest who broke the chalice, begins in a child's words of one syllable, but presently the priest has a handkerchief that is "inefficacious," and he lies "solemn and copious" in his coffin. Everywhere the description and evocation have a precision and economy and sensitiveness that constitute the reality of the book's style just as the "scrupulous meanness" constitutes its appearance. The style is in fact ironic, contriving to expose what it affects to accept.

A striking use of this technique occurs at the end of "Ivy Day in the Committee Room." We are introduced to a group of canvassers in a Dublin municipal election. They are working only for the money they hope to get from their candidate, whom they despise and distrust and would be quite ready to desert. This, with much more of the degradation of civic and national life that they represent, emerges through the medium of conversation, which eventually turns on Charles Stewart Parnell, the leader of the Irish nationalist movement, who had died shortly after being driven out of political life by opponents who had exploited his involvement in a divorce case. One of those present is persuaded to recite an appropriate poem of his own composition. It begins:

> He is dead. Our Uncrowned King is dead.
> O, Erin, mourn with grief and woe
> For he lies dead whom the fell gang
> Of modern hypocrites laid low.

The verses, which continue in a vein of facile patriotic sentiment and factitious indignation against the treachery that had brought Parnell to ruin, read as if they might have been picked out of a forgotten popular newspaper, but they are a clever fabrication by Joyce himself. And the effect achieved is subtle. The poem is fustian; and its massed clichés and threadbare poeticisms declare it to belong to the same world of impoverished feeling conveyed in the preceding conversations. But that is not quite all. There is a ghost in the poem, the ghost of generous enthusiasms and of strong and sincere attachments to large, impersonal purposes. We respond both ways, as we are later to do to analogous outcrops of romantic clichés in the reveries of Dedalus.

It is in the last and longest story in *Dubliners*, "The Dead," that Joyce's stature as a writer first declares itself unmistakably. Two old ladies and their niece, all obscure figures in the musical life of Dublin, are giving their annual party, and to this their nephew Gabriel Conroy, a schoolmaster with literary tastes, brings his wife, Gretta. The party, which is an undistinguished, rather vulgar, but entirely human affair, is described with a particularity in which the influence of Flaubert may be supposed. Gabriel takes prescriptively a leading part, although his superior education and his sensitiveness prevent his doing it easily, and he makes a speech that we are given in full. This speech, like the poem in "Ivy Day in the Committee Room," is an example of Joyce's deftest double-talk. It is full of trite and exaggerated sentiment, dwelling on spacious days gone beyond recall, absent faces, memories the world will not willingly let die, and so forth; and Gabriel is himself aware of its insincerity as he speaks. But we ourselves are correspondingly aware that it represents a kindly attempt to perform a duty and give innocent pleasure; and our attitude to Gabriel remains sympathetic even while we are being afforded a searching view of him.

After the party Gabriel and his wife drive through the snow to the hotel where they are to spend the night. He is full of desire for her, but she does not respond, and presently he learns that a song heard at the party has reminded her of a boy, Michael Furey, of whom he has never heard, and who died long ago as the result of a passionate vigil he had kept for Gretta when he was already very ill. Gabriel's realization that he has been a stranger to what is thus revealed as the deepest experience of his wife's life now becomes the deepest experience of his:

A shameful consciousness of his own person assailed him. He saw himself as a ludicrous figure, acting as a pennyboy for his aunts, a nervous, well-meaning sentimentalist, orating to vulgarians and idealizing his own clownish lusts. . . .

Generous tears filled Gabriel's eyes. He had never felt like that himself towards any woman, but he knew that such a feeling must be love. The tears gathered more thickly in his eyes and in the partial darkness he imagined he saw the form of a young man standing under a dripping tree. Other forms were near. His soul had approached that region where dwell the vast hosts of the dead. He was conscious of, but could not apprehend, their wayward and flickering existence. His own identity was fading out into a grey impalpable world: the solid world itself, which these dead had one time reared and lived in, was dissolving and dwindling.

A few light taps upon the pane made him turn to the window. It had begun to snow again. He watched sleepily the flakes, silver and dark, falling obliquely against the lamplight. . . . Yes, the newspapers were right: snow was general all over Ireland. It was falling on every part of the dark central plain, on the treeless hills, falling softly upon the Bog of Allen and, farther westward, softly falling into the dark mutinous Shannon waves. It was falling, too, upon every part of the lonely churchyard on the hill where Michael Furey lay buried. It lay thickly drifted on the crooked crosses and headstones, on the spears of the little gate, on the barren thorns. His soul swooned slowly as he heard the snow falling faintly through the universe and faintly falling, like the descent of their last end, upon all the living and the dead.

"The Dead" mingles naturalism and symbolism with a new confidence and richness; tragic ironies play across it subtly and economically; its parts are proportioned to each other strangely but with brilliant effectiveness. And if its artistry looks forward to a great deal in Joyce's subsequent writings, its charity and sympathy are qualities to which he was never to allow so free a play again.

V

*A Portrait of the Artist as a Young Man*, essentially the story of Joyce's own break with the Catholic church and discovery of his true vocation, was published in 1916, at the end of a process of gestation covering many years. Joyce had begun an autobiographical novel while still in his teens, and he persevered with it until it was 150,000 words long and could be regarded as approximately half finished. About 1908 he decided to rewrite the book on a smaller scale and different method, and it appears probable that the greater part of the original manuscript was then destroyed. The only considerable fragment certainly preserved, which has been published under Joyce's original title of *Stephen Hero* (1944), is rather longer than the whole perfected work but corresponds to only the final third of it.

The technique of *Stephen Hero* is objective, explicit, and ploddingly documentary. It is the only one of Joyce's works self-evidently and at once to rebut Wyndham Lewis' charge that here is a writer stimulated only by ways of doing things, and not by things to be done. It thus has some claim to be considered as a substantive work, with an illuminating place in the development of Joyce's writing, and it certainly possesses the curious interest of closely defining the whole basic structure of Joyce's personality. Nevertheless the mature *Portrait* is of altogether superior artistic significance. Its opening sentence exhibits the new technique: "ONCE upon a time and a very good time it was there was a moocow coming down along the road and this moocow that was coming down along the road met a nicens little boy named baby tuckoo."

Our knowledge of Stephen is now going to come to us mediated through his own developing consciousness. That consciousness is to be the theater of whatever drama the book attempts to present, and at the same time a territory sufficiently broad for the exercise of the vigorous naturalism that Joyce has been learning from continental masters. Yet with a quite bare naturalism he is no longer to be content, and on the second page we come upon him putting unobtrusively into operation a different sort of machinery:

The Vances lived in number seven. They had a different father and mother. They were Eileen's father and mother. When they were grown up he was going to marry Eileen. He hid under the table. His mother said:
—O, Stephen will apologise.
   Dante said:
—O, if not, the eagles will come and pull out his eyes—
   Pull out his eyes,
   Apologise,
   Apologise,
   Pull out his eyes.

The whole *Portrait* is an apologia: at the same time its cardinal assertion is that Stephen will *not* apologize; rather he awaits the eagles. Joyce's eyes, moreover, were in actual fact threatened from the first; presently in the *Portrait* Stephen as a schoolboy is going to be unjustly punished as a consequence of defective vision; the master who beats him has just declared twice over that a boy's guilt may be seen in his eyes; the complex of ideas thus established remains with Stephen and is several times resumed in *Ulysses*—in a manner fully intelligible only to a reader equipped with the relevant memories of the *Portrait*.

This technique of weaving elusive symbolic themes percurrently through the strongly realistic fabric of his writing is something that Joyce is to exploit more and more. His prose at length becomes a vast hall of echoes—and one fatally adapted (the toiling inquirer must feel) to the conflicting voices of scholiasts. Eventually Joyce appears to have enjoyed playing up to his commentators. "Eins within a space," we read in *Finnegans Wake*, "and a weary-wide space it wast, ere wohned a Mookse.'" The relationship of the mookse to the moocow opens a wide field for conjecture.

The development of young men destined to be artists was already in Britain, as on the Continent, a prolific field of fiction, but this scarcely qualifies the large originality of the *Portrait*, which is as much a landmark in the English novel as is *Joseph Andrews* or *Middlemarch* or *The Way of All Flesh*. We have only to think of the novel's line of representative young men—Roderick Random, Tom Jones, David Copperfield, Arthur Pendennis, Richard Feverel—to realize that Stephen Dedalus is presented to us with a hitherto unexampled intimacy and immediacy. It is true that this is achieved at some cost to the vitality of the book as a whole. Here, as later in parts of *Ulysses*, we are locked up firmly inside Stephen's head; and there are times when we feel like shouting to be let out. What Stephen takes for granted, we have to take for granted too; and as he is aware of other people only as they affect his own interior chemistry, there is often something rather shadowy about the remaining personages in the book. But the picture is always clear and hard in its exhibition of Stephen's successive predicaments. The imaginative and unathletic small boy, hard pressed by the narrow orthodoxies and hovering brutalities of a Jesuit boarding school; his growing realization of his family's drift into squalor, and the pride and arrogance that he progressively summons to his aid; the overwhelming sense of sin into which the severity of Catholic doctrine precipitates him upon the occasion of his untimely sexual initiation; the breaking of his nerve and his phase of anxious and elaborate religious observance; his stumbling but implacable advance, through reverie and through conversation with whatever acquaintances will listen, upon an understanding of the realm of art and his elected place in it; the crisis of his break with church and family, and the exalting moment of revelation and dedication on the strand: all these are vividly realized and rendered experiences.

In the *Portrait* Joyce abandons that aggressively frugal and monotonous prose, pervasive in *Stephen Hero*, out of which he had evolved the highly expressive "scrupulous meanness" of *Dubliners*. Vocabulary, syntax, rhythm are now boldly varied to accentuate the contours of the underlying emotion, and Joyce is thus beginning to deploy his resources as a master of imitative form. *Ulysses*, considered in point of prose style, is to reveal itself quite frankly as a museum displaying, as in a series of showcases, all the old ways of using English and a great many new ones as well. The *Portrait*, although in some degree looking forward to this, renders an overriding impression of unity, since each of the styles reflects one facet of Stephen, who is a highly unified creation. "He chronicled with patience what he saw," we are told, "detaching himself from it and tasting its mortifying flavour in secret."

This Stephen is best represented in some of the conversations—which, as in *Dubliners*, are based upon an ear and intellect so alert as to combine a maximum of significant statement with a minimum of apparent selection. The early scene in which Stephen's father and Mrs. Riordan quarrel over Irish politics during dinner on Christmas day is Joyce's early masterpiece in this kind. When Stephen ceases to be merely a recording intelligence and responds actively to the challenge of a world he finds so largely inimical, the style reaches out at once for weapons and armor, its whole tone becoming an extension of Stephen's most caustic and arrogant condemnations: of Dublin, which has "shrunk with time to a faint mortal odour," of Ireland, "the old sow that eats her farrow," of her church, which is "the scullery-maid of christendom." Stephen himself is "a priest of the eternal imagination," and he speaks in cold exalted phrases consonant with the role.

But there is yet another Stephen in the book, the Stephen who ceaselessly communes with himself on solitary walks about Dublin. It is here—it is in the style Joyce largely employs in rendering Stephen *chez lui*—that the success of the *Portrait* trembles in the balance. The hazard is not the consequence of any simple miscalculation of effect; it is a necessary risk involved in the complexity of what Joyce attempts. There are always two lights at play on Stephen. In the one he is seen as veritably possessing the sanctity and strength he claims—for he has been set aside, not of his own will, to serve the highest. In the other he is only the eldest of Simon Dedalus' neglected children, and his aspirations have the pathos he is to discern in his sister Dilly, when she shyly produces the tattered French grammar she has bought from a stall. Moreover, he is an adolescent as well as an artist; and the emotions of adolescence are often both disturbingly self-indulgent and much in excess of their specific precipitating occasions—expressing themselves in maudlin tags, conventional postures, phrases, and cadences caught up out of books, sometimes hovering agonizingly between sublimity and absurdity, hysteria and inspiration. It is because of all this that Stephen is represented as outrageously sentimentalizing himself and regularly clothing his poignantly felt nakedness in the faded splendors of a bygone poetic rhetoric:

> He heard the choir of voices in the kitchen echoed and multiplied through an endless reverberation of the choirs of endless generations of children: and heard in all the echoes an echo also of the recurring note of weariness and pain. All seemed weary of life even before entering upon it. And he remembered that Newman had heard this note also in the broken lines of Virgil, "giving utterance, like the voice of Nature herself, to that pain and weariness yet hope of better things which has been the experience of her children in every time."
>
> (ch. 4)

In this kind of writing the key is regularly pitched not to the objective scale of its occasion, but to the dimensions of that occasion as they exist at the moment for the boy. Thus Stephen takes part in some theatricals in the presence of the girl he admires, and the situation excites and disturbs him. So we have:

> He hardly knew where he was walking. Pride and hope and desire like crushed herbs in his heart sent up vapours of maddening incense before the eyes of his mind. He strode down the hill amid the tumult of sudden risen vapours of wounded pride and fallen hope and baffled desire. They streamed upwards before his anguished eyes in dense and maddening fumes and passed away above him till at last the air was clear and cold again.

Before passages like this, or those far more highly wrought pages of the same sort that describe the boy's miserable frequenting of the brothels of the city, one of Joyce's best critics is surely wrong in speaking of "purple passages that have faded considerably." They remain highly expressive, like Juliet's hysteria or Hamlet's rant in Ophelia's grave.

At the book's crisis this boldly heightened writing is employed with great skill. Stephen's coming to his true vocation is by way of successive sensuous impressions, each of which has a sort of trigger action upon forces that have been building themselves up in his mind. The piety that he has evinced since abandoning and repenting his carnal sins has suggested that he is apt for the priesthood, and the question of whether he has indeed a vocation is put to him temperately and wisely by a Jesuit director. His pride and arrogance are brought into play; he is tempted by the thought of secret knowledge and power. He is tempted, too, without clearly knowing it, as an artist: the "vague acts of the priesthood" attract him "by reason of their semblance of reality and of their distance from it." On the threshold of the college the director gives Stephen his hand "as if already to a companion in the spiritual life." But Stephen feels the caress of a mild evening air, sees a group of young men walking with linked arms, hears a drift of music from a concertina. And these impressions are reinforced by memories of his schooldays:

> His lungs dilated and sank as if he were inhaling a warm moist unsustaining air and he smelt again the moist warm air which hung in the bath in Clongowes above the sluggish turfcoloured water.
> Some instinct, waking at these memories, stronger than education or piety, quickened within him at every near approach to that life, an instinct subtle and hostile, and armed him against acquiescence.
> (ch. 4)

Yet still his mind oscillates. He is entered at the university and celebrates the occasion with comical portentousness in an elaborately harmonious reverie. But this in turn brings to his mind "a proud cadence from Newman":

> Whose feet are as the feet of harts and underneath the everlasting arms

and "the pride of that dim image brought back to his mind the dignity of the office he had refused. . . . The oils of ordination would never anoint his body. He had refused." Why? The answer—the positive answer—comes as he walks on the beach. It is, in fact, the secular artist's reply to the "proud cadence" of Newman: "He drew forth a phrase from his treasure and spoke it softly to himself:—A day of dappled seaborne clouds." This is Stephen Dedalus' moment of apocalypse. He realizes that he has apprehended something beautiful. Soon he will be able to write in his diary the final truth about himself: "I desire to press in my arms the loveliness which has not yet come into the world." It is only a shallow irony that would remark that this loveliness is to be represented by Leopold and Molly Bloom in *Ulysses*. Nor need we contemn, in the name of sophisticated restraint, the pitch of the prose in which this moment, a moment at once of final release and final submission, is celebrated:

> Where was his boyhood now? Where was the soul that had hung back from her destiny, to brood alone upon the shame of her wounds and in her house of squalor and subterfuge to queen it in faded cerements and in wreaths that withered at the touch? Or where was he?
> He was alone. He was unheeded, happy, and near to the wild heart of life. He was alone and young and wilful and wildhearted, alone amid a waste of wild air and brackish waters and the seaharvest of shells and tangle and veiled grey sunlight and gayclad lightclad figures of children and girls and voices childish and girlish in the air.
> (ch. 4)

The whole hymn of praise and dedication and pride has still its aspect of precariousness and pathos; it preserves, for all its gorgeousness, the poignancy of the boy's cry in *Stephen Hero:* "Mother . . . I'm young, healthy, happy. What is the crying for?" Stephen, in the last analysis, is singing only as his brothers and sisters have been singing a few pages earlier, when that could be detected in their voices which Newman had heard in the broken lines of Vergil.

VI

In the penultimate section of *Ulysses*, which takes the form of a long catechism, Leopold Bloom is described in bed at the end of the day. He is curled up, we are told, like a child in the womb. And the section concludes thus:

> Womb? Weary?
> He rests. He has travelled.
>
> With?
> Sinbad the Sailor and Tinbad the Tailor and Jinbad the Jailer and Whinbad the Whaler and Ninbad the Nailer and Finbad the Failer and Binbad the Bailer and Pinbad the Pailer and Minbad the Mailer and Hinbad the Hailer and Rinbad the Railer and Dinbad the Kailer and Vinbad the Quailer and Linbad the Yailer and Xinbad the Phthailer.
>
> When?
> Going to dark bed there was a square round Sinbad the Sailor roc's auk's egg in the night of the bed of all the auks of the rocs of Darkinbad the Brightdayler.
>
> Where?

Bloom has traveled as the whole crowd of us must travel. But the final question *Where?* is unanswered and ambiguous. If we stress the all-life-in-a-day aspect of *Ulysses*, it is a question about futurity, and there is no answer to it on any premises that Joyce admits. If we think simply of 16 June 1904, then Bloom's journey is from the waking world to the world of dream, and there is a sense in which *Where?* receives its answer in Joyce's next book. Bloom has fallen asleep; we have accompanied him just over the threshold and thereby gained a preliminary glimpse of the vast territory of the unconscious mind into which we are to be conducted in *Finnegans Wake*. The jingle of names (as well as making the statement "Bloom=Everyman=Us") is hypnoidal, and the syntactical obscurity of a *square round Sinbad* and the strange resonance in *Dirkinbad the Brightdayler* expresses the violence done by the unconscious and its queer categories to the logic of waking life.

A positive response to Joyce's writing as a whole depends upon the ability to accept such uses of language as this passage adumbrates. Some readers find it endlessly fascinating. Others declare it boring and assert Joyce to be simply one who, solemn and wide-awake, adds Finbad to Ninbad till the cows come home. There can be no doubt that he became compulsively addicted to letting words fool around, and that his brain was the most elaborately equipped playground for the purpose that has ever left a record of itself in literature. Whether he is to be indicted for progressive artistic irresponsibility makes a hard question not likely to be well answered either by fanatical Joyceans or by those who turn away from his books in disgust and indignation.

The action of the *Portrait* extends over many years, in a manner traditional enough in the novel. *Ulysses* is revolutionary in this regard, being a work of great length in which the entire action is organized, as in a classical play, so as to fall within a single revolution of the sun. Yet it begins precisely as if it were a continuation of the *Portrait*, with the thread taken up after the hero's brief absence from Ireland. In fact, it represents a curious amalgam of just such a sequel with a wholly different project that Joyce had entertained during the period of *Dubliners*. "Ulysses" was to have been the title of a short story descriptive of a day's wandering about Dublin on the part of a certain Mr. Hunter. The ironic association of this personage with the Homeric hero was later enriched through a further association with the Wandering Jew, and from this fusion Leopold Bloom was born. Then Joyce, having hit upon the notion of a loosely organized structural correspondence with the *Odyssey*, perceived that he could begin with a *Telemachia* in which the central figure would still be Stephen Dedalus.

But the opening pages, although they have indeed an unforgettable largeness as of great painting, scarcely persuade us that we want to hear much more about Joyce's former hero. Stephen has not been improved by his residence in France. Indeed, we are already more likely to have admired the art of the *Portrait* than the personality of its protagonist. And although that criticism is obviously defective which depreciates the book on the score that Stephen is a prig or a cold fish, it yet remains true that part of a novelist's material, however austere a realist he be, consists in the sympathy of his reader; that he must learn to manipulate this like everything else; and that to miscalculate here is to invite disaster.

In *Ulysses* Stephen is more insufferable than his creator appears disposed to admit. His weariness, his hauteur, his curiously hinted proneness to indulge a dream life in the University of Oxford, his disposition to speak "quietly," "coldly," "bitterly" ("It is a symbol of Irish art. The cracked looking-glass of a servant"), even his dislike of water and presumably of soap: all these are facets of his character that invite fairly enough the jibes of Wyndham Lewis. When presently Stephen is discovered teaching school, we find ourselves disposed to question his declared unfitness for the task, since his mental habit is represented as almost wholly pedantic. This impression is intensified in the succeeding section, which presents us with Stephen's highly allusive and recondite stream of consciousness as he walks on the strand, and which begins thus:

Ineluctable modality of the visible: at least that if no more, thought through my eyes. Signatures of all things I am here to read, seaspawn and seawrack, the nearing tide, that rusty boot. Snotgreen, bluesilver, rust: coloured signs. Limits of the diaphane. But he adds: in bodies. Then he was aware of them bodies before of them coloured. How? By knocking his sconce against them, sure. Go easy. Bald he was and a millionaire, *maestro color di che sanno*. Limit of the diaphane in. Why in? Diaphane, adiaphane.

Part of the obscurity results from Joyce's demand that our consciousness should be steadily at play over the entire surface of his work, so that phrases and associations are intelligible only in the light of others scores or hundreds of pages away. This is a legitimate device, and the extent of its use is a matter of literary tact: the more serious the undertaking, the more vigorous the cooperation we may fairly be expected to bring to it. But so much in Stephen's reverie is resistant to any ready elucidation that we come to wonder whether all this showing off to himself (if it is that) might have been more succinctly accomplished had his creator been less concerned to show off to us.

Certainly Stephen is a Telemachus to whom Ulysses, in the figure of Bloom, comes decidedly to the rescue, so far as the general artistic success of the book is concerned. Whether, within the fable, Bloom ultimately means much to Stephen, or Stephen to Bloom, is a question that has been variously answered by critics. Considered as an action, *Ulysses* ends in obscurity, whether inadvertent or deliberate. But considered as a theater of novel design, constructed mainly for the exhibition of a comic character of striking vitality and verisimilitude, it is an unchallengeable even if dauntingly labored success.

For Lewis, once more—always the best devil's advocate when we are judging Joyce—Bloom is a walking cliché; beneath a vast technical elaborateness in the presentation is an orthodox comic figure of the simplest outline. It is certainly true that the lifelikeness of Bloom does not proceed from his being very directly observed from the life. He is a highly evolved literary creation, and his complexity—for he is complex—is literary. Some aspects of him exist only because a body of Anglo-Irish humor existed; others, only because Flaubert's last and unfinished novel, *Bouvard et Pécouchet*, existed. But his principal derivation is surely from the mock-heroic tradition. It has been asserted on eminent authority that the *Odyssey* provided Joyce merely with a scaffolding that a reader may disregard. This is not so. To anyone who has got the hang of the book, Ὀδυσσεὺς πολύτροπος, the much-traveled Ulysses, is sufficiently present to make Bloom seem absurd and diminutive. Yet, as with the best mock-heroic, the reference is capable too of working the other way. Bloom's positive qualities, his representative character, his pathos, all take point from his original.

An elaborate and considered craft is evident too in the medium in which Bloom is presented to us. Joyce had found in Édouard Dujardin's *Les Lauriers sont coupés*, a short novel published in 1887, a technique of internal monologue that in *Ulysses* he develops with immense resource and cunning. Once more he is far from drawing directly on life. Bloom never stops talking to himself—except just occasionally when he talks to someone else—and we are bound to feel that this assiduity in verbalization, although convenient both to his creator and to us who would make his acquaintance, is something quite outside nature. Yet Joyce achieves with it a vivid and deep illusion. The content of Bloom's mind, his interests, his responses to stimuli, are depicted with deliberation as very much those of any vulgar, curious, kindly man. To give just that with unexampled fullness is largely the idea of the book, and it carries with it the danger of a rather boring lack of particularity. Yet we become convinced that Bloom's mind is not quite like any other mind. It is indeed with his mind as with his hat. On 16 June 1904, many Dubliners must have been wearing a high-grade hat from Plasto's, but only Bloom can have been wearing a high-grade ha. We suspect a misprint (as we often do) but are in the presence of a device. Bloom's internal idiom, too, is consistently and not too obtrusively idiosyncratic. A traditional literary resource—one exploited alike by the creators of Hamlet and Mr. Jingle—has been deftly transferred to a new theater.

Bloom admits us more generously to his intimacy than does almost any other figure in fiction. Yet he is a small man; neither nature nor nurture has given him much; his moral being, which is amebic, and his intellectual interests, which if lively are circumscribed, prove alike unrewarding to exploration on the scale proposed by the book. Bloom thus comes, for all his liveliness and attractiveness, to shoot his bolt with us just as Stephen has done. His environment threatens to swamp him; he ceases to float upon the current of his creator's abounding imaginative vitality and is felt as battling rather desperately against it. It is perhaps by way of redressing a balance here that Joyce offers us finally, and so much at large, the figure of Molly Bloom, the sadly faithless Penelope of the story.

Mrs. Bloom is essentially passive. In the morning, she accepts breakfast in bed from the hands of her husband; in the afternoon, again in bed, she entertains the irresistible Blazes Boylan; in the small hours, in bed still, she indulges herself in the enormous reverie with which the book concludes. The sustained erotic tension of this, which takes about two hours to read, reflects more credit upon Joyce than upon Mr. Boylan. Totally without punctuation (although, for some reason, divided into eight enormous paragraphs), it appears concerned to carry the technique of internal monologue to something near its theoretical limit. And it does achieve, for all its psychological implausibility, an exhibition as of some vast sprawled and monolithic image of female sexuality. Bloom, on the other hand, is throughout in restless motion: he visits the pork butcher, feeds the cat, attends a funeral, pursues his profession as an advertisement tout, has a row in a pub, misconducts himself on a beach, and so on. His most characteristic motion is a wriggle—through inhospitable doors and past averted shoulders. He remains symbolically, if not very impressively, male.

If the Blooms have anything in common it is a retrospective turn of mind. Characters or events in *Dubliners* frequently recur to them. Bloom, engaged on one of his morning duties, recalls how, long ago, he used to jot down on his cuff what his wife said when dressing. "What had Gretta Conroy on?" she had once asked. Bartell d'Arcy, whose singing of "The Lass of Aughrim" called up for Gretta the shade of Michael Furey, has been among Mrs. Bloom's lovers; and so has Lenehan, once the admirer of that Corley who wheedled the gold coin from a servant girl. Mrs. Bloom during her vigil recalls, among numerous other prominent citizens, "Tom Kernan that drunken little barrelly man that bit his tongue off falling down the men's WC drunk in some place or other." Two of the friends who took Kernan to a retreat for businessmen join Bloom at the funeral at Glasnevin; and Bloom reflects that his last visit there was for the funeral of Mrs. Sinico—of whose unfortunate end we have read in a short story called "A Painful Case." Simon Dedalus—another of Mrs. Bloom's bedfellows—is perhaps a little changed, even as his family is further degraded; in some regards an engaging character, he now speaks with a violent foulness and out of a deep venom absent from the *Portrait*.

All this reminiscence reflects Joyce's own mind, which we feel to repose in the Dublin of his youth in a quite extraordinary way. He is nowhere able, or at least disposed, to set out for the past as upon an act of exploration. He has carried the past along with him in his consciousness—as he carried, it is said, its newspapers and tram-tickets along with him in his trunks. It is not indeed wholly true that, as Lewis avers, his thought was "of a conventional and fixed order" that remained unchanged since his early days. *Ulysses* differs from the *Portrait* not merely in elaboration, display, technical variousness, and virtuosity. It mirrors deeper responses to the whole spectacle of enjoying and suffering humanity. But the spectacle itself is confined to the same stage; the old props are trundled on and off; and we are progressively aware of an inflexibly willed, rather desperate resourcefulness as the sustaining principle of the whole. And the resourcefulness is—surely to a hazardous degree—linguistic and stylistic. *Ulysses* is quite staggeringly full of language. The stuff comes at us in great rollers, breakers, eddies, and tumbles of spume and spray. It is wildly exhilarating. It is also rather buffeting, bruising, exhausting long before the end.

There is evidence that Joyce gave anxious and sustained thought to the form and structure of his work. He certainly let his disciples suppose so; they are fond of expounding the successive episodes in terms of an intricate superimposition of framework upon framework: organs, arts, colors, symbols, and technics. Read, however, without all this instruction, *Ulysses* may strike us as a large-scale improvisation, a hand-to-mouth progression from stunt to stunt— with nearly all the stunts coming off quite brilliantly—but to a final effect of agglomeration before which any summing up, any secure arriving at a right aesthetic total, is singularly hard to achieve.

A curious encylopedism, such as may be found in certain medieval poets, obsesses the author of *Ulysses*. He seems to feel, for instance, that his book should contain not only his own sort of English—or rather his own sorts of English in their almost inexhaustible variety—but every other sort of English as well; and so he writes one long section, that in which Bloom visits the National Maternity Hospital in Holles Street and meets Stephen, in a succession of parodies tracing the whole evolution of English prose. Some of these are presented out of order; and we are told by the commentators that as this evolution of styles is being appropriately exhibited in a context of development from unfertilized ovum to birth, and as, in an embryo, one or another organ may in fact develop prematurely, there is a particular grace in setting the parodies too in an occasional chronological confusion. Joyce's mind, we must recognize, is as tortuous and pedantic as it is prodigal and—in essentials—poetic. And its prodigality seems to render very uncertain its sense of measure.

Between the longest section of the book, the unparalleled and astounding fantasia of the unconscious, thronged and farced with specters of preternatural vigor and overpowering horror, which opens at "the Mabbot street entrance of nighttown" —between this and the contrasting but equally unexampled long slow earthen pulse of Mrs. Bloom's concluding reverie, there is obviously required some episode of relaxed tension. Joyce provides two such episodes in succession. First, Bloom and Stephen are to be represented as sitting in a cabmen's shelter, exhausted. This exhaustion is to be conveyed, on the governing principle of the book, by recourse to an exhausted, a jejune prose. Joyce therefore contrives what is best described as a sustained cliché of some twenty thousand words. Next the two men—casually thrown together but symbolically regarded as profoundly in search of each other—make their way to Bloom's kitchen. They are isolated individuals, souls struggling toward some obscure self-realization through and against the recalcitrant medium of matter. This recalcitrant medium Joyce evokes overwhelmingly by a yet longer and denser device: an interminable, inexorable catechism, couched almost exclusively in a flat scientific jargon, exhaustively tabulating not only Bloom's present physical environment but also that of the dream-cottage to which he aspires to retire:

> What homothetic objects, other than the candlestick, stood on the mantelpiece?
> A timepiece of striated Connemara marble, stopped at the hour of 4.46 a.m. on the 21 March 1896, matrimonial gift of Matthew Dillon: a dwarf tree of glacial arborescence under a transparent bellshade, matrimonial gift of Luke and Caroline Doyle: an embalmed owl, matrimonial gift of Alderman John Hooper.

There are more than three hundred such answers to questions, and some of them describe with minute particularity as many as ten or twenty separate objects. Joyce is said to have taken more pride in this part of *Ulysses* than in any other. Certainly it cannot be called idle or even—strangely enough—boring, and there is no reason to suppose that the precise effect it produces could be produced in any other way. Yet this massive accumulation, this enormous stasis, is presented to us at a point where we suppose ourselves to be moving toward the resolution of a fable. What, we ask, is this resolution? The mountain has labored. But where is the mouse?

Stripped and viewed as an action, *Ulysses* reveals itself as being much what it started out to be: a short story in *Dubliners*. We need not suppose that Mr. Hunter's wanderings about Dublin were to have been no more than a small exercise in the picaresque. That was never Joyce's way. Something always happens in his stories—but it is generally a small, muted, problematically or evanescently significant thing. Most characteristically, it is an encounter—an encounter with some circumscribed hinted consequence that is not pursued. And this is the formula of *Ulysses*, the spare skeleton that has been given so much flesh and so many clothes. None of the great elaborative works of literature—Milton's *Paradise Lost*, Goethe's *Faust*, Mann's *Joseph und seine Brüder*—has made do with quite so little.

Yet this strange book—so *voulu*, so willfully tedious, so dirty, often smelling so queerly of pedagogy and examination papers—is one to which mature readers will return again and again. We revisit it—Edmund Wilson has excellently said—as we revisit a city, a city animated by a complex inexhaustible life. Its material may be "consciously the decay of a mournful province"—the words are Lewis' once more—but it is not itself mournful. And it is not negative. It closes, with passion, on a basic affirmation: "yes I said yes I will Yes."

VII

*Ulysses*, the record of a single day, exhausts the exploration of the waking mind. *Finnegans Wake*, the formidable work to the elaborating of which Joyce devoted the last fifteen years of his life, is correspondingly the record of a single night; and it proposes to interpret, with an equal exhaustiveness, the nature and content of the mind asleep. To this tremendous proposal Joyce was in part driven by the logic of his own achievement, in part encouraged by the drift of contemporary psychological speculation, and in part lured by the unparalleled opportunities that the fabricating of a dream-language would afford to his remarkable logopoetic faculty.

As if conscious that he had revealed no genius for that sort of large-scale fiction that has significantly a beginning, a middle, and an end, Joyce framed this final work upon a peculiar principle. It begins: "riverrun, past Eve and Adam's, from swerve of shore to bend of bay, brings us by a commodius vicus of recirculation back to Howth Castle and Environs." And it ends: "A way a lone a last a loved a long the."

The last sentence, in fact, runs straight into the first. Ideally, the text should be disposed not in a bound volume but in a single line of type round an enormous wheel. History, Joyce now believed, is such a wheel, and its revolution has been explained by the eighteenth-century Italian philosopher Giambattista Vico. The "commodius vicus of recirculation" introduces us to Vico and his theory, as well as to a pleasant *giro* (round trip) that may be taken round

Dublin bay. Howth Castle and Environs display initial letters preluding the entry of the book's central character, Humphrey Chimpden Earwicker. But as Earwicker is a universal figure, the initials may also stand for "Haveth Childers Everywhere" or "Here Comes Everybody." Eve and Adam's is the popular name for a church on the banks of the Liffey, which is the river that is running in the opening word; but as we are already talking about the stream of history, we are no doubt being invited, incidentally, to consider that stream's first welling-up in the Garden of Eden.

Joyce is said to have declared in a moment of arrogance (which may indeed have been softened by humor) that the demand he made upon his reader was no less than the application of a lifetime. Certainly he now had little regard for anything that can be approximated to lucidity, a fact that becomes apparent as soon as we go on from the first paragraph to the second:

Sir Tristram, violer d'amores, fr'over the short sea, had passencore rearrived from North Armorica on this side the scraggy isthmus of Europe Minor to wielderfight his penisolate war: nor had topsawyer's rocks by the stream Oconee exaggerated themselse to Laurens County's gorgios while they went doublin their mumper all the time: nor avoice frou afire bellowsed mishe mishe to tauftauf thuartpeatrick: not yet, though venissoon after, had a kidscad buttended a bland old isaac: not yet, though all's fair in vanessy, were sosie sesthers wroth with twone nathandjoe. Rot a peck of pa's malt had Jhem or Shen brewed by arclight and rory end to the regginbrow was to be seen ringsome on the aquaface.

"The first impression," Joseph Campbell and Henry Morton Robinson say of this in the volume that they have devoted to a preliminary exegesis of *Finnegans Wake*, "is one of chaos, unrelieved by any landmark of meaning or recognition." But this impression they assert to be totally mistaken, since the passage holds nothing that need shake our faith in Joyce "as a wielder of the most disciplined logic known to modern letters." It is surely abundantly clear, however, that as long as we assert the traditional canons of what constitutes discourse, Joyce *is* producing nonsense. The passage is logical—or claims to be logical—only in the very special sense in which (according to certain psychological theories) the most phantasmagoric dream must be logical; in the sense, that is to say, that its constituting elements are chosen and concatenated not fortuitously but as the designed product of unconscious mental processes in which may be detected the working of intelligible laws. When eventually we discover that Earwicker has a wife and daughter, and that he has reached a phase of sexual involution in which his relations with them are ambiguous, we realize the appropriateness with which the dream-logic calls up both Tristram, who had two Iseults, and Swift ("nathandjoe" being an anagram for Jonathan), who had Stella and Vanessa. If we ask why Vanessa is disguised as "in vanessy" we may find ourselves thinking of "Inverness" and so recalling Macbeth, who, like Earwicker, fell into some moral danger as a consequence of his relations with females.

It will be evident that *Finnegans Wake* offers much scope to the interpreter. The reader's first endeavor, however, should be less with the larger significances that the book is conjectured to embody than with the linguistic technique that it indubitably employs. If one considers, still in the above passage, the phrase "penisolate war," one quickly sees that it is simply "Peninsular War" (the title commonly given by historians to the Napoleonic campaigns in Spain) so distorted as to carry more secondary suggestions than one. For example, if hyphenated as "pen-isolate war" it may call up a whole complex of thoughts about Joyce himself, who certainly fought with a pen—and did so from the isolation of Trieste or Zurich. It was maintained by Freud and his followers that language regularly takes on this ambiguous character—whether in wit or in slips of the tongue or pen—under pressure of conflicting unconscious forces. Psychoanalytic literature, moreover, reports many instances of such obscurely significant disguisings and telescopings of words being remembered from dreams; and it is evident that from this Joyce derived the notion that it should be possible to excavate—or if not to excavate, to invent—a whole dream-language of this sort.

It is certain that *Finnegans Wake* is not, in any simple sense, the product of a psychic automatism. Joyce wrote much of it in comparatively plain language, which he then with great labor elaborated until he had achieved his complex final product. Of some sections of the work early and intermediate versions have been published, and at least some of these have been judged by many readers to be more successful than the later versions evolved from them. Once again we have to question Joyce's sense of measure; he overdoes it, and the eventual effect is of something mechanical or synthetic. But the mere fact that he worked over his text again and again is irrelevant in judging its merits as an artistic evocation of the world of dreams. The more one reads the book, the more one is disposed to acknowledge in it an authentic imaginative correspondence with what we know of unconscious mental life.

But *Finnegans Wake* remains a very hard book. Joyce does nothing to help us. It is only in the penultimate section that we gain anything but the most obscure and fragmentary intimations of what, in any common sense, it is all about. Moreover, to the obscurities of one psychological system Joyce has cheerfully added the obscurities of another. Earwicker, the Dublin publican, dreams obediently on Freud's principles—but when he dreams deeply enough he dreams on Jung's as well, so that his dream becomes anybody's or everybody's dream; universal knowledge, fragmented and distorted, drifts in and out after a fashion that none of the Earwicker family could conceivably compass: and we are presumably being invited to believe that we have penetrated to something like a Great Memory, or collective unconsciousness of the race. Such an exploration must almost necessarily, one supposes, be attended by a large obscurity. But it is sometimes possible to feel that we are in the presence of something much more circumscribed, and that the reduplication of darknesses in *Finnegans Wake* represents simply veil upon veil that Joyce has spun round some personal predicament, some obliquity of the private or domestic life such as had always haunted his writing and that he is now at the last unwilling to exhibit directly either to others or to himself.

*Finnegans Wake*, then, if enigmatic at a first entrance, is yet largely susceptible of elucidation both as a cunningly contrived and disposed phantasmagoria of near-dreamlike material and as an inexhaustibly subtle, even if at times depressingly dogged, campaign upon the farthest boundaries of language. What is most accessible in it is its often hauntingly beautiful melody, which is perhaps best illustrated by the famous ending of the section originally published under the title "Anna Livia Plurabelle." Anna Livia is the Liffey, and the Liffey is the symbol of the feminine, just as the Hill of Howth is ("Howth Castle and Environs") of the masculine. Here two washerwomen—who as well as being washerwomen are a stone and an elm, death and life—are gossiping about Anna in the gathering dusk. And their gossip—to quote Edmund Wilson—"is the voice of the river itself, light, rapid, incessant, almost metrical, now monotonously running on one note, now impeded and syncopated, but vivaciously, interminably babbling its indistinct rigmarole story, half-unearthly, half-vulgarly human, of a heroine half-legendary, half-real":

And ho! Hey? What all men. Hot? His tittering daughters of. Whawk.

Can't hear with the waters of. The chittering waters of. Flittering bats, fieldmice bawk talk. Ho! Are you not gone ahome? What Thom Malone? Can't hear with bawk of bats, all thim liffeying waters of. Ho, talk save us! My foos won't moos. I feel as old as yonder elm. A tale told of Shaun or Shem? All Livia's daughtersons. Dark hawks hear us. Night! Night! My ho head halls. I feel as heavy as yonder stone. Tell me of John or Shaun? Who were Shem and Shaun the living sons or daughters of? Night now! Tell me, tell me, tell me, elm! Night night! Telmetale of stem or stone. Beside the rivering waters of, hitherandthithering waters of. Night!

Yet many who have turned to the whole work with excitement after hearing Joyce's own recorded reading of this must have been baffled and disappointed by the indigestible matter they found there. It will never conduce to Joyce's reputation to assert that *Finnegans Wake* is, in any ordinary sense, a readable book. It is not; it is in the main a closed book even to most persons of substantial literary cultivation. But if not readable it may yet be seminal; and it seems possible that, for many generations, its frequentation by a small body of writers and students will indirectly enrich the subsequent stream of English literature.

SELECTED BIBLIOGRAPHY

(Compiled by Jeri Johnson)

I. BIBLIOGRAPHY. A. Parker, *James Joyce: A Bibliography of His Writings, Critical Material and Miscellanea* (Boston, 1948), see also W. White, "James Joyce: Addenda to Alan Parker's Bibliography," in *Papers of the Bibliographical Society of America*, 43 (First Quarter 1949), pp. 93–96, and 43 (Fourth Quarter 1949), pp. 401–411, W. White, "Addenda to James Joyce Bibliography, 1950–1953," in *James Joyce Review*, 1, no. 2 (June 1957), pp. 9–25, and W. White "Addenda to James Joyce Bibliography, 1954–1957," in *James Joyce Review*, 1, no. 3 (September 1957), pp. 3–24; J. J. Slocum and H. Cahoon, *A Bibliography of James Joyce: 1882–1941* (New Haven, Conn.–London, 1953), the standard bibliography, listing all publications of Joyce's own work up to 1950, see also A. M. Cohn, "Corrigenda to the Joyce Bibliography (Slocum and Cahoon D 1-2), and a Possible Addendum," in *Papers of the Bibliographical Society of America*, 65 (Third Quarter 1971), pp. 304-307, R. M. Kain, "Supplement to Joyce Bibliography," in *James Joyce Review*, 1, no. 4 (December 1957), pp. 38-40, and A. M. Cohn, "Further Supplement to James Joyce Bibliography, 1950-1957," in *James Joyce Review*, 2, nos. 1 and 2 (Spring-Summer 1958), pp. 40-54; T. E. Connolly, *The Personal Library of James Joyce* [in the Lockwood Memorial Library in the University of Buffalo]: *A Descriptive Bibliography*, University of Buffalo Studies, 22, no. 1 (April 1955), records some marginalia and evidence of use.

R. E. Scholes, *The Cornell Joyce Collection: A Catalogue* (Ithaca, 1961); P. Spielberg, *James Joyce's Manuscripts and Letters at the University of Buffalo: A Catalogue* (Buffalo, 1962); D. Hayman, ed., *A First Draft Version of "Finnegans Wake"* (London, 1963), includes a catalog of the *Finnegans Wake* MSS in the British Museum; the *James Joyce Quarterly* (University of Tulsa), checklists of Joyce criticism, comp. by A. M. Cohn at least annually since 1963, the best listings of material published since the first ed. of Deming's *Bibliography*; R. H. Deming, *A Bibliography of James Joyce Studies* (Lawrence, Kans., 1964; rev. ed., Boston, 1977), the standard annotated checklist of critical material on Joyce complete to December 1973; M. Beebe, P. F. Herring, and A. W. Litz, "Criticism of James Joyce: A Selected Checklist," in *Modern Fiction Studies*, 15 (1969), pp. 105-182.

M. Groden, *James Joyce's Manuscripts: An Index* (New York-London, 1980), the most complete checklist of all extant MSS, typescripts, and proofs of Joyce's works.

II. SELECTED WORKS. *Introducing James Joyce* (London, 1942; repr. 1973), a sel. of Joyce's prose with an intro. by T. S. Eliot; H. Levin, ed., *The Portable James Joyce* (New York, 1947), published in England as *The Essential James Joyce* (London, 1948), contains *Dubliners, A Portrait of the Artist as a Young Man, Exiles, Collected Poems,* "The Holy Office," "Gas from a Burner," and sections from *Ulysses* and *Finnegans Wake*.

III. SEPARATE WORKS PUBLISHED BEFORE 1941. *Note:* In each case the date and place of the first ed. is followed by the same information for the most correct, accepted, or standard ed.

*Chamber Music* (London, 1907), ed. with notes by W. Y. Tindall (New York, 1954), see *Collected Poems; Dubliners* (London, 1914), ed. by R. Scholes in consultation with R. Ellmann (New York, 1967); *A Portrait of the Artist as a Young Man* (New York, 1916), ed. by R. Ellmann, definitive text corrected from Dublin holograph by C. G. Anderson (New York, 1964), first published serially in the *Egoist* (2 February 1914-1 September 1915); *Exiles* (London, 1918; New York, 1951).

*Ulysses* (Paris, 1922; New York, 1961), first published serially in the *Little Review* (New York, 1918-1920) and the *Egoist* (London, 1919), but Joyce rev. the text substantially before its final publication in Paris in 1922; many eds. now available, all error-ridden; work on a definitive critical ed. is currently in progress in Germany; *Pomes Penyeach* (Paris, 1927), see *Collected Poems; Collected Poems* (New York, 1936; New York, 1957), includes *Chamber Music, Pomes Penyeach,* and "Ecce Puer"; *Finnegans Wake* (New York-London, 1939), first published in fragments as "Work in Progress" from April 1924, in various pamphlets and periodicals, notably *transition* (Paris).

IV. POSTHUMOUS WORKS. T. Spencer, ed., *Stephen Hero* (New York, 1944), with an intro. by Spencer, rev. with additional MS material and a foreword by J. J. Slocum and H. Cahoon (New York, 1956), further rev. with further manuscript material, and ed. by Slocum and Cahoon (New York, 1963), the surviving part of the first draft of *A Portrait of the Artist; Letters of James Joyce,* S. Gilbert, ed., vol. I (New York, 1957), reiss. with corrections by R. Ellmann (1966); R. Ellmann, ed., vols. II-III (New York, 1966); E. Mason and R. Ellmann, eds., *The Critical Writings of James Joyce* (New York, 1959), includes Joyce's essays "Ibsen's New Drama," "James Clarence Mangan," and "The Day of the Rabblement," book reviews, "The Holy Office," and "Gas from a Burner"; T. E. Connolly, ed., *James Joyce's Scribbledehobble: The Ur-Workbook for "Finnegans Wake"* (Evanston, Ill., 1961), transcript of one of Joyce's largest notebooks in the Wickser Collection at the University of Buffalo Library, with photographs of some pp.; *Daniel Defoe* (Buffalo, 1964), Joyce's lecture at Trieste, Italian text with a trans. and notes by J. Prescott; R. Scholes and R. M. Kain, eds., *The Workshop of Daedalus* (Evanston, Ill., 1965), includes Joyce's *Epiphanies*, his Paris, Pola, and Trieste notebooks, and the autobiographical essay "A Portrait of the Artist," written when he was twenty-one; R. Ellmann, ed., *Giacomo Joyce* (New York, 1968), facs. repro. of a Joyce notebook, written while he was in Trieste, much of which was previously published in Ellmann's *James Joyce*; P. F. Herring, ed., *Joyce's "Ulysses" Notesheets in the British Museum* (Charlottesville, Va., 1972), transcription, annotation, and discussion of the notesheets Joyce compiled in writing *Ulysses; James Joyce: "Ulysses." A Facsimile of the Manuscript,* 2 vols. (New York, 1975), intro. by H. Levin, bibliographical preface by C. Driver, a photo-repro. of the holographic MS now at the Rosenbach Foundation in Philadelphia.

*James Joyce: "Ulysses." The Manuscript and First Printing Compared* (New York, 1975), ann. by C. Driver, photo-repro. of the text as printed in the *Little Review,* marked to show the differences between it and the Rosenbach MS; issued in a three-vol. set with the above; R. Ellmann, ed., *Selected Letters of James Joyce* (New York, 1975), containing several new letters not published in the three-vol. ed.; P. F. Herring, ed., *Joyce's Notes and Early Drafts for "Ulysses": Selections from the Buffalo Collection* (Charlottesville, Va., 1977), transcription, some photographs; M. Groden, ed., *The James Joyce Archive,*

63 vols. (New York–London, 1978) (index published separately as Groden, ed., *James Joyce's Manuscripts: An Index* (New York, 1980), facs. photo-repro. ed. of Joyce's entire "workshop": all extant and available notes, drafts, MSS, typescripts, and proofs of his work; vol. I: *Chamber Music, Pomes Penyeach, and Occasional Verse*; vols. II–III: *Notes, Criticism, Translations, and Miscellaneous Writings*; vols. IV–VI: *Dubliners*; vols. VII–X: *A Portrait of the Artist as a Young Man*; vol. XI: *Exiles*; vols. XII–XXVII: *Ulysses*; vols. XXVIII–LXIII: *Finnegans Wake*.

V. BIOGRAPHICAL STUDIES. F. Budgen, *James Joyce and the Making of "Ulysses"* (London, 1934), repr. with additional material (London, 1972), about Joyce while he was living in Zurich, best account of him as a friend and writer; H. Gorman, *James Joyce* (New York, 1939; rev. ed., New York, 1948), the first full-length biography of Joyce, written with his help, contains material not available elsewhere; J. F. Byrne, *Silent Years: An Autobiography, with Memoirs of James Joyce and Our Ireland* (New York, 1953), an account of Joyce as a young man by the "Cranly" of *A Portrait of the Artist*; M. Colum and P. Colum, *Our Friend James Joyce* (New York, 1958; ppbk. repr., New York, 1961), describes meetings with Joyce the established writer; S. Joyce, *My Brother's Keeper* (New York, 1958; ppbk. repr., New York, 1964), ed. and with an intro. by R. Ellmann, preface by T. S. Eliot; K. Sullivan, *Joyce Among the Jesuits* (New York, 1958), provides information about Joyce's early education; S. Beach, *Shakespeare and Company* (New York, 1959), includes account of Joyce during his Paris days and the publication of *Ulysses*; R. Ellmann, *James Joyce* (New York, 1959), rev. with additional material (New York–London, 1982), the standard biography; W. Y. Tindall, *The Joyce Country* (University Park, Pa., 1960; ppbk. repr., New York, 1972); S. Joyce, *The Dublin Diary of Stanislaus Joyce* (Ithaca–London, 1962), G. H. Healey, ed., rev. and published as G. H. Healey, ed., *The Complete Dublin Diary of Stanislaus Joyce* (Ithaca, 1971); C. G. Anderson, *James Joyce and His World* (London, 1968), concise account, many pictures; C. P. Curran, *James Joyce Remembered* (New York–London, 1968), Joyce during his Dublin and Paris student days; J. Lidderdale and M. Nicholson, *Dear Miss Weaver: Harriet Shaw Weaver, 1876–1961* (New York–London, 1970), a portrait of the founder of the Egoist Press, which published *A Portrait of the Artist* and *Ulysses*, valuable information on Joyce's early struggles for recognition; S. G. Davies, *James Joyce: A Portrait of the Artist* (London, 1975).

VI. GENERAL CRITICAL STUDIES. E. Pound, "Joyce," in the *Future* (May 1918), pp. 161–163; repr. in T. S. Eliot, ed., *Literary Essays of Ezra Pound* (London, 1954); W. Lewis, *Time and Western Man* (London, 1927), especially "An Analysis of the Mind of James Joyce," pp. 91–130, led to Joyce's collaboration with Stuart Gilbert and a ch. of *Finnegans Wake*.

C. Connolly, "The Position of Joyce," in *Life and Letters*, 2, no. 11 (April 1929), repr. in C. Connolly, *The Condemned Playground* (New York, 1946); E. Wilson, *Axel's Castle: A Study in the Imaginative Literature of 1870–1930* (London, 1931), contains ch. on Joyce; D. Daiches, *The Novel and the Modern World* (Chicago, 1939; rev. ed., 1960), contains chs. on Joyce; E. Wilson, *The Wound and the Bow: Seven Studies in Literature* (New York, 1941; repr. 1959), contains discussion of *Finnegans Wake*; H. Levin, *James Joyce: A Critical Introduction* (Norfolk, Conn., 1941; London, 1944), still one of the best general intros. to Joyce's work; S. Givens, ed., *James Joyce: Two Decades of Criticism* (New York, 1948; rev. ed., 1963), contains a number of important essays, including T. S. Eliot's "Ulysses, Order and Myth" (1923), S. F. Damon's "The Odyssey in Dublin" (1929), and P. Toynbee's "A Study of James Joyce's *Ulysses*" (1947).

W. Y. Tindall, *James Joyce: His Way of Interpreting the Modern World* (New York, 1950); G. Melchiori, "Joyce and the Eighteenth-Century Novelists," in M. Praz, ed., *English Miscellany*, 2 (1951); F. Russell, *Three Studies in Twentieth Century Obscurity* (Aldington, 1954), contains attack on Joyce's later work; H. Kenner, *Dublin's Joyce* (Bloomington, Ind.–London, 1956; repr. Gloucester, Mass., 1969), intelligent and original interpretations of Joyce's work; M. Magalaner and R. M. Kain, eds., *Joyce: The Man, the Work, the Reputation* (New York, 1956), assembles and comments upon a large body of critical material; M. Magalaner, ed., *A James Joyce Miscellany* (New York, 1957), followed by the more important *A James Joyce Miscellany, Second Series* (Carbondale, Ill., 1959) and *Third Series* (Carbondale, 1962), contains wide variety of articles, some of great value; W. T. Noon, S.J., *Joyce and Aquinas* (New Haven, Conn., 1957), sympathetic account of Joyce's use of Aquinas; J. M. Morse, *The Sympathetic Alien: Joyce and Catholicism* (New York, 1959), considers Joyce's use of Aquinas and other patristic writers; W. Y. Tindall, *A Reader's Guide to James Joyce* (New York, 1959), places great emphasis on Joyce's use of symbols; M. J. C. Hodgart and M. Worthington, *Song in the Works of James Joyce* (New York, 1959), contains lists of songs in Joyce's works.

S. L. Goldberg, *The Classical Temper* (London, 1961), Joyce as a novelist, with special attention to *Ulysses*; A. W. Litz, *The Art of James Joyce: Method and Design in "Ulysses" and "Finnegans Wake"* (London, 1961), landmark study in the analysis of Joyce's methods of composition; V. Mercier, *The Irish Comic Tradition* (London, 1962); J. I. M. Stewart, *Eight Modern Writers* (Oxford, 1963); H. Kenner, *Flaubert, Joyce and Beckett: The Stoic Comedians* (London, 1964); J. Prescott, *Exploring James Joyce* (Carbondale, Ill., 1964), essays focusing on Joyce's powers of rev.; A. W. Litz, *James Joyce* (New York, 1966; rev. ed., 1972), short, introductory survey intended for American college students; A. Goldman, *The Joyce Paradox* (London, 1966), an artful discussion of Joyce's methods and philosophy; F. Read, *Pound/Joyce: The Let-*

ters of *Ezra Pound to James Joyce, with Pound's Essays on Joyce* (New York, 1967), very good, essential to an understanding of the crucial relationship between Pound and Joyce.

R. H. Deming, *James Joyce: The Critical Heritage*, 2 vols. (New York–London, 1970), vol. I: *1907–1927*, vol. II: *1928–1941*, invaluable collection of over 300 articles, some abr., from various viewpoints, very good for a historical perspective on Joyce's reception; H. Cixous, *The Exile of James Joyce*, S. Purcell, trans. (New York, 1972); F. Senn, *New Light on Joyce from the Dublin Symposium* (Bloomington, Ind.–London, 1972), various important articles, especially J. P. Dalton's "The Text of *Ulysses*"; A. Burgess, *Joysprick: An Introduction to the Language of James Joyce* (London–New York, 1973); Z. Bowen, *Musical Allusions in the Works of James Joyce* (Albany, N.Y.–Dublin, 1974); J. Garvin, *James Joyce's Disunited Kingdom and the Irish Dimension* (New York–Dublin, 1976); B. Benstock, *James Joyce: The Undiscover'd Country* (New York–Dublin, 1977); R. Ellmann, *The Consciousness of Joyce* (New York–London, 1977), includes in appendix a complete list of Joyce's Trieste library; C. H. Peake, *James Joyce: The Citizen and the Artist* (London, 1977), especially good on *Ulysses*; H. Kenner, *Joyce's Voices* (Berkeley, Calif.–London, 1978), a stimulating and entertaining rationale for Joyce's varying styles.

D. Manganiello, *Joyce's Politics* (Boston–London, 1980); B. Benstock, ed., *The Seventh of Joyce* (Bloomington, Ind.–Sussex, 1982), includes the best of the papers presented at the Seventh International Joyce Symposium, Zurich, 1979.

VII. Critical Studies of Early Works. E. Pound, "*Dubliners* and Mr. Joyce," in the *Egoist*, 1 (15 July 1914), repr. in T. S. Eliot, ed., *Literary Essays of Ezra Pound*; M. Magalaner, *Time of Apprenticeship: The Fiction of Young James Joyce* (New York, 1959), reproduces the first version of "The Sisters" and contains interesting notes on the factual bases of Joyce's stories.

T. E. Connolly, ed., *Joyce's "Portrait": Criticisms and Critiques* (New York, 1962; London, 1964), essays by Harry Levin, Dorothy van Ghent, Richard Ellmann, and others; W. E. Morris and C. A. Nault, eds., *Portraits of an Artist: A Casebook* (New York, 1962), wide variety of critical material, with full critical apparatus and bibliography; D. Gifford, with assistance of R. J. Seidman, *Notes for Joyce: "Dubliners" and "Portrait of the Artist"* (New York, 1967; rev. ed., 1982); C. G. Anderson, ed., "*A Portrait of the Artist as a Young Man": Text, Criticism and Notes* (New York, 1968), Viking Critical ed.; W. M. Schutte, ed., *Twentieth Century Interpretations of "A Portrait of the Artist as a Young Man"* (Englewood Cliffs, N.J., 1968), see especially the articles by Wayne Booth, Hugh Kenner, and S. L. Goldberg; J. R. Baker and T. Staley, eds., *James Joyce's "Dubliners": A Critical Handbook* (Belmont, Cal., 1969), contains essays by such critics as Robert Penn Warren and Lionel Trilling; C. Hart, ed., *James Joyce's "Dubliners": Critical Essays* (New York–London, 1969), essays by A. Walton Litz, Fritz Senn, Adaline Glasheen, and others; R. Scholes and A. W. Litz, eds., *James Joyce's "Dubliners": Text, Criticism and Notes* (New York, 1969), Viking Critical ed., standard text and solid criticism.

M. Beja, *Epiphany in the Modern Novel* (Seattle, 1971), especially his discussion of Joyce's epiphanies; M. Beja, ed., *James Joyce, "Dubliners" and "A Portrait of the Artist as a Young Man": A Selection of Critical Essays* (London, 1973), essays by Hugh Kenner, Richard Ellmann, Anthony Burgess, and others; T. F. Staley and B. Benstock, eds., *Approaches to Joyce's "Portrait": Ten Essays* (Pittsburgh, 1976), see especially Hans Walter Gabler's "The Seven Lost Years of *A Portrait of the Artist as a Young Man*."

VIII. Critical Studies of *Ulysses*. E. Pound, "*Ulysses*," in the *Dial*, 72 (June 1922), repr. in T. S. Eliot, ed., *Literary Essays of Ezra Pound*; V. Larbaud, "James Joyce," in *Nouvelle Revue française*, 24 (April 1922), trans. in *Criterion*, 1 (October 1922), the first explanation of the "structure" of *Ulysses*; S. Gilbert, *James Joyce's "Ulysses"* (London, 1930; rev. ed., 1952), written with the help of Joyce, gives an account of the Homeric parallels; C. G. Jung, "*Ulysses*: Ein Monolog," in *Europaische Revue*, 7 (1932), trans. in *Nimbus*, 2 (1953); M. L. Hanley et al., *Word Index to Joyce's "Ulysses"* (Madison, Wis., 1937).

R. M. Kain, *Fabulous Voyager* (Chicago, 1947), Joyce's uses of "facts" (i.e., newspapers, street maps, directories) in the writing of *Ulysses*; W. M. Schutte, *Joyce and Shakespeare: A Study in the Meaning of "Ulysses"* (New Haven, Conn., 1957); R. M. Adams, *Surface and Symbol: The Consistency of James Joyce's "Ulysses"* (New York, 1962); S. Sultan, *The Argument of "Ulysses"* (Columbus, Ohio, 1965), account of the narrative of *Ulysses*; H. Blamires, *The Bloomsday Book* (London, 1966), page-by-page narrative paraphrase, at times wrong; W. Thornton, *Allusions in "Ulysses"* (Chapel Hill, N.C., 1968), most useful.

D. Hayman, *"Ulysses": The Mechanics of Meaning* (Englewood Cliffs, N.J., 1970), first to give name to the Arranger as narrative device in *Ulysses*; T. F. Staley and B. Benstock, eds., *Approaches to "Ulysses"* (Pittsburgh, 1970), especially David Hayman's "The Empirical Molly"; R. Ellmann, *Ulysses on the Liffey* (New York, 1972); E. R. Steinberg, *The Stream of Consciousness and Beyond in "Ulysses"* (Pittsburgh, 1973); D. Gifford, with R. J. Seidman, *Notes for Joyce: An Annotation of James Joyce's "Ulysses"* (New York, 1974); C. Hart and D. Hayman, eds., *James Joyce's "Ulysses"* (Berkeley, Calif.–London, 1974), eighteen essays, one for each ch. of *Ulysses*, most of which are excellent; T. F. Staley, ed., *"Ulysses": Fifty Years* (Bloomington, Ind.–London, 1974); M. French, *The Book as World: James Joyce's "Ulysses"* (Cambridge, Mass.–London, 1976); M. Seidel, *Epic Geography: James Joyce's "Ulysses"* (Princeton, N.J., 1976), exploration of Joyce's use of Victor Bernard's *Les Pheniciens et l'Odyssée*; M.

Groden, *"Ulysses" in Progress* (Princeton, N.J., 1977), a complete account of the development of the text of *Ulysses;* J. H. Maddox, *Joyce's "Ulysses" and the Assault upon Character* (New Brunswick, N.J., 1978).

E. B. Gose, *The Transformation Process in Joyce's "Ulysses"* (Toronto-Buffalo, N.Y.-London, 1980), Freudian psychoanalytic theory applied to *Ulysses;* H. Kenner, *Ulysses* (London, 1980), interesting and stimulating general introduction to *Ulysses;* J. Gordon, *James Joyce's Metamorphoses* (Dublin-New York, 1981); K. Lawrence, *The Odyssey of Style in "Ulysses"* (Princeton, N.J., 1981), extremely good account of the stylistic "problems" of *Ulysses.*

IX. Critical Studies of *Finnegans Wake.* S. Beckett et al., *Our Exagmination Round His Factification for Incamination of Work in Progress* (Paris, 1929), reiss. with additional material (1961), Joyce said he "stood behind" the twelve authors, presumably directing their work; J. Campbell and H. M. Robinson, *A Skeleton Key to "Finnegans Wake"* (New York-London, 1944; ppbk. ed., New York, 1961), first attempt at page-by-page explication, still very good.

M. J. C. Hodgart, "Shakespeare and *Finnegans Wake,"* in *Cambridge Journal,* 6 (September 1953); J. S. Atherton, *"Finnegans Wake":* The Gist of the Pantomime," in *Accent,* 15 (Winter 1955); A. Glasheen, *"Finnegans Wake* and the Girls from Boston, Mass.," in *Hudson Review,* 7 (Spring 1955); A. Glasheen, *A Census of "Finnegans Wake"* (Evanston, Ill., 1956), followed by *A Second Census of "Finnegans Wake": An Index of the Characters and Their Roles* (Evanston, Ill., 1963), and *A Third Census of "Finnegans Wake"* (Berkeley-Los Angeles-London, 1977), very useful; D. Hayman, "From *Finnegans Wake:* A Sentence in Progress," in *PMLA,* 73, no. 1 (March 1958), a careful study of thirteen stages in Joyce's composition of a sentence.

J. S. Atherton, *The Books at the Wake: A Study of Literary Allusions in James Joyce's "Finnegans Wake"* (New York, 1960; rev. ed., 1974); F. H. Higginson, *"Anna Livia Plurabelle": The Making of a Chapter* (Minneapolis, 1960); F. Senn, "Some Zurich Allusions in *Finnegans Wake,"* in *Analyst,* 19 (December 1960), a thorough account by a native of Zurich; C. Hart, *Structure and Motif in "Finnegans Wake"* (London, 1962); C. Hart, *A Concordance to "Finnegans Wake"* (Austin, Tex., 1963; rev. ed., 1974); D. Johnston, "The Non-Information of *Finnegans Wake,"* in *Massachusetts Review* (Winter 1964), the entire issue is devoted to writers of twentieth-century Ireland; B. Benstock, *Joyce-Again's Wake: An Analysis of "Finnegans Wake"* (Seattle, 1965; repr. 1975); J. P. Dalton and C. Hart, eds., *Twelve and a Tilly: Essays on the Occasion of the 25th Anniversary of "Finnegans Wake"* (Evanston, Ill.-London, 1966), essays by A. Walton Litz, David Hayman, Richard M. Kain, and others; M. C. Solomon, *Eternal Geometer: The Sexual Universe of "Finnegans Wake"* (Carbondale, Ill., 1969); C. Hart and F. Senn, *A Wake Digest* (Sydney-University Park, Pa.-London, 1969), essays by Hart, Senn, Jack P. Dalton, Adaline Glasheen, and others; W. Y. Tindall, *A Reader's Guide to "Finnegans Wake"* (New York-London, 1969), a report on twenty years of studies at Columbia University.

M. Norris, *The Decentered Universe of "Finnegans Wake": A Structuralist Analysis* (Baltimore-London, 1977); R. McHugh, *Annotations to "Finnegans Wake"* (New York-London, 1980); D. Rose and J. O'Hanlon, *Understanding "Finnegans Wake"* (New York-London, 1982).

X. Special Joyce Journals. *Note:* Several periodicals have been devoted entirely to the task of interpreting Joyce's works. Among them are the following: *James Joyce Review* (New York), ed. E. Epstein, appeared in four quarterly numbers in 1957 and as a single "double number" in 1958, and in 1959, when it ceased publication, several important articles were published in it; the *Analyst,* ed. Robert Mayo, published occasionally by the Department of English, Northwestern University, has devoted many issues entirely to Joyce and published articles, sometimes lengthy ones, by John V. Kelleher, Adaline Glasheen, Fritz Senn, and others; *A Wake Newslitter,* ed. Clive Hart and Fritz Senn, now published in Colchester, England, through the Department of English, University of Essex, first eighteen numbers (March 1962-March 1963), which had no official support, contained articles by Thornton Wilder, M. J. C. Hodgart, Adaline Glasheen, Nathan Halper, the eds., and many others; *James Joyce Quarterly* (University of Tulsa), ed. T. F. Staley, has been appearing since autumn 1963, now the official publication of the James Joyce Society.

# JOHN KEATS
(1795-1821)

## Miriam Allott

### INTRODUCTION

JOHN KEATS was born in London on 31 October 1795 and died of tuberculosis in Rome, where he had been sent for recovery, on 23 February 1821, having been unable to write any poetry during the last fourteen months of his life because of his illness. His brief poetic career falls roughly into four stages: 1816–1817, when he wrote most of the thirty-three poems in his first collection; 1817, when he was chiefly engaged in writing *Endymion*; 1818, a year bringing crucial personal experiences that deeply affected his imagination and that closed with his first attempts at *Hyperion*; and 1819, when he wrote his major poems. The precipitating events of 1818 included his parting with his brother George, who emigrated to America that June; the loss of his other brother, Tom, who died of tuberculosis in December, aged nineteen; his first sight, during his summer walking tour with his friend Charles Brown, of the dramatic mountain scenery in the Lake District and Scotland; and his introduction in the autumn to Fanny Brawne, the girl he loved and whom he was unable to marry, first because they lacked means and later because he was too ill.

Keats had little longer in which to discover his individual poetic voice and learn something of his craft than many students need to study for a first arts degree in a British university; but he lived to see published his two collections, *Poems* (1817) and *Lamia, Isabella, The Eve of St. Agnes, and Other Poems* (1820), and, in the interval between these, his lengthy *Endymion: A Poetic Romance* (1818). Much of the rest of his work, including a selection of his remarkable letters, appeared posthumously in two small volumes published in 1848 by Richard Monckton Milnes as *Life, Letters and Literary Remains of John Keats*. Milnes added to these in 1856 by printing for the first time *The Fall of Hyperion*, a reworking of the earlier, unfinished *Hyperion*.

The total output is not large and its quality is uneven; but it became a seminal influence for other poets in the nineteenth century, remains widely familiar today, even if only by hearsay, and receives from modern scholars the serious critical attention given to major writers. It is the product of a young talent wholly dedicated to its poetic calling and to poetry as a supreme expression of the beautiful, approaching perfection only with the writer's approach to maturity. This was a state reached, as Keats saw it, by growing away from unreflecting delight in external nature and into a wise understanding of the harsher realities of existence and the annihilation of self-regarding impulses through empathic identification with others. This he called "negative capability" and associated it above all with the Shakespearean creative imagination. He did not reach it in his own poetry, though the quick human intelligence and breadth of feeling in his letters make us think that with time he might have done so.

But Keats constantly sought to further the dual development of his poetic and his personal selves by working hard at his craft, experimenting with different genres and metrical structures, submitting himself to various literary influences, and searching for a balance between what he called "sensations"—responsiveness to the concrete particulars of life—and "thoughts"—the exercise of his powers of intellect and understanding, and the nourishing of them by wide reading and varied personal experience.

If we look in turn at Keats's first collection of verse, his narrative poems, his major odes, his final effort to forge a new kind of poetic statement by reworking his abortive "epic," *Hyperion*, into a highly personal "vision," and certain passages in his letters, we can distinguish, at least in outline, the movements of this self-discipline and something of the quality of the work it helped to produce. Critical judgments of Keats have sometimes been drawn out of true, partly because the human appeal of an existence haunted by poverty and fatal disease, which nonetheless finds compensation in the activity of a vivid creative intelligence, can distract attention from the work to the life (the tendency is still common in some modern studies of the Brontë sisters).

In the case of Keats it encouraged the legendary image of a chlorotic youth too sensitive to withstand hardship and done to death by hostile reviewers. Readers fastened on passages that suggested exclusively the poet of luxurious "sensations" and exquisite longing for death, a habit that encouraged a simplistic view of romanticism in general and of Keats's romanticism in particular. It became easy to isolate his confession in the "Ode to a Nightingale":

> ... many a time
> I have been half in love with easeful Death,
> Called him soft names in many a musèd rhyme,
> To take into the air my quiet breath,
> Now more than ever seems it rich to die,
> To cease upon the midnight with no pain,[1]
> (st. 6, 1–6)

to overlook his recognition that death, after all, means insentience:

> Still wouldst thou sing, and I have ears in vain—
> To thy high requiem become a sod.
> (st. 6, 9–10)

and with this to ignore the entire movement of thought and feeling that at first carries the poet from "The weariness, the fever and the fret" into an ideal world of beauty and permanence, and finally returns him to what is actual and inescapable.

This curve of feeling shapes, in some degree, all Keats's major poetry. It is connected with that side of his creative temper where a flexible intelligence seeks to penetrate feeling with the vitality that certain Victorian readers anticipated modern criticism in recognizing. An arresting instance is William Howitt's remark, in a book published in 1847, that Keats's poetry was "a vivid orgasm of the intellect." David Masson, in his long article of November 1860 for *Macmillan's* magazine (he was then its editor), saw as outstanding in Keats "the universality of his sensuousness," but found the true sign of poetic greatness in the evidence, even in early poems, "of that power of reflective and constructive intellect by which alone so abundant a wealth of the sensual element could have been ruled and shaped into artistic literary forms."

This "potentiality" adds to our difficulties. In longer-lived and more prolific writers we can follow the individual imagination developing in accordance with its own laws of growth and movement. In Keats we catch little more than a glimpse of these laws and of how they might have come to order and direct his work. Had he lived, he would probably have suppressed or destroyed a great many early poems and, judging by certain comments in his letters, perhaps even some of those we most admire. As it is, we have to understand a talent that made many false starts; produced hundreds of journeyman lines; took time to shake off the insipidities of various unfortunate adoptive styles (especially the current neo-Elizabethanisms most damagingly influential in Leigh Hunt); and produced only a handful of fully achieved poems. Among these are "The Eve of St. Agnes" and the major odes of 1819; one or two unfinished works that, paradoxically, convey a sense of fine poetic accomplishment, notably the first *Hyperion* and (on a different scale) "The Eve of St. Mark"; and a few passages elsewhere—outstandingly the description of Moneta in *The Fall of Hyperion*—that hint at the approach of a new poetic maturity.

But we must remember that except for poets of the very first rank, and perhaps even here too, there is in the canon a relatively small area in which the shadow falling between conception and execution is dispelled by a high noon of creative intensity. Keats had his own feelings about the not fully achieved work of art as early as March 1817, when, at the age of twenty-one, he wrote a sonnet on first seeing the Elgin Marbles, the celebrated sculptures from the Parthenon brought to England by Thomas Bruce, seventh earl of Elgin, and bought for the nation in 1816, when they were housed in the British Museum. "I never cease to wonder at all that incarnate delight," he once said, when he was discovered gazing at them with his customary intentness.

> My spirit is too weak—mortality
> Weighs heavily upon me like unwilling sleep,
> (1–2)

he begins, expressing in the sonnet his baffled consciousness of his own artistic inadequacy, his long-

---

[1] Quotations from the poems are from M. Allott, ed., *The Poems of John Keats* (London, 1970).

ing to overcome it and the "dim-conceivèd glories of the brain," which "Bring round the heart an indescribable feud." "These wonders," broken but still withstanding the erosions of time, irradiate the imagination with gleams of something greater than either he or they, in their present form, can convey. They mysteriously mingle

> ... Grecian grandeur with the rude
> Wasting of old Time, with a billowy main,
> A sun, a shadow of a magnitude.
> (12–14)

The architect Charles Robert Cockerell, contemplating Michelangelo's unfinished tondo of the Holy Family in 1823, found it "striking in its unfinished state ... the subject seems growing from the marble and emerging into life ... you trace and watch its birth from the sculptor's mind. ..." A similar sense of emergent power distinguishes the "shadow of a magnitude" in Keats's unfinished *Hyperions* and the individual intelligence struggling to realize itself in the 1819 odes and the vivacious letters. We cannot scrutinize here what is "classical" and what "romantic," but Keats's writings remind us that incompleteness is a characteristic of one kind of romantic art. The aesthetic experience offered suggests "nature naturing," *natura naturans*, rather than "nature natured," *natura naturata*, which affords another kind of experience, one that we might be forgiven for identifying with what is "classical."

## EARLY YEARS AND POEMS

THE prelude to Keats's poetic career runs from his birth in 1795—Thomas Carlyle was born that year, which should remind us that Keats would have been a man in his forties at the time of the Oxford movement, the last flare-up of Chartism, and Matthew Arnold's first volume of poems—to 1815, when he entered Guy's Hospital as a medical student; he had left the Clarke School at Enfield in 1811 to be apprenticed to Thomas Hammond, a surgeon and apothecary of Edmonton.

The events of a writer's life sometimes seem in retrospect to be designed exclusively for the needs of his creative imagination. Certainly Keats's early years suggest a necessary "set." On one side is the schoolboy, small in height—Keats was always rueful about his want of inches—and sensitive to hurt, who yet was robust, affectionate, and mettlesome; there are stories of his squaring up to boys who bullied his brothers and his routing of a butcher's boy who was cruel to a cat. On the other side are the experiences that constantly tested these qualities: fatal family illnesses, deaths, separations, material losses.

Keats's father, the head ostler at a local inn, died in an accident in 1804; his mother, for whom he felt deeply, remarried shortly after being widowed, and six years later died of tuberculosis, which also killed his brother Tom in 1818. His grandmother, who since 1804 had cared for the three brothers and their young sister, Fanny (the recipient of some of Keats's gayest and most tender letters), died in 1814. By this time Keats was away at Hammond's, and George—Tom accompanied him later—was taken on as a clerk by Richard Abbey, one of the two guardians appointed for the young family. Their latest loss brought more financial hardship because Abbey seemingly was slow to hand over money placed in trust for them. At this stage, though, he did keep on George and Tom, take Fanny into his home, and continue in the belief that he had secured a good professional opening for his eldest ward.

Keats's true calling announced itself in 1814, at the end of his eighteenth year, when, fired by *The Faerie Queene* and "enamoured of its stanza," he composed his first known poem, "Imitation of Spenser"; the calling was confirmed on 3 March 1817, when C. & J. Ollier published his *Poems* and set the seal on his abandonment of medicine for poetry. In intervals of walking the wards at Guy's Hospital, attending lectures, and passing, in July 1816, his qualifying examinations at Apothecary's Hall, he wrote most of the thirty-three poems in the collection. They reflect little of his student life except the loneliness and oppression he felt on leaving the Edmonton countryside to live in lodgings in the crowded capital.

> O Solitude, if I must with thee dwell,
> Let it not be among the jumbled heap
> Of murky buildings, ...
> (1–3)

he writes in "To Solitude" (1815), picturing the wooded places

> ... where the deer's swift leap
> Startles the wild bee from the foxglove bell.
> (7–8)

These two lines, with their Wordsworthian ring, are the best in this youthful piece, but it is momentous as his first published work. Its appearance in Leigh Hunt's *Examiner* for 5 May 1816 signaled his entry into the literary world.

Hunt, whom Keats admired not only for his verses but also for his liberal idealism and his admirable periodical (it served Keats as a kind of Open University), had been a hero since school days. The 1817 volume is suffused with his influence, and opens with a dedicatory sonnet rejoicing that though "Glory and loveliness have passed away," the author can feel

> ...a free,
> A leafy luxury, seeing I could please
> With these poor offerings a man like thee.
> (12–14)

The first of the three sections of the *Poems* consists of eleven pieces, usually saluting in Hunt's sugary style the "Spenserian" delights of chivalric love and a natural world filled with "leafy luxury," white-handed nymphs, and "bowery" glades designed for poetic reverie. Two pieces, "Specimen of an Induction to a Poem" and "Calidore," inspired by Hunt's tripping style in *The Story of Rimini* (1816), are Keats's abortive first attempts at narrative poetry.

Of the three verse epistles in pentameter couplets in the second section, "To My Brother George" and "To Charles Cowden Clarke," composed in August and September 1816, show an advance on the earlier and more flowery "To George Felton Mathew," addressed to a poetaster associate of still more youthful days. (Clarke was the estimable schoolmaster and friend who fostered Keats's early enthusiasm for poetry and introduced his poems to the Hunt circle.) They emulate Hunt's informal verse letters recently published in the *Examiner* but, as elsewhere in the volume, are distinguished by the intermittent accents of an individual voice struggling for expression.

> With shattered boat, oar snapped, and canvas rent,
> I slowly sail, scarce knowing my intent,
> (17–18)

says Keats despondently in the epistle to Clarke, but his manner gathers buoyancy as he recalls the poetry that his friend taught him:

> The grand, the sweet, the terse, the free, the fine;
> What swelled with pathos, and what right divine;
> Spenserian vowels that elope with ease,
> And float along like birds o'er summer seas....
> (54–57)

In the third section Keats grouped seventeen Petrarchan sonnets, mostly celebrating recent literary friendships and artistic enthusiasms. Among them are "On Seeing the Elgin Marbles," "Great Spirits Now on Earth Are Sojourning . . . ," which praises Hunt, William Wordsworth, and the painter Benjamin Haydon, and "On First Looking into Chapman's Homer," unquestionably the finest performance of this early period. He closed the volume with his reflective, confessional "Sleep and Poetry," running to some 400 lines in pentameter couplets and linked with "I Stood Tip-toe," written in the same meter and printed in the first section. Unequal in quality and awkward in meeting the simultaneous demands of sense, syntax, and rhyme, these nevertheless foreshadow later achievements. "I Stood Tip-toe" is a first gesture toward *Endymion*. Foremost among nature's "luxuries" that quicken poetic inspiration is the moon:

> O Maker of sweet poets, dear delight
> Of this fair world....
> (116–117)

It was "a poet, sure a lover too" who, from his post on Mount Latmus,

> Wept that such beauty should be desolate.
> So in fine wrath some golden sounds he won
> And gave meek Cynthia her Endymion.
> (202–204)

Touched by Wordsworth's account of Diana, Apollo, and other rural deities in book IV of *The Excursion*, which was a profoundly influential work for the second generation of romantic poets, Keats too finds that myths originate in imaginative response to the beauties of nature, and "I Stood Tiptoe" singles out the haunting legends of Eros and Psyche (141–150), Pan and Syrinx (157–162), and Narcissus and Echo (163–180). The theme recurs in "Sleep and Poetry," which brings together for the first time central ideas concerning the interdependence of sleep, reverie, and poetic creativity; the vitalizing of the natural world through classical myth; and individual progress from what Keats later termed, in a letter of 3 May 1818 to John Hamilton Reynolds, the "Chamber of Maiden-Thought" to the darker world of "Misery and Heartbreak, Pain, Sickness and oppression." "Byron says, 'Knowledge is Sorrow,'" reflects Keats in the same letter, "and I go on to say that 'Sorrow is Wisdom.'"

The influence of Wordsworth's "Tintern Abbey," working on his own views about personal development, mitigates to some degree the debilitating prettinesses of Keats's poetic language.

> Oh, for ten years, that I may overwhelm
> Myself in poesy . . .
> (96–97)

he writes in "Sleep and Poetry," looking for the time when simple delight in "the realm . . . of Flora and old Pan" will yield to

> . . . a nobler life
> Where I may find the agonies, the strife
> Of human hearts—
> (123–125)

Keats conjures up an image of the creative imagination, partly inspired by the portrayal in certain of Nicolas Poussin's paintings of a chariot driven across the sky by Apollo, who was always an immensely potent figure for him. A charioteer descends to earth and communes with nature, but then focuses on the "shapes of delight, of mystery, and fear" embodied in the procession of men and women now passing before him. The conception is sufficiently striking, but ultimately eludes his poetic reach. At this stage of his career, the distance between Keats's available resources and his high sense of poetic vocation began to narrow when he freed his language from its fustian clutter by concentrating on "the object as in itself it is": in "To Charles Cowden Clarke" the moon seen among clouds,

> As though she were reclining in a bed
> Of bean blossoms, in heaven freshly shed,
> (95–96)

the uneven sound of Clarke's parting footsteps at night, sometimes resonant on the "gravelly" path, sometimes muffled as he stepped on the grass verge; or the attaching particularity found in his sonnet "To My Brothers,"

> Small, busy flames play through the fresh-laid coals,
> And their faint cracklings o'er our silence creep,
> (1–2)

and felt again in his description of setting out at night after the warm gathering at Hunt's Hampstead cottage:

> Keen, fitful gusts are whispering here and there,
> Among the bushes, half leafless and dry;
> The stars look very cold about the sky,
> And I have many miles on foot to fare.
> ("Keen, Fitful Gusts," 1–4)

The clarity and immediacy usually peter out too soon; but the promise of poetic vigor is sustained in the Chapman sonnet, where the creative imagination as a "golden" realm filled with "wonders" generates the poem's unifying imagery of exploration and discovery and, for once (it was long before this happened again), the poem's structure and style are consistent with the movement of thought and feeling. Keats wrote it rapidly one October night in 1816, after he and Clarke had spent many hours poring excitedly for the first time over George Chapman's translation of Homer. (Homer had been familiar to them hitherto only in Alexander Pope's version, which never afforded Keats the keen delight he found, for instance, in his favorite line from Chapman on Odysseus shipwrecked: "The sea had soaked his heart through. . . .") In another sonnet of the period, "How Many Bards," Keats records the "thronging" in his mind of recollections from his favorite poets, which "make pleasing music" like the mingling of evening sounds—birdsong, "the whispering of the leaves," "the voice of waters"—as they lose their individual identity in the distance.

This sonnet vividly describes the working of Keats's densely associative literary memory, and the Chapman sonnet is a rare early illustration of his successful "alchemizing" of these recollections into his own idiom. It draws on wide literary memories, many of them probably half-conscious, some gathered from contemporary authors (Wordsworth included) and most of them echoed from his schoolroom reading: the most influential were accounts, in William Robertson's *History of . . . America*, of Balboa, Cortez, and the discovery of gold in the New World, and, in a schoolbook on astronomy, of the first sighting by William Herschel of the planet Uranus in 1781. The individual instances in the sestet of man's encounters with dazzling new experience and knowledge reinforce the fine opening breadth of the octave. Leigh Hunt celebrated the "prematurely masculine" vein in this "noble sonnet," which closed "with so energetic a calmness and which completely announced the new poet taking possession."

### NARRATIVE POEMS

WITH his first volume of poems in print, Keats devoted the rest of 1817 to *Endymion*, the "Poetic Romance" that was to be "a test, a trial of my Powers of Imagination and chiefly of my invention by which I must make 4,000 lines out of one bare circumstance," the "circumstance" being the legend that the moon goddess—known variously in classical myth as Diana, Phoebe, and Cynthia—fell in love with the shepherd Endymion as he lay asleep on the mountain heights of Caria.

For his first major literary enterprise Keats obeyed the narrative impulse that prompted his fragmentary Huntian-Spenserian tales in 1816 and led him, in 1819 to compose "The Eve of St. Agnes," "La Belle Dame Sans Merci," and the more ambitious and uneven "Lamia." But, as A. C. Bradley saw in his *Oxford Lectures on Poetry* (1909), the "long poem" in the romantic period, adding its weight to a progressive breakdown of genres, contains lyrical, confessional, and reflective elements as well as a narrative interest. Keats usually relates a love story that expresses personal ideas and feelings rather more urgently than it arouses interest in "what happens next" to the lovelorn characters. *Endymion* uninhibitedly dramatizes his current aspirations for the supreme experience of an ideal passion. Later (as with William Butler Yeats, who met Maud Gonne after celebrating the legendary Niamh in *The Wanderings of Oisin*) his relationship with what he called in "Lamia" a "real woman" gave his work a new emotional charge.

"The Eve of St. Agnes" was written in January–February 1819, a few weeks after Keats's first "understanding" with Fanny Brawne on Christmas Day, and celebrates the warmth of a requited passion but, characteristically, cannot forget its attendant hazards or its vulnerability to time. His young brother had just died, and love and death are inextricably bound together in his imagination. In "La Belle Dame Sans Merci" and "Lamia," written, respectively, on 21 April and between about 28 June and 5 September in the same year, where the destructiveness of passion is expressed as keenly as its delight, the emotion is still more ambivalent and the presence of death yet more haunting. The earlier "Isabella, or the Pot of Basil," on the other hand, written during March–April 1818, before the most overwhelming personal experiences of that year, is in spite of its authorial interpolations the least "personal" of these love stories. It led Keats a step or two along a road not taken elsewhere in his poetic life.

All these poems are consciously exploratory in their diverse techniques and source materials. *Endymion* continues in the pentameter couplets used for its precursor, "I Stood Tip-toe"; but Keats also handles ottava rima for his Italian "Isabella," Spenserians for "The Eve of St. Agnes," ballad-style quatrains for "La Belle Dame Sans Merci," octosyllabic couplets freely interspersed with seven-syllable lines for the fragmentary "The Eve of St. Mark," and Drydenesque couplets for "Lamia." The first and last draw on classical, the rest on medieval, sources. The latter suited Keats's liking for rich pictorial effects and, as it turned out, provided themes that allowed him to balance the inner and the outer, so that the work could be quickened by personal feeling without falling into disabling subjectivity.

*Endymion*, with more flats than elevations in its four long books, which here we can only glance at in passing, is for many readers a monument of misdirected effort. But its general style is an improvement on *Poems* (1817), reflecting (as in the fine April 1817 sonnet "On the Sea") the first effects of Keats's simultaneous disenchantment with Hunt and renewed passion for Shakespeare, whom he now saw as his "Presider." Some passages, especially the "Hymn to Pan" in book I, which is his first major ode (the "Ode to Sorrow" in book IV is less distinguished), look forward to the work of 1819. New ground is broken in his use of a narrative medium to express current ideas about human experience, while his poetic creativity is stimulated afresh by his "thronging" literary recollections, now chiefly from George Sandys' translation of *Ovid* and classical reference books "devoured" (as Clarke put it) at school; allusions to Endymion and the moon in the Elizabethans, particularly Shakespeare, Edmund Spenser, and Michael Drayton; and details of magical journeys from *The Arabian Nights* and colorful modern verse narratives including Walter

Savage Landor's *Gebir* (1798) and Robert Southey's two lengthy poems, *Thalaba the Destroyer* (1801) and *The Curse of Kehama* (1810).

Endymion's journeys—he seeks the shining amorous girl of his dream vision on the earth (book I), beneath it (book II), under the sea (book III), and in the air (book IV)—rework the stages of individual development outlined in "Sleep and Poetry." From his carefree existence among his native woods and hills, he passes into melancholy obsession with the difference between the ideal and the actual, and is finally admitted to unshadowed bliss only after learning selfless identification with the pain of others. Since love appears in this poem as the supreme good, its frustration is the type of all pain. Endymion's succoring of Glaucus and the drowned lovers in book III, and his sacrifice of his "dream" for the lovelorn Indian maid in book IV, ensure the transformation of this dusky girl into his fair divinity (in context this has a startling and somewhat perfunctory effect that suggests the author's growing fatigue), who summons him to share with her "an immortality of passion."

The poem follows too many side winds of inspiration to qualify as a sustained allegory, as it is sometimes mistakenly described; but the ordering of the story implies—perhaps as an answer to Shelley's gloomy "Alastor" (1816)—that the ideal is indeed attainable, provided one first enters into and accepts the bliss and bale of everyday life. This suggestion is strengthened by the famous "pleasure-thermometer" passage in *Endymion*, book I (777-842), tracing the gradations of human happiness, which rise from delight in nature and art to the human ties of friendship and, supremely, physical love. The driving force throughout is man's longing for "fellowship with essence," by which he will ultimately

> ... shine
> Full alchemized, and free of space....
> (I. 779-780)

The mystery of an ultimate knowledge, felt but not realizable in words, is conveyed in the "Hymn to Pan," where the god of universal nature is invoked as the "unimaginable lodge/For solitary thinkings" that

> ... dodge
> Conception to the very bourne of heaven....
> (I. 294-295)

The lines anticipate the "silent form" in the "Ode on a Grecian Urn" that teases the poet

> ... out of thought
> As doth eternity....
> (44-45)

Keats's fine preface shows that he judged the immaturity of *Endymion*, which is very noticeable in its boyishly succulent love scenes, more penetratingly than its many unfriendly reviewers in the Tory periodicals, who disliked Keats on principle as a member of the "Cockney" school associated with Leigh Hunt. He found similar weaknesses in "Isabella"—"what I should call were I a reviewer 'A weak-sided poem'"—and in "The Eve of St. Agnes," only "not so glaring," but thought "Lamia" was stronger and had more "fire."

His readers generally take a different view: "Isabella" is flawed but represents an advance from adolescence to adulthood;[2] "The Eve of St. Agnes" imaginatively blends with its sumptuous Elizabethan opulence individual feeling for what has "no joy, nor love, nor light"; while "Lamia," with some highly accomplished versification to its credit, uneasily mingles virtuoso pictorial effects, intense feeling, and would-be sophisticated satire, a mode in which Keats was never at home—as the quasi-Byronic "The Cap and Bells," also of late 1819, unhappily demonstrates at some length.

It can be argued that Keats's need to assimilate the experiences of 1818 and 1819 worked as much against as for his success in narrative poetry. "Isabella," which hints at the possibility of a different kind of achievement, was written before George's departure, Tom's death, and the arrival in his life of Fanny Brawne. It was undertaken in obedience to a "public" impulse—the suggestion in William Hazlitt's February 1818 lecture, "On Dryden and Pope," that modern translations of Giovanni Boccaccio's tales, "as that of Isabella," might win a popular success. It is less poised than its successor, "The Eve of St. Agnes," and matches *Endymion* in its lush love scenes and awkward attempts at naturalistic dialogue. "Those lips, O slippery blisses," says Keats in *Endymion*; and Lorenzo's lips "poesy" with Isabella's "in dewy rhyme." "Goodbye! I'll soon be back" is one of several bathetic touches in the lovers' conversation; and the rodomontade in the stanzas

---

[2] See F. W. Bateson, *English Poetry* (London, 1950), p. 222 n.

castigating Isabella's brothers, who kill Lorenzo because he is too poor, is out of keeping with the fine plangency in the rest of the tale.

Yet Keats's modern fellow poet Edward Thomas praised the ottava rima stanzas, with their "adagio" effect, for making "Isabella," appropriately, "a very still poem" and for accommodating, better than his early couplets, Keats's "choiceness of detail." Thomas could have added that this detail is more purposefully employed to focus both the events in the narrative and the feelings they generate. The dead Lorenzo, appearing to Isabella in a dream, mourns his lost love and the small, touching sounds of life in the world she inhabits. The chestnut leaves and "prickly nuts" fall onto his grave, a "sheep-fold bleat" reaches him from beyond the river, he hears "the glossy bees at noon . . . fieldward pass"; but

> . . . those sounds grow strange to me,
> And thou art distant in humanity.
> (st. 39, 311–312)

The "immortality of passion" sought in *Endymion* yields to another order of feeling:

> Thy beauty grows upon me, and I feel
> A greater love through all my essence steal.
> (st. 40, 319–320)

A year later, in "The Eve of St. Agnes," Keats's growing concentration on "the object as in itself it is" seems for most of the story to be at the service of a less universalizing vision. But the hostile setting, which includes Madeline's family, who play Capulet to Porphyro's Montague, the bleak winter and rising storm, and the chill of age and death stiffening the figures of the Beadsman and old Angela, provide an oblique commentary on the stolen night in Madeline's room, where Keats introduces the richest "luxuries" yet, exquisitely indulging the senses with music, delicacies from "silken Samarkand to cedared Lebanon," and a love effortlessly consummated in a dream in which the actual and the ideal "melt" deliciously into one another. This interplay of warmth and cold, color and paleness, love and death, constitutes the "criticism of life" in the poem—this time, it seems (since Madeline escapes with Porphyro to his home "over the southern moors"), with a measured optimism about reaching a longed-for good here and now. But the oppositions suggest a more restless preoccupation with the difference between ideal and actual experience than one might have expected after the touching quietude briefly achieved in "Isabella."

Technically, Keats is no less at home with Spenserian stanzas than with ottava rima, commanding in them the peculiarly rich pictorial details that enliven his improvisation on the "popular superstition" that a girl who goes fasting to bed on St. Agnes' Eve will see her future husband in a dream. The medieval coloring, which is more lavish than in "The Eve of St. Mark," the unfinished poem that William Morris saw as a main inspiration behind the Pre-Raphaelite movement, paradoxically owes much to contemporary rather than earlier writers, especially Sir Walter Scott's *The Lay of the Last Minstrel* (1805), Ann Radcliffe's "Gothick" tales, and Samuel Taylor Coleridge's "Christabel" (1816). It owes something, too, to Keats's recent visits to Chichester Cathedral and the newly established chapel at Stansted. Of course the family feud and the role of Madeline's aged attendant Angela come straight from *Romeo and Juliet*, one of the many plays densely marked in his copy of Shakespeare (now at the Keats House in Hampstead).

It is impossible to represent adequately here the textural richness nourished by these currents of literary and personal experience, but the following is an instance of the contrasts between warmth and encompassing cold that make the poem something more than a pretty piece of medievalism inspired by wishful erotic fantasy. The Beadsman, "meagre, barefoot, wan," opens the poem, returning after prayer along "the chapel aisle":

> The sculptured dead, on each side, seemed to freeze,
> Imprisoned in black, purgatorial rails . . .
> (st. 2, 14–15)

And his death ends it:

> The Beadsman, after thousand aves told,
> For aye unsought for slept among his ashes cold.
> (st. 42, 377–378)

In the interval are the events in Madeline's room, which open with the hidden Porphyro secretly watching her say her prayers and prepare for bed, a description much worked over in the manuscript (the self-criticism revealed by Keats's habits of revision is a subject on its own). The final version, with its suggestions of warmth, youth, and physical immediacy, marvelously counterpoints the aged

Beadsman's solitary devotions and his approaching death:

> Full on this casement shone the wintry moon,
> And threw warm gules on Madeline's fair breast
> As down she knelt for heaven's grace and boon;
> Rose-bloom fell on her hands, together pressed,
> And on her silver cross soft amethyst,
> And on her hair a glory, like a saint.
> She seemed a splendid angel, newly dressed,
> Save wings, for Heaven. Porphyro grew faint;
> She knelt, so pure a thing, so free from mortal taint.
>
> Anon his heart revives; her vespers done,
> Of all its wreathèd pearls her hair she frees;
> Unclasps her warmèd jewels one by one;
> Loosens her fragrant bodice; by degrees
> Her rich attire creeps rustling to her knees.
> Half-hidden, like a mermaid in sea-weed,
> Pensive awhile she dreams awake, and sees,
> In fancy, fair St Agnes in her bed,
> But dares not look behind, or all the charm is fled.
> (st. 25–26, 217–234)

As I have said elsewhere, in "La Belle Dame Sans Merci," written on 21 April 1819, and "Lamia," written in September of the same year, when Keats had left London to "wean" himself from his passion for Fanny Brawne, so that he could try to make his way with his writing:

The moderate "wishful" optimism of "The Eve of St. Agnes" is rejected for something much more uncompromising. The "knight-at-arms" awakens "on the cold hill side," and Lycius is destroyed. The lady encountered "in the meads," and the "maiden bright" whom Lycius finds "a young bird's flutter from a wood," both turn out to be fatal enchantresses who spell disaster for their victims and are themselves somehow doomed.[3]

Formally, though, there is no similarity between the two narratives. The earlier, perhaps Keats's most magical and self-sufficient poem, is very short; and its austere ballad stanza, forbidding the indulgence of luxuriant detail, relies on compression and spare figurative imagery for emotional effect. The density of imaginative experience that helped to bring this deceptively simple little poem into being makes it barely easier to comment upon in a short space than *Endymion*. But it can be said at once that, in contrast

[3] "'Isabella,' 'The Eve of St. Agnes' and 'Lamia,'" in K. Muir, ed., *John Keats: A Reassessment* (London, 1958; repr., 1969), p. 56.

with Keats's earlier narratives, where love is a kind of dream that quickens and delights every sense and is constantly threatened by the hard realities of the ordinary world, the enchantment is now itself a threat, and from the beginning carries the seeds of its own destruction. The poem opens, like "The Eve of St. Agnes," with winter images that affect us the more because the absences recall what once existed in a happier season:

> The sedge has withered from the lake,
> And no birds sing!
> (st. 1, 3–4)

The "lady" and her enchantment are identified with "winter" even more than with "summer," for her thrallèd knights have caught from her an everlasting cold:

> I saw their starved lips in the gloam
> With horrid warning gapèd wide,
> And I awoke, and found me here
> On the cold hill side.
> (st. 11, 41–44)

The echoes in the poem arrive most resonantly, perhaps, from Spenser and Chatterton; but the resemblance to the traditional ballad of True Thomas the Rhymer, victim of another enchantress, makes it almost certain that Keats's preoccupation with the destructiveness of love and the inevitability of death is closely associated with fears for his own poetic destiny. His treatment of the three central characters in the much longer "Lamia" and his general uncertainty of direction in that poem suggest his continued concern with an increasingly unsettling dilemma.

Keats based his new story on an anecdote in Robert Burton's *Anatomy of Melancholy*. Lycius, a student of philosophy and "twenty-five years of age," is beguiled by a beautiful woman who leads him to her house in Corinth with promises of music, song, feasting, and eternal love—the pattern of the Keatsian enchanted dream. They live blissfully until Lycius insists on a public wedding; thereupon the philosopher Apollonius appears among the guests, recognizes the lady as an enchantress, "a serpent, a lamia," and all about her "like Tantalus's gold . . . no substance but mere illusions."

In the source she vanishes "in an instant," together with her house and everything in it. In the poem the destiny of both lovers is tragic. Lamia has the power "to unperplex bliss from its neighbour pain" (which the "dreamer" certainly cannot do, according to the argument in *The Fall of Hyperion*, where he "vexes mankind"), and is herself the victim as well as the caster of spells. And when she is destroyed, Lycius is destroyed too.

> And Lycius' arms were empty of delight,
> As were his limbs of life, from that same night.
> . . .
> . . . no pulse, or breath they found,
> And, in its marriage robe, the heavy body wound.
> (II. 307-308; 310-311)

Here, then, is the problem posed in the 1819 odes. Where does the "truth" lie? In ideal experience or everyday reality? At the far end of the spectrum from the "dream" is "cold Philosophy," though this is not to be confused with the "wisdom" that Keats elsewhere sees nourished by imaginative response to life and art. Matthew Arnold felt that the romantic poets "did not know enough." This was Keats's worry, too. But to "know enough" might mean exercising processes of ratiocination and abstract thought inimical to the poetic imagination. Keats had seen in 1817 and early in 1818 that "a gradual ripening of the intellectual powers" was essential "for the purposes of great productions," and had felt that the way lay through "application, study and thought"; at the same time he had always found it difficult to see "how any thing can be known for truth by consequitive reasoning." Hence his vivid simile "The Imagination may be compared to Adam's dream—he awoke and found it truth" and his call "O for a Life of Sensations rather than of Thoughts."

Torn between Apollonius' "consequitive reasoning" and the quickening "sensations" of Lamia's enchanted dream, he produced a poem interesting to dissect thematically but compelling imaginative assent only in relatively few phrases and passages. To set against his awkward shifts of tone and his stylistic gaucheries, especially his attempted worldly manner in describing "a real woman" as "a treat" and love as always short-lived,

> Love in a hut, with water and a crust,
> Is—Love, forgive us!—cinders, ashes, dust,
> (II. 1-2)

are Hermes seen as "the star of Lethe"; Lamia described first in her brilliantly marked "gordian shape . . . rainbow sided, touched with miseries" and later in her quasi-Miltonic transmogrification, "convulsed with scarlet pain" as she assumes her human form; the ritualistic and inventive construction of her magic palace; and, expanded from a few hints in Burton, the portrait of Corinth:

> And all her populous streets and temples lewd,
> Muttered, like tempest in the distance brewed,
> . . .
> Men, women, rich and poor, in the cool hours
> Shuffled their sandals o'er the pavement white,
> Companioned or alone; while many a light
> Flared, here and there, from wealthy festivals . . .
> (I. 352-353; 355-358)

The latter makes a first-rate companion piece for the cool and charming account of Bertha's quiet cathedral town in the tantalizingly fragmentary "The Eve of St. Mark":

> The city streets were clean and fair
> From wholesome drench of April rains,
> And, on the western window panes,
> The chilly sunset faintly told
> Of unmatured green valleys cold,
> Of the green thorny bloomless hedge,
> Of rivers new with spring-tide sedge,
> Of primroses by sheltered rills,
> And daisies on the aguish hills.
> Twice holy was the Sabbath-bell;
> The silent streets were crowded well
> With staid and pious companies,
> Warm from their fireside orat'ries,
> And moving with demurest air
> To even-song and vesper prayer.
> Each archèd porch, and entry low
> Was filled with patient folk and slow,
> With whispers hush and shuffling feet,
> While played the organ loud and sweet.
> (4-22)

### THE 1819 ODES

CERTAIN anxieties underlying "Lamia" became explicit in lines that Keats wrote for Fanny Brawne on their reunion in October 1819. He mourns his lost liberty and the tyranny of a love that impedes his "winged" Muse, in earlier days

> . . . ever ready . . . to take her course
> Whither I bent her force,
> Unintellectual, yet divine to me.

> Divine, I say! What sea-bird o'er the sea
> Is a philosopher the while he goes
> Winging along where the great water throes?
> ("To Fanny," 12–17)

But in the interval since "The Eve of St. Agnes" Keats had written his famous odes, which could not be what they are without their "intellectual" components and the interpenetration in them of feeling and thought. With Wordsworth's "Ode: Intimations of Immortality," John Milton's "On the Morning of Christ's Nativity," and Coleridge's "Dejection," these are probably the best-known odes in English, and they have generated a quantity of critical and scholarly discussion so vast that it is impossible now to compute its scale. Yet Keats singled out the weakest, "Ode on Indolence," as the poem he most enjoyed writing in 1819, and pushed the manuscript of the "Ode to a Nightingale" behind some books (whence it was rescued by Charles Brown). Although he copied out or mentioned most of his recent poems in his journal-letters to his brother George in America, only the "Ode to Psyche" and "To Autumn" received comment.

The circumstance adds to the mysteriousness of Keats's achievement in these poems. They display a sudden advance in his mastery of poetic skills and in his use of them to explore, more concentratedly than in the narratives and with a stronger gnomic effect, the relationship between human suffering, the ideal in art and individual aspiration, and the role of the poet, whose representations of the beautiful and enduring "tease us out of thought" because we cannot be sure whether they constitute a vision of truth or a wishful dream. At the heart of the odes is the necessity to accept suffering and the transience of youth, beauty, and love, and to do so without destroying imaginative order and harmony.

Earlier, in the "Epistle to John Hamilton Reynolds," written during March 1818, Keats had wished that "dreams" of poets and painters could take their coloring "From something of material sublime" rather than from gloomy inner conflict and, longing for wisdom, had grieved that he was too untutored to "philosophize" without despondency:

> ... It is a flaw
> In happiness to see beyond our bourn—
> It forces us in summer skies to mourn;
> It spoils the singing of the nightingale.
> (82–85)

A year later, in "Ode to a Nightingale," the singing is not "spoilt"; rather, its intense delight sharpens the poet's pain in the everyday world,

> Where youth grows pale, and spectre-thin, and dies,
> Where but to think is to be full of sorrow,
> (26–27)

but that still compels a movement of necessary assent. The mental and emotional processes that prepared the way for these poems were reinforced by a bold series of technical experiments. Keats's youthful odes—"Ode to Apollo" is an instance—gesture toward English Pindarics, but his metrical structure in 1819 is entirely new. He evolved his characteristic stanza from long practice with existing sonnet forms. As we have seen, he had a brilliant early success with the Petrarchan kind. He turned after January 1818 to the Shakespearean, which inspired "When I Have Fears" and the "Bright Star!" sonnet, two of his memorable poems on the Shakespearean themes of love, poetic ambition, and the passage of time.

But in April 1819 he set about discovering "a better sonnet stanza than we have," the Petrarchan having too many "pouncing rhymes" and the Shakespearean being "too elegiac—and the couplet at the end ... has seldom a pleasing effect." His experiments—they include the unrhymed sonnet "If by Dull Rhymes Our English Must Be Chained ..." and the understandably often anthologized "To Sleep"—seem not to have satisfied him. Yet they led to his ode stanza's combination of a "Shakespearean" quatrain and a "Petrarchan" sestet and to the form that gave him both discipline and flexibility in a manner removed from the neatly tripping seven-syllable trochaic couplets he had used for his "Fancy" and "Bards of Passion ..." in the previous December. He gives a hint of his future development, though, in his attractive fragment of an "Ode to May" written earlier that year.

Keats acknowledged his renewed concern with craftsmanship when he copied out the "Ode to Psyche" on 30 April 1819 in a journal-letter, claiming that it was "the first and only [poem] with which I have taken even moderate pains—I have for the most part dash'd off my lines in a hurry—this I have done leisurely—I think it reads more richly for it." This is a matter of debate among readers, though it seems true to say that just as "To Autumn" is more complex than the direct statement of reconciliation and acceptance it is often taken to be, so the undertones in Keats's celebration of Psyche make it more interesting than "a pretty piece of Paganism" (Wordsworth's ill-fitting description of the "Hymn to Pan").

Keats, we know from his letter, understood that Psyche meant the soul. Elsewhere in the same letter he images the world as "the vale of soul-making," and its "pains and troubles" as "necessary to school an intelligence and make it a soul." He must have fastened on the resemblance between Psyche's quest for Eros and Endymion's quest for the goddess in his own story, since both are "schooled" by "pains and troubles" before reaching "an immortality of passion." It is Psyche thus translated whom Keats celebrates, picturing her in his first stanza asleep beside Eros in the lush grass and disappointingly—but unsurprisingly, if we accept the association—reverting to the artificial style of *Endymion* ("soft-conchèd ear," "tender eye-dawn of aurorean love"). Yet it is difficult not to detect in his later stanzas—which recall that she came "too late" to "Olympus' faded hierarchy," and so missed "the happy pieties," the "antique vows," and "the fond believing lyre"—mingled tones of regret for the vanished "simple worship of a day" (the phrase is from the "Ode to May") and belief that to the "fond worshippers" Psyche's destiny would mean less than to the hard-pressed poet of a darker age.

All the same, Keats's "pains" serve his themes less than the pictorial effects and the quasi-liturgical incantatory rhythms and repetitions, sometimes echoing Milton's "On the Morning of Christ's Nativity," which he strove to create from his studiedly loose Pindaric form with its irregular verse paragraphs and varying length of line. In the densely worked last stanza, which describes the "fane" to be built for Psyche in some "untrodden region of my mind," the emphasis finally shifts from "the pale-mouth'd prophet dreaming" and returns to an individual idiom, especially in the lines (deeply admired by John Ruskin) about the "dark-clustering pines" that fledge "the wild-ridged mountains"; the conception of "the wreath'd trellis of a working brain," which combines with medical recollections Keats's habitual sense of the "labyrinthine" and "Daedalian" nature of the creative imagination; and the closing reference to the window open at night "To let the warm love in," an allusion to Eros now openly visiting Psyche and perhaps also, as at least one critic has thought, to his feelings about Fanny Brawne. She was living at this time next door to him in Hampstead, and he would have been able to see her lighted window at night.

In his next two odes, both of May 1819, Keats "schools" his intelligence by posing against the "worlds of pains and sorrows" an object suggesting the possibility of permanence: in the first the nightingale's song, unchanged from age to age and identified with the beauty of the natural world; in the second an ancient Greek urn, fresh as when the artist made it, and on its frieze depicted a world of unchanging youth, love, and "happy piety." His interrogation determines a poetic structure based on the flight from everyday reality and the return to it; but the "Ode on a Grecian Urn," because it is more ostensibly a "dialogue of the mind with itself" about the ambiguous relationship between ideal and actual experience—taken up from its predecessor's final line, "Fled is that music. Do I wake or sleep?"—possesses wider tonal range with less textural richness. (Keats printed it after the "Ode to a Nightingale" in his 1820 volume, perhaps as an intended reply.)

The new ten-line stanza serves these diverse effects well, though Keats afterward dropped the short eighth line in the "Ode to a Nightingale," which was possibly meant to accord with the lyrical movement of the bird's song. The melodic pattern of onomatopoeic effects, worked at with "pains" in the Psyche ode largely for its own sake, now enacts successive states of feeling: "drowsy numbness" (a state often prefacing Keats's moods of creativity) induced by excessive pleasure in the bird's song; longing to escape with the singer from "the weariness, the fever and the fret" into the flower-scented woods; delight in his own lullingly rich evocation of them; and back, through thoughts of death, to the solitary self, grieving at the term set to human happiness and puzzled about the validity of the reverie. Death, at first seemingly a "luxury," becomes a repellent finality from which only the bird can escape to comfort with its "self-same song" generations of suffering men and women, "emperor and clown" alike, and also "perhaps," in an unforgettable image of loss and exile,

> ... the sad heart of Ruth, when, sick for home,
> She stood in tears amid the alien corn.
> (st. 7, 66–67)

The celebrated stanza imagining the woods on an early summer night transmutes with the familiar Keatsian alchemy passages about summer sweetness, renewal, and growth remembered from other poets (particularly Coleridge's "To a Nightingale" of 1798 and Shakespeare's "I Know a Bank Whereon the Wild Thyme Grows") into an individual celebration of nature's "luxuries" now entangled with thoughts of death. It is in an "embalmèd" darkness that the poet guesses "each sweet" and summons in his session of silent thought the "white hawthorn and the pastoral eglantine," the "fast-fading violets," and

> . . . mid-May's eldest child,
> The coming musk-rose, full of dewy wine,
> The murmurous haunt of flies on summer eves.
> (st. 5, 48–50)

This ode questions the validity of the poet's "fancy" and not the quality of the song that inspires it, but Keats's urn arouses feelings the ambivalence of which affects the tone of his celebration, as the effort is made alternately to subdue and to define uncertainty. The movement is between contrasts of activity and stillness, warmth and cold, permanence and transience, with the sestet in each of the five stanzas countering or expanding upon the quatrain, which may itself set forward puzzling contrarieties. The opening quatrain defines the "still" perfection of this Attic objet d'art, but the humanizing terms— "unravished bride of quietness," "foster-child," "sylvan historian"—direct attention to a paradoxical union of age and youth, the human and the artificial, while the breathless questions of the sestet—

> What men or gods are these? What maidens loth?
> What mad pursuit? What struggle to escape?
> (st. 1, 8–9)

—clearly no longer suggest stillness. In the sestet of the second stanza, the figures are neither vital nor reposed, but imprisoned:

> Fair youth beneath the trees, thou canst not leave
> Thy song, nor ever can those trees be bare.
> (st. 2, 15–16)

The ostensibly comforting lines

> She cannot fade, though thou hast not thy bliss,
> For ever wilt thou love and she be fair!
> (st. 2, 19–20)

recall the antithetical real world in the nightingale ode,

> Where Beauty cannot keep her lustrous eyes,
> Or new love pine at them beyond to-morrow,
> (st. 3, 29–30)

and lead into the plaintive invocation, "More happy, happy love" (the epithet is equally insistent in the two earlier odes), which conveys the total absence of happiness in the poet himself. Simultaneously the urn becomes remote:

> All breathing human passion far above,
> That leaves a heart high-sorrowful and cloyed.
> (st. 3, 28–29)

The entire stanza risks a damaging self-indulgence, from which Keats rescues himself by the brilliant innovation in his subsequent sestet, which turns from the urn to the "actual" world from which its figures came, a "little town" where empty streets

> . . . for evermore
> Will silent be; and not a soul to tell
> Why thou art desolate can e'er return,
> (st. 4, 38–40)

a conception alien to the creator of the urn but typical of the poet, who—this time obliquely—leads us back through the terms "empty" and "desolate" to his "sole self." From this he modulates into his attempted final summary, where the urn at first becomes no more than an "Attic shape" covered with "marble"—not "warm" or "panting"—figures. Yet his first delight still lingers with his new "reflective" position, and the entire complex that teases "us out of thought/As doth eternity" finds its only possible expressive outlet in the paradox "Cold pastoral."

This may be seen as the true imaginative climax of the poem. The sestet, with its too-much-discussed closing lines,[4] represents Keats's final effort to subdue his doubts about the urn. He had opened *Endymion* with the line "A thing of beauty is a joy for ever," a conception reintroduced with the urn, again humanized, as "a friend to man" that will console future generations "in midst of other woe/Than ours" with the one message it can offer. Its statement—

> "Beauty is truth, truth beauty"—that is all
> Ye know on earth, and all ye need to know
> (st. 5, 49–50)

—may be right or wrong. Keats does not say. It is the offering of the urn, and his decision to close with it brings a moment of repose.

---

[4] For a summary of the principal arguments, see M. Allott, ed., *The Poems of John Keats*, pp. 537–538.

There is a correspondence with these themes and ideas in the "Ode on Melancholy," where the references to spring and early summer in the second of its three stanzas suggest that it too was written in May. The poem is perhaps the most concentrated expression of Keats's belief in the necessary relationship between joy and sorrow.

> Welcome joy and welcome sorrow,
>   Lethe's weed and Hermes' feather;
> Come today and come tomorrow,
>   I do love you both together!

are the opening lines of his "little song" written in October 1818. Earlier he had described his "pleasure-thermometer" in *Endymion*, book I, as "a first step" to his central theme, "the playing of different Natures with Joy and Sorrow," and had linked his "Ode to Sorrow" in book IV with his "favourite Speculation," set out in a letter of 22 November 1817 to his friend Benjamin Bailey: "I am certain of nothing but of the holiness of the Heart's affections and the truth of Imagination—What the Imagination seizes as beauty must be truth . . . our Passions . . . are all in their sublime, creative of essential Beauty."

Keats's youthful ode is attributed to the forlorn Indian maid. The burden of her song is

> Come then, Sorrow!
> Sweetest Sorrow!
> Like an own babe I nurse thee on my breast.
>   I thought to leave thee
>   And deceive thee,
> But now of all the world I love thee best
> (IV. 279–284)

It foreshadows the "Ode on Melancholy" in connecting melancholy with the perception of beauty and its transience. But it has nothing of the later poem's richness or economy. To repeat an earlier summary of mine, Keats's "argument" now runs "Melancholy is not to be found among thoughts of oblivion (stanza 1); it descends suddenly and is linked with beauty and its transience (stanza 2); it is associated with beauty, joy, pleasure and delight and is felt only by those who can experience these intensely (stanza 3)."[5] The three stanzas possess an imaginative consistency and must have "come clear" after Keats had canceled the false start of his original first stanza with its macabre and violent imagery:

> Though you should build a bark of dead men's bones,
>   And rear a phantom gibbet for a mast,
> Stitch creeds together for a sail, with groans
>   To fill it out, blood-stainèd and aghast. . . .
> (1–4)

The climax then is that one would still fail

> To find the Melancholy—whether she
> Dreameth in any isle of Lethe dull. . . .
> (9–10)

The finished poem picks up this allusion in its opening lines,

> No, no, go not to Lethe, neither twist
> Wolf's-bane, tight-rooted, for its poisonous wine;

and thereafter unfolds images and ideas that are integral to Keats's self-communings of May 1819. He speaks of the death moth as a "mournful Psyche": the former has markings that resemble a human skull, and Psyche—the soul, as we know—was frequently represented as a butterfly. He rejects the drugged relief of oblivion—"shade to shade will come too drowsily/And drown the wakeful anguish of the soul. . . ."—because, as he finds in the nightingale ode, awareness, even if it is awareness of pain, is better than insentience; and, what is more, the "wakeful anguish" fosters imaginative creativity just as the "weeping cloud" of an April shower "fosters the droop-headed flowers all." He senses the close kinship of intense pleasure and intense pain: "aching Pleasure nigh,/Turning to poison while the bee-mouth sips. . . ."

And, finally, from this keen sensitivity to suffering and change, Keats seeks to evolve a statement the imaginative order of which provides its own stay against impermanence. More explicit than elsewhere, and on another level from his young eroticism in *Endymion*, is his use, noticeable in the closing stanza, of sexual imagery as a paradigm for the inextricable relationship between joy and sorrow:

> Aye, in the very temple of Delight
> Veiled Melancholy has her sovran shrine.
> (25–26)

As Douglas Bush said,[6] the ensuing lines,

> Though seen of none save him whose strenuous tongue
> Can burst Joy's grape against his palate fine;

---

[5] See M. Allott, ed., p. 358.

[6] *John Keats: His Life and Writings* (London, 1966), p. 147.

His soul shall taste the sadness of her might,
And be among her cloudy trophies hung,

(27-30)

indicate a recollection of *Troilus and Cressida*, marked by Keats in his copy of Shakespeare:

> ... what will it be
> When that the wat'ry palates taste indeed
> Love's thrice-repurèd nectar? Death, I fear me;
> Sounding destruction; or some joy too fine,
> Too subtle-potent, tun'd too sharp in sweetness,
> For the capacity of my ruder powers....
>
> (III. ii. 19-24)

The parallel strengthens the felt presence of sexual elements in the stanza. Moreover, the curve of feeling, familiar from the structure of the other odes and also found in other poems, which takes the poet from languor to intense sensation and out of this to another, sadder, and more anticlimactic state of being, corresponds to the pattern of Keats's moods of poetic creativity.

It is the "languor" alone that Keats celebrates in his "Ode on Indolence." The poem, not surprisingly, lacks the confident order of the other odes, which were written in obedience to a more urgent creative impulse. Keats, it seems, found difficulty even in deciding on the final arrangement of the individual stanzas, which differs in the various manuscripts. Understandably he omitted the ode from his 1820 collection, though he wrote to Sarah Jeffrey on 9 June, "You will judge of my 1819 temper when I tell you that the thing I have most enjoyed this year has been writing an ode to Indolence." Whatever its weaknesses, its first inception represented a stage in the process leading to the "Ode on a Grecian Urn." On 19 March Keats had written in a journal-letter: "This morning I am in a sort of temper indolent and supremely careless.... Neither Poetry, nor Ambition, nor Love have any alertness of countenance as they pass by me; they seem rather like three figures on a greek vase—a Man and two women.... This is the only happiness...."

Keats must have begun the poem some time after rereading this passage before sending the letter off in May (its closing entry is 3 May); there are throughout references to summer warmth, and the adoption of his special ode stanza suggests that it followed the "Ode to a Nightingale" and the "Ode on a Grecian Urn." The theme runs alongside certain ideas belonging to the "half" of Wordsworth that Keats said he greatly admired (the other "half" he connected with Wordsworth's "egotistical sublime"—at the opposite pole to Shakespearean "negative capability"—and with the "palpable design" of his explicit didacticism).

Keats's earlier unrhymed sonnet, "What the Thrush Said" (of February 1818), restates in his own terms the Wordsworthian theme of "wise passiveness," especially as this is expressed in "The Tables Turned" (1798):

> Books! 'tis a dull and endless strife:
> Come, hear the woodland linnet,
>
> (9-10)

and

> ... how blithe the throstle sings!
> He, too, is no mean preacher:
> Come forth into the life of things,
> Let Nature be your Teacher.
>
> (13-16)

Keats's thrush sings:

> Oh, fret not after knowledge—I have none,
>   And yet my song comes native with the warmth.
> Oh, fret not after knowledge—I have none,
>   And yet the evening listens....
>
> (9-12)

His "Ode on Indolence" is less serene. It captures fleetingly the mood of deep passivity in the summer heat,

> ... Ripe was the drowsy hour;
> The blissful cloud of summer indolence
>   Benumbed my eyes; my pulse grew less and less;
> Pain had no sting, and pleasure's wreath no flower
>
> (15-18)

and turns away from the imaginatively quickening delight aroused by the display of energetic feeling celebrated in the "Ode on Melancholy":

> ... glut thy sorrow on a morning rose,
> Or on the rainbow of the salt sand-wave,
>   Or on the wealth of globèd peonies;
> Or if thy mistress some rich anger shows,
>   Imprison her soft hand, and let her rave,
> And feed deep, deep upon her peerless eyes.
>
> (st. 2, 15-20)

As the "three figures" in "Indolence" pass again before him (one guesses that some time has elapsed between the writing of one part of the poem and another),

> . . . like figures on a marble urn,
> When shifted round to see the other side
> (st. 1, 5–6)

he remains, it seems, unmoved:

> The morn was clouded, but no shower fell,
>   Though in her lids hung the sweet tears of May;
>   The open casement pressed a new-leaved vine,
>   Let in the budding warmth and throstle's lay;
> . . .
> So, ye three Ghosts, adieu! Ye cannot raise
>   My head cool-bedded in the flowery grass.
> (st. 5–6, 45–48; 51–52)

A belying want of ease nevertheless weakens the rest of the closing stanza, which falls into the irritable manner that often accompanies Keats's attempts at satirical humor:

> For I would not be dieted with praise,
>   A pet-lamb in a sentimental farce!
> (st. 6, 53–54)

Other instances of stylistic clumsiness affect Keats's discourse about his three visitants—

> Oh, why did ye not melt, and leave my sense
> Unhaunted quite of all but—nothingness?
> (st. 2, 19–20)

—and it becomes increasingly plain that a certain bravado mars his "wise passiveness":

> . . . to follow them I burned
> And ached for wings because I knew the three;
> The first was a fair maid, and Love her name;
> The second was Ambition, pale of cheek,
>   And ever watchful with fatiguèd eye;
> The last, whom I love more, the more of blame
>   Is heaped upon her, maiden most unmeek,
> I knew to be my demon Poesy.
> (st. 3, 23–30)

Like the other odes, this one draws on, even if it cannot organize as they do, the feelings generated by Keats's major concerns in 1819. It assembles what are, in effect, a series of direct personal statements, and so sheds some light on important fluctuations of feeling in his "1819 temper." Its pretensions to detachment present a remarkable contrast with his movement in "To Autumn" toward an unprecedentedly calm acceptance of "the object as in itself it is." He wrote this ode at Winchester about 19 September, when he had not yet returned to London and to Fanny Brawne, and was enjoying a brief mood of quietude and self-containment. "I 'kepen in solitarinesse,'" he said peacefully, quoting his own "imitation of the authors in Chaucer's time" from "The Eve of St. Mark." The weather was mild and tranquilizing. He wrote to Reynolds on 21 September:

How beautiful the season is now. How fine the air. A temperate sharpness about it. Really, without joking, chaste weather—Dian skies—I never lik'd stubble-fields so much as now—Aye better than the chilly green of the Spring. Somehow a stubble-plain looks warm—This struck me so much in my sunday's walk that I composed upon it.

There is no flight from and return to actuality, as in the spring odes. "Where are the songs of Spring," he asks. "Aye, where are they?" And answers, "Think not of them, thou has thy music too." He replaces the images of renewal and growth drawn on for the "Ode to a Nightingale" with images of fullness and completion, for it seems now that "ripeness is all." Autumn is in league with the sun,

> To bend with apples the mossed cottage-trees,
>   And fill all fruit with ripeness to the core;
>   To swell the gourd, and plump the hazel shells
>   With a sweet kernel; to set budding more,
> And still more, later flowers for the bees.
> (st. 1, 5–9)

But the poem depends for its unusual poise on exactly that sense of process and the movements of time that accompanied the evocation of summer in "Ode to a Nightingale" and that is found in all Keats's major poetry. The difference lies in the manner in which it is brought under command. Keats had reached a moment of stillness at the close of his debate about the Grecian urn by reproducing, with a strong desire to suspend disbelief, what he took to be its individual message of consolation and reassurance. In this poem he celebrates the period of time that lies between high summer and the onset of winter, as Collins in his "Ode to Evening" celebrates the period that lies between day and night. For both poets, the subject subsumes ideas of process and change, while saluting a point of repose within that process.

In Keats the balanced, but still contrary, aspects of his chosen time are felt from the beginning, for this is a season of "mists" as well as "mellow fruitfulness," and throughout the poem words that suggest fullness also convey heaviness and the hint of decay. Summer has "o'erbrimmed" the "clammy cells" of the bees. Autumn, personified in the second stanza, watches "the last oozings" of the cider press and, in the guise of a reaper, "Spares the next swath and all its twinèd flowers," so that one senses, along with munificence, the ineluctable destructiveness of the scythe (for if Autumn is a reaper, so is Time). The third stanza has the line "in a wailful choir the small gnats mourn," of which the touchingly vivid visual and auditory effect owes much to the thought that the gnats are lamenting the shortness of their life and the lateness of the season. As Arnold Davenport put it, "The music of Autumn which ends the poem is a music of living and dying, of staying and departure, of summer-winter."[7]

The success of the poem lies in its equipollent balancing of the contraries. The passage

> And sometimes like a gleaner thou dost keep
> Steady thy laden head across a brook . . .
> (19-20)

forms part of Keats's address to Autumn at the end of the second stanza; and the subject, with the subtle metrical movement of the lines, could be taken as a figure for his own poetic control. F. R. Leavis admired the lines because "In the step from the rime-word 'keep', across . . . the pause enforced by the line-division to 'Steady', the balancing movement of the gleaner is enacted." Douglas Bush, also testifying to the metrical and structural skills of the poem, has spoken of the ordered deploying through the three stanzas of Keats's sense responses to the ripeness and fulfillment of the season: "In the first stanza the sense of fullness and heaviness is given through mainly tactile images; in the second they are mainly visual . . . in the last the images are chiefly auditory." It should be added that in this, the last and for many readers the finest, of his 1819 odes, Keats worked further on his own metrical innovations, adding an extra line to his ten-line stanza. This gave him still ampler room to "load every rift with ore" at the same time that it imposed an additional discipline in its demand for another rhyming line.

For all this, I do not think we can say that "To Autumn" represents a decisive new turn in Keats's artistic development. Rather, it seems to enact through its subject and style just such a moment of pause and equilibrium in his "1819 temper" as the tranquilizing season he celebrates may introduce into the cycle of the natural year. For a hint of the direction his genius might have taken, we need to look at the successive stages of his work on *Hyperion*.

### THE TWO HYPERIONS

THESE incomplete poems belong to a different and weightier order of achievement than the rest of Keats's poetry. If we take into account their germination, planning, composition, and reconstruction, they can be said to span his entire poetic career, from his "Ode to Apollo" in February 1815 to his final reworkings in December 1819, after which he wrote little more poetry of any significance. His first recorded references in 1817 are associated with Endymion, who is united with the goddess of the moon, sister to Apollo, the god of the sun, of healing, and, above all, of music and poetry. "Thy lute-voiced brother will I sing ere long," Keats tells his hero (*Endymion*, IV.774); and he refers in his 1818 preface to "the beautiful mythology of Greece," which he wished "to try once more, before I bid it farewell." The projected poem had its title by 23 January 1818, when Keats advised Haydon, who wanted to use a passage from *Endymion* to illustrate a frontispiece, "Wait for . . . *Hyperion* . . . the nature of *Hyperion* will lead me to treat it in a more naked and grecian Manner . . . the march of passion and endeavour will be undeviating . . . Apollo in *Hyperion* being a foreseeing god will shape his actions like one."

Keats began composition in the autumn, but the juxtaposing of the two names shows that his subject matter was already established as the defeat of the Titans by the new race of Olympian gods, with the old and the new gods of the sun as the figures central-

---

[7] "A Note on 'To Autumn,'" in K. Muir, ed., *John Keats: A Reassessment*, p. 98.

ly opposed. The law of progress affirmed by Oceanus in the poem,

> ... 'tis the eternal law
> That first in beauty should be first in might
> (II. 228-229)

and the identification of "beauty" with wisdom and knowledge through suffering, by which Apollo is transfigured and immortalized, continue the arguments about individual development explored in "Sleep and Poetry" and in Keats's letter to Reynolds of 3 May 1818. This presents life as a "Mansion of Many Apartments," beginning with "the infant or thoughtless Chamber" and going on to the "Chamber of Maiden-Thought," which at first is filled with "pleasant wonders" but is "gradually darken'd" as we come to understand "the heart and nature of Man" and the world as a place filled with "Misery and Heartbreak, Pain, Sickness and oppression. . . ." "Knowledge enormous makes a God of me," says Apollo in the presence of Mnemosyne, who has deserted the Titans for his sake,

> ... agonies
> Creations and destroyings, all at once,
> Pour into the wide hollows of my brain,
> And deify me, as if some blithe wine
> Or bright elixir peerless I had drunk,
> And so become immortal. ...
> (III. 115-120)

Keats abandoned the first version of the poem at this climax in April 1819, and went on to write his shorter narratives, his experimental sonnets, and the spring odes. His reconstruction, *The Fall of Hyperion*, at which he worked intermittently from July to September, and seemingly again from November to December, stops short at the entry of Apollo's predecessor Hyperion. Of the various reasons offered as an explanation for this second abandonment of the poem, the most important are connected with Keats's attempt to reconstruct it as a vision in which the defeat of the Titans is related by the priestess Moneta, an august reincarnation of Mnemosyne.

The theme of suffering and its effect on the poetic imagination receives a stronger personal emphasis, with the poet assuming Apollo's role as he drinks the magical "elixir" that induces his vision. It is central to the debate in the first canto, which turns on the general question of the poet's value to humanity and the particular question of Keats's poetic achievement. He is admitted to Moneta's shrine as one of those

> ... to whom the miseries of the world
> Are misery, and will not let them rest,
> (I. 148-149)

but her stern lesson is that this is not enough:

> ... "Art thou not of the dreamer tribe?
> The poet and the dreamer are distinct,
> Diverse, sheer opposite, antipodes.
> The one pours out a balm upon the world,
> The other vexes it." ...
> (I. 198-202)

The poet "pours ... balm" on suffering because of his knowledge and wisdom; the dreamer "vexes" it, adding to it by dwelling on "miseries" without suggesting how to face them. On 21 September Keats told Reynolds that he had given up the poem because "there were too many Miltonic inversions in it—Miltonic verse cannot be written but in an artful or rather artist's humour. I wish to give myself up to other sensations. English ought to be kept up." The same letter records his composition of "To Autumn," his association of Chatterton with the season, and his admiration of him as "the purest writer in the English language."

But clearly there was also the problem of sustaining his exploratory personal statement at the same time as Moneta's "seer's" vision of the past. Above all, there was the intractable fact that in his revised first canto—which takes its direction from the climactic third canto of the original *Hyperion*—Keats had already given vivid dramatic expression to his central themes.

The evolution and expression of these themes in the two versions reflects Keats's imaginative development from the youthful celebrant of "poesy" in "Sleep and Poetry," who yearned to

> ... die a death
> Of luxury and my young spirit follow
> The morning sunbeams to the great Apollo
> Like a fresh sacrifice ...
> (58-61)

to the poet acquainted with the "sharp anguish" of death who in *The Fall of Hyperion* records, in his vision of Moneta's unveiled face, the mystery and dignity of suffering:

> . . . Then saw I a wan face,
> Not pined by human sorrows, but bright-blanched
> By an immortal sickness which kills not.
> It works a constant change, which happy death
> Can put no end to; deathwards progressing
> To no death was that visage; it had passed
> The lily and the snow; and beyond these
> I must not think now, though I saw that face.
> (I. 256–263)

There are no Miltonic inversions in this blank verse, nor is it ostensibly the work of an "epic" poet, though in 1817 the writing of an epical poem probably would have appeared to be a natural sequel to the long trial run of *Endymion*, which had given Keats practice in sustaining a narrative through which to dramatize ideas important to him. Further, in 1817 he had added to his renewed familiarity with Shakespeare by beginning to read Milton seriously for the first time. "Shakespeare and the paradise Lost every day become greater wonders," he wrote to Benjamin Bailey on 14 August 1819, adding in a letter of 24 August to Reynolds, in a similar context, "The more I know what my diligence may in time probably effect, the more does my heart distend with Pride and Obstinacy."

The following month Keats changed his mind—"I have but lately stood upon my guard against Milton. Life to him would be death to me"—and asked Reynolds to "pick out some lines from *Hyperion* and put a mark X to the false beauty proceeding from art, and one || to the true voice of feeling." That his instinct was true as usual to his current poetic needs is apparent from his handling of the new material in *The Fall of Hyperion*, but his former ardor accounts for strength as well as weakness. His Miltonic constructions are certainly intrusive—"thunder . . . rumbles reluctant"; "came slope upon the threshold of the west"; "gold clouds metropolitan"; "Regal his shape majestic." Yet Keats's "stationing" of his figures owes much to the grouping that he praised in a marginal note to *Paradise Lost*, VII. 420–424: "Milton . . . pursues his imagination to the utmost . . . in no instance . . . more exemplified than in his *stationing* or *statury*. He is not content with simple description, he must station. . . ." His own finest instance provides the first *Hyperion* with its impressive opening:

> Deep in the shady sadness of a vale
> Far sunken from the healthy breath of morn,
> Far from the fiery noon, and eve's one star,
> Sat grey-haired Saturn, quiet as a stone,
> Still as the silence round about his lair. . .
> (I. 1–5)

Keats's disposition of the other fallen Titans, situated amid cavernous rocks and "the solid roar/Of thunderous waterfalls and torrents hoarse" in attitudes of anger, grief, and despair, aims, though not with consistent success, for a similar effect, and their ensuing debate obviously derives from the "Stygian council" in Milton's Pandemonium. But inspiration is not imitation, and Keats's poem takes its own course. As always in his work, it is nourished by a wide range of literary and personal experiences. Some of the "Miltonic" grandeur is in fact owed to his enthusiastic response to the scenery in the Lakes and Scotland during his summer walking tour. He wrote then a number of slight poems and many lengthy, vivid letters, among them a description for Tom of Fingal's Cave, which he called "this cathedral of the sea"—"suppose the Giants who rebelled against Jove had taken a whole Mass of black Columns and bound them together like bundles of matches—and then with immense Axes had made a cavern in the body of these columns"—and which he remembered later in his "stationing" of Saturn and Thea in *Hyperion*:

> . . . these two were postured motionless,
> Like natural sculpture in cathedral cavern.
> (I. 85–86)

Keats's reading on the tour was confined to the 1814 edition of Dante's *Divine Comedy*, which added its own contribution to the solemnity of the first *Hyperion* and was instrumental in shaping the second, for it stimulated Keats's eager study during the following summer of the original Italian—especially, to judge by the cadences and echoes in *The Fall of Hyperion*, the *Purgatorio*, which certainly affected his own purgatorial "vision" and gave his portrayal of Moneta some of the flavor of the mingled awe and benignity surrounding Dante's Beatrice.

The "shaping force" at work upon these diverse elements is still unequal to a sustained flight, and is at its most disappointing in the handling of the pivotal theme. The Titans are beings of power and identity; their successors, the Olympians, whose qualities are epitomized in Apollo, have no identity and represent Keats's idea of the poetical character as he expressed it in a letter to Richard Woodhouse of 27 October 1818:

> ... the poetical Character ... that sort distinguished from the wordsworthian or egotistical sublime ... is not itself—it has no self. ... A Poet is the most unpoetical of any thing in existence; because he has no Identity—he is continually ... filling some other Body.

He had written to Benjamin Bailey the previous November: "Men of Genius are great as certain ethereal Chemicals operating on the Mass of neutral intellect ... they have not any individuality, any determined Character. I would call the top and head of those who have a proper self Men of Power."

Keats knew from his classical reading that although Hyperion preceded Apollo as god of the sun, he was endowed with no power over music and poetry. In the first *Hyperion*, although he makes his Titan less consistently magnificent than the gorgeous palace he inhabits (it takes some hints from Wordsworth's cloud palace in *The Excursion*, II. 839–840, and the halls of Eblis in William Beckford's *Vathek*), he succeeds nevertheless in making him unmistakably a "Man of Power."

> He entered, but he entered full of wrath;
> His flaming robes streamed out beyond his heels,
> And gave a roar ...
>     ...
>         ... On he flared,
> From stately nave to nave, from vault to vault ...
>         (I. 213–215; 217–218)

His self-centered rage is the expression of his threatened "identity":

>             "... Why
> Is my eternal essence thus distraught
> To see and behold these horrors new?
> Saturn is fallen, am I too to fall?
> Am I to leave this haven of my rest,
> This cradle of my glory ..."
>             (I. 231–236)

This invests the figure with at least sufficiently appropriate poetic force; but on the entry of Apollo in canto III, Keats reverts disastrously to the fruity manner of his *Endymion*. Apollo, deified by "knowledge enormous" of the suffering of the world and supposedly endowed with the imaginative power dependent on such knowledge, remains an effeminate figure who "weeps and wonders somewhat too fondly," as Leigh Hunt said in 1820, though Hunt also thought that "His powers gather nobly on him as he proceeds." The "nobility" belongs, in truth, only to the few lines, quoted earlier, that record the accession of his visionary insight. The poem closes with a semierotic description:

> Soon wild commotions shook him, and made flush
> All the immortal fairness of his limbs,
>         ...
>         ... So young Apollo anguished;
> His very hair, his golden tresses famed,
> Kept undulation round his eager neck.
>         (III. 124–125; 130–132)

Mnemosyne the while holds up her arms "as one who prophesied," and

>         ... At length
> Apollo shrieked—and lo! from all his limbs
> Celestial ...
>         (III. 134–136)

And there it ends, with the poet seemingly (and understandably) stumped and the entire war of the Titans against the Olympians yet to record. A year later Keats had transformed this material into the intensely imaginative personal statement of the first canto of *The Fall of Hyperion*.

If we try to hold the two versions together in our mind as one poem, it is apparent at once that they represent two totally different kinds of poetic impulse. Keats's themes and his creative temper could never have lent themselves fully to expression through an epic conflict in the high Miltonic style, for which he had tried in his first version. He makes, it is true, a valiant, and far from unsuccessful, effort to dramatize his ideas about suffering and creativity in his Titans, especially when he differentiates between the grief of the fallen Saturn and Thea, whom sorrow has made "more beautiful than Beauty's self"; the rage of "huge Enceladus," whose words boom among his fellows

>         ... like sullen waves
> In the half-glutted hollows of reef-rocks,
>         (II. 305–306)

and the different kinds of pain felt by the stoical Oceanus, who understands the law by which he must perish, and the simpler Clymene, who alone has heard the song of Apollo, felt the "living death" of its melody, and knows what it is to be

> ... sick
> Of joy and grief at once....
> (II. 288-289)

But Keats's recasting of the material for *The Fall of Hyperion*, whatever the rights and wrongs of moving from a more "objective" to a more "subjective" kind of writing, is entirely consistent with two strong impulses seen at work in his poetry from the beginning. There is the confessional impulse, which found early expression in "Sleep and Poetry," and there is the impulse toward a more oblique expression of important personal themes that shapes in some degree all the narrative poems and the major odes.

Looked at in this way, *The Fall of Hyperion*, with its mixture of earnestness about the importance of the poet's "public" role, its jealous feeling nevertheless for the poet's individual voice, and its projection of personal themes through a fictional situation, not only is seen to build on these impulses but also offers an early example of the tendency toward the fictionalized spiritual autobiography so common in Victorian prose and poetry.

Carlyle, as we said, was born in the same year as Keats, and his *Sartor Resartus* is often regarded as the first major example of the Victorian habit of disguising as a fiction the history of pressing inner conflict. Other examples, dealing especially with the role of the creative writer in his struggle to penetrate the romantic dream, run from Tennyson's "The Lady of Shalott" to Matthew Arnold's *Empedocles on Etna*. It could be said that all these have an early precursor in *The Fall of Hyperion*, and that Keats's "vision" hints at a potential development of the youthful romantic poet into a writer who might have been a particularly eminent Victorian.

### THE LETTERS

At about the time of his last attempts to rework *Hyperion*, Keats wrote to his publisher John Taylor, on 17 November 1819:

I have come to a determination not to publish any thing I have now ready written; but for all that to publish a Poem before long and that I hope to make a fine one. As the marvellous is the most enticing and the surest guarantee of harmonious numbers I have been endeavouring to persuade myself to untether Fancy and let her manage for herself—I and myself cannot agree about this at all. Wonders are no wonders to me. I am more at home amongst Men and Women. I would rather read Chaucer than Ariosto—The little dramatic skill I may as yet have however badly it might show in a Drama would I think be sufficient for a Poem—I wish to diffuse the colouring of St Agnes Eve throughout a Poem in which Character and Sentiment would be the figures to such drapery—Two or three such Poems, if God should spare me, written in the course of the next six years, would be a famous *gradus ad Parnassum altissimum* ... they would nerve me up to the writing of a few fine Plays—my greatest ambition when I do feel ambitious.[8]

This is one of the last major statements about his poetic intentions in Keats's letters, and it demonstrates the shrewdness of his self-knowledge and the consistency of his debate with himself about his poetry since at least late 1816. Behind his wide range of poetic experimentalism is the unchanging impulse to overcome his native longing for an ideal "romantic" world, in order to reach a Shakespearean understanding and acceptance of the world as it is. In June 1819, a few months before his letter to Taylor, he had distinguished Matteo Boiardo from Shakespeare as "a noble Poet of Romance; not a miserable and mighty Poet of the human Heart." His gifts, at the stage we see them, and particularly in his narratives where he tries to present the passions of "Men and Women," are plainly not in keeping with his ambitions. We find Keats less the "Poet of the human Heart" that he wished to be than the poet of the "wonders" he wanted to grow away from. It is hardly surprising that his one play, the melodramatic *Otho the Great*, written in collaboration with Charles Brown and worked on in the months when he was composing "Lamia" and revising *Hyperion*, is not "fine" at all, nor that the quality of the fragmentary *King Stephen* of the same period, which also was designed as a vehicle for his admired Edmund Kean, rests exclusively on its few but by no means unimpressive passages of quasi-Shakespearean blank verse.

As a writer of prose, on the other hand, Keats is

---

[8]Quotations from the letters are from H. E. Rollins, ed., *The Keats Circle: Letters and Papers and More Letters and Poems of the Keats Circle* (Cambridge, Mass., 1965).

often several jumps ahead of his poetic practice. His letters are perhaps the most vivacious expression of lively and unpretending intelligence in English literary history (there is no eye to posterity in them). They mirror from day to day, and sometimes from hour to hour, the rapid movements of his thinking and feeling, his excited gaiety in observing the world around him, and his remarkably knowledgeable, sensitive, and unselfregarding feeling for other people. Few literary figures—few people anywhere—have won so much affection and respect from their associates. Many of his circle—prominently Charles Brown, John Hamilton Reynolds, and Richard Woodhouse—are known to posterity primarily because of his correspondence with them and their own care in preserving copies of his letters and poems (this is one reason there is such a wealth of Keatsian manuscript material in existence). Characteristically, once his brother George had left for America with his wife Georgiana in June 1818, Keats took pains to write long, affectionate, newsy journal-letters, recording daily happenings and copying out with comments many of his recent poems.

Thus his letters provide a magnificent gloss on his poetry; they also help to explain why he has been so fortunate in his modern biographers, who since 1958 have been able to consult them in Hyder Rollins' superb annotated edition. They form, in effect, an integral part of his creative life, and should be required reading for anyone interested in literature, particularly poetry, the poetic process, and the nature of poetic sensibility. If there is immaturity in their volatile expression and flexibility,[9] there is also unusual self-knowledge.

Keats had no doubts about his ultimate goal, only about how to reach it, and recognized that in exploring possibilities he would swing between opposite poles and "take but three steps from feathers to iron." He used this sharp image on 13 March 1818 to Benjamin Bailey, after copying his sonnet "The Human Seasons," which foreshadows the balanced mood, but not the imaginative poise, of "To Autumn." The relaxed, informal prose of his accompanying remarks, with their darting parentheses and sudden flashes of insight, enacts the ebb and flow of his "speculations." "I shall never be a reasoner because I do not care to be in the right," he declares, and persuades his reader through the suggestiveness rather than the logic of his improvisations on the theme that "Every mental pursuit takes its reality and worth from the ardour of the pursuer—being in itself a nothing." There are

Things real—such as existences of Sun Moon & Stars and passages of Shakespeare—Things semireal such as Love, the Clouds &c which require a greeting of the Spirit to make them wholly exist—and Nothings which are made Great and dignified by an ardent pursuit. . . .

Even "poetry itself," in his "very sceptical" moods, may appear "a mere Jack a lantern to amuse anyone who may be struck with its brilliance."

This letter clearly represents a stage in the continued communings by Keats with himself and his friends that carried him from his ideas about "negative capability" at the end of 1817 to his definition in October 1818 of the "poetical character" and his poignant affirmation of his dramatic ambitions in November 1819. As he walked away from a Christmas pantomime in December 1817, he was caught up in "a disquisition with [Charles] Dilke" and "several things dove-tailed in my mind":

at once it struck me, what quality went to form a Man of Achievement, especially in Literature, & which Shakespeare possessed so enormously—I mean *Negative Capability*, that is when man is capable of being in uncertainties, Mysteries, doubts, without any irritable reaching after fact & reason.

A day or two earlier, while admiring a painting by Benjamin West, Keats had missed in it "the excellence of every Art," which lies "in its intensity, capable of making all disagreeables evaporate, from being in close relationship with Beauty and Truth—examine 'King Lear' and you will find this examplified [sic] throughout." He closes his "negative capability" passage with the reflection that he is saying no more than that "with a great poet the sense of Beauty overcomes every other consideration."

A year later his description of "the poetical character" once more emphasizes his openness of response and refusal to tie himself to unexamined axiomatic systems ("Axioms in philosophy are not axioms until they are proved on our pulses," Keats explains in a May 1818 letter to John Reynolds). He is not concerned, he says to Woodhouse in October 1818, with "the wordsworthian or egotistical sublime . . . a thing *per se*," for which he felt mingled ad-

---

[9]And also, one should add, in their engagingly idiosyncratic spelling and punctuation.

miration and distaste. "We hate poetry that has a palpable design upon us," he said in February 1818 when thinking of Wordsworth's "bullying" didacticism. "Poetry should be great and unobtrusive." Yet he was deeply indebted to this elder statesman among contemporary poets, and in the previous month had praised *The Excursion* as one of the few artistic achievements "to rejoice at in this Age." The "poetical character" with which Keats identifies himself in a letter to Woodhouse of 27 October 1818

... has no self—it is every thing and nothing—It has no character—it enjoys light and shade; it lives in gusto, be it foul or fair, high or low, rich or poor, mean or elevated—It has as much delight in conceiving an Iago as an Imogen. What shocks the virtuous philosop[h]er, delights the camelion Poet. . . . A Poet is the most unpoetical of any thing in existence; because he has no Identity—he is continually . . . filling some other Body.

The ability to re-create his own experience of "filling some other Body" is at best fitful in Keats's poems, but the experience itself is constantly displayed in his letters. He is aware of it in his letter to Bailey of 22 November 1817 when he speaks of being "annihilated" when in a room full of other "identities," of being "pressed" upon by the identity of Tom or his sister Fanny; and "if a Sparrow come before my Window I take part in its existence and pick about the Gravel." He responds instinctively to the individual temper of his correspondents. Bailey, the friend who studied theology and took orders, prompted his discussion in this November letter, quoted earlier, about the relative value of "consequitive reasoning" and "sensations" as a means of penetrating truth, and led him on to his celebrated reflections about a possible afterlife, where perhaps "we shall enjoy ourselves . . . by having what we called happiness on Earth repeated in a finer tone."

Keats's letters to Reynolds, including the verse epistle written in March 1818 to cheer him when ill, are stimulated by his responsiveness to this close friend's own interests in writing poetry, and read like continuations of their conversations together. His analysis of life as a "Mansion of Many Apartments" (3 May 1818) is designed to draw Reynolds into its reassuring arguments about the uncertainties of youthful years:

We see not the ballance of good and evil. We are in a Mist—We are now in that state—We feel the "burden of the Mystery", To this point was Wordsworth come . . . when he wrote 'Tintern Abbey" and . . . his Genius is explorative of those dark Passages. Now if we live, and go on thinking, we too shall explore them. . . .

It was Reynolds, as we saw, whom he asked to distinguish the Miltonisms from "the true voice of feeling" in *Hyperion*.

To John Taylor, his publisher, and Richard Woodhouse, the lawyer who faithfully transcribed numerous letters and poems, and sometimes acted as an intermediary with his publishers, Keats writes, so to speak, more "publicly" and informatively about his artistic progress, setting out for Taylor on 27 February 1818, as a kind of apologia, "axioms" about poetry that he thinks *Endymion* has not met ("Poetry should surprise by a fine excess. . . . Its touches of beauty should never be half way. . . . if Poetry comes not as naturally as the leaves to a tree it had better not come at all. . . ."). He adapts himself quite differently to the Reynolds sisters, whom he quizzes inventively while staying with Bailey at Oxford in September 1817: ". . . here am I among Colleges, Halls, Stalls . . . but you are by the sea . . . argal you bathe—you walk—you say how beautiful—find out resemblances between waves and Camels—rocks and dancing Masters—fireshovels and telescopes—Dolphins and Madonas. . . ."

He writes for his brothers vigorously raffish Regency jokes about his dancing and drinking parties in late 1817 and early 1818, when he was released from his dogged labors on *Endymion* and for a short time could indulge his pleasure in company and his liking for claret; cracks awful puns for them and for Charles Brown, who was waggish in this way and encouraged such jokes (not very happily for his poetry) when Keats was walking with him in Scotland and living with him at Hampstead after Tom's death; and he invents amusing fantasies to entertain his young sister Fanny. For his brothers, again, he particularizes the magnificences of the waterfalls, the changing colors of slate and stone, and the mixed exhilaration and discomfort of climbing the vast heights of Ailsa Craig and Ben Nevis during his walking tour with Brown.

This quickness of sensibility made it impossible for Keats to respond to experience or to compose poetry tranquilly. The word "fever" recurs in his accounts of his active creative moods, which were usually preceded and followed by the "indolence" that he celebrates in his 1819 ode ("Thou art . . . a fever of thyself" is Moneta's scathing reproach in *The Fall of Hyperion*). It appears in another context when finally, in late 1819, he begins to speak, circuitously, about his current feeling for women. A beautiful woman, he tells George and Georgiana Keats, can haunt him "as a tune of Mozart's might do," and if she distracts him from poetry, "that is a fever."

About his feelings for Fanny Brawne he was deeply reticent to everyone except her. His letters to her worried Matthew Arnold, who thought them effeminate (this was the later, settled Arnold, who long ago had made his own troubled accommodations about his feelings for Marguerite). But in the context of everything we know about Keats, these love letters, with the generosity of their total emotional commitment, are exactly what we should expect from him. They are at first passionate, tender, and amusingly inventive. Later, when he was torn apart first by fears for his imaginative freedom and afterward by his appalling despair at having been separated from her through illness and the tragically ill-advised journey to Italy, they become the most ravaging of any personal letters to have appeared in print.

We see everywhere in all these extraordinarily attaching human documents the play of a particular kind of creative sensibility that vitalizes everything it contemplates, and does so by the peculiar immediacy with which it simultaneously senses and reflects upon the objects of its experience. Long before T. S. Eliot's remarks about the "dissociation of sensibility," Arthur Hallam, the subject of Tennyson's *In Memoriam* and himself a young poet (he died at twenty-two), saluted in a brilliant article of 1831 the interplay of "sensation" and "thought" in certain modern poets, notably Keats and Shelley. "The tenderness of Keats," he says, "cannot sustain a lofty flight" and, like Shelley, he is a poet "of sensation." Yet "so vivid was the delight attending the simple exertions of eye and ear, that it became mingled more and more with their trains of active thought, and tended to absorb their whole being in the energy of sense." Had he lived long enough to read more of Keats's letters in Milnes's 1848 edition of the *Life, Letters and Literary Remains*, and also *The Fall of Hyperion* when it appeared a few years later, Hallam would probably have emphasized even more strongly the "reflective" components contributing to that "energy of sense" in Keats. Eliot saw "traces of a struggle towards unification of sensibility" in the second *Hyperion*. We could add that there is evidence of such a struggle from the beginning, and that Keats in his letters provides a conscious and continuous commentary upon it.

### SELECTED BIBLIOGRAPHY

I. BIBLIOGRAPHY. Detailed bibliographical information can also be found in the appropriate volumes of the *New Cambridge Bibliography of English Literature* and the *Oxford History of English Literature*. See also the *Keats-Shelley Journal*, which carries annual bibliographies. *Catalogue of a Loan Exhibition Commemorating the Anniversary of the Death of John Keats (1821–1921) Held at the Public Library, Boston, February 21–March 14, 1921* (Boston, 1921); G. C. Williamson, ed., *The John Keats Memorial Volume* (London, 1921), contains T. J. Wise, "A Bibliography of the Writings of John Keats"; T. J. Wise, comp., *The Ashley Library: A Catalogue of Printed Books, Manuscripts and Letters* (London, 1928), printed for private circulation, contains a description of books and MSS by or relating to Keats; J. R. MacGillivray, *Keats: A Bibliography and Reference Guide, with an Essay on Keats' Reputation* (Toronto, 1949); D. B. Green and E. G. Wilson, eds., *Keats, Shelley, Byron, Hunt and Their Circles: Bibliographies from the Keats–Shelley Journal, July 1, 1950–June 30, 1962* (Lincoln, Nebr., 1964).

II. COLLECTED EDITIONS. *The Poetical Works of Coleridge, Shelley and Keats* (Paris, 1829), the Galignani ed.; *The Poetical Works* (London, 1840), in Smith's Standard Library, the first English collected ed.; *The Poetical Works* (London, 1854), with a memoir by R. M. Milnes (Lord Houghton), the first illustrated ed., with 120 designs by G. Scharf; W. M. Rossetti, ed., *The Poetical Works* (London, 1872), with critical memoir by Rossetti; Lord Houghton, ed., *The Poetical Works* (London, 1876), the Aldine ed.; H. B. Forman, ed., *The Poetical Works and Other Writings*, 4 vols. (London, 1883), vols. III and IV contain Keats's letters; G. Thorn-Drury, ed., *The Poems*, 2 vols. (London, 1896), with intro. by R. Bridges; H. E. Scudder, ed., *The Complete Poetical Works and Letters* (Boston-New York, 1899), the Cambridge ed.; H. B. Forman, ed., *The Complete Works*, 5 vols. (Glasgow, 1900–1901), brings the eds. of 1883 and 1889 up to date with new material and biographical notes; E. de Selincourt, ed., *The Poems* (London, 1905; rev. eds., 1907; 1926), with intro. and notes; H. B. Forman, ed., *The Poetical Works* (London, 1906), also in H. W. Garrod, ed. (London, 1956), with intro. and textual notes; J. M. Murry, ed., *Poems and Verses of John Keats* (London, 1930; rev. ed., 1949), arranged in chronological order; H. W. Garrod, ed., *Poetical Works* (London, 1939; rev. ed., 1958), the Oxford variorum ed.; M. Allott, ed., *The Poems of John Keats* (London, 1970; repr. with revs., London-New York, 1972; rev. paperback ed., 1973), the first complete, chronological, annotated ed.; J. Barnard, ed., *John Keats: The Complete Poems* (London, 1973), useful, inexpensive annotated ed., with poems in chronological order.

III. SELECTED WORKS. R. Monckton Milnes, ed., *Life, Letters and Literary Remains of John Keats*, 2 vols. (London, 1848), prints many poems and letters for the first time, including the tragedy *Otho the Great*; *The Eve of St. Agnes, and Other Poems* (Boston, 1876), in the Vest-Pocket series of standard and popular authors; *Odes and Sonnets* (Philadelphia, 1888), with illustrations by W. H. Low; *Selections from Keats* (London, 1889), with preface by J. R. Tutin, includes all the poems from the 1820 vol. and a selection from that of 1817; *The Odes of Keats* (Oxford, 1897; facs. ed., Tokyo, 1965), with notes and analyses and a memoir by A. C. Downer; H. B. Forman, ed., *Endymion and the Longer Poems* (London, 1897); H. Ellershaw, ed., *Poetry and Prose* (Oxford, 1922), with essays by C. Lamb, L. Hunt, R. Bridges, and others; C. W. Thomas, ed., *Poems. With Selections from His Letters and from Criticism* (London, 1932), includes criticism by E. de Selincourt, R. Bridges, and A. C. Bradley; J. A. Walsh, ed., *Selected Letters and Poems* (London, 1954); E. C. Blunden, ed., *Selected Poems* (London, 1955); R. Gittings, ed., *Selected Poems and Letters of John Keats* (London, 1967).

IV. SEPARATE WORKS. *Poems* (London, 1817), facs. ed. in Noel Douglas Replicas series (London, 1927); *Endymion: A Poetic Romance* (London, 1818), type-facs. ed. with intro. and notes by E. C. Notcutt (London, 1927), also in T. Saito, ed. (London, 1931), with notes; *Lamia, Isabella, The Eve of St. Agnes, and Other Poems* (London, 1820; facs. ed., 1970); "La Belle Dame Sans Merci," in *Indicator* (10 May 1820), signed "Caviare"; R. M. Milnes, ed., *Another Version of Keats's "Hyperion"* (London, 1857 [?]), repr. of Milnes's contribution to *Miscellanies of the Philobiblion Society*, 3 (1856-1857), the basic text of *The Fall of Hyperion: A Dream* until the discovery of the Woodhouse transcript in 1904; *Hyperion. A Facsimile of Keats's Autograph Manuscript with a Transliteration of the Manuscript of The Fall of Hyperion: A Dream* (London, 1905), with intro. and notes by E. de Selincourt; R. Gittings, ed., *The Odes of Keats and Their Earliest Known Manuscripts* (London, 1970), with intro. and notes by Gittings.

Students should also consult the *Examiner*, the *Indicator*, *Annals of the Fine Arts*, *Blackwood's* magazine, and other periodicals of Keats's day.

V. LETTERS. *Letters to Fanny Brawne, 1819-1820* (London, 1878), with intro. and notes by H. B. Forman; J. G. Speed, ed., *Letters* (New York, 1883); S. Colvin, ed., *Letters to His Family and Friends* (London, 1891), excludes letters to Fanny Brawne; H. B. Forman, ed., *Letters* (London, 1895), contains every letter of Keats's known at the time; T. Watts-Dunton, G. Williamson, and H. B. Forman, eds., *The Keats Letters, Papers and Other Relics Forming the Dilke Bequest* (London, 1914); H. B. Forman, ed., *Letters*, 2 vols. (London, 1931; 2nd ed., 1935; 3rd ed., 1947), the ed. of 1935 adds 10 letters; H. E. Rollins, ed., *The Keats Circle: Letters and Papers, 1816-78*, 2 vols. (Cambridge, Mass., 1948); H. E. Rollins, ed., *More Letters and Poems of the Keats Circle* (Cambridge, Mass., 1955), new ed. entitled *The Keats Circle: Letters and Papers and More Letters and Poems of the Keats Circle* (Cambridge, Mass., 1965), contains the 1948 and 1955 eds. in 2 vols.; H. E. Rollins, ed., *The Letters of John Keats, 1814-1821* (London, 1958), the definitive ed.; R. Gittings, ed., *Letters of John Keats* (London, 1970), replaces F. Page's selection in the World's Classics. See also under COLLECTED EDITIONS, SELECTED WORKS, and BIOGRAPHICAL AND CRITICAL STUDIES.

VI. BIOGRAPHICAL AND CRITICAL STUDIES. P. B. Shelley, *Adonais: An Elegy on the Death of John Keats* (London, 1821); L. Hunt, *Lord Byron and Some of His Contemporaries* (London, 1828), contains an account of Keats with criticism of his poetry, also in J. E. Morpurgo, ed. (London, 1949); A. Hallam, "On Some of the Characteristics of Modern Poetry," in *Englishman's* magazine, 1 (August 1831), 616-621, discusses Tennyson, with arresting analysis of Keats as his forerunner, repr. in G. Matthews, ed., *The Critical Heritage* (London, 1971); S. C. Hall, ed., *The Book of Gems*, III (London, 1838), contains comment on Keats by L. Hunt; L. Hunt, *Imagination and Fancy* (London, 1844), also in E. Gosse, ed. (London, 1907); T. Medwin, *The Life of Percy Bysshe Shelley*, 2 vols. (London, 1847), contains comment on Keats, based on information from L. Hunt, Fanny Brawne, and Shelley; R. M. Milnes, ed., *Life, Letters and Literary Remains of John Keats*, 2 vols. (London, 1848), reviewed by A. de Vere in *Edinburgh Review*, 90 (October 1849), 388-433, in a perceptive essay comparing Keats, Shelley, and Tennyson; review repr. in G. Matthews, ed., *The Critical Heritage* (London, 1971); E. S. Dallas, *Poetics: An Essay on Poetry* (London, 1852); T. Taylor, ed., *Life of B. R. Haydon from His Autobiography and Journals*, 3 vols. (London, 1853).

D. Masson, "The Life and Poetry of Keats," in *Macmillan's* magazine, 3 (November 1860), 1-16, an important essay anticipating some aspects of modern criticism of Keats, repr. in G. Matthews, ed., *The Critical Heritage* (London, 1971); M. Arnold, *On the Study of Celtic Literature* (London, 1867), ch. 4 refers to Keats's "natural magic"; see also Arnold's essay "Maurice de Guérin," in his *Essays in Criticism* (London, 1865); J. R. Lowell, ed., *My Study Windows* (London, 1871), in Low's American Copyright Series of American Authors; Sir C. W. Dilke, *The Papers of a Critic*, 2 vols. (London, 1875), the memoir contains letters from Keats and other material; C. C. Clarke and M. C. Clarke, *Recollections of Writers* (London, 1878); F. M. Owen, *John Keats: A Study* (London, 1880); T. H. Ward, ed., *The English Poets: Selections* (London, 1880), with general intro. by M. Arnold, vol. IV contains an essay on Keats by Arnold that was repr. in his *Essays in Criticism*, 2nd ser. (London, 1888); S. Colvin, *Keats* (London, 1887; new ed., 1889), in the English Men of Letters series; W. M. Rossetti, *Life of John Keats* (London, 1887), contains a bibliography by J. P. Anderson; W. Sharp, *The Life and Letters of Joseph Severn* (London, 1892); R. Bridges, *John Keats: A Critical Essay* (London, 1895), privately printed, also in the Muses' Library (London, 1896), repub. in Bridges' *Collected Essays*, IV (London, 1929).

*The Bookman*, Keats double number (October 1906), contains original material relating to Keats; A. C. Bradley, *Oxford Lectures on Poetry* (London, 1909), contains essay "The Letters of Keats," followed by a comparison of Keats's *Endymion* and Shelley's "Alastor," repr. with intro. by M. R. Ridley (London, 1965); L. Wolff, *John Keats: Sa vie et son oeuvre, 1795-1821* (Paris, 1910); E. Thomas, *Keats* (London, 1916); D. L. Baldwin, ed., *A Concordance to the Poems of John Keats* (Washington, D. C., 1917); S. Colvin, *John Keats: His Life and Poetry, His Friends, Critics and After-Fame* (London, 1917; rev. ed., 1925); Keats House Committee, *John Keats Memorial Volume* (Hampstead, 1921); H. I'A. Fausset, *Keats: A Study in Development* (London, 1922); A. Lowell, *John Keats*, 2 vols. (Boston, 1925); J. M. Murry, *Keats and Shakespeare: A Study of Keats's Poetic Life from 1816 to 1820* (London, 1925); H. W. Garrod, *Keats* (London, 1926); E. Blunden, *Leigh Hunt's Examiner Examined* (London, 1928); G. L. Marsh, ed., *John Hamilton Reynolds, Poetry and Prose* (London, 1928), with intro. and notes by Marsh; C. Spurgeon, *Keats's Shakespeare: A Descriptive Study* (London, 1928), based on Keats's markings and marginalia in his copies of Shakespeare; T. Saito, *Keats's View of Poetry* (London, 1929); L. Wolff, *Keats* (Paris, 1929).

J. M. Murry, *Studies in Keats* (London, 1930), rev. and enl. as *Studies in Keats, New and Old* (London, 1939), as *The Mystery of Keats* (London, 1949), and as *Keats* (London, 1955); M. R. Ridley, *Keats' Craftsmanship: A Study in Poetic Development* (Oxford, 1933); *Keats House and Museum: An Historical and Descriptive Guide* (London, 1934; new ed., 1966; 7th ed., 1974); E. Blunden, *Keats's Publisher: A Memoir of John Taylor* (London, 1936); C. L. Finney, *The Evolution of Keats's Poetry*, 2 vols. (Cambridge, Mass., 1936); T. Saito, *John Keats* (Tokyo, 1936); C. A. Brown, *Life of John Keats* (Oxford, 1937), D. H. Bodurtha and W. B. Pope, eds., with intro. and notes, the first publication of reminiscences by Keats's friend Charles Brown; D. Hewlett, *Adonais: A Life of John Keats* (London, 1937), rev. and enl. as *A Life of John Keats* (London, 1949; 3rd rev. ed., 1970); W. H. White, *Keats as Doctor and Patient* (London, 1938).

E. Blunden, *Romantic Poetry and the Fine Arts* (London, 1942), Warton Lecture on English Poetry for 1942, first printed in *Proceedings of the British Academy*, 28 (1942), 101-118; G. H. Ford, *Keats and the Victorians: A Study of His Influence and Rise to Fame, 1821-1895* (London, 1944); W. J. Bate, *The Stylistic Development of Keats* (New York, 1945); R. H. Fogle, *The Imagery of Keats and Shelley: A Comparative Study* (Chapel Hill, N. C., 1949); L. Trilling, *The Opposing Self: Nine Essays in Criticism* (New York, 1950), contains "The Poet as Hero: Keats in His Letters"; N. F. Ford, *The Prefigurative Imagination of Keats: A Study of the Beauty-Truth Identification and Its Implications* (Stanford, Calif., 1951); J. Richardson, *Fanny Brawne: A Biography* (London, 1952); R. Gittings, *John Keats: The Living Year, 21 September, 1818 to 21 September, 1819* (London, 1954); R. Gittings, *The Mask of Keats: A Study of Problems* (London, 1956); E. C. Pettet, *On the Poetry of Keats* (Cambridge, 1957), includes an extended analysis of *Endymion*; K. Muir, ed., *John Keats: A Reassessment* (London, 1958; repr., 1969), essays by Muir, K. Allott, M. Allott, A. Davenport, R. T. Davies, J. Grundy, and others; D. Perkins, *The Quest for Permanence: The Symbolism of Wordsworth, Shelley and Keats* (Cambridge, Mass., 1959).

J. Bayley, *Keats and Reality* (London, 1962), lively British Academy lecture; W. J. Bate, *John Keats* (Cambridge, Mass., 1963), highly distinguished and indispensable critical biography; J. Richardson, *The Everlasting Spell: A Study of Keats and His Friends* (London, 1963); A. Ward, *John Keats: The Making of a Poet* (London, 1963), biographical study, making suggestive use of the poems to illuminate Keats's character and temperament; W. J. Bate, ed., *Keats: A Collection of Critical Essays* (Englewood Cliffs, N. J., 1964), in Twentieth Century Views series; R. Gittings, *The Keats Inheritance* (London, 1964), on the question of the Keats family's financial position; W. H. Evert, *Aesthetic and Myth in the Poetry of Keats* (Princeton, N. J., 1965); D. Bush, *John Keats: His Life and Writings* (London, 1966), admirably succinct and informative intro. for the Masters of World Literature series; I. Jack, *Keats and the Mirror of Art* (London, 1967), an examination of Keats's cultural milieu, especially the influence of painters and art critics on his poetic development; J. O'Neill, ed., *Critics on Keats* (London, 1967), extracts from important critical works, arranged in chronological order of Keats's writings; R. Gittings, *John Keats* (London, 1968), impressively detailed biographical study; J. Stillinger, ed., *Twentieth Century Interpretations of Keats's Odes: A Collection of Critical Essays* (Englewood Cliffs, N. J., 1968), includes essays by M. H. Abrams, K. Allott, W. J. Bate, C. Brooks, D. Perkins, R. P. Warren, and others; J. Jones, *John Keats's Dream of Truth* (London, 1969), on Keats and "Romantic feeling."

C. I. Patterson, *The Daemonic in the Poetry of John Keats* (London, 1970), argues that the "daemonic" in Keats is a nonmalicious, pre-Christian, Greek conception, and is in conflict with his personal feeling for the actual world; M. Dickstein, *Keats and His Poetry: A Study in Development* (Chicago, 1971), explores the contrarieties in and the development of Keats's imagination through close reading of the texts, especially *Endymion*, the odes, *The Fall of Hyperion*, and some minor poems; T. Hilton, *Keats and His World* (London, 1971), useful pictorial biography; G. Matthews, ed., *Keats: The Critical Heritage* (London, 1971), invaluable collection of early nineteenth-century and Victorian commentaries on Keats; J. Stillinger, *The Hoodwinking of Madeline and Other Essays on Keats's Poems* (Urbana, Ill., 1971), offers an individual view of Keats's "realism"; T. Redpath, *The Young Romantics and Critical Opinion, 1807-1824* (London, 1973); S. M. Sperry, *Keats the Poet* (Princeton, N. J., 1973), discusses the connection between "sensation" and "thought" in Keats; C. Ricks, *Keats and Embarrassment* (Oxford, 1974), vivacious essay on evidence in Keats's poems and letters of his sensitivity to and intelligence about embarrassment; J. Stillinger, *The Texts of Keats's Poems* (Cambridge, Mass., 1974), offers a detailed analysis of textual problems in Keats and suggests principles for establishing a standard text; reviewed by M. Allott in *Times Literary Supplement* (12 December 1975).

Periodicals containing valuable regular contributions about Keats include *Keats-Shelley Journal* (1952-    ) and *Bulletin of the Keats-Shelley Memorial*: vol. I (1910); vol. II, Sir R. Rodd and H. N. Gray, eds. (1913; repub. 1962); vol. III (etc.), D. Hewlett, ed. (1950-    ).

# RUDYARD KIPLING

(1865-1936)

## A. G. Sandison

The man Kipling, the myth Kipling, is over; but the stories themselves have all the time in the world.

(Randall Jarrell)

FOR decades it has been customary to preface any study of Kipling with either an apology or a highly specific justification for doing anything so displeasing to the clerisy and potentially damaging to the critic's own academic reputation. Yet since the 1960's a number of commentators have struggled to show that to confuse Kipling with the idea of empire is to create a barrier to understanding both. Moreover, time is on the side of those who fight against the confusion. As Britain's imperial heyday becomes more and more remote, Kipling begins to emerge from the imperial shadows as a writer of formidable talent.

This study, therefore, lays most of its stress on Kipling's artistic achievement. He was, quite simply, one of the greatest—some would say *the* greatest— short-story writer England has produced.

*I*

RUDYARD KIPLING was born on 30 December 1865 in Bombay, where his father had gone earlier that year to take up an appointment as a teacher of utilitarian technical crafts (designing and manufacturing terracotta pottery and architectural sculpture) in a recently established school of art. While he labored at these humble tasks in the exotic East, his friends and relatives were spearheading the increasingly successful arts and crafts movement in England.

John Lockwood Kipling was one of many children of a poorly paid Methodist minister. After leaving school he worked as a designer and modeler, and attended art school before becoming assistant to an architectural sculptor in London. In 1865 he married Alice Macdonald, whose father was also a Methodist minister. Hers too was a large family; the daughters were particularly celebrated for their beauty and wit and, ultimately, for their distinguished marriages: one to Edward (later Sir Edward) Burne-Jones, the Pre-Raphaelite painter; another to Edward (later Sir Edward) Poynter, in time president of the Royal Academy; and a third to Alfred Baldwin, an iron manufacturer (their son, Stanley Baldwin, was elected three times as prime minister of Great Britain).

In financial terms, Alice's marriage was not, initially at least, successful, and she herself wrote for magazines and local papers to eke out the family income. But though their position on the Anglo-Indians'[1] social scale was not high, they enjoyed the privileges and comforts that went with being members of the "imperial race." Consequently young Rudyard had not only his *ayah*, or nurse, but also his own manservant; and during the first five years of his life so much of his time was spent with them that they were the people he was most strongly inclined to identify with. Sharing their superstitions and their secrets, attending religious ceremonies and rituals of considerable diversity, he was rather more in their society than that of his parents, and he had learned to speak Hindi before he mastered English.

In 1871 the Kiplings returned briefly to England to leave their two children—Alice ("Trix") had been born in 1868—to be educated there. The practice was common, because of the exceptionally high mortality rate among young European children who remained in India and because of their need for an adequate education. (Sir Angus Wilson, in *The Strange Ride of Rudyard Kipling*, 1977, suggests that there was also a chauvinistic element in such a practice: the children were sent home to "make sure of their roots.")

[1] The term used by Kipling and his contemporaries to signify the British residing in India.

What was extraordinary, however, in such loving—and loved—parents was that they gave no warning of their intentions to the children. Compounding this error, they were easily reassured about the suitability of the selected foster parents. The result was that Rudyard and Trix found themselves inexplicably abandoned by their parents in a dreary house on the south coast of England dominated by a formidably disagreeable lady whom they were obliged to call Aunty Rosa. Whether she was quite as cruel as she is portrayed in "Baa, Baa Black Sheep" and *The Light That Failed* (1890) is not easy to establish, but the small boy was systematically bullied, beaten, and generally victimized by her for the next six years.

From being the center of attention of an entire household, idolized and pampered by servants, Kipling was at the age of six plunged into an environment that was almost the very opposite of the only one he had ever known. Though he survived mentally intact, surprisingly enough, he was far from being unscathed. In all sorts of ways his fiction is colored by the experience, and not just in the relatively superficial sense of dealing much in hallucinations, nightmares, and mental breakdowns. From this early time came, too, the misery of insomnia, with which he was plagued for the whole of his life and which came to play such an important part in his literary imagination.

There was one important source of relief and refuge from "the House of Desolation," as Kipling called Aunty Rosa's establishment. Each Christmas until he was ten, he and his sister went to stay with their Aunt Georgie and her husband, Edward Burne-Jones. These vacations represented an experience so totally at odds with life in Southsea that the Burne-Jones home—"the Grange" in Fulham—took on the character of a magical world. There they met other children, watched magic-lantern shows, played boisterous games (ably led by Burne-Jones himself), joined in the music-making, and generally took part in all the high-spirited fun that characterized the household at this time of year.

But the Grange was a great deal more than just a very good place to spend Christmas. For nearly thirty years it was to be a favorite meeting place of many of the most talented artists and writers of the time. It was at the heart of what might be described as the second wave of the Pre-Raphaelite movement and of that part of the arts and crafts movement which centered on William Morris and his associates in what became known as "the Firm" (actually named Morris, Marshall, Faulkner, and Co., manufacturers and decorators).

Three men closely involved with this radical and innovative group were in a position to influence the young Kipling, and two of them, Burne-Jones and Cormell Price, undoubtedly did so; a third, William Morris, was influential, too, but in a less direct and personal way, even though the children had, at the Grange's Christmas festivities, made him an honorary uncle. Burne-Jones was the closest of all to Kipling. When he died in 1898 Kipling, then living in Rottingdean, wrote to a friend that his Uncle Ned had been "more to me than any other man. He changed my life by his visits down here."

Cormell Price ("Uncle Corm") was a friend of Burne-Jones and had been a painter of promise. More to the point, he was headmaster of the United Services College at Westward Ho! in Devon, which Kipling attended until he was nearly seventeen. Aware of the boy's enthusiasm for literature, Price gave him access to his own exceptionally well-stocked library and quite clearly helped to develop his literary taste.

Charles Carrington in *The Life of Rudyard Kipling* (1955) sums up the young Kipling and his world as he came to the end of his schooldays:

He was a rebel and a progressive which is to say, in 1882 paradoxically—that he was a decadent. His friends, his teachers, were liberals, his tastes were "aesthetic," the writers he most admired were the fashionable pessimists. . . .
In the holidays he vanished into a world that differed profoundly from that known to the average officer's family. . . . At the Poynters' or at the Burne-Jones's, as in his father's house, all the talk was of the fine arts and in the jargon of the studio.

(p. 31)

Carrington refers there to the influence of "his father's house," and John Lockwood Kipling's role in shaping his son's taste must also be acknowledged. Throughout his life Kipling was exceptionally devoted to his parents and eagerly sought his father's help and advice when he wanted to talk over problems of composition. John Kipling is the model of the curator of the Lahore museum in *Kim* (1901), and the role is a peculiarly apt one for him to play; his granddaughter recalled that his "knowledge of every art and craft, even the most unusual, was amazing, while his skill with his hands was a joy to watch."

And he shared the artistic priorities and sympathies of his friends Price and Burne-Jones.

What then did these avant-garde artists, in whose ambience Kipling grew up, stand for? Among the more easily defined objectives of the original Pre-Raphaelite Brotherhood (which had been founded somewhat accidentally in 1848 by a group of young painters very resentful of the power and conservatism of the Royal Academy) was the necessity of turning the eyes of painters and of the public back again to nature and away from what they saw as a sterile classicism. But in "painting directly from nature" they were nonetheless to imbue their work with a strong ethical and narrative content and to choose for their themes subject matter that was explicitly moral and religious. Under the influence of the painter and poet Dante Gabriel Rossetti they were also encouraged to regard poetry, painting, and social idealism as organically linked.

Despite the introspective and mystical bent of much Pre-Raphaelite work, it was the painters' so-called realism, deriving from their close attention to minuteness and precision of detail, that attracted the most censure. Sir John Everett Millais' *Christ in the House of His Parents* was considered typical in its effrontery: "a pictorial blasphemy," the *Athenaeum* called it, from which all decent people would "recoil with horror and disgust." To the *Times* (London) it was "plainly revolting," having the temerity to associate "the Holy Family with the meanest details of a carpenter's shop, with no considerable omission of misery, of dirt, and even disease, all finished with the same loathsome minuteness." Even Charles Dickens, though he later made amends, joined in the general denunciation. Yet in many ways, as John Dixon Hunt points out in *The Pre-Raphaelite Imagination 1848-1900* (1968), painters like Millais and Holman Hunt were Victorian in their attempts, as Holman Hunt put it, to "make more tangible Jesus Christ's history and teaching." Dixon Hunt also makes the point that their exact and detailed representation of objects is less an end in itself than a suggestion of greater things.

In social subjects the Pre-Raphaelites were certainly capable of challenging accepted orthodoxies. Two of Rossetti's pictures have a prostitute as a central figure; Hunt's *The Awakened Conscience* shows the misery of a "kept woman"; and even Burne-Jones published a short story, "The Cousins," which in its depiction of squalor and misery could be taken as a forerunner of Kipling's excellent story—much acclaimed for its originality and frankness—"The Record of Badalia Herodsfoot."

Other characteristics that the Pre-Raphaelite Brotherhood shared were an intensity of both feeling and color, a tendency to look back nostalgically to the past, and—increasingly—a rejection of the ugliness and materialism that industrial success had brought to Britain. Burne-Jones was closely associated with these last-named reactions, declaring uncompromisingly that "the more materialistic science becomes, the more angels I shall paint." When Burne-Jones first fell under John Ruskin's influence while at Oxford, he attempted to rally his friends by calling for "a Crusade and Holy War against this age." In the event, it was his friend William Morris who came nearer to carrying out this crusade, with his complete repudiation of Victorian "mechanism" and his championship of the craftsman.

It was not William Morris who originated the arts and crafts movement, though he is often credited with doing so. However, Morris, Burne-Jones, and other members of what the latter called the Birmingham Colony (Charles Faulkner, R. W. Dixon, William Fulford, and Cormell Price) enthusiastically adopted as central to their creed the principle John Ruskin had defined for the Pre-Raphaelite Brotherhood: "absolute uncompromising truth in all it does, obtained by working everything, down to the most minute detail, from nature only"; and having done so, they began to turn their attention to the applied arts.

In one sense this credo was a deliberate riposte to the aloofness and exclusiveness of the Academy, but it was also a natural development for them. In it they were once again consciously turning away from the materialism of their own age and back to the Middle Ages, when "the artists were more workmen and the workmen were more artists." When the possibility arose of forming a kind of cooperative to make the sort of well-designed household furnishings Morris and his friends had been unable to find for his newly built house, it was Rossetti who exclaimed, "Let's have a shop, like Giotto." Morris took the idea very seriously. He believed strongly in the redemptive force of art upon society: "You cannot educate, you cannot civilize men unless you give them a share in art," he had written.

So "the Firm" was launched in 1861. In addition to Marshall, an engineer introduced to the others by Ford Madox Brown, and the mathematician Charles Faulkner, the company consisted of the architect

Philip Webb, Rossetti, Burne-Jones, and Arthur Hughes. Against all expectations "the Firm" was a success, and its products can still serve to illustrate both the founders' faith in good craftsmanship—notably in the mediums of furniture and glass—and the idealism that found expression in, for example, their fabrics, stained glass, and ceramics.

Morris and his colleagues were attempting to express, according to Gillian Naylor,

the idea of the unity of the arts that had been latent in Pre-Raphaelite theory. To the "painterly" vision of the Pre-Raphaelites, however, there was added the ideal of the vernacular, as expressed by Philip Webb, who saw architecture as a "common tradition of honest building" and who had built [Morris'] Red House, with its great oak staircase, oak beams, red-tiled hall and large brick chimneypieces, as an expression of that vision.
(*The Arts and Crafts Movement*, 1971, p. 101)

For Morris these theories and objectives implied sweeping social changes. When he joined the Social Democratic Federation in 1883, he gave as his reason for doing so the need to "act for the destruction of the system which seems to me mere opposition and obstruction." The position, he felt, was inescapable for an artist like himself: "Both my historical studies and my practical conflict with the philistinism of modern society have *forced on* me the conviction that art cannot have a real life and growth under the present system of commercialism and profit-mongering."

Burne-Jones, though not particularly interested in politics, shared at least something of Morris' radicalism. The two of them, together with Cormell Price, organized the Workmen's Neutrality Demonstration in London in 1878 to oppose British plans to intervene in the Russo-Turkish war. Given the mood of the British public, their action required conviction and courage, for the government's bellicose attitude helped to focus the growing imperialist fervor in the country at large. The word "jingoism" itself came into the language as a direct result of the crisis, from a boastful patriotic song that became a favorite in the music halls: "We don't want to fight, but by jingo if we do. . . ."

Georgiana Burne-Jones was also of an independent and liberal opinion. Her house at Rottingdean came near to being sacked when, amid the general celebration on the night peace was concluded with the Boers, she hung a black banner from her windows with the words: "We have killed and also taken possession." Only the intervention of her nephew Rudyard saved the situation from getting seriously out of hand.

This then was the aesthetic and moral background within which Kipling grew up: forceful and influential in its pioneering of new ideas and the new aesthetic; forceful and influential, too, in its radicalism and idealism. The obvious question is: How could a writer, nurtured in this lively and original milieu, turn into "the laureate of Joseph Chamberlain's designs" (Chamberlain was colonial secretary) and "the banjo-band of empire"? But this begs another question: *Did* he?

It might seem that he did if we follow his biography a little further. In 1882, at the age of seventeen, Kipling returned to India to work as a journalist on the *Civil and Military Gazette* in Lahore. There he rediscovered the India he had known and loved as a child; and he wrote about it, perceptively and affectionately, in his paper—though it is worth noting that Kipling wrote (and thought) mainly of the Punjab. He also wrote about the political scene, drawing on club gossip, listening to the tales that soldiers—privates rather than officers—had to tell. With the arrival of Lord Dufferin as viceroy in 1894 he was even able to catch a glimpse of the innermost corridors of power, for the viceroy befriended the Kiplings and admitted them, in some small measure at least, to his circle.

All of this experience Kipling put to good use in his first volume of poems, *Departmental Ditties* (1886); in *Plain Tales from the Hills* (1888); and in his other Indian stories. But in 1889 he left India, returning only once, briefly in 1891, to see his parents. Though he settled first in London, he stayed there for less than three years. In 1892 he married Caroline Balestier, an American, and went to live in Vermont, where over the next four years he wrote some of his best stories. It was there that he first started to work seriously on *Kim*, but not until he had returned to England in 1896 and talked the subject over with his father at great length was he able to give it final shape. Finally, early in 1901, *Kim* was published. There are many (including the present writer) who believe that *Kim* marks the high-water mark in Kipling's creative achievement. Many excellent stories were to follow, but those written after 1901 lack the energy, the sharpness of eye and ear, the tightness of detail and shape, the sense of easy mastery of *Kim*.

In a number of respects Kipling never repudiated his late-Pre-Raphaelite boyhood; quite the contrary. William Gaunt surely gets the wrong end of the stick when he suggests rather archly that Pre-Raphaelitism had "whispered its enchantment into the ear of the Imperial Muse": "Perhaps some of those little golden fables spun by the painter influenced his 'beloved Ruddy,' turning him back from his sharply realist contemporary vision to those overlapping vistas of a past which was also the present in which paleolithic man, Roman legionaries, mediaeval burgesses still lived."

It is true that Kipling's interest in the past is deep and sustained (witness *Puck of Pook's Hill,* 1906); it also has something in common with the views of Burne-Jones, though a great deal more with those of Morris. Like the latter, Kipling had no solid faith in a God, Providence, or a future life, and, like him too, he found solace in what seemed to him the permanence of the country and the rural life that in his eyes enshrined the history of the race and guaranteed, so far as anything could, its future. In the attention he gives to the past, Kipling reflects a habit of mind characteristic not just of the Pre-Raphaelites but of the Victorians in general: J. S. Mill had concluded that it was their chief preoccupation to compare their own with former ages.

It is equally arguable that it was the Pre-Raphaelite influence that turned him toward what Gaunt calls his "sharply realist contemporary vision"—though some of it, at least, is also the product of continental influences. "The Record of Badalia Herodsfoot," with its emphasis on urban misery, prostitution, and exploitation, is in a direct line from Dickens, as Uncle Ned Burne-Jones's story "The Cousins" shows: "Those were [Badalia's] days of fatness, and they did not last long, for her husband took to himself another woman, and passed out of Badalia's life, over Badalia's senseless body; for he stifled protest with blows." This is really not profoundly different from the early part of "The Cousins" except in its ironic and paraded detachment, which has us at once on our guard against manipulation by what we instinctively recognize to be a very clever writer: a reaction no one is ever likely to have on reading "The Cousins."

Kipling's indebtedness to Pre-Raphaelite realism is more convincingly demonstrated in his precise use of detail, like that of the reins on the sleeping Rissaldar's wrist in *Kim,* the loaded tea-table in "The Wish House," or, paradoxically, his description of the machinery of the lighthouse in "The Disturber of the Traffic." Thomas Carlyle had praised the Pre-Raphaelites for "copying the thing as it is," and it is much the same for Kipling, even in the ideal world:

> . . . each for the joy of the working, and each, in his separate star,
> Shall draw the Thing as he sees It for the God of Things as They are.
> ("When Earth's Last Picture Is Painted")

It is also possible to find other significant signs of indebtedness to Burne-Jones and his circle. There is, for example, the infusion of moral allegory into what is very often a highly pictorial composition (though part of that may also come from the Methodist background of which Kipling was very conscious). There is his overt concern with the art of the painter in so many of his stories, from *The Light That Failed* (1890) to the "Eye of Allah" (1926); and his taste for a brilliant use of color, at its most vivid in *Kim.*

Even more likely to be part of his inheritance is the intense care he took with his own craft, going over his stories again and again, paring out all that was not strictly essential. Like Morris, Kipling believed deeply that art should be committed, not divorced from the concerns of people as they busy themselves with what he considered their best means of salvation—the day's work. He says so explicitly in "The Children of the Zodiac" and in "'Teem.'" Like Morris and his friends, he was also deeply suspicious of the age's materialism and its contentment with "Idols of greasy altars built for the body's ease" ("The Islanders"). Unlike Morris, however, he did not oppose the new technology, though for unexpected reasons, as we shall see.

In one key area Kipling can be seen developing a central preoccupation of the Pre-Raphaelites to a point where it takes on for him a totally different moral significance, one that comes to underlie and give special character to his whole creative endeavor.

As anyone will realize who has ever had occasion to consult that remarkable barometer of the moral climate in nineteenth-century Britain, Thomas Carlyle, an essential consideration in the understanding of these eminent Victorians is their troubled relationship with nature. Pre-Raphaelitism and the arts and crafts movement both embodied the recognition that many of these gifted and creative men shared—most notably Edward Welby Pugin, Ruskin, and Morris—that modern progress, particularly of an industrial and technological kind, threatened to alienate man from nature. To Pugin and Ruskin in particular this meant alienation from God, since they were in no doubt that nature was ultimately a spiritual entity. But all of them believed that man's rightful and accessible domain was indeed in the bosom of nature: it was there, informed by the spirit of the Creator, that man found the roots of his being; and it was through art that he could be brought to realize this and effect a unification or a reunification with nature, thus staving off the recognized threat of alienation.

Kipling likewise is concerned, every step of the way, with man's relation to nature; only he finds the latter hostile to man and he accepts alienation as an inescapable fact of existence. Recognizing this, he sees that life will be one long battle to preserve moral integrity in a universe where there is no order and no refuge.

Kipling's conclusion is much the same as that of his contemporary Joseph Conrad. But Kipling derived his comprehensive symbol for the conflict from the idea of empire, an idea that for the world at large had a concrete and controversial political reality. Thus when he lauded the structure of empire, many of his readers assumed that he was enthralled with the political reality of empire and judged him accordingly. Such a fate was inevitable; to a certain degree there was poetic justice in it, for Kipling was prepared to put flesh, bone, and muscle on his symbol, but a symbol that shoots people and rules countries uninvited can no longer be seen simply as a literary device. One must look beyond literature to appreciate how far, and in whose company, he took part in the age's polemic. This we cannot do unless we also appreciate what he was rooted in.

II

OF Joseph Conrad, Bertrand Russell wrote:

He gave me the impression of a man who thought of civilised and morally tolerable human life as a dangerous walk on a thin crust of barely cooled lava which at any moment might break and let the unwary sink into the fiery depths.
(*Portraits from Memory*, 1956, p. 82)

The description, however, seems equally applicable to Kipling. At the heart of such a response there is an extreme, existential loneliness and fear as well as a deep pessimism.

The signs are there from the beginning, which in itself is remarkable in a man who by the time he was nineteen had already written some of the stories in *Plain Tales from the Hills*.

> A stone's throw out on either hand
> From that well-ordered road we tread,
> And all the world is wild and strange.

So runs the epigraph to "In the House of Suddhoo," but this is the reality that governs nearly all Kipling's actions and reactions. The world of nature is hostile and threatening: it is exactly the world that Conrad's Marlow surveys when he looks over the anarchy of nature represented by the jungle in *Heart of Darkness* and wonders, "Could we handle that dumb thing or would it handle us?" In fact Kipling has something like a horror of what the French social and political theorist Georges Sorel, another distinguished contemporary, defined as "natural nature": "a mysterious, even malignant Fate, an arbitrary and meaningless force that constantly threatens to overwhelm the spheres conquered by human reason." The comparison with Sorel is strengthened by his solution, namely, to seek succor in "artificial nature," which was the construction imposed upon the chaos of reality by scientists and technicians in order to tame it. Interestingly, this is precisely the métier of the favored Kipling character. When his heroes are not literally engineers and technicians, which they frequently are, they are administrators taming the alien and menacing forces of what he calls in *Kim* "great, grey, formless India." A concern for artificial nature and its beneficent powers is also what attracts him to the machine, from which, in turn, we get stories like "The Ship That Found Herself" and ".007." To Kipling, as to Sorel, the machine is a major expression of man's ability to understand and control the forces of nature. "If there is something that is most specifically social in human activity," wrote Sorel, "it is the machine. It is more social than language itself."

So many of his stories allude to this threat from "natural nature" either centrally or peripherally that even a random dip into his works is going to illustrate its importance to Kipling. But one can choose here one or two stories where it is integral to the whole tale.

"The Disturber of the Traffic," first published in 1891, has as its epigraph a verse that is itself characteristic of the vision I have been discussing. The first stanza runs:

> From the wheel and the drift of Things
> Deliver us, good Lord;

# RUDYARD KIPLING

And we will meet the wrath of kings,
The faggot, and the sword.

The story is of a lighthouse keeper, Dowse, who goes mad, seeing in the waters flowing beneath his tower the anarchy of the world. But the tale is, in a manner altogether characteristic of the author, enclosed in a context that greatly extends the power and significance of Dowse's disorienting experience. For the narrator, in true Kipling fashion, first creates an exalted notion of the mystery and exclusiveness of those (principally the lighthouse keepers) in the very special service of the Board of Trinity. He does so because they represent that selfless confederacy dedicated to the preservation of order and integrity the world over: an order that is seen quite clearly to be neither physical nor political but moral.

The great light by which the narrator and the keeper, Fenwick, are sitting when the story begins beams out through the obscurity of the darkness and the fog to bring order into what would otherwise be the chaos of coastal ships blundering about in the English Channel. Interestingly, the lighthouse is described as that of St. Cecilia-under-the-Cliff and the most powerful of the south coast lights. St. Cecilia is, of course, the patron saint of music, and the light, we are told, "when the sea-mist veils all," turns "a hooded head to the sea and sings a song of two words once every minute." But the sound undergoes what one might be forgiven for calling a sea-change: "From the land that song resembles the bellowing of a brazen bull; but off-shore they understand, and the steamers grunt gratefully in answer." Later a ship is described as "bleating like an indignant calf."

All the delicacy, charm, and harmony we might associate with St. Cecilia—backed by a vague picture of a lady of rare beauty and classical drapery—is rudely dispelled. In its place there is very deliberately planted an image of a world of brutes presided over and kept in order by the primitive, pagan force of a brazen bull. The world is a place of marauding animals—an image that recurs in Kipling's stories—dominated and disciplined by the still greater brute energy of a bull. But the fact that the bull is brazen—wrought by man, in other words—tells us something else. To control the disorder of "natural nature" Kipling turns to "artificial nature" and the world of the machine:

One star came out over the cliffs, the waters turned to lead-colour, and St. Cecilia's Light shot out across the sea in eight long pencils that wheeled slowly from right to left, melted into one beam of solid light laid down directly in front of the tower, dissolved again into eight, and passed away. The light-frame of the thousand lenses circled on its rollers, and the compressed-air engine that drove it hummed like a blue-bottle under a glass. The hand of the indicator on the wall pulsed from mark to mark. Eight pulse-beats timed one half-revolution of the Light; neither more nor less.

In the chat that follows between Fenwick and the narrator—though it is pointedly strewn with technical jargon about dynamos, governors, and feed-pipes—the subject is mainly pilots and lights, both servants in the cause of order. As Fenwick tells his tales they are accompanied by "the roller-skate rattle of the revolving lens," the active instrument of order, and, symbolic of the anarchy of the natural world, "the sharp tap of reckless night-birds that flung themselves at the glasses."

The tale that is selected by the narrator to retell to us is of a keeper called—with rather too obvious an intent—Dowse, who is in charge of a light in a quarter of the globe where the currents are depicted as being among the most unruly, inexplicable, and destructive: "they chop and they change, and they banks the tides fust on one shore and then on another, till your ship's tore in two." An excellent example of Kipling's ability to conjure up a vivid, almost allegorical, tableau is the description of Dowse sitting up in his tower "for to watch the tigers come out of the forests to hunt for crabs and such like round about the lighthouse at low tide." This tension between order and anarchy is heightened when we are made aware of another presence in the vicinity of the lighthouse:

"There was another man along with Dowse in the Light, but he wasn't rightly a man. He was a Kling. No, nor yet a Kling he wasn't, but his skin was in little flakes and cracks all over, from living so much in the salt water as was his usual custom. His hands was all webby-foot, too. He was called, I remember Dowse saying now, an Orange-Lord, on account of his habits. You've heard of an Orange-Lord, sir?"

The narrator corrects him: the word is "orang-laut" and means, we are told, a sea-gypsy. This orang-laut, whose name is Challong, has a disturbing affinity with these unruly elements policed by the light:

"Dowse told me that that man, long hair and all, would go swimming up and down the straits just for something to do;

735

running down on one tide and back again with the other, swimming side-stroke, and the tides going tremenjus strong. Elseways he'd be skipping about the beach along with the tigers at low tide, for he was most part a beast; or he'd sit in a little boat praying to old Loby Toby of an evening when the volcano was spitting red at the south end of the strait. Dowse told me that he wasn't a companionable man, like you and me might have been to Dowse."

The splendid irony in the last sentence is typical of Kipling; for it is a datum with him that the wildness may be already in man's soul, whether he is civilized or not. Gradually the anarchy of the waters begins to affect Dowse, whose head "began to feel streaky from looking at the tide so long."

"The streaks, they would run with the tides, north and south, twice a day, accordin' to them currents, and he'd lie down on the planking—it was a screw-pile Light—with his eye to a crack and watch the water streaking through the piles just so quiet as hogwash. He said the only comfort he got was at slack water. Then the streaks in his head went round and round like a sampan in a tide-rip; but that was heaven, he said, to the other kind of streaks—the straight ones that looked like arrows on a wind-chart, but much more regular."

Driven to desperation and goaded by Challong, who "swum round and round the Light, laughin' at him and splashin' water with his webby-foot hands," Dowse decides that he must stop all ships from coming through the straits, because they churn up the water and make the streaks worse. He constructs, with Challong, a number of rafts (taking longer over the job than might have been needed "because he rejoiced in the corners, they being square, and the streaks in his head all running longways") on which he mounts lights so that they will serve as wreck-buoys. The captain of an admiralty survey ship hears of these mysterious buoys and goes to investigate.

When the captain gets Dowse to his ship (pursued by Challong, who "was swimmin' round and round the ship, sayin' 'dam' for to please the men and to be took aboard"), Dowse's madness becomes plain even to himself. Kipling has him suddenly catch sight of his reflection in the binnacle brasses, whereupon he realizes that not only is he stark naked but he has been so for weeks. As the ship bears Dowse away with it, Challong follows "a-calling 'dam-dam' all among the wake of the screw, and half-heaving himself out of water and joining his webby-foot hands together." This image of the creature who "wasn't rightly a man" pursuing the boat, his "webby-foot hands" uplifted in supplication, vividly recalls the native woman's gesture of appeal to the departing Kurtz in Conrad's *Heart of Darkness*; and the significance of the two images is surprisingly similar. Challong may not be "rightly a man," but he is far too close to one for comfort. This creature who, dismayingly, does not merely survive but seems at home in the anarchy of the streaky currents, is *not* different in kind, and thereby reveals what a carefully constucted thing is one's sense of moral order, and how near one lives to what is perhaps the natural state of moral lawlessness. Conrad's Marlow, looking over the jungle landscape, had made a similar discovery:

The earth seemed unearthly. We are accustomed to look over the shackled form of a conquered monster, but there —there you could look at a thing monstrous and free. It was unearthly, and the men were—No, they were not inhuman. . . . That was the worst of it—this suspicion of their not being inhuman.
(*Heart of Darkness*, II)

"The Disturber of the Traffic" is by no means Kipling's best story: he fumbles a little at the beginning, and he does so again toward the end, when Fenwick comes back into the tale; and there are other blemishes, notably in the dialogue. All the same it is a powerful and serious story that for most of its length is extraordinarily well organized despite its density.

Kipling often flaws an outstanding piece of writing quite perversely, and this tale offers a good example. One can accept the slight lack of focus at the beginning because something significant and integral to the tale is going on. But Fenwick's coming into the scene again at the end and meeting up with the guilt-ridden Dowse at Fratton is a mistake. And it is all the more exasperating in that it is quite gratuitous, for there comes after it an excellent, even brilliant, coda, which is all that was needed:

Day had come, and the Channel needed St. Cecilia no longer. The sea-fog rolled back from the cliffs in trailed wreaths and dragged patches, as the sun rose and made the dead sea alive and splendid. The stillness of the morning held us both silent as we stepped on the balcony. A lark went up from the cliffs behind St. Cecilia, and we smelt a smell of cows in the lighthouse pastures below.

Then we were both at liberty to thank the lord for another day of clean and wholesome life.

The story shows something of Kipling's art as well as his disturbing vision of that menacing realm of "natural nature" which lies so close to the surface. It was published in 1891, when Kipling was twenty-five, and its central concern is common to many of his early tales, where the vision seems to find its metaphor with an ease and congruency that is much less obvious in his later work. (I agree with Somerset Maugham's view that by the end of the century and with the publication of *Kim*, Kipling had written his best work.) Of course one also finds the mawkish and the ephemeral in the early stories, just as one finds superbly integrated tales in, for example, *Debits and Credits* (1926).

"At the End of the Passage," first published in 1890, shows Kipling's keen visual sense and technical virtuosity in the very first paragraph:

Four men, each entitled to "life, liberty, and the pursuit of happiness," sat at a table playing whist. The thermometer marked—for them—one hundred and one degrees of heat. The room was darkened till it was only just possible to distinguish the pips of the cards and the very white faces of the players. A tattered, rotten punkah of whitewashed calico was puddling the hot air and whining dolefully at each stroke. Outside lay gloom of a November day in London. There was neither sky, sun, nor horizon,—nothing but a brown purple haze of heat. It was as though the earth were dying of apoplexy.

The men are in effect prisoners—at first, it seems, prisoners of their own sense of duty and stubborn dedication to the job in hand (and the story loses pace when Kipling allows his principals to have too much to say about their particular share of the white man's burden). But as the story unfolds it is clear that they are much more the prisoners of their own loneliness; and that does not mean simply the loneliness of the Englishman in India, nobly sacrificing himself far from his own kith and kin so that "the people" may have efficient administration, railways, irrigation systems, and the like. It means man's essential loneliness and isolation, an inescapable condition of his existence: "The players were not conscious of any special regard for each other. They squabbled whenever they met; but they ardently desired to meet, as men without water desire to drink. They were lonely folk who understood the dread meaning of loneliness."

The absurdist inclination of the tale is heightened when added to the picture of the four men seated in a hut, playing whist in the middle of an inferno with no distinguishable horizon, no heaven and no earth, is Mottram tinkling out London music-hall songs on the broken piano, in the middle of this same nothingness: "A dense dust-storm sprang up outside, and swept roaring over the house, enveloping it in the choking darkness of midnight, but Mottram continued unheeding, and the crazy tinkle reached the ears of the listeners above the flapping of the tattered ceiling cloth."

There is a strong feeling in this story that the chaos already exists within man and is held at bay only by the most stringent application of certain disciplines, such as unremitting work and devotion to duty. The apparent objectives (they are referred to as "trifles" in the epigraph) to which the men sacrifice themselves are ultimately of little intrinsic value: but, trifles though they may be, devotion to them gives structure and a sense of identity to the individual. Isolation, prolonged and tortured, is going to stretch their defenses to the very limit, and the destructive entropic principle that seems the only reality will more easily cause the breakup of that carefully constructed artifact—the self. Kipling's characters are haunted by the knowledge of this possibility, so that when he writes of the four young men understanding "the dread meaning of loneliness," the phrase must not be taken casually. In many stories, including "At the End of the Passage," this fear of the destruction of identity and sense of self is portrayed in terms of the most acute agony. Hummil, one of the men, is gripped by terror that has reached an uncontrollable pitch:

"For three weeks I've had to think and spell out every word that has come through my lips before I dared to say it. Isn't that enough to drive a man mad? I can't see things correctly now, and I've lost my sense of touch. My skin aches – my skin aches! Make me sleep. Oh Spurstow, for the love of God, make me sleep sound. It isn't enough merely to let me dream. Let me sleep!"

Just at a point in the story where we might suspect the author of being too closely identified with his character's crisis, the skill of the storyteller reasserts itself. The injection of morphia Dr. Spurstow administers to Hummil has only a limited effect. Preoccupied in dismantling Hummil's guns, Spurstow is as startled as we are by the engineer's wild cry from the doorway: "You fool!" The degree to which Hummil is beyond all self-control and possibly in the possession of something else is forced on us by the sheer drama of the moment; and it is followed by the deployment of an image that Kipling reserves for moments of ultimate anomic horror:

> As a sponge rubs a slate clean, so some power unknown to Spurstow had wiped out of Hummil's face all that stamped it for the face of a man, and he stood at the doorway in the expression of his lost innocence. He had stept back into terrified childhood.

The doctor leaves, and almost immediately Hummil finds himself haunted again. The tale is well told: "When he came in to dinner he found himself sitting at the table. The vision rose and walked out hastily. Except that it cast no shadow, it was in all respects real."

Spurstow returns a week later and finds Hummil dead: "The body lay on its back, hands clinched by the side. . . . In the staring eyes was written terror beyond the expression of any pen." Again there is the suggestion of his whole being having been usurped by some "power unknown." "Cover up the face!" says Lowndes. "Is there any fear on earth that can turn a man into that likeness? It's ghastly. Oh Spurstow, cover it up!" And Spurstow replies, "No fear—on earth." What follows is generally regarded as a weakness in the story, though some allowance ought to be made for contemporary interest in such phenomena. Spurstow thinks he sees something odd in the dead man's eyes and, despite Lowndes's plea to "leave that horror alone," puts his camera to each eye and photographs it, afterward retreating into the bathroom to develop his film: "After a few minutes there was the sound of something being hammered to pieces, and he emerged, very white indeed."

The story ends with Spurstow turning in the doorway as he leaves (thus recalling the earlier unexpected appearance of Hummil in the doorway of the saddle room and consequently their shared doom) and quoting:

> "There may be Heaven,—there must be Hell.
> Meantime, there is our life here. We-ell?"

This concluding reference to hell raises an interesting question. The Kipling character's fear of moral disintegration quite frequently seems mixed up with a conviction that the hostile force in the universe is not simply its entropic principle but is actually, and actively, evil itself, and that evil expresses itself in man's essential being. This conviction diminishes the existentialist aspect of Kipling's notion of self and replaces it with a double dose of original sin—perhaps in unconscious tribute to his double dose of Methodist ancestry.

"At the End of the Passage" can very easily be read in a way that locates it in limbo. The description in the opening paragraph supports the idea, and the epigraph is explicit:

> The sky is lead and our faces are red,
> And the gates of Hell are opened and riven,
> And the winds of Hell are loosened and driven, . . .

But there are other pointers. Mottram's tinkling on the piano turns into the evening hymn:

> "Sunday," said he, nodding his head.
> "Go on. Don't apologise for it," said Spurstow.
> Hummil laughed long and riotously: "Play it, by all means. You're full of surprises to-day. I didn't know you had such a gift of finished sarcasm."

The others object to Hummil's continued bitter disparagement ("You miss the note of gratitude"; "It ought to go to the 'Grasshopper's Polka'") and launch into a sentimental defense of the hymn as evoking "the most sacred recollections":

> "Summer evenings in the country,—stained-glass window,—light going out, and you and she jamming your hands together over one hymn-book," said Mottram.
> "Yes and a fat old cockchafer hitting you in the eye when you walked home. Smell of hay, and a moon as big as a bandbox sitting on the top of a haycock; bats—roses,—milk and midges," said Lowndes.
> "Also mothers . . ." said Spurstow.
> The darkness had fallen on the room. They could hear Hummil squirming in his chair.

That "darkness had fallen on the room" is worthy of Conrad. Hummil accentuates the gloom *and* gives it a more—and, indeed, curiously—precise spiritual location: "'Consequently,' said he testily, 'you sing it when you are seven fathom deep in Hell! It's an insult to the Deity to pretend we're anything but tortured rebels.'" That last is a surprise: in no way, metaphorical or any other, are they rebels, within the given terms of their setting; only in the context of man's rebelling against God's edict and being cast into hell because of the evil in his nature does it make sense. And though it surprises us, that is perhaps a criticism of our inattentiveness to what has gone before.

A few pages earlier, in a quite dense sentence,

Kipling has unobtrusively prepared the ground: "The piano was indeed hopelessly out of order but Mottram managed to bring the rebellious notes into a sort of agreement, and there rose from the ragged keyboard something that might once have been the ghost of a popular music-hall song."

"At the End of the Passage" is not wholly consistent in its quality, but Kipling shows that he can write with real power and possesses a somber vision that penetrates far below the imperial symbol he uses as a vehicle.

A considerable number of Kipling's stories have hell as their setting, some notably good ones, such as the much later "Uncovenanted Mercies" (1932); and there are others where it is offered as a clear analogue. In "At the End of the Passage," hell is an option and is well defined as such.

In "The Strange Ride of Morrowbie Jukes" (1888), hell is there, though less explicitly. This story again raises the specter of a realm of disorder and anarchy lying just under man's civilized feet. If it is true that the tale derives a good deal from Edgar Allan Poe, it does so via Robert Louis Stevenson, since it is for the most part written with a pace, concentration, and economy typical of the latter. But I see no real reason to assume either mentor, for, as must now be clear, the subject is one that nearly obsessed Kipling.

Jukes—yet another engineer, "with a head for plans and distances and things of that kind"—recovering from an attack of fever, sets out on a wild ride on horseback to silence the dogs that have been baying all night under a full moon. His horse "went forward like a thing possessed," far beyond the dogs, into what seems like uncharted desert, until, cresting a sharp rise, horse and rider find themselves rolling down a steep slope on the other side. Quite literally they have fallen into a pit—or perhaps the Pit. So steep and sandy are the sides that attempts to clamber up to the top fail. We are carefully told that the angle of the slope is about sixty-five degrees, and the sand wall about thirty-five feet high; for Jukes is an engineer and his world is symbolized by just such mathematical order. But the pit is not unpopulated; far from it. Hindu ritual, we are told, requires that when a corpse, on its way to cremation at the burning ghâts, revives from what proves to be not death but merely deep trance or catalepsy, it is not considered proper to return the man or woman to society. Such individuals are secretly transported to such a place as the pit." If you die at home," says Gunga Dass," and do not die when you come to the ghât to be burnt, you come here." One side of the pit opens to the river, but when Jukes seeks to find a way out of the trap in that direction he is fired on from a boat that is anchored in midstream to prevent escapes.

The people who emerge from the caves and holes in the sand wall are filthy and repellent. But what shakes Juke seriously is their reaction to him. He approaches the crowd with all the confidence of a sahib "accustomed to a certain amount of civility from my inferiors," as he unselfconsciously puts it. What actually happens is that they laugh at him; in fact rather more than that: "They cackled, yelled, whistled, and howled as I walked into their midst; some of them literally throwing themselves down on the ground in convulsions of unholy mirth." Kipling properly refrains from anything more explicit, but the reason for this laughter is as obvious to us as it clearly was to the shaken Jukes: a sahib, one of the lords of creation, has been reduced to the same level as themselves. The allusion is expanded when he engages Gunga Dass, whom by chance he had once known when the latter was in charge of a telegraph office, in conversation. Jukes still attempts to invoke the order of the world he has just left: "I turned towards the miserable figure and ordered him to show me some method of escaping from the crater."

Just how much the subject of the story is, in truth, the ever-present threat of the moral anarchy that Kipling sees as the essential character of nature is well established by the detail—some of it extremely subtle—in depicting Jukes's dependence on an ordered universe and in emphasizing its utter absence here. As Dass talks, Jukes is already roughing out in his mind a plan of escape: "He, however, divined my unspoken thought almost as soon as it was formed; and, to my intense astonishment, gave vent to a long low chuckle of derision—the laughter, be it understood, of a superior or at least of an equal." Jukes's character (and those of his kind) is well caught in the phrase "to my intense astonishment" and in the amazed repetition of "laughter." That a native should actually be laughing at him is almost literally world-shattering. (Kipling is by no means uniformly successful in separating himself from his first-person narrator, but here he does so wholly.) In Jukes's very next sentence he notes parenthetically that the word "sir" has disappeared from Dass's vocabulary in his near-contemptuous dismissal of Jukes's escape plans.

A "nameless terror" seizes Jukes, and he rushes blindly and vainly at the sand walls, finally collapsing by the well. There the complete disregard of the other prisoners is made strikingly manifest in all its humiliation: "Two or three men trod on my panting body as they drew water, but they were evidently used to this sort of thing, and had no time to waste upon me." The literal and moral degradation so graphically and yet so laconically described shows Kipling the short-story writer at his most effective. It is well supported in the deft touch that follows.

Jukes realizes he will starve unless he sinks his pride to some degree and gets Dass to help him. What this means in terms of the dangers to his own status and moral integrity is made clear in the sentence "being only a man after all, I felt hungry, and intimated as much to Gunga Dass *whom I had begun to regard as my natural protector.*" Not only the phrase I have italicized, but its predecessor, "being only a man, after all," show Kipling working apparently effortlessly and impersonally, deep within the organic structure of his tale. He continues in this brilliant vein: "Following the impulse of the outer world when dealing with natives, I put my hand into my pocket and drew out four annas. The absurdity of the gift struck me at once." Jukes's accustomed universe has become the *outer* world, and its practices come to be seen as nothing less than absurd when viewed from his new perspective. What makes deftness into something very like genius, however, is what immediately follows. Gunga Dass, resident in the pit for two and a half years, virtually grabs the money.

I have already alluded to Kipling's strong visual sense. Here that sense is evident as the tattered, degraded Dass—he is as conscious of once having been a Brahmin as Jukes is of having been a sahib—long cast out from a world in which money has meaning, greedily snatches at it just the same. The futility of the damned in their hell, quarreling over money, is a vivid, powerful indictment, not just of Gunga Dass, but of man's ineradicably corrupt nature. "Gunga Dass clutched the coins and hid them at once in his ragged loin-cloth, his expression changing to something diabolical, as he looked round to assure himself that no one had observed us."

The nature of the world into which Jukes has entered—the true reality, perhaps, beneath the illusions of the world he has just left—is made still more explicit in the reflection, after he has surrendered all his money, that "one does not protest against the vagaries of a den of wild beasts; and my companions were lower than wild beasts." While he eats, his difficulty in coming to terms with his new status asserts itself again as he notes that the people around him "showed not the faintest sign of curiosity—that curiosity which is so rampant, as a rule, in an Indian village"; and he comes near to thinking—for him—the unthinkable: "I could even fancy that they despised me." His questions to Dass get unsatisfactory answers, though they are illuminating to us. When he asks how long this "terrible village" has been in existence, he is told, significantly, "from time immemorial," and concludes naively that "it was at least a century old." (The truth is that it is as old as man's sins.) Who the "they" are who order and maintain this system, Dass cannot or will not tell him. (In passing it is worth noting the appearance of the shadowy, menacing company who seem to patrol the outer marches of man's ordered universe and convey a sense of complicity with that world of anarchy and chaos which lies beyond. "They" appear in a number of Kipling stories and poems, in a role that reminds us of a more recent poet of law and order, W. H. Auden, with whom Kipling has sometimes been compared for largely the wrong reasons.)

Jukes endures considerable torture at the hands, or rather lips, of Gunga Dass, who takes a malicious pleasure, we are told, in telling him of the hopelessness of his plight and watching him wince. When Juke asks, "And how do you live from day to day?" the answer includes the sardonic observation that "this place is like your European Heaven; there is neither marrying nor giving in marriage."

The bitter and painful lessons that Jukes has to learn are vividly illustrated in a central section of the tale that seems to stand with the best of Kipling's writings in its imaginative insight, control of narrative, and literary tact (the fine balance between suggestive reticence and explicitness). Because of the ramifications of meaning that have been implicit from the start, although we see Jukes's tendency to appreciate the predicament in terms consistent with his more limited imagination, we ourselves are all the time aware of wider perspectives being offered and of pointers to larger dimensions. Though the order he sees repudiated is still that of the sahibs, Jukes's imagery increasingly equates himself with the less-than-human world:

Here was a Sahib, a representative of the dominant race, helpless as a child and completely at the mercy of his native neighbours. In a deliberate, lazy way [Dass] set himself to torture me as a schoolboy would devote a rapturous half-hour to watching the agonies of an impaled beetle, or as a ferret in a blind burrow might glue himself comfortably to the neck of a rabbit.

And he adds, speaking more truly than he knows, "if it were possible to forejudge the conversation of the Damned on the advent of a new soul in their abode, I should say they would speak as Gunga Dass did to me throughout that long afternoon." Then, in a skillful touch so characteristic of Kipling's handling of this tale, Jukes, the rather prosaic engineer of limited imagination, compares his ensuing struggle with "the inexplicable terror" to "the overpowering nausea of the Channel passage." Jukes sees clearly enough, though, to make the important concession that "my agony was of the spirit, and infinitely more terrible."

Kipling, however, juxtaposes this half-realization with the brilliantly conceived and told entrapment of the crows. Jukes's utter absorption in what is happening speaks volumes about his predicament, and for once Kipling resists an intrusion of his own voice in order not to spoil the effect of Jukes's severe, Swiftian understatement: "I was a good deal impressed by this, to me novel method of securing food, and complimented Gunga Dass on his skill." Dass's response is consequently all the more of a jolt, especially since it is modulated in the same cool language: "'It is nothing to do,' said he. 'To-morrow you must do it for me. You are stronger than I am.'"

In fact Dass pushes his demands a little too far, and Jukes reacts by telling him that "there is nothing on earth to prevent my killing you as you sit here and taking everything you've got," which brings Jukes dangerously near Dass's level in our eyes—as it is meant to do. The parenthesis, "I thought of the two invaluable crows at the time," is excellent, not just because of the rightness of the slightly pedantic "invaluable" but because the decoy crows are precisely what value has sunk to—survival on the lowest possible terms. Thus the victim of entrapment becomes the trapper and loses all moral distinctness.

Jukes himself in his supposed retrospective view of his behavior in the pit is explicit enough to confirm Kipling's careful structuring of detail and suggestion:

At the time it did not strike me as at all strange that I, a Civil Engineer, a man of thirteen years' standing in the Service, and, I trust, an average Englishman, should thus calmly threaten murder and violence against the man who had, for a consideration it is true, taken me under his wing.

This averageness is self-evident in the way Jukes can ingenuously employ that last metaphor, despite what, for the reader at least, has been an all-too-indelible picture of the decoy crows going about their ferocious business. Jukes goes on:

I had left the world, it seemed, for centuries. I was as certain then as I am now of my own existence, that in that accursed settlement there was no law save that of the strongest; that the living dead men had thrown behind them every canon of the world which had cast them out.

The unconscious irony in "as I am now of my own existence" is another proof of the sustained level of Kipling's achievement here. Back in his world of sahibs he can now once again be certain of it, but in the pit he had seen its supports begin to crumble; and the reader, flattered by the discreet narrator into a perception more acute than the one by the pedestrian Jukes, has seen much further and has been made to recognize the fictions on which that certainty rests.

"I am not," says Jukes, "of an imaginative temperament—very few Engineers are"; and it is partly through Kipling's insistence on Jukes's limited sensibilities that he achieves some of his best effects: Jukes's plain account of the pegging out of the decoys and their appalling efficiency, for instance; or his account of the slaughter of his horse, Pornic. The killing of the sahib's horse is, of course, a gross violation of the order of things, at least as they were in the world he had come from. Dass rubs the message in: they killed the horse because it was better to eat than crow and "greatest good of greatest number is political maxim. We are now Republic, Mr. Jukes, and you are entitled to a fair share of the beast. If you like, we will pass a vote of thanks. Shall I propose?" Again our knowledge of Jukes's sensibilities as "an average Englishman" stands us in good stead. To him the death of his horse is bad enough (and his "How they had killed him I cannot guess" is far more sinisterly effective than full-blooded detail); but to be invited to eat it would be truly to signal the approaching end of the world: "Yes we were a Republic indeed! A Republic of wild beasts penned at the bottom of a pit, to eat and fight and sleep till we died." To us, with our wider sensibility heavily involved by this time, this sounds like a description of the reality of "natural nature."

Objection has on occasion been taken to the ending of the tale; but the ending seems to me quite justifiable. Abrupt it undoubtedly is, but Jukes, we know, is not one to elaborate even this incident. By ending it almost as though one has been suddenly awakened from a nightmare, Kipling sustains an option for the reader that was there from the beginning:

that all of what has transpired has been indeed a dream. Even the bland first sentence is slightly provocative, challenging our disbelief: "There is, as the conjurors say, no deception about this tale." It also leaves us slightly unsure about the reliability of the narrator. The slant of Jukes's own account makes certain that the door remains open: "In the beginning it all arose from a slight attack of fever." The sentence is quite dense in possibilities: the "in the beginning" is, in a purely narrative sense, syntactically inept or redundant. But Kipling does not make any such blunders in this story, and there is the clearest invitation to recall the opening of St. John's gospel, "In the beginning was the Word." It is typical of Kipling's at times sardonic humor to revise it to read, "In the beginning . . . [was] a slight attack of fever." Fever breeds dreams, and Jukes's feverishness is again alluded to in a sort of second opening (where we should note the date, 23 December, which means that the action takes place over Christmas Eve and Christmas Day). The association of the action of the tale with the birthday celebrations of a redeemer of sins once more offers a deeper perspective on Jukes's experience. Sahib though he is, he may still be of the damned, and in his subconscious, at least, he regards himself as such.

Jukes's "strange ride" has a proper claim to being considered among the best of Kipling's short stories: the control of the narrative's movement is unfailing; incident succeeds incident in a way admirably calculated to manipulate the intensity of the readers' reaction, and each is visualized with a clarity that imprints our eyes as surely as "the horror" recorded itself on Hummil's. So the mesmeric drama of the trapping of the crows gives way to the yet more Stevensonian discovery of the wound in the back of the corpse. At no time are we allowed to forget the moral significance of the story, however exciting the drama: indeed, the moral vision constantly interacts with the physical. There is, too, a plausibility in the behavior and expression of the characters that we readily accept just because these, too, are so organic to the tale's moral structure. When Gunga Dass admits without any remorse that he killed the first Englishman who fell into the pit, his explanation is an impressive indictment of the incorrigible vanity of man: "it is not advisable that the men who once get in here should escape. Only I, and *I* am a Brahmin."

Anyone who is tempted to think Kipling too extravagantly praised in this discussion should remember that when he wrote "The Strange Ride of Morrowbie Jukes," he was just nineteen.

All of the virtues mentioned above are present in yet another excellent early story, which again alludes to those inscrutable forces, inimical or at best indifferent to man, that seem to express the character of his universe. In this story, however, there is an ironic espousal—apparently above everything else—of all forms, conventions, and structures that help to give man's existence some semblance of order.

The story "Beyond the Pale" was first published in *Plain Tales from the Hills,* when Kipling was twenty-two. In essence it is simple enough: an Englishman, Trejago, while aimlessly wandering through the city, finds himself walking down what turns out to be something more like a cattle-pen than the urban cul-de-sac it is. Stumbling over some cattle food he hears a laugh from behind a grating. Since it was "a pretty little laugh," he goes forward and whispers a few lines from "The Love Song of Har Dyal," which are capped by the lady from behind the grating. In due course Trejago and Bisesa become lovers; but her father finds out and, in an exceptionally disagreeable fashion, puts an end to the affair.

One of the extraordinary things about the tale is its economy, an achievement that registers all the more forcefully when we begin to realize the density of meaning compressed within it.

Kipling was criticized in his own time as well as later for an apparent indifference to "good writing." Not only had he a tendency to start his sentences with a relative pronoun, but they could often be almost brutally abrupt. In fact, for all its apparent repudiation of finesse, his style is as carefully wrought in its own idiosyncratic way as was, say, Thomas Carlyle's; and so it is invariably part of the statement he is making. That statement usually starts with the opening paragraph, and "Beyond the Pale" is no exception:

A man should, whatever happens, keep to his own caste, race, and breed. Let the White go to the White and the Black to the Black. Then, whatever trouble falls is in the ordinary course of things—neither sudden, alien, nor unexpected.

But before the liberal reader shuts the book in indignation, he should note the ironic tone, the provocative all-knowing worldliness, the airy espousal of segregation as something conducive to ease of body and peace of mind.

The second paragraph—to literary purists of the

day a structure hardly worth the title—cunningly stresses one word in particular: "This is the story of a man who wilfully stepped beyond the safe limits of decent everyday society, and paid for it heavily." It is hard to read the sentence in any way that does not oblige one to put an emphasis on "wilfully" (with a secondary stress on "safe"). But with the rather swaggering assurance of the narrator still provoking us from the first paragraph, we are a little suspicious of him and what *he* might regard as willful or safe. Quite deliberately Kipling has made his narrator antagonize us, and that antagonism is reinforced in the third, "simplifying," paragraph when he, the all-knowing, criticizes the hero of his tale for knowing too much: "He knew too much in the first instance; and he saw too much in the second. He took too deep an interest in native life; but he will never do so again." The narrator's "knowingness" is applied directly to the tale in a way that is both exasperating and tantalizing: he teases us not just with our own lack of knowledge but also with our strong desire to know. "Neither Suchet Singh nor Gaur Chand approve of their women-folk looking into the world. If Durga Charan had been of their opinion he would have been a happier man to-day, and little Bisesa would have been able to knead her own bread."

After his encounter in Amir Nath's Gully, Trejago receives an object-letter from Bisesa. The components of the object-letter—a broken glass bangle, a flower of the *dhak*, some cardamom seeds, and so on—intrigue us as much as they do Trejago; but he has the knowledge to read them and understand the message he has been sent, even though "no Englishman should be able to translate object-letters." He keeps the suggested assignation, and at the appointed hour the voice behind the grating once more takes up "The Love Song of Har Dyal." The narrator's flaunting of his knowledge is at its most offensive here: "The song is really pretty in the Vernacular. In English you miss the wail of it." So Trejago embarks on a double life. By day he attends to his office work and his social duties, but at night he seeks the hidden world behind the "dead walls" and the grating. The sense of a world beyond our knowing and beyond our finding (indicated partly by the alien vocabulary that helps to describe his journey there) is very well conveyed: the love that flowers in that bare little room is more intensified and sweetened by its being so shut away, so enclosed. And it is love, though the all-knowing narrator is again made to annoy us by referring to it dismissively as "this folly." When news reaches Bisesa that Trejago has been paying particular attention to a lady of his own race—purely in the line of duty, we are given to understand—she flies into a temper, even threatening to kill herself "if Trejago did not at once drop the alien Memsahib who had come between them." Despite Trejago's rather patronizing attempt to explain "and to show that she did not understand these things from a Western standpoint," she insists on breaking off their acquaintanceship.

Trejago stays away for three weeks; then, thinking the rupture has lasted long enough, he returns to the Gully hoping that his rap on the grating will be answered. He is, we are told with heavy irony, "not disappointed":

There was a young moon, and one stream of light fell down into Amir Nath's Gully, and struck the grating which was drawn away as he knocked. From the black dark Bisesa held out her arms into the moonlight. Both hands had been cut off at the wrists, and the stumps were nearly healed.

The effectiveness of Kipling's style could hardly be better illustrated, short sentences and all. Even so, the bland understatement of the last phrase is something of a tour de force. Our lack of knowledge, which the narrator earlier teased us with, is now a little less complete: at least we now know why Bisesa is unable to knead her own bread.

Trejago does not escape unscathed. "Something sharp"—the inexplicitness of the instrument of retribution is quite deliberate—is thrust at him through the window and hits him where retribution in this case ought to—in the groin. The hint is to be added to others that Trejago's love was—far more than Holden and Ameera's in "Without Benefit of Clergy"—compromised by an element of sexual adventuring. It confirms the suspicion raised by Trejago's remark that Bisesa did not understand these things "from a Western standpoint"; and it also allows Kipling one of his most laconic concluding sentences, presented in the syntactical form that so annoyed the guardians of literary propriety:

But Trejago pays his calls regularly, and is reckoned a very decent sort of man.
There is nothing peculiar about him, except a slight stiffness, caused by a riding-strain, in the right leg.

Of more importance, however, are these sentences, immediately preceding:

One special feature of the case is that he does not know where lies the front of Durga Charan's house. It may open on to a courtyard common to two or more houses, or it may lie behind any one of the gates of Jitha Megji's *bustee*. Trejago cannot tell. He cannot get Bisesa—poor little Bisesa—back again. He has lost her in the City where each man's house is as guarded and as unknowable as the grave; and the grating that opens into Amir Nath's Gully has been walled up.

The way that the word "knowledge" or one of its variants is made to echo through this very brief story is masterly. Of course it is a means of enhancing that tightness of organization on which the whole effect really depends, but it also keeps before us with no sense of contrivance the story's deeper moral implications. Trejago's knowledge crossed several borders and so encroached on the wild and the strange that lies on either side "of that well-ordered road we tread." Such an experience is morally shattering, and the anarchy that is the reality of "natural nature" cannot be warded off. In this light the equally knowing narrator is a sardonic young Mephistopheles. He *has* that knowledge, gained presumably by losing himself, as the epigraph has it, and in a worldly-wise manner he lectures those who will come after him against such folly. But he knows, too, that men will go on behaving foolishly, because they will always set love beyond safety, prompted at least partly by what Milton referred to as the twitching of an impetuous nerve. And they will consequently always risk losing themselves as Trejago does with Bisesa, "ignorant as a bird," whose "lisping attempts" to pronounce his name so amused Trejago: "The first syllable was always more than she could manage, and she made funny little gestures with her rose-leaf hands, as one throwing the name away."

It is important to stress that Kipling is *not* writing against an interracial love affair: to reduce it to the crass message that this is what happens to men of imperial blood who dabble with natives is a serious, though not uncommon, misreading. It is in fact about the anarchy and horror of nature and about the sanctity of well-established forms, conventions, and structures, since they are the only bulwark against the former. The self is a fragile, vulnerable, even illusory entity, and without observance of forms it cannot be sustained. Kipling was only taking a little further something that Carlyle, so much the mentor of his age, had written years before: "Formulas? There is no mortal extant, out of the depths of Bedlam, but lives all skinned, thatched, covered with Formulas; and is, as it were, held in from delirium and the Inane by his Formulas."

"Beyond the Pale" rarely gets a place in a Kipling anthology despite all the virtuosity it displays, including its exceptionally adroit manipulation of ironic tone and its innovations vis-à-vis the role of the unreliable narrator, who first offends us and then, once we are hooked, convinces us that those of limited knowledge are the more fortunate.

Another story on a similar theme, "Without Benefit of Clergy," is usually included. Of all Kipling's early stories, this is probably the bleakest. When Holden's butler tries to comfort him after his double bereavement with the words "Moreover the shadows come and go, *sahib*; the shadows come and go," there is no lightening of the gloom for his master; and rightly, for no such equilibrium has been established in the tale. More accurate a summary is Holden's despairing, helpless cry as he rides away from the bungalow that had housed his wife and child and his happiness: "Oh you brute! You utter brute!" It is a cry directed at that hostile nature utterly without order or sympathy or anything that can be appealed to. In no little way it reminds us of Kurtz's last words in *Heart of Darkness*, "The horror! The horror," though its metaphysical pretensions are slighter and its human reality all the greater.

In fact the whole story is about the insignificance of man and the (at best) indifference of his universe toward him. The opening is tightly focused and profoundly personal. Two human beings are discussing in the seclusion of their home that momentous thing, a new birth: "But if it be a girl?" The conclusion, however, is utter desolation: "It shall be pulled down, and the Municipality shall make a road across, as they desire, from the burning ghaut to the city wall, so that no man may say where this house stood." The focus is now broader; man's life is symbolized by the road that leads from the city of his toil to the place where his body will be cremated.

From the start there is an overpowering sense of anxiety and of doom, and from the start the most strenuous efforts are made to seek some avenue of communication with the Powers that rule men's lives in order to propitiate them. But the anxiety is also in the cause of love and relationship, for Ameera finds it hard to accept Holden's protestations of his enduring love for her. Not only do they challenge the gods to do their worst in the "normal" way—by destroying their child—but they presume to sustain an enduring bond across two cultures. Thus, Ameera's confidence that her prayers and her offerings at Sheikh Badl's shrine will ensure them a son paradoxically fills us with apprehension.

Kipling is at his best in suggesting the borderline on which the couple is living. Before Holden leaves for a fortnight's special duty elsewhere—directed there precisely at the time when his child's birth is due—he writes a telegraph message and bids his watchman to send it to him under certain circumstances. All the time he is away, Holden is in hourly dread of receiving the telegram, for it is not notice of whether the child is a boy or girl, but rather notice of his wife's death.

Ameera does not die, however, and Holden on his return finds he has a son. Crossing the threshold of Ameera's room, he steps on a dagger laid on it to avert bad luck. The dagger breaks, and Ameera takes the incident as a hopeful sign: "God is great. . . . Thou hast taken his misfortunes on thy head." Solemnly she assures Holden that their son is "of the Faith" and doubly blessed by being born on a Friday.

When Holden leaves he is stopped by the watchman, who hands him a sword and asks him to kill the two goats he had tethered—"otherwise, the child being unguarded from fate may die." Holden, who knows the necessary Mohammaden prayer for the sacrifice, recites it and kills the goats. The effect of all this ritual and propitiation is, however, to diminish the reader's confidence.

When we next meet Holden and Ameera they are taking their son outside for the first time, onto the flat roof of their house, to count the stars, says Ameera, "for that is auspicious." She observes the correct ritual for such an occasion, wearing her best jewelry and dressing in green. The presence of the caged green parrot—"a sort of guardian-spirit in most native households"—gives them the idea of calling the baby Tota, a word for parrot in Ameera's language. Their utter peace, security, and secluded happiness are described in one of Kipling's highly visualized set pieces:

The two sleek, white well-bullocks in the courtyard were steadily chewing the cud of their evening meal; old Pir Khan squatted at the head of Holden's horse, his police sabre across his knees, pulling drowsily at a big water-pipe that croaked like a bull-frog in a pond. Ameera's mother sat spinning in the lower verandah, and the wooden gate was shut and barred. The music of a marriage-procession came to the roof above the gentle hum of the city, and a string of flying-foxes crossed the face of the low moon.

Ameera breaks the silence by telling Holden that she has prayed both to the Prophet and to the Virgin Mary. "Will my prayers be heard?" she asks Holden. "How can I say? God is very good." Throughout these exchanges there runs Ameera's bitter consciousness of the two cultures, and she speaks "almost savagely" of the Englishwomen, one of whom, she fears, will supplant her. So Kipling with unwonted tenderness shows both the acute fearfulness of the two for their baby and the ever-present cultural barrier that also threatens their security despite the profundity of their love.

Ameera continues to invoke charms for Tota, and one of his first possessions is a silver belt "with a magic square." But, as we have come gradually to suspect, it is all to no avail. Sheikh Badl, the Prophet, the Virgin Mary, the guardian-spirit are all deaf, and Tota dies. He dies, we are told carefully, as the result not of some cataclysmic event but of "the seasonal autumn fever," and the ordinariness of his sickness not only increases the poignancy but also illustrates just how much this family—and mankind—are at the mercy of their pitiless environment.

Kipling writes well of Holden's pain in the aftermath of his son's death; of his inability to declare his sorrow; and of the unfeeling nature of events when he is forced to watch the children of others at the bandstand. At night he now returns to Ameera to go through again "the hell of self-questioning reproach which is reserved for those who have lost a child." But even now Ameera from time to time sees, and refers to, Holden as an alien, though only to correct herself in an excess of self-reproach. Nonetheless the fragility of their relationship, together with the baleful power of a hostile nature, is at once reasserted. Gradually they "touched happiness again, but this time with caution":

"It was because we loved Tota that he died. The jealousy of God was upon us," said Ameera. "I have hung up a large black jar before our window to turn the evil eye from us, and we must make no protestations of delight, but go softly underneath the stars, lest God find us out."

Once again there is attempted propitiation of these jealous and harsh gods, mixed with a recourse to folk magic. Now they hope that "the Powers" will hear their disclaimers of delight and joy in each other. Predictably, however, "the Powers were busy on other things." Famine is followed by pestilence, and "Nature began to audit her accounts with a red pencil":

Then came the cholera from all four quarters of the compass. It struck a pilgrim-gathering of half a million at a sacred shrine. Many died at the feet of their god; the others broke and ran over the face of the land carrying the pestilence with them. It smote a walled city and killed two hundred a day. The people crowded the trains, hanging on to the footboards and squatting on the roofs of the carriages, and the cholera followed them, for at each station they dragged out the dead and the dying. They died by the roadside, and the horses of the Englishmen shied at the corpses in the grass. The rains did not come, and the earth turned to iron lest man should escape death by hiding in her.

Death (always a preoccupation with Kipling) is almost visible in this description as it mows down all before it with irresistible violence. Once again destructive nature seems to be the only reality: pilgrimages, shrines, and all the paraphernalia of religion seem nothing more than a mockery of the devout.

The Englishmen, before entering the war against the rebellion, send their women to the relative safety of the hills. Holden, "sick with fear of losing his chiefest treasure on earth," does his best to persuade Ameera to go away too. Sadly, it is Ameera's consciousness of her "foreignness," declaring itself in her jealousy of the Englishwomen, that makes her refuse all his entreaties. They are going, therefore she will stay; her love for Holden is of a different, higher quality than the love of Englishwomen for their husbands.

There are not many happinesses so complete as those that are snatched under the shadow of the sword. They sat together and laughed, calling each other openly by every pet name that could move the wrath of the gods. The city below them was locked up in its own torments. Sulphur fires blazed in the streets; the conches in the Hindu temples screamed and bellowed, for the gods were inattentive in those days. There was a service in the great Mahomedan shrine, and the call to prayer from the minarets was almost unceasing. They heard the wailing in the houses of the dead, and once the shriek of a mother who had lost a child and was calling for its return. In the gray dawn they saw the dead borne out through the city gates, each litter with its own little knot of mourners. Wherefore they kissed each other and shivered.

The administrative machine of the raj gets rapidly into full gear to deal with the emergency: gaps are made in its ranks, too, and quickly filled. Holden is about to be drafted to fill such a gap when news reaches him that Ameera is dying. The scene in which Holden enters Ameera's room, the one where Tota had been born, is remarkably powerful and effective. It is both tense and subtly poignant:

She made no sign when Holden entered, because the human soul is a very lonely thing and, when it is getting ready to go away, hides itself in a misty borderland where the living may not follow. The black cholera does its work quietly and without explanation. Ameera was being thrust out of life as though the Angel of Death had himself put his hand upon her. The quick breathing seemed to show that she was either afraid or in pain, but neither eyes nor mouth gave any answer to Holden's kisses. There was nothing to be said or done. Holden could only wait and suffer. The first drops of the rain began to fall on the roof, and he could hear shouts of joy in the parched city.

Not for the first time in this story are we aware of what might be called, without disparagement, its operatic strength: emotion is manipulated in an almost formal way so that its modulations seem to transcend language. Words are superfluous as Holden, forgetful of himself, kisses Ameera on the lips, while the growing patter of rain on the roofs and the joyful cries of the populace herald the end of the epidemic. Even now, when Ameera manages a few last words, they betray her anxiety about her claim on Holden's love in the face of what she sees now—as she has all along—the inevitable triumph of her white rivals.

Three days later Holden receives orders to replace a dying colleague and goes to take a last look at his house, now decayed after the torrential rains:

He found that the rains had torn down the mud pillars of the gateway, and the heavy wooden gate that had guarded his life hung lazily from one hinge. There was grass three inches high in the courtyard; Pir Khan's lodge was empty, and the sodden thatch sagged between the beams. A gray squirrel was in possession of the verandah, as if the house had been untenanted for thirty years instead of three days. . . . Ameera's room and the other one where Tota had lived were heavy with mildew; and the narrow staircase leading to the roof was streaked and stained with rain-borne mud.

It is already as though neither they nor their great love had ever existed. But what also disappears with the house, with Ameera and Tota, and the fragile, beautiful bond between the three, is any faith in a God or gods; or indeed in any order in nature. Man is on his own; and Ameera's last words bear stark testimony to the discovery: "'I bear witness—I bear witness'—the lips were forming the words on his ear—'that there is no God but—thee, beloved!'"

Kipling repeats the first phrase for a reason; the repudiation is made all the more harsh and complete by commencing with the formal Moslem statement of faith but substituting, at the end, Holden for Allah. The gods have failed them, and the only salvation is devotion to each other and to the job in hand: to that work, so often just routine, which Holden is driven to immerse himself in after Tota's death and which "repaid him by filling up his mind for nine or ten hours a day."

The title, "Without Benefit of Clergy," refers, of course, to the illicit union of Holden and Ameera, though in no censorious mood. But the words have, or had, another sense, alluding to the law of "benefit of clergy," which allowed the clergy dispensation from prosecution through civil courts. Taken in this sense, it means that there is no dispensation from the common hard fate of mankind for these two lovers, be their love ever so profound, noble, and unselfish.

### III

THE five stories we have discussed show first that Kipling was concerned with the world of "natural nature," and convinced that disorder and not order is the true inclination of his universe. He was as aware as Conrad that anarchy can be held at bay only by the forceful imposition of, and loyal submission to, conventions, codes, and rituals: structures, in other words, that the mind of man must devise for his own protection. Second, they show something of Kipling's characteristic abilities as a writer, and reveal him as a master of the short-story form. Third, they are interesting for their settings, as is *Kim*, which many would place in the first rank of all his writing. One of the five short stories is about the sea, where it serves in a Conradian way as an image of the moral anarchy of the world. The rest of the selections are set in India, and the juxtaposition highlights the fact that the vast subcontinent comes to have precisely the same symbolic function. With this in mind, I would argue strongly that India provides Kipling with his ideal metaphor: the vehicle through which he can best express his essential artistic, rather than political, vision.

The main character in his Indian stories is not the tired, tough administrator, the resourceful subaltern, the resilient Other Ranks, or the ever-present engineer, but India itself. Indeed this has been established in four of the five stories we have considered. "At the End of the Passage" shows four men engaged in a relentless battle against their natural environment—India. With total commitment they throw themselves into the daily routine of work, striving to tame a tiny area of the vast space that continually threatens to engulf them, while preventing the surrounding anarchy from penetrating their own fragile integrity. In this story, however, as in many of the others, there is a whisper that anarchy may already be there, planted perhaps in original sin.

As the pattern is repeated, India comes increasingly to serve as an immensely powerful symbol of the "natural nature" that is so central a component in Kipling's moral and artistic vision: the exact equivalent of Russell's crust of barely cooled lava with the flames of destruction raging underneath. Vast and featureless, it is the enemy of form: "Great, grey formless India," as it is called in *Kim*, overwhelms and crushes, both physically and morally. One's own truths and moral definitions blur and diffuse themselves into meaninglessness, just as they did for E. M. Forster's Mrs. Moore in *A Passage to India* (1924). A character who appears in a number of early Kipling stories, Mrs. Mallowe, has, in fact, occasional flashes of Mrs. Moore's perception, observing very clearly the moral destructiveness of India, where, as she says in "The Education of Otis Yeere," "you can't focus anything." Because it is Kipling, and not Forster, we are inside India looking outward through our bars, rather than outside looking in with Mrs. Moore's cool clarity of mind.

Faced by a country that can destroy them, these beleaguered Anglo-Indians band together in pitiful, blind opposition, doomed to ludicrous failure, however much they speak of Smith as a Bengal man and Jones as a Punjabi. Herded together in the Club, in the Station, in Simla, they insist upon their "difference" from the rest of India; but even in the safety of their own community, they cannot escape the constant awareness of their vulnerability:

Everybody was there, and there was a general closing up of ranks and taking stock of our losses in dead or disabled that had fallen during the past year. It was a very wet night, and I remember that we sang "Auld Lang Syne" with our feet in the Polo Championship Cup, and our heads among the stars, and swore that we were all very dear friends.
("The Mark of the Beast")

It is in the isolated outposts that India's malignant power is to be seen at its most active in its relentless war against the aliens.

> The night-light was trimmed; the shadow of the punkah wavered across the room, and the *"flick"* of the punkah-towel and the soft whine of the rope through the wall-hole followed it. Then the punkah flagged, almost ceased. The sweat poured from Spurstow's brow. Should he go out and harangue the coolie? It started forward again with a savage jerk, and a pin came out of the towels. When this was replaced, a tomtom in the coolie-lines began to beat with the steady throb of a swollen artery inside some brain-fevered skull.
>
> ("At the End of the Passage")

Bound on his wheel, the imperial servant struggles to reduce the hostile mass of India to governable terms, more often than not ending up as "one of the rank and file who are ground up in the wheels of the Administration; losing heart and soul, and mind and strength in the process."

Always the good these expatriates do is seen, by themselves at least, to be short-term: the bringing of some sort of law and order, the relief of famine, the improvement of agriculture, and so on. Surprisingly they show little inclination to speculate about theirs being an enduring contribution and none at all to preach the notion of a thousand-year Reich. In "The Education of Otis Yeere," for example, Mrs. Mallowe has no illusions: "We are only little bits of dirt on the hillsides—here one day and blown down the *khud* the next. . . . we have no cohesion." The raj may seek to impose its institutions on this body and domesticate it, but even they are not proof against India's inexorable power of assimilation. British justice itself is on occasion eroded, as we see in "Gemini," to the level of a useful new pawn in a very old game.

The Pax Britannica had already sowed the seeds of its own destruction:

> said Wali Dad . . . "Thanks to your Government, all our heads are protected, and with the educational facilities at my command"—his eyes twinkled wickedly—"I might be a distinguished member of the local administration. Perhaps, in time, I might even be a member of a Legislative Council."

In this story, "On the City Wall" (1898), even the narrator is, quite brilliantly, shown to be unwittingly taken over (and made a fool of) by India. The collision between the old order and the new is again well illustrated. Wali Dad—who had made "an unsuccessful attempt to enter the Roman Church and the Presbyterian fold at the same time" and been found out by the missionaries who had "called him names . . . but . . . did not understand his trouble"—presents the most complete picture of what has happened in this collision to people like him:

> "India has gossiped for centuries—always standing in the bazars until the soldiers go by. Therefore—you are here to-day instead of starving in your own country, and I am not a Muhammadan—I am a Product—a Demnition Product. That also I owe to you and yours: that I cannot make an end to my sentence without quoting from your authors."

Exhorted to take up his "place in the world," he becomes even more ironic:

> "I might wear an English coat and trouser. I might be a leading Muhammadan pleader. I might be received even at the Commissioner's tennis-parties where the English stand on one side and the natives on the other, in order to promote social intercourse throughout the Empire."

The mordant edge to his critique is worthy of Forster's Dr. Aziz and serves as a reminder of the famous bridge party in *A Passage to India*.

In this discussion of the role of India, however, one acknowledgment is missing: to the fascination that India continued to exert while crushing and annihilating its servants. Mrs. Mallowe sees clearly enough the bars of the cage: "I don't suppose a Russian convict under the knout is able to amuse the rest of his gang; and all our men-folk here are gilded convicts."

Outside Simla, more often than not, there was not even the gilding. Yet the color and seething abundance of life with which their enemy veiled its malevolence could still attract, quite apart from the fact that, so much having been absorbed by it, the colonials could no longer have an independent existence.

Kipling reflects the fascination in many places, but nowhere more so than in the brilliantly colored pictures in *Kim*.

### IV

So far it has been the object of this essay to show how India served Kipling less as an imperial shibboleth than as a token of the anarchy of "natural nature," which was, for him, the ultimate reality. What is above all striking in *Kim* is that here Kipling for the first and only time succeeds in painting a picture of a moral universe that is balanced.

Kipling's best stories are very often those that draw their power from his awareness of the chaos and anarchy that underlie the apparently solid world in which his characters move. Indeed, the Indian empire, far from being treated as substantial and permanently enduring, is shown to be valued simply because it offers a very clear structure through which "natural nature" will be bitted and bridled and a sufficiency of order imposed for the individual to secure some sort of integrity for himself. The vast body and power of India come to stand for this anarchy, and the Anglo-Indian's struggle with India, in the form of its famines, plagues, climate, size, becomes a paradigm of man's constant struggle to retain his integrity and identity in a world where he has no natural (or supernatural) ally: where, to the contrary, he is constantly persecuted and threatened with physical and moral extinction.

To ward off this outcome, the Kipling hero is a dedicated activist, for only in constantly grappling with his enemy will he gain any sense of his own reality. So the Kipling protagonist, often quite literally a builder or engineer, toils wearily on, frequently dying in his tracks but at least having secured self-consciousness for himself in the moment of his activity. Action is seen as the antidote to anarchy, and the man of action as the hero on the side of order against cosmic disorder; those who adopt a passive mode of conduct are seen as fifth-columnists and saboteurs and are denounced by Kipling in vitriolic, at times hysterical, terms.

In *Kim*, however, we find none of this neurotic polarization; and the way in which the lama, who stands for a renunciation of action and the world, is balanced by Kim and Mahbub Ali, with their respective degrees of commitment to the activist ethic, is the best thing of its kind Kipling ever did. For the first time we find in his writing evidence of a generous magnanimity, which ordinarily he is much too fearful for his own soul to indulge in.

The book is framed by Kim and the lama. It opens with Kim sitting outside the Lahore Museum astride the gun Zam-Zammah, and it closes with the lama sitting like Buddha, his quest apparently concluded. This antithesis of activist and quietist principles illustrates a structural pattern in the work that is one of Kipling's principal methods for reinforcing its unity. In the same way, youth is balanced against age, secular against spiritual, individual against communal. Cross-references are continual, and taken together they give the book a firm intellectual shape and a compelling aesthetic symmetry.

The lama's search is the one that overarches the whole design: even Kim's is dwarfed by it, and rightly so, for the significance of Kim's search lies precisely in the fact that it remains firmly committed to life on earth, in sharp contrast to the lama's, which is from the start transcendental. As a result, Kipling is able to move easily between the material and spiritual dimensions and so make a serious comment about the meaning of life without seeming too didactic.

For those who adhere to the lama's form of Buddhism, suffering and misery stem from being bound in the perpetual cycle of life, death, and rebirth. Men are condemned to this cycle by their attachment to earthly desires and ambitions; were they able to break free from these fetters they would successfully interrupt the cycle of reincarnation and reach Nirvana, that blisssful union with the Great Soul which releases them from all suffering and reasserts the oneness of all created beings. It is this cycle the lama refers to when he talks about the Wheel of Life. Those who recognize their predicament and seek to extricate themselves from it by renouncing all earthly interests and following the Buddhist law are described as followers of the Way, and among these, of course, is the lama himself. His objective is the River that was released from the earth at that place where the arrow shot by Buddha landed. The symbolism is clear: the River will wash away sin and mark the final release for this faithful devotee of the Way from the torment of the Wheel.

The Wheel becomes the single most important and pervasive image in the book. In functioning as a symbol, it links everyone and everything in the endlessness of its form. And it emphasizes what the narrative tells us explicitly: that all men are ultimately the same, nursing the same hopes and ambitions and enduring the same fate. When the lama tells the English curator of the Lahore Museum the story of the arrow and the River, the curator acknowledges that "so it is written." But we are told that he replies "sadly." He knows the tale, and his sadness sums up all men's need for this River and the consciousness that it may never come within their reach.

The Wheel of Life is an abstraction, of course, but at the end of the discussion the lama departs, brushing through the turnstile. The effect of Kipling's deft juxtaposition of the abstraction with its concrete prototype (for the turnstile is basically a wheel) is to plant the symbol firmly in the world of men.

The physical world, it is thus made clear, will certainly not be lightly dismissed, for it has a robust argument of its own to put against the lama's asceticism. By linking the Wheel of Life with the turnstile, Kipling might at first seem to be endorsing the lamaistic view of human life on earth as that of an endless, miserable chain gang, groaning under its doom. But the turnstile can also click away merrily, reflecting something of the noise, bustle, and excitement of life: the same sort of bustle and vitality that we encounter among the innumerable wheels of the Grand Trunk Road. At times, indeed, the whole Indian landscape seems to be alive with the creaking sound of well wheels, cart wheels, train wheels. And all are helping man in that activity which Kim's excited and affectionate vision convinces us has great value. In fact Kim's own health is described in terms of a wheel. When he falls ill in chapter 15, he feels that his soul is "out of gear with its surroundings—a cog-wheel unconnected with any machinery." And his return to health is signified when he feels "the wheels of his being lock up anew on the world without."

On the other hand, once seen from the lama's exalted perspective, human activity is never likely to be viewed uncritically, or unthinkingly given absolute value. Also, near the end of the book Kipling focuses the antithesis between these two states or standpoints with great imaginative force, finely contrasting a transcendent and ageless spiritual reality in which all things find themselves in an ideal unity, and the restless flux of an earth-bound, wheel-bound humanity. The delicate, lemon-colored background throws the figure of Buddha into heavy relief, infusing into it a solid reality that reflects the assurance of the lama's faith: "[Kim] peered at the cross-legged figure, outlined jet-black against the lemon-coloured drift of light. So does the stone Bodhisat sit who looks down upon the patent self-registering turnstiles of the Lahore Museum" (ch. 15). So Kipling sympathetically balances a recognition of the vanity of man's earthly ambitions and activity with a sense of life's rich possibilities within its given limits—and symbolizes both with the Wheel.

Kim's nickname, "Little Friend of All the World" —perhaps it sounds less embarrassing in Urdu— clearly identifies him with the idea of human community, and his ready command of vernacular speech and proverbial wisdom, to say nothing of his intimate knowledge of native customs and even native secrets, greatly strengthens the association. Later, when he sets out on his own search along with the lama, he is more than a little inclined to forget all about it in the sheer pleasure of participating in the life going on around him. Given that Kim's physical being remains rather shadowy, the reader is oddly responsive to his sensations. As a result, the countryside and its people have vitality and clarity as well as richness of color, as if the whole world were new. Once more, through his skillful manipulation of perspective, Kipling makes us aware that if Kim is young, India is very, very old: the possessor of a vast history casts a light on man's absurd conceits, as, for example, when man sits astride the spoils of his latest, ephemeral, conquest.

Several of the elements of Kim's love for the life that surrounds him appear in an example of Kipling's excellent description:

The diamond-bright dawn woke men and crows and bullocks together. Kim sat up and yawned, shook himself, and thrilled with delight. This was seeing the world in real truth; this was life as he would have it—bustling and shouting, the buckling of belts, and beating of bullocks and creaking of wheels, lighting of fires and cooking of food, and new sights at every turn of the approving eye. The morning mist swept off in a whorl of silver, the parrots shot away to some distant river in shrieking green hosts: all the well-wheels within earshot went to work. India was awake, and Kim was in the middle of it, more awake and more excited than any one, chewing on a twig that he would presently use as a tooth-brush; for he borrowed right- and left-handedly from all the customs of the country he knew and loved.

(ch. 4)

The lama's search, as I have said, is for the mystical River that gushed out of the earth at the precise spot where the arrow shot by Buddha himself had landed. It is by no means fanciful to discern another parallel here between Kim and the lama, for wherever Kim's glance falls, a river of life springs up. Indeed it is precisely the phrase he thinks of when he first sets foot on the Grand Trunk Road: "The lama, as usual, was deep in meditation, but Kim's bright eyes were open wide. This broad, smiling river of life, he considered, was a vast improvement on the cramped and crowded Lahore streets" (ch. 4). And since what is reality for Kim is also reality for those who embrace an activist creed, it is appropriate that the old Rissaldar should take the same view of "the Great Road which is the back-bone of all Hind": "All castes and kinds of men move here. Look! Brahmins and chumars, bankers and tinkers, barbers and bunnias, pilgrims and potters—all the world going and coming. It is to me as a river from which I am withdrawn like a log after a flood" (ch. 3).

Now we have another river, which is opposed to the mystical River of the lama's search; and another wheel, opposed to the lama's Wheel. In the first of these three quotations, Kipling seems to go out of his way to mention wheels that are altogether mundane. The purpose is clear: the world where this wheel revolves is the workaday world where men live and where action seems to have an intrinsic value every bit as justifiable as renunciation.

One major symbol remains to be considered, that of the Great Game. The Great Game is the rather arch euphemism that Colonel Creighton and Mahbub Ali use to describe their work for military intelligence. In this role they are the vigilantes of empire, omnisciently aware of all that might threaten its security from either outside its borders or within them, and consequently ready to move at once to checkmate any advance by the enemies of law and order. Kim, with his knowledge of the country and its people, and his quick wits, is a natural recruit and is duly inducted into the Game, though with more ambivalence in his attitude to it than he is usually given credit for.

The significance of the Great Game goes beyond the limits of military intelligence, however, for it is an emblem of the deadly serious game that Kipling played all his life to secure a personal identity and integrity. In *Kim* as elsewhere in his writings, India is a metaphor for the artifact of the individual self; an entity that, as we have seen, is perpetually threatened and at risk. So these vigilantes who participate in the Great Game are certainly guarding the political structure of the Indian empire (in particular, the threat from Russian subversion, even invasion, was regarded as a real one), but they are also, once more, acting the roles of guardians of a moral structure.

From my own critical viewpoint, the intrusion of the Great Game nearly brings disaster with it. One recovers, of course, for all the other very good things in the novel are still there at the end; but one's confidence in the writer has been shaken and an element of suspicion and resentment at the damage done to such an imaginative, potentially triumphant work is also, alas, still there. To account for the harm done to the book by the Great Game, it is necessary to recapitulate a little.

Kipling is enormously successful in creating a sense of unity and universality in *Kim*. Binding all together both morally and aesthetically is the lama's overarching search for unity with the Great Soul, whereby man's physical and spiritual destiny is universalized in the pervasive symbols of the Wheel and the River. But the chief source of the effect is Kipling's imaginative capacity for suffusing the narrative with a palpable warmth of sympathy and human love, whereby even a character as thinly drawn as Mahbub Ali becomes most real through his caring and affection for Kim. The warm, human sympathies are most effective in creating the sense of unity and universality when Kim observes the teeming life of India. Life does indeed seem an endless, intricately patterned tapestry.

Then we are subjected to a sudden and unpleasant shock. Up there, somewhere near the home of the Northern Folk, there is a frontier that puts a check on this developing comity of being; and from behind it comes a threat. There are barbarians prowling the outer marches of this "great and wonderful world." At once India seems to shrink within discernible perimeters. The beautiful submission to sense impressions seems suddenly less relaxed, and we wonder in a slightly depressed way whether we are being told that this variety of people, living amicably side by side, are doing so by virtue of the great Pax Britannica, which then becomes the (factitious) source of all unity. Rightly, I think, we suspend judgment, for we experience the more charitable effects of the lama's vision, which makes the idea of empire seem absurd, and those of Kim's humanity, which makes it seem vicious.

Kim's perceptions show us the unity in all this diversity, and as long as this impression stems from his own self-delight, his pleasure in his own senses and in his excited participation in a multitude of different actions, all is well. He is part of what he sees, and this life-affirming spirit in him is reflected in his surroundings. But something of this unity comes from Kim's precocious *knowingness;* and we are at once in what can be only, at best, the world of make-believe and, at worst, the world of the British empire. Either way, the unity seems suddenly much more artificial. Simultaneously we became aware of the reason for our dislike of Kim's nickname, "Little Friend of All the World," for in sentimentalizing the desired universal brotherhood, it compromises the writer's detachment; and we see behind Kim the pressure of Kipling's own needs. So we reject the narrator's attempt to impress us with his omniscience: "If there be one thing in the world that the small Hill-Rajahs deny it is just this charge; but it happens to be one thing that the bazars believe, when they discuss the mysterious slave-traffics of India" (ch. 4). A little of this elaborately casual parading of obscure knowledge goes a long way; and we get a great deal of it: "Few can translate the picture-parable [of the Wheel]; there are not twenty in all the world who can draw it surely without a copy: of those who can both draw and expound are but three" (ch. 11).

What is exposed by this "knowingness" is the strength of Kipling's personal desire to impose his *own* unity on his surroundings. Before, he had been saved by his literary tact, letting a sense of the inherent unity of things breathe through the luminous countryside that materializes under the purifying vision of the youthful Kim; now, his tact deserts him under pressure from his own paramount and neurotic need for security against the anarchy that is always about to destroy him.

In concluding this critique, it is profitable to discuss the ending of the novel. This, too, has been criticized on the ground that nothing has been "settled": Kim has not formally chosen between the lama and government service. Such an expectation is not only a misunderstanding of the nature of the book—which, no more than, say, Henry Fielding's *Tom Jones*, is the sort of book that ties knots or reaches a denouement—it also seems to me an oversight of the true significance and absolute propriety of the ending. Although Kipling may owe something to Miguel Cervantes for the concept of *Kim*, it is not of great help to think of it as picaresque. For Kim and his lama do not stumble out of one adventure into another; in fact the only major adventure in the book is an anticlimax, when, after a brief skirmish, the two intruders fade quickly from the scene and are overshadowed by the lama's flight from the deluding mountains.

What we get, in fact, is not a series of adventures so much as a series of pictures—and certainly not just pretty pictures, for all of them have a moral significance that is ultimately anchored in the creative antithesis provided by the contrasting visions of Kim and the lama.

The novel leaves us with a highly visual memory. Scene after vivid scene has arrested itself until we find ourselves in a superb kind of picture gallery, at the center of which is a magnificent portrayal of the Indian landscape. To paint it Kipling seems to have adopted the technique of J. M. W. Turner, for when we think of this landscape we think of a rich luminosity. Light pours over it: in the brilliant morning, when "all the rich Punjab [lies] out in the splendour of the keen sun"; at noon, when it streams through the shade of the mango tree "playing checkerwise" on the face of the lama; in "the smoke-scented evening, copper-dun and turquoise across the fields." Not even at night is light absent, for with great skill Kipling brings firelight and sunlight cleverly together:

It was a strange picture that Kim watched between drooped eyelids. The lama, very straight and erect, the deep folds of his yellow clothing slashed with black in the light of the *parao* fires precisely as a knotted tree-trunk is slashed with the shadow of the long sun, addressed a tinsel and lacquered *ruth* which burned like a many-coloured jewel in the same uncertain light. The patterns on the gold-worked curtains ran up and down, melting and reforming as the folds shook and quivered to the night wind; and when the talk grew more earnest the jewelled forefinger snapped out little sparks of light between the embroideries.

(ch. 4)

This usually golden light that continually suffuses the landscape has a coalescent effect, bringing all into one focus. It could be said that, in a very large view, the light arrests time, eternalizing Kim's youth and innocence, the lama's search, and the flux of human life, while vaguely suggesting that it has a benevolent source not entirely of this world.

Kipling's Indian pastoral is modified in an interesting and Victorian way, for these subsidiary pictures are remarkably similar to the narrative pictures, or even the parable pictures, favored by so many painters of the time, including Kipling's relatives. The parable picture is, indeed, something that Kipling excelled in, and its appearance in *Kim* links the book with two others in a trio that for many people constitutes his finest work: *The Jungle Books* (1894–1895) and *Just So Stories* (1902).

One of the most eloquent and resonant of all his pictorial compositions occurs near the end of *Kim* and strongly supports the case that the novel depends primarily on a pictorial narrative structure. It is the scene where Mahbub Ali and the lama sit beside the inert figure of Kim, who is sunk in something "deeper than sleep," and talk quietly about his future (or, perhaps, the Future, for the episode is imbued with a more universal significance):

> The ground was good clean dust—no new herbage that, living, is halfway to death already, but the hopeful dust that holds the seed of all life. He felt it between his toes, patted it with his palms, and joint by joint, sighing luxuriously, laid him down full length along in the shadow of the wooden-pinned cart. And Mother Earth was as faithful as the Sahiba. She breathed through him to restore the poise he had lost lying so long on a cot cut off from her good currents. His head lay powerless upon her breast, and his opened hands surrendered to her strength. The many-rooted tree above him, and even the dead man-handled wood beside, knew what he sought, as he himself did not know. Hour upon hour he lay deeper than sleep.
> (ch. 15)

Mahub Ali is anxious to save Kim for the world—which in his interpretation means government service; but the lama, regarding this concern as irrelevant, confidently claims Kim for that Other World to which the lama has dedicated himself.

There they sit, like two presiding (and somewhat imperial-minded) deities, calmly prescribing for unconscious and innocent Youth its destiny. But in this the picture parable does no more than repeat in a concentrated form the moral proposition advanced by the impressive diptych within which the book is enclosed: the picture at the beginning of an even more youthful Kim astride the gun; and the other one, at the end, of the lama seated, like Buddha, under his tree. Nor should it be otherwise, for it is wholly beyond the nature and scope of such a composition to tell us of the degree to which Kim's own life will veer toward one or the other of these poles.

V

KIPLING had, as we now can see, certain prophylactics against the moral disorder that for him expressed the true character of the universe. Chief among these was the day's work, which teaches us what we really ought to thank our creator for:

> Not for Prophecies or Powers, Visions, Gifts, or Graces,
> But the unregardful hours that grind us in our places
> With the burden on our backs, the weather in our faces.
>
> Not for any Miracle of easy Loaves and Fishes,
> But for doing, 'gainst our will, work against our wishes—
> Such as finding food to fill daily-emptied dishes.
> ("The Supports")

Work, routine, discipline, law, these are the principal weapons to ward off anarchy. Without them there is, in Kipling's view, little that can be done to prevent the complete disintegration of that fragile artifact, the self. But Kipling goes a step further and includes art as yet another of the bulwarks, seeing it as the job of the artist both to tell the truth and to bring help and comfort to a mankind free of illusions.

A number of his stories deal either centrally or substantially with the nature and function of art and the role of the artist, stories such as "'Teem,'" "The Bull That Thought," "The Eye of Allah," "The Children of the Zodiac," and, of course, his only full-length novel in conventional form, *The Light That Failed*. There is no doubt that in the latter he is rebutting some of the charges made against his own art when his work erupted on the London literary scene. After the initial raptures over this startling new talent, when critics praised him in particular for his brilliance of color—J. M. Barrie, for example, described his prose as having the effect of a very bright lantern—and his creation of an exotic mise-en-scène for his tales, came the hostile attacks on the uncouthness, vulgarity, brutality, and lack of shading in his portrayal of character and events.

It is not fanciful to find something of Kipling in Dick Heldar in *The Light That Failed*, when in his absence the character is being admonished for apparently assuming that he can "storm up and down the world with a box of moist tubes and a slick brush," or when he is aggressively proclaiming that "real Art" is the ultrarealistic soldier in his own painting "His Last Shot":

> I made him a flushed, dishevelled, bedevilled scallawag, with his helmet at the back of his head, and the living fear of death in his eye, and the blood oozing out of a cut over his ankle-bone. He wasn't pretty, but he was all soldier and very much man.
> (ch. 4)

But this is not what the "art-appreciating" public wants. To them, says Dick with heavy irony, "it was brutal and coarse and violent,—man being naturally gentle when he's fighting for his life. They wanted something more restful, with a little more colour." So he has taken "His Last Shot" back and made a few alterations:

> I put him into a lovely red coat without a speck on it. That is Art. I polished his boots,—observe the high light on the

toe. That is Art. I cleaned his rifle—rifles are always clean on service,—because that is Art. I pipeclayed his helmet—pipeclay is always used on active service, and is indispensable to Art.

(ch. 4)

From this harangue it is fairly obvious what Dick's —and Kipling's—view is of the nature of art. It is emphatically realist, with much stress on detail and no nonsense about shutting one's eyes to what polite society might regard as offensive and unpleasant. Art "smells of tobacco and blood," says Maisie accusingly; and Dick, who knows "what life and death really mean," would not deny it, though he does not regard himself as limited to such themes. To prove it he embarks on a "head" to rival her "Melancolia," but, ironically again, it begins to take shape only when he finds a real-life prostitute to act as a model. (Predictably, and in the best fin-de-siècle manner, Kipling has this "real" creature of the gutter destroy what is possibly Dick's greatest work.)

The novel puts Dick's theory into practice, too, for two of the most memorable descriptions are of a brothel in Port Said and a battlefield that Dick visits again, after the action is over, where there has not been time to bury the twelve hundred dead. Dick says: "The sight of that field taught me a good deal. It looked just like a bed of horrible toadstools in all colours, and—I'd never seen men in bulk go back to their beginnings before."

Realism of this order demands close attention to detail and consequently a complete command over draftsmanship and materials: in Dick's words, "A great deal depends on being master of the bricks and mortar of the trade." At another point he says to Maisie: "You have a sense of colour, but you want form. Colour's a gift,—put it aside and think no more about it,—but form you can be drilled into." As a writer Kipling certainly endorses these views, as he does Dick's respect for inspiration: "Good work has nothing to do with—doesn't belong to—the person who does it. It's put into him or her from outside. . . . All we can do is to learn how to do our work to be master of our material. . . . Everything else comes from outside ourselves."

Kipling believed strongly in his "daemon," as he called his inspiration, also seeing it as something outside himself. This insistence on form and accurate drawing may, however, owe something to Burne-Jones, who, after the somewhat inspirational tuition of Rossetti, was instructed by G. F. Watts, who in turn put much greater emphasis on the discipline of drawing. Watts "compelled me to draw better," Burne-Jones said many years later, and made him realize, according to one critic, "a sounder basis for his art."

The emphasis on craftsmanship and technique is asserted again in "The Bull That Thought" (first published 1924) and "The Eye of Allah" (1926). The latter is one more of Kipling's reticent yet highly organized tales in which a great deal of affective life is going on just under the surface. The Abbot's love for the Lady Anne, now mortally sick; John's deep suffering following the death of his beloved mistress (his gift to the Lady Anne of what can only be his mistress's carnelian necklace is a delicate touch); the frustration and anguish of Roger of Salerno at being too old to make use of new scientific discoveries that the church will suppress if it can: all of this comes to light under the "eye of Allah"—an early microscope—as though the eye itself were revealing an intense world of deep, hidden, private feelings, schooled into concealment by the discipline that the characters, with difficulty and some reluctance, accept.

At the end, the wise and experienced Abbot deliberately smashes the protomicroscope to pieces despite the desperate appeals of Roger Bacon and Roger of Salerno. That it could have been put to the service of humanity there is no doubt; perhaps it could even have helped to heal people as ill as the Lady Anne. But the Abbot knows that the church will not at this time allow it, since the truth it advances would undermine the church's authority. Disorder and death would follow the premature advocacy of the invention: "Fated as dawn, but as the dawn, delayed/Till the just hour should strike." In the meantime the church contributes to a soul-saving serenity, as is noted by the party returning across the roofs of the building after having conducted their experiment on the stagnant puddle: "They walked quietly back along the leads, three English counties laid out in evening sunshine around them; church upon church, monastery upon monastery, cell after cell, and the bulk of a vast cathedral moored on the edge of the banked shoals of sunset."

In the tale, the artist-craftsman John of Burgos is twice made to say that his trade is the outside of things. (The first time there is a slight but significant difference: "There's less risk for the craftsman who deals with the outside of things.") Again it is clear that the sentiment allows some identification with Kipling: in it we find both a reply to those critics (like

Henry James and Francis Adams) who claimed that Kipling was unable to realize characters with convincing interior lives, and a statement of his interpretation of the role of the artist. The latter could *suggest* an interior life but should do so through a concentration on the things of the surface—a modus operandi that inevitably results in an aesthetic with the accent on the public and social dimensions of men's lives.

In "The Eye of Allah" Kipling once again refuses to exempt the artist from the fate of those he writes about or paints. He, too, is under the common doom, and his art will help to ease the pain that is not physical in its origins. When John of Burgos returns to the monastery after the death of his mistress, the Abbott, whose own mistress is dying, shows his understanding in a conversation with him. Of a "cake of dried poppy juice," he says to him: "This has power to cut off all pain from a man's body"; and when John assents, he adds: "But for pain of the soul there is, outside God's Grace, but one drug; and that is a man's craft, learning, or other helpful motion of his own mind." John knows this too and sinks himself "past all recollection" in his great work, the illumination of the Gospel according to St. Luke. And out of his knowledge of intense anguish and suffering comes his best work. When the senior copyist asks him how the great task is proceeding, John knows that he has at last got it fully realized: "'All here!' John tapped his forehead with his pencil. 'It has been only waiting these months to—ah God!—be born.'" Out of the deaths of his mistress and his newborn son comes the proof of his talent.

The story that illustrates most specifically and successfully the "applied" nature of Kipling's view of art, and its relation to human experience and suffering, is without doubt "The Children of the Zodiac" (first published 1891). It is really about death and dying, a subject that looms large with Kipling; but it is without the passion, savagery, and cynicism that the same subject attracts in other stories, such as the bleak and moving "On Greenhow Hill" (1890).

In the tale, the Children of the Zodiac learn mortality, having started with the belief that they were gods and having been treated as such by men. During the time when they persisted in seeing themselves as gods, they understood nothing of human affairs. When stories of death and dying and requests for help were brought to the Bull, he would only "lower his huge head and answer, 'What is that to me?'" Nor could the Children understand laughter, and laughter, like love, is community. The first sign of their growing understanding appears when Leo kisses the Girl.

Through the kiss—the human kiss—they have opened the door to the human world and closed it on the supernatural. Immediately afterward the Girl claims understanding, and almost as soon we see the first intimations of mortality:

"We have come to the end of things," said the man quietly. "This that was my wife—"
"As I am Leo's wife," said the Girl quickly, her eyes staring.

It is the Girl, too, who understands why the old man, after complaining of having to live, tries to escape death. There is the growing realization that they are not immortal:

"Leo we must learn more about this for their sakes."
"For *their* sakes," said Leo very loudly.
"Because *we* are never going to die," said the Girl and Leo together, still more loudly.

Their fears are confirmed when Leo asks Scorpio why he should trouble the children of men and receives the answer in Scorpio's question: "Are you so sure that I trouble the children of men alone?" The Bull, the Ram, and the Twins all admit their ultimate mortality and their need to keep working—though all explicitly find life like this unpleasant. Then Leo finds his own fate in the House of the Crab, though by this time he has realized his identity with the sons of men. There follows the final rejection of their status as gods and of their mythical immortality:

Next morning they returned to their proper home and saw the flowers and the sacrifices that had been laid before their doors by the villagers of the hills. Leo stamped down the fire with his heel, and the Girl flung the flower-wreaths out of sight, shuddering as she did so.

And when the villagers visited them they found not gods but simply "a man and a woman with frightened white faces sitting hand in hand on the altar-steps."

Leo—it is impossible to dissociate Kipling from him here—finds it hard to accept the reality of death; and after an evening of pleasant, happy company, redolent of health, life, and vigor, he wakes up with the poignant realization:

"Every one of those people we met just now will die—"

"So shall we," said the Girl sleepily. "Lie down again, dear." Leo could not see that her face was wet with tears.

But Leo's fears cannot be stilled, and he goes in search of the Bull, who is so tired after his walk that (happily) all his contemplation is taken up by the beautiful straight furrows he has made that day. "'Well,' said the Bull, "what will you do? . . . You cannot pull a plough. . . . I can, and that prevents me from thinking of the Scorpion.'"

Leo, however, finds that he can sing, and though he would have liked "to lie down and brood over the words of the Crab," he is persuaded to continue singing. First he sings the song of the fearless, but soon discovers another, much more powerful, song.

This was a thing he could never have done had he not met the Crab face to face. He remembered facts concerning cultivators, and bullocks, and rice-fields that he had not particularly noticed before the interview, and he strung them all together, growing more interested as he sang, and he told the cultivator much more about himself and his work than the cultivator knew. The Bull grunted approval as he toiled down the furrows for the last time that day, and the song ended, leaving the cultivator with a very good opinion of himself in his aching bones.

So Leo becomes the Singer, the Poet, the Writer, or simply the Artist, whose job it is to secure just such an effect as the above quotation describes. Boldly he has confronted his destiny, and now, through his efforts, man will be helped toward dignity, integrity, and self-respect, as well as to the modicum of happiness that he is permitted.

It was after this that Leo made the Song of the Bull who had been a God and forgotten the fact, and he sang it in such a manner that half the young men in the world conceived that they too might be Gods without knowing it. A half of that half grew impossibly conceited, and died early. A half of the remainder strove to be Gods and failed, but the other half accomplished four times more work than they would have done under any other delusion.

It remains a delusion, but without it existence would not be possible.

And now the last vestiges of divinity have disappeared from the Children of the Zodiac. The Girl dies, and with her death Leo knows—in terms highly suggestive of the Fall—"all the sorrow that a man could know including the full knowledge of his own fall who had once been a god." But he continues to sing the same song, teaching fortitude and denying any facile, mystic optimism. One of his listeners is struck down:

"It is well for me, Leo that you sang for forty years."

"Are you afraid?" said Leo. . . .

"I am a man, not a God," said the man. "I should have run away but for your songs. My work is done, and I die without making a great show of my fear."

"I am very well paid," said Leo to himself. "Now that I see what my songs are doing, I will sing better ones."

But the Artist in the middle of his work meets his own fate in Cancer, the Crab. And at the end it is emphasized that the Artist makes the same remark as all human beings, "Why have you come for me now?" Then he too draws himself up and, recalling the godhead he once thought he possessed, reaffirms his fearlessness. Kipling with a careful touch completes his story's development: "What is that to me?" said the Crab.

It is, then, the duty of the artist to "draw the Thing as he sees It for the God of Things as They are." Wreaths of marigolds presented to gods who are not gods will do nothing to ameliorate the lot of the children of men; but if the poet, the artist, can show them how to live with the maximum of fortitude and dignity, while doing nothing to minimize the stark certainty or finality of death, his contribution is precious. Above all he must be in the world of men—there is his "proper home."

Go to your work and be strong, halting not in your ways,
Baulking the end half-won for an instant dole of praise.
Stand to your work and be wise—certain of sword and pen,
Who are neither children nor Gods, but men in a world of men!
("England's Answer")

Edmund Wilson's accusation that Kipling lacked faith in the artistic vocation seems to me a strange one, since Kipling's reverence for the artist's enduring contribution is proved in many places—even if the artist is a music-hall singer, as "A Recantation," dedicated to "Lyde of the Music Halls," makes clear:

*What boots it on the Gods to call?*
*Since, answered or unheard,*
*We perish with the Gods and all*
*Things made—except the Word.*

The last verse of "A Recantation" could very well serve as a coda to "The Children of the Zodiac":

*Yet they who use the Word assigned,
To hearten and make whole,
Not less than Gods have served mankind,
Though vultures rend their soul.*

## VI

KIPLING's feeling for humanity as well as his sensitive portrayal of the Anglo-Indian stems from his recognition of the immeasurable preciousness of the individual self in "man," and of the unceasing battle with the Lords of Life to which man is ineluctably joined in defense of the self.

Such a realization, such a concern, can only stem from clear-sightedness. For Kipling, as for Conrad, there is a crisis of realization—such as Leo experiences—when man faces his destiny clearly and without illusions. But whereas Conrad projected this crisis in explicity artistic statements through characters like McWhirr and Mitchell on the one hand and Lord Jim on the other, Kipling leaves it largely unprojected. The crisis is part of his own experience, and though it obviously informs his work, it very rarely becomes the subject of it. (Perhaps what he lacks artistically is a reliable spokesman such as Conrad's Marlow, and Kipling's early development of the technical device we now know as "the unreliable narrator" is his attempt to find a remedy.) The fact that this crisis influences but is scarcely ever realized, in artistic terms, in his writing has an unfortunate effect upon his characterizations. In the presentation of an individual character, all traces are frequently concealed, with the result that the real dynamic of the character is largely denied him in the moment of his appearance; he arrives postcrisis with an upper lip so stiff as to preclude any explanation of his behavior. Consequently his inevitable courage, fortitude, and endurance have too often the dead unreality of a fait accompli. Kipling seems to shrink nervously from bringing the crisis into the public world of his characterization, but his awareness of it cannot be suppressed. Adherence to a code, insistence on work and discipline, are in the Kipling hero indications not of attitudinizing but of a deep sensitivity that has allowed him to see far into "the wheel and the drift of Things."

With his characters living on the Edge of Nothing, Kipling's awareness of the abyss of "natural nature" is acknowledged in one way or another throughout his work. In the later as well as the earlier stories he returns to supernatural themes or to dealing with men who are in some way obsessed—men who are literally taken possession of by something larger and more powerful than themselves. Whether we take "The Lost Legion," "At the End of the Passage," "The Mark of the Beast," "In the Same Boat," or "The Woman in His Life," what is presented is self-possession versus possession—or the threat of possession—by the nonself. Nameless and shapeless, this malignant force, which derives from the moral anarchy that constantly threatens Kipling's carefully constructed identity, haunts his work in capitalized abstractions; it is a "Thing" or an "It"; it is "the Horror passing speech"; it is, very frequently, a Face that is faceless, depersonalized, dehumanized. Such, for instance, are the Faces, mildewed and half-eaten, that Miss Henschil sees in her nightmares in "In the Same Boat," or the Face in "A Matter of Fact," whose "horror . . . lay in the eyes, for those were sightless—white, in sockets as white as scraped bone, and blind," or the one we encounter in "La Nuit Blanche":

*Then a Face came, blind and weeping,
  And It couldn't wipe Its eyes,
And It muttered I was keeping
  Back the moonlight from the skies; . . .*

There are three non-Indian stories that invoke the supernatural in a particularly telling way, though the supernatural event is not what the story is about. In fact all three are about an excessive, even violent, sexual passion: in the case of two of them the principals could be said to be possessed by it. The stories could be prefaced by the poem "Gipsy Vans," which is attached to one of them. Two of these tales, "A Madonna of the Trenches" and "The Wish House," are among Kipling's later work; they were published within a few months of each other in 1924.

Almost from the outset, as has been shown, Kipling's writing is marked by a density of organization, a structuring of detail in which no item is superfluous, and a narrator far more active and independent than has been generally recognized. It is very far from the case, therefore, as has long been implied, that only the later work has sophistication of organization. As proof there is the third of the tales, the celebrated conundrum "Mrs. Bathurst" (published 1904), dense to the point of impenetrability. The effect of the exceptional degree of suppressed narrative in "Mrs. Bathhurst" is, for the most part, to tease us in the right way; that is, in a way that stimulates the reader by increasing the interpretative possibilities in action and event—the sort of thing contemporary novelists and dramatists do a little more crudely, by suggesting several possible endings to their novels and plays.

In "Mrs. Bathurst" Kipling's pictorial sense is active in a particularly dramatic and focal way. The key episode involves a quite literal picture, a new-fangled moving-picture, and the denouement is a picture of another kind: an exceptionally graphic representation of two people turned into charcoal by lightning: he standing up, she (if it is a she) on her knees in an apparent gesture of devotion—with no narrative explanation following. It is a tale, too, in which a recognition of the strength—sometimes the obsessive strength—of sexual desire is made not only explicit but far more convincing than in the conventional fin-de-siècle treatment of such a theme.

Teasing though the tale is, I do not think it is as much of a wild-goose chase as is the pursuit of the Boy Niven (with the besotted reader in the role of the credulous seamen). What few concrete impressions are left, *do* stay with us. They illustrate a permanent concern of the author, as the rest of our reading readily confirms: the power of an obsession to lure man away from the security and discipline of his craft or order to what is wild and strange and ultimately destructive. And the image of the two charcoal figures, lately possessed of such an energy of passion that it has burned them up, and still so full of a mystery from which they resolutely exclude us, is abidingly powerful. I have only one criticism: Pyecroft assumes that the crouching figure was a man; Pritchard that it was Mrs. Bathurst. For Hooper to keep silent is surely to cheat a little; for he was there and saw them.

In this story the inexplicable nature of the universe, unsusceptible to reason and law (that is what makes it such a hostile environment to man), is once more at the forefront of the picture. And here Vickery is representative of what happens when the world's disorder is allowed to enter his own mind: it destroys him, as we see when he is pointedly made to repudiate all the order, discipline, and law that are summed up in the regulations of the Royal Navy, which are recalled on every other page. In this as in other ways, we are forcefully reminded of Conrad's *Lord Jim.* There Captain Brierly also is shaken to the roots of his moral being by what a fellow officer does; whereas Vickery's captain only puts on his court-martial face, Brierly commits suicide. Before he does so, however, he throws away his chronometer. We recall that Vickery's captain is said to have been seen looking like this only once before, when someone threw overboard the gunsights. Both instruments signify order and control.

That anarchy should, in this story, manifest itself in excessive physical passion is of the greatest interest. Elliott Gilbert is right, I think, in *The Good Kipling* (1972), when he relates this directly to Kipling's complex attitude to women:

Women as individuals may be charming and wholly innocent and yet at the same time may be acting, unconsciously, as the agents of a terrible power totally beyond their understanding or control. And though this power may originally have been generated by some overwhelming creative urge, its random, mindless application can just as easily be deadly and destructive.

(p. 102)

Kipling's mother, it is tempting to speculate, had much to answer for when she abandoned her son to Aunty Rosa, in that house of desolation at Southsea. On the other hand, if she had not done so, I doubt that we would ever have had Mowgli and his surrogate family of wolves, let alone Mrs. Bathurst.

In "A Madonna of the Trenches" the supernatural element is more explicit; but again it occurs as the product of an intense and illicit passion. That passion has a fundamentally disorienting effect on the principal observer and comes to reflect once more the moral anarchy that threatens to destroy the foundations of man's conventional universe.

As usual in Kipling, no detail of the environment or what is enacted within it is superfluous. Clem Strangwick, the central figure, is one of Kipling's many broken men who return from the war, their sanity undermined by the horror of their experiences. World War I, though all too real to Kipling (his only son was killed in it), was yet another vehicle for his vision of the world as a place of lawless anarchy where order, personal and cosmic, fights a losing battle against chaos. Randall Jarrell makes an interesting and perceptive remark in this connection. Quoting an observation of William James's—"The lunatic's visions of horror are all drawn from the material of daily fact. Our civilization is founded on the shambles, and each individual existence goes out in a lonely spasm of helpless agony. If you protest, my friend, wait till you arrive there yourself"—Jarrell then adds:

Kipling had arrived there early and returned there often. One thinks sadly of how deeply congenial to this torturing obsessive knowledge of Kipling's the first World War was: the death and anguish of Europe produced some of his best and most terrible stories. . . . The world *was* Hell and India underneath, after all; and he could say to the Victorian, Edwardian Europeans who had thought it all just part of his style: "You wouldn't believe me!"[2]

The framework of "A Madonna of the Trenches" is provided by the story's being set in a Freemason's Lodge—for Kipling, yet another model for order and discipline; and it is within this haven of structure that Strangwick has a recurrence of the breakdown he endured in the trenches. Apparently he cannot get out of his mind the frozen corpses under the duckboards in the bottom of the trenches: "I can't stand it! There's nothing on earth creaks like they do! And—and when it thaws we—we've got to slap 'em back with a spa-ade!"

Keede, the doctor who attends Strangwick now, was, as it happens, the medical officer at the front to whom Strangwick had been brought when he had his first collapse. Then as now Keede believes that Strangwick is using the horrors he had witnessed to protect himself against something still more terrifying; he himself gives a studiedly casual account of the same scene, in even more repellent detail, when he tells of how the French had faced both sides of their trenches with their own dead soldiers "to keep the mud back." Ordinary though he makes the scene sound, this degradation of the human body is an important detail in the story. Gradually we get at the truth.

Strangwick's family is a close-knit working-class group in which a network of relationships binds all together in an apparently solid and unbreakable order. (We are reminded that the Kiplings used to talk about their own unit as the Family Square.) Strangwick's unsettling discovery is that Sergeant Gadsoe, who has been from childhood his honorary uncle, and Strangwick's aunt, Bella Armine, have for many years been deeply in love. Because of the "family square" it is impossible for them to desert their respective spouses and live together, and their only hope is that they will be together after death. Bella is, in fact, dying of cancer, and the brief note that she sends to Gadsoe, telling him of the date by which her "little trouble" will be over, conveys a suppressed, conspiratorial excitement—even jubilation. On the day she has appointed, her ghost appears before Gadsoe *and* Strangwick in the trenches. The latter is appalled, not just at her apparition, but at the behavior of the two lovers as well. Gadsoe's cry, Strangwick recognizes, is both of joy and relief, his "Thank Gawd" referring back to their conversation a few minutes earlier, when he quoted from the burial service, "If, after the manner of man, I have fought with beasts at Ephesus, what advantageth it me if the dead rise not?"

Strangwick's mind cannot cope with the double revelation that Bella's ghost brings with it. A new and unpleasant dimension has been added to his view of the world and its possibilities, hitherto closely regulated by his culture's totems and taboos. The words of the burial service—which have been assimilated into his background as a vaguely consoling piece of mumbo-jumbo that he does not properly understand (he talks about fighting with "beasts of officers")—in effect disturb his sense of being safely anchored. "You see . . . there wasn't a single gor-dam thing left abidin' for me to take hold of, here or hereafter. If the dead *do* rise—and I saw 'em—why —why *anything* can 'appen. Don't you understand?"

He has been permitted a sudden discomposing glimpse of the abyss, then. But what has caused him to see the chaos is almost as important as the view itself: he has discovered that sexual passion can exist on a scale of intensity that puts it outside nature; that is, outside the nature that is circumscribed and tamed by family squares, rituals of love and marriage, and the like, all rounded off with the intonation of a misunderstood burial service. Repeatedly his shock is registered in his reference to the strength of passion that he saw on his aunt's face: "All that time Auntie Armine stood with 'er arms out—an' a look on 'er face! *I* didn't know such things was or could be."

The experience demoralizes him completely: "I saw 'im an' 'er—she dead since mornin' time, an' he killin' 'imself before my livin' eyes so's to carry on with 'er for all Eternity—an' she 'oldin' out 'er arms for it! I want to know where I'm *at*." What crowns

---

[2]"On Preparing to Read Kipling," in E. L. Gilbert, ed., *Kipling and the Critics* (New York, 1965), p. 147.

everything for Clem Strangwick and brings final devastation with it is the fact that these lovers come from his own network of relationships. More than that, they are, so to speak, the elders of the tribe, who by virtue of their age are seen by him to be an organic part of the moral fabric of his community and coterminous with it. And Kipling carefully underlines their age. Early in the story Gadsoe is described as "an elderly bird who must have lied like a parrot to get out to the front at his age"; Bella's offense seems to be summed up in Strangwick's frequently repeated, "An' she nearer fifty than forty an' me own Aunt."

So completely is Clem's faith in women and in a moral order shattered that he has decided to break off his own engagement (and is threatened, ironically, with the law as a consequence). And once more, altogether inconspicuously, Kipling has provided a twist in the closing paragraphs of the story that deepens and complicates its meaning:

Let 'er sue if she likes! She don't know what reel things mean. *I* do—I've 'ad occasion to notice 'em. . . . *No*, I tell you! I'll 'ave 'em when I want 'em, an' be done with 'em; but not till I see that look on a face . . . that look . . . I'm not takin' any. The real thing's life an' death. It *begins* at death, d'ye see. *She* can't understand. . . . Oh, go on an' push off to Hell, you an' your lawyers.

The law and lawyers are not usually associated with hell in Kipling's writing; quite the contrary. The law and loyalty to it are what constitute Kipling's heaven. This can only spell complete demoralization for Strangwick. He, a weak and irresolute character from the start, is not just haunted by the intense, life-consuming passion he has witnessed; he is caught in its toils. Emphatically Clem is not of the Gipsy stock that can, through the intensity of feelings and the formidable strength of essentially lawless natures, survive in such a maelstrom. He, of the Gorgio race, could never inhabit the Romany world and is now unfitted for any other. We have this confirmed when the Brother who had introduced him to the Lodge tells Keede and the narrator at the end that the young lady Clem has rejected is in every way suitable: "an' she'd make him a good little wife, too, if I'm any judge." "That is all that's wanted," says Keede when he discovers the identity of the Brother: he is Armine, the widower husband of that "good little wife," Bella.

Kipling's conception and execution of the tale (dense though his working of it is) are quite remarkably authentic in psychological scope and subtlety. He is wholly convincing, too, in his portrayal of this literally supernatural love, not shrinking from investing it with a dark, grave-defeating lustfulness that has a suggestion of the demonic in it. For their awesomely long-nurtured love does not leave us with the impression of innocence. Gadsoe's carefully worded greeting, for example, as smooth and contained as their passion has been, is eloquent in its understatement: "Why, Bella . . . this must be only the *second* time we've been alone together in all these years" (italics added). And there is the look on Bella's face, which so upsets Clem: "Then he comes out an' says: 'Come in, my dear'; an' she stoops an' goes into the dug-out with that look on her face—that look on her face!"

"A Madonna of the Trenches"—the irony of the title once more cuts in many ways—is not wholly successful. It is too involuted, with its triple framing of the Masonic Lodge, the Front Line, and the Family; it is too wordy, and the clumsily handled dialect gets in the way. But what it lacks in structural clarity it makes up for in moral comprehension and complexity.

It would be unwise to leave this story, particularly considering what has yet to be said about "The Wish House," without making one thing clear. A lot has been made of the poem "Gipsy Vans" (which prefaces "A Madonna of the Trenches"), much of it quite properly approving, for the verse is well done. But it does *not* mean that Kipling is recommending Gipsy morality as a pattern for living and loving; for it leads to suffering and death. He is saying that in love—as he said before in "Beyond the Pale" and "Without Benefit of Clergy"—there are those who, given the strength of their nature and passion, will always embrace such a creed—and suffer and triumph accordingly.

> Unless you come of the gipsy stock
>    That steals by night and day,
> Lock your heart with a double lock
>    And throw the key away.
> Bury it under the blackest stone
>    Beneath your father's hearth,
> And keep your eyes on your lawful own
>    And your feet to the proper path.
>     *Then you can stand at your door and mock*
>       *When the gipsy-vans come through . . .*
>     *For it isn't right that the Gorgio stock*
>       *Should live as the Romany do.*

There are two other stories connected with World War I that are of outstanding merit, "Mary Postgate" and "The Gardener." There is not space to deal with them fully here, but their virtue is now well established, and they rightly find their way into many short-story anthologies. Again there is a considerable if inconspicuous stress on the sexual element.

Of the two, "Mary Postgate" seems the better one. There is an excellent consistency of tone throughout, slightly distanced from the event, as is proper, since it is filtered through the mind of a spinster in her early forties who "prided herself on a trained mind which 'did not dwell on these things'"—"these things" being the less pleasant aspects of life, of which Miss Postgate was by no means ignorant. As the story proceeds, the need for the cool, almost detached tone becomes greater, and the effect of the tone is much richer, both morally and dramatically.

Wynn Fowler, the nephew of Miss Postgate's employer, enlists; and in Kipling's skillful description of this event, war really does seem like the plague in the Indian stories:

It took the Rector's son who was going into business with his elder brother; it took the Colonel's nephew on the eve of fruit-farming in Canada; it took Mrs. Grant's son who, his mother said, was devoted to the ministry; and, very early indeed, it took Wynn Fowler, who announced on a postcard that he had joined the Flying Corps and wanted a cardigan waistcoat.

Mary Postgate silently dotes on Wynn and gladly serves as a slave to the demanding and not particularly grateful youth. The exact nature of Mary's emotional response is not easy to gauge in this reticent and colorless spinster. "What do you ever think of, Mary?" asks Miss Fowler, and when Mary deliberately avoids the bait and starts talking about Wynn's stockings, she persists—"But I mean the things that women think about." When Wynn is killed, however, Miss Fowler, watching as Mary takes his things to the incinerator, says to herself: "Mary's an old woman. I never realised it before." Near the incinerator, as she is about to sprinkle on "the sacrificial oil" and burn Wynn's belongings, Mary discovers the badly injured German airman who that afternoon had bombed the village, killing a child, almost right before her eyes. Repeatedly he pleads with her to get him a doctor, but all she will say is, "Ich haben der todt Kinder gesehn" (I have seen the dead child). She proceeds with her work; Wynn's funeral pyre becomes the stake at which she is burning his enemies and the slaughterers of little children. With powerful Kiplingesque irony, she assures herself with complete confidence that "Wynn for no consideration on earth would have torn little Edna into those vividly-coloured strips and strings." And when the wounded German again calls for help, she replies using one of Wynn's favorite phrases, "Stop that, you bloody pagan." So he dies, and at the sound of his death-rattle Mary "closed her eyes and drank it in."

The story ends brilliantly:

Then the end came very distinctly in a lull between two rain-gusts. Mary Postgate drew her breath short between her teeth and shivered from head to foot. "*That's* all right," said she contentedly, and went up to the house, where she scandalised the whole routine by taking a luxurious hot bath before tea, and came down looking, as Miss Fowler said when she saw her lying all relaxed on the other sofa, "quite handsome!"

Frustrated motherhood is certainly there, but clearly the sensuality in the closing description implies more. Kipling's controlled prose is quite well-matched to the control shown by Miss Postgate.

"The Wish House," which with "Mrs. Bathurst" and "A Madonna of the Trenches" forms a trio of tales dealing with the supernatural and with obsessive physical infatuation, is the best of all his later stories. Its triumph is in part due to its very density; not the sort of opaque density we find in "Mrs. Bathurst," but the concentrated, highly organized detail that binds the story so tightly together that its intensity is communicated to us almost as a physical sensation.

The first paragraph, as so often in Kipling, tells us the most. There is enormous irony in this story of sexual rapacity, of obsessive and violent adultery, starting with the sentence: "The new Church Visitor had just left after a twenty minutes' call." But the first few lines of dialogue give us a clear lead as to the moral nature of the characters; and Grace Archer's powerful, forthright, and unsympathetic personality is etched with the most dexterous economy:

"Most folk got out at Bush Tye for the match there," [Mrs. Fettley] explained, "so there weren't no one for me to cushion agin, the last five mile. An' she *do* just-about bounce ye."

"You've took no hurt," said her hostess. "You don't brittle by agein', Liz."

The grimness of the reply, mediated through the description of her as "hostess," with its pointedly inappropriate invocation of middle-class, conventional tea-table chat, confirms the characterization. Exactly which side of the moral fence she inhabits is brought out in another brief but telling detail: "'What like's this new Visitor o' yours?' Mrs. Fettley inquired.... Mrs. Ashcroft suspended the big packing needle judicially on high, ere she stabbed home. 'Settin' aside she don't bring much news with her yet, I dunno as I've anythin' special agin her.'" The coarseness of the dialect, so well caught and held, has a moral and dramatic significance.

The context of their conversation, too, is well chosen. As the dialogue unfolds, the tale that is told is found to be one of ferocious sexual license and passion. But what is going on over tea in the cottage is not counterpointed against honest rural toil in the surrounding fields:

The tile-sided cottage trembled at the passage of two specially chartered forty-seat charabancs on their way to the Bush Tye match; a regular Saturday "shopping" 'bus, for the county's capital, fumed behind them; while, from one of the crowded inns, a fourth car backed out to join the procession, and held up the stream of through pleasure-traffic.

There is no such thing as rustic innocence here; people are given over to pleasure, of which the tale unfolding within the cottage is simply a denser concentration. It is a world debased and venal, a world of lost innocence.

Mrs. Archer's sixteen-year-old grandson, with "a maiden of the moment in attendance," enters, snatches up the basket his grandmother has been working on, and rushes out without acknowledgment. Mrs. Fettley's response borders on the prurient: "I lay *he* won't show much mercy to any he comes across, either." Speaking, we are told, "with narrowed eyes," she adds, "Now 'oo the dooce do he remind me of, all of a sudden?" Mrs. Archer ignores the question, and her reply to the first part is cool and hard: "They must look arter theirselves—same as we did." Mrs. Fettley concedes that Mrs. Archer always could, and slyly brings up the case of Polly Batten's husband, one of Mrs. Archer's earlier conquests. She does this in a way that suggests the two women are as much adversaries as friends; for the narrowed eyes warn us of her recognition, made explicit later, that Mrs. Archer's grandson bears a strong resemblance to Polly's husband: "Why, 'tis Jim Batten, and his tricks come to life again!" Mrs. Archer's reply is as self-possessed as ever; and she gives as good as she gets: "Mebbe. There's some that would ha' made it out so—bein' barren-like, themselves."

Mrs. Fettley admits, however, that, as Mrs. Archer says, she has had *her* "back-lookin's" too, and pauses as in reverie: "Mrs. Fettley stared, with jaw half-dropped, at the grocer's bright calendar on the wall. The cottage shook again to the roar of the motor-traffic, and the crowded football-ground below the garden roared almost as loudly; for the village was well set to its Saturday leisure." Then she confides her "satisfactions" to Grace Archer, principally, it seems, with a railwayman lover "over the four years 'e was workin' on the rail near us." In turn Mrs. Archer discloses some of her own secrets.

Kipling's introduction to these intimate confidences between the two ladies of such copious appetite is masterly in its ironies of tone and image: "The light and air had changed a little with the sun's descent, and the two elderly ladies closed the kitchen-door against chill. A couple of jays squealed and skirmished through the undraped apple-trees in the garden." There is nothing as genteel as the tone would suggest about the two women: their natures are much better represented in the second sentence of the quotation. Mrs. Archer recounts *her* skirmishing with her husband over their mutual infidelity, and deftly implicates Mrs. Fettley: "for *you* know, Liz, what a lover 'e was." Delicately as it is done, what is conveyed in a few words is a violence of passion bordering on the murderous: Grace Archer confronting Dolly Batten with a pitchfork; her husband being jailed for assaulting to the point of death his mistress's husband.

Mrs. Archer's last affair is the one that is of most significance here, for when Harry eventually falls seriously ill after he leaves her, she discovers a means of relieving him. She has learned, from a little girl who is devoted to her, how to take somebody else's pain upon herself. It is done by making contact with a Token—"the wraith of the dead or, worse still, of the living"—in what is called a Wish House. Grace Archer's wish is to "take everythin' bad that's in store for my man, 'Arry Mockler, for love's sake." From that time Harry's health improves, and the ulcer on Mrs. Ashcroft's leg begins. When she discovers that the method works, and continues to work when Harry is subsequently injured and made well through her sacrifice, Grace is exultant: "I've got ye now, my man. . . . You'll take your good from me 'thout knowin' it till my life's end. O God send me long to live for 'Arry's sake!" But the fierceness of her triumph shows that it is not so much love as jealous passion that possesses her; and indeed her only real fear is that Harry might find another woman. Here she pleads with Mrs. Fettley to reassure her that "the pain do count, don't you think?" and that this will be "counted agin" the possibility of Harry's falling prey to another woman.

Mrs. Archer's sacrifice is complete, for she knows that her ulcer has "turned," that is, it has become malignant and will bring about her death in the near future. And this last confidence provokes another from Mrs. Fettley, who has just asked her how long she has to live.

"Slow come, slow go. But if I don't set eyes on ye 'fore next hoppin', this'll be good-bye, Liz."

"Dunno as I'll be able to manage by then—not 'thout I have a liddle dog to lead me. For de chillern, dey won't be troubled, an'—O Gra'!—I'm blindin' up—I'm blindin' up!"

"Oh, *dat* was why you didn't more'n finger with your quilt-patches all this while! I was wonderin'. . . . But the pain *do* count, don't ye think, Liz?"

It is difficult not to feel a twinge of pity for Mrs. Fettley at her desertion by her thankless children and the onset of her blindness. We now see the significance of her staring so long at the grocer's bright calendar: she can no longer see it properly. But she has no real claims to her children's love or ours, for when it has suited her, she too has wantonly broken the rules that might have given her a place in her family's affections, putting her own sexual desire before loyalty to her home.

Toward Mrs. Archer we do not feel even an inkling of pity. She has gone after her various quarries with a predatory disregard for everything but her own self-satisfaction. Nothing deflects her iron will or softens her disposition. When the little girl offers her real affection or promises to take her headache away, Mrs. Archer misunderstands her: "I told her not to lay a finger on me, for I thought she'd want to stroke my forehead, an'—I ain't that make."

As the last quotation shows, Kipling never loses his command over detail and nuance. That such control should be sustained is, of course, absolutely imperative. It is essential that this passionate, iron-willed woman should be *dispassionate* in her own account, and it is important that we should not identify her with any of our own warmer emotions. And in moral terms the picture remains consistently and appropriately dark, as Kipling ensures with his deft manipulation of perspective. True, this utterly pagan story of a profane love begins with an innocuous reference to a Church Visitor, but it is not a simple opposition between smug orthodoxy and a healthy, rustic, "natural" order. The two ladies are not singular oddities, but are as corrupt as their environment. This is no Hardy-like vision of rustics living in some sort of life-embracing harmony with the rhythms of a sympathetic nature, and there is no way in which Grace Archer's story could be subtitled, like *Tess of the d'Urbervilles*, "The Story of a Pure Woman." Her invocation of the infernal powers of the Wish House to further her aims demonstrates the moral lawlessness of Grace and her community, and leaves us with a feeling that this lawlessness may well be, once more, the reality underlying all appearances.

VII

IN an essay of this sort the problem is what to leave out. In such limited space one cannot do justice either to the full range of Kipling's talent or to the complexity of his moral vision. The present critique has to be seen, therefore, as a contribution to the many excellent studies already in existence, to be read along with them. I particularly regret having to leave out the beautifully elegiac story "They," told with such tenderness and restraint; the totally different tales of the "soldiers three," in which Kipling is so careful to show each of them, underneath their banter, possessed of an acute sensitivity and a capacity for suffering; the somber stories of mental sickness and healing that follow World War I and reveal yet again the fragility of mental and moral integrity; and, of course, *The Jungle Books*. In many ways, if one had been simply concerned to identify Kipling's themes, the latter could have been used to illustrate virtually all of them. In "Mowgli's Brothers," for example, Mowgli shows movingly both his (and the Kipling character's) need for community—and his isolation. On the other hand, "Tiger! Tiger!" provides a succinct summary of what Kipling means by the law, a concept of primary importance to him and one of his most misunderstood subjects: "Lead us again, O Akela. Lead us again, O man-cub, for we be sick of this lawlessness, and we should be the Free People once more."

Whatever the scale of one's enterprise, Kipling is never an easy author to write about; the many prejudices against him make it difficult to present a dispassionate consideration of his literary merit. As Randall Jarrell puts it in his excellent essay: "If people don't know about Kipling they can read Kipling, and then they'll know about Kipling." But the trouble for many years has been that people *have* "known about" Kipling; that is, they have a little, very shallow, knowledge, and for them it is sufficient. Kipling is an imperialist, and that ruins any decent palate.

Now that our pomp of yesterday *is* one with Nineveh and Tyre, and the dust of frontier skirmishes no longer obscures our vision, we are more able to see what his writing really amounts to. In some ways one could say we are beginning to catch up with him and are better able to appreciate the novelty and originality that G. K. Chesterton—so often a perceptive critic of his contemporaries—saw in Kipling's imaginative exploration of new technology and vernacular speech.

More comprehensively, he stands revealed to us as one of the greatest short-story writers England has ever produced. It is a form quite characteristically appropriate to all that he stood for morally and aesthetically, for above all it requires a craftsmanship and a discipline of the most rigorous sort. Somerset Maugham, who was influenced by Kipling and himself became a celebrated short-story writer, endorsed the view generously, perhaps establishing a claim of his own in the style he adopted for his tribute:

The short story is not a form of fiction in which the English have on the whole excelled. The English, as their novels show, are inclined to diffuseness. They have never been much interested in form. Succinctness goes against their grain. But the short story demands form. It demands succinctness. Diffuseness kills it. It depends on construction. It does not admit of loose ends. It must be complete in itself. All these qualities you will find in Kipling's stories when he was at his magnificent best, and this, happily for us, he was in story after story. Rudyard Kipling is the only writer of short stories our country has produced who can stand comparison with Guy de Maupassant and Chekov. He is our greatest story writer. I can't believe he will ever be equalled. I am sure he can never be excelled.

(*Choice of Kipling's Prose*, 1952, p. xxvii)

VIII

*The following section is reprinted from the introduction to Bonamy Dobrée's* Rudyard Kipling, Realist and Fabulist (Oxford, 1967), *by permission of Oxford University Press.*

Now a polo-pony is like a poet. If he is born with a love of the game he can be made.

("The Maltese Cat")

ONE day, when Beetle [Kipling] was browsing in the Head's library, rather idly conning through Isaac D'Israeli's *Curiosities of Literature* [1791–1834], suddenly

... at the foot of a left-hand page [there] leaped out on him a verse of—incommunicable splendour, opening doors into inexplicable worlds—from a song which Tom-a-Bedlams were supposed to sing. It ran:

With a heart of furious fancies
   Whereof I am commander,
With a burning spear and a horse of air,
   To a wilderness I wander.
With a knight of ghosts and shadows
   I summoned am to tourney,
Ten leagues beyond the wide world's end—
   Methinks it is no journey.

He sat mouthing and staring before him, till the prep-bell rang.

("Propagation of Knowledge")

What doors that would open to a boy—he was then about fifteen—poetically endowed! It would suggest that poetry works, not so much through reason, as through the intuitions, guiding our existence by awakening us to the basic, though in our daily commerce, unrecognized assumptions by which we live at all, and stirring unaccustomed levels of consciousness. Furious fancies, a burning spear, and a horse of air.

Born with the love of the game, Kipling was responsible for the verse which enlivened the amateur theatricals at Westward Ho!, jokes on the masters, and so on.[3] Most of his other verses are of the imitative kind to be found in *Schoolboy Verses*, which, unknown to him, his parents had printed in India

[3] *Stalky & Co.*, passim.

before he returned there, though he did write one poem, "Ave Imperatrix," thought by T. S. Eliot worthy of inclusion in his selection; and on one occasion he was paid a whole guinea for some verses, untraced, which he sent up to a paper, so that "the Study caroused on chocolate and condensed milk and pilchards and Devonshire Cream." Rhyme throughout his life was an essential part of verse, and he very rarely wrote anything without it. Having to "do" Horace at school, he rebelled against him and, pretending not to understand classical quantities, declared that "he could do better if Latin verse rhymed as decent verse should." When, as an imposition he was told to send up a translation of Ode III. ix, "he turned 'Donec gratus eram' into pure Devonshire dialect,"[4] the first example of a manner he could later use so effectively. The first two stanzas read:

> *He.* Ez long as 'twuz me alone
>   An' there wasn't no other chaps,
> I was praoud as a King on 'is throne—
>   Happier tu, per'aps.
>
> *She.* Ez long as 'twuz only I
>   An' there wasn't no other she
> Yeou cared for so much—surely
>   I was glad as glad could be.

He did, however, make a by no means despicable attempt at blank verse before his sixteenth birthday.[5]

How important verse was to Kipling for expressing the whole range of his ideas and emotions from the lightest to the most profound is evident from the extent to which it has been appropriate to quote it in the process of trying to elucidate his thought or emotion. It would seem that he turned for expression to verse as readily as to prose, the one medium being as natural to him as the other. As Eliot stressed, he did not try to write "poetry." When the thought lent itself to what we call poetry, or the emotion was deep enough, the "verse" became "poetry."

Thus whether he wrote in prose, or, to invert Dryden's phrase, "in the other harmony of verse," seems to have been with him not so much a matter of indifference as of the mood of the moment, sometimes, of course, of subject-matter. States of mind are not always susceptible of being conveyed in story form, except too clumsily. What could be made of, say, "The Two-Sided Man"? But often, with his thirst to formulate, even project, what he had to say in different ways, he came to accompany his tales with a poem, either as preface or as conclusion, sometimes both. These to some degree elucidate the tale, or the tale explains the poem. Eliot went so far as to say that he invented a kind of dual form, story and poem making one whole, each being incomplete without the other: but this is rare. Occasionally there seems to be little connection. How, for instance, does "Akbar's Bridge" throw a light on "The Debt"? One may well feel that the former, good as it is, would be better as a prose story, perhaps after the manner of "The Amir's Homily."

At all events he labored at his verse as indefatigably as he did at his prose; the briefest study of the manuscripts will show this with their drafts, corrections, scribblings over, and rewriting. One extended example will illustrate the point, "A Song in Storm," already partly quoted. The manuscript version[6] has for first stanza:

> Be well assured that from our side
>   Good luck has taken flight—
> And nosing wind and raging tide
>   Make us their prey to-night.
> Our past so nearly, clearly won
>   Alas! is far removèd:
> Then welcome Fate's discourtesy
>   Whereby it shall be provèd
>     How in all time of our distress
>     (Whatever Fate shall do)
>     The game is more than the player of the game,
>     As Fame is more than the seeker after fame,
>     And the ship is more than the crew.

In the Definitive Edition this has become:

> Be well assured that on our side
>   The abiding oceans fight,
> Though headlong wind and heaping tide
>   Make us their sport to-night.
> By force of weather, not of war,
>   In jeopardy we steer:
> Then welcome Fate's discourtesy
>   Whereby it shall appear
>     How in all time of our distress
>     And our deliverance too,
>     The game is more than the player of the game
>     And the ship is more than the crew!

---

[4] "An English School," in *Land and Sea Tales*.
[5] Neither is included in the Definitive Edition. Printed in *Carrington*, ch. 15, p. 39.
[6] British Museum. Add. MSS 44841.

That was not merely correcting: the change of idea in the first four lines is radical. Nor did he cease revising. Just as in collecting his stories he would make alterations of the magazine versions, so he did when collecting his poems, even from one garnering to another—as has been marginally exampled earlier.

Whatever opinion may be held of him as a poet, it is agreed that he was brilliant in versification. Some of his verse admittedly is jingle, but of set purpose, and always disciplined, prosodically controlled. He could handle all sorts of meters, while his rhythms are complex, sometimes indeed subtle, as quotations already made will have illustrated. He was at home in the heroic couplet, common measure, ballad forms; the iambic or the rollicking anapaest, as well as more difficult prosodic units; the octosyllable or the sixteener; literally "free" verse, though rhymed; a variation of the terza rima, the varied seventeenth-century stanza, or something too readily regarded as Swinburnian, though dating from much earlier. If, however, he excelled in meter, forms beyond that of the stanza did not much attract him. His ballads are poor, his few sonnets, although one or two are good poems, are unimpressive as sonnets, lacking the structural movement, his one triumphant success in an exacting form being "Sestina of the Tramp Royal." His long poems tend to be too protracted, though exception must be made of the great monologues "McAndrew's Hymn" and "The 'Mary Gloster,'" to which may be added the semi-dialogue "Tomlinson."

There is little point in considering influences. After his *Schoolboy Lyrics* and *Echoes,* not collected, there is no trace of the Pre-Raphaelite note, except perhaps in "The Love Song of Har Dyal." It appeared in 1884 as part of "Beyond the Pale," and purports to be a rendering of an Indian poem, very moving in the original: "In English you miss the wail of it. It runs something like this—

> Alone upon the housetops to the North
>    I turn and watch the lightning in the sky,—
> The glamour of thy footsteps in the North,
>    *Come back to me, Beloved, or I die!*
>
> Below my feet the still bazar is laid—
>    Far, far below the weary camels lie,—
> The camels and the captives of thy raid.
>    *Come back to me, Beloved, or I die!*
>
> My father's wife is old and harsh with years,
>    And drudge of all my father's house am I.—

> My bread is sorrow and my drink is tears,
>    *Come back to me, Beloved, or I die!*
>       (*Definitive Edition* differs slightly)

That is clearly influenced by the Rossetti ear; we meet the vaguely evocative phrase, "the glamour of thy footsteps in the North," absent from Kipling's more characteristic verse.

The monologues may have been suggested by Browning, but the attack and versification are different. Only the very early "One Viceroy Resigns" (1888) is obviously after the manner of Browning. Parodies there are: the early one of Swinburne, where he puts the first chorus from *Atalanta in Calydon* to more mundane uses; and those in "A Muse Among the Motors." All that can usefully be said is that, widely read in English poetry, he used, or dropped into, whatever form of rhythm either came to him, or that he felt to be appropriate. When he smote "'is bloomin'" lyre he winked at all the Homers down the road of history.

More general considerations present themselves before embarking on any detailed study. Most readers will be aware of the crucial difficulty Eliot laid finger on when he said in the introduction to his *Selection of Kipling's Verse:*

While I speak of Kipling's work as verse and not as poetry, I am still able to speak of individual compositions as poetry, and also to maintain that there is "poetry" in the "verse."

Admittedly Kipling was a dazzlingly able versifier in the matter of rhythm and meter, as already said; but it will be claimed here that he was a poet in the full sense of the term. Notoriously, to try to define poetry is to rush in where angels fear to tread; it may, finally, depend upon what each person expects poetry to do for him. One may begin, however, by what Moneta said in John Keats's *The Fall of Hyperion:*

> The poet and the dreamer are distinct,
> Diverse, sheer opposites, antipodes.
> The one pours out a balm upon the world,
> The other vexes it.
>       (I.199–202)

Much of what Kipling wrote vexed the world, sometimes by direct attack upon its complacency, but more importantly, and more in Keats's meaning, by forcing the individual to face himself, the conditions of living, or the abyss of darkness which he sometimes feels may engulf him. But before he spoke with those ends in view, he vexed the secluded, self-conscious literary world of his time in a more superficial way, by using the colloquial idiom of the people. His sin was to act on Wordsworth's precept—which is more than Wordsworth did—of writing poetry in the language men (ordinary men) use in speaking to men; or, as Ben Jonson put it, animated by the same cyclical desire to purify the dialect of the tribe, to write poetry in words "such as men doe use." "Tommy" Kipling wrote in plain vernacular, then decried but now seen as contributing to that freedom of "poetic" diction that has been one of the feathers in the cap of present-century metrical writing. His was better than most, for, as Robert Bridges declared, "nothing in [his] diction is common or unclean." We get such pieces as "For to Admire," which opens:

> The Injian Ocean sets an' smiles
> So sof', so bright, so bloomin' blue:

verses in which there may not be much "poetry," except perhaps for the striking

> Old Aden, like a barrick-stove
> That no one's lit for years an' years. . . .

But there was certainly poetry in the later "Sestina of the Tramp Royal," as there was in "Chant-Pagan":

> Me that 'ave been what I've been—
> Me that 'ave gone where I've gone—
> Me that 'ave seen what I've seen—
>    'Ow can I ever take on
> With awful old England again,
> An' 'ouses both sides of the street,
> An' 'edges two sides of the lane,
> And the parson an' gentry between,
> An' touchin' my 'at when we meet—
>    Me that 'ave been what I've been.

"Danny Deever," which appeared first in February 1890, to be included in *Barrack-Room Ballads* later in the year, is now recognized as a poem proper, and a very powerful one.

But he "vexed" more deeply than that. As R. G. Collingwood noted, he 'burst into the stuffy atmosphere of the aesthetes' china-shop not only by his diction, but by writing 'magical' poetry, poetry that is, that 'evokes and canalises the emotions that are to men as the steam in the engine of their daily work, and discharges them into the affairs of practical life.' "[7] That would, naturally, be repugnant in an "art for art's sake" period. There is a deal of this sort of work at a certain period of Kipling's career, "The Islanders" for instance, which vexed more than the aesthetes; "The Dykes," "The Truce of the Bear," and, though this gained considerable support to the tune of many thousands of pounds, "The Absent-Minded Beggar." There is not very much poetry to be found in these pieces, which were mainly the result of irritated impatience rising sometimes to indignation, for if in his case it was true that *facit indignatio versum*, the verse was hardly poetry. The political poems have plenty of "punch," as Mr. Hilton Brown remarks, but one cannot altogether agree with him that they make dull reading now, and would seem to have only an historical interest. Read in the context of their time, as one reads, say, John Dryden's *Absalom and Achitophel*, they take on life, while some, for example "The City of Brass," are startlingly prophetic of today. Yet it is where the "magical" fuses with the philosophic, as, to give an early, and possibly best-known, example, "Recessional," that our minds become receptive in the way that poetry induces.

A major difficulty in treating of Kipling's poetry is that he adventured along so many of the nine-and-sixty ways. He is as varied in the subject-matter of his verse as he is in his story-telling, as also in his manner. To try to simplify the discussion (though this is to be more than a little arbitrary) it might be suggested that in the main, apart from his "magical" verse, he wrote three kinds of poetry. The edges of such things are, however, always *con*fused, Kipling sometimes *fusing* the kinds. These I would call the "lyric-romantic" or dreamer's poems; poems of thought and experience; and, to coin a word, "actuality" poems. It is not possible to separate these into periods. "Romantic" poetry Kipling wrote all through his life; the next group soon appeared and continued to the end; the outstanding "actuality" poems, though mainly related to his later development, are embryonically present at a fairly early date. It is only "magical" poetry that belongs to a period, that during which he was emotionally involved in politics, and it disappeared when he had reached the stage of acceptance.

[7] *The Principles of Art* (Oxford, 1938).

# RUDYARD KIPLING

## SELECTED BIBLIOGRAPHY

I. BIBLIOGRAPHY. E. W. Martindell, *A Bibliography of the Works of Rudyard Kipling, 1881-1921* (London, 1922; rev. ed., 1923); F. V. Livingstone, *Bibliography of the Works of Rudyard Kipling* (New York, 1927), supp. (Cambridge, Mass., 1938); L. H. Chandler, comp., *A Catalogue of the Works of Rudyard Kipling* (New York, 1930), exhibited at the Grolier Club, New York, 1929; J. McG. Stewart, *Rudyard Kipling: A Bibliographical Catalogue*, A. W. Yeats, ed. (Toronto, 1959); *English Fiction in Transition*, Purdue University, vol. III, nos. 3, 4, 5 (Lafayette, Ind., 1960).

II. COLLECTED WORKS. *Edition Deluxe*, 38 vols. (London, 1897-1937); *Outward Bound Edition*, 36 vols. (New York, 1897-1937); *Pocket Edition*, 29 vols. (London, 1907-1938), 32 vols. (New York, 1908-1932); *Bombay Edition*, 31 vols. (London, 1913-1938); *The Complete Works in Prose and Verse*, 35 vols. (London, 1937-1939), the Sussex ed., includes works not previously in book form; *Rudyard Kipling's Verse* (London, 1940; 1960), latest and most complete collection of inclusive eds. published since 1912.

III. SELECTED WORKS. T. S. Eliot, ed., *A Choice of Kipling's Prose* (London, 1941), with intro. by Eliot; W. S. Maugham, ed., *A Choice of Kipling's Prose* (London, 1952), with intro. by Maugham; W. G. Bebbington, ed., *A Kipling Anthology* (London, 1964); R. C. Green, ed., *Rudyard Kipling. Stories and Poems* (London, 1970), Everyman's Library; A. Rutherford, ed., *Rudyard Kipling. Short Stories* (London, 1971), Penguin ed.; C. E. Carrington, ed., *The Complete Barrack-Room Ballads* (London, 1973); J. Cochrane, ed., *Rudyard Kipling. Selected Verse* (London, 1977), Penguin ed.

IV. SEPARATE WORKS. FICTION: *Departmental Ditties and Other Verses* (London, 1886); *Plain Tales from the Hills* (London, 1888), stories; *Wee Willie Winkie* (London, 1888), stories; *Barrack-room Ballads* (London, 1890, enl. ed., 1892), verse; *The Light That Failed* (New York, 1890; rev. ed., 1891), novel; *Soldiers Three* (London, 1890), stories; *Life's Handicap* (London, 1891), stories; *The Naulahka*, in collaboration with W. Balestier (London, 1892), novel; *Many Inventions* (London, 1893), stories; *The Jungle Book* (London, 1894), stories; *The Second Jungle Book* (London, 1895), stories; *The Seven Seas* (London, 1896), verse; *Captains Courageous* (Leipzig-London-New York, 1897), novel; *The Day's Work* (London, 1898), stories; *Stalky & Co.* (New York, 1899), stories.

*Kim* (London, 1901), novel; *Just So Stories for Little Children* (London, 1902), stories; *The Five Nations* (London, 1903), verse; *Traffics and Discoveries* (Leipzig-London-New York, 1904), stories; *Puck of Pook's Hill* (New York, 1906), stories; *Abaft the Funnel* (New York, 1909), stories; *Actions and Reactions* (London, 1909), stories; *Rewards and Fairies* (Garden City, N.Y., 1910), stories; *A Diversity of Creatures* (Garden City, N.Y., 1917), stories; *The Eyes of Asia* (Garden City, N.Y., 1918), fiction; *Twenty Poems* (London, 1918); *The Years Between* (Garden City, N.Y., 1919), verse; *Children's Stories* (New York, 1925), stories; *Debits and Credits* (Garden City, N.Y., 1926), stories; *A Tour of Inspection* (New York, 1928), story; *Thy Servant a Dog, Told by Boots, Edited by R. Kipling* (London, 1930); *Limits and Renewals* (London, 1932), stories; *The Maltese Cat* (London, 1936), story; *"'Teem'"—A Treasure Hunter* (New York, 1938), story.

NONFICTION: *Out of India* (New York, 1895), description; *A Fleet in Being* (London, 1898), history; *From Sea to Sea*, 2 vols. (New York, 1899), travel letters; *A History of England*, in collaboration with C. R. L. Fletcher (Oxford, 1911); "Indictment of the Government" (London, 1914), speech; *France at War* (London, 1915); "Kipling's Message" (London, 1918), speech; *The Art of Fiction* (London, 1926), criticism; *Souvenirs de France* (Paris, 1933), travel; *Something of Myself for My Friends, Known and Unknown* (London, 1937), memoir; M. Cohen, ed., *Rudyard Kipling to Rider Haggard* (London, 1965), letters.

V. BIOGRAPHICAL AND CRITICAL STUDIES. W. M. Clemens, *A Ken of Kipling* (New York, 1899).

R. LeGallienne, *Rudyard Kipling, A Criticism* (London, 1900); G. F. Monkshood [pseud.], *Rudyard Kipling, the Man and His Work* (London, 1902); G. K. Chesterton, *Heretics* (London, 1909); C. Charles, *Rudyard Kipling, Life and Work* (London, 1911); G. A. Borgese, *Kipling e un sui critico* (Turin, 1913); H. Jackson, *The Eighteen Nineties* (London, 1913); D. Mantovani, *Il nuova apologio R. Kipling* (Turin, 1913); R. Durand, *A Handbook to the Poetry of Rudyard Kipling* (London, 1914); G. A. Borgese, *"Kim" di Kipling* (Milan, 1915); C. Falls, *Rudyard Kipling, A Critical Study* (London, 1915); A. Galletti, *Saggi i studi* (Bologna, 1915); H. Jackson, *Rudyard Kipling, A Critical Study* (London, 1915); W. M. Hart, *Kipling the Story-Writer* (Berkeley, Calif., 1918).

A. Chevrillon, *La Poésie de Rudyard Kipling* (Paris, 1920), and *Three Studies in English Literature: Kipling, Galsworthy, Shakespeare* (London, 1923); D. Braybrook, *Kipling and His Soldiers* (London, 1926); *The Kipling Journal*, quarterly publication of the Kipling Society (London, 1927—    ); L. C. Dunsterville, *Stalky's Reminiscences* (London, 1928); M. Brion, *Rudyard Kipling* (Paris, 1929); B. Dobrée, *The Lamp and the Lute* (Oxford, 1929; repr. New York, 1963); R. T. Hopkins, *Rudyard Kipling: The Story of a Genius* (London, 1930); T. G. P. Spear, *The Nabobs: A Study of the Social Life of the English in Eighteenth Century India* (London, 1932); G. C. Beresford, *Schooldays with Kipling* (London, 1936); G. F. MacMunn, *Rudyard Kipling, Craftsman* (London, 1937); L. Lemonnier, *Kipling* (Paris, 1939); A. M. Weygandt, *Kipling's Reading and Its Influence on His Poetry* (Philadelphia, 1939).

E. Shanks, *Rudyard Kipling* (London, 1940); H. E. Bates, *The Modern Short Story* (London, 1943); C. H. Brown, *Rudyard Kipling: A New Appreciation* (London, 1945); G. Orwell (pseud.), *Critical Essays* (London, 1946); J. I. M. Stewart, *Rudyard Kipling* (London, 1946); R.

Croft-Cooke, *Rudyard Kipling* (London, 1948); S. (Nobbe) Howe, *Novels of Empire* (New York, 1949); R. Church, *The Growth of the English Novel* (London, 1951); B. Dobrée, *Rudyard Kipling* (London, 1951; rev. ed., 1966); L. Trilling, *The Liberal Imagination* (London, 1951); E. Wilson, *The Wound and the Bow* (London, 1952); C. C. Carrington, *The Life of Rudyard Kipling* (Garden City, N. Y., 1955); R. A. Scott-James, *Fifty Years of English Literature* (London, 1956); F. Leaud, *La Poétique de Rudyard Kipling* (Paris, 1958); J. M. S. Tomkins, *The Art of Rudyard Kipling* (London, 1959).

R. Cook, *Rudyard Kipling and George Orwell* (London, 1961); R. L. Green, ed., *The Readers' Guide to Rudyard Kipling's Works* (Canterbury, 1961); R. H. Harbord, ed., *The Readers' Guide to Rudyard Kipling's Works*, 7 parts (London, 1961–1972); C. S. Lewis, "Kipling's World," in *They Asked for a Paper* (London, 1962); A. Sandison, *The Wheel of Empire* (London, 1962); J. I. M. Stewart, *Eight Modern Writers* (London, 1963); C. A. Bodelsen, *Aspects of Rudyard Kipling's Art* (New York, 1964); A. Rutherford, ed., *Kipling's Mind and Art* (Stanford, Calif., 1964); E. L. Gilbert, *Kipling and the Critics* (New York, 1965), includes R. Jarrell, "On Preparing to Read Kipling"; R. G. L. Green, *Kipling and the Children* (London, 1965); L. M. Cornell, *Kipling in India* (London, 1966); A. L. Rowse, *The English Spirit* (London, 1966); B. Dobrée, *Rudyard Kipling, Realist and Fatalist* (Oxford, 1967); T. R. Henn, *Kipling* (London, 1967).

R. L. Green, *Kipling. The Critical Heritage* (London, 1971); E. L. Gilbert, *The Good Kipling* (Manchester, 1972); J. Gross, ed., *Rudyard Kipling: The Man, His Work, and His World* (London, 1972); S. Islam, *Kipling's "Law": A Study of His Philosophy of Life* (London, 1975); J. K. Lyon, *Bertolt Brecht and Rudyard Kipling: A Marxist's Imperialist Mentor* (The Hague, 1975); P. Mason, *Kipling: The Glass, the Shadow, and the Fire* (London, 1975); A. Wilson, *The Strange Ride of Rudyard Kipling. His Life and Works* (London, 1977); K. Amis, *Rudyard Kipling and His World* (London, 1978); F. W. F. Smith, Lord Birkenhead, *Rudyard Kipling* (London, 1978).

## LIST OF SHORT STORIES

(The title in italics refers to the volume in which the story appears.)

"The Amir's Homily," *Life's Handicap*; "The Army of a Dream," *Traffics and Discoveries*; "The Arrest of Lieutenant Golightly," *Plain Tales from the Hills*; "As Easy as A.B.C.," *A Diversity of Creatures*; "At Howli Thana," *Soldiers Three*; "At the End of the Passage," *Life's Handicap*; "At the Pit's Mouth," *Wee Willie Winkie*; "At Twenty-Two," *Soldiers Three*; "Aunt Ellen," *Limits and Renewals*.

"Baa, Baa, Black Sheep," *Wee Willie Winkie*; "A Bank Fraud," *Plain Tales from the Hills*; "Beauty Spots," *Limits and Renewals*; "Below the Mill Dam," *Traffics and Discoveries*; "Bertran and Bimi," *Life's Handicap*; "Beyond the Pale," *Plain Tales from the Hills*; "The Big Drunk Draf," *Soldiers Three*; "The Bisara of Pooree," *Plain Tales from the Hills*; "Black Jack," *Soldiers Three*; "The Bonds of Discipline," *Traffics and Discoveries*; "'Bread Upon the Waters,'" *The Day's Work*; "The Bridge-Builders," *The Day's Work*; "The Broken-Link Handicap," *Plain Tales from the Hills*; "The Bronckhorst Divorce Case," *Plain Tales from the Hills*; "Brother Square Toes," *Rewards and Fairies*; "'Brugglesmith,'" *Many Inventions*; "The Brushwood Boy," *The Day's Work*; "Bubbling Well Road," *Life's Handicap*; "The Bull That Thought," *Debits and Credits*; "By Word of Mouth," *Plain Tales from the Hills*.

"The Captive," *Traffics and Discoveries*; "A Centurion of the Thirtieth," *Puck of Pook's Hill*; "The Children of the Zodiac," *Many Inventions*; "The Church that Was in Antioch," *Limits and Renewals*; "The City of Dreadful Night," *Life's Handicap*; "Cold Iron," *Rewards and Fairies*; "The Comprehension of Private Copper," *Traffics and Discoveries*; "A Conference of the Powers," *Many Inventions*; "Consequences," *Plain Tales from the Hills*; "The Conversion of Aurelian McGoggin," *Plain Tales from the Hills*; "The Conversion of St. Wilfred," *Rewards and Fairies*; "The Courting of Dinah Shadd," *Life's Handicap*; "Cupid's Arrows," *Plain Tales from the Hills*.

"Dayspring Mishandled," *Limits and Renewals*; "The Daughter of the Regiment," *Plain Tales from the Hills*; "A Deal in Cotton," *Actions and Reactions*; "The Debt," *Limits and Renewals*; "The Devil and the Deep Sea," *The Day's Work*; "The Disturber of the Traffic," *Many Inventions*; "A Doctor of Medecine," *Rewards and Fairies*; "The Dog Hervey," *A Diversity of Creatures*; "Dray Wara Yow Dee," *Soldiers Three*; "Dream of Duncan Parreness," *Life's Handicap*; "The Drums of the Fore and Aft," *Wee Willie Winkie*; "'Dymchurch Flit,'" *Puck of Pook's Hill*; "The Edge of the Evening," *A Diversity of Creatures*; "The Education of Otis Yeere," *Wee Willie Winkie*; "The Enemies to Each Other," *Debits and Credits*; "An Error in the Fourth Dimension," *The Day's Work*; "The Eye of Allah," *Debits and Credits*.

"Fairy-kist," *Limits and Renewals*; "False Dawn," *Plain Tales from the Hills*; "Fatima," *Soldiers Three*; "The Finances of the Gods," *Life's Handicap*; "Friendly Brook," *A Diversity of Creatures*; "A Friend of the Family," *Debits and Credits*; "A Friend's Friend," *Plain Tales from the Hills*; "The Gardener," *Debits and Credits*; "The Garden of Eden," *Soldiers Three*; "Garm—A Hostage," *Plain Tales from the Hills*; "The Gate of the Hundred Sorrows," *Plain Tales from the Hills*; "Gemini," *Soldiers Three*; "Georgie Porgie," *Life's Handicap*; "A Germ-Destroyer," *Plain Tales from the Hills*; "Gloriana," *Rewards and Fairies*; "The God from the Machine," *Soldiers Three*; "An Habitation Enforced," *Actions and Reactions*; "Hal o' the Draft," *Puck of Pook's Hill*; "The Head of the District," *Life's Handicap*; "The Hill of Illusion," *Wee Willie Winkie*; "His Chance in

"Life," *Plain Tales from the Hills*; "His Majesty the King," *Wee Willie Winkie*; "His Private Honour," *Many Inventions*; "His Wedded Wife," *Plain Tales from the Hills*; "The Honours of War," *A Diversity of Creatures*; "The Horse Marines," *A Diversity of Creatures*; "The House Surgeon," *Actions and Reactions*.

"The Incarnation of Krishna Mulvaney," *Life's Handicap*; "In Error," *Plain Tales from the Hills*; "In Flood Time," *Soldiers Three*; "In the House of Suddhoo," *Plain Tales from the Hills*; "'In the Interests of the Brethren,'" *Debits and Credits*; "In the Matter of a Private," *Soldiers Three*; "In the Presence," *A Diversity of Creatures*; "In the Pride of His Youth," *Many Inventions*; "In the Same Boat," *A Diversity of Creatures*; "The Janeites," *Debits and Credits*; "Jews in Shushan," *Life's Handicap*; "The Judgment of Dungara," *Soldiers Three*; "Judson and the Empire," *Many Inventions*; "Kidnapped," *Plain Tales from the Hills*; "The Knife and the Naked Chalk," *Rewards and Fairies*; "The Knights of the Joyous Venture," *Puck of Pook's Hill*.

"The Lang Men o' Larut," *Life's Handicap*; "The Limitations of Pambé Serang," *Life's Handicap*; "Lispeth," *Plain Tales from the Hills*; "Little Foxes," *Actions and Reactions*; "Little Tobrah," *Life's Handicap*; "The Lost Legion," *Many Inventions*; "'Love-o'-Women,'" *Many Inventions*; "The Madness of Private Ortheris," *Plain Tales from the Hills*; "A Madonna of the Trenches," *Debits and Credits*; "The Maltese Cat," *The Day's Work*; "The Man Who Was," *Life's Handicap*; "The Man Who Would Be King," *Wee Willie Winkie*; "The Manner of Men," *Limits and Renewals*; "The Mark of the Beast," *Life's Handicap*; "Marklake Witches," *Rewards and Fairies*; "Mary Postgate," *A Diversity of Creatures*; "A Matter of Fact," *Many Inventions*; "The Miracle of Saint Jubanus," *Limits and Renewals*; "Miss Youghal's Sais," *Plain Tales from the Hills*; "Mrs. Bathurst," *Traffics and Discoveries*; "The Mother Hive," *Actions and Reactions*; "Moti Guj—Mutineer," *Life's Handicap*; "The Mutiny of the Mavericks," *Life's Handicap*; "My Lord of the Elephant," *Many Inventions*; "My Own True Ghost Story," *Wee Willie Winkie*; "'My Son's Wife,'" *A Diversity of Creatures*; "My Sunday at Home," *The Day's Work*.

"Naboth," *Life's Handicap*; "Namgay Doola," *Life's Handicap*; "A Naval Mutiny," *Limits and Renewals*; "Old Men at Pevensey," *Puck of Pook's Hill*; "One View of the Question," *Many Inventions*; "Only a Subaltern," *Wee Willie Winkie*; "On Greenhow Hill," *Life's Handicap*; "On the City Wall," *Soldiers Three*; "On the Gate: A Tale of '16," *Debits and Credits*; "On the Great Wall," *Puck of Pook's Hill*; "On the Strength of a Likeness," *Plain Tales from the Hills*; ".007," *The Day's Work*; "The Other Man," *Plain Tales from the Hills*.

"The Phantom 'Rickshaw," *Wee Willie Winkie*; "Pig," *Plain Tales from the Hills*; "Poor Dear Mamma," *Soldiers Three*; "'A Priest in Spite of Himself,'" *Rewards and Fairies*; "Private Learoyd's Story," *Soldiers Three*; "The Prophet and the Country," *Debits and Credits*; "The Propagation of Knowledge," *Debits and Credits*; "The Puzzler," *Actions and Reactions*; "The Record of Badalia Herodsfoot," *Many Inventions*; "Regulus," *A Diversity of Creatures*; "Reingelder and the German Flag," *Life's Handicap*; "The Rescue of Pluffles," *Plain Tales from the Hills*; "The Return of Imray," *Life's Handicap*; "The Rout of the White Hussars," *Plain Tales from the Hills*; "A Sahibs' War," *Traffics and Discoveries*; "Sea Constables: A Tale of '15," *Debits and Credits*; "A Second Rate Woman," *Wee Willie Winkie*; "The Sending of Dana Da," *Soldiers Three*; "The Ship that Found Herself," *The Day's Work*; "Simple Simon," *Rewards and Fairies*; "The Solid Muldoon," *Soldiers Three*; "Steam Tactics," *Traffics and Discoveries*; "The Story of Muhammed Din," *Plain Tales from the Hills*; "The Strange Ride of Morrowbie Jukes," *Wee Willie Winkle*; "The Swelling of Jordan," *Soldiers Three*; "'Swept and Garnished,'" *Debits and Credits*.

"The Taking of Lungtungpen," *Plain Tales from the Hills*; "The Tender Achilles," *Limits and Renewals*; "The Tents of Kedar," *Soldiers Three*; "'Their Lawful Occasions,'" *Traffics and Diversions*; "'They,'" *Traffics and Diversions*; "Three and—an Extra," *Plain Tales from the Hills*; "The Three Musketeers," *Plain Tales from the Hills*; "Through the Fire," *Life's Handicap*; "Thrown Away," *Plain Tales from the Hills*; "The Tie," *Limits and Rewards*; "To Be Filed for Reference," *Plain Tales from the Hills*; "Tod's Amendment," *Plain Tales from the Hills*; "The Tomb of His Ancestors," *The Day's Work*; "The Treasure and the Law," *Puck of Pook's Hill*; "The Tree of Justice," *Rewards and Fairies*; "Uncovenanted Mercies," *Limits and Renewals*; "The United Idolators," *Debits and Credits*; "Unprofessional," *Limits and Renewals*; "The Valley of the Shadow," *Soldiers Three*; "Venus Annodomini," *Plain Tales from the Hills*; "The Village That Voted the Earth Was Flat," *A Diversity of Creatures*; "The Vortex," *A Diversity of Creatures*.

"A Walking Delegate," *The Day's Work*; "The Wandering Jew," *Life's Handicap*; "Watches of the Night," *Plain Tales from the Hills*; "A Wayside Comedy," *Wee Willie Winkie*; "Wee Willie Winkie," *Wee Willie Winkie*; "Weyland's Sword," *Puck of Pook's Hill*; "William the Conqueror," *The Day's Work*; "The Winged Hats," *Puck of Pook's Hill*; "'Wireless,'" *Traffics and Discoveries*; "The Wish House," *Debits and Credits*; "With Any Amazement," *Soldiers Three*; "With the Main Guard," *Soldiers Three*; "With the Night Mail," *Actions and Reactions*; "Without Benefit of Clergy," *Life's Handicap*; "The Woman in His Life," *Limits and Renewals*; "The World Without," *Soldiers Three*; "Wressley of the Foreign Office," *Plain Tales from the Hills*; "The Wrong Thing," *Rewards and Fairies*; "'Yoked with an Unbeliever,'" *Plain Tales from the Hills*; "Young Men at the Manor," *Puck of Pook's Hill*.

# D. H. LAWRENCE
(1885-1930)

## *Alastair Niven*

### THE WRITER AND THE MAN

No one attending the birth of David Herbert (Richards) Lawrence on 11 September 1885 could have anticipated that this fourth child and third son of a miner in the Nottinghamshire town of Eastwood would become the most frequently studied English novelist of the twentieth century. As this short study of his work emphasizes, he also became a proficient poet and playwright as well as one of the most prolific literary correspondents of modern times, a combative essayist, and a uniquely atmospheric travel writer. His talents extended to book reviewing, translation, philosophical discourse, painting, and teaching, but it was in the powers of his imagination and in his ability to match these with many appropriate aesthetic forms that his true genius lay. It has taken time to recognize Lawrence as a great writer, and in his own lifetime he often resorted to writing short articles in order to earn some of the money that his full-length works never made. His final and subsequently most famous novel, *Lady Chatterley's Lover* (1928), had initially to be privately published in Florence. If this was principally because of its sexual content, it nevertheless summed up the precarious relationship that Lawrence had with the publishing world. His best books were too controversial to be best sellers, the others too elusive to be categorized alongside the fiction of his time. Only since about 1960 has his work attained the reputation that now makes it a pivot of most modern English literature courses in all kinds of educational establishments throughout the world.

Lawrence is not an easy writer to read, but he never meant to be. At a time when the socially realistic novels of John Galsworthy, Arnold Bennett, and H. G. Wells were in vogue, Lawrence wanted to explore beneath the surface of human behavior in an attempt to gauge the forces that may motivate it. In his essay entitled "Morality and the Novel" (1925) he denounces "the smart and smudgily cynical novel, which says it doesn't matter what you do, because one thing is as good as another, anyhow, and 'prostitution' is just as much 'life' as anything else."[1] Lawrence's work is at all times totally concerned with discriminating between levels of existence. The majority of people live half-lives, failing to develop even a tenth of the potential that they retain inwardly without knowing it. Hence the prevalence in his work of images that suggest stunted growth: seeds within husks, fruits within rinds, roots struggling below stones for light and air, but too often only withering and dying. "A thing isn't life," he continues in "Morality and the Novel," "just because somebody does it. This the artist ought to know perfectly well. The ordinary bank clerk buying himself a new straw [hat] isn't 'life' at all: it is just existence, quite all right, like everyday dinners: but not 'life.'" This view shows how out of line Lawrence was with the age that produced Galsworthy's *The Forsyte Saga*, Bennett's *Clayhanger*, and Wells's *Kipps*.

Lawrence's need to explore man's nature below its surface led him into far franker discussions of sex, religion, and psychology than we find in any English novelist before him. He had the advantage over most of his predecessors in having inherited a scientific terminology for these topics to draw upon when he wished, but more normally he creates his own vocabulary, the authentic Lawrentian voice that is so readily recognizable to the practiced reader of his works. One may fairly doubt, however, whether Lawrence contributed to our knowledge any truly original notion about our basic human impulses. The author of "The Woman Who Rode Away" (short story, 1928), "Democracy" (essay, probably written 1917), the Loerke chapters in *Women in Love* (1920), and *The Plumed Serpent* (1926) could verge

---

[1] Quotations and references are from the Penguin editions of Lawrence's writings.

on the bizarre, but from an empirical point of view he more frequently followed initiatives already taken by other intellectuals. This in no way detracts from his radical importance in the development of English literature, for far more effectively than any other contemporary writer he kept pace with the welter of ideas that transformed society in his lifetime and brought them directly into his work. His subsequent reputation depended a great deal upon critics and readers recognizing how, especially in major achievements like *The Rainbow* (1915) and *Women in Love*, he debates many sides of the major issues of the early twentieth century. His work is highly individualized, as all great art must be; it is often eccentric and sometimes reactionary; but the person who has read his way through all of Lawrence has witnessed the transformation of English attitudes to education, morality, science, and culture through the eyes of someone who accepted nothing uncritically and who retained to the end of his life a deep skepticism about the nature of the changes.

Lawrence's writing may be termed "open-ended," even if it is not always open-minded. Though F. R. Leavis effectively linked his moral concern with Jane Austen's and George Eliot's, Lawrence lacks the sense of a confident overview that permeates the work of his nineteenth-century predecessors. Austen and Eliot, in their different ways, do not doubt their own moral perspective. Lawrence, while superficially appearing to be a more dogmatic and authoritarian writer, constantly extends himself to the limits of his understanding, seeming at times to contradict himself. In *Women in Love*, for example, he paints a powerfully seductive portrait of a society harnessed to science in order to serve man's greed, though his intention is to deplore the mechanical life to which it gives birth; at the end of *The Plumed Serpent* he appears to renounce the thesis upon which the novel has been built; he wrote *Lady Chatterley's Lover* three times because his focal point kept shifting. Indeed, in the sexual descriptions of this last novel, as in the pastoral rhapsodies of his first, *The White Peacock* (1911), or in the mystical ceremonies of *The Plumed Serpent*, the resources of language themselves nearly crack under the strain of expressing feelings that are wholly nonverbal in experience. Neither Austen nor Eliot—indeed, no English novelist before Lawrence, with the possible exception of Emily Brontë—had risked such a stretching of language. Lawrence brings to modern prose an instinct to express the nearly inexpressible that previously only some poets had tried. If his work sometimes threatens to collapse into a heap of rhetorical, repetitive, and inflated utterance, it is more because even the prodigiously flexible English language cannot cope with the moments he is seeking to render than because his art has failed.

Many elements in Lawrence's life story found their way into his writing, for he hardly ever wrote about things he had not witnessed or about situations that did not ultimately derive from personal experience. We know him, however, as a novelist, poet, playwright, or essayist, not as an autobiographer. He would plant allusions to his own life in his books—the Beardsall family in *The White Peacock*, for example, take their name from his mother, Lydia Beardsall, who herself became the basis for Mrs. Morel in *Sons and Lovers* (1913) and partly for Lydia Lensky in *The Rainbow*. However, he never allowed his imagination to be dominated by documentary accuracy. Specific details about Lawrence's life can be found in his writing only when he thought them useful to mention, and one wonders, therefore, if their relevance has not been overstressed by many critics.

D. H. Lawrence was brought up in respectable hardship. The atmosphere of Eastwood in the late nineteenth century is best described in his essay "Nottingham and the Mining Country" (1929), in which he rues the social and aesthetic disaster by which old England was made ugly and dehumanized by the spread of industrialism. The theme of erosion obsessed Lawrence all through his writing career—erosion of nature, erosion of humanity:

Now though perhaps nobody knew it, it was ugliness which betrayed the spirit of man in the nineteenth century. The great crime which the moneyed classes and promoters of industry committed in the palmy Victorian days was the condemning of the workers to ugliness, ugliness, ugliness: meanness and formless and ugly surroundings, ugly ideals, ugly religion, ugly hope, ugly love, ugly clothes, ugly furniture, ugly houses, ugly relationships between workers and employers. The human soul needs actual beauty even more than bread.

Lawrence recognized, moreover, that beauty means different things to different people, and that for this reason his parents' marriage had already drifted into a state of implacable resentment when he, the fourth son, was born in 1885. Mrs. Lawrence came originally from a lower-middle-class family in Kent. She had trained as a schoolteacher and continued until her death in 1910 to venerate study and art. Her husband had little formal education and viewed with suspicion anything that was not fundamentally necessary to the practicalities of living. Such a summary, however, has immediately to be qualified, lest it suggest that Lawrence's father was a puritan fundamentalist and his mother an intellectual dabbler. Almost the opposite was true. Lawrence's father had an instinct for comradeship with his workmates that became stronger as he felt more excluded from the life that Mrs. Lawrence created for herself and her children. He knew little more than the Bible, some hymns, and a few robust ballads, whereas she admired all expressions of learning, but she did so with a seriousness more profoundly puritanical than was evident in his love of plain living and easy friendship. Mrs. Lawrence venerated the Protestant ethic of hard work and Nonconformist morality. Pleasure that was not directed toward self-improvement verged on sin. In her son's novels we find this conflict between two almost opposed views of life expressed many times; though it is most obvious in *Sons and Lovers*, it is the issue upon which Rupert Birkin clashes with Gerald Crich in *Women in Love*, and it underlies every crisis in Lawrence's works where reason and will, intellect and passion are at odds. The source of these differences was partly social, or so Lawrence rationalized it at the end of his life in "Nottingham and the Mining Country," where he talks of the "curious close intimacy" between men in a working community and of the instinct for "possession and egoism" in the women left at home. Men disappear in their working lives into the dark womb of the earth, while the women remain on its surface crust, looking outward and beyond, straining for what might be rather than content with what actually is: it is as though our daily existences in an industrial community embody the gulf that has opened up between male and female.

Lawrence's mother idolized her second son, Ernest, who died in 1901. She cared about the education of all her children, however. Lawrence himself attended a local board school, and then from 1898 to 1901 was a student at Nottingham High School. After a brief period as a clerk in a Nottingham factory he became a student teacher in Eastwood, and from 1906 to 1908 he studied at Nottingham University College. It was in these years that he befriended Jessie Chambers, whom he uncharitably represented as the spiritual Miriam in *Sons and Lovers*. The Chambers family lived on a farm called The Haggs, where Lawrence spent many of his spare moments. For the first time he experienced an environment where love of nature and discussion of serious issues did not have to be indulged defensively. He also came under the influence of William Hopkin, a local bootshop manager who introduced him to the principles of socialism and invited him to attend meetings where he met several Labour leaders. Lawrence always followed political life closely and became increasingly interested in the possibilities of political action in his later novels, but he remained dissatisfied with the values of the British political parties all his life, finding them hierarchical and simplistic.

Jessie Chambers, Alice Dax, Louie Burrows, Hopkin's wife, Sallie, Lawrence's sister Ada—in the years of his young manhood Lawrence was not short of female company. Mrs. Dax is believed to have initiated him sexually, and to Louie Burrows he was briefly and rather unconvincingly engaged. Jessie probably exerted the greatest influence on him because she took the greatest interest in his early attempts at writing, reading his first poems, the earliest draft of his play *A Collier's Friday Night* (published 1934), and the manuscript of *The White Peacock*. In 1908 Lawrence moved to Croydon, just south of London, where for the next four years he taught art, English, and biology at Davidson Road School. He made new friendships—mainly with women—and began tentatively to make contact with the literary world in London. He met Ford Madox Hueffer (later changed to Ford), editor of the *English Review*, Ezra Pound, Edward Garnett; he corresponded with many other writers, gave lectures about some of them, and continually enlarged his reading.

Lawrence's first published work consisted of poems and reviews in the *English Review*. *The White Peacock*, his first novel, was published in January 1911; *The Trespasser*, his second, in May 1912; and *Sons and Lovers*, his masterpiece of self-examination, in May 1913. This rapid production belies the difficulty with which Lawrence perfected his work to his own satisfaction. Each novel and most of his stories and poems went through several drafts. He was, however, a compulsive writer and had been so since the age of nineteen, when he wrote his first poems. For some writers such a prolific output might betoken an inability to relate to the social world, but this was never true of Lawrence. His friendships were sometimes shortlived and quarrelsome, but even in the years when he lived in remote places he enjoyed the fellowship of good company. No modern English writer has had the minutiae of his daily life so frequently observed in the memoirs of the people he met. Though Lawrence left Davidson Road School in 1912 and never again had that kind of regular employment, it would be quite wrong to suppose that he opted out of vigorous social intercourse.

In March 1912 Lawrence met Frieda Weekley, the wife of a Nottingham professor. Only two months later they left England together to visit Germany, where Lawrence was briefly arrested as a spy. Frieda came from a family of minor German nobility called von Richthofen. She was the mother of three children, whom she "abandoned" by going away with Lawrence, but with whom she remained in close contact all her life. It was in every sense an unconventional liaison that shocked contemporary morality, for it not only disrupted the Weekley marriage but it cut across class. When Lawrence and Frieda eventually married in July 1914 they compounded their social unacceptability by going against the current of Anglo-German hostility. The relationship could hardly have been more ill-starred from society's point of view, and this was undoubtedly a major factor in the Lawrences' eventual decision to leave England and live abroad.

By 1914 D. H. Lawrence was an established author, singled out by the elderly Henry James as one of the most promising novelists in England, the friend of many leading intellectuals, and the favored house guest of fashionable patrons. He was at work on his grandest conception, provisionally entitled *The Sisters*, but later to be divided into two quite different works, *The Rainbow* and *Women in Love*. He was flattered by this life and invigorated by his own intellectual capacities. He was, however, wary of being taken over by the Bloomsbury circle, whom he found conceited and soft-centered. He contemplated founding an experimental school with Bertrand Russell, but soon realized how far apart they were emotionally, and the friendship collapsed in cold abuse. He seemed to Russell "a sensitive would-be despot who got angry with the world because it would not instantly obey" (Russell's *Autobiography*, vol. II, 1968, ch. 1). Though Russell's case against Lawrence seems, in the light of Lawrence's complex writings, greatly overstated—"he had no real wish to make the world better, but only to indulge in eloquent soliloquy about how bad it was"—it is only fair to say that many of their contemporaries viewed him in a similar way.

The Lawrences led a peripatetic life during World War I, though regulations prevented them from leaving England. As we shall see in the discussion of his novel *Kangaroo* (1923), Lawrence had the most profound horror at the way the war was conducted. It seemed to him an explosion of all the obscene, violent, destructive, and materialistic characteristics of Western machine-worshiping society, while at the same time he was equally outraged by the loss of young life. He offered himself for war service and was rejected on medical grounds. He and Frieda stayed in London, then in a borrowed house near Padstow, and finally in a house near St. Ives. These were years of conflict with society. When *The Rainbow* was published in 1915 it was abused by the critics and eventually banned as a danger to public morality.

At the end of the war Lawrence at once made plans to leave England, though it was only after Frieda visited her family in Baden-Baden that they left for Italy in November 1919. Here, in various places including Florence, Capri, and Sicily, and with a period of three months in Germany, the Lawrences stayed until February 1922. By the standards of his earlier years this period was not so productive. Lawrence had completed *Women in Love* before he went abroad (it was published in New York in 1920). In Italy he completed *The Lost Girl* (1920) and revised his *Studies in Classic American Literature* (1923); wrote *Aaron's Rod* (1922), drawing on his observations in Florence; composed the poems that became *Birds, Beasts and Flowers* (1923); and produced some of his best short fiction, including "Fanny and Annie," "The Captain's Doll," and "The Fox." None of these works, however, is written on the scale of *Sons and Lovers*, *The Rainbow*, and *Women in Love*. Though there are few signs in this period of Lawrence's imaginative fertility drying up, he was undoubtedly feeling deeply unsettled. At the root of this apprehension was his profound conviction that the war had solved nothing and merely confirmed the wrong course that modern society was taking. He therefore looked around for other societies where alternative options might still be open, or where, perhaps, the people might be confident enough in their own created values not to want to emulate northern Europe and America. Sicily came close to such a society, but the influence of the church was too restricting. Lawrence therefore set sail for Australia, the newest attempt by Western man to start afresh in virginal surroundings; or so he supposed it to be, until he lived there for a few weeks in a house facetiously called "Wyewurk."

From Australia the Lawrences sailed, via New Zealand and Tahiti, to San Francisco, and thence they traveled to Taos in New Mexico. Here a rapacious American *padrona* named Mabel Dodge lived in a state of self-conscious "protection" of the local Indians. Lawrence increasingly resented any form of patronage, but among the descendants of the Aztecs in New Mexico and in Mexico itself he probably came closest to his ideal of discovering a way of life that was still in communion with its own ancestry; this was because the Mexico of the mid-1920's was undergoing a nationalist revival in which it was seriously suggested that the ancient religion of Quetzalcoatl might be a viable alternative to Fascism or to vehement pro-American influences. Lawrence rejoiced in the ruins of the former civilization he saw in Mexico and seriously explored the mystical aspects of the old religion. Out of these experiences came two of his most obscure and symbolic works of fiction, *The Plumed Serpent* and "The Woman Who Rode Away" (1925), but in the end he realized the impossibility of grafting an alien culture onto instincts that had taken centuries to germinate in his own part of the world. He found himself, in other words, as much in touch with the civilization he thought he had rejected, and whose material expressions he would continue to deplore, as the Mexican Indians were in touch with their serpent god.

In 1924 Lawrence made a brief return to Europe, and he finally left Mexico in September 1925, six months after tuberculosis was positively diagnosed as the origin of his continuing physical debilitation. Lawrence had never enjoyed good health, and in his search for other modes of living he always went to warm climates where his condition improved. From 1925 onward, however, his illness prevailed. It affected his creativity. In the last five years of his life he wrote only one novel, *Lady Chatterley's Lover*—though admittedly there are three versions of the book. He wrote some of his best essays, including "Pornography and Obscenity," "A Propos of *Lady Chatterley's Lover*," and "Nottingham and the Mining Country." Poems and stories, the latter including "The Escaped Cock" and "Rawdon's Roof," his philosophical commentary, *Apocalypse* (1931), and many of his best poems also date from these last years. He continued to review books, to write letters, to translate from the Italian, and to see friends. He lived from late 1925 to mid-1928 mainly in Italy and thereafter principally in France, where, at Vence on 2 March 1930, he died at the age of forty-four.

In the last months of his life Lawrence was visited by H. G. Wells, Norman Douglas, Aldous Huxley, Mulk Raj Anand, Mark Gertler, the Aga Khan, and many others. He was very famous but still almost totally unaccepted by the general reader. It took three decades before Lawrence's work automatically appeared on educational syllabi. He remains a controversial figure, not least to the modern feminist movement, which has usually taken issue with him. In 1960 he was the subject of the most publicized literary prosecution in the English courts when Penguin Books successfully defended its unexpurgated edition of *Lady Chatterley's Lover*. Lawrence is now, however, almost certainly the most widely taught twentieth-century writer that England has produced. All his books are in print. A definitive edition of his works is being published by Cambridge University Press. Film versions have been made of *The Trespasser, Sons and Lovers, Women in Love, Lady Chatterley's Lover, The Fox, The Rocking-Horse Winner,* and *The Virgin and the Gypsy;* and in *The Priest of Love* Lawrence's life in Mexico was brought to the screen. An academic journal is devoted to his work. At every point on whatever scale we measure popularity and greatness Lawrence's name appears. More than fifty years after his death he more and more appears as one of the major figures in the history of literature. This account of his work attempts to show why this may be so, and why the questioning and dispute that his name continues to arouse help to justify rather than to undermine his reputation.

## THE WHITE PEACOCK

LAWRENCE's first novel is his only one to be told in the first person. *The White Peacock* came out in 1911, a few months after the death of Lawrence's mother, who was nevertheless able to read an advance copy. The new young author revised his work several times before submitting it to the publisher William Heinemann Ltd., and something of this overrefinement can be detected in the more flamboyantly lyrical passages of the novel. Lawrence always liked to reconsider what he had written once the first draft of a novel was complete, but this was usually because he was battling to find an appropriate form to express complex ideas and had even, on occasion, radically changed his views about what he wanted to say. In *The White Peacock* his revisions tend less to the recasting of thought than to a self-conscious decoration of the prose. This is a novel full of adolescent rhapsodizing about love and nature, but it contains many passages that anticipate the mature Lawrence. Its excesses are characteristic of an ambitious writer finding his feet and of someone wanting to harness his exultation in language to his curiosity about human behavior.

Before Lawrence the opportunities for working-class writers to write about working-class life and then to see their work in print were extremely rare. Lawrence therefore made middle-class people the subject of his first novel; in his next book, *The Trespasser*, the social level is less privileged, but the values against which the protagonists react are still essentially middle class; only in *Sons and Lovers* did he find an authentic voice for working-class aspirations. The three central characters in *The White Peacock*—Lettie Beardsall, George Saxton, and Leslie Tempest—are described to us by Lettie's brother Cyril. Lawrence handicaps himself by using an "I" narrator, for after Lettie marries Leslie it becomes difficult to sustain the intimate observation of their relationship, which Cyril's presence beforehand permits. The novel thus loses much of its impetus in its last chapters. Enough has been established by then, however, for us to recognize the error of Lettie's decision to reject the more sensual George. In doing this she denies fundamental needs within herself in order to do what is socially proper and what will bring the surface rewards of position and wealth. This conflict between self-fulfillment and social gratification reflects the more impersonal battleground of society's encroachment upon nature. In *The White Peacock* Lawrence celebrates the beauties of his native countryside with the extravagant enthusiasm of one who fears it may be threatened with destruction by creeping industrialization, a theme he summarizes symbolically by having the archenemy of materialism, the gamekeeper Annable, crushed by a fall of stones in a quarry.

The opening lines of Lawrence's first novel show his characteristic facility in relating the natural world to the human:

> I stood watching the shadowy fish slide through the gloom of the mill-pond. They were grey, descendants of the silvery things that had darted away from the monks, in the young days when the valley was lusty. The whole place was gathered in the musing of old age. The thick-piled trees on the far shore were too dark and sober to dally with the sun; the weeds stood crowded and motionless. Not even a little wind flickered the willows of the islets. The water lay softly, intensely still. Only the thin stream falling through the millrace murmured to itself of the tumult of life which had once quickened the valley.

At the start of *The Rainbow* and *Lady Chatterley's Lover*, and at some point in all his novels, Lawrence links the contemporary world with the natural and social history out of which it has evolved. Here at the opening of *The White Peacock* he presents an idyllic scene of unperturbed nature, "gathered in the musing of old age." This is a world once tilled by monks where man has come and gone, but to which he now returns only as an onlooker—or a violator. The natural world throughout this novel has a harmony and self-sufficiency that contrast with the disruptions of the social world.

It is not impossible for man to share in this harmony. The harvest episodes and the scene with George and the narrator bathing in the pond show man and nature in almost rhythmic correspondence. "When I began to swim," Cyril records, "soon the water was buoyant, and I was sensible of nothing but the vigorous poetry of action." This sense of man finding complete freedom in a partnership with nature, as the body is supported here by the upthrust of the water, attracted Lawrence throughout his life. His works may largely be read as an exploration of how such a right balance may be found. The passage continues: "I saw George swimming on his back laughing at me, and in an instant I had flung myself like an impulse after him." Through partnership between human beings something of this absorption within nature may be discovered: certainly an ill-balanced relationship (an unhappy marriage, a dominating lover, a possessive parent) will be no way to achieve it. In *The White Peacock* Cyril's obvious attraction toward the manly George has homosexual undertones that no doubt expressed part of Lawrence's own nature, but they are not the essential point of it.

In novel after novel Lawrence seeks for the establishment of right partnership that will accord with nature. The sexual element is only part of this. Significantly in this passage the narrator speaks of flinging himself after George "like an impulse": not "on an impulse," but as though he has actually *become* a force of nature. For one instant true harmony between men and their natural environment has been created: "our love was perfect for a moment, more perfect than any love known since, either for man or woman." If only this moment could become a continuing reality. That is Lawrence's central urge—to find permanence for those isolated moments of perfect interfusion that we experience perhaps only a few times in our lives, but that, as a consequence, we know could be the character of our existences. In *Lady Chatterley's Lover*, at the end of his career, the insistence on trying to describe the pleasure of orgasm is a further attempt to express this deep conviction, at all stages of his career, that a higher kind of experience is waiting for us if we can only find a means of achieving it.

The only certainty is that all the roads upon which society is traveling are taking men away from the realization of this perfect harmony with nature and with each other. Annable, the keeper in *The White Peacock*, who looks forward to Mellors in *Lady Chatterley's Lover*, believes that all civilization is "the painted fungus of rottenness." He has been humiliated by marriage to a pre-Raphaelite lady—an early indication of Lawrence's antipathy to the destructiveness of gentility—and he has tried to drop out of society by living a "natural" life in the woods. Appealing to Cyril though Annable is, not least for his physical endowments, we are not invited to admire his existence as ideal. This Jacques in Arden has too cynical a view of man's failures: "he scorned religion and all mysticism." Though Lawrence had not yet developed a vocabulary for talking at length about them, he felt deeply that there were mysteries within nature ready for man's discovery. If the novel often retreats into poetic excess—"Here was spring sitting just awake, unloosening her glittering hair and opening her purple eye"—this is mainly because Lawrence strives too anxiously to find a lyrical tone for his quasi-religious motif. In *The Rainbow* he writes more confidently, not because he has greatly developed his sense of man's potential interaction with nature, but because his expression of it has its own personality. It no longer seems enslaved by a Pater-like concept of "beautiful prose." Yet many passages in *The White Peacock* also record Lawrence's wonderful eye for natural detail. Not since Hardy—who stopped writing novels in 1894—had an English novelist written so observantly of country life.

*The White Peacock* sets a vivid life of social interaction and of family relationships against its eulogy of the natural world. Several episodes indicate the viciousness in man's nature—George flippantly destroying a bee, and the rabbit hunt, for example—but at the core of each main character a crucial weakness exists like a rot: George's narcissism; Leslie's sexual inadequacy (hinted at: the novel of 1911 was still governed by Victorian restraints), for which he compensates by material display; Lettie's lack of courage to be herself; Cyril's detachment; Annable's bitterness. Lawrence's first novel is a study of failure. So, too, is *The Trespasser*, but in this next novel he at least shows elements of triumph in that the main character refuses to compromise with mediocrity. *The White Peacock* shows a natural world vanishing fast and the possibility of private worlds that might have been, but it does not offer the achievement of any world worth having. Lawrence could sow the seeds of his distinction as a novelist in this kind of young man's pessimism, but he could not bring it to fruition.

### THE TRESPASSER

*The Trespasser* (1912) is the shortest of Lawrence's full-length novels. It is also one of his least known. Lawrence moves away from the familiar world of the English Midlands to London and the Isle of Wight. In 1909 he went on a short summer holiday to the Isle of Wight and from that visit he no doubt gained some of the local color for *The Trespasser*, but many of the circumstances of the novel were derived from a brief love affair between one of his Croydon colleagues, Helen Corke, and a music teacher. Helen Corke kept a journal of her relationship with Herbert Macartney during a week they spent together on the Isle of Wight; it was on this and on his conversations with her that Lawrence based the relationship between Siegmund McNair and Helena Verden in *The Trespasser*. Helen Corke re-created her friendship with Macartney in her own novel *Neutral Ground* (1931), and said more about it in her autobiography, *In Our Infancy* (1975). In both works her version significantly differs from Lawrence's. As with *Sons and Lovers*, however, critics have expended much energy on the biographical elements in the book, without always appreciating that Lawrence was writing a work of imagined experience. Its source lay in fact, but the concerns of the novel show a natural development from *The White Peacock*; Lawrence would no doubt have found some other framework to explore the same issues had he not encountered Helen Corke's account of her bizarre romance.

Whereas *The White Peacock* shows a settled

world being disrupted by emotional tensions and by the creeping malaise of modern life, *The Trespasser* begins in a dull suburban house in London. Lawrence sets a substantial part of only one other novel, *Aaron's Rod*, in the capital city, and in both books the main character escapes from it as soon as possible. As Lawrence says at the end of his essay "Dull London" (1928), "the sense of abject futility in it all only deepens the sense of abject dullness, so all there is to do is to go away." Helena's room, where *The Trespasser* begins, has walls "of the dead-green colour of August foliage" and a carpet that lies "like a square of grass in a setting of black loam." These comparisons with nature only highlight the drabness of the room. Siegmund's home is no different, loveless and lightless when we first read of it. Helena and Siegmund escape from their dreary world of mechanical routine to a brief idyll on the Isle of Wight, but they return to London, she in eventual denial of their love, he to his hollow marriage.

Siegmund is the only one of Lawrence's major protagonists to take his own life. He cannot endure a life without Helena, yet to abandon his wife and children is equally inconceivable:

He was bound by an agreement which there was no discrediting to provide for them. Very well, he must provide for them. And then what? Humiliation at home, Helena forsaken, musical comedy night after night. That was insufferable—impossible! Like a man tangled up in a rope, he was not strong enough to free himself.

(ch. 27)

Siegmund therefore hangs himself. His death requires some courage, but the fact that Lawrence never again used such an ending underlines his dissatisfaction with this solution to the novel, and may account for the relatively low estimation of it that most critics have had. In a novelist so passionately interested in seeing how a fulfilled life may be attained, the extinction of life represents a defeat not only for his main character but for his own conception of fiction. Later heroes like Paul Morel in *Sons and Lovers* and Birkin in *Women in Love* overcome their tendency to despair and reach toward a positive view of life, however difficult this may be to sustain.

*The Trespasser* is not an antifeminist novel—Siegmund's wife, for example, is portrayed with some pity—but it does suggest that between male and female there too often exists an imbalance in the relationship that debilitates both partners. As Siegmund's acquaintance Hampson puts it, "She can't live without us, but she destroys us." This is not Lawrence's view of what has to happen when men and women conjoin, but his notion of what frequently does happen because the right balance has not been struck, give and take has not been proffered. An assertion of wills must lead to one partner's victory over the other. Since the man normally works closer to the land than the woman, whose role has traditionally been domestic, he is more in tune with the natural forces with which humanity has so often lost touch. In later novels Lawrence shows women breaking out of their expected role and thus showing a capacity to achieve with men the two-way sharing, in harmony with the natural world, that they too frequently resist—Ursula Brangwen in *The Rainbow* is the prime example. Helena in *The Trespasser* goes some way in Ursula's direction, but fatally lacks the final intensity of vision that is needed. Hampson has a point, Lawrence intends us to realize, when he goes on to say: "These deep, interesting women don't want *us*; they want the flowers of the spirit they can gather of us. We, as natural men, are more or less degrading to them and to their love of us; therefore they destroy the natural man in us—that is, us altogether."

*The Trespasser* shares with *The White Peacock* a vivid realization of the natural world, though in the former Lawrence indulges less in poetic effect for its own sake. Indeed, it tends to be in his analysis of human behavior that his imagery overreaches itself. Self-conscious phrasing—"She was the earth in which his strange flowers grew" or "She felt herself confronting God at home in His white incandescence"—shows how artificial Lawrence could still be. The novel is full of a slightly adolescent religiosity: Siegmund, for example, derives comfort "from the knowledge that life was treating him in the same manner as it had treated the Master, though his compared small and despicable with the Christ-tragedy." At times the urgency of Lawrence's desire to express his sense of there being a mystic reality that makes human ambitions paltry leads him to be nearly incomprehensible:

... it only happens we see the iridescence on the wings of a bee. It exists whether or not, bee or no bee. Since the iridescence and the humming of life *are* always, and since it was they who made me, then I am not lost. At least, I do not care. If the spark goes out, the essence of the fire is there in the darkness. What does it matter? Besides, I *have* burned bright; I have laid up a fine cell of honey somewhere—I wonder where?

(ch. 21)

Rationally this passage does not make clear sense: how can "iridescence on the wings of a bee" exist, "bee or no bee"? However, it is necessary to accept, because we encounter many such prose moments in later works, that Lawrence is struggling to express a concept that lies beyond the normal restrictions of language—to convey that there is something deeply interfused in the universe that will continue to exist even if mankind should die out, and that certainly continues when each individual man dies. This creative force can be glimpsed at least representatively in nature—the bee's wings—but man normally makes no attempt to understand what it is or how it may be experienced fully. In *Women in Love* Birkin will reflect on what the world would be like if the human race should cease to exist: "a world empty of people, just uninterrupted grass, and a hare sitting up," an image of a nature still flowing (a favorite Lawrentian word) even if man has failed to live up to it. In *The Trespasser* the novelist reaches for a way of expressing his sense of this other life, beside which human life looks ephemeral and irrelevant. It is worth noting, however, that he has not yet sorted out his scale of values. Siegmund feels increasingly "like a slow bullet winging into the heart of life," as though his human existence has no meaning in the "gorgeous and uncouth" natural world. Later novels are life affirming, with Lawrence seeking to accommodate humanity, not to reject it. *The Trespasser* may have been for him a therapeutic novel, for within it he seems to exorcise the debilitating melancholia and nihilism of the young romantic idealist in order to move, in his next novel, to a more robust and emotionally complex contemplation of the world. Eventually, in *The Rainbow* and *Women in Love*, he came as close as he could to defining the right balance that ought to exist between man's sense of his own worth and his understanding of the life forces that he so often fails to perceive because of his self-obsession.

*The Trespasser* is full of themes that Lawrence developed more expressively in maturer novels. In itself it is too patchy to be a complete success, though the opening and closing chapters have a severity that shows Lawrence's eagerness not to use language only for poetic effects. The book is another study in stunted growth. In his next novel, *Sons and Lovers*, he developed beyond this because, for the first time, he imagined his own instincts at the center rather than at the periphery of the experiences he was describing.

## SONS AND LOVERS

*Sons and Lovers* is possibly the most widely read serious English novel of the twentieth century. In some respects it renders commentary of any kind absurd. Who, for example, can read the description of Mrs. Morel's death without being reminded of a grief they themselves have experienced? The novel obviously draws on personal recollections so deeply that it seems impertinent to analyze it. Yet our admiration for it results partly from its imaginative intensity and from its masterly control of feeling. Lawrence's narrative never becomes self-indulgent; even in the moments when he tries to be visionary or mystic the prose becomes only slightly overcolored. Personally felt though *Sons and Lovers* is, Lawrence in some ways makes of it his most orthodox novel. It capitalizes on the *Bildungsroman*, a form of fiction that allows the novelist to re-create through the maturing of his protagonist some of his own remembered intensity of experience. *Sons and Lovers* marks a great advance for Lawrence on the two novels he had written before it, but in terms of the evolution of the English novel its main innovations are less a matter of fictional technique than of topic. It is one of the first wholly authentic novels of English working-class life, set mainly in an industrialized as opposed to an agricultural community and written by someone who had grown up within the society he is depicting. It marks Lawrence's arrival as a great novelist, but it may also mark the end of his ability to speak so straightforwardly of working life, for its success provided him with an entrée into other kinds of society to which he had already started to gravitate from the time he began teaching in Croydon.

"Paul Morel [as he initially planned to call *Sons and Lovers*] will be a novel—not a florid prose poem, or a decorated idyll running to seed in idealism: but a restrained, somewhat impersonal novel." This comment, in a letter dated 18 October 1910, shows how self-critical Lawrence could be, for he planned now to write a work wholly different from *The White Peacock* or *The Trespasser*, both of which, we must conclude from the phrasing, dissatisfied him on account of their exaggerated language. *Sons and Lovers*, one must emphasize, is not an autobiography. If it were then there would be no place in it for an incident such as that where Mrs. Morel names her baby son—"She thrust the infant forward to the crimson, throbbing sun, almost with relief." This may be distantly related to an actual happening about which Lawrence's mother talked, but it is realized poetically and symbolically, an initiation rite, a baptism by fire, an exorcism of guilt. It goes far beyond a mere statement of personal history. This is so with every part of the novel.

In the conflict that develops early on in *Sons and Lovers* between Mr. and Mrs. Morel we see dramatized, in an almost emblematic way, two strains in the English national character. This in no way minimizes the powerful clash of temperaments and wills that makes their marriage so tragic and, in the last chapters of the book, so pathetic. It shows *Sons and Lovers* to be not only a novel of private emotions but a study in late-nineteenth-century social life. Mr. Morel displays qualities of unintellectual male-oriented sociability that contrast with his wife's strict Nonconformist morality, high intentions for her children, and possessiveness. Lawrence, in his later books, came to admire the type of man that he believed his father to have been far more than would appear from his portrait of Walter Morel, who is presented initially as unreasonably ill-tempered, then as weak-willed, and finally as an empty husk from whom the kernel of life has been removed. In *Sons and Lovers* the personality of Mrs. Morel dominates all the early chapters and the end of the novel. Lawrence's account of her as magnificently strong-minded, loving but stifling, is one of the chief glories of the book, though his portrait is critical. She sums up much of the imprisoning morality and vaulting intellectual ambition that he increasingly believed to be instilled in the women of industrialized communities.

Paul Morel's growing up and his awakening to the possibilities of the world is the main subject of *Sons and Lovers*. To convey this, Lawrence achieves a synthesis of social realism and metaphor that may be unparalleled in English fiction. There are many instances to exemplify this—Mrs. Morel's expulsion from her house on the night she becomes aware of Paul's conception is one example; Clara's initiation of Paul is another. We find it at all stages of Paul's relationship with Miriam. Here they are, at springtime, symbolically representing youth and promise, while at the same time tangibly expressing the goodness of nature to which Paul can escape from his industrial home: "Miriam went on her knees before one cluster, took a wild-looking daffodil between her hands, turned up its face of gold to her, and bowed down caressing it with her mouth and cheeks and brow." Her action is sexual yet chaste, loving yet oppressive. It provokes Paul into a cruel denunciation of her possessiveness. "You're always begging things to love you," he says, "as if you were a beggar for love. Even the flowers, you have to fawn on them." The scene thus serves two purposes: to show a pastoral world in which Paul can make contact with pleasures unknown in Bestwood, where he lives, and to use this world for explicitly metaphorical purposes. It is an Eden in which love can be encountered not only as a sexual experience but as something spiritually oppressive, and ultimately life-restricting rather than fulfilling.

Though Miriam is partly based on Jessie Chambers, who was offended by this portrayal of her relationship with Lawrence, she often seems in the novel less a creature of flesh and blood than a "literary" prototype, platonic and allusive. She creates around herself a nunlike and romantic purity, giving herself to Paul more as an act of self-martyrdom than in a spirit of sexual partnership. Her instincts attract her to figures in history and to saints in paintings. She does not like the reality of known experience so much as the chimeras of fiction, and thus she models her relationship with Paul on ideals rather than allowing it to grow out of true instincts. Just as Paul learns to conceal from his mother all his private feelings that do not directly impinge upon her, so he comes to realize how much of his true self has to be held back in his relationship with Miriam.

Like Lettie in *The White Peacock*, Miriam lacks the capacity to grow in harmony with her partner. Paul outstrips her. A modern feminist case against *Sons and Lovers* would center on the manner in which Lawrence presents the women in the novel as only instruments for Paul's awakening to manhood. The charge does not altogether hold true, however. Miriam is inadequate *in her own right*. By the Lawrentian standard she does not permit her repressed sexuality any kind of natural outlet, so that she can give herself only in an act of self-abnegation. She denies the possibilities in her own life as well as in Paul's. Similarly, Paul's mother, though emotionally very affecting for most readers, never knows a life of give and take in equal proportions. She wants to possess or to dominate or to live through the surrogate satisfaction of other people's achievements.

Clara Dawes comes closest to the modern feminist position by making a free choice to return to her husband after initiating Paul into a fuller manhood than Miriam could provide; but Clara's strength contrasts, like Mrs. Morel's and Walter's, with the weakness of her husband. Far from the women of the novel being only staging posts in Paul's progress to adulthood, they loom like intransigent fates who induct him into mysteries only at the threat of extinguishing his personal light. At the end of the novel, when he feels himself "infinitesimal, at the core of nothingness, and yet not nothing," we do not remember Paul as the thwarter of female aspirations. The women of the novel have shown a strength that, alone now, he has to prove he has himself. In his relationships with women, whether as a son or as a lover, Paul has resisted being taken over. It most nearly happens in the natural bond of mother and son, but Miriam and Clara threaten it in different ways. He resists not just to preserve his personal identity but because the right equation cannot be established between a consuming partner, as Lawrence sees each of these women, and a still weak man who has not worked out for himself a conduct of being. The feminist argument has some truth in it if it claims that Lawrence makes the women of *Sons and Lovers* tyrannizing and emasculating, but none at all if the case rests on an accusation that they have no being except to feed Paul Morel's vanity.

In his first two novels Lawrence had tried to deal with sexual feeling in a discreet way. Even in *The Trespasser*, the main subject of which is an adulterous passion, he does not often find a language capable of facing the issues head on. His view of sex sometimes seems more theoretical than intuitive in these early novels, either because of poetic evasions or because of a simple incapacity to talk in a sustained way about sexual feeling. It is therefore astonishing to see how much Lawrence matured as a writer in the few months that separate the final revision of *The Trespasser* in February 1912 and the completion of *Sons and Lovers* in November of the same year. Now when he wants to be poetic the passage does not read as decorative gilding or adolescent extravagance but as a necessary part of the symbolic patterning. Flower imagery is applied with a consciously associative value. Set pieces, like Paul and Miriam beside the ivory-colored roses (in chapter 7) or their lovemaking at the time of the cherry harvest (in chapter 11), are fully integrated into the novel. Naturalistic dialogue is used to explore feeling in a more direct way than perhaps any English novelist had used it before. Here, for example, are Clara and Paul in chapter 13:

"Do you think it's worth it—the—the sex part?"
"The act of loving itself?"
"Yes; is it worth anything to you?"
"But how can you separate it?" he said. "It's the culmination of everything. All our intimacy culminates then."
"Not for me," she said. " . . . I feel," she continued slowly, "as if I hadn't got you, as if all of you weren't there, and as if it weren't *me* you were taking——"
"Who, then?"
"Something just for yourself. It has been fine, so that I daren't think of it. But is it *me* you want, or is it *It*?"

The passage reads calmly and undramatically, yet it conveys so much that Lawrence struggles to articulate in this novel, but that he had hardly ventured to express in his first two books. What is the relationship of love and sex? Must sexual passion entail possessiveness? Is there a chance of creating a balance between partners? How can the awareness of self in one person be matched by a knowledge of the other person's selfhood? Does the oneness of me necessarily prevent me from seeing the youness of you, and if I see it can I seek it out without wanting to crush it? Are Miriam's self-denial and Paul's self-gratification the only ways in which sexual feeling can express themselves? Lawrence explores personal and sometimes mystical experiences through language that carefully balances ordinary speech with poetic intensification. This, as much as its reputation for emotional honesty, is one of the strengths of this great novel.

Though Lawrence analyzes relationships in *Sons and Lovers* so well, we ought not to forget his success in conveying the detail of late-nineteenth-century working life in both a mining and a farming community. The novel moves freely between the two, partly reminding us of how an industrialized village like Bestwood (Lawrence's own hometown, Eastwood) seems like an ugly gash on the landscape. The miners' lives, the petty class distinctions that grow up even in a poor community, the suspicion of books, the attraction of London, the way in which competitions and scholarships provide almost the only avenue of escape for an intelligent young man, all these come fully alive as we read *Sons and Lovers*. Lawrence's self-analysis and his depiction of the halting way in which youth moves into maturity would have far less density and even credibility if the social background were less effectively realized. In *Sons and Lovers* he wrote probably his most immediately approachable book and the one that readers will bother with, even if they cannot tolerate anything else he wrote. If the ability to remind people of their own lives in a way that makes common experiences seem special is the gift of a major writer, then Lawrence proves himself many times in *Sons and Lovers*.

## THE RAINBOW

"I love and adore this new book," Lawrence wrote to Edward Garnett in March 1913. ". . . I think it's great—so new, so really a stratum deeper than I think anybody has ever gone, in a novel." Though he wrote this in the first month of its composition, Lawrence's intention for *The Rainbow* was clear from the start. This was to be a novel not only unlike the three he had written ("It is all analytical—quite unlike *Sons and Lovers*, not a bit visualized," he adds in the same letter) but a new departure for the form of the novel itself. There is immense confidence in the way Lawrence talks of this new book, as though he now felt equipped to tackle something on an altogether larger scale than anything he had attempted before, a novel not drawn from personal experience, as basically both *Sons and Lovers* and *The White Peacock* had been, or from the experience of a friend, as *The Trespasser* was, but concerned with the way in which modern English society had reached its contemporary state. Indeed, more than this, Lawrence took nothing less than the evolution of man as his theme. It shocked him profoundly when *The Rainbow*, published in 1915, met with a disapproving reception and eventual banning on account of its supposed obscenity.

As mentioned earlier, Lawrence conceived *The Rainbow* and *Women in Love* as one novel. Initially he intended calling this work *The Sisters* and subsequently he referred to it as *The Wedding Ring*, a particularly apt title as the central subject of the book was to be the way in which a complete being might be realized, perfectly in union with the chosen partner and at one with a united society. The ring has conventionally been a symbol of union and perfection: in thinking of *The Wedding Ring* as a title for his new work Lawrence intimated his wish to write about the potential perfectibility of man. As he worked further on the novel his bright conception seemed to cloud, and eventually he felt he could no longer sustain the vision in a single book. He thus split *The Sisters* or *The Wedding Ring* into *The Rainbow* and *Women in Love*, linking them principally through the character of Ursula Brangwen, but creating in the second novel almost a modifier of the first. The structure of *Women in Love* is quite different from that of *The Rainbow*, synchronic rather than diachronic (actions happening simultaneously though in different places rather than actions narrated developmentally in a sequence). Though the almost apocalyptic and revelatory images of the first novel carry over into the second, they do so in a less "plotted" way. Whereas the metaphorical patterning of *The Rainbow* seems at times almost in danger of determining the ideas of the novel rather than of expressing already conceived thoughts, there is an even distribution of arguments in *Women in Love* supported by an intricate network of imagery in which no one symbol prevails over the others. *Women in Love* is the more equivocal novel, though in the end the same vision that inspires *The Rainbow* survives the challenges of powerful countervisions. Lawrence seems to have found the imaginative life of *The Rainbow* impossible to maintain into a second volume, for his own intellectual honesty demanded that he be fair to the pervasive forces of materialism, capitalism, and autocracy that his instincts railed against.

*The Rainbow* thus has a clarity of utterance that is sometimes less evident in *Women in Love*. It is a saga novel, but so unlike contemporary works like Galsworthy's *The Forsyte Saga* or Bennett's *Clayhanger* as to create its own genre within English fiction. The links are with Norse sagas, with the Bible, and with *Paradise Lost* if they are anywhere, but Lawrence's achievement is not seriously comparable with these: names and symbols allude to other literatures, some of the language has a Hebraic resonance; but Lawrence does not depend on any imagination other than his own to express the nature of his vision.

*The Rainbow* spans three generations of the Brangwen family. A simplified genealogical plan may help us, with the earliest generation married around 1840.

# D. H. LAWRENCE

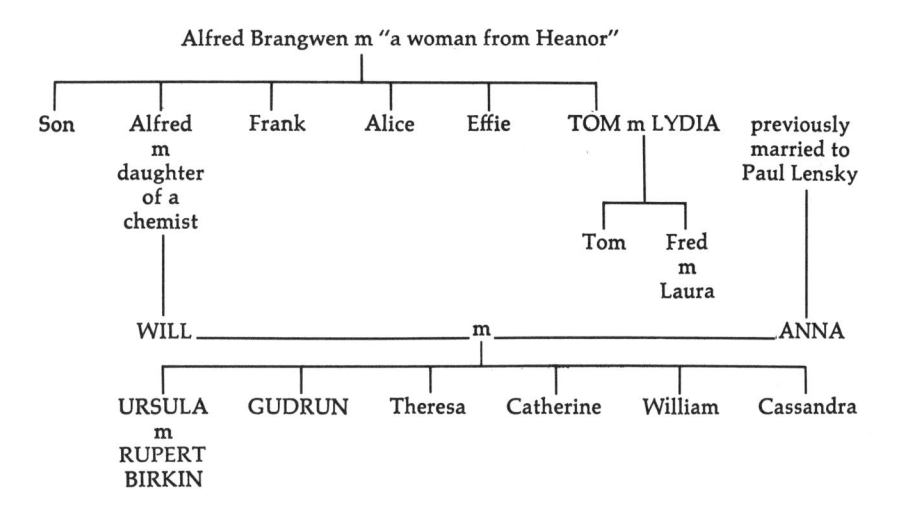

```
                    Alfred Brangwen m "a woman from Heanor"
   ┌────────┬──────────┬─────────┬────────┬────────┬─────────────────┐
  Son     Alfred     Frank     Alice    Effie   TOM m LYDIA    previously
           m                                         │         married to
        daughter                                     │         Paul Lensky
         of a                                    ┌───┴───┐          │
        chemist                                 Tom    Fred         │
           │                                            m           │
           │                                          Laura         │
          WILL ─────────────────── m ───────────────────────────── ANNA
                                   │
   ┌────────┬──────────┬─────────┬────────┬─────────┐
 URSULA   GUDRUN    Theresa   Catherine  William  Cassandra
   m
 RUPERT
 BIRKIN
```

The characters in capital letters in the plan are the principals in *The Rainbow* and *Women in Love*, though Gudrun plays only a minor role in the first novel and Rupert Birkin appears only in the second. Indeed, *Women in Love* concerns the youngest Brangwen generation almost exclusively, Will and Anna having slipped into a passive background and Tom and Lydia being long dead. Though the novels concentrate on the inner lives of these Brangwens, they make their way through a society undergoing such rapid change that this feature itself becomes pivotal to Lawrence's conception. Indeed, the Brangwens in *The Rainbow* have a representational significance, illustrating the movement of solid English farming stock from a wholly agricultural existence to a world in which industrialization and intellectual ambitions have rendered complex and confused their former certainties of belief.

*The Rainbow* opens with a testament to the lost preindustrial world. Lawrence knew that history cannot be reversed, though lessons may be learned from it. This world is irrecoverable. It may, nevertheless, be lamented. He therefore wrote a prologue to the main novel, though in the guise of an opening chapter, for he wanted the final form of *The Rainbow* to be an organic whole, no part outside the integrated entirety:

In autumn the partridges whirred up, birds in flocks blew like spray across the fallow, rooks appeared on the grey, watery heavens, and flew cawing into the winter. Then the men sat by the fire in the house where the women moved about with surety, and the limbs and the body of the men were impregnated with the day, cattle and earth and vegetation and the sky, the men sat by the fire and their brains were inert, as their blood flowed heavy with the accumulations from the living day.

(I.1)

In a free-flowing, almost impressionistic prose Lawrence establishes an image of pastoral harmony. It is the women who disrupt it:

On them too was the drowse of blood-intimacy, calves sucking and hens running together in droves, and young geese palpitating in the hand while the food was pushed down their throttle. But the women looked out from the heated, blind intercourse of farm-life, to the spoken world beyond. They were aware of the lips and the mind of the world speaking and giving utterance, they heard the sound in the distance, and they strained to listen.

(I.1)

Like Eve, their prototype, the early Brangwen women are not content with their settled existence. They glimpse possibilities of knowledge and material achievement beyond it. Here Lawrence implants in the reader's mind an association—it is no more than that—with the Book of Genesis, and he loosely moves to the Book of Revelations at the end of *Women in Love* when Ursula and Birkin set out to seek a new kind of world; but at no time does he permit his own vision to be molded by the biblical parallels. He is more concerned at the start of *The Rainbow* to evoke a preindustrial world and then to establish within it a conflict of ambitions between the sexes, for this will be the central issue of the novel. The men are content to live this life; the women lust for something more. Lawrence extends the issues upon which the Morel marriage founders in *Sons and Lovers*, but he no longer believes it to be merely a struggle between different kinds of moral perception. The women's behavior is virtually instinctive, as though at some primeval point when the sexes separated out of the initial life-mass they were imbued with a biological hunger for knowledge and advancement. The first sentence of *The Rainbow* begins "The Brangwens had lived for generations of the Marsh Farm," as though they have evolved there from the origins of life.

Throughout *The Rainbow* and *Women in Love* Lawrence insists on the difference between the sexes as more than obviously physical; it is mental, emotional, within the beings of men and women. "The man has his pure freedom, the woman hers," he writes in *Women in Love*. "Each acknowledges the perfection of the polarized sex-circuit. Each admits the different nature in the other." If this is so, however, does it necessarily mean an inalienable gulf between men and women and an irrevocable isolation for each individual? Lawrence seems anxious to resist such a conclusion. His conviction that the sexes can ideally live in balanced harmony with each other, neither claiming possession of the other (though in reality both often do), is the thesis of both *The Rainbow* and *Women in Love*. Each relationship in the novels explores ways in which such equilibrium may be established, testing the claims of each kind of partnership in an earnest search for proof that the ideal is realizable. Tom and Lydia, Will and Anna, perhaps most positively Ursula and Birkin show moments of perfected union, though none of these relationships survives without conflict. Lawrence knew from his own marriage that a measure of struggle and argument between both partners was a natural part of a developing relationship, and that once these ceased the union was threatened with extinction. In the various relationships of *The Rainbow* and *Women in Love*, however, he seeks to distinguish between truly creative conflicts and those that, like war, leave only scars and damage.

Tom Brangwen marries Lydia Lensky. He has grown up mainly among women and has a love of poetry and a resentment of "mechanical stupidity" that separates him from the other Brangwen menfolk of his generation. Lydia is Polish, a stranger in religion and in cast of mind from the community into which she marries. Though Lawrence makes little of her Polishness, using it primarily to convey her "otherness" or the distance that must always exist between her and Tom, he nonetheless makes no mistakes historically in talking about her background or her first marriage to a failed radical. The details of *The Rainbow* are always accurate, and the narrative unfolds with a tight control of chronological accuracy.

Tom and Lydia live in struggle with each other but their marriage is ultimately a success in Lawrence's scheme, for it entails a creative kind of self-questioning and a constant move forward. Lydia's daughter, Anna, the child of her marriage to Paul Lensky, grows into a wholly self-sufficient person, inheriting her mother's private instincts but none of her giving nature. Anna is one of Lawrence's most original creations. We follow her from her willful childhood, vexatiously trying to tame the farm geese, to her destructive maturity when she almost voluntarily sloughs her imagination and denies all emotions other than her maternalism. Into her world comes her cousin Will, "a dark enriching influence she had not known before." The potential is there, Lawrence emphasizes, for a fully balanced partnership, he a worker who can make art and beauty shine out of simple wood, she the begetter of children who has yet glimpsed possibilities of a superior life: "Something she had not, something she did not grasp, could not arrive at. There was something beyond her. But why must she start on the journey? She stood so safely on the Pisgah mountain." Anna quite literally cannot make the effort to discover the better world that, imaged by the first appearance of a rainbow in the novel, she has been privileged to glimpse: "She would forfeit it all for the outside things . . . she would throw away the living fruit for the ostensible rind."

There ensues a battle more debilitating than that between the Morels. Will retreats into himself and Anna finds a limited fulfillment in rearing her children. Theirs, however, is a tragedy of wasted opportunity, for both Will and Anna stifle their own growth. A favorite image of Lawrence's is the plant struggling for life above ground only to meet a stone that causes it to twist itself into a half-formed distortion. It can be applied to Will and Anna, who have the capacity to form the kind of balanced relationship that Lawrence seeks to express, but who turn away from this into an existence of destructive conflict and eventual sterility. Even their moments of reconciliation are as though impaired by their self-absorption, opting out of the flow of life.

In their eldest child, Ursula, Lawrence invests the best possibility of creating a new form of life, for she remains always inquiring and, in *The Rainbow* at least, unfettered—"out of nothingness and the undifferentiated mass, to make something of herself!" Her path is partly an intellectual one, partly sexual, but unlike her mother she accepts her destiny as "a traveller on the face of the earth . . . ultimately and finally, she must go on and on, seeking the goal that she knew she did draw nearer to." At times Lawrence seems to echo Charlotte Brontë's imagery in *Jane Eyre* (though in his 1929 essay "Pornography and Obscenity" he calls her novel "slightly obscene" on account of Rochester's need to be emasculated before he is worthy of Jane)—he speaks of Ursula as a bird, an infant crying in the night, a moon-person whose reality is not wholly of this world. Yet her first attempts to make sense of her life are through dedicated service to society. Her days as a schoolteacher show her something of the intractability of human nature, and they allow Lawrence an opportunity to write with scathing accuracy about the English classrooms of his own day, wherein educational ideals almost inevitably fell victim to expediency.

In a perhaps conscious allusion to *Jane Eyre*, Ursula has the opportunity to leave England and go to India. Her relationship with the Polish aristocrat Skrebensky, like Jane's with St. John Rivers, has an almost comic edge to it, for it is wholly out of balance. He is a son of institutional life, restricted by class, by the army, by his code of propriety. She triumphs over him not as Anna triumphs over Will, exulting in being the "Anna Victrix" of chapter 6, but because she is simply too free and too large to be partnered with him for any significant length of time. Skrebensky is a stage in her personal and sexual development, but in the end no more relevant to her fulfillment than her lesbian attraction toward a fellow schoolteacher. Ursula's true consummation comes in *Women in Love*, when it takes almost a mystical and transfiguring form. Lawrence in *The Rainbow* shows the limitations as well as the glories of sexuality.

*The Rainbow* is five hundred pages long, densely and often poetically written. Occasionally this awareness of its own scale leads to some falseness of vision—the final manifestation of the rainbow, though beautiful in rhythm and tone, surely sacrifices truth to symbol, as though Lawrence felt he must end on a high prophetic note when the argument of the novel calls for an open-ended, speculative, anxious conclusion. The novel cannot be satisfactorily summarized in a few pages, but one can be reasonably certain that nowhere else in English fiction does a writer come so close to embodying in his characters the main tensions of industrialized man or the issues that at once separate and bind the sexes.

## WOMEN IN LOVE

IN one of his best-argued and most persuasive chapters in *D. H. Lawrence: Novelist* (1955), F. R. Leavis says of *Women in Love*:

Even a reader who is still far from having grasped the full thematic development must be aware by the time he reaches the end of the book that it contains a presentation of twentieth-century England—of modern civilization—so first-hand and searching in its comprehensiveness as to be beyond the powers of any other novelist he knows of.

(ch. 4)

Here is the immediate difference between *Women in Love* and *The Rainbow*. Its vigorous contemporaneity contrasts with the more grandiose conception of *The Rainbow*, where Lawrence seems at times to be hampered by the lofty symbolism. Though there is a great deal of explicit social detail in *The Rainbow* it does not convey so specific a sense of period as *Women in Love*, with its café society, its smart observation of clothes and decor, its ear for fashionable nuances, and its foreboding of a threat even to the tarnished civilization that modern man has provided for himself.

At the start of the last section I drew attention to the initial conception whereby Lawrence envisaged *The Rainbow* and *Women in Love* as one novel. Relics of this approach remain in the second novel, even though its basic structure fundamentally differs from the first. Lawrence originally intended a saga of man's history from the marshes (hence the name of the Brangwen farm) out of which life evolved up to the present corruptible moment—and beyond that to a future where he will either have established a viable society quite different from the one he now inhabits, or have ceased to exist at all. The latter proposition is seriously countenanced in *Women in Love*, mainly in what Birkin says, though it may be thought that Gerald Crich's materialistic juggernaut is heading for man's extinction too. Birkin does not want to see the end of the human race, but he does not believe it to be either inconceivable or totally disastrous:

"Let mankind pass away—time it did. The creative utterances will not cease, they will only be there. Humanity doesn't embody the utterance of the incomprehensible any more. Humanity is a dead letter. There will be a new embodiment, in a new way. Let humanity disappear as quick as possible."

(ch. 5)

Lawrence by now had arrived at a religious conviction that he never forsook. It has pantheistic elements, but it is too personally felt and totally uninstitutionalized to be given a recognized conceptual name. He sees in the universe a "primal sympathy—which having been must ever be": Wordsworth's words come close to expressing it. This creative presence informs all nature; man is only a detail, more complex than most but not on this account indispensable to the universe. More than once the novel reminds us of the demise of certain mammals that evolution regarded as expendable. Man may go the way of the dinosaur. If so, the universal force will not die. In a famous image of the novel, there will still be a hare sitting up in an empty field.

Lawrence's romantic vision is presented in some of his most high-sounding but ultimately unsatisfactory prose, for it convinces more by rhetoric and poetic diction than by intelligence. Many times in *Women in Love* we have to be on our guard against Lawrence's compulsive language, for it sometimes argues a point of view contrary to the general direction of the novel. Birkin's speeches on the irrelevance of man to the cosmic scheme exemplify this. Phrases like "Let mankind pass away—time it did" and "Humanity is a dead letter" no doubt express Lawrence's own feelings in certain moods, but they do not satisfactorily indicate the beliefs of the novel, though they come dangerously close to diverting the reader from Lawrence's central conviction that life *is* worth living, that it must survive, and that a world without man would be as good as inert; however dynamic the energies that continued to inform it, a globe devoid of humanity would have no vision to perceive it or consciousness to absorb it. It would be living, but it might as well be dead. Lawrence's faith in man, however monstrously wrong the paths he has taken, never profoundly deserts him. It is a weakness of *Women in Love* that we so often worry that it may be about to do so. This is what Leavis means when he talks of places in the novel where "Lawrence betrays by an insistent and overemphatic explicitness, running at times to something one can only call jargon, that he is uncertain—uncertain of the value of what he offers; uncertain whether he really holds it."

*Women in Love* is a novel of ideas, though paradoxically one of its main ideas contends that the world suffers too much from thought and intellect. Indeed, there are points in the book (*pace* the late plays of Samuel Beckett) where Lawrence almost comes to reject language because it is the instrument of cerebral experiences. Birkin expresses this in a passage in which we feel he is not negating the main flow of the novel, as in his speech quoted earlier, but is reaching for a means of saying something that is almost inexpressible. He is speaking to Ursula:

"There is," he said, in a voice of pure abstraction, "a final me which is stark and impersonal and beyond responsibility. So there is a final you. And it is there I would want to meet you—not in the emotional, loving plane—but there beyond, where there is no speech and no terms of agreement. There we are two stark, unknown beings, two utterly strange creatures, I would want to approach you, and you me.—And there could be no obligation, because there is no standard for action there, because no understanding has been reaped from that plane. It is quite inhuman—so there can be no calling to book, in any form whatsoever—because one is outside the pale of all that is accepted, and nothing known applies. One can only follow the impulse, taking that which lies in front, and responsible for nothing, asked for nothing, giving nothing, only each taking according to the primal desire."

(ch. 13)

Here is the kernel not only of *Women in Love* but of all Lawrentian fiction. Characteristically, the truest moments in his prose totally lack rhetoric. This flows naturalistically, like real speech rather than speechmaking. Birkin advocates a meeting of the sexes without the restrictions of morality or custom, the setting up of a new world that quite literally starts afresh. All that language has rationalized and "terms of agreement" defined will be made redundant. It is useless to ask what Lawrence means practically by this: How will such a society be established, where will it operate, how can it preserve privacy? He is writing almost allegorically of the *need* for a better world where the achievements of clever men will not automatically be regarded as the right criteria for human life. He appeals, in other words, for an opportunity whereby the emotional depths in men and women can be allowed to surface. We need not be the slaves of self-restraint.

Ursula aspires to this personal freedom throughout *Women in Love*. "Her spirit was active, her life like a shoot that is growing steadily, but which has not yet come above ground." Within an immensely complex novel Lawrence shows not only Ursula but several other characters striving for personal attainment. Her sister, Gudrun, sees her own salvation within the sophisticated world. Gerald Crich sees it in the triumph of the machine-based society. Both of them wish to discipline their lives, to impose curbs on natural feeling, and to see enforced a set of absolute values that will test people and thus weed out the weak from the strong. Theirs is an antilife belief because it denies nature. We see it most dramatically expressed in the scene where Gudrun exults as Gerald cruelly tries to tame his mare. Eventually Gudrun deserts Gerald for the industrial artist Loerke, who, in the final chapters of the novel, epitomizes the separation of art from life and of reason from instinct.

Lawrence's attitude to Gerald Crich demonstrates his humanity as a novelist. "This is the first and finest state of chaos," says Lawrence of Gerald's beliefs, "pure organic disintegration and pure mechanical organization." Everything that Gerald stands for repels Lawrence, yet his portrait moves us greatly, almost as Milton's Satan makes us weep in pity. Gerald and his father worship the machine, as though it can protect them against a knowledge of death. Terror lies at the center of their beings. They therefore seek power over men, animals, land, and objects, for without it they would topple into the dark abyss. They know no inner life, whereas Ursula and Birkin struggle to release theirs.

Birkin and Gerald are powerfully attracted to each other, and there can be little doubt, if one reads the prologue to *Women in Love* which Lawrence decided to keep back from publication, that the relationship was meant to encompass homosexual feeling. This is presented not with any trace of eroticism, but as one possible means by which men might know each other better. The possibility of love between men (or between women, as suggested in *The Rainbow*) does not appall Lawrence, because he believes it need not exclude the love of men for women. Nor by this is he appealing for bisexuality in men, but for the capacity to love in a brotherly way (this may include touch, hence the wrestling scene, but not homosexual intercourse) even while one loves a person of the opposite sex. Birkin reaches for a relationship with Gerald at the same time that he moves forward with Ursula: the two relationships need not be mutually exclusive, and it would be absurd to talk of them as promiscuous.

*Women in Love*, as Leavis implies, presents a picture of contemporary England. Sometimes this can be seen in its satirical portraiture—Bertrand Russell and the famous society hostess Ottoline Morrell are two of the victims, the latter comically parodied in the extravagant Hermione. On a larger scale, however, Lawrence indicts the capitalist ethos of post-Edwardian England. He does not adopt a socialist or radical stance by which to do so, but portrays working-class existence as demeaning and mechanistic. The problem, however, is that he offers no alternative to it. When Ursula and Birkin go off to seek their own fulfillment they have to do so outside any social context. Lawrence himself wandered away from industrialized society in the years following the writing of *Women in Love*, as we shall explore in the next sections of this study, but he failed to realize that this option simply does not exist for most people.

At the end of the novel, literally in its closing lines, the debate about society and personal freedom continues. *Women in Love* is, like most of Lawrence's major fiction, open-ended and uncommitted when it finishes. Ursula and Birkin wander off, uncertain what they will make of the future. Gudrun and Loerke represent all the life-denying forces that, after Lawrence's own death in 1930, were to manifest themselves in Nazism. Gerald has died, crushed by the forces of nature (symbolically represented by a glacier) that he always tried to control. The novel is about exploring life, but not about reaching destinations. English literature has subsequently had other examples of this technique whereby the author does not seek to express certainties or to define absolutes, but *Women in Love* in its own time created a new form of fiction because it did not move toward a settled conclusion or seek to leave a comprehensive overview in the mind of the reader.

In 1925 Lawrence wrote an essay entitled "Reflections on the Death of a Porcupine" in which he describes an incident when he shot a porcupine. The episode illustrates the natural balance of the world: "the whole of creation is established upon the fact that one life devours another life, one cycle of existence can only come into existence through the subjugating of another cycle of existence, then what is the good of trying to pretend that it is not so?" The passage neatly indicates that Lawrence was not a sentimentalist. Nature is rough and it presupposes the superiority of some creatures over others. At the time he wrote the essay, contemporary with *The Plumed Serpent*, Lawrence no doubt assumed that some men were naturally higher in the cycle of existence than others. It provides an interesting retrospective view of *Women in Love*, for in "Reflections on the Death of a Porcupine" he shows that a certain amount of callousness and aggression are endemic to nature. *Women in Love* shares this view but it indicates, often through examples of human mastery over animals (a cuttlefish, a mare, a rabbit), but also through attempts by one man to subjugate another, that the natural balance can easily be overturned by excess—by delight in cruelty, by greed, and by exploitation of others. Though the novel will strike many readers as Lawrence's most intellectual achievement (despite its wish to depose intellectual gods), it resounds with this deep humanity that deplores any kind of behavior that imbalances nature: accept the savagery that must exist within nature as one accepts death as the end of life, but do not add to it. Gerald and Gudrun go too far, Ursula and Birkin draw back. *Women in Love* is less a novel about opposites than about checks and balances.

## THE LOST GIRL

It is not uncommon for great writers to reach a point of creative exhaustion following the completion of a major work. This certainly happened to Lawrence, who, after finishing *Women in Love*, seriously contemplated abandoning the writing of fiction, perhaps in favor of speculative essays, more book reviewing, translations (he became fascinated with the Sicilian novelist Giovanni Verga), and poems. He had not recovered from the reception given to *The Rainbow* and seriously questioned the value of writing unappreciated novels. "I feel I don't want to write—still less do I want to publish anything. It is like throwing one's treasures in a bog," he declared in April 1919. It was during this period, when he felt so directionless, that Lawrence wrote *The Lost Girl*, a novel that fundamentally changes its character as it develops. Lawrence starts it as though he were trying to concede ground to critics who resented his lack of conventionality. In the first half of *The Lost Girl* he does not complicate his realistic portrait of the English lower middle class with sexual radicalism or metaphysics. We might almost be reading a novel by Galsworthy or Bennett. There are, too, strong echoes of Charles Dickens, particularly of *Hard Times*, in the episodes with the traveling vaudevillians, the absurdly named Natcha-Kee-Tawaras. Yet in the second part of the novel Lawrence seems released from these restraints and finds his own voice. The novel moves to Italy, the relationships become more sexually explicit, a longing for nonurbanized living creeps in.

This almost abrupt change of emphasis used to be attributed to a gap in the composition of the novel, it being assumed that the first part was written before 1914, when Lawrence left the manuscript in Germany, and the second half after 1918, when he was able to take it up again. Keith Sagar, however, in his book *D. H. Lawrence: A Calendar of His Works* (1979), has challenged this suggestion and indicates that the whole of *The Lost Girl* was written after the war. If so, it means that the shifts of view within the novel were planned from the outset. Alternatively, and more probably, Lawrence embarked on this novel with the intention of making it more like the kind of fiction his popular contemporaries were writing; but his natural form of self-expression made it impossible for him to complete the book in such a cut-and-dried manner. As he wrote in his 1928 essay on Galsworthy, defending by implication his own tendency not to be straitjacketed by conventions of morality or technique:

If life is a great highway, then it must forge on ahead into the unknown. . . . The tip of the road is always unfinished, in the wilderness. . . . In the three early novels . . . it looked as if Mr. Galsworthy might break through the blind end of the highway with the dynamite of satire, and help us out on to a new lap. But the sex ingredient of his dynamite was damp and muzzy, the explosion gradually fizzled off in sentimentality.

My belief is that Lawrence found his own writing in the middle stages of *The Lost Girl* becoming "damp and muzzy" and that the redirection of the novel was a consequence of his need to preserve his sense of artistic integrity.

Lawrence contemplated several titles for *The Lost Girl*, each one indicating something of its theme. In its earliest form, the one that Sagar says Lawrence began before the war but subsequently scrapped, it was called *The Insurrection of Miss Houghton*. Later on he thought of *Mixed Marriage, Perdition*, and *The Bitter Cherry* as possible titles. The novel concerns Alvina Houghton, a respectably brought up draper's daughter in a town called Woodhouse. She rejects the conventional world in which she is reared by trying several paths of escape—as a nurse in London, a pianist in her father's cinema, and the lover of an inarticulate vaudeville artist called Francesco Marasca, "Cicio." Cicio's surname derives from a kind of cherry, just as "Alvina" relates to the Italian word for "womb" (*alvo*). Lawrence often intended us to pick up hints from the names of his characters, more because of their associations than for what they specifically mean. In *The Lost Girl* the links between the cherry and the womb indicate the strong sexual theme upon which the novel centers. Alvina finds in the dark, magnetic Italian artist a quality of being that is absolutely unknown in damp, repressed Woodhouse. In the last chapters of the book she goes with Cicio to a mountain village in southern Italy, but Lawrence does not provide the banal and sentimental conclusion that a romantic escapist would offer. Life for Alvina becomes harder as Cicio returns to his enclosed world of male comradeship and strong family ties, but she refuses to be crushed by it. At the end of the novel (which, surely taking something from the pre-1914 first version, is set on the eve of the war) Alvina contemplates a future in America, the "New World," with her Italian soul mate.

The English novel has many examples of main characters awakening to a new consciousness of life. Nineteenth-century convention did not altogether disguise the sexual implication in this. Anne Elliot in Austen's *Persuasion*, Jane Eyre in Brontë's novel, Jude the Obscure in Hardy's, all have to come to terms with their own sexuality. Lawrence handles this subject without inhibition, but whereas in Paul Morel and Ursula Brangwen he presents the sexual aspect as only one part of a carefully balanced equation in their personalities—they are as concerned with finding the right kind of society for themselves—in Alvina Houghton's case the flowering of her sexual self is the mainstream of the novel. We understand this early in the book when she goes down her father's mine, an un-Galsworthian interruption among the first chapters:

There was a thickness in the air, a sense of dark, fluid presence in the thick atmosphere, the dark, fluid, viscous voice of the collier making a broad-vowelled, clapping sound in her ear. He seemed to linger near her as if he knew—as if he knew—what? Something forever unknowable and inadmissible, something that belonged purely to the underground: to the slaves who work underground: knowledge humiliated, subjected, but ponderous and inevitable. . . . She felt herself melting out also to become a mere vocal ghost, a presence in the thick atmosphere. Her lungs felt thick and slow, her mind dissolved, she felt she could cling like a bat in the long swoon of the crannied, underworld darkness.

(ch. 4)

This is a totally different way of writing about the mines from that of *Sons and Lovers*. Lawrence hardly seems interested in the work going on or in the economic state of the mine. It exists as a means of exploring Alvina's inner being, the self we have not had revealed in the early, more socially descriptive chapters. Alvina yearns to subjugate her Woodhouse being and become a reborn person. When she meets Cicio, the means of achieving this rebirth, she changes her name and becomes Allaye, as though disposing of one identity to allow the free flow of another. She is "the lost girl" because she loses her own self to release a new person.

Alvina is "lost" in the different sense of being no longer acceptable to the prim society of her upbringing. In his correspondence at the time of writing *The Lost Girl* Lawrence sometimes refers to it as "a rather comic novel." We ought to remember this when we read about the adventures of Mr. Houghton, a man of grandly impractical schemes, of the pinched Miss Pinnegar, the fussy Mr. May, the hysterical Mrs. Tuke, and the theatrical Madame Rochard, who governs the Natcha-Kee-Tawara troupe. Each one is a comic vignette of considerable style. Together they form a Dickensian world that hovers on the edge of caricature, but the satirical humor with which Lawrence endows them helps to temper the passionate relationship of Alvina and Cicio at the center of the book. Since the novel lacks the semiautobiographical pain of *Sons and Lovers* or the marvelous proliferation of ideas that wells beneath the action of *The Rainbow* and *Women in Love*, we need this comic detail to focus the intense main theme.

In *The Lost Girl* Lawrence makes an effective study of English provincial attitudes toward the foreigner. Cicio seems exotic and animal-like in the context of Woodhouse, but ordinary and even sad in his own village of Pescocalascio. He says very little in the novel. His presence is felt more than observed.

Lawrence suggests that Cicio is inscrutable, that he cannot altogether be summarized as Latinate and foreign or be neatly contrasted as Alvina's physical opposite and the instrument of her sexual liberation. He has an "otherness," a mystery resulting not from the author's lack of interest in his subject but from his deliberate intention to create a character who cannot be fully described. In this respect Lawrence, who introduces Cicio quite late in the novel, is experimenting with the possibilities of characterization in fiction. Having begun *The Lost Girl* in a more orthodox way than any of his previous stories, he ends up by trying to portray a character whose nature partly defies rational description or conventional psychological analysis. He takes the attempt further in *The Plumed Serpent*, particularly with Don Cipriano, but this and his next two novels were to be set either entirely or predominantly outside England, as though he was interested in exploring the nature of foreignness itself. *The Lost Girl* is a bridging novel, but in its own right it ought not to be underestimated, for its mixture of comic observation and exoticism makes it one of Lawrence's most easily read and entertaining works of fiction.

## AARON'S ROD

And the Lord spake unto Moses, saying . . . And it shall come to pass, that the man's rod, whom I shall choose, shall blossom. . . . And it came to pass, that on the morrow Moses went into the tabernacle of witness; and, behold, the rod of Aaron for the house of Levi was budded, and brought forth buds, and bloomed blossoms, and yielded almonds.

(Numbers 17:1, 5, 8)

*Aaron's Rod* is a novel about flowering in a strange land. Its main character, Aaron Sisson, lives in the same kind of domestic dullness as Siegmund in *The Trespasser* and, like him, he earns his living by playing in an orchestra. The first chapter dryly describes the bitterness into which Aaron's marriage and home life have sunk: "The acute familiarity of his house, which he had built for his marriage twelve years ago, the changeless pleasantness of it all seemed unthinkable. It prevented his thinking." In *The Trespasser* the hero escapes from this sort of life by committing adultery and then by killing himself. Neither solution pleased Lawrence, for whatever the strains a marriage might create he did not admire infidelity. The only other major example of it in his work is Lady Chatterley's, though her adultery with Mellors is more a way of attaining a fulfillment that her husband can neither physically nor emotionally supply. As for suicide, we have already seen that Lawrence regarded it as solving nothing. It was an escape *from* life, but not *into* life. In *Aaron's Rod*, however, he begins to examine the possibility that fulfillment may be attained not through sexual means so much as by submission to a dominant person or idea.

Aaron leaves his home and goes to London. Here he encounters Rawdon Lilly, a compulsive philosophizer who befriends him and nurses him back to health when he falls ill. The portrait of Lilly is probably based on John Middleton Murry, the critic and personal friend of Lawrence. Elements of the young Mussolini possibly color the characterization in the Italian chapters of the book, because Lawrence observed at first hand the beginnings of Fascism and heard some of the hectic speeches that accompanied them. Aaron follows Lilly across Europe and at the end of the novel supports such an act of abasement. As Lilly puts it, "there must be one who urges, and one who is impelled." He states this as though it were a natural law like the laws that govern magnetism and gravity.

This thesis of submission of the weak to the strong is a serious attempt by Lawrence to find a way of establishing harmony between human beings. Instead of competition and struggle we should seek for the right balance between people, in sex, in politics, in religion. It fails to convince, however, because Lilly is simply not interesting enough to sustain the role demanded of him by Lawrence. We have to take on trust his charismatic effect upon Aaron. What he actually says and does in the novel is too often bombastic and sometimes confusing. Some critics, therefore, have tried to find a homosexual element in the Aaron-Lilly relationship, but if it is there, as implicitly it may be, it must detract from what Lawrence is centrally asserting, for his point in *Aaron's Rod* is not primarily sexual. He claims that a better balance will be struck in the world if the masses submit to the benevolent will of great leaders. In the early 1920's, when Fascism had not yet been seriously politically tested, this notion appealed to many people; but Lawrence fails to represent it credibly because his embodiment of the leadership impulse lacks intellectual dynamism. Lilly is essentially undistinguished, lacking even the remote otherworldliness of Cicio in *The Lost Girl*.

Though Lawrence led a peripatetic life from 1919 onward, and reflected this in his writing, he did not produce any other work as unrooted as *Aaron's Rod*. Its title and central metaphor betoken wandering, and the novel is wholly concerned with unsettled people. Aaron's companions in London and in Italy are fashionable dilettantes who might as easily have come from the pages of an early Evelyn Waugh novel. Indeed, most of them are based on actual people. Lawrence laughs at them, but without humor. They are butterflies flitting across the surface of Europe, and we can therefore expect little seriousness from them. *Aaron's Rod* is in some ways a tantalizing novel since it raises the specter of deracinated intellectuals abandoning England because it is philistine or because they feel sexually incompatible with its moral climate or simply because they prefer an alternative culture; but it makes little of this theme, even though such a situation was obviously close to Lawrence's own predicament. In his other "travel" novels, *Kangaroo* and *The Plumed Serpent*, he places the wanderer in a context: primeval Australia, Aztec Mexico. In *Aaron's Rod* all the characters seem caught in a vortex relating to nothing outside itself. By setting the novel mainly in London and Florence, Lawrence has the opportunity to create a context for his analysis of leadership and disillusionment, but he avoids it. He provides a civilized setting for his story, only to miss its significance.

*Aaron's Rod* has never been particularly popular among Lawrence's novels. This may be because it is alone among his works in having no prominent female character. The most characteristically Lawrentian element is therefore missing: the assessment of relationships between the sexes. It was probably a necessary novel for him to have written at the most uncertain period of his life, when he was deciding where his future lay, but it is the closest he came to an aesthetic failure. He wrote it in bits, beginning it in November 1917 and not completing it until June 1921. This shows, for the novel has no coherent imaginative design. It allowed him, however, to experiment with an episodic fictional structure and to try out some ideas that he developed more fully in his next book. *Kangaroo*, an altogether more successful novel, capitalizes on the looseness of form and woolliness of thinking that afflict *Aaron's Rod*, making strengths out of their weakness. If Aaron's rod brings forth any blossoms at all, it is in *Kangaroo*.

## KANGAROO

LAWRENCE's decision to leave England had been intimated in his correspondence and had been detectable, as some of his contemporaries realized, in aspects of *Women in Love*, *The Lost Girl*, and *Aaron's Rod*; but it was only on 26 February 1922 that he and Frieda embarked at Naples for his first voyage outside Europe. They called briefly at Ceylon, but their destination was intentionally—and perhaps symbolically—as far from Britain as possible. It is perhaps important to remember how comparatively unknown the antipodes were in the early 1920's to most British people: legends of Ned Kelly and Rolf Boldrewood's novels of hardy outdoor life (the most famous of which is *Robbery Under Arms*, 1888) encouraged a notion of Australia as the antithesis of English suburbia. Lawrence hoped to discover there a kind of precivilization where men, learning by the mistakes of the northern European, would in effect have begun again. He was not to find this "ur-society" among Australian men or women, and he did not make contact with aboriginal Australia, as he would surely have wanted to do had he been visiting it now; but he did discover in the landscape of the outback a scale in nature grander than anything he had seen before, and hence, in his estimation, close to the wellsprings of the universe. Trim England, even the wildness of Cornwall, could not compete with the essence of unrestraint that "the pale, white unwritten atmosphere of Australia" had upon Lawrence. It resulted in writing about which it is difficult to talk without evoking a paradox, for it is at once coolly objective and yet wholly passionate:

To be alone, mindless and memoryless between the sea, under the sombre wall-front of Australia. To be alone with a long, wide shore and land, heartless, soulless. As alone and as absent and as present as an aboriginal dark on the sand in the sun. The strange falling-away of everything.
(ch. 17)

Lawrence's descriptions of landscape in *Kangaroo* are among the best he wrote outside his travel books, and even today many native-born Australian writers fall short of them. His account of the humanity that inhabits this preternatural setting does not have the same concentration: instead of achieving a successfully paradoxical style, Lawrence veers confusingly between extremes of emotion. *Kangaroo* is his most autobiographical novel in that he wrote it while experiencing the events from which the novel takes its life. The autobiographical elements in his other novels, including *Sons and Lovers*, are recollections in comparative tranquillity. In *Kangaroo* the writing of the novel often reflects what Lawrence was doing that day, how he felt about Australia, and on what terms he was with his wife, for all but its last chapter was written during the months of June and July 1922, when he and Frieda stayed in New South Wales. The book thus allows us a unique chance to see Lawrence's volatility transmuted into his prose. The shapelessness of the novel, verging occasionally on incoherence, has led the majority of critics to label it a failure, but it is pertinent to wonder whether any other form would have conveyed so much immediacy of reaction. Chapter 8 of *Kangaroo* is called "Volcanic Evidence" and chapter 14 is called "Bits," headings that sum up Lawrence's intention in this novel not to give a fully rounded interpretation of the Australia he visited but something more exploratory, more rough-hewn, and more like the experience of life as we actually feel it.

Richard and Harriet Somers come to Australia as strangers, a point emphasized in the amusing first pages of *Kangaroo* when the "Aussie" workmen speculate whether they might be "Fritzies" or "Bolshies." This is post–World War I society, but the prejudices remain. Indeed, the molding influence of 1914–1918 can scarcely be overstated in connection with this novel. It comes to the fore most obviously in chapter 12, "Nightmare." Here the Somerses recall the indignities of life in England during the war and the reasons for their disillusionment with Western society. "No man who has really consciously lived through this can believe again absolutely in democracy," Lawrence writes. His "Nightmare" chapter is a crucial though very often unregarded analysis of his reasons for leaving England in search of a better society. The people of England had voluntarily subjected themselves to the mass hysteria, as he saw it, of patriotism, to authoritarianism masquerading as democracy. The war for Lawrence was the obscene culmination of industrialization and science—the tyranny of the mechanical over the natural. Though several poets, most famously Wilfred Owen, had alerted the British public to the horrors of trench warfare, a deep-seated revulsion at how the war had been managed, and particularly how the ordinary people had reacted to the chauvinism of their leaders, had not yet set in. Lawrence was in this respect ahead of his contemporaries in making known his bitterness before it became fashionable to do so:

We hear so much of the bravery and horrors of the front. Brave the men were, all honour to them. It was at home the world was lost. We hear too little of the collapse of the proud human spirit at home, the triumph of sordid, rampant, raging meanness. "The bite of a jackal is blood-poisoning and mortification." And at home stayed all the jackals, middle-aged, male and female jackals. And they bit us all. And blood-poisoning and mortification set in.
(ch.12)

Such writing bears out Lawrence's comment in a letter when midway in creating *Kangaroo*—"the Lord alone knows what anybody will think of it: no love at all, and attempt at revolution." He was describing not just the plot but also the spirit of the book.

Lawrence's own decision to go abroad, dramatized in that of Richard Somers, grew directly out of his conviction that England was dead. As the Somerses leave the coast of England they see it "like a grey, dreary-grey coffin sinking in the sea behind." Lawrence used this image more than once in his fiction, and it presumably captures his funereal feelings as he and Frieda set sail from England in 1919 on the travels that would eventually take them to Australia. In "Nightmare" we trace the source of this bitterness in one of the least known but most trenchant pieces of antiwar writing in modern fiction.

The Australia to which the Somerses come is riddled with political dissension. *Kangaroo* has sometimes been cited as a novel in which Lawrence indicated Fascist tendencies. After the failures of "democracy" in the war, many intellectuals felt the need for tighter political leadership, providing it was based on an ability to heal the dissensions in society. Critics of Lawrence such as Bertrand Russell, who later accused him of setting out on a path leading to Auschwitz, overlook the novelist's constant tendency to self-reappraisal. In *Kangaroo*, and again in *The Plumed Serpent*, Lawrence has by the end reached a point where he is rejecting charismatic autocracy. The novel considers it seriously, and examines too the claims of the trade unions on the left, but at no point can Lawrence seriously be seen as a precursor of the Fascism of the 1930's, with its determination to perfect the machinery of society, or of Soviet-style Communism under Stalin. He poses for his readers a problem of discrimination, for he was genuinely attracted by the notion that mankind would be able to see its way out of its current malaise only if it followed the guidance of a great leader; but he also saw how easily this could lead to perversions of power and to the possibility that people would then surrender the last vestiges of their individualism. If Lawrence saw the seductive side of absolute political movements, he was also a prophet of their evils.

Ben Cooley and Willie Struthers are the two leaders through whom Lawrence debates the merits of individual and mass action. Cooley is the "Kangaroo" of the novel's title, conceived lovingly, associated often with flowers, the phoenix, fire, and Christ, as though filled with goodness and life. Yet this born leader of men closes his mind to views different from his own. His message to the world is one of love and hope for change, but it verges on threat. Somers' disillusionment grows stronger and he finally denies Kangaroo a deathbed reconciliation. The novel ends in doubt and confusion as the Somerses leave Australia. The new country has not offered them the political revelations or the social developments they hoped to find there, though as a time to take stock of each other, to see primeval and petit bourgeois worlds in contact, and to become more positively directed toward spiritual regeneration when political and social impulses have failed them, the Australian weeks have been essential. On his last day Somers reflects that "one of his souls would stand forever out on those rocks beyond the jetty," and so it was for Lawrence, who, in a letter dated 22 June 1922, wrote that "Australia would be a lovely country to lose the world in altogether." At no point in his life, however, could Lawrence make such a remark approvingly. He was too concerned with finding the world to delight in the possibility of losing it.

THE PLUMED SERPENT

LAWRENCE's travels to Mexico took him among stranger human relics than he had ever seen before. If in Sicily he had glimpsed the possibilities of an ancient civilization surviving in an even more ancient physical setting and in Australia witnessed the conjunction of a primeval landscape with vulgar bourgeois encroachments, in Mexico he saw not only scenes of undisturbed beauty but the evidence of a religious revival. Mexico, he believed, was regenerating itself. When Lawrence arrived in 1926 the country was racked by a dispute between church and state that broke out into open conflict; the same year

*The Plumed Serpent* was published. The expulsion of Christian images from the churches and the revival of dance rites in honor of the ancestral gods actually took place as he describes them in the novel. The religion of Quetzalcoatl (whose name is a compound of Nahuatlan words meaning "plumed serpent") had been a great unifying myth in ancient Mexico. There are different versions of the legend, but undoubtedly Lawrence knew about the religion in detail and was not—as a few critics have supposed him to be doing—weaving a spurious fantasy of his own. He was attracted to the Quetzalcoatl myth because it dealt only in the present, asserting life and rebirth and seeming to deny the finality of death. As Don Ramón puts it in the novel, "There is no Before and After, there is only Now." Its symbol was the phoenix, which Lawrence adopted as his own (it appeared on his grave in France before his ashes were removed to New Mexico). He hoped that in the revival of faith he saw at work in Mexico there might exist a viable formula for mankind as a whole.

Lawrence was forty years old when he wrote *The Plumed Serpent*, the same age as Kate Leslie, its main character. Like her, he was torn between abandoning Europe forever by settling in an unsophisticated community and returning to where he knew his cultural roots would always be. We know from Lawrence's correspondence at the time he first went to Mexico that he felt exactly as Kate does, and that the minor characters at the start of the novel—Owen, Villiers, Mrs. Norris, for example—were based on Mabel Dodge and her associates, with whom Lawrence frequently stayed. The character of the novel changes, however, when he introduces Don Ramón and Don Cipriano, the two main advocates of the Quetzalcoatl revival.

Lawrence does not entirely resolve the problem of how to make Ramón and Cipriano credible as human beings when they spend so much of their time adopting the personae of Aztec deities, Ramón as Quetzalcoatl himself, Cipriano as the war-god Huitzilopochtli. Ramón seems especially remote from real experience, for Lawrence expects him to figure as the repository of an enlightened philosophy—a kindly parent, and, at least with his second wife, Teresa, a loving husband—while at the same time he exacts bloody retribution on those who defy Quetzalcoatl, drives his first wife, Carlota, to her death, and participates in strange ceremonies of invocation to the Morning Star and the wind. He also mouths some of the most repugnant sentiments that Lawrence ever put on paper. Some of these have to do with race, some with the subjection of women to men, some with the need for great individuals to preside over the destiny of the masses. "I would like," Don Ramón says, "to be one of the Initiates of the Earth . . . forming a Natural Aristocracy of the World." Natural Aristocrats, he continues, "can be international, or cosmopolitan, or cosmic. It has always been so. The peoples are no more capable of it than the leaves of the mango tree are capable of attaching themselves to the pine."

This spiritual pride in Ramón does not prevent him from having much of the aura and mystic interest that Rawdon Lilly fatally lacks in *Aaron's Rod*. Though *The Plumed Serpent* may seem faintly absurd to the modern reader, with its elaborate accounts of ritual worship verging on biblical pastiche, it is more likely to be the resonant prophetic tone of the novel rather than the content that alienates people. Lawrence, through Ramón, speaks of the need for a regeneration of mystery in the world: "And a new Hermes should come back to the Mediterranean, and a new Ashtaroth to Tunis; and Mithras again to Persia, and Brahma unbroken to India, and the oldest of dragons to China." In other words, if each community in the world, led by the inspiration of great leaders, could resurrect what is true to its culture, temperament, and climate, then no one religion would be more important than any other, yet all would be part of a global renewal of the spirit. Then, Ramón insists to Cipriano:

"I, First Man of Quetzalcoatl, with you, First Man of Huitzilopochtli, and perhaps your Wife, First Woman of Itzpapolotl, could we not meet, with pure souls, the other great aristocrats of the world, the First Man of Wotan and the First Woman of Freya, First Lord of Hermes, and the Lady of Astarte, the Best-Born of Brahma, and the Son of the Greatest Dragon?"

(ch. 17)

On the surface this may seem rhetorical and obscure, but it is no more than a plea for the coming together of mankind in common resistance to the age of the machine and the tyranny of materialism. Many of the subcultures of the 1960's and 1970's pleaded for the same ideal through not dissimilar means.

*The Plumed Serpent* must not be altogether exonerated from criticism, however. There is in the book a peculiar doctrine of blood separatism whereby the races of the world should remain pure from the corruption of intermingling. It also asserts more nakedly than any other Lawrence novel the doctrine of male supremacy. When Kate marries Don Cipriano the ceremony enacts the subjection of woman to man, just as Teresa serenely accepts her servility to Ramón. The very landscape of Mexico, with its phallic cacti and "sperm-like water," is evoked in terms of male sexuality. Ramón and Cipriano share an affinity of spirit that, in the episode where Cipriano is initiated into the role of the war-god, becomes explicitly physical. The general thesis of the novel argues for a positive will to revive our dormant spirituality, and thus it increasingly seems in tune with many people's attitudes today; but within this broad idea many of the particular doctrines in *The Plumed Serpent* remain peculiarly resistible. I suspect that Lawrence came to feel this himself, for the novel loses some of its coherence toward the end. Kate, even in marriage, does not wholly commit herself either to Mexico or to Cipriano. Lawrence likewise becomes less convincing in his presentation of the revivalism as the novel moves to its close. Surely it is he who speaks through Kate in an italicized section on the last page: "*What a fraud I am! I know all the time it is I who don't altogether want them. I want myself to myself. But I can fool them so that they shan't find out.*"

*The Plumed Serpent* cannot be easily absorbed as an organic whole. Too many ideas proliferate, some almost contradicting others. There are long passages of ritual incantation. Yet the novel has a vigorous dramatic quality. Sometimes, as in the chapter entitled "The Attack of Jamiltepec" or in the description of the bullfight at the beginning, it arises from the same kind of powerful physical observation that Lawrence so often displays in his travel writings or in such essays as "Reflections on the Death of a Porcupine." It comes, too, from the urgency of his concern for a new world. Though *The Plumed Serpent* is unlikely now to be read with wholehearted seriousness, it would be wrong to dismiss it as some kind of theatrical extravaganza. This is not the world of the Natcha-Kee-Tawaras but an earnest attempt to see what relevance a wholly different culture from our own may have to the kind of society we are still constructing.

## LADY CHATTERLEY'S LOVER

For many, *Lady Chatterley's Lover* probably still arouses the sniggers that surrounded it in 1960 when its publishers were taken to court on a charge of purveying obscenity. The novel made D. H. Lawrence a household name but for entirely the wrong reasons. He became identified with "free love," "permissiveness," and "four-letter words," trends in the 1960's that might well have appalled the morally serious Lawrence. As a penalty for his new fame he became erroneously linked with sexual emancipation and frequently trivialized by people who did not understand his work. Even now it needs to be asserted that there are three central themes in *Lady Chatterley's Lover* that make nonsense of the myth that it offers a kind of intellectual's pornography. These themes are fidelity in human relationships, the erosion of old England, and the capacity of the English language to express more than conventional morality wishes it to say. Lawrence had touched on them all in earlier novels, but in *Aaron's Rod*, *Kangaroo*, and *The Plumed Serpent* his intense concern with the possibilities of reforming society through different kinds of leadership had diverted him from any straightforward discussion of England, its mores, its society, or its language. In his last novel (though he did not know it to be so), Lawrence wrote his most fully English work apart from *Sons and Lovers*. There are no Lydia Lenskys, Loerkes, or Cicios here, no excursions abroad. Altogether abandoning the exotic territories of his previous three novels, Lawrence writes now of an England in which pastoralism and industrialization exist in uneasy conjunction.

There are three versions of *Lady Chatterley's Lover*. *The First Lady Chatterley*, as William Heinemann Ltd. termed it when publishing it for the first time in England in 1972, is the shortest. Lawrence wrote it between October 1926 and March 1927. His next version, completed in the summer of 1927, is much longer. In its published form it is known as *John Thomas and Lady Jane* (1972). Both these earlier versions of *Lady Chatterley's Lover*, like the familiar third version, were first printed outside of England. *The First Lady Chatterley* was published in America in 1944, and *John Thomas and Lady Jane* appeared in an Italian translation (by Carlo Izzo) in 1954. No version was legally available in Britain before 1960, when the uncut Florence edition of 1928 was republished. This checkered writing and publishing history reflects the self-questioning attitude with which Lawrence approached his subject. He had always been an avid reviser of his own work, but he clearly intended *Lady Chatterley's Lover* not only to be satisfactory in the form it took but to be explicit in its meaning. The three versions are thus cast in very different ways.

Frieda Lawrence, in her introduction to *The First Lady Chatterley*, expresses her preference for it because, she implies, it is the truest statement of what Lawrence wished to say: "*The First Lady Chatterley* he wrote as she came out of him, out of his own immediate self. In the third version he was also aware of his contemporaries' minds." He kept adjusting the novel, Frieda tells us, because he was frightened that his critics would dismiss the book as mere mysticism (as *The Plumed Serpent* is still sometimes dismissed). He seems not to have bargained for the comparative indifference with which all three versions were treated for thirty years.

*The First Lady Chatterley* is the gentlest of the three, *John Thomas and Lady Jane* the most detailed, and *Lady Chatterley's Lover* the most polemical. Between the first and the second version Lawrence seems to have worried that the novel would be too dissociated from recognizable daily life. In the second, therefore, he emphasizes the effects of industrialization upon the beauties of England, he peoples the novel with more characters, and he balances pastoral lyricism with some degree of satire. The third version, the one most of us read first, is less changed from version two than version two is from its predecessor, even though it is only now that Lawrence's famous gamekeeper acquires the name Mellors (he is Parkin in the earlier versions). *Lady Chatterley's Lover* does, however, have a franker sexual vocabulary than either of the other versions. In a review in the *Times Literary Supplement* (27 April 1973) the anonymous writer maintains, at the end of an intelligently hostile assessment of the three works, that

there is little point in offering an order of preference between the three versions. Certainly the first, comparatively free from jargon and overt bullying, is the least offensive: lacking the crudely opposed contrasts of *John Thomas and Lady Jane* and more especially of *Lady Chatterley's Lover*, it is more honest in observation, though correspondingly more obscure in purpose. But it does not make enough difference.

The reviewer takes this point of view because he does not regard any version of *Lady Chatterley's Lover* as a major work of art, concluding, indeed, that "much hatred lies within its assumption of tenderness." I believe it does matter, however, which version we like best, for all three attempt different things. My own preference is for the familiar third version because it seems to possess a clarity of statement that, while it may be less "honest" in the sense that it is less fair-minded than the previous drafts, overtly says what Lawrence primarily wanted to get across: namely that contemporary society in the Western industrialized world is based on false values and that until we establish the right kind of relationships between individuals there can be no serious prospect of man fulfilling himself in anything but a mechanical way.

*Lady Chatterley's Lover* in its final form has the diagrammatic straightforwardness of a fable. Lady Chatterley, Mellors, and Sir Clifford Chatterley have been pared down to prototypes, as though in an allegory. Lawrence had been moving toward this view of character in all his novels since *The Rainbow*, but in his final novel, in its final form, he has come to regard three-dimensional complexities of character as mere accretions. The novelist's task is to be spare, functional, and explicit, as the earliest storytellers were. *Lady Chatterley's Lover*, in this respect, looks forward to the formal experiments of modernism in fiction and back in time, as is appropriate in a novel eulogizing the English past, to the simple structure of primitive storytelling.

Of the three themes mentioned at the start of this discussion of *Lady Chatterley's Lover*, that of fidelity requires most explanation. Is not this a tale of marital infidelity? In a purely legal sense it is, but Lawrence creates in this novel a world so deeply private between Connie Chatterley and Oliver Mellors that it would be virtually sacrilegious to impose judicial restraints upon it. Clifford Chatterley embodies inherited privilege, atrophied power, and sexual denial. He is socially boorish, insensitive to nature, and physically impotent. He has no life in the novel (or in any version of it) other than as the symbolic manifestation of the mechanical will. To insist upon married fidelity between him and Connie would be to assert the superiority of social forms over instinctual behavior. In the serious evaluation of right relationships Lawrence appropriately looks for trueness of feelings, not for conventions approved by a society he believed to be dying.

Connie's life as the lady of Wragby Hall is described early in the novel as "void ... spectral, not really existing." When she gives herself sexually to Michaelis, a house guest, it means nothing to her, only confirming the emptiness of her being. Lawrence describes the episode with reticence, in obvious contrast to the flowing rhythms with which he later writes of the lovemaking between Connie and Mellors. These early chapters define a world where talk is a substitute for action and where Sir Clifford can seriously intellectualize "this sex thing" as a minor adjunct to "the slow building up of integral personality."

At the conclusion of this conversation we meet Mellors for the first time, "like the sudden rush of a threat out of nowhere." He betokens a new kind of life, isolated from the social world but in obvious harmony with the natural environment, whose right balance it is his duty, as a gamekeeper, to ensure. Though their first encounters are wary, the relationship that develops between Connie and Mellors intensifies to a point where Sir Clifford and his world become extraneous to the needs that the two lovers can fulfill in each other. At the end of the novel Connie is pregnant, awaiting her divorce, and anticipating a future of true personal freedom.

In the *Times Literary Supplement* review already quoted, this ending is reviled as escapism into a "story-book future—for those who are lucky enough to be able to live the forest life. As for the rest, why, their future is none of our concern: they are simply the world which Connie will jettison for her own personal salvation." The implied criticism of Lawrence's scheme has to be faced, and it is best to do so by remembering that though few individuals have the pastoral opportunities of Connie and Mellors, we all have the capacity to form relationships. In getting the private world right we may collectively come closer to a changed society. Having failed in *Kangaroo* and *The Plumed Serpent* to find a practical solution to the malaise in modern society, Lawrence approaches the problem from the other end, through private experience rather than public action.

The family of Chatterley "stood for England and St. George," Lawrence tells us in the first chapter, and "never knew there was a difference." For Lawrence the true England is in the woods and valleys, not in the great houses. Ironically Sir Clifford also sees the woods as a symbol of England, even though his father had cut the trees to supply the war effort. We think back to the crass leadership in the war that Lawrence indicts in *Kangaroo*. Sir Clifford's woods, however, would always be private, untrespassed. They are "property." For Connie and Mellors they are the place where they make love, teeming with natural life and undestroyed beauty. Around them the spread of industrial England blots out more and more of the agricultural landscape. It is as though a black monster has been unleashed, feeding only on England's past:

It was as if dismalness had soaked through and through everything. The utter negation of natural beauty, the utter negation of the gladness of life, the utter absence of the instinct for shapely beauty which every bird and beast has, the utter death of the human intuitive faculty was appalling.

(ch. 11)

*Lady Chatterley's Lover* is a cry of lamentation for disappearing England. "Ours is essentially a tragic age, so we refuse to take it tragically," Lawrence says in the opening line of the novel. The tragedy is that modern industrialized man has not been the innocent victim of malevolent gods, but has chosen this form of evolution. The only hope for him is that he will see how the process of destruction is not yet complete. The natural world has been contained but not destroyed. When Connie and Mellors place forget-me-nots on each other's sex-parts they express not only the tender intimacy of their love for each other, but their knowledge of a remembered England whose pattern of life was "organic," not "mechanical." In a simple summary this sounds like nostalgic sentimentality, but the import of *Lady Chatterley's Lover* is severe, even brutal. Man must rescue himself or be blotted out. Lawrence hopes, surely, that we will see in Connie and Mellors the same archetypal representation of human possibilities that John Milton intended in the expelled Adam and Eve.

Lawrence, in the third version of the Lady Chatterley story, writes an uncluttered prose that he steers into lyricism when he believes the theme requires it. He is in total command of his language now, with none of the poetic overwriting of his first novels, overurgent didacticism of some passages in *The Rainbow* and *Women in Love*, or confused rhetoric occasionally detectable in the "leadership" novels. *Lady Chatterley's Lover* does not have a single style, but finds at each stage an appropriate correspondence between language and subject. Since some of the novel describes sexual intercourse and explicit responses to sex, Lawrence needs to find an unequivocal language. The best sexual descriptions in the novel achieve a rhythm that conveys the sense of a wholly sensual experience: "And it seemed she was like the sea, nothing but dark waves rising and heaving, heaving with a great swell, so that slowly her whole darkness was in motion, and she was ocean rolling its dark, dumb mass."

At moments such as this Lawrence is extending English prose in an attempt to realize virtually unrealizable sensations. Language can perhaps only be retrospective. When we burn ourselves we feel the pain, and only then do we articulate it. Sexual orgasm likewise lies beyond language, though almost every love poet has tried to recall it in a form of words that may capture the sense of the moment. Lawrence tries to realize the moment itself, to leave out the time gap between experience and recollection. It leads him to adopt the kind of vocabulary that, sparsely used though it is, took the novel into the law courts. He rejoiced in his opportunity to release the English language from some of its prudery—none of the words that caused offense were less than several hundred years old—but he did not really find a way of making them seem less than quaint and archaic. Mellors is a fairly educated man, and his switches into regional speech where sexual words are supposed to sound natural smack too much of a literary device. Lawrence may not have succeeded, therefore, in realizing a new form of English capable of expressing nonlinguistic sensations, but he was defeated more by the limitations of language itself than by his own approach to it.

*Lady Chatterley's Lover* was written by an ill man who could see almost nothing admirable in the way his society was moving. One might expect in the circumstances a cry of bitter despair, but the novel insists not only that the world is worth saving but that it can still be saved. Lawrence shows himself still interested in the power of the novel as an aesthetic form, experimenting almost dramatically with new methods of presenting character and using English. It is the final major work of fiction in his career, but it shows an artist in full command of his gifts, capable of reviving past strengths that more recent work had obscured, while at the same time inching his talents into new territory. Lawrence died in the midstream of his creative flow, not at the point where the river widens into the dark sea.

## LAWRENCE'S OTHER FICTION

THOUGH his ten novels must always be regarded as the basis of his claim to greatness as a writer, Lawrence is also the author of innumerable other works of fiction. Some critics have thought his shorter fiction better art than his full-length works because he necessarily denied himself the elaborations and diversions, the repetitions, and the flights of metaphysical fancy that are integral to his novels. In a short account of these writings it is impossible to mention more than a few of the stories, novellas, and other fictions unless this section is to degenerate into a mere list of titles, for they amount to well over seventy separate creations. None of them lacks interest; some of them are crucial to his development.

Not content to write novels of his own, Lawrence in 1923 spent a considerable amount of time reworking other people's fiction. The most famous outcome of this is *The Boy in the Bush* (1924), a revision of "The House of Ellis," an unpublished novel by M. L. Skinner. He was honest with Mollie Skinner: "You have no constructive power," he told her. He gave the novel (or so we must presume) the qualities that make it an engrossing if lightweight account of a young Australian's growth into manhood in the 1880's. "The only thing was to write it all out again, following your MS almost exactly, but giving a unity, a rhythm, and a little more psychic development than you had done," he told the original author, and she unresistingly accepted his amendments. At the same time Lawrence was translating a novel by the Sicilian writer Giovanni Verga, revising *Dragon of the Apocalypse* by Frederick Carter (published as an essay entitled simply *Apocalypse*, 1931), and continuously reviewing fiction for various London journals.

In his correspondence Lawrence occasionally mentions a book he is currently working on but that never finally saw the light of day or that was later published in another form. Almost every novel he wrote started with a different title. It would be an engaging quiz to ask who wrote the following novels, and by what other names they are known: *Laetitia, The Saga of Siegmund, Paul Morel, The Sisters, The Bitter Cherry, Quetzalcoatl,* and *Tenderness,* for only *Aaron's Rod* and *Kangaroo* seem to have survived under the titles Lawrence first planned for them. One of the novels that never came to anything was to be about Robert Burns, a Lawrentian hero in embryo. It may have been a good thing that Lawrence never took it very far, because he intended to transplant the Scottish poet to a Derbyshire setting. A more determined attempt to write a novel that eventually came to nothing is "Mr. Noon," a vivacious comedy that Lawrence started immediately after completing *The Lost Girl.*

Lawrence's first major story was "The White Stocking" (1907), a prototype of the stories he was to write more maturely in later years, wherein a young wife is torn between decency toward her husband and her natural attraction to a man she meets at a dance. His first published tale was a slight piece entitled "A Prelude," which he had submitted under Jessie Chambers' name for a literary competition in Nottingham. The first story to be printed under his own name was "Goose Fair" (1910).

Lawrence's rapid development as a writer can be seen if we compare these comparatively tenuous early stories with works like "Odour of Chrysanthemums," a tale of grief in a mining community, and "Daughters of the Vicar," in which he explores the social gulf that divides the English middle class from the working class. Only a few months separate all these works, but the intensity of Lawrence's writing has deepened immensely. They were published together in *The Prussian Officer, and Other Stories* (1914), which for many people remains his most satisfactory collection. The title story presents a relationship between an officer and his orderly as concentrated and sensual as any we encounter in the novels. It is tempting in a group of stories such as this to trace the links with other works, but each one has an individual power that bestows on it a separate existence. Though "The Prussian Officer," for example, anticipates something of the Birkin-Crich relationship in *Women in Love,* it has its own kind of violent imagination. We reduce the stories if we see them only as antecedents of larger works.

The same must be said of the stories that appeared in the second collection published during his lifetime, *England, My England, and Other Stories* (1922), of which at least three—the title story, "The Horse Dealer's Daughter," and "Fanny and Annie" —are among the best he wrote. In "England, My England" Lawrence means us to see Egbert, the main character, as a symbol of effete but not altogether impotent English gentility. Lawrence possibly asks too much if he intends us to read the whole plight of this class into one short story, but in the final pages of this loosely constructed tale he manages to conjure up for us the barbarity of war. By contrast "The Horse Dealer's Daughter" creates a private world between a doctor and the girl he rescues from suicide. An intense but not altogether humorless climax brings the two of them to the point of marriage, as though their love has been fanned by the flames of the fire before which they have been drying themselves. Within its own terms the story works well because Lawrence does not deviate from his tight control of atmosphere.

"Fanny and Annie" may serve as a representative example of Lawrence's short-story technique at this middle point in his writing career. It opens with characteristically Lawrentian vocabulary: "Flame-lurid his face as he turned among the throng of flame-lit and dark faces upon the platform. In the light of the furnace she caught sight of his drifting countenance, like a piece of floating fire." A woman returns from a far place where she has been a lady's maid to be met by her first love. The setting is industrial and the theme as much a conflict of attitudes within class as that between the Morels in *Sons and Lovers*, though Fanny does not have Mrs. Morel's different background. This is a coming home to claim her last opportunity to be a wife. She arrives "with her umbrella, her chatelaine, and her little leather case," a mock lady with mock gentility. Harry, by contrast, "had waited—or remained single—all these years." Lawrence carefully balances irony and pathos, for that is the skill of this story. Fanny has to learn humility during the course of it and feels "dragged down to earth, as a bird which some dog has got down in the dust," but the ending leaves it ambiguous as to whether Fanny's final assimilation into her old community is a resignation to the second-rate or a decent alternative to the nonlife she has had as a maid. Lawrence is entirely fair to the Morley villagers in the tale, satirizing them lightly but never dismissively. It is a decent community, proud of its standards, its festivals, its cleanliness. Is not Fanny's return the moment of her release, not least sexually, for Harry has the gruff sexuality of Lawrence's natural man? However we interpret Fanny's history, this story displays Lawrence's technique at its sharpest. Image and theme constantly interrelate so that in only fifteen pages we have met a vivid group of people with the qualified hopes and unexpressed frustrations of countless numbers like them.

In 1923 "The Ladybird," "The Fox," and "The Captain's Doll" were published together. These three novellas were deeply admired by the most influential of Lawrence's critical advocates, F. R. Leavis. In *D. H. Lawrence: Novelist* he wrote:

The inspiration, the *raison d'être*, of The Captain's Doll entails the convincing presentment of the Lawrentian themes in an action that shall affect us as belonging, not to a poetic-prophetic Sabbath-world, as The Ladybird does, but to the everyday reality in which we live, though, unlike The Fox, to a milieu of educated and sophisticated people.

Leavis admired "The Captain's Doll" for its "common sense," but many readers are more likely to be struck by its humor and by the way in which Lawrence appears to be parodying some of his own attitudes toward the relationship of the sexes. "The Fox" is a study in tortured sexual relations, linking the human world with a symbolic value placed on animal behavior. "The Ladybird," in a much more stylized way, explores the kind of territory that *Lady Chatterley's Lover* successfully makes its own, contrasting sexless, almost euphuistic love with true passion.

"St. Mawr" (1925) was described by Leavis as having "a creative and technical originality more remarkable than that of *The Waste Land*, being, as that poem is not, completely achieved, a full and self-sufficient creation. It can hardly strike the admirer as anything but major." "St. Mawr" extends the symbolism of animals much further than the "Rabbit" chapter in *Women in Love* or "The Fox," for St. Mawr is a stallion resentful of the ignoble men who try to master him. The novella suffers from irrelevant Lawrentian diversions about "the secret evil" in men that indulges their greed and death wish, so that Leavis' judgment on it is now likely to seem overstressed for most readers, but it undoubtedly makes a vigorous case against Western civilization. Along with "The Woman Who Rode Away" (1928), an unpleasant but brilliantly sustained tale of female submission to alien gods, it evokes a wholly foreign world that, repellent though it may be to many people, holds total conviction while we read of it.

Lawrence went on writing stories even in the less energetic final years of his life. They include "The Virgin and the Gipsy" (1926; published 1930), which embodies almost definitively the theme of sexual attraction across class and even ethnic barriers, powerfully conveyed through an insinuatingly erotic use of imagery. "Love Among the Haystacks" came out in 1930 (though drafted much earlier); "The Man Who Died" (originally "The Escaped Cock," 1928), "The Man Who Loved Islands" (1927), and several pieces not published until after his death show a writer constantly probing for new ways of expressing his concern for man's future and his fascination with human relationships. These late stories are sometimes too symbolically wrought to seem other than obsessional, but we seldom feel that Lawrence repeats himself. Even when the themes are familiar the imaginative form they take is usually unique.

Some critics claim that the short story and the novella differ from the full-length novel not just in length and scope but in their essential aesthetic being. If this is so, then D. H. Lawrence proves the exception to the rule, for his shorter writings normally parallel themes and concepts in his novels. They are neither less nor more effective at their best, complete achievements in their own right that cast light on the novels only if that is how we want to use them. Though Lawrence maintained close contact with Katherine Mansfield, the main artist of the English short story in the early part of the century, he never imitated her style. Nor did he borrow from the classic continental short-story writers. He found a voice so uniquely his own that one can open almost any page of one of his tales and recognize it as distinctively Lawrentian: urgent prose, with carefully placed emphases and recurring key words; background detail fully creating the intended world yet corresponding to the emotional nature of the protagonists; private moods evoking public themes and metaphysics. It does not always work, but when it does, in a naturalistic tale such as "Odour of Chrysanthemums" or in a ritualistic piece such as "The Woman Who Rode Away," we see in Lawrence a complete master of the shorter narrative.

### LAWRENCE AS A TRAVEL WRITER

ALMOST everything Lawrence wrote after *The White Peacock* reflects his personal odyssey. The early novels are full of excursions to English places such as the Isle of Wight (in *The Trespasser*) and Lincoln Cathedral (in *The Rainbow*). In *Women in Love*, *The Lost Girl*, and *Aaron's Rod*, the novels of his middle period, Lawrence gives increasing emphasis to "abroad." In the early 1920's his correspondence becomes very bitter as he talks about England as a graveyard. There can be little doubt that he regarded the war as a historical disaster that totally failed to arrest the decline of moral wisdom he perceived throughout northern Europe. In 1928 he summed up his true feelings about England in the essay "Dull London." The hostility has gone and he expresses instead a profound distaste for the passionless nature of English society as he saw it. The tone is regretful rather than aggressive:

Of course, England is the easiest country in the world, easy, easy and nice. Everybody is nice, and everybody is easy. The English people on the whole are surely the *nicest* people in the world, and everybody makes everything so easy for everybody else, that there is almost nothing to resist at all. But this very easiness and this very niceness become at last a nightmare. It is as if the whole air were impregnated with chloroform or some other pervasive anaesthetic, that makes everything easy and nice, and takes the edge off everything, whether nice or nasty. As you inhale the drug of easiness and niceness, your vitality begins to sink. Perhaps not your physical vitality, but something else: the vivid flame of your individual life. England can afford to be so free and individual because no individual flame of life is sharp and vivid. It is just mildly warm and safe. You couldn't burn your fingers at it. Nice, safe, easy: the whole ideal. And yet under all the easiness is a gnawing uneasiness, as in a drug-taker.

Apart from *Kangaroo* and *The Plumed Serpent*, Lawrence's main travel writings are three short books dating from the same period: *Sea and Sardinia* (1921), *Mornings in Mexico* (1927), and *Etruscan Places* (1927; published 1932). He wrote one earlier volume of travel pieces, *Twilight in Italy* (1916), in which there is much Christology and also some first-rate observation of Italian domesticity in which pagan associations are evoked. *Sea and Sardinia* is a more substantial attempt to render what Lawrence was constantly seeking, a society "outside the circuit of civilization," which before he left Europe he instinctively felt would most probably be encountered in the remoter parts of Italy. "The name of Athens hardly moves me," he writes in *Sea and Sardinia*, but on his journey to Sardinia from Palermo he begins to hear the "terrible echo" that calls "from the darkest recesses of my blood." Athens, the ancient seat of reason and learning, leaves him cold, but the territory in which he travels in *Sea and Sardinia*, real places rather than remembered notions, brings him into contact with unspoiled peasant communities where manly virtues still thrive. The Sardinian days are recalled with humor and vitality. There are almost no incursions into philosophical generalization. The result is a book that places Lawrence more straightforwardly as a romantic writer than perhaps anything else he wrote, antirational, marrying instinct and intelligence:

This Sunday morning, seeing the frost among the tangled, still savage bushes of Sardinia, my soul thrilled again. This was not all known. This was not all worked out. Life was not only a process of rediscovering backwards. It is that, also: and it is that intensely. Italy has given me back I know not what of myself, but a very, very great deal. She has found for me so much that was lost: like a restored Osiris. But this morning in the omnibus I realize that, apart from the great rediscovery backwards, which one *must* make before one can be whole at all, there is a move forwards. There are unknown, unworked lands where the salt has not lost its savour. But one must have perfected oneself in the great past first.

(ch. 6)

Perfecting oneself in the great past is the author's dedicated intention in *Mornings in Mexico* and *Etruscan Places*. These sketches, though still in the episodically descriptive manner of the first two books, do not have the same kind of humanity. The interest is more abstract, more abstruse. The readers of *Sea and Sardinia* know the ship's passengers, the bus drivers, the peasants, and the urchins whom we meet in Lawrence's vivid immediate style. He might be in great demand today as a travel commentator, implying social conclusions from anecdotal observations in the way that V. S. Naipaul and Paul Theroux do in their travel books, but in the manner of *Sea and Sardinia* rather than that of the two later books.

*Mornings in Mexico* ought to be read partly as a companion piece to *The Plumed Serpent*, though it differs in some of the details of ancient rites. The book comprises eight descriptions of Mexican or New Mexican life, the core of which are three essays on Indian dances. Dramatic and vigorous though these undoubtedly are, often discovering a prose rhythm to match the movement of the dance ("Mindless, without effort, under the hot sun, unceasing, yet never perspiring nor even breathing heavily, they dance on and on"), our principal interest in them today may be for the light they throw on the strange doctrines of Lawrence's Mexican novel. Here he defines his attraction to the animistic credo of the Aztec descendants, with their insistence on "the mystic, living will that is in man." The Christian believes in a lost paradise and a future redemption, but in Lawrence's view he despises the present moment. Man feels himself unworthy of God. He is always, in the Western tradition, exorcising his original sin and seeking future grace, so that he has no immediate vitality. This, ultimately, explains the "pervasive anaesthetic" he describes in "Dull London" as a feature of English life: it derives not just from the northern temperament climatically, but from the religious sources of Western man, with their insistence on past error, future need, and present imperfectibility.

*Etruscan Places*, published posthumously, is incomplete, being six sketches toward an intended cycle of twelve. In 1927 Lawrence visited the four sites he describes in the book. They are Cerveteri, Tarquinia, Vulci, and Volterra. Here he seeks knowledge of a civilization even more ancient and "lost" than that of the Aztecs, for the Etruscans have left nothing behind but paintings, tombs, and the memorabilia of a people doomed to extinction through the colonizing power of brutal Rome (Lawrence's dislike of Roman classicism was as strong as his negative sentiments toward the Greeks). *Etruscan Places* is the work of an art critic rather than a novelist, though even here Lawrence's imagination constantly re-creates the personae of Etruscan life. At this point in his life Lawrence turned to painting as his main form of expression—his last ten years teem with pictures he made himself, pictures about which he wrote, and pictures he went long distances to see. In paintings from the heyday of Etruscan civilization he finds evidence of naturalness and feeling, though these qualities were gradually eroded by rationality, skepticism, and science, Roman qualities that deny "red blood" and "consciousness."

In Lawrence's correspondence, which is now being edited in its entirety for the first time and published by Cambridge University Press, proliferate comments and ideas about the places he visited from his first travels to Germany to his last days in France, supplements not only to his imaginative work but to his travel documentaries. Rootlessness and self-exile have become increasingly familiar to writers in the twentieth century, betokening the breakup of a shared assurance about permanent values in society. Lawrence is a major contributor to the literature of exile and though his travel writings do not especially add to our regard for him as a great writer, they undoubtedly make available details and evidence about him that considerably help our reading of his novels and poetry. In their own right they contain some of his finest prose moments, bringing to life alien landscapes and other cultures. "I am English, and my Englishness is my very vision. But now I must go away, if my soul is sightless for ever. Let it then be blind, rather than commit the vast wickedness of acquiescence," wrote Lawrence in a letter in October 1915. Through his travel writings we can perhaps find the clearest indication of how he avoided the blindness he feared might result from leaving the country of his birth.

# D. H. LAWRENCE

## LAWRENCE THE POET

LAWRENCE's first published works were some poems selected on his behalf by Jessie Chambers and sent to the *English Review*, where they appeared in November 1902.

> I have opened the window to warm my hands on the sill
> Where the sunlight soaks in the stone: the afternoon
> Is full of dreams, my love, the boys are all still
> In a wistful dream of Lorna Doone.

These opening lines from his first printed poem, "Dreams Old and Nascent," are addressed to Jessie Chambers. If they do not announce the arrival of a great writer, they certainly indicate the young Lawrence's love of plain, natural pleasures. Stillness and warmth, with the same mellowness as the pastoral chapters of *The White Peacock*, flood through the early part of the poem, but then "The surface of dreams is broken" and the poet reaches almost in panic toward "the terror of lifting the innermost I out of the sweep of the impulse of life." We might detect some echoes of Gerard Manley Hopkins and William Butler Yeats in the early Lawrence poems, but he is astonishingly free from other influences. Overwritten and imprecise though he can occasionally be, he nevertheless writes with the confidence that what he has to say matters.

Lawrence wrote poetry all his life. Eight collections were published in his own lifetime: *Love Poems and Others* (1913), *Amores* (1916), *Look! We Have Come Through!* (1917), *New Poems* (1918), *Bay* (1919), *Tortoises* (1921), *Birds, Beasts and Flowers* (1923), and *Pansies* (1929), in addition to the two volumes of his *Collected Poems*, which came out in 1928. Three more volumes were published posthumously: *Nettles* (1930), *Triumph of the Machine* (1930), and *The Ship of Death, and Other Poems* (1933). His writings in this area amounts to an abiding concern for poetic expression, though just as one finds the word "poetic" necessarily coming to mind when talking about so much of his prose, so it is impossible not to read some of his verse without feeling it is only rhetoric or metered prose. This reaction would not have dismayed Lawrence, who regarded divisions among literary genres as arbitrary and banal.

Lawrence's early poems, from 1906 to 1911, are almost entirely autobiographical. Though their lyrical vocabulary is conventionally Georgian, their tone and what he does with the words he chooses show a poet eager to express a personal vision. When he describes a snapdragon

> Strangled, my heart swelled up so full
> As if it would burst its wine-skin in my throat,
> Choke me in my own crimson. I watched her pull
> The gorge of the gaping flower, till the blood did float
> Over my eyes, and I was blind.

or a water hen

> Oh, water-hen, beside the rushes
> Hide your quaint, unfading blushes,
> Still your quick tail, lie as dead,
> Till the distance folds over his ominous tread.

we see as explicitly as we do in any of the novels how attentive Lawrence was to the details of nature and how sympathetic to the struggle of small creatures before rampant man. These extracts come from "Snap-dragon" and "Cruelty and Love," two of Lawrence's best early poems.

In *Look! We Have Come Through!* Lawrence begins to experiment more drastically with form. Though many of the poems in this collection still rhyme and still retain the combination of ballad clarity and unaffected lyricism that characterizes the earlier work, others flow freely and meanderingly like spoken narratives:

> But why, before
> He waters the horses does he wash his heel?
> Jesus!—his spurs are red with shining blood!
> ("The Young Soldier with Bloody Spurs")[2]

This dramatic, seminaturalistic quality becomes stronger in Lawrence's poetry. The poet's "I" persona speaks up more frequently and the invocations to the life forces in the universe are sounded as though in urgent conversation:

> Come quickly, and vindicate us
> against too much death.
> Come quickly, and stir the rotten globe of the world
>     from within,
> burst it with germination, with world anew.
>                 ("Craving for Spring")

Lawrence's poems read well in poetry recitals because of this personalized vigor. Some poems, main-

---

[2] Published in some editions as "A Servant Girl Speaks."

ly in the *Birds, Beasts and Flowers* collection, are therefore standard anthology pieces:

> A snake came to my water-trough
> On a hot, hot day, and I in pyjamas for the heat,
> To drink there.
> ("Snake")

The poem, beginning casually, goes through a small moment of horror, "a sort of protest against his withdrawing into that horrid black hole," before leaving the observer with "something to expiate;/ A pettiness."

The animal world can teach man much about the dignity of life or the naturalness of behavior in an unscientific mentality. Always Lawrence admires unconscious instinctive being in the creatures he observes: "Fish, oh Fish/So little matters!" ("Fish"); "She watches with insatiable wistfulness./Untold centuries of watching for something to come." ("Kangaroo"); "Such silence, such suspended transport." ("Mosquito"). These creature-poems are told with humor, for Lawrence sees the comedy in his attempts to outwit an insect, a bat, or a wolf; but beneath them all lies a vast admiration of forms of life that float freely in the world without responsibility or ambition. Lawrence does not sentimentalize his subjects—as his title essay in *Reflections on the Death of a Porcupine* (1925) indicates, he understood the predatory instincts in all living things (even in plants, he might have added)—but he achieves in *Birds, Beasts and Flowers* his twin aim of making observed nature dramatic and symbolic. Each subject lives in his poems individually, but each manifests the dark powers of the universe with which he constantly seeks to make contact.

As one would expect, the poetry that Lawrence wrote in the 1920's (though between 1923 and 1928 he wrote very little) matches the grand exploratory themes of his novels in the same period. It is summed up in "Terra Incognita":

> There are vast realms of consciousness still
>     undreamed of
> vast ranges of experience, like the humming of
>     unseen harps,
> we know nothing of, within us.
>
> Oh when man has escaped from the barbed-wire
>     entanglement
> of his own ideas and his own mechanical devices
> there is a marvellous rich world of contact and sheer
>     fluid beauty
> and fearless face-to-face awareness of now-naked
>     life.

Urgent, free-flowing verse of this kind can hardly escape an accusation of repetitiousness, even of boring the reader, but at its best (in "Thought" or in "Bavarian Gentians") Lawrence disciplines his language so that his prophetic desperation about mankind carries conviction. His last poems are so strongly shadowed by the possibility of death that even when they lose much poetic concentration in terms of form they still exert a powerful emotional force. "But still I know that life is for delight," he says in "Kissing and Horrid Strife." Here, as in his poems of triumph over death, "The Ship of Death" and "Shadows," he discovers a gravity of diction and calmness of utterance that are deeply affecting. All rhetoric is gone now and only his strict need to go on insisting that life is worth fighting for in a dying world—the world's death, not his own—keeps him from silence:

> then I must know that still,
> I am in the hands of the unknown God,
> he is breaking me down to his own oblivion
> to send me forth on a new morning, a new man.
> ("Shadows")

The last poems of Lawrence have this religious sobriety because the mood is intense and the language unstrained. He was a poet capable of greatness only in a few animal poems and in these last pieces on mortality; but in everything he wrote for his poetry collections he expressed himself as though the poem in hand was all that really mattered. We never feel that he is being a dilettante or that his verses are idle compositions on a rest day. They vary wildly in quality but they can never be said to lack conviction or to be less than full of passionate intensity.

## LAWRENCE AND THE THEATER

LIKE Henry James, Lawrence was a great novelist who hankered for recognition in the theater but failed even remotely to attain it in his own lifetime. Unlike James, whose work remains largely untouched in the standard repertoire today, Lawrence has since the mid-1960's undergone considerable re-estimation as a dramatist, and at least one of his plays, *The Daughter-in-Law* (1912), was regularly performed in British provincial playhouses in the early 1980's. He wrote eight plays in all, though only three of them were published in his own lifetime: *The*

*Widowing of Mrs. Holroyd* (1914), *Touch and Go* (1920), and *David* (1926). They span his entire writing career, probably starting with *A Collier's Friday Night* ("written when I was twenty-one, almost before I'd done anything, it is most horribly green") and concluding with his biblical epic, *David*, at the point in his career when he was most obsessed with old religions. His other plays are *The Merry-Go-Round* (probably 1910), *The Married Man* (1912), and *The Fight for Barbara* (also 1912). He also, when in New Mexico in 1924 and 1925, began two other plays, tentatively called "Altitude" and "Noah's Flood," though these are hardly more than fragments.

The theater plays quite a central part in Lawrence's fiction. In *The White Peacock* he writes of George and Meg "shaken with a tumult of wild feeling" at a performance of *Carmen*, as though the combination of music and drama has brought them into contact with a special kind of life: "their eyes were blinded by a spray of tears and that strange quivering laughter which burns with real pain." Siegmund in *The Trespasser* and Aaron in *Aaron's Rod* play in theater orchestras. The Natcha-Kee-Tawara troupe is the catalyst in *The Lost Girl*. Many of the rituals in *The Plumed Serpent* are presented dramatically, with an emphasis on formal speech and patterned action. Lawrence wrote about the theater in *Twilight in Italy* and about dance in *Mornings in Mexico*. He is also known to have taken a practical interest in stage production when teaching at Croydon, was concerned to have the respect of the leading playwright of the day, Bernard Shaw ("one of those delightful people who give one the exquisite pleasure of falling out with him wholesomely," he wrote in 1908), and made efforts, normally without success, to see his own plays staged. On the other hand, he wrote almost nothing on contemporary European theater, even though his lifetime saw the introduction of a regional repertory movement, the rise of German expressionism, the main impact of Henrik Ibsen and Anton Chekhov after their deaths, and a revolution in ways of producing Shakespeare that endorsed precisely those qualities of natural feeling and unmannered simplicity that Lawrence sought for in his own work.

Lawrence's plays were ignored for so long that it has become customary to think of them as diversions, scripts he wrote because he was a compulsive writer taking time off from his more serious work in the novels and essays. Recent productions, however, have suggested a real dramatic ability in these works. They act well and are therefore likely to be seen more frequently. The process by which they have become accepted in the theater has been extraordinarily slow. In his lifetime only two were staged; *The Widowing of Mrs. Holroyd*, initially in an amateur performance and eventually, in 1926, professionally, and *David*, in a 1927 production by the Stage Society. An adaptation of *The Daughter-in-Law* by Walter Greenwood, entitled *My Son's My Son*, was given in London in 1936, but the unadulterated play itself had to wait until 1967, when Peter Gill, a young director who is himself an accomplished playwright, staged it at the Royal Court Theatre.

There followed in 1968 a Lawrence season at the Royal Court when Gill revived *The Daughter-in-Law* alongside *A Collier's Friday Night* (which he had staged without decor for a single performance at the same theater in 1965) and *The Widowing of Mrs. Holroyd* (televised in 1961 but unstaged since 1926). This brilliantly successful season radically altered the standard view of Lawrence as lumpily unstageable. It became apparent that the British theater had an important dramatist of working-class attitudes writing at a time when the bourgeois taste of almost every playgoer prevented his work from being performed. We know that Harley Granville Barker had politely declined to stage *The Widowing of Mrs. Holroyd* in 1911, three years before its publication, at a time when he was attempting (ironically also at the Royal Court) to inject more social realism into the English theater, but it is very strange that between then and the 1960's there was such a total absence of response to Lawrence's plays.

Lawrence's other plays have not been widely performed. Gill staged *The Merry-Go-Round* at the Royal Court in 1973. It is a sleeker play than the earlier trio that he had directed, and on this occasion he "doctored" the text substantially. A production of *The Fight for Barbara* was presented at London's Mermaid Theatre in 1967 as part of a Lawrence evening, but the non-naturalistic elements in this rather stylized play surprised the critics, who received it badly. The Oxford Playhouse staged a first production of *Touch and Go* in 1979. *The Married Man* has not received a recorded performance, nor have the two unfinished pieces. *David*, too, would seem to demand another opportunity to be seen on the stage since Robert Atkins' production in 1927 was mounted without the necessary resources, and at a time when critics and public were less inclined to take Lawrence's religiosity seriously.

Though the priority at the moment must be to see

Lawrence's plays given a chance to establish themselves in the theatrical repertoire, it is already impossible to see or read them without relating them to the novels that were being written at the same time. Indeed, Lawrence perhaps used his plays as a chance to work out some of the issues and characters with which he was struggling simultaneously in his fiction. The most obvious example of this is *Touch and Go*, a play about the relationship between workers and managers that he created while writing *Women in Love*. Though the social debate in this play forms its core, the Lawrentian desire to see "a new freedom, a new life" enshrined in each individual gives it a metaphysical element too. The main male character in *Touch and Go*, Gerald Barlow, sympathetically extends our understanding of men like Gerald Crich.

Lawrence's lasting reputation as a dramatist will probably rest on the first three plays he wrote, for in these he captures the spirit of industrialized livelihood without resorting to sentimentality. In *The Daughter-in-Law* especially, the clash between two generations of women for the possession of Luther Gascoigne is realized through a vigorous use of dialect. The themes of this play, *A Collier's Friday Night*, and *The Widowing of Mrs. Holroyd* echo elements in *Sons and Lovers*, but the dramatic presentation has a muscularity of its own, for in each case Lawrence eschews the poeticizing language and semimystic elaborations that suit passages in his fiction but that would seem theatrically stilted. Indeed, *The Fight for Barbara* and *The Married Man* are unlikely to gain the same kind of place in the theater because they are more artificial and theoretical. *David*, being the story of David, Saul, and Jonathan, makes no attempt at naturalism and might have a hieratic credibility if given a careful production. More probably, though, it will remain principally known on the page, an adjunct to the leadership novels. It is another study in male friendship and the possibilities of autocracy.

If one has a preconception that novelists and poets stray into drama only to the embarrassment of their reputations, then Lawrence proves one wrong. He will almost certainly not now be neglected on the stage as he was for forty years. The case for his drama must not be overstated, however. He always wrote lively, argumentative dialogue in his fiction and he gave careful consideration to the structure of each plot he devised, but though these are dramatic strengths they do not by themselves make for a great playwright. Lawrence's plays lack the tight unfolding of the best naturalistic drama. They flare into life with marvelous intensity on some occasions—the opening section of Act III of *The Daughter-in-Law*, for example, where Minnie and Mrs. Gascoigne talk about their menfolk, or scene 11 of *David*, where Samuel prays for Saul—but the effects are intermittent. "The actual technique of the stage is foreign to me," Lawrence said in 1927, when writing to a possible producer of *David*.

He was partly right, but we ought to remember that the two kinds of plays he handled best, working-class naturalism and stylized religious pastiche, have never been greatly popular in the theater. Though the former has been in vogue for some years now, it may be that Lawrence's regionalism will vitiate his impact, for the Nottinghamshire dialect of the early plays is difficult to reproduce credibly. As for *David*, it requires an epic form of presentation that will always mean it is rarely performed even in the unlikely event of a return to favor of biblical drama. *David* is Lawrence's most ambitious play and in some ways the one he cared about most—he even wrote the music for its original production. His durability in the theater will center, however, on *The Daughter-in-Law* and perhaps on *The Widowing of Mrs. Holroyd*. They will be performed partly out of curiosity value, as minor works of a great novelist, but in their own right they would eventually have achieved some kind of status, even if their author had written nothing else.

### LAWRENCE'S ESSAYS AND CORRESPONDENCE

"Essays" is a poor word for these brilliantly varied writings, since "an essay" unhappily implies something formal and academic and highbrow, whereas Lawrence was always intensely personal and spontaneous, with such a horror of pedantry and the university manner that he vastly preferred to be slangy and jaunty. "Non-fictional prose" is worse than "essay," so until somebody coins a better word we must stick to essays, though in Lawrence's case the word is more like a reference number than a description of literary form.

So writes Richard Aldington in his introduction to the 1950 Penguin edition of Lawrence's *Selected Essays*. But the word "essay" derives from the French *essayer*, to try, and in this sense completely justifies its use for Lawrence. His essays are attempts at definition, struggles to articulate complex attitudes to society, literature, sex, religion, education, and philosophy. In almost every one the academic pen can cross out paragraphs as redundant because the point has already been adequately made, but to do this is to bring ruination to a style that relies on underlining and insistence. Against the charge that he is dogmatic, preachy, or rhetorical Lawrence could validly reply, "Who listens to me?" He forces home his points for fear of being ignored. He is ignored less because of the manner in which he speaks —though few of his champions would want to maintain that his essays demonstrate his best prose—than because what he has to say so often seems unpalatable.

Many of Lawrence's essays disappeared from sight during his own lifetime, buried in obscure journals or remaining unpublished. Now, however, virtually everything is in print. Not all of it requires apology or explanation. Essays like "Nottingham and the Mining Country" and "Dull London," to which I have referred in accounts of his imaginative work, are hardly likely to evoke controversy; even though the point of view is distinctively Lawrentian, essays of this kind obviously record a personal response to remembered experience, and it would be as inappropriate to challenge them as to say that Andrew Marvell had no right to speak thus to his coy mistress or that John Keats was wrong to insist that a thing of beauty is a joy forever.

Two of Lawrence's longer treatises, *Pyschoanalysis and the Unconscious* (1921) and its continuation, *Fantasia of the Unconscious* (1922), argue the case for harmony between man and his environment. In them he denounces "the mechanical principle" that he saw prevailing in modern society and that he felt vitiated many of the procedures of Freudian psychoanalysis. These works are best read now as illuminating adjuncts to his novels, particularly to *The Rainbow* and *Women in Love*.

Lawrence is on more vulnerable ground with his literary criticism. His "Study of Thomas Hardy" (1914), for example, contains a number of factual inaccuracies about Hardy's work as well as some silly dismissive statements. On form, however, Lawrence can be crisply perceptive, as he is when pointing out Hardy's main greatness:

> His feeling, his instinct, his sensuous understanding is, however, apart from his metaphysic, very great and deep, deeper than that perhaps of any other English novelist. Putting aside his metaphysic, which must always obtrude when he thinks of people, and turning to the earth, to landscape, then he is true to himself.
>
> (*Phoenix: The Posthumous Papers*, ch. 9)

Lawrence felt impassioned about literature, particularly about the novel. He did not care if a writer lacked the limited particularity of an Arnold Bennett providing he was "man alive," that is, fully responsive to the currents that provide life to the body and significance to the universe. When he insists on "blood consciousness" in so many of his works he is basically seeking a metaphor to express this sense of currency, or flow, within living things. "Let us learn from the novel," he says in "Why the Novel Matters"—the same essay in which he talks of "man alive." "In the novel, the characters can do nothing but *live*. If they keep on being good, according to pattern, or bad, according to pattern, or even volatile, according to pattern, they cease to live, and the novel falls dead." This is his charge against Galsworthy, Bennett, even, obscurely, against Dostoyevsky. "A character in a novel has got to live, or it is nothing." Hence Lawrence's verdict on Joseph Conrad ("I can't forgive Conrad . . . for giving in"), on E. M. Forster ("Life is more interesting in its undercurrents than in its obvious; and E. M. does see people, people and nothing but people: *ad nauseam*"), on James Joyce ("utterly without spontaneity or real life"). I glean these last remarks from letters he wrote, for it is often in his correspondence that a chance observation crystallizes something that pages of overstatement in the essays have blurred.

Lawrence wrote several letters a day almost all his life. As the majority of these went to fellow writers, or to publishers, or to editors, they obviously document a living dialogue between him and the literati of his day. He was personally friendly with Aldous Huxley, H. G. Wells, Compton Mackenzie, and Katherine Mansfield, and even when strains came into the relationships he would write an honest view of their work.

Some of Lawrence's literary subjects deviate wildly from the topic apparently planned. His essay on "Pornography and Obscenity," for example, lampoons *Jane Eyre* as "much nearer to pornography than is Boccaccio" only a couple of pages before it goes on excessively about masturbation as "certainly the most dangerous sexual vice that a society can be afflicted with." Juxtaposition of ideas in this way can work only if there is a tight controlling argument, but Lawrence is thinking with his heart, battering us with unsubstantiated generalizations. Within the framework of a novel, even one as extravagantly ritualized as *The Plumed Serpent*, such a technique may carry weight. It fails to do so in many of the essays. It fails partly because Lawrence forgets at these times his central belief that nothing in life should be stationary or fixed, that the flow must always proceed, nothing be totally defined because even the word, liberator of expression though it is, can also be a jailer. As he says of reading books, "once it is *known,* and its meaning is fixed or established, it is dead."

This last statement comes from *Apocalypse.* This was Lawrence's final major work, completed a few weeks before he died. Beginning as an introduction to a book by Frederick Carter, it developed into a free-flowing commentary on the Book of Revelation, imagery from which he had used in *The Rainbow* and to which he now returned in the passionate conviction that beneath what he understood to be a mainly allegorical structure the last book of the Bible held part of the key to an interpretation of life. Some of *Apocalypse* is almost incoherent, some of it pretentiously numerological, but the kernel carries on from where *The Plumed Serpent* drifted unconvincingly to a close. "All religion, instead of being religion of *life,* here and now, became religion of postponed destiny," he writes. In his last and longest essay he once again appeals for a regenerated religion that will inform the life at hand and not the possibly mythical life to come.

Many of Lawrence's essays will strike the reader as idiosyncratic; some of his prolific correspondence is quirky or ill-tempered. Surely, however, we are fortunate to have this extra body of material to throw sudden illumination on the major texts, or simply to enlarge our knowledge of Lawrence's place in the contemporary literary world. A work of art is entire in its own right, and I am not suggesting that *Sons and Lovers* cannot be read independently of "Nottingham and the Mining Country," or that *The Plumed Serpent* will be any the less obscure because one has encountered *Apocalypse.* Even *Lady Chatterley's Lover* does not need the essay "A Propos of *Lady Chatterley's Lover*" that Lawrence wrote as an explanation of the novel's "phallic reality." He meant these essays to be read, however, by anyone who wanted to follow his chain of thought. Sometimes they are too strident to be helpful, but on balance they clarify far more than they cloud. As for his letters, we find in them a record of a major novelist reacting to the world as he experienced it day by day. Often they have a beauty of language as controlled as famous passages in the novels, but these come to us as sudden moments of wonder. Almost alone among his writings Lawrence wrote letters without ever intending to revise them. Here, very often, we detect the immediate Lawrence, the man of spontaneous feeling who has not fretted for the right phrase or channeled the observation into a distorting theoretical mold. In his letters we can approach the real man, and in the essays we often find the artist with his defenses down. Both are indispensable.

### CRITICS ON LAWRENCE: A NOTE

LAWRENCE wrote so trenchantly about other writers and about the art of fiction that it can only be with the greatest trepidation that anyone writes about his work. After his death a number of generally critical reminiscences about him were published by people he liked to consider his friends. The fairest and most pertinent of these is *The Savage Pilgrimage* (1932) by Catherine Carswell. F. R. Leavis pioneered the academic study of Lawrence's work, eventually placing him in a line of great novelists descending from Austen. Leavis' interest in Lawrence was primarily moral. For all its convoluted prose and occasionally weird judgments Leavis' *D. H. Lawrence: Novelist* (1955) remains essential reading. *Thoughts, Words and Creativity* (1976) elaborates upon, but does not greatly add to, the emphases of the earlier book, but it shows how even in old age Leavis regarded Lawrence as the consummate twentieth-century English writer. In recent years there have been many accounts of Lawrence's writing, including "casebook" studies of individual texts. Among the best of the general studies are Keith Sagar's *The Art of D. H. Lawrence* (1966), Frank Kermode's *Lawrence* (1973), an intelligently provocative Freudian critique, and F. B. Pinion's *A D. H. Lawrence Companion* (1978). Émile Delavenay's *D. H. Lawrence: The Man and His Work* (revised 1972) and Harry T. Moore's *The Priest of Love* (1974; revised edition of *The Intelligent Heart: The Story of D. H. Lawrence,* 1955) are the best biographies, with Martin Green's *The Von Richthofen Sisters* (1974) a useful adjunct. I have personally found Sagar's *D. H. Lawrence: A Calendar of His Works* (1979) as invaluable a contribution to the study of a great writer as any produced in recent years. It documents on a day-to-day basis the course of Lawrence's writing, publication schedules, and travels, authenticating evidence that was previously only supposition and discrediting some long-established falsehoods.

# D. H. LAWRENCE

SELECTED BIBLIOGRAPHY

I. BIBLIOGRAPHY. E. D. McDonald, *A Bibliography of the Writings of D. H. Lawrence* (Philadelphia, 1925); E. D. McDonald, *A Bibliographical Supplement* (Philadelphia, 1931); L. C. Powell, *The Manuscripts of D. H. Lawrence* (Los Angeles, 1937); E. W. Tedlock, *The Frieda Lawrence Collection of D. H. Lawrence Manuscripts* (Albuquerque, 1948); W. Whyte, *D. H. Lawrence: A Checklist* (Detroit, 1950); M. Beebe and A. Tommasi, "Criticism of D. H. Lawrence: A Selected Checklist with an Index to Studies of Separate Works," in *Modern Fiction Studies*, V, 1 (Spring 1959), 83–98; W. Roberts, *A Bibliography of D. H. Lawrence* (London, 1963), the standard bibliography, includes details of periodical publications; K. Sagar, *The Art of D. H. Lawrence* (Cambridge, 1966), includes a useful chronology at the head of each ch. and information on periodical publications.

II. COLLECTED WORKS. *The Collected Poems of D. H. Lawrence* (London, 1928), vol. I: "Rhyming Poems," vol. II: "Unrhyming Poems"; *The Phoenix Edition of D. H. Lawrence*, 20 vols. (London, 1954–1964); E. D. McDonald, ed., *Phoenix: The Posthumous Papers* (London, 1936), with intro., contains "Study of Thomas Hardy," "The Reality of Peace," "Introduction to These Paintings," "Democracy," "Education of the People," "John Galsworthy," and many essays, reviews, and intros; Penguin ed. (New York–London, 1978), more reliable ed.; *Complete Poems*, 2 vols. (London, 1964); *Complete Plays* (London, 1965); W. Roberts and H. T. Moore, eds., *Phoenix II: Uncollected, Unpublished and Other Prose Works by D. H. Lawrence* (London, 1968, with intro. and notes, includes "The Crown."

A complete edition of Lawrence's works (see LETTERS below) is in progress at Cambridge University Press.

III. SEPARATE WORKS. *The White Peacock* (London, 1911), novel; *The Trespasser* (London, 1912), novel; *Love Poems and Others* (London, 1913); *Sons and Lovers* (London, 1913), novel; *The Widowing of Mrs. Holroyd: A Drama in Three Acts* (New York, 1914); *The Prussian Officer, and Other Stories* (London, 1914), contains "The Prussian Officer," "The Thorn in the Flesh," "Daughters of the Vicar," "A Fragment of Stained Glass," "The Shades of Spring," "The Soiled Rose," "Second Best," "The Shadow in the Rose Garden," "Goose Fair," "The White Stocking," "A Sick Collier," "The Christening," "Odour of Chrysanthemums"; *The Rainbow* (London, 1915), novel; *Twilight in Italy* (London, 1916), travel sketches; *Amores: Poems* (London, 1916); *Look! We Have Come Through!* (London, 1917), verse; *New Poems* (London, 1918); *Bay: A Book of Poems* (London, 1919).

*Touch and Go: A Play in Three Acts* (London, 1920); *Women in Love* (New York, 1920), novel; *The Lost Girl* (London, 1920), novel; *Movements in European History* (London, 1921), essays written under pseud. Lawrence H. Davison; *Psychoanalysis and the Unconscious* (New York, 1921), essay; *Tortoises* (New York, 1921), verse; *Sea and Sardinia* (New York, 1921), travel; *Aaron's Rod* (New York, 1922), novel; *Fantasia of the Unconscious* (New York, 1922), essay; *England, My England, and Other Stories* (New York, 1922), contains "England, My England," "Tickets, Please," "The Blind Man," "Monkey Nuts," "Wintry Peacock," "You Touched Me," "Samson and Delilah," "The Primrose Path," "The Horse Dealer's Daughter," "Fanny and Annie"; *The Ladybird* (London, 1923), stories, contains "The Ladybird," "The Fox," "The Captain's Doll"; *Studies in Classic American Literature* (New York, 1923), criticism; *Kangaroo* (London, 1923), novel; *Birds, Beasts and Flowers: Poems* (London, 1923); *The Boy in the Bush* (London, 1924), novel written with M. L. Skinner; *St. Mawr: Together with "The Princess"* (London, 1925), stories; *Reflections on the Death of a Porcupine, and Other Essays* (Philadelphia, 1925); *The Plumed Serpent: Quetzalcoatl* (London, 1926), novel; *David: A Play* (London, 1926); *Sun* (London, 1926), story; *Glad Ghosts* (London, 1926), story; *Mornings in Mexico* (London, 1927), travel sketches; *Rawdon's Roof: A Story* (London, 1928); *The Woman Who Rode Away, and Other Stories* (London, 1928), contains "Two Blue Birds," "Sun," "The Woman Who Rode Away," "Smile," "The Border Line," "Jimmy and the Desperate Woman," "The Last Laugh," "In Love," "Glad Ghosts," "None of That"; *Lady Chatterley's Lover* (Florence, 1928), novel; *Sex Locked Out* (London, 1929), essay; *The Paintings of D. H. Lawrence* (London, 1929); *Pansies: Poems* (London, 1929); *My Skirmish with Jolly Roger* (New York, 1929), essay; *Pornography and Obscenity* (London, 1929), essay; *The Escaped Cock* (Paris, 1929), story.

*A Propos of "Lady Chatterley's Lover": Being an Essay Extended From "My Skirmish with Jolly Roger"* (London, 1930); *Nettles* (London, 1930), verse; *Assorted Articles* (London, 1930); *The Virgin and the Gipsy* (Florence, 1930), story; *Love Among the Haystacks, and Other Pieces* (London, 1930), stories and sketches, contains "Love Among the Haystacks," "A Chapel Among the Mountains," "A Hay Hut Among the Mountains," "Once"; *Triumph of the Machine* (London, 1931), verse; *The Man Who Died* (London, 1931), extended version of *The Escaped Cock*; *Apocalypse* (Florence, 1931), essay; *A Letter from Cornwall* (London, 1931); *Etruscan Places* (London, 1932), sketches; *Last Poems* (Florence, 1932); *The Lovely Lady* (London, 1933), stories, contains "The Lovely Lady," "Rawdon's Roof," "The Rocking-Horse Winner," "Mother and Daughter," "The Blue Moccasins," "Things," "The Overtone," "The Man Who Loved Islands"; *We Need One Another* (New York, 1933), essays; *The Ship of Death, and Other Poems* (London, 1933); *A Collier's Friday Night* (London, 1934), play; *A Modern Lover* (London, 1934), stories, contains "A Modern Lover," "The Old Adam," "Her Turn," "Strike Pay," "The Witch à la Mode," "New Eve and Old Adam," "Mr Noon"; *Foreword to "Women in Love"* (San Francisco, 1936), not originally published with the novel, first included with Modern Library ed.

*Fire and Other Poems* (San Francisco, 1940); *The First Lady Chatterley* (New York, 1944; London, 1972), first version of *Lady Chatterley's Lover*, 1972 ed. includes intro. by F. Lawrence; A. Arnold, ed., *The Symbolic Meaning* (London, 1962), uncollected versions of *Studies in Classic American Literature*; *John Thomas and Lady Jane* (London, 1972), second version of *Lady Chatterley's Lover*.

IV. WORKS TRANSLATED BY D. H. LAWRENCE. L. Shestov, *All Things Are Possible* (London, 1920), trans. by S. S. Koteliansky, with collaboration of D. H. Lawrence; I. A. Bunin, *The Gentleman from San Francisco and Other Stories* (London, 1922), trans. by S. S. Koteliansky and L. Woolf, title story co-translated with D. H. Lawrence; G. Verga, *Mastro-Don Gesualdo* (New York, 1923), trans. by D. H. Lawrence; G. Verga, *Little Novels of Sicily* (New York, 1925), trans. by D. H. Lawrence; G. Verga, *Cavalleria Rusticana, and Other Stories* (London, 1928), trans. with intro. by D. H. Lawrence; A. F. Grazzinini, *The Story of Dr. Manente* (Florence, 1929), trans. with intro. by D. H. Lawrence.

V. LETTERS. A. Huxley, ed., *The Letters of D. H. Lawrence* (London, 1932); H. T. Moore, ed., *D. H. Lawrence's Letters to Bertrand Russell* (New York, 1948); H. T. Moore, *The Collected Letters of D. H. Lawrence*, 2 vols. (New York, 1962); J. T. Boulton, ed., *Lawrence in Love: Letters from D. H. L. to Louie Burrows* (Nottingham, 1968); M. Secker, ed., *Letters from D. H. Lawrence to Martin Secker, 1911-1930* (London, 1970); G. J. Zytaruk, ed., *The Quest for Rananim: D. H. Lawrence's Letters to Koteliansky, 1914-1930* (Montreal, 1970); G. M. Lacey, ed., *D. H. Lawrence: Letters to Thomas and Adèle Seltzer* (Santa Barbara, 1976); *The Letters of D. H. Lawrence*, J. T. Boulton, ed., vol. I: *1901-1913* (Cambridge, 1979), G. J. Zytaruk and J. T. Boulton, eds., vol. II: *1913-1916* (1981); in progress are J. T. Boulton and A. Robertson, eds., vol. III: *1916-1921*; W. Roberts and E. Mansfield, vol. IV: *1921-1924*; D. Farmer, ed., vol. V: *1924-1927*; G. M. Lacy, ed., vol. VI: *1927-1928*; K. Sagar and J. T. Boulton, eds., vol. VII: *1928-1930*.

VI. BIOGRAPHICAL AND CRITICAL STUDIES. H. J. Seligmann, *D. H. Lawrence: An American Interpretation* (New York, 1924); F. R. Leavis, *D. H. Lawrence* (Cambridge, 1930); R. West, *D. H. Lawrence* (London, 1930); J. M. Murry: *D. H. Lawrence: Two Essays* (Cambridge, 1930); J. M. Murry, *Son of Woman: The Story of D. H. Lawrence* (London, 1931); A. Lawrence and G. S. Gelder, *Young Lorenzo: Early Life of D. H. Lawrence* (Florence, 1931); C. Carswell, *The Savage Pilgrimage: A Narrative of D. H. Lawrence* (London, 1932); A. Nin, *D. H. Lawrence: An Unprofessional Study* (Paris, 1933; reiss. London, 1961); D. Brett, *Lawrence and Brett: A Friendship* (London, 1933); H. Corke, *Lawrence and "Apocalypse"* (London, 1933); J. M. Murry, *Reminiscences of D. H. Lawrence* (London, 1933)); E. Brewster and A. Brewster, *D. H. Lawrence: Reminiscences and Correspondence* (London, 1934); H. Gregory, *Pilgrim of the Apocalypse: A Critical Study of D. H. Lawrence* (London, 1934); F. Lawrence, *Not I, But the Wind* (New York, 1934); E. T. [Jessie Chambers], *D. H. Lawrence: A Personal Record* (London, 1935); K. Merrild, *A Poet and Two Painters: A Memoir of D. H. Lawrence* (London, 1938).

R. Aldington, *Portrait of a Genius, But . . . : The Life of D. H. Lawrence, 1885-1930* (London, 1950); W. Tiverton, *D. H. Lawrence and Human Existence* (London, 1951); D. Kenmare, *Fire-Bird: A Study of D. H. Lawrence* (London, 1951); V. de S. Pinto, *D. H. Lawrence: Prophet of the Midlands* (Nottingham, 1951); W. Bynner, *Journey with Genius: Recollections and Reflections Concerning the D. H. Lawrences* (New York, 1953); M. Spilka, *The Love Ethic of D. H. Lawrence* (Bloomington, 1955); H. T. Moore, *The Intelligent Heart: The Story of D. H. Lawrence* (London, 1955), reissued with some additional material as *The Priest of Love* (London, 1974); M. Freeman, *D. H. Lawrence: A Basic Study of His Ideas* (Gainesville, 1955); F. R. Leavis, *D. H. Lawrence: Novelist* (London, 1955); G. Hough, *The Dark Sun: A Study of D. H. Lawrence* (London, 1956); E. Nehls, ed., *D. H. Lawrence: A Composite Biography* (Madison, Wis., 1957-1959), vol. I: *1885-1919*, vol. II: *1919-1925*, vol. III: *1925-1930*.

R. L. Drain, *Tradition and D. H. Lawrence* (Groningen, 1960); F. Lawrence, *The Memoirs and Correspondence* (London, 1961), ed. by E. W. Tedlock; A. Beal, *D. H. Lawrence* (Edinburgh, 1961); L. D. Clarke, *Dark Night of the Body: A Study of "The Plumed Serpent"* (Austin, Tex., 1964); G. H. Ford, *Double Measure: A Study of the Novels and Stories of D. H. Lawrence* (New York, 1965); H. M. Daleski, *The Forked Flame: A Study of D. H. Lawrence* (London, 1965); K. Sagar, *The Art of D. H. Lawrence* (Cambridge, 1966); B. Russell, *Autobiography*, vol. II: *1914-1944* (London, 1968); C. Clarke, *River of Dissolution: D. H. Lawrence and English Romanticism* (London, 1969).

R. P. Draper, ed., *D. H. Lawrence: The Critical Heritage* (London, 1970); K. Alldritt, *The Visual Imagination of D. H. Lawrence* (London, 1971); E. Delavenay, *D. H. Lawrence: The Man and His Work—The Formative Years, 1885-1919* (London, 1972), trans., rev., and abridged from the French by K. M. Delavenay (1969), a work of massive research, but not always reliable in its comprehension of Lawrence's language; S. J. Miko, *Toward "Women in Love": The Emergence of Lawrentian Aesthetic* (New Haven, Conn.-London, 1972); H. Coombes, ed., *D. H. Lawrence: A Critical Anthology* (Harmondsworth, 1973); F. Kermode, *Lawrence* (London, 1973); M. Green, *The Von Richthofen Sisters* (London, 1974); S. Sklar, *The Plays of D. H. Lawrence* (London, 1975); M. Black, *The Literature of Fidelity* (London, 1975); F. R. Leavis, *Thought, Words and Creativity: Art and Thought in Lawrence* (London, 1976); F. B. Pinion, *A D. H. Lawrence Companion* (London, 1978); K. Cushman, *D. H. Lawrence at Work: The Emergence of the "Prussian Officer" Stories* (Hassocks, 1978); A. Niven, *D. H. Lawrence: The Novels* (Cambridge, 1978); P. Delany, *D. H. Lawrence's Nightmare: The Writer and His Circle in the Years of the Great War* (New York, 1978); A. Smith, ed., *Lawrence and Women* (London, 1978); A. H. Gomme, ed., *D. H. Law-*

rence (Hassocks–New York, 1978); K. Sagar, *D. H. Lawrence: A Calendar of His Works* (Manchester, 1979); J. Worthen, *D. H. Lawrence and the Idea of the Novel* (New York–London, 1979); C. L. Ross, *The Composition of "The Rainbow" and "Women in Love": A History* (Charlottesville, Va., 1979); G. H. Neville, *A Memoir of D. H. Lawrence: The Betrayal*, C. Baron, ed. (Cambridge, 1981); H. Simpson, *D. H. Lawrence and Feminism* (Croom Helm, 1982).

*Note:* Further information about Lawrentian criticism is available in K. Sagar, *The Art of D. H. Lawrence*, and from the checklist compiled by M. Beebe and A. Tommasi in *Modern Fiction Studies*, V, 1 (Spring 1959). For an account of the nature and chronology of Lawrence's literary development in the years 1913–1915 that differs in important ways from that put forward in the present essay, the reader is referred to M. Kinkead-Weekes, "The Marble and the Statue: The Exploratory Imagination of D. H. Lawrence," in M. Mack and I. Gregor, eds., *Imagined Worlds* (London, 1968).

# JOHN LE CARRÉ
(1931–        )

## *George J. Leonard*

SINCE SMILEY AND the other spies in his novels use so many cover names, somehow it is satisfying to learn that "John le Carré" is itself only a cover name, adopted by the author, one reads, because people working in the Foreign Office were not allowed to publish under their real names. Another sound reason for the pseudonym would be le Carré's disinclination to have his bosses read, in *Call for the Dead* (1961), his first book, descriptions of themselves like these: "the professional civil servant from an orthodox department . . . , a man who could reduce any colour to grey . . . , the Head Eunuch" (ch. 1); and "a barmaid's dream of a real gentleman" (ch. 2). When *The Spy Who Came In from the Cold* (1963) was a hit, le Carré instructed his banker to notify him when his account reached a certain sum; when the call came, he gleefully resigned.

"There are few people more dishonest," le Carré has warned us, "than writers professing to recall how they came to do things." His pen name, he said, "came from nowhere that I can really remember," but he finally began telling "persistent" interviewers that he stole it from a shoe shop he used to pass en route to work. The shoe shop has never been located. He has stopped telling the story. Much of the information about him is of that quality, even when it comes directly from him.

So that is not his name. Later one discovers he never even worked "in the Foreign Office." Britian does not officially admit to having an FBI and a CIA for, respectively, domestic and international espionage—though everyone knows that such agencies exist. When a person is a domestic spy the British press writes, by long-standing gentlemanly agreement, that "he works in the Home Office"; if he spies on other nations, they write, "he works in the Foreign Office." (Everyone understands, just as they understand that "his constant companion" means "his mistress.")

We start then, fittingly, by removing his cover name and his cover job. We still have a long way to go. Like Peer Gynt peeling the onion to find its center, when we try to learn about le Carré we continually find cover stories within cover stories.

The cover name, in French, means "John the Square" and though the critics who long pondered it—John the Stolid? John the Straight Dealer?—have finally dismissed it as unsymbolic, it is not insignificant. He once remarked he wanted an upper-class-sounding name: that desire for upper-class status has been an obsession of his characters. He is also, almost in spite of his friendliest critics, exceptionally self-conscious of himself as the heir of the great spy novelists and loves to make filial allusions to them. One of the first stars of the genre was William LeQueux, whose *The Great War in England in 1897* appeared in 1894. John Buchan's famous *The Thirty-Nine Steps,* a pioneering 1913 spy novel, was first published under the pseudonym "H. de V." Too remote to have interested him? Le Carré has a scholar's love of allusion. One of Smiley's cover names, "Mr. Standfast," is the title of a 1919 Buchan novel.

The real-life David John Moore Cornwell was born on 19 October 1931. Before the stories about his father began to surface, Americans frequently assumed that Cornwell, an Oxford graduate and former Eton don, was a pillar of the Establishment, and they projected those politics onto his novels and his hero Smiley. Nothing could be further from the truth. He registers Labour party. Le Carré, although he has the old-boy manners and credentials, lived in that world, he has told us, virtually as a "spy." When he was three his mother left his father, Ronald Cornwell, a high-living professional swindler who, despite a prison sentence during David's youth, managed to accumulate two more wives and defraud enough people to achieve a spectacular bankruptcy, in debt about thirty million contemporary dollars. All the while David was in the exclusive Sherborne School he knew that "there was absolutely no money," and that "there was a lot to hide: women, the past, the present." His father sent him to school not to educate him but to turn him into "fake gentry," to plant him in the Establishment like a Russian "mole" in the secret services, to become useful later. To make a "gentleman" out of David, "my father always said he was prepared to steal; and I'm afraid he did."

It sounds like a novel and it eventually provided material for one: *A Perfect Spy* (1986). (In colloquial American English, the title means "a born spy" or "a natural spy.") If we were studying Dickens, it would make sense, at this point, to let the similarly autobiographical *David Copperfield* (1852) flesh out the sketchy notes on his childhood Dickens left his biographer, Forster. In le Carré's case, we have no less than four novels I consider autobiographical—indeed, nearly confessional, sometimes obsessive. The plots of *A Perfect Spy*, *A Murder of Quality* (1962), *A Small Town in Germany* (1968), and *The Naive and Sentimental Lover* (1971) are perfunctory. The writer seems intent on reliving an experience, understanding it, and exorcising it. "Factual" biographical data is, he himself warns us, hard to come by. For years his life involved matters still covered by Britain's Official Secrets Act. One thinks of the narrator/lawyer of *The Russia House* (1989), who carries the Act around, forcing people to sign. There are family considerations: he has been able to speak about his father only since Ronnie Cornwell died, and even so it caused strain in the family. Also, le Carré scholarship is in a primitive state: no autobiography, no standard biography, no collected letters or even collected essays, no bestselling exposé by an ex-wife. But we are not at a loss for evidence. What does a born spy, a habitually self-disguising person do when he has a need to "exorcise" experiences? This one writes novels.

Enough is now known about our man to help us glean from the novels what we need—not names and dates, but something we want even more and which novels supply even better than a witness could: what certain events meant to the young David Cornwell *emotionally;* how they colored his novels; and how they probably led him to his most famous creation, George Smiley. When we see le Carré, at thirty, sit down to create Smiley, we will know who he is. I will hold discussion of *The Naive and Sentimental Lover,* his novel of mid-life crisis, till its appropriate place in the middle of the story.

A PERFECT SPY

A PERFECT SPY is only superficially the story of Magnus Pym/Titch/Sir Magnus/Canterbury. (Le Carré's critics usually cope with his characters' many names by resorting to slashes.) Clearly, the author's purpose in writing the book was to depict his father, Ronnie (revealed in the book in the character of Rickie), and whenever this character is offstage the tension drops.

*A Perfect Spy* is an endless novel written in le Carré's lamented late lax style; its main interest is autobiographical. At the book's start Magnus has holed up in a room he keeps in Devon and is beginning a long memoir addressed to his son Tom. Meanwhile his wife, Mary, and his father-figure boss, Jack Brotherhood, ransack his home, because the CIA is claiming "the Firm" has been infiltrated by a Czech double agent, and Magnus has promptly disappeared. Inside Magnus' chimney they find a "small, clever-looking" Czech camera used for photographing documents (ch. 3). With this discovery all suspense ends, although the book will not for another four-hundred-odd pages. Unfortunately Jack and Mary, both in love with Magnus, need hundreds of pages to arrive at the same conclusion the reader has, and sitting with them while they come to their senses takes patience.

Crosscuts to Magnus' letter to Tom slowly reveal that Jack Brotherhood, when he recruited Magnus to the Firm in Berne, after the war, persuaded him to finger his best friend, the charismatic, war-wounded Axel, as a possible Russian agent. Magnus heard Axel taken away in the night. When he joyfully found Axel/Sgt. Pavel later in Austria, both of them were minor Army intelligence agents, but on opposite sides. They started trading secrets, advancing each other's careers. Some years later, a full-fledged agent, Magnus was arrested in Czechoslovakia and saved by Axel, who claimed him as a double agent, and since then he has been one, partly to take revenge on Jack Brotherhood—mostly, however, to sweep away, as Axel says, "the churches, the schools . . . , the class systems" and all the corrupt institutions and people who have produced "such sad little fellows as Sir Magnus" (ch. 15). Particularly people like Magnus' father, Rickie.

After his parents' separation, le Carré stayed with his father, whom he describes as a "colorful and curious personality" and, more significantly, as "a Micawber character." But Micawber was lovable. Ronald Cornwell, by contrast, was (his son has said) "perhaps a schizophrenic." Like Rickie in *A Perfect Spy*, Ronald was "the only son of religious lower-middle-class parents." And Ronald was "tremendously ambitious to get out, by any means."

Rickie gets out by knocking up the mousy daughter of Sir Makepeace Watermaster, pottery factory owner and chief minister in his workers' Tabernacle, a "dissenting" fundamentalist Protestant church. (The English Establishment belongs to the Church of England, headed by the monarch. The lower-middle and working classes belong to many small sects, often called simply "chapel.") Rickie had embezzled all the Tabernacle's funds and Magnus, it seems, is conceived as insurance because Rickie guesses—correctly—that Sir Makepeace will discover the theft. Magnus, like le Carré, grows up a "millionaire pauper," living in a succession of unpaid-for fine houses and hotels, his father surrounded by courtiers and "lovelies." For his mother, Dorothy (Dot), Magnus (Titch) has only pity, not love. All seven-year-old Magnus' love, even sexual interest, is wrapped up in the magical Annie Lippschitz called "Lippsie." "Life began with Lippsie, Tom," he writes to his son in chapter 4. Lippsie, a "German Four-by-Two . . . cockney rhyming slang for Jew," is a refugee Rickie acquires to be a maid of all work. A beauty, she eventually becomes the "trois" in a ménage à trois with Rickie and Dot. Rickie's man, Syd Lemon, says, "She was lonely, Titch. Adored the kids. Adored you." Magnus recalls this time as "Paradise" (ch. 4).

In jail and out, in trouble and out, Rickie bilks widows and old people of great sums of insurance and investment money. Le Carré has not sentimentalized his father here. Magnus prays Rickie will marry Lippsie. But Lippsie's "deepening melancholy" disturbs him. Her family is dead, she is sure—"Old Lippsie's on about her Jews," Syd Lemon says, "another lot's been done" (ch. 4).

At this time "Rick formed the determination to turn Pym into a gentleman" (ch. 4) and sends him to Grimble's school (based on St. Andrew's in Pangbourne). "And so we arrived," le Carré said later, "in educated, middle-class society feeling almost like spies," knowing there was "a great deal to conceal. . . . We learned to dissemble and be very watchful." The born spy. As a result, although institutions fascinate him, le Carré has "never felt at home in any social structure really." All through his novels le Carré does not conceal his hatred for the smugness of the Establishment, represented in *A Perfect Spy* by insufferable little Sefton Boyd and his gang. He will always identify with Jews or anyone else who, like himself, does not fit in.

Rickie sends Lippsie with Titch to school, to labor as a kind of payment. He knows too that Lippsie is only "held to the world" through Titch. Lippsie teaches him his first German lessons, a language he loves throughout his life. But she tells Rickie "you made me to be a *teef*" (ch. 4)—a thief—and not long after, leaps from a school tower to her death. Syd leads us to think it is a case of survivor guilt: she has "the guilts she isn't dead" like her family (ch. 4). Sefton Boyd claims to have seen her vagina as she lay dead. Titch carves Boyd's initials in the beautiful wooden walls of the master's lavatory and Boyd is flogged. It is Pym's first important act of deceitful rebellion; later he betrays his father, and finally he betrays hated Establishment England. At the novel's end, he commits suicide.

Since Rickie is based on le Carré's real father—what of Lippsie? Could le Carré actually have had, in his youth, a Jewish surrogate mother who committed suicide because of his father? Amazingly, no one has ever asked him. Yet imagine the effect on his fiction. We have been searching through le Carré's books in emulation of his hero, Smiley, and here Smiley would pause, and mumble, "A Jewish heroine named Lippsie. . . ." He would think of *The Spy Who Came In from the Cold* and say, "Jewish heroine named Liz." Lippsie and Liz resemble each other physically; both die tragic deaths as a result of their Jewishness. He would reach for *The Honourable Schoolboy* whose heroine, Lizzie, is sometimes called Liza Worth (Liz Gold = Liza Worth?) and sometimes, most oddly, Liese, pronounced "Leesa" although it is a German name and she is not German. The wealthy man who keeps her, Drake Ko, makes her call herself that. Connie Sachs, with her "frightening" sixth sense, uncovers that Ko, orphaned young, was taken in by a German woman named Liese.

Lippsie, Liz, Lizzie, Liese—there is too much of this for it all to be coincidence. In a letter written 20 August 1990, le Carré confirms that there was a real-life original. After his mother left, he was for a while "entrusted" to a German Jewish girl named Annaliese. She was, he later decided, one of his father's conquests. Lippsie commits suicide. Annaliese, "most likely . . . as the consequence of a love affair" with his father, returned home to Germany just before the war—in retrospect, a kind of suicide, and his father's fault. Le Carré writes,

> I was still in school in 1945, when the scale of the Holocaust became known. British newsreels at the cinema, and the British tabloid press, carried an almost unbearable diet of pictures of the atrocities, and they made an impact on all of us. I cannot tell you how much I was aware of the Holocaust before that, but I do remember that my fears for Annaliese grew as the war continued and the fate of the Jews in Central Europe became clearer.

Le Carré hunted for Annaliese after the war, when he was doing his national service as a lieutenant in the Intelligence Corps. "I spent most of my time interrogating and classifying refugees from all corners of Central and Eastern Europe. Some of these were survivors from the Holocaust, others claimed to be. All of them had tragic tales to tell." He visited the Dachau concentration camp, and Bergen Belsen, and "many" camps for refugees. Le Carré reports that he "used the military network in Austria and Germany to try to trace her, but I was unsuccessful."

Annaliese became Annie Lippshitz, "Lippsie." This is a figure of whom the novelist has written, "Life began with Lippsie...." Knowing that the novelist, abandoned by his natural mother, acquired a beloved Jewish surrogate mother whom he believed died at the hands of the Nazis, a mother-figure he searched for among the concentration camp survivors, throws a whole new light on his novels. He has named three heroines after her, but that is almost superficial compared to the deep effects on his work. Finally we understand how le Carré, though not born Jewish, has written more about Jews than most Jewish novelists. He was a pioneer in what is now called Holocaust Studies. A large part of his work has been the empathetic study of what it means to be Jewish in the modern world.

His works contain, in particular, portraits of Jewish women strikingly at odds with current stereotypes. Lippsie and Liz Gold are almost supernaturally gentle, and nurturing, fantasy Jewish mothers. They are the most reverent portraits of Jewish women in contemporary literature and they stand shockingly alone. Le Carré writes counter to such tradition as exists—particularly within the Jewish community—a perplexing, scandalous situation. Woody Allen, Philip Roth, and Bruce Jay Friedman have popularized an image of the Jewish woman as "yenta" (nag or harridan) or "kvetch" (complainer).

Le Carré's beautiful portraits stand in lonely contrast. Though he never stereotypes, he is intensely conscious of both women as Jewish, and their Jewishness is central to their goodness, to the attractive parts of their personality. In *A Murder of Quality* one reads of masters telling British schoolboys that to show emotion is lowerclass. Le Carré's Jewish women are oases in an emotional desert: loving, emotionally expressive, volatile, nurturing, caring. In *A Perfect Spy*, Lippsie is warmer, more giving to a little English child starving for maternal love, than his own poor mother knows how to be. When he joins her in a bath, a beloved memory, it is more than a rebaptism, it is a rebirth.

## A MURDER OF QUALITY

In *A Perfect Spy*, Magnus, at seventeen, like le Carré runs away from the Establishment idiocies of an English school to Bern, Switzerland, where he holds odd jobs and perfects his German at the university. Following military service (1950–1952) le Carré took a degree at Lincoln College, Oxford, studying German and French, graduating with first-class honors. His father's bankruptcy made the newspapers in 1954. That year le Carré married Alison Ann Veronica Sharp; together, they had three sons.

From 1956 to 1958 he taught German at Eton, most famous of the exclusive British private schools (called "public" schools). Eton is the heart of the Establishment, the old-boy network that has long run English life. "Let anyone who derides the notion of the Establishment," le Carré has warned—in his introduction to *The Philby Conspiracy* (1968), by Bruce Page, David Leitch, and Phillip Knightley—consider how it covered for the spy Kim Philby. During the Suez crisis, le Carré recalls most of the cabinet ministers were old boys from Eton. David Cornwell, the secret outsider, the born spy, loathed the place. Le Carré has been frank about it, but the best way to know the surprising intensity of his hatred is to read *A Murder of Quality*, which is otherwise of little interest.

Just as le Carré used the secret services as a "microcosm of the British condition," as he wrote in his introduction to *The Philby Conspiracy*, he tries to use Eton—or rather, Carne—as a microcosm of the British Establishment, a way to plunge quickly to its heart. On the first page we learn that the famous school Carne was "founded by obscure monks, endowed by a sickly boy king, and dragged from oblivion by a Victorian bully." In chapter 1, two boys in uniform discuss Stanley Rode—"You can tell he's not a gentleman"—and Terence Fielding, a senior don about to retire—"My Pater says he's a queer." Perkins, Fielding's head boy, quotes Fielding: "Emotionalism is only for the lower classes." Giving you the feel of this atavistic, oppressive little world, and making sure you hate it, is the novel's true goal. The plot is more of a tour—a short tour that other books have done better. In the end it turns out Fielding killed Rode's wife, to stop her from blackmailing him about a wartime incident with a boy. To solve the crime, Smiley must decipher the Hardyesque ramblings of Mad Janie, who lives in an abandoned church. A bad book.

## A SMALL TOWN IN GERMANY

FAR more deserving of our attention is *A Small Town in Germany*. This book, published in 1968, is set about two years ahead in the future. It deals with the rise of a neo-Nazi movement, led by Dr. Klaus Karfeld, while Britain, anxious not to offend Germany during certain trade negotiations, looks the other way. Le Carré shows us a British Establishment amoral and spineless as ever, once again desperate for peace at any price. At one point Karfeld's "mindless" crowds, "mediocre, ponderous and terrifying," shuffle pointedly toward "Chamberlain's hill" (ch. 17). Neville Chamberlain, British prime minister in 1938, had sold Europe out to Hitler. Chamberlain's speeches are some of le Carré's strong early memories.

During this crisis Leo Harting, a low-level diplomat, a "temporary" employee of the British Embassy in Bonn (the "small town" of the title) has disappeared with forty sensitive files, including an ultrasensitive Green File. Le Carré has written that although he left Harting's religion "ambiguous," he "never doubted" Harting was Jewish (unpublished letter, 20 August 1990). Harting had been a prewar child refugee in England with a certain member of the German parliament later known to be a Communist. The Foreign Office assumes that another Communist mole has decamped and sends in a Security man to investigate.

Foreign Office investigator Alan Turner, though an Oxford man, is defiantly working-class, Northern, and venomously anti-Establishment. He flies in from London and interrogates the embassy staff. The novel, little more than the record of Turner's inquest, offers the reader primarily a gallery of grotesques. *A Small Town in Germany* is a comparatively straightforward warm-up for the brilliantly intricate mole hunting in *Tinker, Tailor, Soldier, Spy* (1974).

Since le Carré had been, like Harting, a "second secretary" in the Bonn embassy, the novel is of considerable biographical interest. All le Carré's novels rest on his claim that "the British secret services" are "microcosms of the British condition, of our social attitudes and vanities" (introduction to *The Philby Conspiracy*). Turner and his creator reveal their disgust for the doglike complicity of all classes that keeps the effete Establishment secure. Le Carré describes, with a hatred bordering on relish, the diplomatic wives who manage to enter the English Church on Sunday, following, "quite by accident, the order of succession which protocol, had they cared about such things, would exactly have demanded" (ch. 2).

These institutional workaday fools are no match for the genius of Leo Harting, who, like a German Ronnie Cornwell, detaches their secret files from them simply by drinking with the men, flirting and sleeping with the women, listening to everyone's pathetic confidences, and—a brilliant touch—giving everyone hair dryers, then an expensive vanity item. There is something so tawdry about bribing people with hair dryers. *A Small Town in Germany* could have been titled after the Mann novel le Carré alludes to, *Confessons of Felix Krull, Confidence Man* (1954). Not even *A Perfect Spy* gives us a better feel for Ronnie Cornwell. There is rare knowledge behind le Carré's tour-de-force portrait of Harting's chameleon turns into each target's fantasy friend: with old Gaunt, the guard, Harting is the democratic aristocrat happy to sit like a regular chap and drink some tea and chew the fat; with dowdy Jenny Pargiter, he is a continental lover, a man of burning glances and barely bridled romantic passions; to bourgeois Cork, he becomes a sad and comic sidekick, flatteringly envious of Cork's wife and kids; with Mickie Crabbe the boozer, he is a drinking buddy to go whoring with; for Hazel Bradfield, his boss's wife, Harting becomes Lady Chatterley's lover, more sensitive and genuine than anyone from her class; to Rawley Bradfield, he is a present to appease his discontented wife. When Turner at last uncovers Harting's private lair deep inside the embassy, only we, looking at his mundane props, his thermos, his foot warmer, his hair dryers, finally envision him, like Laurence Olivier backstage: oddly colorless and normal, a small hard-working man.

Turner discovers, at book's end, that Leo Harting, no Communist mole, stole the files that proved Karfeld took part in the Chemical Research murder of thirty-one "hybrid" (half-Jewish) slave laborers. When Turner realizes the British decided to keep Karfeld's secret so that they could blackmail him if he came to power, his disgust and ours is complete. Turner only sees Harting at the instant Harting is murdered, while trying, critics claim, to assassinate Karfeld at a Nazi rally.

Le Carré's account of Leo Harting's lonely passion shines a great light backward on an experience we know le Carré to have had. One of le Carré's persistent themes is the presence of unpunished Nazi war criminals in Germany and the continued danger of naziism. A second is the Holocaust and its aftermath, including the state of Israel and contemporary Jewish unease. Obviously the two themes connect. Knowing more of le Carré's biography will help us understand why they fascinate him.

Drafted in 1949, le Carré was sent to Austria, where his good German was put to use interrogating DPs, "displaced persons," including former prisoners from concentration and slave labor camps. "Lippsies in the making," le Carré calls them in a scene from *A Perfect Spy* that depicts this time. Some "spoke of death and torture so casually that he became indignant at their unconcern.... If they described a night crossing over the hills, Pym crossed with them, lugging their Lippsie suitcases and feeling the icy mountain air" (ch. 13).

The interviews the twenty-year-old le Carré had with these survivors were some of the great formative experiences of his life. We know he was searching for Annaliese and probably picturing everything he heard happening to her. The marks of these interviews are all over his novels. *A Small Town in Germany* hangs on them: le Carré gave Leo Harting his own old job. Harting's youthful confrontation with the Holocaust so sears him that it produces the obsession still driving him two decades later. Le Carré wrote the 1968 *A Small Town in Germany* just before the deadline that motivates Leo: the twenty-year statute of limitations for Nazi war crimes was about to run out. "What's so damn holy about twenty years?" Praschko says Leo had shouted at him; Praschko's response was to say that we have gotten "old" and "tired" of remembering. Leo, Praschko relates, said he had "seen the living witness of evil," felt he was a "privileged" person who must bear witness (ch. 17); and so must le Carré. Leo dies in Turner's arms as Turner sees "his own life, his own face" in Leo's (epilogue).

The ghastly experiences available to most of us only through a movie like Claude Lanzmann's *Shoah* (1985), le Carré, at twenty, endured daily, and in the flesh. I helped an Auschwitz survivor write his memoirs fifteen years ago, and it is not an experience one can forget. ("Where were you standing when your mother fell off the train?") Le Carré was seeing Holocaust victims, while the wounds and memories were still fresh and emotions strong. In le Carré's first published novel, the very first thing Smiley does is visit a concentration camp survivor, Elsa Fennan, and interview her, "a slight, fierce woman" with hair "the colour of nicotine."

Although frail, she conveyed an impression of endurance and courage, and the brown eyes that shone from her crooked little face were of an astonishing intensity. It was a worn face, racked and ravaged long ago, the face of a child grown old on starving and exhaustion, the eternal refugee face, the prison-camp face....
(*Call for the Dead*, ch. 3)

A face le Carré knows well. Interviewing her, Smiley feels "sick and cheap." She does not resent him. "He was an oppressor, but she accepted oppression." His quest for Annaliese led le Carré to write more about the Holocaust and its aftereffects than most Jewish novelists. The strongest pejorative in le Carré's characters' vocabularies to this day is "fascist." Indeed, the youthful le Carré probably, like Harting, acquired through his interviews information about Nazi war criminals, then watched the Western Occupation forces decide it was impolitic to prosecute them. "The war crimes investigation units themselves were near to disbandment," we learn in *A Small Town in Germany*. "There was pressure from London and Washington to bury the hatchet and hand over all responsibility to the German courts" (ch. 16). That is what motivates Elsa Fennan's spying in le Carré's first novel. At the end of the sequel, *The Spy Who Came In from the Cold*, we discover Elsa to have been correct. The entire British operation has been staged to protect a murderous former Nazi who is selling information to the British. A dedicated Jewish Communist is about to expose him, and the British discredit him, even accidentally unleash a new current of anti-Semitism. The Nazi even murders the hero's Jewish Communist girlfriend, Liz Gold. A few years later, as the Statute of Limitations approached, le Carré, who had been a "privileged" witness, wrote his only "message novel," challenging the Statute, telling what he had seen, arguing that Nazis still prominent in Germany could start all over again. When le Carré wrote of Israel later in *The Little Drummer Girl* (1983), he was only continuing his meditations on the Holocaust in another part of the world. It was hardly the ill-informed meddling in Jewish affairs that critics like Harold Bloom assumed it was at the time. When le Carré interviewed survivors in Israel twenty-five years after his original interviews, he was a person who—from the deepest personal interest—had spent much of his life work reflecting on what it meant to be a Jew after the Holocaust, a person who had written to warn against persistent Nazi strains operating in Germany.

## CALL FOR THE DEAD

CALL FOR THE DEAD was published by a small house, Walker, in the United States, so many Americans who read *The Spy Who Came In from the Cold* did not realize that that novel was actually a sequel to the successful earlier book. *The Spy Who Came In from the Cold* reads differently, and its impact is even stronger, when it is read in the context of *Call for the Dead*. "In one of those old sixpenny note books" in which he wrote his first Smiley story, le Carré remembers, he made a sketch of that character as he "first imagined him. Tubby and perplexed, the weary pilgrim is struggling up a stony hill, carrying his exhausted horse on his shoulders."

Smiley is one of the great suggestive names in literature. Not only does the name make you instantly picture him, but even to pronounce it leaves your face in his polite, perpetually embarrassed smile. Although le Carré's concept of Smiley deepens, the center of the myth is present from *Call for the Dead's* first sentence: "When Lady Ann Sercombe married George Smiley," she described him to her amazed upper-class friends as "breathtakingly ordinary." In the second sentence she leaves him for a "Cuban motor racing driver." Smiley's appearance will not alter from this first page on: "Short, fat and of a quiet disposition, he appeared to spend a lot of money on really bad clothes, which hung about his squat frame like skin on a shrunken toad."

If the essence of popular literature is wish fulfillment, whose wish would be fulfilled by becoming George Smiley? One could understandably wish to be James Bond, but why would one identify with this unhappy little cuckold? Le Carré now admits, he did use a "model" for his depiction, at least for its "externals": the Reverend Vivian Green, his Oxford "tutor," who, like his student, knew Sherborne, having been chaplain there. Le Carré told the Book-of-the-Month Club Green was "tubby, bespectacled and in manner very quiet." Like Smiley, he dressed expensively but terribly, "white silk shirts that crumpled the moment he put them on." We recognize deeper Smiley traits: "When [Green] started a conversation he seemed to begin in the middle, as if he had read your thoughts thus far." He had the "ability to empathize, to affiliate himself with you without appearing to intrude."

In creating Smiley, le Carré was, I think, using an old father figure to create for himself the ideal father he never had. He acknowledged this when he told Joseph Lelyveld, in a 1986 interview for the *New York Times Magazine*, in reference to *A Perfect Spy*, that "it was only when I took leave of Smiley in my own mind" after *Smiley's People* (1980), "that I was able to address myself to my real father." He clearly implies that Smiley had long been his fictional one. Smiley may be the opposite of James Bond, but he is even more the opposite of Ronnie Cornwell: as faithful as Ronnie was fickle, as solid as Ronnie was shoddy. That gave Smiley his emotional fascination for his creator, who could write with all the power of a child's wish. Smiley is, unlike Ronnie, kind, gentle, sexually faithful (indeed, chivalric), respectable if not patrician—normal. He *belongs,* as Ronnie never did, and as Ronnie's children, by extension, never did. Ronnie's legacy of social ambiguity and the burden of all his lies are a theme throughout le Carré's novels. It intensifies le Carré's fury at the Establishment. We start to see how unreal, how dreamlike Smiley is when we realize he fits all of St. Paul's criteria for the perfect human being: Smiley suffereth long, and is kind; Smiley envieth not, doth not behave himself unseemly, is not puffed up; Smiley beareth all things, believeth all things, hopeth all things. And le Carré's fantasy father proved to be very close to the international reading public's.

Already, in this first book, Smiley works essentially alone, and wins. The individual still counts. Although he has been written of as an "organization man," whenever we actually see him he is as alone as a cowboy, as a samurai *ronin,* as a novelist. He returns from retirement, often, or works solo, only physically inside a corrupt organization. The spy in Western literature had been a sneak. During this century he became an affirmation of the individual's power against the megastate or megacorporation—the Circus (le Carré's term for the British secret service) or the Centre (his term for the Russian secret service)—which all others bow to as the sun. "It is sheer vanity," Smiley lectures himself in *Tinker, Tailor, Soldier, Spy,* "to believe that one fat middle-aged spy is the only person capable of holding the world together" (ch. 10). Le Carré dares to say it because he knows we will say "Not vanity at all!" We are readers and thinkers like Smiley, and his victories give us new faith in our own powers.

*Call for the Dead* begins when a Foreign Office employee, Samuel Fennan, whom Smiley had routinely questioned about Party membership in Oxford in the 1930's, kills himself, leaving a typed suicide note saying Smiley hounded him to death. Smiley is aghast. Fennan had known he was closing the file. "Half the Cabinet were in the Party in the '30s." The suicide seems unbelievable. "What was he like?" Peter Guillam asks, and readers who have not spent the time we have on le Carré's biography will flinch at Smiley's answer: "To look at, obviously a Jew" (ch. 2). The omniscient narrator sums up Smiley's thoughts later: "Samuel Fennan, the eternal Jew" (ch. 8). "I'm the wandering Jewess," his wife Elsa tells Smiley at the end of chapter 12.

Now that le Carré's reputation as a writer of serious literature has grown, and he is included in standard works like this one, people who never read *Call for the Dead* will become aware of it. Knowing nothing of le Carré, I fear they will misunderstand it, as many did *The Little Drummer Girl.* The important critic Harold Bloom—who is, alas, no le Carré expert—in a 1987 introduction he wrote to what is still the only collection of essays about le Carré, spent half the introduction blasting him for insensitivity to Jews. When le Carré writes that Israeli jets "bombed the crowded Palestinian quarter of Beirut," killing many children, Bloom retorts the passage "just won't do": "[it] makes me want to shout at le Carré" about the "rabbis and old men massacred by Palestinians last week in an Istanbul synagogue." Le Carré's sympathy, Bloom says, is "essentially . . . with the Palestinians in a very English tradition of choosing sides in that terrible and perpetual war."

I contend, on the contrary, that le Carré's extraordinary personal experience of the Holocaust, dramatized in Leo Harting's quest to bring Nazi murderers to justice, convinced him that the Holocaust was the most significant moral subject of his time. This conviction, and his deep personal identification with Jews—like himself, outsiders in Establishment England—have consistently drawn le Carré to where most gentile angels fear to tread. The narrator describes "the eternal Jew" in *Call for the Dead* this way: "cultured, cosmopolitan, self-determinate, industrious and perceptive: to Smiley, immensely attractive" (ch. 8).

Bloom is entirely right to hint at an English tradition of anti-Semitism. "We all knew who the Jews were in school," le Carré said with disgust later, "and made sure they knew it too." Anti-Semitism had been, le Carré well knew, particularly strong in the English thriller, which tended to play on spy mania and xenophobia. Sapper's (H. C. McNeile's) series character Bulldog Drummond led bands of black-shirted thugs to beat up Jews and foreigners. "The Jew is everywhere," a character tells Richard Hannay in chapter 1 of Buchan's seminal *The Thirty-Nine Steps* (1915) "but you have to go far down the backstairs to find him." Once you get past the gentile front men and "get to the real boss, ten to one you are brought up against a little white-faced Jew in a bathchair with an eye like a rattlesnake. Yes sir, he is the man who is ruling the world just now," and he wants a "return match for the *pogroms . . .* because his aunt was outraged and his father flogged" "Krauts. *Bloody* Krauts. God, I hate them!" Mendel says in *Call for the Dead.* "Forgive and forget.

*Why* bloody well forget? ... Krupp and all that mob—oh no" (ch. 6). Superficially identical scenes. The difference is, le Carré's Mendel isn't "ruling the world," he is a retired police inspector. He is also Smiley's closest friend through all the novels. When Smiley is injured, Mendel even takes over as *Call for the Dead*'s protagonist for several chapters. And, the Jewish character here is not spoken about, described, but speaks *for himself*. Finally, Mendel's anger is, I will show, also le Carré's.

*Call for the Dead* treads on particularly dangerous ground for le Carré, since it is not a "Philby" novel (it does not deal with an Establishment mole) but a "Rosenberg" novel. The most famous American espionage case of the 1950's, still a bitterly sensitive subject in the Jewish community, was the prosecution of Julius and Ethel Rosenberg, American Communists, at the height of the McCarthy anti-Communist hysteria. They died in the electric chair as spies on 19 June 1953. Pablo Picasso painted them, scores of books and novels have been written about them. The American Jewish community has long considered them innocent martyrs to chauvinist hysteria. Smiley, investigating the case of Samuel and Elsa Fennan, will discover that Elsa is indeed guilty. What is more, her motive is her sense of herself as "the wandering Jewess," and she has even helped kill her husband because he endangered her mission.

That sounds as bad as Harold Bloom could fear. Pieced together with the widespread opinion that *The Little Drummer Girl* is anti-Semitic, it could suggest a very different le Carré than the one I see. But to read it as anti-Semitic one must know nothing of le Carré's biography or the "Never forget!" passions of *A Small Town in Germany*. Remembering that novel, we realize that Mendel's opinion about never forgiving Krupp is le Carré's. Le Carré wrote *A Small Town in Germany* to warn us that a policy of "forgive and forget" could lead straight to Klaus Karfeld's neo-Nazi crowds shuffling once more toward Chamberlain's hill, while the coward British Establishment seeks peace in our time. Le Carré plants a newspaper headline in *Call for the Dead* about the lynching of a Jewish shopkeeper in Dusseldorf to underline the reality behind Elsa's fears. What makes *Call for the Dead* so interesting is that le Carré thinks Elsa Fennan is *right*, but that nothing corrupts like being right, and being absolutely right has corrupted Elsa absolutely. Smiley, at the end, pictures Elsa and her Jewish controller, Dieter, tragically: "They dreamed of peace and freedom. Now they're murderers and spies" (ch. 18). The double irony is that Smiley, too, is a spy; and he has just killed Dieter.

Dieter Frey, Elsa's controller from the Abteilung, the East German Intelligence Service, is not only a Jew—he was once Smiley's star pupil. "A tall, handsome, commanding cripple," Smiley says, "the idol of his generation; a Jew" (ch. 11). Change the last phrase to "a homosexual" and you have Bill Haydon, the mole of *Tinker, Tailor, Soldier, Spy*. During the war, Smiley, running a network of agents in Germany, recruits Dieter and trains him. Dieter somehow escapes the gas chambers and after the war follows his Socialist sympathies to East Germany.

Elsa survives a death camp, but is hospitalized for three years following. In the mid 1950's she watches the ascent of the "New Germany" and sees, like Mendel, that the "old names had come back, names that had frightened us as children. The dreadful, plump pride returned.... They marched with the old rhythm" (ch. 12). She becomes Dieter's agent, begins stealing her husband's Foreign Office papers and passing them to the Abteilung. When Dieter sees George Smiley interviewing Samuel Fennan, he fears the worst and has his "silent killer," Hans-Dieter Mundt, murder Fennan. Mundt is an ex-Nazi, and Dieter's association with him (symbolized by their shared name) is the mark of Frey's corruption. As for Elsa, her fear of a Nazi resurgence has led her to help a Nazi kill a Jew—her own husband.

In the end, Smiley tracks Dieter onto a bridge, Dieter pulls his gun, and they grapple. Dieter cannot bring himself to shoot his old mentor and Smiley, desperate, knocks him off the bridge. The crippled Dieter drowns while Smiley cries, "Oh dear God what have I done, Oh Christ, Dieter ... why didn't you shoot?" Looking back on the way Dieter, not he, had honored their human connection with each other, Smiley muses, "Who was then the gentleman ... ?" (ch. 16).

THE SPY WHO CAME IN FROM THE COLD

BUT what of Dieter Frey's "silent killer," Hans-Dieter Mundt? His escape from England at the end of *Call for the Dead* is hard to believe; and after he has killed Samuel Fennan and Adam Scarr and nearly killed Smiley, it is a strangely unsatisfying way for

*Why* bloody well forget? . . . Krupp and all that mob—oh no" (ch. 6). Superficially identical scenes. The difference is, le Carré's Mendel isn't "ruling the world," he is a retired police inspector. He is also Smiley's closest friend through all the novels. When Smiley is injured, Mendel even takes over as *Call for the Dead*'s protagonist for several chapters. And, the Jewish character here is not spoken about, described, but speaks *for himself*. Finally, Mendel's anger is, I will show, also le Carré's.

*Call for the Dead* treads on particularly dangerous ground for le Carré, since it is not a "Philby" novel (it does not deal with an Establishment mole) but a "Rosenberg" novel. The most famous American espionage case of the 1950's, still a bitterly sensitive subject in the Jewish community, was the prosecution of Julius and Ethel Rosenberg, American Communists, at the height of the McCarthy anti-Communist hysteria. They died in the electric chair as spies on 19 June 1953. Pablo Picasso painted them, scores of books and novels have been written about them. The American Jewish community has long considered them innocent martyrs to chauvinist hysteria. Smiley, investigating the case of Samuel and Elsa Fennan, will discover that Elsa is indeed guilty. What is more, her motive is her sense of herself as "the wandering Jewess," and she has even helped kill her husband because he endangered her mission.

That sounds as bad as Harold Bloom could fear. Pieced together with the widespread opinion that *The Little Drummer Girl* is anti-Semitic, it could suggest a very different le Carré than the one I see. But to read it as anti-Semitic one must know nothing of le Carré's biography or the "Never forget!" passions of *A Small Town in Germany*. Remembering that novel, we realize that Mendel's opinion about never forgiving Krupp is le Carré's. Le Carré wrote *A Small Town in Germany* to warn us that a policy of "forgive and forget" could lead straight to Klaus Karfeld's neo-Nazi crowds shuffling once more toward Chamberlain's hill, while the coward British Establishment seeks peace in our time. Le Carré plants a newspaper headline in *Call for the Dead* about the lynching of a Jewish shopkeeper in Dusseldorf to underline the reality behind Elsa's fears. What makes *Call for the Dead* so interesting is that le Carré thinks Elsa Fennan is *right*, but that nothing corrupts like being right, and being absolutely right has corrupted Elsa absolutely. Smiley, at the end, pictures Elsa and her Jewish controller, Dieter, tragically: "They dreamed of peace and freedom. Now they're murderers and spies" (ch. 18). The double irony is that Smiley, too, is a spy; and he has just killed Dieter.

Dieter Frey, Elsa's controller from the Abteilung, the East German Intelligence Service, is not only a Jew—he was once Smiley's star pupil. "A tall, handsome, commanding cripple," Smiley says, "the idol of his generation; a Jew" (ch. 11). Change the last phrase to "a homosexual" and you have Bill Haydon, the mole of *Tinker, Tailor, Soldier, Spy*. During the war, Smiley, running a network of agents in Germany, recruits Dieter and trains him. Dieter somehow escapes the gas chambers and after the war follows his Socialist sympathies to East Germany.

Elsa survives a death camp, but is hospitalized for three years following. In the mid 1950's she watches the ascent of the "New Germany" and sees, like Mendel, that the "old names had come back, names that had frightened us as children. The dreadful, plump pride returned. . . . They marched with the old rhythm" (ch. 12). She becomes Dieter's agent, begins stealing her husband's Foreign Office papers and passing them to the Abteilung. When Dieter sees George Smiley interviewing Samuel Fennan, he fears the worst and has his "silent killer," Hans-Dieter Mundt, murder Fennan. Mundt is an ex-Nazi, and Dieter's association with him (symbolized by their shared name) is the mark of Frey's corruption. As for Elsa, her fear of a Nazi resurgence has led her to help a Nazi kill a Jew—her own husband.

In the end, Smiley tracks Dieter onto a bridge, Dieter pulls his gun, and they grapple. Dieter cannot bring himself to shoot his old mentor and Smiley, desperate, knocks him off the bridge. The crippled Dieter drowns while Smiley cries, "Oh dear God what have I done, Oh Christ, Dieter . . . why didn't you shoot?" Looking back on the way Dieter, not he, had honored their human connection with each other, Smiley muses, "Who was then the gentleman . . . ?" (ch. 16).

THE SPY WHO CAME IN FROM THE COLD

BUT what of Dieter Frey's "silent killer," Hans-Dieter Mundt? His escape from England at the end of *Call for the Dead* is hard to believe; and after he has killed Samuel Fennan and Adam Scarr and nearly killed Smiley, it is a strangely unsatisfying way for guard tells Liz, he will be shot. "Comrade Mundt knows what to do with Jews" (ch. 24). Mundt's rival is gone; he is stronger than ever.

And Leamas realizes that Mundt in fact *was* an English agent. He had not miraculously escaped after the Fennan affair. Captured, he had been "turned," given the choice of hanging or turning double agent and getting rich. To help Mundt rise to replace Dieter Frey, Control let him discover and kill Leamas' East German agents—to Control nothing more than a bunch of expendable Communist traitors, to be used any way that best advanced British interests. But—as we saw at the Wall—Mundt had to kill them on capture, before Fiedler could sweat them and learn anything valuable about the Circus or its methods. That aroused Fiedler's suspicions. So Leamas was duped. "We are witnessing," Leamas tells Liz, ". . . a filthy, lousy operation to save Mundt's skin. To save him from a clever little Jew. . . . They made us kill him, do you see, kill the Jew" (ch. 24). Control and Smiley only needed Liz and Leamas to be together "for a day" so that by bringing her money later they could make it look as if the Circus was paying for an agent's affair.

Mundt arranges a car for Leamas and Liz's escape. As they flee toward the Wall, Liz puts the book in so strange a light that le Carré's 1963 American readers probably took it as so much Communist nonsense. I know I did. The misleading Establishment image we had of le Carré also made it impossible to think he might in any way agree with Liz: "Fiedler was . . . doing his job," she tells Leamas, "and now you've killed him. Mundt is a spy and a traitor and you protect him. Mundt is a Nazi . . . he hates Jews. What side are you on?" (ch. 25). The one absolute in le Carré's world is anti-Semitism. Characters may act for communism or against it, but no character associated with anti-Semitic violence is ever excused.

Liz says it seems "odd" that Mundt let her go—"a Party member knowing all this." It isn't "logical" (ch. 25). They're given clear instructions on when to scale the Wall. They follow them, but the lights go on: only Liz is shot. Mundt—and Control—did not go through all this only to let this smart little English Communist endanger the entire operation. Smiley is shouting from the other side, "The girl, where's the girl?" so he obviously played his role thinking that she would be rescued with Leamas. Control will abuse Smiley's trust again in the next book. The guards were instructed to kill only her, for when Leamas, coming "in from the cold" to side with his love, goes back down the Wall on the chance that she might still be alive, at first no one fires. She is dead. He stands, "glaring around him like a blinded bull in the arena" till they shoot.

*The Spy Who Came In from the Cold* is one of the best novels written in the second half of the twentieth century, a fusion of emotion and intellect that recalls the best work of Dickens. The style is more beautiful than Dickens, a unique compound of twentieth-century imagist descriptions and the elegant dialectical conversations of Jane Austen or Bernard Shaw.

THE LOOKING GLASS WAR

THE LOOKING GLASS WAR is one of le Carré's least read novels and the easiest to understand, so I will be brief—regretfully, for it is excellent. Le Carré is supposed to have said that the operation in *The Spy Who Came In from the Cold* was too brilliant, and he wanted to write of a normal operation in which everything goes wrong. That project is this book. The first scene, in which the silly ass Taylor accidentally gets drunk waiting for a film drop, parodies *The Spy*'s great tense opening. Accidents abound. People forget their orders or are too proud to say they never understood them.

Leclerc, a bureaucrat right down to his name, tries to find reasons for "the Department," a leftover arm of Military Intelligence, to exist. They do not even rate a staff car anymore. He decides he believes some hokey photographs suggest that the Russians are putting nuclear missiles in East Germany—another Cuban Missile Crisis? That threat pries loose some funding, not only for a car, but to reactivate one field agent. They train and send a trusting Pole, Fred Leiser, into East Germany. Leiser is caught and killed. Control, at the Circus, has been giving Leclerc enough rope to hang himself, as Smiley, who was liaison, realizes in horror at the end. Leiser was caught because Control gave Leiser outdated World War II radio equipment that Leclerc was too ignorant to refuse. (The way Control manipulates Smiley reinforces our sense of how things went in *The Spy Who Came In from the Cold*.) At book's end, Leclerc seems to have become senile from the shock, and the department will probably be disbanded.

The prose is beautiful but the book's real beauty lies in the delicacy of the characterizations, the portraits of average men trying to find some purpose in their lives. Le Carré quotes, ironically, from Rupert Brooke's early, innocent prowar poem, "1914," at the beginning of part 3: "To turn as swimmers into cleanness leaping / Glad from a world grown old and cold and weary." *The Russia House* is in some ways a heavy-handed replay of this theme. Organizations exist to perpetuate themselves, not to serve; Cold War organizations exist to perpetuate the Cold War, which they must feed on as if it were a host. Members of the Russian Writers' Union, in a 1989 interview with le Carré, expressed their fascination with *The Looking Glass War*. In the post–Cold War era, this fine book will be read intently, and we will all wonder how much of the Cold War was only Russian, American, and British Leclercs trying to save the departments they loved.

## THE NAIVE AND SENTIMENTAL LOVER

THE year 1968 saw the publication of *A Small Town in Germany*. Two years later there was a "time out," in *Lover*'s own words. *The Naive and Sentimental Lover* was supposedly le Carré's attempt at a "straight novel" but is actually something less than that. *The Naive and Sentimental Lover*, both a critical and commercial failure, is a familiar male mid-life crisis novel, published in 1971, the year of le Carré's divorce from Ann, his wife of nineteen years.

The novel is the story of Aldo Cassidy, a youthful "tycoon" in his late thirties, a graduate, like le Carré, of Sherborne and Oxford. Nearing forty, Aldo runs away from wife and career to experience the joys of bohemian freedom. The novel is a period piece. There were countless like it in those years as the "silent generation" that had come of age in the sober 1950's and been good organization men for twenty years hit forty at the very minute that the hippie generation seemed to be having all the fun. One movie had the memorable title, *Middle-Aged Crazies*, and *The Naive and Sentimental Lover*, despite the pretentious title from Friedrich von Schiller, is about the same subject. "Cassidy," le Carré explained, "is the victim not of society, but of himself . . . a dreamer obliged to conform. But with this difference: he could, he really could, be free. What defeats him is . . . the impossibility of middle-class love." Merely to read such sentiments, in all their dogged honesty, snaps one back to love beads and *Sgt. Pepper*.

It helps very little to know that the book was based on le Carré's actual ménage à trois with Susan and James Kennaway, the latter a fine Scottish novelist who died prematurely in 1968. (*The Looking Glass War* is dedicated to Kennaway.) If *The Naive and Sentimental Lover* had dealt with le Carré's feelings about Kennaway's death it might have been a deeper book, but le Carré confines it to domestic adventure. Parts are quite funny. Aldo's pride at having cleaned up by inventing a better baby-carriage brake is *very* funny. Le Carré worked hard on the novel, and in a somewhat pathetic letter to the bookstores before publication warned them that there would be, for once, no spies.

In *Rabbit Redux* (1971) John Updike, le Carré's contemporary, sends white-bread Rabbit off to learn about the free life from an African American named Skeeter. Aldo's mentor is the Irish artist Shamus, who addresses him as "lover." Shamus' beautiful wife, Helen, is first seen naked. Shamus says uncompromising things like, "Who wants the twilight when he can have the fucking sun?" (ch. 17). Le Carré's eye for English mores fails him for once: the artists use slang that sounds twenty years out of date, and Cassidy's naked fantasy girl, Helen, is first seen listening to Frank Sinatra! In a series of painfully familiar scenes, Cassidy gets his horoscope read, looks guiltily at his children as he reads them bedtime stories, sleeps with a hippie vegetarian with "broad, hard thighs" under a poster of Che Guevara: "She adored Castro but her greatest single regret was that she had not fucked Che Guevara before he died." The narrator is moved: "Time out; borrowed Time; a past unlived, too long imagined, belatedly made real . . . Cassidy stripped, stood in the fountain, and felt the edges of his existence" (ch. 29). This is the only time le Carré, that precise stylist, will write anything that sounds like Beatles lyrics.

After various mild *Walpurgisnacht* scenes, Shamus and Helen give him their last kisses. In chapter 38 Helen tells him to "put a value on *yourself*." Shamus says, "Keep trying, lover. Never regret, never apologize"—which Henry Ford II once said was his father's motto. Critics who lamented the prose as self-indulgent did not understand that the whole novel is in praise of self-indulgence. In an epilogue Shamus becomes a successful serious artist and Cassidy goes back to his wife, although he allows himself some infidelities: "For in this world, whatever there was left of it to inhabit, Aldo Cassidy dared not remember love."

*The Naive and Sentimental Lover* was not for naught. Years later, when le Carré decided to draw the left-wing actress Charlie in the opening half of *The Little Drummer Girl,* he would satirize the hippie artist world with deadly, knowing accuracy.

## TINKER, TAILOR, SOLDIER, SPY

SADDENED, perhaps chastened by the failure of *The Naive and Sentimental Lover,* le Carré returned to his forte, the secret world of spies, and created one of the most memorable characters in twentieth-century literature, his mature conception of George Smiley.

Dostoyevsky gives us a clue about Smiley in a letter appraising Smiley's precursor, Mr. Pickwick—a letter written when he was creating his "idiot," the gently charismatic Prince Myshkin. The most difficult thing in the world for the novelist to do, Dostoyevsky writes, is to "portray a *positively* good man." That was the challenge le Carré faced, too. The two successes Dostoyevsky says he knows of are Don Quixote and Pickwick, who succeed because they are "good only because at the same time . . . ridiculous." Pickwick, whom Dostoyevsky calls an "immense" conception, is "ridiculous and succeeds by virtue of this fact." So Smiley, in direct line of descent from that other British hero he so physically resembles, is good, ridiculous, and ultimately successful.

In recognizing that Smiley is an heir to Pickwick, we ascribe to him his legitimate fictional father: Dickens, not Graham Greene. Although they both use the same subgenre to write serious literature, in every important way le Carré is the opposite of Greene. Greene's most famous character, Pinkie, is a revelation of human evil; le Carré's George Smiley is a revelation of human virtue. Greene creates plausible evil characters; le Carré creates plausible good—almost saintly—characters. Greene has the imagination of sin and le Carré of human goodness: Even Smiley's antagonist Karla is a relative stick figure till *Smiley's People,* when le Carré can imagine him as a distraught father transformed by "excessive love." Even Karla!

Since Greene accepts human evil he is friendly to coercive systems wherever he finds them: critics should not be bewildered by his friendliness to Catholicism *and* communism, even Stalinism. Greene understands anyone who wants to make us be good. Le Carré is an instinctive anarchist, so deeply does he believe in the goodness of the individual. He hates all organizations: his villains often seem to be not actively bad, merely mediocre wills an organization has soured or corrupted. *The Naive and Sentimental Lover* celebrated his own brief personal flouting of all social and sexual mores during the 1960's. Flower-child philosophy suited him well, brought out the most mawkish part of him. A central scene in all his novels concerns two people trying to make love while some bureaucrats refuse to leave them alone. Le Carré's version of glasnost in *The Russia House* sometimes seems to be little more.

At the beginning of *Tinker, Tailor, Soldier, Spy* Smiley is summoned from retirement for the third time straight to confer secretly with "Whitehall's head prefect" (p. 28), Oliver Lacon (ch. 3). The Circus has been betrayed. At Lacon's Ascot estate he shows Smiley a Far East gunrunner and Circus agent, "Tarr, sir. Ricki Tarr from Penang" (ch. 4), who has had a romance with Irina, a Russian agent. She has been executed, but not before passing Ricki her diary. One sentence introduces us to a new name and sets Smiley off on his great "quest": "Have you heard of Karla?" (ch. 8).

In the 1930's, Irina claims, Karla recruited a Communist university student, who became a deep-penetration agent, a mole in the Circus. (Le Carré has admitted to making up most Circus terms, although real spies have now adopted many of his inventions; the Circus itself never existed, though London tourists, thinking it as real as the Pentagon, try to find it.) As *Call for the Dead* used the Rosenberg case for a springboard, so *Tinker, Tailor, Soldier, Spy* uses the Philby case. Many novels did. In fact, the year before *Tinker, Tailor, Soldier, Spy* was published there was Brian Freemantle's *Goodbye to an Old Friend* (1973), the same year, Alan Williams' *Gentleman Traitor* (1974), and four years later Greene's pro-Philby pro-Communist reply, *The Human Factor* (1978).

Karla's origins may be traced to 1968, when le Carré wrote a lengthy, furious preface to *The Philby*

*Conspiracy* (1968, published in Great Britain as *Philby: The Spy Who Betrayed a Generation*). As he struggled to find the "apt phrases of outrage," he started to think that "none of us is yet equal to the dimensions of this scandal. Like a great novel, and an unfinished one at that, the story of Kim Philby lives on in us." *Tinker, Tailor, Soldier, Spy*, begun three years later, was his shot at finishing that great unfinished novel. In 1968 le Carré, reading, began to see Philby as the epitome of everything he had long hated about the British Establishment. "Let anyone who derides the notion of the Establishment read this book," he writes.

Guy Burgess, Donald Maclean, and Kim Philby were three leftist Cambridge students recruited in the 1930's to be Moscow's moles in SIS (British intelligence). Philby's father, St. John Philby, had been a man of the Empire, a more successful version of Lawrence of Arabia, a famous explorer and soldier who rose to become the Saud dynasty's general liaison with the West. Kim, born in India, nicknamed with amazing precognition after Rudyard Kipling's boy spy, had the British version of "the right stuff": he "was of our blood and hunted with our pack." He rose to become a master of the SIS and Britain's representative to the CIA. For ten years anything Britain (and maybe America) knew went to Moscow, and Moscow fed back disinformation. "In place of an all-seeing eye," SIS became "a credulous ear and a misleading voice."

When Burgess and Maclean's covers were blown in 1951 and the two fled to Moscow, all signs pointed to Philby as their protector. But the Establishment intervened, reasoning, le Carré fumed, " 'This Club does not elect traitors, therefore Kim is not a traitor.' This Establishment is a self-proving proposition." One might as well have suggested a Roosevelt had been spying. Prime Minister Harold Macmillan publically exonerated Philby in 1956. When, in 1963, the British "turned" the chief of Polish Intelligence, Philby was identified. But the Establishment/SIS (le Carré argues that the two are "identical") became so embarrassed that Philby, even after a confession, was virtually put on his honor as a gentleman not to flee; he fled. So the Colonel Blimps had dithered away even his interrogation, the last chance at some repair.

In his preface le Carré goes beyond the book about Philby, claiming the "principal character" was still "missing": the Soviet controller who had "consciously seduced" the three boys. "We discern his hand, his influence, his shadow: never once do we . . . hear his name." That will be le Carré's appointed task. The preface's suddenly dramatic prose, at this point, the rush of emotional energy, marks le Carré's first vision of a grand antagonist for George Smiley, the Hamletic English liberal, the man of agonizing conscience: Karla, equally brilliant but utterly convinced, as secure in his ideology as a twelfth-century heretic burner, Totalitarian Man.

"Have you heard of Karla?" Smiley has met him before, he tells Guillam after they have left Rickie Tarr. In a cell in Delhi, years before, he had tried to convince a Russian "calling himself Gerstmann" to defect (ch. 23). This Gerstmann was Karla. Smiley tried to reach him on an emotional level, even let him borrow his wife Ann's cigarette lighter, which Gerstmann kept: "I had convinced myself that Gerstmann ultimately was accessible to ordinary human arguments." Smiley had never faced a figure of such massive "philosophical repose," a priest without doubts, a monk beyond family or individual desire. Smiley, not yet aware, trying to make some "human" contact, exposes his own humanity, his doubts, his insecurity. "The political generality [is] meaningless," he tells Karla. "Don't you think . . . that there is as little worth on your side as there is on mine?" Smiley later understands that the supernaturally calm little figure only saw him as "the very archetype of a flabby Western liberal" (ch. 23). Smiley, notice, was in all ways temporarily mistaken: there *are* great differences between the two sides, he will insist in the end.

Now, to track Karla's mole, Smiley hides out in the Islay Hotel. With Guillam and Mendel as legmen, he conducts a sedentary paper chase, a scholar's exercise in reason. The mole he ultimately uncovers is Bill Haydon. Haydon's character is based upon Philby; he is also bisexual, like Guy Burgess. Smiley recognizes that Karla has had Bill sleep with his wife, Lady Ann, knowing that Smiley, the liberal endlessly attempting to be "fair," would, if he ever suspected Bill's treason, instantly doubt himself instead as a biased judge. Bill's Oxford schoolmate and lover, Jim Prideaux—whom he betrayed when Control, sensing there was a mole, sent Prideaux on a mission into Czechoslovakia—shadows Smiley and Guillam when they capture Bill, guesses the truth, gets into the prison, and breaks Bill's neck for him. Philby—who read that scene—commented wryly before his death that he suspected le Carré didn't like him, but was glad to have "contributed to his amazing affluence."

Bill, captured, is full of "half-baked political assertions" (ch. 38). Philby, le Carré had written, was not a political animal, but a vain, deceitful, self-important child frustrated by the diminished roles the diminishing Empire offered him to play. Kim (and Bill) loved "the great game," as Kipling termed spying in, fittingly, *Kim*. He loved deceit; above all, he loved the figure he cut as the grand betrayer. His half-baked politics were but an excuse to accept the starring role the Russian "seducer" had offered the boy. Le Carré will use this motive again in *The Little Drummer Girl*, when the born actress Charlie shifts her political loyalties 180 degrees to land a starring part in the "theatre of the real."

Smiley, at the end, is no more ideologically assured than when he first faced Karla. Le Carré hates Philby, but Smiley is someone else, and he does not hate Bill; he feels a "wasting grief" (ch. 38). Opposite Karla, "whatever intellectual or philosophical percepts he clung to broke down entirely now that he was faced with the human situation" (ch. 36).

### THE HONOURABLE SCHOOLBOY

THE HONOURABLE SCHOOLBOY (1977) was le Carré's self-conscious attempt at "the Eastern novel," as one of the book's own characters styles it (ch. 5), giving learned references to Graham Greene *(The Quiet American)*, André Malraux *(Man's Fate)*, and Joseph Conrad *(Lord Jim* in particular). However much le Carré belongs in that company artistically, one telling difference immediately comes to mind: those men really knew something about "the East."

What would tempt le Carré to try this, when he had always been so careful to stay in his own backyard? He wrote of English spies operating in London, Germany, or "Czecho." They were almost always bookish, even academic, and the plots involved them with people connected in some way to the Holocaust. Although le Carré seemed a man of the world, it was a small world he was the man of. For him to decide to branch out by attempting a novel about the East (as in "Mysterious East"? how dated a concept, by 1977) was more radical a departure than his previous attempt at a romance.

He was driven to take such a chance because he had been drawn back to the problem dramatized in *The Spy Who Came In from the Cold*. *The Honourable Schoolboy* is the second of what, since *The Russia House*, we see to be a pattern: I will call *The Spy Who Came In from the Cold*, *The Honourable Schoolboy*, and *The Russia House* his "star-crossed lovers" books. In all three, the characters, the theme, even the final plot twist show such deep structural similarities that if he had staged all three in Germany, the second two would be too familiar. In both later books, to reuse his Romeo and Juliet pattern le Carré has had to restage the action in another country, to give the pattern as much surface dissimilarity as possible.

The "star-crossed lovers" dramatize in the most moving and human way the central dilemma of his fiction: the conflict between personal and civic morality. Critics oversimplify when they say he writes of "ends and means." The wider civic morality, which Smiley has decided, with great reluctance, is worth upholding, frequently requires the individual to trespass against his or her personal morality. Le Carré has cited the English saying about a diplomat being an honest man "who lies for the good of his country." How much more dramatic a test case, then, is the spy, required to cheat and betray for his country. Le Carré never loses his sense that spying is sneaking. He is never interested in the genuine sneaks who do it, but only the "honest man" like Smiley who must descend even lower than the diplomat for the civic good. Smiley makes that moral descent in the first book, when he kills a former surrogate son, Dieter, and is forced to question himself thus: "Oh, God, who was then the gentleman?" Throughout the books le Carré's method will be to take his Pickwick and force him to act like a Fagin. "Smiley," le Carré told an audience at Johns Hopkins University in 1986, "sacrifice[s] his own morality on the altar of national necessity."

The star-crossed-lovers novels give the knife an extra twist. Here is their equation. Let Smiley, in his inevitable moral agony, take up the dirty sword to defend the civic good; then poise against him a surrogate son like Leamas or Westerby. Let the son, like Romeo, fall in love with a Juliet from the other side. He must then decide if Smiley's Way, the civic good, is worth betraying Juliet—must decide whether to betray his father or his wife, and whether to betray himself. Had the first novel, *Call for the Dead*, been written from Dieter's point of view, we might have seen how similar even *it* was to the later pattern.

Le Carré is *not* repeating himself. Rather, he debates his earlier self, and even repudiates himself. As he has come to different conclusions about this, his central moral conflict, he has been drawn back to this poignant knot. Each time he has returned to the star-crossed lovers, he has grown bolder in declaring for individual morality above the civic good.

Le Carré sought, in Hong Kong, a stage for his Romeo and Juliet at the maximum distance from the Berlin Wall. He needed new background shots, new clothes, new accents for his lovers, in short, new "nuts and bolts," as novelists contemptuously call all that. Most readers were charmed. Although many groaned at the glacial pace, *The Honourable Schoolboy* won a slew of prizes, and now forms the central book in le Carré's trilogy, retroactively dubbed *The Quest for Karla*. Really it is a reportorial tour de force: much of what seems cultural analysis is actually beautifully rendered surfaces, meticulous travelogues. The biggest card le Carré held was that his readers, like the aristocrats who bought Watteau's fantasies of the Chien Lung court, knew even less about the East than he did.

For his plot, le Carré has transplanted other familiar themes. Karla has had a high-ranking mole, Nelson Ko, inside the Chinese Communist hierarchy, just as he had Bill Haydon inside the Circus. Nelson's brother Drake is a filthy-rich, rags-to-riches, racehorse-owner, airline managing director, and opium smuggler working for Moscow Centre. The plot hangs on his stop-at-nothing Eastern determination to spring his brother from Communist China—which le Carré seems to picture surrounded by a Berlin Wall, manned by Chinese Mundts determined to shoot Chinese Liz Golds as they crawl to safety.

German efficiency was a poor paradigm with which to imagine China, 80 percent peasant, chaotic and corrupt, run by *ho-murr* ("back door" influence). Anyone with Drake Ko's money could have bought an exit visa for his brother. Enough complaining. Accept the book as a romantic fable, *orientalia,* or pass it by.

Smiley's patient tracking has uncovered a Russian "gold seam" (a flow of bribe money) leading to Drake Ko. Jerry Westerby becomes Smiley's Eastern agent and surrogate son, telling him, "You point me and I'll march" (ch. 5). Smiley and Jerry soon realize that Drake is holding Moscow's money in trust for his brother the mole.

Smiley plans to kidnap Karla's mole as he escapes from China to Drake's brotherly embrace. However, just as Leamas' conscience was awakened by his love for Liz Gold, Jerry's conscience is awakened by his love for Lizzie Worthington, Drake's mistress. Liz and Lizzie, Gold and Worthington, both women connected with the other side: the parallel seems deliberate. At the critical moment, Jerry's honor makes him side with the personal moral demands of his love against the moral demands of the state, even a state personified by Smiley.

Jerry betrays Smiley and tips off Drake, but, as the brothers are rejoined, the Americans shoulder Smiley's forces aside and snatch the mole for questioning. Le Carré, perhaps aware that the American readership might be less than outraged, considering the Circus' record, has Jerry rather pointlessly shot, either by Fawn, the Circus' most dangerous "silent killer," or by some faceless American in the departing black helicopters. We are supposed to expect a motive from neither.

Smiley drops into retirement, le Carré's favorite position for him. In the trilogy's last novel, the excellent *Smiley's People,* he can, yet again, be recalled to work from outside the system to save it.

### SMILEY'S PEOPLE

Le Carré came home to London, Paris, and Bern, the city of his student days, regaining his form to write the superb *Smiley's People*. This novel, the conclusion of *Quest for Karla,* is a central and satisfying book in the canon, but the reader is so familiar now with Smiley's world it can be sketched in very few words. As with *Tinker, Tailor, Soldier, Spy* we enter through a fun house of mysterious visits, multiple identities, false leads. When Smiley exposes the right path, we find that Karla has paid the price for his inhumanity. In the ultimate act of the Organization Man, that selfless, nonindividual assented to the purge of his lover. Communism, like all totalitarian systems since Plato's *Republic,* has resented the family. People are to identify with no cause but the state's. Karla purges his love, but his daughter, Tatiana, knows nothing of theory and she goes insane. His child's agony proves too much for whatever residual genetic cues in Karla still make him a human being. For the first time in his life he acts as an individual, breaks secretly with Party discipline, breaks rules, and even embezzles to find treatment for his daughter. Like the bloody Macbeth, he is left begging, "Cans't thou not minister to a mind diseased?"

First he makes a (for him) shockingly clumsy attempt to convince an old émigré, Maria Ostrakova, that Tatiana is Alexandra, the daughter she bore to "the Jew Glikman" and left in an orphanage twenty years ago when she fled Russia. Alexandra needs "the assistance of a mother," one of Karla's hoods, Kirov/Kursky, tells Ostrakova. Karla is willing to give Tatiana up to save her. Ostrakova looks at "several muddy photographs" and knows they do not depict her child (ch. 1). She alerts the old Estonian General Vladimir in London, who, after obtaining evidence, begs a meeting with the Circus. Vladimir is killed en route and power-broker Lacon brings Smiley back from retirement. When he uncovers the situation, he goes to Bern, blackmails the Russian diplomat, Grigoriev, who keeps Tatiana in a mental hospital there, and gets the evidence of Karla's corruption into the sin of paternal love.

There is the tremendously moving moment when Grigoriev, interrogated by Smiley, tells how the hard man he still does not realize is Karla had lapsed into emotion: "You must be a friend to this child. . . . Her father's twisted life has had a bad effect on her" (ch. 25). This had been the man Smiley once envied as utterly convinced, a rock of "philosophic repose." This only too plausible end reveals that Smiley's way, always to trust to one's individual conscience, "never acquiescing in a facile orthodoxy of [another], or of our own"—as Walter Pater put it (The Renaissance, 1868)—is a safer path than accepting the peace that dogma brings. It only remains to use Grigoriev's evidence to blackmail Karla: all is known, we are your only friends now, come to us and we will provide for you, care for Tatiana.

The last scene is at the Berlin Wall, the "icon of the cold war," where, two decades before, we and Leamas had waited for Reimeck, only to see him shot. After great suspense, Karla crosses safely to the West, a defection immeasurably greater than Bill Haydon's. He pauses and drops Ann's cigarette lighter—that reminder of their first meeting—at Smiley's feet. Smiley does not bother to pick it up. "George, you won," his disciple Guillam says. Smiley, with characteristic restraint, finally replies, "Did I? Yes. Yes, well I suppose I did" (ch. 27).

Le Carré, writing in 1980, had no way of knowing that he had now written the last great Berlin Wall scene, as well as the first one. The Wall would not long outlast Karla, and it would crumble from within in a similar, inevitable, human way. All through the Cold War le Carré's novels argued that Karla's way, running against the human grain, could not endure.

### THE LITTLE DRUMMER GIRL

IN 1983, when le Carré wrote *The Little Drummer Girl,* the problem with his prose that had been evident in *The Honourable Schoolboy* became a crisis. Buried beneath the flab of le Carré's late style is the muscle of a fine novel. He simply stopped editing. In *The Spy Who Came In from the Cold,* the crackpot Bayswater Library for Psychic Research, an important locale where Liz falls in love with Leamas, is captured in three perfect sentences:

The Library was like a church hall, and very cold. The black oil stoves at either end made it smell of paraffin. In the middle of the room was a cubicle like a witness box and inside it sat Miss Crail, the librarian.

(ch. 4)

Three and one-half lines of type, yet we have the look of it, chill of it, smell of it; plus the mental associations of churches, courtrooms, and prim older ladies who go by "Miss." In *The Little Drummer Girl,* by contrast, almost any location gets line after line of irrelevant, distracting detail, like this:

Their operations room in Freiburg city centre was a hastily rented ground-floor office in a busy main street, their cover the Walker & Frosch Investment Company, GmbH, one of dozens that Gavron's secretariat kept permanently registered. Their communications equipment had more or less the appearance of commercial software; in addition they had three ordinary telephones, courtesy of Alexis, and one of them, the least official, was the Doctor's own hot line to Kurtz.

(ch. 24)

That is only the start. The question is, why did le Carré omit the street name? Was it because it wouldn't mean a thing to the development of the story? *That* is a good reason. But by that logic, why include that this office was "ground-floor" or that the main street was "busy" or that its specific cover name was "Walker & Frosch"? From all this verbiage one does not learn as much as from the description in *The Spy Who Came In from the Cold,* not how it smells or how it feels on the back of your neck to stand there. "Walker & Frosch" or "busy main street" does not have the emotional resonance of "cubicle like a witness box." The description in *The Spy Who Came In from the Cold* tells us only what we need in order to feel how Liz feels, laboring in that hole with Miss Crail observing from her witness box. That mattered. When Liz jumps at the first live man to ever enter that chilly church hall we understand. Le Carré pruned away all else as potential distraction.

*The Little Drummer Girl* paragraph, a mere list, shows the unsuccessful replacement of inspiration by industry. One pictures le Carré, newly serious about his research, scribbling in his notebook about the exact color—"olive"—of the Dreisam, and noting the exceptional width of the window, and its Venetian blinds. It takes great self-discipline to throw out so much labor later, when you realize that readers want to know what will happen to Charlie and do not give a damn if it happens on the Dreisam or the Rhine. After *Tinker, Tailor, Soldier, Spy,* le Carré lacked that self-discipline. Writing *The Little Drummer Girl* he forgot that ten years earlier, even when he needed technical terms about spying, he had not done any research—he simply made them up, nearly two hundred of them. Not only did it not matter, but real spies, like the rest of the world, began to use them.

*The Spy Who Came In from the Cold* is a Rembrandt—one beam of light on St. Bartholomew's knife, another on his thoughtful forehead, the rest, darkness. *The Little Drummer Girl* is a pre-Raphaelite painting, every woodshaving on the carpenter's floor illuminated equally with Christ. The late novels, if they were stripped of unnecessary verbiage, would actually be the same length as the earlier ones. *The Little Drummer Girl* might have been *The Spy Who Came In from the Cold,* but it remains forever two months' work away from it.

No one has remarked how similar Magnus, "the perfect spy," is to Charlie. When le Carré used his left-leaning half sister Charlotte, an actress, as the model for the leftist actress Charlie in *The Little Drummer Girl,* he quite reasonably provided her with a father much like the one who made his sister what she was. Not surprisingly, Magnus Pym, who shared that father, seems her brother. *The Little Drummer Girl* could have been called "A Perfect Actress." A confidence man like Ronald—an actor, essentially—would produce, as children, a pair of actors like Charlie and Magnus, both playing multiple roles under multiple names, Charlie on stage and Magnus in the "theatre of the real" as the novel terms it (ch. 12). Both are observers and mimics who use their skills to manipulate an audience (much as a novelist does, we note). Swindler, Actress, Novelist, Spy: Le Carré has now biopsied each profession, and shown them to be a family.

At the end of *The Little Drummer Girl,* Charlie can no longer act on stage, for she has "no stomach any more—and, worse, no understanding—for what passed for pain in Western middle-class society" (ch. 27). The book is meant to be her, and the middle-class audience's, education in the true depth of tragic suffering. The book begins with a suitcase bomb blowing apart an Israeli diplomat's home in West Germany. A child dies. Enter a team of experienced Israeli investigators, headed by a man we will later know as Kurtz. Critics rightly call him a Jewish version of Smiley. In the book he quests for the master terrorist Khalil, whose name is about as close as Arabic can get to Karla, particularly as le Carré pronounces it.

Khalil, the childkiller, is one villain; the next chapter brings out the other, Misha Gavron, Kurtz's chief, a Control-like figure. Gavron, like Smiley's feared American "Cousins," sees life in terms of good and bad groups, not individuals. Smiley wants to remove Karla, but the Cousins are endlessly ready to "bomb 'em all back to the Stone Age" (in the famous words of an American general about the North Vietnamese). Gavron too loves "American-style power-plays." Kurtz races to remove Khalil, before his terrorist provocations win Gavron the votes to bomb entire refugee camps back to the Stone Age. When the operation succeeds too late, "Kurtz's worst fears and Gavron's worst threats were fulfilled" (ch. 27) and the (historical) massive Israeli drive into Lebanon takes place.

American Jews were horrified when, after writing the book, le Carré met with PLO leader Yasir Arafat and decided he was "maligned," a "moderate." Le Carré is speaking in favor of moderation; if he mistakenly (I think) believed Arafat a moderate, that does not change what le Carré's values are.

Similarly, if readers think le Carré mistaken about the Lebanon expedition's strategic necessity, they should notice they are not arguing with le Carré about whether Jews or Israelis are "good" or "bad." Le Carré, emotionally involved with Jews all his life, is far beyond seeing Israel as a monolith. (People who argue that Jews or Israelis are "good" create, I submit, a historically dangerous precedent: the habit of picturing Jews as other than normal disagreeing individuals, as a kind of eerily cohesive mass.) *The Little Drummer Girl* is, in fact, specifically about a battle between factions and individuals—the same factions le Carré described battling in England, and almost the same individuals. Le Carré has even been criticized for doing a Middle Eastern Smiley and Karla Show, but he does it obviously, to bring out our feeling of eternal archetypes in battle everywhere. When Gavron's star ascends, Kurtz's body "seemed to shrink to half its size," his "Slav eyes lost all their sparkle" (ch. 27). Then, after a month of retirement, he "had vigorously resumed his strange running feud with Misha Gavron." Kurtz and Gavron are eternal enemies—how could anyone jell them into one political entity, "the Israelis"? Indeed, if le Carré's works have any single point, it is to express the need to see people as individuals, not as Jews, Germans, Russians, Palestinians.

Gavron's impending invasion is the deadline before which Marty Kurtz must remove the provocateur Khalil. Khalil is as much an enemy of the moderates as Gavron is, and for the rest of the book he will plan to kill the dovish Israeli professor Minkel. First Kurtz locates Khalil's skirt-chasing baby brother, Salim (also known as Michel), who, with a blonde groupie companion had delivered his brother's suitcase bomb. Khalil is kidnapped. Then the dashing Gabi Becker, an Israeli agent, beds a parlor Marxist and Palestinian sympathizer, the actress Charlie (short for Charmian).

The 1970's world le Carré took so seriously in *Naive and Sentimental Lover,* he now, in 1983, finds insufferable. Charlie's commitment to revolution has entailed reading some magazines, sleeping around, taking some drugs, and exchanging politically correct views with her theater friends. A type familiar to, sometimes prominent in, the theatrical and academic worlds, she is mercilessly anatomized. Kurtz and Becker know that she's been to some weekend introductions to "radical thinking" in which she was primarily introduced to "group sex." She and her actor-lover Alastair attended a seminar on "bourgeois Fascism in Western capitalist societies" and signed a resolution against Zionism (ch. 7): "Charlie . . . knew the protest folk songs, and sang them in an angry mannish style." She's gung-ho, the little drummer girl herself. " 'You wait till my revolution dawns,' she'd warn them" (ch. 3). Le Carré means to give this middle-class radical, and the audience, an education in what the tough words Charlie uses so casually actually mean. Charlie will be forced to act in the "theatre of the real." "You've read Frantz Fanon," Kurtz baits her. "Violence is a cleansing force, remember?" (ch. 7).

Becker, torso covered with the scars of real violence and mideast battles, appears among Charlie's friends on a beach filled with middle-class "radicals" at play. " 'Isn't he *fabulous?*' said Lucy loudly. 'I'd have *him* with my salad any day.' 'Me too,' said Willy, louder still" (ch. 3). Becker, the first man of violent action Charlie has personally met, seduces her easily. It is no great achievement, nor is converting this perfect actress to the Israeli cause, once she is in love with him. Becker and Kurtz replace her surrogate family of actors with a new one of friendly young Israeli agents, then offer her what they make out to be the starring role in Kurtz's theatre of the real. Le Carré's concept, reminiscent of Hermann Hesse, is so surreally compelling one becomes furious with him for burying it under an endless drizzle of street locations, window widths, and river colors. The audience has to make out the action as if through a windshield spotted with rain. *The Spy Who Came In from the Cold* was complete by the time *The Little Drummer Girl* has reached the ninth of twenty-seven chapters.

Love letters between Salim/Michel and Charlie are forged—letters that show Michel has told Charlie compromising details about Khalil. Michel, when captured, had been traveling with two hundred pounds of Russian plastic explosives in his car. He is put back into the car, along with the blonde friend he bombed the diplomat's house with, and it is detonated. Terrorists Mesterbein and Helga use Michel's letters to find Charlie, to see what she knows. By stages she persuades them to accept her as Michel's replacement. She is trained in a Lebanese terrorist camp. Charlie, now acting in the theatre of the real, pretends to aid Khalil in blowing up the dovish Israeli Minkel; then, through a planted transmitter, brings Becker to where Khalil has been rewarding himself with her. "She saw Khalil's face burst" as the bullets hit. "She had gone deaf, so she could only vaguely hear her own screaming" (ch. 26). Covered with blood and vomit, she is taken to an ambulance. Reality is too much for this middle-class comedienne. Her mind breaks beneath the weight.

Charlie cannot continue to act in the theatre of the real but, literally and figuratively, she can no longer return to the romantic fluff of Western middle-class life: she cannot say her lines. Kurtz provides for her financially and Becker comes to be her lover at the end, but her last words in the book are "I'm dead, Jose. You shot me, don't you remember?" (ch. 27). *The Little Drummer Girl*'s great success is in making real the oceans of suffering the first world, like a ship, floats on. It makes the word "violence" real again. If the reader is in a university, leaving the book to go back to that world is, oddly, not like leaving a work of art for reality, but like leaving reality to watch people like the younger Charlie acting in a middle-class romantic play.

## THE RUSSIA HOUSE

In the last few weeks of 1989 the Berlin Wall fell, the governments of Czechoslovakia, Poland, Hungary, and Bulgaria broke free of both communism and the Russians, and Romania captured and executed its tyrant of twenty-three years, Ceaucescu. All Europe was in upheaval. *Newsweek* said, "The cold war is over and we have won." The 1 January 1990 edition of *Time* magazine had Mikhail Gorbachev on its cover: "Man of the Decade"; inside, in a photo section titled "Icons of the Cold War," between a picture of Fidel Castro during the Cuban Missile Crisis and one of Senator Joe McCarthy conducting a Communist witch-hunt, appeared Richard Burton as the spy Leamas, from Martin Ritt's 1966 film version of le Carré's *The Spy Who Came In from the Cold*.

The photo shows the moment in which Leamas tries to pull his lover across the Berlin Wall, that icon of the Cold War and the centerpiece of so many le Carré novels. Burton pulls her up desperately by the wrists. The border guards are about to shoot them dead. A few weeks before the article appeared, the Berlin Wall, to the world's astonishment, had been demolished; in the television news the dreaded "Vopo" Wall guards accepted flowers from girls and waved for the cameras.

In that moment all le Carré's novels changed. The Wall, falling, revised them all. They had been novels about a present, about a nuclear stalemate, a balance of terror that the world assumed would persist for hundreds of years, if not forever. When the Wall fell le Carré's novels became historical novels, available to *Time* for use as "icons of the Cold War," icons of the past. The novels were revealed to have been war novels, and the war he wrote about had ended. One might have wondered if le Carré, nearly sixty, his war finished, was finished as well.

But he had already embarked on a new phase. His prophetic *Russia House*, published four months before the Communist bloc collapsed, had the distinction of being the first novel of the post–Cold War era. *The Russia House* is the third of le Carré's star-crossed lovers novels, his ultimate declaration for individual morality above the civic good. Smiley, who had personified that good, has fittingly left the scene. Only the CIA Cousins have any power now, although they politely make use of a few British Establishment pawns like the narrator, a drone called Palfrey. Le Carré's distaste for everything American has become a phobia; all an apologist can say is that the Americans he has been forced to work with all his life have all been agents, either CIA, literary, or Hollywood. Someday he may discover the rest of the country.

Russia, however, he judged extremely well. Rupert, le Carré's half brother, was the London *Independent*'s man in Moscow during the 1980's. He undoubtedly helped. Le Carré also traveled there twice. When he stood by the book in a June 1989 interview predicting "the visible crumbling of power in the Soviet Union, the fragmentation of the Empire," the amazed interviewer wondered if "the cynical le Carré has simply gone soft."

The Leamas/Westerby role is now filled by Barley Blair, a saxophone-playing playboy, heir to a small-time publishing firm which sometimes sends him to Moscow for book fairs. The beautiful, committed Liz Gold role is played by the Russian Yekaterina Orlova ("Katya"), an editor and emissary of Professor Yakov Savelyev ("Bluebird" or "Goethe"), her Sakharov-like lover. Barley nicknames him "Goethe" because of his vision of European unity, beyond the claims of all nation states. Goethe's question is, do we dare to be traitors in order to be faithful to humankind? He sends Barley, via Katya and Niki Landau, a plucky Polish-English Jew, secrets he wants Barley to publish in the West—all on the strength of a drunken conversation they had had years before. Barley, a patriot, instead agrees to work for the "Russia House" wing of the British secret services, who want to acquire Goethe for themselves as a source.

But the Cousins turn out to have completed their acquisition of the British secret services. Barley is to be run not by London but by the people Bill Haydon once called "fascist puritans." When the arrangement leaves Katya in Liz Gold's unprotected position, and the Cousins do not care any more than Control did, Barley does something Leamas and Westerby never dared: he defects to Russia. He makes it seem Katya had been running him as a double agent, instead of vice versa, hands over the CIA's "shopping list" of questions (showing "the Sovs" exactly what the United States does not know) and saves Katya and her children. Like Goethe, he has left the "safe bastion of infinite distrust" and chosen the "dangerous path of love" (ch. 17).

In this, le Carré's third and probably final return to the star-crossed lovers, an ultimate point has been reached. In 1989 Barley acts out treason for his love, which Leamas, in 1963, must have thought of, but suppressed in horror; and his author did too. Love brought Leamas "in from the cold" yet he continues to function as agent until Liz's death. Then all he can do is attempt a suicidal gesture of rescue. Jerry betrays the Circus for the woman he loves, just as Barley betrays it for his Russian lover. Jerry will die. Barley will be allowed to survive. We see a clear progression from Leamas, who in 1963 doubts but obeys, to Jerry, who in 1974 disobeys but must die, to Barley, who in 1989 disobeys but is allowed to live happily ever after. At book's end he is living in Portugal, waiting confidently for Russia to complete its reforms and let Katya join him. The Berlin Wall fell a few months after the novel was published. He probably got his wish.

In *The Russia House,* then, le Carré, following his conscience, finally carries his lifelong individualism to virtually an anarchist position. If individuals follow their consciences, the civic good will take care of itself. The "state" does not exist; it is merely the sum total of its individuals, and if *they* act morally, it must in turn be moral.

In 1991's *The Secret Pilgrim,* le Carré reviewed, in linked stories, his own pilgrimage through the Cold War, and let George Smiley say good-bye. The book topped best-seller lists. Critics applauded his return to his old terse style. Chapter 10, Smiley's adventure with some cufflinks, is as sentimental as Dickens' "Christmas Carol" and as successful.

Like Barley Blair at the end of *The Russia House,* John le Carré looks forward to the future confidently. He is more than sixty now, the Cold War of which he was *the* master novelist is concluded, and one might have pictured him about to enter a decline. Instead, he seems rejuvenated, and has already begun writing about a new era.

## SELECTED BIBLIOGRAPHY

I. COLLECTED WORKS. *The Incongruous Spy* (New York, 1963), includes *Call for the Dead* and *A Murder of Quality,* also published as *The le Carré Omnibus* (London, 1969); *The Quest for Karla* (London and New York, 1982), includes *Tinker, Tailor, Soldier, Spy, The Honourable Schoolboy,* and *Smiley's People.*

II. SEPARATE WORKS. *Call for the Dead* (London, 1961; New York, 1962), republished as *The Deadly Affair* (Harmondsworth, Eng., 1964); *A Murder of Quality* (London, 1962; New York, 1963); *The Spy Who Came In from the Cold* (London, 1963; New York, 1964); *The Looking Glass War* (London and New York, 1965); "Dare I Weep, Dare I Mourn?" in *Saturday Evening Post* (28 January 1967), short story; *A Small Town in Germany* (London and New York, 1968); "What Ritual Is Being Observed Tonight?" in *Saturday Evening Post* (2 November 1968), short story; *The Naive and Sentimental Lover* (London, 1971; New York, 1972); *Tinker, Tailor, Soldier, Spy* (London and New York, 1974); *The Honourable Schoolboy* (London and New York, 1977); *Smiley's People* (London and New York, 1980); *The Little Drummer Girl* (London and New York, 1983); *A Perfect Spy* (London and New York, 1986); *The Russia House* (London and New York, 1989); *The Secret Pilgrim* (London and New York, 1990).

III. SCREENPLAYS. *Smiley's People,* with J. Hopkin (BBC/Paramount Pictures, 1981).

IV. INTRODUCTIONS AND ARTICLES. "To Russia, with Greetings: An Open Letter to the Moscow *Literary Ga-*

zette," in *Encounter,* 26 (May 1966); "The Spy to End Spies: On Richard Sorge" in *Encounter,* 27 (November 1966); introduction to B. Page, D. Leitch, and P. Knightley, *Philby: The Spy Who Betrayed a Generation* (London, 1968; published in New York as *The Philby Conspiracy,* 1968); "At Last, It's Smiley," in the *London Sunday Telegraph Magazine* (21 October 1979); "Was There a Real George Smiley? Yes. No. Maybe," in *Book-of-the-Month Club Newsletter* (1979); introduction to D. McCullin, *Hearts of Darkness* (London, 1980; New York, 1981); "Memories of a Vanished Land," in *Observer Magazine* (13 June 1982); "The Betrayal," in *Observer Magazine* (3 July 1983); "Exiles in the White Hotel," in *Observer Magazine* (3 July 1983); "Hughes of Hong Kong," in the *London Sunday Times* (8 January 1984); "Le Carré: The Dishonourable Spy," in *Harper's Magazine* (December 1986), excerpt from "The Clandestine Muse," a speech given by D. Cornwell at Johns Hopkins University, Spring 1986; "The Unbearable Peace," in *Granta* 35 (Spring 1991).

V. INTERVIEWS. M. Dean, "John le Carré—The Writer Who Came In from the Cold," in *The Listener* (5 September 1974); J. Cameron, "The Case of the Hot Writer," in the *New York Times Magazine* (8 September 1974); M. Barber, "John le Carré: An Interrogation," in the *New York Times Book Review* (25 September 1977); S. Kanfer and D. Fischer, "The Spy Who Came In for the Gold," in *Time* (3 October 1977); G. Hodgson, "The Secret Life of John le Carré," in *Washington Post Book World* (9 October 1977); M. Gross, "The Secret World of John le Carré," in the *London Observer* (3 February 1980); H. McIlvanney, "The Secret Life of John le Carré," in *Observer Magazine* (6 March 1983); A. Gelber and E. Behr, "A Stellar Spymaster Returns," in *Newsweek* (7 March 1983); J. Lelyveld, "Le Carré's Toughest Case," in the *New York Times Magazine* (16 March 1986); P. Assouline, "Spying on a Spymaster," in *World Press Review* (August 1986); V. Orlik, "Spies Who Come In from the Cold War: A Session Between John le Carré and the Soviets," in *World Press Review* (October 1989); A. P. Sanoff, "The Thawing of the Old Spymaster," in *U.S. News and World Report* (19 June 1989), C. R. Whitney, "I Was Heartily Sick of It," in the *New York Times Book Review* (6 January 1991).

VI. CRITICAL STUDIES. R. J. Ambrosetti, "A Study of the Spy Genre in Recent Popular Literature," Ph.D. dissertation, Bowling Green State University, 1973; G. Grella, "John le Carré: Murder and Loyalty," in *New Republic* (31 July 1976); A. Burgess, "Peking Drugs, Moscow Gold: *The Honourable Schoolboy,*" in the *New York Times Book Review* (25 September 1977); C. James, "Go Back to the Cold!: *The Honourable Schoolboy,*" in the *New York Review of Books* (27 October 1977); P. Vaughn, "Le Carré's Circus: Lamplighters, Moles, and Others of That Ilk," in the *Listener* (13 September 1979).

J. Halperin, "Between Two Worlds: The Novels of John le Carré," in the *South Atlantic Quarterly,* 79 (Winter 1980); R. W. Noland, "The Spy Fiction of John le Carré," in *Clues: A Journal of Detection,* 1 (Fall/Winter 1980); V. S. Pritchett, "A Spy Romance: *Smiley's People,*" in the *New York Review of Books* (7 February 1980); J. Kennaway, *The Kennaway Papers* (New York, 1981), a memoir largely concerning le Carré; A. Rothberg, "The Decline & Fall of George Smiley: John le Carré and English Decency," in *Southwest Review,* 66 (Autumn 1981); J. Wolcott, "The Secret Sharers: *The Little Drummer Girl,*" in the *New York Review of Books* (14 April 1983); J. Atkins, *The British Spy Novel: Styles in Treachery* (London and New York, 1984); L. O. Sauerberg, *Secret Agents in Fiction: Ian Fleming, John le Carré, and Len Deighton* (New York, 1984); P. E. Lewis, *John le Carré* (New York, 1985); D. Monaghan, *The Novels of John le Carré: The Art of Survival* (Oxford and New York, 1985).

T. Barley, *Taking Sides: The Fiction of John le Carré* (Philadelphia, 1986); F. Conroy, *"A Perfect Spy,"* in the *New York Times Book Review* (13 April 1986); S. Knight, "Re-Formations of the Thriller: Raymond Chandler and John le Carré," in *Sydney Studies in English,* 12 (1986–1987); D. Monaghan, *Smiley's Circus: A Guide to the Secret World of John le Carré* (London 1986); H. Bloom, ed., *John le Carré* (New York, 1987); M. Denning, *Cover Stories: Narrative and Ideology in the British Spy Thriller* (London and New York, 1987); K. M. Radell, "The Triumph of Realism over Glamour: Martin Ritt's Realization of le Carré's *The Spy Who Came In from the Cold,*" in D. Radcliff-Umstead, ed., *Transformations: From Literature to Film* (Kent, Ohio, 1987); P. Wolfe, *Corridors of Deceit: The World of John le Carré* (Bowling Green, Ohio, 1987); A. Bold, *The Quest for le Carré* (New York, 1988); J. R. Cohn, "The Watch on John le Carré," in *Studies in the Novel,* 20 (Fall 1988); J. Geoghegan, "The Spy Who Saved Me: A Thriller Starring John le Carré," in the *New York Times Book Review* (4 December 1988); W. Walling, "John le Carré: The Doubleness of Class," in *Columbia Library Columns,* 37 (February 1988); G. Hempstead, "George Smiley and Post-Imperial Nostalgia," in R. Samuel, ed., *Patriotism: The Making and Unmaking of British National Identity,* vol. 3 (London, 1989).

*Critique: Studies in Contemporary Fiction,* 31 (Winter 1990), issue dedicated to le Carré.

# DORIS LESSING
(1919– )

## Michael Thorpe

### LIFE AND ATTITUDES

DORIS LESSING was born of British parents in Kermanshah, Persia, on 22 October 1919. Her father was then managing a bank for the Imperial Bank of Persia; in 1924, disillusioned with business life, he made the romantic retreat to a farm on the high veld in Rhodesia, now Zimbabwe. From Lessing's autobiographical and fictional writings it is clear that, while the farm turned out to be no happy haven for her parents, it became their imaginative daughter's lucky spiritual home. A "neurotic" child, she wasted no more time than she could help in the classroom, at a convent school in Salisbury. She left school at fourteen and became a nursemaid for a time before returning to the farm. Like Olive Schreiner, her nineteenth-century forerunner as novelist of Southern Africa and of an isolated, aspiring girl's life—and her fictional heroine Martha Quest—she was formed on the one hand by her intense response to the living body of Africa, on the other by independent reading and reflection.

A deeply felt recollection of that early life occurs in the second chapter of *Going Home* (1957), an account of her last visit to Rhodesia, in 1956 (after which the Rhodesian government did her the honor of declaring her a prohibited immigrant). There she comments: "The fact is, I don't live anywhere; I never have since I left that first home on the kopje. I suspect more people are in this predicament than they know." It was a house literally made of the earth to which it had long since returned; in her loving, detailed description of it the reader who may have begun with the later Lessing, whose characters insecurely inhabit an urban wilderness—"I have lived in over sixty different houses, flats and rented rooms during the last twenty years and not in one of them have I felt at home"—may be surprised in working back to discover her afresh as one of the major artists of the African landscape and seasons.

Having written two bad novels on the farm and destroyed them, she returned to Salisbury in the guise of a telephone operator. Her life sharply changed direction, turning outward into the flux of the brashly provincial settlers' capital. She immersed herself, she says, in "the kind of compulsive good time described in *Martha Quest."* This led to marriage with a civil servant and the birth of a son and a daughter. When this marriage broke up, she had to leave the children. She remarried, to a German exile named Lessing, who was an active Communist in Rhodesia during the war. When this marriage also failed, she brought out of it with her to England a second son and retained her husband's name.

Establishing herself in London was a struggle at first. In those drab postwar years it was "a nightmare city," but so it might have seemed anyway to one who had known nothing during her first thirty years but bright light, sun, and clean air. Still, it was "the old country": her mother was a Londoner; her father, an Essex man, had talked nostalgically of the tamed, eternally green countryside. In any case, London was the inevitable launching point for an African writer at that time. In an autobiographical sketch opening her contribution to *Declaration* (1957), a symposium of authors' "positions," Lessing notes that she had already written and destroyed six novels, but the one she brought with her, *The Grass Is Singing,* was accepted at once and acclaimed as one of the outstanding novels by a postwar English writer. It was reprinted seven times within five months, and by 1971 the Penguin edition alone had sold 70,000 copies. Her early experiences in London were saved for semiautobiographical treatment until *In Pursuit of the English* appeared in 1960. In tone it is the lightest of her

833

books. By the time it appeared it could already be considered "dated," but it remains a convincing impression of London working-class life in those gray years of postwar austerity and well illustrates the author's insight into people's ordinary lives. The sympathetic outsider's bias is less marked than in the documentaries of George Orwell, but it is there, and mention of it points to some preliminary consideration of her political and social concerns.

Like Martha Quest, the heroine of her *Children of Violence* novels, Lessing had been involved in leftist politics in Rhodesia as a Marxist but not as a card-carrying Communist. Three years after coming to England she joined the Communist Party, but although she left the party in 1956, it was not, she has informed me, simply because of the Soviet invasion of Hungary—"I didn't leave in the sense of some dramatic event, I simply let the thing fade away . . . there were many reasons." In 1954 her first novel dealing explicitly with Martha's political involvement, *A Proper Marriage,* had come out. Her previous books about Africa had, however, all implied a strong concern, humanitarian rather than political, to expose the sterility of white "civilization" in Rhodesia and its unjust dealings with the Africans.

It must be admitted that the English reader who comes to her writing about politics with a knowledge of the literature of the 1930's and 1940's, which reflects a similar swing from optimistic commitment to utter disillusion, will often have a sense of déjà vu. But it is the themes and attitudes that will seem overfamiliar, not the mode of presentation. What Lessing set herself to do, she tells us in her preface to a new edition (1972) of *The Golden Notebook*—and the statement applies equally well to the *Children of Violence* novels—was "to give the ideological 'feel' of our mid-century," and it is hard to think of any other English novelist who has matched her achievement in this respect. Dated such work must be, as her preface concedes, for "'Marxism' and its various offshoots have fermented ideas everywhere, and so fast and energetically that, once 'way out,' it has already been absorbed, has become part of ordinary thinking." Later in the preface she makes the point that takes us to the heart of her political concern: "I think it is possible that Marxism was the first attempt, for our time, outside formal religions, at a world-mind, a world ethic." This was its appeal to her, as it was to the six famous contributors to *The God That Failed,*[1] and to millions without a name.

Her search for "a world ethic" did not end with the recognition that the Marxist dream had turned into a nightmare; unlike many disenchanted writers, at no time had she compromised her artistic integrity in the service of a narrow creed. In her contribution to *Declaration,* "The Small Personal Voice," she justly attacked critics for failing to see that the theme of *Children of Violence* was "a study of the individual conscience in its relations with the collective." The Marxist word "collective" should not mislead: the unity she seeks is older than any political dogma and is the goal of the questing artist, not the politician. She looks back in *Declaration* to the great realists, praising their "humanity" and "love of people"—Leo Tolstoy, Honoré de Balzac, Feodor Dostoevsky, Stendhal—and names Thomas Mann as the last of those whose work was capable of "strengthening a vision of a good which may defeat the evil" (today she would surely add Alexander Solzhenitsyn). It may be noted that these names are all European; there is, partially excepting D. H. Lawrence, little precedent in English fiction for the kind of visionary sweep over society, evoked in numerous individual lives, that she aims at. Comparing the English novelists of the 1950's, she criticizes their parochialism; the anti-heroes of John Wain and John Braine are "petty" (her own heroine, Martha, feels alienation but fights it). She accuses the more seriously influential work of Albert Camus, Jean-Paul Sartre, Jean Genet, and Samuel Beckett of a "tired pity," "emotional anarchy," and indulgence in "the pleasurable luxury of despair." Her positive claim for the novelist, on the face of it modest, in fact asks as much of him as can be hoped: "In an age of committee art, public art, people may begin to feel again a need for the small personal voice; and this will feed confidence into writers and, with confidence because of the knowledge of being needed, the warmth and humanity and love of people which is essential for a great age of literature." More recent developments beyond this humanistic attitude will be discussed in the latter parts of this essay, but it remains central to her view of the writer's value, as is shown

---

[1] *The God That Failed: Six Studies in Communism,* by Arthur Koestler, Ignazio Silone, André Gide, Richard Wright, Louis Fischer, and Stephen Spender, edited by Richard Crossman, 1950.

in her lectures of thirty years later, *Prisons We Choose to Live Inside* (1986).

## THE GRASS IS SINGING *AND OTHER AFRICAN STORIES*

WHEN it appeared in 1950, *The Grass Is Singing* at once joined the company of *Heart of Darkness, Mister Johnson,* and *Cry, the Beloved Country* as one of the few profound explorations of the tragedy of the white man's presence in Africa. Lessing's characteristic strength was already refined and matured. Though the subject cries out for the liberal's moral indignation, her narrative is controlled throughout. There is commentary, but we are so completely immersed in the inward study of a claustrophobic "double solitude" ("The world was small, shut in a room of heat and haze and light") that it never obtrudes. It is restricted to the barest details, and seldom does Lessing even allow herself irony; the story could speak for itself.

The epigraphs from *The Waste Land* and the "Author Unknown" point at the novel's double purpose: to show the true nature of "white civilization" in settled Africa and to write a parable of the coming overthrow of white oppression by black force. To achieve these aims Lessing took the clichés of white supremacy, especially that of white infallibility, and exposed them to the implicit judgment of fallible lives. The whites can survive only so long as the fiction of infallibility sustains them, as Charlie Slatter and the Police Sergeant realize when they seek to cover up the Turners' weakness.

The Turners, neither pioneers nor Boer trekkers, represent the commonplace middle of any class or color; lacking "guts," they find no prop in belonging to a superior race, but above all they are cursed with fatal weaknesses of temperament. This stems from lives that have taught them a fear of insecurity and a hopeless dependence; they are temperamentally unsuited to either enter the settlers' enclave or relieve each other's loneliness. Yet they must make a pretense of strength—Mary in her fatalistic "struggle" with her servants, Dick in imposing his will on both native and fickle land. Their shared tragedy shows them all too human: Dick lacks the absoluteness of a Charlie Slatter, who "like the natives he despised" recklessly rapes the land, bullies his "niggers," and passes on, seeing in Africa no abiding home. Mary and Dick, though conditioned to acceptance of their white role, are nevertheless sensitives, dreamers whom the system cannot afford. In portraying them Lessing evokes a sympathy with which we can see them beyond the stereotype of oppressors as victims themselves—pitiably failing to live up to the inhuman image their race has created. We pity Dick, nursing his grove of young gum trees, his tribute to the land, or clutching a handful of the soil he must forsake. Mary, too, is pitiable; for her hot Africa has been the perpetual antagonist, yet the same country can offer every cool June, as it does on her last morning, a glimpse of delusory peace, even a transcendent vision: "as if she were holding that immensely pitiful thing, the farm with its inhabitants, in the hollow of her hand."

*The Grass Is Singing,* tracing every stumbling step of this couple's fated life together, builds up an almost intolerable tension like their own. We inhabit with them the heat-choked house, watch Moses, the epitome of black force, loom through Mary's eyes, feel how the bush bars escape and only waits to complete the final violation, when bush and native merge in her "last thought." Mary's obsession with Moses, which lesser novelists would have vulgarized, develops as in a dream; she herself never understands it. Ironically, it is with an inferior native that Mary is forced for the first time in her life—with white or black—into "the personal relation." "It was like a nightmare where one is powerless against horror: the touch of this black man's hand on her shoulder filled her with nausea; she had never, not once in her whole life, touched the flesh of a native." What does Moses feel? Jealousy, clearly, of the new white assistant who stands between him and Mary, but at the end Lessing retires, like Joseph Conrad in his Malayan stories—though without Conrad's rhetoric—from the incomprehensible: "what thoughts of regret, or pity, or perhaps even wounded human affection were compounded with the satisfaction of his completed revenge, it is impossible to say."

*The Grass Is Singing* was soon followed by Lessing's first collection of short stories with an African setting, *This Was the Old Chief's Country* (1951), *Martha Quest* (1952), and *Five* (1953)—five novellas, of which four are set in Africa. (*Martha Quest,* the first volume of *Children of Violence*, will be discussed later.) The early African stories and novellas were in 1964 combined with other stories published or written up until 1963 to form a collection of thirty pieces entitled *African Stories* (reprinted in two volumes in 1973).

In a preface to *African Stories* Doris Lessing recalls that her first two books "were described by reviewers as about the colour problem ... which is not how I see, or saw, them." The reviewers' bias was, of course, symptomatic of what was in the early 1950's an awakening interest in the problem. Her deeper concern, already evident in the compassionate handling of her first novel, was with the *human* problem: "colour prejudice is not our original fault, but only one aspect of the atrophy of the imagination that prevents us from seeing ourselves in every creature that breathes under the sun." This perception is reinforced by her vision of "Africa which gives you the knowledge that man is a small creature, among other creatures, in a large landscape." This attitude infused her work from the beginning; only once does a narrow didacticism limit her achievement, in the long story from *Five* entitled "Hunger," a failure, as she recognizes in the preface, because she deliberately set out to write a story of social purpose. Although she is convincing in her attempt to bring us close to Jabavu's experience from primitive hut to city shebeen, the story as a whole conforms to the "Joe comes to Jo'burg" morality tale, of the native "child's" corruption by the evil white city. Ironically, perhaps because of its very predictability, "Hunger" has been, she thinks, "the most liked."

Another reason why "Hunger" may seem to fail is the reader's inevitable doubt about the authenticity of the white writer's adoption of the African's viewpoint. Nowhere else, if one excepts so universally intelligible a story of sexual jealousy as "The Pig," does Lessing attempt this. As with Moses in *The Grass Is Singing*, she confines herself to what she has observed and, within plausible limits, imagined. Her main business is with the white settlers she knows best; in portraying their lives she inevitably includes, but does not concentrate upon, racial problems.

In fact two-thirds of the African stories are about the personal lives of the white settlers, with the natives in the background. Lessing refuses to limit herself to the doctrinaire viewpoint that because the monstrous shadow of the racial conflict blots out the African sun, it is impossible to write on any other topic or to treat the white oppressor as an ordinary human being. In Africa, as elsewhere, ordinary people are preoccupied with their own loves, ambitions, and dreams: great sensitivity in these areas may lie side by side with an indifference, conditioned from infancy, to the quality of the lives of those considered "inferior." (Consider the irrelevance of the relatively modern concept of "social conscience" to our response to the novels of Jane Austen and much of the work of Henry James and even George Eliot.) Few can become heroes or self-sacrificing martyrs in any condition of life—and few indeed can be masters of their own lives. The pathetic, sometimes moving, ordinariness of the supreme race is one of the abiding impressions these stories leave; in their fears and insufficiency they are simply and vulnerably human. This is brought out in a wide range of subtle studies: "Eldorado," where the possessed dreamer represents those hundreds who fail for every one who succeeds in converting the far country into the material stuff of dreams; "Old John's Place" and "Getting Off the Altitude," in which the child's unblinking eye searches out the shabbiness of adult lives behind the prosperous, full-living face; "Lucy Grange" and "Winter in July," taut studies of the emotional cost to those numerous lonely women sacrificed to the obsessed settlers' lust for the land; and, at a lower social level, we meet in "A Road to the Big City" the white counterparts of Jabavu, no less than he prey to a cruelly deceptive dream.

That loose political category, "white," is broken down under the novelist's eye into a spectrum of shades of opposition and difference. Two of her most complex renderings of this awareness are "The Second Hut" and "The De Wets Come to Kloof Grange." We find in these not only the traditional antagonism between Englishman and Afrikaner but a deep exploration of the pathetic inner lives of people struggling, as all do, to build themselves a secure world to live in. There are no simple contrasts. In "The Second Hut" the English pair and the Afrikaners alike are struggling to cling to the last shreds of dignity and what they call life in an Africa—natural as well as human—bent on expelling them. Although the Van Heerdens, living "native," obviously have the greater capacity for survival, for both pairs of white intruders the country offers only an ironic promise and fertility and a passage to a further "grey country of poverty." In both this story and "The De Wets Come to Kloof Grange," as in so much of the African writing, the isolated women attract strongest feeling. Major Carruthers' wife takes to her bed, while Major Gale's has built a more soothing, but nonetheless fragile, retreat in her eighteenth-century English room and tamed two acres of garden—"she had learned to love her isolation." Upon this intrudes the unwanted presence of the new Afrikaner overseer's young wife, Betty, bringing with her the passion and disquiet Mrs. Gale has long since shed. She brings, too, a disturbing affinity for the Africa beyond the English garden, for the river in the "green-crowded gully," with its "intoxicating heady smell": this Mrs. Gale has learned to ignore, raising her gaze to *her* hills," but to the brash girl it is "a lovely smell" and she walks alone through the bush to seek it rather than Mrs. Gale's reluctant companionship. Just as Van Heerden's wife in "The Second Hut" finds content in her droves of children: it is they who collaborate, however crudely, with "Africa," while the finer whites pale behind their gentlemanly ideal. Mrs. Gale glimpses this truth when, after Betty has pretended to run away, she "hated her garden, that highly-cultivated patch of luxuriant growth, stuck in the middle of a country that could do this sort of thing to you so suddenly"; but when she learns the girl's flight was faked, a provoking demand for her husband's love, she rejects her insight and labels it "savage." In such stories Lessing is as powerful as Lawrence, blending revelation of her characters' inner lives with an intense evocation of setting and atmosphere to expose simultaneously the flaws in both character and society.

Where Lessing does write explicitly of the "color problem," what interests her most is not the crass exercise of white power, but the complex predicament of the "good" white. Excellent examples are "Little Tembi," "No Witchcraft for Sale," and the ironic novella from *Five*, "A Home for the Highland Cattle." "Little Tembi" explores the pathetic outcome of a well-intentioned white mistress' nursing of a sick African boy, who later develops so jealous a dependence upon her affection that he turns into a petty criminal, stealing to gain attention. It brings out with moving irony the risk involved in the stock attitude the Jane McClusters adopt when they approach the native sympathetically—"They are just like children, and appreciate what you do for them." In "No Witchcraft for Sale," as in "Little Tembi," the good mistress' humane treatment of her cook is at bottom dangerously self-gratifying—"she was fond of the old cook because of his love for her child." The cook, a "mission boy," collaborates in his mistress' comfortable view of the white-black relation as "God's will." When a tree-snake spits in the little baas's eye, Gideon heals it with a mysterious root from the bush, but afterward, when the whites want him to lead them to where it can be found, he hoodwinks them. It remains Gideon's secret, "the black man's heritage," which lies deep below the white man's shallow possession of the land. Gideon has the last, unconsciously ironic word: "Ah, Little Yellow Head, how you have grown! Soon you will be grown up with a farm of your own."

Lessing's most sustained ironic treatment of the dilemma of the newer-minted white liberal is "A Home for the Highland Cattle." Marina Giles

was that liberally-minded person produced so plentifully in England during the thirties... somewhere in the back of Marina's mind had been a vision of herself and Philip living in a group of amiable people, pleasantly interested in the arts, who read the *New Statesman* week by week, and hold that discreditable phenomena like the colour-bar and the black-white struggle could be solved by sufficient goodwill... a delightful picture.

It all comes down to something more basic—the servant problem, dear to our Victorian forebears, but which nowadays one goes abroad to encounter. While Philip, her agriculturist husband, pursues the African's well-being in his practical, worthwhile way, Marina struggles in their semidetached box at 138 Cecil Rhodes Vista (wicked name) to practice human equality upon her "boy," Charlie. From the beginning Charlie is groping to comprehend this new variety of "madam," and clearly it will not be long before he takes advantage of her weakness.

As a central serio-comic symbol, Lessing has chosen one of those Victorian pictures of highland cattle ("Really, why bother to emigrate?"), left in Marina's keeping by Mrs. Skinner, her landlady. Marina, naturally, abhors it, but Charlie seems to admire it—an admiration dimly connected, she supposes, with the part played by cattle in tribal life "that could only be described as religious." This part is the use of cattle as *lobola*, or bride-price, now as shown in this story in a pathetic state of decay. Gradually, Marina works herself into a false position: her attempts to treat Charlie more humanely "spoil" him; she becomes so embroiled in his personal life that she lands in the ancient role of white paternalist, with the African as foolish child. Her attempt to get him married to Theresa, his pregnant girlfriend, brings the picture into play. Thinking it valuable, Charlie has the bright idea of presenting it to Theresa's father in lieu of *lobola;* and Marina, betraying her white integrity, agrees to give it to him. She and Philip drive the pair and the picture out to the wretched location where the father lives, only to receive from the broken-down old man a nostalgic homily on the degeneration of the old ritual and courtesies. Nevertheless, he accepts the picture. Philip and Marina drive back, grim but little wiser, leaving the couple unbeknown to them to celebrate in an illicit liquor den.

The sequel is no less sordid. When Mrs. Skinner gets an inkling on her return what those "white kaffirs" have done with her precious picture, she has no difficulty in getting Charlie arrested for stealing a few worthless objects, including a "wooden door-knocker that said *Welcome Friend.*" Later Marina, by now a truly colonial madam in a smarter suburb, passes a file of handcuffed prisoners in a street "in this city of what used to be known as the Dark Continent," thinks she recognizes Charlie among them but, intent on discovering that "ideal table" at once, dismisses the thought. Her well-intentioned but amateurish meddling has caused both his misfortune (although he accepts it with easy philosophy) and her tired indifference. In this story, exercising a light but firm ironic control comparable to E. M. Forster's in *A Passage to India,* Lessing has, like that earlier analyst of the inner contradictions of imperialism, subtly exposed the perils of liberal efforts at "connection," if unsupported by extraordinary character and intelligence.

Marina is a "liberal" outsider; if she utterly fails, what more can be expected of those who grow up conditioned to acceptance of the system? We glimpse in "No Witchcraft for Sale" how the white child is formed to rule; he is unlikely ever to begin to imagine affinity with the native. More deeply, "The Old Chief Mshlanga" exposes through the eyes of a sensitive, solitary girl, who has herself never known any home but Africa, the ignorant assumptions that perpetuate master racism. It is an intense moment of wakening for her to realize that "this was the Old Chief's Country" and a painful stage in her maturing to recognize her inherited guilt for dispossessing him. The child's-eye view provides a naive naturalness of response and a strong focus of values; its advantages are most fully explored in "The Antheap," from *Five.* At its center is a sensitive white child, Tommy Clarke, who questions the double standard he is expected to live by as he grows older; forbidden to play with "a lot of dirty kaffirs . . . now you're a big boy," he feels something vital is lost and "wept bitterly, for he was alone." While his father's boss, Macintosh, grubs a fortune from the antheap, Tommy forms substitute playmates from clay and gives them names—a striking contrast in the exploitation of the African earth. One figure Tommy names Dirk —after a "kaffir" boy whose lighter color intrigues him. It is fitting that Dirk should be one of Macintosh's half-caste children: as the illicit bond between these boys strengthens, through their hard-won friendship Lessing is naming the price that the Macintoshes of Africa should be made to pay for their reckless abuse of the land and its people. The forced union between the two worlds has produced that most tragic being, the "colored," accepted by neither; he is in the flesh inextinguishable witness to the whites' double standard. In tracing the boys' love-hate relationship through the years and the baffled response of old Macintosh, Lessing concentrates on the play of emotion among groping, passionate people, letting our sense of the "problem" emerge without insistence. The boys' "victory" is equivocal: "now they had to begin again, in the long and difficult struggle to understand what they had won and how they would use it."

"The Antheap" is the one story in which connection is really achieved, and then it is between white and colored, not white and black—in the circumstances the only probable connection. Elsewhere, the most that can be hoped for is a fair give-and-take in the master-servant relationship, such as exists in " 'Leopard' George" until the white master blunders ignorantly through his favorite African's sensibilities. And, ultimately, through his own: for that "undeveloped heart" (E. M. Forster's phrase) is tragically immature, slow to grasp connections, not nonexistent. In a story similar in theme to " 'Leopard' George" but more strongly dramatized, "The Black Madonna," Lessing uses in a way reminiscent of Forster the Italian artist Michele to point to the want of "heart" in "a tough, sunburnt, virile, positive country contemptuous of subtleties and sensibility." In her portrayal of the Captain we see how the double standard divides mind and heart against each other: "You can't have a black Madonna," the Captain protests, seeing no contradiction in his assumption that you *can* have a black mistress, his "bushwife" Nadya. "Black peasant Madonna for black country," answers Michele simply. Under the skin the Captain senses the true meaning of this—in human as in spiritual love— but fears to let it out. So it remains at the end; Michele, like Forster's Italians, is potentially a liberating agent, but the offer is declined. The Captain, when Michele visits him in hospital, refuses to accept the picture of the black girl, but, when the white-haired Italian leaves, turns his face to the wall and silently weeps. After an acid beginning, "The Black Madonna" develops into one of Lessing's most compassionate portrayals of the white man's tragedy. The necessity to maintain an impregnable front before "the lesser breeds," the male drive needed to "tame" the land, must warp the personal life at its deepest levels.

Together, *The Grass Is Singing* and *African Stories* provide a complex inner portrait of an anachronistic society, which has failed to adjust to the pace of change; they make us see and feel that it consists of people little different from ourselves, who demand understanding, even sympathy, as well as judgment. This can surely be more deeply felt by English readers today in what has itself become, since Lessing's African writing first appeared, a multiracial society.

## CHILDREN OF VIOLENCE

THE *Children of Violence* quintet (1952–1969) takes us from an African experience as remote and closed as that of Schreiner's *The Story of an African Farm* through layer upon layer of Anglo-colonial society, out of Africa altogether to London, where Lessing's heroine's life closes in again, a life of rooms, flats, decaying claustrophobic houses, in each phase deepening the study of "the individual conscience in its relation with the collective." Lessing's narrative owes nothing to structural experimentation and supplies little debatable symbolism. As her heroine's Bunyanesque name, Martha Quest, and the title of the series suggest, she does not mask her intentions. Several modern novelists, following Marcel Proust, have used the novel sequence, centering upon one character's experience but giving a detailed impression of movement through time. In English we think of Ford Madox Ford, Evelyn Waugh, Joyce Cary, Anthony Powell, Lawrence Durrell, C. P. Snow; and the form continues in Edward Upward's political trilogy and the work of younger novelists such as Frederic Raphael. How can we distinguish Doris Lessing's series from these? Most obviously, for its African subject matter, as a narrative of the never-to-be-repeated experience of growing up in an isolated white settlers' enclave and striving, like Schreiner's Lyndall in the nineteenth century, to move outward into a world of fuller experience and wider values. Second, in centering upon a woman's experience, to a degree unmatched in intensity since Virginia Woolf. Further, while "feminist" would be a less dubious label to attach to Lessing than Woolf, her fiction stands in a *critical* relation to the question of the position of women and is no mere instrument of it. The sequence is also (like Cary's and Upward's) one of those rare works that treat politics seriously, without reducing the characters to puppets.

All these aspects except the political (initially relatively slight) combine in the strong first volume, *Martha Quest* (1952), which covers the period from Martha's critical awakening in adolescence to her first marriage. The opening pages indicate the major themes and sketch Martha's heavy consciousness of herself—derived from books—in relation to them and the spirit of her time:

She was adolescent, and therefore bound to be unhappy; British, and therefore uneasy and defensive; in the fourth decade of the twentieth century, and therefore inescapably beset with problems of race and class; female, and obliged to repudiate the shackled women of the past.

We watch her seeking to thrust outward away from her parents' "ironic mutual pity" and her father's "dream-locked" existence, but see that she is —as so many of Lessing's protagonists will be—a dreamer too, and will have a hard journey toward her "noble city" where there is "no hatred or violence"; the traditional symbol of the ideal city lives in Martha's imagination until her death, and provides the binding symbol of the series (discussed at length in this author's "Martha's Utopian Quest," *Commonwealth*, 1972). While lucidly defining Martha's typical dilemma, Lessing nevertheless gives us a complex awareness of the "many selves" Martha must choose from in her individual effort to take "the responsibility of being one person, alone," together with a sympathetic insight into the baffled lives of those who surround her. Although she sees the colony as in "a sickness of dissolution," Martha, a child of her time and place, is infected herself. One self is drawn to the false unity, the "system of shared emotion," of the Club —this is the modern girl who "knew everything was allowable"; another, deeper self responds to individuals whom she sees as trying like herself to forget a painful separateness. Hence the shameful affair with the despised Jew, Adolph King, and her marriage out of tenderness and a willed conviction of a shared aspiration to freedom to Douglas Knowell. Yet beneath all is a deeper self:

the gift of her solitary childhood on the veld; that knowledge of something painful and ecstatic, something central and fixed, but flowing . . . a sense of movement, of separate things interacting and finally becoming one, but greater—it was this which was her lodestone, even her conscience.

(pt. 4, ch. 1)

This description of Martha's "individual conscience" is reinforced more strongly in this than in the later books by Lessing's passionate recollection of the body of Africa; it links her heroine with the romantic impulse of aspiration toward a cosmic unity beyond the reach of any political or social idea—a link we may lose sight of as the series progresses but which the final novel confirms and carries forward.

Of the first four novels, *Martha Quest* leaves the most rounded impression: we see Martha's restless development against the permanent reality of her spiritual Africa; African setting and atmosphere are dense, suggesting a true point of departure and potential return. The next three novels trace her erratic movement through flawed relationships in the makeshift colonial capital toward the desired but distant establishment of herself as a "free spirit"—in which attempt, despite her modern advantages, she is hardly less hampered by convention and conformity than are George Eliot's Dorothea or James's Isabel Archer. Disenchantment with the suburban "bourgeois" marriage, which threatens to reduce her to wifely dependence, has become a stock theme now, but it was not so in the 1950's. *A Proper Marriage* (1954) remains distinguished for its calm characterization and objective analysis of a subject too often treated by later writers with feminist indignation; we see that Douglas, no less than Martha, is the victim in this dishonest marriage, and both are guilty. (Lessing is no bigoted feminist in her portrayals of men: see in *The Habit of Loving* [1957] "The Witness" and "He," and in *A Man and Two Women* [1963] the title story, and even "One Off the Short List" with its distasteful compulsive seducer.)

At the end of the second novel Martha has shed husband and daughter and temporarily, at least, substitutes for the failed personal relationship attachment to the "collective," influenced by the young Communists in the Royal Air Force, a new and utterly alien element in Zambesia. Although she has a brief, happy affair with one of them, *A Ripple from the Storm* (1958) mainly explores the ramifications of love for "the people," which for Martha may also be seen as an outlet for her romantic "passion for the absolute" (to quote the novel's epigraph from Louis Aragon). As such, it is destined for disillusion. Unlike mid-1930's Europe, the colony offers the tiny Communist group no footing in the "mass"; it is cut off from its natural base among the Africans by their ignorance and suspicion. Repeating recent European history, the group forms a reluctant alliance with the Social Democrats and becomes fragmented, but it is the flaws of its members that Lessing brings out so shrewdly. She shows how political purism may betray individual weakness and, in practice, destroy the individual it pretends to serve. Even Anton Hesse, who may be termed Martha's ideological second husband, a German who has suffered for his Marxist beliefs, becomes insidiously seduced by bourgeois "furniture." Only Athen, the doomed Greek, who is presented sympathetically but unsentimentally, possesses a felt, unselfish Communism. Futility is the mood of *A Ripple from the Storm*, and it will repel readers who crave romance with their politics (which would have been a fictional combination indeed for that place and time); but since neo-Marxist revolutionism continues to sacrifice the individual to a "collective" absolutism, it remains a valuable cautionary tale.

While the political theme continues in *Landlocked* (1965), which covers the late 1940's, it is felt increasingly as mere background to Martha's revitalized emotional life. This novel is the least satisfying of the series, largely because of its very success in reflecting through a fragmented narrative the tedium and frustration, the truly "landlocked" condition of the reactionary colonial backwater. The old political scene is dissolving and new African radicals and white extremists are taking over, but Martha has discovered love and "from this centre she now lived." Her love for Thomas Stern, the Polish Jewish peasant, snatched at intervals in the loft at the foot of his brother's garden, is insulated from the world of argument at first and reaches a lyrical intensity; it is the most obviously "Lawrentian" episode in her work. It cannot last: Thomas, a child of violence, goes to Israel to fight for the Promised Land and when he returns is utterly changed. After his death, of blackwater fever, caught in an equivocal Kurtz-like involvement with tribal Africans, Martha has no reason to remain; her father dies too, so ending a chapter in the "quicksand" of Martha's irritable, compassionate embroilment with her parents, which is tenderly drawn throughout the series. Martha now yearns toward the liberating sea, and beyond it England—the traditional bourne of the "free spirit." Africa has shrunk to a backdrop of arid immensity; Zambesia is abandoned to the "enemy," the racist settler Sergeant Tressell.

The title of *The Four-Gated City* (1969), the final volume in the series, harks back to Martha's youthful vision of a utopian city upon the veld (suggestive in shape of Campanella's fifteenth-century utopian republic, City of the Sun—though this was unknown to Lessing), but, though Africa reappears in the prophetic appendix as a refuge from nuclear holocaust, London is the novel's city.

At first it is shabby postwar London, physically and psychically desolate. There, inevitably, Martha seeks the working class, the mythical "proletariat" Africa denied; she finds them warm but depressing, no ideal beings (a realization *In Pursuit of the English* had already expressed, more lightly, in 1960). Martha's renewed quest is neither political nor sexual in emphasis: neither can "create" her now; more active and independent than before, she embarks on inward self-exploration, now clearly her chief concern. Yet at the same time her life at the center of the distraught, liberal Coldridge household is a focus of widening responsibility toward and understanding of others, not an engrossment with self. There are no absolutes now, individually or collectively. The novel's great length is justified by its intensive exploration of the most complex and vital experience. Particularly impressive are the portrayals of "this remarkable traffic between parents and children," in both Martha's last painful confrontation with her mother and the conflict between the adults and the questioning youth of the 1960's, and the tracing of Martha's anguished inner probing whose pace is set for her by Mark Coldridge's "mad" wife, Lynda. Not since Virginia Woolf has an English novelist explored so thoroughly the labyrinth of the strained sensitive mind, or pleaded so strongly for a more enlightened science of the mind than a dogmatic psychiatry provides. In this area Martha's individual conscience reaches out toward a deeper connection with the needs of the "collective" than any abstract cause could offer, probing "this strange disease of modern life" (Matthew Arnold's phrase) at its root. We may be unable to share Martha's newfound hope in extrasensory powers or Lessing's prophetic vision of the survival, after atomic devastation, of a scattering of "new children" with an inborn telepathic capacity to "see" and "hear" more finely: "grown up . . . mentally and emotionally . . . they are beings who include that history [of this century] in themselves and who have transcended it." To them the dying Martha consigns the guardianship of the "four-gated city" some future race will build. The climax offers as the only hope a faith in evolutionism derived, in Lessing's version, not from positive Darwinism but (as several of the novel's epigraphs indicate) from her study of Sufism[2] in the writings of Idries Shah. However skeptically one views this "solution"—Shah too closely resembles the Shaw of *Back to Methusaleh*—*The Four-Gated City* is an admirable attempt to "strengthen a vision of a good," to make us see and feel how we do and should live now and here. When it appeared, it seemed likely to become her most influential work, but fascination with break-

---

[2]Sufism is an Islamic form of mystical monism; in recent years it has had, like Hindu mysticism, a growing appeal in the West. See A. J. Arberry, *Sufism,* 1950, and Idries Shah, *The Way of the Sufi,* 1968.

down as "higher sanity" has cooled: it seems more likely that *The Golden Notebook* will stand as her major novel.

## THE GOLDEN NOTEBOOK

UNTIL *The Four-Gated City* appeared, *The Golden Notebook* (1962) had stood for several years as Lessing's most ambitious work. It may remain her best known; the interest it has aroused as one of *the* novels of our time was marked by its reissue in a hardback edition with a lengthy author's preface in 1972.

In this preface she states that her intention was to follow the great European—not English—novelists of the last century in producing a comprehensive work "describing the intellectual and moral climate" of her time, not to produce (as weekly critics eagerly assumed) a feminist broadside. She had already demanded in her *Declaration* essay, "Why should the sex war be offered as a serious substitute for social struggle?" She aspired instead to meet the need for the more varied view of the human condition such as a Tolstoy or a Stendhal could provide. *The Golden Notebook,* with a writer now as protagonist, is about this need and how hard it is in our time for the novelist to meet it. The action is a purgative process that may—or may not—fit Anna to convey "a vision of a good."

Being a "free woman" is certainly a strong twin theme—and the more general one; it is "the disease of women in our time," especially for those who like Anna attempt to "live the kind of life women never lived before." But this is inseparable from the universal theme of the individual's isolation: in a world that supplies no dependable values, Anna, like Martha Quest, must make her life as she goes along, or be torn and fragmented by it. Like many people, she knows "I'm scared of being alone in what I feel" and fears emotion in a hostile world, but as an artist, "driven to experience as many different things as possible," she has to face the question of responsibility. If literature is concerned with the self, it is also concerned with self-control: in the beginning Anna cannot write because she fears spreading her feelings of "disgust and futility" (contrast the contemporary anti-hero's indulged alienation); by the end she has learned to "live through" her divided selves, "naming" the horrors. This, for a writer, is also her duty. We do not see Anna's predicament as separate from her society, its ideals and failures; she does reflect these, the frustration and sterility of "living like this" without "a central philosophy," but, forced like Martha to accept the fading of the Marxist dream, she seeks a new center.

Her search is reflected in the book's unusual structure, which despite its bulk is no Victorian "baggy monster" or rag-bag of writer's scraps. There is ample precedent for dislocated narrative in such modern novelists as André Gide (*Les Faux-Monnayeurs* also includes a novelist as a character writing a novel about his experience within the novel), Woolf, James Joyce, Aldous Huxley and, more recently, in the *nouveau roman*. In *The Golden Notebook* the discontinuity reflects not only the novelist's viewpoint but the lack of unity in Anna's life and life as she sees it: hence her writer's block. By means of the Notebooks Anna "divided herself into four" to avoid facing up to the chaos; in one, the Blue, she tries to be honest, and this especially is in the end superseded by the Golden, *all of me in one book*.

The Notebooks punctuate installments of a conventional novel entitled "Free Women," in which Anna herself is a character, using experience in the Notebooks selectively. If "literature is analysis after the event," the Notebooks represent event, "Free Women" the literature or fiction. If we read the Notebooks, then the novel, in that order, we would see how Anna, the unblocked writer of "Free Women," is using her fragmented experience recorded in the Notebooks, compelling it into a *positive* whole, with control, not raw subjectivity. The African material of the Black Notebook that she cannot "use," though it describes some of her most deeply felt experience, disappears. At the center of "Free Women" is the Richard-Tommy-Marion triangle, from which, in the Notebooks, Anna appears excessively detached. The Notebooks are used in Anna's novel as a crucial factor behind Tommy's suicide attempt—absent from the "real," but central in the fiction: thus Tommy becomes Anna's surrogate, he goes through the experience she evaded. After his blinding, Molly comments with tragic irony, "he's all in one piece for the first time in his life." The suicide motif had already been approached by Ella in the Yellow Notebook "novel," but as a fictional projection of her own despair; in placing the Notebooks as a power for evil in "Free Women," Anna is accepting moral responsibility for them.

Previously in the Yellow Notebook we have seen Anna trying to fictionalize her experience, making Ella a simplified, more coherent version of herself. Ella is "not interested in politics"—all the Red material, Anna's albatross, is cast off. In this Notebook occur anticipations of themes that will be converted to positive use in the more integrated Golden Notebook: for example, Paul's image denoting his split attitude to his profession when he tells Ella, "We are the boulder-pushers ... we are the failures" recurs in an almost identical passage in which Anna envisions Paul and Michael merged in a single heroic figure who reassures her, "But my dear Anna, we are *not* the failures we think we are" —the boulder-pushers are needed by the prophets at the summit; finally, Anna can tell Saul that they are both boulder-pushers, and in doing so implicitly accepts for herself the attitude of Mathlong, the African nationalist, described in the Blue Notebook: "He was the man who performed actions, played roles, that he believed to be necessary for the good of others, even while he preserved an ironic doubt about the results of his actions ... this particular kind of detachment was something we needed very badly at this time."

Anna has been blocked as a writer because excessive self-concern has distorted her vision. Parallel with this theme is her struggle toward a fulfilled love, to achieve which she must recognize, as in the artistic sphere, that she cannot "force patterns of happiness or simple life." In the Yellow Notebook the story Ella must write, of "a man and a woman ... at the end of their tether ... cracking up because of a deliberate attempt to transcend their own limits," yet winning "a new kind of strength," foreshadows the "acceptance" born of Anna and Saul's stormy relationship, the subject of the unified Golden Notebook. Although the devils that dominate the first page of the Black Notebook are exorcized on the first of the Golden, this is almost the latter's solitary indication of "happiness." This, Anna notes, is left out, and we are caught up in the violently fluctuating emotions of two people seeking transcendence, breaking each other down, yet building out of mutual self-recognition a new acceptance and control. This is reflected in the reduction of ninety emotional pages of the Golden Notebook to barely ten in the Milt episode of "Free Women": the Anna there, like Ella, is more "intelligent"; Milt, like Saul, can "name" her and she him. They part to write the works they inscribe to each other, to push their boulders as best they can; Anna (with some irony?) also to take up marriage welfare work.

If we see "Free Women," as these comments suggest, as representing Anna's positive reshaping of her experience, we are bound to ask how good a novel it is. Could it stand alone? It is doubtful whether this is a very useful question: we do not read it alone, but as a skeletal piece of fiction whose flesh in "life" the Notebooks provide. They flesh in the depth and complexity of Anna's experience— most strongly evoked in many passages, especially the African Mashopi episodes, which the selective, conventionally shaped novel omits. *The Golden Notebook* must be judged as a whole, whose aim is to explore the plight of the socially responsive and responsible writer in the phase of disorientation and alienation in which we live. The fact that it also explores in depth the dilemma of the "free women," woman's most intimate experience (as in the clinically faithful description of Anna's day, 17 September 1954), is incidental though indispensable to this theme. Lessing's "free spirits," no less than those of the Brontës or George Eliot, have to love and be loved: this need creates the muddle that makes them human—and humanity, no single segment abstracted from it, is the novelist's business. The fact that many readers eagerly abstracted from *The Golden Notebook* ammunition to fight their own local battles is symptomatic of the author's succeeding in what she set out to do. Her protagonist as artist is no remote being, but one who has an uncommon responsiveness to common experience; this is recorded with such fidelity that some readers have overlooked Anna Wulf's primary significance *as artist*—if this is lost sight of, it is impossible to respond adequately to the novel's larger meaning.

*JOURNEYS WITHIN:* BRIEFING FOR A DESCENT INTO HELL; THE SUMMER BEFORE THE DARK; THE MEMOIRS OF A SURVIVOR

*The Golden Notebook* could be done only once. Having made a statement that throws serious doubt on the value of art, the artist might be expected to fall silent. Nevertheless, Lessing, like her fictional "creature," has continued boulder-pushing. We have already considered *Landlocked* and *The Four-Gated City*, the novels that followed *The Golden Notebook* in the 1960's. In these we can trace an intensifying concern with exploring the mind's frontiers: relatively limited in *Landlocked*, in the episode of Thomas Stern's paranoia and breakdown before death, this becomes central in the inner Golden Notebook, where Anna and Saul break down into each other and form new self-knowing personalities, and in the characterization of Lynda and of Martha's arduous struggle to achieve self-transcendence in *The Four-Gated City*. Looking further back, we can see early indications of this development in the portrayal of the unbalanced Mary in *The Grass Is Singing* and in the fluid presentation of Martha's many selves in the earlier novels of the series. (Outside the novels it is at the heart of the African stories about lonely women and is strongly sustained in later "English" stories such as "To Room Nineteen" in *A Man and Two Women*.) It is not, therefore, surprising that this novelist so often loosely associated with such rationalist obsessions as Marxism and feminism should in 1971 publish *Briefing for a Descent into Hell*, a concentrated study of a middle-aged man's mental breakdown and, reflecting her interest in the ego-extinguishing inward vision of Sufism, his confrontation with the God within.

The descent motif, symbolizing man's perilous exploration of inner space in his search for truth, is, of course, as old as literature. The novel's title points back to the heroic journeys to the Underworld of classical literature; in modern times, the fictional prototype is Dostoevsky's *Notes from the Underground* (1864), followed by variations in Joseph Conrad, Franz Kafka, Samuel Beckett, Albert Camus, and many more. Today, under the ever-increasing evidence of civilized man's tragic self-division, few themes are more compelling for the responsible novelist than the dubious meanings of "sanity" and "normality"; he is strongly supported in this by the work of humanist psychologists such as C. G. Jung and, more recently, Michel Foucault and R. D. Laing.

In *Briefing for a Descent into Hell* Lessing cast as protagonist an outwardly successful and established professor of classics, Charles Watkins. We meet him confined to an observation ward, suffering from amnesia. Under sedation, cut off from the social world that gave him identity, he undergoes an inner voyage of great imaginative richness, exploring both the horrors of his journey and its risks of transcendental illumination. In these dreams the perfect city is threatened (as was Martha's) by Yahoo-like creatures that inherit and—like us—degrade it. From above, borne by a blessed White Bird, he looks down upon a warring Earth exposed beneath the Moon's full light, then undergoes a descent into corruption and possible forgetfulness. Interspersed with these inner searchings are the disconsolate voices of Doctors X and Y, who label his dreams religious paranoia and labor to restore his sense of "reality": their role, like Mother Sugar's in *The Golden Notebook*, is treated critically as undermining in its attempt to explain away individual pain by means of a witchcraft of rationality. To Watkins his dreams form a vision of "Knowing. Harmony. God's law," but he cannot cling to the fable. His doctors probe after his outer identity, recruiting through letters the witness of wife, colleagues, friends. These demonstrate both how little he had liked or communicated with others and throw ironic light upon the idea of "personality." The most significant letter, in Watkins' pocket when he is found, is from Rosemary Baines, a woman who had seen him only once, lecturing in a humdrum local hall, but who was moved by some submerged quality in him. It is this quality, unexplored by his outer self, that his "schizophrenia" offers him a chance to approach—but the ego has its defense. Self-deceivingly, Watkins submits to shock treatment, hoping to "remember properly," but as another intuitive observer, the patient Violet Stoke, fears, it turns out "just that—you are Professor Watkins." "Sanity" triumphs and Watkins, "in possession of his faculties again," writes letters in his turn, disengages himself from Rosemary Baines, and returns to the insincerities of his outer life.

*Briefing for a Descent into Hell* is no mere casebook (it may be contrasted in this respect with the fragmentary account of the "ten-day voyage" of Jesse Watkins in R. D. Laing's *The Politics of Experience* [1967]). The fabular night journey within is a vividly imagined divided universe in which anarchy and harmony blend, dissolve, and confront each other in dynamic tension. Counterpointed against this are the studied rationalizations of the doctors and the self-entangled prejudices of the "normal." If, compared to previous novels, it seems under-dramatized, this serves the purpose of deepening its protagonist's isolation. It is a novel strong and forceful in both theme and structure, as economical and self-contained as *The Grass Is Singing*.[3]

*The Summer Before the Dark* (1973) continues the search for the undivided self through a more realistic narrative reminiscent of the early Quest novels, into which is woven an inner motif of dream-discovery. The narrator, who continually interprets the narrative and the protagonist's representative significance, introduces Kate Brown in mid-life, "queen termite" to a family who now need her decreasingly. Confronting "this truth, that the faces and movements of most middle-aged women are those of prisoners or slaves," she senses she must change to meet the cold wind blowing from the future, but—a less individual figure than Martha Quest—she is less apt to choose for herself. During her husband's lengthy absence abroad, she accepts the chance to put her translating ability to work for Global Food, only to become there, as in her family, "tribal mother," a valued organizer of others' lives. She travels to Turkey, then Spain, having drifted involuntarily into an affair with Jeffrey, a thirtyish drop-out who "did not know how he wanted to live." The affair almost comically fails to answer her need: Jeffrey is fretful, restless, yearning after his slipping youth; he falls ill and Kate becomes again the maternal slave. After much patient waiting, she too falls ill, but wills herself back to London and retreat into one of those solitary rooms where Lessing's women confront themselves. Her prolonged illness involves shedding the superficial images of self: "she, Kate Brown, Michael's wife, had allowed herself to be a roundly slim red-head with sympathetic eyes for thirty years." Wasted and unkempt, she achieves, moving into the north-facing room of a basement flat shared with Maureen (another dropout), a potent nullity, free of the sex-shaped cocoon of "other people's recognition of what she had chosen to present." What she is emerging from is pointed at by the dilemma of Maureen's ineffectual escapism, fluctuating between infantile regression, her desire to be herself, or many selves, and a compulsive attraction to rival males in Philip and William, each of whom would impose a "male" order upon her life. Whatever Maureen's choice—if she can choose—it remains uncertain at the novel's close, and Kate scarcely influences it.

The real action of the summer, for Kate, has been her "serial dream" of a stranded seal she must drag through the Arctic waste to the life-restoring sea: "What I think has really been going on," she tells Maureen, "is my dream. It hasn't been all the other things, at all." She feels when her journey is complete in a sun that "seemed to sing" in front of, not behind, her that she has accomplished an act for others, not just herself (the seal she has felt symbolizes her life), but Maureen cannot profit by it: "cages and being shut in are much more my style" (women's lot?). Kate herself can return, strengthened by discovering "the self behind," the capacity to struggle toward self-recognition and survive—to a home that will no longer cage her because she can say, "No: no, no, no, NO—a statement which would be concentrated in her hair." That, untinted now, will image her true stage of life and acceptance of "the dark": aging and death.

The narrative of *The Summer Before the Dark* is tightly controlled, its psychological and psychic meanings constantly pointed: character and action in the literal world are subordinated to the novel's purposeful exploration of midlife crisis. The control excludes the potent threat of schizophrenia in *Briefing*, making a novel that can reach readers at a level closer to the "normal." Kate Brown's apprehension of impending cataclysm at the opening of *The Summer* remains undeveloped but is experienced by her successor (or, more aptly, Martha's), the narrator of *The Memoirs of a Survivor* (1974), a woman living alone who is, significantly, nameless, almost impersonal. Her significance is concentrated not in her "real" life or in the concretely realized action, but in her psychic receptivity and growth.

Marooned in her rooms in a decaying apartment block, in a London through which Kate Brown's cold future wind is blowing, the narrator is witness and interpreter of that breakdown of urban order envisioned in *The Four-Gated City* and *Briefing*. Disorder is no longer elsewhere, "out there": it is in the gangs and migrating bands of the homeless, the slackening powers of government and police, the disintegration of family loyalties and the ethical norms of community. The narrator lives this experience by proxy in the forced growing up of the adolescent Emily, whom a stranger mysteriously leaves with her—together with Hugo, the cat/dog,

---

[3] This discussion of *Briefing for a Descent into Hell* repeats parts of this author's two reviews of the novel in *Encounter* (September 1971) and *The Journal of Commonwealth Literature* (June 1972).

embodiment of fidelity and fearful intuition, whose fate is at risk throughout. The external action focuses upon Emily; with Gerald, her hero of the pavement life, she struggles to build a center of order, to provide a caring center for the outcast children who are slipping into unrestrained savagery. Like Martha in the Coldridge house, the narrator observes the trials of youth with mingled emotions, an anxious compassion for their efforts pitted against her conviction of their futility against "it"—"above all a consciousness of something ending," beyond human control.

The bizarre internal action is the narrator's: more comprehensively than the serial dream of *The Summer*, it is another world of consciousness she can enter, through and beyond her flat's limiting wall. An extension of the complex self, it is inevitably no ideal world, is like the outer world subject to chaos and destruction; its scenes centering upon the young Emily, loveless and oppressed, image the perverted relations that have always obstructed possibilities of wholeness. Yet it also offers a sustaining vision of plenitude: "Gardens beneath gardens," and a personal "presence . . . as pervasive as the rose scent." As the outer action approaches utter breakdown, Emily, who at fourteen has the disenchanted understanding of a Kate Brown, "the jaded woman of our dead civilization," realizes she can "give" no more. A few survivors huddle in the stricken, almost airless room, then the walls dissolve and the worlds converge: "one person I had been looking for . . . was there," "that One who went ahead showing them the way out of this collapsed little world into another order of world altogether." Clearly, this ending is not realistic: the narrator's history, which records the absorption into the transcendent world of the diverse figures foremost in her consciousness throughout, suggests that the whole narrative—"an attempt at autobiography," according to Lessing's words quoted on the dust-jacket—may be read as occurring within a mind struggling to achieve "integration." One uses a Jungian term, but Lessing's acknowledged bent is toward Sufism, which "says that you cannot approach [it] unless you are able to think that a person quite ordinary in appearance and in life can experience higher states of mind. . . . 'Be in the world, not of it,' is the aim" (*Encounter* [August 1972], p. 62). The narrator and her experience accord with this description; mystical vision is indeed scarcely communicable, but it has one striking element: the maternal or Earth Motherly aspect of the "One" renders as beneficent an image that, in human terms, Lessing's fiction has devalued.

### "SPACE FICTION": THE CANOPUS IN ARGOS, ARCHIVES

LESSING prefaces *The Sirian Experiments,* the third volume of the *Archives,* with comments on her intentions and expectations in making her contribution to "this genre of space fiction."[4] Her central concern is shared with that novel's protagonist: "ideas must flow through humanity like tides. Where do they come from?" Her wish, as an imaginative writer, is that "reviewers and readers could see this series . . . as a framework that enables me to tell (I hope) a beguiling tale or two; to put questions, both to myself and to others; to explore ideas and sociological possibilities." As in the Sufi tradition, she (a living "sage") seeks to enlighten by means of teaching-stories whose inner meaning transcends the literal interpretations to which familiar elements may tempt the reader.

The first archive, *Shikasta* (1979), like so much of her earlier work, is a comprehensive diagnosis of our world's condition, but new in its thirty-thousand-year span of vision and the antidote prescribed. Shikasta, "the hurt, the wounded one," put in its humble place in the universal scheme as a colony of Canopus, is viewed compassionately through the eyes of Johor, the Canopean visitor and secret healer. Such, we infer, must be the visionary writer's role—within, yet not of, her human community. Like Johor in the novel, Lessing sees our Earth as in its Last Days, closing a century of destruction; her mission, like his, is to alert a saving remnant who will ensure the continuity and regeneration of life after the apocalypse. The latter part of *Shikasta* enlarges upon and refines the message of the brief appendix to *The Four-Gated City*. It finally banishes her ideal urban vision and points in Old Testament fashion the way back to renewal in desert places.

Those who may have expected Lessing, the Sufi

---

[4]Not her first: the story "Report on a Threatened City" adopts the viewpoint from outer space, chronicling through progress reports by invisible visitors from another planet our insouciant acceptance of inevitable annihilation (in *The Story of a Non-Marrying Man,* 1972).

convert, to have turned aside from our political and social realities, of which she does despair, will find in the Canopean history of Shikasta an authoritative analysis of modern world history. This stresses exploitation of the globe by "the narrow fringes of the north-west" and the iniquitous class system of the dominant nation, the breaking of its power in the World Wars, to be succeeded by "The Age of Ideology." As in *The Golden Notebook* we find vivid symptomatic histories of individuals (thwarted idealists, oppressed women, perverted terrorists) and an exposition of the significance of the generation gap, updated from *The Four-Gated City*. The indictment of *Shikasta* in the book's mock trial of the offending White Races is historically even-handed: while the "shadow city" of *The Four-Gated City* has now engulfed the Western metropolis, Third World resentments are not flattered. Their skeletons—the homemade slave-trade, or entrenched Indian injustice to untouchables—rattle loudly too.

However, the sweep of vision and the ideas are more telling than the fictional effects. The central figure, Johor, in his guise of George Sherban, the inspiring youth leader, is a kind of holy man, whose influence is in inverse proportion to a capacity for persuasive talking, which the reader must take almost wholly on trust. His goodness and the Sufi mystical sense of oneness beyond our straitened reality—reflected in the SOWF (Substance-of-we-feeling) that has drained away from erring Shikasta—remain incommunicable articles of faith, lacking fictive realization. Goodness, like evil, is not readily communicable: evil is an almost melodramatically present malign force whose agents, the Empire Puttiora and its rogue planet Shammat, so far answer all too readily the stereotypes of conventional science fiction.

*The Marriages Between Zones Three, Four and Five* (1980) has little or nothing to do with *Shikasta* and is in no way a sequel; this is typical of the series as a whole. In *Shikasta* the three Zones are mentioned in passing by Johor as "lively and for the most part agreeable places, since their inhabitants are those who have worked their way out of and well past the Shikastan drag and pull." What this means is unclear. The Zones are governed, respectively, by a pacific matriarchy (Three), a militaristic, male-dominated hierarchy (Four), and a combative Amazonian queen (Five). The leaders and the ways of life they nurture correspond to certain stereotypes of human personality. The subject matter is ahistorical: government, war, racism, power struggles, and areas of influence are not particularized. Male and female qualities, struggle and compromise, monopolize action.

More than *Shikasta* the narrative "beguiles," with the qualities of fable, legend, and myth. "Anon" might have written it, though with a clearly personal tone that is serene, humorous, tolerant of man's (and woman's) posturings in the search for love and dominance. The central episode, and the main subject of the Zone Three chroniclers' narrative, is the account of the marriage ordained by "The Providers" between Al-Ith, the queen of their Zone—peaceable, paradisiac (man the animals' friend, understanding their language), artistic, and intuitive—and the warrior king, Ben Ata, of Zone Four. Al-Ith, the unifying feminine, labors to soften her boorish husband, who slowly responds to his utmost; their son will rule Zone Three and perhaps combine his parents' best qualities. Ben Ata must subsequently obey a new ordinance to marry the wild and willful queen of Zone Five, where anarchy rules; he eases this difficult union with the deeper understanding Al-Ith has nurtured —while she, believing "we must find out what we are for," withdraws, finally to disappear into Zone Two, the country of higher consciousness few dare explore.

The familiar quest is not this novel's focus: its main action is animated by Lessing's warm and tolerant reexploration of pleasures, pains, and errors by a man and a woman seeking a balanced, understanding union. Masculine and feminine dissolve into a complex, volatile striving; the "sting of otherness" allows no relaxed consummation. The *Marriages* can be relished with the free commitment proper to myth and fable, beyond the pressures of contemporary sexual politics. It is both new and familiar, a distillation of the stuff of myth filtered through a ripened imagination. The Providers, like the traditional gods, impose harsh demands upon or succor their chosen ones; a warrior people chafe restlessly against an inner sense of deprivation, while their hedonistic and sensitive opposites grow "fat and mindless." Both share an unwillingness to attempt the mountains of longing and aspiration; their leaders must undergo the agonies of ascent and descent. Interwoven into this traditional scheme are numerous minor classical echoes, as when a faithful intuitive horse awaits his mistress' return before giving up the ghost. The narrative flows, sweetened with Lessing's mature spirit of concern for human complexities.

The third archive, *The Sirian Experiments: The Report by Ambien II, of the Five* (1981) is an illustrative memoir, composed in exile by Ambien II, a disgraced high colonial administrator and social scientist of the Empire Sirius (an anagram for U.S.S.R.?). She finds herself writing, uncharacteristically, "a history of the heart, rather than of events"—in effect, a narrative of the soul's search for perfection. She shows how her colonial work of social engineering, controlling and conditioning the satellites of the Sirian Empire, had turned under the mysterious compulsion of her encounters with representatives of a higher system, Canopus, into a quest for the ultimate meaning and source of what Sirius "compassionately," yet mechanically, does. Ambien II is well equipped as omniscient narrator to embody Lessing's aims. She is virtually immortal: "We of the superior Sirian mother-stock . . . do not expect to die except from accident or a rare disease." Through Ambien's timeless perception, as both actor and observer, Lessing allows herself the utmost freedom to pursue her manifold quest.

Lessing's quasi-allegorical fictive cosmology embraces legendary, pre-, or factual world history; myths and beliefs about good and evil; an eclectic range of social and political ideas. The action centers again upon Shikasta (in Sirian, Rohanda) and leads up to that of the first archive, Shikasta's Last Days. "Good" (Canopus) and "evil" (Puttiora/Shammat) come more fully into focus now, yet constantly, tantalizingly beyond their struggle for ascendancy in Shikasta lies the Canopean recognition of the hidden Necessity (a Sufi concept) that governs all. Earth-visiting gods, immaculate conceptions, UFOs, talismanic magic, Wellsian echoes combine with freely shuffled episodes from our world's history—Aztecs and conquistadores, Mongol invasions, the modern global wars—to form an imagined whole whose metaphysical direction remains open, and intriguing, to the end. However, meaning and message, as in *Shikasta,* tend to smother fictional effect; one is seldom taught by indirection.

*The Making of the Representative for Planet 8* (1982) is told again by a single, involved narrator, and the narrative is the most firmly integrated and the most compelling of the first five archives. The doom The Ice threatens is evident from the outset in the narrator's use of the past tense and in the prospect held out by the Canopean agent, Johor again, of transferring the threatened population of the planet to Rohanda, "a beautiful plane"; readers of *Shikasta* already know the news Johor will later break to Doeg, the narrator: "Rohanda is . . . Shikasta, the broken one, the afflicted." The narrative, then, is of hope and despair, and beyond, of seeking to understand and accept an inevitable fate. Canopus is not omnipotent; yet salvation is not where Doeg and the other Representatives expect it: it is not in life, but through death. Those who are fitted to learn this, who are attuned to "a general and shared consciousness" beyond the solipsistic "I" (one recalls the SOWF of *Shikasta*), are led by Johor's questioning and the struggle to the end he shares with them to "earn" their return to an original world, inwardly apprehended: "A world of dazzling light, all a shimmering marvel—where the colours you yearn to see are shining—from whence you came." (One recalls the luminous imagery of Henry Vaughan, a seventeenth-century devotional poet). They become, finally, one Representative, a mystical "new being" in a transcendent otherness. The action, the struggles against The Ice, the contrivances of survival, the wrestling with bodily and spiritual limitation are all concretely rendered. In her afterword Lessing reveals that her imagination was deeply imbued with the accounts of Robert Scott's expeditions to the Antarctic, in writing both this novel and *The Sirian Experiments.* She quotes from Apsley Cherry-Garrard's *The Worst Journey in the World* (1922) and George Seaver's biography *Wilson of the Antarctic* (1933)—Wilson died with Scott. The lesson of their example is less, for her, in their sense of duty (unfashionable today) than in their obeying the "need to break out of our ordinary possibilities. . . . This need may well be the deepest one we have." In Wilson she finds united a noble selflessness with an urge to use his life to the utmost in the pursuit of knowledge. Thus, the legendary Antarctic expedition of 1910–1913 inspired in *The Making* a myth of endurance and faith, of simplicities by no means modern.

The fifth archive, *Documents Relating to the Sentimental Agents in the Volyen Empire* (1983), is not among the more "beguiling" tales. The narrative mode, Klorathy's reports to Johor in Canopus on the events surrounding the collapses of the Volyen Empire, distances the reader; the opening sections, clotted with reference to persons, place, and events, handicaps initial response. As in *Shikasta* the play of ideas and political allegory, rather than of character or character conflict, is dominant. The motif of the sentimental agents, Canopeans not fully tempered by experience of inferior worlds, focuses upon the errors of Incent (the Innocent) in a vein of obvious comedy that palls in the telling. The School of Rhetoric and the Hospital for Rhetorical Diseases, alias the Institute for Historical Studies, and the therapeutic technique of Total Immersion are, however, worthy of the Third Book of *Gulliver's Travels*. The revolutionary is the ultimate sentimentalist. As in the first archive, in Volyen's history and politics we recognize much of our world: the relations between developed and underdeveloped countries, imperial mission and its decline, accompanied by an influx of unwanted immigrants; in the role of Sirius, Soviet Russia and the link between revolution and empire. Volyen, treated more sympathetically than Shikasta, suffers from markedly English afflictions: though comparatively pleasant, its idealistic youth agitate to undermine it; Sirian agents are (like the Cambridge Communists of the 1930's) members of Volyen's privileged classes. As with the trial that closes *Shikasta*, the Indictment of Volyen's vulnerably open society produces an acute and stimulating conflict of ideas and attitudes. Behind all, gifted with foresight, though aware that solutions are bound by Necessity, hovers Canopus. It is the arbiter of ultimate value—what our world lacks, certainly—and the source of choice (free will); Klorathy, on duty in a Volyen afflicted, like Shikasta, with "self-destructive dementia," sometimes pines for its unnameable quality. While it is perhaps essential that Lessing should preserve Canopus as a vague principle of justice, it threatens to become a fine-spun abstraction, a romantic figment closer in spirit to Shelley's *Prometheus Unbound* than to those eighteenth-century rationalists her political satire recalls.

### THE DIARIES OF JANE SOMERS

"SINCE writing *The Golden Notebook* I've become less personal. I've floated away from the personal. I've stopped saying, 'This is *mine*, this is my experience. . . . I don't believe any more that I have a thought. There is a thought around'" ("Doris Lessing at Stony Brook" [1970], reprinted in *A Small Personal Voice* [1974]). Her ensuing work has been faithful to this piece of self-analysis until the surprising news, broken in 1984, that parallel with her writing the *Canopus* series Lessing had published two linked novels in her earlier "realistic" style under the pseudonym of Jane Somers. In 1984 these were reprinted as her work in one volume, with a tart preface where Lessing explains that she had made the experiment to combat publishers' and reviewers' entrenched prejudices in favor of established and against unknown writers. *The Diary of a Good Neighbour* (1983) and *If the Old Could . . .* (1984) were both written in the most personal of forms, the diary, self-preoccupied and self-revealing. Yet this is only technically a return to the personal mode: the preoccupation is not with a thinly disguised authorial self, but with crises of experience and understanding readily apprehensible, one supposes, to middle-aged women like Janna Somers, established in her career but emotionally unfulfilled. Janna is again that familiar, pre-Canopean heroine, a representative figure akin to such as Kate Brown who in *The Summer Before the Dark*, facing the "cold wind" of solitude, age, and irrelevance, had found the resources within herself to live beyond the roles she had outgrown.

If in their pseudonymous guise these novels were not detected as Lessing's this may partly be due to her protagonist's unlikely identity and striking authenticity as a women's magazine editor and romantic novelist. Yet Janna Somers' pattern of life and anxiety for change will be familiar: she preserves a careful face in her public world, but while apparently self-contained and successful, is conscious, like all Lessing's heroines, of her incompleteness. Having failed both husband and mother as they neared death, she resolves "to learn something else," to change. The opportunity comes from an unexpected quarter—the very old Maudie, one of the unnoticed, unnoticeable old women who merely survive in the crannies of the metropolis, a London that belongs to the young, the healthy life-forcers. Realizing "how afraid we are of age," instinctively Janna allows herself to be drawn into this subterranean world, where she falls in love with Maudie's indomitable spirit. The theme is not entirely new: one recalls the story "An Old Woman and Her Cat" in *The Story of a Non-Marrying Man* (1972), a deeply felt but unsentimental sketch of a homeless old woman's dogged evasion of society's efforts to put her and her pet to sleep. The emotional intensity this story shares with Lessing's treatment of the Janna-Maudie relationship does stem, one may infer, from the personal attachment she mentions in the afterword to *The Making of the Representative for Planet 8,* a book finished the day "after the death of someone I had known a long time.... It took her a long cold time to die, and she was hungry too, for she was refusing to eat and drink, so as to hurry things along. She was ninety-two, and it seemed to her sensible."

The faithfulness to every detail of Maudie's struggling, squalid existence, the close delineation of Janna's ambivalent responses, and the broad insight into the nature of this contemporary London Underworld are all conveyed in a brisk, concrete style, alive with Janna's shrewd commentary upon her fluctuating feelings—an index of ours—reminiscent of such earlier journal-novels as *The Golden Notebook* and *The Memoirs of a Survivor* (1974). However remote from the Lessing of Canopus, it now seems odd that her hand escaped detection (the novels escaped this writer altogether on first publication). In both novels another familiar element is the scrupulous, even dogged fidelity with which the close relations between women are captured.

In *If the Old Could . . . ,* Maudie's death having closed The Diary, Janna the romantic novelist becomes caught up in a middle-aged romance that reality—Richard's duty to wife and family, Janna's chastened sense of the claims of self—denies. In the margin Annie, Maudie's less appealing aged counterpart, persists as a reminder of "a world ... few of us, ever, want to think about until we have to." This novel is weighted with Janna's burden of obligation to young and old alike; the negative emotions of guilt and self-doubt vitiate self-realization and the urge to self-gratification in both Janna and Richard. Personal relations are stifled by the moral imperatives and uncertainties of familial ties. Some relief is felt in the harmonious colleagueship of Janna's editorial office, or in her delight with Richard in discovering the pleasures of London and its "salty and original" people, recapturing at times the exuberant flavor of the early *In Pursuit of the English.* These novels often refreshingly revisit ordinary life with gusto, curiosity, and engaged social concern: their strength, in relationship, is in that between Janna and Maudie; if one feels as a weakness in the second book a diminution of interest in a character who is acted upon rather than embodying a positive force, this is nevertheless symptomatic of Lessing's fidelity to Janna's unslaked search for satisfaction and her own refusal to impose a neat romantic resolution.

While Lessing may value *The Diaries* below her *Canopus* series, their appearance arrested a growing perception that a preoccupation with the figment of a transcendent absolute had led to the shedding of common reality. Yet even in that series of generally less admired works, at their best one is engaged and moved by Lessing's consistent twin concern with the individual in himself and in relation to society; while in her best work, she achieves insight simultaneously into the private life and the "wider public life" by which, George Eliot commented in *Felix Holt,* the private is determined. *The Golden Notebook* is the modern counterpart to *Middlemarch.* Like Eliot, Doris Lessing does not shrink from earnestness and unblushing didacticism, and although (especially in her "English" short stories) she more often lightens her narrative with a teasing humor, she frequently employs a similarly authoritative, astringent irony, the "dryness" she aptly notes in her preface to *The Diaries.* Like Eliot, too, she insists on keeping absolute values before us. So serious and prolific a writer, always responsive to the pressure of the time, is likely to be uneven. I have not stressed the lapses, even in her best work, into protracted documentary or circumstantial narrative and slack, unrevised prose. Ultimately, these defects matter little, because of the power of the mind that creates. Lessing is worthy to be spoken of in the company of those great novelists before her who used the novel not to divert with a sensational or aesthetic experience, but to change us —Eliot, Hardy, Conrad, Lawrence. If she shares with them also—as with her nearest comparable contemporary, Patrick White—the unevenness of writers who reach for the utmost inclusiveness, this is redeemed by the unteachable quality of keeping the reader morally alive. No English novelist today is more responsibly concerned with keeping literature critically in touch with life, as it is and as it should be.

Literature and history, these two great branches of human learning, records of human behaviour, human thought, are less and less valued by the young, and by educators, too. Yet from them one may learn how to be a citizen and a human being. We may learn how to look at ourselves and at the society we live in, in that calm, cool, critical and sceptical way which is the only possible stance for a civilized human being, or so have said all the philosophers and the sages.

(*Prisons We Choose to Live Inside*, 1986)

## POSTSCRIPT: THE GOOD TERRORIST

THE unattributed epigraph to her first novel, *The Grass Is Singing*, would stand aptly at the beginning of *The Good Terrorist* (1985): "It is by the failures and misfits of a civilization that one can best judge its weaknesses." Another could be Hannah Arendt's dictum on the sources of the kind of situation the novel attempts to capture: "loneliness and the logical-ideological deducing the worst that comes from it represent an anti-social situation and harbour a principle destructive for all human living-together" (*The Origins of Totalitarianism*, New York, 1973, p. 478).

Lessing's new "children of violence," founders of the C.C.P. (a would-be independent Communist Center Party), are emotional amateurs, not ideologues, stemming from several varieties of alienation in contemporary England—unemployment, miseducation, child abuse, family breakdown, color prejudice; they are gays, lesbians, narcissists, idlers, and one fiercely righteous bomb maker, who find an uneasy unity in their disaffection, however deviously it is reached. Their conspiracy to overthrow a "stinking" society is mostly a tragicomedy of errors, which escalates almost involuntarily into a tragedy in earnest (reminiscent of the Oxford Street bombings in 1977) for which none is quite prepared, least of all Alice, Lessing's protagonist: "Had she not believed the bombing was serious, then? No, not really; she had gone along with it, while feeling it was not right—and behind that was the thought that *serious* work (whatever that might turn out to be) would come later." The millenium is never today. Alice is the only "revolutionary" whose mind and past life we enter, yet she is probably the least typical. She is neither merely sentimental nor fanatical, but "good" in a Lessing succession we recognize; closest to her among "caring" heroines is the Martha of *The Four-Gated City*—and indeed she might have borne the same name, as one "cumbered about much serving . . . careful and troubled about many things" (Luke 10:40–41).

Until near the end, revolutionary acts are peripheral to Lessing's detailed exploration of the personal and political relations among the young people, at whose center the frenetic Alice works (and steals, from her "fascist" parents: thus, no guilt) to convert their condemned North London Victorian house, or "squat," into a decent habitation for the "family" she would have them become. In this apparently contradictory "bourgeois" behavior her "Comrades" both deride and depend upon, she sublimates the split between her parallel lives, the yearning for order and calm beneath the outbursts of hatred and anger the once good girl, good daughter, had suppressed. Behind her stand Dorothy, her mother, and her friend Zoë, hangovers from the fruitless demonstrations of the 1960's, from whose now merely intellectual concern the book-hating activist Alice early learned to block herself off—as also from sex, which means chaos and violation of the self. A professional Comrade (a Russian agent) distinguishes her from Lenin's "useful idiots" (her fellow revolutionaries) as a "pure good woman," by which perhaps he cynically means both credulous and susceptible, a vessel of pure faith, while the reader sees in her a naive, warped compassion for the marginal people whom life defeats. She drifts, with deadly innocence, into connivance with Lenin's cynical dictum, "Morality has to be subdued to the needs of Revolution." Too late she foresees the consequences but never reaches understanding.

The intense focus upon Alice allows little scope for broader vision. From her perspective society is bureaucratic, arbitrary, bullying; she has learned, using her intuitive, girlish self, to manipulate its softer-hearted functionaries, but her encounters with the police and members of the tired or simply uncomprehending older generation yield no hint of more fruitful possibilities beyond her grasp. The only somewhat constructive figures in this negative portrayal of disaffected youth, who join safe Greenpeace "demos" and plan their partnership in a flat for two, are ironically treated. The concentration upon Alice, who is no typical revolutionary, is difficult to explain: in symbolic terms she embodies a universal conflict between the desire to conserve and the impulse, springing from twisted and thwarted idealism, to destroy; more realistically, through her concentration on one who poignantly expresses wasted human quality in a "lost" generation, Lessing could sympathize rather than condemn. One is reminded of Conrad's problems, frankly expressed in his preface to *The Secret Agent:* his choosing the "ironic method" to enable him to speak "in scorn as well as in pity," and his focus upon Winnie Verloc, who tragically suspects that "life doesn't stand much looking into." But while *The Good Terrorist* lacks the control and concentration of Conrad's novel and of Lessing's earlier work, it reestablishes her challenging role as, to quote from *The Golden Notebook,* "a central point of awareness."

## SELECTED BIBLIOGRAPHY

I. BIBLIOGRAPHY. C. Ipp, comp., *Doris Lessing: A Bibliography* (Johannesburg, 1967); S. R. Burkom, ed., "A Doris Lessing Checklist," in *Critique,* 11 (1968), includes a guide to reviews; A. N. Krouse, "A Doris Lessing Checklist," in *Contemporary Literature,* 14 (1973).

II. COLLECTED AND SELECTED WORKS. *African Stories* (London, 1964), contains the short stories in *This Was The Old Chief's Country,* reprinted together with the African stories from *The Habit of Loving* and *A Man and Two Women* and the four novellas from *Five* with an African setting ("The Other Woman" omitted), also "Traitors," first printed in *Argosy* (May 1954), "The Black Madonna," from *Winter's Tales* (London, 1957), and two early stories, "The Trinket Box" and "The Pig," printed for the first time; *Martha Quest and A Proper Marriage* (London, 1965); *Children of Violence* (London, 1966–); *Nine African Stories* (London, 1968), selected by M. Morland from *African Stories,* with intro. by the author written in 1967; *Collected African Stories* (London, 1973), vol. I: *This Was the Old Chief's Country,* vol. II: *The Sun Between Their Feet; Collected Stories,* vol. I: *To Room Nineteen* (London, 1978), vol. II: *The Temptation of Jack Orkney* (London, 1979).

III. SEPARATE WORKS. *The Grass Is Singing* (London, 1950), fiction; *This Was the Old Chief's Country* (London, 1951), short stories; *Martha Quest* (London, 1952), vol. I of *Children of Violence; Five* (London, 1953), short novels, includes "A Home for the Highland Cattle," "The Other Woman," "Eldorado," "The Antheap," "Hunger"; *A Proper Marriage* (London, 1954), vol. II of *Children of Violence; Retreat to Innocence* (London, 1956), fiction; "Myself as Sportsman," in the *New Yorker,* 31 (January 1956), personal narrative; *The Habit of Loving* (London, 1957), short stories; *Going Home* (London, 1957; rev. ed., 1968), personal narrative; "A Small Personal Voice," in T. Maschler, ed., *Declaration* (London, 1957), gives her writer's "position"; *A Ripple from the Storm* (London, 1958), vol. III of *Children of Violence; Each His Own Wilderness* (London, 1959), play, pub. in *New English Dramatists,* three plays introd. and ed. by E. M. Browne; *Fourteen Poems* (Northwood, 1959); *In Pursuit of the English: A Documentary* (London, 1960), personal narrative; *The Golden Notebook* (London, 1962), fiction (new ed. with author's preface, 1972); *Play with a Tiger: A Play in Three Acts* (London, 1962); *A Man and Two Women* (London, 1963), short stories; "What Really Matters," in the *Twentieth Century,* 172 (Autumn 1963); *Landlocked* (London, 1965), fiction, vol. IV of *Children of Violence; Particularly Cats* (London, 1967), personal narrative; "Afterword," in O. Schreiner, *The Story of an African Farm* (New York, 1968); *The Four-Gated City* (London, 1969), vol. V of *Children of Violence.*

*Briefing for a Descent into Hell* (London, 1971), fiction; "In the World, Not of It," in *Encounter,* 39 (August 1972), an article on Sufism; *The Story of a Non-Marrying Man* (London, 1972), short stories; "What Looks Like an Egg and Is an Egg?" in the *New York Times Book Review* (7 May 1972); "An Ancient Way to a New Freedom," in L. Lewin, ed., *The Elephant in the Dark* (London, 1972); *The Summer Before the Dark* (London, 1973), fiction; *The Memoirs of a Survivor* (London, 1974), fiction: *A Small Personal Voice: Essays, Reviews, Interviews* (New York, 1974), ed. by P. Schlueter; "If You Knew Sufi," in the *Guardian* (8 January 1975); "A Revolution," in the *New York Times* (22 August 1975); "The Ones Who Know," in the *Times Literary Supplement* (30 August 1976); *Re: Colonised Planet 5, Shikasta* (London, 1979), vol. I of *Canopus in Argos, Archives;* "My First Book," in *Author,* 91 (Spring 1980); *The Marriages Between Zones Three, Four and Five* (London, 1980), vol. II of *Canopus . . . ; The Sirian Experiments: The Report by Ambien II, of the Five* (London, 1981), vol. III of *Canopus . . . ; The Making of the Representative for Planet 8* (London, 1982), vol. IV of *Canopus . . . ;* "Our Minds Have Become Set in the Apocalyptic Mode," in the *Guardian* (14 June 1982); *Documents Relating to the Sentimental Agents in the Volyen Empire* (London, 1983), vol. V of *Canopus . . . ; The Diaries of Jane Somers* (London, 1984), fiction, with a preface by Lessing, previously pub. under the pseudonym Jane Somers as *The Diary of a Good Neighbour* (London, 1983) and *If the Old Could . . .* (London, 1984); *The Good Terrorist* (London, 1985); "Impertinent Daughters," in *Granta,* 14 (1985); "Autobiography (Pt. II): My Mother's Life," in *Granta,* 17 (1985); *Prisons We Choose to Live Inside,* CBC Massey Lectures (Toronto, 1986); *The Wind Blows Away Our Worlds* (London, 1987), personal narrative on Afghanistan.

IV. INTERVIEWS. R. Rubens, "Footnote to *The Golden Notebook,"* in the *Queen* (21 August 1962); R. Newquist, in R. Newgrist, ed., *Counterpoint* (Chicago, 1964); F. Howe, "Talk with Doris Lessing," in the *Nation* (6 March 1967); J. Raskin, "Doris Lessing at Stony Brook," in the *New American Review,* 8 (1970); L. Langley, "Scenarios of Hell," in the *Guardian Weekly* (24 April 1971); F. Howe, "A Conversation with Doris Lessing (1966)," in *Contemporary Literature,* 14 (1973); "The Doors of Perception," in the *Sunday*

*Times* (18 November 1979); M. Thorpe, "Interview," taped, for The British Council (London, 1980).

V. BIOGRAPHICAL AND CRITICAL STUDIES. J. Gindin, *Postwar British Fiction: New Accents and Attitudes* (London, 1962), contains a chapter, "Doris Lessing's Intense Commitment"; D. Brewster, *Doris Lessing* (New York, 1965); M. Tucker, *Africa in Modern Literature* (New York, 1967); S. R. Burkom, " 'Only Connect': Form and Content in the Works of Doris Lessing," in *Critique*, 11 (1968); M. Thorpe, "Martha's Utopian Quest: Doris Lessing's *Children of Violence* Quintet," in A. Rutherford, ed., *Commonwealth* (Aarhus, 1972); P. Schlueter, *The Novels of Doris Lessing* (Carbondale, Ill., 1973); C. J. Driver, "Profile of Doris Lessing," in the *New Review*, 1 (1974); A. Pratt and L. S. Dembo, eds., *Doris Lessing: Critical Essays* (London, 1974); E. Showalter, *A Literature of Their Own: British Women Novelists from Brontë to Lessing* (Princeton, N.J., 1977); Mary Ann Singleton, *The City and the Veld: The Fiction of Doris Lessing* (Lewisburg, Pa., 1977); M. Thorpe, *Doris Lessing's Africa* (London, 1978); R. Rubinstein, *The Novelistic Vision of Doris Lessing* (Urbana, Ill., 1979); I. Holmquist, *From Society to Nature: A Study of Doris Lessing's "Children of Violence"* (Gothenburg, 1980); L. Sage, *Doris Lessing* (London, 1982); M. Green, *The English Novel in the Twentieth Century: The Doom of Empire* (London, 1984), contains a chapter, "Doris Lessing: The Return from Empire"; J. Taylor, ed., *Notebooks, Memoirs, Archives: Re-reading Doris Lessing* (London, 1982); C. Tomalin, "Mischief: Why a Famous Novelist Played a Trick on the Literary World," in the *Sunday Times* (23 September 1984); P. Harrison, "Seeking Mrs. Lessing," in the *Bookseller* (24 September 1984); A. Beck, "Doris Lessing and the Colonial Experience," in the *Journal of Commonwealth Literature*, 19 (November 1984).

*N.B.*: A *Doris Lessing Newsletter*, ed. by D. Seligman, at 35 Prospect St., Sherborn, Mass., 01770, is put out occasionally and contains research notes, essays, and reviews.

# C. S. LEWIS
(1898–1963)

## Sanford Schwartz

AN OXFORD DON AND author of several distinguished books on English literature, C. S. Lewis is best known for his literary fantasies and for the apologetic tracts he composed in defense of traditional Christian doctrine. Lewis began to gain public recognition during the 1930s, but he became an overnight celebrity in 1941, when a series of BBC radio broadcasts made him a household name in England. During and after World War II he also published a highly applauded series of books, including his celebrated cycle of children's stories, *The Chronicles of Narnia* (1950–1956), which established his reputation throughout the English-speaking world. Altogether he published some forty books in his lifetime, and, as a consequence of his enduring popular appeal, more than twenty volumes of stories, poems, essays, and letters have appeared since his death in 1963. With his gift for spiritual fable and for finding the illuminating image, Lewis has not only survived his midcentury vogue but is now generally regarded as one of the most influential Christian apologists of the twentieth century.

### LIFE

CLIVE Staples ("Jack") Lewis was born in Belfast on 29 November 1898. His father, Albert, was a solicitor descended from Welsh immigrants who prospered in Belfast's shipbuilding industry. His mother, Florence Hamilton Lewis, was the daughter of a minister from an established Protestant family. The first of their two children, Warren ("Warnie"), was born a year after their marriage in 1894. He was Jack's best childhood friend, and after 1930 his permanent companion.

The most vivid portrait of Lewis' early life is his own autobiography, *Surprised by Joy* (1955). Lewis depicts the life of a flourishing middle-class family in the suburbs of Belfast, a dirty but thriving city still unravaged by sectarian strife. Warnie and Jack (his lifelong nickname) constructed their own playland in the attics and crawl spaces of their large, rambling house. Anticipating things to come, they created a sprawling imaginary kingdom, "Boxen," populated with human and animal figures derived from the rich world of Edwardian children's fiction. This blissful existence, as Lewis describes it, came to a sudden end with the death of their mother in 1908. Soon afterward, the grieving widower sent his children to various boarding schools, the first of which was tyrannized by a headmaster whose meanness (actually incipient madness) reached Dickensian proportions. (Conditions were better elsewhere, but in later life Lewis never missed an opportunity to witness to the horrors of the British public school system.) Finally, in 1914, Lewis was sent to his father's former teacher, William T. Kirkpatrick ("Kirk"), in whose home he spent two happy years learning the languages and literature that provided the basis for his later career.

Lewis' entrance to university was delayed by enlistment in the army. During military training Lewis was introduced to Janie Moore, the mother of a fellow recruit, E. F. C. ("Paddy") Moore, and a divorcée in her forties. Lewis and Mrs. Moore quickly took to one another, and after Paddy's death in France they remained together for more than thirty years. No one—including Lewis' brother, who purchased a house with them in 1930—knew the precise nature of their relationship. In *Surprised by Joy*, Lewis restricts himself to the remark that "one huge and complex episode will be omitted.... All I can or need say is that my earlier hostility to the emotions was very fully... avenged" (p. 198).

In January 1919 Lewis finally entered Oxford, where he read classical philosophy, history, and

855

literature ("Greats") for three years and then spent an additional year studying English literature. After another two years of uncertainty over his future, he received an offer of employment as a tutor in English from Magdalen College, Oxford, where he remained for the next three decades. During his early years at Oxford, Lewis established a number of significant friendships: with Owen Barfield, who gained an early reputation with *History in English Words* (1926) and *Poetic Diction* (1928); Nevill Coghill, a promising scholar of medieval literature; Hugo Dyson, an Oxford wit and later lecturer at Reading University; and J. R. R. Tolkien, another rising medievalist, who was transforming his knowledge of Celtic, Germanic, and Norse mythology into an ample fictional world of his own. Together with the London-based Charles Williams (whom Lewis met in 1936), they eventually formed the nucleus of the now-celebrated circle known as the Inklings, which gathered each week to listen to its members' work in progress. Dyson and Tolkien were particularly instrumental in the final stage of Lewis' conversion to Christianity. In *Surprised by Joy*, Lewis recalls that his long trek through agnosticism, philosophical idealism, pantheism, and abstract theism came to an end as the result of a late-night walk in September 1931, when his two companions overcame his last reservations to Christian belief.

Lewis examined his spiritual awakening in *The Pilgrim's Regress* (1933), an allegory of his own journey to faith. Three years later he published his classic study *The Allegory of Love: A Study in Medieval Tradition* (1936), which secured him a solid reputation as a literary scholar. In the ensuing years he published several additional books, and by the end of World War II he was regarded as one of the most distinguished literary scholars in England. In the later 1930s Lewis had also returned to fiction, and over the next half decade or so he composed a trilogy of science-fiction novels: *Out of the Silent Planet* (1938), *Perelandra* (1943; reissued as *Voyage to Venus* in 1953), and *That Hideous Strength* (1945). In 1939 he was invited to contribute to a series of religious books, Christian Challenge, and wrote *The Problem of Pain* (1940), which launched his career as an apologist for Christianity. The book caught the attention of the director of religious broadcasting for the BBC, James Welch, who asked Lewis to consider a set of radio talks to a national audience. *Right and Wrong: A Clue to the Meaning of the Universe?* was broadcast in fifteen-minute segments each Wednesday evening in August 1941. Delivered during the darkest hours of World War II, these broadcasts proved so popular that Lewis was asked to continue. He disliked the medium of radio, but his spectacular success resulted in three sequels: *What Christians Believe,* which aired in January and February 1942 (published with the first series as *Broadcast Talks,* 1942; in the United States as *The Case for Christianity*); *Christian Behaviour,* which aired September through November 1942 (published in 1943); and *Beyond Personality,* which ran February through April 1944 (published in 1944). (The entire collection now circulates in a revised four-part edition, *Mere Christianity,* published in 1952.) As a result of these broadcasts, Lewis became a major celebrity. His reputation was compounded by the appearance of other works of apologetics—*The Screwtape Letters* (1942), *The Abolition of Man* (1943), *The Great Divorce* (1945), and *Miracles* (1947)—and by the end of the decade Lewis enjoyed a major following in Christian circles throughout the English-speaking world.

In 1948, Lewis began to compose the celebrated cycle of children's stories, *The Chronicles of Narnia,* which appeared over a seven-year period: *The Lion, the Witch, and the Wardrobe* (1950); *Prince Caspian* (1951); *The Voyage of the Dawn Treader* (1952); *The Silver Chair* (1953); *The Horse and His Boy* (1954); *The Magician's Nephew* (1955); and *The Last Battle* (1956). Around the same time he wrote his autobiography, *Surprised by Joy: The Shape of My Early Life* (1955), and his most intriguing though least appreciated work of fiction, *Till We Have Faces* (1956). Lewis' private life also changed during these years. In the late 1940s Mrs. Moore became increasingly infirm; she died in 1951 at the age of seventy-nine. In the following year Lewis was visited by one of his many American admirers, Helen Joy Gresham (née Davidman), a writer and a Jewish convert to Christianity, who was at the time estranged from her husband, the author William Lindsay ("Bill") Gresham. Lewis eventually married Joy Davidman in a civil ceremony in 1956, and after she was diagnosed with cancer, they were wed in a religious ceremony in 1957. The story of their later relationship—the sudden remission of the disease, their three happy years as husband and wife, and the pathos surrounding her death in 1960—has been dramatized in William Nicholson's BBC teleplay *Shadowlands*

(1985) and the stage and film versions based upon it. Lewis registered his own sense of loss in a book of anguished meditations, *A Grief Observed* (published in 1961 under the pseudonym N. W. Clerk), which departs dramatically from the buoyant tone of his other religious writings.

The other major change of this period was his departure from Oxford. After several unsuccessful bids for a professorship, Lewis accepted a new chair of Medieval and Renaissance English at Magdalene College, Cambridge, in 1954. From then on he commuted between the two university towns, returning home to Oxford each weekend. The move to Cambridge was also accompanied by a new flurry of scholarly work. His monumental *English Literature in the Sixteenth Century, Excluding Drama*, volume 3 of the *Oxford History of English Literature* (or *OHEL*, as he called it), appeared in 1954, followed by *Studies in Words* (1960), *An Experiment in Criticism* (1961), and *The Discarded Image: An Introduction to Medieval and Renaissance Literature* (1964). At the same time Lewis composed a new set of religious writings: *Reflections on the Psalms* (1958); *The Four Loves* (1960); *A Grief Observed* (1961); and *Letters to Malcolm: Chiefly on Prayer* (1964). But soon after Joy's death, Lewis' own health began to deteriorate. After a long struggle with complications from a prostate condition, he died on 22 November 1963, one week before his sixty-fifth birthday.

## SCHOLAR AND CRITIC

THE foundations for Lewis' achievement were laid in the long years of study prior to his religious conversion. His early letters, especially the correspondence with his lifelong friend Arthur Greeves (1895–1966), indicate the breadth and focus of his reading: his attraction to epic tradition from Homer to Wagner; the discovery of George Macdonald's *Phantastes* (1858), William Morris' *The Well at the World's End* (1896), and other fantasy narratives; the metaphysical questions provoked by his extensive reading in philosophy; and the fortunes of his various poetic projects. By comparison to Barfield and Tolkien his scholarly career began slowly, but by the early 1930s Lewis was publishing the articles that would culminate in *The Allegory of Love: A Study in Medieval Tradition* (1936), still his most influential work of scholarship. Several other books appeared over the next few years: *Rehabilitations* (1939), a collection of essays on a variety of literary subjects; *The Personal Heresy: A Controversy* (1939), a debate with a well-known scholar, E. M. W. Tillyard, over the role of the author's "personality" in the construction and interpretation of a text; and *A Preface to Paradise Lost* (1942), which was instrumental in resituating Milton's poem in the traditions of classical epic and Christian theology. By the early 1940s Lewis was widely regarded as Oxford's most popular lecturer and one of England's most renowned literary critics.

Lewis' major scholarly achievement of this period was *The Allegory of Love*, which also sheds light on his fiction and apologetics. It is a book of broad historical scope, extending from the birth of allegory in late antiquity to its flowering in the Middle Ages and the Renaissance. Lewis begins with the death of the pagan gods and the concomitant birth of a new sense of interior consciousness, common to both pagan and Christian authors, in the late Roman Empire. The revolutionary nature of this development is epitomized by Saint Augustine's amazement at the sight of Bishop Ambrose reading without stirring his lips (*Confessions*, book 6). According to Lewis, allegory emerges when poets begin to use the obsolete pantheon of pagan gods to personify internal conflicts within the newly discovered "soul." But it is not until the advent of a second spiritual revolution—the birth of "romantic" love in eleventh- and twelfth-century France—that allegory develops into a sophisticated means of exploring a new domain of sensibility. This literature often oscillates between a new worldliness and the traditional demand for sensual renunciation, but Lewis is most drawn to authors who envision "a *tertium quid* between the courtly and the religious conceptions of the good life" (p. 102). He finds this reconciliation in the twelfth-century Platonism of the School of Chartres and in the literary development of "the 'other world' not of religion, but of imagination; the land of longing, the Earthly Paradise, the garden east of the sun and west of the moon" (pp. 75–76). Lewis traces the allegorical elaboration of this "third world of myth and fancy" (p. 82) from the *Romance of the Rose* in the thirteenth century to its final flowering in Edmund Spenser's *The Faerie Queene* at the end of the sixteenth. By that point the worldview supporting such a phenomenon was already yielding to currents that would alter the character of European literature.

*The Allegory of Love* breaks off abruptly after Spenser, but Lewis has already informed us that several centuries after the demise of allegory as a dominant mode, "that free creation of the marvellous which first slips in under the cloak of allegory" (p. 82) would be reconstituted by the Romantics under the aegis of symbolism. Thus the Romantics perpetuate the "third world of myth and fancy," but with a significant difference: whereas allegory is merely a poetic device for expressing passions by means of fictional personifications, symbolism—or "sacramentalism" (p. 45)—is a mode of thought implying the presence of a higher reality:

> The difference between the two can hardly be exaggerated. The allegorist leaves the given—his own passions—to talk of that which is confessedly less real, which is a fiction. The symbolist leaves the given to find that which is more real. . . . There is nothing "mystical" or mysterious about medieval allegory; the poets know quite clearly what they are about and are well aware that the figures which they present to us are fictions. . . . Symbolism comes to us from Greece. It makes its first effective appearance in European thought with the dialogues of Plato. The Sun is the copy of the Good. Time is the moving image of eternity. All visible things exist just in so far as they succeed in imitating the Forms. . . . But of course the poetry of symbolism does not find its greatest expression in the Middle Ages at all, but rather in the time of the romantics.
>
> (pp. 45–48)

This convergence of symbolism, sacramentalism, and Platonism is crucial to all of Lewis' works. From his conversion until his death, Lewis held to a form of Christian Platonism that had as its central tenet a belief "in an 'other' world . . . that Nature, the totality of phenomena in space and time, is not the only thing that exists" (*Studies in Medieval and Renaissance Literature*, p. 144). Christianity and Platonism, in common with the particular conception of romanticism he was prepared to defend, point to a higher reality of which the natural world is merely the confused and partially spoiled copy.

### THE PILGRIM'S REGRESS

PRIOR to his conversion, Lewis' literary publications were confined to two slender volumes of verse: *Spirits in Bondage* (1919), an assemblage of forty loosely related lyrics, and *Dymer* (1926), a long mythical narrative. Out of step with the innovative techniques of modernist poetry, Lewis' verse was ignored at the time, and even now its interest lies primarily in the anticipation of his later work. Both volumes focus on "immortal longings" for a higher reality that transcends mundane existence. This desire (or *Sehnsucht*, as he called it) is awakened by a brief vision of "wondrous islands" or a "Hidden Country" (prologue, *Spirits in Bondage*), which imbues the soul with a permanent longing to retrieve and retain its fleeting state of joy. The pre-Christian Lewis is haunted by the specter that these flashes of transcendence are empty illusions, and that Divinity, if it exists, is indifferent or even hostile to our aspirations. *Spirits in Bondage* struggles toward a timid affirmation of the "Country of Dreams" (p. 75), while *Dymer* passes through the most frightful earthly calamities, produced ironically by the very quest for the "sacred shiver / Of joy" (*Narrative Poems*, p. 24), to achieve a final slim ray of hope. The Christian Lewis would close this gap between aspiration and reality. But he retained the notion of *Sehnsucht*, elaborating this romantic longing into the more complex "dialect of Desire" (preface, *The Pilgrim's Regress*, 3d ed.) that informs his subsequent writings.

This new development appears in Lewis' first work of prose fiction, *The Pilgrim's Regress: An Allegorical Apology for Christianity, Reason, and Romanticism* (1933), written in the manner of John Bunyan's *The Pilgrim's Progress* (1678) soon after Lewis' conversion. The pilgrim personifies the spiritual condition of Everyman, but in fact his particular trials follow Lewis' own journey to faith. The story begins in Puritania, a thinly veiled Ulster administered by the Steward on behalf of the stern absentee Landlord. John, the pilgrim, knows that the Landlord's Castle lies in the nearby mountains to the east, but his focus is directed to the distant west where he briefly glimpses a beautiful island and feels "a sweetness and a pang so piercing that instantly he forgot his father's house, and his mother, and the fear of the Landlord, and the burden of the rules" (book 1, chap. 2). Smitten by *Sehnsucht*, John leaves home in quest of the island, even though he recognizes "with one part of his mind . . . that what had befallen him was not seeing at all. . . . that it was not entirely true" (book 1, chap. 2). His subsequent adventures allegorize the propensity of the soul to wander from its true objective by settling on lesser objects (idolatry), by trying to reproduce the emotion in the absence of its correlative object (some versions of romanticism), or by abandoning the quest altogether (the way of modern naturalism). Only at the end of his pilgrimage does he discover that the island in the west is in reality the other side of the mountains to the east, and to reach his true destination, the Landlord's Castle, he must journey back the way he came. It turns out that spiritual progress is also a regress—a circle perhaps, though not a vicious one, since it is only by means of the journey that the soul discovers the reality it has left behind.

Between the beginning and the end of his travels, Lewis' pilgrim encounters allegorical figures personifying modern forms of intellectual seduction. He reckons with the seemingly antithetical temptations of the Enlightenment and romanticism—the former personified by Mr. Vertue's commitment to morality without God, the latter by harp-playing Mr. Halfways, who dissolves the supernatural into a mere state of mind: "the Landlord they dreamed to find, we find in our hearts: the Island you seek for, you already inhabit.... it is an Island of the Soul" (book 2, chap. 5). Geographically, Enlightenment and romanticism lie on either side of the Main Road that divides this fictional world into northern and southern zones. In the north dwell the excesses of intellection, in the south the lures of emotional satisfaction. The Main Road represents a desirable middle way, since "we were made to be neither cerebral men nor visceral men, but Men. Not beasts nor angels but Men—things at once rational and animal" (preface, 3d ed.). The pilgrim errs in both directions, but Lewis regarded the ascetic north as the characteristic terrain of his own disillusioned age and devotes much of the book to contemporary sins of the intellect: cynical postwar poets who scorn the "immortal longings" of their predecessors; disciples of Freud who reduce the soul to elemental mechanisms of desire— "the Island was the pretence that you put up to conceal your own lusts from yourself" (book 3, chap. 6); and, perhaps surprisingly, various modern conservatives—neoscholastics, neohumanists, and neoclassicists—who trample on human emotion by formulating hyper-rational defenses of traditional religious values. The hostility directed at the neoconservatives is significant in pinpointing Lewis' own position. If Mr. Halfways' romanticism offers emotional satisfaction without objective foundation, Lewis found the antiromanticism of moderns such as T. S. Eliot far more dangerous. Properly understood, romanticism expresses our natural longing for the reality beyond the material realm. Lewis could agree with certain articles of the neoconservative creed, but he saw the solution not in the renunciation of emotions but in the recovery of their transcendent object.

As his sojourn continues, John learns of trouble stirring to the far north, where multitudes of angry "revolutionary sub-men" (book 6, chap. 6), at once the victims of the modern malady and its most aggravated symptom, are assembling for a great invasion. But Lewis is concerned less with fascism and communism than with his own pilgrimage to faith, and he sends his pilgrim south to encounter less harsh dispositions of the soul. The story of John's adventures now follows Lewis' own passage through a variety of philosophical and spiritual allegiances until his final acceptance of Christianity. As Lewis marches his pilgrim through some rarefied academic debate, many readers find themselves in the dark, struggling to decode an allegory based on the concerns of a few Oxford intellectuals in the 1920s. But in a certain respect this is the most profound section of the book. Lewis discriminates among some deceptively similar philosophies, identifying seemingly small but crucial differences in their ontological commitments. As a result of this process, John arrives at Christianity not by a sudden lurch into faith but through a carefully measured progress of the mind toward the reception of what would otherwise seem the most improbable of doctrines.

Having discovered that his true goal lies to the east, the converted pilgrim quickly begins his "regress" home. The surprise is that the same terrain looks so different on the return journey. Ideas that once loomed large in his thinking have shriveled into insignificance. "Your eyes are altered. You see nothing now but realities" (book 10, chap. 2), John learns from a reliable guide. The finale takes place in Puritania, where the pilgrim is instructed to prepare for death. Believing he had transcended his attachment to worldly things, John is surprised to find himself weeping over his imminent departure from this world and over the news that many of his family and friends have died. Lewis' point is that we are at once cursed and blessed by "the tether and pang of the particular." He modulates into verse to express the mingling of sorrow and joy that not only "turns all / Spirit's sweet water to astringent soul," but also draws us closer to the divine suffering so that we may

> . . . not reflect merely,
> As lunar angel, back to thee, cold flame.
> Gods we are, Thou hast said: and we pay dearly.
> (book 10, chap. 10)

The author's poetic gifts are limited, but the tension between irrecoverable loss and redemptive hope at the end of *The Pilgrim's Regress* achieves an emotional depth equal to anything in his more mature works.

*The Pilgrim's Regress* made considerable demands on its audience. The book sold reasonably well, though the archaic style, allegorical form, and philosophical exposition limited its appeal. Lewis addressed these difficulties in the 1943 edition, to which he appended an illuminating preface and explanatory headlines for each chapter (absent from some later editions). At the same time he acknowledged the irreparable difficulties of a book that required such ancillary apparatus. *The Pilgrim's Regress* remains an oddity in the Lewis canon, but it also anticipates the structure and thematics of the major fiction. Most of Lewis' later stories are journeys of the soul toward the recognition of a transcendent reality. Like *The Pilgrim's Regress*, they are voyages through imaginary landscapes that reveal the shortcomings and expand the horizons of their protagonists, culminating in their spiritual transformation. For Lewis the imagination is a means of awakening the mind to new possibilities of thought, feeling, and action. In this respect the literary voyages to the alternative worlds of Puritania, Mars, or Narnia are designed to detach us from habitual patterns of thought and allow us "to see with other eyes, to imagine with other imaginations, to feel with other hearts, as well as with our own" (*An Experiment in Criticism*, p. 137).

## SPACE TRILOGY

AFTER completing *The Pilgrim's Regress*, Lewis devoted himself primarily to scholarly activities, but in the late 1930s and early 1940s he returned to fiction and composed a series of novels—*Out of the Silent Planet* (1938), *Perelandra* (1943), and *That Hideous Strength* (1945)—that are now well established classics of science fiction. The new venture was influenced by the popular scientific romances of H. G. Wells and Olaf Stapledon, but its principal source of inspiration was David Lindsay's *Voyage to Arcturus* (1920), which used interplanetary travel as a means for exploring spiritual issues. Lewis' unlikely protagonist, Elwin Ransom, is a Cambridge philologist who becomes entangled in spiritual warfare on Mars, Venus, and finally Earth. Ransom is a Christian from the outset, but until his departure from Earth he is only dimly aware of the true glory of creation and the terrible plight of our own "silent planet." Over the course of the trilogy Ransom develops from a perplexed spectator to an anointed agent of divine redemption, confronting the demonic powers that threaten the beneficent order of the universe, which is overseen by a loving God (Maleldil) and his angelic ministers (*eldila*) but imperiled by the abuse of the very freedom that consummates the creation.

*Out of the Silent Planet* is the story of Ransom's adventure on Mars. It pits the hero against two villains—Weston, a brilliant physicist, and Devine, a rapacious businessman—who are preparing to conquer the red planet, the former out of a twisted view of human destiny, the latter out of sheer lust for power. The two schemers kidnap Ransom in the mistaken belief that the Martians, whom they equate with primitive tribesmen, have demanded an earthling as a sacrificial victim. As a prisoner on their spaceship, Ransom experiences the first of many surprises. The vast regions beyond our world are not the dark, alien void envisioned by popularizations of modern physical theory, but an ocean of radiant light:

A nightmare, long engendered in the modern mind by the mythology that follows in the wake of science, was falling off him. He had read of "Space": at the back of his thinking for years had lurked the dismal fancy of the black, cold vacuity, the utter deadness, which was supposed to separate the worlds. He had not known how much it affected him till now—now that the very name "Space" seemed a blasphemous libel for this empyrean ocean of radiance in which they swam. . . . No: Space was the wrong name. Older thinkers had been wiser when they named it simply the heavens—the heavens which declared the glory.

(p. 32)

The planets, as Ransom now sees them, are "mere holes or gaps in the living heaven . . . formed not by addition to, but by subtraction from, the surrounding brightness," and perhaps "visible light is also a hole or gap, a mere diminution of something else. Something that is to bright unchanging heaven as heaven is to the dark, heavy earths" (p. 40).

After landing on Malacandra, Ransom experiences a second reversal of expectations. Influenced by H. G. Wells, he had imagined Mars as a desolate expanse or a labyrinth of monstrosities. Instead he discovers a world of great beauty populated by initially odd-looking but peaceful and rational beings. Escaping from his captors, Ransom learns from the planet's inhabitants that Malacandra possesses three species of rational beings. Thematically, the crucial point about Martian society is that for all their differences in appearance, custom, and skill, none of these species seeks to exercise control over the others. Unlike their counterparts on Earth, who enslave other members of their own species, or even define them as members of a lesser species, the three types of Martian humanity dwell separately but harmoniously in the same world. Dreams of colonial conquest never cross their minds. All three species pay homage to another type of being, the angel-like *eldila*, who are plainly visible to the Martians though at first barely discernible to Ransom.

The rest of the plot is simple. Ransom is summoned before the chief *eldil*, or Oyarsa, who rules Malacandra on behalf of Maleldil the Young (analogous to the second person of the Christian Trinity). Here Ransom is instructed in cosmic history—how the once magnificent Oyarsa of Earth rebelled against Maleldil; how his attempt to ruin Mars damaged the surface of the planet and forced the construction of the canals visible from Earth; and how he was eventually driven back to his own planet, where "he lies to this hour, and we know no more of that planet: it is silent" (p. 121). At this point Weston and Devine are led in with the bodies of several Martians whom they have killed. Still regarding Oyarsa as little more than a savage chieftain, they are sent back to Earth, punished by the fear that they will perish on the voyage. Ransom, offered the opportunity to remain on Mars, elects to return home, and enters the spaceship protected by the "unseen presences" (p. 146) that fill the heavens.

The cosmic struggle continues in *Perelandra*, where the scene shifts from the aging civilization of Mars to the newly created world of Venus. In the first novel, Ransom's involvement seems accidental; in the second, he sets out on a divinely appointed though unspecified mission. When he reaches Venus he finds himself in the midst of a pleasurable flux:

It looked exactly as though you were in a well-wooded valley with a river at the bottom of it. But while you watched, that seeming river did the impossible. It thrust itself up so that the land on either side sloped downwards from it; and then up farther still and shouldered half the landscape out of sight beyond its ridge; and became a huge greeny-gold hog's back of water hanging in the sky and threatening to engulf your own land, which was now concave and reeled backwards to the next roller, and rushing upwards, became convex again.
(p. 51)

These vertiginous descriptions are not simply a display of their author's visionary gifts. In part Lewis is attempting to counter the common view of paradise as an intolerably static condition of being. But more important, his portrayal of the unfallen world as a ceaseless flux is a means of examining the human predicament in our own fallen world, where temporal progression is distorted by insecurity and the specter of death.

This theme moves to the foreground when Ransom notices his desire to freeze the perpetual movement around him. The impulse appears initially as a temptation to repeat a pleasant experience:

This itch to have things over again, as if life were a film that could be unrolled twice or even made to work backwards... was it possibly the root of all evil? No: of course the love of money was called that. But money itself—perhaps one valued it chiefly as a defence against chance, a security for being able to have things over again, a means of arresting the unrolling of the film.
(p. 48)

In other words, our attempt to deny the temporal conditions of our existence and control our own destiny is the very basis of our fallen state. Lewis underscores this point when Ransom meets the Green Lady—the Eve of this new Eden—who simply accepts the "unrolling of the film" and never imagines that the stream of life could be anything other than it is. The one prohibition in her fluid world—its Tree of the Knowledge of Good and Evil—is that she must not settle on the Fixed Land.

Perelandran paradise is soon disturbed by the arrival of Weston, or as Ransom comes to realize, the diabolical Un-man who is taking possession of Weston's body. The physicist is now espousing a theory of creative evolution—the postulate of an immanent Life-Force (Bergson's *élan vital*) that impels creation to ever-higher forms of development—and declares himself the instrument through which this vital impulse will take its next leap forward. Lewis sees major dangers in this theory. By placing humanity at the forefront of cosmic development, the idea of creative evolution can turn into a means of rationalizing our worst impulses. In Weston's hands it is a mere excuse for interplanetary conquest, but closer to home it gets twisted into a pseudotheory that justifies the domination of one sector of humanity over another. From this perspective, the theory of creative evolution is simply another expression of our desire to usurp control over the conditions of our existence. It is a parody of true temporality, a theory of flux that paradoxically reveals our inability to accept the natural flow of time.

The real aim of the Un-man's mission is to extend the dominion of evil. In a reprise of the biblical story, the Un-man urges the Green Lady to inhabit the Fixed Land. (Lewis published *A Preface to* Paradise Lost a year before *Perelandra*, and the Un-man's arguments derive much of their ingenuity from the tempter in Milton's poem.) Ransom tries to assist the Lady, who in her innocence proves nearly as shrewd as her adversary. But fearful that they are no match for the Un-man's tireless casuistry, Ransom despairs of reasoning and resorts to physical combat. The Un-man turns out to have no more physical strength than the body he inhabits, and in extended combat Ransom succeeds in destroying it.

*Perelandra* concludes with a celebration of Deep Heaven, though for many readers the finale fails to dispel the bad odor left by the recourse to physical violence. Lewis had his reasons for this resolution. Like many of his compatriots, he looked back on his nation's reluctance to use force against Nazi Germany as the fatal error of the 1930s. He had little patience for Christian pacifism and wished to remind his contemporaries that some of the Lord's work might require the virtues of Saint George. The problem of *Perelandra*, however, is not physical combat per se, but the fact that the violence is initiated by Ransom out of despair over the impotence of discourse. Lewis had his reasons for this as well, but it left him with a morally problematic and artistically unsatisfying resolution.

The conflict returns to Earth in *That Hideous Strength*, the final and by far the longest volume of the trilogy. The plot revolves around a callow young couple—Mark Studdock, a fellow in sociology at a small provincial university, and his wife, Jane—who drift into opposite sides of a monumental conflict. Mark, a member of his college's "progressive" faction, is lured into a powerful organization—the National Institute of Co-ordinated Experiments (N.I.C.E.)—whose real aim is control of the planet, while Jane is drawn into the small spiritual remnant left to combat the seemingly irresistible force of the enemy.

N.I.C.E. first appears as a vaguely benign research center, but it soon consolidates its hold on the region by employing techniques of violence and fraud reminiscent of the Nazi rise to power. N.I.C.E.'s scientists are attempting to resurrect the dead: their aim is to conquer the basic conditions of life and replace humanity with "the New Man, the man who will not die, the artificial man, free from Nature" (p. 177). They seek to locate and revive the corpse of the ancient magician Merlin in the hope of combining the lost art of magic with the power of modern science. And peering beyond the limits of scientific rationalism, the N.I.C.E. elite has intimations of superhuman intelligences (*macrobes*) that may be harnessed to consolidate the reign of evil. In a scientific manner they are groping toward their true masters—the *eldila* that have turned Thulcandra into "the silent planet." This macabre stew of scientism and demonism is the "hideous strength" poised for final conquest of humanity.

Opposed to N.I.C.E. is a motley assemblage of Christians centered in a nearby village. When certain members of this group discover that the initially non-Christian Jane is having dream visions of the impending struggle, they introduce her to their director, Elwin Ransom, now Pendragon of Logres, anointed by Maleldil to battle the power of N.I.C.E. The office of Pendragon descends in a kind of apostolic succession from King Arthur; it serves the secret kingdom of Logres that has kept the spirit of Maleldil alive in Britain for many dark centuries. Merlin, Ransom tells us, was "the last vestige of an older order in which matter and spirit were, from our modern point of view, confused. . . . After him came the modern man to whom Nature is something dead—a machine to be worked, and taken to bits if it won't work the way he pleases. . . . In a sense Merlin represents what we've got to get back to in some different way" (pp. 285–286). Ransom's immediate goal is to find Merlin's body before it falls into the hands of the enemy. The ultimate goal is to refashion the way modern humanity conceives itself and the world around it.

Once the various elements of main conflict are in place, the resolution is vigorous if distressingly clumsy. Merlin is recovered, and the Christian remnant, inspired by an impressive display of cosmic pageantry, marches to a lopsided victory over N.I.C.E. Lewis ties this reunion of Heaven and Earth to the restitution of right relations between the sexes. Mark's eleventh-hour rejection of his demonic masters exempts him from their fate, and the chastened couple look forward to the real beginning of their marriage.

By 1945, Lewis had a large and receptive audience, but many readers considered *That Hideous Strength* a flawed book and a disappointing conclusion to the trilogy. The shift in locale from imaginary worlds to our own is accompanied by an irreparable loss in inventiveness. The development of the plot is painfully slow and aggravated by constant shuffling from place to place within each chapter. The strains of integrating Arthurian legend, along with the jumble of ideologies fused together in the army of evil, make the final showdown something of a hash. Moreover, Lewis' message was an offense to a portion of his audience. From his perspective the novel is an attempt to depict the ultimate consequences of Enlightenment rationality, which has despiritualized the natural order and given us the arrogance to believe that we can refashion the world to our liking. In this respect, the apparent benevolence of social engineering is only one step away from the open coercion of fascism. Composed as the tide began to turn against the Axis powers, *That Hideous Strength* is a warning that the threat posed by modern naturalism will not disappear with victory over Germany. But many readers did not take kindly to this near equation between a progressivist social agenda and fascism. Even under ordinary circumstances the book would have met considerable resistance; but appearing at the very moment when Britain was mobilizing for its own ambitious experiment in social reform, Lewis' novel was dramatically out of step with the times.

## APOLOGETICS

FOR nearly thirty years Lewis bore witness to Christianity in a stream of books, essays, sermons, poems, and letters. But the period around World War II may be distinguished for his commitment to apologetics—the reasoned defense of Christianity designed to answer objections, dispel doubts, and win the assent of a general audience. In addition to his radio broadcasts and the openly apologetical elements of his space trilogy, Lewis published *The Problem of Pain* (1940), *The Screwtape Letters* (1942), *The Abolition of Man* (1943), *The Great Divorce* (1945), and *Miracles* (1947). His wartime audience was struck by the vitality of his prose, the cogency of his reasoning, and the images, metaphors, and analogies he relied on to clinch an argument. His paragraphs flowed with such ease that readers missed, or were prepared to forgive, the missteps in argumentation: the miscasting and trivializing of objections, the use of an unproven conclusion from one argument as the premise for the next, the reduction of complex issues to either/or alternatives equally embarrassing to the opposing side, or the slippery equation between Christianity's case against naturalism and Britain's struggle against fascism. But to Christians eager for a spirited defense of the faith, and an embattled populace receptive to moral justifications of its cause, Lewis possessed an immense appeal.

His first effort at apologetics, *The Problem of Pain*, is one of his most controversial. The Judeo-Christian tradition has long struggled with the problem of reconciling the goodness of an omnipotent creator with the suffering of the innocent and just in this world. From Job to the present, the integrity of this tradition has depended in part on the reluctance to brush away the scandal of human suffering. Lewis opens safely enough by claiming that pain ("suffering" would have been the more appropriate term) is a scandal only because we possess the notion of originary goodness and therefore regard affliction as an aberrant state of being. While naturalism dismisses religion as a defensive reaction to the terrors of insecurity, suffering, and death in this world, Lewis contends that these terrors are not so much the cause as the effect of our apprehension of the supernatural. In other words, the supernatural "creates, rather than solves, the problem of pain, for pain would be no problem unless, side by side with our daily experience of this painful world, we had received what we think a good assurance that ultimate reality is righteous and loving" (p. 24). To explain the rift between ultimate reality and our existing condition, Lewis adopts the Augustinian view that attributes evil to mankind's misuse of free agency, a willful defection that has produced "a radical alteration of his constitution, a disturbance of the relation between his component parts, and an internal perversion of one of them" (p. 84).

The argument begins to creak, however, when Lewis jumps from this traditional explanation to the conclusion that God sanctions pain for our own benefit. At the point where a Christian might have expected him to turn to the redemptive act of divine suffering, Lewis dwells instead on the divine use of human suffering. Pain is the means by which God "shatters the illusion that all is well" (p. 95), disrupting our slide into complacency with the world we have arranged for ourselves. At this stage Lewis is on the verge of transgressing the limits of Christian doctrine by positing a "tribulational system" (p. 105) in which suffering becomes the "sterilised or disinfected evil" (p. 116) through which God summons his wayward creatures back to himself. It is no accident that even sympathetic readers prefer the tormented sufferer of *A Grief Observed*. (Nor is it an accident that William Nicholson begins his play *Shadowlands* with a self-assured Lewis paraphrasing *The Problem of Pain* before he tastes the bitter cup of grief.) The original audience found much to praise in the book, but the metaphors were misleading, the prose too glib for so sensitive an issue, and the notion of a beneficent "tribulational system" bore spiritual and social implications that Lewis himself would have deplored.

No such problems beset the fictional *Screwtape Letters*, where the agency of tribulation shifts from a real heaven to an imaginary hell. The book comprises epistles from a senior devil to his nephew Wormwood, an apprentice in the art of temptation who is cutting his teeth on a new convert to Christianity. Screwtape has a nose for human folly and a knack for exploiting the favorable conditions of modernity. He advises Wormwood to capitalize on the novice's petty foibles and secret pride:

Work hard, then, on the disappointment or anticlimax which is certainly coming to the patient during his first few weeks as a churchman.... What he says, even on his knees, about his own sinfulness is all parrot talk. At bottom, he still believes he has run up a very favourable credit-balance in the Enemy's ledger by allowing himself to be converted, and thinks that he is showing great humility and condescension in going to church with these "smug," commonplace neighbours at all. Keep him in that state of mind as long as you can.

(pp. 13–14)

Although the young man's faith survives these early trials, Screwtape knows that every stage of spiritual growth offers fresh opportunities for seduction. If the patient shows signs of true humility, tempt him to become proud of it; if he begins to amend his life, "let the reflection 'My feelings are now growing more devout, or more charitable' so fix his attention inward that he no longer looks beyond himself to see our Enemy or his own neighbours" (p. 30). The trick at any stage is to attenuate our focus on the reality external to ourselves—"the taste for the *other*" (*The Problem of Pain*, p. 123)—and elevate the self into the principal object of its own attention.

Self-glorification, according to Screwtape, is the very essence of the infernal "Lowerarchy":

The whole philosophy of Hell rests on the recognition of the axiom that one thing is not another thing, and, specially, that one self is not another self. My good is my good and your good is yours. What one gains another loses.... for us, it means the sucking of will and freedom out of a weaker self into a stronger. "To be" *means* "to be in competition."

(p. 81)

The self-giving nature of divine love is beyond demonic comprehension, though Screwtape is confident that infernal science (another slap at naturalism) will one day penetrate the mystery: "If we could only find out what He is *really* up to! Hypothesis after hypothesis has been tried, and still we can't find out. Yet we must never lose hope; more and more complicated theories, fuller and fuller collections of data, richer rewards for researchers who make progress, more and more terrible punishments for those who fail" (p. 87). Unable to fathom or contain the Enemy, Screwtape grows short-tempered with his nephew as the new Christian repeatedly slips out of his net. By the time the young man dies in a bombing raid, he is beyond the grasp of his tempters, who in accord with their own nature have also turned on one another.

Christian tradition has generally pitched itself between privative and positive conceptions of evil. On one side is the Augustinian view that evil is ontologically void, and therefore nothing other than a defection of the will from God. On the other side is the dualist view that evil has the kind of substantial being implied by figures such as Satan and his brood. Each of these conceptions entails certain consequences, and each has been used at times to offset the excesses of the other. Lewis himself was an Augustinian and knew that the pragmatic advantage of the privative notion is that it checks the temptation to displace evil onto forces external to ourselves. In *The Screwtape Letters* he takes an imaginary excursion in the opposite direction to make playful use of the dualist element in Christian doctrine. By objectifying evil as an external power we can treat our own frailties as the effect of a power alien to our essential nature and better mobilize ourselves against them. The key to Lewis' success is that the objectifying mirror provokes much laughter and a little sympathy for our fragile condition.

In *The Abolition of Man* (1943), Lewis continues to reflect on suffering and evil in the modern world. Roughly contemporaneous with *That Hideous Strength*, the book situates the horrors of totalitarianism in the context of the more fundamental change associated with naturalism. In *The Abolition of Man*, Lewis attributes this change to the modern dissociation between mind and nature, emotion and object, values and facts—which has drained morality of its objective foundations and transformed external reality into a measurable and purely material domain. In line with contemporaneous critiques from the other end of the ideological spectrum, such as Theodor Adorno and Max Horkheimer's *Dialectic of Enlightenment* (1947), Lewis claims that in the modern era, rationality has been reduced to an instrumental mechanism for the conquest of Nature. Paradoxically, this rationality becomes a monstrous irrationality when it turns its gaze on humanity itself:

We reduce things to mere Nature *in order that* we may "conquer" them.... But as soon as we take the final step of reducing our own species to the level of mere Nature ... the being who stood to gain and the being who has been sacrificed are one and the same.... It is the magician's bargain: give up our soul, get power in return. But once our souls, that is, our selves, have been given up, the power thus conferred will not belong to us. We shall in fact be the slaves and puppets of that to which we have given our souls. It is in Man's power to treat himself as a mere "natural object" and his own judgements of values as raw material.... not raw material to be manipulated, as he fondly imagined, by himself, but by mere appetite, that is, mere Nature, in the person of his dehumanized Conditioners.

(pp. 82–84)

Humanity's conquest of Nature has turned into Nature's reconquest of humanity, and the very agency of humanity's emancipation has become the instrument of its re-enslavement. The political implications of this process are as frightening as they are obvious: "the power of Man to make himself what he pleases means ... the power of some men to make other men what *they* please" (p. 72).

Against this self-destructive rationality Lewis marshals the perennial wisdom of the ages. Reversing the modern tendency to subjectivize values, Lewis draws on the sages of various traditions, pagan and Christian, Western and non-Western, to demonstrate the universality of moral law—"the doctrine of objective value, the belief that certain attitudes are really true, and others really false, to the kind of thing the universe is and the kind of things we are" (p. 29). Lewis is enough of a philosopher to know that mere agreement on certain principles does not demonstrate their inherent validity. Nevertheless, by gathering diverse testimonials as evidence of common rationality based on principles of justice, kindness, loyalty, and courage, he portrays modern rationality as a grisly aberration from the human norm. A demonstrable proof may be beyond our grasp, but as Lewis sets up the alternatives, the consequence of denying the moral law will be the "abolition of man" as envisioned in the inner sanctum of N.I.C.E.

In *The Great Divorce* (1945), Lewis returns to the fictional mode of *The Screwtape Letters* and lays out his Augustinian view of evil. The book is a dream vision based on the medieval idea of the *Refrigerium* (p. 66)—the speculative notion that God continues to woo the damned in Hell by offering them periodic glimpses of Heaven. At the outset an unnamed narrator finds himself boarding a bus with some inhabitants of a dull sprawling town. Before long he realizes from their incessant griping that his fellow riders belong to the infernal regions, and when their bus arrives at the outer precincts of Heaven, he notices that they appear insubstantial by comparison to the bright solid people they encounter. In a series of exchanges with former colleagues, friends, and relatives, most of the visitors reaffirm the choice they have already made: a former bishop maintains his conviction that "to travel hopefully is better than to arrive" (p. 43); a hard-bitten cynic asserts that Heaven and Hell are run by the same Combine; a woman fixated on the child she has lost remains indifferent or hostile to God.

At the center of the book the narrator meets his venerable mentor, George Macdonald, who unravels the meaning of the dream vision. Heaven is the only Reality, Macdonald explains, while Hell is a but a "state of mind." The damned are those who have chosen to reject or ignore God, and "without that self-choice there could be no Hell" (p. 72). The freedom to decide remains open to them even beyond the grave, and nothing but their own will prevents them from staying forever in the company of the blessed. The consequences of choice, according to Macdonald, transcend mortal conceptions of time and space. For the individual who turns to God, the past itself "begins to change so that his forgiven sins and remembered sorrows take on the quality of Heaven" (p. 68). At the same time, Hell dissolves into nothing so that "the Blessed will say, 'We have never lived anywhere except in Heaven'" (p. 68). By the end of the book the privative conception of evil has been pushed so far that the infernal dominion has dwindled into a minute crack in Deep Heaven, and Macdonald declares that the tiniest element in the Real World is more substantial than Hell in its entirety. In language ascending to an almost mystical plane, Macdonald affirms the eternal significance of freedom—"the gift whereby ye most resemble your Maker" (p. 125)—and in suggesting that true freedom may transcend our mortal understanding of choice he hints at the universalist position that ultimately every soul will be redeemed. Nevertheless, he reminds the narrator that Hell is real enough for those who continue to choose it. Or as Lewis puts it in the preface: Hell may be ontologically void, but we should resist the "false and disastrous" conclusion "that everything is good and everywhere is Heaven" (p. 7).

In his last major work of apologetics, *Miracles* (1947), Lewis abandons the more conversational manner of previous books and attempts a sustained philosophical treatise to demonstrate "the possibility or probability of the miraculous" (p. 4). His initial assault on naturalism runs into trouble, however, and in the view of some readers, he never quite recovers. In *The Abolition of Man*, Lewis considered the dualistic element of naturalism and successfully picked apart its dissociation between value and fact, mind and matter. In *Miracles* he approaches naturalism as a monistic system that reduces everything to matter governed by deterministic laws. Few would quarrel with this formulation, but Lewis goes on to argue that naturalism is caught in a vicious circle, since it calls into question the integrity of the rational processes upon which it (or any conceptual system) depends. By employing this argument Lewis walks into the midst of a long and complex debate over the relationship between mind and reality, a debate involving a host of issues that he never bothers to address.

Lewis has better success in later sections of the book, where he offers a vivid if not entirely original reconception of miracles as the fulfillment rather than the disruption, or "invasion," of the natural order: "Our whole picture of Nature being 'invaded' (as if by a foreign enemy) was wrong. When we actually examine one of these invasions it looks much more like the arrival of a king among his own subjects" (p. 32). In other words, Lewis naturalizes the miraculous not by eliminating the supernatural but by subsuming the natural into a more inclusive reality in which the common distinction between natural and supernatural no longer holds. But as compelling as this vision may be, the argument of *Miracles* is hobbled throughout by the casual use of problematic terms, inferences, and analogies. Lewis himself was dissatisfied with the book, particularly after it received a drubbing from the philosopher G. E. M. (Elizabeth) Anscombe during a now-legendary Oxford debate in February 1948 (chapter 3, the main target of her attack, was revised for the 1960 edition). It is difficult to say whether this incident affected the subsequent course of Lewis' career, but never again did he attempt a treatise on the order of *Miracles*, and it was nearly a decade before he returned in a serious way to religious exposition of any sort. When *Reflections on the Psalms* appeared in 1958, Lewis made it clear from the start that he had left behind apologetics for a more intimate mode of spiritual reflection.

# C. S. LEWIS

## THE CHRONICLES OF NARNIA

LEWIS may have been disappointed by *Miracles* and its reception, but part of the ill-fated book proved fertile for his next venture into fiction. At one point in *Miracles*, Lewis speculates on the possibility of natural systems other than our own. For the modern naturalist, he claims, the system of nature as we know it is the only existent reality; for the supernaturalist, however, there is a higher reality transcending nature, and the latter "may, or may not, be the only reality which the one Primary Thing has produced" (p. 9). Lewis goes on to imagine that God might bring two natures into partial contact at some point, and "if this occurred each of the two Natures would be 'supernatural' in relation to the other. . . . It would be one kind of Miracle" (p. 10). For Lewis, this notion of alternative worlds serves several ends: first, it establishes the point that our spatiotemporal system is a derived, contingent, and relative arrangement; second, it suggests that we may live in a created universe far richer than we ordinarily assume; and finally, it holds out the possibility that our own nature may be influenced by other natures, or, as Lewis indicates elsewhere, by the power of imagination to disrupt and transform the "natural" order of things.

These ideas came to fruition in *The Chronicles of Narnia*, begun in 1948 and published in seven installments between 1950 and 1956. They relate the stories of several English children who find themselves transported periodically to the world of Narnia. The children become leaders and agents of redemption at crucial points in Narnian history, and in this respect their exploits are a kind of miraculous intervention in the affairs of a different natural order. At the same time the sudden translation to another world is a kind of miracle in the lives of the children, who return home tested and transformed by their adventures. The fact that these journeys take up no earthly time—the children return to the same place at the same time they departed—underscores their "miraculous" character.

Narnia is at once the name of the world and of a particular kingdom within it. The latter is inhabited by the Talking Beasts, the Waking Trees, and a variety of other creatures such as the Fauns, Naiads, Satyrs, and Centaurs. Like the Malacandrans of *Out of the Silent Planet*, the various inhabitants of Narnia possess rational intelligence. Once again, Lewis is imagining what it would be like to dwell in a world where rationality is not confined to a single species but permeates the entire creation. The Waking Trees play a minor role in Narnian affairs, but they illustrate the mingling of consciousness and matter associated with Merlin in *That Hideous Strength* and presumably lost to nature as we now conceive it. The Fauns and other mythological beings exemplify Lewis' hypothesis that the myths of one world may be the realities of another, as if to say that the mythopoeic imagination has an objective foundation in the cosmic order. Together these creatures constitute a natural system that is corrupted not by willful rebellion from within, as is our world, but by external intervention from beyond. Throughout its history Narnia has kings and queens imported primarily from our world, and while the virtuous monarchs reign on behalf of the lion Aslan—creator and sovereign of this alternative world—others exercise tyrannical control, muting the Talking Beasts and polluting the Narnian landscape. (Late in the cycle Lewis introduces another source of evil in the mighty, despotic empire of Calormen, inhabited by humans of unexplained origins and alien customs, to the south of the Kingdom of Narnia. Unfortunately, Lewis depicts the difference between free and imperial societies in terms of a transparent contrast between fair-skinned, northern followers of Aslan and dark-skinned, desert dwellers who worship the bloodthirsty Tash.) Aslan himself appears periodically in Narnian history, and though he may disappear for centuries at a time, he returns at the end as judge and redeemer.

In *Miracles*, Lewis speculates that "other Natures might not be spatio-temporal at all" (p. 9). Narnia is a spatiotemporal world, but it is governed by natural laws different from our own. Physical conditions are similar, but the sudden metamorphoses confined to mythology in our world are literal in Narnia: witches transform living beings into stone; a greedy child turns temporarily into a dragon; Aslan turns a stiff-necked prince into a braying donkey. Narnian time is also slightly different. Altogether *The Chronicles* span a half century of Earth time—approximately 1900 to 1950—corresponding to roughly twenty-five hundred years Narnian years. But compared to our world, Narnian time runs not only faster but also at an uneven rate: one year on Earth may correspond to a Narnian millennium, another year to a Narnian decade, and whenever the children are in Narnia no time transpires in our world. By relating the two temporalities in this asymmetrical manner, Lewis attempts to disrupt our ordinary sense of time and hints at the possibility of unexpected disruptions in the rhythm of temporal progression. The sense of the uncanny is highlighted by the fact that the children cannot enter Narnia at will. They are translated by Aslan without warning and have no foreknowledge of the span of Narnian time that has transpired since their previous visit.

The plots of the first five books are relatively simple: overcoming the tyranny of a wicked witch (*The Lion, the Witch, and the Wardrobe*); delivering Narnia from foreign overlords (*Prince Caspian*); journeying to the End of the World (*The Voyage of the Dawn Treader*); recovering a lost prince (*The Silver Chair*); and alerting the kingdom to a surprise invasion (*The Horse and His Boy*). The first story is Christological—an archetypal tale of redemption and sacrifice resembling the story of the crucifixion and resurrection of Christ. The next four stories focus on issues of moral development: trust, loyalty, and steadfastness in *Prince Caspian*; temptations of flesh and spirit in *The Voyage of the Dawn Treader*; wisdom and discernment in *The Silver Chair*; and confidence and humility in *The Horse and His Boy*. The last two books—*The Magician's Nephew* and *The Last Battle*—provide a mythic frame for the cycle by telling the story of Narnia's creation, destruction, and final transfiguration.

Lewis' Christian Platonism underlies the entire sequence. Christian myth is at the center of the first tale; Platonism is introduced in the fourth tale, and synthesized with Christianity in the finale. In *The Lion, the Witch, and the Wardrobe*, four children enter Narnia to find a land tyrannized by the White Witch, who has "made it always winter and never Christmas" (p. 102). The Witch quickly seduces the boy Edmund into betraying his siblings, but the other three children are drawn to the figure of Aslan, who has returned to restore his kingdom. In her climactic encounter with the Lion, the Witch lays claim to Edmund, invoking the Deep Magic by which "every traitor belongs to me as my lawful prey" (p. 139). Offering his own life in exchange for the boy, Aslan is bound to the Stone Table, muzzled, and killed by the exultant Witch and her crew. Lewis' depiction of the children's grief over Aslan's death, and their joy over his reappearance, is skillful enough to offset the element of predictability and recapture some of the wonder of the original resurrection story. As the Lion explains, the Deep Magic of the law has been superseded by the Deeper Magic of grace: "It means," said Aslan, "that though the Witch knew the Deep Magic, there is a magic deeper still which she did not know. . . . when a willing victim who had committed no treachery was killed in a traitor's stead, the Table would crack and Death itself would start working backwards" (pp. 159–160). The Narnianism of death "working backwards" conveys the sense of the miraculous but in the concrete terms of a natural process in reverse. Once the point is made, Lewis provides the satisfaction of watching Aslan rout his adversaries and install the children as monarchs of the realm.

*The Silver Chair* introduces the Platonic elements that loom large at the end of *The Chronicles*. Two children are assigned to recover the lost Prince Rilian, who was ensnared by a beautiful witch ten years earlier. Armed with instructions from Aslan and a shrewd, skeptical guide, the children are compelled at every turn to exercise vigilance and remain attentive to the signs that will lead them to their destination. Eventually they descend into the gloomy, subterranean Underland where they find the enchanted Prince. Unaware of his own identity, Rilian believes that the Witch protects him from a curse that sends him into a frenzy once each night. In fact, it is during his nocturnal fits, when he is bound to a silver chair, ostensibly to keep him from harming others, that Rilian briefly recovers his true identity and demands his release. Echoing Plato's allegory of the cave (*Republic*, book 7), the Witch uses her powers of enchantment to lull her new adversaries into believing that the world outside her kingdom is only a dream. Employing the logic of naturalism, she explains away their appeal to the "sun" and other elements of the Overworld:

When you try to think out clearly what this *sun* must be, you cannot tell me. You can only tell me it is like the lamp. Your *sun* is a dream; and there is nothing in that dream that was not copied from the lamp. The lamp is the real thing; the *sun* is but a tale, a children's story. . . . There is no Narnia, no Overworld, no sky, no sun, no Aslan.

(pp. 155–157)

The Witch reverses image and archetype, copy and original, claiming that the Underland is the reality and the Overland an illusory extrapolation.

It is the children's guide, skeptical as always, who summons his last ounce of strength and breaks the metaphysical spell:

> Suppose we *have* only dreamed, or made up, all those things—trees and grass and sun and moon and stars and Aslan himself. Suppose we have. Then all I can say is that, in that case, the made-up things seem a good deal more important than the real ones. . . . I'm on Aslan's side even if there isn't any Aslan to lead it. I'm going to live as like a Narnian as I can even if there isn't any Narnia.
>
> (p. 159)

This response is more the tentative reasoning of William James's "The Will to Believe" (1896) than the credo of an assured believer. But for Lewis the guide is expressing an intuitive apprehension of a true homeland beyond the confines of the natural world. His gesture proves potent enough to overcome the enchantment, since the Witch instantly turns into a serpent and is put to death. Lewis reiterates the Platonic theme when the triumphant company returns to the Narnian Overland. The old Narnian king dies in the midst of the reunion with his son, but anticipating the miraculous conclusion of the final book, the children are briefly transported to Aslan's country to witness the king's awakening, or as Lewis would put it at the end of *The Chronicles*, "the beginning of the real story" (*The Last Battle*, p. 184).

Christian eschatology and Platonic metaphysics come together in *The Last Battle*. For readers of the first six stories, the tale of Narnia's downfall is a particularly grim affair. External enemies overrun the kingdom, while moral confusion erodes it from within, as an insidious ape dupes a gullible donkey into posing as Aslan and holding court inside in a stable. The always skeptical Narnian Dwarfs become more suspicious than ever in this deceitful atmosphere and finally desert their countrymen. For the first time the arrival of children from our world fails to rescue Narnia. Moreover, in the midst of this consuming chaos the children begin to recall that on earth their train was crashing at the moment they were translated to Narnia, and they gradually realize that their own lives are coming to an end. Lewis is drawing together his two worlds.

Just as all hope of temporal deliverance vanishes, the scene of the final battle turns into the site of redemption. The stable of the false Aslan becomes the judgment seat of the true Aslan, and its door the gateway to eternity. In a vivid account of cosmic devolution the stars fall from the sky, the last living things are gathered into the stable, and the land, the sea, and the sun dissolve into darkness. But following the de-creation of Narnia comes its final transfiguration. It begins with some signs of Aslan's mercy—the salvation of a virtuous worshiper of Tash and the poor donkey who posed as Aslan. The intensity rises steadily in anticipation of the discovery that the Narnia left behind "was only a shadow or copy," and the world beyond death is "the real Narnia, which has always been here and always will be here" (p. 169). "It's all in Plato" (p. 170), we are reassured, as Lewis tries to capture his characters' mixture of astonishment and recognition upon arrival in the "deeper country": "I have come home at last! This is my real country! I belong here. . . . The reason why we loved the old Narnia is that it sometimes looked a little like this" (p. 171). In the final chapter, "Farewell to Shadow-Lands," the limitations of space and time are suspended as the newcomers swim up the face of a waterfall, and their pace continues to quicken "till it was more like flying than running" (p. 175). The children are reunited with old Narnian and earthly friends, and catching a glimpse of "the real England" they learn from Aslan that indeed they have all died in a railway accident. But the Lion quickly puts it in the right light, welcoming them to their true home beyond the contingencies of the natural order: "'The term is over: the holidays have begun. The dream is ended: this is the morning.' . . . the beginning of the real story" (pp. 183–184).

On the basis of the lukewarm early reviews, it would have been difficult to predict the remarkable response to the Narnia tales. *The Chronicles* are among the most celebrated children's stories in circulation, and the attraction seems to extend well beyond childhood. Since they have achieved classic status, it has become common either to expect too much from them or to fall prey to the suspicion such popularity breeds. Lewis himself never took these stories as seriously as either his followers or his disappointed detractors. But if the Narnia stories are no foundation for a degree in theology, they are wise and edifying. If they fail to rise to the level of the most distinguished modern fiction, they are still masterpieces of a more limited kind, and in their moments of highest mythopoeic intensity they far transcend the limitations of their genre.

## TILL WE HAVE FACES

For many years Lewis had dreamed of refashioning the tale of Cupid and Psyche as it appears in Apuleius' second-century romance, *The Golden Ass*. The story had obvious appeal as an allegory of the soul's search for love, but in Lewis' reworking (*Till We Have Faces*, published in 1956) it becomes a portrait of the corruption of love and the ease with which love can turn into its own opposite. The narrator and main protagonist is not Psyche but her sister Orual, a minor figure in Apuleius. Her narrative is divided into two sections. In part 1 she tells the story of her life in the form of a complaint against the gods, who have left her embittered in old age. In the brief part 2, written as she approaches death, Orual relates the eleventh-hour transformation of soul that compels her to reinterpret her life and reconciles her to the mysterious ways of the divine. Whether or not Lewis intended it, the relation between the telling and the retelling of her story is not simply a matter of error and correction of error. Orual's initial self-portrait is sufficiently persuasive, and her complaint against the gods sufficiently cogent, to make this work of fiction the most complex in the Lewis canon.

The novel takes place in the pagan kingdom of Glome, "a little barbarous state," as Lewis later described it, "on the borders of the Hellenistic world with Greek culture just beginning to affect it" (*Letters of C. S. Lewis*, 1993 ed., p. 462). Orual describes her upbringing as a physically unattractive but intelligent princess who is tutored by a wise Greek—the Fox—with clear ties to Stoic philosophy. Orual's principal attachment, however, is to her beautiful younger stepsister, Psyche, whose mother died while giving birth to her. Psyche's beauty is "'according to nature'; what every woman, or even every thing, ought to have been and meant to be, but had missed by some trip of chance. Indeed, when you looked at her you believed, for a moment, that they had not missed it. She made beauty all around her" (p. 22). The relationship between the two sisters changes dramatically when a ruinous plague afflicts the kingdom. The priest of the goddess Ungit (Lewis avoids the name Aphrodite) descends from the sacred mountain and demands the sacrifice of royal blood to the mysterious shadow known as the Brute. When the Fox argues that the demand for human sacrifice is irrational and barbaric, the Priest responds with a chilling but prophetic statement:

We are hearing much Greek wisdom this morning.... but it brings no rain and grows no corn; sacrifice does both.... They demand to see such things clearly, as if the gods were no more than letters written in a book. I, King, have dealt with the gods for three generations of men, and I know that they dazzle our eyes and flow in and out of one another like eddies on a river, and nothing that is said clearly can be said truly about them. Holy places are dark places. It is life and strength, not knowledge and words, that we get in them. Holy wisdom is not clear and thin like water, but thick and dark like blood.

(p. 50)

At this point it is tempting to identify with the humane position of the Fox, who resists the pagan demand for human sacrifice, and after the lot falls on Psyche we also identify with the plight of Orual, who is threatened with the loss of her sister. But to Orual's dismay Psyche seems to welcome her fate:

I have always—at least, ever since I can remember—had a kind of longing for death.... The sweetest thing in all my life has been the longing—to reach the Mountain, to find the place where all the beauty came from.... All my life the god of the Mountain has been wooing me.

(pp. 74–76)

This is vintage *Sehnsucht*, and Orual's response—"I only see that you have never loved me" (p. 76)—takes us to the thematic crux of the book. If the exchange between the Fox and the Priest defines the conflict between natural and supernatural points of view, the encounter between Orual and Psyche establishes a parallel but more problematic opposition between human and divine love. Orual's control over the narrative keeps the reader sympathetic to her and to the Fox, but the course of subsequent events will reveal the shortcomings of her passionate attachment to Psyche and confirm the sacred wisdom of the Priest.

After Psyche is led away to sacrifice, Orual journeys to the Mountain to give her a proper burial. She is shocked to find her sister alive and is perplexed by Psyche's report that she is now dwelling in a palace with an unnamed god whose face she is forbidden to see. In her account of the situation, Orual recalls her own uncertainty over her sighting of the palace:

It might have been a true seeing; the cloud over my mortal eyes may have been lifted for a moment. It might not.... Either way, there's divine mockery in it. They set the riddle and then allow a seeming that can't be tested and can only quicken and thicken the tormenting whirlpool of your guess-work. If they had an honest intention to guide us, why is their guidance not plain?

(pp. 133–134)

After consulting the Fox, who shares her suspicions, Orual returns to her sister and threatens to take her own life unless Psyche will "set all our doubts at rest" (p. 162) by looking at the face of her lover. Out of love for her sister Psyche reluctantly agrees, lamenting "that I am betraying the best of lovers" (p. 166). Soon afterward Orual has a fleeting recognition that "from the beginning, I had known that Psyche's lover was a god," and hears a voice tell her, "Now Psyche goes out in exile.... You also shall be Psyche" (pp. 173–174). She then returns home, and hiding her face with a veil—symbolic of the suppression of her wounded soul—she commits herself to serving the kingdom.

Part 1 ends many years later when the aging Orual, after a long and successful reign as queen of Glome, travels abroad and hears a priest relate a distorted version of Psyche's story. In this account (essentially Apuleius'), Orual's decision to compel Psyche to gaze on her lover's face is motivated by sheer envy:

It was as if the gods themselves had first laughed, and then spat, in my face.... For if the true story had been like their story, no riddle would have been set me; there would have been no guessing and no guessing wrong. More than that, it's a story belonging to a different world, a world in which the gods show themselves clearly and don't torment men with glimpses, nor unveil to one what they hide from another.... In such a world (is there such? it's not ours, for certain) I would have walked aright. The gods themselves would have been able to find no fault in me. And now to tell my story as if I had had the very sight they had denied me.

(pp. 243–244)

Orual returns home to write her indictment of the gods, who will neither leave us alone nor "show themselves openly ... what is all this but cat-and-mouse play, blindman's buff, and mere jugglery? Why must holy places be dark places?" (p. 249). Her narrative ends with a demand for a response from the gods in the expectation that "they have no answer" (p. 250).

In part 2, the dying Orual relates the events that transform her life and bring about a recantation of her earlier narrative. "The gods' surgery" (pp. 253–254) begins with the memories awakened by the very act of composing part 1, proceeds to the recognition of her past insensitivities to family and friends, and culminates in two significant dream visions. In the first, Orual looks into a mirror and beholds the loathsome face of Ungit. Tearing the veil from her own face, she confronts the spiritual ugliness that she has concealed for so long. In the second, Orual is led into a divine courtroom and instructed to read her complaint against the gods. In the course of this testimonial she becomes aware of the true beauty of the gods, though it merely fuels her resentment and betrays the selfish nature of her love for Psyche:

Do you think we mortals will find you gods easier to bear if you're beautiful? I tell you that if that's true we'll find you a thousand times worse. For then (I know what beauty does) you'll lure and entice. You'll leave us nothing.... The girl was mine. What right had you to steal her away into your dreadful heights? ... Oh, you'll say you took her away into bliss and joy such as I could never have given her, and I ought to have been glad of it for her sake. Why? What should I care for some horrible, new happiness which I hadn't given her and which separated her from me? Do you think I wanted her to be happy, that way? It would have been better if I'd seen the Brute tear her in pieces before my eyes.... She was mine. *Mine.*

(pp. 290–292)

Orual does not need the judge to pronounce the verdict. Condemned by her own selfishness, she knows that "the complaint was the answer. To have heard myself making it was to be answered" (p. 294). She now understands that the failure to understand the divine is closely tied to the failure to know ourselves: "I saw well why the gods do not speak to us openly, nor let us answer. Till that word [the truth at the center of our being] can be dug out of us, why should they hear the babble that we think we mean? How can they meet us face to face till we have faces?" (p. 294).

Exposed to the depths of her own soul, Orual hears the voice of the Fox, who instructs her in divine wisdom and leads her to the threshold of Psyche's palace. Hand in hand with her sister she is prepared to come before the presence of the sacred:

The air was growing brighter and brighter about us; as if something had set it on fire. Each breath I drew let into me new terror, joy, overpowering sweetness. I was pierced through and through with the arrows of it. I was being unmade.... The most dreadful, the most beautiful, the only dread and beauty there is, was coming. The pillars on the far side of the pool flushed with his approach. I cast down my eyes.

(p. 307)

After the voice of the god fulfills the old prophecy by declaring, "You also are Psyche" (p. 308), the vision fades and Orual prepares for death. Her narrative breaks off in the midst of a final prayer that replaces the divine silence at the end of part 1 with the recognition, echoing the conclusion of the Book of Job, that "You are yourself the answer. Before your face questions die away" (p. 308).

*Till We Have Faces* met a confused and rather cool reception. Lewis himself could not understand his readers' difficulties. In his view Orual presented a case of "human affection in its natural condition: true, tender, suffering, but in the long run, tyrannically possessive and ready to turn to hatred when the beloved ceases to be its possession. What such love particularly cannot stand is to see the beloved passing into a sphere where it cannot follow" (*Letters of C. S. Lewis*, 1993 ed., p. 462). Lewis provides a sufficiently accurate gloss, but it fails to take into account the uncharacteristically sharp opposition between reason and faith, human and divine knowledge, that cuts through this text. Nor does it acknowledge the tricky and sometimes equivocal relations between the meaning and the vehicle used to convey it. Consider, for example, Orual's physical appearance. The use of facial ugliness to signify a spiritual condition may be an acceptable convention in certain genres, but in this work of mixed and almost indefinable genre Orual's unsightly face—a brute fact of her existence—is a misleading figure for spiritual "ugliness," which implies a disposition of the will and therefore a condition for which we are ultimately responsible. Similar difficulties arise in the relationship between the pagan setting and the Christian meaning. Given the initial contrast between the humane rationality of the Fox and the barbaric rituals of Glomian religion, it should come as no surprise that readers identify with Orual's complaint against the gods, or that they sense something monstrous in the Priest's call for human sacrifice and in his victim's eagerness to offer herself. In other words, it is not just a lack of discernment that prompts certain readers to prefer Orual's love for Psyche to Psyche's love of death, and to feel a bit deceived or even cheated when the former is declared tyrannically possessive and the latter divinely inspired. At the end of *The Pilgrim's Regress*, Lewis carefully mediated between otherworldly *Sehnsucht* and the recognition that human beings do not possess the "angelic indifference" to detach themselves entirely from "the tether and pang of the particular." Perhaps those readers who are troubled by the austere detachment of the Priest, and Psyche's all-too-angelic compliance with his demand, are defending Lewis' own deeper sense of the doubleness of the human condition.

### LATER WORKS

LEWIS remained a prolific writer until his death, despite the wearing effects of illness in his final years. In his last decade he published four scholarly works: His classic survey, *English Literature in the Sixteenth Century, Excluding Drama* (1954); *Studies in Words* (1960), an analysis of axial terms such as "nature," "sense," and "conscience" (and their cognates in other languages) from the Greeks to the present; *An Experiment in Criticism* (1961), an essay on the practice of reading; and *The Discarded Image* (1964), an introduction to medieval cosmology. The last, designed as a practical guide for students, is characteristic of the workmanlike, almost offhand style of his later prose. Occasionally mistaken for fatigue or laziness, the new style proceeds from an attempt to adopt a less declamatory and more companionable voice.

This stylistic change is also evident in the religious writings to which Lewis returned after nearly a decade—*Reflections on the Psalms* (1958), *The Four Loves* (1960), *A Grief Observed* (1961), and *Letters to Malcolm: Chiefly on Prayer* (1964)—which depart from the platform manner of the 1940s. The very choice of topics indicates the new direction. Lewis is no longer the public orator demonstrating the truth of Christianity to a general audience. As he states in the opening of *Reflections on the Psalms*, "A man can't be always defending the truth; there must be a time to feed on it" (p. 7). His voice becomes warmer and more personal. The genial *Four Loves*, originally commissioned for broadcast on American radio, reflects candidly on the pleasures of natural affection, friendship, and sex (for which it ran into trouble). *A Grief Observed* is openly confessional, and *Letters to Malcolm* (an imaginary friend) has the ambling manner of "two people on the foothills comparing notes in private" (p. 63). Whether or not it is attributable to the intimacies of his relationship with Joy Davidman, a new recognition of the more personal recesses of faith, already apparent in *Till We Have Faces*, underlies the style and substance of these works. Never far from view is a concern with the images, fictions, and illusions that mask us from our own selves and from the divine reality beyond us. Echoing Orual's realization of the difficulty of meeting God "face to face" (*Till We Have Faces*, p. 294), Lewis tells Malcolm in his final book that "the prayer preceding all prayers is 'May it be the real I who speaks. May it be the real Thou that I speak to'" (*Letters to Malcolm*, p. 82).

*A Grief Observed* is the most intimate and rhetorically complex of these religious writings. Originally published under a pseudonym, it comprises several notebooks expressing the author's anguish after the death of his wife. The risk of such a book is that it courts the inauthentic at every turn. The problem is apparent in the double meaning of the title: the experience or "observance" of mourning is threatened by the very act of observing it. The reader is alert to any hint that the writer is glancing over his shoulder at a prospective audience or, worse still, using the situation as another occasion for writing. Lewis confronts these difficulties by representing the process of mourning as a ceaseless struggle against the very temptation to lapse into the counterfeit. He expresses disgust with his own efforts to dramatize his grief, to reduce it to something less painful or to produce more self-satisfying images of his wife:

Slowly, quietly, like snow-flakes—like the small flakes that come when it is going to snow all night—little flakes of me, my impressions, my selections, are settling down on the image of her. The real shape will be quite hidden in the end.... The rough, sharp, cleansing tang of her otherness is gone.... As if I wanted to fall in love with my memory of her, an image in my own mind! It would be a sort of incest.

(pp. 21–22)

As he grows more concerned with the fictions that cloud his relations to other persons and to God, the cross becomes the image for the shattering of images: "Images of the Holy easily become holy images—sacrosanct. My idea of God is not a divine idea. It has to be shattered time after time. He shatters it Himself. He is the great iconoclast. Could we not almost say that this shattering is one of the marks of His presence?" (p. 76). A similar gesture leads to the final recognition that in the process of nullifying our efforts to explain its mysteries, "Heaven will solve our problems, but not, I think, by showing us subtle reconciliations between all our apparently contradictory notions. The notions will all be knocked from under our feet. We shall see that there never was any problem" (p. 83). Paradoxically, it is this iconoclastic demand for the real that allows Lewis to portray his grief, and project a vision of the afterlife, without seeming to fictionalize them in the process.

## LEGACY

SEVERAL decades after Lewis' death it is still difficult to assess the significance of his achievement. From one perspective he seems a relatively minor figure in twentieth-century letters: his scholarly works are still read but are no longer in vogue; his fiction receives scant attention in mainstream literary histories; and his religious writings cater primarily to sectarian interests. But this assessment ignores the fact that Lewis retains a huge following that has shown no sign of slackening. In particular it overlooks the extraordinary and enduring appeal of the Narnia tales, and the esteem in which his religious writings are held in many Christian churches. In other words, Lewis has left a divided legacy that reflects more basic divisions within our culture.

Lewis' influence as a scholar and critic has lasted several generations. *The Allegory of Love* restored appreciation for a literature alien to twentieth-century ears, and though its main premises have been successfully challenged, the book remains the *locus classicus* of a still-influential view of medieval literature. Lewis' second major study, *English Literature in the Sixteenth Century*, is a standard work in the field and an indispensable guide to the less-celebrated authors of the period. These books, supported by *A Preface to* Paradise Lost, *Studies in Words, The Discarded Image,* and any number of influential articles, constitute one of the century's most imposing interpretations of medieval and Renaissance literature.

As a writer of fiction, Lewis stood apart from the literary realism that was still dominant in the first half of the century, and to a degree he has suffered from his allegiance to narrative modes that are only now securing their share of cultural prestige. In 1947 (the year prior to the birth of Narnia) Lewis expressed a forlorn hope for "a better school of prose story in England: of story that can mediate imaginative life to the masses while not being contemptible to the few" ("On Stories," in *Of This and Other Worlds*, p. 42). As a member of the Inklings, he was struggling to create the taste for an alternative fictional tradition that looks back to Macdonald and Morris and within a few years would include Tolkien's *The Lord of the Rings* and his own *Chronicles of Narnia*. At that point it would have been difficult to envision the spectacular success of his enterprise. But it is also hard to imagine that he would have relished the mutation of his "better school of prose story" into a major popular industry with Tolkien as high priest and Lewis as his prophet.

In the realm of popular Christian apologetics, Lewis seems to have no peer. His books are steeped in the ethos of a bygone era, but the audience first stirred by his wartime books and broadcasts now makes up only a tiny portion of his vast readership. His extraordinary popularity in the United States, especially among evangelical Protestants, has given rise to a substantial industry (see the bibliography) sustained by Christian publishing houses, enterprising author societies, and the establishment of a major archive in Wheaton, Illinois. Such lionization produces its own frictions, but it should not obscure the fact that the Lewis mystique transcends many of the prevailing divisions within contemporary Christendom. To many who are unfamiliar or unmoved by the discourse of modern theology, he holds out the prospect of a rationally sustainable Christianity in an age when it can no longer rely on its traditional metaphysical supports. Although his defense of Christian doctrine skirts some of the difficult questions raised by modernity, his appeal to the mind through the imagination has made him the most influential apologist of our time.

## SELECTED BIBLIOGRAPHY

I. BIBLIOGRAPHIES. Joe R. Christopher and Joan K. Ostling, *C. S. Lewis: An Annotated Checklist of Writings About Him and His Works* (Kent, Ohio, 1974); Walter Hooper, "A Bibliography of the Writings of C. S. Lewis: Revised and Enlarged," in *C. S. Lewis at the Breakfast Table and Other Reminiscences*, ed. by James T. Como (New York, 1979; London, 1980); Susan Lowenberg, *C. S. Lewis: A Reference Guide, 1972–1988* (New York, 1993).

II. SEPARATE WORKS. *Spirits in Bondage: A Cycle of Lyrics* (London, 1919), pub. under pseudonym Clive Hamilton; *Dymer* (London, 1926), poem pub. under pseudonym Clive Hamilton; *The Pilgrim's Regress: An Allegorical Apology for Christianity, Reason, and Romanticism* (London, 1933; 3d ed. 1943); *The Allegory of Love: A Study in Medieval Tradition* (Oxford, 1936); *Out of the Silent Planet* (London, 1938); *The Personal Heresy: A Controversy*, with E. M. W. Tillyard (London, 1939); *Rehabilitations and Other Essays* (London, 1939).

*The Problem of Pain* (London, 1940); *Broadcast Talks* (London, 1942; pub. as *The Case for Christianity*, New York, 1943); *A Preface to* Paradise Lost (London, 1942); *The Screwtape Letters* (London, 1942; New York, 1943; repr. with additional letter in *The Screwtape Letters and Screwtape Proposes a Toast*, London, 1961; New York, 1962); *The Abolition of Man; or, Reflections on Education with Special Reference to the Teaching of English in the Upper Forms of Schools* (London, 1943); *Christian Behaviour: A Further Series of Broadcast Talks* (London and New York, 1943); *Perelandra* (London, 1943; New York, 1944; repub. as *Voyage to Venus*, London, 1953); *Beyond Personality: The Christian Idea of God* (London, 1944; New York, 1945); *The Great Divorce: A Dream* (London, 1945; New York, 1946); *That Hideous Strength: A Modern Fairy-Tale for Grown-Ups* (London, 1945; abridged as *The Tortured Planet [That Hideous Strength]*, New York, 1946); *Miracles: A Preliminary Study* (London and New York, 1947; repr. with revised chapter 3, London, 1960); *The Arthurian Torso: Containing the Posthumous Fragment of "The Figure of Arthur" by Charles Williams and "A Commentary on the Arthurian Poems of Charles Williams" by C. S. Lewis* (London, 1948); *Transposition and Other Addresses* (London, 1949; pub. as *The Weight of Glory and Other Addresses*, New York, 1949; rev. and exp., 1980).

*The Lion, the Witch, and the Wardrobe: A Story for Children* (London and New York, 1950), book 1 of *The Chronicles of Narnia*; *Prince Caspian: The Return to Narnia* (London and New York, 1951), book 2 of *The Chronicles of Narnia*; *Mere Christianity* (London and New York, 1952; repr. with some original broadcast material, New York, 1981), a revised and amplified edition, with a new introduction, of *Broadcast Talks* (1942), *Christian Behaviour* (1943), and *Beyond Personality* (1944); *The Voyage of the Dawn Treader* (London and New York, 1952), book 3 of *The Chronicles of Narnia*; *The Silver Chair* (London and New York, 1953), book 4 of *The Chronicles of Narnia*; *English Literature in the Sixteenth Century, Excluding Drama* (Oxford, 1954), *Oxford History of English Literature*, vol. 3; *The Horse and His Boy* (London and New York, 1954), book 5 of *The Chronicles of Narnia*; *The Magi-*

cian's Nephew (London and New York, 1955), book 6 of *The Chronicles of Narnia*; *Surprised by Joy: The Shape of My Early Life* (London, 1955; New York, 1956); *The Last Battle: A Story for Children* (London and New York, 1956), book 7 of *The Chronicles of Narnia*; *Till We Have Faces: A Myth Retold* (London, 1956); *Reflections on the Psalms* (London and New York, 1958).

*The Four Loves* (London and New York, 1960); *Studies in Words* (Cambridge, Eng., 1960); *The World's Last Night and Other Essays* (New York, 1960); *An Experiment in Criticism* (Cambridge, Eng., 1961); *A Grief Observed* (London, 1961), pub. under pseudonym N. W. Clerk; *They Asked for a Paper: Papers and Addresses* (London, 1962); *The Discarded Image: An Introduction to Medieval and Renaissance Literature* (Cambridge, Eng., 1964); *Letters to Malcolm: Chiefly on Prayer* (London, 1964), first appeared as *Beyond the Bright Blur* (New York, 1963), a limited edition of chaps. 15–17.

III. POSTHUMOUS COLLECTIONS. (All collections edited by Walter Hooper unless otherwise noted.)

*Poems* (London, 1964); *Screwtape Proposes a Toast and Other Pieces* (London, 1965); *Of Other Worlds: Essays and Stories* (London, 1966); *Studies in Medieval and Renaissance Literature* (Cambridge, Eng., 1966); *Christian Reflections* (London and Grand Rapids, Mich., 1967); *Spenser's Images of Life*, ed. by Alastair Fowler (Cambridge, Eng., 1967); *A Mind Awake: An Anthology of C. S. Lewis*, ed. by Clyde S. Kilby (London, 1968); *Narrative Poems* (London, 1969); *Selected Literary Essays* (Cambridge, Eng., 1969).

*God in the Dock: Essays on Theology and Ethics* (Grand Rapids, Mich., 1970), pub. as *Undeceptions: Essays on Theology and Ethics* (London, 1971); *Fern-Seed and Elephants, and Other Essays on Christianity* (London, 1975); *The Dark Tower and Other Stories* (London and New York, 1977); *The Joyful Christian: 127 Readings from C. S. Lewis*, with a foreword by H. W. Griffin (New York, 1977).

*The Visionary Christian: 131 Readings from C. S. Lewis*, ed. by Chad Walsh (New York, 1981); *Of This and Other Worlds* (London, 1982), pub. as *On Stories, and Other Essays on Literature* (New York, 1982); *The Business of Heaven: Daily Readings from C. S. Lewis* (London and San Diego, 1984); *Boxen: The Imaginary World of the Young C. S. Lewis* (London and San Diego, 1985); *First and Second Things: Essays on Theology and Ethics* (London, 1985); *Present Concerns* (London and San Diego, 1986); *Timeless at Heart: Essays on Theology* (London, 1987); *The Essential C. S. Lewis*, ed. by Lyle W. Dorsett (New York, 1988); *The Quotable Lewis*, ed. by Wayne Martindale and Jerry Root (Wheaton, Ill., 1989).

*Christian Reunion and Other Essays* (London, 1990); *Daily Readings with C. S. Lewis* (London, 1991).

IV. LETTERS AND DIARIES. *Letters of C. S. Lewis*, ed. with a memoir by W. H. Lewis (London and New York, 1966; rev. and enlarged edition, ed. by Walter Hooper, San Diego, 1993); *Letters to an American Lady*, ed. by Clyde S. Kilby (Grand Rapids, Mich., 1967), to Mary Willis Shelburne; *They Stand Together: The Letters of C. S. Lewis to Arthur Greeves, 1914–1963*, ed. by Walter Hooper (London and New York, 1979); *Letters to Children*, ed. by Lyle W. Dorsett and Marjorie Lamp Mead (London and New York, 1985); *Letters—C. S. Lewis and Don Giovanni Calabria: A Study in Friendship*, trans. and ed. by Martin Moynihan (Ann Arbor, Mich., and London, 1988); *All My Road Before Me: The Diary of C. S. Lewis, 1922–1927*, ed. by Walter Hooper (London and San Diego, 1991).

V. BIOGRAPHICAL STUDIES. Carolyn Keefe, ed., *C. S. Lewis: Speaker and Teacher* (Grand Rapids, Mich., 1971); Roger Lancelyn Green and Walter Hooper, *C. S. Lewis: A Biography* (London and New York, 1974); Sheldon Vanauken, *A Severe Mercy: C. S. Lewis and a Pagan Love Invaded by Christ, Told by One of the Lovers* (London and San Francisco, 1977); Humphrey Carpenter, *The Inklings: C. S. Lewis, J. R. R. Tolkien, Charles Williams, and Their Friends* (London and Boston, 1978); *C. S. Lewis at the Breakfast Table and Other Reminiscences*, ed. by James T. Como (New York, 1979); Walter Hooper, *Through Joy and Beyond: A Pictorial Biography of C. S. Lewis* (London and New York, 1982); W. H. Lewis, *Brothers and Friends: The Diaries of Major Warren Hamilton Lewis*, ed. by Clyde S. Kilby and Marjorie Lamp Mead (London and San Francisco, 1982); Lyle W. Dorsett, *And God Came In: The Extraordinary Story of Joy Davidman, Her Life and Marriage to C. S. Lewis* (New York, 1983); Brian Sibley, *Shadowlands: The Story of C. S. Lewis and Joy Davidman* (London, 1985); William Griffin, *Clive Staples Lewis: A Dramatic Life* (San Francisco, 1986); Lyle W. Dorsett, *Joy and C. S. Lewis* (London, 1988); Douglas H. Gresham, *Lenten Lands: My Childhood with Joy Davidman and C. S. Lewis* (New York, 1988); George Sayer, *Jack: C. S. Lewis and His Times* (London and San Francisco, 1988); Owen Barfield, *Owen Barfield on C. S. Lewis*, ed. by G. B. Tennyson (Middletown, Conn., 1989); A. N. Wilson, *C. S. Lewis: A Biography* (London and New York, 1990).

VI. CRITICAL STUDIES. Chad Walsh, *C. S. Lewis: Apostle to the Skeptics* (New York, 1949); Clyde S. Kilby, *The Christian World of C. S. Lewis* (Grand Rapids, Mich., 1964); Jocelyn Gibb, ed., *Light on C. S. Lewis* (London, 1965); Peter T. Kreeft, *C. S. Lewis: A Critical Essay* (Grand Rapids, Mich., 1969).

Kathryn Ann Lindskoog, *C. S. Lewis: Mere Christian* (Glendale, Calif., 1973; rev. ed., Downers Grove, Ill., 1981; rev. ed., Wheaton, Ill., 1987); Corbin S. Carnell, *Bright Shadow of Reality: C. S. Lewis and the Feeling Intellect* (Grand Rapids, Mich., 1974); Peter J. Schakel, ed., *The Longing for a Form: Essays on the Fiction of C. S. Lewis* (Kent, Ohio, 1977); Lionel Adey, *C. S. Lewis's "Great War" with Owen Barfield*, English Literary Studies monograph series no. 14 (Victoria, B.C., 1978); Gilbert Meilaender, *The Taste for the Other: The Social and Ethical Thought of C. S. Lewis* (Grand Rapids, Mich., 1978); Peter J. Schakel, *Reading with the Heart: The Way into Narnia* (Grand Rapids, Mich., 1979).

Paul F. Ford, *Companion to Narnia* (San Francisco, 1980); Evan K. Gibson, *C. S. Lewis, Spinner of Tales: A Guide to His Fiction* (Grand Rapids, Mich., and Washington, D.C., 1980); Martha C. Sammons, *A Guide Through C. S. Lewis' Space Trilogy* (Westchester, Ill., 1980); Donald E. Glover, *C. S. Lewis: The Art of Enchantment* (Athens, Ohio, 1981); Margaret P. Hannay, *C. S. Lewis* (New York, 1981); Robert H. Smith, *Patches of Godlight: The Pattern of Thought of C. S. Lewis* (Athens, Ga., 1981); Stephen Schofield, ed., *In Search of C. S. Lewis: Interviews with Kenneth Tynan, A. J. P. Taylor, Malcolm Muggeridge, and Others Who Knew Lewis* (South Plainfield, N.J., 1983); Dabney Adams Hart, *Through the Open Door: A New Look at C. S. Lewis* (University, Ala., 1984); Peter J. Schakel, *Reason and Imagination in C. S. Lewis: A Study of* Till We Have Faces (Grand Rapids, Mich., 1984); John Beversluis, *C. S. Lewis and the Search for Rational Religion* (Grand Rapids, Mich., 1985); James Patrick, *The Magdalen Metaphysicals: Idealism and Orthodoxy at Oxford, 1901–1945* (Macon, Ga., 1985); Joe R. Christopher, *C. S. Lewis* (Boston, 1987); Thomas Howard, *C. S. Lewis, Man of Letters: A Reading of His Fiction* (Worthing, Eng., 1987); Colin N. Manlove, *C. S. Lewis: His Literary Achievement* (Basingstoke, Eng., and New York, 1987); Bruce L. Edwards, ed., *The Taste of the Pineapple: Essays on C. S. Lewis as Reader, Critic, and Imaginative Writer* (Bowling Green, Ohio, 1988).

Colin Duriez, *The C. S. Lewis Handbook: A Comprehensive Guide to His Life, Thought, and Writings* (Eastbourne, Eng., and Grand Rapids, Mich., 1990); Peter J. Schakel and Charles A. Huttar, eds., *Word and Story in C. S. Lewis* (Columbia, Mo., and London, 1991); David C. Downing, *Planets in Peril: A Critical Study of C. S. Lewis's Ransom Trilogy* (Amherst, Mass., 1992); Kath Filmer, *The Fiction of C. S. Lewis: Mask and Mirror* (Basingstoke, Eng., and New York, 1993); Colin N. Manlove, The Chronicles of Narnia: *The Patterning of a Fantastic World* (New York and Toronto, 1993); Doris T. Myers, *C. S. Lewis in Context* (Kent, Ohio, 1994).

VII. ARCHIVES The Marion E. Wade Center at Wheaton College, Wheaton, Ill., holds the papers and letters of Lewis' brother, Major Warren Lewis, including his vast compilation of family history entitled *Lewis Papers*. The collection also includes manuscripts, first editions, a major collection of letters, and other Lewis memorabilia. The Department of Western Manuscripts at the Bodleian Library, Oxford, Eng., has an extensive collection of Lewis' books and articles, plus some manuscripts and letters. Each of the two centers has photocopies of the unique manuscripts in the possession of the other.

NOTE: Several C. S. Lewis societies publish journals: *CSL: The Bulletin of the New York C. S. Lewis Society* (1969– ); *Chronicle of the Portland C. S. Lewis Society* (1972–1984); *The Lamp-Post of the Southern California C. S. Lewis Society* (1977– ); and *The Canadian C. S. Lewis Journal* (1979– ). Other journals devoted to Lewis and friends: *Mythlore: A Journal of J. R. R. Tolkien, C. S. Lewis, Charles Williams, General Fantasy, and Mythic Studies* (1969– ); *Seven: An Anglo-American Literary Review* (1980– ); and *Inklings: Gesellschaft für Literatur und Asthetik* (1983– ).

# SIR THOMAS MALORY
(d. 1471)

## M. C. Bradbrook

IN his study W. B. Yeats kept a scrap of silk from a Japanese lady's dress, and a Samurai sword, as "things that are/Emblematic of love and war." These two themes are fundamental to the work of Sir Thomas Malory. Religion—the third of the great epic themes—is admittedly and nobly subordinated; only at the end, Guinevere, in expiation of her guilt in destroying the Round Table, becomes a nun; and Lancelot, for love of her and not for love of God, takes on himself the habit of perfection.

For nearly five hundred years, since its publication by William Caxton at Westminster on 31 July 1485, Malory's *Morte Darthur* has stood at the center of English literature. It has been read, and it has nourished the work of other writers; but it has been little discussed. This is one of the silent areas in English criticism, but such deceptively simple works, which offer little to be clever about, are the centers of high creative activity. Spenser's debt to Malory is clear; and throughout the nineteenth century he was used as a quarry. For the poetry of Tennyson and the Pre-Raphaelites he provided an essential basis; in our own day T. S. Eliot has described Malory as one of his favorite authors. Chaucer in the fourteenth century and Malory in the fifteenth together laid the foundations of modern English narrative; the scale of their work as well as its excellence, its breadth combined with its individuality, established and fortified the art of the imaginative story, in poetry and in prose. They are the only two English medieval writers who have been continuously and widely known from their own day to the present.

The differences between them are more obvious than the likeness. Chaucer, a diplomat and civil servant, writing for the elegant and sophisticated court of Richard II, with a cosmopolitan taste and a fine tact, a delicate malice and a most urbane wit, might have felt there was some rusticity about Malory, who did in fact begin his work by turning into prose an alliterative English poem of the fourteenth century, of the kind that Chaucer would certainly have thought exceedingly provincial. In *The Canterbury Tales*, it is the middle-class wife of Bath who tells an Arthurian fairy story, while Chaucer burlesques the whole tradition of romance in the delicious *Tale of Sir Thopas*, which he gives to himself to tell in his role of boring and incompetent simpleton. This is, of course, a burlesque of the popular and not of the courtly romance; but it suggests that in Chaucer's mind tales of wandering knights had already turned into old wives' tales.

Malory belonged to the next age, that turbulent fifteenth century whose disorder Shakespeare depicted in the trilogy of *Henry VI*, where the civil strife of the Wars of the Roses culminates with the scene of a lamenting king, set between a son who has killed his father and a father who has killed his son. Whether the Wars of the Roses were really disastrous for any but the small class of barons and knights is very problematic; but it was just this class, the remnants of an earlier society, from which Malory sprang, and which is idealized in the Round Table. Malory belonged to that older order of chivalry which finally went down on Bosworth Field in 1485, the year in which his work was published, 14 years after his own death.

Until 1966, Sir Thomas Malory was generally identified with a knight of Newbold Revell, in Warwickshire, who in his youth served with the great Richard Beauchamp, earl of Warwick. Later, however, he turned to a life of violence and died in Newgate Prison, 14 March 1471. Many scholars felt some embarrassment at thus identifying the author of "the noble and joyous book," and in 1966 William Matthews produced a rival candidate from the North. However, his case against the knight of Newbold Revell is much stronger than his case for any alternative figure.

Defenders of the Warwickshire knight have pointed out that in the fifteenth century it was too easy to frame a charge against political enemies. Thomas Malory was accused of breaking into an abbey and on two occasions of feloniously ravishing Joan, wife of Henry Smyth of Monks' Kirby—which need not mean more than abduction. As C. S. Lewis remarked, "He might, on the evidence, have been as good a knight as Tristram; for what should we think of Tristram himself if our knowledge of him were derived only from King Mark's solicitors?" Or indeed, what if we compare Malory with that pattern of chivalry, John Tiptoft, earl of Worcester? Otherwise known as the Butcher of England, in 1470 it was with great difficulty that he was brought to the scaffold through the London mob thirsting for his blood. His translation of *Controversia de nobilitate* was also published by Caxton.

Thus Malory's generally accepted identity as the knight of Newbold Revell should not merely be brushed aside.

Fortune's wheel whirled Malory continually lower and lower, in contrast to successful climbers like the Paston family, whose letters show them rising in the social scale throughout the fifteenth century by methods sometimes as violent as Malory's but more skillfully timed. The landless knight, the man-at-arms who followed his lord to foreign wars, often turned to violence when loosed upon his native soil, as the disbanded soldier took to begging or highway robbery. Though Malory himself was not landless, he behaved as one of this class, and some of his imprisonments were for debt. His story of violence, disaster, and stormy veerings to and fro may seem at variance with the modern notions of chivalry; but Malory seems to have retained the first chivalric virtue, that of loyalty to his lord. Here, however, his allegiance illustrates once more the decline of chivalry. Richard Beauchamp, earl of Warwick, whom he followed as a young man to Calais, was a pattern of courtesy as well as a great lord. Richard Neville, the Kingmaker, who succeeded to the title after his marriage to Beauchamp's granddaughter, and who made and unmade kings in Malory's later years, was the father of a queen, and himself greater than a king in possessions; but his rapid changes of party, his merciless slaughter of conquered enemies, above all his unnatural position of superiority and domination towards his lord the king seem to epitomize all that Malory and later even Shakespeare dreaded as the supreme evil of evil times—the dissolution of harmony, order, and degree which a divided rule may bring.

Malory wrote his work in prison. At the end of *The Tale of King Arthur*, standing first in the book, the Winchester MS has a note that it was written "by a knight prisoner, Sir Thomas Malleorré, that God send him good recover." At the end of the *Tales of Sir Gareth*, the writer appeals:

And I pray you all that readeth this tale to pray for him that this wrote, that God send him good deliverance soon and hastily.   Amen.

At the end of Caxton's printed version comes the paragraph entreating all gentlemen and gentlewomen "pray for me while I am on live that God send me good deliverance. And when I am dead, I pray you all pray for my soul." The writer himself adds such a prayer ". . . by Sir Thomas Maleoré knight as Jesu help him for His great might, as he is the servant of Jesu both day and night." This piteous little jingle suggests that by the ninth year of the reign of King Edward IV Malory had lost hope in an earthly deliverance.

Those who have seen works of art produced by prisoners during their confinement will not be surprised at the immense care and pains that are shown in *Le Morte Darthur* by the development of the style. Painfully and slowly Malory evolved his own prose, learned an eloquence, a craftsmanship, and a power of organization that could not have come easily to one who was not a clerk. He had all the time in the world in which to learn.

### THE KNIGHTLY ROMANCE

STORYTELLING was the great art of the Middle Ages, and the romance was a special form of this art. It was a long-continuing and popular form; the stories that Malory told were also in substance many hundreds of years old. They were ennobled by long tradition; they were, too, believed to be true history. But they represented at the same time an enlarged picture of contemporary life. This seems one way of defining the romance. It gives an idealized version of the life of the knightly class; it is the warrior's daydream, designed for recreation (or "solace"), not instruction (or "doctrine"), and representing the average sensual man's point of view. Such stories might also reflect and celebrate contemporary events; Malory in *The Tale of the Noble King Arthur that was Emperor himself through Dignity of his Hands* seems to shadow the glorious campaigns of Henry V, as his source-poem had those of Edward III and the Black Prince. But it is quite exceptional for romances to carry religious overtones, as in the great fourteenth-century poem of *Sir Gawain and the Green Knight*. In Malory, the *Tale of the Sankgreal* is a separate story, in which the religious is simply a particular department of the marvellous. Miracles or legends of the saints are the religious equivalent of the knightly romance; the marvellous was allowed a very large share in both kinds.

Romance differs from epic in its readiness to include the fantastic, magical, and wishful elements largely within the action. In epic, though the world presented is enlarged and ennobled, it remains the world of everyday. It has been suggested that the epic material of one race or culture becomes romance when it is handed over to another race or culture and needs to be reinterpreted; when it has lost its social roots. Romance therefore presupposes epic; Malory recreated an epic story from romance.

The hero of a medieval romance, whatever the age in which he lived, always becomes a knight. In the romances of Troy, Hector is described as a knight, the "root and stock of chivalry"; Alexander becomes a medieval king. So, too, Arthur the Romano-British chieftain was seen as a contemporary ruler surrounded by his chivalry, the knights of the Round Table. The heroic early French epic of Charlemagne and the Twelve Peers of France underwent a similar transformation.

The medieval epic poem, such as *Beowulf* or the *Song of Roland*, dealt with the war leader and his band or *comitatus*; ultimately the structure of feudal society was based upon such bands, united by personal oaths of fidelity which bound vassal to lord and lord to vassal. The strong personal unity of a group of fighting men, in which unshakable loyalty and courage were essential for survival, developed into the feudal state in which the barons were bound to their lord the king, the lesser tenants to their own lords, and the whole structure depended upon a network of loyalties, all of a personal kind. The society depicted in the romances is the uppermost stratum of this social order. There is very little sense of the underlying and supporting levels of society. In Malory this is particularly noticeable. The churls who appear are churlishly treated, as when Lancelot strikes an uncooperative carter "a reremain," a blow over the back of his neck with a mailed fist, and summarily stretches him dead. Manners consist in giving each man his due; and the Lady Lionesse thinks a kitchen knave deserves nothing but insults.

The characters in romance are elected by age as well as class. They consist almost entirely of fighting men, their wives or mistresses, with an occasional clerk or an enchanter, a fairy or a fiend, a giant or a dwarf. Time does not work on the heroes of Malory; they may beget sons who grow up to manhood, without seeming to change in themselves: it is impossible to think of an old age, still less a late middle age, for Lancelot or Guinevere. There are very few old men or women, almost no infants or children. It is also a world in which family relationships, though they exist, are usually of comparatively little significance. Fathers are finally supplanted by sons (Lancelot by Galahad, Arthur by Mordred); the relation of husband to wife is a feudal and not a personal one. Brothers are related chiefly as brothers-in-arms; sisters and mothers hardly exist. The deep relationships in this world are those of knight and vassal, or its mirror image of lady and lover; and of these, the former is in Malory the most important, the last exhibiting the same virtue of fidelity which is more amply mirrored in the comradeship of arms. There is no doubt that even in the loves of Arthur, Lancelot, and Guinevere, the masculine loyalties triumph. When the strife between Gawain and Lancelot breaks out, Arthur cries:

> Wit you well, my heart was never so heavy as it is now. And much more I am sorrier for my good knights' loss than for the loss of my fair queen; for queens I might have enow, but such a fellowship of good knights shall never be together in no company.
> (Vinaver, p. 833[1])

It is the mature recognition of responsibility for their guilt toward society that keeps Lancelot and Guinevere apart in the end. After Arthur is dead, and she has betaken herself to the nunnery at Amesbury, the queen is sought out by Lancelot, and to her ladies she addresses herself before she speaks to him, and sends him away forever:

> Through this same man and me hath all this war be wrought, and death of the most noblest knights of the world; for through our love that we have loved together is my most noble lord slain.
> (p. 876)

So later still Sir Lancelot laments over the two he had loved. Guinevere dies and is buried beside Arthur.

> For when I remember of her beauty and her noblesse, that was both with her king and with her, so when I saw his corpse and her corpse so lie together, truly mine heart would not serve to sustain my careful body. Also when I remember me how by my defaute and mine orgule and my pride that they were both laid full low, that were peerless ever was living of Cristen people, wit you well, said Sir Lancelot, this remembered, of their kindness and my unkindness, sank so to mine heart that I might not sustain myself.
> (p. 880)

Even such lovers as Chaucer's Troilus and Criseyde, the delicacy and complexity of whose relationship is a matter of finest adjustment, are governed instinctively by the social demands that put marriage between a prince and the widowed daughter of the traitor Calchas quite out of court. Chaucer did not need to explain this; in Malory's day, when Edward IV married Elizabeth Woodville, Warwick the Kingmaker deserted him. For Malory, the story of Lancelot and Guinevere is one of divided loyalties; it is the social results of the love even more than the love itself which concern him, while the passionate story of Tristram and Isold fails to awaken his deeper interest, and remains episodic. Here the tragic end is missing, and the lovers are left happily together at Joyous Garde, Lancelot's castle, whither they have fled: their end is briefly mentioned by Lancelot, as the time of his own fall draws near (Vinaver, p. 828). This may be quite deliberate; the end of a well-known story could be suppressed to make a particular interpretation clearer, as Chaucer himself suppressed the death of Criseyde. Tristram and Isold are not faced by the same dilemma as Lancelot and Guinevere, since Mark cannot claim loyalty, being himself so treacherous; and the magic potion which they have drunk takes from their love the guilt and the glory of a voluntary choice. Theirs is a blind trancelike passion; Lancelot and Guinevere, though the queen's stormy rages and jealous outbursts may complicate the story and drive Lancelot like Tristram into madness, prove for each other a kind of fidelity that belongs not to the world of fancy but to the world of men.

In the great hymn in praise of fidelity in love, which opens Section IV of *Lancelot and Guinevere*, "The Knight of the Cart," Malory indulges in a rare lyric outburst. True love is likened unto summer; and in words which owe nothing to his "French book," though something perhaps to the joyous French songs that celebrate the coming of spring, he unites the love of man and woman with the great rhythms of the world and the seasons.

> . . . For, like as winter rasure doth alway arace and deface green summer, so fareth it by unstable love in man and woman, for in many persons there is no stabylité; for we may see all day, for a little blast of winter's rasure, anon we shall deface and lay apart true love, for little or naught, that cost much thing. . . .
> Wherefore I liken love nowadays unto summer and winter; for, like as the one is cold and the other is hot, so fareth love nowadays. And therefore all ye that be lovers, call unto your remembrance the month of May, like as did Queen Guinevere, for whom I make here a little mention, that while she lived she was a true lover, and therefore she had a good end.
> (pp. 790–791)

The pathos of Malory's "dying fall," the cadence dropping to a minor chord, is his tribute

---

[1] For convenience, the page references are to Vinaver's one-volume edition in the Oxford Standard Authors; but the spelling has been modernized throughout the quotations.

to those inward feelings which in his masculine world receive so little direct expression. As always, the supreme virtue is truth.

The most famous and most magnificent passage in all Malory's work is the lament that closes it, the lament of Sir Ector de Maris over his brother, Sir Lancelot. Here the word "truest," sounds twice, like a tolling bell. It is the final picture of the perfect knight, the summary of all the paradoxical virtues of gentleness and sternness, all the defeated hopes that the knight prisoner had strengthened himself with in his prison.

Ah, Lancelot! he said, thou were head of all Cristen knights! And now I dare say, said Sir Ector, thou Sir Lancelot, there thou lyest, that thou were never matched of earthly knight's hand. And thou were the courteousest knight that ever bare shield! And thou were the truest friend to thy lover that ever bestrad horse, and thou were the truest lover of a sinful man that ever loved a woman, and thou were the kindest man that ever strake with sword. And thou were the goodliest person that ever came among press of knights, and thou was the meekest man and the gentlest that ever ate in hall among ladies, and thou were the sternest knight to thy mortal foe that ever put spear in the rest.

(p. 882)

### THE ENGLISH ROUND TABLE

IF, then, the inner core of feeling which lies at the center of Malory's world is the masculine bond of fidelity, the old loyalty of the band of fighting men, we should expect him to encounter some difficulty in dealing with the French romances upon which his work is for the most part based, since in these the love of knight and lady was often the leading motif. The elaborate and fanciful code of manners which in theory governed the behavior of courtly lovers, involving the absolute subjection of the knight to the lady, with all the artifice of courtly etiquette, and all the exotic ritual of a mock religion, was never really acclimatized in England. The lovely dream of the garden of the rose, which Guillaume de Lorris wrote and Chaucer translated, had indeed inspired some of Chaucer's love poetry; and early in the fifteenth century also had inspired that of a nobler prisoner than Malory, James I of Scotland, who, looking out of his prison tower, beheld a fair lady walking in a springtime garden, when

> suddenly my heart became her thrall
> For ever, of free will. . . .

But the courtly manners of royalty required a setting that most readers and writers of romance did not know; they remade the stories, so that the kings, queens, and knights became enlarged versions of themselves, with manners to correspond. Probably the most courtly poem in English about Arthur's knights is the fourteenth-century *Sir Gawain and the Green Knight*, in which a society as elegant as Chaucer's is depicted, and in which the maneuvering of the lady who tempts Gawain is as sophisticated as that of any heroine of Restoration comedy. A keen battle of wits between her and the knight (whom she takes at the greatest disadvantage by visiting him in bed) ends with the victory of the stronger sex; without discourtesy, Gawain repulses her, thus keeping his obligation as guest towards his host, the lady's husband.

This story was retold in rougher form as *Sir Gawain and the Carl of Carlisle*, and here the knight's adventures with his hostess take on a much cruder and more primitive form. In some cases, courtly romances ended as popular ballads, with all the fine-drawn sentiments, all the rich descriptions pared away, to leave the simple structure, the bare bones of some tragic story, told perhaps with noble simplicity, or perhaps only with confused, dull repetition and a plentiful use of well-worn phrases. Chaucer's *Tale if Sir Thopas*, though cruel, is not unjust to the popular romance which at its worst is unbearably boring.

Most of these English Arthurian romances deal with the adventures of some single knight. Sir Gawain, Sir Percival, Sir Launcefal and the rest are each shown as the center of a series of adventures. Some of the material belongs to the perennial world of the fairy tale; thus, tales of the fairy bride who rewards the knight with riches, with magic means to overcome his enemies, and sometimes with a fairy kingdom, are obviously popular subjects for a masculine daydream. Other tales tell of ordeals, the overcoming of magic obstacles, or war with giants, Saracens, devils. These are the two basic forms for the romantic adventures of a knightly hero.

In Malory, however, we meet a whole world of knights. Sir Lancelot is its undisputed champion, but Percival, Tristram, Galahad, Gawain, Gareth, and many others take for a while the center of the stage. Malory's great work, as it would appear from the Winchester MS, which came to light in 1934 in the library of Winchester College, is a collection or anthology of tales about the Round Table. It is not a single narrative, but a group of narratives, like the *Decameron* or the *Canterbury Tales*; based, however, on a different principle of selection, that of a common subject: all the tales are about Arthur's knights. To see the work in this way enables the reader to measure Malory's progress and his growing power in shaping his material.[2] Caxton, when he printed the work as if it were a single continuous narrative instead of an anthology, destroyed the perspective and blurred the outlines of Malory's work. By the recovery of their plan, the stories have acquired new shape and cohesion. First to be written was *The Tale of the Noble King Arthur that was Emperor himself through Dignity of his Hands*. This is a story of military triumph in which Arthur sets out to conquer Rome; which he does, and is crowned Emperor there, thus anticipating the glories of Charlemagne among epic heroes, and reflecting for Malory the triumphant conquests of Henry V. Professor Vinaver has shown how Malory modifies the course of Arthur's French campaign to correspond with the course of Henry's. This part of Malory's work is based on an English heroic poem, *Le Morte Arthur*; but here, as in the story of Tristram, Malory has cut out the tragic ending, and uses only the first part of the poem, which deals with Arthur's triumph. At the very end of his work he was to return to another English poem to help him in depicting *The Most Piteous Tale of the Morte Arthur Saunz Guerdon*. But in the interval he relied on various "French books," prose romances of great length, which he shaped and reorganized with increasing skill. Only for one or two stories, particularly *The Tale of Sir Gareth of Orkeney that was called Bewmaynes*, are the sources of his work unknown. To trace the history of the stories of King Arthur is a lifetime's task; and the majority of scholars who give themselves to the study of Malory or of his originals are concerned mainly with constructing genealogical trees for the stories and disputing various theories of descent. This, though a fascinating game, is sometimes a way of evading the duty—at once more simple and more difficult—of seeing them as literature. But the idea of the Round Table is so central to Malory's work, and in itself so especially English a development of the story, that a brief sketch of it may be attempted.

### MALORY AND THE HEROIC TRADITION

THREE hundred years before Malory, the poet Layamon gave an account of the founding of the Round Table. Arthur held a great feast at which his vassals from Britain, Scotland, Ireland, and Iceland assembled. A squabble about precedence developed. At first bread and cups were thrown and fists used. Then a young hostage of Arthur's household snatched up the carving knives from before the king, and the killing began. It took Arthur and a hundred armed men to quell the fight, under the most terrifying threats of instant death for men and mutilation for women related to those who began the brawl. If any sought revenge for what had happened, he would be torn in pieces by wild horses. The body of the man who began the fight was to be thrown out to rot unburied.

As a result of these measures, the dead were carried off and the feast went merrily on; but the cunning smith who offered to make Arthur a wondrous table at which sixteen hundred might sit without question of precedence seems to be catering less for the vassals of an overlord than for the members of some primitive horde. Arthur, however, appears as the dominant figure. In his words:

Sit down! sit down at once! or your lives will pay

is heard the authentic voice of command.

Precedence at feasts, and the order of service at the lord's table, was a matter of signifi-

---
[2] C. S. Lewis, *Essays on Malory* (Oxford, 1963), p. 23.

cance throughout the Middle Ages. The long narrow table on the dais in the opening scene of *Sir Gawain and the Green Knight* is set in customary fashion with the king in the middle, and his principal guests on each side. A round table would in fact have been a great curiosity and departure from custom, in one of those ceremonious occasions which the romances loved to depict; and in all stories, the feast which so frequently opens or closes them (the symbol of good fellowship and unity) is described in the usual sort of medieval hall with the usual high table on a dais. What generally happens is that the King is feasting his knights and declares that he will not eat till he sees a marvel. Instantly some damsel in distress or some strange apparition like the Green Knight appears and the adventure begins.

Although in most of the earlier romances the story is concerned with the adventures of a particular knight, there is a sense of the brotherhood of the Round Table given by these feasts at the beginning and end of the story; after a series of combats, it is usual for the valiant enemy of the hero to be accepted as a member of the Round Table. By the fourteenth century it was thought of as a fellowship akin to that of some knightly order, such as the Garter, or the Bath, and certain kinds of tournament became known as "round tables."

The Great Tournament is in Malory the last and supreme moment of unity and good fellowship for the Round Table; it is the expression of the bond which is about to be dissolved by the quarrel between Lancelot and Gawain, Arthur's champion and his nephew and heir. Tournaments, or mock battles, in which knightly qualities were displayed without the risk of real battle, had become something like a fifteenth-century Olympic Games; they were great pageants at which fortunes were spent upon equipment, and to which champions would travel from all over Europe. The last and most gorgeous occasion of this kind to be generally remembered is the encounter between Henry VIII and Francis I of France, known as the Field of the Cloth of Gold.

Such tournaments gave opportunity for the writer of romance to indulge in long descriptions of splendor, with detailed accounts of the dishes at the feasts, the armor of the knights, and the order of combat. Here Malory departs from the habits of the age. He is not interested in descriptions but in action; and he does not do more than note the color of the knights' armor. Combat excites him, but his world lacks the stateliness and the ritual of Chaucer's and the Gawain poet's, the true courtly ceremoniousness.

He has, on the other hand, a very strong sense of the fellowship, which enables him to rise to the heights of the last books. This sense of the fellowship dominates one or two other works; such as the poem of *Lancelot du Laik* and the alliterative *Morte Arthur* on which Malory based the first of his tales. These poems imitate the literary form of the Chronicle History. Here there is an account of the king's challenge to lordship of a foreign land; then an invasion and a series of battles are described, very closely akin to the English wars in France. In each battle, a list of the eminent warriors taking part on both sides is given, and a list of those who fell. Such poems are no longer pure romance of adventure; they are histories. In Malory, too, there is this strong sense of history, implying the epic rather than the romantic style.

After his early tale of Arthur's conquest of Rome, Malory turned back for a time to the more primitive and wilder stories about Merlin. These belong to the oldest traditions of romance. In general, the more primitive the stories, the larger the part played by magic; thus, in the one Arthurian tale in the *Mabinogion* (a collection of Welsh tales in prose dealing with Celtic mythology), all the knights are possessed of superhuman powers, and are frankly figures of magical rather than human kind.

After his excursion into the realms of magic, Malory tells a number of tales about individual knights, in the same form roughly as the romances of adventure that have been described. These are tales of wanderings, in which the hero rides away on a quest. The quest for the Holy Grail includes five such tales of individual knights. The tragic tale of *The Knight with the Two Swords* and the tale of Gareth have each a strong and shapely coherence; others follow rather the interlacing and interweaving technique of the long French romances. The story of Tristram is of this kind, containing in itself several minor stories, such as the tale of Alexander le Orphelin.

The adventures of individual knights in their quests show them freed from all restrictions of ordinary life. Armor and tournaments may be realistic, but in a romance there is suppression of all the usual laws of cause and effect in action. The knightly champion has to meet giants, dragons, monsters, the king's enemies, sorcerers, and mysteries of all kinds. Heads that are cut off may be stuck on again; marvels and wonders are the rule and not the exception. The appearance and manners of the knight are familiar, merely an enlargement of the everyday, but he has no responsibilities, no followers. He rides through vast and shadowy landscapes and forests, where only the cities of Caerleon and Carlisle remind the listener that this is England. The modern reader may see a parallel in the world of science fiction, in which the admired technical apparatus which commands most prestige today is used to decorate the wildest fantasy. Romance indulges in the same mixture of the fanciful and the up-to-date. It allows the listener to identify himself with a hero of almost superhuman prowess, yet matches him against forces that stress his humanity and normality. Monsters from outer space are the modern equivalent of the fairy-tale giant.

Most romances of individual knights arrive at a happy ending; feasts and weddings wind them up. When the theme is the Round Table itself, however, the story ends with the great epic battle, the unsuccessful fight against odds. Whereas incidents of the individual romances defy cause and effect, in the epic of the Round Table morality is always felt behind the action; the ideal is a social and ethical one. It was to this graver subject that Malory finally turned at the end of his work, joining the tale of his great hero Lancelot with the fate of the whole fellowship.

The stories of Arthur and his knights can thus be seen to undergo a development not unrelated to the society that in an idealized form they reflect. In the earliest tales, magic and violence predominate; then the image of a society based on feudal ties of loyalty emerges; the adventures of individuals follow, with, in the more courtly versions, much stress on manners and on wooing, and in the popular versions, simply on adventure and marvels. In both, the ideal knight in quest of adventure undergoes a great variety of different trials, from which he usually emerges victorious. Finally, something akin to the older epic style reappears, reflecting also the form of contemporary chronicles and, in Malory, tinged with some shadowing from contemporary struggles. At his greatest, in the final passages dealing with the last battle and death of Arthur, he seems to reflect in an enlarged form all the troubles of his own society, the ruin that civil strife had brought upon him and his kind. This is imaginatively seen in the dissolution of the Round Table, the bond and fellowship of knighthood. Conquest, like true and faithful love, belongs to the past: the first and last campaigns of Arthur represent for Malory a youthful hope of the past contrasted with a tragic present.

The unity of "the hoole book" as Malory finally achieved it depends on unity of atmosphere and underlying concepts, leading finally to unification of statement and theme. In recent years, scholars have restressed the unity of Malory's work, and even the natural continuity of Caxton's additions as being like

a great cathedral where Saxon, Norman, Gothic, Renaissance and Georgian elements all co-exist and all grow together into something strange and admirable which none of its successive builders intended or foresaw.
(*Essays on Malory*, p. 25)

*TRAGIC THEMES IN MALORY*

MALORY was, of course, not depicting the troubles of his time directly; he only was giving an imaginative form to them. Unlike the poets of the alliterative tradition, Langland and the rest, he has no counsel to give. The grace and beauty of the *Morte Darthur* spring largely from its freedom from any reflection, any complicated tangle of social or of emotional repercussions. It is a splendid holiday from all such teasing questions as our living in the daily world implies.

The fights are sheer trials of strength and skill; the love-making is free from sentimentality, complaint, or evasion—as the healthy union of animals. There is something extraordinarily clean about Malory's world. Nearly all the knights are good except Kay (who appears chiefly in the early books), Mark, Mordred, and a few characters like Breuntz sauns Pitié; but these are so clearly labelled, and their churlishness is so obvious, that the listener is quite untroubled by their fulfilling of their customary roles. Morgan le Fay, the wicked queen and Arthur's sister, is the villainess of the piece, a figure at once more remote and more powerful.

Blood flows very freely. Two strange knights meet, "and as soon as either saw other they made them ready to joust." When they had fought for half a day and nearly killed each other, they ask each other's name and discover that they are Sir Percival and Sir Ector de Maris, both in search of Sir Lancelot, who has run mad in the woods. Both feel themselves to be dying and are unable even to seek a priest for shriving. But Percival kneels and prays, and on a sudden appearance of the Holy Grail "forthwith they were as whole of hide and limb as ever they were in their life" (Vinaver, p. 603). An action that resembles nothing so much as the instinctive rushing together of two wild boars (Malory's favorite simile for his warriors) thus ends with a miracle that does not at all differ from the magic spells of the Lady Lionesse, who restored the heads of decapitated knights by enchantment. The knights are suitably chastened.

Then they gave thankings to God with great mildness

and gravely discuss what can have happened to them. Sir Ector explains to Sir Percival that they have seen the Holy Grail.

"So God me help," said Sir Percival, "I saw a damsel, as me thought, all in white, with a vessel in both her hands, and forthwith I was whole."
So then they took their horses and their harness, and mended it as well as they might that was broken; and so they mounted up and rode talking together. And there Sir Ector de Maris told Sir Percival how that he had sought his brother Sir Lancelot, long, and never could hear witting of him: "In many hard adventures have I been in this quest." And so either told other of their great adventures.
(pp. 603–604)

This condition of complete simplicity, a combination of violence and innocence, was presumably taken for granted by Malory himself and by his contemporaries. Vinaver points out how new is delight in the inarticulate assurance of the fighting man when King Arthur asks his knights for counsel. "They had no counsel, but said they were big enough." There is pathos in the loyalty of Sir Lancelot's kinsmen, when they warn him "insomuch as ye were taken with her, whether ye did right other wrong, it is now your part to hold with the queen," and he asks them "Wherefore, my fair lords, my kin and my friends, what will ye do?"

And anon they said with one voice:
"We will do as ye will do" (p. 827)

Taciturnity could go no further than the comment of the hermit when his salutary counsel to do penance is rejected by Gawain, on the plea that the life of a knight-errant is sufficiently hard in itself.

"Well," said the good man and then he held his peace. (p. 651)

*Tacit et fecit* might be the motto of any of Arthur's knights.

A knight finds his mother in bed with another knight. He strikes off her head. A lady whose knight is slain kills herself with his sword. Elaine gets Lancelot to her bed by enchantment, even within Arthur's court, and knowing that he thinks he is abed with Guinevere. Such a trick, which destroys all depth in the action when Shakespeare uses it in *All's Well that Ends Well* and *Measure for Measure*, does not jar in Malory. He comments:

And wit you well this lady was glad, and so was Sir Lancelot for he wende that he had had another in his arms. (p. 593)

After Lancelot has fled, being driven mad by the anger of Guinevere, the two ladies from mutual reproaches fall to common lament.

"As for that," said dame Elaine, "I dare undertake he is marred for ever and that have you made. For neither you nor I are like to rejoice him, for he made the most piteous groans when he leapt out at yonder bay window that I ever heard a man make. Alas!" said fair Elaine, and "Alas!" said the queen, "For now I wot well that we have lost him for ever."

(p. 595)

It is left to Sir Bors to rebuke both of them; he spares neither Elaine nor the queen, who proceeds to send out knights in quest for Lancelot, with "treasure enough" for their expenses—a fact that is duly recorded to Lancelot himself when he returns to his right mind.

"And therefore, brother," said Sir Ector, "make you ready to ride to the court with us. And I dare say, and make it good," said Sir Ector, "it hath cost my lady the Queen twenty thousand pounds the seeking of you."

(p. 616)

This, as Vinaver observes, is the only time an Arthurian quest is assessed in money terms. "There's beggary in the love that can be reckon'd," as Antony says, but perhaps it is not unfitting that one who knew the inside of a debtor's prison should use the hateful unfamiliar terms for once, to reckon the worth of Lancelot.

Set against Elaine the mother of Galahad, is Elaine the Maid of Astolat, whose story is perhaps the most inward and pathetic of all Malory's tales. Elaine of Astolat shares with her young brother Lavaine a kind of compulsive and enthralled devotion to Lancelot; it is at once completely innocent and frankly sensuous. She speaks to Lancelot in the voice of Miranda.

"Why, what would ye that I did?" said Sir Lancelot.
"Sir, I would have you to my husband," said Elaine.
"Fair damsel, I thank you heartily," said Sir Lancelot, "but truly," said he, "I cast me never to be wedded man."
"Then fair knight," said she, "will ye be my paramour?"
"Jesu defend me!" said Sir Lancelot, "For then I rewarded your father and your brother full evil for their great goodness."
"Alas then," said she, "I must die for your love."

Lancelot's attempt at consolation is a model of tactlessness. He informs her that he has had many other offers, and says that he would like to reward her for her kindness, which he will do by settling up her a dowry of a thousand pounds a year.

And so he departs, attended by Lavaine:

"Father," said Sir Lavaine, "I dare make good she is a clean maiden as for my lord Sir Lancelot; but she doth as I do, for sithen I first saw my lord Sir Lancelot I could never depart from him, neither nought I will, and I may follow him."

(p. 778)

The death of Elaine, justifying her love against the counsel of her ghostly father, who bade her leave such thoughts ("Why should I leave such thoughts? am I not an earthly woman?") by submitting herself to God, is perhaps a more truly religious occasion than all the episodes of the Holy Grail. There is the clearest acceptance of bodily death; she asks her brother to write a letter "and while my body is hot let this letter be put in my right hand, and my hand bound fast to the letter until that I be cold." This letter containing her plaint to Lancelot and her last request that he would bury her and offer her mass-penny is delivered in the scene that is the most dramatically and picturesquely described in all Malory; the barge hung in black samite, hove to upon the Thames; the silent boatman; and the corpse on a fair bed, covered to her middle with cloth of gold.

And she lay as she had smiled.

(p. 780)

Death is the one fact that is emotionally charged in Malory. Again and again, when he records the deaths of Balin, of Gawain, of Arthur, and finally of Lancelot, he rises to heights of passion and of eloquence that are not matched elsewhere in the *Morte Darthur*. Although life is cheap and wounds are so frequent that the chief knights seem to be sorely wounded about an average of once a week, yet in the moment of death which is also the moment of truth, a life may be summed up, a judgment given, and a garland bestowed.

In the last tales, the emotionally charged fact of death and the imaginatively perceived disruption of the social order are combined, as Malory describes the mutual destruction of the Round Table and the death of his chief heroes. There is still nothing that could be called reflection, comment, or entanglement in daily living; there is, of course, the fully apprehended physical horror of battle.

> Then Sir Lucan took up the king the one party and Sir Bedwere the other party, and in the lifting up the king swooned and in the lifting Sir Lucan fell in a swoon, that parts of his guts fell out of his body. . . . And when the king awoke, he behold Sir Lucan how he lay foaming at the mouth and part of his guts lay at his feet. (p. 869)

But beyond this, there is the deeper pain that arises from remorse, from the failing of the Fellowship, and above all from the sense of mystery, which comes with the passing of Arthur in the black barge tended by the weeping queens. The good end of Lancelot and of Guinevere, and of the remnant of the knights, who took the cross and "died upon a Good Friday for God's sake"—the last words of the book—are in the nature of a *coda*. For the men and women of Malory are earthly men and women; and for them, the good life of earth, the active life of loving and fighting, and the unlimited horizons of Arthur's kingdoms are all.

### THE DAY OF DESTINY

THE ancient heroic tradition of English poetry—the tradition of *Beowulf* and of *The Battle of Maldon*—descended to Malory through the English alliterative poetry of the fourteenth century upon which he based his earliest story, *The Tale of the Noble King Arthur that was Emperor himself through Dignity of his Hands*. His own shaping of the Arthurian tales, which had already undergone so many changes in the course of the three hundred years in which they had been the common property of writers all over Western Europe, was grave, masculine, and at its deepest levels concerned with personal relationships as part of the social structure and not as the private, secret joy and pain of man or woman. Elaine of Astolat, though a touching figure, is yet a minor one in his great tapestry. The French books had developed the subtlety and the fineness of courtly love, and had overlaid the primitive simplicities of the stories. The author of *Sir Gawain and the Green Knight* had fused adventure and morality; at the center of his poem is a description of the emblem of the Five Wounds of Christ and the Five Joys of Mary which the good knight bears upon his shield. Malory's world is rougher and simpler than either of these. In the last two tales, *The Book of Sir Lancelot and Queen Guinevere* and *The Most Piteous Tale of the Morte Arthur Saunz Guerdon*, he attains to his full heroic theme.

In the intervening tales, his characters have a kind of depth and stability which the figures of English romances do not usually possess. Where interest is concentrated upon a marvellous succession of adventures, characters retain a fairy-tale flatness and remain simply types, upon which the fantasy of the listeners can be easily projected, and with whom they can readily identify themselves. The central figure in the warrior's daydream must be fairly indeterminate, if he is to act as an idealized self for all and sundry. Slowly, Arthur, Gawain, and Lancelot have become, if not characters in the full dramatic sense, at least figures defined by their existence in a mutual relationship to each other. They have social if not individual identities.

In *The Tale of the Noble King Arthur*, it is the king himself who is the hero. Here, instead of a quest, Malory depicts a whole campaign. There is nevertheless a magnificent preliminary description of Arthur's single-handed combat with the giant of St. Michael's Mount. A weird and terrifying scene first greets him as he climbs to the summit of the crag—a weeping woman by a new-made grave, two fires "flaming high" at which the bodies of little children, "broched in a manner like birds," are being roasted and tended by three captive damsels. In such a setting there is a tremendous hand-to-hand encounter. At the end of this, locked together, the king and the sorely wounded giant roll from the top to the bottom of the mountain.

> With that the warlow wrath Arthur under, and so they waltred and tumbled over the crags and bushes, and either cleght other full fast in their arms. And other whiles Arthur was above and other whiles under, and so weltering and wallowing they rolled down the hill, and they never left till they fell thereas the flood marked. But ever in the waltring Arthur

smites and hits him with a short dagger up to the hilts, and in his falling there brast of the giant's ribs three even at once. (p. 147)

The rough wit by which he is greeted by his comrades, "I have mickle wonder and Michael be of such making, that ever God would suffer him to abide in Heaven," is matched by Arthur's own, when in the fight with the Emperor he cuts off a giant by the knees: " 'Now art thou of a size,' said the king, 'like unto our fairies' and then he struck off his head swiftly" (Vinaver, p. 159). But the King's prowess having been established in his fight with the giant, others are permitted a large share in the victorious advance upon Rome.

In Arthur's campaign there is the first glimmering of a national pride, which was quite foreign to the knightly society of the Middle Ages, and to the medieval romance. It is manifest in the opening scenes, with the brilliant picture of an invading fleet setting out from England and making its way across to France. Only in the first and the last of the tales does geography become significant; and it does so because in both these parts of the story Malory is depicting the fate, not of individuals, but of a nation.

At the end there is a regression from the more civilized social bonds of the fellowship to the primitive ones of kinship. In the final books, rival brotherhoods to that of the Round Table appear. It is the five nephews of Arthur who in different ways oppose Lancelot—Aggravayne and Mordred by treachery, Gawain, Gaherys, and Gareth from mischance. These last dissociate themselves strongly from the plots of the other two, who lead a little band of twelve "and they were of Scotland, and other else of Sir Gawain's kin, other well-willers to his brother." On the other hand, Lancelot's danger draws togeher "all we ben of your blood and your well-willers," as Sir Bors tells him. Roused by a common sense of alarm, they had all wakened from sleep and come together at the moment when the treacherous assault upon the queen's chamber was made. The issue is clear to Lancelot.

"And therefore, my fellows," said Sir Lancelot, "I pray you all that ye will be of heart good, and help me in what need that ever I stand, for now is war comen to us all."

"Sir," said Sir Bors, "all is welcome that God sendeth us, and as we have taken much weal with you and much worship, we will take the woe with you as we have taken the weal."

And therefore they said, all the good knights.

"Look ye, take no discomfort! for there is no bond of knights under heaven but we shall be able to grieve them as much as they us, and therefore discomfort not yourself by no manner. And we shall gather together all that we love and that loveth us, and what that ye will have done shall be done. And therefore let us take the woe and the joy together."

(p. 825)

The knightly virtue of loyalty has turned against itself. From this point all the efforts of Lancelot to avoid that which he knows is inevitable are doomed. Gawain refuses to oppose Lancelot; as a consequence his two younger brothers, sent as guards to the queen's trial, and going reluctantly and unarmed, are slain unawares by Lancelot in his rescue of the queen; and so the blood feud between himself and Gawain begins. Gawain denies what he well knows, that the deaths were sheer mischance; Lancelot will not defend himself at the cost of injury to Arthur or Gawain; he makes the most stupendous offers of penance for the deaths of Gaherys and Gareth, including a pilgrimage barefoot and in his shirt, from Sandwich to Carlisle, but Gawain will not be reconciled.

The pope finally intervenes and ends the war. The queen is returned to Arthur, and Lancelot is banished from the realm. To point the moral, here in his lament ancient examples of a tragic fall are evoked.

"Fortune is so variant, and the wheel so mutable, that there is no constant abiding. And that may be proved by many old chronicles, as of noble Ector of Troy and Alysaunder, the mighty conqueror, and many mo other. . . ." (p. 847)

So Sir Lancelot departs to Bayonne, and Arthur and his knights once again invade France, no longer as conquerors but in pursuit of vengeance. Then swiftly follows the treachery of Mordred, Arthur's nephew and bastard son, gotten upon his sister Morgawse, queen of Orkney. Mordred, left as regent in England, revolts against Arthur. The sin at the heart of Arthur's court is finally embodied in this dark figure. The fruitless attempt to destroy Lancelot fails, and Gawain dies repentant; the final battle, that between Arthur and the dark powers, draws on. Even here, at the last moment, a bid is made for peace; Arthur and Mordred hold a parley between their armies, but each in such mistrust that they warn their followers if any sword is drawn, they should advance and slay. Success seems imminent; but Fortune turns her wheel, and the Day of Destiny falls upon the chivalry of Britain.

And so they met as their poyntement was, and were agreed and accorded throughly. And wine was fetched and they drank together. Right so came out an adder of a little heath bush, and it stung a knight in the foot. And so when the knight felt him so stung, he looked down and saw the adder; and anon he drew his sword to slay the adder, and thought none other harm. And when the host on both parties saw that sword drawn, then they blew beams, trumpets and horns, and shouted grimly, and so both hosts dressed them togethers. And King Arthur took his horse and said, "Alas, this unhappy day!" and so rode to his party, and Sir Mordred in like wise.
(p. 867)

There is very little left of either army by the end of the day, when the father and son confront each other, afoot and weary, over the heaps of dead. Arthur drives his spear through Mordred's body, but Mordred thrusts himself forward to the butt end of the spear, to give Arthur his death's wound by the sword.

The growth of treachery and mistrust, and the vanity of all efforts by men to stay the course of fortune as it carries them to destruction give to these last books of the *Morte Darthur* an ironic unity and a singleness of action that are new to Malory, and far beyond the world of romance. He had achieved something of the same effect upon a smaller scale in his early tale of *Balin or the Knight with Two Swords*. Balin, a knight out of wild Northumberland, rough and uncouth, by his impulsive acts of vengeance brings down ruin upon himself and his house. Confronted by magic dangers, and invisible foes, he is a human figure imposed on a legendary background, whose very confusion and portentous horror enhances his rude and simple courage. Throughout the story the sense of doom is felt in the phrase so often applied to Balin, "he may not long endure"; in his last battle he rides forward at the challenging sound of the horn, with so ominous and savage a comparison that he seems like Roland riding to the Dark Tower.

And so he heard an horn blow as it had been the death of a beast. "That blast," said Balyn, "is blowen for me, for I am the prize and yet am I not dead."
(p. 67)

So he goes forward into combat, only to find, in the hour of death, that he has fought his own brother Balan, and that they have slain each other.

The slaying of the kinsman, here as in Arthur's last battle, is an act at once profoundly unnatural and yet felt to be inevitable; it marks the disruption of the last and deepest social bond. What symbolism might be seen in this act by more sophisticated ages is irrelevant to Malory, whose greatness lies in his literal significance, and in the boldness with which he faces the unshirkable mysteries of anger and fidelity, courage and grief, love and death. In Arthur's death scene there is a foreshadowing of Shakespeare's tableau in *Henry VI*: the civil strife, the lamenting king who is also the father killing the son, while the son also kills the father. Whether in the single story of Balin, or in the ruin of a kingdom, it is in depicting heroic tragic action that Malory attains his full stature. There are more purely romantic pleasures to be gained from his work, including, even for modern readers, the pleasures of the daydream; but there is no sickliness in his dreams, as there is no malice in his violence. His is a mirror of the active life, untouched by contemplation.

### SELECTED BIBLIOGRAPHY

The bulk of the writing on Arthurian romance is to be found in learned journals, some of which are not readily accessible. Such articles have, therefore, not been listed here; anyone who wishes to do so will find a bibliography of periodical literature in the *Romantic Review* and in *Speculum*, the journal of the Medieval Academy of America (Cambridge, Mass.), together with reviews and notices. Much useful material will also be found in *Medium Aevum*, the journal of the Society for the Study of Medieval Language and Literature (Oxford).

I. TEXTS. H. O. Sommer, ed., *Le Morte Darthur*, 2 vols. (London, 1889–1891), a line by line reprint of the first edition (1485), with an introduction and glossary; E. Vinaver, ed., *The Works of Sir Thomas Malory*, 3 vols. (Oxford, 1947; 2nd ed. 1967; repr. with corrections, 1971), a critical and annotated ed. incorporating the readings of the Winchester MS. A one-volume ed., without the critical apparatus but with brief introduction and glossary, was published in 1954.

Only two copies are recorded of William Caxton's first edition of *The Noble and Ioyous Book Entytled Le Morte Darthur Notwythstondyng It Treateth of the Byrth Lyf and Actes of the Sayd Kyng Arthur of his Noble Knyghtes of the Rounde Table Theyr Mervayllous Enquestes and Adventures Thachyevyng of the Sankgreal and in Thende the Dolorous Deth and Departyng out of Thys World of Them Al Whiche Booke was Reduced in to Englysshe by Syr Thomas Malory Knyght* (Westminster, 1485) (John Rylands University Library of Manchester and the Pierpoint Morgan Library, New York). Only two copies exist (Rylands and Bodleian libraries) of the 2nd ed., printed by Wynkyn de Worde (Westminster, 1498).

Modernized texts include those by A. W. Pollard (London, 1902) and E. Rhys (London, 1910), each in two volumes. See also Derek Brewer, ed., *The Morte Darthur*, paperback, York Mediaeval Texts Series (1968, rev. ed., 1976). The valuable introduction, especially the treatment of Shame and Honour, has been highly influential; the notes and glossary make this the most useful compact edition of these great last books. *The Death of Arthur*, from Vinaver's work, has been published as a separate volume, *King Arthur and His Knights* (Oxford, 1975), also available in paperback.

II. CRITICAL AND BIOGRAPHICAL STUDIES. G. H. Maynardier, *Arthur of the English Poets* (Boston, 1905), a study of the influence of Malory upon subsequent writers; V. D. Scudder, *The Morte Darthur and Its Sources* (London, 1917); J. D. Bruce, *Evolution of Arthurian Romance to 1300*, 2 vols. (Göttingen, 1923–1924), the most complete study of the early evolution of Arthurian legend; E. K. Chambers, *Arthur of Britain* (London, 1927), a more condensed study of Arthurian legend, which contains also a useful bibliographical note; E. Hicks, *Sir Thomas Malory, His Turbulent Career: A Biography* (Cambridge, Mass., 1928); E. Vinaver, *Sir Thomas Malory* (Oxford, 1929), a general study, written before the discovery of the Winchester MS in 1934; R. S. Loomis, ed., *Arthurian Literature in the Middle Ages* (Oxford, 1959), mainly on earlier work, but contains an essay on Malory by Vinaver; J. A. W. Bennett, ed., *Essays on Malory* (Oxford, 1963), a valuable collection of essays by W. Oakshott, C. S. Lewis, E. Vinaver, D. S. Brewer, P. E. Tucker, F. Whitehead, and S. Shaw, with biographical note by R. T. Davies, giving a reassessment in the light of the Winchester MS. The unity of "the hoole book" is defended by Lewis and Brewer; R. S. Loomis, *Development of Arthurian Romance* (London, 1963), defends the unity of Malory's work; W. Matthews, *The Ill-framed Knight* (Berkeley, Calif., 1966; London, 1967), a skeptical enquiry into the identity of Sir Thomas Malory, which on linguistic grounds suggests that the author of *Le Morte Darthur* may have been a Yorkshireman; R. T. Davies, ed., *King Arthur and His Knights of the Round Table* (London, 1967); P. J. C. Field, *Romance and Chronicle, A Study of Malory's Style* (London, 1967), a first attempt to deal with the prose style; Mark Lambert, *Malory, Style and Vision in The Morte Darthur* (New Haven, 1975), develops from Field, a valuable close reading of the text illustrated with comparisons from a wide field; Larry D. Benson, *Malory's Morte Darthur* (Cambridge, 1976), a well-documented, scholarly survey of Malory's relation to earlier romance, and also to the chivalry of his age.

# KATHERINE MANSFIELD
(1888-1923)

## Ian A. Gordon

*I*

For some centuries now the Englishman has been a considerable traveler. War, adventure, commercial instincts, empire building, the selfless missionary spirit, a profound faith in the English way of life (and at times a profound distaste for it), sometimes mere curiosity have all sent generations of Englishmen beyond the seas. Most of these wrote nothing except letters to their families; many of them not even that. But from all these centuries of foreign adventures English literature has profited, emerging always with fresh experiences and on occasion with new insight. Two main themes can be detected in this literature of life overseas. The first, and more obvious, is the undisguised and uninhibited delight in expanded horizons that gives freshness and gusto to writers otherwise as different as Tobias Smollett, Frederick Marryat, and Graham Greene. The second appears in more introspective writers, who—placed in a foreign setting—turn their eyes resolutely homeward: Robert Louis Stevenson in Samoa remembering Edinburgh with affection, James Joyce in Switzerland fascinated though appalled by his native Dublin, the usually unsentimental Rudyard Kipling recalling his Devonshire schooldays. The theme of exile with its elegiac undertones is seldom far from the thoughts of the apparently confident Englishman on his journeys.

To this second group belongs Katherine Mansfield, though her affinity to these manifest exiles has seldom been recognized. It is, however, the key to a full understanding of her writing. She was a third-generation New Zealander who received her childhood education in her own country. After further schooling in London, she went back unwillingly to New Zealand with the single-minded intention of returning with all speed to the literary capital. Wearing down her family's resistance, she was back in London within a couple of years. The remainder of her life was spent there and in the south of England, with longer and longer periods on the Continent as her health deteriorated. She did not return to New Zealand and for some years felt little but her adolescent contempt for the narrow round of colonial life in its early-twentieth-century capital of seventy thousand inhabitants. But events caught up with her. The glittering prizes came her way only when they had ceased to matter. Life, if it never singed her wings, certainly burned her fingers, not once but several times. A reunion with her brother, shortly afterward killed in World War I, completed her enlightenment, and in her middle twenties, a mature and experienced—almost too experienced—woman, she came to recognize that a New Zealander can be as much of an exile in England as an Englishman on an island in the Pacific. From the moment of that discovery the note of elegy entered her work, and she turned for her themes to her origins. All of her best work dates from this point.

The editions of her writings do not make it easy to follow this development. Her earliest volume, *In a German Pension* (1911), was brought out by an obscure publisher and, attracting little attention, went out of print. After her death in 1923, when her reputation was probably reaching its highest point, this resentful and ill-natured volume was reprinted, in 1926, somewhat to the disturbance of readers who were then familiar only with her finished and sensitive work in New Zealand stories like "The Garden Party." Meanwhile the publication in 1924 of *Something Childish, and Other Stories* (in America entitled *The Little Girl*), which contains a mixture of stories of various dates, from some written shortly before her death at the age of thirty-four to one written when she was nineteen, had further confused any but the most careful reader bent on following the pattern of her development, whether in technique or in theme. The collected edition of her work casts no further light. It merely reprints, still as separate en-

891

tities, each of her separately published volumes; most of the stories are undated, and the dates on others are demonstrably false. In any subsequent edition, one hopes that the stories will be printed in the order of composition, or at least that this information will be made available in a brief but accurate appendix.

It is not that the precise date of composition of any one story matters in itself. But it is important before making a critical judgment on a story to know where it fits into her work. The chronological sequence is important for another reason. Katherine Mansfield, to a degree almost unparalleled in English fiction, put her own experiences into her stories. She wrote of nothing that did not directly happen to her, even when she appeared to be at her most imaginative and fanciful. Her stories, read in their order of composition, gain force and significance, and are illuminated at all points, by the events of her own history. Her whole work read in this manner emerges as a kind of *recherche du temps perdu*, a remembrance of things past in a distant dominion.

## II

KATHLEEN BEAUCHAMP was born in 1888 in Wellington, New Zealand. Her father, Harold (later Sir Harold) Beauchamp, was a merchant who combined a shy sensitivity at home with a ruthless drive in his business affairs. She grew up in a family group of two older sisters and a younger brother, with a grandmother and unmarried aunts among the adult members. From the village school she went via the Girls' High School to a private school for young ladies, and then (the family ambition and fortunes still rising) to four years at Queen's College, Harley Street, London. Returning to Wellington in 1906, her head filled with Oscar Wilde and the glamour of the literary life, she sulked and refused to play the part of the accomplished middle-class daughter back from finishing school. She undertook a strenuous six-week camping trip in rough and sometimes primitive conditions and showed her new independence by taking courses in bookkeeping and typing in the Wellington Technical College. The family capitulated. With an allowance from her father (which continued throughout her life) she left for London in 1908 to establish herself as a writer. She was nineteen. She had published a few sketches. All she required was experience. The process was not pleasant. Within a short time she was in retreat, seeking one refuge after another. What she could not know at the time, and came to recognize only after years of despair, was that when she left her own country at the age of nineteen she had already experienced all that she required. The material for her finest work lay in the family group she had abandoned and in the colonial town she had so contemptuously left behind.

Within a year of her arrival in London she was pregnant. She married George Bowden, although he was not the father of her child, left him abruptly, and was packed off to Bavaria by her mother, who was on a hurried visit to England. The child was miscarried, and so the incident was closed. But all of this lay behind the snarling ill humor of her stories of this period. They were first printed in periodicals during 1910, after her return from Bavaria, and (if one excepts "The Modern Soul") form the first seven stories in her 1911 volume, *In a German Pension*. The Germans are observed with loathing. But the Germans are not the real target. What she is depicting is the grossness of the male, guzzling and drinking, pressing his unwanted attentions on the young girl in "At Lehmann's" and on the middle-aged wife in "Frau Brechenmacher Attends a Wedding." Katherine Mansfield's own situation at the time, the pregnant girl surrounded by curious middle-aged matrons, is underlined in "Frau Fischer." For all their German background and variety of characters, these stories are almost autobiography.

Back in London by early 1910, she found temporary refuge with Ida Baker, a friend from her Queen's College days who was to become her guardian angel thereafter. She placed her Bavarian stories with A. R. Orage's the *New Age* and shortly after embarked on a new love affair. The results were almost but not quite as disastrous as the first, and the young man faded from the picture. She began on more stories, some based on her Bavarian memories, two of them—"The Journey to Bruges" and "A Truthful Adventure"—springing from a brief visit to Belgium. The *New Age* published both stories (they did not appear in book form until 1924) and a Bavarian one, "A Birthday." These stories of 1911, though five of them are printed in *In a German Pension*, show a mellower spirit than the 1910 stories. There is a certain genial and kindly humor in "The Advanced Lady"; and love, in "The Swing of the Pendulum," in spite of the intrusion of a predatory male, leads to a conclusion acceptable to the central woman character. But nothing shows the change of attitude so clearly as "A Birthday." The theme is the birth of a child, and the father, Andreas Binzer, is shown as (being a male, inevitably) selfish, but sensitive, nervous, and finally overjoyed. There is nothing of the disgust with childbirth so clearly enunciated in "At Lehmann's" of the previous year.

What caused the change? Partly, one can only suspect, the happier love affair during 1911. But there is a deeper reason. In "A Birthday," Katherine Mansfield is for the first time drawing on her own family. In spite of the German names, "A Birthday" is set in Wellington and Andreas Binzer is a preliminary sketch for the mostly true-to-life picture of her father that was to dominate so many of her later stories. In "A Birthday" there is a harbor, there are ferns in a glass case, there is a gully, the wind shakes the window sashes: the scene is Wellington, so accurately depicted that one can today identify even the streets and the actual house in the story.

### III

A few months after the publication of her first book, Katherine Mansfield moved on to her final love affair. This time it was permanent. The story of her meeting John Middleton Murry in 1912 and of their life together (they could not marry until 1918, when her husband divorced her) has been fully recorded by Murry and by Katherine Mansfield in her published letters. Henceforth, she had a center to work from, and her early disastrous affairs, though they continued to provide a few themes for stories, sank below the horizon. But it is not mere gossip-mongering to record them. Without a knowledge of them the critic must read her early stories as mere literary exercises. They are more than that. They are a first beginning at the recording of experiences often little transmuted in the telling.

During the next two years Katherine Mansfield wrote stories for the two journals that Murry successively edited, *Rhythm* and the *Blue Review*. Most of these are based on New Zealand material. They fall into two groups. First, three tales of violence, all involving murder—the sort of thing that English readers readily associate with a rough colonial background. The best known of these is "The Woman at the Store." The second group begins where "A Birthday" left off. The New Zealand Burnell family begins to emerge, though they are not yet given a name: the little daydreaming girl in "How Pearl Button Was Kidnapped" (at first glance a mere fairy tale); the bullying father, the tender grandmother, the mother, and the family of little girls in "New Dresses" and "The Little Girl."

Early 1914 saw the collapse of Murry's journals. During the year that followed, Katherine Mansfield wrote two of her best stories to date, "Something Childish but Very Natural," a love story that is evidently her and Murry's love-in-a-cottage situation projected back to a couple of youngsters, and "An Indiscreet Journey," based on a visit she paid to Paris in early 1915 to renew acquaintance with an old admirer. To these months also belongs "The Little Governess," a longer story on several of her recurring themes—the young woman alone in the world, the predatory male, the unsympathetic foreign official. Katherine Mansfield had known them all. The story represents a technical advance. For the first time she is inside her character. We are at the beginning of that sensitive feeling for characters portrayed through their own fleeting thoughts that lies at the basis of all her mature work.

### IV

In 1915 occurred one of the several crises that determined her life. Her brother arrived from New Zealand on his way to the army. The exchange of old memories led to the writing of two short New Zealand sketches, "The Apple Tree"[1] and "The Wind Blows." Before the end of the year her brother was dead. When the first shock was over, she knew what lay before her—the *recherche du temps perdu:*

I want to write recollections of my own country. Yes, I want to write about my own country till I exhaust my store. Not only because it is a sacred debt that I pay to my country because my brother and I were born there, but also because in my thoughts I range with him over all the remembered places.

She was ill, and she and Murry moved for a time to the south of France. There at Bandol she completed in early 1916 her first major story, "The Aloe," a recollection of New Zealand. It was not published in

---

[1] In *The Scrapbook* (1939); not included in *Collected Stories* (1945).

its original form until 1930. She laid it aside for revision. Emotion and nostalgia were not enough. Technique required an intellectual effort that demanded more time and cooler reflection. The revision was published as "Prelude" in 1918. It is the story that set the standard and established the pattern for all her later work. The Burnell family are evoked in their early days, the little girls still small children, Stanley Burnell at the opening of his prosperous career, the whole told "in a kind of special prose" (the phrase is her own) that is one of the secrets of her originality.

During the two years following "The Aloe" she was increasingly oppressed by illness. She had seldom been completely in health since her first arrival in London. By the end of 1917 her illness was diagnosed as tuberculosis and in early 1918 she was back in Bandol again. The year between the two visits to Bandol saw her returning on ten occasions to the *New Age*, but not with New Zealand stories. While "Prelude" was maturing in her mind as her major work, she was content to publish only lighter stuff, perceptive but not very deeply felt. "Mr. Reginald Peacock's Day," with its simpering hero, and "A Dill Pickle," the story of the meeting of two disillusioned lovers, are typical of the group. The best of these is "Feuille d'Album," an adolescent love story, remarkable because it is her first full use of the interior monologue. In 1917 that meant being in the forefront of technical experiment.

Her writing of 1918 includes two New Zealand stories, "Sun and Moon," on the surface an allegory but in fact a Burnell family story of the "Prelude" group, and the unfinished "A Married Man's Story," an interior narrative in a Wellington setting. Her best two stories of the year are "Bliss," with its innocently happy wife who recognizes in a moment of horrified insight her successful rival, and the polished "Je ne parle pas français." This last represents a return to old experiences, handled with a technical competence that is approaching its peak. She revives her old memories of the woman on her own, abandoned in Europe by her lover. The situation of her earlier experience was reinforced by the circumstances in which she was writing. Murry was in London—where he had to earn a living. Katherine Mansfield, ill and alone in Bandol (except for the faithful Ida Baker), bombarding him with urgent and not always fair accusations of neglect, felt as abandoned as Mouse, who is finally deserted by her lover in Paris, in the caustic but effective ending of "Je ne parle pas français."

By spring 1918 she was in London again. She was married to Murry in May. Illness prevented much writing, and in later 1918 it had to be the Continent again for the winter. "The Man Without a Temperament," with its theme of a sick wife and coldly patient husband, is her comment on the period. It is of peculiar significance that its original title was "The Exile." The summer was spent back in England. After arranging for the publication of a volume of her stories of the last few years—they were published as *Bliss, and Other Stories* in late 1920 and included the subtle and evocative "Prelude"—she left again for the south of France. It was the final break with England, to which she was henceforth but a fleeting visitor. If she had to be an exile, it might as well be where her failing health had some expectations.

V

FROM then on, for a space of less than two years, Katherine Mansfield worked with the concentrated fury of a woman who has only a little time left. She had been publishing since she was nineteen. She was now thirty-two. The critics had ignored her first book in 1911. Her second, *Bliss*, was acclaimed on all sides. But she was dissatisfied with it: "A great part of my Constable book is *trivial*."[2] This is a harsh judgment. But in view of what she planned—and what she achieved in these remarkable two years—it was true.

The writing of these two final years was to yield a total almost as great as all the work of her previous career. It was done in two bursts of fertile activity, the first at Menton in the south of France during the winter of 1920–1921, and the second from the middle of 1921 till the middle of 1922, when she was with her husband in Switzerland and later was undergoing treatment in Paris. The last half-year of her life (she died on 9 January 1923) understandably produced nothing that has survived.

At Menton she wrote six stories. With her reputation rising rapidly, she found that the solider literary journals were now waiting for her, and all six were published variously in the *Athenaeum*, the *Nation*, and the *London Mercury*. Three are on her leitmotiv of the woman on her own in an unfriendly world. The central situations in "The Lady's Maid," "Miss

---

[2]Constable & Co. were Katherine Mansfield's publishers.

Brill," and "Life of Ma Parker" are variations on this theme, with the lonely woman now slipping into middle age. "The Daughters of the Late Colonel" is a magnificently envisaged story of two women devastated by the death of their father. In life he took everything from them, and his disappearance leaves them without a reason for existing. Constantia, the younger of the sisters, is based on Ida Baker, who (as revealed in *Letters*, 1951) drove Katherine Mansfield to alternate fits of exasperation and gratitude. Both aspects are present in Constantia. "The Young Girl," a slight but sensitive sketch of adolescence, and "The Stranger" complete the group written at Menton. "The Stranger" is a New Zealand story. Stanley Burnell (what matter if he is now called John Hammond, who had been Andreas Binzer?) waits on the Auckland waterfront for the liner bringing home his wife. Burnell is aging, as so many of Katherine Mansfield's characters are at this time, but he is the same man, bustling in public, sensitive and vulnerable in his private relations. His wife has been delayed at the bedside of a dying passenger, and Burnell jealously resents the intrusion: "They would never be alone together again."

When Katherine Mansfield moved to Switzerland, the pressure of work mounted: 1921 was the busiest year of her life. Stories poured from her pen, finished and ready for the publisher, sometimes within an evening, though the themes had often been dormant for years. This is the great year of the Burnell family sequence, lovingly remembered at various periods of their lives. "Sixpence" (excluded from *The Garden Party* volume of 1922 as "sentimental") shows Burnell punishing his small son and then relenting. The father-image has ceased being merely a big bully. In "An Ideal Family" he is sympathetically conceived (now "old Mr. Neave") as an old, failing man, swamped by his three daughters and his son, who has taken over the business. In "Her First Ball," daughter and son are young people, brought face to face with the cynicism of middle age. "The Voyage" recounts an earlier memory, the heroine a mere child with her beloved grandmother. The series culminated toward the end of the year with the magnificent perception of "At the Bay," where the children are youngsters at the family's seaside cottage, and "The Garden Party" (they are now the Sheridans), where the girls and their brother are almost grown up, and they meet for the first time the horror of death—and life—on the other side of the street. Katherine Mansfield in these sensitively felt stories is not merely recording experience. She is expressing a view of life on a basis of recorded memories.

All of this group and the six Menton stories were published in *The Garden Party, and Other Stories*. They do not exhaust its contents. Along with some earlier work there is the love story "Mr. and Mrs. Dove," delicately poised between mockery and sentiment, and a vicious delineation of a brittle woman rejecting the love of a devoted husband, "Marriage à la Mode," written perhaps in contrition to make peace with herself for having written "The Man Without a Temperament." *The Garden Party* evoked a chorus of praise on both sides of the Atlantic. By the end of the following year it had been reprinted once in England and seven times in America. If Katherine Mansfield wanted either popular fame or critical reputation, they both were hers now.

VI

It was too late to matter. Her illness was progressing, but she pushed ahead with her writing. Between the end of 1921 and the middle of 1922, when she ceased writing, she wrote sufficient stories for her final volume, *The Dove's Nest*, published in 1923, a few months after her death. It contains several stories on the relationship of husband and wife—"A Cup of Tea," "Honeymoon," "Widowed," "All Serene!" —and one on her recurring theme of the lonely woman, here deserted even by her pet bird, "The Canary." But the strength of the volume lies once again in the stories of her own town, preeminently in the classic re-creation of childhood "The Doll's House." The childhood is Katherine Mansfield's, the family is the now familiar Burnell group, the scene is an authentic Wellington suburb, where the creek and the house she describes are still discernible. But, like all her best New Zealand stories, it transcends mere locality. Her accurate rendering of background is only part of her larger accuracy in the rendering of life. To this final group of Wellington memories recalled belongs "Taking the Veil," with its adolescent daydreams, and, among the unfinished stories in the book, "A Bad Idea," "A Man and His Dog" (which is an appendix to "Prelude"), and "Susannah."

Two stories, both among the last things she wrote, bring the series to a close and complete the theme on which the death of her brother had launched her, the final repayment of the "sacred debt." The first is "Six Years After"—the title is self-explanatory for anyone with a knowledge of her life history—in which Stanley Burnell (he is now simply "Daddy") and his wife start on a voyage. For him the bustle of shipboard is enough. For his wife the memory of the dead son makes the experience of the journey intolerable. "Six Years After" provides a clue to "The Fly," which was assessed by that masterly critic of the short story E. J. O'Brien as one of the fifteen finest short stories ever written, "as inevitable as the passage of time." "The Fly," written in early 1922, when she knew that the finish was not far off, is often asserted to be her indictment of life. It is, rather, her clear-eyed admission that life goes on. Two old men, retired businessman and boss (both, aspects of Burnell), linger over the memory of the boss's son, killed "six years ago" in the war. When the old man goes, the boss plays with a fly ink-soaked on the blotting-paper, until the fly finally gives up the struggle:

The boss lifted the corpse on the end of the paper-knife and flung it into the waste-paper basket. But such a grinding feeling of wretchedness seized him that he felt positively frightened. He started forward and pressed the bell for Macey.

"Bring me some fresh blotting-paper," he said sternly, "and look sharp about it." And while the old dog padded away he fell to wondering what it was he had been thinking about before. What was it? It was . . . He took out his handkerchief and passed it inside his collar. For the life of him he could not remember.

This may be an indictment of life, but it is much more an admission that the dead pass on, and the living must live their own life. "The Fly" is full of symbolism that the author may not herself have recognized. The spirit of her dead brother, which had driven her on to such urgent activity, was finally at rest. The debt was paid.

## VII

MUCH of the above could not have been written in the years immediately following her death, and criticism of Katherine Mansfield has tended to fasten on what could be judged solely from her published stories—her prose style, insight, technique. All of these are important both for an appreciation of her work and in view of the great influence she had on the art of the short story. She had the same kind of directive influence on the art of the short story as James Joyce had on the novel. After Joyce and Katherine Mansfield neither the novel nor the short story can ever be quite the same again. They beat a track to a higher point from which others can scan a wider horizon.

Criticism of her published stories, however, is powerfully reinforced and given a deeper significance by a knowledge of the sources of her material. Such a knowledge has become increasingly possible with the publication of Katherine Mansfield's own background writing—her *Journal* in 1927, her *Letters* in 1928, and in 1951 the full text of her letters to her husband. The importance of the New Zealand themes (for example) is clear enough to any careful reader of her later stories. But when we turn to her *Journal* of that period and find her haunted night after night with dreams that she is on shipboard sailing back to her own country, we do not need to be psychoanalysts to see the connection between "The Garden Party" and "The Doll's House" and the recurring dream pattern.

Until quite recently Katherine Mansfield's *Journal* and *Letters* have been the best commentary on her stories. But they are sometimes fragmentary and leave unexplained considerable passages in her own history. Biographical studies, which should expand and supplement her own account, have been largely hampered by the 12,000-mile separation between the two parts of her life and also because so many of her associates who are still alive have been chary of discussion. Ruth Mantz's study of 1933, although the author visited New Zealand, is slight, is based on partial evidence, and leaves her subject with all her major stories still to write. Sylvia Berkman's study of 1951 is a much more impressive piece of work, based on an accurate knowledge of the printed materials, of which there were many more available than in 1933, but had the bad luck to be written and published before the full text of the letters was available.

Antony Alpers, who published a biography in 1953, used the 1951 edition of the letters, and, as a New Zealander with substantial residence in England, he was in a position to both overcome the difficulties that earlier biographers had encountered and follow the pattern of her development. He was able to persuade several people to give accounts who had hitherto kept silence, notably Ida Baker, the French poet and novelist Francis Carco, and George

Bowden, Katherine Mansfield's first husband. His information on her father was faulty, however, and he portrayed him in a bad light. Since 1953 others have dug into bank accounts, family and school archives, and Katherine Mansfield's own manuscripts and have corrected the record in significant detail. Meanwhile, Ida Baker has published her memoirs, and numerous firsthand accounts of the London literary scene of Katherine Mansfield's time have appeared. Alpers published a completely rewritten version of his biography in 1980. It is as near to a standard biography as we are likely to see.

### VIII

THE material of Katherine Mansfield's stories, based so directly on her own experiences, is in the central tradition of the English novel, the affairs of every day heightened by sensitivity and good writing. Her range is even more restricted than Jane Austen's few families in a country village. For her, one family and a few relationships were enough to express a universality of experience. Essentially the stress is on character and the subtle interrelationships of people in small groups, bound together by bonds of emotion. To express these she concentrates her writing, discarding the heavy lumber of narration and descriptive background. In the end she has not more than half a dozen themes. First, there is the woman alone in the world, as she had been in her younger days. As Katherine Mansfield grew older, so did this character age, a girl in "The Tiredness of Rosabel," a woman in "Life of Ma Parker" and "The Canary." Second, there are the stories of the man and woman for whom a happy relationship seems impossible because the woman is the victim of a predatory or an indifferent male, as in "The Little Governess," "This Flower," "The Man Without a Temperament," and "Je ne parle pas français."

In a small group of stories, the situation is reversed. In "The Black Cap," "The Escape," and the bitter "Marriage à la Mode," it is the husband who is loving and trusting and the wife who deserts him. Indeed, in Katherine Mansfield, a happy marriage relationship is apparent only in those stories that she based on her parents—Stanley and Linda, under these and other names, face life with confidence and together, in the pages of "Prelude," "At the Bay," and "The Garden Party," and can clearly survive the marital crises depicted in "The Stranger" and "Six Years After."

Her other major theme is children in their relationships with one another and with the adults in the family. The child-father bond is subtly drawn in a series of magnificent studies, starting with the resentment of the young child against the omnipotence of the parent in "Sixpence," "A Suburban Fairy Tale," and "New Dresses"; through relief at his departure from the house and indifference toward him, expressed most clearly in "At the Bay"; to a recognition, in "The Little Girl," that he is "Poor father! Not so big, after all"; and finally to a growing sympathy for him and, as child and parent grow older, a recognition of his adult problems, in "An Ideal Family." This sequence is rounded off with the warning conveyed in "The Daughters of the Late Colonel," where the daughter-father bond has persisted until life without the parent becomes impossible.

All of these relationships may be found in other writers. But in the delineation of children together Katherine Mansfield stands alone. Her lifelong discipline in entering into the mind of her subject ("I have just finished a story with a canary for a hero, and almost feel I have lived in a cage and pecked a piece of chickweed myself") is nowhere more essential than when the writer enters the mind of a child. If an adult writer portrays the mind of an adult character, only the most percipient critic can detect where the character is not fully realized and is "contaminated" by the writer's own personality. Because of this, the delineation of adult character and the impact of adult on adult is, by comparison, easier. The writer may "contaminate" his character with something of himself and still create on paper a credible personality. But the least "contamination" by the adult writer's personality of the character of a child he is creating on paper shows up immediately. Few children are drawn in literature without some adult perception showing through. The author's feeling of adult condescension or regret for his own lost childhood usually comes across. The very titles of books like *The Golden Age* or *When We Were Very Young* imply an adult assessment. But Mansfield portrays children as children, seen through their own eyes and the eyes of other children. Kezia and Lottie and Isabel Burnell and the Trout boys, Pip and Rags (and their dog, a uniquely children's dog), in "Prelude" and "At the Bay," with the unforgettable Lil and Our Else in "The Doll's House," are creations that stand by themselves in English writing.

## IX

THE technique of the stories of Katherine Mansfield's maturity lies partly in their construction and partly in her lyrical use of language. Straightforward chronological narration is seldom favored, but rather an alternation of time present and time past (and sometimes time future), with scenes juxtaposed to heighten the emotional effect. In "The Daughters of the Late Colonel" the two tenses of the story (past, the happiness of life with father; present, the desolation of life without him) are implicit from the opening sentence, every apparently simple word of which has been written and placed with craftsmanlike care: "The week after was one of the busiest weeks of their lives."

The remainder of the story is an expansion of the implications of these opening words, in scenes alternating between present and past, with occasional shuddering glances into the empty future. The story opens with the two women anxiously discussing the disposition of their dead father's effects; it slips back a few days (Nurse Andrews will stay on for a week as guest); a few days further back, to the death of Father; forward to the present—the visit of the clergyman; back to the past—the scene at the funeral; forward to the present, and the problem again of Father's things: should his watch go to their brother, Benny, or to Cyril, the grandson? The question has the effect of sending the story to the past again—a former visit by Cyril; and this merges into Cyril's visit to his grandfather, the old man presented not as a memory but living and grimly in action. The story finally returns (through an interior monologue by one of the sisters) and remains in the bleak present. This manner of presenting a story is familiar enough today. Virginia Woolf and Joyce, to name but two major figures, have made it a commonplace in the novel. But "The Daughters of the Late Colonel" was written in 1920. *Ulysses* did not appear till 1922, and *Mrs. Dalloway* was published in 1925. Katherine Mansfield's handling of time and of interior monologue is her own.

Writing in her *Journal* of another story she is quite explicit about her method of construction: "What I feel the story needs so particularly is a very subtle variation of 'tense' from the present to the past and back again—and softness, lightness, and the feeling that all is in bud, with a play of humour over the character."

This play of time backward and forward is done with great narrative skill. She discards the clumsy mechanism of scene-shifting of the typical novel of the nineteenth and early twentieth centuries, and recaptures a narrative economy in transition from scene to scene that English fiction had lost since Jane Austen. In the story just mentioned, Cyril has written a note of condolence to his two aunts:

Dear boy! What a blow his sweet, sympathetic little note had been! Of course, they quite understood; but it was most unfortunate.
"It would have been such a point having him," said Josephine.
"And he would have enjoyed it so," said Constantia, not thinking what she was saying.
However, as soon as he got back he was coming to tea with his aunties. Cyril to tea was one of their rare treats.
"Now, Cyril, you mustn't be frightened of our cakes. Your Auntie Con and I bought them at Buszard's this morning. We know what a man's appetite is."
("The Daughters of the Late Colonel," viii)

This skillfully written passage starts in the present, glimpses an unattainable future that is already past, shifts to the real future, and then, without a word of transition, introduces a long scene from the past.

The "subtle variation of 'tense'" is a notable feature of all Katherine Mansfield's later stories. It is often used with peculiar appropriateness as one of her means of quietly unfolding character. In "At the Bay" and "Prelude" Stanley Burnell and his mother live in the bustling present; his wife, Linda, dreams in her steamer chair beneath the manuka tree in a timeless past; Kezia and the children occupy the eternal present of childhood; and Beryl, the unmarried girl, lives in a continually imagined future.

## X

THE second part of the passage quoted from her *Journal* emphasizes the care with which Katherine Mansfield contrived the feeling of each situation and character. Whether her people are the little girls of "The Doll's House" or schoolboys (like Hennie in "The Young Girl") or selfish young men and women (like the hero of "A Dill Pickle" and the heroine of "Revelations") or the older men and women of stories like "The Fly" and "The Voyage," the author never allows herself to come onstage as a presenter of whose intrusion we are conscious. She sinks herself inside each of her characters, thinking or speaking in their tone of voice. "Prelude" opens with the family disputing for space in the buggy:

There was not an inch of room for Lottie and Kezia in the buggy. When Pat swung them on top of the luggage they wobbled; the grandmother's lap was full and Linda Burnell could not possibly have held a lump of a child on hers for any distance.

That "lump of a child" is not Katherine Mansfield's comment. It is Linda's unexpressed thought, beautifully worked into the structure of a sentence that in its opening words had the simple function of carrying the narrative and now carries the tone of voice of one of the central characters.

This sense of always being inside the character is one of Katherine Mansfield's greatest contributions to the craft of fiction. Her interior monologues are, for contemporary readers, readily recognizable, though there is nothing mechanical or obvious about her use of them. In addition to examples already mentioned, "The Little Governess," "Feuille d'Album," "Taking the Veil," and "The Doll's House" (to cite stories both before and after she achieved her mature technique) all contain characters who are revealed through their own thoughts. But the innerness of her character-drawing goes beyond the interior monologue. In her best stories the world is always seen through the eyes of one of her characters. Where she describes scenery, it is not merely the background of a situation. It is conveyed to the reader emotionally, and uniquely, as only the person in the story can feel it. Episode vii of "At the Bay" is introduced by such a scene:

Over there on the weed-hung rocks that looked at low tide like shaggy beasts come down to the water to drink, the sunlight seemed to spin like a silver coin dropped into each of the small rock pools. They danced, they quivered, and minute ripples laved the porous shores. Looking down, bending over, each pool was like a lake with pink and blue houses clustered on the shores; and oh! the vast mountainous country behind those houses—the ravines, the passes, the dangerous creeks and fearful tracks that led to the water's edge.

The rocks like great beasts, the pool clustered round with "houses" backed by mountains, the sense of fear and danger—this is not the confident and factual downward-looking view of the adult; it is the viewpoint of a small child seeing objects larger than herself, rendered even larger and more fearful by her fancy. The reader has in this manner been introduced to Kezia, the daydreaming little girl, though he must read another full page before she appears in person. But she is there already. We have approached the beach through her eyes.

Subtler still is Katherine Mansfield's remarkable (one might even dare to say unique) ability to shift the point of view (and so introduce several characters) within the confines of a single sentence. The opening of "Prelude" has already shown a narrative sentence shaping itself into the color of a person's thoughts. In "The Daughters of the Late Colonel" the two sisters ring for the maid: "And proud young Kate, the enchanted princess, came in to see what the old tabbies wanted now." Here within less than twenty words we shift from the point of view of the two sisters, awed and obscurely envious of the girl's dazzling youth, to the viewpoint of the maid, haughtily resentful of her elderly mistresses' having once again rung the bell. Not a word need be added. Not a word could be dropped. And yet it is all there.

XI

SEVERAL critics have pointed out the poetic qualities of Katherine Mansfield's writing. The American critic Conrad Aiken as early as 1921 in a review of *Bliss, and Other Stories* made the essential point. Katherine Mansfield writes a short story with the resources and the intention of lyrical poetry. Her stories should not be (and were not written to be) read as narratives in the ordinary sense, although considerable narrative movement is implied in the majority of them. She conveys, as a lyric poet conveys, the feeling of human situations, and her stories have all the unity and shapeliness and the concentrated diction of implied emotion that characterize the well-wrought lyric. As with the lyric, her stories yield their full meaning only on rereading, when the reader can link up the implications of phrase upon phrase that are not always apparent on the first runthrough. And like the lyrics of a poet the stories illuminate each other. An early critic, G. S. Street, writing in the *London Mercury* in 1921, confessed how he found his clue to the apparently fragmentary "Bliss" when he reread the conclusion of "The Daughters of the Late Colonel." This illumination of one story by another is particularly evident in the

New Zealand family sequence, which, when read *as a sequence*, not in the order of composition but in the internal time-order of the family's own history, is one of the most sensitive and finely conceived writings of our time.

Each separate part, even each separate phrase and word, of her best stories contributes to the final emotional impression of the whole. In "Mr. and Mrs. Dove," the hero is young, insecure, impressionable, and romantic. How well this is captured in a few lines, as Reggie walks toward the house of the girl he is in love with:

"And where are you going, if your mother may ask?" asked the mater.

It was over at last, but Reggie did not slow down until he was out of sight of the house and half-way to Colonel Proctor's. Then only he noticed what a top-hole afternoon it was. It had been raining all the morning, later summer rain, warm, heavy, quick, and now the sky was clear, except for a long tail of little clouds, like ducklings, sailing over the forest. There was just enough wind to shake the last drops off the trees; one warm star splashed on his hand. Ping!— another drummed on his hat. The empty road gleamed, and the hedges smelled of briar, and how big and bright the hollyhocks glowed in the cottage gardens.

("Mr. and Mrs. Dove," in *The Garden Party*, p. 120)

This is admirably done. It is not so much the articulation of the narrative as the implications of the words used that convey the impression of the very ordinary young man ("mater" and "top-hole") who with a sense of release enjoys sensuously the sights and sounds and smells of the fresh afternoon. The fanciful duckling image, the sailing image, the "gleam" of the road, and the "one warm star splashed on his hand": the whole summer afternoon and his sense of elation are compressed into poetic language implicit with emotive overtones, the achievement of the aim Katherine Mansfield had, years earlier, set before her: "Perhaps not in poetry. Nor perhaps in prose. Almost certainly in a kind of *special prose*." One of her greatest achievements lay in this, the creation of a prose style that could borrow from poetry but nevertheless remain prose, firmly based on a simple and even colloquial movement.

## XII

Since the language—one might almost say the diction—of Katherine Mansfield's writing, with its subtle evocation of mood and scene and its poetical use of overtones, is such an important part of her meaning, it is important for the English—or, for that matter, any—reader to remember that certain of her words are used in a sense peculiar to New Zealand and not current in England. In her letters these words and phrases are freely used. There she talks of "swags" of strawberries; a good issue of a journal is "a perfect corker"; depressed by the winter weather of Italy she "had a rare tangi over this climate"; she will do better reviews and send two "bonzers." "Corker" and "bonzer" are both New Zealand slang words corresponding roughly to the current English "smasher"; "swag" is the swagman's bundle; and "tangi"—the word is Maori—is standard New Zealand usage for a general lamentation.

In the stories also there is an occasional New Zealand colloquialism, but only where it is appropriate—among small children, or on the lips of a workman:

"Say, cross my heart straight-dinkum."
The little girls said it.
("At the Bay," in *Collected Stories*, p. 216)

But when they reached the top of the hill and began to go down the other side the harbour disappeared, and although they were still in the town they were quite lost. Other carts rattled past. Everybody knew the storeman.
"Night, Fred."
"Night O," he shouted.
("Prelude," in *Collected Stories*, p. 16)

New Zealand words or usages of a more general nature are introduced to evoke the local scene. The "piece of loose iron" that bangs on the roof in several stories tells the reader snug under slates or tiles that the early colonial houses were roofed with corrugated iron, invariably referred to simply as "iron." The "creek" that runs through "Prelude" is a little stream, not an arm of the sea as it would be in British English. The "bush-covered hills" at the opening of "At the Bay" are covered with heavy forest, not small bushes. Perhaps no word of Katherine Mansfield's, with her insistence on the importance of half-tones and quarter-tones, is so likely to convey the wrong tone as the "paddocks" that surround the houses of her characters. "Paddock" in British usage implies horses, with an undertone of hunting or at least a pony club. Nothing could be further from Katherine Mansfield's meaning. "Paddock" in New Zealand is simply the normal word for field—a grassy meadow into which Kezia and the children can run.

On occasion the setting of the scene in New Zealand is done obliquely, without the use of local language, and yet with quiet precision. In "Prelude" toward the end of the day Kezia waits in the empty house:

> Kezia liked to stand so before the window. She liked the feeling of the cold shining glass against her hot palms, and she liked to watch the funny white tops that came on her fingers when she pressed them hard against the pane. As she stood there, the day flickered out and the dark came.

This is not the close of an English day with its slow twilight and its imperceptible gradation to night. It is the quick oncoming of night that Katherine Mansfield remembered from the latitude of her childhood.

### XIII

THIS essay has been confined to Katherine Mansfield's life-story so far as it seems to be of importance for an understanding of her work and a critical examination of the literary quality of her stories. There has been considerable writing on her (since the publication of her *Journal*), on her mysticism, her "secret," her isolated "purity," which would make her a vaguely symbolic and saintly figure. It cannot be denied that chapter and verse can be found for much of this kind of thing in the later entries in her *Journal*. It is well to remember that in her final year she was a very sick woman, facing death with only the rags of a Christian faith and ready to grasp at dubious philosophic alternatives; she was, too, throughout her whole life in many ways (though never in her craft) naive. She had the intellectual gaps of the self-educated woman that she was. The final scenes of faith-healing under the guidance of a crazy Russian while she formulated a spiritual creed can hardly be the basis for a fair judgment either of her real quality or of her view of life. Katherine Mansfield the writer had laid down her pen many months before that melancholy final passage.

There is nothing vague or nebulous—or naive—about her writings. She is assured in her craft, and knowledgeable even to the placing of a comma. She writes with precision, knowing the effect she intends and achieving it in all her best work with an accuracy and an inexplicable rightness in prose expression that is perhaps in the end the only real secret that died with her.

### XIV

THE disparity between the assured professionalism of the short stories and the otherworldliness that emerges from the *Journal* is something that I have always found difficult to reconcile. Yet there, published in the *Journal* of 1927 and the expanded definitive edition of 1954, are her own comments on life and letters, clearly a primary—if not indeed *the* primary—source for both biographer and critic. It is up to each to effect his own reconciliation of the two Katherine Mansfields or to ignore the wraith of the *Journal* and focus attention on the meticulous craft of the storyteller.

There the matter might have rested. But after the death in 1957 of John Middleton Murry there came on the market a large collection of Katherine Mansfield's notebooks and manuscripts. These were bought by the New Zealand government for the Alexander Turnbull Library, Wellington. They consist of four diaries (for 1914, 1915, 1920, and 1922), which (like most other people's diaries) peter out somewhere between February and March, some thirty notebooks filled with story fragments, ideas for stories varying from a few words to several pages, quotations, personal observations, notes on her reading, lists of household expenses kept in meticulous detail, accurately kept income and expenditure accounts (she was very much, as it appears, the banker's daughter), and some hundred single sheets onto which are copied poems, vignettes, a section of her abortive novel "Maata," an unfinished play, and some finished stories copied out ready for the printer. It is a remarkable record of a writer at work.

A close comparison of this heterogeneous mass of material with the books published after her death has revealed some interesting facts. From this untidy heap of material Murry created the *Journal* of 1927; from some of the leftover pieces he created *The Scrapbook* of 1939; and working over it once again a decade later he created the definitive *Journal* of 1954. Murry was a brilliant editor, and his most brilliant work was the synthesis of his wife's loose papers in what became—justifiably—recognized as a minor classic.

But synthesis it was. Katherine Mansfield did not keep a journal in any usual sense of the word. She bought occasionally a pocket diary and for a few weeks made brief entries. In her working notebooks, among the drafts of stories and notes on possible situations and characters, she made from time to time a personal entry or observation. Something like half of the published *Journal* consists of passages that were in no recognized sense journal material; indeed one or two of them are demonstrably story fragments, fiction, not personal records. The editor has interpolated these pieces, often at precise dates, even where his own penciled notes on the source material reveal that he has doubts about the date. He regularly salvages passages of poetry (by herself and others) that she had copied out—sometimes on a single undatable sheet—and inserts them at appropriate places, to expand and illuminate a diary entry that originally stood in isolation. Occasionally a passage from one notebook is run together, without indication, with a passage from another notebook of different date. The omissions, even in the "definitive" edition, are considerable. The working writer, the businesswoman—the banker's daughter—drop out of sight. There is nothing in the published versions of the *Journal* that is not by Katherine Mansfield. But by selection and by maneuvering the raw material, particularly by the juxtaposition of passages originally unconnected and by printing diary entries continuous with scraps of story-drafting without indication of the change in his material, the editor has created something that was not in the manuscripts and notebooks, a persona, an idealized picture of his dead wife.

It is a curious business so to dismember a book that many readers have come to cherish. And one must be fair. Murry is absolutely scrupulous in his own penciled annotations on the Mansfield manuscripts. He indicates his omissions, and sometimes even writes in his reasons for the omission. He handled the actual documents like a scholar. He published what he decided to transcribe as a creative editor. He was, after all, writing a memorial portrait, not a biography.

But whatever the literary value of the published *Journal*, its value to biographers and critics is severely limited by the editorial method. Any further biographical or critical work on Katherine Mansfield will have to be based on the notebooks and not on the *Journal*, which no longer can retain the status of a primary document. The Katherine Mansfield of the *Journal* is an intense and over-rarefied spirit, conjured up by piety and affection. From the notebooks, as a full edition will show, she emerges as what must be a truer and certainly a more interesting figure, the writer in the workshop with her nose to the grindstone.

There was, as one had always suspected, only one Katherine Mansfield. She is not as pleasant a creature as the persona. She is more businesslike, ruthless on occasion, and sometimes quite cold-blooded. Further confirmation of this emerged some years ago, when her three surviving sisters were asked for their memories of her in a radio interview. The text was published in 1963 (see the bibliography). One sister said, "I think she was very selfish at times," and the second responded, "She was completely self-centered, she was ruthless." This is not the Katherine Mansfield of the legend; but it is the Katherine Mansfield of the notebooks, a single-minded writer—and a more credible human being.

## SELECTED BIBLIOGRAPHY

I. BIBLIOGRAPHY. R. E. Mantz, *The Critical Bibliography of Katherine Mansfield* (London, 1931), some inaccuracies corrected in Berkman's 1951 study, listed below.

II. COLLECTED WORKS. *Collected Stories* (London, 1945); D. M. Davin, ed., *Selected Stories* (London, 1953); I. A. Gordon, ed., *Undiscovered Country: The New Zealand Stories of Katherine Mansfield* (London, 1974).

III. SEPARATE WORKS. *In a German Pension* (London, 1911), stories, repr. (New York, 1926); *Prelude* (Richmond, Eng., 1918), story; *Je ne parle pas français* (London, 1918), story; *Bliss, and Other Stories* (London, 1920); *The Garden Party, and Other Stories* (New York–London, 1922); *The Dove's Nest, and Other Stories* (New York–London, 1923); *Poems* (London, 1923; New York, 1924); *Something Childish, and Other Stories* (London, 1924), published in U.S. as *The Little Girl*; J. M. Murry, ed., *Journal* (London, 1927), autobiography, rev. and enl. ed. (1954); *The Aloe* (London, 1930), story, original form of *Prelude* of 1918; J. M. Murry, ed., *Novels and Novelists* (London, 1930), reviews contributed to the *Athenaeum* 1919–1920; J. M. Murry, ed., *The Scrapbook of Katherine Mansfield* (London, 1939), miscellany; I. A. Gordon, ed., *The Urewera Notebook of Katherine Mansfield* (Wellington, N.Z.–London, 1978), a fully annotated ed. of her 1907 travel diary; M. Scott, ed., "Katherine Mansfield: The Unpublished Manuscripts," in *Turnbull Library Record* (January 1940–November 1962; n.s. March 1967– , Wellington, N.Z.), a continuing series of transcripts from the library's MSS holdings, seven parts published to date, most recent one in 1979.

IV. LETTERS. J. M. Murry, ed., *Letters*, 2 vols. (London, 1928); J. M. Murry, ed., *Letters to John Middleton Murry, 1913–1922* (London, 1951), contains full texts of letters given partially in earlier ed. of letters; "Forty-six Letters by Katherine Mansfield" (to Anne Estelle Rice and Sydney and Violet Schiff), *Adam International Review*, no. 300 (1965).

*Note:* An edition of Mansfield's letters, including hundreds of unpublished ones, is in progress at Oxford University Press under the editorship of Margaret Scott, assisted by Vincent O'Sullivan.

V. BIOGRAPHICAL AND CRITICAL STUDIES. J. W. N. Sullivan, "The Story-Writing Genius," *Athenaeum* (April 1920); C. Aiken, "The Short Story as Poetry," *Freeman* (May 1921); M. Armstrong, "The Art of Katherine Mansfield," *Fortnightly Review,* 113:484 n.s. (March 1923); G. S. Hubbell, "Katherine Mansfield and Kezia," *Sewanee Review* (July–September 1927); E. Wagenknecht, "Katherine Mansfield," *English Journal* (April 1928).

R. E. Mantz and J. M. Murry, *The Life of Katherine Mansfield* (London, 1933), chiefly her early years; F. Carco, *Souvenirs sur Katherine Mansfield* (Paris, 1934), recollections by a writer on whom Katherine Mansfield based a character in several of her French stories; E. Schneider, "Katherine Mansfield and Checkhov," *Modern Language Notes* (June 1935); A. Maurois, *Poets and Prophets: Portraits and Criticism* (London, 1936); W. A. Sewell, *Katherine Mansfield: A Critical Essay* (Auckland, N.Z., 1936); W. Cather, *Not Under Forty* (London, 1936); J. M. Murry, *Between Two Worlds: An Autobiography* (London, 1936); H. Beauchamp, *Reminiscences and Recollections* (New Plymouth, N.Z., 1937), contains ch. on Katherine Mansfield by G. H. Scholefield; W. Orton, *The Last Romantic* (London, 1937); A. D. M. Hoare, *Some Studies in the Modern Novel* (London, 1938); D. Daiches, *The Novel in the Modern World* (Chicago, 1939).

H. E. Bates, *The Modern Short Story* (London, 1941); I. A. Gordon, "Katherine Mansfield, New Zealander," *New Zealand New Writing* (1943, Wellington, N.Z.); L. E. Rillo, *Katherine Mansfield and Virginia Woolf* (Buenos Aires, 1944); V. S. Pritchett, "Review of *Collected Stories*," *New Statesman and Nation* (February 1946); "Katherine Mansfield's Stories," *Times Literary Supplement* (March 1946); P. Lawlor, *The Mystery of Maata* (Wellington, N.Z., 1946); J. M. Murry, *Katherine Mansfield and Other Literary Portraits* (London, 1949).

S. Berkman, *Katherine Mansfield: A Critical Study* (New Haven, Conn., 1951), excellent study, contains a detailed life, with information from one of Katherine Mansfield's sisters, good bibliographical notes; A. Alpers, *Katherine Mansfield: A Biography* (New York, 1953), at the time of its publication the fullest biography, with new material from Katherine Mansfield's associates, but contains errors on Sir Harold Beauchamp that were corrected in 1980 ed. (see below); I. A. Gordon, "The Editing of Katherine Mansfield's Journal and Scrapbook," *Landfall* (March 1959, Christchurch, N.Z.).

B. Brophy, "Katherine Mansfield," *London* (December 1962); O. Leeming, "Katherine Mansfield and Her Family," *New Zealand Listener* (29 March and 11 April 1963, Wellington, N.Z.), text of radio interview with Katherine Mansfield's sisters, revealing and important; C. A. M. Mortelier, "Origine et développment d'une legende: Katherine Mansfield en France," *Études Anglaises* IV (1970), excellent survey of French critical opinion; I. Baker, *Katherine Mansfield: The Memories of LM* (London, 1971), the memoirs of Katherine Mansfield's schoolfellow at Queen's College and lifetime companion; I. A. Gordon, "The Banker and the Banker's Daughter," *New Zealand Listener* (27 November 1972, Wellington, N.Z.), concerned with Sir Harold Beauchamp's lifelong financial support of Katherine Mansfield; V. O'Sullivan, "The Magnetic Chain: Notes and Approaches to K.M.," *Landfall* (June 1975, Christchurch, N.Z.); I. A. Gordon, "Warmth and Hydrangeas: Katherine Mansfield's Wellington Years," *New Zealand Listener* (8 May 1976), sheds new light on the years 1907–1908 with documentation of Katherine Mansfield's enrollment in a technical college for commercial subjects; A. Alpers, *Katherine Mansfield* (London, 1980), a completely rewritten version of the 1953 biography, with fuller documentation and correction of misapprehensions contained in the first version; now the standard biography.

## LIST OF SHORT STORIES

(The title in italics refers to the volume in which the story first appeared. Stories marked with an asterisk were published as unfinished stories in *The Dove's Nest.*)

"About Pat," *Scrapbook*; "The Advanced Lady," *In a German Pension*; *"All Serene!" *The Dove's Nest*; "The Aloe," see "Prelude"; "The Apple Tree," *Scrapbook*; "At Lehmann's," *In a German Pension*; "At Putnam's Pier," *Scrapbook*; "At the Bay," *The Garden Party*; "Baby Jean," *Scrapbook*; *"A Bad Idea," *The Dove's Nest*; "Bains Turcs," *Something Childish*; "Bank Holiday," *The Garden Party*; "The Baron," *In a German Pension*; "A Birthday," *In a German Pension*; "The Black Cap," *Something Childish*; "A Blaze," *In a German Pension*; "Bliss," *Bliss*; "By Moonlight," *Scrapbook*; "The Canary," *The Dove's Nest*; "Carnation," *Something Childish*; "Cassandra," *Scrapbook*; "The Child-Who-Was-Tired," *In a German Pension*; "A Cup of Tea," *The Dove's Nest*.

*"Daphne," *The Dove's Nest*; "The Dark Hollow," *Scrapbook*; "The Daughters of the Late Colonel," *The Garden Party*; "A Dill Pickle," *Bliss*; "The Doll's House," *The Dove's Nest*; "The Dressmaker," *Scrapbook*; "The Escape," *Bliss*; "Father and the Girls," *The Dove's Nest*; "Feuille d'Album," *Bliss*; "The Fly," *The Dove's Nest*; "Frau Brechenmacher Attends a Wedding," *In a German Pension*; "Frau Fischer," *In a German Pension*.

"The Garden Party," *The Garden Party*; "Germans at Meat," *In a German Pension*; "Her First Ball," *The Garden Party*; *"Honesty," *The Dove's Nest*; "Honeymoon," *The Dove's Nest*; "How Pearl Button Was Kidnapped," *Something Childish*; "An Ideal Family," *The Garden Party*; "An

Indiscreet Journey," *Something Childish*; "Je ne parle pas français," *Bliss*; "The Journey to Bruges," *Something Childish*; "Kezia and Tui," *Scrapbook*.

"The Lady's Maid," *The Garden Party*; "Last Words to Youth," *Scrapbook*; "Late at Night," *Something Childish*; "Life Is Not Gay," *Scrapbook*; "Life of Ma Parker," *The Garden Party*; "The Little Girl," *Something Childish*; "The Little Governess," *Bliss*; "The Lost Battle," *Scrapbook*; "Love-Lies-Bleeding," *Scrapbook*; "The Luft Bad," *In a German Pension*; *"A Man and His Dog," *The Dove's Nest*; "The Man Without a Temperament," *Bliss*; "Marriage à la Mode," *The Garden Party*; *"A Married Man's Story," *The Dove's Nest*; "Millie," *The Garden Party*; "Miss Brill," *The Garden Party*; "Mr. and Mrs. Dove," *The Garden Party*; "Mr. and Mrs. Williams," *The Dove's Nest*; "Mr. Reginald Peacock's Day," *Bliss*; "The Modern Soul," *In a German Pension*; "New Dresses," *Something Childish*.

"Pension Séguin," *Something Childish*; "The Pessimist," *Scrapbook*; "Pictures," *Bliss*; "Poison," *Something Childish*; "Prelude" ("The Aloe," rev.), *Bliss*; "Psychology," *Bliss*; "The Quarrel," *Scrapbook*; "Revelations," *Bliss*; "Rose Eagle," *Scrapbook*; "The Scholarship," *Scrapbook*; *"Second Violin," *The Dove's Nest*; "See-Saw," *Something Childish*; "Sewing-Class," *Scrapbook*; "The Sheridans," *Scrapbook*; "The Singing Lesson," *The Garden Party*; "The Sister of the Baroness," *In a German Pension*; *"Six Years After," *The Dove's Nest*; "Sixpence," *Something Childish*; "Sleeping House," *Scrapbook*; "Something Childish but Very Natural," *Something Childish*; "Spring Pictures," *Something Childish*; "Strange Visitor," *Scrapbook*; "The Stranger," *The Garden Party*; "A Suburban Fairy Tale," *Something Childish*; *"Such a Sweet Old Lady," *The Dove's Nest*; "Sun and Moon," *Bliss*; *"Susannah," *The Dove's Nest*; "The Swing of the Pendulum," *In a German Pension*.

"Taking the Veil," *The Dove's Nest*; "Tea on the Train," *Scrapbook*; "There Is No Answer," *Scrapbook*; "This Flower," *Something Childish*; "The Tiredness of Rosabel," *Something Childish*; "The Toothache Sunday," *Scrapbook*; "A Truthful Adventure," *Something Childish*; "Two Tuppenny Ones, Please," *Something Childish*; "Violet," *Something Childish*; "The Voyage," *The Garden Party*; *"The Weak Heart," *The Dove's Nest*; *"Widowed," *The Dove's Nest*; "The Wind Blows," *Bliss*; "The Woman at the Store," *Something Childish*; "The Wrong House," *Something Childish*; "The Young Girl," *The Garden Party*.

# W. SOMERSET MAUGHAM
(1874-1965)

## *Anthony Curtis*

*I*

"THE lucidity of Maugham, last of the great professional writers..." wrote Cyril Connolly in *Enemies of Promise* (1938). It is a curious distinction that, one feels, could have been made only by an English critic writing about an English author. Who, pray, are the great amateur writers? Yet one knows what Connolly meant. Maugham always looked to the market and wrote to supply the needs of the market. "No man but a blockhead ever wrote, except for money," Dr. Samuel Johnson declared forthrightly on 5 April 1776, so Boswell tells us in his *Life of Johnson*, and Maugham's life might be described as one long "Hear, hear!" in support of Johnson's declaration.

What, you may ask, is wrong with writing for the market? Did not Shakespeare write for the market? Did not Dickens write for the market? Yes, if one dare mention them in the same breath as Maugham, they did; but literate society was more homogeneous in their day than in his. By the end of the nineteenth century a hairline fissure had begun to appear between the popular and the serious reading public that in the twentieth was to widen to an apparently unbridgeable gap.[1] Maugham remains the test case of whether it could at any point be bridged.

Maugham desperately wanted to be both a popular writer and a serious writer. He wanted to become rich by his pen, and he wanted to be praised by the best judges. After about ten years of struggle he achieved the former aim; only intermittently did he achieve the latter. Against the praise of Desmond MacCarthy and Cyril Connolly, the leading London critics of their time, both of whom had some personal acquaintance with Maugham, we must put the devastating attacks on Maugham by D. H. Lawrence and Edmund Wilson. Enough time has passed since Maugham's death, perhaps, to make a fresh view possible, one that is less clouded by the animosity that Maugham the man aroused in his contemporaries.

Maugham made no secret of the importance he attached to money in literary life. Money, he often said, is like a sixth sense without which you cannot fully use the other five. This sounds good, but it is not really confirmed by his own prose, which though admirably lucid, as Connolly says, is noticeably weak in the re-creation of sense experience, one of the most immediate pleasures we receive from literature. Although we read through the eye, imaginative writing often comes to life by arousing other senses—aural, tactile, olfactory. The first obvious difference between Maugham and those writers we think of as "modern" in the first half of the twentieth century is his indifference to all but the visual sense, his lack of sensuousness. Even a writer whom he greatly admired, Herman Melville, Maugham castigates for his overindulgence in sensuous exuberance. The American novelist strained every nerve in *Moby Dick* (1851) to communicate the sights, the sounds, and especially the smells experienced by his characters: "But few thoughts of Pan stirred Ahab's brain, as standing like an iron statue at his accustomed place beside the mizzen rigging, with one nostril he unthinkingly sniffed the suggary must from the Banshee isles (in whose sweet woods mild lovers must be walking), and with the other consciously inhaled the salt breath of the new found sea...." Maugham's comment on this passage, in *Ten Novels and Their Authors* (1954), is: "To smell one odour with one nostril and at the same time, another with the other; it is more than a remarkable feat; it is an impossible one." If Maugham is at his weakest when it is a question of smells, sounds, touch, he showed from his earliest days as a writer a quick and sure eye for surroundings, ap-

---
[1] See Q. D. Leavis, *Fiction and the Reading Public* (London, 1935).

pearances, belongings. He is infallible when it comes to material possessions, solid structures, things. It is no surprise that the novelist whom Maugham admired most was Balzac, who showed how to reveal character through the cumulative description of possessions. Maugham wrote:

I believe he was the first novelist to dwell on the paramount importance of economics in everybody's life. He would not have thought it enough to say that money is the root of all evil; he thought the desire for money, the appetite for money, was the mainspring of human action.
(*Ten Novels and Their Authors*)

It is not my purpose in this essay to deal with Maugham's obsession with money as fully as a biographer might wish to, but I propose to consider the question briefly. Obviously Maugham's loss of both his parents before he had reached the age of ten had a great deal to do with it. Life for young Willie Maugham was a precarious business; however rich and eminent he subsequently became, it never ceased to be a precarious business. His boyhood environment, his uncle's vicarage at Whitstable, in Kent, was not poor, but it was grim, austere, parsimonious. As soon as he arrived there Maugham felt deprived, a feeling exacerbated by the instant dismissal of the woman who had looked after him in Paris. His position in the family as the youngest brother, with a big age gap between him and his next of kin, his smallness, his stammer, all contributed to his feeling of insecurity and caused him, as a precociously intelligent child, to look forward to the day when, in the words of Malvolio in *Twelfth Night*, he would be revenged on the pack of them. The choice of authorship as a profession was a break with the tradition of the Maughams: the family had risen to eminence through the law. Maugham's writing confirmed him in his isolation as well as offering him opportunities to overcome the humiliations, fancied and real, of childhood. Fearful, though, of suffering financial insecurity, he played it safe by first providing himself with an alternative profession, medicine, training at St. Thomas' Hospital, in South London. But when the moment came for him to set up as a fully qualified practitioner, he decided to write as his sole means of earning a livelihood. His office was his home, an apartment he shared in Victoria with a friend, Walter Payne, who was an accountant. When *Liza of Lambeth* was published in 1897, Maugham was twenty-three.

II

In that year Payne gave him a present, James Boswell's *Life of Johnson* in six volumes. The work must have struck a chord in Maugham. The situation of the young Johnson, coming to London from Lichfield to make his way by literature and wit, was similar to his own. Here was a supreme example of a man who had worked in isolation, cut off from the academic life, in which his abilities would have enabled him to excel; staking everything on acquiring a reputation; beginning by attracting a small circle of admirers until his fame spread. But what Maugham required was not only a patron saint but practical models of the art of writing. He had an infinite capacity to learn by example, blessed as he was with formidable energy and determination; and he had a further resource in an enviable facility for languages. Maugham's father had been the lawyer in charge of the affairs of the British embassy in Paris. By a quirk of fate Maugham had been born inside the embassy building. French came almost as naturally to him as English. His first literary enthusiasms were for French writers. Maugham described in *The Summing Up* (1938) how he haunted the galleries of the Odéon, standing there reading the novels and short stories of Guy de Maupassant, cutting the pages of books he could not afford to buy. Apart from France —a country with which Maugham always had a special relationship, going there to live after he became successful—he was exposed to other continental influences as a young man. Before taking up medical studies, Maugham had been educated in Germany, at the University of Heidelberg. He heard talk of Wagner and the new music drama, and he saw performances of plays by Henrik Ibsen and Henri Becque, both of whom were bringing a new kind of realism to the theater. While a medical student, Maugham had begun to learn Spanish and Italian, after visiting Spain and Italy for long periods.

With so much to read and so much to take in, Maugham could hardly have had a more bewildering choice of models. Without benefit of an official tutor—such as he would have had if he had gone to Cambridge like his brother Freddie[2]—to monitor his undergraduate essays, whom should he elect as his unofficial tutor? One of the masters of English prose, such as Jeremy Taylor or Jonathan Swift? Or one of

[2] Frederic Herbert Maugham (1866-1958), first Viscount Maugham, Lord Chancellor of England (1938-1939).

the French realists, who earlier in the nineteenth century had wrought major changes in the art of the novel, such as Émile Zola, Gustave Flaubert, or their most brilliant disciple, Guy de Maupassant? In fact, he elected them all, and many others. Such freedom is one of the advantages of belonging to a one-pupil university administered by oneself. Maugham read widely, insatiably, greedily. He was then, and always remained, receptive to good prose wherever he found it. Toward the end of his life he wrote essays on both the seventeenth-century English divine Archbishop Tillotson and the American mystery writer Raymond Chandler. The period of the 1890's offered almost as extreme contrasts between the lofty and the popular. Inevitably, the aesthetic cult, then at its height in England thanks to the genius of Oscar Wilde (1854-1900), made an impression on Maugham.

Wilde and other men of letters, through whom thoughts of the new, ill-educated reading public sent shudders of horror, argued that literature could survive only by becoming more demanding, more remote from ordinary life, more artificial. For the Wildean aesthetes the common enemy was vulgarity. One of the gilded young men who took this view was the essayist and caricaturist Max Beerbohm, a friend of Maugham's, some of whose work had appeared in *The Yellow Book,* a review associated in the public mind with the spirit of decadence. Several of its writers took their tone from Walter Pater, the high priest of the aesthetic movement, who had died in 1894. In his studies of the art of the Italian Renaissance and his imaginary portraits Pater wrote some of the most ornate prose ever penned by an English writer. Maugham dutifully studied Pater and attempted for a time to write like him. There are faint traces of the Pater manner in some of his early work, and some set-piece descriptions survive in *A Writer's Notebook* (1949).

But he soon abandoned this enervating prose style for a plainer approach. Afterward he would mock his youthful Pateresque pretensions. Perhaps, though, he never completely suppressed the aesthete in himself. There is a portrait of Maugham, "The Jester," by his friend the painter Gerald Kelly, made after Maugham's first successful plays were produced, that shows him immaculately attired in tophat and frock coat as a typical English dandy of the 1890's. Maugham's urbanity; his love of that most civilized form, the essay; his insistence on the terrible sacrifices demanded by art, in many stories and novels, not least *Of Human Bondage* (1915) and *The Moon and Sixpence* (1919), demonstrate the lasting influence of the aesthetic ideal.

III

THAT ideal suffered its most grievous setback with the public humiliation and downfall of Oscar Wilde in 1895. Although Wilde's performance under prolonged cross-examination at his trial was a brilliant one, the aesthetic approach to life was thoroughly discredited; and not only aestheticism but homosexuality, with which it often coexisted. All this, one may be sure, made a deep impact on young Maugham, who was just discovering his own homosexual nature in the company of English Wildean aesthetes who lived in Italy. In consequence, part of his most intimate experience would be closed to him when he began to write fiction. One of Maugham's contemporaries, E. M. Forster (1879-1970), solved this problem by writing fiction about homosexual love but not permitting it to be published until after his death. Although the subject deeply preoccupied Maugham and conditioned the whole course of his life, it rarely crops up in all the voluminous pages of his work (save impersonally in discussions of Melville and El Greco), until his notorious newspaper confessions, *Looking Back* (1962).

Early in his career Maugham cast himself in the part of the observer, the noncommittal recorder of experience. This, after all, was what Maupassant had been. It was the perfect stance for an astute literary artist who wished never to give his deepest secret away. There were examples much nearer than Maupassant of the telling effect that could be made by a quasi-documentary approach, of seeming merely to record events and conversations with the greatest possible verisimilitude. The outlook of the French realists had been shared on the English side of the Channel by George Gissing (1857-1903) and by the Anglo-Irish novelist George Moore (1852-1933). Both had made working people, and their sufferings, the main characters in stories and novels. But Maugham's immediate model was a rather more obscure contemporary, Arthur Morrison (1863-1945), whose *A Child of the Jago* (1896) and *Tales of Mean Streets* (1894) had given vivid, firsthand accounts of the lives lived by people caught in the poverty trap of late-Victorian England. Morrison's work had appeared originally in magazine form and had appealed to the railway bookstall public, which did not want to read only stories about cozy village life and people in fashionable drawing rooms. Edward Garnett, T. Fisher Unwin's literary adviser, spotted Maugham's model immediately, but also the talent and individuality. He wrote in his report that Maugham's story *Liza of Lambeth* was not as powerful a study as *A Child of the Jago*, but that it was

*a very clever realistic study of factory girl and coster life.* The women; their roughness, intemperance, fits of violence, kind-heartedness, slang,—all are done truthfully, Liza and her mother Mrs Kemp are drawn with no little humour and insight. The story is a dismal one in its ending, but the temper and tone of the book is wholesome and by no means morbid. The work is *objective*, and both the atmosphere and the environment of the mean district are unexaggerated.

(George Jefferson, *Edward Garnett: A Life in Literature*, 1982)

Morrison had himself been raised in the East End, though he afterward concealed the fact. He knew a great deal more than Maugham about the criminal underworld of London. Where Maugham scored was through his penetration of the slum interior at its most frequent moment of emergency—the delivery of a baby, unplanned and unwanted; for obstetrics was the practical work Maugham had undertaken as a medical student. Morrison had given no hint of extramarital romance in these dim regions; Maugham made such a romance the core of his tale. Its first cynical title was "A Lambeth Idyll." The stirring of love in the resplendent Liza on the one hand, the horror of her death as an unmarried mother on the other provide Maugham's story with its time scale. It has the organic movement of a single life, *une vie* (as Maupassant called one of his novels). The natural rhythm of the seasons accompanies the heroine's passage through life. We first see her on a bright day of early summer; she dies in the winter of the following year. One of the aims of the realist writers was to capture a natural process—the rise and fall, growth and decay, flowering and withering of a human organism, an individual, a group, a family, a society, even a whole nation—and to trace its course with scientific accuracy. The terms *realism* and *naturalism* are sometimes used more or less interchangeably when referring to writers of this kind. But with realism the emphasis is on the method (objective description), with naturalism on the subject (a natural or inevitable progression seen in its entirety). Maugham practiced both. He sought to create an illusion of objective reality in his fiction, and he saw his subjects as in bondage to the processes of nature.

The publication of *Liza of Lambeth* confirmed Maugham in his decision to abandon medicine for professional authorship. The largely favorable notices that the story attracted gave him the confidence in his powers that was to see him through the next decade of hard work, until he established himself as a fashionable writer of comedies for the London theater. During that period he was to experiment with tales long and short, with novels set in the present and the past, with domestic and exotic backgrounds, with travel writing and essay writing as well as fiction. From all this industry he learned two things: that he possessed an uncommon gift for narrative, for arousing the reader's curiosity at the start of a book and sustaining it until the end; and that the style of writing best suited to exploiting that gift was a plain, serviceable, simple prose in which the sentences were never too long and the vocabulary was largely that of ordinary conversation. The dandified style of Beerbohm, now writing a weekly essay on the current theater for the *Saturday Review*, was not for Maugham. Like many writers, he kept a journal, jotting down ideas for stories, fragments of description, snatches of dialogue, insights into the personalities of his friends, notes toward a philosophy of life. Eventually it extended to fifteen volumes. Most of it he destroyed as part of a general strategy of covering his tracks and frustrating the task of a future biographer, but enough survived to make a book of 350 pages, published with a preface by Maugham in 1949 as *A Writer's Notebook*. It is illuminating to read the entries for the end of the nineteenth century and to compare the Gallic aphorisms ("Respectability is the cloak under which fools cover their stupidity") and moral aperçus with the pieces of descriptive prose, enshrining Green Park in London in winter or the fields of Kent in summertime. Maugham worked assiduously to fashion the lucid, easy manner that suited him best.

Above all he used his eyes. Little escaped his clear-sighted vision. He was always looking for those telltale details that give the game away. The profession of intelligence agent into which he was recruited during World War I, being posted on a secret mission to Russia, came naturally to him because he was a practiced observer of the stratagems of people who wish to avoid exposure. In the stories he wrote featuring the British agent Ashenden, based on his own experience, he showed what potential for entertainment there was in tales of espionage, and he may be said to have unwittingly invented the genre that became so hugely popular after World War II. As a young man, it was just such a genre that he was looking for after he had launched his career with *Liza*. Maugham studied the market and tried his hand at various forms. He wrote short tales aimed at magazines; some were accepted by *Punch* and the *Strand*. He wrote one—an exceedingly brief one—for the *Daily Mail*, the newspaper started in 1896 whose short, topical items required minimum effort on the reader's part. As an author, Maugham endorsed this approach.

Soon he had enough short stories for a book, *Orientations* (1899). He also set to work producing different kinds of currently popular novels. He wrote a historical novel set in Italy during the Renaissance; another about a soldier returning from the Boer War; another concerning a white man leading an expedition into deepest Africa; another about the marital problems of a farmer's wife in rural Kent. This apprentice work need not detain us, save perhaps for *Mrs. Craddock* (1902), which with its disillusioned heroine, a martyr to sexual passion, is the real successor to *Liza*. The novel opens in the naturalistic mode, with gray skies mirroring the heroine's moods. The countryside is that of Kent, where Maugham grew up, and there is mention of Blackstable (Whitstable) and Tercanbury (Canterbury), places to which he returned when his talent had matured.

He has no difficulty in painting this rural landscape in the somber and subdued tones favored by his naturalistic masters. Where he fails is in bringing to life the passion felt by his lady of gentle birth for the rough, virile, insensitive, socially ambitious yeoman farmer whom she marries. The subject demands the inward, incandescent, sensually aware manner of D. H. Lawrence. But when Maugham observes the social awkwardness, the flouting of the unwritten codes governing social behavior prompted by such a union, he is on his home ground. He may not be convincing in depicting the heroine's passion, but he leaves us in no doubt about her disillusionment when the true nature of the man she has married becomes apparent to her. Although the novel was written in the last years of Victoria's reign, Edwardian heartlessness is already apparent. There is among the characters an elderly spinster, the maiden aunt beloved of writers of this period, who possesses a pithy turn of phrase and a refreshingly candid manner. She could easily have stepped out of a comedy by Oscar Wilde. A perceptive reader might have thought that the young man who wrote this novel had it in him to write an effective play. Indeed, the playwright Henry Arthur Jones (1851–1929), one of whose daughters was to provide Maugham with the model for Rosie, in *Cakes and Ale* (1930), had thought so on reading *Liza;* and it was toward the theater that Maugham's ambitions were now directed.

IV

MAUGHAM's first play to be produced, *A Man of Honour* (1903) (which he did not include later in his *Collected Plays*), explores the consequences of social suicide. The hero, a young man of gentle birth, marries a common barmaid whom he has made pregnant, a marriage that ensures his exile from polite society. The play was harrowing but dramatically effective, according to contemporary critics. The pain was mitigated by some moments of comedy between the hero's genteel friends and the heroine's coarse relations. Noting how well these scenes performed, Maugham decided that it was with comedy that his immediate future lay. He then wrote several plays in the *fin-de-siècle* Wilde mold. Titled personages, mute footmen, orchidaceous epigrams are all in evidence, but there is a mellower tone than in the work of Maugham's predecessors, as if the great social taboos had by now become a bit of a joke, more honored in the breach than the observance; and there appears too a greater willingness to be frank about money and the part it may play in affairs of the heart.

A favorite device of the earlier writers had been a bundle of letters, tied up with ribbon, suddenly produced from the attic at about the end of Act II, providing incontrovertible evidence of the sexual lapses of the respected patriarch, this somehow getting into the possession of the ostracized heroine. Maugham used this motif in *Lady Frederick* (written 1903, performed 1907), his first great hit. In a brilliant *coup de théâtre* he makes the heroine nonchalantly throw the letters into the fire in the sight of her enemies, whom they could harm, out of sheer goodness of heart. This prepares the audience for the even more effective scene, a sensation in its day, in which she deliberately disillusions her young lover by admitting him to her morning toilette, so that he can see the ravages time has made on her face before cosmetics have done their work.

The success of *Lady Frederick* marked a turning point in Maugham's life. The royalties from its long run gave him the income he craved, enabling him to live like a gentleman instead of a struggling literary hack, while the many appreciative reviews led the hitherto indifferent theatrical managements to fall over one another in the rush to produce his work. Artistically, Maugham felt that his work was part of the long tradition of English comedy in which amorous misunderstanding is exposed in elegant conversation pieces, and current attitudes about sex and money are dissected. The tradition stretched back past Arthur Wing Pinero (1855–1934) and Henry Arthur Jones, his immediate predecessors, through Wilde, to Richard Brinsley Sheridan, to John Dryden, and even to Shakespeare, as in the loving quarrels of Beatrice and Benedict in *Much Ado About Nothing*. When Maugham succeeded in having four plays running simultaneously in London's West End, *Punch* published a caricature showing a pensive Shakespeare standing beside the billboards advertising Maugham's four hits. Maugham was gratified, but he kept his head amid the ballyhoo. No one knew better than he that triumph and disaster were both impostors. He had a long-term strategy for his career of which this was merely a preliminary phase. Today, reading the texts of Maugham's early comedies, *Lady Frederick*, *Mrs. Dot* (1904), and *Jack Straw* (1905), in the austere surroundings of a university library may induce considerable puzzlement as to why anyone ever thought they were at all funny.

This view may be modified if one has the opportunity, as occasionally occurs, to see one of them in production, where the neatness of the repartee and the author's cunning control of the audience's reactions become apparent. Maugham always insisted that his plays were written not to be read but to be performed. As he grew in stature and confidence, he imperceptibly stopped giving audiences what he thought they wanted and gave them instead what he thought they ought to have, keeping his sights focused on contemporary society but widening their range to take in sections other than the impoverished aristocracy—although, as he revealed in *Our Betters* (1915), he had not yet finished with them. Maugham's first theatrical assault on the middle class was in *Smith* (1909), where he made an example of one bridge-playing Kensington set. Here we are in stockbroker-land, with the husband away at his office, while the wife occupies her afternoons playing rubbers of bridge with a man who in a Latin country would be called her gigolo, a penniless woman friend whose bridge earnings are her sole means of subsistence, and a woman who is married to a rich Jewish man and who neglects her newborn baby because of her love of the game and the gossip that goes with it. Maugham paints these typical English middle-class people before World War I in pretty harsh tones.

In one of his final plays, *For Services Rendered* (1932), a portrait of an English middle-class family during the Depression, Maugham offers no alleviation of the general misery; among the characters there is no one whose life is not a hideous mess. But in *Smith* there are two such: the sturdy young parlormaid who gives the comedy its name, and Tom Freeman, the hostess's brother, who has returned home from Rhodesia, where he has a farm. The misalliance across the class barrier that was shown to bring such tragic consequences in *A Man of Honour* here yields a happy ending. Tom lightly vaults over the divide, repelled by the behavior of his sister's bridge set, and takes Smith back with him to Rhodesia, where no doubt she will make him an excellent wife.

The dramatist's manipulation of the basic antithesis is, as often in Maugham, a trifle crude; babies do not often die as a result of their mothers' playing too much bridge. Nonetheless, there are moments of realistic observation that render the play an authentic comment on its period. Gone is the epigrammatic never-never-land of Edwardian England; in its place we have an insight into the Great Britain over which George V will shortly reign, with its appalling waste of human energy, its crumbling class structure, its unashamed anti-Semitism, its incredible complacency, its colonial opportunities.

Today the most often performed of Maugham's plays is the one entitled *Home and Beauty* in England and *Too Many Husbands* in America, written in 1919 while he was ill with tuberculosis in a sanatorium in Scotland, after his espionage activities in World War I. Maugham may have been confined to his room, but he seems to have been keenly aware of what was going on in the country at large. We can, if we like, see the heroine, Victoria, an unwitting bigamist, as a wicked symbol of the Britain of the Armistice—a more self-centered individual never existed—but in doing so we stifle by critical solemnity one of Maugham's most delightful works. There is a Mozartian gaiety in the to-ings and fro-ings of the main trio, a young prima donna of a wife with a pair of gallant husbands, both bent on escaping from her clutches.

A fragment of dialogue in a scene between the heroine and her mother touches on a central concern of many of Maugham's plays, the nature of marriage:

*Mrs. Shuttleworth:* The difference between men and women is that men are not naturally addicted to matrimony. With patience, firmness, and occasional rewards you can train them to it just as you can train a dog to walk on its hind legs. But a dog would rather walk on all fours and a man would rather be free. Marriage is a habit.
*Victoria:* And a very good one, Mother.
*Mrs. Shuttleworth:* Of course. But the unfortunate thing about this world is that good habits are so much easier to get out of than bad ones.

Many of Maugham's plays show people in one way or another getting out of the habit of marriage. Maugham observed among the French and in French novels, not to mention among his smart friends in London, how marriage as a social institution could have its limits stretched. He himself had made a marriage in America, in the early part of World War I, to Syrie, the daughter of Dr. Thomas John Barnardo. This formidable lady, who became known internationally as an interior decorator of impeccable taste, was to be a kind of facade of respectability for Maugham in society; at least that seems to have been his bizarre intention. At the same time he had a male lover, his secretary, Gerald Haxton, with whom he traveled the world. It need scarcely be added that this arrangement, if one may so dignify it, did not work at all harmoniously for either Syrie, Haxton, or Maugham. He did, though, while under considerable stress from the breakdown of his marriage, write a series of successful plays in which he showed people adopting various tactics to avoid altogether, or escape from, the imprisonment of socially respectable marriages. He introduced a new, more ferocious tone in the working out of this well-tried comic formula, one that he may have found in Henri Becque's *La Parisienne* (1885), which he had seen as a student in Heidelberg. One finds it in comedies like *Penelope* (1908), *Caroline* (1915), and *The Constant Wife* (1926), growing in ferocity with the years. His most savage play is *Our Betters* (1915), in which he pitches into the world of Syrie and her friends, including the millionaire store-owner Gordon Selfridge, who had been her protector; this kept the play off the London stage until 1923. It was a sensation in its day, but recent revivals in the provinces suggest that it may have aged as much as its American-born heroine; whereas *The Circle* (first produced in 1921), by common consent Maugham's best play, continues to flourish whenever it is performed. With its shapely symmetry of construction and its generous parts for the elderly, it contains a perfect balance of astringency and sentiment. Maugham has the best of both worlds, the Edwardian and the modern. He gazes nostalgically upon his own youth and remembers that great society beauty, his own mother, in the scene in which Lady Kitty turns the leaves of the photograph album. And Maugham looks at the world around him when the young wife deliberates over whether or not to bolt from her humorless husband, an ambitious politician. If there was a model for this character Maugham never divulged it. Let us remember the pact that Winston Churchill made with Maugham: Maugham would not put him into one of his works. They thus succeeded in staying friends for life.

The theater suited Maugham. The lack of sensuous urgency in his prose, which I have already noted, never worried the actors; his innate sense of dramatic form and timing made up for it. Before he was through, he had covered a wide variety of subjects within the conventions of the well-shaped comedy or drama, including pioneering in Manitoba (*The Land of Promise*, 1913), mercy killing (*The Sacred Flame*, 1928), and disbelief in God (*The Unknown*, 1920). His settings included China (*East of Suez*, 1922), Egypt (*Caesar's Wife*, 1918), and Malaya (*The Letter*, 1926). The last named was the only play that Maugham adapted from one of his own short stories. Usually he left that task to lesser hands, as in the case of *Rain* (1922).

V

THE kinship that exists between the arts of playwriting and short-story writing has often been noted; consider Anton Chekhov or Luigi Pirandello, or, for that matter, Noel Coward. In both forms the writer has to convey a vast amount of information in a minimum number of words; the signals are often multiple while seeming to be simple. You can be a born novelist but lack the ability required to execute either the play or the short-story form successfully. By contrast, you can be a novelist who escapes occasionally into the short story like a man snatching a weekend's break away from home; and you can be by vocation a short-story writer who occasionally attempts the novel. On this question Graham Greene, in the introduction to his *Collected Stories* (1972), writes:

I remain in this field a novelist who has happened to write short stories, just as there are certain short story writers (Maupassant and Mr V. S. Pritchett come to mind) who have happened to write novels. This is not a superficial distinction—or even a technical distinction as between an artist who paints in oil or watercolour; it is certainly not a distinction in value. It is a distinction between two different ways of life.

Maugham happened, like Maupassant, to write novels; one or two of them have become famous. But he was a born short-story writer, one of the most skillful and fertile ever to have practiced the art. He appeared to be able to conjure stories out of the air. His *Notebook* abounds in excellent ideas for stories he never bothered to write up, and so, according to those closest to him, did his table talk. He destroyed one unpublished group, relating to his espionage activities, for security reasons. Many of the earliest he never bothered to reprint after their magazine appearances. Nevertheless, there remain readily accessible in different editions about ninety stories. They range from the very short ones collected in *Cosmopolitans* (1936), written originally to be printed on opposite pages of *Cosmopolitan* magazine, such as "Mr Know-All" and "Salvatore," to those occupying some forty to fifty printed pages, including such famous tales as "Before the Party," "The Outstation," "P. & O.," "The Alien Corn," "Gigolo and Gigolette," and "The Colonel's Lady."

The magazine origin of these stories is not fortuitous. The Maugham short story is a form of journalism: the point at which journalism becomes literary art. Let us pick one to look at closely. I have selected "P. & O.," from *The Casuarina Tree* (1926), almost at random. The whole of the action occurs on board an elegant Peninsular and Orient liner that is carrying an assorted group of British passengers back home after their tour of duty as planters or members of the administration of the Federated Malay States. Maugham fixes on one of the passengers, a Mrs. Hamlyn, as the mediating consciousness for his tale. In her early forties, she is returning to England without her husband, from whom, it soon emerges, she is estranged. He has fallen in love with the wife of a business colleague who, to Mrs. Hamlyn's mortification, is considerably older than she is. At the beginning of the story, Mrs. Hamlyn sits in her deck chair in the early morning, while the ship is tied up in Singapore. Like the good journalist he is, Maugham rapidly establishes the multiracial background, the structure of ethnic strains, that is so relevant to his story:

Singapore is the meeting place of many races. The Malays, though natives of the soil, dwell uneasily in towns, and are few; and it is the Chinese, supple, alert and industrious, who throng the streets; the dark-skinned Tamils walk on their silent, naked feet, as though they were but brief sojourners in a strange land, but the Bengalis, sleek and prosperous, are easy in their surroundings, and self-assured; the sly and obsequious Japanese seem busy with pressing and secret affairs; and the English in their topees and white ducks, speeding past in motor-cars or at leisure in their rickshaws, wear a nonchalant and careless air. The rulers of these teeming peoples take their authority with smiling unconcern. And now, tired and hot, Mrs. Hamlyn waited for the ship to set out again on her long journey across the Indian Ocean.

It is that long journey that provides Maugham with the natural linear progression for his story. By the time the ship sights land at Aden, Mrs. Hamlyn will have come to terms with her life of separation, and a fellow passenger will have died a mysterious death. He is an Irishman named Gallagher who has made his money from the rubber boom and is on his way back home for an early retirement. Mrs. Hamlyn learns from his Cockney foreman, one of the second-class passengers on the ship, that while working upcountry Gallagher had lived for some ten or twelve years with a Malay girl who, on being abandoned, put a curse on him. Here, as in the play *The Circle*, we have a neat symmetry of construction: the situations of Mrs. Hamlyn and Mr. Gallagher mirror each other.

The material of firsthand observation in this story has been arranged with precision to make a number of dramatic points. As soon as the ship leaves port Mr. Gallagher begins to suffer from uncontrollable attacks of hiccups. At first this is treated as a joke by the other passengers, but his condition becomes so serious that he has to retire to the sick bay under the care of the ship's doctor (who, incidentally, is having a flirtation with the wife of one of the other passengers). The curse has started to take effect; Gallagher's life may be in danger. One senses that the germ of the story lay in some traveler's tale that Maugham (or Haxton) overheard. By showing the impact of Gallagher's mortal sickness on the whole shipboard community, passengers and crew, Maugham gives us a portrait of British society in the last days of the colonial era. The irony in his initial statement, "The rulers of these teeming peoples take their authority with smiling unconcern," reverberates as the ship plows its way home.

The class divisions ruling on board between the first-class passengers, the second-class passengers, and the lower decks, containing the humble members of the crew, lascars and others, correspond neatly to those within the British Empire. The first-class passengers are planning a fancy dress ball for Christmas. The great question is, should they drop the protocol for once and invite the second-class passengers? Some argue in favor, but the majority are against. All are concerned lest the death of Mr. Gallagher—if it occurs—cause the ball to be canceled. It is only a second-class passenger, the Irishman's Cockney assistant, who goes out of his way to do something practical that might help his employer. He takes the unprecedented step of applying to the third- and fourth-class citizens, the native members of the crew, to perform a magical ceremony to exorcise the curse Gallagher's mistress has cast over him. They agree to the assistant's request and slit the throat of a cockerel, intoning curious chants. "We're no match for them, us white men, and that's a fact," he tells Mrs. Hamlyn in explanation. But the exorcism does not work, and Gallagher continues to languish.

As his death approaches, "a definite malaise" overcomes the entire ship, and the reader senses a deeper malaise still: it is as though Maugham had foreseen the collapse of the whole paternalistic imperial system some thirty years before it happened. Mrs. Hamlyn observes two Japanese passengers playing deck quoits: "They were trim and neat in their tennis shirts, white trousers and buckram shoes. They looked very European, they even called the score to one another in English, and yet somehow to look at them filled Mrs. Hamlyn with a vague disquiet."

Maugham's stories had a huge readership. They seemed to appeal to all classes throughout the world save one, the professional literary critics. Turning through the pages of the prewar *New Statesman* we can find plenty of critical attacks on Maugham's tales by people like Rebecca West; let us turn instead to the view taken by Cyril Connolly in *The Modern Movement: 100 Key Books from England, France, and America, 1880–1950* (1965):

In these Far Eastern short stories . . . and in the secret service tales of *Ashenden* (1928), Maugham achieves an unspoken ferocity, a controlled ruthlessness before returning to sentimentality with Rosie in *Cakes and Ale*. He tells us—and it had not been said before—exactly what the British in the Far East were like, the judges and planters and civil servants and their womenfolk at home, even as *Ashenden* exposes what secret service work is really like. That would not be enough without his mastery of form, if not of language. His bloodless annexation of the Far East pays off in *The Casuarina Tree*, which includes "The Yellow Streak," "The Out Station," "Before the Party" and "The Letter"—about a coward, a snob, a murderess and a blackmailer.

Nor was it only the Far East, and Europe on the eve of the Bolshevik revolution, to which Maugham applied his "controlled ruthlessness" in short-story form. He viewed the exiled aristocracy and the nightclub entertainers of the French Riviera, where he had made his home, the smart world of Syrie's friends, the inmates of a French penal colony, and a dozen other milieus across the world in the same manner. As far back as his medical student days he had been a great traveler, and now, as a rich man, he toured the world at will. His travel books have the same easy readability, the same journalist's flair for an arresting incident, as his best stories, but they rely more on direct observation and less on manipulation of the material. No one who wishes to know Maugham should neglect books like *On a Chinese Screen* (1922), *The Gentleman in the Parlour* (1930), or *Don Fernando* (1935).

Maugham found a statement of the aims of the short-story writer in Edgar Allan Poe's review of Nathaniel Hawthorne's *Twice-Told Tales*. "In the whole composition," Poe wrote, "there should be no word written, of which the tendency, direct or indirect, is not to the pre-established design." After quoting Poe, Maugham gives his own formulation of a good short story in his 1939 selection:

It is a piece of fiction, dealing with a single incident, material or spiritual, that can be read at a sitting; it is original, it must sparkle, excite or impress; and it must have unity of effect or impression. It should move in an even line from its exposition to its close.

(Introduction to *Tellers of Tales*)

This formulation admirably suits the Maupassant-Poe-Maugham type of story, but not those by Chekhov or Joyce or Lawrence or Katherine Mansfield: these writers reacted against the short story based on a single anecdote, with its dramatic manipulation and linear development. They favored an approach that allowed the writer freedom within the confines of his tale to follow the inner consciousness of his characters, to allow those characters to behave in a spontaneous fashion instead of always behaving in a way determined by the pre-established design. They sought not to spring neat dramatic surprises on the reader but to lead him poetically toward the perception of sudden moments of universal truth about the human condition.

In considering Chekhov, Maugham had no doubt that he was dealing with a great master of the short story, although one who had a completely different conception from his own. "I find," he wrote of Chekhov's stories, "that the impression they make on me is powerful but indeterminate." Chekhov's people are "shadowy." He goes on:

I despair of making myself clear when I say that they strike me less as persons than as human beings. Each one is as it were a part of everyone else, and the hurt that one does to another is bearable because in a way it is a hurt that he does to himself. And because they are shadowy they remain secret. We understand them as little as we understand ourselves. And so Chekhov gets the effect which is perhaps the most impressive that the writer of fiction can achieve: he fills you with an overpowering sense of the mystery of life.

(Introduction to *Tellers of Tales*)

VI

THIS, if evasive, is generous: Maugham profoundly disliked and mistrusted the indeterminate in fiction. He felt that, great as Chekhov was in his native Russia, his influence abroad, especially on the short story, was unfortunate. Maugham had made what he called experiments. He had written one early novel, *The Merry-Go-Round* (1904), with a multiple plot, and in middle age he developed a literary persona in his fiction that permitted the introduction of passages of authorial comment; but he was suspicious of anything that broke the immaculate surface of the prose or muddied the logical connections of the narrative. His literary conservatism blinded him to the importance of the experiments in the art of fiction that Virginia Woolf and others were attempting. Nor did Virginia Woolf and her friends, in their turn, think much of Maugham's fiction. "Class Two. Division One," wrote Lytton Strachey crushingly, on finishing one of Maugham's novels. Influential critical opinion—the intelligentsia (to use the Marxist term of the time), the review pages in papers like the *Times Literary Supplement* and the *Statesman*—tended, whether consciously or not, to take its tone from Bloomsbury. Maugham felt aggrieved, while continuing to publish more books than ever. "I must bear my misfortune with fortitude," he told himself. He brooded on the whole process through which literary reputations were made in London.

The literary salons and the literary press were full of a method of developing character that seemed suddenly to have become available to the novelist, "the stream of consciousness"; it had been seen in Proust and Joyce, although its antecedents could be traced back to more obscure writers, and it had continued in England with Dorothy Richardson and Virginia Woolf. Looking back on all this after half a century with the wisdom of hindsight, it is clear to us, as it was not in the first intoxicated flush of this discovery, that the exploration of a character's inner being by a novelist through an association of thoughts and feelings is not incompatible with linear narrative. On this point I should like to quote part of a discussion I had with Iris Murdoch in the BBC Radio series *Novels Up to Now*. She said:

Tolstoy produces the most tremendous amount of stuff, exhibiting to us the immediate thoughts and feelings of Natasha and Pierre and Prince Andrew and so on.... I am interested in the relationship between immediate thoughts and feelings and the whole of the person, whatever the whole of the person may be, and I like to write and read novels in which the interior of somebody's mind is explored in enormous detail.... A lot of people, I think, rather object to this. I think there has been a reaction against the sort of Virginia Woolf version of this, which isn't just a case of stream of consciousness but is a case of a certain very highly wrought, semipoetic method of presenting it.

Maugham, although dedicated to realism and linear narrative, was by no means uninterested in "the relationship between immediate thoughts and feelings and the whole of the person" and wished at least once to explore the interior of somebody's mind in enormous detail. The "somebody" was himself, especially as his mind and the whole of his person had developed from the time of the death of his mother in Paris, when he was six, to the time when, as a young man on his own in London, he embarked on his literary career. Many novelists in their early days produce a novel describing, under the cover of a fictional story, their own early years; Maugham was no exception. He wrote it first after he had given up medicine. Written about 1898, it was then named "The Artistic Temperament of Stephen Carey." It opens with his nurse informing Stephen that his mother has died; tells of his unhappy years at Tercanbury School (the King's School, Canterbury, where Maugham was educated); and then is occupied with a protracted, self-destructive love affair between Stephen and a waitress in a London tea shop, here named Rosie Cameron. Maugham sent it to his publisher, T. Fisher Unwin, and presumably Edward Garnett had some doubts about it. At any rate, it was rejected and failed to find a publisher elsewhere. After World War II Maugham presented the manuscript to the Library of Congress (where it may be read by students of Maugham) with an embargo on its ever being published.

Although the manuscript languished in a drawer after its tour of rejections, as Maugham wrote comedies and less personal novels, the notion of writing a longer and fuller autobiographical novel, using the "Stephen Carey" script as a first draft, preoccupied him. There was so much in his youth of which he wished to disburden himself. He regarded the opportunities for such private catharsis as one of the main compensations for the hardships of a writer's lot. The result was his longest, most deeply felt work, *Of Human Bondage,* published in 1915.

Far from renouncing or modifying his naturalist principles in approaching this highly subjective material, he applied them as rigorously as ever. Here is Maugham in the person of Philip Carey from the age of about six to twenty-six—as seen by Maugham, aged about forty. Of course, much is omitted. There are no homosexual encounters, for example, and the hero's isolating disability is attributed to a club foot—not, as in real life, a stammer. Some Maugham-watchers have even suggested that the character of Mildred may in real life have been a man, a waiter instead of a waitress. Possibly, but we have no means of confirming this; and certainly Maugham did have some affairs with women before he married Syrie. In spite of alterations, however, the novel is remarkably faithful to the history and the spirit of his youth.

If you wish to learn the facts about Maugham's upbringing by the vicar of Whitstable and his German-born wife, about his years at the King's School, Canterbury, about his bohemian existence in Paris among expatriate artists, about his training as a doctor at St. Thomas' Hospital, this novel must be your first port of call, however many biographies you may wish to consult later on. Sometimes he includes an episode—like Philip's time as a floorwalker in a department store—based on hearsay. As far as is known, Maugham himself never actually went hop-picking, as the hero does in the rather unconvincing happy ending; but as a Whitstable boy Maugham must have had many opportunities to observe the annual hop-picking festival in Kent. He probably exaggerates the extent of his unhappiness when he was young, but we all do that, especially when we know that we have a sympathetic audience. The book stands, in the first instance, as a remarkably interesting social document. Very occasionally Maugham steps forward and summarizes Philip's developing philosophy of life, or lack of it (as after the Paris episode, when he ponders on the meaning of the figure in the carpet), but these pauses in the continuing action are rare and not without their own dramatic point.

However, *Of Human Bondage* is not merely a historical record; it is a novel, a work of art with its own inner life, and it must ultimately be judged as such. The first thing to be said about it artistically is that it seems to have gotten out of hand. Overwhelmed by the abundance of material he finds in his own past, the author has been deserted by his habitual sense of overall form. He keeps his chapters short, and they certainly grip us individually, but they do not fit together in the satisfying architectural proportions of his short stories and plays. This tends to be true in general of Maugham's longer fiction. He solves the structural problem by breaking up the novels into separate short-story sequences, connected only by the fact that each sequence involves the principal character in some way; in a true novelist, someone for whom the novel is a "way of life" in Greene's sense, the sequences are much more organically interrelated, or they are indistinguishable from the whole.

The main sequence, from which the book derives

its title, is the affair with Mildred, a harrowing account of the degrading bondage of one human being to another. This by itself might well have provided enough material for a complete novel, with its own extended linear progression. The novel, as it were, that precedes it is the account of Philip's relations with his adoptive parents, containing the unforgettable figure of the Reverend Carey—one of the most ironic portraits in English fiction—and his efforts to achieve independence from them. Then there is at least one further novel in the episodes concerned with the peculiar joys and sorrows of a life dedicated to art and centered on the Left Bank in the happy-go-lucky days of Paris before World War I.

Maugham had treated this milieu earlier in a novel called *The Magician* (1908). The preposterous figure of Aleister Crowley (1875-1947), exponent of black magic and prolific author, dominated that book, whereas in *Of Human Bondage* Maugham drew on the whole circle of his formative acquaintances at this time, including the painters Gerald Kelly, James Morrice, and Roderick O'Connor, and the connoisseur Ellingham Brooks. All of them engage in a dialectic with Philip Carey through which he arrives at the stoical, agnostic position that he reaches at the end of the book, having at last liberated himself from the rigorous, mean-spirited Anglican upbringing of the rectory. In the Parisian section, the agonies of students who yearn to become artists but lack the requisite amount of talent offer the author yet another self-contained dramatic theme. He dealt with it again in terms of music and anglicized Jews in the story "The Alien Corn," published originally in *Six Stories Written in the First Person Singular* (1931), where, because it is the whole of the predetermined pattern, it has more power.

To write *Of Human Bondage* may have been a liberating act for the author, but it is less of one for the reader. The Darwinian struggle for survival in which all the characters are engaged (Darwin's "great book" is mentioned as coming as a revelation to Philip) communicates itself all too depressingly; and, if the hero just barely holds our sympathy as he makes his way through life in search of his identity, he never becomes endearing. It is a book that one is glad to have read but to which one is reluctant to return.

In Maugham's next novel, *The Moon and Sixpence*, there emerges someone who is to be our constant companion through the rest of Maugham's work. How shall I describe him? As "Somerset Maugham"? Or as the "I" in the story? Or, pompously, as "the authorial presence"? Or simply as "the narrator"? It matters little which term I choose, because every reader of Maugham will know who I mean: that wise and waspish fellow who has knocked about the globe a good deal and who in his own leisurely but compelling fashion has a story to tell us.

Maugham has not abandoned naturalism even now, but he has stretched its limits to include his own observations, conditioning our response to the narrative. While he was baring his soul in the figure of Philip Carey he remained invisible, telling the story in the third person; but now that he is bent on baring the souls of his fellow men he feels free to come before the footlights himself in the role of a one-man chorus. There came a time in 1938 when he decided to hold the stage alone as a one-man show. This was *The Summing Up*, where he distilled into a single volume the observations of a lifetime devoted to successful authorship. In the same vein are the later volumes of essays: *The Vagrant Mood* (1952), *Ten Novels and Their Authors*, and *Points of View* (1958).

It is this author-narrator who holds together the different parts of the narrative in Maugham's last three major novels, *The Moon and Sixpence*, *Cakes and Ale*, and *The Razor's Edge* (1944). The Maugham we meet in these books is no longer the awkward misfit of *Of Human Bondage*; he is the professional author (hence Connolly's description), completely at ease among both the highest and the lowest in the land, and at many levels between those extremes. Even when he does look back on his own youth, either as a scholar or as a young writer with a name still to make, he does it with an amused tolerance. As a boy Maugham may have been bored having to listen every Sunday to his uncle's sermons, but in his own mature work he is by no means averse to adopting a homiletic tone. In one sense Maugham's novels are parables for people who no longer believe in God, nor in anything very much, apart from their own respectability and innate superiority. His favorite text is that of the world well lost, not for love, which he presents as an ephemeral thing killed by habit, but for a sense of vocation, a calling, or even just a whim, provided it turns into a commitment.

I do not know whether the Reverend Maugham ever preached on the theme "If any man come to me, and hate not his father, and mother, and wife and children, and brethren, and sisters, yea, and his own life also, he cannot be my disciple" (Luke 14:26), the saying of Jesus that is so hard to reconcile with the sanctity of the family. Perhaps not; but it became by implication, and in his way of life, his nephew's favorite text. Maugham's heroes abandon their loved ones to follow not the Christian God but the god of their own creativeness, although a Christian might not see a great distinction there. At any rate, his heroes follow their daimons—the need to paint (Strickland, in *The Moon and Sixpence*), to discover the eternal philosophy (Larry, in *The Razor's Edge*), or just to live within one's own artistic strength (Driffield, in *Cakes and Ale*)—with the single-mindedness, the inflexibility, the utter ruthlessness that Maugham applied to his own life.

Maugham was himself Strickland, telling everyone and everything who got in the way of his work to go to hell, but he was also the courteous narrator-figure, full of fun, good advice, and scandalous stories, capable of forming friendships with men and women of many different types, particularly if they had a title of some kind. The personalities of most artists are bifurcated in this way, but few have shown the two sides of themselves in their work with such compulsive clarity. Charles Strickland is in essence much closer to Maugham than to Paul Gauguin, even though the painter's life suggested the book, the last part of which was researched in Tahiti.

*The Moon and Sixpence* is Maugham's most uncompromising statement of this attitude in the form of a novel. More than any other work of art it has spread the myth of the artist as someone who ruthlessly severs all human claims and emotional ties to be able to follow the dictates of his genius with single-minded commitment. It seems strange that Maugham was planning and researching this particular book at precisely the time he himself was embarking on matrimony.

When it appeared, most of the reviewers rejected Charles Strickland as being too much of a monster to be credible; yet at the same time they praised Maugham's narrative technique. One critic, particularly infuriated by Strickland's antics, was the New Zealand–born short-story writer Katherine Mansfield, who had begun reviewing books for the *Athenaeum*, of which her lover, J. Middleton Murry, had recently been appointed editor. Her view was that a genuine artist does not sever human ties in the way Maugham describes, and that anyone who felt compelled to behave in that fashion should not try to become an artist. She wanted to say to him: "If you have to be so odious before you can paint bananas, pray leave them unpainted." Several reviewers failed to make a connection between the book and Gauguin; the writer in the *Saturday Review*, for instance, described Strickland as "a crypto-Monet." As Maugham was the first to admit, there are as many differences between Strickland and Gauguin as there are similarities.

The main difference is that Strickland is an Englishman, and what he escapes from is the genteel world of the near-rich in fashionable London, a world manipulated by women and centered on the tea party, the dinner party, and the drawing room. Maugham had acquired a great distaste for this world, which he had frequented when he first went to London. His rudeness at social functions became legendary and increased with his age and celebrity, although on home ground among his friends he could be a most charming host. *The Moon and Sixpence* should be read as a social satire as well as an apologia for artistic selfishness and intolerance.

If we look at its structure, again we see the familiar Maugham scheme of separate narratives, connected only by the presence of the hero (or anti-hero) mediated through the consciousness of the author (who appears in the first person, sometimes narrating events of which he has no direct knowledge). These distinct narrative sections may be seen in terms of their settings. There is the London setting, preceded by a fine parody of the art of biography in the Max Beerbohm manner, followed by sections set in Paris, Marseilles, Tahiti, and Papeete. Each of these locations represents a different stage of Strickland's journey to artistic martyrdom. In Tahiti Maugham uses material he acquired on his tour there (possibly in part an intelligence mission) during World War I in the company of Haxton. In Marseilles he relies on literary sources and cleverly fakes the scruffy society of sailors' bars and doss-houses, with the help of Captain Nichols, a likable old ruffian Maugham was to use again, more centrally, in a later novel with an exotic backdrop, *The Narrow Corner* (1932). In Paris and London Maugham is drawing directly on his own youthful memories. In the French capital Maugham introduces a figure necessary to any account of a genius: the disciple. Dirk Stroeve, an amiable clown, is one of Maugham's most accomplished comic creations. The twist in the narrative, in which Stroeve so willingly cooperates, is that instead of the disciple betraying the master, the master betrays the disciple.

The novelist's insight into the behavior of both during this crisis seems highly accurate.

Maugham scores some telling points when he describes the effect made on strangers by the reconstructed Strickland. He is even more accurate in describing the effect of the unreconstructed, about-to-become-reconstructed Strickland upon his own kith and kin. The initial drama of Strickland's disappearance, the total misunderstanding of his motivation on the part of his wife, her sister, and the sister's husband, is a fine example of Maugham at his most ironic. Here he wickedly apologizes to the reader for a certain "shadowiness" in his description of the Stricklands at home:

> My only excuse is that the impression they made on me was no other. There was just that shadowiness about them which you find in people whose lives are part of the social organism so that they exist in it and by it only. They are like cells in the body, essential, but, so long as they remain healthy, engulfed in the momentous whole. The Stricklands were an average family in the middle class. A pleasant, hospitable woman, with a harmless craze for the small lions of literary society; a rather dull man doing his duty in that state of life in which a merciful providence had placed him; two nice healthy-looking children. Nothing could be more ordinary. I do not know there was anything about them to excite the curious.

Maugham's sense of remoteness from such people in England was exacerbated by the decision of the authorities to classify Haxton, an American, as an undesirable alien and to refuse him entry. For this and other personal reasons Maugham removed himself to the French Riviera, where he had bought a villa at Cap Ferrat, the Villa Mauresque. It became his permanent residence. He was forced to leave during World War II, which he spent largely in the United States, but returned to France as soon as the war was over. After the war his appearance in London was usually confined to a visit of a few weeks in the summer, when he would stay in a private suite at the Dorchester Hotel.

As a story writer and novelist, Maugham picked up plenty of ideas along his beat in the south of France, on his regular travels with Haxton, in the Far East, and among his many friends in America. However, by 1930 he had not completely finished with the world of his childhood in Whitstable, Kent; nor had he quite finished with those hospitable English women of the middle class who had a compulsion for the small and not-so-small lions of literary society.

Maugham's continuing, horrified fascination with these women becomes apparent in *Cakes and Ale*. This novel, he tells us in the preface to the Everyman's Library edition, started out as a short story about Rosie, its voluptuous heroine; and it kept growing. The lady who is supposed to have suggested the character of Rosie has been identified as Ethelwyn Sylvia Jones, the second daughter of the playwright Henry Arthur Jones.[3] She jilted Maugham in the early days of his fame, some time before he met Syrie; and the pain of his rejection stayed with him, waiting to be put to some good literary use.

In spite of the trauma that contributed to its conception, *Cakes and Ale* is one of the most life-enhancing of Maugham's novels. The satirical description of the lionizing literary hostesses and all the wheeling and dealing in literary reputations that goes on within their drawing rooms alternates with a much more genial mood of romancing about the world of the author's boyhood. He re-creates for us the prosperous, gossipy oyster port, with the full-throated and full-bosomed Rosie presiding over the bar of the local tavern, and the raffish rascal "Lord George" paying court to her.

This is the childhood Maugham never had but would have liked to have had—carefree, athletic, exhilarating. It is all a retrospective daydream, but these happy-go-lucky scenes set in Blackstable provide a pleasant corrective to the harsher portrait of Whitstable in *Of Human Bondage*. The novelist's basic plan is linear: he tells the story of a moderately successful writer (based on Maugham himself in the days before he succeeded in getting his plays produced) who becomes involved in the biography of a grand old man of literature. Maugham makes us aware of the pressures brought to bear on the writer-character to conceal or doctor the truth; and in addition he reveals to us the charmed circle of a literary salon, with its ephemeral admirations and its ruthless mode of operation.

However, these ironic scenes of metropolitan life alternate with those set some twenty years earlier in Blackstable. The narrator boasts a previous acquaintance with the "grand old man," and he knows the full story of his youthful follies and indiscretions. Hence the subtitle: "The Skeleton in the Cupboard." Had Maugham been reading Proust and decided to

---

[3] See R. L. Calder, *W. Somerset Maugham and the Quest for Freedom* (London, 1972).

turn Blackstable into his Combray? At any rate he handles smoothly the shifts from past to present in the narrative, and through this technical device he escapes from the linear mode of story-telling.

Apart from the narrator himself, and the splendidly vulgar, erotic figure of Rosie, the other main characters in the novel are the two novelists at the center of it, Alroy Kear and Edward Driffield. The former has perfected a way of "buttering up" the book reviewers and employs other dubious means of promoting his own career with great energy. By contrast, Driffield does not appear to care about the critics or about promoting his career. He leaves all that to the second Mrs. Driffield, who is Kear's great friend. Driffield sprang from the soil, the people. He has total self-possession, a natural genius whose present eminence has been achieved, Maugham cruelly suggests, largely by reason of his longevity rather than any great intrinsic talent.

The novel created a sensation when it was first published. The London literary world thoroughly relished being told by Maugham that the emperor had no clothes. Kear and Driffield were said to have been suggested by Hugh Walpole and Thomas Hardy. Certainly the caps fitted them, as the expression goes. Walpole, who read an early copy for the Book Society, of which he was on the selection committee, felt as if he were looking into a mirror. Maugham denied that any single author was the model for either novelist, claiming that both were composite portraits with aspects borrowed from different individuals, including himself. But after Walpole's death he admitted in the preface to an American reissue of *Cakes and Ale* that he had indeed had him in mind.

The cause of Maugham's animus against Walpole —who had been a friend and had helped him in his younger days and who was also a fellow alumnus of the King's School, Canterbury—has never been fully explained. It hardly matters at this distance of time any more than the supposed identification of Hardy, with whom the resemblances are just as cogent. Hardy covered his own tracks with a posthumously published biography, which he had written himself but which was published under his wife's name. What matters is the enduring account of making a reputation in literary London. Maugham's description prompted (Mrs.) Q. D. Leavis to make a comparison between his novel and Gissing's *New Grub Street*,[4] which observes the same society slightly earlier in its evolution. Gissing's may be the greater novel of the two; Maugham's is undoubtedly the more readable.

## VII

WITH *Cakes and Ale* Maugham settled his literary account with London. He went on writing plays for another few years. His farewell drama, *Sheppey* (1933), reworked the theme of a very early short story about a working man who, suddenly possessed of a fortune, decides to give it to the poor in emulation of Jesus. His family is furious and tries to have him declared insane. The play is full of beautifully controlled irony, but it was not a success and has rarely been revived. Maugham was glad to depart from the theater at the age of sixty. Writing plays, he said, was work for a younger man, and he hailed the era of Noel Coward. Maugham had not, however, finished, as a writer, with the theme of the world well lost. He returned to it in at least two more novels. In *Christmas Holiday* (1939), set in Paris on the eve of World War II, a young man from a family background not unlike the Stricklands' has an eye-opening encounter with the French criminal underworld. In his case the world is not wholly lost because he does at the end return to respectability. The book closes with the author reflecting: ". . . only one thing had happened to him, it was rather curious when you came to think of it, and he didn't just then know quite what to do about it: the bottom had fallen out of his world."

For the hero of *The Razor's Edge*, which Maugham wrote while he was in America, the bottom falls out of his world early on, and he takes possession of another one through his knowledge of Vedanta. Larry is an early example of the drop-out in twentieth-century fiction. Maugham had been in contact with Aldous Huxley and Gerald Heard in California, and he had been on an extensive tour of India in 1936 (see his essay "The Saint," in *Points of View*), but for much of the plot he re-uses the story line of an unperformed and still unpublished play entitled "The Road Uphill."

Maugham was a much more effective satirist than he was a describer of religious experience, and the real triumph of *The Razor's Edge* is the preposterous figure of Elliott Templeton, the American "socialite" of the Riviera, with his indomitable snobbery and keen nose for a smart party. He stands alongside

---
[4] See *Scrutiny*, vol. VII (1938).

Alroy Kear as one of Maugham's most brilliantly malicious achievements.

At the beginning of *Cakes and Ale* Maugham attempts to place himself in the literary world of prewar England, intellectually dominated as it was by Bloomsbury. He once compared his own position with that of the Reverend George Crabbe, who persisted in his habit of writing narrative poems in rhymed couplets well into the heady, revolutionary romantic era of the young William Wordsworth. This is rather too flattering a comparison, but it may nonetheless help us to view Maugham in relation to his contemporaries. He was a literary conservative who believed in the power of linear narrative and descriptive realism at a time when other, greater, writers were breaking with this tradition. Although claiming to be no more than a mere entertainer, Maugham showed how much was worth conserving in the tradition.

### SELECTED BIBLIOGRAPHY

I. BIBLIOGRAPHY. F. T. Bason, *A Bibliography of the Writings of W. Somerset Maugham* (London, 1931), with a preface by Maugham; K. W. Jonas, *Bibliography of the Writings of W. Somerset Maugham* (New Brunswick, N. J., 1950); R. T. Stott, *Maughamiana. The Writings of W. Somerset Maugham* (London, 1950), with an intro. by Stott; R. T. Stott, *The Writings of William Somerset Maugham* (London, 1956), a supp. (1961; rev. ed., 1973).

II. COLLECTED WORKS. *The Collected Plays*, 6 vols. (London, 1931-1934), in 3 vols. (London, 1952); *The Collected Edition*, 25 vols. (London, 1934-1959); *Altogether* (London, 1934), with a preface by Maugham and an appreciation by D. MacCarthy; *The Pocket Edition*, 14 vols. (London, 1936-1938); *The Complete Short Stories*, 3 vols. (London, 1951); *Collected Short Stories*, 4 vols. (London, 1975-1976).

III. SELECTED WORKS. *Six Comedies* (New York, 1937), contains *The Unattainable, Home and Beauty, The Circle, Our Betters, The Constant Wife*, and *The Breadwinners; The Round Dozen* (London, 1940), stories selected by Maugham; *Here and There* (London, 1948), stories that appeared in *Cosmopolitans, The Mixture as Before*, and *Creatures of Circumstance; The Selected Novels*, 3 vols. (London, 1953); *The Partial View* (London, 1954), contains *The Summing Up* and *A Writer's Notebook; The Travel Books* (London, 1955); *Selected Plays* (London, 1963), contains *Sheppey, The Sacred Flame, The Circle, The Constant Wife*, and *Our Betters; Selected Prefaces and Introductions* (London, 1964).

IV. SEPARATE WORKS. *Liza of Lambeth* (London, 1897), novel; *The Making of a Saint* (London, 1898), novel; *Orientations* (London, 1899), short stories.

*The Hero* (London, 1901), novel; *Mrs Craddock* (London, 1902; new, rev. ed., 1928), novel; *A Man of Honour. A Play in Four Acts* (London, 1903); *The Merry-Go-Round* (London, 1904), novel; *The Land of the Blessed Virgin: Sketches and Impressions in Andalusia* (London, 1905); *The Bishop's Apron: A Study in the Origins of a Great Family* (London, 1906), novel, founded on his play *Loaves and Fishes* (London, 1924); *Flirtation* (London, 1906), short story; *The Explorer* (London, 1908), novel; *The Magician* (London, 1908), novel.

*Lady Frederick. A Comedy in Three Acts* (London, 1912); *Jack Straw* (London, 1912), drama; *Mrs. Dot* (London, 1912), drama; *Penelope* (London, 1912), drama; *The Explorer* (London, 1912), drama; *The Tenth Man* (London, 1913), drama; *Landed Gentry* (London, 1913), drama; *Smith* (London, 1913), drama; *The Land of Promise. A Comedy in Four Acts* (London, 1913); *Of Human Bondage* (London, 1915; new ed., 1946); *The Moon and Sixpence* (London, 1919), novel.

*The Unknown* (London, 1920), drama; *The Trembling of a Leaf. Little Stories of the South Sea Islands* (London, 1921), also issued under titles *Sadie Thompson and Other Stories of the South Sea* (London, 1928) and *Rain and Other Stories of the South Sea Islands* (London, 1931); *The Circle. A Comedy in Three Acts* (London, 1921); *Caesar's Wife* (London, 1922), drama; *On a Chinese Screen* (London, 1922), travel and sketches; *East of Suez* (London, 1922), drama; *Our Betters. A Comedy in Three Acts* (London, 1923); *Home and Beauty. A Farce in Three Acts* (London, 1923); *The Unattainable. A Farce in Three Acts* (London, 1923); *Loaves and Fishes. A Comedy in Four Acts* (London, 1924); *The Painted Veil* (London, 1925), novel; *The Casuarina Tree* (London, 1926), short stories; *The Letter. A Play in Three Acts* (London, 1927); *The Sacred Flame. A Play in Three Acts* (London, 1928); *Ashenden; or, The British Agent* (London, 1928), short stories.

*The Gentleman in the Parlour: A Record of a Journey from Rangoon to Haiphong* (London, 1930); *Cakes and Ale; or, The Skeleton in the Cupboard* (London, 1930), novel; *The Breadwinner. A Comedy in One Act* (London, 1930); *Six Stories Written in the First Person Singular* (London, 1931); *For Services Rendered. A Play in Three Acts* (London, 1932); *The Book Bag* (Florence, 1932), short story, later included in *Ah King* (London, 1933); *The Narrow Corner* (London, 1932), novel; *Sheppey. A Play in Three Acts* (London, 1933); *Ah King* (London, 1933), short stories; *The Judgment Seat* (London, 1934), short story, later included in *Cosmopolitans* (London, 1936); *Don Fernando: or, Variations on Some Spanish Themes* (London, 1935, new, rev. ed., 1950), travel; *Cosmopolitans* (London, 1936), short stories; *My South Sea Island* (Chicago,

1936), essay; *Theatre* (London, 1937), novel; *The Summing Up* (London, 1938), autobiography; *Christmas Holiday* (London, 1939), novel.

*Books and You* (London, 1940), essays; *France at War* (London, 1940), essay; *The Mixture as Before* (London, 1940), short stories; *Up at the Villa* (London, 1941), novel; *Strictly Personal* (New York, 1941; London, 1942), autobiography; *The Hour Before the Dawn* (London, 1942), novel; *The Unconquered* (New York, 1944), short story, later repr. in *Creatures of Circumstance* (London, 1947); *The Razor's Edge* (London, 1944), novel; *Then and Now* (London, 1946), novel; *Creatures of Circumstance* (London, 1947), short stories; *Catalina. A Romance* (London, 1948), novel; *Quartet* (London, 1948), short stories, contains "The Facts of Life," The Alien Corn," "The Kite," and "The Colonel's Lady"; *A Writer's Notebook* (London, 1949), belles lettres.

*Trio* (London, 1950), short stories, contains "The Verger," "Mr. Know-All," and "Sanatorium"; *The Writer's Point of View* (London, 1951), lecture; *Encore* (London, 1952), short stories, contains "The Ant and the Grasshopper," "Winter Cruise," and "Gigolo and Gigolette"; *The Vagrant Mood* (London, 1952), essays; *A Choice of Kipling's Prose* (London, 1962), selected by Maugham, his intro. contains valuable observations on the short-story genre; *The Noble Spaniard* (London, 1953), drama, first produced in London in 1909; *Ten Novels and Their Authors* (London, 1954), criticism; *Points of View* (London, 1958), essays; *Purely for My Pleasure* (London, 1962), color plates of Maugham's pictures, with an account by him of how he came to buy them.

V. BIOGRAPHICAL AND CRITICAL STUDIES. C. H. Towne et al., *W. Somerset Maugham* (New York, 1925); P. Dottin, *W. Somerset Maugham et ses romans* (Paris, 1928); S. Guéry, *La Philosophie de Somerset Maugham* (Paris, 1933); D. MacCarthy, *William Somerset Maugham—The English Maupassant. An Appreciation* (London, 1934); C. S. McIver, *William Somerset Maugham. A Study of Technique and Literary Sources* (Upper Darby, Pa., 1936); R. H. Ward, *W. Somerset Maugham* (London, 1937); R. A. Cordell, *William Somerset Maugham* (Edinburgh, 1937; rev. ed., 1961); P. Dottin, *Le Théâtre de W. Somerset Maugham* (Paris, 1937); R. Aldington, *W. Somerset Maugham. An Appreciation* (New York, 1939); K. W. Jonas, ed., *The Maugham Enigma. An Anthology* (London, 1954); R. Mander and J. Mitchenson, *Theatrical Companion to Maugham* (London, 1955), with an appreciation by J. C. Trewin, a pictorial record of first performances of Maugham's plays; K. W. Jonas, ed., *The World of Somerset Maugham. An Anthology* (London, 1959); L. Brander, *Somerset Maugham* (London, 1963); R. Maugham, *Somerset and All the Maughams* (London, 1965); G. Karin, *Remembering Mr. Maugham* (London, 1966); A. Curtis, *The Pattern of Maugham* (London, 1974); F. Raphael, *Somerset Maugham and His World* (New York–London, 1977); A. Curtis, *Somerset Maugham* (London, 1977); R. Fisher, *Syrie Maugham* (London, 1978); T. Morgan, *Somerset Maugham* (London, 1980).

LIST OF SHORT STORIES AND SKETCHES

(The titles in italics refer to the volumes in which the stories appear. If a story is included in *The Complete Short Stories*, the appropriate volume number is given in parentheses.)

"Adios," *The Land of the Blessed Virgin*; "The Alcazar," *The Land of the Blessed Virgin*; "The Alhambra," *The Land of the Blessed Virgin*; "The Alien Corn," *First Person Singular, The Round Dozen, Quartet* (II); "The Altar of Heaven," *On a Chinese Screen*; "The Ant and the Grasshopper," *Cosmopolitans, Here and There, Encore* (I); "Appearance and Reality," *Creatures of Circumstance, Here and There* (I); "Arabesque," *On a Chinese Screen*.

"The Back of Beyond," *Ah King* (III); "Bad Example," *Orientations*; "The Beast of Burden," *On a Chinese Screen*; "Before the Bull-Fight," *The Land of the Blessed Virgin*; "Before the Party," *The Casuarina Tree* (I); "Behind the Scene," *Ashenden*; "Boabdil the Unlucky," *The Land of the Blessed Virgin*; "The Book Bag," *Ah King* (III); "The Bridge of Calahorra," *The Land of the Blessed Virgin*; "The Bunn," *Cosmopolitans* (II); "By the Road," *The Land of the Blessed Virgin*.

"The Cabinet Minister," *On a Chinese Screen*; "Cadiz," *The Land of the Blessed Virgin*; "Calle de las Sierpes," *The Land of the Blessed Virgin*; "A Casual Affair," *Creatures of Circumstance* (III); "The Cathedral of Seville," *The Land of the Blessed Virgin*; "A Chance Acquaintance," *Ashenden*; "Characteristics," *The Land of the Blessed Virgin*; "Choice of Amyntas," *Orientations*; "The Churches of Ronda," *The Land of the Blessed Virgin*; "A City Built on a Rock," *On a Chinese Screen*; "The Closed Shop," *Cosmopolitans* (II); "The Colonel's Lady," *Creatures of Circumstance, Quartet* (II); "The Consul," *On a Chinese Screen* (II); "Cordova," *The Land of the Blessed Virgin*; "Corrida des Toros," *The Land of the Blessed Virgin*; "The Court of Oranges," *The Land of the Blessed Virgin*; "The Creative Impulse," *First Person Singular, The Round Dozen* (II).

"Daisy," *Orientations*; "The Dance," *The Land of the Blessed Virgin*; "The Dark Woman," *Ashenden*; "Dawn," *On a Chinese Screen*; "De Amicitia," *Orientations*; "Democracy," *On a Chinese Screen*; "The Dining-Room," *On a Chinese Screen*; "Dinner Parties," *On a Chinese Screen*; "A Domiciliary Visit," *Ashenden*; "Don Juan Tenorio," *The Land of the Blessed Virgin*; "The Door of Opportunity," *Ah King, The Round Dozen* (III); "The Dream," *Cosmopolitans* (II); "Dr. MacAlister," *On a Chinese Screen*.

"Ecija," *The Land of the Blessed Virgin*; "El Genero

Chico," *The Land of the Blessed Virgin;* "The End of the Flight," *Cosmopolitans, Here and There* (III); "Envoi," *The Trembling of a Leaf;* "Episode," *Creatures of Circumstance, Here and There* (III); "The Escape," *Cosmopolitans* (I).

"The Facts of Life," *The Mixture as Before, Here and There, Quartet* (I); "Failure," *On a Chinese Screen;* "Faith," *Orientations;* "The Fall of Edward Barnard," *The Trembling of a Leaf* (I); "The Fannings," *On a Chinese Screen;* "Fear," *On a Chinese Screen;* "A Feast Day," *The Land of the Blessed Virgin;* "The Flip of a Coin," *Ashenden;* "Flotsam and Jetsam," *Creatures of Circumstance, Here and There* (I); "Footprint in the Jungle," *Ah King* (III); "The Force of Circumstances," *The Casuarina Tree, The Round Dozen* (I); "The Four Dutchmen," *Cosmopolitans* (III); "The Fragment," *On a Chinese Screen;* "French Joe," *Cosmopolitans* (II); "A Friend in Need," *Cosmopolitans* (II).

"A Game of Billiards," *On a Chinese Screen;* "Gaol," *The Land of the Blessed Virgin;* "German Harry," *Cosmopolitans* (III); "Gigolo and Gigolette," *The Mixture as Before, Here and There, Encore* (I); "The Giralda," *The Land of the Blessed Virgin;* "The Glory Hole," *On a Chinese Screen;* "God's Truth," *On a Chinese Screen;* "Granada," *The Land of the Blessed Virgin;* "The Grand Style," *On a Chinese Screen;* "The Greek," *Ashenden;* "Giulia Lazzari," *Ashenden* (II); "Gustav," *Ashenden.*

"The Hairless Mexican," *Ashenden* (II); "The Happy Couple," *Cosmopolitans, Here and There* (I); "The Happy Man," *Cosmopolitans, Here and There* (I); "Henderson," *On a Chinese Screen;* "Her Britannic Majesty's Representative," *On a Chinese Screen;* "His Excellency," *Ashenden* (II); "Home," *Cosmopolitans, Here and There* (I); "Honolulu," *The Trembling of a Leaf* (I); "The Hospital of Charity," *The Land of the Blessed Virgin;* "The Human Element," *First Person Singular* (II).

"In a Strange Land," *Cosmopolitans, Here and There* (II); "The Inn," *On a Chinese Screen.*

"Jane," *First Person Singular, The Round Dozen* (II); "The Judgment Seat," *Cosmopolitans* (I); "The Kite," *Creatures of Circumstance, Quartet* (III).

"The Last Chance," *On a Chinese Screen;* "The Letter," *The Casuarina Tree, The Round Dozen* (III); "A Libation to the Gods," *On a Chinese Screen;* "The Lights of the Town," *On a Chinese Screen;* "The Lion's Skin," *The Mixture as Before* (I); "Lord Mountdrago," *The Mixture as Before, Here and There* (II); "Los Pobres," *The Land of the Blessed Virgin;* "The Lotus Eater," *The Mixture as Before, Here and There* (III); "Louise," *Cosmopolitans, Here and There* (I); "Love and Russian Literature," *Ashenden;* "The Luncheon," *Cosmopolitans, Here and There* (I).

"A Man from Glasgow," *Creatures of Circumstance* (I); "A Man with a Conscience," *The Mixture as Before* (III); "The Man with the Scar," *Cosmopolitans, Here and There* (II); "A Marriage of Convenience" (III; see "The Wash-Tub"); "Masterson" (III); "Mayhew," *Cosmopolitans* (III);

"Medinat Az-Zahra," *The Land of the Blessed Virgin;* "Metempsychosis," *On a Chinese Screen;* "Mirage," *On a Chinese Screen* (III); "Miss King," *Ashenden* (II); "The Missionary Lady," *On a Chinese Screen;* "Mr. Harrington's Washing," *Ashenden, The Round Dozen* (II); "Mr. Know-All," *Cosmopolitans, Trio* (I); "The Mongol Chief," *On a Chinese Screen;* "The Mosque," *The Land of the Blessed Virgin;* "The Mother," *Creatures of Circumstance* (I); "My Lady's Parlour," *On a Chinese Screen.*

"Neil MacAdam," *Ah King, The Round Dozen* (III); "Nightfall," *On a Chinese Screen;* "The Normal Man," *On a Chinese Screen;* "The Nun," *On a Chinese Screen.*

"An Official Position," *The Mixture as Before, Here and There* (III); "The Old Timer," *On a Chinese Screen;* "On Horseback," *The Land of the Blessed Virgin;* "One of the Best," *On a Chinese Screen;* "The Opium Den," *On a Chinese Screen;* "The Outstation," *The Casuarina Tree, The Round Dozen* (III).

"The Pacific," *The Trembling of a Leaf;* "P. & O.," *The Casuarina Tree* (III); "Puerta del Puente," *The Land of the Blessed Virgin;* "The Philosopher," *On a Chinese Screen;* "The Picture," *On a Chinese Screen;* "The Plain," *On a Chinese Screen;* "The Poet," *Cosmopolitans* (I); "The Point of Honour," *On a Chinese Screen, Creatures of Circumstance* (I); "The Pool," *The Trembling of a Leaf* (I); "The Portrait of a Gentleman," *Cosmopolitans* (III); "Princess September," *Gentlemen in the Parlour* (III); "The Promise," *Cosmopolitans* (I); "The Punctiliousness of Don Sebastian," *Orientations;* "The Question," *On a Chinese Screen.*

"'R,'" *Ashenden;* "Rain," *The Trembling of a Leaf, The Round Dozen* (I); "Raw Material," *Cosmopolitans* (III); "Red," *The Trembling of a Leaf* (III); "The Rising of the Curtain," *On a Chinese Screen;* "Romance," *On a Chinese Screen;* "The Rolling Stone," *On a Chinese Screen;* "Romance," *On a Chinese Screen;* "The Romantic Young Lady," *Creatures of Circumstance* (I); "Ronda," *The Land of the Blessed Virgin;* "The Round Dozen," *First Person Singular, The Round Dozen* (II).

"Salvatore," *Cosmopolitans, Here and There* (III); "Sanatorium," *Creatures of Circumstance, Here and There, Trio* (II); "The Sea-Dog," *On a Chinese Screen;* "The Servants of God," *On a Chinese Screen;* "The Seventh Day Adventist," *On a Chinese Screen;* "Seville," *The Land of the Blessed Virgin;* "The Sinologue," *On a Chinese Screen;* "The Skipper," *On a Chinese Screen;* "The Social Sense," *Cosmopolitans, Here and There* (II); "The Song," *The Land of the Blessed Virgin;* "The Song of the River," *On a Chinese Screen;* "The Spirit of Andalusia," *The Land of the Blessed Virgin;* "Straight Flush," *Cosmopolitans* (III); "The Stranger," *On a Chinese Screen;* "A String of Beads," *Cosmopolitans, Here and There* (I); "The Stripling," *On a Chinese Screen;* "A Student of Drama," *On a Chinese Screen;* "Sullivan," *On a Chinese Screen;* "The Swineherd," *The Land of the Blessed Virgin.*

"The Taipan," *On a Chinese Screen;* "The Three Fat

Women of Antibes," *The Mixture as Before, Here and There* (I); "The Traitor," *Ashenden* (II); "The Treasure," *The Mixture as Before* (II); "A Trip to Paris," *Ashenden*; "Two Villages," *The Land of the Blessed Virgin*; "The Unconquered," *Creatures of Circumstance, Here and There* (I).

"The Verger," *Cosmopolitans, Here and There, Trio* (II); "The Vessel of Wrath," *Ah King, The Round Dozen* (I); "The Vice-Consul," *On a Chinese Screen*; "Virtue," *First Person Singular* (II); "The Voice of the Turtle," *The Mixture as Before* (I).

"The Wash-Tub," *Cosmopolitans* (appears in III as "A Marriage of Convenience"); "Wind and Storm," *The Land of the Blessed Virgin*; "Winter Cruise," *Creatures of Circumstance, Here and There, Encore* (III); "A Woman of Fifty," *Creatures of Circumstance* (III); "Women of Andalusia," *The Land of the Blessed Virgin*; "The Yellow Streak," *The Casuarina Tree* (I).

# JOHN MILTON
(1608-1674)

## E. M. W. Tillyard

*I*

In *Paradise Lost*, Milton described his Adam as formed for "contemplation and valour." He could thereby have been describing both his own nature and his own ideals. Milton was a natural Platonist, a natural seeker after perfection by high contemplation; but he also believed, with Sidney, that the "ending end of all earthly learning" was "virtuous action." Living before Rousseau and the age when men dreamed of human perfectibility, he believed that in this world action would always fall short of the high aims to which contemplation pointed, and he would have followed Sidney in maintaining that "our erected wit maketh us know what perfection is, and yet our infected will keepeth us from reaching unto it." Nevertheless, Milton's nature both craved forms of action that would not be quite unworthy of their moving principles and was sanguine enough to make him think that a great betterment of earthly conditions was possible despite the entrance of sin into the world. That he could combine and harmonize the elements of contemplation and of action in himself and in his poetry is one of his chief claims to greatness. But his high hopes of approximating action to ideals and of living to see a better England than the one into which he was born exposed him more nakedly to the cruelty of fate than someone more skeptical and pessimistic. His final greatness consists both in the primary wealth and vitality of his nature and in the way he adjusted to the worst that fate could bring him.

Gifted with that ultimate simplicity of mind that Thucydides in his history and Mencius in his aphorisms called the mark of the truly great man, desiring to see life in strong, clear outline, more attracted by the gold pieces than by the small change of thought, Milton was unlucky in the period of history that his life covered. It was an age of transition, belonging neither to the Renaissance confidence that went before nor to the Augustan confidence that came after, an age in England of political division, philosophical skepticism, and a literature ingenious, ornate, and sophisticated rather than strong and simple. Milton was very close to his age; and the more scholars discover about him, the more sensitive they find him to the currents of contemporary thought. Yet behind this sensitivity we can detect the impression of Milton's not being spiritually attuned to his setting. Fundamentally he was a Christian humanist, a kind of rear guard of the great Renaissance army, prolonging the Renaissance faith in man into a less noble age, as Thomas Hardy, though bred in an England by then predominantly industrial, succeeded in using the relics of an older rural England for the material of his novels.

But if Milton's life span proved thus unfortunate, it was long before it definitively revealed itself to be so. Looking back, we may note that he was born three years after the ominous Gunpowder Plot of 1605, that the ill-starred Charles I came to the throne at the time Milton entered college, and that Milton's early manhood coincided with the gradual split of the active elements of the nation into two hostile parties. But in thus looking back and knowing what those various happenings actually led up to, we are in a different position from Milton, who was no more aware of the approach of civil war and all its accompanying ills than an Englishman born in 1885 was aware of the coming outbreak of war in 1914. To those living in them, the years in England before 1639 and 1914 seemed good years and full of hope for better things to come. And most of Milton's poems from before the Civil War breathe not only the vitality of youth but also contentment with the England he inhabits. In no poems more than "L'Allegro" and "Il Penseroso" does this contentment show itself. He wrote them probably near the end of his college career at Cambridge, when he was an important figure there, and in them he describes the joys first of the cheerful, and then of the thoughtful, man. And the England that provides these joys is still the united England of the days of Elizabeth, the England that, in the words of Shakespeare, was "true to herself":

> Sometimes with secure delight
> The upland hamlets will invite,
> When the merry bells ring round,
> And the jocond rebecks sound
> To many a youth, and many a maid,
> Dancing in the chequered shade;
> And young and old come forth to play
> On a sunshine holy day. . . .
> ("L'Allegro," 91-98)

Nor does the young Anglican Puritan yet see anything wrong in the artistic and musical adornments of the church service:

> But let my due feet never fail,
> To walk the studious cloisters pale,
> And love the high embowed roof,
> With antique pillars' massy proof,
> And storied windows richly dight,[1]
> Casting a dim religious light.
> There let the pealing organ blow,
> To the full-voiced choir below,
> In service high, and anthems clear,
> As may with sweetness through mine ear,
> Dissolve me into ecstasies,
> And bring all heaven before mine eyes.
> ("Il Penseroso," 155-156)

A little later, in "Arcades" and *Comus*, Milton seems to have enjoyed writing the words for that costly and aristocratic entertainment of mixed poetry, music, dancing, and scenic ingenuity called the masque. This is how he turns his delicate lyric vein to compliment the countess dowager of Derby, ancestress of many grandchildren, in whose honor "Arcades" was performed:

> Mark what radiant state she spreads,
> In circle round her shining throne,
> Shooting her beams like silver threads,
> This this is she alone,
>   Sitting like a goddess bright,
>   In the center of her light.

[1] Adorned.

> Might she the wise Latona be,
>  Or the towered Cybele,
>  Mother of a hundred gods;
> Juno dares not give her odds;
>   Who had thought this clime had held
>   A deity so unparalleled?
> (14-25)

Though a strong minority of the English nobility was on the side of Parliament against the king, the masque, along with other dramatic shows, came to be countenanced by the royalists alone. Milton, the future Cromwellian, writing the words for two masques so gaily and serenely, shows that men little understood the storm that threatened.

*Comus*, by far the longer of the two masques and the longest of Milton's early poems, reveals not only the still-persisting harmony of contemporary England but also the two poles of Milton's own nature, the contemplative and the active. The Attendant Spirit first pictures the earth from without, from the point of view to be reached only through meditation, talking of

> . . . the smoke and stir of this dim spot,
> Which men call earth, and, with low-thoughted care
> Confined, and pestered in this pinfold here,
> Strive to keep up a frail, and feverish being
> Unmindful of the crown that virtue gives
> After this mortal change, to her true servants
> Amongst the enthroned gods on sainted seats
> (5-11)

But he turns into an active character and rescues the benighted children from their danger. The Lady, at her first entrance, varies her speech from pure, active drama:

> This way the noise was, if mine ear be true,
> My best guide now, methought it was the sound
> Of riot, and ill-managed merriment,
> (170-172)

through the shudders of romantic superstitions

> What might this be? A thousand fantasies
> Begin to throng into my memory
> Of calling shapes, and beckoning shadows dire,
> And airy tongues, that syllable men's names
> On sands, and shores, and desert wildernesses
> (205-209)

to the contemplative rapture of

> O welcome, pure-eyed Faith, white-handed Hope,
> Thou hovering angel girt with golden wings,
> And thou unblemished form of Chastity,
> I see ye visibly ....
> (213-216)

*Comus* may not succeed completely as a whole, but it shows Milton free to indulge the wealth of his nature and full of the promise of great things. Indeed, in many details he has attained greatness. The second passage quoted from the Lady's speech is a poem in its own right, legitimately anthologized by Robert Bridges in *The Spirit of Man*. Only a major poet could have thought of using "syllable" as a verb in this context. "Syllable" is very effective onomatopoeia, but, through its uniqueness in verbal use, it also startles and makes a climax that gives the whole passage a convincing shape.

"Lycidas," published in 1637, is a rhymed poem lamenting the death of a college friend by drowning, in the strict tradition of the pastoral elegy of Greece and Rome. In it Milton at once achieves poetry of the highest order and expresses an incidental foreboding of the bitter times that are to come. There are the same large elements as in *Comus*. The element of rapturous contemplation, expressed in Lycidas' apotheosis, is there just as surely and more intensely:

> So Lycidas sunk low, but mounted high,
> Through the dear might of him that walked the waves;
> Where other groves, and other streams along,
> With nectar pure his oozy locks he laves,
> And hears the unexpressive nuptial Song,
> In the blest kingdoms meek of joy and love.
> (172-177)

Milton indulges his vein of romantic description with the utmost brilliance in imagining where the body of his drowned friend may have drifted:

> ... Whilst thee the shores, and sounding seas
> Wash far away, where 'er thy bones are hurled,
> Whether beyond the stormy Hebrides
> Where thou perhaps under the whelming tide
> Visit'st the bottom of the monstrous world;
> Or whether thou to our moist vows denied,
> Sleep'st by the fable of Bellerus old,
> Where the great vision of the guarded Mount
> Looks toward Namancos and Bayona's hold....
> (154-162)

And the urge to action, the will to match ideals with deeds, comes out with all the force of Milton's now mature power in the description of fame and its precariousness in this world:

> Fame is the spur that the clear spirit doth raise
> (That last infirmity of noble mind)
> To scorn delights, and live laborious days;
> But the fair guerdon[2] when we hope to find,
> And think to burst out into sudden blaze,
> Comes the blind Fury with th' abhorred shears,
> And slits the thin-spun life.
> (70-76)

But there is another side to "Lycidas," not found in *Comus*: the political. And this side is the more important because it comes out not only in a direct manner through St. Peter's attack on the degenerate clergy of the day and his grim reference to the inroads of the Roman church:

> Besides what the grim wolf with privy paw
> Daily devours apace, and nothing said,
> (128-129)

but also through a mere hint in another context: proof that Milton's mind was running on politics at this time. The two resounding lines from the end of the passage quoted about the drifting of Lycidas' body, sometimes cited to prove Milton's love of the mere sound of grandiose names, are actually packed with meaning, political included. The "guarded Mount" is the rock fortress of St. Michael's Mount in Cornwall and the "great vision" is the archangel himself, so called because he appeared in a vision to some fishermen at this site. Namancos and Bayona, unidentified for many years after Milton's death, are in Galicia, the Spanish Land's End. Michael, the chief warrior-angel in heaven, is on duty on his own mount near the English Land's End, fixing his defensive gaze on the Spanish Land's End to prevent both a recurrence of the Spanish Armada and the spread through Continental influence of popery in England, of which the Puritan wing of the English church thought there was danger through the High Church doctrines of William Laud, then at the height of his power as archbishop of Canterbury.

In "Lycidas," then, Milton hints at the troubles to come but is far from believing them inevitable. These enrich rather than overshadow the poem.

[2]Reward.

The troubles are, indeed, an important item in the matters that burdened Milton's mind at that time and made him wonder whether his hopes for the future were justified. But they are subordinate to the great theme of the poem, the theme that coexists with the elegiac theme and of which the elegiac theme is the symbol. Milton saw that action in this world is precarious, that the good die young, that great preparations for high and virtuous deeds often miscarry, that the wicked often prosper. It was a painful vision, but he faced it and overcame it by the hard-won admission that results in this world do not matter and that what does matter is the state of mind behind the attempt, whether successful or not, to achieve results. Lycidas died young and achieved little; yet his state of mind was one of integrity, and his "mounting high" into heaven symbolizes the ultimate victory of that state over what he failed to achieve by earthly action. Such were the mental conflict and the victory Milton achieved in "Lycidas." He was destined to fight the same fight more than once in his life—and it is a fight that cannot be avoided by anyone who believes in the necessity at once of contemplation and of action—but having won it on the first occasion, he was not likely to be defeated thereafter.

## II

SHORTLY after writing "Lycidas" (and the last line of the poem, "To-morrow to fresh woods, and pastures new," may refer to it), Milton set out to complete his education in the Renaissance manner through the grand tour. His journey was a happy interlude between the anxieties revealed in "Lycidas" and the imminent Civil War, and its circumstances help us to understand Milton himself. He had no liking for France and did not linger there, and his anxiety about political events at home prevented him from carrying out his plan to visit Greece. Thus his grand tour pretty well resolved itself into a long residence in different parts of Italy. There is every indication that Milton adored Italy and that he was a great success there. Certainly the actual country left its mark on his later poetry. Here, for instance, is a reference to a scene in Tuscany: in the first book of *Paradise Lost*, Satan, having painfully reached the beach of the fiery lake where he had lain prone:

> ... stood and called
> His legions, angel forms, who lay entranced
> Thick as autumnal leaves that strew the brooks
> In Vallombrosa, where the Etrurian shades
> High overarched imbower....
>                               (300–304)

It has been argued very plausibly that the landscape of Milton's Hell derives its details from the volcanic region near Naples known as the Phlegraean Fields; and I have little doubt, though I have not met the notion elsewhere, that the garden of the Villa d'Este at Tivoli, with its abundance of water drawn from the Anio, its slopes and terraces, and its luxuriance, was at the back of Milton's mind when he created his Paradise. But there were more things than the landscape to attract Milton to Italy. By 1638, when Milton reached Italy, the cultural center of Europe had shifted to France; and Italy was living on its past rather than facing the future. The spirit of the Renaissance, prevalent so much earlier in Italy than in the rest of western Europe, lingered there the longest; and it was here above all that Milton could find an intellectual temper really to his taste. Not that we should make Milton's success in Italy a small matter or underestimate his remarkable powers of adaptation to a foreign setting. It speaks very highly indeed for the flexibility and richness of his temperament that he, bred in a Puritan family and in the more Puritan of the two English universities, strongly opposed politically to the Roman church and to any romanizing tendencies in his own, and professing an austere morality, should have grown so much at home in the center of Catholicism and in a land where morals were far from austere. And he did so at no sacrifice whatever of his own private standards.

Upon returning to England in 1639, Milton was caught in the uprush of enthusiasm that carried away the Parliamentary party and the reforming wing of the English church. There was the chance, he believed, that food might after all be provided for the "hungry sheep" of England, who, he had complained in "Lycidas," "look up" and are "not fed." So believing, he could not hold back. "Virtuous action" for him now lay in the region of politics, and not of poetry, where he had wanted it to be. When Milton committed himself, he did so with all his heart, and he devoted himself to politics instead of poetry for many years to come. And his return to poetry was along the sad road of political disillusionment.

But at first his hopes ran high. He believed, with other sincere and ardent men, that if the English church could be further reformed—if, in particular, the episcopacy could be abolished—a new golden age would be established in England; and he pictured himself as the poet chosen to celebrate the new order:

Then, amidst the hymns and hallelujahs of saints, some one may perhaps be heard offering at high strains in new and lofty measures to sing and celebrate thy divine mercies and marvellous judgments in this land throughout all ages; whereby this great and warlike nation, instructed and inured to the fervent and continual practice of truth and righteousness, and casting far from her the rags of her old vices, may press on hard to that high and happy emulation to be found the soberest, wisest, and most Christian people....

("Of Reformation")

This is superbly said, but it shows the weakness of Milton as politician. Such fervor befits ideals, but not acts of Parliament. And when the Presbyterian superseded the Episcopal form of church government in England, Milton was forced to admit that the change did not bring in the millennium and that "new Presbyter was but old Priest writ large." Under the Commonwealth, Milton worked for what we now call the Foreign Office and, after the precedent of Chaucer and Spenser, was an efficient government servant; but he was too much of an idealist to be able to hedge and compromise over the large issues that concern the high politician and that have to be reduced from their utopian potentialities to the scanty proportions of what will work in the shabby, mean-principled world of every day. Milton's pamphlets, his major expression of high political opinion, are not successful as practical tracts for the times. When he is exalted, he is too remote from the real world; when he forces himself to be controversial and lowers his tone, he carries abuse too far to be effective. Nevertheless, considered not as effective political writing but as independent prose works, Milton's pamphlets, uneven as they are, form a wonderful body of vivid and varied and powerful prose, illustrating, like his earlier poetry, his belief in both contemplation and action, and presenting certain sides of his character that might not, though surely there, have been detected in his verse.

I need not dwell on the theme of action in Milton's prose, for most of it is in itself a form of action, and efforts to persuade men to follow this or that course. What is to the point is to show how Milton's belief in contemplation keeps breaking out in contexts that should be severely practical. Thus, in one of his pamphlets against the bishops, *The Reason of Church Government Urg'd Against Prelaty* (1641–1642), he inserts a long personal passage in which he talks of his poetic plans and of his conception of the poet's high office. A true poem, he holds, is

... not to be raised from the heat of youth, or the vapours of wine, like that which flows at waste from the pen of some vulgar amorist or the trencher fury of a rhyming parasite; nor to be obtained by the invocation of Dame Memory and her siren daughters, but by devout prayer to that eternal Spirit, who can enrich with all utterance and knowledge and sends out his Seraphim with the hallowed fire of his altar to touch and purify the lips of whom he pleases....

And if the "eternal Spirit" is ready to inspire, he will inspire the man who has, by the act of contemplation, prepared his heart for the inspiration, for Milton goes on to talk of "beholding the bright countenance of truth in the quiet and still air of delightful studies." Milton is here remote indeed from the grasping and opportunist world of political action.

What are the sides of Milton's nature that his prose makes especially clear, and that readers might overlook in his verse?

First, the man's uncommon exuberance. Milton's total poetic output is not large, and we might be tempted to think that he wrote slowly and painfully. If we heed the torrent of his prose, with its immensely wealthy vocabulary, we can be sure that Milton wrote comparatively little poetry only because he rejected so much and selected so fastidiously. By nature he had the exuberance of a Rubens, but it was checked and compressed by the severity and the scrupulousness of a Racine. In prose, however, Milton felt no obligation to curb his magnanimity or to comb out his vocabulary. He bursts out into vivid metaphors and allows his sentences to grow to great lengths through sheer sustention of vitality. Here, for instance, is his invective, from his tract *Of Education* (1644), against the system of studies still prevalent at the universities with its disastrous effect on the undergraduates' future careers:

And for the usual method of teaching arts, I deem it to be an old error of universities, not yet well recovered from the scholastic grossness of barbarous ages, that instead of beginning with arts most easy (and those be such as are most obvious to the sense) they present their young unmatriculated novices at first coming with the most intellective abstractions of logic and metaphysics, so that they having but newly left those grammatic flats and shallows, where they stuck unreasonably to learn a few words with lamentable construction, and now on a sudden transported under another climate to be tossed and turmoiled with their unballasted wits in fathomless and unquiet deeps of controversy, do for the most part grow into hatred and contempt of learning, mocked and deluded all this while with ragged notions and babblements while they expected worthy and delightful knowledge, till poverty or youthful years call them importunately their several ways and hasten them with the sway of friends either to an ambitious and mercenary or ignorantly zealous divinity: some allured to the trade of law, grounding their purposes not on the prudent and heavenly contemplation of justice and equity, which was never taught them, but on the promising and pleasing thoughts of litigious terms, fat contentions, and flowing fees; others betake them to state affairs with souls so unprincipled in virtue and true generous breeding that flattery and court-shifts and tyrannous aphorisms appear to them the highest points of wisdom instilling their barren hearts with a conscientious slavery, if, as I rather think, it be not feigned; others, lastly, of a more delicious and airy spirit retire themselves, knowing no better, to the enjoyments of ease and luxury, living out their days in feast and jollity, which indeed is the wisest and safest course of all these unless they were with more integrity undertaken—and these are the errors, these are the fruits of misspending our prime youth at the schools and universities as we do, either in learning mere words or such things chiefly as were better unlearned.

This is at once a single sentence and a whole paragraph. Milton's ardor presses on, unremitting to the end.

Second, there appears in Milton's prose—fitfully, it is true—a sense of humor. This comes out at odd moments and in chance phrases, at times when his feelings have cooled and he is not concerned with a main argument. At the end of *Colasterion* (1645), a hot piece of controversy on the subject of divorce, Milton says how glad he is to have done with his adversary:

At any hand I would be rid of him; for I had rather, since the life of man is likened to a scene, that all my entrances and exits might mix with such persons only whose worth erects them and their actions to a grave and tragic deportment and not to have to do with clowns and vices. But if a man cannot peaceably walk into the world but must be infested, sometimes at his face with dorrs and horseflies, sometimes beneath with bawling whippets and shin-barkers . . . have I not cause to be in such a manner defensive as may procure me freedom to pass unmolested hereafter . . . ?

The general tone is scornful, but no man without a sense of humor could have coined the phrase "bawling whippets and shin-barkers." In *Areopagitica* (1644), the most lively and varied and readable of all the pamphlets, there occurs a delightfully humorous description of the wealthy merchant who finds "religion to be a traffic so entangled . . . that . . . he cannot skill to keep a stock going upon that trade" and who solves his problem by hiring a tame clergyman to deputize, resigning "the whole warehouse of his religion, with all the locks and keys, into his custody . . . ."

If the prose tells us certain things about Milton, so do his sonnets, written, like the prose, mostly between "Lycidas" and *Paradise Lost*. Like some of Horace's *Odes* (on which they are partly modeled) and many of Thomas Hardy's lyrics, they are occasional poems dealing with people or contemporary events. That Milton should write sonnets to Thomas Fairfax, Cromwell, and other Parliamentary leaders is not surprising, and accords with his prose. What most adds to our knowledge of the man are the feelings he displays in the personal sonnets: his tenderness toward his second wife, now dead; his uncomplaining humility in the sonnet on his blindness; the urbanity with which, in the following, he invites his friend Lawrence to dinner:

> Lawrence, of virtuous father virtuous son,
>   Now that the fields are dank, and ways are mire,
>   Where shall we sometimes meet, and by the fire
>   Help waste a sullen day; what may be won
> From the hard Season gaining: time will run
>   On smoother, till Favonius reinspire
>   The frozen earth; and clothe in fresh attire
>   The lily and rose, that neither sowed nor spun.
> What neat repast shall feast us, light and choice,
>   Of Attic taste, with wine, whence we may rise
>   To hear the lute well touched or artful voice
> Warble immortal notes and Tuscan air?
>   He who of those delights can judge, and spare
>   To interpose them oft, is not unwise.
>                              (Sonnet 17)

I have written thus far of the pamphlets and the sonnets as isolated works possessing certain literary qualities and telling us things about Milton's nature. They also, when taken in sequence, tell the story of how his hopes of national betterment through high action came to grief, and of his personal disasters or disappointments. Milton did not abandon his hopes lightly. It is true that the defeat of the episcopacy and the victory of Presbyterianism did not produce the wonderful betterment he expected. But Presbyterianism had not come to stay, and better things might issue from the professions of greater religious toleration put out by the Independents. Moreover, the richness and fervor of religious controversy gave Milton grounds for hope. *Areopagitica*, written after the first decisive victory of the Parliamentarians at Marston Moor and when there was the promise of opposition to the now-established Presbyterians, utters this hope. This pamphlet, the classic plea in literature for liberty of the press, is also an utterance of hope that England is about to enter a new era of free vitality when, unrestricted by the harsh decrees of ecclesiastical orthodoxy, she may both face the full truth of God's word and be strong and virtuous enough to draw sustenance and life from it:

Methinks I see in my mind a noble and puissant nation rousing herself like a strong man after sleep and shaking her invincible locks: methinks I see her as an eagle mewing her mighty youth and kindling her undazzled eyes at the full midday beam, purging and unscaling her long-abused sight at the fountain itself of heavenly radiance....

Note once again in this passage the union of action and contemplation: the references first to Samson with his uncut hair, the man of great deeds, and then to the eagle, symbolizing, in its supposed power to envisage the sun, the mind that has the strength to contemplate the Platonic ideas or God himself.

The story of Milton's disillusion is the story of England between *Areopagitica*, written in 1644, and the Restoration in 1660. Parliament won the war but failed to win the hearts of the English people. Representing at first a majority of the population, the Parliamentary rulers became fewer and represented an ever-dwindling minority. Of that minority Milton was an absolutely loyal member, his high idealism drawing him to those who, for whatever reason, were willing to go to extremes. Here, he felt, were real men and not time-servers or Laodiceans; and in some of his sonnets and in his great Latin prose work, *The Second Defence of the People of England*, he celebrated their virtues and gave them high advice. But all the time Milton knew that these heroic men did not have the country behind them, and he experienced a great revulsion from the sentiments expressed in the passage quoted from *Areopagitica*. He believed that lethargy was the besetting vice of most of his countrymen. It was lethargy, he thought, that caused them to sympathize with Charles for all his misdeeds and to withdraw their support from the men who had dared to put him to death; for lethargy cannot bear change, however called for, and the desire for a king was of long and rooted growth. Not that Milton despaired when men regretted Charles; on the contrary, he vented his hopes and his energies in writing in support of the regicides. His vehement efforts were the final reason for his loss of sight. But he never regretted the sacrifice, as he told Cyriack Skinner in a sonnet; nor did he argue

> Against heaven's hand or will, not bate a jot
> Of heart or hope; but still bear up and steer
> Right onward....
(Sonnet to Mr Cyriack Skinner Upon His Blindness)

This is indeed to apply the lesson of "Lycidas," the lesson that the motive of the deed, not its result, matters.

### III

Milton's blindness had the effect of detaching him gradually from his position as government servant. Through his Latin defenses of the regicides he earned the gratitude of the government at home and fame abroad; but as a blind man he could no longer be of the same use. Released from regular employment, though still good for an occasional pamphlet, he returned to his plans for a great poem some four years before the Restoration.

His other personal trouble was the unhappy beginning of his first marriage. His wife returned to her parents probably a little more than a year after the wedding. But we must remember that she returned to him and bore him children, and that his two other marriages were happy. With little knowledge of the feminine heart before marriage, he acquired a sufficiency by the time he came to write *Paradise Lost*.

With Cromwell's death and the plain imminence of the restoration of the Stuarts, Milton still refused to give up hope, and risked his life by writing last-minute appeals to the English people not to submit their necks to a tyrant. The actual shock of the Restoration must have been terrible. There is no record of his feelings unless, as has been conjectured, he composed *Samson Agonistes*[3] while in hiding and in danger of execution. But if Samson's dejection reflects, as it may well do, feelings that Milton at one time experienced, it may plausibly concern the loss of sight that was common to them both. We shall be safer if we reconstruct Milton's feelings at the time of the Restoration from his more firmly dated works. However great the shock of the Restoration (and its magnitude must have corresponded roughly with the vehemence of Milton's pamphleteering immediately before it), I believe he must have faced beforehand the failure of his hopes, just as a good commander will have faced the problem of extricating his troops, should the victory he so passionately desires be denied him.

The evidence is the general scheme of *Paradise Lost*, begun, and hence, we may be certain, in the case of so rigorously architectonic a poet as Milton, already planned, some four years before the Restoration. The general scheme of *Paradise Lost* embodies the moral of "Lycidas": that results matter less than states of minds. Satan's apparently decisive act in causing man's fall, an act based on an envious and cruel state of mind, ends by being less strong than the small, sound human acts of mutual generosity and of repentance performed by Adam and Eve after they have fallen. If Milton had staked everything on the results of his political hopes, he could never have framed his poem in this way. That he cared greatly about the Restoration is proved by his pamphlets; that he had also learned not to care is proved by the scheme of *Paradise Lost*. That it cost him dear to learn not to care, and that he did suffer mental torment when his hopes failed, we cannot doubt.

Milton planned to make a single great poem the crown of his life, to do for his own country what Homer, Virgil, Luís de Camões, and Torquato Tasso had done for theirs. I believe that in *Paradise Lost* he succeeded, and hence I have intended my remarks so far to lead up to this poem. All the qualities so far enumerated find a place there. As I shall point out in detail, it largely concerns action and the proper grounds for it. The side of contemplation is included partly through the many shifts of distance from which action is viewed, partly through descriptions that suggest a static condition of eternity rather than the shifting phenomena of this world. The pageants of earthly history that Michael shows to Adam are seen as if from a distance, and Adam's comment on them at the end fixes this impression:

> "How soon hath thy prediction, seer blest,
> Measured this transient world, the race of time,
> Till time stand fixed: beyond is all abyss,
> Eternity, whose end no eye can reach...."
> (XII. 553-556)

The account of Paradise, though in the first instance borrowed from an actual garden, ends by speaking of an imagined world of incredible static beauty and felicity. Politics, though subordinated to a moral theme that goes far beyond it, is included through the infernal debates in the second book and through the characters of the different speakers. I shall refer later to instances of humor and generally to the diversity of the poem, to Milton's success in including in its compass all experience as he knew it.

Up to *Paradise Lost* the facts of Milton's life sometimes help us to understand his writing; and *Paradise Lost* itself is clearer if we know the conditions that led up to it. But after 1660, Milton lived anything but a public life, and there is little profit in connecting poetry and biography. Thus, from now on, I am concerned with his poetry alone.

The fall of man was not Milton's first choice for the subject of his great poem. At the time of his Italian journey he intended to write on King Arthur, and there are passages in his earliest pamphlets that show the kind of poem it would have been. It would have been partly religious and moral, partly patriotic. Arthur would have borne something of the character of Spenser's Prince Arthur in the *Fairie Queene*, uniting the contemplative and active virtues; but unlike Spenser's prince, he would have

---

[3]The date of composition of *Samson Agonistes* has been much disputed among modern scholars. The case for an early dating (1647-1653?) is set out by W. R. Parker, *Philological Quarterly*, 23 (1949) and *Notes and Queries*, 5 (1958).

been the center of action in defeating the heathen Saxon invaders. British history, again as in Spenser, would have been narrated in prophecy, culminating in the defeat of the Spanish Armada. The main emphasis would have been on heroic action. If there had been no civil war and Milton had been free to write his Arthuriad around the time of *Areopagitica*, he would have given us a divinely energetic poem, but one less varied and less mature than *Paradise Lost*. He might have gone on to a second, more mature poem; and the two together might have had an even wider scope than *Paradise Lost*. But if the choice were between an Arthuriad and *Paradise Lost*, we should be content with what we have.

Milton's very earliest critics served him well. Sir Henry Wotton, commenting on *Comus* in 1638, spoke of "a certain Dorique delicacy in your Songs and Odes, whereunto I must plainly confess to have seen yet nothing parallel in our Language." Wotton was thinking of all the parts of *Comus* not in dramatic blank verse, but "Dorique delicacy" describes, like no other phrase, the mixture of austerity and sensuous sweetness that generally marks Milton's early poetry. Andrew Marvell supplied a set of commendatory verses to the second edition of *Paradise Lost* that show a just appreciation of its scope and versification. He described the scope of Milton's subject thus:

> Messiah crowned, *Gods* reconciled decree,
> Rebelling angels, the forbidden tree,
> Heav'n, hell, earth, chaos, all: . . .

This shows that Marvell saw that the actual loss of Paradise was but a fraction of the whole. His account of Milton's style follows:

> At once delight and horror on us seize,
> Thou singst with so much gravity and ease;
> And above human flight dost soar aloft
> With plume so strong, so equal, and so soft.

Softness and ease: these are the qualities of style in *Paradise Lost* often unrecognized by those who are too intent on Milton's gravity and sublimity. Dryden, who praised *Paradise Lost* unstintingly, was also the first critic to interpret it wrongly. He said in 1697 that Milton would have a better claim to have written a genuine epic "if the Devil had not been his hero instead of Adam, if the giant had not foiled the knight and driven him out of his stronghold to wander through the world with his lady errant." There you have that undue narrowing of the poem's scope to the episode of the Fall and the triumph of Satan: a narrowing that has become traditional and still continues to close the eyes of many readers and critics to the full significance of the poem. It is true that Milton himself gave countenance to this narrowing by the title he gave his epic, though I sometimes think that he was being ironical and meant us to think of *Lost* as in quotation marks. But Dryden's witty contention that the giant foiled the knight is quite at odds with the poem itself.

*Paradise Lost* in its grand outlines is founded on a simple irony. And we need not be surprised, for irony is one of the qualities Milton gives to God the Father. When, near the beginning of the third book, the Father looks down and sees Satan "coasting the wall of Heav'n" and about to penetrate the universe, he addresses the Son as follows:

> "Only begotten Son, seest thou what rage
> Transports our adversary, whom no bounds
> Prescribed, no bars of hell, nor all the chains
> Heaped on him there, nor yet the main abyss
> Wide interrupt can hold? . . ."
>
> (III. 80-84)

One critic accused Milton of inconsistency here because when, in the first book, Satan raised himself from the burning lake, Milton tells us he did so only through the "will and high permission of all-ruling Heaven." Of course there is no inconsistency, for in the passage quoted the Father speaks ironically, adopting Satan's foolish assumption that he raised himself from the lake and set out to ruin mankind on his own initiative and responsibility alone. If we grasp God's ironical words at Satan's expense, we may be the readier to believe that irony is central to the whole plot. The irony is as follows. Satan succeeds in tempting mankind to transgress God's commandment, and he believes that his success can have only one result: as Satan and his fellows have brought complete ruin on themselves by disobedience, so must Adam and Eve by theirs. But he has made a false comparison. Satan's sin was self-motivated; that of Adam and Eve was partly motivated from without. For Satan there is no hope, for he is corrupt throughout his whole being; for Adam and Eve there is hope, because theirs was not the whole responsibility. And in the end humanity finds itself able to attain an inner paradise better than the paradise it must give up; Dryden's knight and lady errant have in fact the key to a better stronghold than the one from which the giant has driven them. Such is the irony at Satan's expense. There is the further irony that Adam and Eve are as mistaken as Satan about their ultimate fate. When, exhausted by their quarrels and bereft of their pride, they become reconciled in very simple human companionship and fellow feeling, they are quite unaware that they are following the promptings both of heaven and of the residue of good thoughts that have survived the Fall, and that, by so following, they have attained salvation: just as the Ancient Mariner blessed the watersnakes unaware, not knowing that thereby he had broken the evil spell.

There are important consequences of this fundamental irony. First, the weight of the plot is put not on the mere episode of Eve eating the apple in the ninth book but on the whole process of temptation, Fall, the judgment by the Son of the Serpent, Adam, and Eve; on the corruption of the world through the entry of Sin and the consequent despair of Adam and Eve; and then, unexpectedly evolved out of all these varied and vast happenings, their mutual reconciliation, their penitence before God, and their salvation. These happenings occupy the whole of books IX and X. Such a weighting of the plot is of the first moment. The fall of Eve, adequate enough in a larger ironic context, is nowhere near weighty enough, as described by Milton, to be the center of the poem, the point to which all earlier happenings lead and from which all subsequent happenings derive.

But read books IX and X as a unit, treat the events after the Fall not as appendixes to a completed climax but as a sequence leading up to the real climax in man's regeneration, and you find them a brilliantly diversified and massive area of high poetry, a principal glory of the English tongue. It may be asked whether the climax as thus described will really bear the weight put on it any more than will the traditionally assumed climax, the eating of the apple. Can this purely human scene of man and wife forgetting their quarrels, coming together again, and confessing their sin to God stand the tremendous test? First, it can be retorted that Milton undoubtedly intended it to do so. Near the end of the poem there is a conversation between Adam and Michael that follows the vision of future world history Michael has given to Adam for his instruction. From its all-important position and its intensely concentrated and earnest tone, it is clearly crucial to the meaning of the poem. Adam has at last learned wisdom, and this is his statement of some of the things hard experience has taught him:

> "Henceforth I learn, that to obey is best,
> And love with fear the only God, to walk
> As in his presence, ever to observe
> His providence, and on him sole depend,
> Merciful over all his works, with good
> Still overcoming evil, and by small
> Accomplishing great things, by things deemed weak
> Subverting worldly strong, and worldly wise
> By simply meek...."
>
> (XII. 561-569)

This is high moralizing verse that would be irrelevant in a narrative poem if it did not repeat in its own abstract form what had already been transacted in concrete, dramatic action; and it points precisely to the true climax of the poem, where by their "small" decent action Adam and Eve accomplish great things and in their apparent weakness subvert the apparently "strong" machinations of the prince of this world. Whether Milton not only intended to make this part of the poem his climax but also succeeded in making it a worthy one can be decided only by the verdict of competent readers. But to me, at least, the account of Adam's black despair, his ferocious and cruel repulse of Eve, her persistence, Adam's softening toward her, their coming together, Eve's still distraught state of mind and inclination to suicide, Adam's strong and comforting words, and their final resolution to confess their sins to God is true to the fundamental simplicities of human nature and composes one of the most moving dramatic episodes in literature; it can bear a very heavy weight.

The second consequence of recognizing the fundamental irony of the poem is that it puts Satan in his proper place. Dryden has had many distinguished successors in his heresy that Satan is the hero; and as long as Adam and Eve were denied heroic action in their recovery after the Fall, it was natural to fill the resulting vacuum with any other action that had heroic pretensions. And that action was the escape of Satan from the fiery lake in Hell, and his courage in undertaking alone the journey to

Earth for the ruin of mankind. But Milton's Satan is never a hero; he is an archangel ruined: that terrible thing—a being with great potentialities of good corrupted; graced, indeed, to heighten the drama, with some relics of good feelings but doomed to turn those relics to even greater evil. Those who have sentimentalized Satan have failed to see the coarseness and the vulgarity that accompany and darken these lingering relics of good feelings. Here is Milton's description of Satan reviewing the army of devils now mustered in Hell:

> ... he through the armed files
> Darts his experienced eye, and soon traverse
> The whole battalion views, their order due,
> Their visages and stature as of gods;
> Their number last he sums. And now his heart
> Distends with pride, and hardening in his strength
> Glories ....
> (I. 567–573)

It is a most damning description. How significant the juxtaposition of number and pride. Satan is revealed as the vulgarian who is thrilled by mere quantity. No wonder he commits a fundamental error in his estimate of what fate awaits disobedient man. All this is not to deny Satan's grandeur. It is just because he combines grandeur with vulgarity, a commanding intellect with a fundamental stupidity, not to speak of other discrepant qualities, that he is so true to life and so eternally fascinating a figure.

The fundamental irony at Satan's expense and at the apparent expense—but to the ultimate profit—of Adam and Eve is surpassingly powerful because it grew out of Milton's life experience and provided the most authentic material for his supreme poetic gift, a gift both congenital and improved by intense study. Milton condemns pride with such authority because he was himself strongly tempted to it. Compare him in this matter with Shakespeare. There is in literature no finer indictment of pride than Isabella's speech to Angelo in *Measure for Measure*:

> Could great men thunder
> As Jove himself does, Jove would ne'er be quiet,
> For every pelting, petty officer
> Would use his heaven for thunder;
> Nothing but thunder ... Merciful heaven,
> Thou rather with thy sharp and sulphurous bolt
> Split'st the unwedgeable and gnarled oak
> Than the soft myrtle; but man, proud man,
> Drest in a little brief authority,
> Most ignorant of what he's most assured—
> His glassy essence—like an angry ape,
> Plays such fantastic tricks before high heaven
> As make the angels weep ....
> (II.ii. 111–122)

In his history plays, too, Shakespeare gives convincing pictures of proud and ambitious and unscrupulous men. But Isabella's speech and Shakespeare's quarreling nobles are passionately observed, not created out of the personal stuff of Shakespeare's mind. He could objectify them from the beginning, unhampered by any unusual personal involvement. But, as his pamphlets clearly show, Milton did suffer from that impatient pride that revolts against the nature of things and demands quick results; he had an element of Satan in him, and he experienced the despairing bafflement in which such pride is bound to end. But, as "Lycidas" showed, he was also aware of this side of his nature and hated it, believing even more passionately in the need for humility. And always the victory of humility was complete. It is because of this personal conflict, absent from Shakespeare in this acute form, that the basic irony of *Paradise Lost* has its peculiar power. Milton did objectify his material: we do not, in reading *Paradise Lost*, think of Milton the man. But he objectified with greater difficulty and at a later stage of the poetic process than Shakespeare did; and his poetry makes a different impression. Shakespeare was very close to life; Milton, to his own life. And the Miltonic closeness has its own superb authenticity.

I have asserted that the basis of *Paradise Lost* is a great irony expressive of a great piece of simple morality and that Milton's own total experience of this morality makes his poem authentic. We are reluctant, however, to accept a piece of simple morality as authentic unless it is supported by a great mass of detail. We require a poet to talk about many things before we are ready to accept what he most has to say. So I come now by a quite natural sequence to the various parts of *Paradise Lost*. These are so many that I will have to select; and I will do so by dealing only with those things that have either been denied to Milton or, if granted to him, ignored or slurred over or deprecated.

First, there is the theology. While the eighteenth century was too prone to see in *Paradise Lost* a simple orthodoxy, the late nineteenth and early twentieth centuries were too prone to cut out the theology altogether as an unfortunate accretion dictated by the conditions of seventeenth-century England. The truth is that Milton's theology is not entirely orthodox and that it is inseparable from the poem. If, as I assert, the main theme of the poem has to do with pride and humility, these qualities are not independent and uncircumstantiated, but bear the form, inescapable in the postclassical tradition in Europe, given them by Christianity. However much Milton had tried to free himself from theological ties, Pride, as he presented it, would in some sort have remained the chief of the Seven Deadly Sins, and humility a quality exemplified in the story of Christ as told in the New Testament. When Milton implies the doctrine of disinterestedness in "Lycidas," he gives us neither the abstracted doctrine nor the form of it found in the *Bhagavad-Gita*. However universal the doctrine, Christian and Indian writers had to present it in the ways they had inherited. Readers today are better placed to accept Milton's theology because recent scholarship has been teaching them a great deal about the theological tradition Milton inherited. So long as readers conceived it as a narrow fundamentalism of the kind described in the Mark Rutherford novels, they had to free Milton the poet from it. But if they realize that for Milton, as for his predecessors, theology included all philosophy and a great deal of natural science, they will see that such severance is not only unnecessary but also disastrously weakening to the range of Milton's interests.

One of the great theological doctrines was that a main way to approach God was through studying the beautiful variety of his creation. I have already mentioned the exuberance of Milton's nature as something fundamental. Possessing it, he was bound to find the bounty of nature both exciting and satisfying. Living when he did and brought up as he was, he could conceive of this bounty in other than theological terms. He must see it in terms of the great orderly arrangement of the total creation pictured as a great hierarchical chain stretching from the seraph nearest the throne of God to the meanest speck of inanimate matter. Even when Comus, the champion of disorder, speaks of the bounty of God's creation, that he may tempt the Lady to license, he does so with an enthusiasm that can best be matched in the panegyrics of orthodox divinity:

> Wherefore did Nature pour her bounties forth,
> With such a full and unwithdrawing hand,
> Covering the earth with odors, fruits, and flocks,
> Thronging the seas with spawn innumerable....
> (710–713)

And when, in *Paradise Lost*, Milton writes of free will, he colors a doctrine that was essential to his own nature with traditional disputes over predestination and with the special Protestant doctrine of Christian liberty based on the writings of St. Paul. Milton's theology, far from being a tie, an alien thing, was a great world of thought where an immensely wide range of passions could find their natural embodiments.

Great poets are often the subject of large popular misconceptions. Chaucer has been thought of as hearty, Shakespeare as uneducated and unacademic, Shelley as weakly neurotic, Milton as inhuman and humorless. And these misconceptions die hard. It may be difficult, therefore, to gain the reader's ear if one points to humor and a delicate human perception in *Paradise Lost*. Humor, indeed, is not what one is led to expect in the straight epic from Virgil onward; nor could humor be advertised in the uniform meter of the epic with the clarity possible in a play using both verse and prose like Shakespeare's *Henry IV*. But Milton expects his readers to be fit as well as few; and fitness indicates close reading, which in its turn reveals, perhaps as a great surprise, these qualities of humor and delicate human perception. I mentioned earlier as a humorous figure the wealthy city merchant in *Areopagitica*, who hired a divine to manage his religion for him; and I fancy he reappears in a passage of *Paradise Lost* that has been cited as an example of Milton's seeking to be funny with disastrous results. It occurs just before the great description of Paradise and is a comparison with the way Satan overleaped the leafy barriers of that place, scorning entry by the proper way:

> Or as a thief bent to unhoard the cash
> Of some rich burgher, whose substantial doors,
> Cross-barred and bolted fast, fear no assault,
> In at the window climbs, or o'er the tiles....
> (IV. 188–191)

The point of the passage is to lower the dignity of Satan, who a little earlier has struck a highly dramatic attitude, by homely comparisons, so that the reader may have his mind cleared for the coming description of Paradise; but the actual lines are a piece of satirical humor at the expense of the rich merchant who is imaginative enough to guard against direct assault but not imaginative enough to forestall a cat burglar.

I remarked earlier that Milton acquired a knowledge of women during the years of the Commonwealth, and in *Paradise Lost* this knowledge comes, as we might expect, in the later books, where the action has converged from Hell and Heaven to the universe and finally to the narrow human stage of the mount of Paradise. It is in the long scene near the beginning of book IX, when Adam and Eve discuss whether they shall garden separately or jointly, that the human comedy is most evident. That Milton dared to introduce comedy immediately before the great disaster in human history is quite amazing; and, if that disaster had been irreparable, comedy would have been out of the question. But I do not see how any careful and honest reader can miss the comedy; and I fancy Milton introduced it because he wished to relieve the disaster of the Fall itself of too stark an emphasis and to prepare for the basic irony of the poem.

The dispute between Adam and Eve is as delicate a piece of domestic comedy as you could find. Eve proposes separate gardening on this particular morning, not because she really wants that but because she wants Adam to say that he loves her too much to bear separation from her. Adam falls into the trap and replies with a heavy piece of moralizing. Eve gets her own back by saying that Adam does not trust her. Adam grows seriously concerned and argues earnestly, even impressively; and, if only he could see it, Eve is by now quite satisfied with the effect that her stratagem has produced. But Adam does not see, and refuses the responsibility of keeping Eve at his side. Finally Eve feels that after all this she cannot refuse the offer of a freedom she did not really want at any time, and now less than ever. And so they part, and Eve is exposed alone to the wiles of Satan. It is a perfect picture of the sort of misunderstanding that can afflict any ordinary, well-intentioned married couple; and it is proof that Milton had an eye for ordinary human traffic as well as for God's empyrean. Most remarkable is the stylistic skill by which he keeps the comedy from being cheap, so that it can slide into the tragic; for Adam's failure to assert himself at the right moment is not only comedy but also a tragic moral lapse.

But Milton's success in passing from comedy to tragedy is possible only within a restricted area of contrast. Obliged by writing in the epic form to observe a certain kind of uniformity, he has to pitch his comedy in a higher style than is required for the drama; his conversational cadences have to blend with a modicum of pomp. The conversational cadence of Eve's reprimand to Adam:

But that thou shouldst my firmness therefore doubt
To God or thee, because we have a foe
May tempt it, I expected not to hear.
(IX. 279-281)

with its stresses on "thou" and "my" is perfect, but it is delicately, not blatantly, conveyed; and the dignity of the passage does not fall below the standard expected from epic writing in the seventeenth century. It is this delicacy and lack of blatancy that both separates Milton's art from that of the metaphysical poets and exaggerates that separation. The metaphysicals founded their art on surprise and advertised what they were doing with much emphasis. Milton resembled them in being full of surprises, but he was extremely discreet about them. Had he not been full of surprises, he would have been untrue to the age in which he lived; had he paraded the fact, he would have been intolerable as an epic poet.

The matter of surprise is connected with another: that of realism. Milton's epic has the remotest possible setting, yet he wished its application to be entirely modern. To achieve his end he constantly refers in passing to contemporary events or interests, and slips the homely and the sensuous into contexts that are grandiose and remote. In the high description of Satan's lieutenants in book I, Milton suddenly inserts his reference to the riotous young men who made the streets of London dangerous in the later years of his life:

. . . and when night
Darkens the streets, then wander forth the sons
Of Belial, flown with insolence and wine.
(I. 500-502)

It is a startling piece of realism, but slipped in so coolly and quietly that it does not impair the epic texture. In the last lines of the poem, which give the vast picture of the angels thrusting Adam and Eve out of the gates of Paradise, occurs a reference of the greatest possible homeliness: to an ordinary peasant returning home to supper on a misty evening. I give it in its setting.

> So spake our mother Eve, and Adam heard
> Well pleased, but answered not; for now too nigh
> The archangel stood, and from the other hill
> To their fixed station, all in bright array
> The cherubim descended; on the ground
> Gliding meteorous, as evening mist
> Risen from a river o'er the marish glides,
> And gathers ground fast at the laborer's heel
> Homeward returning. High in front advanced,
> The brandished sword of God before them blazed
> Fierce as a comet; which with torrid heat,
> And vapor as the Lybian air adust,
> Began to parch that temperate clime; whereat
> In either hand the hastening angel caught
> Our lingering parents, and to the eastern gate
> Led them direct, and down the cliff as fast
> To the subjected plaine; then disappeared.
> They looking back, all the eastern side beheld
> Of Paradise, so late their happy seat,
> Wav'd over by that flaming brand, the gate
> With dreadful faces thronged and fiery arms. . . .
> (XII. 624-644)

I quote this passage to illustrate how successfully Milton could insinuate the homely and the realistic into the grandiose, but it will serve also to prompt a final general comment on *Paradise Lost*. It is one of the great passages, and it is typical of the poem generally in uniting so many strands and grades of feeling: the huge, almost monstrous picture of the thronged gate and the miniature picture of the two human beings; the archangel matched by the peasant; the particularity of description of the "eastern gate" set against the symbolic significance of the "subjected plaine." And these many strands are made to cooperate through their common subordination to a unifying though never monotonous type of verse. Such is the general nature of *Paradise Lost*, and it corresponds to the primary wealth and vitality of Milton's own nature, as well as to the mental discipline through which he accepted and held together the good and the ill that life brought him.

*Paradise Lost* is exacting because it is a long, highly concentrated poem, but not so exacting as to be beyond the reach of a wide public. In the eighteenth century it was extremely popular, partly because, along with the Bible and *The Pilgrim's Progress*, it was legitimate Sunday reading for Puritans, but also partly because readers of that time were willing to give steady attention to a few great works. And it could regain such a vogue whenever a wide public cared to give it similar attention; the potential attraction, the perennial human appeal, are there all the time. *Paradise Regained* is a different case; it has always been a poem for the few. But those few have found it, in some strange way, immensely attractive. Why Milton wrote it we do not know. The old idea that it is a sequel to *Paradise Lost* does not work, because the earlier poem had included the recovery of Paradise through Christ in its scope and had taken world history far beyond the period of time to which *Paradise Regained* is confined. What is certain is that *Paradise Regained* deals once again with the dominant Miltonic theme of the prime importance of the state of mind and the dependence of action on that state.

*Paradise Regained* is a narrative version of Christ's temptation by the Devil in the wilderness; and in choosing this episode as the chief one in the gospels, Milton was following an earlier tradition particularly dear to Puritan thought. Puritanism loved to picture the Christian life and the chief events leading up to it as a battle. The Christian was a warrior, clad in the spiritual armor listed by St. Paul; and there had been two principal battles that had decided his fate. First, the Devil had fought with and defeated Adam, the Old Man, in the Garden of Eden; and second, Christ, the New Man, had fought with and defeated the Devil in the wilderness. And the wilderness was necessary for the proper correspondence. As Adam had lost a garden for a wilderness, so must Christ conduct his battle in a wilderness to win back the paradisiac garden. Milton accepted this rather surprising preference of the Temptation to the Crucifixion partly because he liked to work in the tradition of the religious party to which, generally, he belonged and partly because the Temptation was, in his view, the episode that marked the formation of the state of mind that governed all Christ's subsequent action, the acceptance of crucifixion included. Once Christ had acquired that state of mind, he had only to act in accordance with it, and action would take care of itself—or, rather, God in heaven would take care of it. Christ's victory in the wilderness symbolized the general moral truth that the state of mind comes first and results are subordinate.

Milton's heart was therefore thoroughly in his theme, and in his treatment of it he seems to have consulted his own inclination rather than his readers' applause, in a way different from *Paradise Lost*. There are long speeches and few deeds. The poem is more of a debate than a narrative; and it is likely that the Book of Job was Milton's model here. The language is less ornate and more restricted to simple words than that of *Paradise Lost*, and the rhythm more subdued and closer to quiet conversation. This is the cool, quiet, and yet passionately concentrated way in which Milton ends the first book. Satan has just asked, with assumed humility, permission to come and talk with Christ in the wilderness:

> To whom our Saviour with unaltered brow.
> Thy coming hither, though I know thy scope,
> I bid not or forbid; do as thou find'st
> Permission from above; thou canst not more.
>    He added not; and Satan bowing low
> His gray dissimulation, disappeared
> Into thin air diffused: for now began
> Night with her sullen wing to double-shade
> The desert, fowls in their clay nests were couched;
> And now wild beasts came forth the woods to roam.
>                                            (I. 493–502)

It is those already familiar with Milton who will appreciate this kind of writing. For them the leanness of Christ's speech will not indicate starvation or poverty, but the leanness of the perfectly trained athlete whose body is free from every trace of superfluous fat and consists of operant bone and muscle. It will further resemble the athlete's body when in gentle, not violent, motion—gentle, but containing the promise of the fiercest violence, should violence be required. It is also those already familiar with Milton who will appreciate the delicate conversational cadence of many of the speeches. This is Christ speaking of worldly glory:

> But why should man seek glory? who of his own
> Hath nothing, and to whom nothing belongs
> But condemnation, ignominy, and shame?
> Who for so many benefits received
> Turned recreant to God, ingrate and false,
> And so of all true good himself despoiled,
> Yet, sacrilegious, to himself would take
> That which to God alone of right belongs;
> Yet so much bounty is in God, such grace,
> That who advance his glory, not their own,
> Then he himself to glory will advance.
>                                            (III. 134–144)

There is no unusual word here, no simile, scarcely a metaphor. The effect depends on the verse, the rise and fall of emphasis within narrow limits, the occasional flicker of feeling as in the word "sacrilegious," as if the poet were addressing an intimate reader, one who could catch much meaning from mere hints, one who could take so very much for granted.

If the conversations are quiet and delicately cadenced, the landscape is of twilight and suggests less a real scene than a symbol of the working of the mind. But into this dimness Milton projects brilliant visions that, whether by accident or by design, resemble the infernal creations that in medieval romance tempted Sir Galahad in his quest for the Holy Grail. Here is the description of the phantoms that attended the banquet Satan raised in the wilderness.

> And at a stately sideboard by the wine
> That fragrant smell diffused, in order stood
> Tall stripling youths rich-clad, of fairer hue
> Then Ganymede or Hylas; distant more
> Under the trees now tripped, now solemn stood
> Nymphs of Diana's train, and Naiades
> With fruits and flowers from Amalthea's horn,
> And ladies of the Hesperides, that seemed
> Fairer then feigned of old, or fabled since
> Of fairy damsels met in forest wide
> By Knights of Logres, or of Lyonesse,
> Lancelot or Pelleas, or Pellenore,
> And all the while harmonious airs were heard
> Of chiming strings, or charming pipes and winds
> Of gentlest gale Arabian odors fanned
> From their soft wings, and Flora's earliest smells.
>                                            (II. 350–365)

*Paradise Regained* is unusually compounded of twilight, trancelike descriptions, conversations remote from the marketplace or senate house or inn, yet delicately suggesting the cadences of real talk, and brilliant visions. It is a varied and startling composition, but it is strange too; and it is not surprising that in general readers have not been able to take *Paradise Regained* to their hearts.

The case is very different with the other poem published along with *Paradise Regained* in 1671, *Samson Agonistes*. Milton's Samson, blind and in Philistine captivity, is, like Chaucer's Wife of Bath or Shakespeare's Macbeth or Dickens' Mrs. Gamp, one of those figures that helps to compose what can be called a nation's literary mythology. Anthony

# JOHN MILTON

Trollope, in *The Last Chronicle of Barset*, makes Mr. Crawley, himself a tragic figure, talk of Milton's Samson as if he were an accepted national inheritance, the common property of all intelligent readers. Mr. Crawley has been making his daughter read about the blinded Polyphemus in the *Odyssey*, and he stops her and comments:

The same story is always coming up; we have it in various versions, because it is so true to life.

> Ask for this great deliverer now, and find him
> Eyeless in Gaza, at the mill with slaves.

It is the same story. Great power reduced to impotence, great glory to misery, by the hand of Fate. At the mill with slaves! Can any picture be more dreadful than that? The mind of the strong blind creature must be so sensible of the injury that has been done to him! The impotency, combined with his strength, or rather the impotency with the memory of former strength and former aspirations, is so essentially tragic.

Aldous Huxley chose *Eyeless in Gaza* for the title of one of his novels. And T. S. Eliot assumed a response he could not assume if he had referred to *Paradise Regained* when he wove references to "*Samson Agonistes* into the texture of "East Coker":

> O dark dark dark. They all go into the dark,
> The vacant interstellar spaces, the vacant into the
>     vacant . . . .

Trollope's Mr. Crawley was right. Milton's Samson is a terrible yet compelling figure of human suffering, reminding one of Sophocles' Philoctetes, Shakespeare's Lear, and one or two of Hopkins' most poignant sonnets. Milton is surely thinking of the physical pangs of Philoctetes when he makes his Samson burst into this lyrical complaint:

> O that torment should not be confined
> To the body's wounds and sores
> With maladies innumerable
> In heart, head, breast, and reins;
> But must secret passage find
> To the inmost mind,
> There exercise all his fierce accidents,
> And on her purest spirits prey,
> As on entrails, joints, and limbs,
> With answerable pains, but more intense,
> Though void of corporal sense.
>     My griefs not only pain me
> As a lingering disease,
> But finding no redress, ferment and rage,
> Nor less then wounds immedicable
> Rankle, and fester, and gangrene,
> To black mortification.
> Thoughts my tormentors armed with deadly stings
> Mangle my apprehensive tenderest parts,
> Exasperate, exulcerate, and raise
> Dire inflammation which no cooling herb
> Or med'cinal liquor can assuage,
> Nor breath of vernal air from snowy alp.
> Sleep hath forsook and given me o'er
> To death's benumbing opium as my only cure.
> Thence faintings, swoonings of despair,
> And sense of heaven's desertion.
>                                         (606–632)

But if Samson the sufferer is part of English literary mythology, what of the whole play? Here the answer is in some doubt. Milton cannot have written the play to be acted; Samuel Johnson accused it of defective action, and a general notion has prevailed that as a whole it is insufficiently dramatic. And yet *Samson Agonistes* has been played in amateur performances with great success. The general notion and the specific event do not concur. The truth is that Samson is indeed dramatic, but in a way unusual in English drama. There is little action on the stage, the most important being reported. But there is sufficient action in Samson's mind. Even so, that action is unusual. Motives on the stage are usually more obvious than they would be in life. However, mental action in Samson does not consist in obvious changes and transitions, but in the spread of an unconscious temper into consciousness. At the beginning of the play Samson is in the same case as Adam is in book X of *Paradise Lost*, when he is in despair and thinks God has quite cast him off. Actually, both Adam and Samson have accepted complete responsibility for what they have done, and thereby have touched the humility that means salvation. *Samson Agonistes* reveals the mind of its protagonist in its various stages of testing, awakening, comprehension, and finds its end in the death of a forgiven and redeemed hero. As a psychological drama it is a wonderful and satisfying piece of work. And now that the technique of choric speech has been improved (mainly through productions of T. S. Eliot's verse drama), there is no reason why *Samson Agonistes* should not take its place as one of the great acted English classics.

I have written of *Samson Agonistes* after *Paradise Regained* as if the facts of simultaneous publication and the sequence within that publication indicated the same order of composition. But, as already stated, there is no certain proof of when *Samson* was written. Nevertheless, it does supplement *Paradise Regained* very remarkably; and even if Milton wrote *Samson* earlier, he may have recast it for publication. In any case, if he chose to publish the two poems together, we are safer in considering them together than in plumping for earlier dates of composition for which there is no scrap of firm evidence. Like *Paradise Regained*, *Samson Agonistes* deals with the regions of reflection and action. Christ rejected all temptations to achieve quick results. He knew his own powers and wondered whether he should lead Israel to revolt against Rome. But he knew too that such was not his true fate. And he waited until, in the fullness of time, he achieved a state of mind that insured that all his actions would be soundly based. Samson, on the other hand, chose a life of physical action; and up to a point he was right, because he had been gifted with unusual strength. But success corrupted him and made him overvalue his gift. Through this pride he fell into misfortune, but he recognized his error and fell into the extremes of despair and humility:

> O impotence of mind, in body strong!
> But what is strength without a double share
> Of wisdom, vast, unwieldy, burdensome,
> Proudly secure, yet liable to fall
> By weakest subtleties, not made to rule,
> But to subserve where wisdom bears command.
> (52–57)

Once Samson has realized that the state of mind comes first, once his own state of mind is sound, God allows him yet again to put his gift of unusual physical strength into action. The idea of the two poems is the same; but in the first the climax is the achievement of a state of mind implying perfect actions to come, while in the second it is a piece of action based on a sound state of mind already achieved.

I think that *Paradise Lost* is worth more than all the rest of Milton's works put together, but fewer readers than in former times have the patience to master a long poem. The almost superstitious reverence for the successful epic has disappeared. It may be that for some years to come the early poems, fragments of *Paradise Lost*, *Samson Agonistes*, and perhaps *Areopagitica* will be the operant portions of his works. It is to be regretted if this should be so; but even if thus truncated, Milton survives as a major poet of surpassing power and variety.

SELECTED BIBLIOGRAPHY

I. Bibliography. J. Bradshaw, ed., *A Concordance to the Poetical Works of John Milton* (London, 1894; repr. 1965); W. A. Wright, pub., *Facsimile of the Manuscript of Milton's Minor Poems Preserved in the Library of Trinity College, Cambridge* (Cambridge, 1899), partly reproduced by F. A. Patterson (New York, 1933; Menton, 1970); L. E. Lockwood, *Lexicon to the English Poetical Works of John Milton* (New York, 1907); *Milton, 1608–1674: Facsimile of the Autographs and Documents in the British Museum* (London, 1908); E. N. S. Thompson, *John Milton: A Topical Bibliography* (New Haven, 1916); A. H. Gilbert, *A Geographical Dictionary of Milton* (New Haven, 1919); L. Cooper, ed., *A Concordance of the Latin, Greek and Italian Poems of John Milton* (Halle, 1923); J. H. Hanford, *A Milton Handbook* (New York, 1926; 5th rev. ed., 1970); D. H. Stevens, *Reference Guide to Milton from 1800 to the Present Day* (Chicago, 1930); H. F. Fletcher, ed., *Contributions to a Milton Bibliography, 1800–1930: Being a List of Addenda to Stevens's Reference Guide* (Urbana, Ill., 1931); V. de S. Pinto, *The English Renaissance 1510–1688* (London, 1938; 3rd rev. ed., 1966), contains a bibliography; C. Huckabay, *John Milton: A Bibliographical Supplement, 1929–1957* (Pittsburgh—Louvain, 1960), also in rev. ed., *John Milton: An Annotated Bibliography, 1929–1968* (1969); E. S. Le Comte, *A Milton Dictionary* (New York, 1960; English ed., 1961); William Ingram and Kathleen Swain, eds., *A Concordance to Milton's English Poetry* (Oxford, 1972).

II. Collected Works. J. Tolland, ed., *A Complete Collection of the Historical, Political, and Miscellaneous Works of Milton*, 3 vols. (London, 1694–1698); P[atrick] H[ume], ed., *Poetical Works, Together with Explanatory Notes on Each Book of the Paradise Lost, and a Table Never Before Printed*, 5 pts. (London, 1695), the first collected ed. of the poetry; H. J. Todd, ed., *Poetical Works. With the Principal Notes of Various Commentators*, 6 vols. (London, 1801; 7 vols., 1809, with additions and a verbal index), a variorum ed. using the work of some of the best-known eighteenth-century editors of Milton, including R. Bentley, T. Newton, and Thomas Warton, and critical appreciations of Milton by Andrew Marvell, John Dryden, Joseph Addison, James Thomson, Samuel Johnson, Thomas Gray, William Cowper, and others; W. Hayley, ed., *Cowper's Milton, with Notes by William Cowper*, 4 vols. (Chichester, 1810); J. A. St. John, ed., *Prose Works*, 5 vols. (London, 1848–1853); J. Mitford, ed., *Works, in Verse and Prose*, 8 vols. (London, 1851), complete except for "Of Christian Doctrine" and minor items; R. C. Browne, ed., *English Poems* (London, 1866), also with notes by H. Bradley (London, 1894); D. Masson, ed., *Poetical Works*, 3 vols. (London, 1874; rev. ed., 1890), the Globe one-volume ed. has an intro. by Masson (London, 1877); A. W. Verity, ed., *The Cambridge Milton for Schools*, 11 vols. (London, 1891–1899); H. C. Beeching, ed., *The Poetical Works of John Milton* (Oxford, 1900; rev. ed., 1938); W. Aldis Wright, ed., *Poetical Works* (London, 1903); H. J. C. Grierson, ed., *The Poems of John Milton, Arranged in Chronological Order*, 2 vols. (London, 1925); M. W. Wallace, ed., *Milton's Prose*, (London—New York, 1925); F. A. Patterson, ed., *The Student's Milton* (New York, 1930), contains the complete poetry and most of the prose, plus early biographies of Milton—the revised edition (1933) contains annotations to the poetry and prose; F. A. Patterson, gen. ed., *Works*, 18 vols. (New York, 1931–1938), issued by Columbia University, is the only complete edition of Milton's works, the last vol. contains previously uncollected writings and marginalia, and there is a two-vol. index, F. A. Patterson and F. R. Fogle, eds. (New York, 1940), that forms an invaluable work of reference; *Private Correspondence and Academic Exercises*, P. B. Tillyard, trans. (Cambridge, 1932), with intro. and commentary by E. M. W. Tillyard; J. H. Hanford., ed., *The Poems of John Milton* (New York, 1936); E. H. Visiak, ed., *Complete Poetry and Selected Prose* (London, 1938); H. F. Fletcher, ed., *Complete Poetical Works* (Boston, 1941), a new text ed., with intro. and notes, of the Cambridge ed., W. V. Moody, ed.; H. F. Fletcher, ed., *Complete Poetical Works*, 4 vols. (Urbana, Ill., 1943–1948), reproduced in photographic facs.: M. Y. Hughes, *John Milton, Complete Poems and Major Prose* (New York, 1957), with notes by Hughes; K. M. Burton, ed., *Milton's Prose Writings* (London—New York, 1958); Helen Darbishire, ed., *Poetical Works* (London, 1958), in the Oxford Standard Authors ed.; J. T. Shawcross, ed., *The Complete English Poetry of John Milton* (London, 1963); D. M. Wolfe et al., eds., *The Complete Prose Works*, 5 vols. (New Haven, 1953–1970); D. Bush, ed., *Complete Poetical Works* (Boston, 1965; English ed., 1966); J. Carey and A. Fowler, eds., *The Poems of John Milton* (London, 1968).

III. SELECTED WORKS. *Poems of Mr. John Milton. Both English and Latin. . . . Printed . . . for H. Moseley* (London, 1645; facs. repr. of English poems, 1968), the minor poems: "On the Morning of Christ's Nativity," "L'Allegro," "Il Penseroso," sonnets, and others; *Poems, Etc. upon Several Occasions. By Mr. John Milton: . . . With a Small Tractate of Education to Mr. Hartlib* (London, 1673); W. Hayley, ed., *Latin and Italian Poems of Milton*, William Cowper, trans. (Chichester, 1808), also W. MacKellar, ed., *Latin Poems*, MacKellar, trans. (New Haven, 1930); O. Elton, ed., *Minor Poems*, 5 vols. (Oxford, 1893–1900); J. S. Smart, ed., *Sonnets* (Glasgow, 1921; repr. 1966), with original notes and new biographical matter; M. Y. Hughes, ed., *Paradise Regained, the Minor Poems and Samson Agonistes* (New York, 1937); D. Bush, ed., *The Portable Milton* (New York, 1949), with intro. by Bush; *Poems of Mr John Milton* (New York, 1951; reiss. London, 1957), the 1645 ed., with analytical essays by Cleanth Brooks and J. E. Hardy; N. Frye, ed., *John Milton: Paradise Lost and Selected Poems* (London–New York, 1951); E. Le Comte, ed., *"Paradise Lost" and Other Poems* (New York, 1961); M. Y. Hughes, ed., *Paradise Lost* (New York, 1962); I. G. MacCaffrey, ed., *John Milton: Samson Agonistes and the Shorter Poems* (New York–London, 1966); C. Ricks, ed., *John Milton: Paradise Lost and Paradise Regained* (New York–London, 1968).

IV. SEPARATE WORKS. "An Epitaph on the Admirable Dramaticke Poet, W. Shakespeare," first published in the Second Folio of Shakespeare's *Plays* (London, 1632); "A Maske Presented at Ludlow Castle, 1634. . . . " (London, 1637), the title *Comus* was first used in the stage version of 1738; "Lycidas," in *Obsequies to the Memory of Mr. Edward King* (London, 1638), a collection of memorial verses in Latin, Greek, and English; *Epitaphium Damonis* (London, ca. 1640), unique copy in British Museum; *Of Reformation Touching Church-Discipline in England: . . .* (London, 1641); *Of Prelatical Episcopacy . . .* (London, 1641); *Animadversions upon the Remonstrants Defence Against Smectymnuus* (London, 1641); *The Reason of Church-Government Urg'd Against Prelaty* (London, 1641); *An Apology Against a Pamphlet Call'd A Modest Confutation of the Animadversions upon the Remonstrant Against Smectymnuus* (London, 1642); *The Doctrine and Discipline of Divorce . . .* (London, 1643; 2nd ed., rev. and enl., 1644); *Of Education. To Master Samuel Hartlib* (London, ca. 1644); *The Judgement of Martin Bucer . . .* (London, 1644); *Areopagitica . . .* (London, 1644); *Colasterion: A Reply to a Nameles Answer Against the Doctrine and Discipline of Divorce* (London, 1645); *Tetrachordon: Expositions upon the Foure Chief Places in Scripture Which Treat of Mariage, or Nullities in Mariage* (London, 1645); "Sonnet to Henry Lawes," in Henry and William Lawes, *Choice Psalmes, Put into Musick for Three Voices* (London, 1648); ΕΙΚΟΝΟΚΛΑΣΤΗΣ: In Answer to a Book Intitl'd Εἰκὼν Βασιλικὴ, the Portrature of His Sacred Majesty in His Solitudes and Sufferings (London, 1649; 2nd ed., enl., 1650); *Observations upon the Articles of Peace with the Irish Rebels . . .* (London, 1649); *The Tenure of Kings and Magistrates* (London, 1649); *Pro Populo anglicano defensio . . .* (London, 1651), translated by J. Washington (London, 1692); *A Letter Written to a Gentleman in the Country, Touching the Dissolution of the Late Parliament and the Reasons Thereof* (London, 1653); *Pro populo anglicano defensio secunda* (London, 1654), translated by F. Wrangham (London, 1816); *Joannis Miltonii pro se defensio . . .* (London, 1655); *Considerations Touching the Likeliest Means to Remove Hirelings out of the Church* (London, 1659); *A Treatise of Civil Power in Ecclesiastical Causes . . .* (London, 1659); *Brief Notes upon a Late Sermon, Titl'd, The Fear of God and the King . . .* (London, 1660); *The Readie & Easie Way to Establish a Free Commonwealth . . .* (London, 1660); *Paradise Lost* (London, 1667; 2nd ed., 12 bks., rev. and enl., 1674), facs. of 1st ed. with intro. by D. Masson (London, 1877), also in A. Fowler, ed. (London, 1971), MS of bk. I edited by H. Darbishire (Oxford, 1931); *The History of Britain . . .* (London, 1670); *Paradise Regained* (London, 1671), to which is added "Samson Agonistes"; *Of True Religion, Haeresie, Schism, Toleration, and What Best Means May Be Us'd Against the Growth of Popery* (London, 1673); *Mr. John Milton's Character of the Long Parliament and Assembly of Divines . . .* (London, 1681), originally part of bk. III of *The History of Britain*; *A Brief History of Moscovia . . .* (London, 1682); *Letters of State, Written by Mr. John Milton . . . from the Year 1649 till 1659 . . .* (London, 1694), includes a biography by E. Phillips, several poems, and a catalog of the works; C. R. Sumner, ed., *De doctrina christiana* (Cambridge, 1825), also translated by Sumner (Cambridge, 1825).

V. SOME BIOGRAPHICAL AND CRITICAL STUDIES. Early biographies of Milton by John Aubrey, Anthony Wood, Edward Phillips, John Toland, Jonathan Richardson, and Thomas Ellwood are collected in *The Student's Milton* (1930). See also Helen Darbishire, *Early Lives of Milton* (London, 1932).

Works of the seventeenth and eighteenth centuries are Andrew Marvell, "On Paradise Lost," a poem in praise of Milton prefixed to the 1674 ed. of *Paradise Lost*; John Dryden, "Apology for Heroic Poetry" (1677), in W. P. Ker, ed., *Essays* (Oxford, 1900); Joseph Addison, papers on *Paradise Lost*, in *Spectator* from 31 December 1711 to 3 May 1712 (no. 267, and on Saturdays until no. 369), twelve papers discuss the beauties of each of the twelve books, and six discuss *Paradise Lost* as a whole; Jonathan Richardson, *Explanatory Notes and Remarks on Milton's Paradise Lost* (London, 1734); J. Warton, *An Essay on the Genius and Writings of Pope* (London, 1756), an interesting estimate of Milton in relation to Pope; Samuel Johnson, "Life of Milton," in his *Lives of the Poets* (London, 1779).

Nineteenth-century writings include W. S. Landor, *Imaginary Conversations* (London, 1824–1829), contains two "conversations" between Milton and Marvell, which were edited by C. G. Crump (London, 1891); S. T. Coleridge, *Literary Remains*, H. N. Coleridge, ed. (London, 1836–1839), contains a lecture on Milton delivered in 1818, also see Coleridge's comparison of Milton and Shakespeare in his *Biographia literaria* (London, 1817), ch. XV; D. Masson, *The Life of John Milton*, 7 vols. (London, 1858–1881; with index, 1894); T. B. Macaulay, *Critical and Historical Essays, Contributed to the Edinburgh Review*, 3 vols. (London, 1843), contains the famous essay on Milton published in August 1825, also see his *Miscellaneous Writings* (London, 1860); M. Arnold, *Mixed Essays* (London, 1879), see also his *Essays in Criticism, Second Series* (London, 1888); W. Bagehot, *Literary Studies*, R. H. Hutton, ed. (London, 1879), contains a study of Milton; M. Pattison, *Milton* (London, 1879), in the English Men of Letters series; R. Garnett, *Life of John Milton* (London, 1890); R. Bridges, *Milton's Prosody* (Oxford, 1893; rev. ed., 1901), a revised version of two essays (1887 and 1889), also another ed. with a chapter on accentual verse, and notes (1921).

During the first three decades of the twentieth century appeared Sir W. A. Raleigh, *Milton* (London 1900); C. G. Osgood, *The Classical Mythology of Milton's English Poems*, Yale Studies in English no. 8 (New Haven, 1900; repr. Oxford, 1925); Lascelles Abercrombie, *The Epic* (London, 1914), contains important criticism of Milton's epics; R. D. Havens, *The Influence of Milton on English Poetry* (Cambridge, Mass., 1922); Denis Saurat, *Milton: Man and Thinker* (New York, 1925), a translation and adaptation of essays earlier published in French that contains a bibliography of criticism of Milton; J. H. Hanford, *A Milton Handbook* (New York, 1926; 5th rev. ed., 1970), see also Hanford's *The Youth of Milton*, in the series University of Michigan Studies of Shakespeare, Milton, and Donne (New York, 1925); H. J. C. Grierson, *Cross Currents in English Literature of the XVIIth Century* (London, 1929), the Messenger lectures, delivered at Cornell University, 1926–1927.

Works of the 1930's are E. E. Stoll, *Poets and Playwrights: Shakespeare, Jonson, Spenser, Milton* (Minneapolis, 1930); E. M. W. Tillyard, *Milton* (London, 1930; rev. ed., 1966), a full treatment of Milton's literary and mental development; T. S. Eliot, *Selected Essays, 1917–1932* (London, 1932), contains observations on Milton that were later amplified in the British Academy's "Annual Lecture on a Master Mind" (1947); Rose Macaulay, *Milton* (London, 1934; rev. ed., 1957); B. Willey, *The Seventeenth Century Background: Studies in the Thought of the Age in Relation to Poetry and Religion* (London, 1934); F. R. Leavis, *Revaluation* (London, 1936), contains an important essay on Milton, see also his *The Common Pursuit* (London, 1952); H. J. C. Grierson, *Milton and Wordsworth, Poets and Prophets: A Study of*

*Their Reactions to Political Events* (Cambridge, 1937); J. H. Finley, *Milton and Horace: A Study of Milton's Sonnets*, Harvard Studies in Classical Philology, XLVIII (1937); E. M. W. Tillyard, *The Miltonic Setting, Past and Present* (Cambridge, 1938), a study of Milton's seventeenth-century setting and his present poetic status; J. S. Diekhoff, ed., *Milton on Himself* (London, 1939; new ed., 1965).

During the 1940's there appeared W. R. Parker, *Milton's Contemporary Reputation* (Columbus, Ohio, 1940); G. McColley, *Paradise Lost: An Account of Its Growth and Major Origins* (Chicago, 1940); M. Kelley, *This Great Argument: A Study of Milton's De doctrina christiana as a Gloss upon Paradise Lost* (Princeton, 1941); D. Wolfe, *Milton in the Puritan Revolution* (New York, 1941), a study of the political significance of Milton's work; A. E. Barker, *Milton and the Puritan Dilemma, 1641-1660* (Toronto, 1942; repr. 1956); C. S. Lewis, *A Preface to Paradise Lost* (London, 1942), a study of the Christian background of the poem; C. M. Bowra, *From Virgil to Milton* (London, 1945; New York, 1946); D. Bush, *Paradise Lost in Our Time: Some Comments* (Ithaca, N. Y., 1945), a defense of Milton against his modern detractors; C. R. Buxton, *Prophets of Heaven and Hell: Virgil, Dante, Milton, Goethe: An Introductory Essay* (Cambridge, 1945); J. S. Diekhoff, *Milton's Paradise Lost: A Commentary on the Argument* (New York, 1946); B. Rajan, *Paradise Lost and the Seventeenth Century Reader* (London, 1947); I. Samuel, *Plato and Milton* (Ithaca, N.Y., 1947); A. J. A. Waldock, *Paradise Lost and Its Critics* (Cambridge, 1947), an able and coolly provocative statement of doubt whether the poem is a consistent whole; R. Warner, *John Milton* (London, 1949); J. M. French, ed., *The Life Records of John Milton*, 4 vols. (New Brunswick, N.J., 1949-1958); J. H. Hanford, *John Milton, Englishman* (New York, 1949; London, 1950).

Works of the 1950's include: M. M. Mahood, *Poetry and Humanism* (London, 1950); J. Thorpe, ed., *Milton Criticism: Selections from Four Centuries* (New York, 1950; London, 1951); B. Rajan, *The Lofty Rhyme: A Study of Milton's Major Poetry* (London – Coral Gables, Fla., 1970); E. M. W. Tillyard, *Studies in Milton* (London, 1951), aims largely at supplementing and correcting some matters in Tillyard's *Milton*, while a study on the crisis of *Paradise Lost* corrects a common assumption and advances a general interpretation of books IX and X; S. E. Sprott, *Milton's Art of Prosody* (Oxford, 1953); A. Stein, *Answerable Style: Essays on Paradise Lost* (Minneapolis-London, 1953); D. C. Allen, *The Harmonious Vision: Studies in Milton's Poetry* (Baltimore-London, 1954; enl. ed., 1970); J. Arthos, *On a Mask Presented at Ludlow Castle* (Ann Arbor, Mich., 1954); F. T. Prince, *The Italian Element in Milton's Verse* (Oxford, 1954), an original study, embodying new discoveries; R. M. Adams, *Ikon: Milton and the Modern Critics* (Ithaca, N.Y.-London, 1955); A. E. Dyson, "The Interpretation of Comus," in *Essays and Studies*, 21 (London, 1955); W. Haller, *Liberty and Reformation in the Puritan Revolution* (New York-London, 1955); K. Muir, *John Milton* (London-New York, 1955; rev., 1960); W. B. Watkins, *An Anatomy of Milton's Verse* (Baton Rouge, La., 1955); L. A. Cormican, *Milton's Religious Verse*, in B. Ford, ed., *From Donne to Marvell* (New York-Harmondsworth, England, 1956); H. F. Fletcher, *The Intellectual Development of John Milton*, 2 vols. (Urbana, Ill., 1956-1961); E. M. W. Tillyard, *The Methaphysicals and Milton* (London, 1956); D. Daiches, *Milton* (London-New York, 1957); J. F. Kermode, *Romantic Image* (London, 1957); R. Tuve, *Images and Themes in Five Poems by Milton* (Cambridge, Mass., 1957); A. Stein, *Heroic Knowledge: An Interpretation of Paradise Regained and Samson Agonistes* (Minneapolis-London, 1957); I. MacCaffrey, *Paradise Lost as Myth* (Cambridge, Mass.-London, 1959).

During the 1960's there appeared J. B. Broadbent, *Some Graver Subject: An Essay on Paradise Lost* (London, 1960), a penetrating analysis of the way *Paradise Lost* evolves; J. F. Kermode, ed., *The Living Milton: Essays by Various Hands* (London, 1960), an honest and erudite attempt to define what is left of *Paradise Lost* when its many defects are taken into account; W. Empson, *Milton's God* (London, 1961; rev. ed., with new appendix, 1965); J. B. Broadbent, *Milton, Comus and Samson Agonistes* (London, 1961); E. S. Le Comte, *A Milton Dictionary* (New York, 1961); J. Hollander, *The Untuning of the Sky: Ideas of Music in English Poetry, 1500-1700* (Princeton, N.J., 1961); G. Williamson, *Seventeenth Century Contexts* (Chicago-London, 1961); G. A. Wilkes, *The Thesis of Paradise Lost* (Melbourne, 1961); D. Bush, *English Literature in the Earlier Seventeenth Century, 1600-1660* (vol. 5 of *The Oxford History of English Literature*, New York-Oxford, 1962); J. H. Summers, *The Muse's Method; An Introduction to Paradise Lost* (London, 1962); J. H. Sims, *The Bible in Milton's Epics* (Gainesville, Fla., 1962); B. A. Wright, *Milton's Paradise Lost* (London, 1962); D. A. Ferry, *Milton's Epic Voice: The Narrator in Paradise Lost* (Cambridge, Mass., 1963); J. Arthos, *Dante, Michelangelo and Milton* (London, 1963); C. Ricks, *Milton's Grand Style* (Oxford, 1963); R. Daniells, *Milton, Mannerism and Baroque* (Toronto, 1963); M. H. Nicolson, *John Milton: A Reader's Guide to His Poetry* (New York, 1963); J. Blondel, *Le Comus de John Milton: Masque Neptunien* (New York-London, 1964); D. Bush, *John Milton: A Sketch of His Life and Writings* (New York, 1964); R. D. Emma, *Milton & Grammar* (The Hague, 1964); P. Hagin, *The Epic Hero and the Decline of Epic Poetry* (Berne, 1964); A. E. Barker, ed., *Milton: Modern Essays in Criticism* (New York-London, 1965); M. Y. Hughes, ed., *Ten Perspectives on Milton* (New Haven, 1965); J. Thorpe, ed., *Milton Criticism: Selections from Four Centuries* (London, 1965); N. Frye, *The Return of Eden: Five Essays on Milton's Epics* (Toronto-London, 1965); I. Williamson, *Milton and Others* (Chicago-London, 1965); J. H. Summers, ed., *The Lyric and Dramatic Milton* (New York-London, 1965); H. Gardner, *A Reading of Paradise Lost* (Oxford, 1966), the Alexander lectures, delivered at the University of Toronto, 1962; L. L. Marle, ed., *Milton: A Collection of Critical Essays* (Englewood Cliffs, N.J., 1966); B. K. Lewalski, *Milton's Brief Epic: The Genre, Meaning and Art of Paradise Regained* (Providence, R.I.-London, 1966); A. Rudrum, *Milton: Paradise Lost* (London, 1966); K. W. Gransden, *Paradise Lost and the Aeneid*, in *Essays in Criticism*, 17 (1967); P. Murray, *Milton: The Modern Phase. A Study of Twentieth-Century Criticism* (London, 1967), C. A. Patrides, *Milton and the Christian Tradition* (Oxford, 1967); C. A. Patrides, ed., *Milton's Epic Poetry: Essays on Paradise Lost and Paradise Regained* (Harmondsworth, 1967), contains a useful bibliography; A. Rudrum, *Comus, and Shorter Poems* (London, 1967); I. Samuel, *Dante and Milton: The Commedia and Paradise Lost* (London, 1967); J. M. Steadman, *Milton and the Renaissance Hero* (London, 1967); S. E. Fish, *Surprised by Sin: The Reader in Paradise Lost* (London-New York, 1967); J. Arthos, *Milton and the Italian Cities* (London, 1968); J. G. Demaray, *Milton and the Masque Tradition . . .* (Cambridge, Mass.-London, 1968); W. G. Madsen, *From Shadowy Types to Truth: Studies in Milton's Symbolism* (New Haven-London, 1968); H. Reesing, *Milton's Poetic Art: A Mask, Lycidas and Paradise Lost* (Cambridge, Mass.-London, 1968); A. Rudrum, *Milton, Modern Judgments* (London, 1968); E. L. Marilla, *Milton and Modern Man* (University, Ala., 1968); C. A. Patrides, ed., *Approaches to Paradise Lost* (London, 1968); John Carey, *Milton* (London, 1969); *Critical Essays from E. L. H.* (Baltimore, 1969), reprints articles from *Journal of English Literary History*; J. B. Leishman, *Milton's Minor Poems*, G. Tillotson, ed. (London, 1969); B. Rajan, ed., *Paradise Lost: A Tercentenary Tribute* (Toronto-Buffalo-London, 1969); J. D. Simmonds, *Milton Studies*, vol. I (Pittsburgh, 1969), vol. II (Pittsburgh, 1970); C. V. Wedgwood, *Milton and His World* (London, 1969).

Works of the 1970's include J. Halkett, *Milton and the Idea of Matrimony* (New Haven, 1970); J. H. Hanford, *A Milton Handbook*, 5th ed. rev. by J. H. Hanford and J. G. Taaffe (New York, 1970); J. T. Shawcross, ed., *Milton: The Critical Heritage* (London, 1970); *A Variorum Commentary on the Poems of John Milton* (London, 1970- ), vol. I: "The Latin and Greek Poems" by E. Bush, and "The Italian Poems" by J. E. Shaw and A. Bartlett Giamatti; L. Ryken, *The Apocalyptic Vision in Paradise Lost* (Ithaca, N.Y.-London, 1970); H. Blamires, *Milton's Creation: A Guide Through Paradise Lost* (London, 1971); J. P. Hardy, *Reinterpretations: Essays on Poems by Milton, Pope and Johnson* (London, 1971); L. Potter, *A Preface to Milton* (London, 1971); J. A. Wittreich, ed., *The Romantics on Milton* (Cleveland, 1971); B. R. Rees, *Aristotle's Theory and Milton's Practice: Samson Agonistes* (Birmingham, 1972); L. Brisman, *Milton's Poetry of Choice and His Romantic Heirs* (Ithaca, N.Y., 1973); C. Grose, *Milton's Epic Process: Paradise Lost and Its Miltonic Background* (New Haven, 1973); G. Bouchard, *Milton: A Structural Reading* (London, 1974); J. D. Simmons, ed., *Milton Studies* (London-Pittsburgh, 1975); G. M. Crump, *The Mystical Design of Paradise Lost* (Lewisburg, Pa., 1975); J. H. Steadman, *Epic and Tragic Structure in Paradise Lost* (London-Chicago, 1977); A. Stein, *The Art of Presence: The Poet and Paradise Lost* (London-Berkeley, 1977).

VI. MISCELLANEOUS. *Milton's Illustrators*: William Blake made 53 illustrations for Milton's poetry, including 2 sets of watercolor drawings for *Comus* (1801), 12 watercolor drawings for *Paradise Lost* (1807) and a second set of 9 drawings (1808), 6 watercolor drawings for the "Nativity Ode" (1809), 12 designs illustrating "L'Allegro" and "Il Penseroso" (*ca.* 1816), and 12 watercolor drawings for *Paradise Regained* (*ca.* 1816). See Geoffrey Keynes, ed., *John Milton, Poems in English with Illustrations by William Blake* (London, 1926). Other major illustrators of Milton were Jean-Henri Füssli (1802) and John Martin (1824-1826).

*Milton's Poetry Set to Music*: Henry Lawes composed the music for *Comus* in 1634. Milton's "Sonnet to Henry Lawes" was set to music by Henry and William Lawes and appeared in their *Choice Psalmes, Put into Musick for Three Voices* (London, 1648). In 1677 Dryden wrote a rhymed opera, *The State of Innocence*, based on *Paradise Lost*.

*Portraits of Milton*: G. C. Williamson, *Milton Tercentenary: The Portraits, Prints and Writings of John Milton, Exhibited at Christ's College, Cambridge, 1908* (Cambridge, 1908); R. S. Granniss, *The Beverley Chew Collection of Milton Portraits* (New York, 1926).

# GEORGE ORWELL
(1903-1950)

## Tom Hopkinson

### I

GEORGE ORWELL's reputation as a writer rests largely on his novels, but his gifts are not those of a novelist, and, if the novel had not happened to be the prevailing literary form during the twenty years when he was writing, he would probably never have been attracted to it. Orwell had little imagination, little understanding of human relationships; his sympathy was with humanity in general rather than with individual human beings. His gifts were an inspired common sense and a power of steady thought; a wary refusal to be taken in by attitudes and catchwords; the courage of the lonely man who is not afraid of being lonely and has learned, in his loneliness, to regard himself with some detachment. These, however, would have made Orwell no more than an unusual citizen in the tradition of English individuality, a tradition which, happily, still survives despite the pressure exerted by both the main political parties—a pressure toward convention and conformity from the Right, and pressure toward leveling and uniformity from the Left. Orwell's distinction is that these gifts in his case were supported by a talent for writing nervous, flexible, and lucid prose: so deeply indeed was writing a part of Orwell's nature that qualities are manifest in his work which did not reveal themselves in his life.

Orwell, for example, was a good talker in a somewhat didactic manner, but no one, I think, would have called him witty. His writings, however, particularly his essays, are full of wit, and his masterpiece, *Animal Farm* (1945), is a river, or at least a sparkling brook, of witty observation and lively, vigorous expression.

These gifts of Orwell's implied—as gifts do—their certain defects. His common sense could degenerate into pawkiness. His habit of lucid thought led him at times to brush the other person's, or the other side's, arguments out of his way, disposing of opposition not by reasoning but with a kind of comprehensive sideswipe: "In spite of his [Swift's] enormously greater powers, his implied position is very similar to that of innumerable silly-clever Conservatives of our own day—people like Sir Alan Herbert, Professor G. M. Young, Lord Elton, the Tory Reform Committee, or the long line of Catholic apologists from W. H. Mallock onwards...."[1] His wariness sometimes became suspicion—as when he fancied a leading London publisher was persecuting him by trying to prevent *Animal Farm* from being published. And his lonely courage involved a concentration on himself that had two unsatisfactory results.

First, all his novels are alike. They are all tales of solitary characters, each in one way or another an expression of Orwell himself, seen against backgrounds that are taken from his own experience. These solitary characters seek to make contact with others but are usually rebuffed, slighted, or betrayed. The backgrounds are vividly drawn, often with a painful grittiness which implies that the author is doing his utmost to be fair about what was really an intolerable situation. But the essence of the novels is that they are unforgiving, and the author's own anger conveys a sense of discomfort to the reader, who feels he is being nagged at for something which is only very indirectly his fault and resents that an author of such uncommon talents should care so little whether he conveys enjoyment to his readers.

Second, Orwell's concentration on himself leads him to see the outside world as an enlarged projection of his own personal problems. He was, from childhood—indeed from infancy—hampered by lack of money, and he came to see the world as a succession of money rackets. He was by birth and up-

---

[1] From "Politics vs. Literature: An Examination of *Gulliver's Travels*," in *Shooting an Elephant, and Other Essays* (London, 1950).

bringing—or, rather, through an upbringing strangely ill-suited to his birth—acutely sensitive to class distinctions, and he supposed everyone else to be as painfully affected by them as he was himself. Because they had conditioned his own life, he regarded them not as temporary phenomena doomed to disappearance, but as part of the basic order of human existence, at least in the British Isles.

Moreover, in his work he tends to dwell on relatively unimportant subdivisions of society, as when, in *A Clergyman's Daughter* (1935), he makes the grim headmistresss class her pupils in three categories—those who may be ill-treated to any extent, those with whom some care should be exercised, and those who must on no account be touched and whose work must always be described as excellent—according to how promptly the parents pay their bills.

Orwell's strength and weakness relate to a single source; he was without historical perspective. He saw the world of his day with peculiar intensity because he saw extremely little of its past and tended to regard the future as simply a continuation and extension of the particular present that he knew. In his essay "Wells, Hitler, and the World State" (in *Critical Essays*, 1946), Orwell derides H. G. Wells for having completely misunderstood Hitler and the course that World War II would take because his mind was stuck in the early 1900's, so that he was still slaying paper dragons at a time when real ones were ravaging the world. But in his last book, *Nineteen Eighty-Four* (1949), Orwell shows that his own mind was similarly stuck, so that his picture of the future resembles the present—but in a more stupid, oppressive, miserable, dirty, and ill-fed form.

This concentration on the present, this belief that the historic moment is *now*, led Orwell—backed by his uncommon courage—to do at any point in life the thing that seemed to him most important. If fear of poverty is the enemy, the thing to do is to face it, reducing oneself to the lowest state, learning what happens when the last coat is pawned, the last franc is spent, the bugs on the wall are massing in battalions, and one's temperature indicates pneumonia. If on the Spanish Civil War hangs the hope of human freedom, then the inevitable step is to take part: the fact that one may be an incompetent soldier, and that one will certainly come under the suspicion of authority for the rest of one's life for having done so, can be neither here nor there.

This direct connection between what he felt to be the situation and his own response to it is Orwell's strength—a manner of acting that truly deserves the word "magnificent," deserving it all the more because Orwell was not naturally a man of action. On the contrary, his contacts with the physical world were ineffective: if he painted a room, the walls were smeared; if he cleaned a lamp, it caught fire; even the cigarettes he rolled continually fell to pieces. But his concentration on the present moment is his weakness too, because though this particular moment is historic, it is no more so than any other moment. Every hour is both man's finest and his feeblest.

Orwell's preoccupation with the present acted as a handicap to his understanding of the past and his perception of the future. And his preoccupation with his own experience and his own duty, besides being a source of strength, served also as a limitation since it prevented his enlarging that experience by a sympathetic understanding of others. He could endure the company of a derelict in the next hospital bed by conscious effort, but the moment conscious effort was relaxed, his fellow human beings appeared odious and detestable. And the closer they were, the more odious they usually appeared. Orwell was a writer and a highbrow, but "The modern English literary world, at any rate the high-brow section of it, is a sort of poisonous jungle where only weeds can flourish." Orwell was a Socialist, but

the typical Socialist . . . is either a youthful snob-Bolshevik who in five years' time will quite probably have made a wealthy marriage and been converted to Roman Catholicism; or, still more typically, a prim little man with a white-collar job, usually a secret teetotaller and often with vegetarian leanings, with a suspicion of nonconformity behind him, and, above all, with a social position which he has no intention of forfeiting.

In the second part of *The Road to Wigan Pier* (1937), from which these extracts are taken, Orwell seems able to loathe his fellow men for such varied reasons as that they are bald, or hairy; their clothes are good, or bad; they have an accent, they have none, or, if they had one, they have given it up; they smell—or else, having abandoned the honest simplicity of a working life, they have ceased to do so.

If one were forced, after a study of Orwell's gifts and limitations, to say in what form of literature he could deploy them best, one would suggest in Swiftian satire against mankind, or in the recording of frustrating personal experience. Certainly if one had given such an answer, its truth would have been amply proved. Orwell, besides novels and essays, wrote two admirable records of misfortune—*Down and Out in Paris and London* (1933) and *Homage to Catalonia* (1938), his picture of the Spanish Civil War—as well as one satire, *Animal Farm*.

Masterpieces are never the result of happy chance but are always the full flowering of a nature; this is true even when, as is often the case with poets, they are written in youth, before contact with life. Concerning the few, the very few, writers who produce a masterpiece, there is always one question of supreme interest: How did he come to do it? We can seek the answer in two places: in Orwell's books and in his life. Each of his books contains a section of autobiography; we can therefore follow the progress of his life and examine his production as a writer at the same time.

## II

ORWELL was born Eric Arthur Blair at Motihari, in Bengal, on 23 January 1903. His father was a minor official in the Indian Customs who retired on a small pension when his only son was a few years old. There were also two daughters, one older than the boy and one younger. Orwell later placed his family with typical precision as belonging to "the lower-upper-middle class," and he clearly felt this as a misfortune, though in fact the combination of a sparse upbringing with a reverence for intellectual values which distinguishes this class has produced a quite disproportionate number of notable men and women. It does not as a rule produce characters of grace and charm, but it does produce characters—and Orwell himself was among them.

From the first, as he remembers in *Such, Such Were the Joys* (1953), human relationships were not easy for him:

Looking back on my own childhood, after the infant years were over, I do not believe that I ever felt love for any mature person, except my mother, and even her I did not trust, in the sense that shyness made me conceal most of my real feelings from her.... I merely disliked my own father, whom I had barely seen before I was eight and who appeared to me simply as a gruff-voiced elderly man forever saying "Don't."

A fashionable preparatory school on the south coast was chosen for the small boy. There his parents managed to keep him, at considerable sacrifice—and, Orwell adds, at reduced fees because the headmaster hoped he would win a scholarship. This school, in which the other boys were so much better off than he was and in which prestige attached only to those gifts and qualities he did not have, set in his mind, he believed, a pattern of failure and depression:

I had no money, I was weak, I was ugly, I was unpopular, I had a chronic cough, I was cowardly, I smelt.... The conviction that it was *not possible* for me to be a success went deep enough to influence my actions till far into adult life. Until I was thirty I always planned my life on the assumption not only that any major undertaking was bound to fail, but that I could only expect to live a few years longer.

Despite this conviction of failure, Orwell was awarded at the age of thirteen not one but two scholarships. He chose the more distinguished, to Eton, and was there from 1917 to 1921. Of this time he later wrote: "I did no work there and learned very little, and I don't feel that Eton has been much of a formative influence in my life." There is, in my opinion, a non sequitur in those few lines. The fact that Orwell did little work at Eton may have been the result of his school's influence rather than evidence that it had none. Many young Englishmen do no work at their universities, but acquire a broadening of outlook and a confidence in the power of the mind to solve complex problems, an ability which is far more valuable than academic learning. Orwell certainly acquired these gifts from somewhere: Eton, in its tolerant attitude toward the individual and its appreciation of intellectual freedom, is much more like a university than a school and probably deserves more credit than he gave it. Most other schools would have expelled a boy who, holding a scholarship, chose to do no work.

When the time came to leave Eton, the natural course for Orwell would have been to go to Cambridge, to which he could almost certainly have won a scholarship. He did not do so, and it is clear that he resented the fact and felt that those who did gained an easy advantage over him.[2] Instead, he was advised by one of his tutors to break free from a way of life he found so painful, that of a poor boy among those richer than himself, and take a job abroad. By

---

[2] In *Keep the Aspidistra Flying* (1936) the hero, Gordon Comstock, has a manuscript rejected and ruminates, "'The Editor regrets!' Why be so bloody mealy-mouthed about it? Why not say outright, 'We don't want your bloody poems. We only take poems from chaps we were at Cambridge with. You proletarians keep your distance'?"

the time he was forty he would have saved money and earned the right to a good pension; he could then choose his own way of life. A post in the Indian Imperial Police was open. Orwell took it and spent the years 1922–1927 in Burma.

He embodied this experience in *Burmese Days*, which was published in New York in 1934. It is a moving story of frustration and humiliation—the humiliation, associated with social snubs, being rather more pressing than the frustration, which derived from the difficult and painful official relationship between the English and the Burmese.

Malcolm Muggeridge, who knew Orwell and was living in India at the time Orwell was in Burma, wrote:

The ordinarily-accepted view is that Orwell was deeply revolted by what was expected of him as a member of the Burma Police Force, and that his subsequent political views were to some extent a consequence of the great revulsion of feeling thereby induced in him. Personally, I consider that this is an over-simplification. It is perfectly true that Orwell was revolted by . . . police duties in Burma, . . . and, indeed, to a certain extent by authority as such; but it is also true that there was a Kiplingesque side to his character which made him romanticize the Raj and its mystique.

In this connexion, it is significant that one of the most vivid descriptive passages in *Burmese Days* is of the hunting expedition that Flory (the "hero") went on with Elizabeth. Another is of the attack on a small handful of Englishmen in their club by an enraged Burmese mob. Flory was the hero of this occasion. . . .

("Essay on *Burmese Days*," in *World Review*, June 1950, pp. 45–48)

In Burma Orwell also wrote, or found material for writing, his essay "Shooting an Elephant," which was to rank as a classic within his lifetime and gives an example of his prose style at its most lucid and precise. An elephant runs amok, and Orwell, as the British official of the district, has to take action. Carrying a borrowed rifle, he follows the beast to the fields, where it is standing peacefully, recovered now from its attack of madness:

As soon as I saw the elephant I knew with perfect certainty that I ought not to shoot him. It is a serious matter to shoot a working elephant—it is comparable to destroying a huge and costly piece of machinery. . . .

However, the pressure of the crowd's will, all determined to witness a shooting, is too strong, and Orwell fires:

In that instant, in too short a time, one would have thought, even for the bullet to get there, a mysterious, terrible change had come over the elephant. He neither stirred nor fell, but every line of his body had altered. He looked suddenly stricken, shrunken, immensely old, as though the frightful impact of the bullet had paralysed him without knocking him down. At last, after what seemed a long time—it might have been five seconds, I dare say—he sagged flabbily to his knees. His mouth slobbered. An enormous senility seemed to have settled upon him. One could have imagined him thousands of years old. I fired again into the same spot.

To this period also probably belongs the short essay "A Hanging," which appeared in the *Adelphi* in 1931. Into these six-and-a-half pages Orwell has concentrated his falcon's power of observation and his living sympathy with mankind, but they are under the control of an artist's impartiality and detachment.

Between victim and executioners Orwell takes no side; he understands the Superintendent's grim responsibility equally with the victim's agony:

We stood waiting, five yards away. The warders had formed in a rough circle around the gallows, and then, when the noose was fixed, the prisoner began crying out to his god. It was a high, reiterated cry of "Ram! Ram! Ram! Ram!" not urgent and fearful like a prayer or cry for help, but steady, rhythmical, almost like the tolling of a bell. The dog answered the sound with a whine. The hangman still standing on the gallows, produced a small cotton bag like a flour bag and drew it down over the prisoner's face. But the sound muffled by the cloth, still persisted, over and over again: "Ram! Ram! Ram! Ram!"

Finally, when all is over, comes the jocular relief that dissolves even racial barriers; this too Orwell accepts without moral indignation: "We all had a drink together, native and European alike, quite amicably. The dead man was a hundred yards away."

Because of the detachment that is so often lacking in his novels, the result—in spite of its tiny scale—is a complete work of art. No more on the subject need ever be said.

### III

In 1927 Orwell came home, ostensibly on leave:

I was already half determined to throw up the job, and one snuff of English air decided me. I was not going back to

be part of that evil despotism. But I wanted much more than merely to escape my job.
("How I Became a Socialist," in *The Road to Wigan Pier*)

Either because he saw the situation more clearly than others, or else for reasons of his own temperament, Orwell felt deep guilt over his experience in Burma. His conviction that the British ought to withdraw from the country would be regarded as outrageous when voiced by him in 1934—but it is worth recalling that, little more than ten years later, it had become the official policy of the British government. This guilt was one of the reasons Orwell gave for the next, most extraordinary, change in his life.

He went to Paris, ostensibly in order to write books and articles; but no one wants the books and articles of an unknown writer in a foreign country and it is clear that his real motive must have been different. Orwell went to Paris in order to plunge himself into the destructive element he had been brought up to dread; to experience failure in its most painful form; to rub shoulders with mankind at its lowest and dirtiest; to commit an act of public defiance against the money values of our world, and particularly of those wealthier than himself, by whom he had been surrounded and, he felt, humiliated at his schools.

Besides guilt over his Burmese experience ("For five years I had been part of an oppressive system.... I was conscious of an immense weight of guilt that I had got to expiate"), Orwell records the desire, which many men feel, to test himself in hardship. There is, he says:

a feeling of relief, almost of pleasure, at knowing yourself at last genuinely down and out. You have talked so often of going to the dogs—and well, here are the dogs, and you have reached them, and you can stand it. It takes off a lot of anxiety.

Another reason that he sometimes gave was the actual difficulty in the years 1927–1928 of finding any kind of job. It is certainly true that, in the late 1920's, thousands of young men in Orwell's position (and hundreds of thousands in worse ones) struggled in vain to find any kind of work. But I think the pressure was indirect: not that Orwell himself literally could not obtain paid employment, but rather that by identifying himself with the underdogs of every given moment, he deliberately sought to equate the suffering of his life with theirs.

There are two further reasons for his down-and-out life that were not stated by Orwell but that ought, I think, to come into the reckoning. First, Orwell's impression of working-class life (it appears particularly strongly in *Nineteen Eighty-Four*) was as a kind of warm feather bed into which one could sink, abandoning all pretensions. His own family, he seemed to feel, had only recently and with great difficulty hauled itself up into the middle classes. The enterprise of a grandparent, the foothold gained by his father as a minor official, his own sufferings at school, and the sacrifices made by parents and sisters to keep him there had led only to this: a police job that was more than he could stomach. Since the whole upward fight had been in vain, the sensible thing to do was to relax and go down. The resulting hardship would be well compensated for by peace of mind.

Second, there is the reason that governs so much of a writer's life, though it is a reason which he must often conceal from himself: the hope that out of this dramatic, even desperate, change of circumstance would come a book. Orwell could not say to himself, "I will fall through the bottom of society and live the life of a complete outcast. Then I will write my experiences," for this would have given too journalistic a color to his project. What he quite naturally did was to invite the experience for other reasons and make a record of it when the experience was complete.

*Down and Out in Paris and London*, Orwell's first book, was published in January 1933. It is a remarkable and fascinating work, somewhat scrappy, but containing a succession of curious portraits and a flow of practical comments on the outcast's life. The first words set the note:

The Rue du Coq d'Or, seven in the morning. A succession of furious choking yells from the street. Madame Monce, who kept the little hotel opposite mine, had come out onto the pavement to address a lodger on the third floor. Her bare feet were stuck into sabots and her grey hair was streaming down.
*Madame Monce:* "Salope! Salope! How many times have I told you not to squash bugs on the wallpaper? Do you think you've bought the hotel, eh? Why can't you throw them out of the window like everyone else? *Putain! Salope!*"
*The woman on the third floor:* "*Vache.*"

For eighteen months Orwell endured abysmal poverty in Paris rather than apply to friends who could, and would, gladly have helped him. His best days during this period were when he succeeded in getting a job as a dishwasher in a large Paris hotel. Then, quite suddenly, in a manner he does not explain, Orwell felt free to ask help of an English friend, who at once sent him five pounds and the promise of a job. Back in London, he learned that the job could not begin for a month and, once again, the mysterious barrier fell: "Sooner or later I should have to go to B. for more money, but it seemed hardly decent to do so yet, and in the meantime I must exist in some hole-and-corner way."

So there begins an English workhouse and doss-house life to supplement his recent French experience, in which a cup of tea, a slice of bread and butter, and shelter for the night are the deepest concerns of life. This life is described in as matter-of-fact a way as if Orwell were writing a tramp's handbook or doss-house guide; and it ends as suddenly as his Paris life, when Orwell feels free to apply again to B. and borrow a few pounds more.

*Down and Out in Paris and London* did not sell well, but it received high praise from the critics and must have established Orwell in his own eyes as a writer. It is notable that, from the start, his work was noticed and praised by leading critics. In 1934, when the first book had been followed by *A Clergyman's Daughter* and *Burmese Days*, Compton Mackenzie wrote: "No realistic writer during the last five years has produced three volumes which can compare in directness, vigour, courage, and vitality, with these three volumes from the pen of Mr George Orwell." However, until the great popular success of *Animal Farm* eleven years later, this critical approval was not translated into cash. Over the ten years 1930–1940, Orwell himself, in the sort of calculation he was fond of making, reckoned his literary earnings at not quite three pounds a week.

## IV

BETWEEN 1929 and 1935 Orwell kept himself afloat with difficulty as a private tutor and a teacher in cheap private schools—of which *A Clergyman's Daughter* gives a horrifying picture—as well as by books and journalism.

*A Clergyman's Daughter* is a book Orwell himself came to dislike heartily. He ceased to include it in his list of published works and is said to have bought and destroyed any copies he could find. It has a different flavor from any of his other works: first, because of its theme and teaching, which appears to be that faith is what matters, regardless of whether one can believe in the faith or not; second, because its central character is a woman. Orwell identifies himself with a clergyman's daughter who shrinks from and has a horror of sex, manifested in a ceaselessly nagging conscience; and there can be no doubt—when one recalls the two painful seduction scenes in *Keep the Aspidistra Flying* and *Nineteen Eighty-Four*—that this corresponded to a strong side of his own nature. Indeed it would be possible to regard the novel as in essence the story of an attempt on the part of one who feels fear and loathing for the world to make contact with it. This contact is so painful that it can be brought about only through loss of memory, involving the loss of everything else as well, including reputation. Finally, the one seeking to make contact abandons the attempt and retreats into the shelter of a faith—any faith, no matter what, being better than exposure to life without protection.

In construction the book follows the picaresque convention, being simply a series of adventures in which the heroine moves about from place to place while different things happen to her. Orwell was thus able to use his own experiences of hop-picking in Kent, of London doss-houses, and of the worst kind of private school to provide gloomily impressive backgrounds and give his work the reforming message that he seldom failed to introduce.

There is one quite extraordinary scene, vivid and disastrous as a glimpse into a corner of hell, in which the clergyman's daughter finds herself homeless in Trafalgar Square on a freezing night with a handful of characters as lost as but more desperate than herself. Their talk forms a kind of litany of the damned, with the defrocked parson, the woman whose husband has locked her out, the louse-ridden old tramp, the lads from the north singing round the pubs for a living—and, every now and then, the policeman coming to move them all on just as they are beginning to experience an illusion of warmth.

Orwell's next book, *Keep the Aspidistra Flying*, published in 1936, is essentially the same mixture of a gloomy setting—implying angry criticism of the way life is organized—with an analysis of the values around which that life is built. This time the theme is money.

Gordon Comstock, a solitary young man of literary leanings, gives up an opportunity in an advertising firm and takes a job as a bookshop assistant at two pounds a week in order to have time for writing. Inevitably, his poverty so dominates his thoughts that he cannot get on with his literary work—a fact he never faces, living in a kind of envious haze of all who have inherited or achieved a more workable adjustment to life than he has. Most of the miseries of Comstock's life spring directly from his own confusion: he regards himself as at war with money and respect for money, yet suffers deeply when a waiter is insolent because he is poor.

"In love" with a girl called Rosemary, he does his best to pass his humiliations on to her and reproaches her for not bringing into his life the warmth and comfort he lacks; but his manner of bringing about the desired fulfillment is to ask complainingly, "Are you *ever* going to sleep with me?" or else to make love to her on the ground in a copse in outer suburbia. When for a sufficient reason she rejects him, he ascribes the rejection to his poverty.

The book ends on a more positive note. Rosemary is about to have a baby; the couple decide to marry; and Comstock discovers the commonplace pleasures of owning some furniture and a place to put it, and the commonplace virtues of paying one's way, raising a family, and putting the best face on life one can. It is from this that the book takes its title, with that almost indestructible potted plant, the aspidistra, as a symbol of middle-class endurance and sense of personal responsibility. These virtues, Orwell seems to say, are constantly sneered at, but the sneerers themselves would often be in a poor way unless these same virtues were at work, making their world at least reasonably orderly and solid.

*Keep the Aspidistra Flying* was not a success, but Orwell was pleased by the number of young men who wrote to tell him that his hero's experience—taking a girl out for the day on a few shillings and wondering the whole time whether the money would last out—had often enough been their own.

In making his central figure a bookseller's assistant, Orwell once again was using his own experience. For about eighteen months, between 1932 and 1934, he worked as an assistant in a Hampstead bookshop, and was also at this time writing for various magazines, in particular the *Adelphi*, edited by his friend Sir Richard Rees. However, Orwell had always detested London, and when he married in 1936 he moved to Hertfordshire. His wife was Eileen O'Shaughnessy, described by Rees, who knew her well, as "a charming and intelligent women." The cottage they took together was also the village shop, the idea being that Orwell should write in the mornings and see to the shop in the afternoons. As a business venture it was not a success—the profit from the store was a bare one pound a week—but this was clearly a happy period in his life. "Outside my work," he once wrote, "the thing I care most about is gardening, especially vegetable gardening. . . . My wife's tastes fit in almost perfectly with my own."

During this time, however, he also became active as a Socialist, and his publisher, Victor Gollancz, who had founded and was running the Left Book Club, invited him to make a journey through one of the depressed areas of Britain, setting down what he saw. The result was *The Road to Wigan Pier* (1937), which takes its title from a North Country joke. "Pier" suggests the seaside, holidays, gaiety. Wigan is a somewhat forbidding inland town whose pier is a derelict wharf on a canal.

*The Road to Wigan Pier* is Orwell's worst book. It is made up from his habitual blend of immediate impressions with past personal experience, but in this case the blend is particularly uneasy. The first section gives his impression of life in the depressed area and is, in a curious way, misconceived. It is clear that Orwell largely failed to make the close contact with the working class which was the purpose of his journey. John Beavan, who was later editor of the *Daily Herald*, had lived in Wigan for years on the low pay then earned by a reporter on a local paper, and wrote of it:

> He attacked the class barrier at its thickest and highest point. He tried to get into the manual working class and into a very special section of it—the miners. He chose, moreover, a sub-section of the miners—those out of work; and he chose a sub-section of the unemployed: those who lived in the worst slums.
> ("*The Road to Wigan Pier*," in *World Review*, June 1950, pp. 48-51)

Had the choice been a more reasonable one, Beavan adds, Orwell

> would have been accepted and he would have learned something from the inside of the worker's enormous zest for life, the richness of his humour, the breadth of his ambitions, and the simple philosophy which sustains him so long in adversity. But the barrier here was too low. There was no expiation to be found along this easy path.

In the early part of the book Orwell shows an exaggerated, sometimes an undignified, humility toward the working class. "If there is one man to whom I do feel myself inferior, it is a coalminer," he writes. But the artist has no business feeling himself inferior to his subject matter, and the guilt Orwell expresses over his expensive education and middle-class background serves rather to embarrass the reader than to win sympathy for those whose life Orwell is describing.

In the second part there is much that is interesting about the writer's own life, but again Orwell seems to misconceive the way in which good relations between classes come into being and are, on the whole, maintained—that is, by each person accepting as naturally as he can the position in which he finds himself, while being ready to accept changes that are for the general benefit.

Because he lacked historical sense and could not allow for the element of time that dominates every human calculation, Orwell wanted an immediate resolution of all class differences. This was to be obtained by himself and other middle-class people identifying themselves with the manual worker—not merely with his political aspirations but with his choice of pictures and his taste in food:

> It is no use clapping a proletarian on the back and telling him that he is as good a man as I am; if I want real contact with him, I have got to make an effort for which very likely I am unprepared. For to get outside the class-racket I have got to suppress not merely my snobbishness, but most of my other tastes and prejudices as well. I have got to alter myself so completely that in the end I shall hardly be recognizable as the same person. What is involved is not merely the amelioration of working-class conditions, nor an avoidance of the more stupid forms of snobbery, but a complete abandonment of the upper-class and middle-class attitude to life.

In other words, what Orwell is asking for is not "real contact" but identification. Though in argument the book is often misguided (and marred by resentful criticism of the Labour party, the middle classes, the working man who has made money, and many other dummy figures put up to be knocked over), it was a natural reaction from a man of sympathy and courage to the sight at close quarters of honest, capable men living on a pittance in enforced idleness because their country's financial system could not see how to make profit from their labor.

*The Road to Wigan Pier* was published as a "choice" (the term used for an officially recommended book) of the Left Book Club, which had at that time tens of thousands of members and some influence. It appeared with a foreword by Victor Gollancz, who on behalf of himself and his fellow selectors, John Strachey and Harold Laski, criticized strongly the work he was recommending and recorded that he had "marked well over a hundred minor passages about which I thought I should like to argue with Mr Orwell in this Foreword." However, by the time the book came out, early in 1937, it was too late for its publisher to argue with its author. Orwell had already gone to Spain.

V

It was Orwell's way, as we have seen, to do at any moment the thing he found most important. In the early part of 1936 it seemed most important to investigate firsthand the life of a depressed area; by Christmas, it was to observe the Spanish Civil War. In each case the backing of a publisher was needed; and since Orwell had now changed publishers, it was the firm of Secker and Warburg that supported his Spanish journey. However, if one wished to see anything when one got to Spain, political contacts were as necessary as money: Orwell's chief connections in England were with the Independent Labour party, a rather forlorn offshoot of the Labour party. The ILP lined up not with the Spanish Communists but with a much smaller group known as the POUM (Partido Obrero de Unificación Marxista), which had Anarchist affiliations. Orwell went with a group that included Bob Smillie (the grandson of a noted miners' leader) and some former gunmen of the Irish Republican Army. Because of his different contacts, his experiences were quite different from those of most foreigners, who went to Spain under Communist auspices and who, if they fought at all, probably joined the International Brigades.

Orwell's behavior when he reached Spain was as typical of him as the manner in which he went. In *Homage to Catalonia*, written after he returned in 1938, he recalled:

> I had come to Spain with some notion of writing newspaper articles but I had joined the militia almost im-

mediately, because at that time and in that atmosphere it seemed the only conceivable thing to do.

After a brief parody of training, decked in uniforms so various that Orwell says they should have been called "multiforms," and armed with such weapons as rusty Mausers stamped "1896," he and his fellow militiamen found themselves at the front:

And quite half the so-called men were children—but I mean literally children, of sixteen years old at the very most. Yet they were all happy and excited at the prospect of getting to the front at last.

Fortunately the fighting lines were too far apart for either side to make much contact.

Later, near Huesca, his unit was involved in serious fighting, and it was there at five o'clock one May morning that Orwell was hit. The bullet, according to the Spanish doctors, missed severing Orwell's windpipe and carotid artery "by about a millimetre," passing right through his throat. For two months after this he could not speak above a whisper; then the other vocal chord "compensated" for the one that had been paralyzed. His voice, always flat, had from then on a strange cracked quality of which he was probably unaware.

The wound put an end to Orwell's fighting, but it did not prevent his experiencing the true horror of the war—the ferocious internal dissensions and, in particular, the ruthlessness and treachery of the Communists, which ended by destroying the government side's resistance and paving the way for Franco's victory. It was Orwell's bitter experience to be recovering from a wound in Barcelona when his party, the POUM, was denounced by the Communists, its offices seized, and its leaders imprisoned or liquidated. Militiamen on leave were prevented from returning to the front lest they lower the morale of fellow soldiers fighting, ill-armed and quarter-trained, by letting them know they were accused by men at home (nominally their allies) of being "Fascist spies" and "traitors." Orwell and his wife, who was with him, both took serious risks to help certain of his friends, before themselves escaping across the border into France.

However, the confusion and treachery that it was his lot to meet in Spain exercised an entirely clarifying and strengthening effect on Orwell. Much of his painful concern over class and money values had now been shrugged off in the face of grimmer troubles. There are also glimpses throughout *Homage to Catalonia* of a new capacity to make contact with his fellow men; true, these are only slight encounters—an Italian militiaman met for a moment in the barracks, an officer who shakes his hand when Orwell risks his liberty on behalf of a fellow member of the POUM. But they are real:

This war, in which I played so ineffectual a part, has left me with memories which are mostly evil, and yet I do not wish that I had missed it.... Curiously enough, the whole experience has left me with not less but more belief in the decency of human beings.

The reason for this is clear. It is that Orwell had now a more firmly based confidence in his own essential decency and courage.

*Homage to Catalonia* is a first-rate piece of reporting—vivid, dramatic, remorselessly objective—but an objective picture of the Spanish Civil War had no attraction for the supporters of either side. Those of the Right preferred stories about the desecration of dead nuns' bodies; those of the Left demanded a heroic picture of unity and courage. Of the fifteen hundred copies printed, no more than nine hundred had been sold by the time of Orwell's death; and in America the book was not published until 1952. Its reputation has increased so much that it is now rightly regarded as one of his finest books.

VI

RETURNING home, Orwell lived quietly in Hertfordshire for the two years before World War II broke out, except for one winter he spent in Morocco, probably because his wound and the hardships he had undergone in Spain had aggravated the lung trouble from which he suffered all his life. The novel he published during 1939—*Coming Up for Air*—was the first book of his to meet with some success, and went into several editions. Once more it is the story of a "solitary," but in this case the solitary is a fat, good-natured man with a ripe and easy humor. George Bowling, a middle-aged insurance salesman, wins a few pounds on a horse and succeeds in concealing it from his wife. He decides to spend the money on a visit to the little country town where he was brought up, which has remained for him the symbol of idyllic peace and rural beauty. He gets there only to find that it has been submerged in the hellish "development" that destroyed so much more of Britain during the twenty years between the wars than the enemy attacks did later and that has continued at an accelerated pace since the last war ended.

The book is written with dash and some enjoyment. Though the insurance man's life is dreary, he is not a dreary character himself. Not until George reaches his hometown does Orwell's passion for "rubbing the reader's nose in it" overcome him and us. When George looks down on Little Binfield, he sees at a glance the hateful transformation that has overtaken his birthplace. So do we. But then for page after page the reader is obliged to accompany George round the town, while he sees what has happened to the old marketplace, the old High Street, the old horse trough, the teashop, the corn merchant's, the churchyard, and, finally, to the girl he once loved and to the most cherished memory of his childhood, the pool where the great fish used to lie.

The book is incidentally memorable for a vivid picture of the effects of bombing, soon to become painfully familiar to millions of Britons, and probably a memory of something Orwell had seen in Spain. The bomb on Lower Binfield (it has fallen by accident in peacetime) sheers away the front of a house, leaving its contents exposed but strangely undisturbed, as intimate and complete as a doll's house with the door open.

This bomb is the open statement of an undercurrent that runs through the book and that had been running through Orwell's writing for some time—a warning of the imminence of war. "I have known since about 1931," he wrote in a war diary of 1940, "that the future must be catastrophic.... Since 1934 I have known war between England and Germany was coming, and since 1936 I have known it with complete certainty. I could feel it in my belly."

Before we come to the war and the two books of Orwell's that grew out of it, we should take note again of his essays. Orwell wrote four books of essays: *Inside the Whale* (1940), *Critical Essays* (1946), and two volumes that appeared after his death, *Shooting an Elephant* (1950) and *England Your England* (1953). The latter appeared in the American edition as *Such, Such Were the Joys*, this being the title of an autobiographical essay about his preparatory school life that was left out of the English edition because of possible libel proceedings.

He also wrote *The Lion and the Unicorn* (1941), a sociological tract in the form of a long essay, as well as the text for a picture book, *The English People* (1947), that is descriptive rather than illuminating.

Many of the essays in these books are slight, but there are some that show Orwell's unique qualities to advantage. Because of his sympathy with the lives of ordinary men and women, he chose subjects other writers overlooked; two of the most famous deal with the so-called comics then read by schoolboys and the humorous postcards seen in newsagents' shops at the seaside. His own ambivalent attitude to the empire helped him to write penetratingly, if incompletely, about Kipling; and he makes certain points about Dickens with clarity and force. A delightful humor gleams out at times; of Gandhi's insistence that to take animal food is a sin, even if life is in danger, even if the life is that of a wife or child, Orwell comments, "there must be some limit to what we will do in order to remain alive, and the limit is well on this side of chicken broth."

To many readers a chief interest of the essays will be that they contain the seeds of much of Orwell's other work. "Politics and the English Language" foreshadows his invention of "Newspeak" in *Nineteen Eighty-Four*, and his study of Swift in "Politics vs. Literature" points in the direction of *Animal Farm*.

Once war began, Orwell made repeated efforts to join the army. When these failed, he volunteered for the Home Guard, became a sergeant, and took his duties very seriously, though he was never really at home in his dealings with the physical universe. In the autumn of 1941, by which time the life of an independent writer had become almost impossible, he joined the Indian service of the BBC. Throwing himself into this work with devotion, he insisted on delivering almost all the talks to Malaya, his special field of action, himself.

For the whole period of the war, Orwell consistently overworked; moreover, the conditions of the time affected him far more seriously than they would a person of normal health. Most London offices had their windows largely bricked-up against bombardment, so that one worked always by artificial light in airless rooms. It was common to work far into the night, and not unusual to remain all night, lie down for a few hours on a camp bed, and start the day again. Such conditions were harmful enough for anyone whose lungs had been affected, but in Orwell's case there was another source of weakness. In the last year of the war, Orwell's wife died, collapsing after a quite minor operation. To a friend who visited him, he remarked that this was probably due to lack of strength; both of them, he said, had consistently gone without their rations or part of their rations, "so that there should be more for other people."

## VII

IN May 1945, the month war with Germany ended, *Animal Farm* was published. By far Orwell's finest book, it did not have an easy passage into print. It had been written between November 1943 and February 1944—"the only one of my books I really sweated over," Orwell said of it. Certainly it is the only one of his books that shows not the least sign of having been sweated over, flowing absolutely clear from start to finish, as though the author had needed to do nothing but copy it out. Four publishers refused it on the ground that at that time it was not possible to print a book attacking a military ally. As events turned out, however, the book's appearance could not have been better timed and it was quickly a best-seller; in America its success was even greater than in Britain.

*Animal Farm* is a ninety-page satire on Stalinist dictatorship. The animals on a farm unite against their master, Jones. They are successful in getting rid of the tyrant and in managing the practical work of the farm, but they are disastrously unsuccessful in something they had never regarded as a problem—their dealings with each other. The revolution is hardly complete before differences appear: "The pigs did not actually work, but directed and supervised the others. With their superior knowledge it was natural that they should assume the leadership." With the leadership they also assume the buckets of milk yielded by the cows and the apples from the orchard.

"Comrades!" [cried Squealer.] "You do not imagine, I hope, that we pigs are doing this in a spirit of selfishness and privilege? Many of us actually dislike milk and apples. . . . Milk and apples (this has been proved by Science, comrades) contain substances absolutely necessary to the well-being of a pig. We pigs are brain-workers. The whole management and organisation of this farm depend on us. . . . It is for *your* sake that we drink that milk and eat those apples. Do you know what would happen if we pigs failed in our duty? Jones would come back! . . . Surely, comrades," cried Squealer almost pleadingly, skipping from side to side and whisking his tail, "surely there is no one among you who wants to see Jones come back?"

Once there is no longer any danger of Jones's return, a new threat must be found to keep the other animals working their hardest, contented in submission to the pigs. The new threat is himself a pig, Snowball, who believes that the proper strategy is to "send out more and more pigeons and stir up rebellion among the animals on the other farms." This is opposed by the pigs' leader, Napoleon, backed by Squealer, who insists that "what the animals must do was to procure firearms and train themselves in the use of them." Long after Snowball has been driven into exile, his name serves as a slogan of hatred: his machinations are held responsible for every failure on the farm, and every animal suspected of disaffection is denounced as an emissary of Snowball:

a goose came forward and confessed to having secreted six ears of corn during the last year's harvest and eaten them in the night. Then a sheep confessed to having urinated in the drinking pool—urged to do this, so she said, by Snowball. . . .

At last the farm is established as a going concern, but the animals are surprised to find that—except for the pigs and their protectors, the watchdogs—life is exactly as hard and painful as it always was. Even their sense of pride as animals is destroyed when, on returning from the fields one evening, they find that the pigs have taken to walking on two legs and carrying whips; meantime, the basic principle of the revolution, "All Animals Are Equal," inscribed on the barn wall after the expulsion of Jones, has been given a qualifying clause: "But Some Animals Are More Equal than Others."

*Animal Farm* is conceived and written in the classic tradition of satire, the tradition of receding planes, which gives it precisely the depth of every reader. Like *Gulliver's Travels* or *Aesop's Fables*, it makes a delightful children's story. It is manifestly an attack on Stalinism. It can be read as a lament for the fate of revolutions. But it is also a profound and moving commentary on the circumstances of human life: each of us is forced to combine with others in order "to get things done," but must compromise with his own truth and honesty in every combination that he makes. It may be of interest here to mention that *Animal Farm*, like *Nineteen Eighty-Four*, was one of the books used for English instruction in the training of African journalists at the centers in Nairobi and Lagos run by the International Press Institute. *Animal Farm* exercised just the same magic in Africa that it does in Britain and America, and more than one student told me that he was convinced Orwell must have known and been writing about the African state from which he had come.

One question that arises is: How was Orwell, a somewhat irritable man whose writings tended to overemphasize the gloomy aspects of every subject and experience he treated, able in this one book to achieve such admirable good humor and detachment, which at once raises his satire to a higher plane? Disillusion with Communism was a common complaint among Orwell's generation, that is, among those of Orwell's generation whose minds had been at any time receptive. But as a rule this disillusion was expressed in a form either violent or peevish; Orwell himself had contributed to a symposium called *The Betrayal of the Left* (1941), published before the Nazi attack on the USSR caused a swing back in many minds (though not in Orwell's) in favor of the Soviet system.

Part of the answer lies, I think, in Orwell's Spanish experience, which had purged his mind of much personal rancor, enabling him to see events of the day with a new detachment. A friend of Orwell's and a fellow author, T. R. Fyvel, has made the ingenious suggestion that part of the answer also may lie in his having chosen to write about animals rather than human beings. Orwell actively liked animals. "Most of the good memories of my childhood, and up to the age of about twenty," he wrote, "are in some way connected with animals."

Besides money and an international reputation, Orwell achieved with *Animal Farm* something he had been seeking all his life—contact with ordinary people, to whom for the first time he really got across. A mere succès d'estime would never have satisfied him. "I would far rather have written 'Come Where the Booze Is Cheaper' or, 'Two Lovely Black Eyes,'" he declared once in the *Tribune* (the left-wing London magazine of which he was literary editor), "than, say, *The Blessed Damozel* or *Love in a Valley*."

For two more years Orwell, now a successful author and an established journalist, worked on in London. Then in 1947 he left for the remote island of Jura, off the west coast of Scotland. He was tired. He wished to get on with the writing of *Nineteen Eighty-Four;* and he was anxious, if one takes his own statements seriously, to get away, with his adopted son, from possible atomic war. My own impression of Orwell, from the evidence of his life and work and from some personal knowledge, is that if he had expected atomic war, he would certainly have remained in London.

From the point of view of scenery, Jura was delightful, but as a place of recovery for a consumptive he could scarcely have chosen worse. The house was twenty-five miles from the island's only shop, eight of them almost impassable by car. Conditions were primitive and in damp weather the house dripped. Before long he was obliged to go into a hospital near Glasgow; after his release he had to continue making periodic visits to be medically checked, and from Jura every journey was an undertaking.

By 1949 Orwell was ordered by his doctor to go south. He entered a sanatorium in Gloucestershire, from which friends who visited him regularly urged him to come up to London; he was removed before long to University College Hospital. Meantime, by an immense effort, he had succeeded in finishing *Nineteen Eighty-Four:* "It wouldn't have been so gloomy," he said, "if I hadn't been so ill."

*Nineteen Eighty-Four*, as its title implies, is Orwell's version of the future awaiting mankind. The scene is England, now known as "Airstrip One," which forms part of "Oceania." A ceaseless, pointless war goes rumbling on, a war in which Oceania is in alliance with Eastasia against Eurasia—at least that is the statement put out by the Ministry of Truth. However, nobody any longer feels certain about anything; it is fairly clear that only four years previously Oceania had been in alliance with Eurasia against the common enemy, Eastasia, and by the end of the book the situation has switched back. Though the war is unending, and the population continually stimulated by news of overwhelming victory or sensational defeat, nothing actually happens. An occasional rocket falls. A few prisoners are escorted through the streets. Life becomes steadily a little grimmer, a little meaner; the houses become dirtier and more overcrowded, the food worse. A daily Two Minutes' Hate, directed against the mythical Goldstein (a Trotsky or Snowball figure), distracts people from their sufferings. Everything is controlled by the Party, which is itself controlled by the secret Inner Party; the Party's three slogans are "War Is Peace," "Freedom Is Slavery," and "Ignorance Is Strength."

All apparatus of government is concentrated into four ministries. The Ministry of Truth concerns itself

# GEORGE ORWELL

SELECTED BIBLIOGRAPHY

I. BIBLIOGRAPHY. I. R. Willison, *George Orwell: Some Materials for a Bibliography* (London, 1953); Z. G. Zeke and W. White, "George Orwell: A Selected Bibliography," in *Bulletin of Bibliography*, 23, no. 5 (May–August 1961); Z. G. Zeke and W. White, "Orwelliana," in *Bulletin of Bibliography*, 23, nos. 6–7 (September–December 1961 and January–April 1962); I. R. Willison and I. Angus, "George Orwell: Bibliographical Addenda," in *Bulletin of Bibliography*, 24, no. 8 (September–December 1965); J. Meyers, "George Orwell: A Bibliography," in *Bulletin of Bibliography*, 31, no. 3 (July–September 1974).

II. COLLECTED WORKS. *The Uniform Edition* (London, 1948–1960); *The Orwell Reader: Fiction, Essays, and Reportage by George Orwell* (New York, 1956); *Selected Essays* (London, 1957); G. Bott, ed., *Selected Writings* (New York, 1958); *Collected Essays* (London, 1961); S. Orwell and I. Angus, eds., *The Collected Essays, Journalism and Letters of George Orwell* (New York–London, 1968), vol. I: *An Age Like This, 1920–1940*, vol. II: *My Country, Right or Left, 1940–1943*, vol. III: *As I Please, 1943–1945*; vol. IV: *In Front of Your Nose, 1945–1950*.

III. SEPARATE WORKS. *Down and Out in Paris and London* (London, 1933), autobiography; *Burmese Days* (New York, 1934), novel; *A Clergyman's Daughter* (London, 1935), novel; *Keep the Aspidistra Flying* (London, 1936), novel; *The Road to Wigan Pier* (London, 1937), sociology; *Homage to Catalonia* (London, 1938), history; *Coming Up for Air* (London, 1939), novel.

*Inside the Whale, and Other Essays* (London, 1940), contains "Inside the Whale," "Charles Dickens," "Boys' Weeklies"; *The Lion and the Unicorn: Socialism and the English Genius* (London, 1941), pamphlet; *Animal Farm: A Fairy Story* (London, 1945), satire; *James Burnham and the Managerial Revolution* (London, 1946), pamphlet; *Critical Essays* (London, 1946), contains "Charles Dickens," "Boys' Weeklies," "Wells, Hitler, and the World State," "The Art of Donald McGill," "Rudyard Kipling," "W. B. Yeats," "Benefit of Clergy: Some Notes on Salvador Dali," "Arthur Koestler," "Raffles and Miss Blandish," "In Defence of P. G. Wodehouse"; *The English People* (London, 1947), essay, in the "Britain in Pictures" series; *Nineteen Eight-Four: A Novel* (London, 1949).

*Shooting an Elephant, and Other Essays* (London, 1950), contains "Shooting an Elephant," "A Hanging," "How the Poor Die," "Lear, Tolstoy and the Fool," "Politics vs. Literature: An Examination of *Gulliver's Travels*," "Politics and the English Language," "Reflections on Gandhi," "The Prevention of Literature," "Second Thoughts on James Burnham," "I Write as I Please," "Confessions of a Book Reviewer," "Books vs. Cigarettes," "Good Bad Books," "Nonsense Poetry," "Riding Down from Bangor," "The Sporting Spirit," "Decline of the English Murder," "Some Thoughts on the Common Toad," "A Good Word for the Vicar of Bray"; *Such, Such Were the Joys* (New York, 1953), contains "Such, Such Were the Joys," autobiography, and the following essays: "Why I Write," "Writers and Leviathan," "North and South," "Notes on Nationalism," "Anti-Semitism in Britain," "Poetry and the Microphone," "Inside the Whale," "Marrakech," "Looking Back on the Spanish War," "Down the Mine," "England Your England"; *England Your England, and Other Essays* (London, 1953), the English edition of *Such, Such Were the Joys*, without the autobiography.

*Note:* Orwell contributed to V. Gollancz, ed. *The Betrayal of the Left* (London, 1941), an examination and refutation of Communist policy from 1939 to January 1941, and to *Talking to India* (London, 1942), a series of broadcasts. He wrote an introduction to Jack London's *Love of Life and Other Stories* (London, 1941) and to the first two vols. of selections from *British Pamphleteers* (London, 1948). The Orwell archive at University College, London, contains, among other things, letters and unpublished Ph.D. theses on Orwell. A wartime diary by Orwell appeared in a special number of *World Review* (June 1950) that also contains a number of personal and critical tributes to him.

IV. BIOGRAPHICAL AND CRITICAL STUDIES. J. Atkins, *George Orwell: A Literary Study* (London, 1954; new ed., 1971); L. Brander, *George Orwell* (London, 1954); C. Hollis, *A Study of George Orwell: The Man and His Works* (London, 1956).

R. Heppenstall, *Four Absentees* (London, 1960), reminiscences of Orwell and others; R. Rees, *George Orwell: Fugitive from the Camp of Victory* (London, 1961); R. J. Voorhees, *The Paradox of George Orwell* (Lafayette, Ind., 1961); J. Strachey, *The Strangled Cry, and Other Unparliamentary Papers* (London, 1963), contains an essay on Orwell; S. J. Greenblatt, *Three Modern Satirists: Waugh, Orwell and Huxley* (New Haven, Conn., 1965); R. A. Lee, *Orwell's Fiction* (Notre Dame, 1965); E. M. Thomas, *Orwell* (Edinburgh, 1965); G. Woodcock, *The Crystal Spirit: A Study of George Orwell* (Boston, 1966); B. T. Oxley, *George Orwell* (London, 1967); J. Calder, *Chronicles of Conscience: A Study of George Orwell and Arthur Koestler* (London, 1968); K. Alldritt, *The Making of George Orwell: An Essay in Literary History* (London, 1969).

M. Gross, ed., *The World of George Orwell* (London, 1971); S. Hynes, ed., *Twentieth Century Interpretations of "1984": A Collection of Critical Essays* (Englewood Cliffs, N. J., 1971); R. Williams, *Orwell* (London, 1971); D. L. Kubal, *Outside the Whale: George Orwell's Art and Politics* (Notre Dame, 1972); P. Stansky and W. Abrahams, *George Orwell. The Transformation* (London, 1972); P. Stansky and W. Abrahams, *The Unknown Orwell* (London, 1972); H. Ringbom, *George Orwell as Essayist: A Stylistic Study* (Åbo, 1973); J. Buddicom, *Eric and Us: A Remembrance of George Orwell* (London, 1974); A. Sandison, *The Last Man in Europe: An Essay on George Orwell* (New York–London, 1974); R. Williams, ed., with education, news, the arts—all boiling down in practice to propaganda. The Ministry of Love maintains law and order, largely through the dreaded Thought Police. The Ministry of Plenty keeps everyone down to the barest necessities of life, continually announcing increases in rations that are actually reductions. The Ministry of Peace is occupied with the conduct of the war.

Orwell's central character, Winston Smith, works in the Ministry of Truth, where his job is largely the rewriting of history to suit the shifts of Party policy and removing from previous records the names of persons who have since been "vaporized." In secret revolt against the Party and his own miserable life, Winston Smith keeps a diary in which his private thoughts and feelings are recorded—not an easy matter when there is a telescreen in every room through which the smallest action may be observed. He also permits himself the folly of being attracted to Julia, a girl in another department of his ministry.

One day as he is passing her in the office corridor (it was in an office corridor that Comstock met Rosemary in *Keep the Aspidistra Flying*), she passes him a scrap of paper on which is written "I love you." They succeed in spending a day together, and make love in the open (again like Rosemary and Comstock). From that time on they arrange meetings, usually in a room that he rents above a junk shop. Here they plan conspiracy against the Party and, believing on very little evidence that a fellow member of their staff—a senior called O'Brien—is also a revolutionary, they confide in him. O'Brien proves to be a pillar of the existing order, and Winston is imprisoned, beaten, and tortured until all resistance is burned out of him, and he finally betrays Julia, who has already betrayed him.

The weakness of *Nineteen Eighty-Four* is a double one. Orwell, sick and dispirited, imagined nothing new. His world of 1984 is the wartime world of 1944, but dirtier and more cruel, and with all the endurance and nobility that mankind shows in times of stress mysteriously drained away. Everyone, by 1984, is to be a coward, a spy, and a betrayer.

Even technically, the world has not moved on. The war of 1984 is fought with the weapons of 1944, rockets and tommy guns; all that has happened is that they are now less effective than they used to be, and the horror that distorts life in the future is merely the horror that hung over existence in the author's lifetime. Totalitarianism, with its ceaseless witch-hunts, its secret police—whose charges are never formulated and can therefore never be answered—covers the whole world instead of only a large part of it, and all alleviating aspects have been removed.

The book's second weakness is another expression of the first. By amputating courage and self-sacrifice from his human beings, Orwell has removed any real tension from his story. The only challenge to totalitarianism must derive from the individual's assertion of personal values and beliefs against mass standards, and from the upholding of human love against artificially stimulated hate. This Winston Smith is incapable of doing: he is a feeble creature in himself and can draw no strength from his relationship with Julia, since what he feels for her is not love; it is not even lust, but merely a tepid mixture of attraction and contempt.

Though these two failures undermine the interest of the book, it has importance for our age as a warning: this is what happens if the state is allowed to become all-powerful. It also contains one notable invention that has contributed words and phrases to our common speech. This is Newspeak, the version of the English language approved by the Party:

> The purpose of Newspeak was not only to provide a medium of expression for the world-view and mental habits proper to the devotees of Ingsoc [English Socialism] but to make all other modes of thought impossible. It was intended that when Newspeak had been adopted once and for all and Oldspeak forgotten, a heretical thought—that is, a thought diverging from the principles of Ingsoc—should be literally unthinkable, at least so far as thought is dependent on words. . . . To give a single example. The word *free* still existed in Newspeak, but it could only be used in such statements as "This dog is free from lice" or "This field is free from weeds." It could not be used in its old sense of "politically free" or "intellectually free," since political and intellectual freedom no longer existed even as concepts, and were therefore of necessity nameless.

During the last months of his life Orwell married again. His second wife was Sonia Brownell, whom he had known for some years and who, as editorial assistant on the magazine *Horizon*, had been involved in the publication of some of his essays. With her Orwell discussed his plans for future work: he intended to make a complete break from his former polemical, propagandist way of writing and to concentrate on the treatment of human relationships. He had actually roughed out a story in the new manner, but it was destined never to be completed.

George Orwell died on 23 January 1950, a few minutes following a tubercular hemorrhage. He was not yet forty-seven.

*George Orwell: A Collection of Critical Essays* (Englewood Cliffs, N. J., 1974), in the "Twentieth-Century Views" series; Alex Zwerdling, *Orwell and the Left* (New Haven, Conn., 1974); J. Meyers, *A Reader's Guide to George Orwell* (London, 1975); C. Small, *The Road to Miniluv: George Orwell, the State and God* (London, 1975); J. Meyers, ed., *George Orwell: The Critical Heritage* (London, 1975); W. Steinhoff, *The Road to "1984"* (London, 1975), published in the U.S. as *George Orwell and the Origins of "1984"* (Ann Arbor, Mich., 1975), includes a bibliography; A. Burgess, *Nineteen Eighty-Five* (London, 1978), the first half is a searching criticism of *Nineteen Eighty-Four* and the second consists of Burgess' own predictions.

B. Crick, *George Orwell: A Life* (London, 1980); L. Smyer, *Orwell's Development as a Psychological Novelist* (St. Louis, 1980); T. R. Fyvel, *George Orwell: A Personal Memoir* (New York, 1982).

# ALAN PATON
(1903–1988)

## *Randy Malamud*

THE WORK OF South African writer Alan Paton is uniformly about the racial injustice of his country's society. From the time his first novel, *Cry, the Beloved Country*, was published in 1948 until his death in 1988, Paton was an unrelenting advocate of liberal reform. He was preeminently a moralist, secondarily a political activist. He considered writing to be his profession, but he gladly exploited his literary talent for his cause.

Paton is not essentially a *personal* moralist, though his fiction certainly is based on the personal, the individual character suffering in an oppressive society. His focus, always beyond the personal, is clearly on the larger social structure that must be changed. He is insistently pragmatic and proudly propagandistic in his writing. He is, stylistically, a better and more engaging writer of novels than of political essays, or newspaper broadsides, or South African biographies (and autobiography), but there is no change of focus as Paton moves from one of these genres to another; he uses whatever forum is available to advance a moral challenge to his country and to the world. "I should like to write books about South Africa which would really stab people in the conscience," he told an interviewer the year after his first novel was published; his mission, as he saw it, was "simply a question of stating an overwhelming truth that a man just cannot deny" (Breit, p. 92).

Paton's readers cannot help being drawn into the murky and anguished world of twentieth-century South Africa's ethical abyss. His fiction, however, does not present an exhaustive political overview of that country's condition; instead, it leads the readers to read more sophisticated and detailed political studies, historical sources, and even, at present, daily newspaper dispatches about the ongoing turmoil. As literal as Paton's scenarios are, they are at the same time a bit impressionistic: Paton is most successful when he distills into one consciousness (as he does with the Reverend Stephen Kumalo in *Cry, the Beloved Country* or Lieutenant Pieter van Vlaanderen in *Too Late the Phalarope*) varied sensibilities and impressions of the country's complex institutionalized racism. Certain political aspects may be highlighted or deemphasized to suit the narrative at hand. A political overview, however, is finally incomplete in his novels. It is more fully realized in his essays and biographies, but these, like his novels, tend to focus on isolated elements of politics and society. Paton's work, therefore, is not ultimately a self-sufficient entity. Rather, its success is marked by the extent to which it draws his audience into the turbulence of South African society. At that point of being drawn in, the difficult task of understanding (and, ideally, working to improve) South Africa's situation has only begun.

Virginia Woolf, in "Mr. Bennett and Mrs. Brown," complained about books that "leave one with so strange a feeling of incompleteness and dissatisfaction. In order to complete them it seems necessary to do something—to join a society, or, more desperately, to write a cheque. That done, the restlessness is laid, the book finished; it can be put on the shelf, and need never be read again." Woolf meant this criticism as derisive of her contemporary novelists; she felt the novelist should be interested "in things in themselves; in character in itself; in the book in itself" (*Collected Essays*, London, 1966, vol. 1, p. 326). That Woolf could write this way reflected a luxury Paton could not afford. Certainly, through her inspection of the enlightened and liberated consciousness, Woolf, too, advances a social vision, but Paton's work reflects an urgency that cannot brook her aesthetic subtlety. His writing is manifestly and intentionally the kind that, as Woolf writes, leaves the reader needing to do more, after finishing the book, to complete the experience.

It is perhaps also true, as Woolf asserts, that once such literature has raised one's consciousness, it need never be read again. Woolf's aesthetic is still potent three-quarters of a century after she crafted it. Paton's writing may well date more quickly. Even forty years after he began writing, the specific scenarios on which he based his fiction were relatively obsolete—sadly, they are not yet rectified, but immeasurably more intricate as the discrimination caused by apartheid has increased vastly. Still, Paton's characterizations of oppressed humanity retain their poignancy, even if the nature and scale of oppression have changed. If and when a democratically representative government is instituted in South Africa, his writing may lose much of its fascination, except as a reminder of the past. Paton certainly would not have minded such a turn of events.

Harvey Breit, interviewing the newly acclaimed writer in 1949, found him "small and wiry and with a lean and hungry look.... His mind is lucid and tough, his speech is precise, unembellished and neutral, yet nevertheless touched as though with a bitter memory. The over-all sense of him is of iron—iron-minded, iron-willed and iron-muscled" (p. 90). This is exactly the kind of author that a reader would infer from the persona through which Paton narrates his novels. For several decades Paton was the most important and most publicized white South African voice for reform.

It is certainly a consequence of South Africa's racism that Paton cannot be said to be the transracial voice of reform: as morally forceful as he may be, he is constrained within the European viewpoint, which is—as all Africans know—the viewpoint of the oppressor, however mitigated it may be by Paton's personal goodwill. Paton writes essentially of whites, and for whites. Even his African characters are white people's Africans. The black South African writer Richard Rive categorizes two strains of writing about his country's troubled history: liberal writing by whites and protest writing by Africans. Liberal writing, of which *Cry, the Beloved Country* was the early international triumph, draws upon a tradition reaching as far back as Olive Schreiner's nineteenth-century stories that confronted the moral dilemma of racism; William Plomer and Laurens van der Post also predate Paton in this liberal South African literature, which is, Rive explains,

> written by concerned, enfranchised white citizens for other white citizens in order to emphasize their moral, social and political responsibility toward blacks. The appeal is directed at those who have the power to effect change or at least have the power to keep the controversy alive. The theme is the discrimination implicit in the black–white situation and the writing . . . is critical of white, racial domination. Concern, trusteeship and guardianship of the less privileged are amongst its primary concerns.
>
> (p. 26)

Liberal writing reflects the indignation of those who are outraged by institutional injustices, though they are not directly affected by them—and certainly may, though unwillingly, benefit from white dominance. In the essay "Apartheid in Its Death Throes," Paton admits:

> Do you want to know what it is like to live under apartheid? Then you should really ask a Black person. I am White and the laws of apartheid are made by White people to preserve the privileges of White people. . . .
>
> The law also weighs heavily on White people—some White people—who hate apartheid, who try to reject it in their own lives, who are every day reminded of the cruelty of the laws that they cannot change.
>
> Your cynical Black friend will say to you: "I am very sad about your suffering, but you continue to enjoy all the protection of the apartheid laws, all the days of your life." And he will be right too.
>
> (*Save the Beloved Country*, p. 66)

Protest writing, such as that of Paton's contemporary Peter Abrahams, embodies the forthright political imperative of those who are actually being oppressed, and whose need to fight that oppression is not simply moral but pragmatic and immediate. Paton's "seeming emphasis of moral issues at the expense of political ones" in *Cry, the Beloved Country* is the basis of much African criticism of his writing. Rive argues: "They claim that Paton is preaching for a revolution of hearts rather than for a revolution in the social and political structure. They prefer the hard-line militant approach to that of the religious idealist" (p. 27).

As effective as Paton may be in capturing and publicizing the experience of the nonwhite South African, those who are themselves oppressed find a lack of substantial protest. "The liberal novel often has a strong moralistic streak and a didacticism which is superimposed on the work rather than emerging from it" (Rive, p. 28)—a self-righteous and possibly gratuitous morality. "There is little room in the protest novel for any form of didacticism. The anger flows directly out of the narrative sequence and often obscures it, so that in its rush of recrimination there is no time to ponder over the morality of what is happening." Liberal didacticism, Rive continues, often leads to a "built-in paternalism, an understanding at a level removed from those with whom it is concerned" (p. 29). Paton presents an example of such paternalism in his biography of Archbishop Clayton, published in 1973. He quotes the churchman in opposition to a policy of white supremacy, speaking of the need to allow Africans to transcend the oppressed position of inferiority in which the government had kept them: "It is a temptation to parents to prevent their children growing up and losing their endearing ways. But it is a temptation that has to be resisted. The children must grow up" (*Apartheid and the Archbishop: The Life and Times of Geoffrey Clayton, Archbishop of Cape Town,* p. 188). Paton shows at least some sensitivity to charges such as Rive's about paternalism; in a footnote to Clayton's quotation, he writes, "This was in 1949. One could not use such metaphors today" (p. 188). Still, when Paton began writing, in the late 1940's, he was certainly susceptible to the same paternalistic instincts as Clayton.

South Africa's institutionalized racism is so pervasive that even those whites who most strongly reject it cannot escape its taint; Paton, however well-meaning, cannot ultimately speak for those with whom his work is most concerned, because he is not one of them. Mitigating his charges of didactic paternalism, Rive admits that the commitment of liberalism "is a genuine one although not of the brand that more radical opinion, especially by blacks, would prefer.... It must be remembered that [Paton] grew up in an era before South African race politics had hardened into its present intransigence and that *Cry, the Beloved Country* appeared at a time when liberalism seemed to provide many answers to South Africa's problems" (p. 30).

The two primary groups of European settlers in South Africa were the Afrikaners (or Boers, Dutch for "farmers"), descended from Dutch, German, and French settlers who began coming to the continent in the seventeenth century, and the British, who bought parts of the country from the Dutch and seized others from the Boers in the nineteenth century. Paton's ancestry was British—his maternal grandparents settled in Natal in the 1850's, and his father came from Scotland in 1901, during the Boer War. Paton's parents called Britain home; he writes that he is proud never to have used that expression. Paton's heritage and culture were strongly British, but a brand of colonial British that was firmly rooted in Africa. As Afrikaners' nationalistic culture grew and came to dominate the country throughout the twentieth century, they regarded English-speaking South Africans as intrusively foreign; and they have resented, for generations, their humiliation and barbarism by the British during the Boer War. Paton was proud that he had a working knowledge of the Afrikaner language, Afrikaans, and recognized the value of the strong national sensibility that tied these people to the country they loved as fiercely as he did; yet throughout his career, he viewed Afrikaners as more susceptible to racial hatred, and as more responsible than English South Africans for the country's problems. Paton certainly did not wish to imitate the Afrikaners in their chauvinism; nevertheless, he promoted, gently but constantly, the contributions he felt British South Africans could offer: a presence that he saw as desirably reform-minded and beneficial for the future.

## LIFE

ALAN STEWART PATON was born in Pietermaritzburg, Natal, on 11 January 1903. His parents were James Paton, a civil servant, and Eunice Warder James, a teacher. He attended high school at Maritzburg College and studied physics at Natal University College (now the University of Natal), where he became involved with religious and civic groups such as the Students' Christian Association and the Students' Representative Council. This involvement anticipated the mixture of religious and civic activism Paton was to embrace throughout his life, and his energetic leadership roles in these groups prefigured his later career.

On 2 July 1928, Paton married Doris Olive Lusted; their son David was born in 1930 and their son Jonathan in 1936. In *Kontakian for You Departed,* a tribute to Dorrie, who died of cancer in 1967, Paton makes clear how important his wife's life and death were as a source of inspiration for his work. Paton's secretary while he was writing that book, Anne Margaret Hopkins, became his second wife in 1969.

Paton's career can be divided into three phases: he was a teacher and schoolmaster from 1924 to 1935, a reformatory principal from 1935 to 1948, and a writer and political activist from the publication of his first novel in 1948 until his death on 12 April 1988, at Botha's Hill in Natal. During the public phase of his life, he was internationally acclaimed and honored—the institutions that awarded Paton honorary degrees include Harvard University (1971), Yale University (1954), Kenyon College (1962), and Edinburgh University (1971), along with such African institutions as Rhodes University (1972) and the University of the Witwatersrand (1975). His literary and humanitarian accolades included the American Ainsfield–Wolf Award and the London *Sunday Times* Special Book Award in 1949; the Benjamin Franklin Award in 1955; the American Freedom Award in 1960; and the Pringle Award in 1973.

### TALES FROM A TROUBLED LAND

IN the early years of his career, Paton was only vaguely concerned with social welfare. He was thrust much more forcefully into the arena of South Africa's social turmoil when he was named principal of Diepkloof reformatory at Potchefstroom, outside Johannesburg. Four hundred African boys, aged as young as seven, were incarcerated there for offenses ranging from trivial acts to murder. (When Paton applied for a principalship, he had expressed a preference *not* to work in an institution for Africans.) Paton spent thirteen years at Diepkloof, leaving shortly after the publication of *Cry, the Beloved Country*—the demands of life as a writer and political participant, he felt, necessitated that he give up his work in the reformatory. In many ways the novel grew out of his work at Diepkloof: he wrote it while on an extensive foreign trip in 1946 and 1947 to inspect prisons and reformatories in Europe and America, and to discover techniques he could implement in South Africa.

As principal, Paton learned to work with Africans. The reformatory's staff included Africans, to many of whom Paton grew quite close and to whom he credited the successes he was able to achieve there. For the first time, he developed a keen sensitivity to the African people at large through his extensive contacts with the boys. He learned the important lesson of making the best of an imperfect system in an imperfect society: juvenile African offenders and misfits certainly did not evoke great concern or sympathy on the part of white government officials and departments, yet Paton was able to improve reformatory conditions significantly. He worked hard and effectively to make the reformatory experience one that would prepare the inmates for a better life after they were released, instead of simply punishing and hardening them, as had been the case before his tenure.

Paton carried out urgently needed improvements in Diepkloof's physical plant: installing latrines to eliminate the putrid smell of the buckets for urination and defecation that had rested in the middle of each cell; getting rid of intimidating security fences and walls. He treated the boys with dignity and paternal affection. He implemented job-training programs and granted temporary furloughs. Morale increased greatly, and Paton gained a wide reputation as a pioneer in liberal reformatory administration. Paton's fiction, especially his collection of short stories called *Tales from a Troubled Land* (1961), is populated with numerous youthful offenders of whom the author offers sympathetic and understanding portraits. At Diepkloof, Paton learned to appreciate the touchingly delicate humanity of young Africans; he also learned how victimized the impoverished African homes and families were in a society dominated by white rulers whose policy was, at best, one of benign neglect.

The stories in *Tales from a Troubled Land* provide insights into harshly broken African families that evoke the cruelty described in nineteenth-century American slave narratives. Because the stories are often modeled closely on Paton's reformatory experiences, many of the characters are criminals. While they all dream of successful and meaningful lives, their opportunities constantly vanish in this "troubled land"—sometimes destroyed by others, sometimes sabotaged by themselves. In these stories, the reformatory principal—obviously an incarnation of Paton—narrates, looking on empathetically but impotently. The authority figure wrestles with the anguish of trying to "reform" people whose world is itself unreformable.

Paton certainly had some success with his charges, but these stories are more about the failures, who indicate the pervasively inhospitable world of South Africa. It is disquieting that so many of Paton's Africans are criminals, recidivists—constantly fighting, stealing, lying. This focus on Africans as criminals and misfits reflects one facet of his inability to escape whites' inherent limitations in viewing Africans. Still, the reformatory authority does not condemn them—he understands them, and somehow takes some of the guilt upon himself, as the representative of white society. Paton's Africans are imprisoned, yet, in a sense, freer of spirit than he is—one dreams of being a preacher, even though he is constantly in jail. Paton disturbs his readers, and means to, by creating a personal sympathy for these characters, then showing the pain in which their lives seem fated to end.

"Death of a Tsotsi" shows what Paton is constantly asserting in these stories: that omnipresent racism generates social corruption. Spike, a well-intentioned graduate of the reformatory, cannot escape involvement in the conflicts of local gangs. He has a good job and a concerned family, yet ends up pointlessly stabbed to death. At his funeral, the head of the reformatory reflects:

We were all of us, white and black, rich and poor, learned and untutored, bowed down by a knowledge that we lived in the shadow of a great danger, and were powerless against it. It was no place for a white person to pose in any mantle of power or authority; for this death gave the lie to both of them.

And this death would go on too, for nothing less than the reform of a society would bring it to an end. It was the menace of the socially frustrated, strangers to mercy, striking like adders for the dark reasons of ancient minds, at any who crossed their paths.

(pp. 105–106)

In "The Waste Land," Paton depicts the tenuous tightrope that any African continually walks in hoping to survive:

The moment that the bus moved on he knew he was in danger, for by the lights of it he saw the figures of the young men waiting under the tree. That was the thing feared by all, to be waited for by the young men. It was a thing he had talked about, now he was to see it for himself....

His wages were in his purse, he could feel them weighing heavily against his thigh. That was what they wanted from him. Nothing counted against that. His wife could be made a widow, his children made fatherless, nothing counted against that. Mercy was the unknown word.

(p. 58)

Though the young men are African, that does not mitigate Paton's assertion that the story's "waste land" is created by white oppression. Whites have created a world in which Africans have to fear even themselves; a world reduced, through poverty and institutional inhumanity, to a vicious jungle in which a man can never attain security for himself and his family, no matter how hard he works or how good he is—a world corrupted, and beyond the control of its victims.

## CRY, THE BELOVED COUNTRY

IN "South Africa Today," a pamphlet Paton wrote in the 1950's to explain his country's plight to the rest of the world, he pinpoints the causes of the corruption and disintegration of African society, in what could be a précis of his first novel:

Many urban parents are at a total loss to understand the wayward behavior of their children, being too simple to recognize how they themselves were sustained.... The truth is that the impact of the cities on tribal life was shattering. Both fathers and mothers had to go out to work, the schools were full, and most children were educated in the streets. Prostitution began, and illicit liquor was obtainable.... law and custom began to wither away.... Theft and housebreaking became the occupations of the shiftless, often carried out with violence and murder.... It is then not to be wondered at that African tribal life has undergone a process of disintegration, and that crime, illegitimacy, and drunkenness disfigure African urban life. A whole nation has been rocked to its foundations.

(p. 18)

*Cry, the Beloved Country* brought Paton immediate international fame when it was published in 1948. It is a fusion of the eloquent rhythms of English, Zulu, Xhosa, and even Afrikaans speech and thought; of the African priest, the Anglican missionary, the prodigal son, the Sophiatown street urchin and prostitute, the European gentleman farmer—all are captured poetically and intertwined tenuously but insistently. Just as all these strands of social culture comprise South Africa's panorama, so they contribute to Paton's symphonic convergence of souls in *Cry*. Paton's vision of all these forces is incisively journalistic and sociological, but more prominently lyrical—with the lyricism, perhaps, of the Old Testament psalmist, cognizant of oppression and injustice, invoking hope for a soothing salvation. Maxwell Anderson and Kurt Weill confirmed Paton's lyrical force when they adapted the novel for their Broadway musical production, *Lost in the Stars:* the opening chorus is taken verbatim from the beginning of Paton's delicate prose narrative:

> There is a lovely road
> that runs from Ixopo into the hills.
> These hills
> are grass covered and rolling, and they are lovely beyond any singing of it.

*Cry, the Beloved Country* brought international attention to the violent and depressing plight of Africans living under white oppression; it is widely credited with bringing South Africa's shame to the world's attention—attention, of course, that was to increase drastically throughout the century, leading to the international isolation of the white South African government and a worldwide moralistic call for reform. Significantly, the novel was conceived and written abroad—in a burst of energy and inspiration Paton felt on his international tour of prisons and reformatories. He became inspired in a cathedral in Trondheim, Norway, as he describes in the autobiographical *Towards the Mountain:*

> It was now almost dark, and the cathedral itself was in darkness.... It has ... one of the most beautiful rose windows in the world, and when we had finished our tour we sat down in two of the front pews and looked at it. There was still enough light in the sky to see its magnificent design and its colours. We did not speak, and I do not know how long we sat there. I was in the grip of a powerful emotion, not directly to do with the cathedral and the rose window, but certainly occasioned by them. I was filled with an intense homesickness, for home and wife and sons, and for my far-off country.
> (pp. 267–268).

Returning to his hotel room, Paton wrote the first chapter before dinner; later, he wrote, "I do not even remember if I knew what the story was to be" (p. 268). As he continued on his fact-finding tour, he completed the novel over the next four months, mostly while in America, and had it enthusiastically accepted by Scribners a month later—after a flurry of manuscripts rushed by mail back and forth across America. Newly made friends and enthusiastic supporters of this novel that he had dashed off hurried to help Paton complete all the arrangements before his return to Africa. The novel is significantly a product of the perspective Paton gained while abroad—his next novel, too, was written while he was on a trip to England—though he never acknowledged (or, perhaps, even recognized) this fact. While he described the novel as an expression of his homesickness, it is a homesickness in (temporary) exile. Other writers more consciously recognized the need to escape from the homeland in order to write about it without becoming mired down in it—James Joyce writing on Ireland from Paris, Doris Lessing writing about Rhodesia from London. Africa, as Paton has often written, is a land of mesmerizing beauty—and certainly of a grandeur that allows one to lose sight of human vanities. The predominant success of *Cry* is that, in it, Paton escapes from the limitations inherent in an uneasily inequitable society and presents for the world at large a picture of its suffering. The novel certainly could not have been written in South Africa.

*Cry* presents the wrenching moral consciousness of a liberal white man groping for answers, for reconciliation, for an antidote to the growing racism that is beginning to sunder a hapless African society. The novel is not about apartheid—apartheid did not begin, institutionally, until the victory of the white supremacist Nationalist Party almost four months after the release of the novel. Paton was not oblivious to the coincidental timing of these events—he wrote in *Towards the Mountain* that the publication of his novel "could justly be called one of the two decisive events in my life. The extraordinary thing is that the second decisive event happened soon after.... the event of May 26, 1948, brought my intention to nothing, and condemned me to a struggle between literature and politics" (pp. 303–304). Legislated apartheid proliferated in the early 1950's, a few years after *Cry* was published—yet it is not a mistake to associate the publication and reception of *Cry* with the origins of, and reaction against, apartheid.

Through fortuitous timing, and certainly with a kind of prescience on the author's part, *Cry* presents the anguishing challenge that South Africa would pose to the world as apartheid quickly crystallized into the brutal system of discrimination that has led the country to the crisis of the late twentieth century. As the situation became more complex over the next decades, he was increasingly criticized by some for maintaining a simplistic and unrealistic perspective on the country's problems. In defense of Paton, it can only be said that at the formative moment of his moral triumph, his country's later complexities had not yet burgeoned.

As in much African writing, the landscape is predominant in *Cry:* the vast veld, the rich soil, the dramatic valleys and rivers, the sights and sounds of birds and animals that seem to be more vitally conscious within the landscape than in any other national literature. In *Towards the Mountain,* Paton's boyhood memories of his country are lushly Edenic:

I cannot describe my early response to the beauty of hill and stream as anything less than an ecstasy.... As often as not a small stream ran down the kloof, and on its banks grew ferns and the wild begonia whose soft stems we would chew for their acid juice.... A glade of clivias in flower, in one of the larger stretches of bush that might be called a forest, is a sight not to be forgotten. ... And one might, though perhaps only once in a lifetime, catch a glimpse of the small mpithi antelope, shy and delicate.

(pp. 4–5)

Paton begins *Cry* with a paean to this land: "Stand unshod upon it, for the ground is holy, being even as it came from the Creator. Keep it, guard it, care for it, for it keeps men, guards men, cares for men. Destroy it and man is destroyed" (p. 3). Yet the covenant between the Africans and their land had been abrogated by the intrusions of a society not their own, one that did not foster their symbiotic harmony with the ecosystem: "But the rich green hills break down.... Too many cattle feed upon the grass, and too many fires have burned it" (p. 3). The land "is not kept, or guarded, or cared for, it no longer keeps men, guards men, cares for men. ... The great red hills stand desolate, and the earth has torn away like flesh.... The men are away, the young men and the girls are away. The soil cannot keep them any more" (pp. 3–4).

Reverend Stephen Kumalo, the respected *umfundisi* of the small Natal village of Ndotsheni, lives in one of the quickly disappearing places where Africans are still in touch with their land and able to control their own lives with relative stability. This control dissipates, though, as Kumalo is forced to forsake the peace of Ndotsheni for a journey to the urban chaos of Johannesburg, where his son, Absalom, and his sister, Gertrude, have gone in search of different lives: lives perhaps more immediately stimulating but also inestimably more uncontrollable and ultimately destructive. Kumalo is entreated, in a letter from a fellow priest in the Johannesburg African slum of Sophiatown, to rescue his sick sister. Kumalo's quest represents his awakening to the sordid urban world that heralds the Africans' unpromising future. To pay for this trip, he must spend the small sum of money that had been scrupulously saved to send Absalom to St. Chad's, "to learn that knowledge without which no black man can live" (p. 9)—the knowledge for which Africans must fight so hard, against whites' intentions that they stay uneducated and unable to challenge white authority. But Kumalo's wife knows the implication of her son's having disappeared in Johannesburg without having sent any word home: "Absalom will never go now to St. Chad's" (p. 8).

The quest begins with a draining and dizzying train journey, on which Kumalo's countrypeople already start to lose their identities: in the train carriage he sees "some with strange assortments of European garments, some with blankets over their strange assortments, some with blankets over the semi-nudity of their primitive dress, though these were all women. Men travelled no longer in primitive dress" (p. 13). In his trip to the city, Kumalo learns of the other world that is increasingly attracting hordes of Africans—"All roads lead to Johannesburg" (p. 10). The train takes Kumalo away from the safe and the familiar, and toward the hostile and entropic world of the city:

One must catch buses too, but not as here, where the only bus that comes is the right bus. For there there is a multitude of buses, and only one bus in ten, one bus in twenty maybe, is the right bus. If you take the wrong bus, you may travel to quite some other place. And they say it is danger to cross the street, yet one must needs cross it. For there is the wife of Mpanza of Ndotsheni, who had gone there when Mpanza was dying, saw her son Michael killed in the street. Twelve years and moved by excitement, he stepped out into danger, but she was hesitant and stayed at the curb. And under her eyes the great lorry crushed the life out of her son.

(p. 12)

When Kumalo finally sees Johannesburg, it is as a terrifying dynamo:

Railway lines, railway-lines, it is a wonder. To the left, to the right, so many that he cannot count. A train rushes past them, with a sudden roaring of sound that makes him jump in his seat. And on the other side of them, another races beside them, but drops slowly behind. Stations, stations, more than he has ever imagined. People are waiting there in hundreds, but the train rushes past, leaving them disappointed.

(pp. 16–17)

In Johannesburg, Kumalo finds a remnant of kindness in Msimangu, who had sent him the letter, and others who are not yet corrupted; but the city is predominantly a place where Kumalo learns firsthand "of the sickness of the land, of the broken tribe and the broken house, of young men and young girls that went away and forgot their customs and lived loose and idle lives" (p. 22). As Msimangu explains, "The white man has broken the tribe. . . . It suited the white man to break the tribe. . . . But it has not suited him to build something in the place of what is broken" (pp. 25–26). South Africa's hegemonic white power structure has divided and conquered the country's original inhabitants; Paton's scenario evokes the government's seizure of Africans' lands, dispersion of tribal and cultural strengths, and enforced economic dependence on the meager wages that African laborers receive from the country's vast natural wealth (the profits of which accumulate in white hands). Paton weaves such underlying causes of Africans' troubled lives into the background of his narrative when they do not directly fit the plot. In several interpolated choric passages, Paton shows Africans facing extreme housing shortages, discussing the politics of economic exploitation and oppressive antilabor tactics, planning strikes and boycotts, nurturing incipient stirrings for self-control and self-rule.

Kumalo, attempting to find and reunify his dissolving family, learns from Msimangu that Gertrude "has no husband now. . . . It would be truer to say, he said, that she has many husbands" (p. 23). She makes and sells "bad liquor . . . made strong with all manner of things that our people have never used. . . . These women sleep with any man for their price. A man has been killed at her place. They gamble and drink and stab. She has been in prison, more than once" (p. 23).

Paton learned of these neighborhoods, these worlds, from the inhabitants at Diepkloof. He knew how insidiously seductive they were, how dangerous, how inescapable. And as Paton reached out to the victims of these worlds at the reformatory, so Kumalo ventures deeper and deeper into Johannesburg's slums with only compassion for those it has overcome, and determination to bring his family out of it.

He is unsuccessful at extricating Gertrude and Absalom. Though he finds his sister, and convinces her to return home, she disappears just as they are about to leave Johannesburg; she is addicted to its depravity, unable to escape its lure. Kumalo does, though, bring home the son she has had in the city, representing the potential of a better life for the next generation and a hope that his people can learn from and surmount the oppressive lives of this generation. Similarly, Kumalo's son is no longer able to return to his home, having complicated and lost control of his life even more horribly than Gertrude. Absalom has been in the reformatory and, like the reformed Spike in *Tales from a Troubled Land,* has been unable to sustain his innocence in a world of violence. Following vague hints about where his wandering son has gone (unwillingly given by suspicious and fearful urban Africans), Kumalo spends wearying days trying to follow the faint trail Absalom left as he moved from shanty to shanty. As Kumalo traces each step in his son's odyssey, he learns more about Absalom's descent into the troubled, shady world of Johannesburg. Ironically, after Kumalo has spent a great deal of energy and money tracing his son, Paton shows the police retracing the same steps, quickly and easily. They intimidate all the people who know of Absalom's whereabouts, and extract from them the information they were so hesitant to give his father. The police are seeking Absalom because he is a suspect in the murder of a white engineer.

The murder of Arthur Jarvis, a fighter for justice, rocks Johannesburg. Jarvis, whose character is a composite of Paton himself and the contemporaries he admired, had been a popular speaker at liberal functions. In a paper on which he was working moments before he was killed, Jarvis explores the dynamics of South African society in the unmitigated terms of Paton's own moral sensibility:

It is not permissible to develop any resources if they can be developed only at the cost of the labour. It is not permissible to mine any gold, or manufacture any product, or cultivate any land, if such mining and manufacture and cultivation depend for their success on a policy of keeping labour poor. It is not permissible to add to one's possessions if these things can only be done at the cost of other men. Such development has only one true name, and that is exploitation....

... Our natives today produce criminals and prostitutes and drunkards, not because it is their nature to do so, but because their simple system of order and tradition and convention has been destroyed.

(pp. 145–146)

Kumalo, as he reads of the killing in the newspaper, remembers that Jarvis' father is a farmer in the hills above Ndotsheni: "I know him well by sight and name, but we have never spoken"; he remembers Arthur, too, as "a small bright boy" (p. 72). Kumalo and his son are finally reunited in prison: brought together by the police rather than by a father's loving quest, and when it is too late to avert Absalom's tragedy. Absalom had carried a revolver, "For safety, he says. This Johannesburg is a dangerous place. A man never knows when he will be attacked" (p. 98). Kumalo poses many questions while trying to discover what happened—what Absalom was doing at Jarvis' house, why he has led the life he has. Presumably, Absalom was robbing the house, but all the precise questions his father poses "cannot be answered"—there are no neat answers, or reasons, in Absalom's profoundly unreasonable world. Absalom's only defense or explanation is "I was frightened when the white man came. So I shot him. I did not mean to kill him" (p. 98).

Kumalo and the elder Jarvis, who had never spoken, are now cruelly thrust together in this social morass. The novel's second book switches from Kumalo's perspective to Jarvis'. It begins identically to the first book: "There is a lovely road that runs from Ixopo into the hills. These hills are grass-covered and rolling, and they are lovely beyond any singing of it" (p. 129). It is, of course, the same country that Kumalo and Jarvis inhabit, and they are forced to acknowledge this bond through the sorrow their sons have brought them. For the rest of the novel, though the narrative extensively follows Absalom's trial, his contrition, his death sentence and ultimate execution, Paton concentrates more hopefully on the two fathers, and how they must confront their pain constructively and together. Paton is not a nostalgist—clearly, he would have preferred to explore the future of his country through the lives of the young men, Absalom Kumalo and Arthur Jarvis, but both are dead. Paton leaves only the less satisfying recourse of considering, in the third and final book of the novel, how the fathers cope: how they try, in spite of their losses, to continue in a humanistic progression toward justice even in view of the pervasive injustice that afflicts both their lives; how they learn to communicate with each other, willingly and productively, instead of only through the necessity of the tragedy that brought them together.

Absalom, before his incarceration, had lived with a young woman in Pimville—an orphan, as badly off as everyone in the ramshackle satellite settlements outside Johannesburg—whom he planned to marry, and who is pregnant with his child. Kumalo reaches out to her with love, arranges for her to marry his son as he awaits execution, and brings her back to Ndotsheni; though he cannot bring his son, he brings the promise of a grandchild, rescuing mother and child from the misery of the city. When he returns to Ndotsheni, Kumalo is broken by what he has experienced in the city; nevertheless, he works to improve his people's lives, to uplift his village, to care for what is left of his family, in the hope that the sins of the parents will not be visited on the children rescued from Johannesburg.

Kumalo confronts drought and desolation in Ndotsheni, partly the result of the lack of agricultural education and partly of forced exploitation of land resources. The young son of the murdered Jarvis has returned to rural Natal, and reminds Kumalo of Arthur Jarvis as a boy. The murdered man's son wanders into the Africans' village and, with the innocence and kindness of youth, connects freely with them. Seeing their desolation, the boy acts as an intermediary to his grandfather, who delivers to the village much-needed milk, the gift of life, to help the Africans through the period of drought. The elder Jarvis, having learned the importance of his son's work to improve the lives of Africans, carries on this work by hiring an "agricultural demonstrator" to teach Africans how to farm more scientifically and productively. At the end of the novel, the continuation of Kumalo's and Jarvis' efforts to work for a better society heralds regeneration, the coming of dawn in this land of sublime beauty mixed with pervasive misery—not yet the time "of our emancipation, from the fear of bondage and the bondage of fear" (p. 277), for that hope is, Paton knows, still uncertain; but a dawn that may lead to that better dawn. The novel, as Edward Callan writes,

offers no blueprint for a utopian society. It offers instead recognition of personal responsibility. The crucial development in the characters of both Jarvis and Kumalo is that each comes to recognize how individual fear or indifference infects society with moral paralysis; and that the antidote for this paralysis is individual courage willing to go forward in faith.

(p. 41)

Horton Davies, in a 1959 study of the role of Christian ministry in the modern novel, finds that *Cry, the Beloved Country* asserts that "the ultimate reconciliation of racial tensions is to be found in Christian humility, forgiveness, and compassion" (*A Mirror of the Ministry in Modern Novels,* p. 129)—that is, in the spirit of religious transcendence embodied in the African Reverend Kumalo and the English Father Vincent (who assists Kumalo and Msimangu with their quest in the city, and whose character is based on a close friend of Paton's, an Anglican priest from Johannesburg). The novel, through its focus on the biblical motifs of the prodigal son, the redemptive value of suffering, the compassion shown by Reverend Kumalo, and the sublime forgiveness embodied in the elder Jarvis, finds its spirit of reassurance in Christian faith, Davies asserts; and Father Vincent stands out as the consummate spirit of understanding and Christian salvation. This interpretation illustrates grounds for criticism of Paton's vision based on this religious emphasis (which, for Marxist critics, will certainly appear as a kind of opiate in the strikingly unreligious world of the novel's victims and its immoral society) and on the depiction of benevolent whites. Though whites are marginal to the social morass that the novel describes, they are, as Davies and others have found, in some ways supremely omniscient and transcendent, paternalistic and possessed of a larger Christian humanity, compared with the noble but stumbling African protagonists. Edmund Fuller writes, "The primary story is pathetic, in that the suffering characters are more bewildered victims than prime movers in their difficulties" (*Books with Men Behind Them,* p. 95). As Richard Rive reminds us, the African tradition of protest literature finds this pathos belittling.

The novel's British edition bears the subtitle *A Story of Comfort in Desolation.* Paton finds this comfort in Absalom's repentance, Jarvis' forgiveness, and the promise of the children. Would a real-life Absalom have found comfort in this? Is it too tidy to look for comfort in the decadent and oppressive world in which Absalom falls? A. A. Monye rejects the sensibility of *Cry, the Beloved Country,* finding that its emotions

do not offer any positive solution to the problems of racism and colonial brutality in South Africa. We are merely invited to cry for a bruised and bleeding land and people. But the question is: Should we merely Cry? Is crying all we can do for these unfortunate victims of apartheid? . . . [Paton's sermon] is meaningless in a society where the basic requirements of life are denied a section of it. It is useless in a system where a negligible number of the population arrogate to themselves certain privileges and rights which they deny an integral part of that same just because of the pigmentation of the skin. To preach love to a people who are denied all their human rights, a people, who denied their ancestral heritage, are forced to the shanties and ghettoes by aliens who now occupy the richer part of the land, is quite unrealistic. Love in this society will only be realistic when what has been denied the Black South African is restored to him.

(pp. 74–75)

Monye, criticizing Paton from the tradition of protest writing, finds the characterizations of Africans naive and pointless:

I think this journalistic exercise—showing us a weeping people and expecting us to respect and pity them—is quite inadequate a solution to the reality of the Black man's predicament in racist South Africa. It could, at best, give us cue for action, but it is not positive action in itself. Today, the African writer is not content with only exposing the sufferings of his people for the world to see. He is now concerned with how to devise a positive solution to the problems of his people.

(p. 76)

Kumalo, Monye feels, is

like the absurd man in the proverb who leaves his burning house to pursue a rat fleeing from the flames. . . . [he] leaves reality and pursues shadows. He weeps when he should confront the enemy. He prays when he should use his position to lead his people in an organised revolt against the oppressive system of his country.

(p. 76)

## TOO LATE THE PHALAROPE

PATON followed his first novel with *Too Late the Phalarope* in 1953. Here he focuses more intently on the portrait of an Afrikaner rather than an African. Pieter van Vlaanderen is the victim of social disintegration, and an emblem of the torturously confused personal morality that is a consequence of living in a society that is in moral turmoil. Taken as a companion to *Cry, the Beloved Country*, *Too Late the Phalarope* shows that great suffering (though not, of course, equal blame) lies on both sides of the color bar. Van Vlaanderen's tragedy is that "he was always two men" (p. 3) at the same time. One of his personalities is strictly in accord with the Afrikaner ideal: a police lieutenant, dispassionately enforcing law and order, oblivious to the social harm his people are inflicting. But the other person is a man with "strange unusual thoughts in his mind, and a passion for books and learning" (p. 2)—a person whose passion cannot be limited by the narrow-minded thinking of the Afrikaner Nationalists, and who knows that the law he enforces is wrong, that he cannot live by it. His aunt, narrating the story, records that it is "the story of our destruction" (p. 3); the outside world crashes down on van Vlaanderen's character just as it did on Kumalo's. Paton initially presents van Vlaanderen in his first role, as enforcer of apartheid: he stops a British boy who had been having some sort of possibly subversive (in the eyes of the police lieutenant) encounter with Stephanie, a young African woman. Van Vlaanderen stresses for the boy the importance of the Immorality Act:

> The police have had instructions to enforce the Immorality Act without fear or favour. Whether you're old or young, rich or poor, respected or nobody, whether you're a Cabinet Minister or a *predikant* or a headmaster or a tramp, if you touch a black woman and you're discovered, nothing'll save you.
>
> (p. 13)

The act, instituted in 1927 and strengthened by the Nationalists in 1950, was the cornerstone of apartheid, legislative "racial purity"; it reflected the fear and disgust its architects felt toward nonwhites. Afrikaners viewed the possibility of love between African and white people as extremely dangerous; their fear of such love seems to reveal their unease with their situation in Africa—a recognition of how fragile their condition is. In *Towards the Mountain*, Paton confirms that the terror of the Immorality Act had not lessened in the decades since he wrote of it in his novel:

> If a white man of any substance, a minister of religion, a professor, a lawyer, a schoolmaster, is found guilty of breaking this law, his life is ruined, even if the court suspends his punishment. At the time I write this, three white men have committed suicide in the last few weeks rather than face trial.
>
> (p. 16)

With the rise of the Nationalist government in Pretoria came the firmest commitment to legislated racial separation, and a conviction that such separateness was God's will. Paton writes in *Too Late the Phalarope*:

> They set their conquered enemies apart, ruling them with unsmiling justice, declaring "no equality in Church or State," and making the iron law that no white man might touch a black woman, nor might any white woman be touched by a black man.
> And to go against this law, of a people of rock and stone in a land of rock and stone, was to be broken and destroyed.
>
> (p. 17)

Such is the incarnation of the "first person" that van Vlaanderen is—but the other person, a man of thought and passion, naturally cannot bridle his passion according to the cruelly irrational laws of a totalitarian government. When Pieter was a young boy, his father tried to raise him to be a stern, dispassionate, and unfeeling Afrikaner: he forbade the boy to pursue his hobby, his passion, of collecting stamps, which the father viewed as unmanly. Though Pieter was forced to repress this passion, he never abandoned it; and though the South African government tried to forbid interracial love, the older Pieter is similarly unable to forsake this passion when it comes his way.

He develops an infatuation for Stephanie in spite of his love for his wife and children, and in spite of his firsthand knowledge of the uncompromising way the police force and the government deal with such love. Stephanie has often been jailed, for the same kinds of offenses as Gertrude's in *Cry*, and she risks losing custody of her young child; she therefore allows the romance to develop, hoping to gain some power over Pieter that will enable her to keep her child. As Pieter gives Stephanie a little money, and tries to arrange a job for her, she lets him know where she will be at a certain time in the evening, in a deserted place. He is wrenchingly torn between the two people that he is, in a society that will not allow for such a range of personality; he cannot repress his "second person," but instead follows his impulse and passion: he goes to the place Stephanie had mentioned:

where it is dark, away from the three pools of light. And he came to the place where the blue-gums are, and the *kakiebos* weed in the vacant ground. And he stood there waiting in the dark, with the mad sickness and the fear.
And there, God forgive him, he possessed her.
(p. 153)

From that point, Pieter lives a nightmare of psychological terror and paranoia. When he returns home, a note pinned to his door states I SAW YOU, and he lives in constant fear of exposure. The note turns out to be a joke played by his friend Japie, a welfare worker, which referred to a trivial flirtation Pieter had had with a white woman. Nicholas H. Z. Watts observes that the phrase, in the present tense, is a traditional Zulu greeting "that acknowledges and respects the identity of the other. Pieter's reaction is a measure of how far apart he has drifted from those around him" (p. 253). He is tormented by the certainty that the society in which he has progressed so successfully according to its rules will turn on him. Yet in spite of his torment, he continues his relationship with Stephanie. Through this characterization, Paton asserts that Afrikaners—at least some—are not merely racist automatons, but have another aspect to their personalities, an individual pursuit of passion that defies legislated hatred.

J. B. Thompson asserts that Pieter's infatuation with Stephanie is not emotional: "Stephanie is no soul mate of Pieter's and not even a 'playmate,' but is joylessly used by him as a sexual object for sinister psychological purposes of his own" (p. 38): to undermine his people's blind faith in the force of racial purity. All Pieter feels for Stephanie, Thompson argues, "is the sort of benevolence he feels towards all members of 'the black nation' " (p. 38). Pieter's intent in the affair is to bring to the surface the second person that he is, and to destroy the first. "If his aim were to bring the maximum disgrace upon his family," Thompson writes, "he could not have made a better choice, and that, I feel, is precisely the point. It is a sort of blind irrational retaliation. . . . The consequence is an eruption of defiance" (pp. 40, 41). Myrtle Hooper, though noting, as Thompson does, the impersonal objectification of Stephanie, criticizes Paton for complicity in enforcing her silence, which represents the "elusion [of her character] of both author and reader" (p. 62). She asks, "As a prominent and respected member of his community, as a policeman, is [Pieter] not simply exploiting someone weaker than himself, disadvantaged, and voiceless?" (pp. 58–59). She argues that a character from J. M. Coetzee's novel *Foe* illustrates the same void that Stephanie represents in *Too Late the Phalarope*: "Many stories can be told of [Robinson Crusoe's "manservant"] Friday's tongue, but the true story is buried within Friday, who is mute. The true story will not be heard by art till we have found a means of giving voice to Friday" (p. 61).

The novel's enigmatic title comes from an episode in Pieter's relationship with his father, representing the dilemma of the Afrikaner who is in his prime trying to come to terms with the stoic and stubborn tradition of his people. For his father's birthday, Pieter has bought him a book—a dangerous gift, because the anti-intellectual old man scorns any literature except the Bible. This book, *The Birds of South Africa*, meets with some approval from the elder van Vlaanderen, who is, like all good Afrikaners, a lover of the land. It represents a potential connection between the "second" Pieter—the thinker, the member of a generation that is different from his father's—and the elder van Vlaanderen. But the book is by an Englishman, which offends the father's anti-British prejudices. The old man delights in finding mistakes in the book:

—Pieter, have you ever seen the phalarope?
—The what, father?
—The phalarope.
[His father] added impatiently, a bird.
Then his son, for politeness sake, took a step or two also until he stood by his father, but his father still did not turn to him, but stood as he was before.
—No, father.
—That Englishman of yours says they're birds of the coasts. Have you ever seen the *ruitertjie*, at the farm at Buitenverwagtig?

—Yes, father.

—And you've seen the phalarope there too, but you always thought it was the *ruitertjie.*

—It could be, said his son doubtfully.

His father turned to him.

—I didn't say it could be, he said, I said it was. Do you think I was blind when I was young?

—No, father, but . . .

But his father had turned round and faced us all. It gave him pleasure that we were all listening to him, but I write down here that it was not a vain pleasure, it was more a kind of mischief.

(pp. 115–116)

Much later, while on a family picnic, the father (whose incapacity for intimacy with his son mirrors Paton's relationship with his own father) spots a phalarope, and points it out to Pieter—confirming his own expertise and the Englishman's mistake—trying to share a moment of natural communion, the phalarope's flash of grace, with his son.

These are the novel's only references to the phalarope. From the title, the reader must infer that this is all too late—that is, the son tries to share the Afrikaner naturalist passion with his father through the son's medium, a book. The father also tries to share a part of his son's life by buying him a block of stamps for his birthday, decades after he had forbidden his son to collect them. But the essential connections have been lost; the time for possible understanding has passed, and Pieter has already taken the step that will earn his father's unrelenting hatred.

With an Afrikaner subordinate of van Vlaanderen's (who hates Pieter because he should have been his superior, but is of lower rank because he refused to fight with the English in World War II, as Pieter had), Stephanie conspires to reveal Pieter as her lover. When the father learns of Pieter's transgression with Stephanie, he crosses out his son's name in the family Bible, destroys every photograph and reminder of Pieter, and locks the front door, saying, "The door shall not be opened again" (p. 251). Pieter's wife and children leave him, and his father dies of shame eight days later. At the end of the story, Pieter receives a prison sentence, but the emphasis is not on society's punishment of him; rather, it is on the horrible crumbling of his family, their inability to survive the maelstrom of their country's irrational system, their unwillingness to face the human reality of uncontrollable passion. Pieter has lived his life unable to find comfort in the sober religion, the stern self-satisfaction, and the self-righteousness of his father.

Earlier, Pieter had heard a story told by a schoolmate of his who came to the aid of a woman in an auto accident: he rescued her from the car, holding her in his arms, until he saw that it was a Malay woman.

And he could not hold her any more; he let her go in horror, not even gently, he said, and even though a crowd was there. And without a word he pushed through the crowd and went on his way. For the touch of such a person was abhorrent to him, he said. . . .

(p. 126)

Pieter envies his friend's idiotic racism, his horror of nonwhites, "for to have such a horror is to be safe" (p. 126)—safe from confronting the unstable reality around him and the schizophrenic inclinations of his own character. But to be a thinking and feeling member of Afrikaner society, Paton asserts, is to be tormented. And, as in *Cry, the Beloved Country,* the beauty of the phalarope, and of the land, is no longer a sufficient force to overcome the turmoil that people have wrought in the land—it is too late.

## AH, BUT YOUR LAND IS BEAUTIFUL

PATON's next novel, *Ah, But Your Land Is Beautiful* (1982), followed *Too Late the Phalarope* by nearly three decades—time Paton spent writing biographies and essays, and participating extensively in South African politics. In the novel (part of a planned trilogy, never completed), Paton returns to the 1950's, perhaps because that was a time he felt he understood better than the 1980's; a time when, in retrospect, the murky situation seemed clearer, and when it seems one could have done something, and found a clearer way out of the situation than was imaginable in the 1980's.

Paton's narrative becomes immensely more intricate in *Ah, But Your Land Is Beautiful* than in his earlier novels: numerous plots are intertwined and deal more explicitly with the political issues of the 1950's than in the earlier novels (which used these issues more as a backdrop against which an emotional human story was set). Among the issues discussed are civil disobedience, Indian resistance, the establishment of African homelands (and the usurping of more attractive African land by whites), the Group Areas Act (segregating living areas, and fragmenting African families and homes), "Bantu education" (the meager educational system for Africans), mixed worship laws, sanctions, segregation of sports associations, and, again, the Immorality Act and the idea of racial purity.

The various stories that encompass all these issues are, at first, difficult to follow and link together, but appreciating discrete individual stories is not the point of this novel: Paton succeeds at what he means to do, bombarding his readers with a pastiche made up of a vast range of anatomies of oppression and struggles to surmount this oppression. The reader gets not so much a feeling of empathy (as is evoked for Kumalo or van Vlaanderen) as a general sensitivity to the tenor of South African racism. Thematically, the novel indicates Paton's more mature view of apartheid. It depicts the years when the South African government constructed the harshest measures of apartheid with the most enthusiasm and dedication to isolating the different races and keeping nonwhites subordinate. No longer does Paton see the simple enduring spirit of a noble protagonist as a viable weapon against discrimination; instead, he points his readers toward the overwhelming panorama of oppression, all of which must be taken in and confronted by various members of the opposition, acting in some kind of unity. This novel is more aggressive and forthrightly activist than his first two, and more inspirational for direct political involvement in the specific issues Paton depicts in detail.

The voice of the oppressed is more authentic, more self-controlling, and more angry in this novel than in the earlier ones. Paton tells, for example, of a nurse–missionary who has devoted her life to the care of Africans in the slums, and who is killed during a riot provoked by the police:

Of course it is said, and how could it not be, that the Defiance Campaign is responsible for her death. And of course it is said, and how could it not be, that the real causes of her death are the laws of apartheid, and the poverty, and the frustrations, and the belief that the white rulers of South Africa know only one language, and that is the language of violence. It is the language they speak, and therefore it is the language in which they must be spoken to. It is not a campaign of protest, it is a war, and therefore everything white must be destroyed, even the sisters and their hospitals and their clinics and their schools.

(p. 26)

While this confidently accusatory voice is not the only voice in the novel, it is for Paton newly radical, newly strong. Like *Cry, the Beloved Country,* the novel is a fusion of the various voices of South Africa; but in contrast with those in his first novel, the voices are more extreme, more directly combative, more isolated from each other in their own camps. African protesters proudly and fiercely chant, "Mayibuye! Afrika! Afrika! Afrika!" ("Come back, Africa," or, "Give Africa back to us.") At the other extreme, the voice of a woman who writes obscene letters signed "Proud White Christian Woman" to the liberal white reformer Robert Mansfield (who is, like Jarvis in *Cry, the Beloved Country* and the reformatory director in *Tales from a Troubled Land,* another incarnation of Paton), embodies a compulsive psychological sickness:

I have read about your speech in Cape Town. So you are against the Immorality Act. That's nothing to wonder about, because every time you poke your black dolly girls, you must be afraid of getting caught. What do they say? Caught in the act, ha! ha! I can see it, you and your dolly girl pawing at each other like two animals, breathing, panting, stinking of sex and sweat.

I bet you wake up at night and can imagine it all. How can you imagine such filth? You call yourself a Christian. How can you imagine such things? And that fuzzy hair, above and below.

Has your wife found any hair on the pillow yet? Or has she got her own black lover? You would both stoop to anything, I am sure.

(p. 99)

Another series of anonymous letters, from "The Preservation of White South Africa League," further explores the taint of such perverse hatred:

This is a letter of warning to you. It should be taken very seriously. We note that you have accepted the chairmanship of the Natal region of the Liberal Party. We regard your party as anti-Christian, and anti-White South African, and we have taken the decision that all the regional chairmen of the party, and all those who are foolish enough to become their successors, would be eliminated.

Do you know the meaning of the word *eliminated,* Mr. Mansfield? It has the same meaning as it had in Germany, under the great Führer Adolf Hitler.

(p. 77)

(In 1960, Paton had his passport suspended when he said, "We are not a Nazi country, but we are not a bad imitation of one" [*New York Times*, 12 April 1988]. It was not restored until 1970.) The novel presents pervasive conflict and tension: not just interracially but also whites against whites, Afrikaners against Afrikaners, party members in conflict with each other—Paton thus demonstrates the unavoidable turbulence and dissension that is ripping his society apart.

Paton's authorial voice is more aggressively critical of the government than in his earlier work, and totalitarian government leaders are more pointedly exposed as Orwellian villains. The obvious hypocrisy of this government is exposed, for example, through its opposition to the Freedom Charter (which demands basic rights for Africans—free education, abolition of apartheid, right to a fair trial, freedom of travel, abolition of pass laws and permits, and so forth—which the government views as treasonable, communistic). The government responds to this with language that evokes *Animal Farm*: Apartheid is "Dr. Hendrik's Great Plan for peaceful and harmonious separate coexistence" (p. 110); the government acts to protect "peaceful natives who appreciated that the apartheid laws were made for their advancement" (p. 168) from the supporters of the Freedom Charter. Paton's Orwellian sarcasm is evident in the attempts to prove that the Freedom Charter is a communist document, undertaken by three Afrikaner scholars who "are probably the greatest experts in the world on communism. Dr. Munnik's works in particular are said to be so profound that the number of people who understand them is small" (p. 143). And Nationalists fantasize about their own leadership: "Never in history have so few legislated so thoroughly and devotedly for so many divergent peoples, nor ever before in history have rulers shown such a high sense of purpose or idealism" (p. 67).

The novel is intentionally fragmented; while many of these fragments are even more propagandistic than Paton's earlier fiction, some are as incisively moving as anything Paton has written: a kindly white judge, for example, is asked to participate in the ceremony of washing feet at an African church's Maundy Thursday service. He agrees to be called to wash the feet of the elderly African woman who had nursed all of his children; when he begins to do this, he remembers how kind she has been to his family, and how she used to kiss their feet after bathing them, and he does the same for her. A white newspaper reporter happens to witness this, and writes the story for his newspaper, causing a tremendous scandal and reactionary hostility among white society:

In the first place the judge's action at Bochabela ran counter to the racial policy of the Government.... Mixed worship is not compatible with racial separation, and racial separation is the mandate that was given to the Government in 1948, and renewed even more strongly in 1953. . . .

[His action] is repugnant to most white Christian opinion, and certainly to most Afrikaner Christian opinion. The performance was melodramatic and tasteless.
(pp. 249–250)

Paton paints the scene as he depicted van Vlaanderen's transgression: as a simple act that rocks the false complacency of racist society; as a kind of personal tragedy for the transgressor but, more depressingly, as a ridiculously unnecessary trauma for society. Though these traumas fester unresolved in Paton's fiction, there seems to be a tentative hope that beyond the scope of the novel these traumas will awaken South Africans to the precarious state of their country and, after enough such traumas have taken place, will spur them to forsake and atone for their prejudices.

### LIBERAL PARTY ACTIVITY

PATON did not exhort reform solely through his writing. For fifteen years, from 1953 until 1968, he was heavily involved in the formation and guidance of South Africa's strident, though often quixotic, Liberal Party. At the far left of the (white) political spectrum, the Liberals eventually called for universal adult suffrage, unqualified and regardless of race. The party attempted to be multiracial, thus drawing the condemnation of the vast majority of white South Africans, though in practice most politically active nonwhites found a more effective forum in such nonwhite groups as the African National Congress, the Pan-African Congress, and various Indian congresses. Some of these groups, Paton writes, "accused us of weakening the only true opposition in the country" (*Journey Continued*, p. 68). The party finally disbanded in 1968, when the government prohibited interracial organizations. Paton was vice president of the party at its formation, and became its national chairman in 1956 and its president in 1958. The Liberals suffered a battery of criticism, and Paton's descriptions of his party's work in his autobiographies illuminate the profoundly chaotic state of any South African political movement that challenges the status quo: In *Journey Continued*, he writes:

The critics of the right viewed our racial policies with abhorrence. What kind of people called for the repeal of the Mixed Marriages Act and the Immorality Act? We were obviously sex-obsessed, and we were particularly attracted by the thought of sex across the colour line.

Our critics on the left regarded us as useless. They accused us . . . of "blunting the edge of the revolution." They were angry with us for not joining the grand Congress movement. We were preventing black and coloured and Indian people from joining their own congresses, by offering them this pie-in-the-sky non-racialism.

We were accused . . . of making promises that we could never keep. I do not remember any of these promises. We promised blood and toil and tears and sweat, and that is what many of us got.

(p. 117)

The Liberal Party polled only one-third of one percent in the 1961 national elections, and did not run a candidate in the 1966 elections. Clearly, the party was based on an idealism that found only a negligible constituency in the real-life world of South African politics. Liberals were criticized for their political innocence and what seemed to opponents to be a willfully naive disregard for "the dynamics of history, the imperatives of economics, or the strategic devices of power. Liberals have tended to respond that the first are obscure, the second debatable, and the third are often morally dubious," writes Douglas Irvine (p. 120). African leaders, such as the African National Congress' president Chief Albert Luthuli, resented "white liberals' initial concern in the 1950s with 'civilization' as a criterion for voting rights, and impatience as well with what often seemed too great a regard for respectability and legality" (p. 118)—even the Liberals did not advocate full universal suffrage until 1960.

While the Liberals never found the groundswell of support they sought, they tenaciously forbore to engage in extensive government harassment, bannings, police raids, and bombings, and used their platform as a soapbox from which to denounce the South Africans' increasing embrace of apartheid. At the party's final meeting in 1968, Paton admitted, "The party was small and not powerful. But it was formed to give expression to ideas that were not small, and were full of power": ideas such as freedom of the individual, of association, of employment, of residence. "The government was afraid of them. Therefore, it took merciless steps against those who held them" (quoted in Irvine, p. 133). Paton's energetic commitment to actual change through political involvements added to his writing the force of one who was not merely an idle or theoretical observer of events, but of one who had done everything within his power to affect them. Paton's historical overview in *Hope for South Africa* (1958), and his copious essays from the 1960's through the 1980's, collected in *Save the Beloved Country* (1989), embody a bitterly pessimistic assessment of South African society and government; but his bitterness reflects the experience of one who, though he has failed, has made a valiant effort to extend the moral vision of his literature into the world outside it.

## BIOGRAPHIES

PATON wrote two full-length biographies: *Hofmeyr* (1964), abridged in an American edition as *South African Tragedy: The Life and Times of Jan Hofmeyr*, and *Apartheid and the Archbishop: The Life and Times of Geoffrey Clayton*. Paton knew both subjects personally and fairly intimately—he worked with both, and recorded in his autobiography that they were two of the most profound influences on his life and career. In his study of the politician Hofmeyr, whom Paton acclaims as a relatively positive moral force in the 1920's through the 1940's, Paton demonstrates the extremely dubious relativism that has always marked even the liberal end of the white South African political spectrum. (Certainly, his homage to Hofmeyr helps to explain Paton's own relativism and—in the eyes of Africans and the West—occasional deficiencies in his activism.) Hofmeyr was founding principal of the University of Witwatersrand; minister of finance, mines, education, interior, and public health; a leader of the United Party, a compelling statesman, and deputy prime minister during the Smuts era. Paton is adulatory of his boyhood schoolmate, and demonstrates in this work the biographer's stamina and dedication to factual precision; the work as a whole, though, concentrates on extreme technicalities and nuances of politics, often overdone. Paton shows Hofmeyr as a man possessing some degree of conscience in an unconscionable government. By tracing one man's (sometimes mild) opposition to racist legislation, he succeeds in intricately exploring the decades of development of what would become apartheid.

Hofmeyr, an Afrikaner, was rejected by more fiercely nationalist Afrikaners because he had been a Rhodes scholar at Oxford, where he learned to admire the British character, and because he was bilingual. He was, Paton writes, raised as a culturally committed Afrikaner, but "of a gentle kind"—not one of those xenophobes hardened by England's defeat and humiliation of South Africa in the Boer War. Especially in the earlier sections of the biography, Paton's role seems to be apologist. In a very tame rebuke of Afrikaner racism in the 1920's, he writes, "In those days, not only Hertzog, but also Smuts and Hofmeyr, entertained an idea of the white man's role in Africa which has proved erroneous" (pp. 95–96).

Paton believed that Hofmeyr always had the betterment of the nonwhite South African population in mind; at the same time, he is forced to admit that Hofmeyr largely accepted white dominance—he was perhaps critical of it, but never challenged it, because he was consummately a politician and represented a constituency committed to some kind of perpetuation of *baasskap,* white supremacy. Paton argues that when, for example, Hofmeyr fought for a small increase in the funds allotted to African education (which did not appreciably change the seven-to-one ratio in favor of education funds for whites), he was doing better than any other politician who hoped to keep his parliament seat and his ministry could do.

Hofmeyr was, seemingly, the least of many evils. Still, he frequently voted in support of bills that restricted the rights of non-Europeans and expressed a determination to keep them in an inferior position. Like many other South Africans, Hofmeyr envisioned extending European dominance in Africa as far north as Kenya. He unilaterally rejected claims for racial and social equality in his own country; his most liberal rapprochement to nonwhites was the institution of a kind of benevolent Christian trusteeship, in which a preeminent white race would do its best to uplift the rest of the population. And again, when Hofmeyr asserts, "We are revolted by the notion of social equality," Paton apologizes: "It seemed that he was talking of something felt by others . . . something that a politician could not ignore" (p. 192). Late in his career, Hofmeyr finally expressed his opposition to the color bar (and was blamed, as a result, for his party's loss of power in 1948, and the coming to power of the Afrikaner Nationalists, who immediately begin constructing apartheid). At the same time, however, Hofmeyr wrote to those (whites) who served as advocates for nonwhites in parliament, "saying he understood the reasons for their impatience and admitting that there were discriminatory laws. But to ask for their repeal forthwith was to ask for the impossible; while working for their repeal one had to live with the laws and, of course, obey them" (p. 338).

Hofmeyr never responded to calls from the Left to leave the compromising United Party and form his own; Paton, with his Liberal Party work in the 1950's and 1960's, seems personally to have picked up the mantle from Hofmeyr, and to have done what he imagined Hofmeyr would have done had he had another few decades to move forward at the slow pace palatable to his constituency. Paton's faith in Hofmeyr, and his respect for him, inspired his intense dedication to the biography over eleven years. In *Journey Continued* he writes, "I am often asked, 'Which do you regard as your best book?' To that I answer, 'I would not place *Hofmeyr* second to any of the others' " (p. 13). Current readers and critics would be unlikely to concur with that judgment, but it does point to Paton's belief that political efforts are of paramount importance in South Africa, and that Hofmeyr was, in Paton's estimation, a politician who had the unique attributes of being as enlightened and as successful (within the system as it stood) as was pragmatically possible.

Like *Hofmeyr, Apartheid and the Archbishop* (1973) provides, through a focus on one man, an intricate overview of a fundamental South African institution (the Anglican Church, but with considerable discussion of other religious institutions as well) over several decades. Also like the earlier biography, the study of Geoffrey Clayton is technically detailed, covering the church's personalities, political involvement, missionary activity, and social role as exhaustively as *Hofmeyr* explored the nuances of the United Party and Parliament.

Archbishop Clayton, whom Paton lauds for a commitment to the same kinds of values he admired in Hofmeyr—liberal tolerance and at least theoretical opposition to the color bar—seems to have had a greater degree of freedom in acting on his values. Though he, too, was to some extent co-opted by South Africa's racially oppressive society, a churchman's necessary compromises were less insidious than a politician's, and Clayton's platform in the church allowed him greater freedom of conscience than did Hofmeyr's in Parliament. Clayton solved his dilemmas about how to achieve moral results in a less-than-moral society by learning to compromise, or attain limited victories, just as Hofmeyr had often had to choose the lesser of two evils. Paton describes Clayton's philosophy: "When you could not see clearly how you would reach your objective, then *you must do the next right thing*" (p. 116). As Hofmeyr had had to make concessions to the status quo, voting for and upholding discriminatory laws that he knew were wrong, so under Clayton's rule, African Anglican priests were paid about one-third (or less) the stipends of white clergy. To put this in the context of "the lesser of evils," though, it must be remembered that in the Afrikaners' church, it was preached that racial segregation was divinely ordained.

Through Clayton, Paton further explores the dilemma of English-speaking South Africans' dual allegiances (and the consequent hostility on the part of Afrikaners). Clayton was a native of Leicester, England—like most officials in South Africa's Anglican Church, he was sent to serve for a few years in the "colonies," then expected to return to England. Clayton, however, spent his life serving in South Africa and, Paton notes to the archbishop's credit, never referred to England as "home," firmly adopting South Africa as his nation. South Africans of English ancestry were generally more liberal than the descendants of people from other European nations; consequently, Paton saw it as imperative that they be firmly rooted in South Africa and work there to proliferate their values.

With Hofmeyr's death in 1948 and the rapid passage of the most oppressive apartheid laws, Clayton was driven to carry on Hofmeyr's reformist work and became increasingly prominent as an activist opposed to apartheid. As Clayton became more outspoken, he became more alienated from the ruling Afrikaners and was charged with spreading, personally and through his church, anti–South African propaganda overseas. After earlier personal resistance to civil disobedience, he finally came to support it. Finally, at age seventy-three, after extensive deliberation, he wrote a letter to the prime minister announcing that he would urge his clergymen, from their pulpits, to entreat blatant disobedience of a proposed law: a clause in the Native Laws Amendment Act that explicitly extended the province of apartheid to the churches and mandated that church officials enforce segregation. Clayton saw this as a challenge to religious freedom, and took his strongest stand against apartheid; he died, however, before the letter was mailed. It was subsequently sent out and ignored by the prime minister. The law was passed, though in part through Clayton's publicized opposition to it, it was widely challenged and ignored.

In his decision to spend years researching and writing on Hofmeyr and Clayton, Paton showed his commitment to what he saw as the two most important callings in his career. *Hofmeyr* was a complement to Paton's own career in the Liberal Party and as a political reformer. *Apartheid and the Archbishop* confirmed Paton's strong religious faith and his commitment to bringing about, through that faith, the salvation of his country.

### INSTRUMENT OF THY PEACE

PATON further demonstrated his faith in *Instrument of Thy Peace* (1968), a series of meditations on the prayer of St. Francis of Assisi: "Lord, make me an instrument of Thy Peace. Where there is hatred, let me sow love; where there is injury, pardon; where there is doubt, faith; . . ." The small book is an expansion on this theme. He writes:

I say to myself, this is the only way in which a Christian can encounter hatred, injury, despair, and sadness, and that is by throwing off his helplessness and allowing himself to be made the bearer of love, the pardoner, the bringer of hope, the comforter of those that grieve.

(p. 2)

The meditations make some reference to the troubles of Paton's society, and explain the Christian motivation behind his reformatory work: as St. Francis wrote, "It is in pardoning that we are pardoned," so Paton explains how his work at Diepkloof refuted "the extraordinary theological view that when a man commits an offence he rends the moral order of the universe, and that this damage is repaired only by his punishment" (p. 22). Instead of the sequence of "offence–punishment," Paton exhorts "offence–forgiveness–restoration." Primarily, though, Paton wrote these meditations not with reference to specific social problems but as a moral exhortation to persevere: "for those who are inclined to melancholy, for those who are inclined to withdraw rather than to participate, for those who are tempted to retreat into pietism because they are afraid of active engagement in the world" (p. v).

## AUTOBIOGRAPHICAL WORKS

PATON's three explicitly autobiographical works—*Kontakion for You Departed* (1969), which focuses on his wife's death, *Towards the Mountain* (1980), and *Journey Continued* (1988)—are essentially a gloss on everything else he has written. The first of these is marked by a strong sense of loss and a tremendously vital and moving personal passion; the second embodies the energetic and idealistic optimism that Paton felt in his earlier years, as it follows his life up to the publication of *Cry, the Beloved Country*; and the third, finished just before his death, deals with the later period of political turmoil and frustration, and is thus more hardened. All three show not an advancement nor a development of his ideas but, rather, a commitment to saying the same thing over and over, never abandoning his moral onus. One senses, as in his novels and biographies, the writer's commitment to directing whatever topic is at hand—in this case, his own life—toward the enlightenment of those who believe in social inequity; and, at the same time, the ever-present implacable reality that Paton's voice is ultimately too small: the people who are causing the most harm in South Africa simply will not listen to him, and continue to live their lives in what often seems to be a universe that has no points of moral connection with his own.

"We Must Act Quickly" (1971) is the kind of essay that leaves Paton vulnerable to charges of tame activism, and perhaps even collaboration with the Nationalist government. Discussing the government's philosophy of "separate development" for whites and nonwhites (through which the South African government attempted to appease the nonwhite population with the same kind of paltry concessions that were given to American minorities until the "separate but equal" doctrine in *Plessy* v. *Ferguson* was declared unconstitutional in 1954), Paton equivocates on the potential of that maneuver. Tellingly, he structures the essay as a dialogue between "Alan" (representing idealism) and "Paton" (a pragmatic respondent), showing that he realizes he is espousing compromises that are arguably contradictory, hypocritical. "Alan" asks, "Do you honestly foresee the day when there will be eight or nine independent States, all economically strong, living in harmony together, in what we now call the Republic of South Africa?" "Paton" responds, "Of course not. Nobody does. But"—a word that recurs uncomfortably often throughout the essay—"I believe that the attempt to achieve such a goal may bring improvements in the conditions of Black men which they would never have achieved . . . in a supreme White Government" (*Save the Beloved Country*, p. 56).

The pragmatist "Paton" acknowledges that South Africa will not see racial harmony until the gap between white and nonwhite incomes is closed, but then sidesteps an activist attitude toward fulfilling this ideal; instead, he says, "All I can say is that [Africans'] moral case is extremely strong. And it is my belief that White South Africans are growing more vulnerable to moral demands" (*Save the Beloved Country*, p. 57). Any African activist could have told Paton that the oppressed majority had given up the hope that any change would come about through the moral conscience of a white South African government. Paton espouses a tentative stance, waiting and hoping that some positive results, even limited gains, can come from the Nationalists. By the 1970's, it was clear to most observers that the hope for liberation arising from limited tidbits thrown out by the ruling government was ephemeral. The Nationalists were in no essential way reform-minded throughout the 1970's and 1980's, but were merely stalling for time.

On other issues, too, Paton rejected stances of extreme confrontation with the government or full support of the country's increasingly radical elements. He seems jealous of, and unnecessarily confrontational with, Bishop Desmond Tutu in an essay entitled "Your Philosophies Trouble Me." (In response to Tutu's receiving the Nobel Peace Prize, Paton writes, "I have never won a prize like that. I am afraid that my skin is not the right colour" [*Save the Beloved Country*, p. 183]). Of Tutu's support for a political agenda that aggressively challenges the Nationalists, Paton writes, "I think your morality is confused just as was the morality of the Church in the inquisition, or the morality of Dr. Verwoerd [the architect of apartheid] in his utopian dreams" (*Save the Beloved Country*, p. 185). In "Indaba Without Fear" (1987), he is condescending toward Winnie Mandela; he calls her demand for the Nationalist government to abdicate and hand over power to the black majority "a forthright but quite useless suggestion" (*Save the Beloved Country*, p. 165). In "Where They Are Wrong" (1975), about student movements, he writes, "I am against the stupid kind of activism that demands everything NOW" (*Save the Beloved Country*, p. 221).

Paton had once occupied a position that seemed to the world to be the epitome of liberal reform-mindedness. As African movements caught up with and surpassed Paton's, other activists increasingly attacked him. Stephen Biko, the leading voice of the Black Consciousness movement that arose at African universities in the 1970's, specifically rejected Paton's involvement in his activism: while Biko felt Paton was generally committed to the same principles he himself espoused, he believed that the writer, like many white liberals, was insensitive to the proud and aggressive self-orientation of his group. While white leftists advocated improving Africans' lives, Biko asserted, they did not accept that this must adversely affect their own positions of privilege.

In the 1980's, in the face of a growing international movement to isolate and boycott South Africa economically by withdrawing investment in that country (support of which movement the government had made illegal), Paton demurred: "There is only one firm statement I can make on disinvestment—I will have nothing to do with it. I will not, by any written or spoken word, give it any support whatsoever" (*Save the Beloved Country*, p. 6).

Certainly, on this issue in Paton's camp there were other liberal politicians who feared, as Paton wrote, "that those who will pay most grievously for disinvestment will be the Black workers of South Africa" (*Save the Beloved Country*, p. 7). (In the event, as early 1990 saw major victories in the campaign for African liberation, the effects of international divestment were widely credited with having generated significantly important pressure on the white regime.)

Paton's stance on this issue, however, reflects his inclination in his later years to avoid the harshest possible criticism of the status quo and the hegemonic white power structure. He defends himself, somewhat simplistically, by analogy with his reformatory experience: he had learned in that phase of his life that "punishment was not the proper treatment for delinquent children. Punishment failed totally to treat the cause of delinquency. Punishment could change behaviour, but it was not a true reformatory instrument. . . . Punishment is no proper treatment for erring children, nor is it the proper treatment for erring countries" (*Save the Beloved Country*, p. 9). Again, he repeats the conviction, or at least the hope, that "the Afrikaner Nationalist is ready to behave better" (*Save the Beloved Country*, p. 9); presumably, Paton feels the rest of the world should simply wait for such improved behavior to be manifested. The fallacy in Paton's analogy is that racist totalitarian governments with extensively demonstrable records of harsh opposition to the human rights of tens of millions of their citizens are not like children. From his experience with children, Paton had learned to give a second chance, to forgive and hope for a better later effort. With the Nationalist government and its record, the stakes are different.

The older Paton, though, seemed oblivious to the differences in scale, and to the fact that the vast majority of South Africans had, over the decades of Nationalist rule, grown weary of waiting quietly on the sidelines for the white minority to improve the moral stance of their own accord. For these oversights, Paton lost some credibility and respect in the reform movement he once so influentially dominated. The force of his writing endures, however—if not as an effective contemporary manifesto, then as an acute psychological portrait of the human character torn by social hatred, and as a fiercely moral defiance of South African oppression.

## SELECTED BIBLIOGRAPHY

I. BIBLIOGRAPHIES. E. Callan, "Selected Bibliography," in his *Alan Paton* (New York, 1968; rev. ed., 1982); and L. Bentel, comp., *Alan Paton: A Bibliography* (Johannesburg, 1969).

II. COLLECTED WORKS. *The Long View*, edited by E. Callan (New York, 1968); *Knocking on the Door*, edited by C. Gardner (New York and Cape Town, 1975); *Save the Beloved Country*, edited by H. Strydom and D. Jones (New York, 1989).

III. SEPARATE WORKS. *Cry, the Beloved Country* (New York, 1948); *South Africa Today*, Public Affairs Committee Pamphlet No. 175 (New York and London, 1951); *Too Late the Phalarope* (New York, 1953); *South Africa in Transition* (New York, 1956), with photographs by D. Weiner; *Hope for South Africa* (London, 1958); *Tales from a Troubled Land* (New York, 1961); *Hofmeyr* (Cape Town and Oxford, 1964), abridged as *South African Tragedy: The Life and Times of Jan Hofmeyr* (New York, 1965); *Instrument of Thy Peace* (New York, 1968); *Kontakion for You Departed* (New York, 1969); *Apartheid and the Archbishop: The Life and Times of Geoffrey Clayton, Archbishop of Cape Town* (New York, 1973); *Towards the Mountain* (New York, 1980); *Ah, But Your Land Is Beautiful* (New York, 1982); *Go Well, My Child* (Washington, D.C., 1985), with photographs by C. S. Larrabee; *Journey Continued* (New York and Oxford, 1988).

IV. DRAMATIC ADAPTATIONS. *Lost in the Stars* (1949), Broadway musical based on *Cry, the Beloved Country*, book by M. Anderson and music by K. Weill; *Cry, the Beloved Country* (1951), film directed by Z. Korda; *Sponono* (1964), Broadway play based on stories from *Tales from a Troubled Land*, adapted with K. Shah.

V. BIOGRAPHICAL AND CRITICAL STUDIES. H. Breit, *The Writer Observed* (Cleveland, 1956); H. Davies, *A Mirror of the Ministry in Modern Novels* (New York, 1959); E. Fuller, *Books with Men Behind Them* (New York, 1962); E. Callan, *Alan Paton* (New York, 1968; rev. ed., 1982); J. B. Thompson, "Poetic Truth in *Too Late the Phalarope*," in *English Studies in Africa*, 24, no. 1 (1981); S. Watson, "*Cry, the Beloved Country* and the Failure of Liberal Vision," in *English in Africa*, 9 (May 1982); A. A. Monye, "*Cry, the Beloved Country*: Should We Merely Cry?" in *Nigeria Magazine*, 144 (1983); T. Morphet, "Alan Paton: The Honour of Meditation," in *English in Africa*, 10, no. 2 (1983); R. Moss, "Alan Paton: Bringing a Sense of the Sacred," in *World Literature Today*, 57, no. 2 (1983); R. Rive, "The Liberal Tradition in South African Literature," in *Contrast: South African Literary Journal*, 14 (July 1983); R. J. Linnemann, "Alan Paton: Anachronism or Visionary?" in *Commonwealth Novel in English*, 3 (Spring–Summer 1984); N. H. Z. Watts, "A Study of Alan Paton's *Too Late the Phalarope*," in *Durham University Journal*, 76 (June 1984); D. Irvine, "The Liberal Party, 1953–1968," in J. Butler, et al., eds., *Democratic Liberalism in South Africa: Its History and Prospect* (Middletown, Conn., 1987); M. Hooper, "Paton and the Silence of Stephanie," in *English Studies in Africa: A Journal of the Humanities*, 32, no. 1 (1989).

# HAROLD PINTER
## (1930– )

### John Russell Taylor

*I*

IN his published writings Harold Pinter contrives to tell us remarkably little about himself, his life, and his background. It is part of his method. As against dramatists like John Osborne or Arnold Wesker, who unashamedly write plays as a sort of spiritual autobiography, with characters often little more than mouthpieces for their author's ideas or slightly adapted self-portraits, Pinter believes in covering his tracks, writing plays that are completely separated from himself to stand as independent, self-sufficient works of art. Perhaps Pinter is his plays, but he is certainly not in any obvious sense in them, and any deductions one might make from them about him are in the realm of speculative psychology.

Of course, equipped with a basic chronology of his life one might make a few reasonable guesses. He was born in Hackney, East London, on 10 October 1930; his parents were Jewish (of remotely Portuguese origin) and he an only child. He was educated in Hackney, and his first theater-going experience was to see Sir Donald Wolfit in *King Lear.* Though he had seen very little theater, he had ambitions to become an actor and studied at the Royal Academy of Dramatic Arts. He also, in connection with his national service, stood two trials as a conscientious objector. When he was nineteen he began an eight-year career as a repertory actor, playing all over the country and spending eighteen months with Anew McMaster's touring company in Ireland, a period recalled in his affectionate reminiscence of McMaster, *Mac* (1968). Meanwhile, he began to write: poems, mainly, plus a few short unpublished prose pieces and a semi-autobiographical novel, "The Dwarfs," which he finally abandoned as unsatisfactory, though it contributed elements (not recognizably autobiographical) to his later radio play of the same title. In 1957 he had an idea for a one-act play, and when suddenly faced with a request from an old friend to write a play for student production, he wrote *The Room* in four days. The experience of writing it and seeing it produced was sufficiently stimulating to make him embark right away on a full-length play, and the result was *The Birthday Party.* This, on its first production in London (fairly disastrous in terms of audience and critical response), established him as someone to be reckoned with in the booming new English theater of the time. Two years and four plays later *The Caretaker* became one of the big successes, commercial as well as critical, of the new movement, and since then Pinter's life, so far as it is known by and concerns the public at large, has been simply the succession of his writings—for the stage, for radio and television, and latterly also for the cinema.

And behind them all the man himself remains enigmatic, largely, I suppose, because he considers that he is and ought to be irrelevant to the appreciation of his work. Naturally his dramatic material, the characters and situations, must come from somewhere. In an interview, for example, he has told us that *The Birthday Party* had its beginnings in a situation and an atmosphere he encountered in a lodging house where he stayed in his acting days. But to the further question of why, in developing this material, he did not include a character representing himself in the play, he answered: "I had— I have—nothing to say about myself, directly. I wouldn't know where to begin. Particularly since I often look at myself in the mirror and say 'Who the hell's that?'"

In the same way, on the level of "interpretation" Pinter has constantly insisted that he has nothing to say, that he is in no more privileged a position than anyone else to say what his plays are about. At most he will sometimes volunteer that he did not consciously intend some particularly weird interpretation, such as that which sees the three characters in *The Caretaker* as God the Father, God the Son, and God the Holy Ghost, and the shed that one of them intends to build as Christ's Church on Earth. But, he will probably add, conscious intentions may well have little to do with it. The play is there, independent of him, to work as it may on audiences. If it works it will need no interpretation. If it does not work, all the interpretation in the world will not improve it.

The urge to interpret is nevertheless inescapable. Pinter tells us that he wants to write plays that tell a story, chronicle a series of happenings, without the artificial becauses and therefores of drama, but simply in the basic childlike terms of "and then . . . and then . . . and then." But his plays, while doing this very effectively, always have the teasing air of meaning more than they say, having resonances that hang disturbingly on the air and vibrate in the memory long after the tale has been told. It would, admittedly, be absurd to look in Pinter's work for a philosophical system or for "ideas" that can be taken out of context and considered on their own independent merits—as, for instance, one may do with the plays of Arnold Wesker. Pinter's plays are not conceived that way. Rather, they must be studied with the same sort of techniques we would bring to bear on lyric poetry, or on music: they define their own terms of reference, working not by the elaboration of ideas but by the development and transformation of themes and images, which take their value and significance entirely from their context.

## II

OF all the drama produced in Britain since the inauguration of the dramatic revival with John Osborne's *Look Back in Anger* in 1956, Pinter's is the most completely, obsessively about nothing but itself, self-defining. Like Lewis Carroll's *The Hunting of the Snark*, his plays tend toward a conclusion that is entirely satisfactory in terms of their own logic, their own internal structure: "For the Snark was a Boojum, you see." Related to any reality outside the reality of the theatrical experience, they may mean anything or nothing. And yet just to describe this process involves one in interpretation. In other words it is impossible to describe without ipso facto interpreting, whether we are dealing with John Keats's "Ode on a Grecian Urn" or Pinter's *Old Times*. In each case, any attempt to say what the work is about, however well worth making, will select and distort; it may even murder to dissect. Ultimately there is no substitute for the poem but the poem, the play but the play. The best the critic can hope to do is indicate certain lines of continuity, to lay bare to some extent the mechanics of the work and suggest why it affects us as it does, when there seems to be no reasonable reason why it should.

In Pinter's case the critic's task is made easier by the unswerving logic with which each play follows from the one before, taking up, elaborating, or modifying themes and images with such ruthless concentration and precision that it would probably be possible, knowing nothing of Pinter and confronted with his complete oeuvre all jumbled up, to rearrange it in chronological order on internal evidence alone. In broader outline one may trace a number of major themes and images that run through his work, now one, now another taking the most prominent place in the composition. The most obvious are the Room, Menace, Communications, the Family, the Woman, Personality, Perception, and Memory—in approximately that order. It is some measure of the coherence of Pinter's imaginative world that all of them are present, embryonically at least, in the first tiny piece of dramatic dialogue of his that we know, a short, elusive sketch called *Kullus*, which dates back as early as 1949. Hence the elements are of the simplest. The narrator lets an outsider, Kullus, into his room. Kullus at once starts to take over: he calls in a girl who is waiting outside and without more ado they climb into the narrator's bed. This new situation carries the seeds of its own dissolution; the narrator is now the outsider, the menace to the status quo, and before long the girl, seemingly passive yet actually the determining element in the situation, is inviting the narrator to reverse it. In the process the characters of Kullus and the narrator seem to blur, combine, and exchange places; memory is annihilated as the three characters co-exist in a mysterious, ambiguous present.

All of which is no doubt a lot to read into three small pages of dialogue and narration. And yet every element, here only lightly, indirectly suggested, comes up for development and elaboration in Pinter's later work, so that, seen in the perspective of his plays, every word is full of significance.

# HAROLD PINTER

To begin with, there is the classic situation of Pinter's early plays: the room, representing warmth in the cold, light in the darkness, a small safe area of the known, apparently secure, peaceful existence of those inside. These are the principal constituents of Pinter's "comedy of menace," a term coined just when, at the time of *A Slight Ache* (1959)[1], it was ceasing to have any central relevance to his writing. But even if it bedeviled for a while discussion of *The Caretaker* and later plays (it is still trotted out occasionally, as though it pigeonholes everything Pinter has done), it remains a very apt and exact description of *The Room, The Birthday Party, The Dumb Waiter,* and *A Slight Ache,* the group of plays Pinter wrote in rapid succession in 1957–1958.

All these plays are both frightening and funny, creating an atmosphere of nameless, undefined terror and at the same time shocking us into laughter, shocking us sometimes by the very amiability, jollity even, with which the most alarmingly destructive attacks on the human mind are launched, which creates something very like complicity between audience and menace, as well as imaginative identification between audience and menaced. In *The Room* (1960), which remains Pinter's least mature and satisfactorily shaped play, the room itself is inhabited by a married couple, the Hudds. The play opens with a long monologue by Mrs. Hudd, during which we learn that her husband is a lorry driver and is about to go out on the icy roads. They are visited by their landlord, who gives a deliberately confusing account of himself, his home, and his family. Mr. Hudd leaves shortly after the landlord, and almost immediately another couple arrive, the Sands. They are looking for a room and have been told, or so they say, by someone in the basement that this room is vacant. Next the landlord returns and says that the man in the basement is eager to see Mrs. Hudd while her husband is out. Finally she agrees, and the man arrives. He proves to be a "a blind Negro" named Riley, who claims to know Mrs. Hudd, despite her denials, and begs her to come home with him. At this point Mr. Hudd returns, and quite casually kicks and beats up Riley. Mrs. Hudd is struck blind, and the curtain falls.

The play is prodigal of incident and diffused in its effect, as Pinter's work will never be again. But certain things are already apparent in it. First, the image of security and the threat from outside: the room is the Hudds' guarantee of security, and any intrusion is potentially menacing. The landlord exerts some control over their tenancy of it and could perhaps put them out (when asked where his bedroom is now he answers evasively, "Me? I can take my pick"). The Sands are rivals for the room, and bring worrying word that elsewhere in the house it is already regarded as vacant. Riley, on the other hand, wants to lure Mrs. Hudd out of the room's warmth and security, calling on some undefined loyalty or obligation to persuade her (is he in fact meant to be, or suggesting that he is, her father?). And attack is not a completely reliable way of defending the room and the security it confers: even within the room Mrs. Hudd can be struck blind, taking on, as it were, the disadvantages of her least powerful-seeming adversary. The trouble with the play is that it seems too evidently teasing, too deliberately mysterious: we find ourselves forced to ask questions that are probably irrelevant, to suppose that the characters have some sort of quasi-allegorical significance we cannot quite fathom. Why, for instance, is the last intruder "a blind Negro"? If the play were completely self-defining we would not ask; we would instinctively accept Pinter's statement that he does not know himself: at that stage in writing the play a door opened and a blind black man walked in, almost in his creator's despite.

If *The Room* is regarded as a rough sketch, *The Birthday Party* (1957) is Pinter's first finished work of art. In it he concentrates his attention on the central image of the Room and explores it in detail. Here the principal character is Stanley, idle, spoiled, content to do nothing and be pampered and fussed after by Meg, his stupid, doting, suffocatingly motherly landlady, who irritates him but is still very useful in making his life as comfortable as possible. The location of this room is particularized, as it never is in *The Room*—a down-at-heel boarding house in a seaside town—and the daily routine of its inhabitants' lives are observed in minutely realistic detail. All the more frightening, then, when into this familiar, humdrum household come two mysterious creatures straight out of lurid fiction, hired killers, it seems, out to get Stanley. But what for, exactly? That we never know. Perhaps even Stanley never knows. We gather that he

---

[1] Dates in text refer to first stage production; dates in bibliography refer to publication date.

may have been a pianist sometime in his life, but otherwise his past is a mystery, and so are the motives of those who threaten him, Goldberg and McCann. Not because they refuse to explain themselves; on the contrary, they offer far too many irreconcilable explanations. McCann, Irish and brooding, refers always to politics and religion, heresy and treachery to "the organization." Goldberg, jolly and Jewish, one of nature's traveling salesmen, is preoccupied instead with sex and property, suggesting that Stanley embezzled, murdered his wife, abandoned his fiancée, and so on.

GOLDBERG: What's your trade?
McCANN: What about Ireland?
GOLDBERG: What's your trade?
STANLEY: I play the piano.
GOLDBERG: How many fingers do you use?
STANLEY: No hands!
GOLDBERG: No society would touch you. Not even a building society.
McCANN: You're a traitor to the cloth.
GOLDBERG: What do you use for pyjamas?
STANLEY: Nothing.
GOLDBERG: You verminate the sheet of your birth.
McCANN: What about the Albigensenist heresy?
GOLDBERG: Who watered the wicket in Melbourne?
McCANN: What about the blessed Oliver Plunkett?
GOLDBERG: Speak up, Webber. Why did the chicken cross the road?

(Act II)

The total picture created from these individual details is as inscrutable as the menace with which Stanley teasingly torments Meg at the beginning of the play: the men with a van, and in it a wheelbarrow, and the "certain person" they're looking for.

The lesson is obvious. The more particularized a menace is, the more it is a particular response to a specific transgression, the less imaginative effect it is likely to have, the easier it is for each member of the audience to dissociate himself from it. But we all have, somewhere, a hidden fear, an undefined sense of guilt, a consciousness of original sin or a Big Brother superego watching over us, which can in the right circumstances be played upon. Whatever it is in Goldberg and McCann, or in his own mind, which breaks Stanley down, leads to his ritual humiliation at his own birthday party and his reduction to silent conformity as he is led away the next morning, we never know—and therefore we are left all the more disquietingly with the feeling that the same thing could well happen to us. What Pinter has done, technically, with his material is to write a complete well-made play, except that the exposition and the denouement are left out: we get process and conclusion without explanation or revelation. And not merely as a trick to mystify, but because precise explanations and credentials would be destructive of Pinter's whole dramatic purpose.

Do his characters have any credentials; could they explain themselves if they wanted to? Pinter would probably say no:

The assumption that to verify what has happened and what is happening presents few problems I take to be inaccurate. A character on the stage who can present no convincing argument or information as to his past experiences, his present behavior, or his aspirations, nor give a comprehensive analysis of his motives, is as legitimate and as worthy of attention as one who, alarmingly, can do all these things.

("Writing for the Theatre," *Plays: One*, p. 11)

But before Pinter can go on to explore the further implications of this by delving more deeply into the nature and even the possibility of communication, let alone the definition of human personality in terms of human beings' relations with one another, he has just one loose end from *The Birthday Party* to tie up, and he does so in *The Dumb Waiter* (1960). *The Birthday Party* leaves us, perhaps, asking what exactly are Goldberg and McCann? Are they in fact beings from another world, one of highly colored sensational fiction, or perhaps largely figments of Stanley's overheated imagination? The latter in many respects they may be, but Pinter suggests that their menacing aspects, as apart from Stanley's own personal reading of them, are supplied by their context rather than inherent; that is, that they are menacing only in relation to Stanley's special situation. *The Dumb Waiter* shows a very similar couple off duty, nonmenacing, vulnerable. When the dumbwaiter in their basement room starts relaying intricate and unreasonable orders for exotic foods from aloft, it is their turn to be menaced, to placate the mysterious force above as best they can. And even then they are not safe together in their room-womb. Finally the menace invades the sacred domain itself, when they are ordered to kill each other, each thereby becoming in context the other's prime menace. And, no doubt, if we were ever to encounter whoever is at the other end of the dumbwaiter, he too, according to context, could be menace or menaced, and so on in an infinite Kafkaesque chain.

But this leaves another aspect of the question to be explored. In any given situation there is the menace and there are those who let themselves be menaced. Why do they let themselves be menaced? Do they know? Need there be two sides to the situation, or is one side's readiness to be menaced, willingness if necessary to invent a menace for himself, enough? To such questions Pinter's next works, the play *A Slight Ache* and its companion piece, the story-monologue *The Examination* (1961), provide some hint of his answer. Both of them present a menace-situation that is in effect one-sided, a breakdown, such as Stanley's, that is now unmistakably self-induced. In *A Slight Ache* a married couple, Edward and Flora, become aware of a passive, mysterious presence outside their gate, a matchseller who never seems to move, day or night. Each of them reads his nature and purpose according to his or her own fears and desires. For Flora he is the husband she really wanted, the pet she can fuss over, the child she can mother. For Edward he is an impostor; he may be someone returned from the past; he is sly and cunning, and after something he will get if Edward makes one false move. The intruder (who was anyway freely invited in) never says anything, never does anything (indeed, in the play as originally written for radio, it was uncertain whether he was really there at all). And faced with this monumental, unresponding presence, Edward gradually breaks himself down, until at last he changes places with the matchseller, Flora calmly accepting and even in a measure directing the exchange (shades of Kullus, again).

*The Examination* shows us precisely the same process from the inside. The narrator is the examiner, examining a character called Kullus for some undisclosed purpose. And just as Edward in *A Slight Ache* gradually breaks down faced with the mere presence of the other man, so here "I" breaks himself down in the presence of Kullus, for all that Kullus seems to be in every way obedient and submissive to his orders and arrangement of procedure. At the beginning the examination is taking place in "my room"; by the end it has become unarguably "Kullus' room," as in the long-previous sketch called *Kullus*, and as in the later television play *The Basement*, which turns on exactly the same balance of emotional power exemplified by changing ownership of "the room."

With *The Examination* Pinter completed one cycle in his writing, having worked his way pertinaciously through a wide group of associated images in various aspects and combinations. Though the room and menace do not disappear completely from his later work, they will not from now on be dominant themes. If up to now his characters have been, as he put it, "at the extreme edge of their living, where they are living pretty much alone," from *The Examination* onward they come nearer in to the center; they engage, if guardedly, in social intercourse, and so the focus shifts from the naked conflict of wills, the battle, even, of one individual will to retain its integrity and identity, to wider issues: the means of communication between people (if communication is possible), the definition of character through interrelation, the viability of the very idea of personality as something definable, recognizable, consistent.

### III

THE first play he wrote in the second cycle of his work (after a few brief sketches for popular West End revues) points to this change of emphasis by its very title: *A Night Out* (1960). This was written originally for radio and television, and while it seems unlikely that the fact that it was destined from the start for a mass medium made any essential difference to its style or content, it is no doubt significant that at this stage in his career Pinter felt ready to tackle a mass audience directly. In the play Pinter develops a number of his earlier images in new ways, and most immediately he breaks away from the formerly inescapable room-womb in which the action of his early plays takes place. Admittedly Albert, the protagonist, has some difficulty in breaking free for his "night out." To his possessive mother, a development of Meg in *The Birthday Party*, home represents safety, sanity, and clean living: if he wants to get out, even for one evening, it must be because he is leading an unclean life and "mucking about with girls." All the same, he insists on going to a party given by the firm he works for, and finds that everything goes wrong, since he is blamed, quite unjustly, for a "liberty" taken by someone else with one of the girls. Maddened by his mother's renewed reproaches he storms out and falls in with a genteel prostitute. Though he goes home with her, they never really connect, since she persists in weaving her own fantasies about her life, while he cannot dissociate her from his mother, so that she becomes the indirect victim of his impotent rage against his mother. When finally he returns, having worked off his aggressions on the prostitute, nothing has changed: his relationship with his mother stands just where it always was.

The difference of approach between *A Night Out* and the earlier plays is at once apparent. The effect of the story depends upon the interplay of characters. In a situation that is never really mysterious or designed to create menace we learn about the people by watching their attempts to communicate with one another, and sometimes their inability or refusal to be communicated with. Albert's mother is impervious to communication; she just will not listen to anything that does not fit in with her established idea of things. The prostitute does not want to communicate too much; all she wants is something to bolster up the precarious fantasies that make her life bearable. Albert wants to communicate, but is too tied up in his stifling relationship with his mother to get through, either to her or to anyone else. All this involves them in some intense situations, but the tone of the play is much lighter than before, and none of the characters is entirely enclosed in private desperation. Compared with what has gone before, *A Night Out* represents a much more relaxed Pinter developing his images in terms of a sort of psychological comedy-drama, humanized and demystified.

With this in mind it is easier to "read" his next play, *The Caretaker*, than it was at the time of its first appearance in 1960. We are seemingly back to the room, the occupant and the outsider who comes to menace the existing state of affairs. But it does not work like that. Now there are three characters, of about equal weight, and all are provided with quite suffering backgrounds. There is Aston, the occupier of the room, living a more or less vegetable existence since (as we eventually learn in the play) he underwent electric shock treatment to alleviate a mental disorder. There is Davies, the shifty, opportunistic tramp he brings back to share his home. And there is Mick, Aston's volatile brother, whose game is more elusive, and who eventually succeeds in turning Davies' wiles against himself, so that the long-suffering Aston is moved, of his own accord, to turn him out.

But the word "succeeds" already implies interpretation. More ink has probably been spilt about the "meaning" of *The Caretaker*, what interpretation we should put on it, than on all Pinter's other plays put together. And in fact it does occupy a strange middle position in Pinter's work, neither so gnomic nor (if one chooses to see it that way) so willfully mystifying as his "comedies of menace," nor so blandly self-contained, so coolly observant of its own curious rules, as his later drama. It leaves the sort of loose ends that it is inviting to unravel and then knit up again into some new explanatory pattern. And even if we are content, as seems reasonable, to take Pinter's word for it that he had no allegorical intentions, that it is just about "three men in a room," then we are still left with enough information and enough fair ground for surmise to start speculating on the play's meaning in the more elementary terms of character motivation, of objectives and intentions in the mind of each character.

It is, in fact, virtually impossible to describe the happenings of the play without the description taking on color from one hypothesis or another. To say that Mick "succeeds" in ousting Davies obviously implies the assumption that he intends to do this and works toward it. If we choose to see the relationship between the brothers in this play as the first clear inkling of Pinter's later interest in the dynamics of the family unit (most clearly expressed in *The Homecoming*), then we may see the line of continuity in Mick's behavior as concern for his brother's health and happiness, encouragement at Aston's relationship with Davies as a first sign of Aston's return to the world, and (justified) mistrust of Davies as a suitable friend and support for Aston. If he wants to retain the mental advance Aston has made, but at the same time dispose of Davies, the unconscious agent of that advance, then all his behavior falls understandably into place. And, provided this reading works, it does not really matter whether it is "true," what the author primarily had in mind, or the only possible reading. The play, after all, can sustain an infinite number of readings, all of them more or less consonant with what happens before our eyes.

This is perhaps both its strength and its weakness. "Chekhov himself could not have devised a more satisfying finale," said one reviewer. True, and yet in a way disappointing. *The Caretaker* is a far more conventional play than any of Pinter's others, more approachable by traditional paths, more anecdotal almost. The speech in which Aston tells us of his hospital treatment is a distinguished piece of writing in itself, but somehow too explicit, lacking the richness and indirection of Pinter's best work. And not just because Pinter ought to be "Pinteresque," that is, in popular critical parlance riddling and obscure, but because Pinter's plays, even at their most explicit—and in many respects they grow more and more direct and explicit as we go on—make their effect not by direct, immediately analyzable appeals to our minds or our emotions, but by much more intricate, insidious workings on our instinctive responses. They are essentially poetic drama, with all the subtlety and ambiguity that implies. *The Caretaker* is an admirable play in itself and represents a stage that Pinter no doubt had to pass through in the course of his artistic development. But on the whole its means are not the means of poetry, but the means of prose.

However, a return to poetry was already in preparation: Pinter's radio play *The Dwarfs,* which followed after only a few months, and the unimportant interlude of *Night School,* a very slight television play that really only rearranged the constituents of *A Night Out* rather less effectively. If *The Caretaker* is Pinter's easiest, most approachable play, *The Dwarfs* is in many ways his most obscure and yet haunting. It uses the medium of radio to the full to take us inside its characters' minds, or rather inside the mind of one of its characters, Len, who seems to be on the brink of a nervous breakdown. There are three characters in the play, Len, Pete, and Mark. (A fourth in the novel, a girl, has been eliminated.) Pete and Mark are friends of Len, and nominally of each other, except that each mistrusts the other and regards his influence on Len as bad. Pete is slightly suggestive of Mick in *The Caretaker,* quick-witted, hard, and unpredictable: Len's image for him is that of a seagull, cruel and predatory, digging under stones in the mud. Mark is smooth and complacent, roused only when his vanity is affronted by the news that Pete thinks him a fool: Len's image for him is that of a spider waiting in his web. In effect, we see Pete and Mark largely through Len's eyes, refracted through his consciousness. And he, whether because he is perhaps going mad, or whether because Pinter already

wishes to suggest that this is the way things are, consistently denies the possibility of knowing anything for certain about either of them, or himself, or anyone else. In a great speech, one of the high points of Pinter's writing, Len sums up the theme of the play, and provides the keynote for Pinter's further explorations into the nature of personality in *The Collection, The Lover,* and *The Basement:*

Occasionally I believe I perceive a little of what you are but that's pure accident. Pure accident on both our parts, the perceived and the perceiver. It's nothing like an accident, it's deliberate, it's a joint pretence. We depend on these accidents, on these contrived accidents, to continue. It's not important then that it's conspiracy or hallucination. What you are, or appear to be to me, or appear to be to you, changes so quickly, so horrifyingly, I certainly can't keep up with it and I'm damn sure you can't either. But who you are I can't even begin to recognize, and sometimes I recognize it so wholly, so forcibly, I can't look, and how can I be certain of what I see? You have no number. Where am I to look, where am I to look, what is there to locate, so as to have some surety, to have some rest from the whole bloody racket? You're the sum of so many reflections. How many reflections? Whose reflections? Is that what you consist of? What scum does the tide leave? What happens to the scum? When does it happen? I've seen what happens. But I can't speak when I see it. I can only point a finger. I can't even do that. The scum is broken and sucked back. I don't see where it goes. I don't see when, what do I see, what have I seen? What have I seen, the scum or the essence?

This raises, as the entire play raises, a quite different question of character verification from that raised in *The Birthday Party* or from that raised in *The Caretaker.* In *The Birthday Party,* as a matter of fact, the question is not raised within the play itself, and perhaps only suggests itself on more abstract consideration afterward. Within the confines of the play we accept that Stanley has some reason to fear Goldberg and McCann, and that Goldberg and McCann have some reason to come after him. We accept, equally, that it is not the play's purpose that we should be told these reasons; the question of verification therefore never really comes up. In *The Caretaker* we are invited to find a more everyday explanation for the contradictions and evasions of Davies and Mick (Aston is always straightforward) in what they say about themselves. When Aston asks Davies if he is Welsh and he replies, after a pause, "Well I been around, you know," it is not necessarily because his antecedents and place of birth are unknown, let alone unknowable, but simply that he is by nature untruthful and evasive. Despite what Pinter has said about characters who cannot give a complete account of themselves, this seems to be a refusal to verify, which is in ordinary psychological terms perfectly believable. Len's questions (addressed to Mark) are something else again: what he is denying is the whole basis of our relations with each other, the existence of a consistent, coherent core of personality underlying all the various facets and reflections we offer different observers on different occasions of our life. This assumption is merely the "joint pretense" on which we depend to continue, or, as Pinter has elsewhere said: "There are no hard distinctions between what is real and what is unreal, nor between what is true and what is false. The thing is not necessarily either true or false; it can be both true and false" ("Writing for the Theatre," *Plays: One,* p. 11).

Such a view, if sternly applied to character in drama, would seem likely to make the dramatist's job very difficult. Nevertheless, having logically arrived at this position, Pinter could not do otherwise than follow his apprehension through, if necessary into silence. But if it was to be silence, that would not come yet awhile; and before a period of silence he wrote three of his most striking plays, all produced in the first instance on television: *The Collection* (1961), *The Lover* (1963), and *The Basement* (written in 1963 as a film script). The first is an elaborately worked-out social comedy, based on a mystery surrounding what exactly, if anything, actually did happen between fashion designers Bill and Stella during the presentation of a collection in Leeds. Stella has told her husband, James, that Bill slept with her. James sets out to terrorize Bill into admitting it (a faint echo of the old menace situation), and, after denying everything, Bill agrees and begins to elaborate. Meanwhile Harry, the older man with whom Bill lives, is persuading Stella to retract her story. This done, Bill breaks down and admits that nothing really happened, though it might have. But is even this true? James presses Stella for an answer, but she remains enigmatic. Perhaps it is true, perhaps it is not true, perhaps it is both true and untrue. The pattern of the play prevents Bill and Stella, who are the only ones who might know the truth, from coming together to reveal it, if there is any truth to be revealed. The business of verification, in fact, has been moved into the play itself, instead of remaining something that no one in the play worries about but that might perhaps worry an audience. It is all an elaborate game, with its own rules, through which the various people in the play try to trap each other into revealing the one coherent person beyond the confusing and contradictory reflections. It may be a game, but it is carried on for all the sophistication of the participants in deadly seriousness.

*The Lover* shows us the game a stage further on. A husband says a fond farewell to his wife and goes out, casually asking her if her lover is coming that afternoon. Once he has gone she changes her clothes and assumes a new, "mistress" personality, and prepares to greet her lover, who, when he appears, proves to be the husband, suitably transformed. It is all a game they play to keep their marriage happy and successful; or to put it another way, it is their realistic response to the observed fact that every individual is really a number of different, contradictory individuals, and that, once this is recognized, once the contrived accidents can no longer be sustained, the only thing to do is to accept and come to terms with life's contradiction. *The Basement* goes a step further still: using the basic plot of *Kullus,* it refines the play of conflicting realities even more by showing not only people changing alarmingly, unrecognizably from moment to moment, but also their physical surroundings, the coveted basement flat, following suit.

IV

At this point one might fear that Pinter had worked himself, as a dramatist, into a logical and emotional impasse. And indeed, for a couple of years he devoted his energies primarily to film adaptations of other writers' work—two of them, *The Pumpkin Eater* and *The Quiller Memorandum,* essays in writing technique; the other two, *The Servant* (based on Robin Maugham's story) and *Accident* (from a novel by Nicholas Mosley), taking on the character of Pinter creations, especially in the gradual reversal of the master/servant relationship in the first and in the enigmatic, feline character of the girl in the second, a Pinter woman in the process of definition between *The Collection* and *The Homecoming.* Then in 1965 came another television play, *Tea Party,* in which Pinter actually dramatizes his escape from the impasse his exploration of the nature of personality had brought him to. The play shows us an initially ambiguous situation such as we have encountered in the last three plays: the businessman Disson feels that around him things remain unspoken. His new wife's relationship with her brother, for instance, seems strangely intimate. Is he in fact her brother, and, even if he is, does that mean their relationship is innocent? Other things, such as Disson's highly charged relationship with his secretary, are almost equally ambiguous, but as he becomes increasingly engrossed in his own particular problems of verification, we, as it were, pull away from him; we accept that he is unable to find a coherent, consistent pattern in things, not because no such pattern exists to be found, but because he is going mad. And so at the end of the play, when his irrevocably fractured view of the world about him has driven him to total withdrawal, in a catatonic trance, we are left outside, observing him from a world in which familiar appearances can, after all, be adequately trusted.

This play led the way to one of Pinter's finest works, his third full-length stage play, *The Homecoming* (1965). Technically it is the end product of all Pinter had learned in his writing career: tight, compact, stripped down to bare essentials, seeming to conceal nothing, hold nothing back, and yet remaining as mysterious in its nightmarish clarity as the densest and most obscure of his early plays. It is the perfect embodiment of Pinter's ideals, the story told quite directly, without explanation, in terms of "and then . . . and then . . . and then." The long-absent son of an East End family returns equipped, as he hopes, to impose his own idea of himself on his family at last with the evidences of his worldly success, and with his beautiful wife. But none of it is to any avail: they walk over him, as they have always done, and then his wife, cool, feline, imperturbably in control of the situation, proceeds to walk over them. The play's dramatic inevitability is not in question. It may haunt the spectator, or it may say nothing to him at all. It is, either way, impregnable in its monumental detachment from what the spectator thinks: a monolithic statement of its own right to exist.

In the process it refers, fleetingly, to such familiar Pinter images as the room (all that we see of the family home); menace (the homecomer Teddy as a possible menace to his family; them, individually and collectively, as a menace to his sanity and well-being); the problem of verification (how much of Teddy's glowing account of his successful life in America shall we believe; how much of what his father, Max, and brother, Lennie, tell us about their own appalling exploits?). It is also about six people in a room, just as Pinter has said *The Caretaker* is about three people in a room, except that there he could not prevent audiences from doubting his word, whereas there is no doubt of its literal truth. But, more important, it brings to the fore some new themes in Pinter's work, or themes at any rate that have not received anything like such elaborate treatment before. These are the family as a unit (a subject one might expect to have particular significance for a Jewish writer, already hinted at in *The Caretaker* and developed more fully in *Tea Party*), the role of the female in the power-game of life, and the significance of memory. The most prominent of these themes is that embodied in the character of Ruth, Teddy's wife and the only woman in the play. She is the synthesis of all Pinter's sexually attractive women: the prostitutes/hostesses of *A Night Out* and *Night School,* Stella in *The Collection,* Sarah in *The Lover*, Anna in *Accident.* They all seem to be passive, enigmatic, and yet all of them, except the first, get what they want, regulate the game they will play with the men around them, dominate by their speed of reaction. Men who act will always dominate men who stop to think; women think and act simultaneously, as though with some deep unquestioning instinct, and therefore dominate both. And perhaps, too, it helps that, like cats, they have no remembered loyalties, no encumbering ties with the past. Memory—which is just the problem of verification seen from another angle—is likely to be a liability, committing one always to live out and relive the past instead of living in and taking full advantage of the present. All the men in *The Homecoming*, even the stupidest, are in some way debilitated by memory; only Ruth is free.

V

MEMORY is the main theme of the three short plays Pinter wrote after *The Homecoming: Landscape* (1968), in which an old couple seem to exchange recollections but actually go on living in their independent worlds, sublimely unaware of each other; *Night* (1969), in which a married couple, recalling the occasions of their first meeting and early happiness, are obviously so far from connecting that they might be talking about entirely different people; and *Silence* (1969), in which three characters, two men and a young woman, muse, mostly in separation, about a mysterious triangular relationship they have, haunted by fleeting images of an almost forgotten past. In all three short pieces (*Night* is only a seven-minute sketch) the tone is quiet, meditative, of emotion recollected, if not in tranquillity, at least in a state where all passion is spent, and the characters seem to be perennially waiting.

They are still waiting in *Old Times* (1971), which stands in the same sort of relation to *Landscape* and *Silence* as did *The Homecoming* to the group of one-act plays that preceded it. But if *Landscape* and *Silence* are about the shackles of memory, *Old Times* is in a sense about triumph over memory. As Anna, the old friend refound, says: "There are some things one remembers even though they may never have happened. There are things I remember which may never have happened, but as I recall them so they take place." But if *Old Times* takes as its starting point the material of *Landscape* and *Silence*, it transforms it into something very much more dynamic; as a full-length play (even a very short full-length play), it cannot afford to be merely meditative.

The play starts with deceptive directness and simplicity (or perhaps not so deceptive; Pinter's plays are direct and simple, the responses they evoke complex). Kate and her husband, Deeley, talk about an expected guest, Anna, of whom we learn that Kate once shared rooms with her, that she was not only Kate's best but her only friend, and that on occasions she would steal Kate's underwear. To be precise, Deeley talks about her, eliciting brief, gnomic answers from Kate, whose role almost throughout the play is that of a dreamy, uncommunicative object off whom the others bounce thoughts and feelings. It sounds like a conventional piece of exposition, preparing us for a classic Pinter situation, in which the interloper arrives to disturb what we presume to be the settled peace of an existing domestic situation. Except that Anna is there already, a palpable presence in the background—as though she has always been there, always a psychological presence in the marriage, even before she walks forward as the lights come up to become a physical presence.

Once the three characters are in conversation together, the play quickly becomes an exchange, and then a battle, of memories. Anna chatters on about the past she shared with Kate, when both were young secretaries in the culture-filled London of twenty years ago, and already we begin to wonder how accurate her memories are: do we really believe that these two people ever sat up half the night reading Yeats? Deeley hits back with a long recollection of his first meeting with Kate, who he picked up at some deserted suburban fleapit where they were showing *Odd Man Out*, so that their relationship began, as it were, under the patronage of Robert Newton. Anna's immediate reaction to this is the mysterious statement about memory already quoted, and then a long story about the inexplicable appearance and disappearance of a man one night in their room, hers and Kate's. After which she drops in casually that she went with Kate that hot afternoon to see *Odd Man Out*.

And behind and beneath all this there seems to be something more: a battle over Kate, conflicting claims of ownership, conflicting definitions of her nature. Even something so apparently innocent as a medley of recollections from the good old songs they don't write any more becomes subtly a jockeying for position; it is fundamentally Anna's recollection, but Deeley keeps capping each quotation, taking it over and by implication making it his own. And meanwhile Kate remains more or less passive, withdrawn, the object. She even complains at one point that they both speak of her as though she were dead, so preoccupied are they with redefining their past, her past, to their own ends. And right at the end of the first act Anna seems to be winning the battle for Kate, by taking the conversation with a wrench back to the old times, speaking as though they are back in their flat together, telling Kate what to wear, suggesting one man or another to her attention. But Kate at the last makes her own move: she will run her bath herself. Anna and Deeley are left alone as the lights go down.

But if the first act seems to be mainly a battle between Deeley and Anna for power over Kate, there are also implications of something else, a growing interest felt by Deeley in Anna. In the second act this comes to the fore, with Deeley insisting that he knew Anna too, in the old times, even before he knew Kate, and that in his experience she was not at all the genteel, cultivated figure she now represents herself as being. Gradually more and more memories are brought out and exchanged, canceling one another out, or seeming to ("the thing is not necessarily either true or false; it can be both true and false"). Anna and Kate blur, change places, until there is no knowing what happened to and with which.

At the end, when Kate at last speaks out, it seems to be an assertion of her existence, independent of Anna, her own choice of Deeley in place of Anna: Anna, in Kate's recollections, is seen as dead, smeared with dirt; but then she remembers trying to smear Deeley's face (if it was Deeley in her room) with dirt also. Only he refused, and suggested a wedding instead, and a change of environment. But by now the three are locked into some sort of erotic unity that cannot be broken quite so easily. In the silence after the last word spoken (by Kate) Deeley reenacts the scene remembered (or imagined) by Anna in the first act, when she saw, or thought she saw, a man in their room, cradled by Kate. And at the end Anna is still there, as at the beginning—the three of them are there, separate but inescapably together. Has time been regained and conquered, or is it a trap human beings can never escape?

Pinter's next full-length play (after a brief, slight television piece for one actor, *Monologue,* 1973) seems to represent a moment of stasis in this particular argument. In *No Man's Land* (1975) one old man, seemingly prosperous and established, has got into conversation with another, ferrety and rather disreputable, on the heath and brought him home for a drink. The play consists mainly of the fencing between the two, each guarded, each trying in some way to get the better of the other, in this "no man's land" that is also a *temps mort.* The very last words of Spooner, the visitor, in the play are: "You are in no man's land. Which never moves, which never changes, which never grows older, but which remains for ever, icy and silent." If time must have a stop, evidently it stops here. This is Pinter's winter piece: much of the imagery is of cold and silence, and it portrays the winter of life, presenting incidentally a splendid occasion for two of the British theater's grand old men, John Gielgud and Ralph Richardson, to demonstrate yet again that the fires of life never completely die down. In most respects the play seems to be a taut and economical long one-actor about the two old men in a room, but there are also some interludes of "early Pinter" concerning the host Hirst's two vaguely menacing sidekicks, who sometimes act like his keepers, sometimes like his servants, and indulge in the barbed cross-talk Pinter has always done so well, though here they seem to be around more to make the play into a full evening's theater than as an integral part of the original concept. In this sense *No Man's Land* is formally the least satisfactory of Pinter's major plays, though in the main section of the piece his dramatic logic continues to explore obsessive themes with the same inexorable precision as before.

In his next play, *Betrayal* (1978), all is from the formal point of view highly *soigné,* and the subject is again, glancingly, time, as well as the tangle of human relations and reactions suggested by the title: it depicts the course of an affair that involves husband, wife, and husband's best friend and agent over a period of some ten years, and the twist to it is that the play's nine scenes move backward in time, so that we start with the latest meeting of wife and ex-lover, ex-lover and husband, and then little by little uncover how the final situation came about. In terms of the Pinter we have known there are remarkably few ambiguities or mysteries: everything that is revealed seems to be revealed pretty unequivocally, and though we discover that the people in the play have been keeping all sorts of secrets from one another, they do not appear finally to have many secrets left from the audience. Except, of course, the ultimate, unrevealable secret of human nature and why people do the things they do. But then those have been enough for playwrights to be going on with since the beginnings of theater as we know it, and *Betrayal* certainly showed no weakening in the spell Pinter has always been able to weave around his audiences, drawing them inexorably into his own world. That his world had grown a bit closer to that the rest of us think we live in did not betoken any perceptible falling off in interest, but the play certainly made one wonder if it heralded a new "classicism" in Pinter's work.

The answer to that, as one might expect with Pinter, was at once yes and no. In 1980 he finally let a play he had written back in 1958, right after *A Slight Ache,* and had at various times mentioned in interviews as unsatisfactory and shelved, be performed with minimal revisions. *The Hothouse*, which concerns a lot of somewhat sadomasochistic goings-on in a mental hospital, with the usual dramatic doubts about which are sane and which are mad, proved to be, as Pinter had judged it, inferior to the mainline works he had presented to the public at the time of composition; but at the same time it demonstrated conclusively that even second-rate Pinter is better than first-rate most-other-people, as well as being, naturally, a field day for students of Pinter anxious to fill in all the available pieces. To aid in this process—for thesis-writing about Pinter had by now become a major academic industry on both sides of the Atlantic—he published all his screenplay adaptations, filmed and unfilmed, of novels as improbably varied as John Fowles's *The French Lieutenant's Woman*, F. Scott Fitzgerald's unfinished *The Last Tycoon*, and *A la recherche du temps perdu*, for which, in *The Proust Screenplay*, he accomplished miraculously the inherently self-defeating task of boiling down all of Marcel Proust's major themes and incidents into one dramatic unit denied the essential dimension of sheer length of time passing.

But his original work is really the thing, and in the period from 1981 to 1984 he fulfilled all possible requirements with a series of four short plays produced either singly or, at different times, in two groups of three and one double bill. The two groups of three were both called *Other Places:* at the National Theatre *Other Places* consisted of *Family Voices, Victoria Station,* and *A Kind of Alaska;* in the West End *Family Voices* was replaced by *One for the Road,* previously seen in a lunchtime double bill with *Victoria Station.* Significantly enough, in consecutive years Pinter won the *Drama* award for the best new play with a one-acter, *A Kind of Alaska,* in 1984 and with *One for the Road* in 1985, which would seem conclusively to bear out the oft-repeated judgment that he is England's "best living playwright."

*Family Voices* is, in a familiar Pinter manner, two intercut monologues by a mother and absent son who claim to be very concerned with each other but never actually connect, with brief interventions from the dead father. *Victoria Station* is a radio conversation between a taxi driver apparently undergoing some kind of nervous breakdown and the man who directs him from back at base, trying to get some information, any information, out of him about where he is and what he is doing. But the most substantial of the four are *A Kind of Alaska* and *One for the Road.* The first was inspired by casehistories in Oliver Sacks's book *Awakening*, about the effects of the new drug L-DOPA in arousing patients who had been comatose with sleeping sickness for upwards of fifty years. Obviously Pinter, with his long-established obsessions with identity, communication, and the subjectivity or otherwise of time, would find the subject fascinating, and his imagined awakening is handled very straightforwardly but with amazing subtlety and tact, so that the woman patient's return to life becomes—a quality one has not particularly associated with Pinter before—intensely moving. *One for the Road* was widely touted as a document of another kind of awakening, Pinter's first explicitly political play. But if Pinter were in fact to write anything like a piece of agitprop, then surely the less Pinter he. And sure enough, though the play does concern an apparently political interrogation and the techniques of intellectual intimidation and brainwashing, it is really about just the same ways in which one human being may seek to dominate another as is, say, *The Birthday Party.* What has changed is mainly his technical skill and sense of dramatic economy: everything seems to be absolutely explicit, stated quite directly, and yet the mystery and the totally compulsive quality of the drama remain completely intact. As ever, we never know what Pinter is going to do until he does it, and once he has done it, it proves to have the sort of inevitability that half-convinces us that we must have known all the time.

VI

In discussing the thematic development of Pinter's work from play to play we have largely left his style aside from consideration. And yet that in many ways is the most remarkable thing about his writing. His methods are the methods of poetry: he never preaches, never argues, but makes the significance of what he does emerge from the totality of the work. And yet any notion that "poetic" in his work means vague, generalized, avoiding awkward particularities, would be impossibly wide of the mark. The extraordinary effect of his dialogue comes not from its obvious richness and elaboration, its removal from everyday norms of speech, but from the opposite, the skill with which he captures the rhythms of modern English as it is really spoken, the rigorous discipline with which he cuts everything down to its essential. He gives us, in effect, not an artificial pattern of speech, but everyday speech patterns put under the microscope, examined in such minute detail that they seem, after all, as weird and unfamiliar as the speech of another planet. He has observed, as no one else has, the constant tugs-of-war in normal speech, such as that between the quick-witted talker whose ideas race on ahead of what he is saying and the slower-witted who is still stumbling along a couple of steps behind; or that between the inquisitive inquirer who wants to find out as much as he can while giving nothing away and the wary victim of his interrogation, who cannot or will not bring the conversation to an end but is determined to show himself as little as possible in what he says. Witness the following passage of dialogue from *The Caretaker*:

MICK. ... Look! I got a proposition to make to you. I'm thinking of taking over the running of this place, you see? I think it could be run a bit more efficiently. I got a lot of ideas, a lot of plans. *(He eyes DAVIES.)* How would you like to stay on here, as caretaker?
DAVIES. What?
MICK. I'll be quite open with you. I could rely on a man like you around the place, keeping an eye on things.
DAVIES. Well now ... wait a minute ... I ... I ain't never done no caretaking before, you know. ...
MICK. Doesn't matter about that. It's just that you look a capable sort of man to me.
DAVIES. I am a capable sort of man. I mean to say, I've had plenty offers in my time, you know, there's no getting away from that.
MICK. Well I could see before, when you took out that knife, that you wouldn't let anyone mess you about.
DAVIES. No one messes me about, man.
MICK. I mean, you've been in the services, haven't you?
DAVIES. The what?
MICK. You been in the services. You can tell by your stance.
DAVIES. Oh ... yes. Spent half my life there, man. Overseas ... like ... serving ... I was.
MICK. In the colonies, weren't you?
DAVIES. I was over there. I was one of the first over there.
MICK. That's it. You're just the man I been looking for.
DAVIES. What for?
MICK. Caretaker.
DAVIES. Yes, well ... look ... listen ... who's the landlord here, him or you?
MICK. Me. I am. I got deeds to prove it.
DAVIES. Ah ... *(Decisively)*. Well, listen, I don't mind doing a bit of caretaking, I wouldn't mind looking after the place for you.
MICK. Of course, we'd come to a small financial agreement, mutually beneficial.
DAVIES. I leave you to reckon that out, like.
MICK. Thanks. There's only one thing.
DAVIES. What's that?
MICK. Can you give me any references?
DAVIES. Eh?
MICK. Just to satisfy my solicitor.
DAVIES. I got plenty of references. All I got to do is to go down to Sidcup tomorrow. I got all the references I want down there.
MICK. Where's that?
DAVIES. Sidcup. He ain't only got my references down there, he got all my papers down there. I know that place like the back of my hand. I'm going down there anyway, see what I mean, I got to get down there, or I'm done.
MICK. So we can always get hold of those references if we want them.
DAVIES. I'll be down there any day, I tell you. I was going down today, but I'm ... I'm waiting for the weather to break.

(Act II)

The problem of communication, so much commented on in Pinter's plays, is after all seldom failure or inability to communicate so much as unwillingness: as Pinter himself has put it:

I think that we communicate only too well, in our silence, in what is unsaid, and that what takes place is continual evasion, desperate rearguard attempts to keep ourselves to ourselves. Communication is too alarming. To enter into someone else's life is too frightening. To disclose to others the poverty within us is too fearsome a possibility.

("Writing for the Theatre," *Plays: One*, p. 15)

And so, his plays work quite as much on what they do not say as on what they do. In this sense they are not primarily literary theater at all.

So often, below the words spoken, is the thing known and unspoken.... There are two silences. One when no word is spoken. The other when perhaps a torrent of language is being employed. This speech is speaking of a language locked beneath it. That is its continual reference. The speech we hear is an indication of that we don't hear . . . when true silence falls we are still left with echo, but are nearer nakedness.

(pp. 13–14)

Therefore, the relations between Pinter's characters are always more complex than the words in which they seem to be expressed. The purely literary level of the dialogue is only the surface beneath which move strange and unpredictable monsters of the deep. And this is where Pinter's extraordinary poet's instinct comes in. The job of the poet is as much as anything to direct and define his reader's sensibilities, to use the relevant associations and cut off the irrelevant. Pinter has few equals among dramatists in this subtle, almost imperceptible direction of his audience. In his plays we never know quite what is hitting us or why, but it hits us with full force nevertheless, and with no waste of energy either. The supreme example of this process is *The Homecoming*, where nothing is implied and yet everything is implied, everything is stated and yet nothing is stated.

LENNY. And now perhaps I'll relieve you of your glass.
RUTH. I haven't quite finished.
LENNY. You've consumed quite enough, in my opinion.
RUTH. No, I haven't.
LENNY. Quite sufficient, in my own opinion.
RUTH. Not in mine, Leonard.
*Pause.*
LENNY. Don't call me that, please.
RUTH. Why not?
LENNY. That's the name my mother gave me.
*Pause.*
Just give me the glass.
RUTH. No.
*Pause.*
LENNY. I'll take it, then.
RUTH. If you take the glass . . . I'll take you.
*Pause.*
LENNY. How about me taking the glass without you taking me?
RUTH. Why don't I just take you?
*Pause.*
LENNY. You're joking.
*Pause.*
You're in love, anyway, with another man. You've had a secret liaison with another man. His family didn't even know. Then you come here without a word of warning and start to make trouble.
*She picks up the glass and lifts it towards him.*
RUTH. Have a sip. Go on. Have a sip from my glass.
*He is still.*
Sit on my lap. Take a long cool sip.
*She pats her lap. Pause.*
*She stands, moves to him with the glass.*
Put your head back and open your mouth.
LENNY. Take that glass away from me.
RUTH. Lie on the floor. Go on. I'll pour it down your throat.
LENNY. What are you doing, making me some kind of proposal?
*She laughs shortly, drains the glass.*
RUTH. Oh, I was thirsty.
*She smiles at him, puts the glass down, goes into the hall and up the stairs.*
*He follows into the hall and shouts up the stairs.*
LENNY. What was that supposed to be? Some kind of proposal?
*Silence.*

(Act I)

VII

ALLIED with this minute concern for the texture of his drama is, naturally but not inevitably, a passionate care for the shaping and structure of the piece. Pinter is, we know, extremely careful and fastidious in the writing and rewriting of his plays, especially in constantly refining them down, removing superfluities until only the absolute essential is left. It has been claimed that he is therefore necessarily a miniaturist. But while his concern for the minutest detail of expression is as great in one of his full-length plays as in the briefest sketches such as *Last to Go* (1959) or *The Black and White* (it is recorded that when asked if the Broadway production of *The Homecoming* was much different from the London one he replied, "I think we changed one comma"), this does not necessarily imply that his technique is any less suited to the full-length play, or any less capable of meeting its special demands. On the contrary, *The Birthday Party*, *The Caretaker*, and *The Homecoming* all demonstrate him entirely capable of articulating with perfect skill and confidence a long and complex structure. All his plays, from the longest to the shortest, are, if not in the historical sense at least in the literal sense of the term, impeccably well made.

It is all too easy, discussing Pinter's work in terms either of its recurrent images or of its supreme technical awareness and conscious mastery, to leave out of consideration altogether its quite individual flavor. To begin with, Pinter, though deadly serious in his approach to his art, is anything but solemn. His "comedies of menace" are real comedies, in which the humor has to match the horror every step of the way: when this has been lost, as in the first production of *The Dumb Waiter* (which took place in Frankfurt, in German), the results are disastrous, for much of his effect comes from lightness and speed, underlining nothing. In this he is, surprisingly enough, a very English playwright: if some influence from Samuel Beckett can be observed in his early plays, it is balanced in the later by a real kinship with Noel Coward, a dramatist whom he also vocally admires. His relationship with the Theater of the Absurd, as represented especially by Beckett and Eugene Ionesco, was clear enough in his "comedies of menace," but since *A Slight Ache* has grown very tenuous: *The Caretaker* is hardly absurdist drama at all, either in its theme or in its technique, and the later plays, while recognizably post-, shall we say, *Waiting for Godot*, are totally personal in their language and structure, refusing any neat pigeonholing with this or that school.

For Pinter is, unmistakably now, sui generis. It is easy just to make approving (or maybe disapproving) noises about his work, far harder to place him in any dramatic hierarchy, in Britain or in the world at large. Debate as to whether he is a "major" dramatist, for example, seems not only premature —who can know until posterity has decided the matter?—but heavily dependent on the criteria brought to bear, some of which, central to you, may seem totally irrelevant to me, and vice versa. Is clear moral commitment a necessary ingredient of "major" drama? If so, Pinter's drama is not major, for whatever Pinter the man may care about and stand for in the world of everyday moral decision (we remember, inter alia, his two trials as a conscientious objector), his plays resolutely steer clear of taking up any position in such matters, or even of handling subjects that seem to require commitment of that sort (even *One for the Road* is at best a dubious exception to the rule). They avoid, that is, the recognized "big subject," and stick instead to the obsessive exploration of a private world, of individuals living very much on the edge of their being. In his concentration on human relations abstracted to an almost "pure" state, Pinter seems far closer to Jean Racine than to any of his expansive, voluble contemporaries, or even to the great compressionist of our own time, Samuel Beckett.

It would, I am sure, be misleading to suggest that this is part of any conscious program. If *The Homecoming* takes place in a world where the dead mother can be referred to from moment to moment as an angel or a whore, without any suggestion that the characters subscribe to a hierarchy in which an angel is superior to a whore or indeed noticeably different, that is because that is the way that Pinter sees his world, not because that is intellectually the pattern he wishes to impose on it. Indeed, Harold Pinter, most intelligent of British dramatists, is just about the least intellectual. That is to say, all his conscious exercise of intelligence goes into the shaping of the material itself, or a cool inquiry into its sources and significance. Instinct clearly plays an enormous part in his work, and his refusal to provide explanations reflects a very real need to take his instinct on trust, rather than mere perversity on his part. Technically he has few peers: in that sense he knows absolutely what he is doing and what effect he wants to create as he writes. But in the realm of ideas he really does not have any special knowledge of his own meaning; he chooses not to have, for fear, perhaps, of killing the goose that lays the golden eggs.

*VIII*

So, Pinter's plays give the critic little foothold, few rough patches that can be neatened by applying a coat or two of his ideas or convenient rifts through which the critic can insert himself into the body of the work. And the further on in Pinter's career we get, the more complete and self-sustaining the plays are, the more sublimely careless of exegesis. The most, finally, that the critic can do is describe, retell the story in less effective terms, and hope thereby to convey something of its quality. In Pinter's work, uniquely in the modern theater, there is really no substitute for the poem but the poem, the play but the play. We can observe the paradoxes—that Pinter is at once the least realistic and the most minutely realistic of contemporary British dramatists; that his world seems the smallest and most private, and yet covers a wider range of English society, a greater variety of human emotions, than anyone else's—and still come back to an elementary take-it-or-leave-it judgment of the finished plays. After all the complexities, subtleties, and refinements have been pointed out, it is still open to the spectator to say "So what?" and if he does there is no meaningful way of arguing with him. But to others it is this very self-contained quality in Pinter's work, its steadfast refusal to be considered in anything less than its own integrity, which makes him not only the most inescapably haunting of our modern dramatists, but the most likely to survive as a permanent part of our dramatic literature.

## SELECTED BIBLIOGRAPHY

I. COLLECTED WORKS. *The Birthday Party and Other Plays* (London, 1960), includes *The Room* and *The Dumb Waiter*; *A Slight Ache and Other Plays* (London, 1961), includes *A Night Out*, *The Dwarfs*, and revue sketches; *The Collection and The Lover* (London, 1963), includes *The Examination*; *Tea Party and Other Plays* (London, 1967), includes *The Basement* and *Night School*; *Landscape and Silence* (London, 1969), includes *Night*; *Five Screenplays* (London, 1971), includes *The Servant*, *The Pumpkin Eater*, *The Quiller Memorandum*, *Accident*, and *The Go-Between*; *Plays: One* (London, 1976), includes *The Birthday Party*, *The Room*, *The Dumb Waiter*, *A Slight Ache*, *A Night Out*, *The Black and the White*, and *The Examination*; *Plays: Two* (London, 1977), includes *The Caretaker*, *The Dwarfs*, *The Collection*, *The Lover*, *Night School*, and five revue sketches; *Poems and Prose 1949–1977* (London, 1977); *Plays: Three* (London, 1977), includes *The Homecoming*, *Tea Party*, *The Basement*, *Landscape*, *Silence*, *Night*, and five sketches; *Plays: Four* (London, 1981), includes *Old Times*, *No Man's Land*, *Betrayal*, *Monologue*, and *Family Voices*; *Other Places* (London, 1982), includes *Family Voices*, *Victoria Station*, and *A Kind of Alaska*.

II. SEPARATE WORKS. *The Birthday Party: A Play in Three Acts* (London, 1959; rev. ed. 1965); *The Caretaker: A Play* (London, 1960; 2nd ed. 1962); *The Dumb Waiter: A Play in One Act* (London, 1960); *A Night Out: A Play* (London, 1961); *A Slight Ache: A Play in One Act* (London, 1961); "Pinter Between the Lines," in the *Sunday Times* (4 March 1962), based on a lecture delivered in Bristol to the Seventh National Student Drama Festival; *The Collection: A Play in One Act* (London, 1963); *The Dwarfs, and Eight Revue Sketches* (New York, 1965); *The Homecoming* (London, 1965; rev. ed. 1968); *The Lover: A Short Play* (London, 1966); *Poems* (London, 1968), with *Kullus*, 2nd ed. with additional poems (London, 1971); *Landscape* (London, 1968); *Mac* (London, 1968); *Old Times* (London, 1971); *Monologue* (London, 1973); *No Man's Land* (London, 1975); *The Proust Screenplay* (London, 1976); *Betrayal* (London, 1978); *The Hothouse* (London, 1980); *Family Voices* (London, 1981).

III. BIOGRAPHICAL AND CRITICAL STUDIES. M. Esslin, *The Theatre of the Absurd* (London, 1962; rev. ed. 1968); J. R. Taylor, *Anger and After* (London, 1962; rev. ed. 1969); C. Leech, "Two Romantics: Arnold Wesker and Harold Pinter," in *Contemporary Theatre, Stratford-on-Avon Studies*, no. 4 (1962); G. E. Wellwarth, *The Theatre of Paradox and Protest* (New York, 1964); A. H. Hinchcliffe, *Harold Pinter* (New York, 1967); "The Art of the Theatre, III," in the *Paris Review* (January 1967), interview by L. M. Bensky; W. Kerr, *Harold Pinter* (New York, 1967); R. Hayman, *Harold Pinter* (London, 1968); D. Salem, *Harold Pinter: Dramaturge de l'ambiguïté* (Paris, 1968); J. R. Hollis, *Harold Pinter: The Poetics of Silence* (Carbondale, 1970); M. Esslin, *The Peopled Wound: The Plays of Harold Pinter* (London, 1970), rev. ed. under title *Pinter: A Study of His Plays* (London, 1973); L. G. Gordon, *Strategems to Uncover Nakedness: The Dramas of Harold Pinter* (Columbia, Mo., 1970); A. Sykes, *Harold Pinter* (Quebec, 1970); J. Lahr, ed., *A Casebook of Harold Pinter's "The Homecoming"* (New York, 1971); J. R. Brown, *Theatre Language: A Study of Arden, Osborne, Pinter and Wesker* (London, 1972); S. Trussler, *The Plays of Harold Pinter: An Assessment* (London, 1973); A. Ganz, ed., *Pinter: A Collection of Critical Essays* (Englewood Cliffs, N.J., 1973).

# ALEXANDER POPE
(1688-1744)

## *Ian Jack*

WHEN William Hazlitt began his fourth lecture on the English poets by saying that John Dryden and Alexander Pope were the great masters of the artificial style of poetry in English, as Geoffrey Chaucer, Edmund Spenser, William Shakespeare, and John Milton were of the natural, he lent his authority to a false distinction that survived in literary histories until the other day. The legend has grown up—and few territories of human thought are as fertile in legends as literary criticism—that between the Restoration and the late eighteenth century English poetry was diverted from its main channel. Matthew Arnold went so far as to rule that Dryden and Pope, "though they may write in verse, though they may in a certain sense be masters of the art of versification . . . are not classics of our poetry, they are classics of our prose." As late as 1933, A. E. Housman asserted that "there was a whole age of English in which the place of poetry was usurped by something very different which possessed the proper and specific name of wit." In making this statement he was not only taking his cue from Arnold; he was also (whether consciously or not) harking back to Hazlitt's unsatisfactory distinction between poetry that is "natural" and poetry that is "artificial."

The change that has come over English poetry in the last fifty years has brought with it a revolution in critical perspective. In reaction against what they feel to have been the excessive respect of the later nineteenth century for the work of the romantics, modern poets have turned to the age of John Donne for their inspiration. As a result, such features of decadent romantic theory as the exaggerated insistence on "inspiration" and on the difference between the genius and the ordinary man, the distrust of imitation in poetry, the preference of emotion to thought, of spontaneity to controlled form—all these have begun to be cleared away into the lumber-room of discarded ideas. This explains the fact that the new enthusiasm for the poetry of the metaphysicals has brought in its wake a new and vital interest in the poetry of the Augustans.

Attempts have even been made to trace a close affinity between the poetry of Pope and that of Donne. In an influential essay on William Collins, Middleton Murry claimed that Pope was not only a master of wit "in the Augustan sense, the verbal epigram of an extraordinarily alert mind," but also of "Wit in the best Metaphysical sense—namely, the striking expression of deep psychological perceptions." And in the chapter on "The Line of Wit" in F. R. Leavis' *Revaluation*, Pope occupies an honorable place beside Ben Jonson, Donne, and Andrew Marvell. Yet a moment's reflection will show that Murry's definitions of "wit" are inadequate, and that such resemblances as exist between Pope and Donne are greatly outweighed by the differences. I suggest that it may be more profitable to reverse the position of Hazlitt and to consider Pope as belonging to the same great tradition of English poetry as Spenser and Milton: what may be termed, in the widest sense, the Renaissance tradition. The true contrast, as it seems to me, is not between Pope and the poets who preceded him, but between Pope and his successors of the romantic age. That English poetry will never return to the romantic tradition it is perhaps too early to be certain; but at the moment all the omens are against it, and the modern reader can approach the poetry of Pope unhindered by the preconceptions that misled the readers of the nineteenth century.

In nothing is the contrast between Pope and the greatest of the romantic poets more evident than in their attitudes to earlier poetry. William Wordsworth despised most of the poetry written in the century before his own, and came to regard it as his mission to lead English poets back to the forceful simplicity of an earlier age. If Pope had written an essay on poetry as a preface to a volume of his own work, it would have been very different in tone from the celebrated preface to the second edition of *Lyrical Ballads*. As the *Essay on Criticism*, his letters, and the records of his conversation make abundantly clear, Pope considered the development of poetry in the age before his own as a matter for rejoicing. He shared the view of his contemporaries that Dryden had evolved a poetic idiom superior to that of any earlier poet, and proclaimed that he had learned the art of versification wholly from him. This does not mean that he was ignorant of the poetry written before the Restoration, or contemptuous of it (as Nicolas Boileau-Despréaux was of most of the poetry written before his own time). On the contrary, it would hardly be an exaggeration to say that Pope had read everything of value in earlier English poetry, so far as it was available in his day. Spenser was one of his earliest favorites; with Milton he was intimately conversant; Shakespeare he came to know with the familiarity of an editor. He was something of a collector of old books, numbered among his friends several of the scholars who were beginning to chart the course of English literary development, and himself made notes toward what would have been the first history of English poetry.[1] But it did not occur to him to turn back from the road along which Dryden had traveled with such acclamation; he rather felt that it was his task to use Dryden's discoveries as a basis for further exploration.

As we read Pope's early poems, in which we are watching one of the readiest learners English poetry has ever known serving his apprenticeship, we are fortunate in being able to turn (for a background) to the *Anecdotes* collected by his friend Joseph Spence. This has proved a disappointing book to those who have looked in it for something comparable to the indiscretions of Samuel Pepys or the rounded humanity of James Boswell's portrait of Samuel Johnson; yet to the student of poetics it is an invaluable document, for it gives us, in Pope's own words, an account of his early education, his reading, and his opinions. It is largely due to Spence that Pope is the first English poet of whose methods of composition we have reliable information.

If it were not for Spence, the fact that Pope's first considerable publication was his *Pastorals* might suggest that his career as a writer opened almost too discreetly. But the *Anecdotes* make it clear that Pope was as ambitious as any poet could be in his boyish experiments. When he was about twelve, he told Spence, he "wrote a kind of play, which I got to be acted by my schoolfellows. It was a number of speeches from the *Iliad*; tacked together with verses of my own" (*Anecdotes*, ed. Singer, p. 276). Soon afterward he began an epic poem that was yet more ambitious, including as it did "an under-water scene in the first book." In this poem, of which some 4,000 lines were written, Pope "endeavoured to collect all the beauties of the great epic writers into one piece: there was Milton's style in one part, and Cowley's in another; here the style of Spenser imitated, and there of Statius; here Homer and Vergil, and there Ovid and Claudian." Imitation was of the essence of these early attempts, and when Pope wrote his *Pastorals* imitation remained his lodestar. These four poems mark his arrival at years of poetic discretion. It had become clear to him by now, one may suppose, that his boyish rage for rhyming was to lead to his lifetime's vocation; it was time for him to lay aside the grandiose imaginings of boyhood and settle down to study his art in earnest. Precisely when the *Pastorals* were written, we do not know: they were published in Jacob Tonson's *Miscellany* in 1709, but they were written at least in part three years earlier, when Pope was seventeen or eighteen. Early work as they are, these poems in watercolor reveal a poet who has already made himself master of one sort of versification, and whose descriptive powers—as in this passage from "Autumn"—are astonishingly mature:

> Here where the *Mountains* less'ning as they rise,
> Lose the low Vales, and steal into the Skies;
> While lab'ring Oxen, spent with Toil and Heat,
> In their loose Traces from the Field retreat;
> While curling Smokes from Village-Tops are seen,
> And the fleet Shades glide o'er the dusky Green.
>  (59–64)

Pope's descriptive power is one of the striking features of his early poems, and it is interesting to notice that he was not only a good judge of painting but was actually a painter himself. In his middle twenties—a fact emphasized by the late Norman Ault—he spent some eighteen months studying in the studio of his friend Charles Jervas, who was a fashionable portrait painter. The letters he wrote at this time contain some amusing references to his own apprenticeship to the art. "They tell us," he

---

[1] Printed in Ruffhead's *Life of Alexander Pope* (London, 1769), pp. 424–425.

wrote to one friend, "when St. Luke painted, an Angel came & finish'd the work; and it will be thought here after, that when I painted, the devil put the last hand to my pieces, they are so begrimed and smutted. 'Tis however some mercy that I see my faults. . . ."

While it is interesting to speculate about Pope's attainments as a painter, what is permanently significant is the value to his poetry of this apprenticeship to paint. "I begin to discover Beauties that were till now imperceptible to me," he wrote in another letter. "Every Corner of an Eye, or Turn of a Nose or Ear . . . have charms to distract me." In *Windsor Forest* it is his interest in landscape painting that is most evident:

> There, interspers'd in Lawns and op'ning Glades,
> Thin trees arise that shun each others Shades.
> Here in full Light the russet Plains extend;
> There wrapt in Clouds the blueish Hills ascend;
> Ev'n the wild Heath displays her Purple Dies,
> And 'midst the Desart fruitful Fields arise.
> (21-26)

The same interest in colors and effects of light and shade is one of the features of *The Temple of Fame*:

> Of bright, transparent Beryl were the Walls,
> The Friezes Gold, and Gold the Capitals:
> As Heaven with Stars, the Roof with Jewels glows,
> And ever-living Lamps depend in Rows.
> (141-144)

Throughout Pope's work one finds passages that betray the painter's eye, and his references to the technique of painting are numerous and exact.

When the first collection of his poems appeared, in 1717, Pope's love of luxury and color could not have been overlooked, nor his growing mastery of the heroic couplet. A number of the poems included, however, went far beyond exhibiting his mastery of technique. The epistle "Eloisa to Abelard," to which both Joseph Warton and Johnson assigned a very high place among Pope's poems, is interesting because it deals with a subject with which he was not often to deal, passionate sexual love: the whole poem has a hectic quality that is dramatically appropriate. Even finer is the "Elegy to the Memory of an Unfortunate Lady"; whoever the lady may have been, if she existed at all, this is one of the greatest elegiac poems in the language. As she has died at her own hand, the lady may not be buried in consecrated ground; but what of this? asks the poet:

> What tho' no sacred earth allow thee room,
> Nor hallow'd dirge be mutter'd o'er thy tomb?
> Yet shall thy grave with rising flow'rs be drest,
> And the green turf lie lightly on thy breast:
> There shall the morn her earliest tears bestow,
> There the first roses of the year shall blow;
> While Angels with their silver wings o'ershade
> The ground, now sacred by thy reliques made.
> (61-68)

Pope never wrote more tenderly than in this poem, or with a surer control of tone.

Yet the gem of the 1717 edition remains to be mentioned, *The Rape of the Lock*, of which the original version had been published in 1712, and the much expanded version (which we read now) two years later. This is the poem that Hazlitt described as "the most exquisite specimen of *fillagree* work ever invented" and that even Housman thought possibly the most perfect long poem in the language. The description on the title page, "An Heroi-Comical Poem," has misled some readers into imagining that the comic assault is leveled against heroic poetry; but in fact a mock heroic poem is no more a satire on heroic poetry than mock turtle soup is a satire on real turtle soup. The suggestion for the poem came from a quarrel that had arisen between two wealthy Catholic families in consequence of a stolen curl. When Pope was asked to write something that would restore everyone to good humor, it occurred to him to emphasize the triviality of the whole affair by describing it in the full pomp and splendor of epic verse. No poet has ever succeeded so well in "using a vast force to lift a feather" (as Pope himself described it in the postscript to his translation of the *Odyssey*). The style of the closing lines of canto II, for example,

> With beating Hearts the dire Event they wait,
> Anxious, and trembling for the Birth of Fate,

would be splendidly appropriate at a crucial moment in an epic poem; when we realize that "the Birth of Fate" is to be no more than the snipping off of a lock of hair, the result is high comedy. And yet something of the mastery of the poem is due to the fact that it is not simply and wholly ironical. When Pope wrote the line,

> *Belinda* smil'd, and all the World was gay,
> (II. 52)

he was not being as directly ironical as Dryden had been when he described the "goodly Fabrick" of Thomas Shadwell. The effect of comparing a fat poetaster to Hannibal and Augustus is bluntly sarcastic: that of comparing a beautiful girl to the sun is (in this instance) satirical, yet the comparison has its own imaginative truth. In *The Rape of the Lock* Pope plays with the traditional imagery of lovesick poets, and while his treatment hints at the absurdity of their conventions it is clear that he is enjoying the license this gives his imagination. He demonstrates the superficiality of Belinda's world of fashion and scandal, of petty vanities and trivial, mean absurdities; but he does not deny its transitory beauty—the beauty of which the sylphs, the inspired addition to the later version, are in some sort the symbol. Satire is absent from some of the descriptive passages of the poem, for, as Pope pointed out, "since inanimate and irrational beings are not objects of censure . . . these may be elevated as much as you please, and no ridicule follows." This is true of the description of the coffee-equipage in canto III, which is reminiscent rather of Vergil's use of epic style in the *Georgics* to describe the lives of bees than of the directly satiric method of *MacFlecknoe*:

> For lo! the Board with Cups and Spoons is crown'd,
> The Berries crackle, and the Mill turns round.
> On Shining Altars of *Japan* they raise
> The silver Lamp . . .
>
> (105–108)

Any satirical intention that there may be here is unimportant: the reader enjoys the game by which the things of everyday become transformed into objects of an unfamiliar beauty.

It would be a great mistake to ignore the moral of the poem, which is explicitly stated in Clarissa's speech in the last canto, and which holds the component parts in a close-knit unity; yet seldom has a moral been enforced with more delicacy and tact. Lytton Strachey wrote of Pope as if he were above all things the poet of hatred; but it is partly because there is no hatred in this poem that it is so assured a masterpiece.

In the *Epistle to Dr. Arbuthnot* Pope looks back at his own career and claims in his defense:

> That not in Fancy's Maze he wander'd long,
> But stoop'd to Truth, and moraliz'd his song,
> (340–341)

and earlier in the same poem he contrasts the "pure Description" of his early work with the "Sense" that is now his aim. The contrast between the two halves of his career would be more complete were it not for the perfect union of Fancy and Truth, Description and Sense, in *The Rape of the Lock*, which forms a sort of bridge between his early work and his late, but there is no gainsaying the fact that in the later years of his life he held his Fancy in strict subordination to the claims of Truth. Although many critics have regretted this, it was inevitable that Pope should have "moraliz'd his song." No poet has taken his art more seriously: it would not have occurred to him to be merely "the idle singer of an empty day": his was the dedicated life of Spenser, of Milton, and of Wordsworth, who told Lady Beaumont that he desired to be regarded as a teacher or as nothing.

It was fated to be principally in satire that Pope fulfilled his moral function, but this was not his original intention. The clue to much that is puzzling in his poetic career lies in a poem that was never completed—his epic, *Brutus*. The plan of this poem is printed in Ruffhead's *Life of Pope*, and it is there stated that the author has part of the manuscript, in blank verse, lying before him. Although it is difficult to believe that *Brutus* would have been a great poem—it seems unlikely that anyone could have written a successful epic at the middle of the eighteenth century—it is essential to an understanding of Pope to remember that he, like Dryden before him, shared the Renaissance ambition of writing a great heroic poem. The notion that the Augustans were content to disport themselves on the lower slopes of poetry, ridiculing the soaring ambitions of the more vigorous race of writers who had preceded them, is a travesty of literary history. It was because Pope had thought so much about heroic poetry that he was able, in a *pièce d'occasion* that chanced to become his masterpiece, to write the greatest of all mock heroic poems. From the age of twelve onward his object was to write an epic poem, and the great epics of the world, with the yet more intoxicating Idea of the Epic, were the constant subjects of his meditation. He knew Vergil and Milton almost by heart, and spent more than a decade producing his triumphant translations of Homer. This continual devotion to the greatest of all poetic forms confirmed him in his exacting estimate of the moral function of the poet.

There was one poetic kind that was felt to share

something of the dignity of the epic while sparing the poet the difficulty of finding an acceptable myth: didactic poetry. The suggestion that Pope should write a poem in this kind, justifying the ways of God to man, may have come from his friend Henry St. John, Viscount Bolingbroke: much of the philosophy in it certainly did. But the evidence of the poem itself suggests either that there was some conflict between the philosophy that Bolingbroke expounded to Pope and that which took form in the poet's own mind, or that Pope's understanding of his friend's philosophy was incomplete. It was the somber implications of Bolingbroke's philosophy that touched Pope's mind and heart most deeply. Like Jonathan Swift's, Pope's spiritual roots lay deep in the seventeenth century: he was accessible, to a degree in which Joseph Addison (for example) was not, to the terror and despair that lie beneath the surface of human life. In this Lucretian poem it is not when he is celebrating the power of man that he is at his greatest, but when he is emphasizing the paradoxes and perils of the human situation:

> Plac'd on this isthmus of a middle state,
> A being darkly wise, and rudely great:
> With too much knowledge for the Sceptic side,
> With too much weakness for the Stoic's pride,
> [Man] hangs between; in doubt to act, or rest,
> In doubt to deem himself a God, or Beast;
> In doubt his Mind or Body to prefer,
> Born but to die, and reas'ning but to err.
>
> (II. 3-10)

It is, indeed, as Paul Hazard has said, "déisme impur" that we find in the *Essay on Man*, "déisme où persistaient quelques-unes des données psychologiques que, précisement, on voulait proscrire: un effort de volonté, plus qu'une évidence rationelle; et une acceptation du mystère."[2]

The *Essay on Man* attracted a great deal of attention, becoming a center of religious controversy and making Pope a European celebrity. Yet, though the poem contains many brilliant passages, it might have been as well for his reputation if it had never been written. For no other of his poems—unless it be the *Essay on Criticism*, an early and successful attempt at a humbler sort of didactic poetry—has done so much to lend credence to the notion that Pope was a gnomic versifier of genius, and that his work is "poetry of the surface" characterized by the directness of prose rather than the complex suggestiveness of great poetry. For all its brilliance, the *Essay* should not be taken as an example of his greatest work.

Heroic and didactic poetry are two of the forms in which a poet may embody his teaching: there remains the reverse of the medal, satire, in which he sets out to teach us what is good by painting evil in its true colors. To this form of writing, in which he had already shown himself a master, Pope devoted the best of his remaining energies.

One has only to remember Aristophanes, Miguel de Cervantes, Swift, and Jane Austen to acknowledge that the satiric impulse has been the inspiration of much of the world's greatest literature. Yet it remains true, perhaps because we are still in some respects the heirs of the romantics, that critics are apt to let intrusive biographical and ethical considerations confuse them in their attempt at assessing satiric writings. In its most naive form the objection to satire seems to be an objection to grumbling, and the only answer to it is that man has a great deal to grumble about. Before the Fall there was no satire, because there was no need of it; anyone who still feels that there is nothing to cry out against in life will find satire little to his taste. Satire is born of the impulse to protest: it is protest become art. If Voltaire and Swift had never lost their tempers, the world would be an immeasurably poorer place.

While the work of every satirist is liable to be misunderstood by those who dislike satire, even among satirists Pope has been particularly unfortunate. That critics during his lifetime should too often have discussed his character instead of his poetry is at least understandable; that this tendency should have continued for almost two centuries after his death is striking evidence of the difficulty, in literary criticism, of keeping to the point. The common reader of the late nineteenth century was too often content to read the hysterical condemnation of Pope's character in Thomas Macaulay's mendacious essay on Addison, and to reflect that only a very limited satisfaction could be derived from the work of a man as deformed in mind and body as Alexander Pope.

In the last thirty years various factors—including, no doubt, the increased sympathy for the

---

[2]"A modified deism in which there persisted some of the very psychological data which the deists wished to proscribe: an effort of the will rather than a rational demonstration; and an acceptance of mystery."

unfortunate that psychology has brought with it, as well as a growing body of accurate information about his life and times—have combined to lead critics toward a more favorable estimate of Pope's personality. Edith Sitwell's enthusiastic biography was followed by George Sherburn's scholarly account of Pope's early life, and the researches of a number of scholars have now obscured the bogeyman of the Victorians, putting in his place a human being who is often attractive and always comprehensible. Pope had a great deal to contend with. As a Roman Catholic, he was debarred from the principal careers, as well as being liable to double taxation and other species of legal persecution; while his poor health and wretched physique—he was only four feet six inches tall and suffered from severe curvature of the spine, apparently due to a tubercular infection—made of his whole life one long disease. It is hardly surprising that he was touchy and liable to fits of moroseness and to unfounded suspicions. What is astonishing is that he was able to rise above his disabilities, to support his parents and himself by being a pioneer in the independent profession of a man of letters, and to behave (on occasion) with great forbearance and generosity, as well as becoming the greatest poet of his century.

The ultimate justification of Pope's satire lies in the sincerity of his purpose and the soundness of his code of values. He is a moral satirist in a sense in which Dryden is not. (Of Dryden's three main satires, two are essentially political pamphlets, while the third is an attack on a personal enemy.) But this central fact about Pope's satire has frequently been obscured by two things: his habit of centering much of his satire in attacks on individuals, often individuals who had given him personal offense (a method traditional to satirists, and wholly justifiable); and the fact that his longest satire, *The Dunciad*, is less securely based on moral premises than most of his work. In its original form, as a poem in three books, *The Dunciad* is essentially a satire on bad writing. Pope would have agreed with the later critic who said that "the number of books has increased—is increasing—and ought to be diminished." The poem is many times the length of its model, *MacFlecknoe*, and all the brilliance of individual passages cannot prevent the feeling that it is too long. No doubt it was because he felt this that Pope's friend William Warburton suggested he should widen the scope of the poem. The result was a new book, *The New Dunciad*, written more than a decade later, in which the satire is of the widest possible sort—moral and political as well as literary. From the opening lines:

> Yet, yet a moment, one dim Ray of Light
> Indulge, dread Chaos, and eternal Night!
> Of darkness visible so much be lent,
> As half to shew, half veil the deep Intent

to the sublime conclusion:

> Lo! thy dread Empire, CHAOS! is restor'd;
> Light dies before thy uncreating word;
> Thy hand, great Anarch! lets the curtain fall;
> And Universal Darkness buries All

this continuation far transcends the first three books, and it is not surprising that Pope himself considered it his masterpiece. Unfortunately, however, he was not content to leave *The New Dunciad* to stand by itself, but made an attempt to weld the four books into one poem. He substituted Colley Cibber for Lewis Theobald as his hero, introduced strokes of moral and political satire into the first three books, and endeavored to give Dullness a much wider connotation than it had had before, until (as Warburton explained) it did not stand for "mere Stupidity" but for "all Slowness of Apprehension, Shortness of Sight, or imperfect Sense of things." But a much more comprehensive revision would have been necessary to make a perfect unity of the four books (if indeed the feat was possible), and *The Dunciad* as it now stands is flawed by this uncertain direction.

It is fortunate for us that Pope completed the original *Dunciad* in 1728 and laid it aside, for it was in the years immediately following this that he wrote most of the poems that, with *The Rape of the Lock* and *The New Dunciad*, constitute the summit of his achievement. In these he left mock heroic poetry for satire in the Latin sense of the word. Instead of embodying his criticism of life in narrative form, he turned to the form of *satura* used by Horace and Juvenal, and in modern times by Boileau and Edward Young. In this he was doing something that Dryden had never done, although (characteristically) he is hardly less clearly Dryden's pupil in these poems than elsewhere. Perhaps because it was too personal a form for him, Dryden never made use of the classical form of satire on his own account, although he translated part of Juvenal and the whole of Persius.

Everything about this epistolary form of satire suited Pope. There was no need to find a plot: the poem could be long or short: the poet was free to move from one subject to another, as in conversation, so long as an underlying continuity was preserved: swift changes of tone and temper were expected: while the accommodating freedom of the form made it possible for him to find a home in these discursive poems for the detached passages that he was forever writing. In particular this sort of poem provided a perfect setting for the satiric "character." The creation of these was an art that Pope learned from Dryden, and if anyone has excelled the creator of Achitophel and Zimri it is he. He is extraordinarily skillful in adapting the scope and tone of his "character" to the nature and vulnerability of the person attacked. It is instructive, for example, to compare the direct loathing of the assault on Lord Hervey,

> This painted Child of Dirt that stinks and stings,
> *(An Epistle to Dr. Arbuthnot,* 310)

with the covert malice of the lines on Addison in the same poem. Remembering, perhaps, the touch of genius with which Dryden had rendered his attack on the earl of Shaftesbury yet more lethal by inserting a passage praising his integrity as a judge, and so giving the illusion of impartiality, Pope moves to the attack with a well-turned compliment to a man,

> Blest with each Talent and each Art to please,
> And born to write, converse, and live with ease,
> (195-196)

before he brings the charge that Addison will

> Damn with faint praise, assent with civil leer,
> And without sneering, teach the rest to sneer;
> Willing to wound, and yet afraid to strike,
> Just hint a fault, and hesitate dislike.
> (201-204)

From the narrow prison of such interlocking antitheses a man's reputation can hardly escape. It should be noted that when Pope revised these "characters" he often eliminated the merely particular in favor of the universal: Addison becomes Atticus, and what began as an attack on a personal enemy is transformed into an eternal type of the petty jealousy of a man of letters. When Pope satirizes an individual it is as if he set fire to an effigy: the effigy crackles, blazes, and is burned up; but in the process it ignites a wider conflagration, and in the flames we see, brightly illumined, the hateful figure of Folly or Vice itself. Personal hatred often provides Pope's impetus, but it is the sanity of the position from which the attack is launched that gives his satire its penetration and permanence. We will not do justice to his fierce sincerity unless we understand that his feeling for order, "Nature," the sane norm of the good life, was as passionate and as personal as John Keats's love of Beauty or Wordsworth's love of a Nature very differently defined.

Satire in the modern sense of the word was not the only ingredient of the Latin *satura*, nor is it of Pope's satiric epistles. There are also eloquent passages in praise of his friends, such as the lines on John Gay:

> Blest be the *Great!* for those they take away,
> And those they left me—For they left me GAY,
> Left me to see neglected Genius bloom,
> Neglected die! and tell it on his Tomb;
> Of all thy blameless Life the sole Return
> My Verse, and QUEENSB'RY weeping o'er thy Urn!
> *(Arbuthnot,* 255-260)

and the moving description of his father:

> Unlearn'd, he knew no Schoolman's subtle Art,
> No Language, but the Language of the Heart.
> *(Arbuthnot,* 398-399)

Literary criticism is ubiquitous, as is an element of autobiography and self-justification:

> Ask you what Provocation I have had?
> The strong Antipathy of Good to Bad.
> When Truth or Virtue an Affront endures,
> Th' Affront is mine, my Friend, and should be yours.
> Mine, as a Foe profess'd to false Pretence,
> Who think a Coxcomb's Honour like his Sense;
> Mine, as a Friend to ev'ry worthy Mind;
> And mine as Man, who feels for all mankind.
> *(Epilogue to the Satires,* dial. II, 197-204)

Whether one turns to the *Moral Essays,* which bear a close relation to the *Essay on Man* and are constructed comparatively systematically, or to the more loosely organized *Imitations of Horace,* one finds Pope in these epistolary poems writing at the top of his bent. Never did he handle words more surely, or with more extraordinary economy. Words are like people: you can get them to do almost anything, if only you understand them well enough. You get your way with them not by bullying but by studying their natures. This Pope did, and made words his slaves. He could take two sets of familiar substantives and arrange them in a couplet that says all about pedants that there is to say:

> Pains, reading, study, are their just pretence,
> And all they want is spirit, taste, and sense.
> (*Arbuthnot*, 159-160)

With five of the commonest words in the language he could conclude the most terrible of all epitaphs:

> See how the World its Veterans rewards!
> A Youth of frolicks, an old Age of Cards,
> Fair to no purpose, artful to no end,
> Young without Lovers, old without a Friend,
> A Fop their Passion, but their Prize a Sot,
> Alive, ridiculous, and dead, forgot!
> (*Moral Essays*, II, 243-248)

In considering Pope's poetry as a whole, one is struck by the fact that a remarkably high proportion of it is written in one meter—the heroic couplet. This was not a premeditated self-denial on his part, and he did not consider this meter the only satisfactory one for English verse. His epic was to be written in blank verse, he wrote a number of poems in stanzas of various sorts, while the squibs and occasional poems that he was forever throwing off were most often in ballad meter or tetrameters. Yet it remains true that no English poet of comparable stature is to the same degree a poet of one meter. Why is this?

To answer the question one must remember the revolution in English poetry that followed the Restoration. It is the function of poetic idiom to enable poets to express their own sensibility and that of their age with the greatest possible accuracy. As sensibility changes from one age to another, it follows that the need arises, from time to time, for a revolution in the idiom of poetry. When this takes place one usually finds that each of the main constituents of the new idiom—diction, imagery, syntax perhaps, rhythm and meter almost always—has undergone some alteration; but in any particular revolution the change in one of these constituents is often found to be of primary importance, to be in a sense the root from which the other changes are derived. In the Wordsworthian revolution a change in diction was the heart of the process; in the Augustan revolution it was the discovery of a new rhythm that was vital. The discovery of the rhythmical possibilities of the heroic couplet had an effect as electrical as the discovery of "sprung rhythm" by Gerard Manley Hopkins when his poems were published in 1918. When Pope began to write, the heroic couplet (as developed by Dryden) was still a recent discovery, and he was intoxicated by it.

One of the attractions of the new meter for Pope was its almost endless adaptability. When he aspired to rhythmical or syntactical effects that could better be achieved in some other measure, he was prepared to use another measure; but he found that he had so mastered the heroic couplet that he could compass in it an extraordinary variety of effect. Compare the description of the foolish man-about-town in *The Rape of the Lock*:

> With earnest Eyes, and round unthinking Face,
> He first the Snuff-box open'd, then the Case,
> And thus broke out—"My Lord, why, what the devil?
> Z—ds! Damn the Lock! 'fore Gad, you must be civil!
> Plague on't! 'tis past a Jest—nay prithee, Pox!
> Give her the Hair".—he spoke, and rapp'd his Box.
> (IV. 125-130)

with the translucent beauty of the lines that describe the sylphs:

> Soft o'er the Shrouds Aerial Whispers breathe,
> That seem'd but *Zephyrs* to the Train beneath,
> Some to the Sun their Insect-Wings unfold,
> Waft on the Breeze, or sink in Clouds of Gold.
> Transparent Forms, too fine for mortal Sight,
> Their fluid Bodies half dissolv'd in Light.
> Loose to the Wind their airy Garments flew,
> Thin glitt'ring Textures of the filmy Dew.
> (II. 57-64)

Compare the romantic melancholy of this passage from "Eloisa to Abelard":

> But o'er the twilight groves and dusky caves,
> Long-sounding aisles, and intermingled graves,
> Black Melancholy sits, and round her throws
> A death-like silence, and a dread repose:

> Her gloomy presence saddens all the scene,
> Shades ev'ry flower, and darkens ev'ry green,
> Deepens the murmur of the falling floods,
> And breathes a browner horror on the woods
> (163–170)

with the precise satiric observation of the Epistle to Miss Blount, "On Her Leaving Town after the Coronation":

> To part her time 'twixt reading and bohea,
> To muse, and spill her solitary tea,
> Or o'er cold coffee trifle with the spoon,
> Count the slow clock, and dine exact at noon.
> (15–18)

If one sets these passages beside the quotations already given from *The New Dunciad* and the *Epistle to Dr. Arbuthnot*, the absurdity of the notion that all poems in heroic couplets are monotonously similar becomes very evident. All that is necessary is to read Pope's verse aloud, taking care to find the correct tempo for each passage.

Great as is the variety of Pope's work in tone and style, there is one quality that may be found almost everywhere, and that is a remarkable conciseness. Another master of condensed expression, Swift, paid Pope the compliment of saying that he could

> . . . in one couplet fix
> As much sense as I can in six.

A Mr. Dobson who won a brief fame by translating Matthew Prior's *Solomon* into Latin verse was asked by Pope himself or by Lord Oxford to do the same for the *Essay on Man*, but he abandoned his attempt "on account of the impossibility of imitating its brevity in another language"—a remarkable testimony, in view of the habitual brevity of Latin. It is clear that this conciseness was the result of deliberate effort on Pope's part, and that he took pride in it. In the design prefixed to the *Essay on Man* he says that he chose to write this poem in verse instead of prose partly because "I found I could express them [his principles] more *shortly* this way than in prose." Reading his letters and other prose writings, we often come on confirmation of this claim; for we find numerous reflections and images that were later incorporated in a poem, and comparison of the prose and the verse always reveals the superior brevity of the latter—a brevity that is often accompanied by an increase in point and wit. This conciseness provides a reason why Pope's poetry should usually be read slowly, and read more than once; only so will the full meaning (in his favorite phrase) "open" itself to the reader's mind.

And what of the end to which all this skill in words and rhythms was employed? If Pope was a serious poet as well as a poet of extraordinary technical accomplishment, what was his "message"? Of course a great writer does not offer us a message that can be detached from his work; the greater he is, perhaps, the less does he do so. It is for us to read what he has written, and so to see life as he sees it. But two generalizations may be made about Pope's vision of life. The first is that it is less personal and private than that (for example) of Wordsworth. Just as it would not have occurred to him to write a poem of epic length and seriousness about the development of his own mind, as Wordsworth did in *The Prelude*, so it would have seemed to him ridiculous to offer his readers a reading of life as idiosyncratic as that of the "Immortality Ode." The values on which his work is based, and that he regarded it as his poetic duty to promulgate, are values that have a longer history than those of Wordsworth: they would have been understood and accepted, in general terms, by Socrates, by Cicero, and by Jean Racine, as well as by civilized people in his own day and in ours. Secondly, the fallacy that Pope was a shallow optimist should be allowed to go into honorable retirement. Even in the *Essay on Man* he is an optimist only in a specialized and technical sense that makes the word highly misleading, while the greatest passage of the poem is a somber "diminishing" of man's estate reminiscent rather of a medieval *contemptus mundi* than of the thought of the more shallow among the thinkers of the Enlightenment. Hazlitt was right when on reading *The Rape of the Lock* he did not know whether to laugh or to cry. Pope often reminds one of Mozart: there is in his work the same depth of emotion, perfectly restrained by the strict patterning of art

> . . . since Life can little more supply
> Than just to look about us and to die.

Charles Augustin Sainte-Beuve said of Molière, "Il a au coeur la tristesse": the same words might form the epitaph of Pope.

# ALEXANDER POPE

SELECTED BIBLIOGRAPHY

I. BIBLIOGRAPHY. Detailed bibliographical information can also be found in the *New Cambridge Bibliography of English Literature*, vol. II. R. H. Griffith, *Alexander Pope: A Bibliography* (Austin, Tex., 1922; repr. London, 1962), vol. I, part i, *Pope's Own Writings, 1709-1734*; vol. I, part ii, *Pope's Own Writings, 1735-1751*; vol. II, intended to be "a record of books about Pope," has not appeared; additional bibliographical information may be found in the standard modern eds. of Pope's writings, notably in the Twickenham ed.; E. A. Abbott, *A Concordance to the Works of Alexander Pope* (London, 1875; facs. repr. New York, 1965).

II. COLLECTED EDITIONS. W. Warburton, ed., *The Works of Alexander Pope . . . with His Last Corrections*, 9 vols. (London, 1751); J. Warton, ed., *The Works of Alexander Pope with Notes and Illustrations*, 9 vols. (London, 1797); W. Elwin and W. J. Courthope, eds., *The Works of Alexander Pope, Including Several Hundred Unpublished Letters and Other New Materials*, 10 vols. (London, 1871-1889); J. Butt, gen. ed., *The Twickenham Edition of the Poems of Alexander Pope* (London, 1939-1969), an admirable ed. that is unlikely to be superseded for a long time; a less elaborate ed., based on the text of the Twickenham ed. and also edited by J. Butt, appeared in 1963 (paperback ed., 1965); vol. IV: J. Butt, ed., *Imitations of Horace, with an Epistle to Dr. Arbuthnot and the Epilogue to the Satires* (1939; 2nd ed., 1953), also includes the two adaptations from Donne and *One Thousand Seven Hundred and Thirty Eight*; vol. II: G. Tillotson, ed., *The Rape of the Lock and Other Poems* (1940; 2nd ed., 1954; 3rd ed., 1962), includes both texts of *The Rape of the Lock*, as well as translations, *The Temple of Fame*, "Eloisa to Abelard," and "An Elegy to the Memory of an Unfortunate Lady"; vol. V: J. Sutherland, ed., *The Dunciad* (1943; rev. ed., 1953), gives the texts of *The Dunciad Variorum* and *The Dunciad in Four Books*; vol. III, pt. i: M. Mack, ed., *An Essay on Man* (1950); vol. III, pt. ii: F. W. Bateson, ed., *Epistles to Several Persons (Moral Essays)* (1951; 2nd ed., with new material, 1961); vol. VI: N. Ault, ed., *Minor Poems* (1954), completed by J. Butt; vol. I: E. Audra and A. L. Williams, eds., *Pastoral Poetry and the Essay on Criticism* (1961), also includes "The Messiah," *Windsor Forest*, and Pope's translations from Ovid and Statius; vols. VII-X: M. Mack. et al., eds., *Homer's Iliad and Odyssey* (1967); vol. XI: M. Mack, ed., *Index* (1969); H. Davis, ed., *Pope: Poetical Works* (London, 1966), an admirable ed. in the Oxford Standard Authors series, includes everything except the Homer translations; with a new intro. by P. Rogers (paperback ed., 1978).

III. SELECTED WORKS. G. Sherburn, ed., *Selections . . .* (New York, 1929), reissued as *The Best of Pope* (1931); H. V. D. Dyson, ed., *Poetry and Prose* (Oxford, 1933), brief selections; W. K. Wimsatt, ed., *Alexander Pope: Selected Poetry and Prose* (New York, 1951); R. P. C. Mutter and M. Kinkead-Weekes, *Selected Poems and Letters of Alexander Pope* (London, 1962), a well-annotated volume that makes an excellent intro. to Pope.

IV. PROSE AND LETTERS. Various writings in prose, including prefaces to Shakespeare and Homer as well as numerous letters, appeared during Pope's lifetime. They are listed in the *New Cambridge Bibliography*; only a selection is listed here. N. Ault, ed., *Prose Works* (London, 1936), vol. I of an uncompleted collected ed., covering the years 1711-1720; C. Kerby-Miller, ed., *Memoirs of . . . Martinus Scriblerus*, written by Dr. Arbuthnot, Pope, Swift, Gay, Parnell, and Robert Harley (earl of Oxford) (New Haven, 1950); E. L. Steeves, ed., *The Art of Sinking in Poetry: Martinus Scriblerus' ΠΕΡΙ ΒΑΘΟΤΣ* (New York, 1952); G. Sherburn, ed., *The Correspondence of Alexander Pope*, 5 vols. (London, 1956), an admirable ed. that throws a good deal of new light on Pope's career; J. Butt, ed., *Letters of Alexander Pope* (London, 1960).

V. PRINCIPAL POEMS AND TRANSLATIONS. A much fuller and more detailed list may be found in Griffith and in the *New Cambridge Bibliography*. *Poetical Miscellanies, the Sixth Part* (London, 1709), vol. VI of Dryden's collection, *Miscellany Poems*, published by Tonson, which contains pastorals and other poems by Pope; *An Essay on Criticism* (London, 1711); *The Rape of the Lock and Other Poems*, in Lintott's *Miscellaneous Poems and Translations* (London, 1712), two cantos, 334 lines; see 1714 below; *Windsor Forest* (London, 1713); *The Rape of the Lock, in Five Cantos* (London, 1714), 794 lines. The sylphs, and much else, have now been added; this is the text usually reprinted; *The Temple of Fame: a Vision* (London, 1715); *The Works of Mr. Alexander Pope* (London, 1717-1735), contains "Verses to the Memory of an Unfortunate Lady," "Eloisa to Abelard," and other poems; *The Iliad of Homer*, vols. I-VI (London, 1715-1720); *The Odyssey of Homer*, vols. I-V (London, 1725-1726), books II, VI, VIII, XI, XII, XVI, XVIII, and XXIII were in fact by William Broome, and books I, IV, XIX, and XXII by Elijah Fenton; most reprints of these translations omit the footnotes and other interesting material; *The Dunciad* (London, 1728), in three books, with Theobald as hero, see 1729, 1742, and 1743; *The Dunciad Variorum* (London, 1729), an expanded text, with elaborate satirical prolegomena, footnotes, and other "scholarly" apparatus; *An Epistle to the . . . Earl of Burlington* (London, 1731), often called *Moral Essays, IV*; *Of the Use of Riches, an Epistle to . . . Bathurst* (London, 1732), often called *Moral Essays, III*; *The First Satire of the Second Book of Horace, Imitated* (London, 1733), other *Imitations of Horace* appeared between 1734 and 1738, but not separately listed here; *An Essay on Man* (London, 1733-1734), Epistles I-III appeared separately in

1733, Epistle IV appeared in 1734, followed by a collection of the four in the same year; *An Epistle to Cobham* (London, 1733), often called *Moral Essays, I*; *An Epistle . . . to Dr. Arbuthnot* (London, 1735), later called *Prologue to the Satires*; *Of the Characters of Women: An Epistle to a Lady* (London, 1735), often called *Moral Essays, II*; *Epilogue to the Satires, in Two Dialogues* (London, 1738), published separately in the same year, the first under the title *One Thousand Seven Hundred and Thirty Eight*; *The New Dunciad* (London, 1742); *The Dunciad in Four Books* (London, 1743).

VI. BIOGRAPHY. Throughout his life Pope was involved in controversy. The resultant "Popiana" have often little relevance to his poetry, and they are not listed here. J. V. Guerinot's *Pamphlet Attacks on Alexander Pope, 1711-1744: A Descriptive Bibliography* (London, 1969) gives an admirable account of them. W. Ayre, *Memoirs of the Life and Writings of Alexander Pope, Esq.*, 2 vols. (London, 1745); O. Ruffhead, *The Life of Alexander Pope* (London, 1769; repr. Hildesheim, 1968), the value of these and other early biographies is discussed by Sherburn in the preface to his *Early Career of Alexander Pope* (London, 1934); S. Johnson, *Prefaces, Biographical and Critical, to the Works of the English Poets*, 10 vols. (London, 1779-1781), often reprinted as *Lives of the English Poets*; the best ed. is that of G. Birkbeck Hill, 3 vols. (London, 1905), vol. III: 'The Life of Pope"; the biographical part of the Life is sometimes inaccurate and inevitably out of date; but the assessment of Pope's character is shrewd and refreshingly free from the tendency to confuse a man's personality with his merit as a poet; the critical part is of the greatest interest to anyone who reads Pope's poetry; S. W. Singer, ed., *Anecdotes, Observations, and Characters of Books and Men Collected from the Conversation of Mr. Pope and Other Eminent Persons of His Time by the Rev. Joseph Spence* (London, 1820), indispensable; an admirable ed. in 2 vols. by J. M. Osborn, with full annotation, was published in 1966; C. W. Dilke, *The Papers of a Critic*, 2 vols. (London, 1875), most of vol. I consists of a series of scholarly investigations of Pope's writings; L. Stephen, *Alexander Pope* (London, 1880), in the English Men of Letters series; W. J. Courthope, *The Life of Alexander Pope* (London, 1889), in vol. V of the Elwin-Courthope ed.

E. Sitwell, *Alexander Pope* (London, 1930), unusual in its day for its sympathetic approach; G. Sherburn, *The Early Career of Alexander Pope* (Oxford, 1934), the standard biography "to about 1726 or 1727"; N. Ault, *New Light on Pope with Some Additions to His Poetry Hitherto Unknown* (London, 1949), a series of studies of Pope's life and the canon of his poems; some of the attributions are very uncertain; the chapter on Pope as a painter throws interesting light on the poems; W. K. Wimsatt, *The Portraits of Alexander Pope* (New Haven-London, 1965), a beautifully produced book that throws a great deal of light on Pope and his background; J. V. Guerinot, *Pamphlet Attacks on Alexander Pope 1711-1744: A Descriptive Bibliography* (London-New York, 1969).

VII. CRITICISM. J. Spence, *An Essay on Pope's Odyssey*, 2 parts (London, 1726; repr. Hildesheim, 1968), in the "Anglistica and Americana" series; J. Warton, *An Essay on the Writings and Genius of Pope*, vol. I (London, 1756), vol. II (London, 1782), this digressive study, in which each of Pope's principal poems is considered in turn, is still illuminating. Warton is often called a "pre-romantic," and his admiration of Pope was less wholehearted than Johnson's, but the extent of his reservations is often exaggerated; S. Johnson, *Prefaces . . . to . . . the English Poets* (London, 1779-1781), see "Biography" above; P. Stockdale, *An Inquiry into the Nature and Genuine Laws of Poetry, Including a Particular Defence of the Writings and Genius of Mr. Pope* (London, 1778); W. C. Hazlitt, *Lectures on the English Poets* (London, 1818); D. Masson, ed., *The Collected Writings of Thomas De Quincey* (London, 1889-1890), vols. IV and XI contain interesting criticism of Pope; much of this is reprinted in H. Darbishire, ed., *De Quincey's Literary Criticism* (London, 1900); L. Stephen, *Hours in a Library*, vol. I (London, 1874), contains the essay "Pope as a Moralist"; L. Stephen, *History of English Thought in the Eighteenth Century*, 2 vols. (London, 1876), a pioneering study that is still of great interest, see particularly vol. II, pp. 348-365; A. Beljame, *Le Public et les hommes de lettres en Angleterre au dix-huitième siècle, 1660-1744: Dryden, Addison, Pope* (Paris, 1881), translated by E. O. Lorimer as *Men of Letters and the English Public in the Eighteenth Century, 1660-1744: Dryden, Addison, Pope* (London, 1948), edited with an intro. and notes by B. Dobrée; L. Stephen, *English Literature and Society in the Eighteenth Century* (London, 1904), the Ford lectures, 1903; L. Strachey, *Pope* (Cambridge, 1925), the Leslie Stephen lecture, 1925, repr. in *Characters and Commentaries* (London, 1933), in *Literary Essays* (London, 1948), and in A. S. Cairncross, ed., *Modern Essays in Criticism* (London, 1938); an entertaining and stimulating lecture based on an imperfect understanding of Pope's character; A. Warren, *Alexander Pope as Critic and Humanist*, Princeton Studies in English, no. 1 (Princeton, N. J., 1929), a pioneering study, now inevitably out of date; E. Audra, *L'Influence française dans l'oeuvre de Pope* (Paris, 1931); F. R. Leavis, *Revaluation: Tradition and Development in English Poetry* (London, 1936), still of interest; A. O. Lovejoy, *The Great Chain of Being: A Study of the History of an Idea* (Cambridge, Mass., 1936), see particularly chap. 6; G. Tillotson, *On the Poetry of Pope* (Oxford, 1938), an enthusiastic and stimulating introduction; R. K. Root, *The Poetical Career of Alexander Pope* (Princeton, N. J., 1938); G. Wilson Knight, *The Burning Oracle: Studies in the Poetry of Action* (London, 1939), unusual and often suggestive, see chap. 5; H. Sykes Davies, *The Poets and Their Critics: Chaucer to Collins* (London, 1943; rev. ed., 1960), brief passages of criticism on Pope's poetry by critics from Pope's own time onward; *Essays on the Eighteenth Century Presented to David Nichol Smith* (Oxford, 1945), see particularly G. Sherburn's "Pope at Work"; C. Brooks, *The Well Wrought Urn; Studies in the Structure of Poetry* (New York, 1947), chap. 5 is an interesting study of *The Rape of the Lock*; J. Sutherland, *A Preface to Eighteenth Century Poetry* (Oxford, 1948), an excellent introduction to the period of Pope and that which followed it; J. L. Clifford and L. A. Landa, *Pope and His Contemporaries: Essays Presented to George Sherburn* (Oxford, 1949), see particularly M. Mack's "Wit and Poetry and Pope: Some Observations on His Imagery"; J. Butt, *The Augustan Age* (London, 1950), contains admirable brief introductions to Dryden, Addison, Swift, Pope, Johnson, and others; D. M. Knight, *Pope and the Heroic Tradition: A Critical Study of the Iliad* (New Haven, Conn., 1951); I. Jack, *Augustan Satire: Intention and Idiom in English Poetry, 1660-1750* (Oxford, 1952), chaps. 5-7 deal with Pope; R. W. Rogers, *The Major Satires of Alexander Pope*, Illinois Studies in Language and Literature: vol. XL (Urbana, Ill., 1955), makes some use of MS material; A. L. Williams, *Pope's "Dunciad": A Study of Its Meaning* (London, 1955); G. Tillotson, *Pope and Human Nature* (Oxford, 1958), deals with "the material Pope expresses" rather than with his manner of expressing it, the subject of Tillotson's earlier study; J. H. Hagstrum, *The Sister Arts: The Tradition of Literary Pictorialism and English Poetry from Dryden to Gray* (Chicago, 1958), a general study of great interest; R. Sühnel, *Homer und Die Englische Humanität: Chapmans und Popes Ubersetzungkunst im Rahmen der humanistischen Tradition* (Tübingen, 1958); R. A. Brower, *Alexander Pope: The Poetry of Allusion* (Oxford, 1959), illustrates the fact that an awareness of the allusions throughout Pope's poetry enriches our experience as we read it; J. L. Clifford, ed., *Eighteenth-Century English Literature: Modern Essays in Criticism* (New York, 1959), reprints three important articles in convenient form: M. Mack, "Wit and Poetry and Pope," E. Niles Hooker, "Pope on Wit: the Essays on Criticism," and J. Butt, "Pope Seen Through His Letters"; B. Dobrée, *English Literature in the Early Eighteenth Century, 1700-1740*, vol. VII: *Oxford History of English Literature* (Oxford, 1959), two long chaps. contain a full account of Pope's poetry; U. Amarasinghe, *Dryden and Pope in the Early Nineteenth Century* (Cambridge, 1962), the reputation of these two poets in the romantic period; T. R. Edwards, *This Dark Estate: A Reading of Pope* (Berkeley-Los Angeles, 1963); M. Mack, ed., *Essential Articles for the Study of Alexander Pope* (London, 1964), essential for the advanced student; M. Price, *To the Palace of Wisdom: Studies in Order and Energy from Dryden to Blake* (New York, 1964); R. Trickett, *The Honest Muse: A Study in Augustan Verse* (Oxford, 1967), an interesting account of "the underlying ethos of Augustan poetry" that has a long chapter on Pope; E. Jones, "Pope and Dulness," *Proceedings of the British Academy*, vol. LIV (1968), the Chatterton lecture delivered 13 November 1968, reprinted as an offprint (1970); P. Dixon, *The World of Pope's Satires* (London, 1968); M. H. Nicolson and G. S. Rousseau *"This Long Disease, My Life": Alexander Pope and the Sciences* (Princeton, N. J., 1968); G. S. Rousseau, ed., *Twentieth Century Interpretations of "The Rape of the Lock": A Collection of Critical Essays* (Englewood Cliffs, N. J., 1969); J. A. Jones, *Pope's Couplet Art* (Athens, Ohio, 1969); M. Mack, *The Garden and the City: Retirement and Politics in the Later Poetry of Pope, 1731-1743* (Toronto-London, 1969), the most important and interesting of recent books on Pope; D. H. White, *Pope and the Context of Controversy: The Manipulation of Ideas in "An Essay on Man"* (London, 1971); J. Barnard, ed., *Pope: The Critical Heritage* (London, 1973); P. Rogers, *An Introduction to Pope* (London, 1975); H. Erskine-Hill, *The Social Milieu of Alexander Pope* (New Haven, Conn., 1975); M. Leranbaum, *Alexander Pope's "Opus Magnum," 1729-1744* (London, 1977); M. R. Brownell, *Alexander Pope and the Arts of Georgian England* (London, 1978).

# WILLIAM SHAKESPEARE
(1564-1616)

## Stanley Wells

WILLIAM SHAKESPEARE was baptized in the great church of Holy Trinity, Stratford-upon-Avon, on 26 April 1564. Probably he was born no more than two or three days previously; 23 April, St. George's Day, traditionally celebrated as the date of his birth, is as likely to be correct as any. At the time, his father was an up-and-coming young man who took a prominent part in administering the town's affairs. He had married Mary Arden, who came from a family of higher social standing, about 1552, the year in which he was fined 12d. for failing to remove a dunghill from outside his house. For years after this, as his children were born and as some of them grew up, his position among his fellow townsmen improved. He was a member of the glovers' guild, and also dealt in wool and probably other commodities. In 1556 he was appointed an ale taster, with responsibility for the price and quality of the bread and ale offered to the town's two thousand or so inhabitants. He moved upward in the hierarchy: as constable (1558), principal burgess (about 1559), chamberlain (1561), alderman (1565), and, in 1568, bailiff, or mayor, and justice of the peace.

At this high point in his career he was the father of two sons, William and Gilbert (1566–1612). Two daughters, Joan and Margaret, had died in infancy. Another Joan was born in 1569; a Richard born in 1574 lived, apparently in Stratford and as a bachelor, until 1613. A late child, Edmund, came in 1580; he became an actor in London and died early, aged twenty-seven.

When young William was four years old, he could have had the excitement of seeing his father, dressed in furred scarlet robes and wearing the aldermanic thumb ring, regularly attended by two mace-bearing sergeants in buff, presiding at fairs and markets. Perhaps a little later, he would have begun to attend a "petty school" to acquire the rudiments of an education that would be furthered at the King's New School. We have no lists of the pupils at this time, but his father's position would have qualified him to attend, and the education offered was such as lies behind the plays and poems. The school had a well-qualified master, with the relatively good salary of £20 a year, from which he had to spare £4 to pay an usher, or assistant, to teach the younger boys. At the age of about eight Shakespeare would have begun a regime that might well have sent him "unwillingly" on the quarter-of-a-mile walk from his father's Henley Street house to the schoolroom above the Guildhall and next to the Guild Chapel. Classes began in the early morning, and hours were long. The basic medium of instruction was Latin. A charming scene in *The Merry Wives of Windsor* (IV.i), hardly required by the plot, shows a schoolmaster instructing young boys in their grammar, and must be an amused recollection of the dramatist's own schooldays. From grammar the pupils progressed to rhetoric and logic, and to works of classical literature. They might read Aesop's *Fables* and the fairly easy plays of Terence and Plautus, on one of which Shakespeare was to base an early comedy. They might even act scenes from them. They would go on to Caesar, Cicero, Virgil, Horace, and Ovid, who was clearly a favorite with Shakespeare in both the original and Arthur Golding's translation published in 1567.

But there was a life beyond school. Shakespeare lived in a beautiful and fertile part of the country; the river and fields were at hand; he could enjoy country pursuits. He had younger brothers and sisters to play with. Each Sunday the family would go to church, where his father as bailiff and, later, deputy bailiff, sat in the front pew as his rank required. There he would hear the sonorous phrases of the Bible, in either the Bishops' or the Geneva version, the Homilies, and the Book of Common Prayer, all of which made a lasting impression on him, as well as lengthy sermons that may have been less memorable. Sometimes groups of traveling players came to Stratford. Shakespeare's father would have the duty of licensing them to perform, and probably the boy saw his first plays in the Guildhall immediately below his schoolroom.

As he grew into adolescence, his father's fortunes waned. John Shakespeare fell into debt, and after 1576 stopped attending council meetings. His fellows treated him leniently, but in 1586 felt obliged to replace him as alderman. In 1592 he was listed among those persistently failing to go to church, perhaps for fear of arrest for debt.

But by this time William was in London, already displaying the genius that would enable him to recoup the family fortune. How he kept himself after leaving school we do not know. In 1582, at the age of eighteen, he married Anne Hathaway of Shottery, a mile or so from his home. The marriage was hasty, the bride, eight years older than her husband, pregnant. The clerk of the Worcester court, to which application for a special license was made on 27 November, wrote her name, mistakenly, it seems, as Anne Whateley of Temple Grafton. A daughter, Susanna, was baptized in Holy Trinity on 26 May 1583, and twins, Hamnet and Judith, on 2 February 1585.

The seven years that follow are a blank in our knowledge. Shakespeare may, as Aubrey reported a century later, have become a "schoolmaster in the country." He may have followed one or more of the innumerable other avocations—lawyer, soldier, sailor, actor, printer—that have been foisted upon him. He may have traveled overseas. All we know is that at some point he left Stratford, joined a theatrical company, went to London, and began to write—not necessarily in that order. The first certain printed allusion to him shows that, as actor turned playwright, he had aroused the envy of the dying Robert Greene who, in 1592, wrote scornfully of an "upstart crow" who thought himself "the only Shakescene in a country."

Parodying a line from *3 Henry VI*, Greene conveniently helps to establish a date by which that play was written. His malice provoked a defense of Shakespeare by a minor playwright, Henry Chettle, who wrote of him as one whose "demeanor" was "no less civil than he excellent in the quality he professes. Besides, divers of worship have reported his uprightness of dealing, which argues his honesty, and his facetious grace in writing, which approves his art." Evidently he was well established in London by this time. But apparently he lived always in lodgings there, setting up no household. He seems to have felt that his roots were in Stratford. His family stayed there. How often he visited them we cannot tell. He had no more children. Perhaps he was gradually able to help his father who, in 1596, applied successfully for a grant of arms, and so became a gentleman. In August of the same year, William's son, Hamnet, died. In October, William was lodging in Bishopsgate, London, but in the next year he showed that he looked on Stratford as his permanent home by buying a large house, New Place, next to the Guild Chapel and the grammar school.

Over the following years, his growing worldly success can be followed in both Stratford and London records. In 1598 a minor writer, Francis Meres, published a book called *Palladis Tamia: Wit's Treasury*, which includes the passage:

As Plautus and Seneca are accounted the best for comedy and tragedy among the Latins, so Shakespeare among the English is the most excellent in both kinds for the stage; for comedy, witness his *Gentlemen of Verona*, his *Errors*, his *Love Labour's Lost*, his *Love Labour's Won*, his *Midsummer's Night Dream* and his *Merchant of Venice*: for tragedy, his *Richard II*, *Richard III*, *Henry IV*, *King John*, *Titus Andronicus* and his *Romeo and Juliet*.

We do not know what he meant by *Love Labour's Won*. It may be a lost play or an alternative title for a surviving one. The main importance of the list is that it gives us a date by which all these plays had been written. Add to it the two narrative poems, the three parts of *Henry VI*, *The Taming of the Shrew*, and (perhaps) the sonnets, and it is a remarkable output for a man of thirty-four, especially one who is usually regarded as a late starter.

# WILLIAM SHAKESPEARE

In October 1598 Richard Quiney, whose son was to marry Shakespeare's daughter Judith, went to London to plead with the Privy Council on behalf of Stratford Corporation, in difficulties because of fires and bad weather. He wrote a letter, never delivered, to Shakespeare asking for the loan of £30, a sum large enough to suggest confidence in his friend's prosperity. In 1601 Shakespeare's father died. In May of the following year he paid £327 for 127 acres of land in Old Stratford. In 1604 he was lodging in London with a Huguenot family called Mountjoy, and became mildly involved with their daughter's marital problems. In the same year, through a lawyer, he sued for recovery of a small debt in Stratford. In 1605 he paid £440 for an interest in the Stratford tithes. In June 1607 his daughter Susanna married a distinguished physician, John Hall, in Stratford; his only grandchild, Elizabeth, was christened the following February. In 1609 his mother died there.

About 1610, Shakespeare's increasing involvement with Stratford suggests that he was withdrawing from his London responsibilities and retiring to New Place. He was only forty-six years old, an age at which a healthy man was no more likely to retire then than now. Possibly he had a physical breakdown. If so, it was not totally disabling. He was in London in 1612 for the lawsuit from which we know of his involvement with the Mountjoys. In March 1613 he bought a house in the Blackfriars for £140; he seems to have regarded it rather as an investment than as a domicile. In the same year the last of his three brothers died. In late 1614 and 1615 he was involved in disputes about the enclosure of the land whose tithes he owned. In February 1616 his second daughter, Judith, married Thomas Quiney, causing William to make alterations to the draft of his will, which was signed on 25 March. By now, surely, he knew that he was mortally ill. He died, according to his monument, on 23 April, and was buried in a prominent position in the chancel of Holy Trinity Church.

This selection of historical records shows clearly that Shakespeare's life is at least as well documented as those of most of his contemporaries who did not belong to great families. The identification of the Stratford worthy with the world's playwright is confirmed, if any confirmation is necessary, by the inscription on the memorial in the parish church, erected by 1623, which links him with Socrates and Virgil, and by much in the far greater memorial of that year, the First Folio edition of his plays, in which his great contemporary and rival, Ben Jonson, calls him "Sweet Swan of Avon."

### SHAKESPEARE'S INTELLECTUAL AND THEATRICAL BACKGROUND

FOR a poetic dramatist, Shakespeare was born at the right time. He grew up during a period of increasing stability and prosperity in England. Queen Elizabeth was unifying the nation. Patriotic sentiment was increasing. Continental influences were helping in the transmission of classical knowledge which we call the Renaissance. The arts in general were flourishing; those of literature and drama bounded forward far more rapidly than in the earlier part of the century. The years between Shakespeare's birth and his emergence in London saw the appearance of the first major translations of Ovid, Apuleius, Horace, Heliodorus, Plutarch, Homer, Seneca, and Virgil; Shakespeare seems to have known most of these, and those of Ovid and Plutarch, at least, had a profound influence on him. During the same period appeared William Painter's *Palace of Pleasure*, an important collection of tales including some by Boccaccio that Shakespeare used; Holinshed's *Chronicles*; Lyly's *Euphues*; Sidney's *Arcadia* and *Astrophil and Stella*; early books of Spenser's *Faerie Queene*; Lodge's *Rosalynde*; prose romances and other pamphlets of Robert Greene; the early writings of Thomas Nashe; and other books that Shakespeare either used or must have known. Indeed, it is no exaggeration to say that almost all Shakespeare's major sources are in books written or first translated into English during the first thirty years of his life, though of course he could have read the Latin works, and, probably, those in French and Italian, even if they had not been translated. The greatest earlier English author known to him was Chaucer, and he was considerably influenced by the publication in 1603 of Florio's translation of Montaigne's *Essays*.

# WILLIAM SHAKESPEARE

English dramatic literature developed greatly in Shakespeare's early years. Four years before his birth, blank verse was introduced as a dramatic medium in Sackville and Norton's *Gorboduc*. When he was two years old, George Gascoigne's *Supposes*, a translation from Ariosto and the first play written entirely in English prose, was acted; he was to draw on it in *The Taming of the Shrew*. These are early landmarks. He was already a young man before the pace of development really accelerated. John Lyly's courtly comedies, mostly in prose, began to appear in 1584, the year in which George Peele's *The Arraignment of Paris* was presented to the queen. The pace increased in the later 1580's, with Kyd's *The Spanish Tragedy*, Greene's *James IV*, and, above all, the emergence of Christopher Marlowe. Shakespeare was finding his feet in the theater. Our knowledge of the exact ordering of events in this period is so uncertain that we cannot always say whether he was influenced by the writers of these plays or himself exerted influence on them. What is undeniable is that English drama was rapidly increasing in range, scope, and power. Prose was for the first time becoming a rich dramatic medium—all the more so for its intermingling with verse styles that were immeasurably enriched by the ever more flexible uses that writers were making of blank verse. Growth in the size of acting companies and in the popularity of theatrical entertainment encouraged the writing of more ambitious plays, interweaving plot with subplot, tragedy with comedy, diversified with songs, dances, masques, and spectacular effects in ways that were unknown only a few years before.

The rapid progress of dramatic literature was thus inextricably linked with equally important developments in the theatrical arts. Shakespeare was twelve when James Burbage, already the father of the boy who was to become the greatest actor of Shakespeare's company, erected the Theatre, the first building in England designed primarily for theatrical performances. Before this, acting companies had roamed the land, the better ones under noble protection, playing where they could—in halls of great houses, at the Inns of Court, in guildhalls, and in innyards. Now one company, at least, had a permanent building; it was followed by others. The companies grew in size. They had the facilities to perform increasingly ambitious plays. They were encouraged by enthusiastic audiences and by the pleasure taken in drama by the queen and her court, even though they had also to resist the opposition of Puritan forces. They were, at the least, highly competent. Some gained international reputations. Boy actors, progressing through a system of apprenticeship, played female roles in a fully professional manner.

The Elizabethan theater, with its open roof, thrust, uncurtained stage, absence of representational scenery, rear opening, and upper level, was a sophisticated, if fundamentally simple, instrument. Modern theater designers are returning with excitement to its basic principles. It could accommodate spectacle and machinery, yet many plays written for it could be performed also in the unequipped halls that companies had to use on tour. It was a nonrepresentational, emblematic medium, shaped by and shaping the poetic dramas that prevailed on its stages.

We do not know when Shakespeare joined a company of players. In 1587 the Queen's Men lost one of their actors through manslaughter in Oxfordshire. They visited Stratford soon afterward. That they there enlisted Shakespeare is no more than an intriguing speculation. Some evidence suggests that he may have belonged to Pembroke's Men, first heard of in 1592. Certainly he was one of the Lord Chamberlain's Men shortly after they were founded, in 1594, and remained with them throughout his career. Rapidly this became London's leading company, outshining its main rival, the Lord Admiral's Men, led by Edward Alleyn. With the Chamberlain's Men, Shakespeare became a complete man of the theater: actor, businessman, and dramatic poet. He is the only leading playwright of his time to have had so stable a relationship with a single company. He wrote with their actors specifically in mind, and the conditions in which they performed helped also to shape his plays. They flourished; built the Globe as their London base from 1599; survived the competition of the successful children's companies in the early years of the new century; acquired King James I as their patron in 1603, soon after his accession; increased in size while remaining relatively stable in membership; and by 1609 were using the Blackfriars as a winter house—a "private" theater, enclosed, smaller, more exclusive in its patronage than the Globe. Perhaps it affected Shakespeare's playwriting style; yet his plays continued to be performed at the Globe and elsewhere.

### EARLY SHAKESPEARE

THE beginnings of Shakespeare's career as a writer are obscure. We have no juvenilia, sketches, or drafts. Yet beginnings there must have been. Even his earliest plays demonstrate a verbal power that suggests a practiced writer. Problems of chronology bedevil attempts to study his development. Regrettably, the editors of the First Folio did not print the plays in order of composition but imposed on them an arrangement into kinds: comedies, histories, and tragedies. The divisions are imperfect. Some of the tragedies are historical; some of the histories are tragical; and Shakespeare's greatest comic character appears in one of the histories. Shakespeare was no neoclassical respecter of the limits of dramatic genres. By reference to external evidence, such as contemporary allusions, and internal evidence, mainly stylistic development, scholars have attempted to determine the order of the plays' composition. The chronology proposed by E. K. Chambers is still accepted, with slight modification, as orthodox; but it remains partially conjectural. To treat the works in the assumed order of their composition would suggest more certainty about this order than is justified. To adopt the Folio's grouping would risk losing all sense of Shakespeare's development. In these pages the works will be divided into four groups: those written by about 1594, then those written between about 1594 and 1600, 1600 and 1607, and 1607 and 1612. Within these divisions the plays will be grouped by genre.

### EARLY HISTORIES

ONE of the earliest theatrical projects in which Shakespeare was engaged was also one of the most ambitious: to transfer to the stage Edward Hall's narrative, in the last part of *The Union of the Two Noble and Illustre Families of Lancaster and York* (1548), of events, spanning over fifty years, that led to the founding of the Tudor dynasty in the marriage of Henry VII to Elizabeth of York. The resulting plays were printed in the First Folio as *1, 2,* and *3 Henry VI* and *Richard III*. The first three seem to have been written by 1592, when Greene alluded to a line from the third. Bad texts of the second and third appeared in 1594 and 1595 respectively, as *The First Part of the Contention Betwixt the Two Famous Houses of York and Lancaster* and *The True Tragedy of Richard, Duke of York*. It has often been doubted whether *1 Henry VI* is entirely by Shakespeare. He may have revised someone else's work in order to form a dramatic sequence, but the plays are so closely related to one another that they are easily conceived of as the product of a single mind.

The enormous cast lists of the *Henry VI* plays reflect the difficulty of concentrating and focusing the mass of historical material. Some of the exposition of dynastic issues is labored, some of the action sketchily represented. Shakespeare's powers of individual characterization through language were not yet fully developed, and in *Henry VI* he was saddled with the liability of a passive hero. Perhaps in deference to decorum, Parts One and Three are composed entirely in verse; it does not avoid monotony. And some of the theatrical conventions employed are very much of their time, as the direction "Enter the KING with a supplication, and the QUEEN with Suffolk's head" (Part Two, IV.iv) is enough to show.

Nevertheless, these plays have many merits. They examine England's past in the light of its present at a time of national self-consciousness, of pride in national unity, and of fear that it might be dissipated, as Henry V's had been. On the way, they entertain and teach. They also display a deeply serious concern with political problems: the responsibilities of a king, his relationship with his people, the need for national unity, the relationship between national welfare and self-interest, the suffering caused by dissension, whether between nations or opposing factions within a nation, often mirrored in the image of a family, royal or not.

These concerns are bodied forth with much artistic success in the dramatic form and style. Part One, for example, opens with masterly thematic appropriateness in its portrayal of the ritual of national and personal mourning over the body of Henry V, nobly expressed, but rapidly degenerating into a family squabble. The scene ends with Winchester's declaration of personal ambition, just as the play ends with similar sentiments from Suffolk:

> Margaret shall now be Queen, and rule the King;
> But I will rule both her, the King, and realm.

Though the poetic style of these plays is often formal and declamatory, with extended similes and frequent classical allusions, there are also vivid, deflationary moments of colloquialism, as when Joan of Arc answers the enumeration of Talbot's honors with:

> Him that thou magnifi'st with all these titles,
> Stinking and fly-blown lies here at our feet.
> (Part One, IV.vii. 75–76)*

Part Two has some excellent prose. The scenes of Cade's rebellion show at an early stage Shakespeare's capacity for serious comedy. The horrifying episode in which Cade comments on the severed heads of Say and Cromer (IV.iii) justifies this Senecan device, because it combines with situation and language to provide an entirely convincing representation of the savagery of mob rule.

At times Shakespeare withdraws from the hurly-burly of violent action into reflective scenes of great beauty. The pastoral idea is expressed as well as anywhere in the remarkable scene of the Battle of Towton (Part Three, II.v), which, for all its stylization, forms a perfect dramatic emblem of the personal consequences of war. Henry, dismissed from the battle as useless, envies the shepherd's life. To one side of him appears a son carrying the body of a man he has killed, whom he discovers to be his father; to the other, a father carrying the body of a man he has killed, whom he discovers to be his son. Henry joins in their grief, and adds his own:

> Was ever King so griev'd for subjects' woe?
> Much is your sorrow; mine ten times so much.

*All quotations are from Peter Alexander, ed., *The Complete Works* (London–Glasgow, 1951).

Many of the most powerful scenes in these plays are of mourning, especially of children and parents. Yet the plays are memorable also for their portrayal of energetic evil, sometimes in figures of amoral wit, even charm. Especially remarkable are the duke of York's sons: Edward, later King Edward IV; George, duke of Clarence; and Richard, duke of Gloucester. Richard grows rapidly in menace in Part Three, emerging as the complete antihero in the splendid soliloquy in which he declares his ambitions:

> I'll drown more sailors than the mermaid shall;
> I'll slay more gazers than the basilisk;
> I'll play the orator as well as Nestor,
> Deceive more slily than Ulysses could,
> And, like a Sinon, take another Troy.
> I can add colours to the chameleon,
> Change shapes with Protheus for advantages,
> And set the murderous Machiavel to school.
> Can I do this, and cannot get a crown?
> Tut, were it farther off, I'll pluck it down.
> (III.ii. 186–195)

The rhetorical patterning, the end-stopped lines, the classical allusions, often regarded as limitations of Shakespeare's early style, contribute to a wonderfully energetic portrayal of the flights of Richard's imagination, which leads naturally to his dominance in *Richard III*. This play, of which a bad quarto appeared in 1597, cannot have been written much later than its precursors; but in it Shakespeare creates from his chronicle sources an aesthetically and morally satisfying pattern that shows him as the complete master of his material, able to subdue the world of fact to that of art.

Again, family relationships are important. Richard's engineering of Clarence's murder is ironically contrasted with their elder brother Edward's deathbed efforts to reunite the family. Richard bustles his way to the throne, overcoming all obstacles in a gloriously entertaining display of cynical hypocrisy, intelligence, and wit. But the forces of retribution grow in strength and are especially associated with women's mourning for the victims of past crimes. Murders of innocent children are seen in these plays as ultimate crimes against humanity. Richard's downfall begins when he alienates his chief supporter, Buckingham, by asking him to arrange the murder of his young nephews, the princes in the Tower. Tyrrel's description of their deaths (IV.iii) is an emotional climax. Opposition to Richard is focused in the idealized figure of Richmond, and the grand climax to the ritual of this and all these plays comes as the ghosts of Richard's victims appear to him and to Richmond. Richard's waking soliloquy shows that his self-sufficiency has defeated itself:

> I shall despair. There is no creature loves me;
> And if I die no soul will pity me:
> And wherefore should they, since that I myself
> Find in myself no pity to myself?
> (V.iii. 200–203)

He dies fighting, and Richmond's closing speech restates the image of England as a family:

> England hath long been mad, and scarr'd herself;
> The brother blindly shed the brother's blood,
> The father rashly slaughter'd his own son,
> The son, compell'd, been butcher to the sire.

Now he, as Henry VII, and Elizabeth, heirs of the houses of Lancaster and York, will bring unity to the kingdom. This patriotic climax, spoken by Elizabeth's grandfather, must have been peculiarly satisfying to the plays' first audiences.

Shakespeare is also concerned with dynastic issues in *King John*, a play about an earlier period of English history, first printed in 1623 but apparently written in the early 1590's. It is based in part on *The Troublesome Reign of John, King of England*, printed anonymously in 1591. As in the *Henry VI* plays, there is a strong sense of the futility and wastefulness of war. Shakespeare portrays a conflict in which neither side is right. King John knows that his claim to the English throne is weak. The French king, Philip, withdraws his support of the rival claimant, Prince Arthur, when John offers to make an advantageous match between his niece and the French dauphin. On both sides, selfishness, scheming, and personal greed put "commodity"—self-interest—before the common good. Shakespeare treats the situation ironically in, for instance, the scene before Angiers (II.i). The French Herald calls on the citizens to admit Arthur,

> Who by the hand of France this day hath made
> Much work for tears in many an English mother,
> Whose sons lie scattered on the bleeding ground.
> (II.i. 302–304)

The English Herald immediately calls on them to admit John and his soldiers,

> all with purpled hands,
> Dy'd in the dying slaughter of their foes.
> (II.i. 322–323)

The blood of both sides is wasted, for neither has won. There is a farcical element in the impasse and in John's acquiescence in the suggestion that the opposing armies should unite to

> lay this Angiers even with the ground;
> Then after fight who shall be king of it.
> (II.i. 399–400)

The ironical attitude finds personal embodiment in the figure of the Bastard, Philip Faulconbridge, who serves for the first half of the play as an ironic commentator. But grief is important here, too. Prince Arthur's mother, Constance, gives powerful expression to suffering and loss, and Arthur's threatened blinding and his death form an emotional focus. The discovery of his body turns the Bastard from a commentator into a participant, committed to humanity and England's welfare; and he ends the play as his country's spokesman:

> This England never did, nor never shall,
> Lie at the proud foot of a conqueror,
> But when it first did help to wound itself. . . .
> Come the three corners of the world in arms,
> And we shall shock them. Nought shall make us rue,
> If England to itself do rest but true.

### EARLY COMEDIES

THE mode of the history play was new when Shakespeare began to work in it; he may even have originated it. Comedy, however, had a long ancestry; and his early plays in this kind draw heavily on traditional modes and conventions, as if he were consciously experimenting, learning his craft by a process that included both imitation and innovation.

*The Two Gentlemen of Verona*, not printed until 1623, is clearly an early play. It derives partly from the prose romances popular in the late sixteenth century. The simple plot comes, perhaps indirectly, from a Portuguese romance, *Diana*, by Jorge de Montemayor. Shakespeare's craftsmanship in shaping it for the stage often falters. The play reveals his limited capacity at this period to orchestrate dialogue. Thirteen of its twenty scenes rely exclusively upon soliloquy, duologue, and the aside as comment. Scenes requiring the ability to show a number of characters talking together are generally unsuccessful. Most of the characters are only two-dimensional; some are laughably unrealized.

But *The Two Gentlemen of Verona* is full of charm and promise. It uses many motifs that Shakespeare was to develop in later plays. Those episodes in which he works within his limitations are often entirely successful. An example is the delightful scene (IV.ii) in which Proteus serenades his new love with "Who is Silvia?", while his old love looks on in disguise. The ironic wordplay of Julia's dialogue with the Host suggests real depth of character. Valentine and Proteus, too, have some human substance; and Proteus' servant, Launce, is the first in the great line of Shakespearian clowns. His monologues are masterpieces of comic dramatic prose, constructed with an artistry consummate enough to give the impression of artlessness. Some of the verse, too, is masterly; witness the astonishing matching of sound to sense in Proteus' tribute to the power of poetry:

> For Orpheus' lute was strung with poets' sinews,
> Whose golden touch could soften steel and stones,
> Make tigers tame, and huge leviathans
> Forsake unsounded deeps to dance on sands.
> (III.ii. 78–81)

*The Two Gentlemen of Verona* shows Shakespeare as already a great writer, though not a great playwright.

*The Comedy of Errors*, also printed in 1623, was written by Christmas 1594, when it was played at Gray's Inn. Its dramatic economy is much superior to that of *The Two Gentlemen of Verona*. Here, Shakespeare draws heavily on the traditions of Roman comedy. The action takes place in Ephesus within a single day and is based on Plautus' farce *Menaechmi*, which tells of a man accompanied by his slave and in search of his long-lost twin brother. Shakespeare turns the slave into a servant, Dromio, and gives him, too, a twin, who serves his master Antipholus' brother. The identical twins have identical names, and the result is a great increase in the possible errors of identification. Shakespeare frames the classically derived main action within an episode based on the romantic story of the wanderings of Apollonius of Tyre, which he was to use again in *Pericles*. This gives the Antipholuses a father, Egeon, and the comic complexities of the main action are overshadowed by his being condemned to die at five o'clock unless he can find someone to redeem him. By this and other means Shakespeare interfuses what might have been a merely mechanical farce with pointers to the potentially serious consequences of the misunderstandings. The untying of the comic knot is preceded by a moving lament from Egeon, about to be executed, who is not recognized by the man he believes to be the son he has brought up from birth. The resolution is effected by an Abbess who turns out to be Egeon's wife, a surprise to the audience paralleled in Shakespeare's work only by the apparent resurrection of Hermione in *The Winter's Tale*.

The ending of *The Comedy of Errors* is not just a solution of an intellectual puzzle, it is charged with emotional power. This play is a kind of diploma piece. In it Shakespeare outdoes his classical progenitors. He adapts his style admirably to his material. He modifies the intellectual complexity of his plot by infusing romantic motifs into it, and by relaxing the pace of the action from time to time to allow for the inclusion of discursive set pieces such as Dromio of Syracuse's marvelous prose description of the kitchen wench who was "spherical, like a globe." There is no faltering here.

*The Taming of the Shrew*, printed in the Folio, has a problematic relative, a play printed in 1594 as *The Taming of a Shrew*, once looked on as Shakespeare's source, now more generally regarded as a corrupt text of his play. It includes a rounding off of the Christopher Sly framework, which corresponds with nothing in the Folio. Perhaps that text is damaged too. Editors and directors sometimes, justifiably, add these episodes to the Folio text on the grounds that they may derive from lost Shakespearian originals.

In *The Comedy of Errors* Shakespeare shows people losing their sense of identity when recognition is withheld from them and acquiring a sense of reaffirmed identity when normality returns. In the Induction to *The Taming of the Shrew* he suggests how changes in external circumstances may join with the power of rhetoric to create a sense of changed identity. This play draws partly on conventions of Roman comedy, partly on English folk tale and drama. It owes a distinct debt to *Supposes*, George Gascoigne's prose translation of Ariosto's *I Suppositi*. "Supposes" is as much a key word in *The Taming of the Shrew* as is "errors" in *The Comedy of Errors*. The Induction displays the trick by which Sly is made to suppose that he is not a tinker but "a mighty lord." In the play performed for Sly's amusement, Lucentio, wooing Bianca, employs various "counterfeit supposes," but they are superficial. He, the shallowly romantic lover, is opposed to the unromantic Petruchio, who comes

> to wive it wealthily in Padua;
> If wealthily, then happily in Padua.
> (I.ii.73–74)

Petruchio is offered Kate, the shrew, apparently a far less attractive match than Bianca. And the most vital part of the play demonstrates the "suppose" by which he transforms the shrew into the ideal wife. The process is partly physical, partly mental. But its effect is not to reduce Kate to a state of subjection. Rather it teaches her the importance in human relationships of the ability to participate imaginatively in other people's lives. The play's final scene derives warmth and joy from the fact that Kate, in her new relationship with Petruchio, feels a freedom and wholeness that were previously outside her grasp. The achievement of Petruchio the realist is a romantic one: he creates an illusion and turns it into reality.

*The Taming of the Shrew* is a robust play that acts splendidly. It shows Shakespeare experimenting with techniques of structure and language in order to integrate a variety of diverse materials. It is interesting in the critical attitude that it adopts to romantic conventions. It contains much fine verse and prose; but, in the surviving text, it lacks the subordination of all the parts to the whole, which causes a less ambitious play, such as *The Comedy of Errors*, to seem a more rounded work of art.

*Love's Labour's Lost* is so different as to remind us forcibly of the uncertainties in the chronology of the early plays. Here Shakespeare seems to be writing for a more sophisticated, even courtly audience. The influences of earlier comedy appear to have been filtered through the plays of John Lyly, the leading court dramatist. The play contains topical allusions, some no longer explicable, which may also suggest that it originally had a coterie audience. It was first published in 1598, "as it was presented before her Highness this last Christmas," when it was said to be "newly corrected and augmented." But it was also acted in the public theaters—according to the title page of the second quarto, of 1631, "at the Blackfriars and the Globe"—and a court performance of 1605 suggests that it was not purely topical in its appeal.

In this play Shakespeare employs an exceptionally wide range of verse and prose styles, demonstrating his command of verbal artifice. This is appropriate, for the play is much concerned with artificiality. The king and his three lords have imposed unnatural restrictions on themselves. Beside them Shakespeare places Holofernes, the pedant who stands as an awful warning of what they may become if they persist in their denial of nature, and Costard and Jaquenetta, unspoiled children of nature. The arrival of the Princess of France and her three ladies offers an immediate challenge to the lords' resolutions, and the play's patterned, dancelike progress charts their slow acceptance of their own natures, their acknowledgments of the demands of society, and of the need for a proper and courteous use of the intelligence. Artificial behavior is reflected in artificial language. Significantly, the most important communication in the play does not need to be put into words:

> *Marcade* . . . the news I bring
> Is heavy in my tongue. The King your father—
> *Princess*

# WILLIAM SHAKESPEARE

>     Dead, for my life!
> *Marcade*     Even so; my tale is told.
>                                          (V.ii.706–709)

Artifice gives way before the ultimate reality of death. The lovers are forced into new relationships with one another, and Shakespeare shows that the adjustment is not easy.

The subdued ending of *Love's Labour's Lost* represents one of Shakespeare's most daring experiments with comic form. Usually the comic climax brings happiness; this one brings grief. After it there comes a slow movement toward resignation and hope, but the happy ending lies in the future, at least twelve months away; and that, says Berowne, is "too long for a play." *Love's Labour's Lost* offers its audience full enjoyment of artifice but also invites a critical attitude toward it. The play grows from intellectual playfulness to a warm humanity that comes to full, disturbing flood at the close. It is a play of ideas, a brilliantly dramatized debate; though in some senses it is of its age, it can still reach out vividly to us.

Shakespeare's early experiments in comedy have their perfect outcome in *A Midsummer Night's Dream*, printed in 1600 but probably written by 1595. No single influence is dominant. The design of the play came from Shakespeare's imagination, as it had for *Love's Labour's Lost*, with which it has much in common. It too has a patterned structure, a wide range of prose and verse styles, comedy springing from the follies of young love, a play-within-the-play. It has a similar grace of language, less intricacy and self-conscious brilliance. The theory that it was written for an aristocratic marriage is unsupported by external evidence; but marriage is central to the play's design, linking each of the distinct groups of characters. Theseus is to be married; the lovers wish to be, and finally are; the fairies, who have marital problems, are to intervene in the human plans for marriage and to deliver the concluding epithalamium; the laborers are to provide the entertainment for the multiple marriages, and one of them is bemusedly to receive the amorous attention of the Fairy Queen.

Though marriages form the natural conclusion to the action, there are, in the usual way of comedy, obstacles to be overcome. Misunderstandings among the young lovers are exacerbated by Puck's mischief; dissension between the Fairy King and Queen must be settled before human happiness can be achieved. The supernatural world is lightly suggestive of inexplicable influences upon human behavior, especially in love—"reason and love keep little company together now-a-days." And Shakespeare is led to explore the relationship between reason and the imagination in a way that suggests an affinity between love and artistic responsiveness. The inexperienced lovers are bewildered by their own emotions. The laborers are hopelessly confused by the problem of distinguishing between appearance and reality. But the lovers, temporarily released from the bands of society, come out of the dream world of the wood wiser than they had gone into it. Bottom is taken out of himself by his encounter with the Fairy Queen and, though he regards it as a dream, acknowledges it as "a most rare vision." Theseus looks with the eye of reason, but Hippolyta knows that

>              all the story of the night told over,
> And all their minds transfigur'd so together,
> More witnesseth than fancy's images,
> And grows to something of great constancy.
>                                          (V.i. 23–26)

The last act is a glorious celebration, a dance in which the shifting relationships between the performers of the interlude, the images they try to present, and their audience mirror the conflicting claims of illusion and reality, the world of the imagination—in which openness to experience can lead to wisdom—and the need to acknowledge the hard facts of life. The performance ends in goodwill and courtesy, on which the fairies bestow their blessing; and Puck, in his closing lines, reminds us that we are at liberty to take what we have seen as either truth or illusion:

>     If we shadows have offended,
>     Think but this, and all is mended,
>     That you have but slumb'red here
>     While these visions did appear.

The goodwill of the audience can help the players to "mend." As Holofernes had shown, imaginative detachment is "not generous, not gentle, not humble"; and, as we had witnessed in *The Taming of the Shrew*, imagination can turn illusion into reality.

### EARLY TRAGEDIES

SHAKESPEARE was more tentative in his early explorations of tragic than of comic form. Tragedies were conventionally based on history, and *Titus Andronicus* is set in the fourth century A.D., but the story, like that of his other early tragedy, *Romeo and Juliet,* is fictitious. Shakespeare may have adapted it from an earlier version of *The History of Titus Andronicus*, which survives only as an eighteenth-century chapbook. Ovid, whose *Metamorphoses* appears on stage (IV.i), is an important influence, as is Seneca. Except for Act Three, Scene Two, which first appeared in print in 1623, the play was printed in 1594; and it may have been written several years earlier, perhaps in collaboration with George Peele, perhaps merely under his influence. Popular in its time, it can now be enjoyed only with an exercise of the historical imagination, for its presentation of physical horror can easily seem ludicrous. The disjunction between action and language can bewilder, as when Marcus, seeing his niece with "her hands cut off, and her tongue cut out, and ravish'd" (II.iv), delivers nearly fifty lines of beautifully modulated blank verse; or, still more surprisingly, when Titus, having persuaded Aaron to cut off his hand, betrays no more emotion in what he says than if he had taken off a glove. Nevertheless, it is in the portrayal of suffering that the play justifies itself, and more than one production has shown that, given the right kind of stylized presentation, its ritualistic tableaux of suffering and woe can be profoundly moving. As in the early histories, Shakespeare is most successful in the expression of grief and the portrayal of energetic evil. Titus' lament over his mutilated daughter is elemental in a way that looks forward to Lear:

> I am the sea; hark how her sighs do blow.
> She is the weeping welkin, I the earth;
> Then must my sea be moved with her sighs;
> Then must my earth with her continual tears
> Become a deluge, overflow'd and drown'd.
> (III.i. 226–230)

Aaron, the Moorish villain, displays an enjoyment of evil and a cynical intelligence that relate him to Richard III and Iago; he develops into the play's most complex character. The final horrifying bloodbath, in which Titus serves Tamora with her two sons' heads baked in a pie, kills his own daughter and Tamora, and is himself killed by the emperor, who is then killed by Titus' son, is skillfully engineered; but the events are efficiently rather than imaginatively presented, and tragic emotions are not stirred.

Shakespeare took the well-known story of Romeo and Juliet from Arthur Brooke's long poem *The Tragical History of Romeus and Juliet,* published in 1562 and reprinted in 1587. The play is more markedly experimental than *Titus Andronicus*. It is not set in antiquity but in the sixteenth century. It has affinities with romantic comedy, telling of wooing and marriage. Its poetical center is the balcony scene, perhaps the most celebrated expression of romantic love in our literature; the romance is offset by much witty and bawdy comedy. The tragic outcome of the lovers' passion is the result of external circumstances: the still timelessness of Romeo and Juliet's inward experience, perfectly conveyed at the end of the balcony scene, is threatened and finally destroyed by the time-tied processes of the public feud between their families. The play, first printed in 1597, seems from its verbal styles to have been written several years after *Titus Andronicus*. For the first time among the plays discussed so far, we feel, not merely that the design is ambitious, but that Shakespeare's fecundity overflows the measure. Every rift is laden with ore, and the finished work delights and astonishes by its inventiveness, variety, complexity, and generosity. But it is not undisciplined. Indeed, this play is "early" in the sense that it still relies partly on formal verse structures—the lovers' first conversation, a moment of private communion in the public bustle of the ball, is cast in the form of a sonnet—and on clearly patterned action. Public strife is counterbalanced by private communion; the Prince, the civic governor, has his counterpart in Friar Lawrence, the personal confessor; Romeo's confidant, Mercutio, is matched by Juliet's, her Nurse. Characterization is both brilliant and functional. Shakespeare's verbal virtuosity makes marvelous individuals out of Mercutio and the Nurse, but they too are part of the pattern, each failing one of the lovers in understanding, pushing them still further into isolation. In their bawdy physicality, too, they act as foils to the lovers, whose passion includes but transcends the physical. Romeo and Juliet are gradually destroyed by the world of external reality: the world of uncomprehending relatives and friends, in which the senseless family feud—a symbol of misunderstanding, of the failures in human communication—destroys the most precious representatives of the families. Romeo and Juliet had achieved understanding and union; they had risked—and, in a sense, lost—all for the values of personal love. In this sense comedy is banished from the end of the play. The Prince calls together the heads of the opposing families and speaks of general woe. But out of the suffering comes a hard-won reconciliation. As in some of Shakespeare's later comedies, the union of lovers accompanies the healing of breaches among members of the older generation; but here the lovers are dead.

### THE POEMS

BECAUSE of plague, London's theaters were closed for almost two years between June 1592 and June 1594. Shakespeare turned to nondramatic writing, perhaps because he feared that he might need an alternative career. A new kind of narrative poem was coming into vogue: tales of love based on Ovidian stories and techniques. Thomas Lodge's *Scilla's Metamorphosis* (1589) is an early example. Another, perhaps the finest, is Christopher Marlowe's *Hero and Leander*. Marlowe died in 1593, but the poem was not published until 1598. *Venus and Adonis* was printed in 1593, with the author's dedication to Henry Wriothesley, earl of Southampton, calling the poem "the first heir of my invention"—presumably meaning either his first poem or his first work to be printed. It was extraordinarily popular; at least eleven editions appeared before 1620, and five more by 1640. Partly it had a succès de scandale; Shakespeare makes Venus the suitor, Adonis her reluctant victim, which adds a piquant eroticism to Ovid's story.

The poem's success has not been maintained. Like *Love's Labour's Lost*, it is a sophisticated work, drawing attention to its craftsmanship, demanding admiration rather than submission. It will not be enjoyed if it is read for its story alone: Shakespeare takes nearly 1,200 lines where Ovid took about 75. Yet the narrative is unfolded with such order, clarity, and ease of versification that the general impression is one of speed. The style, though artificial, is varied, ranging from metaphysical elaboration to pared simplicity. Adonis provides the main psychological interest. His innocence and idealism contrast with Venus' experience and paradoxically physical, materialist outlook. It is the goddess who represents lust, the human boy who stands up for love. The tension between his youthful withdrawal from sexual experience and her overmature anxiety to rush into it provides the poem's dramatic impetus. Adonis' immaturity, amusing and touching, is appropriate to the essentially nontragic nature of a story with a quasi-tragic ending.

*The Rape of Lucrece*, printed the following year and also dedicated, more warmly, to Southampton, is a contrasting companion piece. The earlier poem is mythological. *Lucrece*, composed in the seven-line rhyme royal, is historical, based not on the *Metamorphoses* but on the *Fasti* ("Chronicles"). It is about people in society; its tone is not that of high comedy, but of tragedy. Like *Venus and Adonis*, it opens with speed in a stanza that carries concentrated suggestions of the power of Tarquin's lust. A long poem could not be sustained at this pitch, nor would the slender story support it. Shakespeare ekes out his material with meditative soliloquies, discursive episodes, and long moralizing passages. The amplificatory technique is less successful here than in *Venus and Adonis*. There we could remain detached enough to enjoy the poet's verbal flights, his decorative ingenuity, his digressive skill. *Lucrece* seems to demand more engagement with the emotions of the characters. Even the least relevant passages are often fine in their own right, but the parts are greater than the whole. Most important from the point of view of Shakespeare's later development seem to be those passages describing how Tarquin against his better nature is drawn inexorably on toward the crime that will destroy him. Just as a basic theme of Shakespearian comedy, the search for and final achievement of self-knowledge, is adumbrated in *Venus and Adonis*, so a basic motif of his tragedies, the problem caused by an absence of self-knowledge so disastrous that it is finally destructive of self, emerges in *Lucrece*. Tarquin, we are told, as he moves toward Lucrece's chamber, "still pursues his fear" (l. 308). Macbeth, before he kills Duncan, imagines Murder moving "With Tarquin's ravishing strides, towards his design" (II.i.55).

It may have been about the time that Shakespeare was writing the essentially public narrative poems that he also wrote his most seemingly private compositions, his sonnets. When they were written is only one of the mysteries about them. In 1598 Francis Meres referred to Shakespeare's "sugared sonnets among his private friends." In 1599 William Jaggard published corrupt versions of two of them in *The Passionate Pilgrim*, a volume of poems that he attributed to Shakespeare and that also includes three extracts from *Love's Labour's Lost*, four poems known to be by other poets, and eleven of unknown authorship that few have ascribed to Shakespeare. The complete 154 sonnets did not appear until 1609, though the title-page declaration "Never before imprinted" implies that they were not new. The publication appears to be unauthorized. It has a dedication by the publisher, Thomas Thorpe: "To the only begetter of these ensuing sonnets Mr W.H. all happiness and that eternity promised by our ever-living poet wisheth the well-wishing adventurer in setting forth." This sentence has been endlessly discussed, but we still do not know who Mr W.H. is, nor in what sense he was the sonnets' "only begetter." The volume also includes "A Lover's Complaint," a narrative poem of doubtful authenticity.

Sonnet sequences were popular in the 1590's, and Shakespeare's interest in the sonnet form is reflected in some of his early plays, especially *Romeo and Juliet* and *Love's Labour's Lost*. The fact that he did not publish his sonnets may imply that he thought of them as personal poems, but this is not altogether borne out by their content. Some are generalized meditations; some are comparatively formal utterances, like the first seventeen, in which he urges a young man to marry and beget children. Some proclaim a public design in the attempt to eternize their addressee. Some hint at a personal drama. The relationship between the poet and his friend is so close that it is sometimes interpreted as homosexual, though this is explicitly denied (20). It is threatened by another poet who seeks to replace the author in his friend's affections; the poet's mistress, a "black" woman (as he calls her), or Dark Lady, seduces the friend: the poet is more concerned for the friend than for his own relationship with the woman, which he frequently deplores. Sonnets 127–152 are mainly about the woman. They include some of the most tortured and introverted of the poems; it is difficult to imagine the poet wishing to show them even to the woman, let alone make them public. This personal drama might be fictional; if so, it is inefficiently projected. The sonnets are partly "dramatic" in the sense that some of them are written as if from within a particular situation, like speeches from a lost play. Some can be related to classical poetry; some draw on poetic conventions of the time; some represent a deliberate reaction against convention: few if any other sonnets of the time are as bawdy or as insulting to their addressees as some of Shakespeare's. A dramatic poet as great as Shakespeare may have written sonnets on imaginary themes that sound personal, but we know of no reason why he should have done so without intending to publish them. Yet as an autobiographical document, the sonnets are most unsatisfactory. Innumerable attempts have been made to rearrange them into a more coherent sequence, to identify the persons involved, and to elucidate topical allusions. None has succeeded.

To read all the sonnets consecutively is difficult. Though almost all of them have, superficially, the same form, this obscures the fact that their wide range of modes, of tone, of variations within the basic form, of intensity, and of interrelationship imposes disparate demands upon the attention. Some, including many of the most popular, are lyrical, confident outpourings of love, conveyed largely through natural imagery; some express the lover's humility and abasement. Some are well-ordered meditations on eternal poetic themes of time, the transience of beauty and of love; on the power of art, the inevitability of death; some are more narrowly, even enigmatically, related to a particular situation. Some are intellectual, witty workings out of poetic conceits; some, no less intellectual, are tortured, introspective self-communings. Though some seem to belong to the world of *The Two Gentlemen of Verona* or *Romeo and Juliet*, others are closer to *Measure for Measure* or *Troilus and Cressida*. Shakespeare the man remains as fascinatingly enigmatic in the sonnets as in the plays.

### LATER HISTORIES AND MAJOR COMEDIES

AFTER his wide-ranging earlier experiments, Shakespeare narrowed his scope and, during several prolific years after about 1594, wrote only comedies and history plays, of which *Richard II* alone is in tragic form. Here Shakespeare steps backward in his dramatization of history to begin a tetralogy, which, by carrying the story up to the reign of Henry V, will complete an eight-play sequence. The plays are strongly linked, yet each has its own individuality. *Richard II*, written about 1595, was printed in 1597. It was of topical interest. Queen Elizabeth was aging. Anxiety about the succession was growing. The queen's indulgence of her favorites caused unrest; comparisons were drawn between her and Richard II. The absence from the play of the deposition scene (IV.i) in the three editions printed during her lifetime must be attributed to censorship, official or not; and the commissioning by Essex's supporters of a special performance on the eve of his rebellion, in 1601, shows that many drew the parallel.

Nevertheless, Shakespeare's play has no obvious topical allusions. He emphasizes the universal rather than the particular elements of Bolingbroke's usurpation. The play is full of moral ambiguity. Richard, a faulty human being and a weak king, has the unquestioned right to the throne. Bolingbroke has no hereditary right but is wronged by Richard and better fitted for kingship. Shakespeare skillfully manipulates the audience's sympathies. In the early scenes we can only condemn Richard's frivolity and irresponsibility, which culminate in his callous and unconstitutional treatment of his dying uncle, John of Gaunt, whose noble speech on England (II.i. 31–68) laments the lapsing values of the old order. But after Bolingbroke becomes king, and also abuses power in the executions of Bushy and Bagot and the arrest of the Bishop of Carlisle—another spokesman for traditional values—and as Richard's expression of his sufferings grows in eloquence, Richard takes on the stature of a tragic hero. Through him Shakespeare orchestrates, in wonderfully melodious verse, all the resonances of the situation; and the play expands from a political drama into an exploration of the sources of power, of the hold that symbols, including words, can have over men's imaginations, of the tensions between the demands of office and the qualities of those who hold office, of private and public values, of the differences and similarities between a "large kingdom" and a "little grave."

Bolingbroke's guilt haunts him throughout the next two plays of the sequence. Carlisle's prophecy that civil war will follow usurpation is fulfilled. *1 Henry IV* (printed twice in 1598 and reprinted five times before 1623) shows the king, wishing to expiate his guilt by a pilgrimage to Jerusalem, anguished by both national and filial rebellion. Just as, in *A Midsummer Night's Dream*, Oberon and Titania must be reconciled before the mortals' course of love can run smooth, so the dissolute Hal must reform and be reconciled with his father before rebellion can be put down. The issue resolves into a personal conflict between Hotspur, the rebel leader, and Hal, who defeats expectation and becomes the victor. Shakespeare has adjusted the facts, chronicled by Holinshed, to create a basically simple foundation on which he builds a history play with a greater social and emotional range than he had so far attempted. Here his genius for character portrayal, achieved largely through an astonishing capacity to deploy and extend the full resources of the English language, is at its greatest. Dominant is Falstaff, Shakespeare's invention, though distantly related to the historical Sir John Oldcastle as portrayed in *The Famous Victories of Henry V*, a minor source play printed in 1598. The character is rich, as the soliloquies particularly demonstrate; but the profundity of the role derives also from its integration into the total design, most subtly in the first tavern scene (II.iv) when Falstaff and Hal in turn take on the role of the king. Behind the game lurks reality, a subconscious and premonitory acknowledgment on Falstaff's part that the "son of England" should not "prove a thief and take purses," and on Hal's that he is bound eventually to "banish plump Jack." The tavern world provides more fully realized representatives of the ordinary folk of England than we have seen before. It is part of Hal's achievement to link this world with the court and the battlefield.

At the beginning of *2 Henry IV*, Hal seems to have returned to his former ways. There is an uncharacteristic element of repetition in the pattern of paternal reproach, filial repentance, and reconciliation. This may result from an initial uncertainty about whether to treat Henry IV's reign in one play or two. But Part Two has its individual tone, darker and more disturbing than its predecessor's. It brings to the surface moral issues only latent in the earlier play. Even there Falstaff at his most contemptible, stabbing Hotspur's corpse, was juxtaposed with Hal at his most heroic. Here, though we may temporarily condone Falstaff's misuse of his powers of conscription and his exploitation of Shallow and his companions, his self-exculpations are less disarming. In the great tavern scene (II.iv) his amorous exchanges with the deplorable Doll Tearsheet are poignant rather than funny, overshadowed by impotence and the fear of death. But Shakespeare does not encourage us to be morally complacent. Mistress Quickly and even Doll are presented in ways that show his delight in normal human instincts, as well as an awareness that they may be dangerous when out of control. Prince John may have right on his side, but the trick by which he betrays the rebels is distasteful; we can warm to Falstaff's condemnation of "the sober-blooded boy." The darker side of tavern life is savagely evident in the tiny scene (V.iv) of Doll's carting—"the man is dead that you and Pistol beat amongst you." The scene is strategically placed just before Hal's entrance as king; we can see the need for his rejection of Falstaff, though we can see the sadness of it, too.

*2 Henry IV* was written about 1598. First printed in 1600, it was, unlike Part One, not reprinted until 1623. At this stage in his career, Shakespeare was using a higher proportion of prose over verse than at any other period and was achieving with it some of his most complex and truly poetical effects. The political scenes of this play use verse, much of it very fine. But the quintessentially Shakespearian parts are the tavern scene and the Justice Shallow episodes, in which prose is handled with a subtlety matched only in Chekhov for the dramatic expression of emotional complexity.

Shakespeare rounded off his second historical sequence with *Henry V*. An apparent allusion to Essex in the Chorus to Act V suggests that it was written in 1599. A corrupt text of the following year omits the Choruses, first printed in 1623. *Henry V*, composed at the zenith of Shakespeare's career as a comic dramatist, brings history close to comic form. It has a wooing scene and ends, as comedies conventionally do, with a marriage, one that will unite realms as well as hearts (V.ii. 351). Our reactions are guided by the Chorus—Shakespeare's most extended use of this device except in *Pericles*—who speaks some of the play's finest poetry. From the "civil broils" of the earlier plays Shakespeare turns to portray a country united in war against France. There is more glory in such a war, and the play is famous—or notorious—as an expression of patriotism. It has less inwardness than its predecessors. But the horrors of war are strongly presented; the goal of war is peace, and the play suggests that inward peace of conscience is necessary in one who would win national peace. Henry shows concern about the justification for his course of action. More than once, and from both sides of the Channel, we are reminded of his "wilder days." The transition from "madcap prince" to the "mirror of all Christian kings" involves loss. Falstaff is dying; "the king has killed his heart." But Henry has accepted the responsibilities of kingship and talks of them, and its hollow rewards, in a speech that recalls one by his father (*2 Henry IV*, III.i. 1–31) and anticipates (historically) one by his son (*3 Henry VI*, II.v. 1–54). "The King is but a man" (IV.i. 103), and this one moves among his men with an honesty unimaginable in Richard II and quite different from his father's "courtship to the common people" (*Richard II*, I.iv. 24). His success in battle removes the guilt of his inheritance. He has become the "star of England" (final Chorus, 6). If in the process he has made difficult decisions with harsh consequences, that, Shakespeare implies, is the price of political success.

### MAJOR COMEDIES

SHAKESPEARE wrote his later histories over the same period as his greatest comedies. *The Merchant of Venice*, dating from about 1596, was entered in the Stationers' Register in 1598 and printed in 1600. Much of the plot material is implausible, deriving from folktale and legend. The wooing story comes from a collection published in Italian in 1558 as *Il Pecorone*, by Ser Giovanni Fiorentino. The pound-of-flesh story was well known. A lost play, *The Jew*, mentioned in 1579, may have been a source, and Shakespeare must have known Marlowe's *The Jew of Malta*.

The plot's sharp conflict between romantic and antiromantic values leads Shakespeare to define, partly by contrast, his first great romantic heroine and his first great comic antagonist. The opposition of Portia and Shylock provides the chief dramatic impetus, culminating in the controlled excitement of the trial (IV.i). It is easy to think of the play in terms of contrasts: between the beautiful, generous, merciful Portia and the scheming, miserly, legalistic Shylock; between their religions, Christianity and Judaism; between their settings, the idealized Belmont and the money markets of Venice; between the heights of lyrical poetry to which Portia can rise and Shylock's harsh prose. There are other tensions, too: the familiar conflict, in Bassanio, between love and friendship; the opposition, in the episodes of the caskets, between attractive but hollow superficiality and the rewards given to those "that choose not by the view" (III.ii. 131).

The oppositions in the play, though strong, are not entirely simple. The world of Belmont is idealized but flawed. The generous Bassanio has been prodigal. Antonio, noble in friendship, admits to treating Shylock with contempt. Gratiano, though ebullient, is vindictive. Even Portia has to adopt Shylock's legalism to achieve her good ends. Shylock, though villainous, has dignity, eloquence, and pathos. We may deplore his values yet respect his tenacity. Despite its lyricism, grace, drama, and high comedy, many people find *The Merchant of Venice* disturbing and express unease with it. Shakespeare portrays here a clash of values rather like that between Henry V and Falstaff. We know which side is right. We have no doubt that Portia should defeat Shylock as King Henry has to reject Falstaff. But in both plays there is pain in the defeat as well as joy in the victory.

*Much Ado About Nothing*, usually dated about 1598—it is not mentioned by Meres and was published in quarto in 1600—is also based on a traditional tale. It places less emphasis on poetry and romance, more on prose and wit. The young lovers of the main plot, Claudio and Hero, are unconvincing advocates for romantic values. Admittedly, Claudio expresses his love for Hero eloquently in the play's first verse passage, but only after he has assured himself that she is an heiress. We never see him alone with her, and their relationship seems as insubstantial as that of Lucentio and Bianca in *The Taming of the Shrew*. Claudio falls remarkably easily into the deception that Don John engineers, and gives Hero no opportunity to defend herself before launching into his bitter denunciations at the altar where they were to have been married. Her apparent death leads him to no real soul searchings, and her forgiveness and their subsequent reconciliation are sketchily presented. Questions are raised that might have been answered if we had more knowledge of Shakespeare's intentions. If Claudio is played as a callow adolescent, we may pity his succumbing to Don John's evil trickery. If he is more maturely presented, we may look on him rather as an illustration of the hollowness of attitudes to love that are based on illusion instead of knowledge and understanding.

Certainly the lovers of the main plot are less convincing than those of the subplot. There is more true poetry in single prose sentences of Beatrice's—"There was a star danc'd, and under that was I born"—than in many lines of Claudio's verse. This overturning of expectations is one of the ways in which romantic values are questioned. Beatrice and Benedick's "merry war," for all its wrangling, suggests a true engagement of personalities. The brief passage in which they declare their love (IV.i. 255-end) is perhaps the best prose love scene in the language, and we believe in them as complex and developing individuals.

In *Much Ado About Nothing* recurrent overhearings become a structural principle. "Nothing" in the title has been taken as a pun on "noting," and certainly the "misprisions" arising from the overhearings create the complications of the action. Almost all are tricked. Yet a fruitful counterpoint arises from the relationships of the different sets of characters. Dogberry and his companions of the watch have already overheard Borachio's confession when Claudio denounces Hero. The presence of Beatrice and Benedick during the scene of the thwarted wedding is an additional reassurance to the audience. Dogberry and his fellows are the most naturally befuddled characters, yet it is their basic goodwill that, in spite of almost insuperable barriers to communication, resolves the action. The play's interpretative problems are not essentially different from those of most stage works for which we have limited knowledge of the author's intentions. And they enhance rather than diminish its theatrical robustness. It withstands varied treatments and is a constant source of pleasure.

There is a legend that Shakespeare wrote *The Merry Wives of Windsor* rapidly, because Queen Elizabeth wanted to see "Sir John in love." A passage in Act Five alluding to the ceremony of the Feast of the Knights of the Garter clearly has topical reference, and the play almost certainly has some connection with special Garter ceremonies, but we cannot be sure in what year. 1597 has been suggested, but the play's relationship with the other Falstaff plays seems to require a later date. It was first published, in a bad text, in 1602; a better text appeared in the Folio. In spite of its superficial naturalism it has a strongly literary background. Several of the characters derive from Shakespeare's own plays about Henry IV; and though no clear source of the plot has been identified, it is closely related to the ribald tales of tricked lovers and husbands included in many contemporary collections.

Legends about the play's origin, and the fact that its central character is called Falstaff, have damaged its critical reputation. It might be more profitably approached as another of Shakespeare's experiments. It is untypical in various ways. It includes proportionally more prose than any other of his plays. It is his only comedy to have an English setting and to be closely related to contemporary life. In Master Ford, Shakespeare comes closer than anywhere else to writing "humours" comedy in the Jonsonian style. But Shakespeare could never commit himself to Jonson's antiromantic view of life. Ford is shamed out of his jealous humor and kneels to his wife for pardon. Falstaff also undergoes a corrective process of castigation leading to penitence. Shakespeare's essential romanticism shows itself too in the subplot of Anne Page and her suitors. The climax of the love plot comes in the verse passage in which Fenton, safely married, not merely defends his deception of Anne's parents but rebukes them for their previous opposition to the match and their willingness to have her married for money (V.v. 207–217).

*The Merry Wives of Windsor* does not belong to the mainstream of Shakespearian comedy but is recognizably Shakespearian. It is a neat, ingenious, witty comedy of situation. It has attributes of the corrective, satirical comedy that Jonson was making popular at the close of the century, but it also displays a strong moral bent and a romantic attitude to love and marriage. The style suits the matter, and much of the writing is delightful, even if it would not be at home in *Henry IV*. The characterization is partly by types, but the major roles offer excellent opportunities to their performers, and there are passages of subtly manipulated dialogue. Critics have patronized the play. Audiences never fail to enjoy it.

Pastoralism, derived from classical models, exerted an important influence on sixteenth-century literature. We have seen how some of Shakespeare's kings envied the shepherd his life attuned to the seasons and the natural processes. Elsewhere, too, Shakespeare plays with pastoral conventions. In *The Two Gentlemen of Verona* and *A Midsummer Night's Dream*, for example, the movement of lovers from their accustomed environment to a place apart assists their self-discovery. But it is in *As You Like It* that Shakespeare conducts his most searching examination of the pastoral ideal. The play, first published in 1623, is based on Thomas Lodge's *Rosalynde*, a prose romance printed in 1590 and reprinted in 1592, 1596, and 1598. Shakespeare's play of the book, written about 1600, is exceptionally literary in its origins, and he does not attempt to conceal its artificiality. He manipulates the relationship between story and dialogue, between the enactment of events and reflection upon the events, between characters as agents of the action and characters as talkers, to permit the introduction of many of the commonplace debating topics of his times: the relationship for instance between nature and fortune, nature and nurture, court and country. These topics are all associated with the pastoral tradition. Related to them is an idea that fascinated Shakespeare: that wisdom is a kind of folly, folly a potential source of wisdom. He seems to have felt that the effort to attain wisdom may result in an overearnestness that can lead to folly, and that the unguardedness of the subconscious, relaxed mind may, for all its dangers, bring the rewards of unsought illumination. He betrays a concern with the proper use of man's time on earth; and in this comedy in which the central character plays so elaborate, extended, and ultimately important a game, the idea of time, of its uses and abuses, is also, appropriately, pervasive.

Rosalind's game is directed toward the attainment of love, and attitudes to love are dominant among the play's concepts. The forest of Arden is inhabited by lovers, actual and potential. Silvius and Phebe are straight out of the Renaissance pastoral convention, unreal but touching, because in them Shakespeare isolates one aspect of love. Opposed to it is the earthy love affair of Touchstone and Audrey. Touchstone's attitude is partly a criticism of Silvius' but is itself criticized: being purely physical, it is, as he perceives himself, temporary. Subsuming both of these attitudes is that of Orlando and Rosalind. Orlando has attributes of the conventional lover. He hangs verses on trees, sighs out his soul in praise of his beloved. Yet his idealism is robust enough to withstand the mockery of Jaques, the professed cynic, whose criticism is seen to be destructive, joyless, self-absorbed, and without love.

The fullest character of the play, the one who embraces most attitudes within herself and resolves them into a rich synthesis of personality, is Rosalind. Aware of the humorous aspects of love, she knows its potency, too. Her awareness of the danger of folly becomes a self-awareness born of experience, her boyish disguise a means of simultaneously revealing and controlling her emotion. She bears secrets; her revelation that she is a woman is an inward as well as an outward resolution of the play's action. In an early scene Amiens congratulates Duke Senior on being able to "translate the stubbornness of fortune / Into so quiet and so sweet a style" (II.i. 19–20). The quality of human experience is determined partly by the character of the experiencer; Jaques will always be melancholy, but Rosalind and Orlando can win quietness and sweetness from adversity by an exercise of the imagination. To this extent, life can be as we like it.

*As You Like It* gains its impetus rather from the juxtaposition of opposed attitudes than from plot tension. In *Twelfth Night*, also written about 1600 and not published until 1623, Shakespeare returns to a tighter structure. Part of the plot is based on a story from Barnaby Rich's *Farewell to Military Profession* (1581), but Shakespeare idealizes its characters and heightens its romantic tone. The romance framework of separation, search, and reunion that he had already used in *The Comedy of Errors* is here more closely integrated into the action, and there is only one pair of twins to cause comic complications. As in *As You Like It*, love is a unifying motif, but it is often a wistful, frustrated, and sometimes nonsexual emotion. The play opens with Orsino's richly romantic expression of thwarted passion. Death overhangs the early scenes: the death of Olivia's brother, to whose memory she is dedicated, and the supposed death of Viola's brother. Olivia is jested out of her mourning, and Viola is more resilient, but passion continues to be thwarted, sometimes because those who declare it are lost in the fantasies of self-love. Olivia, wooed by Orsino, Sir Andrew, and Malvolio, responds to none of them. She also is thwarted, loving Viola in the belief that she is a man. Viola in her disguise can express her love for Orsino only obliquely. The lovers' folly generates comedy, of which Olivia's fool, Feste, makes much capital. From their first appearance together, an opposition is set up between Malvolio, the professed wise man, and Feste, the professional fool. The exposure of Malvolio is engineered by Maria and Sir Toby Belch, the upholder of the festive virtues of cakes and ale. Feste joins in, and the comedy deepens disturbingly as Malvolio remains incapable of seeing the truth. The play's most positive values are embodied in the enchanting Viola, and it is her reunion with her brother, celebrated in a moving antiphon (V.i. 218–249), that resolves the action. Now there are no obstacles to the union of Viola and Orsino, Olivia and Sebastian. For them, the shadows are dispelled; but Malvolio remains unregenerate, and Sir Toby's harshness to Sir Andrew sours our view of him. After the lovers' happiness, we are left with the wise but lonely Feste's song of the wind and the rain.

### UNROMANTIC COMEDIES AND LATER TRAGEDIES

ABOUT 1600, Shakespeare's imagination turned in new directions. Two tragedies, *Julius Caesar* and *Hamlet*, may even have been written before *Twelfth Night*. An isolated elegy, "The Phoenix and the Turtle," dense, plangent, and probably of irrecoverable allegorical significance, appeared in Robert Chester's *Love's Martyr* in 1601. After that, there appears to be a period of uncertainty and experimentation before the full, confident achievement of the later tragedies.

*All's Well That Ends Well*, first printed in 1623, is usually dated 1602–1603 because of its links with *Measure for Measure*, which can more confidently be assigned to 1604. Since about 1900, these plays, along with *Troilus and Cressida*, have frequently been classed as "problem plays." Shakespeare based the main plot of *All's Well That Ends Well* on a story from Boccaccio's *Decameron*, which he probably read in the English translation in William Painter's *Palace of Pleasure* (1566–1567). He added important characters, notably the Countess; invented the subplot of Parolles; and elaborated both the story and the manner of its telling. In his hands the tale of a physician's daughter who healed a king and demanded as a reward the hand of a handsome, rich, and reluctant young nobleman becomes the vehicle for a discussion of many ideas about human life, especially the extent to which human virtue is innate or acquired. The subplot of the cowardly Parolles illumines the ideas cast up by the main plot, and the comedy of his exposure reflects upon the disgraceful behavior of the nobleman, Bertram. Boccaccio's story employs motifs of fairy tale and folk legend. In some ways Shakespeare enhances its romantic nature, adding, for example, the motif of apparent resurrection that recurs frequently in his work. But his treatment of the story is generally unromantic, producing a tension between the conventionality of some of its elements and the reality of the terms in which he presents them. The play's intellectual qualities, the unromantic nature of its despicable hero, and the fact that the heroine is obliged to behave in an unladylike manner to win him, have counted against its popularity; but it fascinates by its comic brilliance, its passages of tender and delicate emotional writing, and its deeply serious concern with the events and characters that it portrays.

*Measure for Measure*, too, betrays a tension between conventional plot elements and psychological verisimilitude. First printed in 1623, it is based on a two-part play, *Promos and Cassandra* (1578), by George Whetstone. In his first three acts Shakespeare involves us intimately in his characters' moral dilemmas. Claudio's sin of fornication is hardly more than a technical offense. It seems monstrous that he is condemned by Duke Vincentio's "outward-sainted" deputy, Angelo. Isabella's scenes of pleading with Angelo are both personally and intellectually involving, and his internal crisis as he discovers his susceptibility to sexual emotion moves us even while we deplore his duplicity. The scene (III.i) in which the Duke advises Claudio to be "absolute for death" and Claudio expresses his fear of death is a masterly demonstration of what Keats called Shakespeare's "negative capability" in its convincing expression of opposed attitudes.

After this point Shakespeare changes the focus. The duke, in his manipulations, becomes a surrogate playwright. Claudio's fate interests us, yet he appears once only and has a single, brief speech. Angelo becomes a subject of argument rather than an object of psychological exploration. In the final scene much is left to the interpreters. Isabella and the brother she had believed dead are given no words to speak on their reunion, nor does she make any verbal response to the Duke's two unexpected proposals of marriage. Yet the scene works up to an exciting climax as the Duke tests Isabella's capacity to exercise mercy, and, as in *All's Well That Ends Well*, a silent moment of kneeling has great theatrical power. *Measure for Measure* is passionately and explicitly concerned with moral issues. Each of the "good" characters fails in some respect; none of the evil ones lacks some redeeming quality. Even Barnardine, the drunken, convicted murderer, is finally forgiven his "earthly faults." We are all, in the last analysis, "desperately mortal."

The problems of *Troilus and Cressida* differ from those of *All's Well That Ends Well* and *Measure for Measure*. We do not know how long it had been written before its entry in the Stationers' Register on 7 February 1603. The statement made then that it had been played at the Globe was repeated on the original title page of the 1609 quarto, but this page was withdrawn and an added, anonymous epistle described it as "a new play, never staled with the stage, never clapper-clawed with the palms of the vulgar, and passing full of the palm comical." In the Folio it was originally to have appeared among the tragedies, but, perhaps because of copyright difficulties, printing was delayed and it was finally placed between the histories and the tragedies.

This draws attention to problems about the play's genre. Its inspiration is partly classical, partly medieval. Shakespeare went to the first installment of Chapman's translation of Homer, published in 1598, and to Caxton, Lydgate, and Ovid, for the material relating to the siege of Troy; but the love story, which is a late accretion, derives largely from Chaucer's *Troilus and Criseyde*, and the underlying assumptions about the Greeks and Trojans are also generally medieval. The plot is partly historical: it deals with what was regarded as the first important event in the world's history. There is some comedy, largely satirical, in Shakespeare's handling of the story. The tone is in many ways tragic, yet no character achieves tragic stature. *Troilus and Cressida* stands alone, a uniquely exploratory work. It is in every way uncompromising. The language is difficult, the action frequently slow, the dialogue philosophical. Great characters of antiquity—Agamemnon, Achilles, Ajax, Hector—are portrayed as all too fallibly human. Helen, the cause of the Trojan War, is shown on her only appearance (III.i) as a silly sensualist. The most poignant figure is Troilus. Shakespeare makes us feel the intensity of his obsession with Cressida as keenly as his bitter disillusionment at her treachery. Yet we also see him, and the other characters, from outside, as through the wrong end of a telescope, distanced, diminished. Then "Love, friendship, charity" are seen as "subjects all / To envious and calumniating Time" (III.iii. 173–174). Agamemnon epitomizes part of the play's effect in his contrast between the "extant moment" and "what's past and what's to come," which is, he says, "strewed with husks / And formless ruin of oblivion" (IV.v. 166). Thersites, the professional fool, is deflating, reductive, savagely bitter, a railer rather than a jester. As he reduces war to its lowest level, so Pandarus reduces love. Pandarus' final, exhausted meditation breaks across the time barrier of the play, linking the past with the present and suggesting a vision of all between as a "formless ruin of oblivion." All that is left of the great events of Troy is a dying old pander, bequeathing his diseases to the audience.

### LATER TRAGEDIES

A Swiss visitor to London, Thomas Platter, saw a play about Julius Caesar on 21 September 1599. Probably this was an early performance of Shakespeare's play, in which he turns again to politics. Drawing heavily on Thomas North's fine translation of Plutarch's *Lives of the Noble Grecians and Romans* (1579), he turns history into drama, unerringly finding the right style for the subject; the language is classical in its lucidity and eloquence. And he succeeds once again in relating the particular to the general. Characteristically, the first scene sounds a basic theme: the citizens "make holiday to see Caesar, and to rejoice in his triumph," yet the Tribunes denigrate him, and their comments on Pompey, the last popular hero, suggest both the transitoriness of human glory and the fickleness of the

## WILLIAM SHAKESPEARE

mob, which will be much exploited later in the play. Caesar dominates the action even after his death, yet Cassius, Brutus, and Mark Antony are of no less interest. Brutus is one of Shakespeare's most problematic characters. He is "with himself at war" (I.ii. 46), and is easily seen as an adumbration of the later tragic heroes. Self-doubt, perhaps subconscious, is suggested by the rhetoric with which he dresses up the inglorious deed in noble but hollow words: "Let's be sacrificers, but not butchers, Caius" (II.i. 166). Soothing self-delusion contrasts with brutal reality as he talks of "waving our red weapons o'er our heads" crying "'Peace, freedom, and liberty!'" (III.i. 110-111). What this leads to is the senseless and ferocious murder of Cinna the poet (III.iii).

The Romans were especially associated with rhetoric; it is also one of the dramatist's instruments. In this play Shakespeare examines its uses and abuses. With it Cassius seduces Brutus, and Brutus deceives himself and hopes to justify his actions. Caesar creates glory for himself by a rhetoric of action as well as words; and the Forum scene (III.ii) magnificently demonstrates the power of emotive speech to sway men, to lower a crowd into a mob, to overwhelm reason by passion. At its climax we take aesthetic pleasure in the rhetorical virtuosity with which Shakespeare's artistry endows Antony as he calmly, intellectually, manipulates the crowd, finally standing at the still center of the storm of his own creation. Words continue to be important: in the quarrel of Brutus and Cassius (IV.iii), in Antony's taunt that Brutus has tried to disguise his guilt with "good words" (V.i. 30), in the fact that false words cause Cassius' death (V.iii). Antony ends the play with fine words about Brutus, but are they true? Do we know Brutus better than Antony did? Does Shakespeare end with a totally affirmative statement, or an implied question?—with an endorsement of the verdict of history, or a hint that history has its own rhetoric, no more to be trusted than any other of the words of men?

With *Hamlet*, we may feel, Shakespeare's return to tragic territory is complete, yet some critics have classed this work, written and acted by 26 July 1602 (when it was entered on the Stationers' Register), as a problem play. Its rapid popularity is attested by the publication of a pirated, seriously corrupt text—the bad quarto—in 1603. A much better text, apparently based on Shakespeare's manuscript, appeared in the following year. This "good" quarto has about 230 lines that are not in the theatrically influenced First Folio text (1623), which however adds about 80 lines. Editors print a composite version. Shakespeare's source may have been a play, now lost and referred to as the Ur-*Hamlet*, known to have existed by 1589.

*Hamlet* is exceptionally long and ambitious. It is far-ranging in linguistic effect. Shakespeare's virtuosity enables him to create distinctive styles with which to individualize characters such as Claudius, Polonius, the Gravediggers, and Osric. The play offers a wide variety of theatrical entertainment, including such well-tried pleasures as a ghost, a play-within-the-play, a mad scene, a duel, and several deaths. Emotionally, too, the range is wide. This is Shakespeare's most humorous tragedy. Yet the comedy is never incidental. Polonius' verbal deviousness and Osric's affected circumlocutions, comic in themselves, are among the many barriers to honest communication that intensify Hamlet's tragic dilemma. The Gravediggers' phlegmatic humor is an essential element in Hamlet's contemplation of death. And Hamlet's own wit has both a princely elegance that adds to the sense of waste evoked by his destruction, and a savage intellectuality that defines his isolation from those around him and serves him as a weapon against hypocrisy and deception.

Hamlet's appeal derives from his youth, intelligence, charm, vulnerability, and, above all, his intellectual and emotional honesty. He is a raw nerve in the Danish court, disconcertingly liable to make the instinctive rather than the conditioned response. Though this cuts him off from those around him, it puts him into a position of peculiar intimacy with the audience. And in his soliloquies, Shakespeare shows us Hamlet's own raw nerves. Hamlet lacks a distinctive style, at least until the play's closing stages. This is a symptom of his inability to identify himself, to voice his emotions from within a defined personality. But it enables him to speak in a wonderful range of styles, reflecting the openness to experience that is an essential feature of his honesty. The language of his soliloquies presents us not with conclusions, but with the very processes of his mind. Never before had dramatic language so vividly revealed "the quick forge and working-house of thought" (*Henry V*, V Chorus. 23).

Hamlet's progress through the play is a dual exploration of outer and inner worlds. The ghost's command requires that he discover the truth about those who surround him; it leads also to intense self-questioning about his own attitudes to life and, especially, death. During this process he both undergoes and inflicts torments. He causes mental suffering to his mother and to Ophelia, for whose death he is indirectly responsible. He kills Polonius and engineers the deaths of Rosencrantz and Guildenstern. He arrives finally at the truth about the world around him. Whether he ultimately reaches a state of self-knowledge and acceptance is less certain. The new quietude that he demonstrates after his return from England suggests to some critics a fatalistic submission to worldly values; for others, it indicates rather a state of spiritual grace reflecting a full integration of his own personality along with an acknowledgment of human responsibility. Generations of readers and spectators share in Hamlet's self-questionings; it is partly because of his openness to disparate interpretation that he continues to fascinate.

*Othello*, given at court on 1 November 1604 and first published in 1622, must have been written in 1602 or 1603. Like *Romeo and Juliet*, it is based, not on history or legend, but on a contemporary fiction. Shakespeare here transforms a rather sordid tale from Giraldo Cinthio's *Hecatommitthi* (1565), which he seems to have read in Italian. Whereas *Hamlet* is discursive and amplificatory, *Othello* is swift, concise, and tautly constructed. Most of Shakespeare's tragic heroes are royal figures whose fate is inextricably bound up with their nations and whose suffering has a metaphysical dimension. Othello is a servant of the state, not a ruler. His play is in some senses a domestic tragedy, in which we are invited to concentrate on individual human beings rather than to see a connection between their fates and universal, elemental forces. All Shakespeare's tragedies show evil at work. Only in *Othello* is it concentrated in one, centrally placed intriguer. Iago is the playwright within the play. He controls the plot, makes it up as he goes along with improvisatory genius; and, also like the playwright, he retreats ultimately into silence. He is several times called a devil, and historians have seen him as a development of the stereotype of the Vice, an allegorical presentation of an abstract concept. On stage he is as much of a human being as any of the other characters.

In some of Shakespeare's plays we are frequently invited to see the stage action as emblematic of a larger dramatic conflict being played out on a universal stage. The significance of *Othello* resides more purely in the passions and fates of the human beings whom we see before us. But Shakespeare does not present the tale as a documentary imitation of reality. We are made conscious of paradox. Iago, who reveals his villainy to the audience, is "honest" to everyone in the play except Roderigo. Othello's physical blackness joins with the traditional symbolism of black and white as a fruitful source of irony and ambiguity. The language draws our attention to general concepts, and causes us to reflect on the varieties of human behavior. Iago is a rationalist. His characteristic language is a cynically reductive prose; he speaks of the act of love as a bestial coupling: "An old black ram / Is tupping your white ewe" (I.i. 89–90). Othello is a nobly credulous idealist. His "free and open nature" makes him think "men honest that but seem to be so" (I.iii. 393–394). His susceptibility to Iago's corruptive power is a concomitant of his virtue. For him, Shakespeare created a magniloquent verse style suggestive rather of imagination than of intellectuality. The contrast between these two, the way that Iago drags Othello down to his own level, and that Othello, too late, shakes himself clear of him, forms the central dramatic action. The universality of the play lies in our consciousness of Iago's plausibility and our sympathy with Othello's insecurities. Inside the most loving human relationship lie seeds that, once germinated, may destroy it. In Claudius' words:

> There lies within the very flame of love
> A kind of wick or snuff that will abate it.
> (*Hamlet*, IV.vii. 114–115)

In *King Lear*, Shakespeare compounded a story from legendary history with one from prose fiction. Holinshed tells briefly the tale of King Lear. Other versions (all ending happily) include a play, *King Leir*, written by 1594, which is one of Shakespeare's sources. Its publication in 1605 may have given him the impetus to write his play, first recorded in a court performance on 26 December 1606 and printed in 1608. His subplot of the earl of Gloucester derives from Sir Philip Sidney's *Arcadia* (1590). His interweaving of the two stories is crucial to his design. Lear and Gloucester are both faulty but not wicked. Lear has two evil daughters and a good one, Gloucester has an evil son and a good one. Each misjudges his offspring, favors but is turned against by the evil ones, wrongs the good one, suffers as a consequence, learns the truth, and dies. Gloucester's error and suffering are mainly physical. His evil son, Edmund, is a bastard, begotten in adultery. The climax of Gloucester's suffering comes when Lear's daughters, Goneril and Regan, put out his eyes. Lear's fault lies in his warped judgment, and his suffering is primarily mental; its climax is his madness after his daughters have cast him out into the storm. Other characters relate to this patterning. The Fool, physically frail, "labours to out-jest" Lear's "heart-struck injuries" (III.i. 16–17) and to bring him to an understanding of his situation by way of his mind, in snatches of song, witticisms, paradoxes, and parables. Kent, the other servant who remains faithful to Lear through the storm, is more practical, ministering rather to his physical needs. Edmund's sexuality, which in his adulterous relationship with both Goneril and Regan brings about his downfall, recalls his father's. Edgar, Gloucester's virtuous son, metamorphosed into Poor Tom, is of both physical and mental help to his father. The callous, skeptical rationality of Edmund, Goneril, and Regan is opposed to the imagination and sympathy of Edgar, the Fool, and Cordelia.

The employment of the two basic components of human life, the body and the mind, as a structural principle reflects the depth of Shakespeare's concern with fundamentals in this play. In his examination of the values by which men live, he stresses the pre-Christian setting of his story, avoiding any suggestion of religious dogma. His play explores the paradoxes of value. Those who are committed to the world and the flesh destroy themselves. They are deceived by false appearances; so, initially, are Gloucester and Lear. But these two come to "see better" (I.i. 157) when they trust the mind rather than the body. Nowhere is this more apparent than in Shakespeare's causing Gloucester's apprehension of the truth about his sons to follow immediately upon his blinding: "A man may see how this world goes with no eyes" (IV.vi. 150–151). Lear and Gloucester go through purgatory and commune with one another in the amazing scene on Dover cliff. Lear's cynical and disillusioned statements here are only one facet of the play. After this comes his return to sanity and his reconciliation with Cordelia, which is also a reconciliation with life. Nor is this negated by Cordelia's death. This relentlessly unsentimental play puts Lear through the greatest mental torment, but ultimately the man who had vowed never again to see Cordelia's face seeks desperately in her eyes for signs of life. He has learned that she is indeed "most rich, being poor; / Most choice, forsaken; and most lov'd, despis'd" (I.i. 250–251). His final outpouring of love is unselfish; she can do nothing for him now. Her body is dead and useless, but the values for which she stood are those that endure.

*Macbeth*, written probably in 1606, is easily Shakespeare's shortest tragedy. Its topic was particularly relevant to the patron of his company, James I, and the only surviving text, of 1623, may have been specially written or adapted for court performance. Holinshed again provided the basic narrative, but, as in *King Lear*, Shakespeare treated it with much more freedom than in the English histories. To a greater extent even than in *King Lear*, he seems more interested in general ideas than in historical accuracy or particularity of characterization. Many of the characters are purely functional. Duncan is primarily a symbol of the values that Macbeth is to overthrow. He is counterbalanced by the equally generalized Weird Sisters. Even Banquo figures mainly as a measure of the norm from which Macbeth deviates. The witches, with their incantations, spells, and grotesque rituals, suggest evil as a universal force that can be tapped and channeled through human agents.

Like her counterparts in *King Lear*, Lady Macbeth, the play's principal human embodiment of evil, attempts to deny the powers of the imagination. A speech from *All's Well That Ends Well* epitomizes this aspect of *Macbeth*. "They say miracles are past," says Lafeu, "and we have our philosophical persons to make modern and familiar things supernatural and causeless. Hence is it that we make trifles of terrors, ensconcing ourselves into seeming knowledge when we should submit ourselves to an unknown fear" (II.iii. 1–6). Lady Macbeth seeks to reduce "supernatural and causeless"—inexplicable—things to the level of the "modern"—commonplace—"and familiar": "The sleeping and the dead/Are but as pictures. . . . A little water clears us of this deed" (II.ii. 53–54, 67). This is the "seeming knowledge" that turns "terrors" into "trifles," and refuses to acknowledge the "unknown fear" of which Macbeth is so vividly conscious. His imaginative visions almost overwhelm his reason. Better for him if they had, for the play acts out the truth of Lafeu's statement. Lady Macbeth's rationalistic urgings of her husband are at odds with her own incantation "Come you spirits. . . ." (I.v. 37ff.), and when her reason breaks down, her self-assurance is seen to be only a "seeming knowledge" that gives way, too late, to the "unknown fear." Her sleepwalking scene, a soliloquy unheard even by its speaker, is a technically brilliant device to reveal the subconscious acknowledgment in her divided being of "things supernatural and causeless."

In his last three tragedies Shakespeare returns to more fully documented periods of history and, in two of them, to a more particularized presentation of it. The exception is *Timon of Athens*, a problematic play. Thematic resemblances to *King Lear* and *Coriolanus* along with stylistic evidence cause it generally to be dated 1606–1608, but the state of the text, first printed in 1623, is such that study of it can be only provisional. As it appears to have been printed from an uncompleted manuscript, it is exceptionally interesting to the student of Shakespeare's working methods. There are signs of the rapidity of composition with which he was credited by his contemporaries. He seems to have been anxious to lay down the groundwork, to evolve a shape and structure that could later have been filled in. He concentrates on the central role, which is long and taxing. Minor characters might have been developed later; there is uncertainty about some of their names, and there are many anomalies in the action. While some of the language, both verse and prose, is polished, other passages are obviously in draft, veering between verse and prose. There are strong lines of recurrent imagery that might later have been more subtly worked into the structure. The acts of eating and drinking, for instance, and the opposition between roots and gold take on heavily symbolic associations. As in *King Lear*, Shakespeare is concerned with the difference between "true need," which can be satisfied by roots, and superfluity, represented by banquets and gold.

We usually read the play in an edited version, in which some of the imperfections have been smoothed away. Much more tinkering is needed to create a performable text. The result is that this play is peculiarly open to interpretation, raising more questions than it answers. Its strongly schematic quality allies it more closely with *King Lear* and *Macbeth* than with *Coriolanus* and *Antony and Cleopatra*. It is based on Plutarch and treats Timon's story as a two-part structure: Timon in prosperity, followed by Timon in adversity. In the first part, the rich, lavish, magnanimous lord is contrasted with Apemantus, the cynic philosopher. As Timon learns that he has spent all he owned, his flatterers are revealed, in skillfully satirical episodes, as a "knot of mouth-friends" (III.vi. 89), and Apemantus is partly justified. An awkwardly unrelated scene, which might well have become the climax of a subplot, shows the Athenians' ingratitude to Alcibiades. The second part, as it stands, is virtually an interrupted soliloquy by Timon, in which he encounters those he had known in his former way of life. In his misanthropy induced by disillusionment he is as extravagant as he had previously been in his generosity. Now he resembles Apemantus, as a fine scene (IV.iii) between them shows, but Apemantus is a contented cynic, whereas Timon needs to give full emotional vent to his rejection of mankind. The appearance of his steward, Flavius, comes as a reminder of the possibility of love, loyalty, and friendship; and Timon himself accepts, though with difficulty, that he is mistaken in his wholesale denunciation of mankind. The final scenes, showing Timon's death and Alcibiades' successful campaign against Athens, are sketchy.

*Timon of Athens* is underdeveloped and inconclusive. Its tone is harsh and bitter, though other attitudes are present in Flavius and other servants, in Alcibiades, even in Timon's tirades, which suggest a desire to be reconciled with humanity by the very force with which he rejects it. The play has pungent invective, clever satire, a few passages of noble poetry, a clear if crude structure, and some profound revelations of humanity. We can only guess what it might have become if Shakespeare had completed it.

His remaining tragedies, *Coriolanus* and *Antony and Cleopatra*, both first published in 1623, are based closely on Plutarch and reflect Plutarch's concern with the idiosyncrasies and oddities of human character and with the way such characteristics shape national as well as human destinies. *Coriolanus* (probably written 1607–1608) tells a story of war and peace, love and hate. The broad framework is one of national warfare, epitomized in a personal conflict between Caius Marcius, later Coriolanus, and the Volscian leader, Tullus Aufidius. Their relationship is ambiguous; after Coriolanus has been banished from Rome, Aufidius welcomes him with "I . . . do contest/As hotly and as nobly with thy love/As ever in ambitious strength I did/Contend against thy valour" (IV.v. 109–113). Strife within Rome also resolves itself into a largely personal conflict, between Coriolanus and the two unscrupulous Tribunes. His arrogance, inseparable from his valor, brings about his banishment, so that from being the enemy within the state he becomes identified with the enemy outside it. He is at conflict, too, within his own family. His mother, Volumnia, eager for his fame, expresses her love for him in terms that might rather betoken hatred: "O, he is wounded, I thank the gods for't" (II.i. 114). Sharing his hatred of the commons, she yet advises him to dissemble with his nature to catch their votes, and so forces a conflict within Coriolanus himself. His efforts to play the part for which she casts him produce some comedy, but the issues of integrity and honor with which the play is concerned are focused in his ultimate refusal to do so, "Lest I surcease to honour mine own truth,/And by my body's action teach my mind/A most inherent baseness" (III.ii. 121–122). In his consequent banishment he has to pretend hatred of those he loves. When his family come to plead with him, he is forced into self-recognition: "I melt, and am not/Of stronger earth than others" (V.iii. 28–29). His mother insists again on the need for compromise, for, if he conquers Rome, he conquers her. He "holds her by the hand, silent" in a moment of submission that is also a moment of self-examination.

> O mother, mother!
> What have you done? Behold, the heavens do ope,
> The gods look down, and this unnatural scene
> They laugh at. O my mother, mother! O!
> You have won a happy victory to Rome;
> But for your son—believe it, O believe it!—
> Most dangerously you have with him prevail'd,
> If not most mortal to him. But let it come.
> (V.iv. 182–189)

Acknowledging that he can no longer maintain a godlike aloofness from natural emotion, he accepts the full burden of his humanity and also the inevitability of his death. "But let it come" is the equivalent in this play to Hamlet's "The readiness is all," and to "Ripeness is all" in *King Lear*. But it is the final paradox of the mother-son relationship in *Coriolanus* that Volumnia, in calling forth a full expression of her son's love, brings about his death. Thus closely are love and hate allied.

*Coriolanus* is a great achievement of the intellect and the historical imagination. Its characteristic style seems to be carved out of granite. *Antony and Cleopatra*, written about the same time (it was entered in the Stationers' Register on 20 May 1608), is less intellectual and even more imaginative. Few of Shakespeare's plays derive their greatness less from their design, more from their characterization and language. Its style is supple, relaxed, and sensuous. Cleopatra rivals Falstaff as Shakespeare's greatest feat of characterization, and her "infinite variety" is created largely by the flexibility and range of the language with which Shakespeare endows her. The scope of *Antony and Cleopatra* is vast. The action takes place over an area that seems particularly large because characters move so easily from one part of it to another, far distant. Empires are at stake; the play is peopled by their leaders. Nevertheless, much of the play's setting is domestic. Many scenes portray the home life of Egypt's queen, and Shakespeare's greatness as a dramatic writer shows itself particularly in a dialogue of nuance, which gives great significance to oblique statements, exclamations, pauses, and silences. So when Cleopatra is brought to comfort Antony after his "doting" withdrawal from battle:

| | |
|---|---|
| *Eros* | Nay, gentle madam, to him! Comfort him. |
| *Iras* | Do, most dear Queen. |
| *Charmian* | Do? Why, what else? |
| *Cleopatra* | Let me sit down. O Juno! |
| *Antony* | No, no, no, no, no. |
| *Eros* | See you here, sir? |
| *Antony* | O, fie, fie, fie! |
| *Charmian* | Madam! |
| *Iras* | Madam, O good Empress! |
| *Eros* | Sir, sir! (III.ix. 25–34) |

Or, in one of Shakespeare's most pregnant monosyllables:

| | |
|---|---|
| *Thyreus* | He [Caesar] knows that you embrace not Antony As you did love, but as you fear'd him. |
| *Cleopatra* | O! (III.xiii. 56–57) |

But when necessary Shakespeare writes to the very height of his eloquence. Language is intimately related to form, and so a double tragedy presents special problems. In Shakespeare's only other one, *Romeo and Juliet,* the hero and heroine at least die in the same scene; here, their deaths are necessarily separated, and Shakespeare averts anticlimax in the second, Cleopatra's, partly by introducing a new character—the Clown who carries the instrument of her death—partly by the richly symbolic nature of her conversation with him, and, above all, by the transcendent poetry of her closing speeches.

The tension between Egyptian and Roman values in *Antony and Cleopatra* is an aspect of Shakespeare's recurrent portrayal of the opposing claims of festivity and austerity, license and discipline, in plays such as *Twelfth Night* and *1* and *2 Henry IV.* Style and imagery cause us to relate this conflict to the divergent claims of the imagination and the reason, and to man's sense of the potential glory of human achievement along with his awareness of the limitations imposed by mortality. So, as in *Julius Caesar* and *Troilus and Cressida,* we can both live in the moment and see it in relation to eternity. Antony is "the triple pillar of the world" and a "strumpet's fool" (I.i. 12–13); "Kingdoms are clay" (I.i. 35); "Royal Egypt" is "No more but e'en a woman . . ." (IV.xv. 71–73); and the instrument of Cleopatra's death is a worm. These extremes are shown not simply in opposition, but sometimes in double perspective, at other times, movingly, in dissolution from one to the other: Antony, dying, "cannot hold this visible shape" (IV.xiv. 14), "The crown o' th' earth doth melt" (IV.xv. 63). Ultimately Shakespeare seems to support the values of sensitivity and the imagination. In Falstaff he had done so covertly; here, he does so openly. Enobarbus learns the limitations of reason and regrets that he has followed its dictates; and Cleopatra's ultimate celebration of the flesh in the spirit creates a vision that may lack substance but is glorious while it lasts. No other tragic character except, perhaps, Wagner's Isolde, dies with such exaltation.

### LATE SHAKESPEARE

We saw that Shakespeare's return to tragedy overlapped with his later experiments in comedy. Similarly, while he was writing his last tragedies his thoughts seem to have been turning again to comedy, though only, as we should expect, because he saw new possibilities in the form. Four of his late plays make up perhaps the most closely interrelated group among his output. All employ motifs of romance literature. Their plots include highly improbable and supernatural elements. They tell of highborn families and lovers separated by catastrophe, sometimes natural, sometimes humanly contrived. They span large areas of space and time, and involve leading characters in great suffering. Settings are remote. The presentation of character tends to the general and the ideal. Suffering is overcome, obstacles to reunion and reconciliation are removed, sometimes as a result of supernatural intervention, and harmony is restored.

All these characteristics can be found in Shakespeare's earlier comedies, but they are present in greater concentration in what are variously known as the Last Plays, the Romances, or the Late Romances. And these plays have more than superficial resemblances. Shakespeare was never one-track minded. Even plays that employ a relatively narrow focus, such as *Richard II* and *King Lear*, have a range of emotional impact. *Timon of Athens* shows the extremes of a man's experience but, as Apemantus says, little between them: "The middle of humanity thou never knewest, but the extremity of both ends" (IV.iii. 299–301). In his late plays Shakespeare shows a wish to encompass the extremes in a yoking of opposites that will confine a full range of human experience within the local and temporal limitations of a play, and will synthesize the disparate elements so as to allow each to exert its energy.

External influences have sometimes been adduced as an explanation of Shakespeare's change of direction. The increased use of spectacle in the late plays has been attributed both to the growing popularity of masques at court and to the acquisition by the King's Men of an indoor theater, the Blackfriars, which would offer increased opportunities for spectacular staging. Yet the company continued to use the Globe, and the late plays were performed there as well. The first, *Pericles*, presents almost as many problems as *Timon of Athens*. It may have been written before both the purchase of the Blackfriars and the composition of the last of the tragedies. It is based on the old story of Apollonius of Tyre, told by John Gower in his *Confessio Amantis* (1385–1393), and on the version of it in Laurence Twine's *The Pattern of Painful Adventures* (1576?). Shakespeare had already used the tale, in *The Comedy of Errors*, and his attention may have been drawn to it again by the reissue of Twine's book in 1607. Like *Antony and Cleopatra*, *Pericles* was entered in the Stationers' Register on 20 May 1608 by Edward Blount, who, however, published neither. A prose romance by George Wilkins, *The Painful Adventures of Pericles, Prince of Tyre*, published in 1608, refers to the play on the title page and borrows from both it and Twine. *Pericles* was very popular on the stage, but the text published in 1609 is corrupt. It was reprinted five times by 1635, but Heminges and Condell omitted it from the First Folio, presumably because they knew how defective this text was and could not find a better. It is so badly garbled, especially in the first two acts, as to have raised doubts about its title-page ascription to Shakespeare, and some scholars believe that it was either his revision of another dramatist's work or a collaboration.

Editors of *Pericles*, as of *Timon of Athens*, smooth away some of its defects. If we read it with sympathy, we can imagine that the authentic play stood high among Shakespeare's achievements. The device of a presenter, the poet Gower, is used to frame and control the far-flung narrative; and the archaic style and naive tone of his choruses induce the proper mood for the reception of a tale of wonder. The initial stages of the action, in which Pericles gains a wife, Thaisa, are episodic; but it gains in concentration with the birth at sea of their daughter, Marina, and Thaisa's apparent death. Even in its damaged state, some of the verse associated with these events has a unique magic. Marina is a mystically ideal portrayal of the power of chastity, and her presence in a brothel, the inmates of which are sketched with truly Shakespearian immediacy, is one illustration of the play's use of extremes. As in all the romances, there is a strong sense that life is controlled by inscrutable, if ultimately beneficent, powers, symbolized by sea and storm. Thus, Marina laments:

> Ay me! poor maid,
> Born in a tempest, when my mother died,
> This world to me is like a lasting storm,
> Whirring me from my friends.
> (IV.i. 18–21)

Out of the tempest comes a calm of which music is the apt symbol. Thaisa, believed dead and committed to the waves, is revived to the sound of instruments, and Marina sings to her father to try to restore him from the coma into which grief has driven him. Their protracted reunion scene, masterly in its control, draws from Pericles' lines in which he expresses two recurrent ideas of these plays: the close relationship between the apparent extremes of pain and joy, and the capacity of the young to renew their parents' lives:

O Helicanus, strike me, honour'd sir;
Give me a gash, put me to present pain,
Lest this great sea of joys rushing upon me
O'erbear the shores of my mortality,
And drown me with their sweetness. O, come hither,
Thou that beget'st him that did thee beget;
Thou that wast born at sea, buried at Tharsus,
And found at sea again!         (V.i. 189–196)

When Marina's identity is established, the music of the spheres induces in Pericles a vision of Diana leading to the revelation that Thaisa is alive and to the miraculously joyful outcome of the action.

Shakespeare appears to have followed *Pericles* with *Cymbeline*, composed probably 1609–1610 and first published in 1623, in which he implausibly yokes together Roman Britain and Renaissance Italy. The historical background is freely based on Holinshed, and the intrigue tale derives from Boccaccio. The play is peopled by antithetical characters: some, such as Imogen, Pisanio, Belarius, and those children of nature, Arviragus and Guiderius, are paragons of virtue; others, such as Cloten and the Queen, are "Too bad for bad report" (I.i. 17). Iachimo moves from outright villainy to penitence; Posthumus from virtue to debasement brought about by Iachimo's deception, and back to virtue again. Some of the characters seem the reverse of their true selves: the Queen conceals her villainy from most of those around her, Posthumus is made to believe that Imogen is false to him; some—Imogen, Cloten, Posthumus—are disguised for part of the action; others—Arviragus and Guiderius—are unaware of their own true identity. The plot is based on both national and personal opposition: Britain and Rome are at war; many of the characters are at enmity with one another. The design of some of the scenes stresses the falsity of appearance, as when Cloten's attendant lords comment upon him in ironical asides (I.ii), or the Queen's villainous plotting is framed by her instructions to her ladies about gathering flowers (I.v). The language, too, is frequently antithetical. The play's oppositions reach their climax in the scene (IV.ii) in which Imogen, disguised as a boy and believed to be dead as the result of the Queen's drugs, is mourned by the two young men who, unknown to any of them, are her brothers, and lain to rest beside the headless body of Cloten. She has said she values him less than the "meanest garment" of her husband, Posthumus; now he is dressed in Posthumus' clothes. The beauty of the verse in which Imogen is mourned and of the flowers with which the bodies are strewn is juxtaposed with the hideous spectacle of the headless corpse; and her waking speech, in which she identifies Cloten with Posthumus, is perhaps the most bizarre and daring in the whole of Shakespeare.

If this scene gives us both heaven and hell simultaneously, the final one gives us heaven alone. It is prepared for by the appearance of Jupiter to the sleeping Posthumus, which raises the action on to a plane of the ideal. The multiple denouements of the final scene, in which all disguises are removed, all identities made known, and all misunderstandings removed, strike with the wonder—and, unless tactfully performed, the implausibility—of the miraculous achievement of the impossible. In the play's closing lines, Cymbeline celebrates the resolution of discord into harmony:

    . . . Let
A Roman and a British ensign wave
Friendly together . . .
. . . Never was a war did cease,
Ere bloody hands were wash'd, with such a peace.

*Cymbeline* is a fantasy, an exercise in virtuosity, intricate in style and self-conscious in its artifice. In *The Winter's Tale*, which Simon Forman saw at the Globe on 15 May 1611 and which was probably written later than *Cymbeline*, Shakespeare engages more closely with reality. The story, based on a prose romance of the 1580's, Robert Greene's *Pandosto*, covers sixteen years and moves in space from the Sicilian court to the Bohemian countryside, and back to the court again. The central character, Leontes, king of Sicily, passes through extremes of emotion, from the near tragedy of his suffering, culminating in the death of his son and the apparent deaths of his wife and daughter, through the "saint-like sorrow" (V.i. 2) of his penitence to the rapture of the ending, in which he is reunited with those he had believed dead.

Shakespeare fully exploits the variety of theatrical entertainment inherent in this material.

But whereas *Cymbeline* works largely through the juxtaposition of opposed elements, *The Winter's Tale* is notable rather for the transitions by which the movement between extremes is controlled. Leontes' obsessive sexual jealousy is vividly experienced, but the audience is partly distanced from it by Paulina's ironical attitude and by the grotesqueness of Leontes' language. The first movement of the play reaches a powerful climax in the trial of his queen, Hermione (III.ii). Shakespeare skillfully guides us into the idealized pastoralism of the middle section by presenting the terrible (and improbable) subsequent events—the abandonment of Leontes' infant daughter, Perdita, on the shore of Bohemia along with the deaths of Antigonus and the entire crew of the ship on which they traveled—through the eyes of the comically uninvolved Clown and with the assistance of the notorious bear (III.iii).

Long gaps of time are inconvenient to dramatists. Shakespeare solves the problem in *The Winter's Tale* by giving Time a prominent place in the play's structure of ideas. The opening scene includes a poetic evocation of childhood illusions of timelessness (I.i. 62–74); Time makes a personal appearance, as the Chorus (IV.i); Florizel's love speech magically suggests that Perdita's beauty and his love for her can suspend the passage of time (IV.iv. 134–143); the concluding episodes show time offering opportunities for repentance and redemption; and a sense of renewal is created by the fact that the son and daughter of the estranged kings bring about their parents' reconciliation by their marriage. Also prominent among the play's ideas is the antithesis, commonplace in the thought of the period, between art and nature. Their relationship is explicitly discussed in IV.iv, and a kind of art is apparent in the exercise of the will by which Leontes expresses his penitence and the lovers control their ardor.

These ideas merge in the final scene. Shakespeare departs from his source in keeping Hermione alive, and the daring stroke of making her pose as her own statue is symbolically appropriate as well as theatrically effective. Hermione's resurrection is a conquest over time. Self-control brings its rewards as art melts into nature and the stone becomes flesh. The play ends in the joy and wonder characteristic of romance, but they are counterpointed by our consciousness of the suffering out of which the miracle has emerged.

Shakespeare's last independently written play, *The Tempest*, published in 1623, was performed at court on 1 November 1611; probably he wrote it during that year. In its composition he drew on his reading of Ovid, Montaigne, and contemporary travel literature; but he wove the plot out of his own imagination, creating a fantasy that is his most overtly symbolic drama. We have no reason to believe that he knew he was coming to the end of his career, but it is easy to see this as an exceptionally personal play. In it he disciplines the sprawling material of romance by confining it within the limits of the neoclassical unities that he had employed only once before, in the early *Comedy of Errors*. Instead of following the events of the tale from beginning to end and place to place, he concentrates the action into a few hours and the locale into a few acres. We see only the end of the story; the earlier stages are recapitulated in Prospero's narration. This creates a tension between form and content that finds many correspondences in the action. Like Oberon, Duke Vincentio, and Iago before him, Prospero is a playwright within the play. He seeks to discipline his erring fellows and needs self-discipline to do so. His power, though magical, is limited. He can create visions, but they are easily destroyed: the masque vanishes into air at his recollection of Caliban's malice. Prospero can exercise moral influence, but only over those who are predisposed to receive it. Alonso and Ferdinand are better for their experiences, but Antonio and Sebastian remain unregenerate.

It is easy to see this as an allegory of the artist and his work. The masque can only fulfill its purpose of pleasing and instructing if it is received with sympathy. The artist needs a fit audience. *The Tempest* itself may be regarded as one of the glories of mankind or a load of wastepaper. To this extent it may properly be considered as an autobiographical document. But it is very much more. The compression of the plot necessitates a high degree of stylization. The resultant symbolic action and generalized characterization open the play to a wide range of interpretation. Though Prospero can be seen as an artist, he can be seen also as a father, a teacher, a scholar, a scientist, a magistrate, an explorer, a ruler, even a god. We can discuss the play in terms of the artist and his public; but it relates also to many of the concepts that we have found recurring in Shakespeare's work: art and nature, nature and fortune, the imagination and reason, justice and mercy, sin and retribution, guilt and repentance, right rule and rebellion, illusion and reality, self-deception and self-knowledge.

*The Tempest* resists clear-cut allegorical readings; this is a measure of its success. It is a supremely poetic drama, not just because it includes some of Shakespeare's greatest poetry, but because it speaks, as the greatest poetry does, on many levels, universally relevant and—if we can hear Ariel's music—universally effective.

### SHAKESPEARE AND FLETCHER

SHAKESPEARE's successor as leading dramatist for the King's Men was John Fletcher (1579–1625), known for his collaboration with Francis Beaumont (*ca.* 1584–1616), who gave up writing for the stage about 1613. At about this time, Fletcher appears to have begun to collaborate with Shakespeare. *Henry VIII*, published as the last of the Histories in the First Folio (1623), was in performance, possibly for the first time, at the Globe when the theater burned down on 29 June 1613. For a long time its attribution to Shakespeare was unquestioned, but in 1850 James Spedding propounded the theory that parts of it are by Fletcher, and many other scholars have followed him in this belief. Certainly in its overall layout it is unlike the history plays that Shakespeare had written during the 1590's, though in its elegiac tone, its generalized characterization, and the sense that it conveys of destiny working itself out through human life, it has something in common with his romances. It has less variety than most of Shakespeare's plays and presents a series of tableaux showing, as the Prologue says, "How . . . mightiness meets misery." We see the falls successively of Buckingham, Wolsey, and Queen Katherine, each of them eloquent in resignation. But the play works toward the birth of Anne Boleyn's child, and the last scene fulsomely celebrates not only the future Queen Elizabeth I, but also her successor, the patron of the King's Men.

So shall she leave her blessedness to one—
When heaven shall call her from this cloud of darkness—
Who from the sacred ashes of her honour
Shall star-like rise, as great in fame as she was,
And so stand fix'd.    (V.v. 43–47)

This speech is not generally attributed to Shakespeare.

*Henry VIII* has been successful in the theater. It offers several strong acting roles and great opportunities for spectacle, which have caused it to be performed particularly at times of national rejoicing, such as coronations. Some of its most effective passages, including Wolsey's well-known "Farewell, a long farewell, to all my greatness!" (III.ii. 351), are attributed to Fletcher. According to a Stationers' Register entry of 9 September 1653, Shakespeare and Fletcher collaborated on a play called *Cardenio*, now lost, which was given twice at court by the King's Men in the season 1613–1614. A manuscript of it may have lain beyond a play called *The Double Falsehood* by Lewis Theobald, one of Shakespeare's editors, which was acted at Drury Lane in 1727 and printed the following year. The last surviving play in which Shakespeare is believed to have had a hand is *The Two Noble Kinsmen*, a tragicomedy written at some time between February 1613 (the date of the performance of a masque by Francis Beaumont from which it borrows a dance) and 31 October 1614 (when Jonson's *Bartholomew Fair*, which contains an allusion to it, was first performed). It was omitted from the First Folio but appeared in 1634 as "written by the memorable worthies of their time, Mr John Fletcher, and Mr William Shakespeare, Gent." The passages generally attributed to Shakespeare make up about one-third of the play and are characteristic of his late verse style.

The works surveyed in the preceding pages have given Shakespeare his status as the greatest writer in English, perhaps in any language. Like most great artists, he built on foundations laid by other men. His genius was not primarily innovative, though, as we have seen, he constantly experimented with dramatic forms and techniques. The theatrical medium appears to have provided a necessary challenge that sometimes constrained him. In plays such as *The Comedy of Errors, As You Like It, Othello,* and *The Tempest* we feel an absolute matching of content and form. In others, such as *The Merchant of Venice, Hamlet, King Lear,* and *Cymbeline,* signs of struggle may be discerned. The teeming fullness of Shakespeare's creativity results sometimes in writing of convoluted, even bizarre, density and in structures that make exceptional demands in both complexity and length on theater audiences.

Yet his powers as an entertainer were such that his plays can appeal on many levels. The best of them are dramatic and linguistic structures of infinite complexity, which explore mankind's most fundamental concerns. Even in so brief a study as this we have seen something of his interest in government of both the individual and the state, in the moral pressures of society upon the individual, in the part played by reason and the imagination in human affairs, in the need for self-knowledge, in the relation between the past and present, and in the power of language. These are philosophical questions. Shakespeare uses the emblematic and metaphorical techniques of the poetic dramatist to body them forth with a wholly human particularity that is as recognizable today as it was to his first audiences.

### THE PUBLICATION OF SHAKESPEARE'S WORKS

SHAKESPEARE seems to have concerned himself with the printing of only two of his works, the poems *Venus and Adonis* (1593) and *The Rape of Lucrece* (1594). These volumes bear his only dedications, both to the earl of Southampton, and are carefully printed. As for the plays, Shakespeare apparently regarded performance as publication. The scripts belonged to the company, which in general was not anxious to release them for performance. But there was a market for printed plays, and several of Shakespeare's appeared first in corrupt texts that seem to have been assembled from memory by some of the actors who appeared in them. These are known as the "bad" quartos. Sometimes, however, printers were able to work from Shakespeare's own manuscripts, or transcripts of them. Texts produced from such authoritative sources are known, even when they are poorly printed, as "good" quartos. Altogether, nineteen of Shakespeare's plays appeared in separately printed editions in his own lifetime, and *Othello* followed in 1622. Some appeared only in bad texts, some only in good ones, and some in both. The Sonnets were printed in 1609 in a good text.

After Shakespeare died, his colleagues John Heminges and Henry Condell undertook a collected edition of his plays. They had at their disposal the printed quartos and a number of manuscripts, some of which had been annotated for theatrical use. They brought them together in the First Folio, which appeared in 1623, with the Droeshout engraving of Shakespeare, their dedication to the brother earls of Pembroke and Montgomery, their epistle "To the Great Variety of Readers," several commendatory poems including the well-known one by Ben Jonson, and a list of the "Principal Actors" in the plays. The Folio included eighteen plays not previously printed but omitted *Pericles* and *The Two Noble Kinsmen.*

No literary manuscript by Shakespeare survives, unless we accept the attribution to him of three pages of a collaborative play, *Sir Thomas More,* of uncertain date. Otherwise the early printed editions give us our only evidence of what Shakespeare wrote. Unfortunately, this evidence is often unreliable and conflicting. There are many misprints both in the quartos and in the Folio, some obvious, some only suspected. When a play survives in both quarto and Folio, there are often divergences that may be attributed to a variety of causes, including errors of transcription; printing errors; theatrical alterations, omissions, and additions; censorship; authorial revision; and so on. Even the Folio-only plays sometimes show signs of departing from the author's manuscript from which they must ultimately derive.

For a long time no systematic attempts were made to correct Shakespeare's texts. In reprints of the quartos, which went on appearing during the seventeenth century, sporadic corrections of obvious misprints were made, but these texts have no independent authority. Nor do the reprints of the Folio of 1632, 1663, and 1685. The second issue (1664) of the third Folio was the first to include *Pericles;* it also added six apocryphal plays.

Only in the eighteenth century was a start made on the process of correcting the early texts and presenting them in newly attractive and helpful ways. In 1709 the playwright Nicholas Rowe issued an edition, in six volumes, which was prefaced by the first formal biography and illustrated with engravings. It was based on the fourth Folio, with some consultation of quartos; but Rowe, like almost all subsequent editors, introduced modernizations of spelling and punctuation. His is the first edition to divide the plays systematically into acts and scenes, and to indicate locations for the scenes. He also made many necessary textual corrections. The process that Rowe began was continued and developed by many later editors with varying degrees of thoroughness and scholarship. For modern readers, editions from Rowe's to those of the mid-nineteenth century are of mainly historical interest; but it is worth remembering that during this period most of the standard emendations were made, and many explanatory annotations that are still current were first offered. Equally, many conventions of presentation were established, some of which continued to be adopted, often unthinkingly, by later editors. Rowe's successors included Alexander Pope (1723–1725); Lewis Theobald (1733); Sir Thomas Hanmer (1743–1744); William Warburton (1747); Samuel Johnson (1765), whose preface and notes put him among the great Shakespeare critics; Edward Capell (1767–1768); George Steevens (1773, 1778, 1785, 1793); and Edmond Malone (1790). Much of the scholarship of these editors was brought together in the second edition of Malone, completed by James Boswell the younger, published in 1823, and sometimes called the Third Variorum. (The First Variorum [1803] was Isaac Reed's, based on Steevens; the Second Variorum was an 1813 reprint of this.)

Of the many complete editions that appeared during the nineteenth century, the most important is the nine-volume Cambridge Shakespeare (1863–1866, revised 1891–1893), edited by W. G. Clark, J. Glover, and W. A. Wright. For many years this edition was the standard text, especially in the single-volume, Globe version of 1864. In 1871 appeared the first volume of the American New Variorum, a play-by-play edition edited originally by H. H. Furness, which is still in progress. W. J. Craig's Oxford edition dates from 1891, and the thirty-seven volumes of the original Arden edition were published from 1899 to 1924.

At the beginning of the twentieth century a revolution in textual studies greatly advanced understanding of the bases of Shakespeare's text and transformed attitudes to the editing of his works. A number of important editions have resulted. *The New Shakespeare* (1921–1966), edited by J. Dover Wilson and others, has valuable notes and other material but is textually eccentric. G. L. Kittredge's (1936, revised in 1970) has a reliable text and excellent notes. Peter Alexander's unannotated, collected edition (1951) is often used for reference, though it follows the line numbering of the Globe. Hardin Craig's annotated text (1951) has been popular in the United States. In 1951 a new Arden began to appear, a one-play-per-volume series with detailed annotation, which in general is now regarded as the standard edition for scholarly purposes. It is still incomplete. C. J. Sisson's one-volume edition (1954) has useful introductions and appendices. The Pelican (1956–1967) and Signet (1963–1968) lightly annotated paperback editions have been reprinted as hardback single volumes; the New Penguin (1967–    ) offers fuller annotation and more extended introductions. The Riverside edition (1974), under the general editorship of G. Blakemore Evans, has an overconservative text, but otherwise its wealth of ancillary material makes it the ideal desert-island Shakespeare.

There is no end to the editing of Shakespeare, partly because an infinite number of solutions can be offered to the problems posed by his text, partly because different methods of presentation and annotation are required for an ever-changing readership, and a little because of advances in scholarship. No satisfactory old-spelling edition has appeared, but those wishing to read the texts as they were originally printed are well served by *The Norton Facsimile of the First Folio of Shakespeare,* prepared by Charlton Hinman (1968), and by the Shakespeare Quarto Facsimiles, edited by W. W. Greg and, later, Charlton Hinman (1939–   ).

### SHAKESPEARE IN PERFORMANCE

WE know little about performances of Shakespeare's plays during the years immediately following his death. Court performances are recorded, and it is clear that some, at least, of the plays remained in the regular repertory of the King's Men. The closing of the theaters in 1642, when Cromwell came to power, is the most decisive break in the history of the English stage. When they reopened, in 1660, conditions changed greatly. The new buildings resembled the closed, private theaters of the earlier period rather than the open, public ones. Women took over the boys' roles. Some of Shakespeare's plays, especially the romantic comedies, were not revived. Patents were given to only two companies, and the plays were distributed between them. Some, such as *Hamlet, Othello,* and *Julius Caesar,* continued to be performed in versions which, if abbreviated, were not substantially altered. Others were radically adapted both to suit the new conditions and to conform to changes in taste. Sir William Davenant (1606–1668), who boasted of being Shakespeare's natural son and who had written for the Caroline stage, led one of the new companies, for which he adapted *Macbeth* (1663) and combined parts of *Measure for Measure* and *Much Ado About Nothing* to make *The Law Against Lovers* (1662). He collaborated with the young John Dryden on an adaptation of *The Tempest* as *The Enchanted Isle* (1667; further revised as an opera by Thomas Shadwell, in 1673). Dryden himself adapted *Troilus and Cressida* (1679); Nahum Tate, *King Lear* (1681); and Colley Cibber, *Richard III* (1699). The *Macbeth* had singing, dancing, and flying witches; additional scenes for the women characters; and a moralistic dying speech for Macbeth. *The Enchanted Isle* added sisters for both Miranda and Caliban; balanced Ferdinand with Hippolito, who has never seen a woman; added a female sprite; and greatly increased the play's spectacular appeal.

Tate introduced into *King Lear* a love affair between Edgar and Cordelia; omitted the Fool; and sent Lear, Gloucester, and Kent into peaceful retirement. Cibber greatly shortened *Richard III*, altered its structure, added passages from other plays, omitted important characters, and increased the relative length of Richard's role. All these authors rewrote and added speeches. Their adaptations, and others like them, are important because they kept the original plays off the stage, some of them well into the nineteenth century. Cibber's influence extends even as far as Sir Laurence Olivier's film (1955).

The greatest actor on the Restoration stage was Thomas Betterton (*ca.* 1635–1710), who played many of the principal Shakespearian roles, most notably Hamlet. No one of comparable stature emerged until David Garrick (1717–1778) made his sensational London debut in Cibber's *Richard III* in 1741. He excelled in roles as varied as Benedick, Richard III, Hamlet, Romeo, King Lear, and Macbeth. Though he restored Shakespeare's language in some passages of the adaptations, he made new versions of *The Taming of the Shrew* (as *Catharine and Petruchio*, 1756), *The Winter's Tale* (as *Florizel and Perdita*, 1756), and *Hamlet* (1772). His great admiration was largely instrumental in establishing the reverential attitude to Shakespeare as England's major classic author, and the Jubilee that Garrick organized at Stratford-upon-Avon in 1769 was the first large-scale celebration.

This attitude intensified during the Romantic period. Like Garrick, John Philip Kemble (1757–1823) was important as actor, manager, and, to a lesser extent, play reviser. He and his sister, Sarah Siddons (1755–1831), were classical performers: he, impressive as Hamlet, Brutus, and Coriolanus; she, as Volumnia, Constance, and, supremely, Lady Macbeth. Far different was Edmund Kean (1787–1833), volatile and electrifying as Shylock, Richard III, Hamlet, and Othello.

Objections to the standard adaptations were increasingly voiced, and among the earliest to put them into practice was William Charles Macready (1793–1873), who in 1838 restored Shakespeare's *King Lear*. But the performances of the greatest integrity since the early seventeenth century seem to be those of Samuel Phelps (1804–1878), the actor-manager who presented all but six of Shakespeare's plays at Sadler's Wells from 1844 to 1862. Increasingly during the nineteenth century attention was paid to visual effect. With Macready and Phelps it was controlled with discretion and taste, but Charles Kean (1811–1868), whose major productions were given at the Princess's from 1850 to 1859, sacrificed textual integrity and even theatrical excitement to pictorialism and archaeological verisimilitude. Sir Henry Irving (1838–1905) was a far finer actor as well as the successful manager of the Lyceum.

Reaction against the spectacular tradition began effectively with the work of William Poel (1852–1934), whose productions with the Elizabethan Stage Society (founded in 1894), though textually impure, attempted with some success to return to Elizabethan staging methods and so opened the way for performances in which better texts could be played without rearrangements necessitated by scene changing. He worked with Harley Granville Barker (1877–1946), whose productions at the Savoy from 1912 to 1914 showed that it was possible to combine textual integrity with scenic appeal.

The period between the two world wars included much experimentation, as in the modern-dress productions of Sir Barry Jackson (1879–1961), Sir Tyrone Guthrie (1900–1971), and others, though disciples of William Poel such as Robert Atkins (1886–1972), W. Bridges-Adams (1889–1965), and B. Iden-Payne (1881–1976) directed performances in a more traditional style. Gradually directors increased in importance, though Sir Donald Wolfit (1902–1968) continued the tradition of the actor-manager, and major players, including Dame Sybil Thorndike (1882–1976), Dame Edith Evans (1888–1976), Sir John Gielgud, and Sir Laurence (later Lord) Olivier, distinguished themselves in Shakespearian roles at the Old Vic, the Stratford Memorial Theatre, and elsewhere.

The dominance of the director increased still further after World War II, with the work of Peter Brook, Peter Hall, John Barton, and Trevor Nunn, all of whom have worked at what is now the Royal Shakespeare Theatre, Stratford-upon-Avon, which, since the closure of the Old Vic in 1963, has become the main center of Shakespearian production in England, although important performances have been given at the National Theatre and by many other companies.

Shakespeare belongs, of course, to far more than the English stage. Books by Charles Shattuck and Robert Speaight listed in the bibliography tell something of the story of his popularity in American and continental theaters. Annual festivals at Ashland, Oregon; Stratford, Connecticut; Stratford, Ontario; and in Central Park, New York City, present his work to the great American public. All over the world the plays are enjoyed in many languages, and through the media of radio, television, cinema, and the phonograph as well as the stage. Shakespeare's wooden O has become the great globe itself.

### SHAKESPEARE'S CRITICS

CRITICAL comment on Shakespeare by his contemporaries is limited to scattered remarks such as Francis Meres's empty eulogy, William Drummond of Hawthornden's reports of Ben Jonson's informal conversation, and the tributes printed in the First Folio. For a century or more after this, most comment is of a general nature, and much of it tells us more about the taste of the time than about Shakespeare. John Dryden wrote the first important criticism, mainly in the *Essay on the Dramatic Poetry of the Last Age* (1672), the preface to *Troilus and Cressida* (1679), his adaptation of Shakespeare's play, and the *Essay of Dramatic Poesy* (1688). Though he found that "the fury of his fancy often transported him beyond the bounds of judgement, either in coining of new words and phrases, or racking words which were in use, into the violence of a catachresis," he praised Shakespeare nobly as "the man who of all modern and, perhaps, ancient poets had the largest and most comprehensive soul." Thomas Rymer's notoriously destructive criticism of *Othello* comes in his *Short View of Tragedy* (1693).

During the eighteenth century, editions of the plays provided an outlet for opinion. Dryden's view that Shakespeare's greatness lies in his successful imitation of nature persisted. Alexander Pope, in his preface (1725), wrote, "His characters are so much nature herself that 'tis a sort of injury to call them by so distant a name as copies of her." Dr. Johnson, in his magisterial preface and in the pithy notes to his edition (1765), enumerated both Shakespeare's faults and his merits. He found Shakespeare's morality unsatisfying: "He sacrifices virtue to convenience, and is so much more careful to please than to instruct, that he seems to write without any moral purpose." But he also praised Shakespeare as "the poet that holds up to his readers a faithful mirror of manners and of life."

During the later part of the century there developed a fascination with Shakespeare's characters as independent creations, evinced in William Richardson's *Philosophical Analysis of Some of Shakespeare's Remarkable Characters* (1774) and Maurice Morgann's fine *Essay on the Dramatic Character of Sir John Falstaff* (1794), which is romantic in its imaginative identification with the character. Walter Whiter's *Specimen of a Commentary on Shakespeare* (1777) anticipates some of the imagery criticism of the twentieth century.

German interest developed early, and August Wilhelm Schlegel probably influenced Samuel Taylor Coleridge, whose detailed appreciations, seminal in their effect, have to be retrieved from a multitude of sources, including notebooks, marginalia, and other people's reports of his lectures. Coleridge encouraged a reverential submission to Shakespeare, finding that the plays have their own organic unity. William Hazlitt's eulogistic *Characters of Shakespear's Plays* (1817), based in part on his theater reviews, reveals a preoccupation with dramatic character that reflects the nature of performances in an age of great acting. Keen theatergoer though he was, Hazlitt shared some of the sentiments that Charles Lamb expressed in his essay "On the Tragedies of Shakespeare Considered With Reference to Their Fitness for Stage Representation" (1811), in which he argued that the plays suffer in performance. The mid-nineteenth century produced little distinguished Shakespeare criticism, but its later decades saw an increase in scholarly interest, which, along with the establishment of English studies as a university discipline, greatly increased the amount of serious writing on Shakespeare. Edward Dowden's *Shakspere: His Mind and Art* (1875) is a thoughtful study of Shakespeare's development that has had deserved popularity. Much of Bernard Shaw's brilliant, sometimes iconoclastic, criticism is found in the reviews of performances written for the *Saturday Review* from 1895 to 1898. Far different is A. C. Bradley's sensitive, scrupulous, philosophical study, *Shakespearean Tragedy* (1904), limited to *Hamlet*, *Othello*, *King Lear*, and *Macbeth*, which is in some respects a culmination of earlier interest in character portrayal.

A reaction against this is found in the work of E. E. Stoll and L. L. Schücking, both of whom sought a more objective approach, insisting that Shakespeare should be considered in the context of his life and the literary conventions of his age. Stoll, in his many writings, asserted the importance of poetry, and the primacy of plot over character. Harley Granville-Barker, in his series of prefaces to individual plays, published from 1927 to 1947, usefully discussed them in terms of the problems and opportunities with which they confront their performers.

In the 1930's the dominance of a school of criticism concerned with close verbal analysis precipitated language-based studies such as Caroline Spurgeon's pioneering *Shakespeare's Imagery and What It Tells Us* (1935), Wolfgang H. Clemen's *The Development of Shakespeare's Imagery* (1936, translated 1951), and the many books of G. Wilson Knight, a verbal critic of great subtlety who has added to our understanding of Shakespeare's symbolism and, more generally, of his imaginative processes. From among the critics of more recent years it is difficult to distinguish equally dominant figures. This may be because we lack historical perspective, but it also reflects the increasing fragmentation of critical approaches to Shakespeare. The bibliography appended to this essay lists important studies of the sources and of the literary and dramatic background by, among others, W. W. Lawrence, M. C. Bradbrook, Geoffrey Bullough, Kenneth Muir, Anne Righter, and Emrys Jones; of the historical background by Hardin Craig, Lily B. Campbell, and E. M. W. Tillyard; writings showing a particular concern with Shakespeare's social environment, by S. L. Bethell and Alfred Harbage; theatrically based studies by Arthur Colby Sprague, Nevill Coghill, John Russell Brown, Marvin Rosenberg, and Joseph G. Price; ones based on psychoanalytical procedures, by J. I. M. Stewart and Ernest Jones;

others grounded in moral preoccupations, by Derek Traversi, L. C. Knights, and Arthur Sewell; some with an anthropological basis, by Northrop Frye, C. L. Barber, and John Holloway; and examples of close stylistic analysis by M. M. Mahood, Harry Levin, and Maurice Charney. Most of these critics, and others, are, to a greater or lesser degree, eclectic in their methods. Shakespeare continues to stimulate not merely professional diploma pieces but challenging criticism, because his works remain alive as an intellectual and imaginative force, constantly creating newly fruitful relationships between themselves and those who experience them whether in the theater or on the page. So long as they are enjoyed, there will be something new to be said about them.

### SELECTED BIBLIOGRAPHY

This bibliography is, necessarily, highly selective. Individual essays, which often contain good criticism, are omitted; they, along with other items, may be traced through the bibliographies listed in the opening section and through the annual bibliographies, critical surveys, and reviews in the Shakespeare periodicals. Reprints are not listed.

I. BIBLIOGRAPHIES. William Jaggard, *Shakespeare Bibliography: A Dictionary of Every Known Issue of the Writings of Our National Poet and of Recorded Opinion Thereon in the English Language* (Stratford-upon-Avon, 1911); W. Ebisch and L. L. Schücking, *A Shakespeare Bibliography* (Oxford, 1931), and *Supplement for the Years 1930–35* (Oxford, 1937); Gordon Ross Smith, *A Classified Shakespeare Bibliography, 1936–1958* (University Park, Pa., 1963); Ronald S. Berman, *A Reader's Guide to Shakespeare's Plays* (Chicago, 1965; rev. 1973); Stanley Wells, ed., *Shakespeare: Select Bibliographical Guides* (Oxford, 1973); and James G. McManaway and Jeanne Addison Roberts, *A Selective Bibliography of Shakespeare* (Charlottesville, Va., 1975).

II. COLLECTED EDITIONS. W. G. Clark, W. A. Wright, and J. Glover, eds., 9 vols. (London, 1863–1866; 2nd ed., 1867; 3rd ed., revised by Wright, 1891–1893), the Cambridge Shakespeare, on which the Globe (1864) was based; H. H. Furness, Jr., et al., eds. (Philadelphia, 1871–1928; New York, 1929–1955), the New Variorum; C. F. Tucker Brooke, ed., *The Shakespeare Apocrypha* (Oxford, 1918); J. Dover Wilson, Sir A. T. Quiller-Couch, *et al.*, eds. (Cambridge, 1921–1966), the New Shakespeare; G. L. Kittredge, ed. (Boston, 1936); W. W. Greg and Charlton Hinman, eds., *Shakespeare Quarto Facsimiles* (London, 1939–1952; Oxford, 1957– ); Peter Alexander, ed. (London–Glasgow, 1951); Hardin Craig, ed. (Chicago, 1951); U. Ellis-Fermor, Harold F. Brooks, Harold Jenkins, and Brian Morris, eds. (London, 1951– ), the new Arden; C. J. Sisson, ed. (London, 1954); Alfred Harbage, general ed. (Baltimore, 1956–1967; one-volume ed. [the Pelican], 1969); Sylvan Barnet, general ed. (New York, 1963–1968; one-volume ed. [the Signet], 1972); *Shakespeare's Poems . . . a Facsimile of the Earliest Editions* (New Haven, 1964), with a preface by Louis M. Martz and Eugene M. Waith; T. J. B. Spencer, general ed. (Harmondsworth, 1967– ), the New Penguin; Charlton Hinman, ed., *The First Folio of Shakespeare* (New York, 1968), a facsimile; and G. Blakemore Evans, ed. (Boston, 1974, the Riverside).

III. TEXTUAL STUDIES. A. W. Pollard, *Shakespeare Folios and Quartos: A Study in the Bibliography of Shakespeare's Plays 1594–1685* (London, 1909); A. W. Pollard, *Shakespeare's Fight With the Pirates and the Problems of the Transmission of His Text* (London, 1917; 2nd ed., Cambridge, 1920); W. W. Greg, *The Editorial Problem in Shakespeare: A Survey of the Foundations of the Text* (Oxford, 1943; rev., 1951–1954); Alice Walker, *Textual Problems of the First Folio: "Richard III," "King Lear," "Troilus and Cressida," "2 Henry IV," "Othello"* (Cambridge, 1933); W. W. Greg, *The Shakespeare First Folio: Its Bibliographical and Textual History* (Oxford, 1955); C. J. Sisson, *New Readings in Shakespeare*, 2 vols. (Cambridge, 1956); Charlton Hinman, *The Printing and Proof-Reading of the First Folio of Shakespeare*, 2 vols. (Oxford, 1963); E. A. J. Honigmann, *The Stability of Shakespeare's Text* (London, 1965); and Fredson Bowers, *On Editing Shakespeare and the Elizabethan Dramatists* (Philadelphia, 1955; 2nd ed., Charlottesville, Va., 1966).

IV. REFERENCE WORKS AND PERIODICALS. *Shakespeare Jahrbuch*, West, vols. 1–99 (Berlin, 1865–1963), vols. 100– (Heidelberg, 1964– ); E. A. Abbott, *A Shakespearian Grammar* (London, 1869; rev. 1871); Alexander Schmidt, *Shakespeare–Lexicon*, 2 vols. (Berlin, 1874–1875; rev. by G. Sarrazin, 4th ed., Berlin, 1923); C. T. Onions, *A Shakespeare Glossary* (Oxford, 1911); F. G. Stokes, *A Dictionary of the Characters and Proper Names in the Works of Shakespeare* (London, 1924); E. H. Sugden, *A Topographical Dictionary to the Works of Shakespeare and His Fellow Dramatists* (Manchester, 1925); Eric Partridge, *Shakespeare's Bawdy: A Literary and Psychological Essay and a Comprehensive Glossary* (London, 1947; rev., 1968); *Shakespeare Survey* (Cambridge, 1948– ); *Shakespeare Quarterly* (New York, 1950–1972; Washington, D.C., 1972– ); W. H. Thomson, *Shakespeare's Characters: A Historical Dictionary* (Altrincham, 1951); F. E. Halliday, *A Shakespeare Companion 1550–1950* (London, 1952), rev. as *A Shakespeare Companion 1564–1964* (Harmondsworth, 1964); Helge Kökeritz, *Shakespeare's Names: A Pronouncing Dictionary* (New Haven, 1959); *Shakespeare Jahrbuch*, East (Weimar, 1965– ); *Shakespeare Studies*, vols. 1–3 (Cincinnati, 1965–1967), vols. 4–7 (Dubuque, Iowa, 1968–1971), vol. 8– (Columbia, S.C., 1972– ); Oscar James Campbell and Edward G. Quinn, *The Reader's Encyclopaedia of Shakespeare* (New York, 1966); Peter J. Seng, *The Vocal Songs in the Plays of Shakespeare* (Cambridge, Mass., 1967); Marvin Spevack, *A Complete and Systematic Concordance to the Works of Shakespeare* (Hildesheim, 1968–1970); Marvin Spevack, *The Harvard Concordance to Shakespeare* (Cambridge, Mass., 1973); Kenneth Muir and S. Schoenbaum, eds., *A New Companion to Shakespeare Studies* (Cambridge, 1971); and Stanley Wells, *Shakespeare: An Illustrated Dictionary* (London–New York, 1978).

V. BIOGRAPHICAL STUDIES. Sir Edmund K. Chambers, *William Shakespeare: A Study of Facts and Problems*, 2 vols. (Oxford, 1930), abridged by Charles Williams as *A Short Life of Shakespeare With the Sources* (Oxford, 1933); Leslie Hotson, *Shakespeare Versus Shallow* (Boston, 1931); J. Dover Wilson, *The Essential Shakespeare: A Biographical Adventure* (Cambridge, 1932); Leslie Hotson, *I, William Shakespeare* (London, 1937); Edgar I. Fripp, *Shakespeare, Man and Artist*, 2 vols. (Oxford, 1938); T. W. Baldwin, *William Shakespere's Petty School* (Urbana, Ill., 1943); T. W. Baldwin, *William Shakespere's Small Latine and Lesse Greeke*, 2 vols. (Urbana, Ill., 1944); Leslie Hotson, *Shakespeare's Sonnets Dated: and Other Essays* (Oxford, 1949); M. M. Reese, *Shakespeare: His World and His Work* (London, 1953); Kenneth Muir, *Shakespeare as Collaborator* (London, 1960); Gerald Eades Bentley, *Shakespeare: A Biographical Handbook* (New Haven, 1961); Mark Eccles, *Shakespeare in Warwickshire* (Madison, Wis., 1961); Peter Quennell, *Shakespeare* (London, 1963); Peter Alexander, *Shakespeare* (Oxford, 1964); S. Schoenbaum, *Shakespeare's Lives* (Oxford, 1970); S. Schoenbaum, *Shakespeare: A Documentary Life* (Oxford, 1975; compact ed., 1977); and Robert Speaight, *Shakespeare: The Man and His Achievement* (London, 1977).

VI. REPUTATION AND HISTORY OF CRITICISM. D. Nichol Smith, *Shakespeare in the Eighteenth Century* (Oxford, 1928); A. Ralli, *A History of Shakespearian Criticism*, 2 vols. (Oxford, 1932); J. Munro, *The Shakespeare Allusion-Book*, 2 vols. (Oxford, 1932), rev. by Sir Edmund K. Chambers; Gerald Eades Bentley, *Shakespeare and Jonson: Their Reputations in the Seventeenth Century Compared*, 2 vols. (Chicago, 1945); Louis Marder, *His Exits and His Entrances: The Story of Shakespeare's Reputation* (Philadelphia, 1963); Oswald Le Winter, ed., *Shakespeare in Europe* (Cleveland, 1963); Alfred Harbage, *Conceptions of Shakespeare* (Cambridge, Mass., 1966); Arthur M. Eastman, *A Short History of Shakespearean Criticism* (New York, 1968); and Brian Vickers, ed., *Shakespeare: The Critical Heritage*, vol. 1, 1623–1692 (London, 1974), vol. 2, 1693–1733 (London, 1974), vol. 3, 1733–1752 (London, 1975), vol. 4, 1753–1765 (London, 1976), in progress.

VII. SOURCES, INFLUENCES, AND BACKGROUND STUDIES. Edward W. Naylor, *Shakespeare and Music* (London, 1896; rev., 1931); D. H. Madden, *The Diary of Master William Silence: A Study of Shakespeare and of Elizabethan Sport* (London, 1897; rev., 1907); Sir Sidney Lee and C. T. Onions, eds., *Shakespeare's England: An Account of the Life and Manners of His Age*, 2 vols. (Oxford, 1916); Richmond Noble, *Shakespeare's Use of Song* (London, 1923; rev., 1931); Richmond Noble, *Shakespeare's Biblical Knowledge and Use of the Book of Common Prayer* (London, 1935); M. C. Linthicum, *Costume in the Drama of Shakespeare and His Contemporaries* (Oxford, 1936); Hardin Craig, *The Enchanted Glass: The Elizabethan Mind in Literature* (Oxford, 1936); W. C. Curry, *Shakespeare's Philosophical Patterns* (Baton Rouge, La., 1937); E. M. W. Tillyard, *The Elizabethan World Picture* (London, 1943); E. C. Pettet, *Shakespeare and the Romance Tradition* (London, 1949); C. W. Scott-Giles, *Shakespeare's Heraldry* (London, 1950); J. B. Bamborough, *The Little World of Man* (London, 1952); J. A. K. Thomson, *Shakespeare and the Classics* (London, 1952); F. P. Wilson, *Marlowe and the Early Shakespeare* (Oxford, 1953); Virgil K. Whitaker, *Shakespeare's Use of Learning* (San Marino, Calif., 1953); Paul A. Jorgensen, *Shakespeare's Military World* (Berkeley, Calif., 1956); Geoffrey Bullough, ed., *Narrative and Dramatic Sources of Shakespeare* (London, 1957–1975); K. M. Briggs, *The Anatomy of Puck* (London, 1959); W. Moelwyn Merchant, *Shakespeare and the Artist* (Oxford, 1959); K. M. Briggs, *Pale Hecate's Team* (London, 1962); F. W. Sternfeld, *Music in Shakespearian Tragedy* (London, 1963); R. M. Frye, *Shakespeare and Christian Doctrine* (Princeton, N.J., 1963); T. J. B. Spencer, *Shakespeare's Plutarch* (Harmondsworth, 1964); Phyllis Hartnoll, *Shakespeare in Music* (London, 1964); A. F. Falconer, *Shakespeare and the Sea* (London, 1964); George W. Keeton, *Shakespeare's Legal and Political Background* (London, 1967); John W. Velz, *Shakespeare and the Classical Tradition: A Critical Guide to Commentary* (Minneapolis, 1968); T. J. B. Spencer, ed., *Elizabethan Love Stories* (Harmondsworth, 1968); Richard Hosley, ed., *Shakespeare's Holinshed* (New York, 1968); Carol Gesner, *Shakespeare and the Greek Romance* (Lexington, Ky., 1970); Peter C. Milward, *Shakespeare's Religious Background* (London, 1973); E. A. C. Colman, *The Dramatic Use of Bawdy in Shakespeare* (London, 1974); Kenneth Muir, *Shakespeare's Sources* (London, 1977); and Emrys Jones, *The Origins of Shakespeare* (Oxford, 1977).

VIII. LANGUAGE AND STYLE. Walter Whiter, *A Specimen of a Commentary on Shakespeare* (1794), edited by Alan Over and Mary Bell (London, 1967); Caroline F. E. Spurgeon, *Shakespeare's Imagery and What It Tells Us* (Cambridge, 1935); Sister Miriam Joseph, *Shakespeare and the Arts of Language* (New York, 1947); Wolfgang H. Clemen, *The Development of Shakespeare's Imagery* (London, 1951); B. Ifor Evans, *The Language of Shakespeare's Plays* (London, 1952); Hilda M. Hulme, *Explorations in Shakespeare's Language: Some Problems of Lexical Meaning in the Dramatic Text* (London, 1962); Brian Vickers, *The Artistry of Shakespeare's Prose* (London, 1968); and G. L. Brook, *The Language of Shakespeare* (London, 1976).

IX. SHAKESPEARE'S THEATER. Sir Edmund K. Chambers, *The Elizabethan Stage*, 4 vols. (Oxford, 1923); Alfred Harbage, *Shakespeare's Audience* (New York, 1941); Irwin Smith, *Shakespeare's Globe Playhouse: A Modern Reconstruction* (New York, 1956); Leslie Hotson, *Shakespeare's Wooden O* (London, 1959); Bertram Joseph, *Acting Shakespeare* (London, 1960); Bernard Beckerman, *Shakespeare at the Globe: 1599–1609* (New York, 1962); Irwin Smith, *Shakespeare's Blackfriars Playhouse: Its History and Design* (New York, 1964); J. L. Styan, *Shakespeare's Stagecraft* (Cambridge, 1967); C. Walter Hodges, *The Globe Restored* (London, 1953; 2nd ed., Oxford, 1968); and Andrew Gurr, *The Shakespearian Stage, 1571–1642* (Cambridge, 1970).

X. SHAKESPEARE IN THE POST-RESTORATION THEATER. George C. D. Odell, *Shakespeare—From Betterton to Irving*, 2 vols. (New York, 1920); Hazelton Spencer, *Shakespeare Improved: The Restoration Versions in Quarto and on the Stage* (Cambridge, Mass., 1927); Arthur Colby Sprague, *Shakespeare and the Actors: The Stage Business in His Plays, 1660–1905* (Cambridge, Mass., 1944); C. B. Hogan, *Shakespeare in the Theatre 1701–1800*, 2 vols. (Oxford, 1952–1957); Arthur Colby Sprague, *Shakespearian Players and Performances* (Cambridge, Mass., 1953); J. C. Trewin, *Shakespeare on the English Stage 1900–1964* (London, 1964); G. Wilson Knight, *Shakespearian Production: With Especial Reference to the Tragedies* (London, 1964); Christopher Spencer, ed., *Five Restoration Adaptations of Shakespeare* (Urbana, Ill., 1965); Charles H. Shattuck, *The Shakespeare Promptbooks: A Descriptive Catalogue* (Urbana, Ill., 1965); John Russell Brown, *Shakespeare's Plays in Performance* (London, 1966); Gámini Salgádo, ed., *Eyewitnesses of Shakespeare: First-Hand Accounts of Performances, 1590–1890* (London, 1975); Charles H. Shattuck, *Shakespeare on the American Stage, From the Hallams to Edwin Booth* (Washington, D.C., 1976); Robert Speaight, *Shakespeare on the Stage: An Illustrated History of Shakespearian Performance* (London, 1973); J. L. Styan, *The Shakespeare Revolution* (Cambridge, 1977); and Stanley Wells, *Royal Shakespeare: Four Major Productions at Stratford-upon-Avon* (Manchester, 1977).

XI. GENERAL CRITICAL STUDIES. William Hazlitt, *The Characters of Shakespear's Plays* (London, 1817); Edward Dowden, *Shakspere: A Critical Study of His Mind and Art* (London, 1875); D. Nichol Smith, ed., *Eighteenth-Century Essays on Shakespeare* (Glasgow, 1903; rev., Oxford, 1963); A. C. Bradley, *Oxford Lectures on Poetry* (London, 1909); L. L. Schücking, *Character Problems in Shakespeare's Plays* (London, 1922); Elmer Edgar Stoll, *Shakespeare Studies, Historical and Comparative in Method* (New York, 1927); Harley Granville-Barker, *Prefaces to Shakespeare*, 5 vols. (London, 1927–1947); T. M. Raysor, ed., *Coleridge's Shakespearian Criticism*, 2 vols. (London, 1930; rev., London, 1960); G. Wilson Knight, *The Wheel of Fire* (Oxford, 1930; rev., London, 1949); G. Wilson Knight, *The Imperial Theme* (Oxford, 1931); G. Wilson Knight, *The Shakespearian Tempest* (Oxford, 1932); Elmer Edgar Stoll, *Art and Artifice in Shakespeare: A Study in Dramatic Contrast and Illusion* (Cambridge, 1933); J. Middleton Murry, *Shakespeare* (London, 1936); Elmer Edgar Stoll, *Shakespeare's Young Lovers* (Oxford, 1937); Mark van Doren, *Shakespeare* (London, 1939); Elmer Edgar Stoll, *Shakespeare and Other Masters* (Cambridge, Mass., 1940); Oscar James Campbell, *Shakespeare's Satire* (London, 1943); S. L. Bethell, *Shakespeare and the Popular Dramatic Tradition* (London, 1944); F. P. Wilson, *Elizabethan and Jacobean* (Oxford, 1945); E. A. Armstrong, *Shakespeare's Imagination: A Study of the Psychology of Association and Inspiration* (London, 1946; rev., Gloucester, Mass., 1963); Alfred Harbage, *As They Liked It: An Essay on Shakespeare and Morality* (New York, 1947); Dame Edith Sitwell, *A Notebook on William Shakespeare* (London, 1948); J. I. M. Stewart, *Character and Motive in Shakespeare: Some Recent Appraisals Examined* (London, 1949); Arthur Sewell, *Character and Society in Shakespeare* (Oxford, 1951); Harold C. Goddard, *The Meaning of Shakespeare*, 2 vols. (Chicago, 1951); M. C. Bradbrook, *Shakespeare and Elizabethan Poetry* (London, 1951); Alfred Harbage, *Shakespeare and the Rival Traditions* (New York, 1952); Patrick Cruttwell, *The Shakespearean Moment and Its Place in the Poetry of the Seventeenth Century* (London, 1954); G. Wilson Knight, *The Sovereign Flower* (London, 1958); L. C. Knights, *Some Shakespearian Themes* (London, 1959); Samuel Taylor Coleridge, *Writings on Shakespeare*, edited by Terence Hawkes (New York, 1959), repr. as *Coleridge on Shakespeare* (Harmondsworth, 1969); W. K. Wimsatt, ed., *Samuel Johnson on Shakespeare* (New York, 1960), repr. as *Dr. Johnson on Shakespeare* (Harmondsworth, 1969); A. P. Rossiter, *Angel With Horns: and Other Shakespeare Lectures* (London, 1961); J. R. Brown and Bernard Harris, eds., *Early Shakespeare*, Stratford-upon-Avon Studies 3 (London, 1961); Anne Righter, *Shakespeare and the Idea of the Play* (London, 1962); Theodore Spencer, *Shakespeare and the Nature of Man* (Cambridge, Mass., 1962); Edwin Wilson, ed., *Shaw on Shakespeare* (London, 1962); Ernest Schanzer, *The Problem Plays of Shakespeare: A Study of "Julius Caesar," "Measure for Measure," "Antony and Cleopatra"* (London, 1963); Jan Kott, *Shakespeare Our Contemporary* (London, 1964; rev., 1967); Nevill Coghill, *Shakespeare's Professional Skills* (London, 1964); Marion B. North, *Dualities in Shakespeare* (Toronto, 1966); J. R. Brown and Bernard Harris, eds., *Later Shakespeare*, Stratford-upon-Avon Studies 8 (London, 1966); A. C. Hamilton, *The Early Shakespeare* (San Marino, Calif., 1967); Norman Rabkin, *Shakespeare and the Common Understanding* (New York, 1967); Arthur Sherbo, ed., *Johnson on Shakespeare*, 2 vols. (New Haven, 1968), which are vols. VII and VIII of the Yale edition of Samuel Johnson; Philip Edwards, *Shakespeare and the Confines of Art* (London, 1968); M. C. Bradbrook, *Shakespeare the Craftsman* (London, 1969); F. P. Wilson, *Shakespearian and Other Studies*, ed. Helen Gardner (Oxford, 1969); Emrys Jones, *Scenic Form in Shakespeare* (Oxford, 1971); J. L. Calderwood, *Shakespeare's Metadrama* (Minneapolis, 1971); Michael Goldman, *Shakespeare and the Energies of Drama* (Princeton, 1972); Wolfgang H. Clemen, *Shakespeare's Dramatic Art* (London, 1972); Kenneth Muir, *Shakespeare the Professional and Related Studies* (London, 1973); Theodore Weiss, *The Breath of Clowns and Kings: Shakespeare's Early Comedies and Histories* (New York, 1971); and David P. Young, *The Heart's Forest: A Study of Shakespeare's Pastoral Plays* (New Haven, 1972).

XII. CRITICAL STUDIES OF THE COMEDIES. W. W. Lawrence, *Shakespeare's Problem Comedies* (New York, 1931); Frances Yates, *A Study of "Love's Labour's Lost"* (Cambridge, 1936); Oscar James Campbell, *Comicall Satyre and Shakespeare's "Troilus and Cressida"* (San Marino, Calif., 1938); H. B. Charlton, *Shakespearian Comedy* (London, 1938); George Gordon, *Shakespearian Comedy and Other Studies* (London, 1944); David Lloyd Stevenson, *The Love-Game Comedy* (New York, 1946); Ronald Watkins, *Moonlight at the Globe: An Essay in Shakespeare Production Based on Performance of "A Midsummer Night's Dream" at Harrow School* (London, 1946); G. Wilson Knight, *The Crown of Life: Essays in Interpretation of Shakespeare's Final Plays* (Oxford, 1947); S. L. Bethell, *"The Winter's Tale": A Study* (London, 1947); E. M. W. Tillyard, *Shakespeare's Last Plays* (London, 1948); E. M. W. Tillyard, *Shakespeare's Problem Plays* (London, 1950); S. C. Sen Gupta, *Shakespearian Comedy* (London, 1950); Leslie Hotson, *Shakespeare's Motley* (London, 1952); Enid Welsford, *The Fool: His Social and Literary History* (London, 1953); Mary Lascelles, *Shakespeare's "Measure for Measure"* (London, 1953); Leslie Hotson, *The First Night of "Twelfth Night"* (New York, 1954); Derek Traversi, *Shakespeare: The Last Phase* (London, 1954); R. H. Goldsmith, *Wise Fools in Shakespeare* (East Lansing, Mich., 1955; Liverpool, 1958); John Russell Brown, *Shakespeare and His Comedies* (London, 1957; rev., 1962); C. L. Barber, *Shakespeare's Festive Comedy: A Study of Dramatic Form and Its Relation to Social Custom* (Princeton, 1959); Bertrand Evans, *Shakespeare's Comedies* (Oxford, 1960); Kenneth Muir, *Last Periods of Shakespeare, Racine, and Ibsen* (Liverpool, 1961); William Green, *Shakespeare's "Merry Wives of Windsor"* (Princeton, 1962); Bernard Grebanier, *The Truth About Shylock* (New York, 1962); D. R. C. Marsh, *The Recurring Miracle: A Study of "Cymbeline" and the Last Plays* (Durban, 1964); Robert Kimbrough, *Shakespeare's "Troilus and Cressida" and Its Setting* (Cambridge, Mass., 1964); Northrop Frye, *A Natural Perspective: The Development of Shakespearean Comedy and Romance* (New York, 1965); T. W. Baldwin, *On the Compositional Genetics of "The Comedy of Errors"* (Urbana, Ill., 1965); R. G. Hunter, *Shakespeare and the Comedy of Forgiveness* (New York, 1965); E. M. W. Tillyard, *Shakespeare's Early Comedies* (London, 1965); David Lloyd Stevenson, *The Achievement of Shakespeare's "Measure for Measure"* (New York, 1966); Peter G. Phialas, *Shakespeare's Romantic Comedies* (Chapel Hill, N.C., 1966); David P. Young, *Something of Great Constancy: The Art of "A Midsummer Night's Dream"* (New Haven, 1966); A. D. Nuttall, *Two Concepts of Allegory: A Study of Shakespeare's "The Tempest" and the Logic of Allegorical Expression* (London, 1967); Joseph G. Price, *The Unfortunate Comedy: A Study of "All's Well That Ends Well" and Its Critics* (Toronto, 1968); M. Bradbury and D. J. Palmer, eds., *Shakespearian Comedy*, Stratford-upon-Avon Studies 14 (London, 1972); L. G. Salingar, *Shakespeare and the Traditions of Comedy* (Cambridge, 1974); and Alexander Leggatt, *Shakespeare's Comedy of Love* (London, 1974).

XIII. CRITICAL STUDIES OF THE ENGLISH HISTORY PLAYS. *An Essay on the Dramatic Character of Sir John Falstaff* (1777), Maurice Morgann, in his *Shakespearian Criticism*, ed. D. A. Fineman (Oxford, 1972); A. W. Pollard, ed., *Shakespeare's Hand in the Play of "Sir Thomas More"* (Cambridge, 1923); J. Dover Wilson, *The Fortunes of Falstaff* (Cambridge, 1943); E. M. W. Tillyard, *Shakespeare's History Plays* (London, 1944); Lily B. Campbell, *Shakespeare's "Histories": Mirrors of Elizabethan Policy* (San Marino, Calif., 1947); Irving Ribner, *The English History Play in the Age of Shakespeare* (Princeton, 1957; rev., London, 1965); M. M. Reese, *The Cease of Majesty: A Study of Shakespeare's History Plays* (London, 1961); Arthur Colby Sprague,

Shakespeare's Histories: Plays for the Stage (London, 1964); H. M. Richmond, Shakespeare's Political Plays (New York, 1967); Wolfgang H. Clemen, A Commentary on Shakespeare's "Richard III" (London, 1968); H. A. Kelly, Divine Providence in the England of Shakespeare's Histories (Cambridge, Mass., 1970); David Riggs, Shakespeare's Heroical Histories: "Henry VI" and Its Literary Tradition (Cambridge, Mass., 1971); Robert Ornstein, A Kingdom for a Stage: The Achievement of Shakespeare's History Plays (Cambridge, Mass., 1972); Moody E. Prior, The Drama of Power: Studies in Shakespeare's History Plays (Evanston, Ill., 1973); Edward I. Berry, Patterns of Decay: Shakespeare's Early Histories (Charlottesville, Va., 1975).

XIV. CRITICAL STUDIES OF THE TRAGEDIES AND ROMAN PLAYS. A. C. Bradley, Shakespearean Tragedy (London, 1904); M. W. MacCallum, Shakespeare's Roman Plays and Their Background (London, 1910); Elmer Edgar Stoll, Hamlet: An Historical and Comparative Study (Minneapolis, 1919); Lily B. Campbell, Shakespeare's Tragic Heroes: Slaves of Passion (Cambridge, 1930); A. J. A. Waldock, Hamlet: A Study in Critical Method (Cambridge, 1931); J. Dover Wilson, What Happens in "Hamlet" (Cambridge, 1935); Robert B. Heilman, This Great Stage: Image and Structure in "King Lear" (Baton Rouge, La., 1948); H. B. Charlton, Shakespearian Tragedy (Cambridge, 1948); Ernest Jones, Hamlet and Oedipus (London, 1949); John F. Danby, Shakespeare's Doctrine of Nature: A Study of "King Lear" (London, 1949); H. N. Paul, The Royal Play of "Macbeth" (New York, 1950); Willard Farnham, Shakespeare's Tragic Frontier (Berkeley, Calif., 1950); D. G. James, The Dream of Learning: An Essay on "The Advancement of Learning," "Hamlet," and "King Lear" (Oxford, 1951); Peter Alexander, Hamlet, Father and Son (Oxford, 1955); Robert B. Heilman, Magic in the Web: Action and Language in "Othello" (Lexington, Ky., 1956); Franklin M. Dickey, Not Wisely but Too Well: Shakespeare's Love Tragedies (San Marino, Calif., 1957); Adrien Bonjour, The Structure of "Julius Caesar" (Liverpool, 1958); Bernard Spivack, Shakespeare and the Allegory of Evil: The History of a Metaphor in Relation to His Major Villains (New York, 1958); H. S. Wilson, On the Design of Shakespearian Tragedy (Toronto, 1959); Harry Levin, The Question of Hamlet (New York, 1959); L. C. Knights, An Approach to "Hamlet" (London, 1960); Irving Ribner, Patterns in Shakespearian Tragedy (New York, 1960); Marvin Rosenberg, The Masks of Othello: The Search for the Identity of Othello, Iago, and Desdemona by Three Centuries of Actors and Critics (Berkeley, Calif., 1961); Maurice Charney, Shakespeare's Roman Plays: The Function of Imagery in the Drama (Cambridge, Mass., 1961); John Holloway, The Story of the Night: Studies in Shakespeare's Major Tragedies (London, 1961); Morris Weitz, "Hamlet" and the Philosophy of Literary Criticism (Chicago, 1965); Maynard Mack, "King Lear" in Our Time (Berkeley, Calif., 1965); William R. Elton, King Lear and the Gods (San Marino, Calif., 1966); Northrop Frye, Fools of Time: Studies in Shakespearean Tragedy (Toronto, 1967); Nicholas Brooke, Shakespeare's Early Tragedies (London, 1968); Dennis Bartholomeusz, Macbeth and the Players (Cambridge, 1969); Maurice Charney, Style in "Hamlet" (Princeton, 1969); Reuben A. Brower, Hero and Saint: Shakespeare and the Graeco-Roman Tradition (Oxford, 1971); Nigel Alexander, Poison, Play, and Duel: A Study in "Hamlet" (London, 1971); Marvin Rosenberg, The Masks of King Lear (Berkeley, Calif., 1972); Kenneth Muir, Shakespeare's Tragic Sequence (London, 1972); and E. A. J. Honigmann, Shakespeare: Seven Tragedies: The Dramatist's Manipulation of Response (London, 1976).

XV. CRITICAL STUDIES OF THE POEMS AND SONNETS. Edward Hubler, The Sense of Shakespeare's Sonnets (Princeton, 1952); G. Wilson Knight, The Mutual Flame: On Shakespeare's Sonnets and "The Phoenix and the Turtle" (London, 1955); J. B. Leishman, Themes and Variations in Shakespeare's Sonnets (London, 1961); Brents Stirling, The Shakespeare Sonnet Order (Berkeley, Calif., 1968); Stephen Booth, An Essay on Shakespeare's Sonnets (New Haven, 1969); and Giorgio Melchiori, Shakespeare's Dramatic Meditations (Oxford, 1976).

XVI. RECORDINGS. The Marlowe Society of Cambridge, with professional players, has recorded the complete works under the direction of George Rylands in Dover Wilson's text for Argo. Most of the works have been recorded by professional players in G. B. Harrison's text on the Caedmon label. There are other recordings of individual plays and extracts that may be traced through the catalogs of the record companies.